THE EARLY CHURCH

CONTRIBUTORS

Volume 1

Karl Baus • Hans-Georg Beck • Eugen Ewig • Josef Andreas Jungmann • Friedrich Kempf • Hermann Josef Vogt

Volume 2

Quintín Aldea Vaquero • Hans-Georg Beck • Johannes Beckmann • Louis Cognet • Patrick J. Corish • Karl August Fink • Josef Glazik • Erwin Iserloh • Hubert Jedin • Oskar Köhler • Wolfgang Müller • Heribert Raab • Burkhart Schneider • Bernhard Stasiewski • Hans Wolter

Volume 3

Gabriel Adriányi • Quentín Aldea Vaquero • Roger Aubert • Günter Bandmann • Jakob Baumgartner • Johannes Beckmann • Mario Bendiscioli • Pierre Blet • Johannes Bots • Patrick J. Corish • Viktor Dammertz • Jacques Gadille • Erwin Gatz • Erwin Iserloh • Hubert Jedin • Oskar Köhler • Rudolph Lill • Georg May • Joseph Metzler • Luigi Mezzardi • Franco Molinari • Konrad Repgen • Leo Scheffczyk • Michael Schmolke • Antonio da Silva • Bernhard Stasiewski • André Tihon • Norbert Trippen • Robert Trisco • Ludwig Volk • Wilhelm Weber • Erika Weinzierl • Paul-Ludwig Weinacht • Félix Zubillaga

Translators

Peter W. Becker (Books 7, 8, and portions of 5) • Anselm Biggs (Books 2, 3, 4, 10, and portions of 5) • Gunther J. Holst (Book 6) • Margit Resch (Book 9)

THE EARLY CHURCH

An Abridgment of
HISTORY
OF THE CHURCH
Volumes 1 to 3

Edited by Hubert Jedin

English Translation edited by John Dolan
Abridged by D. Larrimore Holland

CROSSROAD • NEW YORK

1993

The Crossroad Publishing Company
370 Lexington Avenue, New York, NY 10017

This abridgment copyright © 1993 by The Crossroad Publishing Company consisting of Volumes 1 to 3 of *History of the Church,* edited by Hubert Jedin and John Dolan:

Vol. 1: *From the Apostolic Community to Constantine*
English translation © 1965 Herder KG

Vol. 2: *The Imperial Church from Constantine to the Early Middle Ages*
English translation © 1980 by The Crossroad Publishing Company

Vol. 3: *The Church in the Age of Feudalism*
English translation © 1969 Herder KG

The complete *History of the Church* is a translation of the *Handbuch der Kirchengeschichte,* edited by Hubert Jedin, published by Verlag Herder, KG, Freiburg im Breisgau.

Printed in the United States of America

Library of Congress Cataloging-in-Publication Data

The Early church: an abridgment of History of the church, volumes 1
  to 3 /edited by Hubert Jedin and John Dolan ; abridged by D.
  Larrimore Holland.
      p.   cm. — (History of the church ; v. 1)
    Contents: Bk. 1. From the apostolic community to Constantine —
  Bk. 2. The imperial church from Constantine to the Early Middle Ages
  — Bk. 3. The church in the age of feudalism.
    ISBN 0-8245-1253-7
    1. Church history—Primitive and early church, ca. 30–600.
  2. Church history—Middle Ages, 600–1500.   I. Jedin, Hubert, 1900–
  II. Dolan, Patrick.   III. Holland, David Larrimore.   IV. Series:
  Handbuch der Kirchengeschichte. English (Crossroad (New York, N.Y.)
  : Firm : 1992) ; v. 1.
  BR141.H35132   1992 vol. 1
  [BR162.2]
  270 s—dc20
  [270.1]   92-31414
                                                    CIP

Contents

BOOK ONE
FROM THE APOSTOLIC COMMUNITY
TO CONSTANTINE

Book One / Part One
The Beginnings

Section One
Jewish Christianity

Section Two
The Way into the Pagan World

Section Two
The Last Attack of Paganism and the Final Victory of the Church

BOOK TWO
THE IMPERIAL CHURCH FROM CONSTANTINE
TO THE EARLY MIDDLE AGES

Book Two / Part One
The Development of the Church of the Empire
within the Framework of the Imperial Religious Policy

Book Two / Part Two
The Theological Disputes in East and West
to the Middle of the Fifth Century

Book Two / Part Three
Inner Life of the Church between Nicaea and Chalcedon

Book Two / Part Four
The Early Byzantine Church

Book Two / Part Five
The Latin Church in the Transition to the Early Middle Ages

Section One
The Missionary Work of the Latin Church

BOOK THREE
THE CHURCH IN THE AGE OF FEUDALISM

Book Three / Part One
The Church under Lay Domination

Section One
The Papacy's Alienation from Byzantium
and Rapprochement with the Franks

Section Two
The Greek Church in the Epoch of Iconoclasm

Section Three
The Age of Charles the Great (768 to 814)

Section Seven
Renewal and Reform from 900 to 1050

Book Three / Part Two
The Struggle for the Freedom of the Church

Section One
The Gregorian Reform

Section Two
The Byzantine Church from 886 to 1054

Section Three
Changes within the Christian West during the Gregorian Reform

Abridgment Editor's Preface

Hubert Jedin (1900–1980) is a name which will not sound familiar to most Americans. Even historians of the Church may not know much about him, until, that is, one mentions the Council of Trent, that important gathering of Roman Catholicism in the sixteenth century which was called to face the challenge of the calls for reform from within and the confrontations with the dissidents, the Protestants, from without. Anyone who knows the literature of the Council of Trent cannot fail to know the work of Professor Jedin, for in his *History of the Council of Trent* (4 volumes, 1949–79) he gave us our first modern look at the Council. Professor Jedin's work brought him respectful encomia from all sides and from scholars of all confessional stripes. I still remember vividly hearing Professor Hanns Rückart (one of those rare Protestant historians in that era who were themselves sufficiently expert on Trent to have a scholarly volume on the Council in print) lecturing at the University of Tübingen in 1955–56 on the Council of Trent and speaking in almost reverential tones of the work of Hubert Jedin. But Professor Jedin was more than just an academic specialist on the Council of Trent. He was also a generalist of the finest sort in the field of Church history. And I think that all of us Church historians who are not Roman Catholics breathed a sigh of relief when we discovered that the *Handbuch der Kirchengeschichte* (Handbook of Church History), which was announced by Verlag Herder in Germany, was being done under Professor Jedin's editorship, for we knew that his standards of objectivity and fairness would bode well for us all. And on the whole one must say that our expectations were amply rewarded. When he died on this date thirteen years ago, the scholarly world and Christendom lost a faithful interpreter.

The assignment of abridging these ten massive volumes into three posed a number of questions and problems. How could one let the peculiar genius of these volumes come through? That is, what is it that sets these volumes off from every other Church history? And how can one maintain that uniqueness while cutting almost sixty percent of the text away? Surely it is the quality of the roster of authors whom Professor Jedin attracted to his project which give the work its uniqueness; and the more acquainted I got with the texts they produced, the more loathe I was to cut the products of their mature reflections. And I must confess: I am haunted by the specter of Judgment Day, when colleagues like Karl Baus, Hans-Georg Beck, Erwin Iserloh, and the others whose labors I have so shamelessly cut up are standing there wanting an account for my scissors-and-paste efforts!

The goal I adopted was this: to make this history available to the average U.S. or other English-language public in as nearly its original form as possible. I have therefore tried to adapt the texts of the translations (which were supervised and edited by Professor John P. Dolan) to conform to the foci of concern to the English-speaking readership as I recognize them from my own teaching. This general criterion was responsible for my chopping of most of what was cut away. There is a strong Germanic bias in the conception of this work as a whole. By that I mean that the history of the Church in Germany gets rather more fulsome accounting than does that of the Church elsewhere. This will be especially noticeable by contrast with the paucity of space allotted to England, the United States, Canada and Australia. Inevitably these volumes will need to be supplemented by studies which focus more directly upon the Church in the English-speaking areas. But these volumes do provide the essential supplement to the usual U.S.-oriented histories. All of which is to say that no single interpretation is perfectly suited to anyone's needs.

The translation is uneven. Some of it is done by experts; some is not. I have tried to establish a bit of superficial uniformity in the various chapters in terms of trying to see that the names of the cast of characters were uniformly rendered and that the forms used were those which have become familiar in currently available histories of the Church: e.g., Lorenzo (not Lawrence) Valla; Pierre (not Peter) D'Ailly; and Hieronymous (not Jerome) Bosch. I clearly have not tried to adapt every name to its English equivalent (hence I have left Berengarius without substituting Berengar for it), And I have tried to weed out the phrases which were themselves meaningless in their translationese. I leave it to the reader to judge the success of those efforts.

Finally it remains for me to acknowledge my indebtedness in this work to Frank Oveis of Crossroad Publishing Company for his patience in seeing it through. My debt to my wife, Jill, for her support and indulgence during the months this abridgement has cost is incredible. And to her and to our sons, Robert and Richard, it is affectionately dedicated.

D. L. H.
Portsmouth, Rhode Island
July 16, 1993

Book One

FROM THE APOSTOLIC COMMUNITY
TO CONSTANTINE

Part One

The Beginnings

Karl Baus

Section One

Jewish Christianity

C H A P T E R   1

Judaism in the Time of Jesus

The New Testament account of salvation history tells us that Jesus Christ came into this world "when the fullness of time was come" (Gal 4:4, Mk 1:14). A longing for the promised Messiah was certainly alive in Jewry at that time, but it was more generally rooted in the political distress of the people than in religious motives. For more than half a century the Jewish people had lived under Roman domination, which was all the more hated because it was exercised by a man who had deeply offended their most sacred national and religious feelings. Herod the Great, the son of Caesar's friend Antipater — an Idumaean and therefore a foreigner — had contrived to obtain from the Roman Senate the title of King of the Jews, in return for which he had to pledge himself to protect Roman interests in the politically important Near East, especially against the dangerous Parthians.

He had first to conquer his kingdom by force of arms, and from the moment that he first trod on Palestinian soil he was met by the hatred of the people, who under the leadership of the Hasmonaean prince Antigonus offered violent resistance to him. Herod overcame this with Roman assistance and took Jerusalem in 37 B.C.E. He ruthlessly exterminated the Hasmonaean dynasty, which more than a century earlier, under Judas Maccabaeus and his brothers, had defended Jewish religious freedom in an heroic struggle against Syrian overlordship. Herod managed to hold in check the seething fury of the people, but in his efforts to win the hearts of his subjects by rebuilding the Temple, founding new cities like Caesarea, and promoting the economic and cultural life of his kingdom, he failed. After his death, his territory was divided among his three sons, Archelaus receiving the central portion and the royal title.

However, the change of ruler led in Judaea to serious disturbances, which could be put down only with the help of the Roman army. The Romans, seeing that he was unable to guarantee peace and security, deposed Archelaus in 6 B.C.E.

4

Augustus gave the country a new administration in the person of a Roman procurator who had Caesarea as his official residence and who was responsible, in association with the Roman governor in Syria, for the military security and economic control of the region, while the Sanhedrin, a purely Jewish body under the presidency of the high priest, was made competent for Jewish internal affairs. But even this arrangement failed to bring the awaited civil peace. The Jews' national consciousness was affronted by the stationing of a Roman cohort in Jerusalem and Romans' fixing their taxes; many procurators also overplayed their representing the Roman master-race and so fanned the flames of resentment of foreign domination. The root cause of the continued strained relations between political overlords and subject people is, however, to be found in the latter's unique intellectual and spiritual character, for which a Roman could hardly have had much understanding.

The Religious Situation among Palestinian Jewry

The Jewish people was seen by others as characterized above all by their peculiar religious convictions, which they sought to defend in the midst of utterly different currents of thought and forms of worship. While not avoiding contact with others in every-day life, Jews had held fast to the essential features of their faith and religious life with a remarkable tenacity, even when it cost them heavy sacrifices and resulted in isolating them from other peoples. Central to Jewish religion was its monotheism: Jews were conscious of being led, throughout all the phases of their history, by the one true God, Yahweh, who had revealed himself in word and deed. The belief in the guidance of a just and faithful God could waver in its intensity and immediacy, and could become rigid through rabbinical speculations, yet the people never lost it. Jews knew themselves to have been chosen before all the nations of the world by the Covenant which God had made with them, so that one day salvation for all men might go forth from them. This faith was sustained by the hope in a future Savior and Redeemer, whom the prophets had unwearyingly proclaimed as the Messiah. He was to spring from among them and to establish in Israel the kingdom of God, thus raising Israel above all the kingdoms of the world, and he was to be king over them.

The expectation of the Messiah and of the kingdom of God was the chief source of strength of the Jews. Yet with the merging of religious and political life, the idea of the Messiah easily took on for many the role of predominantly a savior from worldly tribulation or, later, quite concretely, that of liberator from the hated Roman yoke.

But there were also within contemporary Jewry circles which did not lose sight of the essentially religious mission of the Messiah, as foretold by the prophets, and who awaited in him the king of David's stock who would make Jerusalem all pure and holy, who would tolerate no injustice, no evil, who would reign over a holy people in a holy kingdom (cf. Dan 7:9, 13, 27). Out of such a glowing hope were born those religious canticles which are called the psalms of Solomon, and which, following the pattern of the biblical psalms, express in living and convincing accents the longing for the promised Savior.

Besides belief in one God and the expectation of the Messiah, the Law was of decisive importance in Judaism at that time. To observe the Law was the daily task of every pious Jew, and its fulfillment was his most serious endeavor; if he transgressed against it, even unwittingly, he must make atonement. Fidelity to the Law would have its true reward when the Last Judgment confirmed that one had been just on earth and could enter into eternal life. The Law was given to every Jew in Scripture, into which he was initiated by his parents, nurtured in later in school, and kept alive through being expounded in sermons in worship. As the Law did not provide ready-made answers for every problem, its interpretation was entrusted to special scholars (known as Scribes) who became an important institution in the religious life of the Jews.

All Jews were agreed in their fundamental reverence for the Law; yet the Law itself was an occasion of division of the people into parties, differing from each other on the degree of importance they attached to its influence on the whole of life. There were the Hassidim or Hasideans who sought for their religious life the ultimate will of God that lay behind the Law. They wished to serve the Law with an unconditional obedience even unto death, and thus they helped create that attitude of heroic sacrifice which distinguished the people in the time of the Maccabees. The Hasideans did not gain a universal following; the noble families and the leading priests held aloof from them and themselves became the Sadducees met in the New Testament; subscribing to a sort of rationalism, they rejected angels and spirits and ridiculed the notion of the resurrection of the dead. For them, the principal authority was the five books of Moses, the *Torah* proper, and in matters political they inclined toward an opportunistic attitude in dealing with the Romans. They remained a minority party, though an influential one.

The most considerable religious party of the first century C.E., in the esteem of the people if not in numbers, was that of the Pharisees. Although their name means "the separated ones," they sought consciously to influence the whole people and to spread their opinions with much success. They saw themselves as representatives of orthodox Judaism, and their conception of the Law and its observance was typical of Judaism at that time. They accepted from the Hasideans the basic idea of the overriding importance of the Law in the life of the individual as well as of the whole people, but they went further in wishing to lay down the line of conduct required by the Law in every situation in life. This detailed interpretation of the Law found expression in the *Mishna* and in the *Talmud*, in which great emphasis is placed upon the views of earlier teachers, with the result that an incipient role for the subsequent importance of tradition came into the interpretation of the Law. Casuistry was the occasional result of their efforts and it rendered free moral decision on the part of the individual impossible or else gave it a spurious basis. The casuistry practiced by the Pharisaic Scribes led inevitably to differences of opinions and thus to differing schools of interpretation (e.g., the schools of Shammai or of Hillel). In public life, Pharisees took great pains to exemplify fulfillment of the Law and were, often enough, willing to accept certain titles and honors in return, which could produce a vain self-complacency which, in turn, could produce contempt for "sinners" (Jn 7:49).

The Pharisees did not, however, succeed in permeating the whole of contemporary Judaism with their religious opinions. A group known as the Zealots likewise wished to observe the Law faithfully, but their attitude was markedly warlike, ready for martyrdom. They actively rejected all that was pagan and refused to pay tribute to Caesar; they even called for open resistance to heathen domination, on the ground that obedience to the Law demanded such a holy war.

The Qumran Community

Fidelity to the Law and zeal for its complete and pure fulfillment drove yet another group of Jews, the Essenes, out of public life into the wilderness. The numerous literary and archaeological discoveries which have been made since 1947 among the ruins of Khirbet Qumran, west of the Dead Sea (a center of this sect), have greatly enriched the picture which Pliny the Elder and Flavius Josephus drew of them. Their beginnings go back to the time of the Maccabees and they flourished about 100 B.C.E.

The Essenes believed that Belial, as Satan was called at Qumran, had spread three nets over Israel: unchastity, ill-gotten riches, and pollution of the Temple, referring to the enrichment of the leaders by heathen booty, the lax interpretation of the marriage laws (Lev 18:13), and the impossibility of Temple service by those defiled by such practices. Hence the Essenes separated themselves from Temple worship and regarded themselves as a "holy remnant" of the true Israel. Leadership among them was assumed by a "Teacher of Righteousness" to whom is attributed the first organization of their community. This teacher proclaimed a new, completely rigoristic interpretation of the Law as fulfillment of the will of God. There were no half-way measures: one was either with the Essenes or against God on that view.

The Teacher of Righteousness further proclaimed a new interpretation of the Old Testament prophecies. Accordingly, the last age they foretold had already begun; the final struggle between the sons of light and the children of darkness was at hand and was to bring the sons of light, the Essenes, the commencement of an eternity of peace and salvation. The salvation of the children of light was an unmerited grace, however, based upon a notion of predestination.

This radical doctrine and its commensurate practice led to the organization of communities which, in the Qumran group, took on the character of a religious order; indeed, of a quasi-monastic sort. Persuaded of the correctness of their own views and ways, the Essenes had no pity for the godless man; he was regarded with a merciless hatred and the wrath of God was called down upon him.

The non-biblical writings found at Khirbet Qumran show the strong interest of the group in so-called apocalyptic literature, the themes of which are the great events which are to take place at the end of the world: the final victory over evil, the resurrection of the dead, the Last Judgment, and the glory of the everlasting age of salvation. There is evidence of an Essene origin for many of these writings. Some of this literature indicates a change took place in some of the community's attitudes over time: the hate theme recedes into the background in favor of a more merciful attitude toward both the godless and the sinner and of the duty to love one's neighbor.

The literature so far known permits no complete reconstruction of the Essene movement. Only Josephus *(Antiquitates,* 20, 5, 4, sect. 113–17), writing after the destruction of Jerusalem, goes into any detail. It is not known if the Essenes participated in the struggle during the rebellion against Rome in 66–70 C.E., but it seems likely they would have done so, given the possibilities for seeing in it the final conflict between the sons of light and of darkness. There is no evidence of any dependence of either Qumran or Jesus on the other. The monastic center of Qumran was destroyed by the Romans in 68 C.E., and the remnant of the community was probably so decimated during the Bar Cochba rebellion (132–35 C.E.) that reorganization was impossible. The Essene movement thereafter had no importance in Jewish religious history, and the leading role passed to their great opponents, the Pharisees.

The Jewish Diaspora

Large numbers of Jews dwelt outside of Palestine who were decisively to influence the spread of Christianity in the Hellenistic world. By the beginning of the Christian era, the numbers of Jews in the so-called Diaspora, the dispersion of Jews outside of Palestine, was greater than those within Palestine. They located especially in the great centers of Hellenistic culture (Antioch, Rome, Alexandria), and there formed themselves into congregations, with the synagogue at their centers. For it was religion which formed the bond among the Jews of the Diaspora, and they gained special exceptions and privileges for their religious opinions and practices which set them aside in the eyes of society.

Jews, though without infringing the Law, were influenced by their environment. *Koinē* Greek, the international Greek language of the time, became their language in daily life and in synagogue worship. The Septuagint, the Greek translation of the Hebrew Bible which had emerged in Egypt, became their scripture as the whole worship format became Greek.

Hellenistic culture inevitably influenced Jewish thought and religion. This is seen perhaps most acutely at Alexandria, the intellectual center of the Diaspora. In Philo Judaeus (d. ca. 40 C.E.) we see the effects of the different philosophical tendencies of his time. In his works, one finds such influences as the Stoics' allegorical method of scriptural interpretation. Without giving up the literal sense of the biblical texts, he sought a deeper, secret meaning beneath it. More even than the Stoics, the "most holy Plato" influenced the intellectual world of Philo, who took over from him not only his philosophical terminology but also his high esteem for the intellect, his longing for a spiritualized life, and his idea of the imperfection of the material world. Philo's doctrine of creation has a Platonic coloration, especially his notion of the "middle powers" which exist between a perfect God and an imperfect world; the highest among these was the Logos, Reason itself, which was to play such an important part in the theology of the first Christian centuries. Philo also interpreted Jewish ritual laws allegorically and, using the philosophical terminology of Hellenism, developed from these rituals ethical principles, culminating in the demand for ascetic control of the life of instinct.

Despite his enthusiasm for the Hellenistic philosophy of his time, Philo remained a convinced Jew by religion. If the faith of a Jew so receptive to Greek ideas as Philo, was not endangered in its innermost citadel, the loyalty of the average Diaspora Jew was even more secure. An essential part of it was the spiritual and practical attachment to the Palestinian homeland, to Jerusalem and its Temple, which he unwaveringly maintained. The other support for his faith was the close association of all the Diaspora Jews in their congregations, which led to an exclusiveness often criticized by their pagan neighbors.

The Diaspora Jews carried out an enterprising and methodical propaganda for their convictions and their religion which met with considerable success. The literature produced in this effort sought to inform the Hellenistic reader that the original source of all culture, including religious culture, was to be found in Moses and his people (cf., e.g., the so-called Letter to Aristeas and books three to five or the *Oracula Sybillina*). Josephus' *Contra Apionem* was also a piece of this effort at propaganda and proselytism. A measure of the success of this propaganda is the great number of pagans who entered into closer relations with the Jewish religion. There were proselytes, those whose conversions were marked by circumcision and the undertaking of all of the obligations of the Law. A larger number became known as "God-fearing," those who did not accept circumcision but who were attracted to the monotheism and worship of the synagogue and whose children often made a formal conversion to Judaism.

The significance of the Jewish Diaspora for the early Christian missions cannot be overlooked. It laid much groundwork for Christianity in its preparing the Septuagint, Bible to both Jew and Christian, and in its preaching of monotheism and the Commandments of Moses, which were also the foundation of Christian morality. Since the synagogues were often the starting-place of Christian missions, the missionaries found there, above all, among the God-fearing and the proselytes, hearts ready to receive their message. In the competition between Christian missionary and Diaspora Jew for the allegiance of the pagan, the Christian usually enjoyed the greater success, as witness: the Jews' abandonment of the Septuagint, which had been adopted by and was being so successfully used by Christian apologists, for new translations; their rejection of allegorical biblical interpretation, because of the Christians' too successful use of the method in their polemics; and their increasingly rigid emphasis upon the *Torah* and a strictly rabbinical interpretation of it.

CHAPTER 2

Jesus of Nazareth and the Church

The history of the Church has its roots in Jesus of Nazareth, who was born into the intellectual and religious world of Palestinian Jewry just described. His life and work, by which the Church was founded, are therefore a necessary preliminary to a history of the latter.

The sources which tell us of that life and its significance for the Church are of a quite exceptional nature. Apart from a few references in pagan and Jewish works, which are valuable because they place beyond discussion any attempt to deny the historical existence of Jesus, the main sources are the writings of the New Testament, especially the first three gospels, the Acts of the Apostles, and some of the letters of St. Paul. None of these was intended to be an historical biography of Jesus of Nazareth. The three synoptic gospels are the outcome of the apostolic preaching about Jesus and accordingly give the image of him which remained vivid in the minds and hearts of his first disciples when they proclaimed him after his ascension as the crucified and risen Messiah. That image is shaped by the requirements of the apostles' preaching and the faith which supported it. We are not on that account forced to adopt an attitude of radical skepticism about the question whether such sources can ever lead us to a true picture of the "historical" Jesus. True, an actual "Life of Jesus" cannot be obtained from them. But the New Testament writings are always going back to that Life, giving prominence to single facts and events, to actions and words of Jesus in his earthly life which have a special significance for the proclamation of the apostolic message, bearing witness to them at the same time as important historical facts of his life. The preaching of the apostles was expressly intended to prove that the earthly Jesus of Nazareth was the same Christ that they proclaimed, from whom came salvation for all men. Thus a series of individual facts and characteristics can, with all the scrupulous care that historical criticism demands, be built up from these sources and presented as a kind of outline of the life of Jesus.

Four or five years before the beginning of our era, Jesus of Nazareth was born in Bethlehem of the Virgin Mary. Forty days after circumcision the child was presented to the Lord in the Temple as a first-born son, in accordance with Jewish Law, on which occasion two pious Israelites, Simeon and Anna, spoke prophetically of his Messianic mission. Dangers which threatened the infant from King Herod forced his mother and his foster-father Joseph to sojourn for a long period in Egypt, until, after Herod's death, the family was able to settle at Nazareth in Galilee. The boy grew up in this quiet village, perhaps without ever attending a rabbinical school. Only once did something of his future greatness shine forth, when at twelve years of age he spoke with the Scribes in the Temple about religious questions, showing knowledge superior to theirs and excusing himself to his parents with the words: "I must be about my Father's business" (Lk 2:49).

About thirty years after his birth Jesus left his parental home and began his work among the people of his homeland. First he took a remarkable step, seeking out the great preacher of penance, John the Baptist, by the Jordan and accepting baptism from him, whereby God "anointed him with the Holy Spirit," who descended upon him in the form of a dove while the voice of the Father bore witness from Heaven that this was his "beloved Son" (Mt 3:13f.). Conscious of his Messianic mission and his divine sonship, which he was able to confirm by numerous miracles, Jesus now proclaimed in word and deed that the kingdom of God was come, and that all men, not only Israelites, were called to the kingdom, provided they served God with true piety. The supreme law of the religion he preached was the unconditional love of God and a love of one's neighbor that embraced men of all nations. In clearly recognizable opposition to pharisaical practice with its outwardly correct observance of the Law, he declared purity of mind and intention to be the basis of moral behavior, thus giving to the individual conscience the decisive role in the sphere of religion. Jesus furthermore re-established the true priority of obligations, derived from that life of inward union with the Father which he preached as the ideal: more important than scrupulous observance of the Sabbath is a helpful action performed for our neighbor — of more value than the prescribed prayers recited in the Temple is silent converse with the Father in the solitude of one's own room. Shocking for many was his message that publicans and sinners, the poor and infirm, whom God seemed so obviously to have punished, had the first right to expect a welcome in the house of the Father. The self-righteousness of the Pharisees was deeply shaken by the news that there is more joy in Heaven over one sinner who does penance than over ninety-nine just men; they did not understand that in the coming kingdom of God all human actions count for nothing, that only he is just to whom the Father graciously grants it. The poor were called blessed, because they were free from earthly cares about possessions and riches, which all too easily take up in men's hearts the place that belongs to God alone.

But consoling though his message was for those who had hitherto been despised and lowly among the people, great though the effects of his miraculous powers were upon those marked by lameness, blindness, leprosy, and spiritual diseases, no less strict were the conditions which Jesus imposed upon those who would enter the kingdom of God. The whole man was called upon to follow him without regard for previous friendships, family ties, or possessions; he who set his hand to the plough and looked back was unworthy of the kingdom (Lk 9:62). Such demands dispel any idea of a peaceful family idyll; his words cut like a sword through all existing social and familiar bonds. But the new and unique thing in his teaching was this above all: no man could come to the Father except through Jesus. He demanded a discipleship that was quite impossible without painful self-denial; the man who would truly be his disciple must be able to lay aside his own life (Lk 14:26).

All those, however, who made up their minds to follow him and were thus called to the kingdom formed a new community. Jesus' words and deeds tend unmistakably toward the creation and development of such a community. He proclaimed no kind of only individual piety or religion, but a message which binds together those who hear it and are filled by it as brothers in a religious family that prays together to the Father for the forgiveness of its sins. Jesus himself on one occasion called this community his Church, and he claimed that he was establishing it by his work (Mt 16:18). He carefully prepared the ground for the foundation of this religious society. If, at times, because of his miracles, great multitudes greeted him with loud acclamations, it was but a minority of the people who accepted to become his disciples. From this group he selected twelve men, who occupied a special position among his followers; they were the object of his special attention: with them he discussed the special tasks for which he intended them in the community that was to be. They were to take up and continue the mission which the Father in Heaven had entrusted to him; "As the Father has sent me, even so I send you" (Jn 20:21). The Gospels emphasize again and again with unmistakable clarity the special position of the Twelve, who received the name of apostles, envoys. The content of their mission was the proclamation of the kingdom of God; to fulfill it, the apostles were expressly appointed as teachers, whose word the nations must believe and trust like that of Jesus himself (Lk 10:16; Mt 28:20), to whose judgment they must submit as if it were a verdict of the Lord (Mt 18:18). Finally, to the Twelve, who were to carry out his own office of High Priest in the new community, Jesus gave priestly powers (Jn 17:19; Mt 20:28). They were to nourish and sanctify its members through a mysterious, sacramental life of grace. From the group Jesus chose Peter for a special task: he was appointed to be the rock foundation on which his Church should stand. With a singular form of words he was given the mission to feed the sheep and the lambs and to strengthen his brothers (Mt 16:18; Jn 21:15).

Thus the foundation prepared by Jesus before his resurrection received an organic framework, perceptible even from without, which would now grow in space and time, according to laws of growth implanted in it by its founder. Its purely supernatural basis lies indeed elsewhere: it is ultimately founded on the death of Jesus, through which alone salvation can be newly given to men, from which alone the new structure of the salvation community of the redeemed receives its mysterious life. With his death, which completed the work of atonement and redemption, and his resurrection, which gloriously confirmed that work, the founding of the Church was complete, and her historical existence began with the descent of the Spirit.

Jesus had to go to his death because the majority of his people closed their ears to his message. The religious leaders of Jewry decisively rejected his Messianic claims and persecuted him as a sedition-monger with ever-increasing hatred, which finally led them to plan his violent death. The Roman procurator allowed himself, albeit unwillingly, to be won over and he delivered Jesus into their hands to be crucified. The crucifixion took place on the fourteenth or fifteenth day of Nisan in a year between 30 and 33 of the Christian era.

So the labors of Jesus among his own people come to a sudden end, which in the eyes of those who did not believe in his mission meant too the end of the kingdom which he announced. But after three days he rose again from the dead as he had foretold, and during a period of forty days appeared to his disciples on many occasions, until he was taken up into heaven. Belief in his second coming, which was promised to the disciples by two angels at the time of his ascension, was one of the main supports of the young Church's now growing structure.

CHAPTER 3

The Primitive Church at Jerusalem

The External Events and Early Environment

The most important source for the fortunes of the primitive Church immediately after the ascension of our Lord is the account given in the first seven chapters of the Acts of the Apostles. It does not indeed give a complete picture of events, because the author chose for his subject only what served his purpose, which was to show that the tidings of the kingdom, though first addressed to the Jews, were then, in accordance with God's will, to be delivered to the Gentiles, and that the Jewish Christian Paul, with the approval of the apostles and commissioned by them, had become the legitimate missionary to the Gentiles. Thus only about the first fifteen years of the origin and growth of the community are described.

It was the initially almost incomprehensible fact of the resurrection of the Crucified One that brought together the scattered disciples and united them in a community sharing the same belief and profession of faith. Firm in their belief that their Lord who has ascended into heaven will return, they are determined to carry out the instructions he gave them during the forty days between his resurrection and his ascension. The first act of this group of 120 believers was, under the leadership of Peter, to elect a successor to Judas Iscariot for the apostolic college of the twelve.

The events of the first Pentecost, when the Holy Spirit, to the accompaniment of some extraordinary phenomena, descended upon the assembled believers, gave them access to great strength and courage to bear witness in public. The external growth of the community reflected its inward strengthening, and soon the community's numbers measured 5000 (Acts 3–4:4).

Such success disturbed the Jewish authorities, who arrested, examined, threatened, and punished the leaders of the nascent Church at Jerusalem. As the tasks to be carried out in the community increased with the number of members, some organization became necessary; so that the apostles might remain free to preach, seven men were appointed and ordained with prayer and the laying on of hands to serve the tables, to care for the poor and to help the apostles in their pastoral activities (Acts 6:1–6). The Greek names of these men indicate the considerable numbers of Hellenistic Jews among Christians in Jerusalem, as indeed the dispute between the Hellenists and the Palestinian Jewish Christians also attests. After the stoning death of Stephen, a courageous and articulate member of those seven "deacons" (Acts 7), a persecution arose, especially among the Hellenistic Jewish Christians, and many of them left Jerusalem. Those who left the capital spread the Gospel in Judaea and Samaria, with Philip's mission to the latter area being especially successful. This phenomenon brought Peter and John on an inspection trip to the new Christians which confirmed the missionary activities of Philip. In fact, the presence of Jewish Christians in remote locations like Lydda and Joppa are indications of how widespread the movement had become.

After James the Elder had been executed under Herod Agrippa (42/43 C.E.) and Herod's sudden demise in 44 C.E., the Church enjoyed a period of relative peace and used it to spread the Word. Under the leadership of James the Younger, called "the Just" because of his ascetic life and his devotion to Jewish transitions, the Church at Jerusalem flourished for almost twenty years. James had a weighty role as a mediator at the so-called Council of the Apostles (Acts 15:13–21); he met his martyr's death in 62 C.E..

Within a few years, however, the independence of the Jerusalem Church came to an end when the rebellion against Rome turned into a catastrophe for the whole nation. Not wishing to participate in the struggle, the Jewish Christians emigrated in 66–67 to the land east of the Jordan, where some of them settled in the city of Pella. The fortunes of the young Church took a new turn. Under Peter's leadership in Palestine there had already been individual conversions from paganism, but now there were enough to make it clear that the Good News was not for the Jews alone. A considerable number of former pagans had already formed a Christian congregation in Syrian Antioch under the care of the Cypriot levite, Barnabas. Here the term *Christianoi* was first applied to the followers of the new faith (cf. Acts 1:6–8; 1 Peter 4:16). Indeed, the future of the young Church after the destruction of Jerusalem lay with the pagan nations of the eastern Mediterranean area, whose evangelization had already been successfully begun by the Jewish Christian Paul.

Organization, Belief, and Piety

"Sect of the Nazarenes," *hē tōn Nazōraiōn hairesis*, their Jewish opponents called the disciples of Jesus (Acts 24:5), who had formed themselves into a special community; "congregation, assembly," *ekklēsia*, is the name the Jewish Christians had for this community of theirs (Acts 5:11; 8:1; etc.). They were therefore not merely a group of Jews who shared the conviction that Jesus was the true Messiah, but who otherwise led their own individual religious lives; rather that conviction brought them together and caused them to organize themselves as a religious community. From the beginning, the community was a hierarchically ordered society in which all were not of equal rank. There were within the community individuals and groups to whom certain tasks and functions in life of the community were assigned by higher authority. The first of such groups was the college of the apostles, the twelve who were selected and trained for their unique ministries by Jesus himself before his ascension. In the calling of Matthias to replace Judas Iscariot, it became clear that a man could be called to the office of an apostle only on the supreme authority of God (Acts 1:12–26). To the apostles fell the tasks of bearing witness to the life, death, and resurrection of Christ, of leading the community's cultic solemnities (to administer baptism, to preside at the eucharistic feasts, and to lay on hands for the ordaining of others to certain tasks). They also worked signs and wonders in Christ's name (Acts 2:42; 5:12), and exercised authority and discipline in the community (Acts 8:14f.; 15:2). Nevertheless, the apostle was not so much lord as rather servant and shepherd in the Church, which was firmly based upon the apostolic office (Mt 16:18; 24:45; Acts 20:28).

Among the Twelve, it is clear from the evidence that Peter occupied a special position. All through the first nine chapters of the Acts of the Apostles, it is Peter who exercises leadership, whether preaching, acting as spokesman for the apostles before the authorities, exercising oversight of the community and its affairs in Jerusalem and elsewhere, and in opening the promises of the Gospel to the Gentiles. This ministry had a higher authority, too, it is Mt 16:18–19; Jn 21:15–19. Moreover, the Acts' portrait of Peter's position is significantly confirmed by Paul in Galatians. Indeed, the whole of Peter's work in the primitive Church up to the time when he finally left Jerusalem to engage actively in the mission to the Gentiles can be rightly understood only if one regards it as the fulfillment of the task given him by his Master, of which not only Matthew but also Luke and John tell us when they write that Peter was called by the Lord to strengthen the brethren and to feed Christ's flock.

Acts 6:1–7 portrays another office in the primitive Church, namely, that to which the seven were set aside to assist the apostles and to take over service at table and among the poor of the community. These men were set apart through prayer and laying on of hands by the apostles. As Acts attest, their mission went far beyond charitable activities as is clear from the narrations of Stephen's and Philip's activities in the Acts. Their office is given no special designation in the Acts, but they were servers (deacons) whether or not in succession with those called deacons in Paul's correspondence.

A third group, the "elders" (presbyters), were not so sharply delineated in Acts (11:30). In the primitive Church of Jerusalem they are to be found in the company of the apostles or of James as leader of the congregation; they take part in the decisions of the apostolic Council (Acts 15:2ff.). They were, it would thus appear, assistants to the apostles or to the pastor of Jerusalem in the administration of the community.

Only once in connection with the Jerusalem community are "prophets" mentioned (Acts 15:32); these were Judas Barsabas and Silas, who because of their special gifts were chosen to go to Antioch to report on the Council's decisions and to strengthen and encourage the brethren there. It does not seem to have been a permanent office.

The existence of such office-holders, the apostles, the elders, and the seven, shows clearly that already in the primitive Church there was a division of members into groups, consecrated by a religious ceremony for special tasks, apart from the main body of the faithful. Even then there were clergy and laity.

The Lord's resurrection, the formative event for bringing the followers of Jesus into a community, was one of the fundamental elements of the religious faith by which the primitive Church lived, and it was the pivot upon which the apostolic message hinged. It had therefore to be accepted by all who wished to follow the Gospel. The fact of the resurrection was confirmed by the descent of the Spirit at Pentecost (Acts 2:1ff.), which gave its final clarity and direction to the apostolic message, and from that time forward, the apostles' preaching emphasized their conviction that the Risen One whom they proclaimed was none other than the earthly Jesus of Nazareth, and from this identification all that Jesus taught by word and deed before his death derived its validity and its claim to be preached by them. Therefore they bore witness that it was Almighty God who had raised Jesus from the dead, as he had wrought miracles through him during his life on earth.

Equally radical and new compared with current Jewish beliefs was the Christians' conviction that Jesus was the true and promised Messiah. This was proved to the apostles by his resurrection. And their preaching expressed this belief that Jesus was "the Christ," they preached "the Gospel of Jesus Christ" (Acts 5:42); and it was "Jesus Christ" who healed through the apostles (Acts 9:34). Because Jesus was Messiah, he was also called "Kyrios" (Lord), as properly as to God (Acts 2:36; 1:21; 7:59; 9:1, 10ff., 42; 11:17). Several other titles used in the earliest Church place the risen Jesus close to God as well: judge of the living and the dead, the "Holy and Righteous One," the "Servant of God," and finally the *Sotēr,* the Savior called by God to bring salvation to men (Acts 5:31). The tidings of this salvation were called the Evangelium (the Gospel or Good News) and its proclamation "evangelism."

The first Christians' belief in salvation through Jesus Christ was expressed in the most exclusive terms: "...there is salvation in no one else, for there is no other name under heaven given among men by which we must be saved" (Acts 4:12). Only the grace of the Lord could save. The Gospel showed the way; one might either accept or reject it.

The reception of the Holy Spirit was confirmation for the primitive Church that salvation had already begun for its members. After the first Pentecost in the Church the descent of the Spirit was continually repeated in the life of the Church. The Spirit was effective in the individual believer and in causing the missionary zeal of the apostles and other messengers of the Gospel. They were "filled with the Holy Spirit," and therefore they stepped forth boldly.

Other gifts which redemption by Jesus Christ brought to the faithful were (eternal) life and membership in the kingdom of God. The kingdom theme constantly recurs in the preaching of the apostles, just as after the resurrection it was a subject of Jesus' conversations with them. The kingdom and eternal life were not yet fully realized; that would come only when the Lord came again, and therefore they were filled with an ardent hope in the approaching *parousia* of their master. That alone would bring about the restitution of all things, but they believed the final age had already begun.

The religious life of the community was based upon these and similar convictions. Its members lived wholly in the presence of its risen and living Lord, but they did not therefore feel they had to give up their inherited forms of piety. At first they attended prayers in the Temple, the Jewish hours of prayer, and so forth, though there was by no means a universal mind in the primitive Church respecting the binding character of the Old Law, as the discussions at the apostolic Council reveal. But there was no complete break in the primitive Church from the liturgical practices of Palestinian Jewry.

Certain tendencies are observable, however, which were later to lead to independent forms of piety and ritual. Such a new liturgical act was baptism, the basis of membership in the community. And this was not just the taking over of the baptism of John, for it was unequivocally done "in the name of Jesus Christ, for the forgiveness of your sins" (Acts 2:38). Jesus as a person was at the center of the liturgical act. From Jesus baptism got its supernatural efficacy: forgiveness of sins and entry into the community of the faithful. Reception of the Holy Spirit was also bound up with baptism, though the latter was prerequisite to the former.

According to the Acts, the Jerusalem Christians persevered in the breaking of the bread (2:42), probably already a technical term for the eucharistic celebration (cf. 1 Cor 10:16). And this they did now on the first day of the week (Acts 20:7), as opposed to the Sabbath. Sunday was chosen in commemoration of the day on which the Lord rose.

The Christians also chose different fast days from Judaism's, in this case Friday, in honor of the Lord's death, and Wednesday.

James (5:14ff.) also speaks of an anointing of the sick by the elders (the presbyteroi).

The whole religious attitude of the primitive Church was rooted in a courageous enthusiasm, prepared for sacrifice, which manifested itself above all in works of active charity (Acts 4:32). The brotherly love engendered by the enthusiasm of the new faith made the individual believer easily and gladly renounce his private property in order to help the poor of the community. Such enthusiasm was nourished doubtless by the strong expectation of the *parousia.* This generous indifference to the goods of this world which it brought made them inwardly free, unselfish, and thus capable of great deeds. This moral and religious strength, born of the faith and the eschatological outlook of the primitive Church, also gave its members the strength not to give up when the *parousia* failed to arrive, but instead, to open the way for Christianity into a greater future.

Section Two

The Way into the Pagan World

CHAPTER 4

The Religious Situation in the Graeco-Roman World at the Time of Its Encounter with Christianity

In contrast with the political and cultural unity which prevailed in the Mediterranean area at the beginning of the Christian era, we are presented in the religious sphere, with a multiplicity of religions. In all her political conquests Rome had never sought to impose on subject peoples a single religious faith and a single form of worship, rather it was a principle of Roman policy to leave undisturbed all the religious convictions and practices of the tribes and nations included in the empire.

Decline of the Ancient Greek and Roman Religions

In the Hellenistic world of the first century B.C.E., both ancient Greek polytheism and the old Roman religion were in decline. The causes for this development are various and differ for each. In Greece itself, rationalistic criticism of the gods, which had prevailed in the philosophical schools, and especially among Stoics and Epicureans, had had an adverse effect on traditional beliefs. Political developments in the eastern Mediterranean area also played their parts in furthering the decline of the classical Greek religion. With the dissolution of the city-states and their cults, and with the emigrations to the commercially viable new Hellenistic cities of the East, many of the homeland's ancient sanctuaries fell into ruin. More important however was the exchange of religious ideas and forms of liturgical expression with the eastern religions, an exchange which was brought about by the hellenization of the East and in which the gods of Greece and the Orient were to a great extent assimilated to each other but lost many of their original attributes in the process. As the Greek forms spread with the process of hellenization, however, the spirit of the old religion was now missing from them. On the other hand, the oriental cults streamed westward with greater influence and new forms.

Ancient Roman religion underwent dissolution too. Since the Second Punic War there had been a steadily increasing hellenization of Roman religion, promoted very largely through the direct influence of Greek literature on the beginnings of Latin literature. And when toward the end of the Second Punic War the Sibylline books demanded the introduction of the cult of Cybele from Asia Minor, the eastern religions began their ultimately triumphal invasion of Rome and Italy. The cults of Mithras, of the Cappadocian Bellona and of the Egyptian Isis arrived, and Hellenistic philosophies, like Stoicism with its critical stance vis-à-vis the gods and its deterministic world view also appeared. The concomitant skepticism toward belief in the gods which infected the leading classes and filtered down into private family religion, was destructive of the religious spirit. Even Augustus' attempt to halt the disintegration of the Roman religion could do nothing more than to reinstate the external trappings. The lack of deep religiosity could not even be touched by Augustus' assuming (in 12 B.C.E.) the title *pontifex maximus*.

The Emperor Cult

One feature of Augustus' religious policy was to have far-reaching consequences and to be of real significance when it encountered the growing power of Christianity, namely, the adoption of the oriental cult of the ruler and the attempt to include it in his reorganization of the State religion under the modified form of the emperor cult. Religious veneration of the ruler had its origin in the East, where royal power was early regarded as having a religious basis. Alexander and his successors were able to build on this foundation when they added to it elements of Greek hero cult and Stoic ideas about the superiority of the wise man, and thus succeeded in introducing the religious cult of Hellenistic kingship, which flourished in the Near East and Egypt particularly. Such Hellenistic sovereigns received from the Greek cities of Asia Minor, in return for favors and benefits, titles like *Sotēr, Epiphanes,* and *Kyrios.* The idea increasingly prevailed that in the reigning king God visibly manifested himself. And when Rome supplanted the kingdoms of the Near Eastern *diadochi,* it was probably natural to transfer the titles and religious honors to the de facto rulers. And since Rome had no monarch, it was to *Roma* herself to whom the honors were paid. It was easy enough then for Augustus to take advantage of the situation in the East and to have shrines and temples set up to himself alongside those of Roma and not to refuse religious honors to himself. And, because of the *pax Augusta,* he found willingness to grant him these honors, for he was immensely popular.

In Rome and Italy, however, the cult of the ruler had to be introduced more discreetly. There the Senate decided only after the emperor's death whether *consecratio,* inclusion among the gods, should be accorded him for his services to the State. Private citizens were to sacrifice to the *genius* of the emperor in their houses, for in him the divine was made manifest; men swore by the *genius* of the emperor, and breaking such an oath was tantamount to high treason.

During the course of the first century C.E., some emperors cast aside Augustus' restraints and sought divine honors during their lifetimes, irrespective of whether their ways of life and their performances as rulers recommended them for deification, all of which had the effect of cheapening the emperor cult in Rome. However, since the emperor cult was intimately linked with the power of the State, special importance was attached to it when Christianity, which rejected every form of divine honors paid any man, sooner or later came into conflict with the State.

The Eastern Mystery Cults

While the cult of the emperor as part of the State religion was becoming of universal significance both in East and West, though graduated in intensity in different parts of the empire, the oriental mystery-cults always retained their original private character, albeit their influence on all classes was considerable. The chief reason for their attraction lay in their claim to give the individual a liberating answer to one's questions about his or her fate in the next world. They claimed to show the person how, by ordering one's way of life in this world, one could assure one's survival in the next, that is, how one could find one's eternal salvation.

Alexander the Great's campaigns allowed the oriental mystery-cults to begin their conquest in the East. It was the Greeks on the coast of Asia Minor who were both vulnerable to these cults and who were their principal transporters to the West. These cults were syncretistic in both worship and theology, adopting and adapting elements of existing religious systems. The three oriental civilizations that were sources from which the new cults flowed into the Hellenistic world were those of Egypt, Asia Minor and Syria, to which may be added that of Iran, which produced the cult of Mithras.

The Egyptian goddess Isis and her consort Osiris were Egypt's most important contributions. Isis, after generations of development, had become a universal goddess who was believed to have brought morality and civilization to mankind and who was thought to be a benefactress to all mankind. Osiris, her husband, was the ancient Egyptian god of vegetation whose annual dying and rising again was symbolized in the planting and harvesting of crops. In his dying, man saw his own death expressed; in Osiris' rising again to new life, man hoped for his own rising to new life. That was the basic idea of these mysteries: individual salvation to life beyond this world.

During the Ptolemaic period Osiris was pushed into the background by a new god created by Ptolemy I called Sarapis (Serapis), whose purpose was to unite the Egyptians and Greeks of Ptolemy's kingdom. Sarapis too was associated with Isis as a god of life and death, earth-god and sun-god, whose role among men was that of sublime benefactor. Sarapis tended to incorporate all other gods into himself in the monotheistic tendencies of his cult exemplified in the exclamation: "One is Zeus and Hades and Helios, one is Sarapis."

Asia Minor was home to the cult of the Great Mother, the fertility goddess Cybele, who was early known to the Greeks and who was even introduced into Rome by 204 B.C.E. She too was associated with a male divinity, Attis, who also was involved in dying and rising again. And as salvation came to the god, so also will the believer be saved. This promise of salvation was the most powerful motive for joining the cult. Similarly the cult of Atargatis and her husband, Adonis, whose role was also that of a dying and rising-again vegetation deity, was an equally appealing offering from Byblos on the Syrian coast. The symbolism of these cults, with their preoccupation with death and their prospect of a rejuvenating resurrection, were able to attract many people in the later Hellenistic period. In common they had a basic idea: the death and constant renewal observed in nature were symbolically crystallized in the myth of a young god of vegetation, who is torn from the side of the goddess by a tragic death but rises again to new life. This was taken to represent the fate of man, upon whom in Antiquity death weighed heavily. For man too there would be, as there was for the god in the myth, a resurrection into a mysterious hereafter. This hope held out by these cults of a felicitous afterlife was precisely their attraction, for the religions of Greece and Rome had no parallels for it.

Mithraism, Iran's contribution to these mystery religions, also came to be dominated by the notion of a future life, but not, chronologically, until after Christianity was well established. Mithraism had its greatest successes in and around Rome and on the northwestern frontiers of the Rhineland. It was essentially a masculine cult and found most of its devotees among the soldiers of the Roman army. Its central myth involved the Persian god Mithras' slaying a bull and thus the initiate was united with his salvation in the next world through a *taurobolium,* the sacrifice of a bull and being sprinkled with its blood. Initiation involved undergoing various tests of courage and ritual washings, and eventually as an initiate passing through seven grades toward becoming a full disciple of Mithras. As Mithras was taken up by Helios the sun-god in his chariot, so too might his devotees hope to be raised up in the next world. Members of the cult were also united in a sacred meal, which prefigured, to those who partook of it, a happy life together in the hereafter.

We have no precise data on the numbers of devotees of all these cults. We may suppose, from their expansion in the Hellenistic world and their relative density in the larger urban centers, that their numbers were considerable. Probably least represented were the educated upper classes who sought fulfillment of their religious needs among the philosophical schools of the time. It was the middle classes which were most appealed to by the mysteries.

Popular Religion

The great mass of simple folk, however, found neither the emperor cult nor the esoteric mysteries appealing, and they turned in great numbers to various superstitions prevalent in the age.

Chief among these was astrology, which ascribed to the stars a decisive influence on human destiny. A strategic factor in its appeal was the fact that it found an ally in Stoic philosophy, which saw in astrology a confirmation of its doctrine that all things in this world were determined by the laws of destiny. And when Poseidonios managed to give to astrology the aura of a scientific system, the superstition managed to attract for its views the emperors Tiberius, Marcus Aurelius, and Septimus Severus. In an almost slavish fear people were consulting the stars before undertaking great or even trivial actions. The fatalism of astrology had, as every determinism must have, a deleterious effect upon the relationship of man and his gods, for if life was inevitably subject to the fatal power of the stars, there was no point in praying to the gods.

Magic offered a way of escape from the iron compulsion of astrological fate. It undertook by secret practices to bring into the service of man both the power of the stars and all the good and evil forces of the universe. The magical books of antiquity and the numerous extant magical papyri give an instructive glimpse into that world in which primitive human instincts, fear of the obscure and incomprehensible in nature and in human events, hatred of fellow-men, delight in sensation, the thrill of the uncanny all find unrestrained expression. Belief in magic presupposed also belief in demons and spirits, which belief had permeated the entire Hellenistic world from the fourth century B.C.E. onward. Magic was the way to hold in check the ever-increasing numbers of demons who could harm man, but for the magic to be effective one needed first of all to know the demons secret name and employ the prescribed formula exactly, however senseless its text might appear.

The professional magician, who was master of this secret science, could produce any desired effect in the view of the devotee. And the influence of such magic was supported and confirmed by certain philosophical schools, such as neo-Pythagoreanism and neo-Platonism, both of which, with their highly developed doctrines of demons, contributed largely to the demonization of Hellenistic religion. Even Judaism had a contributory role here (Acts 8:9–13).

Connected with magic were the belief in the secret meaning of dreams and the art of interpreting them which subsequently developed. And this phenomenon continued the tradition of consulting oracles. But now it was not just oracles like the famous Delphic oracle, but other oracles developed even greater followings.

Finally, belief in miracles, so powerfully characteristic of the Hellenistic period, belonged primarily to popular religion even though it was shared by many among the educated classes. The miracle most ardently prayed for was the restoration of lost health, and this involved prayer to Asclepios, the great physician and "savior of all." Temples to this god proliferated everywhere, and the emperor Julian "the apostate" sought to set Asclepios up as savior over against the Christians' Savior in the fourth century. And the Church warred against soteriological claims made for Asclepios from the New Testament right through to the fourth century.

When one considers the general religious situation in the Hellenistic world at the beginning of the Christian era, it is clear the Church's missionaries faced a daunting task. The cult of the emperor was bound to prove a great obstacle for many reasons, not least among which was the machinery of repression the State could muster in the event of Christian attacks on the State's cult. Not only did that inhibit the prospects of the Church's acceptance, but so did the general licentiousness of the oriental mystery cults, some of which had orgiastic features. It was a religiously superficial civilization altogether, and its bold and disrespectful criticism of the older religions' gods tended to undermine all reverence for what was sacred.

In opposition to these negative tendencies, however, there were also some positive features in the general picture of Hellenistic religion which could be used as starting-points for preaching the new faith. A feeling of emptiness had undeniably found roots among many reflective and thoughtful men brought about through the failures of the ancient religions. It would not be too difficult to fill that void with a message of lofty moral ideals. Certain features of the mystery cults too exhibit the presence of a deep hunger for redemption among the men of the time, and there was an appeal in the message of eternal salvation offered by a Savior who, stripped of all earthly greatness, was for that very reason superior to one who would bring salvation only in this world. Finally, the strong tendency toward monotheism which was so apparent in the Hellenistic religions, provided Christian missionaries with an ideal bridgehead in the pagan lands, for the peoples of which — as for the Jews — "the fullness of time was come" (Gal 4:4).

CHAPTER 5

The Apostle Paul and the Structure of the Pauline Congregations

Only through a series of shocks could Jewish Christianity abandon their Israelites' sense of being God's chosen people and arrive at the knowledge that they were under an obligation to carry the Gospel into the Gentile world as well. The question catapulted into their purview when Peter baptized the pagan captain Cornelius of Caesarea and his family (Acts 10:1–11:18). For this act Peter was called to account by his community, and only his being able to allude to a direct command from God in a vision was able to reconcile the disturbed Jewish Christians to his action. And even then there was no immediate increase in missionary activity among the Gentiles.

The real impulse for such activity came from a group of Hellenistic Jewish Christians from Cyprus and Cyrenaica who had had to leave Jerusalem after the death of Stephen and had first settled in Antioch. Here they evangelized the Greeks as well as Jews (Acts 11:19ff.) with much success. This successful mission caused the Jerusalem congregation to send Barnabas, a former levite and a Cypriot of the Jewish Diaspora, to Antioch to appraise the situation. Barnabas approved the reception of the Greeks and had the discernment to see that the courage and spirit of Paul (or Saul) of Tarsus were needed for preaching Christ in that place. Paul had withdrawn to Tarsus after his own conversion to Christ, and there Barnabas sought him out and persuaded him to join him in the Syrian city. After the development of the congregation at Antioch, its members were there first given the name "Christians" (Acts 11:22–26).

The Religious History of the Apostle Paul

Paul too was from the Diaspora; his birthplace was Tarsus in Cilicia, where like his father Paul worked as a saddler. His father already possessed hereditary Roman citizenship, which Paul was to invoke later when on trial before the Roman governor. Growing up in Tarsus, a good-sized city on a trade route, Paul knew Hellenistic culture intimately, and he spoke Greek *Koinē,* the common tongue of the Mediterranean region as fluently as his native Aramaic. His family had remained true to the convictions and traditions of Judaism, even of the stricter Pharisaic observance of the Law.

Probably it was after Jesus' death that Paul went to Jerusalem to study at the school of the Pharisee Gamaliel (Acts 22:3). When the disciples of Jesus began to attract the attention of the Jewish authorities, Paul joined zealously in persecuting them (Acts 7:58; 8:3). As he says, "I persecuted the Church of God violently and tried to destroy it ... " (Gal 1:13f.; cf. 1 Cor 15:9).

The sudden transformation from persecutor to ardent disciple in Paul (Acts 9:3–18; 22:3–16; 26:12–30) was brought about by a direct apparition of Jesus which Paul encountered en route to Damascus to persecute Christians there. Paul refers to this event only in restrained terms in his letters (Gal 1:15; 1 Cor 15:9; Phil 3:4), but he makes it clear that in the apparition of the Lord he saw the supernatural call of grace that, by calling him to be an apostle, which he was never to give up and in which he was never to falter. His message became "Jesus is the Messiah and the Son of God" (Acts 9:20–29), and he was certain that he was to concern himself with the pagan world which, no less than the Jews, could find its salvation only in Jesus Christ (Gal 1:16; Rom 15:15f.).

The Mission of Paul

Once convinced he was called to preach to the Gentiles, the entire Roman Empire presented itself as Paul's appointed mission field. Paul worked from a plan on his missionary journeys. For his first missionary period, up to the Apostolic Council in Jerusalem, his base was Syrian Antioch, and his companions were Barnabas and the latter's kinsman, John Mark.

In the Acts, we see that the starting-points for Paul's missionary work were the synagogues of the cities in the Mediterranean provinces. There were to be found the Diaspora Jews and former pagans who had joined the Jewish community as proselytes or "God-fearing ones." Beginning in Salamis on Cyprus and then moving on to the cities of mainland Asia Minor, Paul's preaching was addressed both to Diaspora Jew and to pagan proselyte, and it is clear that his message found both acceptance and rejection in both groups.

The Acts leave us no room to doubt that the majority of the Diaspora Jews rejected Paul's message. In many places it caused excited discussions which occasionally turned into tumults, in the course of which the missionaries were driven out and sometimes mishandled. Setting a pattern for subsequent persecutions, the initiative on these occasions lay with the Jews who occasionally goaded their pagan fellow-citizens into using violence. Nevertheless Paul's and the others' preaching did find some receptive auditors, especially among the "God-fearers" and proselytes, and in most cities visited on this first missionary journey, congregations arose, to which suitable leaders were appointed. These congregations then did further missionary work among the Gentiles, as Paul had intended. Paul's practice was not to stay too long in one place, but to get the message started and then to turn it over to the new local disciples.

In conformity to his own conviction that belief in Christ implied the end of obligations under the Old Law, Paul imposed neither circumcision nor the ritual law on his new converts. This freedom from the Law for new converts, a central part of his message, brought him into sharp conflict with the so-called Judaizers, the extreme wing of Palestinian Jewish Christians for whom circumcision was sine qua non for salvation (Acts 15:1–5). This dispute was decided in Paul's favor by the Apostolic Council, but the issue plagued his ministry for a long time.

The dispute began at Antioch, when "some from Judaea" demanded circumcision of the Gentile Christians in the local congregation. Paul and Barnabas were sent to Jerusalem for consultations, the result of which led to the recognition in principle of the Pauline thesis that the Mosaic Law could have no binding force for Gentile Christians, and so the independence of Paul's mission was acknowledged by the original apostles. Paul simultaneously took up a collection among his Gentile congregations for the poor in Jerusalem, symbolically testifying thereby to the bond between Gentile and Jewish Christians (Gal 2:1–10).

Despite the decision of the Council to impose nothing additional on newly converted pagans, James proposed that they "abstain from things sacrificed to idols and from blood and from things strangled and from fornication" (Acts 15:28f.). And Peter, visiting Antioch felt himself, under constraint of the Judaizers, unwilling to take part in the communal meals there, thus disparaging the authenticity of the Gentile Christians. That led to the severe attack of Paul upon his behavior mentioned in Galatians 2.

The second phase of Paul's missionary work took him into the provinces of Macedonia, Achaea, and proconsular Asia, that is, into the very center of Hellenistic civilization. On this journey, Paul's companions in mission were Silas and Timothy. Congregations at Galatia, Philippi, and Corinth among others were established, the one at Corinth being predominantly Gentile in membership. Corinth became one of Paul's main centers, for he worked there for about eighteen months in the years 51–52 or 52–53 C.E. (Acts 18:12–17).

Paul then moved on to Ephesus, which was to become the center of missionary work on the west coast of Asia Minor, beginning in 54 C.E.. Paul's work at Ephesus was successful, but also was fraught with difficulties as well, and this time they were initiated by Gentiles as well as Jews (as when Demetrius, owner of a business that made small silver models of the local temple of Diana, seeing his profits threatened by Paul's preaching, staged a demonstration against the missionaries). It was from Ephesus that Paul sent letters to Galatia's congregation and also 1 Corinthians, to continue to show his pastoral concerns for his congregations. In 57 he departed for Macedonia and Greece visiting Philippi and, for a few months, Corinth again. From Corinth came his letter to the Romans which signals his desire to go on beyond to Spain.

Upon his return to Jerusalem Paul's missionary work in its familiar form came to an end, for he was attacked by Diaspora Jews in the Temple and only escaped with his life by being taken into protective custody by the Roman guard, who sent him to the governor at Caesarea (Acts 21:27–23:35), from whence he was transferred to Rome (Acts 27–28) because Paul, to avoid trial before the Jewish Sanhedrin, had exercised his right by Roman citizenship to appeal to the emperor. As the lenient conditions of his custody in Rome permitted intercourse with the outside world, Paul resumed his missionary activities in a different form, addressing representatives of the Jewish community of Rome, some of whom converted, some of whom rejected his message. With the statement that "this salvation of God has been sent to the Gentiles; they will listen" (Acts 28:28), Luke ends the final message of Paul in the Acts. And with it his goal is met, namely, describing how the Gospel made its way from Jerusalem to the Roman capital.

The Acts are silent about subsequent events of Paul's life. There is evidence that his trial ended in his acquittal and that he afterward carried out his planned journey to Spain and also visited the Hellenistic East once more. This hypothesis alone can explain the Pastoral Epistles, which tell of events and situations which can only be fitted into such a final period of his life. On this last missionary journey, Paul was especially concerned with giving directions for the organization of his congregations and with warning them against false doctrines. A second imprisonment led to his martyrdom during the reign of Nero, although it cannot with certainty be attributed to the actual Neronian persecution.

Organization of the Pauline Congregations

It is impossible from the sources we have available to give an adequate account of the organization or "constitution" of the Pauline congregations. What we get are not descriptions of principles or a complete system, but rather only matters related to special situations. Nevertheless, even these occasional utterances make it quite clear that an organization existed which regulated and established the congregations' religious life. And it is a special kind of organization, resting on a supernatural foundation, the same as that on which the Church herself is based, her Lord, who guides his Church through his Holy Spirit, the same Spirit who had caused the Church to grow (Acts 2:47; 6:7), had directed Paul's missionary travels (Acts 16:9; 19:21) and crowned his work with success (Acts 19:11; 1 Cor 2:3ff.; Rom 15:17ff.), also created this organization for the life of the community (1 Cor 3:9ff.; 2 Cor 12:19; Eph 4:12–16). To be called for a special task in the Church meant being called by the Holy Spirit, which meant also being in the service of the Lord and needing to fulfill those tasks in and for the community in a spirit of love (Mark 10:42–45). This organization was willingly accepted by the congregations and not felt to be in opposition to the free working of the Spirit in those charismatically gifted, for it was the same Spirit who called all.

In the organization of the congregations, their founder Paul occupied a unique place, ultimately based upon his direct vocation to be the apostle of the Gentiles. Paul was for all his congregations not only the highest teaching authority but also the chief judge and lawgiver, the apex of a hierarchical order, for no matter how unworthy he himself might feel himself to be, he nevertheless clearly felt he had authority and power for the edification of his congregations.

In each congregation, other men were called into this hierarchical order for specific tasks, care for the poor and the conducting of religious worship. Commensurate with their responsibilities was their authority, to which Paul admonished his congregations to be submissive (1 Cor 16:15f.; 1 Thess 5:12; Rom 12:6ff.). Paul placed his own considerable authority behind theirs too, though it is clear that their authority was subordinate to his. Those entrusted with such duties were called presbyters or elders (Acts 14:23), whom Paul ordained with laying on of hands and prayer. To the elders at Ephesus Paul also said they were *episkopoi/* overseers, but it seems obvious that that was another name for elders. In Philippians, deacons are mentioned as well as overseers, and in the later Pastoral Epistles it is clear that the sphere of activities allotted to them is distinct from that of the presbyters and episcopoi (1 Tim 1:1–10; 5:17, 19; Tit 1:5–11). All of these offices were attached to the local congregations; none of their holders held sway over other congregations, as Paul and his fellow-missionaries had done. Their vocations can only be understood as permanent callings if the work begun by Paul in each place was to endure.

Besides these offices with authority, there were in the Pauline congregations the charismatically gifted, whose functions were essentially different. Their gifts, above all prophecy and the gift of tongues (glossolalia), come directly from the Holy Spirit; these gifts were not permanently attached to people and were not essential for the existence of the community. Their function was fundamentally to keep alive the lofty enthusiasm of the new faith; they were not guardians and guarantors of order. At times these charismatic gifts were deleterious of order, as Paul notes in 1 Corinthians 14.

Finally, it was an essential feature of the structure of the congregations established by Paul that they not regard themselves as independent communities free to go their own individual religious ways. Paul, a bond among the congregations in and of himself, also taught his converts one Lord, one faith, one baptism, one God and Father of us all; he also emphasized the debt owed the Jerusalem Church which resulted in the collection he took for the poor in that city's congregation. The unity of the Church — both of Jewish and of Gentile backgrounds — was one of Paul's important achievements.

Religious Life in the Pauline Congregations

The religious life of the Pauline congregations was centered on belief in the risen Lord, which gave a decisive character both to worship and to its everyday life. Christ stands and must stand in the center of Paul's preaching. "If you confess with your lips that Jesus is Lord and believe in your heart that God raised him from the dead, you will be saved" (Rom 10:9). This belief in the Kyrios, the Lord raised up and glorified after the humiliation of the Cross (cf. Phil. 2:5–11), included the conviction that in him dwelt the fullness of deity (Col 2:9f.), that he therefore as Son of God possessed the divine nature together with the Father and was himself "the power and the wisdom of God" (1 Cor 1:24).

Admission to the community of the faithful was by baptism which, far from being a merely external act, made effective the death of Jesus, which he endured for our sins (1 Cor 15:3), through its standing in real relationship to Christ's death on the Cross and to his resurrection. Only because the Christian is buried with Christ and so lets his former self ("the old man") die, does he, like Christ, rise from the dead to new life (Rom 6:2–8); through baptism alone can he win a share in salvation, can one be "born again."

The congregations met for worship on the first day of the week (Acts 20:7) That choice of days, not the Sabbath, signaled a beginning departure from Judaism. Their communal act of worship took place in the private houses of members (1 Cor 16:19; Rom 16:4; Col 4:15) and began with songs of praise, hymns and psalms of thanksgiving (Eph 5:18ff.; Col 3;16).

The central point and the climax of the service was the eucharistic celebration, the Lord's Supper. Paul's letters give us little information concerning how it was conducted, though it apparently had its context in a meal (1 Cor 11:17–27). Paul clearly tried to impart a deeper theological understanding of the eucharistic act. The "breaking of bread" is presented as a real participation in the body and blood of the Lord (1 Cor 10:16–21). And because the body and blood of the Lord are truly received in the bread and wine, whoever partakes unworthily in this fraternal eating and drinking makes himself guilty of betraying the Lord (1 Cor 11:27). Because participation in this meal confirmed to the believer again and again his direct bond with the heavenly Lord, the congregation was filled with joy and thanksgiving (Eph 5:20); it was a pledge of the final consummation his second coming would bring about. Hence the cry at the Eucharist: *"Marana-tha —* Come, Lord Jesus!" (1 Cor 16:22; Rev 22:30). This was the sacrament of unity: as all members had a share in the same bread, which was the body of Christ, all of them formed one body, the community of God (1 Cor 10:17).

"Salvation was preached" also in the assembled congregation, and not just by traveling missionaries (Acts 20:7–11; 1 Cor 1:17; 9:16f.), but also by the congregations' permanent officers (2 Cor 5:18–21) the message of reconciliation with God was heard (Acts 14:22; 1 Thess 2:2–12; 2 Cor 6:1–2; Phil 2:1–11). Finally, there were the speeches of the "prophets" in the worship.

The realization of the new religious ideal confronted the Gentile Christians of Paul's congregations with no inconsiderable difficulties. Unlike life in Jerusalem with its tradition of monotheism and the Jewish moral law which had set the stage for the Christians, the surrounding pagan world, with its customs deeply rooted in family and business life, was often wholly antithetical to the demands of the Christian faith, and the Gentile Christians had to struggle to remain faithful. That some lapsed may be inferred from Paul's reiterated admonitions, but many must have managed it anyway. And the strongest proof of the general success of the Pauline mission is to be seen in the continuance of his congregations in post-apostolic times and later.

C H A P T E R   6

Peter's Missionary Activity
and His Sojourn and Death in Rome

Extra-Pauline Gentile Christianity

Compared with Paul's successful mission, the work of the other apostles in the eastern or western parts of the empire is less easy to follow. Paul himself witness to the existence of such activity when he disavows any intention of preaching Christ where someone else has already made him known (Rom 15:19–20). Acts refers only casually to extra-Pauline missions (as, e.g., when Barnabas, after departing from Paul, goes off to Cyprus for missionary work; 15:40). Elsewhere the existence of a Christian congregation at Puteoli in Italy near Naples is taken for granted when Acts reports that Paul met "brethren" at the port who invited him to stay with them (28:14). Members of the Roman congregation came out to meet him (Acts 28:15); the name of the original Roman missionary is never mentioned. Similarly there is evidence in the opening of Peter's first letter which refers to extra-Pauline mission fields, when mention is made of Pontus, Cappadocia, and Bithynia as having congregations.

The fragmentary nature of our sources for the history of early Christianity is especially apparent when one inquires about the labors or even the lives of the other apostles (with the exceptions of Peter, John, and James the Younger). The sources are silent in respect of their lives and missions until the second and third centuries when the so-called apocryphal acts of the apostles seek to fill in these lacunae with fanciful tales incapable of being checked historically.

Sojourn and Death of the Apostle Peter in Rome

The route Peter followed to Rome, the time of his arrival in the imperial capital and the length of his stay (perhaps with interruptions) are matters upon which we have no definite information. It is certain that Peter was at the Council of Jerusalem about the middle of the century and that shortly afterward he was staying in Antioch (Acts 15:7; Gal 2:11–14.).

The basis of the Roman tradition concerning Peter is formed by three pieces of evidence, chronologically close to one another and forming together a statement so positive as practically to amount to historical certainty. The first is of Roman origin and is to be found in a letter written to the Corinthian Church in the name of his congregation by Clement. In it Clement speaks of those who at Rome had recently suffered and died for their faith, and among them, Peter and Paul stand out (1 Clem 5:1–4; 6:1–2). His evidence points to the Neronian persecution datable to the mid-sixties.

Corroboration of the essential part of this evidence comes in a letter to the Romans, written about twenty years later, from the East by Ignatius of Antioch, bishop of the Gentile community that possessed the most traditions and was most likely to be informed about the careers of the two leading apostles. In his letter (*Rom.* 4, 3) Ignatius implores the Roman congregation not to rob him of his martyr's crown which he expects to receive thereby interceding with the pagan authorities. Then he gives this respectful qualifier: "I do not command you as Peter and Paul did." The apostles thus stood in a special relationship to the Roman congregation, which had given them authority; that is, they had stayed and worked with the congregation for a lengthy period of time.

A third document, the *Ascensio Isaiae* (4:2–3), which in its Christian version dates to about 100 C.E., suggests that one of the Twelve will be delivered into Belial's [i.e., into Nero's] hands. This statement is illumined by another from the *Apocalypse of Peter,* from the beginning of the second century: "See, Peter, to thee have I revealed and explained all things. Go then into the city of fornication and drink the chalice that I have foretold to thee."

This text underscores the reliability of the tradition of Peter's life and work at Rome. Two additional references may be added: The last chapter of John's Gospel (21:18–19) obviously knows of Peter's martyr's death upon a cross, but is silent about where it took place. On the other hand, Rome ("Babylon") is the place of Peter's abode in the final section of I Peter.

The tradition of Peter's residence in Rome continued unchallenged through the second century and was further confirmed by evidence from the most distant regions in which Christianity had been established: e.g., by Dionysius of Corinth (Euseb., *HE* 2, 25, 8.) in the East, by Irenaeus of Lyons (*Adv. Haer.* 3, 1–3), and by Tertullian in Africa (*De praescr. haer.* 36,3). More importantly, there was no rival tradition nor any dissent from the Roman tradition raised by any contemporary voice, and this becomes a decisive factor in critical evaluation of claims made for the Roman tradition.

The Tomb of Peter

If we can be sure of Peter's last residence, we cannot be so about his place of burial and the form it took. In Rome itself, the tradition concerning the location of Peter's tomb in time became divided. There is ample evidence on the one hand that around 200 C.E. the conviction was held in Rome that Peter's tomb was on the Vatican hill, the place of his execution. The counter-tradition appeared before 258 C.E. of both Peter's and Paul's having been buried on the Via Appia under the basilica later known as St. Sebastian's, which in the fourth century was still known as the *ecclesia apostolorum.* Archaeological evidence in the form of *graffiti* shows that the intercession of both apostles was sought by contemporary visitors, so one may recognize that some at least among the Christians were convinced that here were the tombs of Peter and Paul. What is true here is that the Roman congregation of the third century no longer possessed any certain knowledge of the actual burial place of the apostles, and that this was still the situation until after Constantine's time, for he built basilicas in both locations.

Between 1940 and 1949 there were some very important archaeological ex-cavations under St. Peter's basilica. There, in a vast necropolis under the basilica, there is clear evidence that the builders of Constantine's basilica strove against great construction difficulties to orient their building on one tomb. The archaeological evidence persuaded the excavators as well that they located Peter's tomb. The assumption, however, that Peter's tomb has been located must rest upon clues, the worth of which as evidence can be variously assessed. The problems unanswered by this archaeological evidence are legion, and, since all reliable information about the place of Peter's execution and burial is lacking, the possibilities concerning it continue to remain as so many open questions. The body might have been burnt or mutilated after execution, or buried in a common grave; or the authorities might have refused to hand it over to the Christians. The difficulties have not yet been satisfactorily cleared up, and they therefore make it impossible for the present to agree with the opinion that the excavations have with certainty brought to light the tomb of Peter or its original site. They have given us much valuable information, but, lamentably, not this information. The site on the Vatican hill and that on the Via Appia remain a great riddle, to be the subject of further research in the future.

CHAPTER 7

The Christianity of the Johannine Writings

Toward the end of the first century there appears a group of Christian writings which tradition — although not univocally — early ascribed to the apostle John, son of Zebedee and younger brother of James the Elder. In these Johannine writings, which comprise a Gospel, a fairly long admonitory letter, two short letters and an apocalypse, we see a general picture which unmistakably represents a unique step in its development, in many respects more advanced than the primitive Church at Jerusalem and the Christianity of the Pauline congregations. Two features of Johannine Christianity stand out in their importance for Church history: the image of Christ, which is projected in the Fourth Gospel especially, and the image of the Church, which in the Apocalypse acquires new characteristics.

The question of the authorship of the Johannine writings has found no generally satisfactory solution, but there is much literary evidence to assume that the Gospel and the Apocalypse and the first letter of John are datable to the end of the first century, and it can be stated with a high degree of probability that they originated among the Christian communities along the west coast of Asia Minor. There, in that period, the apostle John was the outstanding figure, so even if these writings took their final form from his disciples, his spirit bears heavily upon them.

The evangelist seeks to impart to his readers, believers as well as Jews, an understanding of Christ unique in its depth and grandeur, when he proclaims him as the Logos, who had existed from all eternity, being himself divine, and who, when he took flesh, came into this world out of his preexistence. This is the content of the majestic exordium of the Gospel which serves as a prologue. There is much to support the view that the evangelist was making use of an already extant hymn to the Logos. It was not, however, the hymn of a Gnostic group in praise of John the Baptist, for John's disciples never worshipped him as the Logos. It may have originated in a Christian congregation of Asia Minor. The idea of the Logos had already found there its inalterable and specifically Christian character, which the prologue endeavors to protect from misunderstanding by the insertion of certain phrases. However widespread the Logos-idea was then in different circles — it was known even to early Greek philosophers, to Philo, for whom the Logos was a middle being between God and the world, and to the Gnostics, for whom he was a redeemer, while Jewish wisdom speculation moved in a world of ideas related to that of the Logos — the very attributes given to the Logos by John — divine essence, personal subsistence, and the Incarnation based thereon — are lacking in previous conceptions of it. The specifically Christian achievement consists in having taken over an idea already existing in many variations and in having given it an unmistakably Christian stamp.

The author of the prologue recognized with a sure instinct the significance of this Christianized idea of the Logos and, by putting it into the Fourth Gospel, he assured for it an effect that cannot easily be estimated. Whenever Jews or pagans met the Logos as presented in John's Gospel, they encountered the person of Jesus interpreted in a way that left no doubt as to his real godhead. It was a formulation that was in essential agreement with Pauline Christology, but which, by its conceptual formulation, opened the Gospel to new spheres of influence. The evangelist was deeply rooted in Jewish thought, as the Qumran texts have reemphasized, but he was able, by adapting the idea of the Logos, to create an image of Christ which, without affecting the essential uniqueness of the message of the Gospel, created fresh possibilities of missionary expansion in the Graeco-Roman world.

To this image of Christ the evangelist joins a clear consciousness of the universal mission of Christianity and of its character as a world religion. This Logos is the light of men; with him came into the world the true light "that enlightens every man" (Jn 1:9); he is the "Lamb of God, who takes away the sin of the world" (1:29); he was sent that the world might be saved through him, so that everyone that believed in him might have eternal life (3:16f.). He gave his flesh for the life of the world, and he went to his death that he might unite the scattered children of God into one community (6:51; 11:52). This image of the divine Logos, who brings light and life and therewith salvation to all mankind, is John's bequest at the end of the first century to the next generation of Christians.

Besides this concept of Christ there is also a new image of the Church in the Johannine writings. Indeed the Johannine author possessed a highly individual, deeply thought out concept of the Church which over and over again he sought to impart to his readers. John's Gospel leaves no doubt that people are received into the community of those who by faith in Jesus attain eternal life by means of a sacramental act (3:5). In baptism the Spirit that the Risen Lord sends effects a new birth and gives new divine life. The baptized form the community of believers, cleansed from all sin by the blood of Jesus (1 Jn 1:7). The "anti-Christs" are separated from their fellowship, because they do not hold steadfastly to the true faith of Christ and to brotherly love (1 Jn 2:19–20; 5:1–2; 4:2–3; 2:9–10), and so lose their divine son-ship. Only within this community does one become a partaker in the other source of that life given, as in baptism, by the Spirit, namely, the Eucharist. Participation in the eucharistic meal, at which the faithful receive the real flesh and blood of the risen Lord (Jn 6:53–58), unites them most intimately with him and with one another and strengthens the bonds of their fellowship as nothing else can.

The evangelist seeks to explain and interpret the reality of this fellowship by words and images employed by Jesus, which have always had an ecclesiological significance. The image of the one shepherd and one flock (Jn 10) illustrates above all the inner unity and compactness of the Church, but also her universality; for all people, Jews as well as Gentiles, will one day be members of her flock (11:52; 17:20ff.). The transfer to Peter of the office of shepherd will ensure the unity of the Church in the future as well. The secret inner life of the Church shines forth in the figure of the vine and its branches. Only in close and permanent attachment to the true vine, Christ, do the members of the Church possess life; only if they remain in this community do they remain also in him and are capable of bringing forth fruit.

In the evangelist's view, the Church is called to bear witness, in the midst of a hostile world, to the risen Christ and to the salvation brought by him (15:26–27). This leads to conflict with the world and so inevitably to actual martyrdom: the Church becomes a church of martyrs, and it is to this theme that the Apocalypse constantly returns (Rev. 12; 14:1–5; 13:7–10). This fellowship is strengthened by the examples of the perfect brethren who had overcome the evil one already, thus building a bridge between the earthly and the heavenly churches. This view of the perfected Church was proclaimed, as a message of hope and comfort and encouragement, to the actual Church of the late first century under Domitian's persecution. It was a great help to her whenever she was called upon to renew her steadfastness in the faith by giving concrete witness to it.

Section Three

The Post-Apostolic Age

With the death of the last apostle, the young Church lost the last leading figure who was an eye-witness to the life, death, and resurrection of the Lord. Her life and destiny were now entrusted to a new generation, one which was conscious of its unique need to perpetuate the traditions of the apostles. Thus the post-apostolic age was a direct development of what was already begun. But it was a distinct age in some ways too. The chief development in the post-apostolic age was within the Church, and our primary sources of information concerning it are the writings of the so-called Apostolic Fathers, which began to appear at this time.

One cannot speak of more penetrating theological insights or of development of the central concerns of Pauline theology here. The ongoing controversy with Judaism carried on in an intensely Jewish atmosphere such that one might at first speak of a theology of Jewish Christianity. The religious philosophy of Hellenism appears only in the works of the Apologists. Conflict with it and with Gnosticism (by now a keen rival) necessitated a further theological development and represents a new phase in the history of the early Church.

The religious practice of the post-apostolic age remained, both in the narrower sacramental sphere of baptism and Eucharist and in its daily expression in prayer and asceticism, largely that established by apostolic tradition. Only in the question of discipline did the Church seek solutions to new problems which arose from the lapses of individual Christians during times of persecution. The greatest progress probably lay in ecclesiastical organization, which gave each congregation, as a general pattern, a monarchical episcopate with clearly defined jurisdiction. At the same time there was a growth in the underlying feeling of unity among the various congregations throughout the Roman world, and they found their unity based upon the requirement of the Lord and believed that in the episcopate set up by him and based on the apostolic succession that unity was secure.

CHAPTER 8

The Conflict between Christianity and the Roman State Power

The Beginnings of the Conflict

The nascent Christian congregations were bound to attract unfavorable attention among their pagan neighbors because of their marked aversion to everything connected with pagan worship. Because for the most part the pagans showed good-natured tolerance to other religions and thus this reaction was unusual, its source is to be sought within the Christian faith itself. Ultimately it lay in the claim to absolute truth of an exclusive sort such as could not be tolerant toward any other religion and brought it into a conflict of principles with the Roman State religion. The Christians' view of God as one and as truth and alone as redeemer of the world precluded their participating in much of classical culture, permeated as it was by religion, and thus they began to appear as enemies of culture and of the State.

This hostile atmosphere was nourished by the Jews of the Diaspora, for whom the Christians' apostasy from Judaism could not be forgiven. Christians' shunning of contact with the outside world continually provided fuel for and an appearance of credibility to dark rumors which accused them of sexual immorality in their nocturnal meetings as well as revolting practices in their religious worship. And all of this formed the soil from which grew the opinion that Christianity was peopled by riff-raff and the climate which served to make the Church vulnerable to persecution on almost any trifling occasion. Christians saw themselves as unjustly persecuted and reveal little understanding on their parts of how their opponents could see their new faith as undermining the fabric of society and of culture. As a consequence, the only accounts of the persecutions are those produced by Christian writers (e.g., Lactantius, and Eusebius of Caesarea) who gave a wholly Christian's viewpoint on the persecutions.

With the abandonment of that traditional scheme, a more objective estimate of the question has become possible which recognizes two important points: first, that it will not do to look upon every Roman emperor or provincial governor, under whose rule or administration Christians were put to death, as a man who persecuted them in blind rage solely because of their faith. The individual cases must be separately assessed. Moreover, the initiative for reprisals against the Christians did not come primarily from the State authorities; it was contrary to the principles of Roman religious policy to proceed with the power of the State against the adherents of a religious movement solely because of their beliefs. No doubt, however, the close connection between the Roman religion and the State was regarded as one of the main supports of the empire. The cult of the emperor did become an essential component of State religion, but its external forms, its ritual, developed only slowly, so that the conscious rejection of emperor worship on the part of Christians could only seldom, in the first century, have been the motive for proceedings against them by the State. Only in isolated situations did Nero and Domitian press the prerogatives of the emperor cult and thus provoke conflicts, but these did not affect the Christians exclusively.

The pagan State power took notice of Christianity only after disturbances occurred between Christians and Jews or pagans, and then it stepped in to control the tumults. And only then did the authorities begin to be convinced that the former religious peace was being disturbed by the Christians and that they in fact posed a threat to the customary religious policy of the empire. Then the State became aware of Christians' rejection of Roman State religion and thus, in the minds of some, jeopardized the State itself. Thus, the primary cause of the persecution of Christians lay not primarily in the pagan State power, but rather in the claim to absoluteness made by Christianity itself; a secondary cause was the hostile attitude of the pagan population. Only in the third century did the conflict between Christianity and the Roman State become one of principle, when the latter saw in the new religion a power that threatened its own existence.

The Persecutions under Nero and Domitian

It was an act of the emperor Claudius which apparently was the first instance of a Roman State authority's being concerned with Christians. According to Dio Cassius and Suetonius, Claudius expelled Jews from Rome who were continually in conflict with each other, a conflict being provoked by a man known as Chrestos. An identification of this Chrestos with Christ positively obtrudes itself, and we may here be seeing the first effects of the Christian message among the Jewish community of Rome. The married couple Aquila and Priscilla were included in the expulsion order, and they then took up residence in Corinth where, in 49–50 they gave hospitality to Paul who was preaching there. It may be assumed that the couple had already embraced Christianity, but were included in the expulsion because they were Jewish by origin. Claudius' action then is not yet clearly anti-Christian; it may have been simply to get rid of a pocket of unrest.

Thus the earliest example of Christians' being persecuted by Roman authorities remains the events under Nero after Rome burned in 64. Tacitus' account (Annals 14, 44) provides background here which is very valuable. To quell the persistent rumor that he himself was responsible for the conflagration which consumed much of the city on 16 July 64, reports Tacitus, the emperor diverted blame onto the Christian community, "who on account of their misdeeds were hated" by the people. Large numbers (*ingens multitudo*) of Christians were arrested for their "crime" and executed in the ways reserved for arsonists: some were sewn into the skins of animals and thrown to the wild dogs; others were clothed in inflammable materials and used as living torches by Nero to light his garden, which he opened to the public for the spectacle. Tacitus leaves little doubt he thought the Christians unjustly accused of arson, however worthy of death for their other presumed crimes. From this episode, we learn that the Christians at Rome in the seventh decade of the first century were many in number (*ingens multitudo*); second that Nero persecuted the Christians not because he felt them a threat to the State, but was aimed rather at individual Christians, not, as the Christian Apologists would have it, the extirpation of the religion.

The statements about a persecution made by Clement of Rome in his letter to the Corinthian congregation no doubt refer to the events under Nero. Not only Peter and Paul suffered violent deaths, but a great many others, including women. It seems unlikely, for many reasons, that the persecution under Nero was other than a local phenomenon confined to Rome, and indeed it was later condemned and declared null and void, with one exception: the proscription of the Christian name was the only *institutum Neronianum* which was not removed by his *damnatio memoriae*. In fact, Nero's action against the Christians had no legal foundation, but sprang rather from the arbitrary will of the ruler, who hoped thereby to cleanse himself from suspicion in the matter of the arson. From that time on, however, in the mind of the people, to be a Christian meant living under suspicion of all sorts of dark crimes. It also meant being an outlaw in the eyes of the people, thanks to the name Christian's being proscribed.

We know far less about the persecution under the emperor Domitian. From Dio Cassius' report (67, 14, 1–2), we can ascertain that the charge was godlessness and thus the *crimen laesae majestatis,* which makes intelligible the motive behind Domitian's action: it was the emperor's claim to absoluteness for his own person, expressed in the demands of a cult that knew no limitations. This account also accords well with that in Revelation, where the clash is between emperor worship on Domitian's pattern and the Christian idea of God. In the eastern provinces of Asia Minor, where the imperial cultus flourished, this conflict was devastating, and the pretext for the persecution there was based solely on the accusation of *lèse-majesté* which rejection of emperor-worship involved. The numbers of casualties must have been great before the emperor Nerva stopped the persecution, but our sources give us little concrete data to report.

The Court Trials of Christians under Trajan and Hadrian

Of the legal position of the Christians during the reign of Trajan (98–117) and of the proceedings of the authorities in Asia Minor, in particular, we should know nothing had we only Christian sources to rely on. The official question addressed to the emperor by a governor of Bithynia, as to what principle he should follow in certain border-line cases when dealing with Christians, shows clearly that in that Asiatic province numerous persons were denounced to the authorities as Christians, tried and examined, and, if they remained true to their faith, executed, unless they were Roman citizens, who were, in accordance with law, transported to Rome for their cases to be heard.

The governor, Pliny, who took office in 111/112, met various situations in hearing the trials of Christians which gave rise to doubts in his mind about correct legal procedures. Pliny formulated his scruples in a few precise questions addressed to the emperor (Pliny the Younger, *Ep.* 10, 96, 97). Must the age of the accused be taken into consideration? May one grant pardon if one of them recants? Is it the name (of Christian) alone which is to be punished, even when there are no other crimes? Are only those crimes to be punished which are associated with the name of Christian? Finally, Pliny tried to suggest an answer to the emperor which would enable him to proceed with leniency: if he were indulgent toward the penitent, he might expect to win back a large number to paganism. In his letter, it is clear that Pliny is unaware of any law or State decree which might serve as a norm in proceedings against adherents of the Christian faith. His dilemma is simply this: does the mere name of Christian suffice as grounds for persecution, or must other crimes be proved?

Trajan's response makes it equally obvious that there was no general law regulating proceedings against Christians. He gives Pliny certain directives intended to ease his difficulties: Christians were not to be sought out, anonymous accusations were to be ignored. A man denounced as a Christian was to be examined; if he denied Christianity and confirmed that denial by invoking the Roman gods, he was not to be punished even if formerly he had been a Christian. But if he confessed to being a Christian and persisted in his confession, he was to be punished. The mere fact of being a Christian sufficed for condemnation.

In his rescript, Trajan gives no reasons or justification for these principles; they were clearly self-evident and familiar to the emperor as an expression of the current public opinion about the Christians. To be a Christian had become something which was not allowed. But the contradictions in the rescript are obvious: these criminals were not to be tracked down; no anonymous accusations were acceptable; and one might escape punishment by simple renunciation of the accusation's charge. In fact, great latitude was given and accepted in the rescript. In places there might be extreme persecution, in others none, depending upon the agitation among the population. But we have little information about the effects of Trajan's rescript. Only two martyrs' names have reached us which are traceable to Trajan's persecution: Simeon of Jerusalem, successor to James, and Ignatius of Antioch.

Hadrian (117–38), successor to Trajan, wrote a letter in a similar situation which is preserved by Justin Martyr in his *Apologia* (68, 5–10). Hadrian condemned, even more decisively than his predecessor, anonymous denunciations and mobs' demands for their punishment. Only when someone vouched with his name for the accusations was a Christian to be brought to trial, and only when it could be proved that the accused "had offended against the laws" was sentence to be pronounced "according to the gravity of the offence." According to Justin's interpretation of this rescript of Hadrian, it meant relief for the Christians, for they now had to violate a law. Hadrian does not give full relief however from punishment for the name, but demands proof of criminality. But this applied only to one proconsul in his own province. Another governor might well follow the maxim that the *nomen Christianum* was in itself worthy of punishment. But the evidence is that Hadrian's rescript perceptibly ameliorated the position of the Christians. No executions of Christians can with certainty be attributed to the reign of Hadrian.

The *nomen Christianum* as punishable remained the general norm throughout the rest of the second century. There were several martyrdoms under Hadrian's successor, Antoninus Pius (138–61), as evidence from Justin and the *Shepherd of Hermas* make clear. Bishop Polycarp of Smyrna's martyrdom is also datable to his reign.

We can say, then, on the basis of a survey of the persecutions of Christians from Nero to the mid-second century, that there was no general law governing the attitude of the State toward the Christians. The notion that being a Christian was incompatible with the Roman way of life arose from the hostile feelings of pagans; from this arose a quasi legal maxim which made possible authorities' punishing adherence to Christianity as a crime in itself. The persecutions that resulted were only local and sporadic and directed against individual Christians. These were sparked off by local popular disturbances, and only because of these did the authorities intervene. The number of victims was relatively small.

C H A P T E R   9

The Religious World of the Post-Apostolic Age As Mirrored in Its Writings

If one compares the letters of the New Testament with the writings of the post-apostolic age, one is immediately struck by the vast differences in form and in content between the former and the latter. The writers of the post-apostolic age saw themselves as epigones, and they took up pen to discuss the interpretation and ordering of the Christian life almost hesitantly, for they felt themselves only followers of the great apostles, whose stature they could not possibly achieve. Insofar as we can identify individual personalities among these writers, we label them "Apostolic Fathers," to express the fact that they felt themselves close in time and to the world of the apostles. The post-apostolic writings were largely nourished by the legacy of the apostles; and what they had to say was the echo and result of apostolic tradition.

The series of apostolic fathers begins with Clement of Rome, the author of a lengthy letter addressed by the Roman congregation to the Church of Corinth shortly before the end of the first century. Clement writes as a leader of the Roman congregation, although his position in the list of Roman bishops cannot be determined with certainty. The occasion of the letter was the report of a regrettable schism within the Corinthian Church, which led to the removal from office of presbyters of proved worth by a group of younger churchmen. The Roman Christians felt bound to the Corinthians by strong ties of solidarity, because of which they earnestly admonished them to restore the unity of the Church. Clement's writing reveals a man steeped in both Jewish and Hellenistic (especially Stoic) thought.

The most sharply defined figure among the apostolic fathers is Ignatius of Antioch. This bishop was condemned to be thrown to the wild beasts at Rome and was martyred there in the last years of Trajan's reign. En route to the capital he wrote seven letters, to the churches in Ephesus, Magnesia, Tralles, Rome, Philadelphia, and Smyrna, and one to Polycarp, bishop of Smyrna. The *corpus Ignatianum* was written *extempore* by a man condemned to death and under the watchful eye of his not terribly considerate jailers. These letters are not thus measured theological works, carefully considered and composed, but the outpourings of a man of courage and full of the love of Christ and a longing for martyrdom.

Polycarp, bishop of Smyrna, to whom Ignatius addressed one letter, was a prime bearer and transmitter of apostolic traditions, for, according to his pupil Irenaeus of Lyons, he had had direct contact with several of the apostles, whose eyewitness accounts of the life and teachings of the Lord he knew well. Of the numerous pastoral letters he wrote (Eusebius, *HE*, 5, 20, 6–8; 5, 24, 16), only two have been preserved, which are valuable insight into the problems a pastor found it urgent to address to the faithful of a congregation he knew.

Some among the writings of the apostolic fathers are either anonymous or apocryphal, but they are valuable sources for the religious life of the period. Chief among these is the *Didache* (The Teaching of the Apostles), which was probably written about 100 in Syria and which incorporates a Jewish work on the "two ways." Its purpose is to give new congregations in Syria a guide for the internal organization of their community life.

The so-called *Letter of Barnabas* is an unlearned man's controversy with Judaism, written about 130, in which he employs an allegorizing misunderstanding of the Old Testament basic to his polemic. His own point of view is however Jewish, despite his unfavorable view of Judaism, and he thus represents a Jewish-Christian post-apostolic theology. It is Alexandrian tradition which attributes the letter to Paul's companion; the text gives no hints at its authorship.

The Shepherd of Hermas brings the post-apostolic period to a close. According to the Muratorian fragment, Hermas was a brother of Pius, bishop of Rome (ca. 140–54). A simple believer from a Jewish-Christian background expresses himself here about his own hard lot, interwoven with the description of which are sincere, sometimes naive, pictures of the life of the Church. Troubled about the lives of many Christians, but devoid of theological or speculative interests, the author demands with great earnestness a moral reform of the Christian community. *The Shepherd* is an important source of information about the significance of penance in the life of the Church as a whole.

Finally, there are the so-called Second Letter of Clement, probably the oldest extant example of a sermon preached during a worship service around the middle of the second century, and the *Epistula Apostolorum,* a work in letter-form which purports to give words of Christ to his disciples after his resurrection and then like an apocalypse goes on to speak of the *parousia* of the Lord, of the resurrection of the body, of the last judgment, and of the missionary work of the apostles; it also utters a warning against false doctrines.

There was, in addition to these written documents, a mass of oral traditions, the so-called traditions of "the Elders" (the apostles), attested mainly by Papias and Clement of Alexandria. Papias, according to Irenaeas "a pupil John and a companion of Polycarp", zealously collected sayings from the Elders (probably the elders of the earliest Church at Jerusalem). And Clement says he copied down the oral traditions that went back to the apostles. These dealt with the doctrine of angels, the interpretation of Genesis 1, and chiliastic ideas, thus giving us another window into the nature of post-apostolic theology.

A general account of the theological principles and religious life in post-apostolic Christianity based on the apostolic fathers shows its most characteristic feature is the controversy with contemporary Judaism. The Jews' claim to be God's chosen people and sole heirs to his promises was from the start countered by the Christians' claim that the Jews' failings and apostasies now meant that the Christians were the true Israel, who had taken over the inheritance of the rejected nation.

This thesis is most strongly expressed in Pseudo-Barnabas, but it is also present in Ignatius of Antioch. The rejection of Jesus by the Jews was ultimately due to their misunderstanding of the Old Testament; they failed to see that in him the promises of the Old Law were fulfilled. The Christology of the post-apostolic age was largely characterized by messianic claims from the Old Testament for Jesus.

Whereas Barnabas' strongly anti-Judaic bias hindered his view of the soteriological significance of Christ, it was clearly seen by other post-apostolic writers. Clement of Rome and Ignatius of Antioch, for instance, both saw clearly that Jesus had shed his blood to atone for the sins of the whole world, giving us a new relationship with the Father. Anti-Jewish polemics figure in the *Didache,* although its author uses Jewish elements in his Lord's Supper liturgy. In the *Shepherd* of Hermas, this anti-Judaism even gives way to a cordiality toward Judaism, however.

The central place that the Lord gave to *prayer* in the religious life of his disciples remained unaffected in the Church of post-apostolic times. Christian prayer was still in many respects akin to that of the Jews; it still continued to employ Old Testaments forms. But a fresh note is audible in more than one of the prayers of this time — a note of victorious confidence, of buoyancy arising from the consciousness of being redeemed. Thus the Father is thanked with gladness for the new life which he has given to men in Jesus. In their hieratic restraint these texts unmistakably show their nearness to liturgical prayers as they were formulated by the bishops who conducted the eucharistic celebration. They are therefore addressed exclusively to the Father, according to the example of the Lord in his prayers. Private prayers were also quite early addressed to Jesus Christ; even Pliny (*circa* 112) knew that the Christians sang hymns to their Lord.

The sacraments were still in process of development, but their essential place in the Christian life as a whole is clear. This is especially true of the sacrament of initiation, *baptism.* The *Didache* stresses the importance of carrying out the rite properly; immersion in "living" (flowing) water is desirable, but in exceptional cases it suffices to pour water thrice over the head of the person to be baptized. More important is it that every time baptism should be administered "in the name of the Father, and of the Son, and of the Holy Spirit" — the trinitarian formula is the essential formula of baptism.

The importance of baptism was underlined by the requirement of a preparatory fast, to which both the person to be baptized and the one administering the sacrament were obliged, but in which, if possible, other members of the congregation were also to take part, for baptism concerned them all — a new member was being incorporated into the community of those who were united in belief in the Lord. In baptism Christians receive the seal of the Son of God, without which there is no salvation; only this sealing makes a man a disciple of Christ. It unites all who receive it in one Spirit, in faith and love, and it admits them into the kingdom of God, into the fellowship of the Church. This seal can indeed be broken, the gifts conveyed by baptism can be lost; therefore every baptized person has a moral obligation "to keep the seal intact."

Statements about the *Eucharist* in the writings of the post-apostolic age are rarer and more restrained. It was celebrated on the Lord's Day. The Eucharist has been given to Christians as food and drink which are above all earthly nourishment, for it gives eternal life through Jesus. Ignatius of Antioch sees the Eucharist as a bond uniting all who believe in Christ. For the individual it is an elixir of life, an antidote against death, because it nourishes life in Christ and so guarantees resurrection to eternal life. The man who excludes himself from it, because he will not confess "that it is the flesh of our Savior Jesus Christ," lives under the threat of death. Just as the Eucharist joins the individual to Christ, so it unites all the faithful among themselves, since they all partake of one flesh and one chalice at one altar. But it can effect this unity only when celebrated in the presence of the rightful bishop or his delegate. Eucharistic communion not only symbolizes the unity of the Church, it also creates it.

The outstanding feature of post-apostolic piety is its christocentricity. The will of Christ is the norm for the moral life of Christians. The Son of God himself is now the Law.

Life in Christ and the imitation of him represented an ideal toward which all indeed were to strive, but which many Christians failed to attain. The failure of such Christians faced the young Church with a problem that found its expression with some asperity in the *Shepherd* of Hermas. Most of the members of the Roman congregation had indeed remained faithful to the obligation of their baptism, and some had distinguished themselves in persecution as confessors or martyrs; but others had been unable to bear this trial. They had vacillated, full of fear, considering whether to deny or to confess, and only after lengthy hesitation had they decided to suffer for the Christian name.

Besides this lack of hope and courage in the hour of danger, Hermas saw other failings in the Roman church. Tepidity and slackness had become widespread, because the desire for possessions and riches had seduced many from the practice of religion, and they lived the same kind of life as the pagans; since they preferred earthly possessions to loyalty toward their Lord. Also rife among the Roman congregation was ambition and striving after the first places, with regrettable consequences for the peace and unity of the faithful.

Did there exist a possibility of atoning for such grave failings, or had the offenders finally forfeited their salvation? The Shepherd tells Hermas that God grants to all those who have fallen another chance to repent, for he knows to what trials man is subject on account of his frailty and the wiles of the Devil. However, if a man falls again and again, and every time wishes to atone by repentance, he is not to entertain any deceptive hopes: his salvation is in jeopardy. Hermas does not discuss the problem of the unforgivability of certain sins; but the question of repentance was already a burning one about the year 140.

C H A P T E R   1 0

The Development of the Church's Organization

In comparison with the development of theology in the post-apostolic age, progress in completing the ecclesiastical organization in that period was far more extensive and significant. The links which bound the constitution of the post-apostolic Church to the organization of the Pauline community were still indeed apparent; but everywhere a further development from the early beginnings is observable, leading to more highly organized forms both within the individual congregation and in the Church as a whole. This fact gives the post-apostolic age of the Church a special importance.

First of all, the individual congregation is more clearly defined as regards its significance and function as part of the Church's organism. The Christians of a city were now everywhere joined together in separate congregations or local churches. This joining together of the followers of Christ in a city to form a single congregation differs markedly from the organization of contemporary Judaism in the Diaspora, which had several synagogues in the same place, several congregations but smaller groups.

There was no Christian that did not belong to such a local congregation. He joined with all his brethren in the eucharistic celebration, at which the unity of the post-apostolic congregation is most clearly apparent.

This vital, compact unity of the congregation was a possession to be constantly guarded, for it could be dangerously threatened by the tendency to disputatiousness and petty jealousy which led to divisions in the community, or by self-will in interpreting Christ's teaching. Schism and heresy were therefore regarded as the great enemies of unity in the early Church.

To the apostolic fathers, the danger of heresy was greater. It was Asiatic Christianity in particular that was exposed to danger from heretical groups in post-apostolic times. Ignatius of Antioch directed his attack against spokesmen of Docetism, who said that Christ had not possessed a real body and asserted that the Jewish Law was still valid. There was only one attitude for members of the Christian community to adopt toward them, and that was strict avoidance of all association with them and a closer drawing together of the faithful among themselves. The leaders of the Church organized the campaign against heresy with exhortations and with warnings to other congregations, almost in the same way as they would soon have to do, with all energy, in opposing Gnosticism.

According to what is perhaps the oldest document of the post-apostolic period, the letter of the church of Rome to that of Corinth, the leaders of the congregation were divided into two groups: one bore the double designation of elders (presbyters) and overseers (*episcopi*), the other was represented by the deacons (*diakonoi*). At the end of the post-apostolic age we also meet in the *Shepherd* of Hermas the two names *overseers* or *elders* for the holders of leading offices in the Church, deacons and teachers being mentioned as well. The *Didache* names only overseers and deacons, Polycarp on the other hand only elders and deacons. Only the letters of Ignatius distinguish clearly among the three offices of overseers, elders and deacons. Every congregation had only one overseer or bishop, to whom the college of elders (priests) and deacons was subordinate.

In Antioch and in Asia Minor there existed therefore in the second decade of the second century a monarchical episcopate: the government of the church was assigned to one bishop, whereas elsewhere both previously and subsequently, this development was not complete. The one office, which in apostolic times bore the double designation of episcopos or presbyter, was divided into two and the term overseer or bishop reserved exclusively for the holder of the highest office in the congregation. Soon after 150 the monarchical episcopate seems generally to have prevailed throughout the area of Christian expansion.

The apostolic fathers also partly worked out a theology of ecclesiastical offices, the authority of which is ultimately derived from God. He sent Jesus Christ, who gave the apostles the commission to proclaim the Gospel; they, in accordance with this commission, appointed overseers and deacons, whose places were to be taken at their death by other approved men who would continue their work among the faithful.

Ignatius further developed the theology of the episcopate in another direction; he was the most eloquent advocate of the complete and unconditional bond of union between bishop and congregation. The latter was one with its bishop in thought and prayer; only with him did it celebrate *agapē* and Eucharist. Its members should follow him in obedience as Christ did the Father; nothing should take place in the congregation without the bishop. Even the administration of baptism and the performance of marriage ceremonies were reserved to him. Presbyters and deacons had a share in his authority; the faithful were to obey the presbyters as the apostles, and in the deacons they were to honor the law of God. The bishop could demand such an attitude from his people only because he represented Christ to them; he who rejected the authority of the bishop was a rebel against the Lord, who was the actual if invisible bishop of every congregation.

Two factors then worked together in order that the bishop and his assistants might fulfill their official duty: the apostolic, that is, God-given origin of their authority, and guidance through the divine Spirit. Thus supported, they conducted the eucharistic celebration, presided at the *agapē,* proclaimed the true doctrine and were guarantors of the purity of the Gospel, guardians of the apostolic traditions.

The working of the Holy Spirit was not, however, limited to the leaders of the congregation; it could be felt everywhere among the faithful. Charismatic gifts were also present in post-apostolic times. As teachers, they devote themselves to the service of the poor and they have to "give thanks." But they had to prove before the congregation their claim to special gifts; for there were false prophets who did not preach the truth and were out to make money.

The congregation of post-apostolic times did not exist in isolation and self-sufficiency. It knew itself to be linked with all the others and united in one organism, through which flowed a supernatural principle of life: Christ the Lord. All the congregations together formed a new people, the universal Church, which was made manifest in every individual congregation. All nations were to recognize that Christians were "the people of God and the sheep of his pasture"; under the banner of Christ the faithful, both Jews and Gentiles, were united in one body, the Church of Christ; all who had received the seal were one in the same faith, in the same love; Christ had given his flesh for his new people. Ignatius of Antioch was the first to call this international community of the faithful "the Catholic Church," whose invisible bishop was Christ. Its catholicity was such a striking characteristic that by its presence the true Church could be recognized.

The Christian experienced the unity and catholicity of his Church in many ways in his daily life. All who travelled were welcomed with brotherly hospitality wherever there was a group of Christians. An active correspondence between one congregation and another kept alive the sense of belonging to each other. Long journeys were even undertaken in order that important questions of a religious nature might be discussed in common.

The inner unity of the universal Church was assured by other powerful ties. Christians sought to maintain religious unity by a rule of faith which, beginning with simple forms, gradually acquired more precise and definite expression; it was in essential points the same everywhere and was impressed upon all Christians at baptism. Unity of worship was established in the celebration of the Eucharist, which did indeed show local variations in form and in the text of many prayers, but which was essentially the same central act of the Christian liturgy. Unity in faith and worship was further preserved by the fact that the tradition of the Church was always the standard to be followed. With striking frequency we find the apostolic fathers, even at this early date, invoking tradition, which was looked upon as a legacy from the apostles and therefore inalterable. Unity in belief, worship and apostolic tradition could ultimately be guaranteed only by him who was their Lord and protector, Christ.

Even though the bishop's sphere of activity was his own congregation, he was not exempt from all responsibility for the Church as a whole. It was not only a feeling of solidarity with the faithful of other congregations that prompted bishops like Ignatius and Polycarp to address to them words of encouragement or rebuke; they acted thus from a sense of duty. There was, indeed, no bishop of the post-apostolic age who intervened in the affairs of other local churches with the same authority as in his own congregation, or could give instructions to the whole Church. Even Clement of Rome was too much of a background figure, as compared with the Roman church as such, to make it possible for us to attribute to him, on the strength of his epistle to the church of Corinth, a right to admonish, in the sense of a primacy, supported by a special authority. Rather was it the Roman congregation as such that made a claim exceeding the limits of brotherly solidarity. Noteworthy too is the respect which Clement's first epistle gained in Corinth and in the rest of the Church during the period immediately following, so that it was sometimes regarded as inspired scripture. This implies the existence in the consciousness of non-Roman Christians of an esteem of the Roman church as such which comes close to according it a precedence in rank. In obvious allusion to the epistle to the Corinthians, the letter of Ignatius to the Romans states that the Roman congregation acted as teacher to others. Ignatius does not however mention the bishop of Rome.

CHAPTER　11

Heterodox Jewish-Christian Currents

Quite early there developed alongside the orthodox Jewish Christianity of the Jerusalem community and of the post-apostolic period, other Jewish groups which took over Christian elements in doctrine and worship. But, in contrast with genuine Jewish Christianity, they transformed these elements and thereby separated themselves from it as well as from post-biblical Judaism. With the latter, however, they shared the main ideas of late Jewish apocalyptic literature, and they recognized the Mosaic Law. Their separation from orthodox Jewry was not so much the result of changes in religious practice as of fundamentally different doctrines. These were concentrated on two main questions: Christology and the binding force of the Mosaic Law. The latter question was a cause of considerable conflict in the congregations founded by Paul and was bound sooner or later to lead to the disavowal of the "judaizers" by the Church if they insisted on imposing observance of the Law upon Gentile Christians as necessary to salvation. For the Church as a whole, however, the Christological question grew more and more important and became a criterion of orthodoxy for individual Jewish Christians and Jewish-Christian congregations.

The Christology of Kerinthos was, for orthodox Jewish Christians, a ground for bitterly opposing him. Irenaeus, with his connections with Asia Minor, may well be reporting what is essentially correct when he states that Kerinthos lived toward the end of the first century in western Asia Minor, and that he asserted of Jesus that the latter was the natural son of Mary and Joseph. As Jesus had distinguished himself above all other men by his justice and wisdom, Christ in the form of a dove had descended upon him after his baptism; from then on he had proclaimed the hitherto unknown Father and performed miracles. Before the end, Christ had again left him; only Jesus suffered death and rose again.

This image of Christ, tinged with Adoptionism and Docetism, was bound to be unacceptable to the Christians of Asia Minor; an indication of this is to be seen in the curious note of Irenaeus that the apostle John was prompted to write his Gospel by the teachings of Kerinthos. Kerinthos also had Gnostic ideas, for according to Irenaeus, he distinguished the "highest God" from the creator of the world, who did not know the former.

The Jewish-Christian group that in Irenaeus goes by the name of *Ebionites* was, however, a considerable movement. Early Christian heresiologists derive this name from a person called Ebion, but it is more probable that it comes from the Hebrew word *'ebjon* (poor). The adherents of this movement would, then, have seen in the name a descriptive designation which referred to their simple way of life. However, they began to propound views on Christology and on the binding nature of the Mosaic Law which were heterodox and led to their breaking away from the Church about the year 150.

Among the writings of the Ebionites, a Gospel of their own must first be mentioned. It was probably the Gospel of Matthew, revised in an Ebionite sense; Ebionite ideas are also to be found in a treatise dating from the first half of the second century, containing the "Sermons of Peter."

No uniform picture can be given of the subsequent history of the Ebionite movement. The following characteristics are typical of the Ebionite movement in so far as it was heterodox. In their concept of the origin of the world the Ebionites took a dualistic view. God, in the beginning, set up a good and an evil principle: to the latter was given dominion over the present world; to the former, dominion over that which is to come. The good principle is Christ, the promised messianic prophet. Jesus of Nazareth was consecrated by God as Messiah and supplied on the day of his baptism in the Jordan with divine power. He was not the existing Son of God, but the naturally begotten son of a human couple, raised to the rank of Messiah because of his exemplary fulfillment of the Law of God. His task was to fulfill by preaching the word of God, not, therefore, by an extraordinary act of salvation, nor by dying for man's redemption. The Ebionites rejected belief in his redemptive death, as Christ had withdrawn himself from Jesus at the time of the crucifixion. The Ebionite image of Christ is thus essentially conditioned by its adoptionist character and by its denial of the soteriological significance of his life and death.

Joined to this Christology was the Ebionites' demand for observance of the Law purged of its distortions. Reform of the Law had been effected by Jesus in his teaching; he had shown what was genuine in the Law and in conformity with the will of God, and what contradicted it. Sacrifices were replaced by a life of poverty and community of goods; the Ebionite purified himself by daily washings, by participation in a ritual meal of bread and water, and by celebrating both Sabbath and Sunday.

The Ebionites also showed a certain "anti-Paulinism," expressed particularly in the "Kerygmata Petrou" an Ebionite treatise of the first half of the second century which influenced the pseudo-Clementines. According to it, Paul was the great opponent of the Law, "the hostile man," who falsified the true ideas of Jesus.

Close to the Ebionites stood other Jewish-Christian groups which, on account of certain opinions held by them, can likewise not be regarded as belonging to orthodox Christianity. First, there was the sect of the *Elchasaites,* which, by the third century, had spread to some extent. It was founded by a man named Elchasai, who was active on the borders of Syria and Parthia during the early decades of the second century. The message of the Elchasaites was based upon a holy book to which a supernatural origin was ascribed. In it, two heavenly beings played a principal part, a female one, called the Holy Spirit, and a male one, the Son of God or Christ, who came into the world in repeated incarnations. The sect practiced a baptism, fully clothed, which was believed to effect forgiveness of sins, as well as frequent washings, which delivered from sickness and defects. The foundation of the Elchasaites' way of life was the Law. They exhibited apocalyptic traits; he who, when the time came, was in possession of a mysterious formula would be saved. The teaching of the holy book of Elchasai was to be kept secret since not all were worthy of it.

The question as to the original source of Elchasaitism cannot be definitely answered from the evidence at present available. Jewish elements were clearly present; as were Christian influences. But the treatment of Christ as a mere man and a simple prophet shows the Christianity of the movement to have been undoubtedly heterodox.

The sect of the *Mandaeans* can be included here, inasmuch as it was probably connected originally with heterodox Jewish baptist sects which had grown up in eastern Syria and Palestine. Baptism played a predominant part in their worship. It was carried out by immersing the candidate thrice in flowing water, and it could be repeated several times. Great importance was also attached to the liturgical celebration of the ascent of the souls of the dead to the realm of light. According to the Mandaean mythology, there was a great king of light or Great Mana, besides whom there existed innumerable lesser manas; opposing him was a world of black water peopled by demons. John the Baptist was highly revered by the Mandaeans, whereas Jesus was regarded as a false prophet and liar whom John unmasked.

Finally, the influence of heterodox Jewish Christianity in some early Gnostic groups can be noted, even though the course of these influences is hard to trace.

Such a Gnostic tendency in heterodox Jewish Christianity can be seen in Samaritan Gnosis, which went back to Simon Magus, who was of course not unfamiliar with Jewish Christianity (Acts 8:10).

The so-called "Apocryphon of John" among the Gnostic writings of Nag Hammadi, with its interpretation of Genesis and its doctrine of archons and angels and the part played by them in the Creation, clearly points to kindred speculations in later heterodox Judaism and in heretical Jewish Christianity. The early Church did not have to engage in controversy to a great extent with all these heterodox Jewish-Christian schools of thought, because she did not come into close contact with all of them. Where, however, such disputes did arise, Christianity had an opportunity to clarify and affirm its beliefs.

Section Four

The Church in the Second Century

<small>C H A P T E R   1 2</small>

The Position of the Church under the Emperors Marcus Aurelius and Commodus— Martyrdom of the Congregations of Lyons and Vienne

The writers of early Christian apologetical works ascribed to the emperor Marcus Aurelius (161–80) an edict favorable to the Christians, which Apollinaris of Hierapolis and Tertullian invoked, when they wished to oppose, as unjust, the proceedings of provincial authorities against the Christians of their day.

The reality was otherwise. The emperor's own writings show how much he despised the Christians in his heart, because (as he believed) they threw their lives away for an illusion. That he was determined not to let the State religion be jeopardized by fanatical sectaries and by the introduction of hitherto unknown cults is shown by a rescript of 176–77, which was not indeed specially directed against the Christians, but which could easily be employed against them by provincial authorities. The increase in the number of complaints from the Christians during the reign of Marcus Aurelius, expressed in the apologetical writings of Melito of Sardes, Apollinaris of Hierapolis, and the Athenian Athenagoras, clearly indicate a worsening of their situation.

That such was the situation is confirmed by a series of individual martyrdoms in different parts of the empire which can be dated in the reign of Marcus Aurelius.

The clearest account of the background, circumstances, and course of a wave of local persecution under Marcus Aurelius is provided by a joint letter from the Christian communities of Lyons and Vienne in Gaul, in which they tell their brethren in Asia Minor what befell them in the year 177; Eusebius has included nearly the whole of it in his History of the Church.

<small>49</small>

In the summer of 177, when representatives of all Gaul were assembled in Lyons for the festival of the imperial cult, the popular rage suddenly vented itself on the Christians, who were supposed, as elsewhere in the empire, to be guilty of atheism and immorality. Statements made by pagan slaves in the service of Christians, e.g., accused their masters of heinous crimes; and thus in a few days the elite of both congregations found themselves in prison. During the trial, about ten Christians abjured their faith; the remainder were condemned to death.

When the governor heard that Attalos, a distinguished man, was a Roman citizen, he postponed his execution in order to inquire of the emperor what line of action he should follow. He was told that apostates were to be pardoned; those who stood fast in their profession of Christianity were to be put to death. All proved steadfast, and so the executions continued. The letter gives no exact number of the victims; only a later tradition mentions about fifty names.

Christians under Marcus Aurelius were not always condemned to death, but were sometimes sentenced to forced labor in the mines.

If we seek the reasons for this obviously increased severity of the Roman authorities toward the Christians, fresh legal measures on the part of the emperor cannot indeed be adduced. His decision in reply to the governor's inquiry clearly shows that the legal position remained as it appears in Trajan's rescript and in the resultant practice under Hadrian. It was public opinion under Marcus Aurelius which had become more unfavorable to the Christians. This hostile atmosphere now found expression more frequently and more intensively than under Hadrian, who had still been able to intervene to curb such excesses. If a provincial governor now gave in to the pressure of popular rage oftener than before, in Rome also public feeling was taken more into account and was given an outlet in the baiting of Christians.

The Christian communities, for their part, had, albeit unwittingly, drawn attention to themselves more than usual. The disputes with the Gnostics in particular congregations could hardly remain concealed from the pagans around them; the Church's increased opposition to pagan culture and the Roman State became apparent. Mention might also be made of the Montanist movement, at least in certain cases, if the growing irritability of the pagans is to be understood. The exalted desire for martyrdom that was peculiar to the Montanists, and their fanatical refusal to have anything to do with the pagan culture on which the State was based, could easily be attributed to Christianity as such, with disastrous results.

CHAPTER 13

Literary Polemic against Christianity

The animosity of the pagans with its explosions of popular anger, and the action taken by the State authorities in consequence, brought the Christians more and more into the public eye, especially during the first half of the second century. Accordingly, there developed a new reaction of paganism against Christianity, this time on the intellectual plane. A will to resist arose in pagan intellectual circles. The resources of profane culture were employed in the battle against Christianity. Mocking speeches, pamphlets, and books became the means of carrying on a literary war, which began about the middle of the second century and soon reached its first climax in the satirical writings of Lucian of Samosata and in the "True Doctrine" (*Alēthēs logos*) of the philosopher Celsus.

This was of great significance for the history of the Church, because it was one of the factors that provoked a reaction from the Christian side; the Christians took up the pen and adopted an attitude of defense and counter-attack. The resultant body of apologetical works became a special department of early Christian literature, giving a characteristic note to the second half of the second century.

The first beginnings of a pagan literary polemic are discernible in the report of Tacitus on Nero's persecution.

But from the middle of the second century a growing unrest becomes evident among educated pagans on account of the increase of the Christian movement, which evidently could not be halted in spite of popular tumults and police measures. The representatives of pagan philosophy now had occasion to become more closely acquainted with the intellectual and religious phenomena of Christianity and to engage in controversy with it. An early example of a discussion between a member of the Church and a pagan philosopher is the encounter between the apologist Justin and the Cynic, Crescens, in Rome. Crescens went about proclaiming that the Christians were "atheists and fellows of no religion." In his disputation with Crescens, no doubt conducted in public, Justin did not feel that he had had the worst of it and was quite ready for further debate.

This example shows that the polemic of the educated adopted the reproach of the masses that the Christians were atheists. The pagan rhetor Fronto took up the grave suspicions which the common folk repeated about the Christians: at their gatherings they were supposed, after having indulged in luxurious meals and partaken copiously of wine, to give themselves up to the worst excesses, including incest.

The picture of the Christians which Lucian of Samosata provides cannot strictly speaking be regarded as a polemic against them. For this mocker, who with his sharp pen so readily exposed the weaknesses of his fellow men to the laughter of their contemporaries, was free from hatred against the Christians; he saw in them neither a danger to the State nor a threat to public order, and therefore scorned to repeat the venomous atrocity stories that were current about them. He regarded their religious convictions and their everyday behavior as belonging to the human follies and errors which he enjoyed pillorying; but he regarded the folly of the Christians as particularly harmless.

Through his caricature of the Christian life we see a perceptible glimmer of the real situation. Lucian had heard something of the esteem in which one who professed the faith was held by his brother-Christians; he knew of their solicitude for the imprisoned, of their community spirit, and their courage in the face of death. We cannot fail to notice the lack of depth and the gaps in Lucian's knowledge of essential features of the Christian religion. Of Christ himself he had only the vaguest ideas; what Christ's life and teaching, death and resurrection meant to the Christians of that period was quite unknown to him. Toward a religion whose adherents were indeed harmless, but at the same time naïve fools, and who moreover were completely uncritical with regard to their own traditions of belief, one could scarcely react other than with pitying amusement. Lucian's portrait of Christianity could not fail to produce its effect in the intellectual battle with paganism.

Celsus

Celsus, who wrote in the eighth decade of the second century, raised the controversy to quite a different level in an extensive work to which he gave the equivocal title *Alēthēs logos.* We no longer possess the whole work, but lengthy excerpts quoted by Origen in his refutation of Celsus do give us a clear idea of its basic arguments.

Celsus represented a philosophical creed which rejected monotheism and tolerated, in the Greek manner, popular religion and the mystery cults, provided they in some measure corresponded to the fundamental ideas of his own philosophically based religion. Every new religion must, according to Celsus, justify itself, whether as a popular belief or as a local cult. Christianity appeared to him as a new religious movement, and therefore he subjected it to examination. He had learnt as much as possible about this new religion. He summed up the results of his studies in a learned and substantial work, which does not however limit itself to displaying theoretical knowledge but also draws practical conclusions. Since his conclusions were wholly unfavorable to Christianity and were expressed moreover in a highly aggressive way, Celsus' *Alēthēs logos* was a decisive event in the history of literary polemic between paganism and Christianity. The importance attached to the work and its possible effect on the public can be seen from the fact that the most significant theologian of the third century, seventy years after its appearance, thought it worth while to write a detailed refutation of it.

Celsus' philosophical principles did not allow him to accept either the Christian doctrine of Creation or the idea of Revelation. A world which was created out of nothing and will pass away again was something that did not fit into his cosmology. God, according to the idea of Celsus, sat enthroned at an inapproachable distance from the world and could not reveal himself without changing his nature or subjecting himself to the vicissitudes of history and coming into dangerous proximity to evil. Platonic dualism and Stoic cosmology were the basis of Celsus' attitude; to him the idea of God's becoming man appeared positively shameful: "No God and no Son of God has ever descended to earth, nor ever will" (Fragm. 5, 2).

With this rejection of the doctrine of the Incarnation, Celsus coupled a characterization of the person of Jesus of Nazareth which was bound to offend every Christian deeply. According to him, Jesus was only a man who had gained respect and authority through the means employed by Egyptian sorcerers; but no one would think of giving one of these the title of "God's Son."

Far more effective than his attacks on Christian doctrines was the unfavorable description Celsus gave of the Christians themselves and of their daily life. They were (he said), for the most part, men of limited intelligence, who did not understand their own doctrines and would not discuss them; they even regarded "foolishness" as a mark of distinction. Their faith was the religion of the stupid and of stupidity; their deliberate exclusion of the Logos from their religious life was in itself a condemnation of Christianity in Greek eyes. Christian preaching even warned its hearers against earthly wisdom and thus frightened away those to whom Greek culture represented an ideal.

Celsus based his moral judgment of the Christians as deceivers and liars on their having consciously borrowed ideas from the Greek past, distorting and falsifying them in their propaganda. Thus Christianity sinned against the Logos and was the irreconcilable opponent of the *alēthēs logos,* the "true doctrine" of the Greeks.

The revolt of the Christians against the sacred ideals of Logos and Nomos gave Celsus a pretext for branding them as a gang of lawbreakers who had to shun the light of publicity. Jesus had picked out men of evil repute to be his apostles, men who carried on the unclean businesses of publicans and sailors; he himself was nothing but a "robber chief" at the head of his band of brigands. The successors of the apostles, the Christian preachers of the author's own time, were no better. It was the duty of the State authorities to intervene against a religion which, in a secret and forbidden confederacy, rebelled against all traditional law and order.

Here we must stop to ask the question: how far was such a powerful attack effective? It could hardly count on any appreciable success among the Christians themselves. The distorted picture of Jesus was bound to fill them with disgust. His complete misunderstanding of the Christian concept of sin and of what gave the Christians their inner cohesion was bound to prevent his work from having any profound effect on the members of the Church.

The effect of Celsus' book upon contemporary paganism may well have been different. An educated pagan who, without personal knowledge of Christianity, read this work which described, with pretensions to extensive learning, a movement threatening all that Greek culture held sacred, could with difficulty bring himself to take much positive interest in such a contemptible religion. The book may indeed have done much to strengthen the conviction that severe measures against such a movement were necessary.

CHAPTER 14

The Early Christian Apologists
of the Second Century

Even before the middle of the second century, some writers on the Christian side had begun a task which, because of its purpose, later earned them the name of apologists. In many respects they introduced a new phase in the development of early Christian literature, for the aim of the apologists was intentionally wider than that of their immediate predecessors, the apostolic fathers. They saw clearly that the situation of Christianity in the first half of the century, especially in the Hellenic East, presented its writers with new tasks.

The apologists perceived that the faith was meeting with ever-increasing hostility in every department of public life. This development led them to address their pagan neighbors directly, in order to give them, in more or less extensive explanatory writings, a truer picture of the Christian religion. Thus an unbiased judgment of its adherents and a juster treatment of them would be made possible. Hence such a work was called "apologia" or speech for the defense. But it was not difficult to combine missionary and propagandist intentions, and these authors worked at least indirectly toward the spread of the faith among their readers.

The method and choice of theme varied according to the adversary addressed. In dialogues with the Jews, the main theme was already given: only Jesus of Nazareth could be the true Messiah, for in him alone were fulfilled the messianic prophecies of the Old Testament. In debate with pagan religions and Hellenistic culture there was a wider choice. First of all, the persistent rumors accusing the Christians of sexual immorality, atheism, and inadaptability for social life had to be refuted, for it was these rumors that kept alive the animosity of the pagan masses. More space was devoted to setting forth the truths of the Christians and the ethic on which it was based. Alongside a more or less positive appreciation of the cultural achievements of paganism there was also, however, a purely negative attitude which treated all that Greek civilization had produced with cheap mockery. Repeatedly, the apologists draw the conclusion that the right to existence of such a lofty religion as Christianity could not be denied, and that, therefore, the measures taken against its adherents by the authorities were completely lacking in justice.

The series of apologetic writers begins with the Athenian Quadratus, who, according to Eusebius, addressed an apologia to the emperor Hadrian. The single fragment of his work which is certainly genuine, permits no conclusions about its general character.

On the other hand it has been possible to rediscover complete in a Syrian translation the long-lost work of his fellow-countryman and contemporary, Aristides, and to show that the Greek novel *Barlaam and Joasaph,* in the version of John Damascene, is a free adaptation of it. Aristides was no doubt addressing the same emperor, Hadrian, as Eusebius (who knew his *Apologia* in the original text) was aware. The author, however, did not succeed in presenting and developing his theme effectively. His main argument was that the three races, barbarians, Greeks, and Jews, did not possess the true idea of God; only the fourth race, the

Christians, had the true doctrine and moral code. The fundamental truths of Christianity, for him, consisted in the belief that Jesus Christ as Son of God had come down from Heaven and taken flesh of a virgin, and that after his death and resurrection he had commanded the apostles to proclaim the true God to all nations and to make them observe his commandments; he who obeyed these would become a partaker in eternal life.

Aristides' tone becomes warmer when he speaks of the daily life of the Christians (c. 15), which recommends itself by its lofty purity of morals. He was deeply permeated with the belief that Christianity alone could bring salvation to mankind.

An incomparably higher achievement was the work of Justin, a convert from a Greek family of Flavia Neapolis in Palestine, who as director of a school in Rome, died a martyr's death about the year 165. An Apologia with an appendix, addressed to Antoninus Pius and his son Marcus Aurelius, together with a lengthy *Dialogue with the Jew Tryphon* have come down to us, the remnant of eight works by Justin. The *Apologia* to the two emperors was written about 150.

The career and the superior education of their author give these writings a special importance. Justin belonged to the educated upper class. As a professional philosopher he was acquainted with all the principal intellectual movements of his time, and as an unswerving seeker after truth he had tried them all in turn and found inner peace only when he recognized Christianity to be "the only certain and adequate philosophy" (*Dial.*, c. 8.) He thereupon embraced it and devoted the rest of his life to proclaiming and defending it. He attacked polytheistic mythology with the methods placed at his disposal by the "enlightened" philosophers. To it he opposed the one true God, the "Father of the universe" (*Apol.* app. 6), who is without origin and himself the first cause of the world, and for whom there is no name that can express his nature. He is enthroned above the world, in which he cannot be directly apprehended by the senses. Justin does not argue that this one God is called "Father" because he has favored men with a kind of divine sonship, but, rather, because he is the first cause of creation. He seeks to connect this philosophical idea of God with elements of the Christian doctrine of the Trinity, so that the Christian belief in God is shown as including also belief in Jesus Christ his Son and in the prophetic Spirit. The Logos was in the beginning with God; he was begotten by the Father and appeared in his divine fullness in Jesus Christ, as Holy Scripture had foretold. He has not indeed the same rank as the Father, but, as his Son, he shares the divine nature (*Dial.* 61). Even before his manifestation in Christ, the Logos was active; not only did the Father create the world through him, but he also appeared frequently as the "angel of the Lord," he spoke in the prophets of the Old Testament, and he was active too in such eminent men as Heraclitus, Socrates and Musonios, in whom he was at work as "germinal Logos," so that these and many others who lived in accordance with the Logos working in their reason are actually to be reckoned as Christians.

If in Justin's teaching about God and the Logos Stoic influence is especially evident, his ideas on the activities of angels and demons show a strong affinity with the Platonic philosophy of his time. God gave the good angels charge over men and earthly affairs (*Apol.* 2:5). They are not pure spirits but possess aerial bodies, nourished by a kind of manna (*Dial.* 57). The fall of the angels was caused by their having sexual intercourse with women. Their children are the demons, who from their kingdom of the air exercise their baleful influence on mankind, until at Christ's return they will be cast into everlasting fire. They are the actual founders of the pagan cults; they also made the Jews blind to the Logos and so caused his death on the Cross. They continue by their cunning to prevent the conversion of mankind to him and to God. But in the name of Jesus Christ the redeemer, a power has been given to Christians which protects them against the demons (*Dial.* 307).

Justin's Christianity has another side, less influenced by philosophical abstractions, which appears when he writes of the daily life of the Christians, in which he took part like any other member of a congregation. Its high moral level was for him a convincing proof that the Christians were in possession of the truth. They led a life of truthfulness and chastity, they loved their enemies and went courageously to death for their beliefs, not because they had been persuaded of the importance of these virtues by philosophical considerations, but because Jesus had demanded of them a life in accordance with such ideals. It was for Justin an incontrovertible proof of the truth of Jesus' message that in him all the prophecies of the Old Testament were unequivocally fulfilled.

With the artlessness of a simple member of the Church he speaks of baptism and the eucharistic liturgy as essential components of Christian worship. Baptism, performed "in the name of God the Father and Lord of the universe and of our redeemer Jesus Christ and of the Holy Spirit" (*Apol.* 61), frees us from sins previously committed and creates a new man through Christ; baptism is also called "enlightenment." The purest form of worship is the eucharistic sacrifice, at which the faithful, joined in brotherly union, bring bread and wine over which the head of the congregation utters a prayer of thanksgiving. These gifts are again distributed among the faithful, but now they are no longer ordinary bread and wine but the flesh and blood of that Jesus who himself became flesh (*Apol.* 62). This food the Christians call the Eucharist; it has replaced the Old Testament sacrifices, which God rejects.

In other matters, too, Justin's views reflect the traditional teaching of the early Church, even when this was in contradiction to pagan sensibilities. Quite naturally he speaks of the mystery of the cross and the redemption of mankind by the bloodshed and death of the Son of God. His belief in the resurrection of the body, which would one day bring incorruptibility to the just, was unshakeable. Although, according to his own words (*Dial.* 80), not all good Christians agreed with him in this, he expected a millennium — thousand-year kingdom — in Jerusalem which would begin at the end of time, when the souls of the dead would be delivered from Hades. He did not confine himself to a purely philosophical Christianity; his survey represents a significant advance in the development of early Christian theology when compared with the world of the apostolic fathers and the earlier apologetic of Aristides.

Justin's pupil, the Syrian Tatian, shared with him a similar way to Christian faith, for he too had found his way to the truth only after long searching (he had been initiated into the Mysteries) and by reading the holy books of the Christians (*Orat.* 29). His "Speech to the Greeks," written to justify his conversion, marks a retrograde step in comparison with Justin's *Apologia*. Tatian had, for the cultural achievements of Greece, only mockery and contempt. Such condemnation was not exactly likely to make an educated Greek receptive to what Tatian had to say about the Christian religion.

The center of this religion, he said, was the one God without a beginning, clearly distinct from the material world he created through the Logos. God intended man to rise again after the consummation of all things and would also be man's judge. Man, endowed with free will, could decide to be on the side of goodness and so enter into immortality, in spite of the influence of the demons, who sought to lead him astray. It was they who tried to force upon mankind belief in Fate, and for this they would finally suffer eternal damnation. Man, as God's image, could free himself from their domination if he renounced matter by strict self-mortification. This the Christians did, though they were calumniously accused of every possible vice.

The incomplete and fragmentary nature of Tatian's theology strikes us at once. What is especially noticeable is his failure to give any details about the person and the redemptive action of Christ, particularly when addressing pagan readers. The want of moderation in Tatian's attack on Hellenistic culture was in accordance with his character, namely, his tendency to extremes, which eventually after his return to his native Syria about the year 172 was to lead him outside the Church to become the founder of the Encratites, a Christian sect which rejected marriage as sinful and renounced the use of flesh or wine in any form.

Tatian's other surviving work, which he called *To dia tessarōn euaggelion,* had a much more far-reaching effect than his apologetical work. It was a harmony of the Gospels which was intended to reduce the four separate gospels to a single account. This *Diatessaron,* seems to have been written in Greek, was used as a liturgical book in the Syrian church until the fifth century, and St. Ephraem wrote a commentary on it. It was early translated into Latin, and it evidently influenced the text of the Gospels outside Syria.

Athenagoras, the "Christian philosopher of Athens," wielded a more skilful pen than any of the apologists mentioned above. About the year 177 he addressed a petition to the emperor Marcus Aurelius and his son Commodus, in which he refuted the calumnies against the Christians, claimed for Christianity equal rights with pagan philosophies, and therefore demanded its toleration by the State. The nobility of tone of the work as a whole is matched by Athenagoras' attitude toward the Greek philosophers, many of whom showed monotheistic tendencies without on that account being looked upon as atheists. The reproach of atheism made against the Christians ought therefore to be dropped, for they believed in one God, the Father, the Son and the Holy Spirit, and were convinced of the existence of a world of angels to whom was entrusted the ordering of the universe (*Suppl.* 10). The existence of this one God can be proved even by reason alone (*Suppl.* 8). Revelation shows the divinity of the Logos; the working of the Holy Spirit, who is an emanation of God, is especially perceptible in the prophets (*Suppl.* 7 and 10). The high standard of Christian morality was proved by the purity of their married life and the esteem in which virginity was held among them, a second marriage being regarded as "decent adultery" (*Suppl.* 31–35). The Christian doctrine of the resurrection of the body, so difficult for the Greeks, Athenagoras sought to prove philosophically in a special work. It is clear that in the writings of this apologist the philosophical argument had gained in quality and the theological understanding of Christianity in depth.

Only the *Three Books to Autolykos* survive out of the considerable body of writings left by Theophilos, a man of Hellenistic education who, after his conversion about the year 180, became head of the Christian congregation at Antioch. Autolykos was his pagan friend, to whom he wished to prove, in a pleasing Greek style, that the Scriptures of the Christians (that is, the Old Testament) were superior, both in antiquity and in religious and philosophical content, to everything that the Greek intellect had produced. The line of argument and the defense against pagan calumnies follow the usual course. In Theophilos' account of the faith we meet for the first time in a Christian writer the designation *trias* (Trinity) (2:15), for the persons of which he always uses the terms "God," "Logos," "Sophia" (1:7; 1:10; 2:18). The evangelists were for him, like the prophets, bearers of the Spirit; their writings, with the epistles of Paul, were the "holy, divine word" (2:22; 3:13–14). The human soul was potentially immortal; immortality would be given as a reward for freely choosing to observe the commandments of God (2:27).

Except for a few fragments, the apologia of Bishop Melito of Sardes, as well as the works of the rhetor Miltiades of Asia Minor and Apollinaris, Bishop of Hierapolis, are lost. With courage and dignity Melito pointed out to Marcus Aurelius the unjust plundering and persecution to which the Christians were exposed, whereas the benevolent attitude of the emperor's predecessors, except Nero and Domitian, had brought God's blessing on the Roman Empire. Eusebius has preserved a list of the other works of this much respected bishop, the titles of which show the astonishing range of his interests. A homily preached no doubt at a Paschal celebration of the Quartodecimans, gives important information about early Christian teaching in Asia Minor on original sin, on the redemptive act of Christ, on baptism, and on the character of sermons at that time. A hymn in the same papyrus fits so well with the Easter liturgy of the Quartodecimans and with the ideas of Melito that it too has been claimed for the Bishop of Sardes.

Finally the anonymous *Letter to Diognetus* attracted attention more by its elegant Greek than by its theological content. A short criticism of the Jewish and pagan religions is followed by the oft-quoted hymnic chapter on the Christians' daily life: "Every foreign place is their home, and their home is a foreign place to them; ... they dwell on earth, but their conversation is in heaven; they love all men and are persecuted by all; they are poor and enrich many. They are despised and are thereby glorified. They are insulted and they bless; they are mocked and show honor to those that mock them; punished with death, they rejoice as if they were awakened unto life. In brief, what the soul is to the body, the Christians are to the world" (chapters 5 and 6). The reality, it is true, did not in the year 200 everywhere correspond to the ideal.

A general appreciation of the achievement of the second-century apologists can no longer defend, without qualification, the thesis that their endeavors to make Christianity intelligible to the Hellenistic world played a decisive part in hellenizing the Church. The genuinely Christian content of apologetical literature is too unequivocal to support such a thesis, especially when we remember its purpose. Compared with the apostolic fathers, however, they show a considerable development in their teaching about God, in the christology of the Logos, in the doctrine of the Trinity, and in Christian anthropology. Great progress was made in biblical studies; a start was made at establishing a canon; the doctrine of inspiration began to be developed, and the Old Testament became the foundation of a christology based on the Bible. Finally, in the works of the apologists we get valuable information on the building up of the inner life of the Church in the second century, notably for instance in the liturgical parts of Justin, in the accounts of the relations between Church and State and of the missionary activity of the young Church.

C H A P T E R   1 5

The Dispute with Gnosticism

If the literary polemic of paganism represented no great danger to the Christian community, there arose in so-called Christian Gnosticism an adversary which, from the first decades of the second century, constituted to an increasing degree a threat to her very existence. It was part of the manifestation of late classical religious syncretism which, based on oriental dualism, united Jewish religious ideas with certain elements of the Christian revelation, albeit in distorted forms. Now, as a mighty current bent on sweeping all before it, it came flooding in from the East.

Gnosticism had a great attraction for Hellenistic man; it made a real appeal to him, demanding that he make up his mind. Its impetus was derived ultimately from its claim to bring to religious-minded persons a valid interpretation of the world and of themselves — the claim made by Christianity itself. Its message was expressed in a copious literature, often of considerable stylistic beauty, and proclaimed by teachers and heads of philosophical schools with respected names. With a sure instinct, Gnosticism felt the Church to be a serious competitor, and it made a bold attempt to conquer her from within, to infiltrate into her congregations and to disrupt them by forming Gnostic cells inside them. The existence of ecclesiastically organized Christianity depended on whether the heads of the Christian congregations saw this danger and were able to sustain a defensive struggle that would tax all their energies.

Until recently, the incompleteness of our sources prevented the writing of any satisfactory account of the basic teachings of Gnosticism and of its manifestations. Only a few works of Gnostic origin were known in the original, as, for instance, the *Pistis Sophia,* which is fairly late, and the *Books of Jeû,* containing alleged revelations of Christ to his disciples. The reason for this state of affairs is that after the victory of Christianity a large part of Gnostic literature was destroyed or else perished through lack of interest. To a great extent therefore the only available material was that contained in quotations and excerpts preserved in the works of

Christian anti-Gnostics, especially in those of Irenaeus, Tertullian and Hippolytus, and to a lesser degree in the writings of Clement of Alexandria, Origen, and the later authors, Epiphanius of Salamis and Filastrius of Brescia.

But even anti-Gnostic literature survives only in part. Thus, what was perhaps the earliest work of this kind, Justin's *Against all Heresies,* written at the time when Gnosticism was most flourishing, is now lost.

A completely new situation with regard to source-material was brought about by the discovery in 1945–46 of the extensive library of a Gnostic community near the Upper Egyptian town of Nag Hammadi in the vicinity of the former Pachomian monastery of Chenoboskion. It contained in thirteen papyrus manuscripts more than forty hitherto unknown works in the Coptic language, mostly direct translations from the Greek. These translations belong to the end of the fourth or the beginning of the fifth century; the Greek originals were probably written in the second century. Many of the titles of the newly found treatises at first led to the supposition that they were already known Christian apocrypha; but closer inspection revealed that their contents are quite new. For example, there are apocryphal gospels of Thomas and Philip, a "Gospel of the Egyptians" and a "Gospel of Truth." There are Acts of the apostles Peter and Matthias. Apocalyptic literature is particularly well represented by apocalypses of Peter, Paul, John, James (three), Dositheos, and Seth (Sem). As in many of the manuscripts the prophet Seth plays a central role, we may assume that the library of Nag Hammadi belonged to the Sethian sect, which is often mentioned by early Christian writers. There are moreover, works of Hermes Trismegistos, doctrinal works by Gnostic leaders such as Silvanos and Eugnostes; others claim to be an "Explanation of Gnosis" or an account of the nature of the archons.

Basic Ideas of Gnosticism

On first acquaintance, Gnostic writings convey an overall impression of a confusing mass of ideas and questions, often expressed in strange forms. The question is: How can man find the true knowledge which will explain the riddle of the world and the evil therein, as well as the riddle of human existence? The Gnostic, Theodotos, gave a rough definition of gnosis. Knowledge (Gnosis) of the answers to the following questions gives freedom: "Who were we? What have we become? Where were we? Whither have we been cast? Whither do we hasten? From what will we become free? What is birth? What is rebirth?" In the answers to these questions the same basic ideas recur: man's inmost being longs for union with the true, perfect, but unknown God. Man, however, by a peculiar destiny has been banished to this imperfect world, which is not the creation of the supreme God, but can only be the work of a lesser, imperfect being, who rules it with the help of evil powers. Man can be free of their domination only if he rightly knows himself and is aware that he is separated from the perfect God. Only this knowledge makes possible his return to the upper world of light where the true God dwells.

These elements were connected with one another in a variety of ways, so that Gnosticism continually appears under different aspects according to the regions to which it spread and the formulations of its leading representatives. The observer is not confronted with any compact system of clearly defined concepts or dogmatic teachings, but with a multicolored stream of religious ideas and opinions, which can look different from different points along its banks. Nevertheless, certain currents are discernible which show from which tributaries the river as a whole was formed.

First of all, there already existed a certain substratum of Gnostic ideas independent of any contact with Christianity. Among these was a strongly marked *dualism*, which made an absolute opposition between light and darkness, between good and evil. The home of this dualism is to be found in ancient Iran. When these Iranian ideas met the Genesis account of Creation, this was interpreted in a Gnostic sense. The Creator God of the Old Testament became the Demiurge who did not know the light. Another source whose waters flowed into the Gnostic stream was astrological learning.

The new discoveries at Chenoboskion stress the fact that Egypt was a fruitful soil for the growth of Gnostic ideas. It is true that the influence of Egyptian religion needs to be more closely studied, but the hermetic writings in the library at Nag Hammadi certainly point to an undeniable connection between Egyptian Hermetism and Gnosis. Even though in these writings a demiurge plays no part in the creation of the world and the bizarre figures of the demons are lacking, the opposition which they proclaim between light and darkness, the encounter of a higher being with matter, the liberation of man who is tied to matter and his ascent to God once he is free — all this is part of Gnostic thought, only here the biblical and Christian elements are absent.

The relationship between Judaism and Gnosis constitutes a difficult problem. It is generally admitted that the world of the Old Testament played a significant part in Gnostic literature. The latter is, besides, full of images and ideas such as were current in Jewish apocalyptic works. Biblical influence is particularly strong (even though the Gnostics disagreed with the Bible) in the Gnostic account of Creation. One feels compelled to ask if there were not here and there connecting links between Essenes and Gnostics. The Qumran community imposed, like the Gnostics, a strict commandment of absolute secrecy regarding certain parts of its doctrine; the *Book of Discipline* further teaches that God, when he created man, appointed two spirits to govern him, the spirit of truth and the spirit of wickedness, which could make a man into a son of light or a son of darkness — a fundamentally dualistic conception which is strongly reminiscent of similar ideas in Gnosticism. It has also been suggested that remnants of the Qumran community survived in Gnostic circles.

Lastly there were the religiously tinged philosophical currents of Hellenism, which undeniably found expression in syncretic Gnosticism. Certain themes of Gnostic theology are already foreshadowed in the Platonic doctrine of the fall of the soul and its attachment to the matter of the body. Stoicism too contributed its share to Gnostic thought. The Gnostic writings of Chenoboskion eagerly take up the allegorical interpretations of Homer and Hesiod which Hellenism had developed. Probably, however, the borrowings of Gnosticism from Hellenistic philosophy were in its terminology rather than in its ideas.

When *syncretism* was at the peak of its development, Christianity entered the

Hellenistic world from its Palestinian birthplace and, in the syncretic climate of the time, it became the object of growing interest.

The leaders of such Gnostic communities appealed in support of their teachings to apostolic tradition or to the words of Christ himself; Ptolemaeos, for instance, a pupil of Valentinus, in his *Letter to Flora*. Others incorporated in their systems Christian ideas in a distorted form, as for example the Valentinians when they stressed the need for redemption, without which no man could reach the *pleroma* or "fulfillment"; the baptism of Jesus effected the remission of sins, but only redemption by Christ, who had descended into him, brought perfection. One became a partaker of this redemption by a mysterious rite and certain formulas to be recited during its performance. Thus the redeemed was to say: "I am confirmed and redeemed; I redeem my soul from this aeon and from all that derives from it, in the name of Jao, who redeemed this soul in Christ, the Living One" (Irenaeus, *Adv. haer.* 1, 33, 3–7). Besides echoes of New Testament phraseology, what is remarkable is the splitting of the person of the redeemer into an earthly Jesus and a heavenly Christ in a way quite unacceptable to the Christian Church.

Two factors may have contributed to the success of Gnostic propaganda. First there was the stress laid on ecclesiastical tradition, on which the doctrine of the "true Gnosis" and the salvation to be attained through it alone was supposed to be based.

From this secret source came the abundance of Gnostic scriptures, which invoked now this apostle or disciple, now that, as the specially chosen messenger of revelation. The very fact that the contents of these revelations were so wrapped in mystery was bound to make them interesting to many Christians. Moreover, the success of the Gnostics in winning adherents was founded upon the thesis that they, as Christians of a higher rank, "spiritual men" (*pneumatikoi,*) alone possessed the true interpretation of cosmic events and were thus the only ones capable of attaining to perfect knowledge of God. He who, like the great mass of Christians, tried to work out his salvation merely by faith and good works, remained for ever on a lower level, a lesser Christian or "psychic." It was unavoidable that a far-reaching conflict should arise between the prophets of such a distorted form of Christianity and the leaders of the Church, if the latter did not wish the substance of their faith to be dissolved.

The Principal Manifestations of Gnosticism

Though the different currents in Gnosticism show a certain basis of opinions held in common, they also show equally clearly how much room there was in the movement as a whole for variations and even contradictions.

The Syrian group belongs to the early phase of Gnosticism and it formed around Menander and Satornil (called Saturninus by Irenaeus) with its center at Antioch. Satornil is said to have been the first Gnostic to mention Jesus; but he was also regarded as a pupil of Simon Magus, in whom Christian apologists saw the actual founder of Gnosis.

The Basilidian school owed its origin to the Syrian Basilides. It ushered in the golden age of Gnosticism and attained great influence, especially at Alexandria, but it also had adherents at Rome. Basilides was very active as an author and, among other works, wrote a commentary on the Gospels in twenty-four books, besides hymns and prayers.

The Egyptian Valentinus was evidently Gnosticism's most gifted exponent. In the form in which he preached it, with lofty religious and poetic enthusiasm, it became the most dangerous threat to genuine Christianity. He began to teach at Alexandria about the year 135 and then propagated his opinions in Rome for nearly thirty years. There he seems to have played a leading part in the Christian community, but after a quarrel with the Roman Christians he returned to the East. His teachings were spread by means of letters, hymns, and sermons, and a *Treatise on the Three Natures* is also attributed to him. Irenaeus mentions a *Gospel of Truth* which was said to have been written by Valentinus, and among the finds at Nag Hammadi is a work of this title, the contents of which do not contradict what we know of Valentinus' doctrines. Many of these can be gleaned from writings or fragments of works by his pupils, for example Ptolemaeos, who in his *Letter to Flora* is a moderate propagandist for the Gnostic religion; or Heracleon, who had a predilection for the Gospel of John and wrote commentaries on it which Origen was later to discuss.

Valentinus' Christian opponents reproached him with having borrowed his wisdom largely from Pythagoras and Plato; they rightly saw that the Gnostic's ideas were similar to those of these philosophers. He also, however, frequently follows Pauline lines of thought and employs words of Christ, interpreted in a Gnostic sense, and this gives his teaching a biblical coloring that may have made it seem familiar to many Christians. The basis of his doctrine of the universe is the common Gnostic myth of the invisible Father, from whom the "syzygies" of the emanations proceed, of which the thirty highest aeons form the pleroma. This is the upper spiritual world, wherein all earthly events have their origin, and to return to which is the longing of imperfect creation. The latter is the work of the Demiurge, who created man and breathed into him the psychic or "natural" element which binds him to matter. Unknown to the Demiurge, however, man also received a pneumatic or "spiritual" element; if this has been awakened and formed by the true Gnosis which the Redeemer brought to earth, the spiritual part of man will be saved at the end of the world and can be again united with the light. In order to make possible the ascent of the lower world toward the light, Jesus became man, and upon him at his baptism the Spirit descended. For the passage to the light, which led the soul through the realm of the hostile powers, the dying Gnostic was, among the Valentinians, prepared by anointings and secret formulas, in which he said to the angels of the Demiurge that he possessed the true knowledge (gnosis) about himself and whence he came, so that they could not harm him.

On the fringe of these main Gnostic schools, there existed also various sectarian groups representing a highly popularized Gnosticism in which now this, now that particular doctrine often blossomed forth in the most luxuriant forms. Among such sects, anti-Gnostic literature mentions in particular the Barbelo-Gnostics, the Ophites, Naassenes, and Sethians.

The myth of the triad of world principles is a characteristic of the Sethian sect. As other manuscripts in the library of Chenoboskion refer to the prophet Sem or Seth or claim to have been written by him, it may be presumed that the whole collection belonged to a Sethian community. Even now, a preliminary inspection of its contents shows that its ideas were often clothed in a mantle of Christianity, so that the Sethians can undoubtedly be regarded as representatives of a Christian form of Gnosticism.

Marcion

Even if Marcion cannot be called a Gnostic in the full sense, he nevertheless adopted so much of Gnostic thought in his teaching that he may not unjustly be included here as representing a Christian Gnosticism of his own. The facts of his life show us a man of strong will, energy, and initiative combined with organizing ability. A well-to-do native of Asia Minor (he owned a shipping business at Sinope in Paphlagonia), he came into conflict while still quite young with the leaders of the local Christian community, probably because of differences of opinion about the interpretation of Pauline doctrines. His exclusion from the congregation in his own city was followed by his rejection on the part of leading Asiatic Christians.

About the year 140 Marcion came to Rome, where he joined the Christian congregation, which he supported with generous financial contributions. His connection with the Syrian Gnostic Cerdon, who also lived in Rome, no doubt made him more closely acquainted with Gnostic ideas, from which he took especially his doctrine about the Old Testament Creator. The latter was not for Marcion the true God, the Father of Jesus Christ, but only the strict and just God who in the Mosaic Law laid upon the Jewish people an unbearable yoke. In Rome too, Marcion's peculiar opinions met with no recognition, and in the autumn of 144 he left the Christian Church, albeit unwillingly.

He at once began with skill and energy to win over adherents, to whom he gave a close-knit organization. Everywhere there arose, alongside the Christian congregations, Marcionite associations, governed by bishops who in turn were assisted by presbyters. As their liturgy continued to follow closely the usage of the Catholic Church, the change-over to Marcion's church was for many Christians not too difficult. The strict organization of his establishment distinguished Marcion's community from the other Gnostic groups and gave it a special impetus which made it a serious danger to the Church. She soon recognized this threat, and the majority of ecclesiastical writers from Justin to Tertullian felt obliged to take up the pen against Marcion and his doctrines. Only when their irreconcilability with apostolic tradition was convincingly proved could their attraction for orthodox Christians be neutralized.

Marcion's teaching was based upon a clearly defined canon of scripture, from which the whole of the Old Testament was a *priori* excluded, for therein spoke the God of justice, the creator of the universe, the Demiurge, who was a stranger to goodness and love. The good God revealed himself only when he sent Christ as the Redeemer, who brought to tormented mankind the Gospel of the love of God. Paul was the only apostle who accepted this Gospel without falsifying it. It found expression in his epistles and in the Gospel of Luke, though even these writings had been corrupted by interpolations due to the apostles who adhered to the Old Testament God. Therefore everything had to be removed from them which sought to introduce into the revelation of Christ the justice and legalism of the Old Testament. Marcion wrote a commentary on these purified scriptures, the *Antitheses,* preserved only in a few fragments.

Marcion's thesis, with its dualistic approach, was a direct attack on the Christian concept of God, which did not permit of a division between a strict, merely just Creator and a God of love unknown till the coming of Christ. This doctrine alone might have caused the Christian writers to include Marcion among the Gnostic teachers. But his christology also justified their doing so; it was less its modalistic coloring than its Docetism which provoked their opposition. For Marcion, the idea that the Redeemer Christ sent by the good God should have chosen impure human flesh to be the bearer of the Deity was impossible; a real human birth would have subjected Christ to the dominion of the Demiurge. The Christian adversaries of Marcion, who pointed out that the latter's doctrine of the apparent birth of Christ led to the conclusion that his death on the cross was also apparent and that therefore the redemption was ineffective, were difficult to refute, even though Marcion tried to maintain the reality of the crucifixion. In the eyes of his opponents Marcion was finally placed in the Gnostic camp by his rejection of marriage, which, in consequence of his view of the body as a part of evil matter, he forbade to all baptized persons.

Marcion's theology was indeed free from the bizarre speculations of Gnosticism about the emanations of the *pleroma,* free from astrological beliefs, from fantastic cosmogony and from the overestimation of pure gnosis as opposed to faith with its consequent gradation of Christians into "pneumatic" and "psychic." The Gnostic ideas which he adopted were enough, however, to make him suspect in the eyes of the Church and to make his teaching seem in an increasing degree a grave danger to essential features of the Christian faith. That the Church opposed him and his sect with more determination and energy than she did many other Gnostic groups was due to his disturbing success, to which the gravity of his ascetic demands and, perhaps most of all, his strong personality contributed. Like no other figure in the Gnostic world, Marcion compelled the Church to consider and to reconsider her own attitude to Scripture and criteria of faith, to overhaul her organization and to deploy her whole inner strength in face of such a menace.

The Church's Self-Defense
and the Importance of the Christian Victory

The Church's campaign against the threat to her existence caused by the manifold attractions of Gnosticism was waged in two ways, each supplementing and supporting the other. First, the leaders of individual congregations immediately took practical steps against those Gnostics who endeavored to infiltrate into them, or who, having previously belonged to the congregation, sought from within to win over its members to their new faith. Secondly there were the theological writers of the time, who attacked the Gnostic movement on the literary plane, demonstrating the irreconcilability of its doctrine with Christian revelation and opposing its main theses with the corresponding truths of Christianity, now more precisely formulated as the result of profound study and development.

The defensive struggle at the pastoral level naturally left little evidence in the literary sources and it is therefore harder to reconstruct it in detail. The immediate object was bound to be the exclusion of the bearers of Gnostic doctrine from the community and the prevention, for the future, of the formation of Gnostic cells in their midst. Only the excommunication of Marcion himself found much of an echo in early Christian literature, but it serves as an example for many similar occurrences. Probably it was already his Gnostic convictions at their earliest stage, which led to his expulsion from the Christian congregation of his home town, Sinope. In Rome likewise the leaders of the church came to recognize that the exclusion of such a wealthy and influential man was the only means of protecting the Christians from the errors which he preached. Similar measures were no doubt taken in all places where the danger of the formation of Gnostic cells within Christian congregations was seen. The complaint of many Gnostics that the Catholics would have nothing to do with them and called them heretics, although they held the same doctrines, implies such defensive action on the part of the senior clergy. Other Gnostics voluntarily separated themselves from the Christian congregations when they found themselves isolated and unable to carry on their activities.

The eradication of Gnostic cells was accompanied by sermons explaining the insidious nature of false doctrines, and Christians were warned by their pastors of the danger to the true faith. We are led to suppose that instruction and immunization against the Gnostic menace was the practice of most Christian leaders of the time.

That this form of defense was not merely local is shown by the example of Dionysius, Bishop of Corinth about the year 170. Eusebius devotes some informative lines to his pastoral activities. Dionysius carried on a lively correspondence seeking to build up a broad defensive front against the heresies of the age. He urged the Christians to hold fast to the true doctrine and warned them against false teachings. The heresy of his time was primarily Gnosticism; indeed, his letter to Nicomedia expressly names Marcion, to whose errors he opposed the "Canon of Truth." The special situation in which Christianity found itself placed with regard to Gnosticism made the bishops more fully aware of their duties as guardians of orthodoxy, and the increased activity of the heads of congregations which resulted made the faithful more conscious of the monarchical episcopate and of its significance for the future.

Parallel to this activity of the bishops in combating Gnosticism ran that of the theological writers, to whom the rise and growth of the Gnostic movement acted as a powerful stimulus. An extensive body of literature from the Catholic side supported the Church authorities and provided a theological basis for the counter-attack.

Certain apocryphal writings on the Catholic side, such as the *Acta Pauli* and the *Epistula Apostolorum* were also of anti-Gnostic tendency. To his account of Gnostic systems Irenaeus added a refutation of their errors. He opposed them, using his own exact knowledge of Scripture and tradition, with the true doctrine of the Church. The author's interest in his subject and the soundness of his work make us forget any stylistic failings; his achievement was not surpassed by any of the anti-Gnostic writers who succeeded him. Of equal merit is the author of the *Philosophoumena* or *Refutatio,* which is generally ascribed (though not with absolute certainty) to the priest Hippolytus, who came from the East and was active in Rome at the beginning of the third century. He brought a new point of view into the discussion, inasmuch as he sought to show that the opinions of the Gnostics were not taken from Holy Scripture but from the works of the Greek philosophers, from the mysteries, from writers on astrology and magic — in fact, from non-Christian sources. Hippolytus' account of the catholic attitude is concise and jejune compared with that of Irenaeus and gives little information about the nature of the Church's campaign against Gnosticism.

More important are the works of the only Latin writer who engaged in the controversy with Gnosticism, Tertullian of Carthage, who, however, did not write until the third century. The two short treatises, *De carne Christi* and *De resurrectione carnis* prove positively from Scripture that two of the Gnostics' theses were untenable: their doctrine of Christ's "apparent" body and their rejection of the resurrection of the body. Three other writings were directed against particular Gnostics: Hermogenes, the Valentinians, and Marcion. To the last work, consisting of five books, Tertullian devoted special care; it gives a detailed account of the principal Marcionite doctrines followed by a skilful refutation based on reason and the Bible. In *De praescriptione haereticorum* he explains the meaning and value of apostolic tradition as opposed to the claim of the heretics, especially the Gnostics, to possess the true doctrine of Christ. The language he uses is that of the Roman law courts.

On the basis of this surviving anti-Gnostic literature we are able to give some account of the character and quality of the theological struggle against Gnosticism, at least in its main features. In general one may say that the Church's theologians thought out anew and established on a firmer foundation those points of Christian revelation which were particularly attacked and threatened by Gnostic teachings.

The claim of the heretics to be the sole possessors of the revelation imparted by Christ to his apostles meant nothing less than a depreciation of the Christian scriptures, which dated from apostolic times, and of the other, extra-biblical apostolic traditions; furthermore it implied a rejection of the Christian bishops' claim to be the only lawful witnesses to that body of tradition. If this Gnostic thesis were correct, then the whole foundation crumbled on which the inner cohesion of the Church had hitherto rested. The Christian theologians set to work to prevent the threatened collapse by bringing into the foreground the concepts of *apostolic tradition* and *succession,* and by deciding and confirming what constituted the Christian scriptures. A starting-point for the establishment of a *canon* of New Testament scriptures was already given in the books of the Old Testament, recognized as sacred. It is evident that two originally separate collections, the four Gospels and the Pauline epistles, gradually came closer together, although the latter were not yet accorded parity of esteem with the Gospels. According to Melito of Sardes, in the years 170–80, books of the New Testament were placed on the same level as those of the Old. No doubt the example of Marcion, who declared a clearly defined canon of New Testament writings to be necessary, hastened a development already begun in the Church. She did not however copy Marcion, but, in sharp contrast to him, accepted the Old Testament as sacred scriptures — the Christian understanding of them being made easier by developing allegorical interpretation — and then incorporated in her New Testament canon other books rejected by Marcion, notably the Acts of the Apostles and the Apocalypse. In the controversy with Gnosticism this canon became widely accepted, and in the "Muratorian Fragment," a list (made by the Roman congregation or one closely attached to it) of the New Testament books held to be canonical, it is already approaching its final form before the end of the second century.

In deciding which individual writings were to be included, the Church had to be able to invoke an undisputed, objective principle. This was to be found in ecclesiastical *tradition*. Only those books could be recognized as canonical which went back to apostolic times and had from an early date been particularly esteemed in the traditions of the whole Christian community. The only guarantors of the genuineness of such traditions were those leaders of congregations who could trace their unbroken succession back to the apostles. The positive effect of this principle of apostolic *succession* was to assure the place of *tradition* as an essential element of the Church's faith and theology.

A second principle was employed by the Christian theologians in their war against error, that which Irenaeus calls the *Canon of Truth,* given to the faithful at baptism. This seems to refer to the baptismal "symbol" or profession of faith, or at least to the summary of truths to which the catechumens had been introduced during their instruction before baptism. Whoever compared the teachings of the Gnostics with this norm or rule of faith could immediately see how they contradicted the true doctrine. The profession of faith at baptism had in fact about the middle of the second century been expanded in a christological sense to affirm more emphatically the reality of the human birth and of the Passion and death of Christ. This was a blow at the Docetism of many Gnostic sects and a declaration of the historicity of our Lord's miracles in the face of "spiritualist" attempts to explain them away. The same creed proclaimed the one God and Lord and Creator of the universe and thus rejected all Gnostic speculations about the origin of the cosmos as well as Marcion's doctrine of two gods. The Christian conviction of the resurrection of the body contrasted with the Gnostics' contempt for the body as part of matter, held by them to be radically evil.

During the course of the conflict some individual theologians were moved to lay stress on certain truths of revelation which were endangered or distorted by Gnostic opinions. Thus Irenaeus made it his special concern, in the face of the dualistic misunderstanding of original sin, to expound the true doctrine of the Fall, and in opposition to Gnostic self-redemption to emphasize the gratuitousness of the gift of grace. The exaggeration by the Gnostics of the value of "knowledge" for redemption was later the occasion for Clement of Alexandria and Origen to consider more deeply the relationship between faith and knowledge and to acquire a Christian understanding and a true theological appreciation of Gnosis.

For the Church, the rise of the Gnostic heresy was nevertheless a very efficient stimulus to reconsider the truths she possessed, to formulate some of them more clearly and to emphasize them more decidedly. Marcionitism in particular hastened the process of the development of dogma and of the Church's consciousness of her own identity, and thus it played its part in forming the character of the "Great Church" of the future.

The decisive victory in the Church's favor occurred before the end of the second century; within a few decades the poison had been ejected, and Gnosticism was thrown back upon itself. Marcion's church, because of its strict organization, lasted longer; but the other Gnostic groups lost all cohesion and lapsed into sectarianism, even though their ideas exercised a certain power of attraction upon educated members of Christian congregations in the big cities down to the middle of the third century, as the works of the Alexandrines, of Hippolytus and Tertullian testify. After that time, anti-Gnostic polemic writings appeared only sporadically, and their complete cessation in the fourth century proves that the once so powerful movement had become insignificant. The actual importance of this swift and permanent victory lies in the fact that the Church, faced by the Gnostic attack, preserved her special character as a supernatural community sharing the same faith and way of life and founded by Christ.

CHAPTER 16

The Rise of Montanism and the Church's Defense

The conflict with Gnosticism was not yet over when a new movement arose in the bosom of the Church which called itself the "New Prophecy." Its opponents called it the "heresy of the Phrygians," thus indicating the geographical area which saw its birth. Only in the fourth century was the term "Montanism" invented, when it was desired to emphasize the part played by Montanus in originating it.

The development of the Montanist movement had an early phase, then a period when it underwent modification by Tertullian, and finally a stage of decline after the Church had defeated it. The early phase began about 170, when the recently baptized Montanus, in Phrygia, proclaimed to his fellow-Christians, with ecstatic behavior and in strange, obscure language, that he was the mouthpiece and prophet of the Holy Spirit, who was now, through him, to lead the Church to all truth. At first this message was received with some doubts; but when two women, Priscilla and Maximilla, joined Montanus and in a similar ecstatic manner uttered their prophecies, while Montanus himself promised his adherents a higher place in the approaching heavenly Jerusalem, a wave of enthusiasm swept away all hesitation.

The most prominent feature of it was its *eschatological message:* the second coming of the Lord was at hand and with it the heavenly Jerusalem would be set up in the plain near the Phrygian town of Pepuza. In many parts of the empire men were not unprepared for this message, due to the grave tribulations which pestilence, war, and social distress under Marcus Aurelius had brought in their train. The prophets drew consequences from their alleged heavenly mandate which involved far-reaching interference with the existing practice of the Church and eventually forced the ecclesiastical authorities to condemn the whole movement.

Fasting suggested itself as a means of spiritual preparation for the coming of Christ, for it had long been recognized as a form of inner sanctification, and the official fasts known as "stations" had also been instituted from eschatological motives. Hitherto these fasts had been limited to two half-days in the week and recommended by the Church to the faithful as a voluntary exercise. Montanus went beyond the previous practice when he made continual fasting a matter of precept for all Christians, since Christ's return might be expected at any hour.

The same eschatological attitude lay behind the second demand of the Montanist prophets, that which forbade the Christian who was waiting for his Lord to make any attempt at flight from martyrdom. Evasion would have meant a renewed attachment to this world, which was after all approaching its end. Earthly possessions, too, had no value any more.

The Montanists' demand for the *renunciation of marriage* (as far as this was possible) was bound to have the most decisive effect. In their eyes it was marriage that most strongly attached men and women to this world.

Montanism naturally showed most enthusiasm in its early phase. New communities in Lydia and Galatia soon added to its already numerous adherents in Phrygia. From the provinces of Asia Minor it passed to Syria where it was especially successful at Antioch; soon it appeared in Thrace also. The Gallic congregations of Lyons and Vienne heard about the Montanist movement surprisingly early, as appears from Eusebius, who writes of a correspondence between those congregations and "brethren" in Asia and Phrygia in which it figures. Eleutheros, Bishop of Rome, was independently informed of the rise of the New Prophecy, but he clearly did not regard it as a serious danger, for he uttered no judgment upon it. Perhaps he was confirmed in this attitude by the Christians of Lyons, who sent their presbyter Irenaeus to Rome with a letter which likewise did not condemn the Phrygian movement. Pope Zephyrinus (199–217) also looked favorably upon it at first, for he sent its members letters of peace, which were the expression of fellowship within the Church. Tertullian ascribes the later change in Pope Zephyrinus' attitude to Praxeas of Asia Minor, who had given him more detailed information, admittedly somewhat distorted, about the prophets and their churches. The Roman bishops, then, were at first unaware of the danger which the New Prophecy represented to the existence of the ecclesiastical organization and of an ordered congregational life.

The first setback to the further spread of the movement was the death of the three original bearers of the prophecy. Maximilla died in 179. Perhaps the movement would have declined more rapidly — certainly the conflict with it would have taken a different form on the Church's side — if a man of the stature of Tertullian had not joined it and, on the level of literary discussion at least, given it a new importance.

We have no evidence as to when and how the African writer came into contact with the New Prophecy. From about the years 205–6 onward his writings show not only that he knew its basic teaching and its demands on the faithful, but that he approved of them. Even in a man of the spiritual greatness of Tertullian one might have assumed there would be a period of inner struggle preceding the change from Catholic to fanatical Montanist, for his new faith involved a contrast, patent to all the world, with his previous convictions; he now scorned in unmeasured invective what he had once ardently defended and respected. He found in it an attitude toward the Christian way of life which, in its pitiless severity to all that was mediocre, corresponded to his own rigoristic approach, but which could not in any way be connected with the Gnostic heresy or with the false doctrines of a man like Praxeas.

Tertullian was not, however, the man to accept the New Prophecy quite uncritically. He thought out afresh its doctrines and organization and modified it so much in detail that Tertullian's Montanism is something altogether different from that of the early days. The three great prophets of that first phase were for him no inviolable authority. Women were not to hold any priestly function, nor were they to be allowed to teach or to speak at divine worship, even if they possessed the gift of prophecy; their use of it, if so endowed, was to be confined to private utterances. He disavowed the more concrete prophecies referring to the descent of the heavenly Jerusalem — Pepuza he never mentions. One gets the impression that he wished to detach the New Prophecy from its connection with the personalities of its early phase and its local associations with Asia Minor and to give it a universal character. The movement's real mission consisted, according to him, in bringing Christianity and mankind in general to adult maturity through the working of the Paraclete.

Tertullian's principal Montanist writings repeat the rigoristic demands of the New Prophecy with undiminished severity and in passionate language. He defends the prohibition against flight in time of persecution, and represents one marriage only as a commandment of the Paraclete that admits of no exception (*secundae nuptiae adulterium*). In like manner he proves the obligation to fast, which the "natural men" or "psychics," whom he reviles in unmeasured terms, refused to accept. His attack on the Church's practice in the matter of penance is of ruthless severity toward sinners and the fallen. It was his attitude on this question that made him into an opponent in principle of the episcopal Church and led him finally to break away from ecclesiastical authority based upon the apostolic succession.

It is remarkable that *after* Tertullian's time the sources are at first completely silent about Montanism; in no work or letter of Cyprian is there even a remote echo of it. Evidently the exaggerated rigorism of its African advocate had been unable to gain any large body of adherents among the simple Christian folk of that region. Tertullian's writings, however, undoubtedly found readers; their literary quality and the uniqueness of their contents would have ensured that. But there were only readers, not converts.

The defensive campaign of the ecclesiastical authorities against Montanism began slowly, because the latter's opposition to the Christian way of life and to the tradition of the Church became apparent only on closer examination. In the message of the New Prophecy there was no connection to be seen with the errors the Church had hitherto been fighting against. Only when it became clear that its genuinely Christian aims were distorted by an immoderate exaggeration of their real significance, and that they represented a falsification of Christian tradition, did defensive action become necessary.

The bishops of Asia Minor must sooner or later have had to face the question, which is bound to arise in the case of every enthusiastic movement, whether the claims of the New Prophecy were not based upon an illusion. Some of them therefore tried to test the genuineness of these prophetic gifts, but they were repulsed by the Montanists. The bishops repeatedly took counsel together (the first example of such synods in the history of the Church) and came to the conclusion that it was not the Spirit of God which spoke through the new prophets. They were therefore to be excluded from the fellowship of the Church together with their adherents.

The victory of the Church over Montanism had consequences for her which brought her unique nature into greater prominence and determined her future development. By refusing to make the excessively ascetic program of the Montanists a norm binding on all Christians, she escaped the danger of sinking to the level of an insignificant sect of enthusiasts and preserved herself for the task of bringing the message of Christ to all men and making it possible for that message to be effective in every cultural milieu.

CHAPTER   1 7

The Expansion of Christianity
Down to the End of the Second Century

The question of the Church's expansion in the second century brings us back to Palestine again. The Jewish war of the first century had, for the time being, put an end to the missionary work of the Jerusalem congregation and of the Christians dwelling in the countryside. By the years 73–74 a new period of Palestinian Jewish Christianity had begun. Its center was again at Jerusalem, where the congregation was presided over by Simeon until his martyrdom about the year 107. The new community, like its predecessor, engaged in missionary activity; for Jews in large numbers had settled again in the city after the catastrophe of the seventies, but they now lacked a Temple as a center for their religious life.

Hegesippus states that at this time there were also Christians outside Jerusalem, especially in Galilee, and this information is confirmed by rabbinical sources. The missionary efforts of the Christians certainly encountered enormous difficulties. First of all they had to deal with heterodox Jewish Christianity, which, partly at least, continued to assert that the Law was still binding on all Christians and recognized Jesus of Nazareth as a great prophet indeed, but not as the Messiah and Son of God; moreover, it had been permeated by Gnostic ideas, as formulated by Simon Magus, Dositheos, Menander and Kerinthos.

The Christians met the most determined opposition from orthodox Palestinian

Jewry, based as it was upon a profound hatred of the "apostates" who had renounced the Sabbath and proclaimed as Messiah him whom the Jews had nailed to the cross. According to the evidence of Justin, not only was this hatred deliberately fomented in the synagogues of Palestine, but it led to powerful missionary counter-activity. Accessions from paganism were probably not considerable in Palestine.

As the Jewish war had brought to an end the original community, so did the rebellion of Bar Cochba in the years 132–35 conclude the second phase of Palestinian Christianity and with it the possibility of missionary work among the Jews of Palestine. As no person of Jewish race was allowed to live in the city of Aelia Capitolina, built on the site of Jerusalem, a Christian congregation could be recruited only from pagan converts. The Gentile-Christian congregation of Jerusalem played no remarkable role during the rest of the second century, at the end of which the bishopric of Aelia ranked below that of Caesarea. In the rest of Palestine too, the Christians were now mainly Greeks, dwelling almost exclusively in the towns.

In neighboring Syria the Christian churches dating from apostolic times maintained themselves or increased in importance. The Christians in Damascus, Sidon, and Tyre, likewise had increased in numbers during the course of the second century, while the Phoenician countryside remained largely pagan. In Antioch especially — its earliest important mission-center — Christianity gained in consideration on account of its bishop, Ignatius, and acquired new converts from among the Greek-speaking population.

In the second half of the second century new territory was opened up to Christianity in the east Syrian district of Osrhoëne, when the Jewish Christian Addai began to work in Edessa and its immediate neighborhood. The destruction of a Christian church at Edessa in the flood of 201 is evidence of a well developed ecclesiastical organization. It is characteristic of the young Syrian church that it did not confine itself to the cities, but from the beginning concerned itself with the evangelization of the country folk. From Edessa Christianity penetrated farther east into Mesopotamia, thanks to the labors of the missionary Addai.

Whereas southern Arabia appears to have had no Christians for a long time, northern Arabia or Transjordan shows evidence that Christianity was known there in the first and second centuries. "Arabs" were represented among the Jews and proselytes staying in Jerusalem at the first Pentecost (Acts 2:11). The faith may also have been brought to the lands east of the Jordan by Jewish Christians fleeing from Jerusalem and Palestine. But before the third century there can have been only individual Arab conversions, most likely in cities such as Bostra, which had come into contact with Hellenistic civilization.

The beginnings of Christianity in Egypt are obscure, in spite of the discovery of numerous papyri of the first and second centuries. The fragment of John's Gospel on papyri of the early second century may be regarded as the earliest proof of the presence of Christians on Egyptian soil. We must also bear in mind that the Gnostic mission had more initial success there than orthodox Christianity, of the existence of which in Alexandria we have no clear evidence dating from before the last two decades of the second century.

Both inland and on the west coast, missionaries could continue to build on the foundations laid by Paul. Even by the end of the first century a number of cities in the west of Asia Minor had organized churches (Apoc 2–3) in addition to those founded by the apostle. Ignatius of Antioch maintained relations with these and with the churches of Magnesia and Tralles. The testimony of Pliny is particularly significant: he states that about the year 112 there was in Bithynia a considerable Christian rural population. In the following decades the names of cities in Asia Minor in which Christianity had gained a footing continued to multiply; they are found in nearly all provinces.

In Crete the churches of Gortyna and Knossos are now known by name, as the correspondence of Dionysius of Corinth shows, whereas we have no information about the growth of the Pauline foundations in Cilicia and Cyprus during the second century. Compared with the rapid expansion or of Christianity in Asia Minor, the areas of Greece and Macedonia evangelized by Paul clearly lagged behind. Corinth surpassed all other churches in the intensity of its life, which, under Dionysius, attained a high degree of ecclesiastical organization. Athens at this time gave to the Church the apologist Aristides.

In the Latin West, the growth of the Christian congregation at Rome was probably greatest. The letter of Clement, Bishop of Rome, to the church of Corinth shows that despite the persecutions under Nero and Domitian the Gospel had gained many more believers before the end of the first century, though these may have been largely non-Romans. The respect in which the Roman church was held appears from the powerful attraction it exercised upon the Christians of the eastern provinces; Ignatius speaks of it with expressions of the deepest reverence. Marcion, Aberkios, Hegesippus and Irenaeus, Valentinus and Theodotos, Justin, Tatian, and Polycarp of Smyrna — all travelled for various reasons to the capital in the West; some to seek recognition for their peculiar doctrines, others to learn there the true Christian teaching or to work for the peace of the Church. Hermas, still writing in Greek, gives us a glimpse of ecclesiastical life in Rome with its everyday problems. With Bishop Victor toward the end of the second century the Latin element begins to predominate. The educated Greek Justin set himself a missionary task in Rome when, in a school like those of classical Greece, he taught "the true philosophy" to interested persons among the intellectuals of the capital. From the extensive charitable activity which the Roman congregation was able to carry on in the second half of the century we may conclude that its membership was considerable. There is little evidence concerning Christian advances in other parts of Italy during the second century. At the most, we can say that in the second half of the century some bishoprics had been established south of Rome.

Whereas Sicily does not appear to have been touched by Christian missionaries before the third century, Roman North Africa proved relatively early to be a profitable field for their activity, although we do not know their names nor the route they followed. The first document that gives information about African Christians, the Acts of the martyrs of Scili, already presupposes the existence there of Latin Christianity, for the six Christians who were put to death in July 180 (a later addition to the Acts shows that other Christians of the province fell victims to the persecution) evidently possessed the epistles of Paul in Latin. The place in which a large Christian community first grew up was, naturally enough, the capital, Carthage, where the catechetical and literary work of Tertullian about the year 200 was so extensive that it would have been possible only in a Christian group that was already numerically strong. North Africa is the only large area of the Latin West at this time which can in any way be compared with the mission fields of eastern Syria and Asia Minor.

The populations of the delta and middle valley of the Rhone owed their first contact with Christianity to the commercial relations between Asia Minor and the south coast of Gaul. For the old Greek colony of Massilia this contact must have come quite early. The numerical strength of the churches of Lyons and Vienne, which is implied in the account of forty or fifty Christians of those cities martyred under Marcus Aurelius, also presupposes a long period of development. Irenaeus of Lyons can be regarded as a missionary bishop, concerned for the Celtic population of his adopted homeland. To him too we owe our knowledge of Christian congregations then existing "in the Germanies" — probably in the Rhenish provinces with their chief towns of Cologne and Mainz — and in the Spanish provinces. But if Christianity had already penetrated to the frontier towns on the Rhine, it had certainly also reached Trier, situated further inside the frontier and much more frequented by traders. Its relations with the cities of the Rhone valley suggest too the way by which the faith reached the Moselle.

This survey of the expansion of Christianity in the course of the second century gives a clear impression that the missionary enthusiasm of the primitive Church was still fresh and active. The bearers of the Gospel were primarily the congregations and the enthusiasm of individual Christians; there is no indication of a central direction and organization of missionary work. The names of the missionaries are for the most part unknown.

Besides the type of preaching familiar from the apostolic period, new ways of proclaiming the Gospel were being employed. First there was the written word, used by the apologetical writers of the second century, whose intentions were also missionary and propagandist. Then there were some Christians who made use of the classical system of education; as teachers in private schools, they expounded the Christian faith. Finally, the heroic behavior of the martyrs in times of persecution became a missionary factor of the first importance, gaining for Christianity a body of new adherents which, if not numerically great, was spiritually of the highest quality.

Part Two

The Great Church of Early Christian Times (ca. 180–324 C.E.)

Karl Baus

Introduction

The transition to the third century introduces the period of the early Christian Church in which it finally became the "great Church" through a combination of external expansion and inner development. In a space of some one hundred and thirty years an interior stability was attained in organization, ritual, day-to-day parish life and clarity of aim in theological studies. Upon attainment of external freedom, it was immediately possible for the Church to assume the tasks inherent in the promising new situation.

In the first place the decisive missionary advance within the Roman Empire was successfully continued through the third century. The organization necessary to cope with this growth was supplied by the formation of larger associations of churches. These developed around certain centers: Antioch in Syria, Alexandria in Egypt, Ephesus in Asia Minor, Caesarea in Pontus, Carthage in North Africa, and Rome, which served the rest of the Latin West.

Everywhere within the Church new forms in liturgy and parish life were created and testify to an intense determination to lead the Christian life. Systematic organization of the catechumenate shows a clear pastoral awareness of the importance of serious introduction to the sacramental world of Christianity. The differentiation of the lower grades of the sacramental order illustrates the clergy's ability to adapt itself to growing pastoral demands. The shock resulting from the large number of Christian defections during the Decian persecution led to thorough reflection, and the regulation of the practice of penance. The rise of the order of ascetics and of the early eremitical movement demonstrated a serious striving after Christian perfection, and laid the foundations for the full growth of monasticism in the fourth century. Various ecclesiastical ordinances served to stabilize liturgical forms in the life of the parish communities; and, in addition, there were at least the beginnings of the separate rites and liturgies which were to characterize the greater groupings within the Church. Christian art developed, and testifies to the growing sureness and confidence of Christian feeling and attitude toward life.

The most enduring effect resulted from the further elaboration of Christian theology in the third century. This development received new impulses from pagan opponents and writers, and from controversies within the Church. The encounter with Middle Platonism proved especially valuable, for it contributed to the rise of the theological school of Alexandria, which had Origen as its outstanding creative figure. Through the work of scholars from Alexandria and Antioch the central position of the Bible in the work of theology was recognized, and great commentaries expounded its significance for faith and religious life. The Trinitarian question formed the center of an important theological discussion. The monarchian attempt at a solution to this problem was rejected, but a subordinationism was advanced which held the seeds of the fourth century's great dogmatic controversy.

Section One

The Inner Consolidation of the Church in the Third Century

C H A P T E R   1 8

The Attack of the Pagan State on the Church

The Persecutions under Septimius Severus

With the accession of the Syrian dynasty's founder Septimius Severus (193–211), a tranquil phase of potential development, both internally and externally, seemed to begin for Christianity. This emperor soon publicly demonstrated his goodwill toward individual Christians. His contemporary, and fellow-African, Tertullian gives definite and impressive proofs of this attitude. Christians held influential positions at court, as they had under Commodus. Men and women of Roman senatorial families, whose adherence to the Christian faith was known to the emperor, were openly protected against the mob, while he vouched for their loyalty. It is a further indication of the freedom of Christianity in the first years of his reign that, about the year 196, the bishops were able to meet in synods at which the date of Easter was discussed. It is true that proceedings against individual Christians were not unknown, for the legal situation created by the rescript of Trajan was still unaltered. Tertullian's *Liber apologeticus* (ca. 197) was provoked by the occurrence of such cases. It was not until the tenth year of his reign that Septimius' attitude altered drastically and created a completely new situation for Christianity.

In the year 202 an imperial edict was issued forbidding conversion to Judaism or Christianity under pain of heavy penalties. It was not only the individual Christian who was at the mercy of a denunciation; the Church as an organization was affected. Every activity which aimed at winning new members could be punished; therefore all missionary work would be made impossible and Christianity would slowly die out within the empire.

Proceedings against Christians as individuals were also continued. From oc-

casional references by Tertullian we can infer that the anti-Christian attitude of
various individual Roman officials or the hostility of the pagan populace prompted
renewed recourse to the rescript of Trajan. No reliable information is available on
the course of the persecutions in Rome. They either abruptly ceased or died away
gradually in the last years of Septimius' reign.

Certainly Caracalla (211–17) inaugurated a period of religious toleration which
was of considerable advantage to Christianity, as was recognized by the early
Christian writers themselves. We find Christians once again in influential positions at court and when, on the emperor's accession to the throne, an amnesty
was granted to deportees, Christians were not excepted from it. Under Severus
Alexander (222–35), the intellectual and religious atmosphere of the court was
determined by the emperor's gifted mother, Julia Mamaea. She may be judged to
have had definite leanings toward Christianity. Her tolerance is reflected in the attitude of the young emperor, who accepted numerous Christians among his closer
associates and entrusted the building of the library near the Pantheon to the Christian Julius Africanus. His policy of religious toleration is accurately characterized
by a phrase of his biographer in the *Historia Augusta,* which states that he allowed
the Christians to exist. This assertion is borne out by the unhampered development
of Christian life in the East. Christian inscriptions of this period are found in great
numbers in Asia Minor, and it was possible to erect a Christian place of worship
in Dura-Europos before 234. In the West Christian burial was now organized quite
freely at Rome. It is characteristic that no legal proceedings against a Christian
and no Christian martyrdom can with certainty be assigned to Alexander's time.

A reaction did not occur until the reign of the former guards officer Maximinus
(235–38). The change of policy first affected the numerous Christians at court;
but it was directed principally against the Church's leaders and introduced a new
note into the anti-Christian actions of an emperor. Had this reign lasted longer, it
could have been of grave consequence for the Church. In Rome itself, it can be
established that the two Christian leaders there, namely, Bishop Pontianus and
the priest Hippolytus, were deported to Sardinia, where both died.

The struggle for power by the soldier emperors who followed left them no
leisure to occupy themselves with the question of the Christians. But in Philippus
Arabs (244–49) a ruler came to power who showed such sympathy for the Christians that a complete reconciliation seemed possible between Christianity and
the government of the Roman State. And the emperor's personal inclination and
that of his wife Severa are mirrored in the correspondence between the imperial
pair and Origen.

A retrospective survey of the relations between the Roman State and Christianity in the first half of the third century makes it clear that the phases of really
peaceful co-existence, and sometimes of positive toleration, predominate over
the waves of harsh persecution. Only twice can the features of a systematic policy
against Christianity be observed: first when Septimius Severus made adherence
to Christianity an indictable offence; and secondly when Maximinus Thrax took
action against the leaders of the Christian communities. For the rest, the haphaz-
ard, unsystematic proceedings against individual Christians reveal the vacillating
religious policy of the holders of power in the State and of their subordinate authorities in the provinces. The unsettled course adopted by these officials was

partly a result of the political decline of the empire under the soldier emperors. At the beginning of the second half of the century the emperor Decius came to power and determined to re-establish the old brilliant reputation of the Roman State by restoring its ancient religion.

The Persecution under Decius

The first measures of the new emperor might appear as a typical or common reaction against the rule of a predecessor. Christians were arrested as early as December 249, and in January 250 the head of the Roman community, Bishop Fabian, was put to death. A general edict in 250, however, soon proved that Decius was pursuing aims concerning the Christians which far exceeded those of his predecessors. All the inhabitants of the empire were summoned to take part in a general sacrifice to the gods, a *supplicatio*. But it was significant that, at the same time, exact supervision of the edict's implementation was ordered throughout the empire. Commissions were set up to see that the sacrifice was performed, and to issue everyone with a certificate, or *libellus*. Before a certain date the *libelli* were to be exhibited to the authorities; and anyone refusing to sacrifice was thrown into prison. Although the decree did not explicitly condemn the Christians, their leading representatives and writers rightly considered it to be the most serious attack that their Church had yet sustained. The bitter laments of the bishops Dionysius of Alexandria and Cyprian of Carthage leave no doubt that the number of those who in one way or another met the demand of the edict especially in Egypt and North Africa, far exceeded the number of those who refused it.

In contrast to these, however, there was in every province of the empire an elite ready to answer for their belief with their lives. Cyprian's letters provide the most informative account of the situation in North Africa. He had sought out a place of refuge in the neighborhood of Carthage, but was able to keep in touch with his flock by correspondence and convey words of encouragement and consolation to the Christians who were already under arrest. Those in prison, including many women and children, showed an intense and genuine longing for martyrdom that was not always fulfilled, for many were released even before the end of the persecution. Cyprian deplored the pride and moral lapses by which some of these latter detracted from the worth of their true confession of faith, but he was able to enroll others among his clergy, so exemplary was their behavior. Cyprian does not give exact figures regarding those who offered the sacrifices, and names only a few of the *confessores*. Naturally, the number of those put to death, the *martyres coronati* or *consummati*, was smaller by comparison. Cyprian mentions two by name, but presupposes a larger number. The confessor Lucianus once mentions sixteen by name, most of whom were left to die of hunger in prison. In Rome, too, some Christians were released from jail after resolutely confessing their faith. For Egypt, Bishop Dionysius of Alexandria mentions the kind of death suffered by fourteen martyrs: ten of them died at the stake and four by the sword. But he knew of numerous other martyrs in the towns and villages of that country, just as he knew that many Christians died of hunger and cold while fleeing from persecution. Finally, he mentions also a group of five Christian soldiers who voluntarily confessed their faith when they encouraged a waverer to stand fast; because of their outspoken courage the court left them unmolested. In neighboring Palestine Bishop Alexander of Jerusalem died a martyr's death at that time, as did Bishop Babylas, the leader of the Antioch community. The aged Origen's longing for martyrdom was at least partly satisfied in Caesarea where he was subjected to cruel torture.

The rapid cessation of the Decian persecution is in a sense surprising. The impression gained is that the administrative apparatus was overtaxed by so extensive an undertaking. The departure of the emperor for the Danubian provinces, occasioned by a new invasion of the Goths, halted it completely; and his death on the battle-field prevented its rapid resumption. The great mass of those who had fallen away soon clamored to be received into the Church again, while many *libellatici* atoned for their fault by a new confession of faith shortly after their lapse. The number of former Christians won over to the State religion does not seem to have been particularly high. The Christian community, for its part, recognized that much within it was decayed and ready to crumble. Conscious leaders of communities, like Cyprian, were spurred by this condition to serious reflection, which, after long controversies about the question of penance, was to lead to a regeneration of the Church.

Valerian and Gallienus

The ensuing seven years of tranquillity for the Church (250–57) were disturbed only by a short wave of persecution in Rome. Dionysius, Bishop of Alexandria, reports arrests in Egypt also occurring at that time. Gallus' repressive action was probably aimed at indulging popular sentiment, which blamed the Christians for the plague then devastating the empire. The first years of the reign of his successor, Valerian (253–60) produced for the Church a situation which Dionysius of Alexandria celebrates in enthusiastic tones. No predecessor of Valerian had been so well-disposed toward the Christians. Indeed so friendly was Valerian's attitude that his household was, so to speak, one of God's communities. But the fourth year of the emperor's reign brought a surprising change, introducing a short but extremely harsh and violent persecution. The emperor's minister and later usurper, Macrianus may have suggested The idea of remedying the precarious financial state of the empire by confiscating the property of wealthy Christians. Valerian was probably also impelled by the threatening situation of the empire in general. He sought to counter a possible threat from within by a radical move against the Christians. The plan is clear even in the edict of 257: the blow was to strike the clergy; bishops, priests, and deacons were to be obliged to offer sacrifice to the gods and any of them celebrating divine worship or holding assemblies in the cemeteries were to be punished with death. In North Africa and Egypt, the leaders of the churches, Cyprian and Dionysius, were at once arrested; and, in addition, many Christians of the African provinces were condemned to forced labor in the mines. The edict of 258 took a further decisive step: clerics who refused the sacrifice were immediately to be put to death. But this time the leading laity in the Christian communities were also included. Senators and members of the order of knights were to lose their rank and possessions, as were their wives; the latter could be punished with banishment and their husbands with execution, if they refused to offer sacrifice to the gods. Imperial officials in Rome and the provinces, the *caesariani,* were also threatened with forced labor and the confiscation of their possessions for similar offense. The aim of this policy was clear: the clergy and prominent members of the Christian communities, who enjoyed wealth and position, were to be eliminated; and the Christians, thus deprived of leaders and influence, were to be condemned to insignificance. The victims were numerous, especially among the clergy. The proportion of laity among the victims of the persecution was not inconsiderable: it was probably quite large in Egypt and highest in North Africa.

The persecution ceased with the tragic end of the emperor who was taken prisoner by the Persians in 259 and soon died. The general impression left by the attitude of the Christians on this occasion is far more favorable than in their previous tribulation. Only in one African record of martyrdom is there a mention of lapsed Christians. The Christians met this trial with far more calm determination than they had displayed eight years previously, and withstood it extremely well. Valerian's son and successor, Gallienus was not content, with a merely tacit cessation of the persecution and issued an edict of his own in the Christians' favor. In this the emperor says that he had restored their places of worship to the Christians some time previously, and that nobody was to molest them in these places. This recognition of ecclesiastical property by the highest civil authority represented a far-reaching act of toleration, and had a favorable effect on the future of the Church. Although Christianity was not yet officially recognized thereby as a *religio licita,* nevertheless there began with Gallienus' edict a period of peace which lasted more than forty years.

C H A P T E R 1 9

Further Development of Christian Literature in the East in the Third Century

The Beginnings of the Theological School of Alexandria

The inner consolidation of Christianity in the third century is particularly evident and impressive in the domain of early patristic literature. More and more frequently, members of the ruling classes joined the new faith and felt impelled to serve it by word and writing in ways which corresponded with their level of culture. This created an essential condition for the development of a learned theology. The earliest attempts of this kind are found of course as early as the second century, when educated converts such as Justin and his pupil Tatian presented themselves publicly in Rome as teachers of the "new philosophy," and gave a well-grounded introduction to the understanding of the Christian faith to a relatively small circle of pupils.

The "schools" of these teachers were not, however, institutions of the Roman Christian community itself, but private undertakings by learned Christians. Out of a sense of missionary obligation, and in the manner of philosophical teachers of the time, these men expounded their religious beliefs to a circle of those who might be interested, and substantiated them by constant comparison with other religious trends. In a similar manner Gnostics like Apelles, Synerus, and Ptolemy, appeared in Rome as private teachers; and men like Theodotus from Byzantium and perhaps Praxeas, too, tried within the framework of such private schools to win support for their particular Monarchian views. While no objection was raised against the teaching activities of orthodox laymen like Justin, the authorities of the Roman community took exception to the activities of Gnostic or Monarchian teachers, and finally excluded them from the community of the Church. These problems induced the Roman bishops of the third century to seek to bring private Christian schools under their control and to transform them into a purely ecclesiastical institution which would administer the instruction of the catechumens. No theological school within the proper sense of the word developed either in Rome or elsewhere in the Latin West, because certain conditions of an intellectual kind were just not present. Neither were the personalities to whom they might have been of use. But both prerequisites were existent in great quantity in the East.

In the Greek East the Egyptian capital, Alexandria, with its scientific tradition and the interest generally shown by its educated upper classes in religious and philosophical questions, was to prove the most favorable soil for the development of a Christian theology on a learned intellectual basis. By establishing the two great libraries of the Sarapeion and the Museion, the first Ptolemies had laid the foundation of that lively interest in the most varied branches of learning which had developed in Alexander's city during the Hellenistic period. This cultural development, especially in the areas of Hellenistic literature and neo-Platonic philosophy, helped to create a general atmosphere which was to prove particularly fruitful when it encountered Christianity. Educated Alexandrians who had adopted the Christian religion were inevitably moved to confront it with the intense cultural life around them; and those of them who felt impelled publicly to account for their faith became the first Christian teachers in the Egyptian capital. According to the sources it is impossible to speak of a "school of catechists in Alexandria" as early as the end of the second century.

The first Christian teacher whose name is known is Pantainus, of Sicilian origin, who was giving lessons about the year 180, expounding and defending his Christian view of the world; but he was teaching without ecclesiastical appointment, just as Justin or Tatian earlier had done in Rome. Any interested person, pagan or Christian, could frequent this private school, and the syllabus was entirely a matter for the teacher's judgment. Clement of Alexandria must be considered to have been the second teacher of this kind, but he cannot be regarded as the successor of Pantainus at the head of any school. He publicly taught the "true gnosis" independently of, and perhaps even simultaneously with Pantainus. The first phase of Origen's teaching activity still had this private character. It was only later, perhaps about 215, that he undertook the instruction of catechumens at the request of Bishop Demetrius, and so became the ecclesiastically appointed head of a catechetical school. He provided a circle of educated persons and advanced students with a systematic exposition of the philosophic knowledge of the age, crowned by instruction in the Christian religion. In this respect, Origen had taken a decisive step; the work which Clement before him had undertaken as a private teacher was now placed directly at the service of the church of Alexandria, which thereby received a school of its own in which instruction in the Christian religion was given in no way inferior in quality to the contemporary pagan course of education. This institution alone has a claim to the title of a theological school. And it is not surprising that Origen's bold step was received with some reserve: he soon had to defend himself against the accusation of attributing too much importance to profane philosophy, but the success and enthusiastic support of his students made him keep to the path he had taken. When the rift between Origen and Bishop Demetrius led to his quitting the country, the Alexandrian school of theologians quickly reverted to a simple school for catechumens, giving to those seeking baptism their first introduction to the Christian religion. Origen took the nature and spirit of his foundation with him to Caesarea in Palestine. Here he tried until his death to realize his ideal of a Christian institute for advanced teaching, this time with the full approval of the Palestinian episcopate.

After Origen's death, it is only possible to speak of an Alexandrian theological school in a wider sense; we can only denote a theology bearing the characteristic marks which the two first great Alexandrians, Clement and Origen, gave it: namely, the drawing of philosophy into the service of theology, a predilection for the allegorical method of scriptural exegesis, and a strong tendency to penetrate by speculation on an idealistic basis the supernatural content of the truths of revelation.

Clement of Alexandria

While none of the writings of the first Alexandrian teacher, has come down to us, three longer works and a small treatise survive from the pen of Clement. Though they are merely the remnants of a more extensive production, they permit us to form an impression of his characteristics as a writer, his theological interests, and the aim of his teaching. Clement was the son of a pagan family of Athens, became a Christian in adult life and, after extensive travels, reached Alexandria toward the end of the second century. There he was active as a Christian teacher until the persecution under Septimius Severus forced him to emigrate to Asia Minor about the year 202, and he died still in this area, about 215.

Clement's secular learning is shown by the very title of the first of the three main works mentioned above. He wrote a *Protrepticus,* a discourse of admonition and propaganda, which presupposes educated pagan readers who are to be won over to his "philosophy." His aim is, therefore, in fact the same as that of previous apologists, but his work is far superior to their writings in form and tone. Naturally, in a Christian apologia, polemic against pagan polytheism could not be lacking, but it is conducted by Clement in a calm and thoughtful manner. He concedes that many of the pagan philosophers, Plato above all, were on the way to a knowledge of the true God; but full knowledge, and with it eternal salvation and the satisfaction of all human aspiration, was only brought by the Logos, Jesus Christ, who summons all men, Hellenes and barbarians, to follow him. A level of discourse on the Christian faith was here attained that had not been known before, and one which could appeal to a cultivated pagan.

Anyone who allows himself to be won over as a follower of the Logos must entrust himself absolutely to the latter's educative power. Clement's second main work, the *Paidagogus,* is therefore intended as a guide in this respect, and at the same time as an aid to training in Christian matters. The fundamental attitude required is first developed: the Logos-Paidagogos has provided by his life and commands in Holy Scripture the standards by which the life of a Christian should be directed; the Christian who acts in accordance with them fulfills to a higher degree the "duties" to which, for example, an adherent of the Stoic philosophy knows he is obliged, since the demands of the *Logos* are in the fullest sense "in conformity with reason." Clement illustrates the application of this basic principle with many examples from daily life, and displays a gift of discernment and a balanced and fundamentally affirmative attitude to cultural values. Both Christian ascesis and Christian love of one's neighbor must prove themselves in the actual circumstances of civilization.

Their formal treatment and intellectual structure show that the *Protrepticus* and the *Paidagogus* are essentially related works. The third surviving work, the *Stromata,* cannot be considered as the conclusion of this trilogy, for its themes are quite different from those announced, and in style and form it in no way corresponds to the first and second studies. The title itself indicates its literary category: a number and variety of questions are treated in an informal manner, are intended in the first place to appeal to pagans interested in religious and philosophical matters. One purpose certainly pervades the whole work: to prove by reasoned confrontation with contemporary Gnosticism that the Christian religion is the only true gnosis, and to represent the faithful Christian as the true Gnostic.

At baptism every Christian receives the Holy Spirit and thereby the capacity to rise from simple belief to an ever more perfect knowledge; but only those rise to attain it in fact who perpetually strive to do so, and who struggle for ever greater perfection in their manner of life. Only by an increasing effort of self-education and by penetrating more and more deeply into the gospel, and that solely within the Church, which is the "only virgin Mother," does a man become a true Gnostic and so surpass the cultural ideal of the "wise man" of pagan philosophy. The model of the Christian Gnostic is the figure of Christ, whom he must come to resemble, and by following whom he becomes an image of God. Linked with this is a perpetual growth in the love of God, which makes possible for the Gnostic a life of unceasing prayer, makes him see God and imparts to him a resemblance to God. This ascent from step to step, does not, however, remove the true Gnostic from the company of his brethren to whom such an ascent has not been granted; rather does he serve them, ever ready to help, and summons them to follow his path by the example of the purity of his life. Such practical questions of actual living stand in the center of Clement's thought and teaching. Speculative theological problems occupy only the fringe of his interests. He takes over the idea of the Logos from St. John, but does not penetrate more deeply into it. The Logos is united with the Father and the Holy Spirit in the divine Trias; the world was created by him, and he revealed God with increasing clarity, first in the Jewish Law, then in Greek philosophy, and finally in becoming man. By his blood mankind was redeemed, and men still drink his blood in order to share in his immortality. The Redeemer Christ recedes, for Clement, behind the Logos as teacher and lawgiver. He did not further speculative theology properly so-called, but he is the first comprehensive theorist of Christian striving after perfection.

Origen

Fortune did not favor the life-work of Origen, the greatest of the Alexandrian teachers and the most important theologian of Eastern Christianity. The greater part of his writings has perished because the violent quarrels which broke out concerning his orthodoxy led to his condemnation by the Synod of Constantinople in 553. As a consequence, his theological reputation suffered for a long time, and the reading of his works was proscribed. Few of these works remain in his Greek mother-tongue, and the greater part of his biblical homilies has survived only in Latin translations, notably those by Jerome and Rufinus. Friends and admirers in the third and fourth centuries preserved a little of his canon and this helps to throw light on the aim and purpose of his life's work, the most useful of this evidence being preserved in the sixth book of Eusebius' *Ecclesiastical History.*

The first decisive influence on Origen was that of the Christian atmosphere of his parents' home. There he inherited and never lost the high courage to confess his faith, and the constant readiness to be active in the ecclesiastical community. Quite soon, while instructing interested pagans in the Christian faith on his own initiative, he felt the need of a deeper philosophical training; and this he found in the lectures of the neo-Platonist Ammonius Saccas, whose influence on him was strong and lasting. Journeys in his early manhood took him to Caesarea in Palestine, where he became a friend of the bishop, Theoctistus, and of Alexander, the head of the Jerusalem community, to Arabia at the invitation of the imperial governor; and also to the West, where he travelled to Rome. These journeys gave him a vivid idea of the life of the Church as a whole, and strengthened his inclination to work everywhere through his lectures for a deeper understanding of Scripture and belief.

His appointment as teacher of the catechumens and his duties as head of the theological school in Alexandria brought his rich intellectual and spiritual powers to full development, and initiated the creative period of his life. This was not fundamentally disturbed when, in the years 230–31, conflict with Bishop Demetrius forced him to transfer his activities to Caesarea in Palestine. The ostensible cause of his estrangement from the local bishop was his ordination to the priesthood without the former's knowledge. It was conferred on him by Palestinian bishops, although Origen, being a eunuch (he had castrated himself in a youthful excess of asceticism), was not, according to the views of the time, a suitable candidate. The deeper reason, however, was the bishop's inability to have a man of such high reputation and intellectual quality by his side. The understanding which was shown to Origen in his second sphere of activity, namely, in Palestine, was munificently repaid by him; for, in addition to his actual teaching, he served the life of the Church directly, both by his tireless preaching and by public theological discussions about problems of the day, which repeatedly took him as far as Arabia. He had occasion to crown his fidelity to faith and Church by manfully confessing the faith during the Decian persecution, when he was imprisoned and subjected to cruel torture. About the year 253 or 254 he died in Tyre as a result of this treatment, when nearly seventy years of age.

The kernel of Origen's theological achievement was his work on the Bible, his efforts for its better understanding and the use made of it to create a right attitude in belief and true piety. His literary production took the form of critical and philological work on the text of Scripture, scientific commentaries on individual books, and finally in his abundant discourses on the Bible, which were recorded by stenographers and later published. These are works of edification. The impressive undertaking of the Hexapla served to establish a trustworthy text of the Bible. It presented in six parallel columns the original Hebrew in Hebrew characters, a Greek transcription, the translations by Aquila and Symmachus, the Septuagint and the Theodotion translation. What was probably the only copy of this work was placed in the library of Caesarea, where it could still be consulted in the time of Jerome and even later. A particularly hard fate overtook the great scriptural commentaries; many of which perished completely, or did so with the exception of a few fragments, such as the commentaries on Genesis, the Psalms, Proverbs, Isaiah, Ezechiel, the Minor Prophets, Luke, and most of the Epistles of St. Paul. Larger portions of the commentaries on the Canticle of Canticles, the Gospels of St. Matthew and St. John were preserved, partly in Greek and partly in Latin translations. The works which most frequently survived were homilies, particularly esteemed for their pastoral use of the Old Testament.

It was with an attitude of deepest reverence that Origen undertook this service of Holy Scripture; for in it he encountered the living word of God which it embodies. And just as all events take place in mysteries, so Scripture also is full of mysteries which unveil themselves only to one who implores this revelation in insistent prayer. He knew that this is only found when the deeper spiritual and divine sense is recognized, that which is hidden behind the letter is the treasure hidden in a field. That is why the allegorical interpretation of Scripture was not for Origen merely a traditional and easily applied method, taken over from the exposition of secular texts. It was often a compelling necessity for him, absolutely essential if what is sometimes offensive in the purely literal sense of Scripture is to be transcended. Origen was fully aware that allegory has its limits. Nevertheless, in the hand of the master and despite all errors in detail, this method remains the path that leads him to the very heart of Scripture, affording ultimate religious insight and knowledge.

The daily reading of Scripture, to which Origen exhorts us, became for him the well-spring of his personal religious life; and it also made him a teacher of the Christian ideal of striving after perfection, whose subsequent influence was immeasurable: first on Eastern monasticism, and then in the Latin West, by way of St. Ambrose. The ultimate goal of the ascent to perfection is the resemblance to God, to which man was called when God created him in his own image and likeness. The surest way to this goal is the imitation of Christ; and to be so centered on Christ is the characteristic attitude of Origen's piety, just as later the principle "Christus" was the basic concept of his pupil, Ambrose of Milan. A presupposition for the success of this imitation is correct self-knowledge, which brings awareness of one's own sinfulness; and this, in turn, imposes a stubborn fight against the perils which threaten from world and from one's own passions. Only a person who has reached *apatheia* is capable of further mystical ascent, but this cannot be attained without a serious ascetic effort, in which fasting and vigils have their place just as much as the reading of Scripture and the exercise of humility. The ascent to mystical union with the Logos takes place by degrees. The profound yearning for Christ is fulfilled in a union with him which is accomplished in the form of a mystical marriage; Christ becomes the bridegroom of the soul, which in a mystical embrace receives the *vulnus amoris*. Origen here is not only the first representative of a profound devotion to Jesus, but also the founder of an already richly developed Christocentric and bridal mysticism, from which the medieval Christocentric spirituality of William of St. Thierry and Bernard of Clairvaux derived, and from which it drew considerable substance.

While in Alexandria, Origen wrote a systematic exposition of the chief doctrines of Christianity. He gave this first dogmatic handbook in the history of Christian theology the title *Peri Archōn* (Concerning Principles), and dealt in four books with the central questions concerning God, the creation of the world, the fall of man, redemption through Jesus Christ, sin, freedom of the will, and Holy Scripture as a source of belief. The Greek original has perished; the surviving version by Rufinus, has smoothed down or eliminated entirely many things to which objection might be raised. There is, consequently, some uncertainty about the precise view which Origen held on certain questions.

In his introduction, Origen speaks with great clarity about the principles of method which guided him in his work; Scripture and tradition are the two primary sources for his exposition of Christian doctrine. He knows that they can be approached only with the attitude of a believer. The Old and New Testaments, the books of Law, the Prophets and the Epistles of St. Paul: all contain the words of Christ and are a rule of life for the Christian, because they are inspired. The authority of the Church guarantees that no spurious writings intrude. Only that truth can be received in faith which does not contradict ecclesiastical and apostolic tradition, and this is found in the teaching of the Church which per *successionis ordinem* was handed down from the apostles. She is the true Ark in which men can find salvation: the house which is marked with the blood of Christ and outside which there is no redemption.

As the rule of faith contains only the necessary fundamental doctrines preached by the apostles, without giving further reasons for them or showing in any detail their inner connections, a wide field of activity remains open to theology. According to Origen, this is where the task lies for those who are called to it by the Holy Spirit through the special gifts of wisdom and knowledge. Theirs is the vocation of penetrating deeper into the truths of revelation and of framing by an appropriate method a theological system from Scripture and tradition. The execution of his own project makes it plain that Origen was not a born systematizer. But of much greater weight than this imperfection of form, are the particular theological views which gave rise to the later controversies about their author's orthodoxy. In his doctrine of the Trinity, Origen still thinks in subordinationist terms: only the Father is *ho theos* or *autotheos;* the Logos, of course, likewise possesses the divine nature, but in regard to the Father he can be called *deuteros theos.* Yet Origen clearly expresses the eternity of the Logos and characterizes him as *homoousios;* and so an advance is made here as compared with early subordinationism. Origen, one might say, is on the path that led to Nicaea. In Christology, too, he devises modes of expression which point to the future: the union of the two natures in Christ is so close in his doctrine that the communication of idioms follows from it; as far as can now be traced the term God-man, *theanthrōpos,* first occurs with Origen. Origen also followed paths of his own in the doctrine of Creation; before the present world, a world of perfect spirits existed to which the souls of men then belonged; these were, therefore, pre-existent. Only a fall from God brought upon them banishment into matter which God then created. The measure of their pre-mundane guilt actually determines the measure of grace which God grants each human being on earth.

All creation strives back toward its origin in God, and so is subjected to a process of purification which can extend over many aeons and in which all souls, even the evil spirits of the demons and Satan himself, are cleansed with increasing effect until they are worthy of resurrection and reunion with God. Then God is once more all-in-all, and the restoration of all things (*apochatastasis tōn pantōn* is attained. The eternity of hell was practically abandoned as a result of this conception. That a new Fall would be possible after this process and consequently a new creation of the world and a further series of purifications necessary, was presented by Origen merely as an arguable possibility and not as certain Christian teaching. Origen recognized perfectly the proper value of what pertains to the senses and the body, and in fact, saw its importance precisely in its function as an image of a spiritual world that lies behind it. Consequently, he did not call for its annihilation, but for its spiritualization and transfiguration. He was likewise convinced that every baptized person is called on principle to perfection, but that there are many stages on the way to it, and that every stage can assimilate only an appropriate part of the truth of revelation. He believed in consequence that the full grasp of Christian truth is only possible at the final stage.

Like every theological achievement, that of Origen must be judged according to the possibilities and conditions which the age provided. Viewed as a whole, his theological work, and especially his systematic treatise *Concerning Principles,* represents a creative personal achievement and consequently an enormous advance in Christian theology. For a judgment of the whole, the fact is important that the work was inspired by the purest ecclesiastical spirit. For all the independence and freedom of his theological questioning and inquiry, Origen wanted only to serve the Church, and was always ready to submit to her judgment. Such an attitude should have prevented posterity from proscribing Origen's work as a whole.

Dionysius of Alexandria, Methodius, Lucian of Antioch and His School

Subsequent teachers in the school of Alexandria, which after Origen's departure assumed once more the character of a school for catechumens, are overshadowed by their great predecessors. The orthodoxy of Dionysius' (later bishop of the Egyptian capital [247–48 to 264–65]) teaching on the Trinity was doubted in Rome, and he attempted to demonstrate it in an apologia composed in four books against Dionysius, Bishop of Rome. He opposed chiliastic ideas in his work *On the Promises,* in which he rejected John the apostle's authorship of the Apocalypse. The written works of Theognostus and Pierius, Dionysius' successors at the head of the school for catechumens, drew on Origen's achievement. The *Hypotyposes* of Theognostus was a dogmatic work, while Pierius occupied himself more with exegesis and homiletics.

Other Eastern writers are also found within the range of Origen's influence, and their inferior performances make the greatness of the master stand out in sharper relief. Numbered among them are: his pupil Gregory Thaumaturgus (d. ca. 270), Julius Africanus (d. post 240), Pamphilus of Caesarea, and Methodius who became an opponent of Origen's theology.

The beginnings of the second theological school in the East are no less obscure than those of the Alexandrian school. It sprang up in the Syrian capital of Antioch, an important center of the Hellenic world where conditions were similar to those in Alexandria. Tradition unanimously names the Antiochan priest Lucian as founder of the school. In the time of Bishop Paul of Samosata, a priest named Malchion enjoyed a considerable reputation in Antioch for wide learning, but was a teacher in a secular Greek school. He demonstrated his superior theological training in the controversy with Paul of Samosata at the Synod of Antioch (268) which led to the latter's condemnation. It is only with Lucian that the records in the sources become more precise. The fact that Lucian was one of the clergy of Antioch permits the assumption that his activity as a Christian teacher was authorized by his bishop. His theological learning, which is praised by Eusebius, did not find expression in extensive publications. His real interest was in biblical work. Lucian's exegetical method must be gathered from the biblical works of his pupils; it takes principally into account the literal sense and only employs typological interpretation where the text itself demands it. Similarly, it is only from the works of his pupils that it is possible to form an idea of Lucian's other theological characteristics. He always starts from biblical data, not from theological presuppositions, and attains, among other things, a strict subordinationism in the doctrine of the Logos. This was represented soon after by Arius and some of his fellow-pupils, the so-called Syllucianists, and they expressly referred to their teacher for it. The characteristics of the Antioch school became fully clear only in the great age of the Fathers, in connection with the Trinitarian and Christological controversies.

C H A P T E R   2 0

The Development of Christian Literature in the West in the Third Century

The Rise of Early Christian Latin and the Beginning of a Christian Literature in Latin

The essentially different course taken by the development of Christian literature in the West in the third century, particularly in Rome, was determined by the linguistic tradition of the Roman Christian community, which at first was composed for the most part of Greek-speaking members and consequently used Greek for preaching and the liturgy. Only with the disappearance of the Greek majority did the necessity arise for translating the Holy Scriptures of the new faith into Latin, of preaching in Latin, and finally of using Latin as a liturgical language too. The first traces of the existence of a Latin Bible extend back, as far as Rome is concerned, into the latter half of the second century.

In Africa, at the turn of the century, Tertullian also quoted from a Latin Bible which he had at hand. The unknown translators thereby initiated the development of early Christian Latin, and with this achievement created the conditions for the rise of an independent Christian literature in the Latin tongue. Old Christian Latin was firmly based in one respect on the colloquial language of the common people, to whom the missionaries at first addressed themselves. On the other hand, it borrowed certain words from the Greek, for many Latin words were impossible to employ because of their previous use in pagan worship. And, finally, for many central concepts of Christian revelation and preaching, existing Latin terms had to be given a new content. In this way there arose, by a lengthy and extremely important process, a sector of early Christian Latin within the wider field of later Latin. It is clearly distinct from the language of secular literature, possessing its own unmistakable style. No single person, therefore, created early Christian Latin: not even Tertullian, the first writer to attest its existence through his writings. It is characteristic that the theological discussions in Rome at the end of the second and in the third centuries were still conducted to a large extent in Greek.

A further characteristic of Latin Christian theology in the third century was that it was not developed in theological schools as was its Eastern counterpart. There was no lack of institutions for the instruction of catechumens at key points of christianization such as Rome and Carthage; but schools where important theological teachers of Origen's kind provided an introduction to the Christian religion for cultivated pagans were unknown in the West.

Hippolytus

Hippolytus can be regarded as a link between East and West. His person and work even today present many unsolved problems for research. It can be said that he was not a Roman by birth but a man from the East, thinking Greek and writing Greek, whose home was possibly Egypt and very likely Alexandria. He came to

Rome probably as early as Pope Zephyrinus' time and belonged as a priest to the Christian community there, in which his culture and intellectual activity assured him considerable prestige. His influence is evident in all the theological and disciplinary controversies which stirred Roman Christianity in the opening decades of the third century. His high conception of the functions of a priest, among which he emphatically reckoned the preservation of apostolic traditions, did not permit him to shrink from bold criticism of the Roman bishops when he thought those traditions threatened by their attitude and measures. His rigoristic attitude on the question of penance made him an irreconcilable opponent of Bishop Callistus (217–22), and the leader of a numerically small but intellectually important opposition group. Nevertheless, the conjecture that he had himself consecrated bishop at that time, and so became the first anti-pope in the history of the Church, finds no adequate support in the sources. And there is just as little reliable evidence that it was the writer Hippolytus whom the emperor Maximinus Thrax banished to Sardinia with Pope Pontian, that it was he who was there reconciled to the latter and died in exile. But it is possible that Hippolytus lived on through the period of the Novatian schism, belonged to this movement for a while and after being received once more into the Christian community survived until later than 253. Both Eusebius and Jerome give a list of his writings; and their titles reveal him as a writer having such notable breadth of interest as to suggest comparison with Origen, though certainly he never achieved the latter's originality and depth.

Hippolytus most clearly shares with Origen an inclination to the study of Scripture, which he expounds in the same allegorical way, though a more sober use of this method is unmistakable in his case. It is true that only a small remnant of his biblical writings has survived, but among them is a significant commentary on Daniel in the Greek original, and an exposition of the Canticle of Canticles, complete but in translation. In the Susanna of the Book of Daniel he considers that the Church, the virgin bride of Christ, is prefigured, persecuted by Jews and pagans. Likewise the bride and bridegroom of the Canticle of Canticles are understood as Christ and his Church, and sometimes the bride is considered to be the soul that loves God, an interpretation that was taken up particularly by St. Ambrose in his exposition of Psalm 118, and so transmitted to the Middle Ages.

Anxiety for the preservation of apostolic traditions was the second motive determining Hippolytus' work as a writer. They seemed to him threatened in doctrine and in the performance of divine worship. Consequently, he wrote a *Church Order* designed to ensure the maintenance of traditional forms in the most important rules and formulas for conferring Orders, the various functions of ecclesiastical offices, the conferring of baptism, and the celebration of the Eucharist. This *Traditio Apostolica* no longer survives in its original language, but it forms the kernel of a series of further Church Orders such as the *Apostolic Order,* the *Testament of our Lord Jesus Christ,* the *Canons of Hippolytus* and the eight books of the *Apostolic Constitutions.* Its principal impact was felt in the East, especially in Egypt, as the many translations into Coptic, Ethiopic, and Arabic show, while the Latin version (ca. 500) is incomplete. For Hippolytus, his *Church Order* probably represented an ideal form which was not designed for the needs of a particular community, but intended to provide a norm by which the Church leaders could test the conformity of their liturgical prescriptions with apostolic tradition.

The anti-heretical dogmatic writings of Hippolytus served to safeguard apostolic tradition in doctrine. An early work was his *Syntagma* against thirty-two heresies, treating of the erroneous doctrines which had appeared in the course of history down to his own day. Unfortunately only its concluding part, which refutes the teaching of Noëtus, is extant. Another anti-heretical work is attributed to Hippolytus: *The Refutation of All Heresies,* also called the *Philosophoumena,* which indicated in its first part the errors of pagan philosophers and the aberrations of pagan religions (Book 1–4), and then proceeded to oppose the Gnostic systems in particular (Books 5–9). The Tenth Book provides a recapitulation of the whole work, and adds a brief account of the content of Christian belief. The chief purpose of the author is to demonstrate his thesis that the root of all heresies is that they did not follow Christ, Holy Scripture, and tradition, but reverted instead to pagan doctrines. The historical transmission of this work is extremely confused. The *Philosophoumena* have very much the character of a compilation, and give the impression of being a first draft which did not receive further revision. The polemic is caustic and oversteps all bounds when a personal opponent is attacked, so that an Hippolytus different from the author of his other works seems to be speaking here. The concept of the Church, which the *Philosophoumena* express, is particularly striking. Here in the controversy with Callistus the Church is addressed as the bearer and safeguard of truth, whose purity and authenticity have to be watched over by bishops in legitimate apostolic succession. The author turns passionately against those who forget their task and who, though appointed members of the hierarchy, open too wide to sinners the gate of the Church of the saints.

Novatian

Novatian may be considered as the first Roman theologian of importance, but his culture and gifts had to overcome manifold contradictions within the Roman community. Although he had received only the baptism of the sick, and so, according to the conception of the time, displayed a lack of courage to confess the Faith, Pope Fabian had nevertheless ordained him priest; and about the year 250 he played a decisive role in the Pope's *collegium.* When the papal see was vacant, he continued the correspondence of the Roman Church with other communities abroad, and in two or three letters to Cyprian expounded the Roman position concerning the treatment of those who had lapsed during persecution, a position identical with Cyprian's prudent practice. About 250 Novatian wrote his chief theological treatise on the Trinity. Here he made use of the work of earlier theologians, especially Hippolytus and Tertullian, and carefully formulated the state of the question in clear language of much formal distinction. The theology of Marcion is rejected in his treatise, as well as the Modalist conception of the Monarchians; Novatian propounds a very definite subordinationism, which however much it emphasizes Christ's Godhead subordinates him to the Father almost more strictly than in earlier theology. He expresses himself very briefly on the relation of the Holy Spirit to the Son and the Father, but here too emphasizes the subordination of the Spirit to the Son. He lays great stress on the role of the Holy Spirit within the Church, which is preserved by his gifts inviolate in holiness and truth.

Novatian's other writings are pastoral in character and belong to the later phase of his life when, after leaving the Roman community, he led his own rigoristic, strictly organized society, as its bishop. His separation from the Roman community was due in the first place to personal motives especially aroused when Cornelius was preferred to him in the election of bishop in 251. The rift became irreparable when Novatian tried to justify his own secession by a concept according to which there could be no place for a mortal sinner in the Church of the saints, however ready he might be to atone by penance. While African circles, contrary to Novatian's expectation, ultimately refused him a following, he found numerous adherents in the East. Dionysius of Alexandria had difficulty in preventing a greater defection than occurred, and in the West a synod of sixty bishops under the leadership of Pope Cornelius clarified the situation by excommunicating Novatian and his followers. Regarding Novatian's end, we have only the report of Socrates that he died as a martyr in the persecution by Valerian.

Tertullian

The contribution made by the young African Church to early Christian literature in the third century was of greater weight and consequence. All evidence seems to indicate that Christianity found its way from Rome to these provinces beyond the sea, and that the first missionaries still used Greek in their preaching. Towns provided the earliest points of contact for Christian teaching, especially and above all Carthage. The transition to Latin for preaching and liturgy took place earlier in Africa than in Rome. The *Acts of the Martyrs of Scili,* the first dated Latin document of Christian origin (180 C.E.), probably already presupposes a translation of the Pauline epistles into Latin; a few years later Tertullian used a Latin translation of the Bible, and, about the middle of the third century, Cyprian quoted it so habitually that it must have been generally known by that time.

The Christian literature which begins with Tertullian vividly reflects the special features of the world of African Christianity in the third century. This area was exposed to most grievous tribulations in the persecutions of the time and had to pay a very heavy toll in blood for its steadfastness in the faith, which was rewarded by a proportionately rapid growth of the Church. The African church was characterized to an almost equal extent by the internal controversies which it suffered with the Gnostic sects and Montanism, by the struggles for its unity which it waged against the schismatical movement of Novatian and Felicissimus and, after the middle of the third century, by the quarrel concerning baptism conferred by heretics. All this left its mark on the early Christian literature of North Africa, and gives it its lively and sometimes pugnacious quality. At the same time the first differences which were to divide the Greek and Latin literature more and more sharply from each other are already apparent within it. The latter was not as much concerned as was the East, in grasping the metaphysical content of revelation and demonstrating its superiority over Hellenistic religious trends. Its prime interest lay, rather, in directly practical questions of actual living in pagan surroundings; and it was concerned, furthermore, with the translation of belief into action, which demands a fight against sin, and with the positive practice of virtue.

In Tertullian we meet the first and at the same time the most productive and distinctive writer of pre-Constantinian literature in North Africa. Born about 160 in Carthage, he was the son of a pagan captain, received a solid general education in the humanities, and pursued special studies in law and Greek. He entered the Church as an adult, as a result of the impression made on him by Christians' fidelity to their beliefs under persecution, and immediately placed his wealth of gifts at her service. The sources do not make it clear whether he became a priest or remained a layman. The period of his activity as a writer covers approximately a quarter of a century (ca. 195–220), and comprises two parts of roughly equal length but of quite contrasting nature. Until ca. 207 he was a convinced and declared member of the Catholic Church, but then he joined the Montanist movement and rejected wholesale what he had previously revered. This change accounts for a double feature in Tertullian's nature which is apparent to every reader of his works. He is a man who gives himself utterly and uncompromisingly to whatever he professes at any given moment: anyone who thinks differently from him is not only an opponent of his views but is morally suspect. His temperament, which inclined him to extremes, led him almost inevitably out of the Church when he encountered in Montanism a form of Christian belief in which the utmost rigorism was the law. For the defense of his conviction of the moment, he had at his command a mastery of contemporary Latin such as no other writer of those years possessed. In expounding his own position, he employed an impressive eloquence supported by comprehensive learning in every field, which he drew upon with brilliant effect. He had also the gift of that brief incisive turn of phrase which holds the reader's interest. His acute intellect relentlessly uncovered the weakness of an opponent's argument, and holds up to ridicule those who differed from him. There can be no doubt that Tertullian's work was read, but its power of conviction is open to suspicion. It seems that even Montanism was not in the end sufficient for his excessive and immoderate nature; and Augustine credibly reports that before his death he became the founder of a sect named, after himself, the Tertullianists.

In a series of writings Tertullian tried to place before the pagans a true picture of the Christian religion. The *Apologeticum* is directly addressed to the *praesides* of the Roman provinces, but indirectly to paganism as a whole. Tertullian takes in each case ideas familiar to the pagans as the starting point of his argument, and contrasts them with Christian doctrine and Christian life. He makes it clear that the most grievous injustice is done to the Christians by condemning them without knowing the truth about them. Tertullian therefore asks not for acquittal but for justice based on impartial investigation of the truth.

Tertullian also defended the claim of the Church to truth and her possession of truth against the heresies of the age and especially against Gnostic trends. This he accomplished in a treatise on principles which makes brilliant use of his legal knowledge: the *De praescriptione haereticorum* demonstrates that Christianity, as opposed to heresy, can substantiate a clear legal claim to the possession of truth. Long before heresies appeared, Christian teachers were preaching that message which they had received from the apostles and which had been entrusted to the latter by Christ. Consequently, Holy Scripture is in the possession of the Church alone; only she can determine its true sense and so establish the content of belief. A series of monographs was also directed by Tertullian against individual Gnostics or their particular tenets; such a work was that against Marcion, which refutes his dualism and defends the harmony between Old and New Testaments. He seeks to safeguard the Christian doctrine of Creation, the resurrection of the body and the status of martyrdom against volatilization by the Gnostics; and against Praxeas he expounds the Church's conception of the Trinity with a clarity hitherto unknown. He deals with practical questions of Christian daily life in his short works on the meaning and effects of baptism, prayer, theatrical shows, patience, and the spirit and practice of penance. A rigoristic strain becomes predominant in the works of the Montanist period. In this latter phase he made demands in utter contradiction of his earlier views, as for instance when he opposes second marriages in his *De monogamia,* military service and all trades in any way connected with idolatry in the *De corona* and *De idolatria,* and proclaims the most rigorous practice of fasting in *De ieiunio.* His fight against the Church took particularly harsh forms; he disputed her right to remit sins, which he reserved in the *De pudicitia* to the Montanist prophets alone. Viewed as a whole, Tertullian's interests as a writer were not of a speculative kind, and he gives no systematic exposition of Christian doctrine. His importance in the history of dogma rests on the value of his writings as evidence of the stage of development which various particular doctrines had reached in his time. He was speaking as a Montanist essentially about the nature of the Church when he rejected an official priesthood. A pre-eminent position with the power of binding and loosing belonged only to Peter, and was not therefore conferred on later bishops. The conception of original sin as a *vitium originis* was familiar to him, in the sense that through Adam's sin evil concupiscence has poisoned human nature, but he does not infer the necessity of infant baptism from this. Tertullian thinks in very concrete terms about the Eucharist; those who take part in the *orationes sacrificiorum* receive the body of the Lord which is just as truly the real body of Christ as was the body on the cross; and the soul is nourished on the body and blood of Christ. In Christology and the theology of the Trinity, he employs a terminology which influenced subsequent developments in the Latin West: according to him, Jesus Christ is true God and true man, both natures are united in one person but not confused. The expression "Trinitas" as well as the term "persona," is found for the first time in Latin literature in Tertullian: in this Trinity, Father, Son, and Holy Spirit are "unius substantiae et unius status et unius potestatis." The Logos existed already before the creation of the world, but only became Son at the creation, and consequently as such is not eternal. The more precise relation of Father and Son is viewed in a subordinationist manner: the Father alone has the fullness of the Godhead; the Son has only a derivative part. The Holy Spirit too is thought of as a person: he is the real teacher in the Church, who first of all led the apostles into all truth, but who is also operative as the representative of God and Christ in every Christian community, especially through Holy Scripture which is his work and in which his voice is audible.

Cyprian

A notable influence on posterity was also exercised by Bishop Cyprian of Carthage as a writer of the African Church. The authenticity of his personality and the example of his pastoral care stamped characteristic features on the Christianity of his native land. The interest taken in his writings was likewise due to the deep impression produced by these qualities. In theology he owed much to Tertullian, whom he called his master and whose works he constantly read. His treatises and letters deal mostly with the solution of questions of the day, as they arose through persecution and the threat to ecclesiastical unity from sectarian divisions. A personal note is struck in the little work *Ad Donatum,* in which the religious certainty attained in baptism after long search finds attractive expression. Cyprian as a pastor turned with a word of consolation to the Christians of North Africa in time of plague, and summoned them to be ready to make sacrifices in order to perform works of mercy. This he did in his *De mortalitate* and *De opere et eleemosynis.* He extols the Christian ideal of virginity and utters warnings against the destructive consequences of dissension in the *De habitu virginum* and *De zelo et livore* and here too he takes up the ideas of Tertullian in his writings on the Our Father and on patience. His treatise *On the Unity of the Church* shows greater independence both in content and in the personal position it reveals; and it has greater value as evidence of the concept of the Church held in the mid-third century. The representative and guarantor of ecclesiastical unity is the bishop, who is united with his fellow bishops through the common basis of the episcopate in the apostolic office. Among the holders of the latter, Peter had objectively and legitimately a special position which rested on the power of binding and loosing imparted to him alone. As this was committed by Christ to only *one* apostle, the unity that Christ willed for the Church was established for ever. Cyprian does not yet infer from this an effective jurisdiction of Peter over his fellow apostles, nor a transmission of his personal prerogatives to his successor as Bishop of Rome. Cyprian unambiguously rejects a Roman right of direction, for instance in the question of the validity of baptism for heretics. Cyprian sets a very high value on membership in the Church of Christ: nobody has a claim to the name of Christian who has not his own name in this Church; only in her is his salvation assured, according to the pregnant formula: "salus extra ecclesiam non est." Children, too, should share in the membership of the Church as early as possible, and so infant baptism is a practice which Cyprian takes for granted. Fidelity to the Church in persecution merits the highest recognition; those who in martyrdom have sealed their testimony to Christ and his Church with the sacrifice of their lives obtain immediately the vision of God.

CHAPTER 21

The First Christological and Trinitarian Controversies

The apologists of the second century in their discussions of pagan polytheism emphasized above all strict monotheism which they did not consider imperilled by their conception of Logos-Christology. In the Church's defensive action against Gnosticism, the emphatic stress on the unity of the divine nature was similarly prominent, and so theology in the second century did not concern itself in great detail with the problem of the relation between Father, Son, and Holy Spirit. A deep conceptual penetration of this truth of revelation and a corresponding linguistic formulation of it had not been attained. Theological reflection was now, at the end of the second century, to concern itself precisely with the question of the Trinity. The Logos-Christology presented by the apologists, and further developed by the second-century writers, was defective to the extent that it subordinated the Son to the Father. According to this concept, the Logos, existing from all eternity within God (*logos endiathetos*) came forth from the Father only as Creator and ruler of the world (*Logos prophorikos*), only then was begotten and only then became the personality distinguishing him from the Father; and, therefore, he was not eternal in the same sense as the Father. But this subordinationism at first less disturbed people's awareness of the faith, because they saw in it no direct threat to the divinity of Christ. In fact this Christological subordinationism led at the end of the second century and the beginning of the third to a vigorous reaction by Christian circles who were anxious at all costs to safeguard the divine unity. The movement owed its origin to men of the Greek East; but the controversies about their theories took place chiefly in the West and especially in Rome. We owe the very name Monarchianism, by which we try to characterize this theology, to a Latin theologian: the African Tertullian renders by the formula "monarchiam tenemus" the slogan by which its adherents tried to express their holding fast to the one God and to a single divine principle.

Emphasis on the unity of God, however, necessitated a decision on the Christological problem, and in this process the Logos-Christology was contested in two ways. Some regarded Christ as merely a man, but one born of the virgin Mary and of the Holy Spirit, and in whom God's power (*dynamis*) was operative in quite a special way. This so-called Dynamist Monarchianism safeguarded the one divine principle but virtually abandoned the divinity of Christ. Another solution of the problem was proposed by those who declared that the one God revealed himself in different ways or *modi,* now as Father, now as Son. This theory so effaced the distinction between Father and Son that it was said that the Father had also suffered on the Cross; and the supporters of this attempted solution are therefore called Modalist or Patripassian Monarchians. Dynamist Monarchianism, which is also not inappropriately called Adoptionism, betrays a rationalist attitude which found the idea of God's becoming man difficult to accept. Consequently, it seems to have gained a wider hearing in intellectual circles, but small support among the common people. The sources name as its first exponent an educated leather-merchant called Theodotus of Byzantium, who came to Rome about 190 and there sought support for his theological ideas. He and his followers tried to prove from Scripture, by means of philological textual criticism, their fundamental thesis that Jesus, until his baptism in the Jordan, led the life of a simple but very upright man on whom the Spirit of Christ then descended. A series of disciples — including Asclepiodotos, Theodotus the younger, and later Artemon — transmitted the ideas of its founder and attempted to organize the Adoptionists in a church of their own. About the mid-third century a double argument inspired the Adoptionists' doctrine: on the one hand, they attacked the orthodox view as ditheistic; and on the other, they also claimed that as true guardians of apostolic tradition they would teach regarding Christ only what had always been believed at all times. An exponent of a particularly crude Adoptionism in the East, in the second half of the third century, was Paul of Samosata, a bishop of Antioch in Syria, whose teaching and life preoccupied several synods. It is true that he employed in his theology the Trinitarian formulas of his age, but he divested them of their orthodox meaning by teaching that "the Son" designated only the man Jesus, in whom the wisdom of God had taken up abode; that, furthermore, "the Spirit" is nothing other than the grace which God gave the apostles. And by "wisdom of God," or Logos, Paul did not understand a person distinct from the Father, but an impersonal power. Although at a first synod in the year 264 he skilfully evaded being pinned down to definite views, the learned priest Malchion demonstrated his errors to him at a second assembly of bishops, which removed him from office and expelled him from the Church's community. At the same time, the synod rejected the statement that the Logos is of the same nature as the Father (*homoousios*), because Paul of Samosata meant by this term to deny the Logos a personal subsistence of his own. The Catholic community of Antioch, under the new bishop Domnus, was obliged even to call in the help of the civil authorities against Paul following his deposition, to make him vacate the episcopal residence. Yet, even after his condemnation, Paul had a considerable following.

Modalist Monarchianism

The Modalist attempt at a solution of the Logos-Christological problem spread relatively widely because it obviously appealed more strongly to simple religious minds, for whom the biblical statements about the unity of God and the full divinity of Christ were deep convictions. Any conception which separated the Son or the Word too sharply from the Father seemed suspect here, because it could lead to the existence of two Gods being deduced from it. Once again, the first representative of Modalist teaching whose name is now known was a Greek, by name Noëtus, who came from Smyrna in Asia Minor. He vigorously emphasized the dogma of the one God, the Father, asserted also that Christ is identical with the Father, and affirmed the inference that the Father became man and suffered on the Cross. Noëtus was expelled from the Church, yet nevertheless found supporters for his ideas. His disciples appealed to passages in the Old and New Testaments (such as Exod 3:6; Isa 44:6; 45:14–15; Jn 10:30; 14:8ff.; Rom 9:5), which they construed in the sense of implying an identity of Father and Son. According to Tertullian's polemic against Praxeas, written about 213, the latter taught the complete identity of Father and Son, and denied that the Logos had any subsistence peculiar to himself, so that in reality it was the Father who suffered, died, and rose from the dead.

Another member of the Patripassianists, as the adherents of this doctrine were later called by Cyprian, was Sabellius, who is said to have come to Rome from Libya when Zephyrinus was bishop (199–217). It was probably he who gave Modalist doctrine a more systematic character, when he attributed to the one Godhead three modes of operation, so that the Father was its actual essence which, nevertheless, expressed itself also as Son and Spirit: as Father, God was the creator and law-giver; as Son, he was operative in the redemption; as Spirit, he conferred grace and sanctification. It is impossible to obtain a completely clear and incontestable picture of Modalist ideas, since only their opponents — Hippolytus, Tertullian, and Epiphanius — report them. In Rome, the center of Modalist propaganda, there was at first no clash with the authorities of the community there. But there was a reaction by the leading theologian, the learned Hippolytus, who sharply attacked the Roman bishops Zephyrinus (199–217) and Callistus (217–22), because of their favoring, as he alleged, and even recognizing this false doctrine. Hippolytus' criticism that Zephyrinus entertained Modalist views was probably provoked by the mistrust that the latter felt for Hippolytus' manner of expression, which sounded to him suspiciously ditheistic. That Hippolytus' judgment was far too harsh is plain from his verdict that Callistus had let himself be misled by Sabellius, though it was Callistus himself who expelled the latter from the Church. It is clear that Callistus was also trying to pursue a middle course between the downright Modalism of Sabellius and, in his judgment, the ditheistic tendency of the learned Hippolytus. In opposition to the latter, he laid all emphasis on the unity of God, when he said that Father and Son are not separate beings; in opposition to Sabellius, he held fast to the distinction between the Father and the Logos, who existed before all time and who became man. He was conscious, therefore, of the dubiousness of Modalist doctrine, but he likewise regarded the doctrine of two or three distinct divine "persons" as an even greater danger to the content of faith concerning the one God.

Nevertheless, the struggle of Hippolytus and Tertullian against Modalism bore fruit, as can be seen from the advance in Trinitarian theology in the work of Novatian about the mid-third century. The latter turned Tertullian's thought and preparatory work to account, and clearly moved away from Modalism in saying that the Son begotten of the Father, that is the Word, is not a mere sound but has subsistence proper to him, and thus is a "second person"; that the Son was not begotten in view only of Creation, but existed before all time, since it is in the nature of the Father as such ever to have a Son. Novatian seeks with even greater emphasis to reject ditheistic lines of thought by stressing that the Son is God only in being the Son, who received his Godhead from the Father, and only as Son is distinct from the Father, so that there is no division of the divine nature. But Novatian does not express himself so plainly regarding the "person" of the Spirit, whom he regards as a divine power operative in the prophets, the apostles, and the Church. According to him, the Son is subject to the Father, is less than the Father, and is obedient to the Father. Novatian's manner of expression is, therefore, strongly subordinationist; and his progress beyond Tertullian and earlier theology consists in his recognizing that the personal distinction between Father and Son does not have its ground in the economy of salvation, that the Son was begotten before all time, and that he subsisted, that is as a person, before the creation of the world. This much was achieved, even if Novatian did not yet clearly grasp the doctrine of an eternal generation of the Son.

The discussion about Monarchianism extended beyond the West to other territories where Christianity had penetrated. Attention was further aroused by the controversy in which Bishop Dionysius of Alexandria engaged about the year 260 with Patripassianists of the Libyan Pentapolis. In several letters, of which one was addressed to bishops Ammonius and Euphranor, Dionysius attacked the Modalist theories with an incisive yet reckless manner of expression; and he gave such imprecise formulation to the distinction between Father and Son, whom he termed a creature (*poiēma*), that the unity of essence of both seemed blurred. A denunciation of this doctrine in Rome caused the bishop there, also called Dionysius (259–68), to make a pronouncement which in several respects is important. He requested the Alexandrian bishop to make his views more precise, and at the same time addressed a letter to the community of Alexandria expounding the Roman conception of the Trinity. Without identifying Bishop Dionysius, but with an unmistakably sharp reference to the school of theologians from which he sprang, he said he had heard that there were catechists and teachers of theology in Alexandria who split up the most venerable kerygma of the Church, the monarchy or the unity of God, into three separate hypostases and three divinities, and taught a doctrine diametrically opposed to that of Sabellius. Whereas the latter maintained that the Son was the Father, and vice versa, these men in a certain way preached three Gods. In contrast with this view, the unity of God should be held just as firmly as the divine Trinity; yet, on the other hand, to speak of Christ as a creature, or to assert that there had been a time when he did not exist, was just as blasphemous as it was to call "his divine and inexpressible generation" a creation (*poiēsis*). Dionysius of Alexandria thereupon replied with a detailed apologia, in which he admitted that certain of his formulas were liable to misinterpretation, but pointed out also that justice had not been done to his view as a whole. His résumé of his position, that the unity of God must be maintained but the three persons must also be acknowledged, clearly satisfied Rome, since the discussion was not pursued further. These issues, it is true, involved the problem of correct terminology, of which the differing senses of "hypostasis" afford a typical example, since it could be easily identified in Rome with Tertullian's "substantia." But behind these linguistic problems were the different aspects through which the theology of the Trinity was approached from East and West. In the West, the "dogma" of God's unity was sacrosanct, and it was difficult for people to recognize and acknowledge as "persons" the distinctions in the Trinity, of which they were convinced. The East was more sensitive to the mystery in the Trinity, as a consequence of its familiarity with the world of neo-Platonic thought concerning the hierarchy of being. This difference in mode of theological thought, together with the imperfection of the terminology worked out so far, found clear expression in the following century and gave rise then to a comprehensive discussion of the dogma of the Trinity.

C H A P T E R 2 2

Manichaeism

A few decades after the great Gnostic movement of the second century had passed its peak, there was born the founder of a new religion, which came on the stage with a definite claim to be the most universal of all religions, and promised true redemption to all nations. It took its name from its founder, the Persian Mani or Manes, who is called in the Greek and Latin sources *Manichaios* or Manichaeus.

Mani was born on 14 April 216 C.E., probably in the Parthian capital Seleucia-Ctesiphon. Mani's father belonged to a religious sect, perhaps the Mandaeans, in which strict abstinence from meat and wine was combined with purification ceremonies of many kinds. Mani was at first brought up in this sect, too, but repeated visions revealed to him very early that he was destined to be the missionary and herald of a new universal religion, the content of which was made known to him through further revelations. Mani quickly undertook a missionary journey to India, where, he preached with particular success. After his return home to Persia, he won the favor of his king who permitted him freely to preach his religious message throughout the Sassanid kingdom. Mani now developed a comprehensive missionary activity, was himself engaged as a missionary in the West, as far as Nisibis, and sent out on a systematic plan other messengers of his faith, who, even during his lifetime, gained entry for his teaching into Egypt and the eastern provinces of Iran. Under King Bahram I, however, a radical change occurred affecting Mani's favor at court. It is probable that the priests of the Zoroastrian religion accused him of subversive plans and heresy; and, after a short imprisonment, Mani died in captivity in 277. Upon Mani's death there ensued a powerful wave of persecution against his adherents, some of whom fled to the West, while others emigrated to India and China, where they secured great influence which persisted as late as the fourteenth century.

Mani set down the content of his missionary teaching in a series of writings which soon attained canonical force. The most important of these are: *The Great Gospel from Alpha to Tau,* which was provided with an album of pictures; the *Treasure of Life,* from which Augustine frequently quoted; the *Book of the Mysteries,* in twenty-four chapters; and finally his letters. According to these works, a radical dualism in the doctrine concerning God characterizes Manichaeism: there are two highest beings or principles of equal rank, the one of light and the other of darkness. Both are unbegotten and eternal; both possess equal power but stand in irreconcilable opposition to one another, each in a realm of his own: the region of light or the good, which lies in the North, and the region of evil, which lies in the South. Each realm has a king: the realm of light is ruled by the Father of greatness; the realm of evil by the Prince of darkness who commands numerous demons. Between the two primary principles and their realms a conflict breaks out: the realm of matter seeks to swallow up the light; and, to defend the latter, the Father of greatness creates the first man, who with his five sons goes out to battle, but is conquered by evil. The first man becomes aware of his fate, and begs the Father of greatness for help. The latter emits from himself, after a series of intermediary emanations, the Living Spirit, who frees the first human being from evil matter and so redeems him.

This mythical occurrence is a symbol and image of the way of redemption for man, who is a mixture of light and darkness. As soon as a man becomes aware of this fact, that is to say knows himself, his redemption begins. And thereafter the Father of light helps him to free himself more and more from the darkness in him. For this purpose he sends the heralds of true religion to earth, who give men correct knowledge about themselves. These messengers are Buddha, Zoroaster, Jesus, and Mani. They are representatives of the Manichaean redeemer, the emissary of light, and each of them brings to a part of mankind the true religion or gnosis, whose spread, however, is impeded from the opposite side. Before Mani, the heralds of religion had been assigned only certain parts of the world to which they were to bring true gnosis: Buddha worked in India, Zoroaster restricted himself to Persia, and Jesus to Judaea, or at least to the West. Neither did these three establish their message in writing; and consequently the religions they founded, especially the Christian religion, quickly fell to pieces or were falsified. Against such a background, Mani's mission stands out more sharply in its uniqueness: he is the last envoy of light, the apostle of the ultimate generation, the "seal of the prophet"; his message is the last summons to salvation; the world can now only be converted or for ever perish. Mani preached the highest, the perfect, gnosis; to reject it, is definitively to refuse salvation. The movement founded by Mani is, therefore, also the most universal religion ever known, comprising all earlier religions in itself, and at the same time leading beyond them. It will conquer the East and the West, and will be heard preached in all languages.

From this Manichaean doctrinal system Manichaean ethics necessarily follow, the fundamental characteristic being the demand for abstinence from everything which links men to matter. In man light and darkness mingle; anyone who forgets this condition, or who does not repent, adheres more to matter, persists in *agnōsia*, determined not to recognize his situation, and so rejects gnosis and thereby salvation. Consequently, the perfect Manichee renounces this world, seeks to possess nothing in it and subdues all his appetites; he binds himself by the triple seal of the mouth, the hands, and the womb; that is to say, he refrains from impure words and pleasures, and rejects menial work, for by these things the world of light, fragments of which are present in all visible, tangible things, is violated; he exercises absolute sexual continence and rejects marriage. In practice these lofty demands of Manichaean ethics could not be fulfilled, a condition which led to the division of Manichaean believers into the elect, or *electi,* and the hearers, or *audientes;* and there were special commandments for each according to their capacities. The hearers or catechumens served the elect, gave them food and clothing, and so hoped to be born sometime in the body of an elect and then to attain salvation.

In addition to being divided into such categories as these, the followers of the Manichaean religion were united in a well-organized church, and this factor ensured them considerable impact in their missionary work. At the summit of the Manichaean church was a supreme head, the head of the apostles or the king of the religion, who had his residence in Babylon. The first head was naturally Mani himself, from whom every successor derived his authority. Subject to this supreme head was a hierarchy with numerous members comprising, in a series of grades, twelve apostles, seventy-two bishops or teachers of truth, and three hundred and sixty priests to whom all other members of the elect, both men and women, were attached as deacons. The great mass of hearers represented the last and lowest grade. The elect, particularly in China, were assembled in monastic communities, which were supported by the alms of the hearers. The ascetic exercises of Manichaeism included an elaborate practice of fasting. By fasting they prepared for a sort of confession, in which they acknowledged transgressions of the commandments of abstinence. In their temples the Manichaean faithful gathered for a pure divine service of the word, which consisted of readings from Manichaean writings and the singing of their own hymns, often possessed of high qualities of form. Other rites were rejected, since in them the body, which is bound to matter, is active, and only true gnosis brings salvation.

Of special importance is the marked dependence of Manichaean doctrine on Christian ideas. The high rank that is attributed to the person of Jesus is particularly striking. It is true that Mani lists the heralds of true gnosis, who had preceded Mani himself, as Buddha, Zoroaster, and Jesus and likewise his brethren; but the chief role is ascribed to Jesus. At the beginning of his letters, Mani emphatically calls himself "apostle of Jesus Christ." This Jesus, as a heavenly "aeon," had appeared on earth with the semblance of a body, in order to teach mankind its real origin and true way of redemption. (According to Arius, the Manichees called Christ "a part of the Father having the same nature as he"; and this use of the *homoousios* idea made the Arians their determined opponents.) Finally, this Jesus has sent the Paraclete promised by him, in order to free his teaching from falsification. The Paraclete came down upon Mani, and revealed hidden mysteries to him; and Mani became one with him, so that Mani could now come forward and teach as the promised Paraclete. Neither does Mani pass over and ignore the Holy Scripture of Christianity. It is true that he adopts a critical attitude to the Old Testament, but more important for Mani are the Gospels and Paul's letters: these also he considers as interspersed with Jewish errors, but they contain a rich store from Jesus' message regarding the profound structure of the world, the meaning of human destiny, the battle between light and darkness, and the liberation of the soul from the fetters of matter. Mani recognized these truths in the New Testament writings, singled them out and absorbed them into his preaching. Manichaeism showed particular interest also in New Testament apocrypha, such as the Gospel of Thomas and the legend of Abgar, and made use likewise of a version of the *Shepherd* of Hermas. This considerable adaptation of Christian elements in Manichaean preaching was intended by Mani to facilitate contact with Christians in the West, and to win them over to his movement, just as he made similar use of the ideas of Zoroastrianism or Buddhism for his missionary work in the East. By taking over these various elements, Manichaean doctrine was intended to show that it was the fulfillment of all the religious aspirations of mankind.

The syncretic character of the new religion certainly ensured those initial successes which were everywhere apparent. The fundamental ideal of a safe way to liberation from the evil in the world and of redemption through true gnosis was familiar to men of the third and fourth centuries. The Manichaean religion quickly spread in Mesopotamia, pressed on from there to Syria and Arabia, and soon found a particularly firm base in Egypt which was developed into a propaganda center for the Mediterranean countries. It had marked success in Rome and North Africa. It can be shown to have existed in Rome under Pope Miltiades (311–14); from there it probably found its way to Gaul and Spain, also appearing in the Balkans.

The emperor Constantine was likewise disturbed by the doctrines of the movement, and had special reports drawn up on the subject. Synods of the fourth century had to deal with Manichaeism repeatedly as did very many imperial edicts as well. In North Africa Manichaeism exercised a peculiar fascination, to which the young Augustine succumbed for ten years. After the Vandal invasion, persecution affected them just as harshly as it did the Catholics; the formulas of abjuration for former Manichees on reception into the Church testify to their continued existence in the West extending into the sixth century. The Byzantine church in the East had to fight against them much longer, and the neo-Manichaean movements of the Middle Ages, especially in the Balkans, once again strikingly manifest the vitality of Mani's foundation.

Since Mani did not allow his followers to belong to another religion, the position of the Church in relation to Manichaeism was different from her defensive struggle against the Gnosticism of the second century. Its claim to sole possession of true and unfalsified Christianity, forced the Church authorities to take up a definite attitude and to put the faithful on their guard. Moreover, the Church could not but experience the Manichaean movement as a dangerous rival in her own missionary endeavor among the pagan population. Very detailed formulas of abjuration, which had often to be signed even on the mere suspicion of Manichaeism, were in use both in the Latin West and in the Greek East.

Hand in hand with these pastoral efforts to immunize the faithful against this heresy, there developed the theological defense carried on by writers. This was waged not only as occasion arose in theological studies, but also in special monographs, of which some have been lost. The success which the Manichaean mission very early enjoyed in Egypt especially roused Egyptian authors to counter-measures.

CHAPTER 23

Further Development of the Liturgy

The growth of theological literature within the Church of the third century was accompanied by an equally important development in the liturgical domain. Here, too, new creative impulses are perceptible, from which the forms of divine worship grew, and which answered the needs of the communities of the great Church as they increased in strength.

Easter and the Easter Controversy

The feast of Easter was given an elaboration which made it, in the minds of the faithful, the central and pre-eminent celebration and memorial of Christian redemption. Two factors in particular were responsible for this development: first, the expansion of the Easter celebration itself by increasing the duration of preparation and celebration; and second, by including within the Easter liturgy the administration of the sacrament of Christian initiation. The beginnings of this twofold development lie in the second century, for our third-century sources (such as the Syrian *Didascalia,* some of Tertullian's works, and the *Apostolic Tradition* of Hippolytus) already clearly show this development.

Despite differing emphases in detail, both East and West shared considerable similarity concerning the Easter celebration. It commemorated the fundamental truths and facts of Christian redemption, which were conferred upon mankind by the death and triumphant resurrection of the Lord.

The so-called Easter controversy at the end of the second century is often misconstrued in terms of a dispute over Easter festivals with fundamentally differing contents between the so-called Quartodecimans on the one hand and those who supported the Sunday pasch. It was not. It was a dispute over the date of the Easter festival and about the nature and the duration of the Easter fast. In second-century Asia Minor and a few neighboring regions, a Christian Passover was kept on the 14th day of Nisan, the date's having been kept from Jewish custom. This celebration focussed upon the passion of the Lord, but culminated on the 15th Nisan with a joyous celebration of the resurrection in a Eucharist. Those who celebrated Easter on the Sunday following 14th Nisan (Syria, Egypt, Pontus, the Latin West), the Sunday Passover, likewise in no way excluded the Lord's passion from their joyful celebration of the redemption perfected by the resurrection.

It is clear that Rome already celebrated the Sunday Passover form of Easter in the second century. From the common elements shared with the Christian Passover of the Quartodecimans (the introductory strict fast; the reading of Exodus 12 with homily appended; and, incorporated into a vigil celebration, a concluding eucharistic supper), we may infer that the Sunday Easter celebration was a further development of the Christian Passover of the Quartodecimans, one which made the culmination of the celebration the Sunday after 14th Nisan. The point was to underscore the contrast with Judaism and to focus on the resurrection as crowning the work of redemption.

Disputes took place between followers of the two traditions. Bishop Polycarp of Smyrna asserted the Quartodeciman position against Bishop Anicetus of Rome, as did Melito of Sardis against Bishop Claudius Apollinaris of Hieropolis in ca. 170, a debate in which Clement of Alexandria intervened. Clement used Johannine chronology (that Jesus died and was buried on one day, the day of preparation for the Passover). Against that Melito used the chronology of the Synoptics, according to which Jesus celebrated the Passover before his death.

A few years before the turn of the century, the dispute over the date of the Easter celebration assumed graver forms. The immediate occasion was found in Rome, where one priest sought to introduce Quartodeciman practice, with the support of the Asia Minor community there. In 195 the Roman Bishop Victor wished to establish a uniform practice throughout the Church, and he called for synods everywhere to be held for this purpose. The majority expressed themselves in favor of the Sunday practice; but there was determined contradiction from the province of Asia, the stronghold of the Quartodecimans, who were determined to maintain their peculiar apostolic tradition. Pope Victor moved to exclude the recalcitrants from the ecclesiastical community, without gaining wholehearted support for his attempt. Irenaeus of Lyons resolutely advocated a course of toleration toward the divergent practice, which apparently was followed.

The Quartodecimans remained faithful to their tradition throughout the third century, and were followed by the Novatians in Asia Minor in this. However, the Council of Arles, 314, imposed the Sunday Easter, and the Council of Nicaea expelled the Quartodecimans from the ecclesiastical community. Thereafter they declined continually.

The East and West were fairly uniform in their patterns of the Easter celebration itself, according to our most important third-century sources. It was introduced by a strictly obligatory fast, which according to local custom might last from one day to a week. The heart of the Easter celebration was the nocturnal vigil, for which the whole Christian community gathered. First of all there was a service of prayer and readings (from the psalms, the prophets, and the Gospel mainly) for the first hours. But as the vigil belonged essentially to Easter, it had a joyful conclusion. At the beginning of the third century, the solemn baptism was incorporated into the framework of the Easter liturgy. The crown and conclusion of the vigil was formed by the eucharistic celebration of Easter Sunday.

The third century also produced the first outline of a paschal season which then became the nucleus and the first ritual cycle, of the developing ecclesiastical year. For fifty days beyond Easter, Christians celebrated with joyful hearts the resurrection of the Lord and their own salvation which this bestowed. There is also evidence for the introduction of the octave of Easter at this same time. Pentecost, the final day of Eastertide, was variously handled in the early Churches, with some celebrating it forty days after Easter and others fifty until with the Synod of Elyira in Spain, after which the latter became the usual practice.

The basis for the development of a third-century Christian calendar of feasts can be observed in the commemoration of the martyrs, which was already customary in the Church of the time. The organization of commemorative services and Eucharists at the grave sites of the martyrs and remembering them in one's prayers were more prominent earlier in the East than in the West where only into the third century was it possible for Christians to acquire their own cemetery and thus obtain the right legally to set up a commemorative service.

In North Africa, Cyprian testifies to a cult of the martyrs, regulated by the Church, in which the *confessores* were also included. Architectural elaboration of the tombs of martyrs may date to this same period, but only the *Memoria apostolorum* on the Appian Way outside Rome can be dated certainly to the period of the third century and be claimed as a *martyrion.* The pre-Constantinian memorial under the *confessio* in St. Peter's which is to be identified with the *Tropaion* on the Vatican Hill mentioned by the Roman presbyter Gais, may also be mentioned here. At all events, the organization the cult of martyrs as a whole becomes in the third century a matter for ecclesiastical authority, i.e., of the bishop of the community, whose influence on the development of liturgy is here particularly evident.

Catechumenate and Baptism

With the introduction of the catechumenate under ecclesiastical direction, as an institutional preparation for the reception of baptism, the growing Church at the end of the second century and beginning of the third accomplished one of its most important achievements and one very rich in consequences. Several causes were decisive in the Church's gradual construction of a carefully planned and organized course of instruction, containing provision for moral and religious training of those seeking baptism. The first would be the missionary thrust. The Church's success in missions must have raised the question of how to maintain the previous level in the Christian communities. Deeper insight and understanding were required because of the threatening growth of propaganda from heretical groups, especially from the Gnostics, many of whom had penetrated into the great Church. Finally, a systematic introduction to the world of Christian sacraments was essential, especially in view of the rival mystery cults, whose influence on pagan religious inquirers is not to be minimized.

In the development of the ecclesiastical institution of the catechumenate, one should note that the earliest forms were private and individual, a Christian passed on his faith to an inquirer. These practices were later put under ecclesiastical supervision or were made dependent on ecclesiastical authorization. Justin Martyr and the earlier Alexandrian teachers fit into this scheme. By the beginning of the third century, as shown in Hippolytus' *Apostolic Tradition* 16, the Church had in existence an organized institution of the catechumenate.

From Hippolytus and the works of Tertullian in North Africa, we obtain a general picture of the catechumenate. Admission of catechumens for instruction was controlled by the Church through strict examination of the candidate, especially of his moral qualities. For this reason each candidate needed a guarantor, an active Christian who could vouch for the candidate's life and intentions and would introduce him to the leader of the congregation. The teacher of the catechumens, who might be lay or a cleric, examined the candidate as to his motives, his marital status, profession, and social position. As Hippolytus' *Apostolic Tradition* presents it, the slave of a Christian master had to have both a testimonial and permission from his master. A number of professions were forbidden Christians in the third century, including anything with a connection to pagan worship, service in the army or civil administration, prostitution, and so forth. The Church took her moral ideal seriously and courageously laid down clear conditions for those who wanted to become her members. Clearly some had to change their professions in order to enter the catechumenate.

A favorable outcome of this initial inquiry allowed the candidate to be received into the catechumenate. A *catechumenus* then entered upon a period (often three years in duration) of instruction in Christian belief and practical training in the spiritual life. After this period of formation, the catechumen was examined again, probably by his bishop, a few weeks before Easter and baptism. A guarantor was again required and the catechumen's life was reexamined for his "good works." Arrest for Christ's sake was particularly eminent among them, and should death have been suffered without baptism under those circumstances, the catechumen was nevertheless saved because "baptized in his own blood."

Satisfactory completion of this examination led to the second and final stage of the catechumenate, which prepared the candidates, now called *electi,* directly for baptism. Here exorcism and greater use of liturgical prayer came into use. More intense practices of penance, frequent prayer, and fasting marked this period. A baptismal fast was imposed on the Friday and Saturday before their Sunday baptisms. The *electi* were also now not only permitted, but were obliged to attend the services of the Word at the celebration of the Eucharist, and there to hear the readings from the Gospel and the homily.

Baptism was imbedded in the impressive framework of a night-long vigil, which time was occupied with readings and final liturgical instructions. The break of day, symbolized by a cock's crowing, brought the beginning of the baptism proper. The candidates had set aside their clothing and all ornamentation; they advanced to the font with a flow of clear water. Each candidate renounced Satan and was anointed with the oil of exorcism. Then the candidate went to the priest by the font and was accompanied into the water by a deacon. The officiating bishop or priest then laid his hands upon the candidate and asked him three questions in sequence concerning his belief: "Do you believe in God the Father almighty? Do you believe in Jesus Christ, the Son of God, who was born by the Holy Spirit of the virgin Mary, who was crucified under Pontius Pilate, died, and was buried, who rose alive from the dead on the third day, ascended into heaven, sitteth at the right hand of the Father, who will come again to judge the living and the dead? Do you believe in the Holy Spirit, Holy Church, and the resurrection of the flesh?" To each question, the candidate responded, "I believe"; and as he did so the officiant poured water over his head. After an anointing with oil of thanksgiving, the candidate dressed again and went from the baptistery into the church. There the rite of *consignatio* was carried out for each individual by the bishop. The bishop placed his hand on the newly baptized praying for God's grace for the new member, anointed the head of each with oil, signed their brows with the sign of the cross, and gave each a kiss with the words, "The Lord be with you," to which the confirmed person responded, "And with thy spirit." He then joined the congregation of the faithful for the celebration of the Eucharist for the first time.

The Celebration of the Eucharist

Justin Martyr gives us a description of the Eucharist in about the year 150. He describes (*Apol.* 65 and 66) the ritual's taking place on Sunday and connected with baptism. The celebration opened with a service of readings from the memoirs of the apostles or the writings of the prophets, followed by a homily, the general prayers, and the kiss of peace. The second part of the celebration began with the presentation of the sacrificial gifts of bread and the chalice with wine and water to the president. The important part here is the prayer of thanksgiving, the *eucharistia,* of the presiding man. This is ratified by the congregation with the Hebrew word

Amen. The consecrated gifts were then distributed to all the baptized present to be consumed. Portions were also taken to those who were not present. And this food itself Justin calls Eucharist.

It is worth noting in this context the social character of the liturgical action; all are drawn into it. And the eucharistic great prayer is one of thanksgiving, and *eucharistia* could now become a technical term for the Mass.

The elaboration the eucharistic liturgy underwent from Justin's time until the first half of the third century is most clearly revealed in Hippolytus' *Apostolic Tradition* 4 and 23, where Hippolytus describes the Mass in connection with the consecration of a bishop and with newly baptized members. The chief value of these sources lies in the formulary of the text of the eucharistic great prayer. This is addressed to the Father through his Son Jesus Christ, whom he has sent as savior and redeemer; Christ is the Word through whom the Father created all things; he took flesh of the womb of the Virgin and was born of the Holy Spirit and her; he freely suffered to defeat death and Satan; and made known his resurrection. The congregation is following his example and command at the Last Supper, when it offers to the Father the bread and the chalice, and gives thanks for his considering them worthy to stand in his service. The bishop also prays that the Father may send down his Holy Spirit on the sacrificial offering of the Holy Church. The whole congregation then ratifies the bishop's prayer with its Amen.

Both Hippolytus' liturgy of the Mass and the eucharistic great prayer were intended as guides for the leader of a community, not as an obligatory form for all. The bishops enjoyed great freedom in their own celebrations, and various types of eucharistic prayers are evidenced throughout the third century. But by the third century, there was a fairly uniform practice of the celebration of the Mass throughout the Christian world. And, in addition to the liturgical forms, the ideas of sacrifice and of the real presence are also uniformly present.

Occasional observations by other writers confirm and complete this picture of the eucharistic liturgy drawn by Hippolytus. Tertullian's writings in particular show on many points the identity or similarity of the African Mass liturgy with it. He explicitly stresses that Christ, with the words "Hoc est corpus meum," makes the bread his body.

The first beginnings of the so-called *disciplina arcani* (the discipline of secrecy) can also be traced to the third century. This is a modern term for the early Christian custom of keeping secret from the uninitiated the most important actions and texts of liturgical worship, especially baptism, the Eucharist, the Our Father, and the creed, or of referring to them in the presence of unauthorized persons in veiled terms only. In particular, the nature and form of liturgical initiation were to be kept secret and "discovered" solely through the initiation itself. As this attitude took shape only slowly, it is no longer possible to discern its beginnings with complete clarity. It seems unlikely Tertullian knew of it, although it is quite apparent in Hippolytus' *Apostolic Tradition,* despite Hippolytus' speaking himself in detail of baptism and the Eucharist. Origen evinces acquaintance with and adherence to the discipline of secrecy too. Since most of the early evidence of the discipline comes from the East, perhaps that is the location of its origin.

The Beginnings of Christian Art

A Christianity which had increased in numbers and self-awareness was provided for the first time in the third century with the possibility of engaging in artistic activity inspired by a Christian spirit, for only the longer periods of peace coming at that time afforded the special conditions required. Christian art was, however, initially opposed by a trend of considerable strength within the Church itself that stood in irreconcilable opposition to artistic activity as such. The prohibition of images in the Old Testament (Exod 20:4) was influential in this respect. Origen, Minucius Felix, and Tertullian were all opposed to Christian art for varying reasons. Clement of Alexandria tolerated certain symbols in one's private domain only. It was the needs of liturgical worship in the stronger communities of the Church as a whole, however, which finally obtained for art an official recognition by ecclesiastical authority. Another contributory factor was the inclination of the Christians, surrounded by a widespread pagan cult of the dead, to express in artistic form on the tombs of their dead whatever their faith proclaimed to them concerning death and resurrection.

First of all, the Christians wanted a place where the worthy celebration of the eucharistic liturgy would be possible, when the size of the congregations made this increasingly difficult in private houses. There is literary evidence for the existence of specifically Christian places of worship at the beginning of the third century, in Edessa (Syria), in Carthage, and elsewhere, and for the second half of the century, in Palestine and Sicily as well. By the end of the third century, they were very numerous, in Bithynia, Galatia, Pontus, Thracia, Africa, Spain and Gaul. By contrast, archaeological confirmation has been weak till now. One clearly pre-Constantinian church was that found at Dura-Europos, a Roman frontier garrison on the west bank of the Euphrates, which dates to about 232. This church had frescoes of the Good Shepherd among tombs, the healing of the man born lame, and Christ walking on the water.

New possibilities for Christian art presented themselves when in the first half of the third century the Church came into possession of her own burial grounds, at first called cemeteries. In Rome from the ninth century onward, these were called catacombs (from the name of the field (or *ad catacumbas,* at the cemetery of St. Sebastian on the Appian Way). The *cemeterium Callisti* is the earliest purely Christian underground burial place, and its walls and ceilings of the burial chambers had pictures from Scripture or other Christian themes (as, e.g., Daniel between two lions in the den, Noah in the Ark, Jonah swallowed by the fish and cast out again, or the resurrection of Lazarus). They are all to be understood as references to the biblical accounts of a person's being saved from deadly peril, and signify the Christian hope of entering into an eternal life, safe from all peril and threat from evil's power. Christ as the Good Shepherd is common to early catacomb paintings and epitaphs. As shepherd, he brings life; as teacher, he gives true knowledge of God. In these and other ways, the flourishing Christian art of the following century had been prepared in the third century.

CHAPTER   2 4

Spiritual Life and Morality
in the Communities of the Third Century

If the sources are studied for the essential concepts and convictions which characterized piety in the third century, two ideas and realities stand out, namely, baptism and martyrdom. All writers of the period who discuss in any detail Christian perfection and its actual realization speak so insistently of baptism as the well-spring, and of readiness for martyrdom as the touchstone of the genuineness of a Christian way of life, that devotion to baptism and to martyrdom must be generally considered to be the fundamental twofold attitude to religious life in the early Christian Church.

Baptismal Spirituality

The first attempts of real importance to frame a theory of Christian perfection were undertaken by the early teachers of Alexandria. Clement of Alexandria traced such a theory in the portrait of the Christian Gnostic in his *Paedagogus* and the *Stromata.* The import of baptism is unmistakable for perfection. It brings complete forgiveness of sins and liberates from the dark power of the demons; it is rebirth to new life in the kingdom of the Father and so grants immortality; and by infusion of the Holy Spirit into the soul, it gives true knowledge of God or *gnosis.* This gnosis is imparted to every baptized person, not just to the *pneumatikoi* (spiritually endowed persons); and by it the grace-given root of all perfection is implanted; this must grow throughout life. This knowledge must stand the test of the struggle with evil. In one's baptism, one is really and effectually given what baptism in the Jordan once effected for Christ. Consequently, the life which springs from baptismal grace is an imitation of Christ, with whom the believer is indissolubly united at his baptism.

Origen expounds on this in rich abundance. This is particularly evident in his homilies, in an ardent metaphorical style with insistent kerygmatic appeal. Origen thus became the most zealous preacher of deep-felt baptismal spirituality for the early Christian Church generally. He lays the foundation first of all in a theology of baptism, which bases all exhortations to live in accordance with baptismal grace on the supernatural event which occurs at baptism. His explanations of that event draw upon the Old Testament prefigurations of it (the exodus from Egypt, the passage of the Red Sea, the stages of the wandering in the desert and the crossing of the Jordan, after which the Promised Land is opened to him. Jesus, not Moses, is his guide, and he is freed from the dominion of Satan; and so forth). The Christian is now summoned to follow Christ, the new guide who has been given to him in baptism. Now instead of being an *imitator diaboli,* he is called to become an *imitator Christi,* of the Logos with whom and in whom he sets out on the paths of his spiritual life which is to lead him to the Father. Baptism, the beginning of this new life, has its source of life-giving power in the death of Christ on the cross, and hence the life of baptismal grace derives ultimately from the crucifixion.

But now this baptismal grace must further develop. And only if it is renewed daily can the new life received in baptism prosper. The task set every Christian in his religious life can be expressed for Origen in the concise phrase: to preserve baptismal grace. The obligation to fidelity derives, negatively, from the renunciation of Satan, but more importantly, positively, from the fact that Christ is now the bridegroom and spouse of the soul, and marital fidelity is required by a perpetual battle against the powers of the evil one. In this combat the baptized follow again the example of their master, who likewise was tempted after his baptism in the Jordan; and so the daily practice of a baptismal spirituality is an actual *imitatio Christi.* Truly lived baptismal piety produced abundant virtues, especially genuine love of one's neighbor and readiness for martyrdom.

Origen preached this not to an elite, but to all Christians, and he was aware therefore of the failure of many to realize the lofty goal. Precisely that is why he preached it so. Others besides the Alexandrians taught similarly, if not with such power. Cyprian, e.g., taught Christian life is the continuance of the *renuntiatio saeculi,* which, once expressed in baptism, must then be made effective by following our Lord when God tests the Christians through persecution. It was precisely such views of baptism which led the early Church to prepare candidates for baptism in the catechumenate, and to organize a solemn celebration of it. The whole impact of initiation into the mysteries of the Christian faith was to work itself out in a religious life which never forgot the radiance of that hour nor the gravity of the solemn baptismal vow.

Devotion to Martyrdom

Devotion to martyrdom as the second fundamental attitude in striving for Christian perfection reached its peak in the third century. Closely linked with the idea of the *imitatio Christi,* esteem for martyrdom as the summit and crown of all perfection became the most widespread, and ascetically fruitful, watchword in the world of early Christian spirituality. Anyone who suffers for confessing the name of Christ becomes thereby a sharer and companion of his Passion.

Devotion to martyrdom received a particular force of attraction from the idea that a martyr's violent death led in a unique way to union with Christ. Even confessing Christ under torture was assumed to reveal this union. At that moment it is Christ who strengthens the confessor/martyr, and so fills him with his presence that, in a kind of exaltation, he scarcely feels the pain of torture and execution. It was this idea which culminated in the custom of honoring the martyrs with the title of *Christophorus:* union with Christ attains perfection by suffering martyrdom, hence its becoming almost a desideratum. Martyrdom was a baptism in blood and completely replaced the other baptism, and in fact surpasses it in efficacy, because there is no danger of later relapse. Martyrdom perfects the Christian life because it is the highest form of imitation of Christ, and it produces union with him in the highest degree.

There is no plainer way to prove love of God and of Christ than by suffering violent death under persecution. Consequently, the *exhortatio ad martyrium* was a regular part of early Christian preaching and literature, not a dull cliché, but a very real factor in the actual realities of the third century itself. Its purest advocates are probably Origen and Cyprian.

When actual martyrdom was not available a kind of martyrdom of desire came into play, where moral striving or extraordinary and self-sacrificial service to others were seen as a kind of equivalent.

The Asceticism of the Third Century

Christians of both sexes who renounced marriage, who dissociated themselves more than others from secular life, yet remained with their families and put themselves at the service of the Christian community, are found already in the apostolic age, but by the third century, these ascetics had become so numerous as to represent an important factor in the daily life of the churches of both East and West. They were not yet bound to a definite mode of life with a fixed rule, so most remained with their families. There was also no rite for the reception by the Church of these people into their state of life; they simply bound themselves by a solemn promise to a life of continence. That promise, however, was enforced by the community authorities very strictly, with excommunication the result of transgressing it. But the vow need not bind permanently, and, for good reasons, the ascetic could be released from it.

Within the community and among its rulers, the ascetics enjoyed unique esteem. A new element with increased prestige was ascetic virginity, since this was connected with the idea of the soul's espousal to Christ. At first this notion was at the service of the ideal of virginity, and a theological basis was sought for the worth of the ascetics. Their mode of life was declared to be the worthiest substitute for death by martyrdom; like the latter, it called for total self-sacrifice. Such a lofty ideal is liable to particular perils, especially given the esteem in which they were held in the communities, and Tertullian warned them against pride, the pseudo-Clementine letters against vanity and empty show, and Cyprian demanded of them a high degree of all the virtues. Methodius directed their minds to meditation and the wealth of riches in that; virginity was to be a means of individual sanctification.

Ascetical excess and a disproportion between the individual's moral strength and such lofty idealism explain a grave aberration in Christian asceticism, especially in the third century, the system of the so-called *agapetae,* in which ascetics lived together as "sister and brother," thus imperilling their vows of virginity and exposing the whole system to derision. The widespread aberration goaded bishops and other ecclesiastical authorities into decisive action to punish the guilty, but the practice remained in both East and West and, in Spain, until the sixth century.

The asceticism of the third century not only perpetuated the earlier forms, but provided the matrix of two new developments of importance. From this practice came the early monasticism of the East, which, in its first eremitical phase, was merely a transference of the life and activity of the ascetics from the Christian community into solitude (as, e.g., in Athanasius' account of the life of St. Antony). The baptismal spirituality and devotion to martyrdom of the second and third centuries, in conjunction with ascetical virginity, continued to exert influence as fundamental ideas of monasticism, and so proved their intense vitality. The vows taken by the monk were compared in value with a second baptism, and his life with a spiritual martyrdom which made him, like the actual martyr, an *athleta Christi,* while his continence ranked him in the company of those who are the brides of Christ. The ideal of virginity also prepared the way for priestly celibacy.

Though highly esteemed in the Church as a whole, the manner of life of the ascetics was one which was always freely accepted and then only by a minority among Christians. Whenever anyone attempted to impose the style of life on individuals or groups, it engendered conflicts with the ecclesiastical authorities. The Encratites, followers of the Syrian Tatian, were such a group which sought to impose its own ideals on all and was resisted by the authorities. But the intense attachment of the third-century Church to the ascetical ideal can certainly be taken as a general proof of her high moral quality.

Prayer and Fasting in Early Christian Spirituality

In the third century, prayer, an indispensable element in Christian worship of God, became the subject both of theological reflection and of practical concern for its right performance both liturgical and private. The Alexandrian theologians sought devotedly a theology of prayer and endeavored to incorporate it into their conception of Christian perfection as a whole. The Latins, Tertullian and Cyprian in particular, in their expositions of the Our Father, display the Latin mind's greater interest in the actual practice of the life of prayer and its importance for daily life. For Clement of Alexandria the Christian's duty to pray is self-evident, for the soul must thank God without ceasing for all his gifts; and in the striving for perfection, prayer of petition is likewise indispensable, and it must be used to implore true gnosis and the forgiveness of sins. One must include the enemy as well as the brother and the conversion of the whole world. Clement hazards the definition of prayer that it is "intercourse with God" (*Strom.* 7, 39, 6). For Clement, however, the highest form of prayer is interior mental prayer, which he clearly distinguishes from vocal prayer. He keeps the latter intact, but values the former higher: it needs no words, is unceasing, makes the whole life a holy day; and gives *theoria,* the vision of divine things. In this distinction between vocal and mental prayer the later division of the spiritual life into active and contemplative is already indicated in a purely Christian sense. Clement is its first important pioneer.

Following on from Clement, Origen deepens and carries further what Clement had begun. Origen too is profoundly aware that the life of the Christian must be a perpetual prayer. Origen insists on the proper disposition of the soul for prayer, defense against sin, freedom from emotional disturbance, and finally interior recollection and concentration, which excludes everything that cannot be consecrated to God. Christian prayer then ascends by stages: petition, including that for gnosis and growth in virtue; then the praise of God is linked to petition; and then the summit is reached in interior, wordless prayer in which the soul is united with God in a unique way. This mirrors Origen's basic conception of a spiritual ascent by stages, ending in the loving knowledge of God in which the soul is "divinized." These views are Origen's in his *De oratione* (On Prayer); but in his homilies, he strikes a somewhat different tone in that instead of to God the

Father, his prayers are offered to Christ, and, importantly, this facet of his work on prayer extensively influenced the spirituality of the Eastern Church, particularly in its monasticism, and, through Ambrose, even Western mystical devotion to Jesus down to the time of St. Bernard.

The commentaries on the Our Father by the Latins, Tertullian and Cyprian, disclose a different attitude and atmosphere toward prayer. They work independently of the Alexandrians, but share certain convictions with them: the obligation to pray; the times and conditions of mind necessary for prayer. But the lofty idealistic strain of the Greeks is foreign to the Latins. Interior prayer and stages of ascent are not their concerns. Their urgent concern is, rather, with the actual concrete form of prayer and its place in the daily life of the Christian community. Their preferred form is that of Christ's Our Father. Both Tertullian and Cyprian understand the petition for daily bread in a predominantly eucharistic sense. Humility is the appropriate attitude for prayer for both. They are concerned about the specific times of prayer and about proper posture for it (for Tertullian, it is with hands upraised and extended in imitation of the suffering Lord). Cyprian is heavily dependent upon his earlier compatriot's work, but he adds a note of warmth and persuasiveness to his exposition and contributes an important ecclesiological aspect to his treatment of prayer: "When we pray," he writes, "we do not pray for one but for the whole people of God, for we are all one." (*De dominica oratione* 8, 24, 30). The Christian people at prayer is joined together in the unity of the Father and the Son and the Holy Spirit and to break that unity is to sin grievously and to lack an essential condition for genuine prayer.

All of these theologians recognize improvised prayers besides the Our Father. The early Christians also prayed the Old Testament Psalms after christianizing them through typological interpretations which allowed them to hear Christ as the speaker in the psalms or else heard the voice of the Church speaking to her glorified Lord in the *Dominus psalmorum.* A particularly striking example of the first sort of typology is to be found in Psalm 3:6 (5): *ego dormivi et soporatus sum et exsurrexi* [I lie down and go to sleep; I awaken again because (the Lord) sustains me]. As early as Justin Martyr, this passage was read as having been spoken by Christ on Easter morning. The christianizing of the Psalter, which made it the prayer and hymn book absolutely preferred by the early Church was furthered and facilitated by the importance and extent of prayer to Christ in early Christian popular devotion.

Finally, prayer addressed to Christ was expressed by turning to the East when praying. The coming of the Lord was awaited from the East; Paradise lay to the East; it contrasted with the Jews who prayed toward the Temple in Jerusalem; it had an eschatological significance, especially when combined with prayer standing before a crucifix while facing East, for the cross, as a sign of his triumph, was to proceed his coming from the East.

The ascetical enthusiasm of the third century also led to a considerable practice of fasting. The weekly fasts on Wednesdays and Fridays had been handed down from apostolic times and became more firmly established. At this period the motive for the choice of the two fast days in the week changed; while earlier it emphasized the independence of the Christians from the Jewish practice (Jews fasted on Mondays and Thursdays), now it was the connection of the two days with the events of our Lord's Passion that was indicated: the betrayal by Judas on a Wednesday and Christ's death on Friday. Fasting on those days was thus a fast of mourning and of grief.

Church authorities placed high value on fasting, as is shown in their incorporation of it in the liturgy in various ways. From early times there was a Passover fast in preparation for the feast of Easter, though its length varied from church to church. The baptismal fast, initially only two days, was now extended. It was envisaged in close relation to prayer, which fasting effectively supports; it was also considered a means of atoning for former sins and preparing to receive the Spirit. Finally, fasting also became an important factor in the penitential discipline of the early Church, imposing on the sinner restrictions on food and drink in conjunction with his penance.

Fasting as a means to gaining mastery over concupiscence and unregulated sense pleasure and consequently as a way to higher perfection, found special favor in early Christian ascetic circles. It brought with it the danger of over-emphasis and becoming an end in itself and opposed to aberrations, theologians very early emphasized that what was decisive was the spirit, a genuine penitential attitude and self-denial, which alone could give bodily fasting its value.

Early Christian Morals

Asceticism characterized the lives only of an elite among Christians, and thus only a minority among them. There arises the question, therefore, of how the great majority of Christians in town and country lived their daily religious lives in pagan surroundings and within a secular civilization determined by pagan principles. Unfortunately, the sources, even for the third century, do not provide us with much information of a generally valid sort. It is again the North Africans, Tertullian and Cyprian, with their intense concerns for the practical questions of daily religious life, who are most informative, but Clement and Origen give insights as well for the Egyptian church.

There were, of course, considerable difficulties which any attempt to implement Christian moral ideals inevitably met with day after day. There were first of all the problems of simply being in an environment where paganism encompassed every facet of private and public life. The large number of trades and professions which served polytheism were interdicted to them. The whole pagan atmosphere presented a ubiquitous temptation to relapse into former habits of life, and Christians had to struggle against this. A high degree of self-discipline was necessary in view of the sexual licentiousness of the time.

The sources show that precisely in the third century, the Christian communities were exposed to searching trials which they did not entirely withstand. During the long periods of lack of active persecution, the toxic pagan atmosphere was able to work on the self-discipline of the Church's members, and when the great trials of the Decian and Diocletian persecutions hit, it became evident how slack self-discipline had become for many. Cyprian's picture of 249–50 C.E. speaks for itself, and his is only reinforced by Eusebius' (*HE* 8, 1, 7–9) of the period prior to Diocletian's persecution. There were not only slackenings in moral discipline, but there were lamentable quarrels among Church leaders, such that Eusebius was minded to explain the persecution as a divine judgment. Nevertheless, it is indisputable that Christianity succeeded in the third century in raising the moral level of the various churches and communities high above that of the pagan world around them.

Marriage and the Family

Ignatius of Antioch had already recommended the contracting of marriage be sanctioned by the bishop. In Tertullian's time too, Christians celebrated their marriages in the presence of the *ecclesia,* and had them sealed with a blessing, although this cannot have indicated a liturgical rite or an indispensable participation of the bishop at marriages in that period. The inner harmony of such a marriage derived from the common religious convictions of the partners and drew its strength from common sharing in the eucharistic repast. Intermarriage with pagans was disapproved of by the Church since such sharing could not go on, and since such marriage exposed the Christian to pagan influences too much. The indissolubility of Christian marriage which had since St. Paul found its deepest ground in its symbolical representation the union of Christ and the Church (Eph 5:32; 1 Cor 7:10ff.), is emphasized by most writers of the third century. Conjugal fidelity and reverence for children were emphasized, adultery was strictly punished by penitential discipline, abortion was ruled murder, and exposing children after birth was condemned. These views contravened contemporary Roman customs.

The place of the woman in Christian marriage was that of a partner with equal rights, which was very much more than pagan women enjoyed. Second marriages were frowned upon by the Church, but were not forbidden. With the trend of the age toward asceticism, they were regarded as signs of diminished moral effort. Clerics could not take part in them, and they posed an impediment to continuing in the clerical state.

Early Christian Works of Mercy

One criterion of the value of Christian ethical principles in daily life is provided by the way in which the commandment of Christian love for one's neighbor is fulfilled. Caring for the brother or pagan in need stood in marked contrast to the prevailing pagan attitude. One of the earliest forms of charitable activity was the "agape," meals in the Christian community which were intended to strengthen community spirit, but also providing effective material help among the poor and needy in the community.

In his *Apologeticum,* Tertullian gives an instructive glimpse at the beginning of the third century. There was a common fund for the voluntary contribution of members and from it the poor were fed, old people in need looked after, orphans and destitute children cared for, brethren in prison helped, and those condemned to forced labor in the mines given support (*Apol.* 39). A special sort of charity was the practice of hospitality toward the itinerating brother in the faith. In the fourth century there grew from this charitable obligation a comprehensive organization which established hostels and hospices. The impact of this work on pagan circles is confirmed, in spite of his own rejection of the faith, by Emperor Julian, who wrote that Christianity had been lastingly furthered "by philanthropy to strangers and care for the burial of the dead" (Sozomenos, *HE* 5, 15). Worthy burial of poor brethren in the faith was felt to be a duty of love and distinguished Christian and pagan societies sharply.

Pre-Constantinian Christianity had no slave problem in any sense that would have caused it to work for the abolition of slavery, but its charitable efforts could not fail to be interested in the lot of slaves. Slaves who converted were regarded as equal brothers and sisters with the rest of the faithful and were accorded complete equality of rights, and all ecclesiastical offices, including that of bishop, were open to them. Slaves among the martyrs were regarded with equal esteem. Mistreatment of a slave by a Christian master was severely censured and, if need be, punished with ecclesiastical penalties. On the other hand, slaves were not to misunderstand the meaning of "Christian freedom" either.

Christian brotherly love had really to prove itself in the times of extraordinary catastrophes which were not lacking in the third century. Dionysius of Alexandria records the selfless caring by Christians for brother and pagan alike during an epidemic in 250, a service which cost many their lives. They cared for the sick and buried the dead. When the plague was raging in Carthage, Cyprian summoned his people by word and example into similar caring duties. All of this contrasted notably with pagan attitudes in the same circumstances.

Practical Christian charity was also given to needy Christian communities in any of the territories to which the faith had spread. The churches at Rome and, especially under Cyprian, Carthage were particularly noted for this activity.

The practical accomplishment of the tasks imposed by the duties of brotherly love required, in the bigger communities of the third century, an administrative organization and personnel. Women were used to supplement the work of the deacons who were the appointed helpers of the bishops in charitable welfare work; they were in any case indispensable in the care of their own sex. Widows, regarded as a special order on the basis of 1 Timothy 5:3–16, were first considered for such work. Only approved women were received (the bishop made the judgment) without consecration and without prescribed vows. They did private pastoral and missionary work in the homes among women. They educated orphans, nursed the sick, and sometimes cared for prisoners. From the second century on, unmarried women were also admitted, and the title deaconess was used for those engaged in charitable works. When this order, through adoption of a more ascetical life style withdrew from such work more and more, in Syrian territory especially, the deaconess became a distinct office within the community: the deaconess was now concerned with looking after the women catechumens, in domestic pastoral work with Christian women in pagan families, and in caring for sick women. By the fourth century, the office of deaconess had begun to attain its definitive form and full development. (The office of deaconess has not been shown to have existed in the churches of the Latin West before the fourth century, however, and the order of widows continued those functions there.)

Christian charitable activity inevitably confronted the Church with a series of social problems, such as those of property and wealth, labor and poverty, which obliged her to adopt definite positions. Clement of Alexandria, in his *Quis dives salvetur?* [Who is the rich man that is saved?] as well as in others of his works, gives the most detailed treatment of these matters. One is to remain detached from property and wealth. A very high premium is placed on almsgiving. Almsgiving is elevated by Cyprian to a means of grace by which one can atone for daily faults committed after baptism (De *opere et eleemosynis* [On works and almsgiving]).

For all her welfare work, however, the Church never failed to proclaim the high personal worth of labor and she opposed the view of antiquity which regarded manual labor as an evil and a bitter necessity, as a sign of lack of freedom and of slavery. Church ordinances simply regarded work as a duty and proclaimed that a Christian who was capable of working should not receive any relief from the community. It was only with Augustine, however, that deeper reflection on the moral and religious meaning of labor began and led to the Christian ethic of work.

The Attitude of Early Christianity
to Secular Civilization and Culture

It was in accord with the fundamentally ascetical attitude of early Christianity that it regarded with marked reserve the amenities of late-antiquity civilization. Though Tertullian's rigorism may have gone too far in its radical rejection of most of civilization's benefits as the invention of pagan demons, even level-headed men condemned pagan luxury. Clement opposed the cultivation of beauty and the body which degenerated into luxury-seeking, though he did not oppose reasonable care for health or moderate use of jewelry. And the great threats to Christian morality represented by pagan entertainments, gladiatorial contests, theatrical shows, and dances were shunned deliberately, if for no other reason than their original connection with idolatry.

The estimate of pagan literature and learning by Christian writers of the third century is very mixed. The Greeks with some reservations show themselves far readier than the Latins (excepting Lactantius) to attribute importance to them. Clement and Origen felt that philosophical thought can be a valuable propaedeutic for faith. Origen recognized the importance of secular studies for Christian instruction, but he compared unfavorably the sophistry and rhetoric of many teachers with the simplicity and conscientiousness of the evangelists. The attitude of Hippolytus was much more reserved, for though he preferred Greek literature to Egyptian and Babylonian, he still explained the rise of heresies by their dependence on Greek philosophies.

Among the Latins, Minucius Felix radically repudiated pagan poetry and literature, but he approved the efforts of some philosophers to arrive at a true conception of God. The attitude of Tertullian on this question is peculiarly complex. In his earlier works, he tended to be more favorable to Greek philosophy and quotes it to buttress his own purposes, but when he turns from his apologetical works to polemics, he becomes more skeptical about its value, he holds it partly responsible for the rise of heresies, and he finds its theses useful only when they agree with Christian truth. Tertullian's practical and ascetical writings are hostile to pagan thought which he finds useless in the formation of Christian moral life. There was a contradiction in Tertullian's soul on this: he himself possessed a comprehensive acquaintance with pagan thought and literature which in his writings he uses to his own distinct advantage in making his points; yet he contested in an increasingly radical manner, and, as it were, despite himself, the idea that these studies possessed any worth whatsoever for the culture of a Christian. Cyprian, a man of deeds, primarily, expressed himself on these matters only sporadically, but negatively. It is only shortly before the turning-point under Constantine that in Lactantius we find a Christian writing in Latin whose regard for the greatness of the past of Rome made possible a more favorable estimate of its literary achievements. He saw value in rhetoric and in philosophy, which latter teaches how to distinguish truth from falsity, even though pagan philosophy had often failed.

The counterpart to the predominantly unfavorable estimate of pagan literature and philosophy of the majority of third-century Christian writers was their proud awareness that in the Old Testament, the Gospels, Epistles and other documents of apostolic tradition, they possessed an intellectual patrimony far superior to the wisdom the Greeks. And if Christianity in the third century was as yet unable to articulate any systematic and specifically Christian ideal of culture, it nevertheless laid foundations upon which a later age could build.

The Early Christian Church and the Pagan State

Of particular interest is the relation which developed in the third century between the pagan State and the Church. The Church clearly became aware of her growing inner strength and felt herself to be the "great Church." This increase in strength within and without was not hidden from the pagan State either, and it now reckoned with her as a power that required the adoption of a new attitude. This consciousness existed on both sides and is most strikingly revealed by Cyprian's proud remark that the Emperor Decius heard the news of the rebellion of a rival usurper much more calmly than the announcement of the election of a new Bishop of Rome (Ep. 55, 9). Both sides considered the relationship afresh and the outcome was of far-reaching import for the period that followed. At the beginning of the century, there was among Christians really only one voice that expressed a radical rejection of the Roman State, namely, Hippolytus'. He expressed his views in apocalyptic terms with great vehemence. The position of the Alexandrians was quite different. Clement was fundamentally loyal to the pagan State, affirming the obligations of taxes and military service and recognizing Roman law; and if that State persecuted the Church, the hand of Providence was to be worshipped. The only limit to this recognition was set by the cult of the emperor and the idolatry encouraged by the State. Origen too is loyal. He works out a theoretical basis for the relation of Church and pagan State from Romans 13:1ff. He derives the power of the *Imperium Romanum* from God, who has conferred judicial authority upon it. To the question of how such a State could persecute the Church, Origen's response is that it is an abuse of the power of the State for which those responsible would have to answer before the judgment seat of God. God's providence permitted persecutions, but always gave back peace again. In principle, the Christian was loyal to the State unless the State required something in direct contradiction to the faith, as, e.g., in the emperor cult. Origen and Tertullian are profoundly appreciative of the *pax Romana* and pray for the government, despite their reservations about other facets of the relationship. And this positive relation brought all sorts of increased contacts between Church and State in the third century.

All of this shows that in the third century the relation between Church and State cannot in many spheres be regarded as one of hostility nor, from the point of view of the Church, even as a matter of indifference. A process is perceptible which may be described as one of mutual gradual approach even though the Church unmistakably expressed the limits of her recognition of Roman power. Only twice, under Decius and Diocletian, was this development harshly interrupted, and these occurred only because both emperors still believed in the possibility of a violent solution. How completely their opinions failed to recognize the signs of the times was shown by the enormously rapid change after Constantine's victory. A view of the exhaustive way the foundations of a reconciliation between Church and State were laid even in the third century shows that the events following the failure of Diocletian's persecution were not as revolutionary a turning-point as they have often been interpreted to be.

CHAPTER 25

The Holiness of the Christian and the Church

The faithful of early Christian times had to conduct their religious life on the foundation of a baptismal spirituality and "preserve the seal of baptism," all of which implied a lofty awareness of the obligation of all the baptized to holiness in a holy Church. Despite their vivid knowledge of this duty, and despite all efforts to conform to it, not all members of the various communities lived up to it. Indeed, the writings of the apostolic and sub-apostolic age reveal perfectly clearly that there were no periods in the life of the young Church which enjoyed the complete absence of sin.

This situation created a serious problem for the individual Christian, the individual community, and the Church as a whole. Had the Christian who had lost baptismal grace forfeited salvation for ever, had he definitely left the Church, or was there still a way for him to "recover the [lost] seal of baptism"? Were some sins so grave, perhaps, that no penance, however strict, could atone for them? Were they unforgivable, and did they make return to the Church's society impossible for ever? These questions — always present in the Church — culminated in the third century and were bound up in disputes about penance.

To sketch the background of the problems: Jesus' preaching demanded an absolutely radical renunciation of evil (Lk 9:62; 14:25), and also judged the situation of one who has relapsed as graver than that of the not yet converted (Mt 13:3ff.). On the other hand, he knew the sinfulness of his closest followers and did not exclude those who were even unfaithful to him from reconciliation and responsibility for important tasks in the *basileia* of God. God's readiness to forgive a sinner many times, is the basis for the precept that they must be equally ready to go on forgiving their brethren (Mt 18:22; 6:12; 7:11). With the conferring of the power of binding and loosing on the apostles as bearers of authority, the Church was appointed to pass judgment on the faithful who sinned, to expel them from the community or to free them from their bond, and forgive them their sins (Mt 18:15ff.; Jn 20:21ff.). That authority was given without restriction; no sin was excepted as unforgivable, and so no sinner was excluded permanently from the Church unless he hardened himself impenitently in the "sin against the Holy Spirit" (Mt 12:31ff.). St. Paul acted in accordance with this when he excommunicated the incestuous sinner at Corinth (1 Cor 5:3ff.). In other New Testament writings, the view prevails too that every sinner can obtain forgiveness again if he does penance (Jas 1:21; 5:19ff.; 2 Pet 3:9; 1 Jn 2:1ff.). Only if he refuses penance and atonement does his fault become for him the "sin unto death" (1 Jn 5:16). The sinner's prayer and that of the community praying for him open up the way to forgiveness (1 Jn 5:14ff.; Jas 5:14ff.). And the Revelation recognizes that God can bring any sinner to repentance (Rev 2:2; 2:14ff.; 2:20–23).

This New Testament attitude about forgiveness' continuing to be available to the penitent persisted into the sub-apostolic age as well. Though its writers wince at the disgrace of the ideal of baptismal sanctification brought on by some, they all issue an urgent summons to penance, which will restore salvation to each. By such penance they meant genuine conversion, that is, renunciation of sin and a return to obedience to God's commandments. This is expressed in prayer of repentance, fasting, alms-giving, as well as confession of sin before God and the community of brethren. In the sub-apostolic period too, penance was a community matter, and during his penance the community assisted him with its impetrative prayers. When the Church authorities decided sufficient penance had been accomplished and pardoned and reincorporated him into the community's life, the Church was convinced that he had obtained God's pardon as well.

Penance in the *Shepherd* of Hermas

It is often mistakenly assumed that Hermas' position in the *Shepherd,* which maintains the possibility of a post-baptismal penance for the forgiveness of sin, marks a breech in the Church's penitential theory and practice of maintaining a Church of the saints. Hermas writes in the form of an apocalypse, so his theories and presentation leave an obscure and contradictory residue. But that interpretation is certainly inadequate: it is not Hermas who initiates a theory of post-baptismal penance and forgiveness; the Church had always maintained that, as we have seen. What Hermas contributes to the development, on the basis of the Shepherd's revelation, is the notion that the possibility of penance has a time limit set to it: it lasts until a certain day with a single possibility of penance for sins committed after baptism. The end of the world, heralded by an imminent persecution, is approaching, and no further chance is available for subsequent sins. The modification in the time available for penance is, thus, given eschatological grounds. But the eschatology is not finally Hermas' point: there is only one possibility of post-baptismal penance because that is something which is unrepeatable in principle, probably on the idea that just as there is only one baptism which confers forgiveness, so there is only one penance which blots out post-baptismal sins. The penance of someone who has relapsed a second time could not have been an irrevocable rejection of evil; it could not therefore have been genuine penance; and God could not have thereby granted forgiveness. The principle of the singleness of *paenitentia secunda* is clearly formulated by Hermas for the first time, and it was to remain in force for a long time.

Among penitential practices for the sinner, Hermas reckons confession of sins, prayer, fasting, almsgiving, and the humility with which he takes all these exercises on himself. When the atonement is complete, when it corresponds to the measure of guilt, its double effect supervenes: it brings forgiveness of sins, and healing, while restoring life to the soul, the seal of baptism that had been lost. By his image of the tower, the symbol of the Church, Hermas makes clear that penance is not just between man and God; it also involves the Church. Sinners in penance are outside the tower, the community of the Church; anyone no longer taken into the tower is lost. The Church excluded (excommunicated) adulterers and those who had lapsed into idolatry. Reception back into the tower presupposed an examination on whether the excommunication penance can be regarded as sufficient or "completed." This was the prerogative of the Church authorities to determine.

One ought here to note that Hermas' intention was not completely to describe the ecclesiastical penance of his time, but rather simply to preach penance.

Tertullian's Two Views of Penance

The increased membership of the communities, especially in the phase of intense growth that characterized the latter half of the second century, involved more frequent cases of failure in Christian life and so heightened the importance of the question of penance. Church authorities might choose stricter or milder penitential disciplines depending on whether they emphasized the ideal of holiness or the motive of mercy. Both tendencies could coexist in the same community, and both are perceptible here and there in the sources, too. Against a "laxness" connected with emphasis on mercy, there arose in Phrygian Montanism a rigoristic trend. More than a mere protest, this Montanist position was part of their extremist movement in which Montanus, its first prophet, could claim: "Potest ecclesia donare delicta, sed non faciam, ne et alii delinquant" ["The Church can forgive sins, but I shall not, lest others fall away"]. This amounted to demanding that for the sake of discipline in the community, the Church should refuse sinners the possibility of penance, the granting of which she was in principle admitted to possess. The initial success of Montanism shows a following for an uncompromising emphasis on holiness. And the question of penance became a prime problem at one stroke when Tertullian by his adherence to Montanism made this demand his own.

As a member of the Catholic community in Carthage, however, Tertullian had previously expounded the traditional view of the question of penance in his own works. For instance, in his monograph On *Penance* from his pre-Montanist days, the existence of the possibility of a single penance for the baptized was something of which he had no doubt whatever. Tertullian speaks of this penance reluctantly, for he felt it wrong to mislead others into a careless attitude toward sin. He felt the loss of baptismal grace to be very grave indeed. Moreover, it is only the gravest of sins of which he speaks in penance, as, e.g., adultery, apostasy, and heresy.

A radical change in Tertullian's view about penance is revealed in De *pudicitia* [On modesty], a later open polemic in which he now denies to the Church any right to forgive grave sins and reserves this to the spirituals of the Montanist movement. Tertullian now recants the "error" of his earlier position, namely, the Catholic position, and sets forth a "new" position. Now he finds some sins remissible and irremissible, among which those of idolatry, adultery, and murder (but not these exclusively) play a special role. The forgiveness of the irremissible sins was up to God alone.

The triad of capital sins (idolatry or apostasy, adultery, and murder) are however not part of the Church's penitential discipline as unforgivable before Tertullian's Montanist period, and this triad of unforgivable sins is a construction of Tertullian himself in his polemics against the Catholic Church.

In his *De paenitentia,* and in some parts of his *De pudicitia*, Tertullian becomes the first Christian writer to reveal enough about the penitential discipline to allow us to see how it operated. The first stage was *exhomologesis,* confession. The sinner had to admit openly that he needed to do penance. Just how this worked itself through is unclear. Performance of public penance began with exclusion from participation in the eucharistic service and the prayer of the community; the penitent now no longer possessed *communicatio ecclesiastica*. This was imposed by the Church authorities, but did not correspond to modern excommunication. He stood "outside the Church." He performed his public penance in two stages: First he stood at the entrance to the church, probably in penitential clothes; clerics and laity passed him by and on his knees he sought the help of their prayers and readmission to their society. The second stage brought him inside the church, where he continued to implore impetratory prayer and restoration of his former membership. Though extending a long time in every instance, penance of a life-long sort does not seem to have been imposed in Tertullian's time.

At the end of penance, there was the act of reconciliation through which the bishop granted pardon and "restoration," probably with the imposition of hands in conjunction with prayer, which granted the restored one *pax* with his Church and conferred and guaranteed reconciliation with God.

More serious consequences for ecclesiastical unity seemed at first to portend from a controversy about the practice of penance which took place almost at the same time in Rome, although this conflict had no intrinsic connection with the African disputes. The learned priest Hippolytus took sharp issue with Bishop Callistus (217–22), defending a rigorist position against the alleged laxness of Callistus. But it is clear that it was something other than penance at issue here for

Callistus cannot be shown to have deviated from earlier Church practice in these matters. Hippolytus and his few followers were unable to carry the day, and their "school" did not outlive its founder.

Penitential Discipline in North Africa in Cyprian's Time

Renewed discussion of the penance question was precipitated by Decius' persecution, for by its end, the large numbers of the lapsed forced the leaders of the Church to review their penitential policy. This dispute had severe repercussions for Church unity and led in fact to the divisions which culminated in the extensive anti-Church of the Novatians.

Bishop Cyprian of Carthage, in hiding from the pagan authorities, received word from his flock about certain priests who were extraordinarily lax in receiving back the lapsed, without requiring any works of penance at all. Many of the lapsed produced "letters of peace" (*libelli pacis*) from martyrs before they died which recommended reception of their bearers back into the Church's fellowship. Or they had *libelli pacis* from confessors. Cyprian reacted sharply to regain control, threatening priests with deprivation of office if they received the lapsed and let the authors of the *libelli pacis* understand they were only advising their bishop, not making decisions which were his prerogative. A fair number of Cyprian's people revolted against his positions and, under the leadership of one Felicissimus, who had been appointed deacon in Carthage in Cyprian's absence by a priest called Novatus. This group set itself up as the Catholic Church in Carthage and set up a propaganda campaign against Cyprian.

This was the situation at Easter, 251, when Cyprian returned to the city. He soon published his *On the lapsed* in which he reiterated his position on the question of penance: he opposed strongly the lax practice of his opponents and demanded serious and comprehensive penance from the lapsed as a condition for their reception. The opposition got their own bishop in the priest Fortunatus and sought recognition from Pope Cornelius, who rebuffed them. Cyprian quickly secured to the ecclesiastical authorities alone the matter of penance for the lapsed. A synod of African bishops summoned by Cyprian in 251 confirmed his position. And when a new persecution threatened under Emperor Gallus which seemed likely to be more severe even than Decius', a second synod in Carthage, in 252, dealt again with penitential discipline for the lapsed. For pastoral considerations, it was decided to grant to the lapsed who had begun their penance the day of their lapse, the peace of the Church. When Gallus' persecution did not assume its portended fearful dimensions, the argument about penance for the *lapsi* was settled by the victory of Cyprian's views.

Two questions were involved: first whether peace with the Church could be restored without works of penance, and secondly, if decisions about it belonged to Church leaders or whether a testimonial from a martyr or confessor superseded with binding force the ecclesiastical authority. Cyprian's views ultimately prevailed. It is notable that the remissibility or irremissibility of the sin of apostasy never enters the discussion, for both parties assumed its remissibility. On one point alone did Cyprian minorate his view, namely, in the matter of the dying who had not completed their penance. So long as they possessed a *libellus pacis,* they might be granted reconciliation.

The external form of the institution or liturgy of penance can be gleaned from Cyprian's writings. First came the *paenitentiam agere* or *satisfacere* of the sinner, his works of self-denial done publicly. The second stage was the *exhomologesis,* the part of the penance which took place in the presence of the community. It consisted in the request of the penitent to the bishop, clergy, and congregation for restoration and reconciliation. This presupposed a non-public admission of guilt to the bishop, which Cyprian terms *confessio.* The third act was reconciliation proper through imposition of hands by the bishop. Long the practice in the East, Cyprian's is the first mention of it for the Latin West. The bishop possessed his power in this by reason of the power of binding and loosing committed to him. That the community collaborated in this judgment is clear, but we have no details of how. Reconciliation restored to the penitent *communicatio* with the Church, he again received the *pax ecclesiae.* He was free to take part in and to receive the Eucharist. Furthermore Cyprian was convinced the *pax* of the Church was ultimately significant for salvation, for one had to be in the community of the Church in which alone it is possible to work out one's salvation.

The Roman Controversy on Penance and the Schism of Novatian

While Cyprian opposed laxity in the Church at Carthage, Rome faced a rigorist movement, led by a Roman priest, Novatian. There is clear evidence that Novatian at first held to the traditional view about the remissibility of apostasy, and as secretary for the Roman college of priests, while the see was vacant in 250–51, he even wrote to Cyprian urging lenience for the penitent *lapsi* on the point of death. His letter suggests that for Rome, a final settlement of the matter awaited an episcopal election. Meanwhile, he articulates a principle of Roman practice in questions of law and faith for the first time: *nihil innovandum,* Rome would hold fast to tradition. One other point in his correspondence is that the martyrs and confessors in Rome never gave out *libelli pacis,* and they disapproved both that and the claims made for them by the *lapsi* in Carthage. Two other observations come from reading these letters of Novatian: first, while merciful love is always perceptible in Cyprian's whole outlook on the fallen, it is quite lacking in Novatian; he is cold, almost harsh toward them and appeals with an undertone of pride to the glorious Roman tradition. Second, there is the clear impression that the whole matter of penance for the lapsed would need to await election of a new Roman bishop.

The change in Novatian's attitude on penance dates to the election of a successor to Pope Fabian, which became possible after the end of the Decian persecution, and which elevated not Novatian, but Cornelius to the episcopate. Novatian then set himself up as a rival bishop in Rome with the help of the priest Novatus of Carthage and sought supporters for his platform that readmission of the lapsed into communion with the Church was to be refused on principle. A Roman synod of sixty bishops excommunicated Novatian and confirmed the previous Roman practice of admitting apostates to penance. Novatian, however, set about establishing a counter-Church everywhere. He took the universal Church for his model and moved with energy and with undeniable propaganda skills. He and his movement met little success in Rome and Italy because of the synod Cornelius had called, and he gathered little following in North Africa because of Cyprian's opposition and the conversion of the formerly pro-laxity party, Novatus, to his rigorism. In other regions, however, Novatian had better luck. In Gaul, Bishop Marcian of Arles join his movement and pitilessly refused reconciliation to the lapsed, even on their death-beds, so that many died in despair. Cyprian took up the case and wrote to urge Pope Stephen (254–57) to excommunicate Marcian and replace him. It is probable too that Novatianism pressed beyond into Spain also.

Much more significant, however, was Novatian's influence in the East; his teachings found supporters in Syria, Palestine, in the Asia Minor provinces of Bithynia, Phrygia, Cappadocia, Pontus, Cicilia, and even in Armenia and Mesopotamia. Novatian wrote personally to leading bishops. Dionysius of Alexandria, however, rebuked Novatian, was instrumental in keeping Fabius of Antioch out of Novatianism despite the latter's sympathy for Novatian's position, and otherwise played a major role through his correspondence in preventing Novatianism's becoming even stronger.

Doctrine and Practice of Penance in the East in the Third Century

To begin this sketch one does well to look first to Irenaeus of Lyons, for he came from Asia Minor. Irenaeus still represented the strict ideal of the holiness of the Church inherited from the beginning. On the question of whether there is any salvation at all for a sinner after baptism, Irenaeus gives us no pronouncement, but on occasion makes perfectly clear the possibility of such penance. Only the obdurate, those who persist impenitently in their apostasy, are eternally lost (*Adv. Haer.* 4, 40, 1; 5, 26, 2). In his "rule of faith" (*Adv. Haer.* 1, 10, 1), that summary of ancient belief, Irenaeus comments that God will "graciously grant life to those who persevere in his love — some from the beginning, some since penance — will grant them incorruptibility and surround them with eternal glory." Hence, for Irenaeus too there is the conviction that man can regain the love of God by penance even after baptism. To designate this penance, Irenaeus uses the term *exhomologesis.*

The Alexandrians' views on penance and penitential discipline is formulated away from the heat of controversies. Clement's idea of penance is marked by his idea of purification, which was influenced by Plato; accordingly he presents liberation from sin as a long process, but one which is not possible without penance (*Quis div. salv.* 40, 3–6; 42, 14f.; *Strom.* 7, 10, 56). Similarly to Hermas, Clement holds out the ideal of avoiding all offence, but knows that God will forgive one post-baptismal penance. No sin is irremissible. Like Irenaeus who likewise does not speak of it, but clearly presupposes it, Clement does not talk about reconciliation, readmission to the Church. Clement is the first to mention spiritual guides for the penitent, who helps by prayer and admonition. The efficacy of their help is to be found in their own sanctity of life. Such a one was a *pneumatic,* one who is Spirit-endowed.

Origen too was less interested in the details of penitential practice than in its theoretical basis, but he does not present that systematically either. With his high view of baptism and the effects of its grace, Origen saw the gross contradiction to the ideal patent in the daily life of many Christians. A sinner's grave offences place him in a worse situation than his pre-baptismal state, for such sins can no longer be wiped out by grace alone, but must be atoned for through penance. He clearly taught the forgiveness of such deadly sins as idolatry, adultery, unchastity, and murder, among others, after baptism by penance. He excepts from forgiveness only impenitence.

For Origen, Church authorities were involved in the accomplishment of penance; they are the physicians to whom one must show his wounds so they can supply the appropriate remedy. Admonitory reprimand, *correptio,* is important to him. Its severest form is excommunication, which he finds a bishop must have the fortitude to impose, if appropriate. Penance is not to be so severe as to discourage the sinner, but its duration ought to outlast baptismal preparation. One novelty in Origen's treatment is his interdicting reconciled persons from Church office.

Even more definitely than Clement, Origen contends that the priest's power of remission is tied to his own personal perfection. Even an ordinary Christian, possessing a high degree of personal perfection, can forgive; none but a bishop, however, can confer reconciliation.

The Syrian *Didascalia* (from the first decades of the third century) is a particularly rich lode of information on the penitential liturgy of sinners. The bishop's is the responsibility for excluding the occasional obstinate offender from the ecclesiastical community. His power in the matter of penance is based on the authority of binding and loosing committed to him. He must always have a double aim: to strengthen the community and to give hope to the sinner. No sin is excepted. Penance takes this general course: upon hearing of a sinner in his flock, he confronts him, takes him to task, and excludes him from the community. Members of the community also castigate his sinful behavior. After a time, they then intercede with the bishop in his behalf, especially through the deacons. The bishop examines the penitent, admonishes him, and imposes a penance (in which fasting is an important part) proportionate to his guilt, and with its acceptance, the "liturgical" phase of his official penance is inaugurated, during which period he may also attend the readings and the sermon. Full reconciliation is granted only by the imposition of the bishop's hands; the sinner's membership and the Holy Spirit (lost by sin) are restored to him. The inseparable connection with the bishop in the *Didascalia* makes clear also the sacramental nature of the forgiveness of sin conferred by him.

Notable in the doctrine of the *Didascalia* on penance is the fact that it nowhere suggests that post-baptismal penance is unrepeatable. Neither do the *Apostolic Constitutions* recognize one single unrepeatable post-baptismal penance, and the conclusion becomes inescapable: A single post-baptismal penance was not everywhere current in the East, and cannot be shown to be the original practice. In the West, as noted above, we find it first in Hermas, where it finds pastoral justification. Thus one cannot assume on this evidence that the Church went from original strictness to later laxity.

Other accounts from the East, with one single exception, give no new or variant information on penance. Gregory Thaumaturgus ("the Wonder-worker"), one of

Origen's pupils, attests the division of penitents into classes, as later came to be established. These classes ("hearers," "fallen," "bystanders," "weepers") had as yet no fixed nomenclature.

Disputes Concerning Penance
after the Persecution of Diocletian

The Diocletian persecution once again made the treatment of apostates a topical issue, since, although fewer in numbers than in the Decian persecution, the Church had *lapsi* again. There was a dispute about penance in Rome under Pope Eusebius (310), who demanded penance of the fallen and Heraclius, who "forbade" penance to the *lapsi*. The circumstances are obscure, and it is unclear if Heraclius represented the rigorist or the laxist parties, though the former seems the more likely. As this dispute led to a split in the community, it drew the intervention of the emperor Maxentius, who banished both Eusebius and Heraclius.

The controversy in North Africa connected with this persecution is not strictly over penance. Many Christians had submitted to Diocletian's demand and had handed over their holy books; they were known as *traditores*. The consecrations of bishops by *traditores* were considered by the rigorist parties to be invalid. When in 311, the newly elected bishop of Carthage, Caecilian, was consecrated by Bishop Felix of Aptungi, a suspected *traditor*, the violent Donatist controversy broke out. This story belongs to the fourth century, however.

The problem of the *lapsi* occupied the Alexandrian church also, where its bishop, Petrus, while showing warm sympathy for the fallen, dealt with their situations along Origen's lines. Bishop Petrus was involved as leader of one party in the so-called Meletian schism in Egypt. His opponent was Meletius, bishop of Lycopolis, in the Thebaid, who opposed, with numerous confessors, the readmission of the *lapsi*. The Meletians were concerned with other questions as well, and later joined the Arians against Athanasius.

After the revolutionary change under Constantine, controversies about the problem of penance ceased. It is the lasting merit of the third-century Church, in the often intense struggles for a right understanding of Christian penance in the face of the rigorism that repeatedly flared up, to have defended the spirit of compassionate understanding for the sinner which the founder of the Church had preached, and yet to have prevented the incursion of lax tendencies into her penitential discipline.

C H A P T E R   2 6

The Development of the Church's Constitution in the Third Century

The third century led in many ways to a further development of the Church's constitution. In addition to the three grades of the ministry in the second century, new lower clerical grades develop, the episcopal office is increasingly consolidated and gains in prestige, the organization of the various individual communities becomes more complex, and in the East, in particular, ecclesiastical provinces take form; the system of synods receives new and intense impetus, and finally, the pre-eminent position of the Roman church and its bishop grows unmistakably stronger by recognition and by contradiction. The sum of these developments in the Church's constitution confirms that here, too, Christianity had grown from its origins into the "great Church" of early Christian times.

The Clergy

The existing orders of bishop, presbyter, and deacon remained unchanged in intrinsic significance, of course, but in many ways were more sharply differentiated, and to some extent, too, underwent an extension in the scope of their functions. The conditions for admission to a particular ministry were further developed, and for the office of bishop a deeper theological grounding was attempted. The various problems within the Church, such as the defense against Gnosticism and Montanism, the greater demands made on the authorities by the various waves of persecution, the elucidation of the question of penance, and the struggle against threats of schism, display a monarchical episcopate functioning fully in the third century and in unquestionable possession of the plenary powers that its ministry conferred. The bishop was now the undisputed leader of the ecclesiastical community in all the expressions of its life. He is the guardian of Church discipline and responsible for the observance of the Christian ideal of life by his flock. He guides its works of charity from day to day, and organizes its relief measures in times of need and crisis. He represents his community in its relation with other local churches or at the synodal assemblies of church leaders of a province, or at even larger regional assemblies. In this way the bishop became an important link between the individual community and the Church as a whole, and an effective furtherer of Church unity.

It is understandable that theological reflection, too, turned more and more to an office in the Church, the holder of which occupied so central a position in Church life and in the minds of the faithful. Origen, more than any other writer of the third century, concerned himself with the ecclesiastical ministry. Not for a moment did he doubt the right and justification of the ministry. The bishop's authority is founded on our Lord's words conferring the power of the keys on Peter; consequently, it is God who calls a man to such an office, and the choice should always be left to God when it is a question of appointing a new bishop in a community. The holder of this office has the task of leading men to the kingdom of God, consequently, he should be a model of every virtue. He has to preach the word of God, therefore he must read and meditate upon the Holy Scriptures, not preaching his own ideas, but what the Holy Spirit has taught him. He has to accomplish liturgical worship and he should only raise in prayer hands that are undefiled. Origen evidently holds the view that the efficacy of priestly authority is bound up with the personal holiness of the man who bears it. Hence his unmistakably sharp judgment on the clergy of his time, when he compared the reality with the ideal held out to them. Ambitious men intrigued for these offices which had become a traffic and which were transmitted from unworthy occupants to unworthy successors. In the choice of a new bishop, therefore, the community should be present and take care that the man chosen is outstanding by reason of his learning, holiness, and virtue.

In the West, it was Cyprian who, a few years after Origen, was the first Latin writer to try to determine the nature and function of the office of bishop in the Church. There can be only one bishop in the local church, who is its judge, and takes the place of Christ. The bishop is in the Church, and the Church in the bishop; anyone who is not with the bishop, is not in the Church, either. The Church, by the will of her founder, is an episcopal Church; "it is built up on the bishops and is ruled by them as overseers." But the responsibility is not limited to his own community; it extends to the whole Church. Origen, too, emphasized that a bishop is called to the service of the whole Church. With Cyprian, this responsibility is expressed in the serious concern of the bishop for maintenance of ecclesiastical unity. He links the idea of succession with the office of bishop by saying that it is founded on our Lord's words to Peter (Mt 16:18), and from there proceed the ordination of bishops and the organization of the Church through the changes and succeeding course of time.

On account of the importance of the office of bishop, the appointment of a man to the position had to be ensured by a sound method of choice. Like Origen, Cyprian, too, expects the community to collaborate in it. This was required because the congregation would be acquainted with a candidate who was a member of it, and be able to form a judgment of his manner of life. The bishops of the province were to play a decisive part in the choice, too, and its validity depended on their consent, which included a judgment about the legitimacy of the way in which the election had been carried out. The right of consecrating the chosen candidate also belonged to these bishops.

The Syrian *Didascalia* indicates in a very special way the pre-eminent position of the bishop in his community. In his office as preacher, he is "the mouth of God," encouraging righteousness, urging on to good works, enthusiastically extolling God's benefits, but speaking, too, of the future wrath at God's judgment. The *Didascalia* speaks insistently of the qualities required by the episcopate and the shortcomings that would exclude one from it. The first requirement is close familiarity with Holy Scripture, of which the bishop must be the interpreter. As all his conduct is to be a model to his flock, he must fulfill the highest demands on moral qualities and character. Guarantees of this are more likely to be provided by a certain maturity in age and so the bishop chosen should be fifty years old if possible. Access to episcopal office was barred to a man who had been married more than once; the manner of life of the wife and children had to be in harmony with the high dignity of the head of the family. The presbyters or priests occupy, generally speaking, in the *Didascalia,* the position that the *Letters* of St. Ignatius of Antioch had already assigned to them; they are the advisers and associates of the bishops, and collaborate particularly in judicial proceedings against a Christian, but have no claim to share by right the gifts of the community. The third century, however, also saw signs of increasing importance in the office of priest. Finally, the growth of priestly functions was due to the growth in this century of large Christian communities, often with several thousand members in the more important towns of the Roman Empire such as Rome, Carthage, Alexandria, and Antioch. The frequent mention of priests at the administration of baptism in the rite described by Hippolytus, is just as noticeable in this respect as the emphasis on the part they played in the ordination of new priests, on whom they laid hands with the bishop. In Rome, the setting up of the *tituli* as actual pastoral districts gave a more independent position to the priests to whom they were entrusted than was possible in smaller communities.

In the daily life of an average Christian community, the presbyters, however, were still less prominent than the deacons. As the chief official assistants of their bishops, especially for the care of the poor, and in the administration of funds, they came into more frequent contact with individual members of the congregation and so, as the *Didascalia* says, were the bishop's "ear and mouth, heart and soul."

The growing needs of the communities in the third century finally led to the development of further grades in the series of clerical ministries which, however, all remained below the rank of deacon. There were subdeacons, acolytes, and exorcists, lectors, and doorkeepers, in the Church's service. The holders of these offices mostly figured in a liturgical role, others had special tasks in connection with corporate works of mercy.

Appointment to these offices, as to those of priest and deacon, belonged exclusively to the bishop who, of course, could consult his flock about suitable candidates. The beginnings of the so-called "irregularities," or canonical impediments are already clearly perceptible in the third century.

As the bishop and deacons were completely occupied with their duties, in the larger communities, it was the obligation of the faithful to see to their upkeep; this was a charge on the general gifts of the faithful for the whole needs of the Church. The other clerics were dependent on private means, or on their income from a profession in civil life.

Little information is available about the training of the clergy for its religious and ecclesiastical tasks at this period; it was not yet subject to fixed rules laid down by the Church authorities. The growing variety of ecclesiastical orders provided the possibility of being tested in a lower grade, and of gradually acquiring deeper religious knowledge and increasing familiarity with the tasks of a higher office.

The Bishop and His Church

We have still to speak specifically about the position of the individual church under its bishop as the holder of ecclesiastical property. This, particularly in the large town communities of the third century, was becoming of considerable importance. The gifts of the faithful which were expended on the manifold activities of the local church, were collected in a common fund which probably became a permanent institution quite early. Local churches everywhere acquired property and funds, the control and administration of which ultimately belonged to their bishops. As well as contributions in money and things in daily use (foodstuffs and clothes), there soon came gifts of houses and land, so that even before Constantine's time, the property of the church communities consisted of money and real estate. The existence of this church property was not unknown to the civil authorities. Since this property was not touched by the State, except in the abnormal circumstances of various particular persecutions, this presupposes the recognition of the individual communities as the legal owners in civil law. The decrees of the State authorities after the end of the Diocletian persecution, which provided for the return of the confiscated property to the various Christian communities as its legal owners, similarly indicate that the capacity of the churches to own property was recognized by the State in the third century.

Another development in the sphere of organization was also important for many churches. They grew not only in numbers, but also in geographical extent. When, in Egypt, there were churches in the country which were served either by a resident priest or by a cleric from the bishop's center, it followed that as the communities came into existence, they did not automatically receive a bishop as their head, but remained subject to the bishop of the nearest larger community. A bigger episcopal diocese comprising several Christian communities in town and country, but with only one bishop at their head, and a Christian community which received a pastor of its own for its immediate religious needs came into being; however, whether priest, or, as in a few places, chorepiscopus, he was always subject to the bishop.

Forms of Organization Larger Than the Local Community

The coming into existence of the "great church" is made very tangibly clear by the association of the various individual communities under their bishops into a higher structure, the church province. The rise of this was determined particularly by two factors. One of these followed from the method of the early Christian mission which first tried to gain a footing in populous towns, which would mean the provincial capitals in the Roman Empire, and attempted to found its first communities there. Consequently, all the daughter communities founded by a central episcopal church were bound together by mutual ties. In this association a certain leading role naturally fell to the bishop of the mother-church, and from the fourth century, this was expressed by the title "metropolitan." But more decisive than the link created by such missions, was the formation of ecclesiastical provinces by the establishment of synods which, from the end of the second century, brought together the bishops of specific regions to discuss important Church affairs. Such synods were a regular custom in the East at the beginning of the third century, while in North Africa they were still unknown. It is clear from the list of those who took part in the Council of Nicaea that, at least in the East, the association of the local churches into church provinces was later adapted to the frontiers of the political provinces, for the list follows the order of the latter.

In the Latin West, the tendency for wider associations of this kind only appeared later, and then assumed different forms. What happened was not really the formation of several ecclesiastical provinces in the proper sense, as in the East, but directly a supra-provincial association of all the episcopal sees in North Africa on the one hand and of central and southern Italy on the other. When the Bishop of Carthage summoned synods in the third century, his invitation was addressed to the bishops of all the civil provinces in North Africa, and was so accepted. Similarly, the synods held by the Roman bishops of the third century brought together all the bishops there were in Italy at that time. Consequently, Rome and Carthage were ecclesiastical administrative centers of a rank far superior to that of a mere ecclesiastical metropolis. Two such higher centers also became increasingly prominent in the third century East, Antioch and Alexandria. The missionary interests of the Antioch bishops extended further than the territory of a church province, too. This third-century development was confirmed by the Council of Nicaea: all the bishoprics of Egypt, Libya, and the Pentapolis were made subject to the bishop of Alexandria, and at the same time, express reference was also made to the similar pre-eminence of Rome. Antioch had similar rights. In this way, the occupants of these two eastern episcopal sees were recognized as a sort of higher metropolitans, and so the foundation was laid for the development of later patriarchates.

The Pre-eminent Position of Rome and Its Bishop

The preceding account has repeatedly had occasion to indicate the special influence which the Roman community exercised on questions and events that exceeded the sphere of interest of an average episcopal community. Similarly, too, there was perceptible the echo of a claim to a pre-eminent position, of a kind that revealed special recognition and regard for the Roman community within the Church as a whole.

In the Church's fight to defend herself against Gnosticism, the importance which Irenaeus of Lyons attributed to apostolic tradition for the recognition of true doctrine must be particularly stressed; he ascribed very high value to the Roman church for the ascertaining of apostolic tradition. This latter can, indeed, be established, he maintains, in every church whose bishops can be derived in a genuine series of succession from the apostles. But it is sufficient to prove this succession in the "greatest and oldest church known to all," that of Rome; for "it was founded and built by the two glorious apostles Peter and Paul" and its list of bishops proves that in it, "the apostolic tradition and preaching of the faith" has come down to our time. Here, therefore, a special pre-eminence of Rome is linked with the fact that its church rests on the most distinguished apostolic foundations and has always remained true to the doctrine of the apostles. Consequently, anyone seeking the truth, will find it in Rome; all the Gnostic founders of sects can be refuted by the traditional truth found in Rome. Irenaeus' line of thought is, plainly, as follows: The apostolic tradition is found with certainty in the communities which rest on a directly apostolic foundation; there are several of these and each of them has a stronger power, grounded in its (apostolic) origin, for the ascertaining of truth, than any other Christian community whatever. But Rome stands out even from this series of apostolic foundations, because, as is everywhere recognized, Peter and Paul were its founders. Then Irenaeus summarizes: with such a church of apostolic foundation every individual church must agree, because precisely such a church has always preserved the apostolic tradition. The Jewish Christian Hegesippus, living about the same time as Irenaeus, showed an interest for the succession of Roman bishops, deriving from similar motives.

Consciousness of a pre-eminent position of the Roman church in determining apostolic tradition, was also the basis of the attitude of the Roman Bishop Victor (189–98) in the dispute about the keeping of Easter. He appealed to apostolic tradition to justify the Roman practice of keeping Easter on the Sunday after 14 Nisan. A claim by Rome to leadership is here apparent which goes far beyond the pre-eminence attributed to it as the guardian of apostolic tradition. It is only explained by the Roman bishop's awareness of his ability to intervene authoritatively in the affairs of even distant churches. His instruction that synods were to be held about the matter was followed even by the bishops of Asia Minor, although they held different views from Rome. The majority of the synods decided on the Roman custom. Opposition to the Roman demand was raised by Bishop Polycrates of Ephesus and his fellow bishops, because they also believed themselves bound to an apostolic tradition. When Polycrates, in his answer to Pope Victor, emphatically recalled the great figures of the Asiatic church of the past, this suggests that Victor had supported the Roman claim on the foundation of its church by Peter and Paul; but that Victor also felt himself to be the guardian of orthodoxy, is proved by his excommunicating the Monarchian Theodotus. A few decades later, Sabellius was excommunicated for heresy by the Roman Bishop Callistus.

An unmistakable expression of the bishop of Rome's awareness that he occupied a special position within the Church as a whole, is encountered in various measures of a disciplinary nature taken by Pope Stephen (254–57). A Spanish bishop Basilides had recourse to Rome because he was convinced that it was the place to which he could appeal against the decision of a Spanish synod, and that there, a disciplinary case of this sort could be dealt with and decided with legal authority. Even more significant is the case of Bishop Marcion of Arles, a convinced follower of Novatian, who allowed the lapsed in his community to die without reconciliation, despite their readiness to repent. This time, it was Cyprian of Carthage who turned to Pope Stephen in a very significant letter that demanded from him decisive action against Marcion, that is to say, his deposition and the appointment of a new head of the community, whose name was to be sent to the African episcopate so that they might know with whom they were to maintain fellowship. The whole tenor of the letter implies the view that the Arles case concerned the pope alone, and could only definitively be decided by him, and that Rome could determine authoritatively who was to be granted ecclesiastical fellowship and who was not. The same conviction was current in Gaul, because Cyprian's letter was sent as a result of steps taken by Faustinus, the bishop of Lyons.

This public recognition of the pre-eminent position of the Roman bishop by Cyprian, at least as regards Spain and Gaul, is rather surprising when it is compared with his theoretical standpoint and attitude to Rome in the dispute about baptism by heretics. It is true that in Cyprian's writings there are statements about the Roman church which at first sight seem to amount to recognition of a special authority of Rome. But closer analysis of Cyprian's linguistic usage obliges us to abandon these texts as conclusive proofs that the idea of the Roman primacy existed in the mind of the North African bishop. Cyprian is here still simply expressing a chronological pre-eminence of Peter over the other apostles in the conferring of the power of binding and loosing, for they, of course, according to his own words, possessed the same plenary power as he. Consequently, all the bishops possess, even now, one and the same equal episcopal office. In the *cathedra Petri*, Cyprian sees the well-spring of ecclesiastical unity, which has its beginning in Peter. Cyprian does not, however, voice the consequence that this well-spring even now in his own day, has this function of bringing about unity, in the *cathedra* of the Bishop of Rome. He does not seem to draw it in his own mind either, for he maintains most emphatically the thesis that bishops are responsible to God alone for the administration of their bishoprics. What Cyprian thought in an actual concrete situation about the right of a Roman bishop to issue binding ordinances with decisive authority for the Church as a whole is shown by the test case of the dispute about baptism which may appropriately be described at this point.

The Controversy about Heretical Baptism

The Christian communities first encountered the problem of heretical baptism when heretical (or schismatical) groups of some size formed, and when members of these wanted to enter the Catholic Church. When it was a case of persons who had been pagans, and who had received baptism in the heretical community, the question arose whether the baptism that had been conferred on them was to be considered valid. The same reply was not given in all the Christian communities. It is true that the Alexandrian church under Bishop Dionysius took up the same position as Rome, where persons baptized in an heretical sect were received into the Roman community merely by imposition of hands. The different estimation of heretical baptism and the resulting difference of treatment of those who has received it, could plainly have existed side by side for decades in the Church without one side having felt the practice of the other to be intolerable. But shortly after the middle of the third century a serious clash occurred over the matter, when the various views found unyielding defenders in Cyprian of Carthage and Stephen of Rome. An African bishop, Magnus, had submitted the inquiry to Cyprian whether "those who came from Novatian" had to be baptized again in the Catholic Church. Cyprian's comprehensive answer is clear; baptism is entrusted to the Catholic Church alone and her baptism alone is valid; anyone who has not got the Holy Spirit cannot confer that Spirit. Cyprian attacks the thesis that in such questions appeal should not simply be made to tradition, but the rational reflection should be allowed to have its say; Peter, whom the Lord chose first, did not make any arrogant claims on that account, and did not presumptuously occupy the first place (*primatus*). A synod considered the question again in 256 and Cyprian wrote at its request to Pope Stephen, enclosing the resolutions of the previous year's synod as well as his previous correspondence on the subject. The whole file clearly showed that Cyprian regarded Roman custom, and the view of the validity of heretical baptism on which it rested, as a grave dogmatic error, but he wrote that he did not want to impose his view on anyone, as each bishop was free to administer his own flock.

Pope Stephen's answer to this letter has not survived, but a clear echo of it is found in Cyprian's correspondence. One of his letters describes it as "uninformed and written without due reflection," and Stephen's standpoint is termed an error. Cyprian was particularly up in arms over the principle with which the Roman, bishop justified his standpoint. "No innovation, but stand by tradition," because in intention it stamped Cyprian as an innovator. The letter of Firmilian of Caesarea throws welcome light on the meaning of these remarks. Cyprian was informed that Pope Stephen's initiative in the matter of heretical baptism was not limited to North Africa. A letter had been sent from Rome to the churches of Asia Minor too, demanding that they should abandon their practice of rebaptism, and threatening excommunication. The detailed answer of the Cappadocian bishop shows how deeply concerned they were in Asia Minor over Stephen's action. It is also said that Stephen, in his folly, "glories in his position as a bishop and claims to hold succession of Peter, on whom the foundations of the Church rest." This makes it clear that Stephen was appealing to Matthew 16:18 and claiming for himself, as Peter's successor, Peter's position in the Church. Previous Roman bishops' awareness of a pre-eminence belonging to them in the Church as a whole, which had already been present earlier was, as a matter of fact, now for the first time given a formal basis in that biblical text which in future was to be increasingly regarded as the decisive attestation of the Roman primacy. The two leading bishops of North Africa and Asia Minor did not bow to Stephen's claim. Cyprian had his position confirmed again at a third synod in September 256. The episcopal delegation sent to Rome with the resolutions of the synod was not even received by Stephen, and he went so far as to give instructions that it was not be received in the church community there either. That meant a breach with the church of North Africa led by Cyprian. It was the most important demonstration of Rome's position of pre-eminence yet undertaken by one of its bishops, and Stephen undertook it, even at the cost of a rupture, in the consciousness of occupying and of having to fulfill the office and function of Peter in the Church as a whole. It is not surprising that this claim met with resistance. It seems worthy of note that in the face of contradiction the idea of the primacy prevailed and held its ground.

The question of heretical baptism did not, however, lead to a division of long duration in the early Christian Church. The two leaders of the opposed views in the West, died shortly after one another, Pope Stephen in 257 and Bishop Cyprian as a martyr on 14 September 258. Their followers were not so personally involved in the dispute and at first let it rest, one side tolerating the practice followed by the other. Under Sixtus' successor, Dionysius (260–68), the conflict between Rome and the bishops of Asia Minor seems to have been settled. In the West, after a first approach at the Synod of Arles, a final clarification was achieved by the dogmatic work of Augustine, in the sense of the Roman view and practice.

The Alexandrian Bishop Dionysius, who was so zealously concerned with peace in the Church, experienced personally, however, that the Roman bishop demanded an account of anyone who put forward false or misleading views in matters of faith, when, in about 260, in controversy with the Patripassians, he used insufficiently precise formulas regarding the distinction between Father and Son. The Bishop of Rome not only required of him a precise exposition of his views but directly addressed himself to Dionysius' flock and warned them of teachers who threatened to falsify the previous teaching of the Church about the Trinity.

The pre-eminence of the Roman position also received spontaneous recognition. The lyrical homage of the Christian Aberkios of Phrygia to the Church of Rome dates from the early third century. The visits, delegations and letters which came to Rome frequently had only one purpose, that of obtaining from this Church and this bishop a recognition and confirmation of their aims or views. They testify thereby to the existence of a widespread conviction that both possessed a unique position.

Devotion to the Church in the Third Century

A final feature has to be added to this picture. The Church is not only an object of knowledge, is not only given its theological basis and affirmed with understanding, its very reality is taken up into the affections of the faithful, felt as a gift of grace. Just as there was a spirituality of baptism and martyrdom, there was a spirituality centered on the Church.

This was given most profound expression by the application of one of the fundamental words of humanity to the Church, which was loved as the "mother" of the faithful. This name was prepared for by the personification of "faith" as a maternal figure in Polycarp of Smyrna and by Hermas, to whom the Church appeared as a revered woman. The Christians of Lyons were the first to apply the name "mother" to the Church, like an expression that had long been familiar to them. For Irenaeus the heretics have no share in the spirit of truth; they are not at the breast of Mother Church who, at the same time, is the Bride of Christ. The catechists, in preparing for baptism, clearly liked to represent the Church to the catechumens as a mother who bears her children in baptism and then feeds and guards them. Tertullian speaks with deep feeling especially in his pastoral writings, of *domina mater ecclesia* who, with motherly care, looks after those who are imprisoned, and whose children, after baptism, recite the Our Father as their first prayer in common with their brethren, "in their mother's house," while the heretics have no mother. The same note of deep feeling is found in the terminology of the Alexandrians; for Clement, the Church is the Virgin Mother who calls her children to herself and feeds them on sacred milk. Origen sees her both as *sponsa Christi* and as mother of the nation; bitter sorrow is caused her by impenitence and attachment to evil. The term *mater ecclesia* has become a real expression of filial love and piety in the writings of Cyprian, who sings the joy his mother feels about her virginal children and brave confessors; but he also knows the tears which she sheds for the lapsed. More than any other writer of the third century, he evokes the picture of this mother when the unity of the Church is threatened by schism. His urgently repeated appeals to the faithful to preserve their unity at all costs culminate in one of his most celebrated sayings: "That man cannot have God as his Father who has not the Church as his Mother" (*De eccles. unit.* 6).

As well as this picture of the Church as Mother, which appealed most directly to the feelings of the faithful, early Christian preaching made use of other images, too, in order to make clear to the hearers the reality of the Church and impress it on their hearts. So, according to Hippolytus, the Church is "God's spiritual garden with Christ as its ground," with an inexhaustible stream of water, from which the four rivers of Paradise flow, the four Gospels which announce the Lord to the world. Origen compares the Church with Paradise in which the newly baptized fulfill the works of the Spirit. The Johannine parable of the vine and the branches (Jn 15:1–7), must have proved particularly rich as a catechetical theme; it is applied to the Church by the Fathers repeatedly with far-ranging symbolism. All these metaphors were of a kind to give the Church distinctive emotional associations in the mind of her members and to make the Church dear to them in a sense of very real affection.

A widespread devotion to the Church of this kind in the third century is, like the spirituality of baptism and martyrdom, an important factor in the history of the Church, and must not be passed over unnoticed.

CHAPTER 27

The Extent of Christianity
Prior to the Diocletian Persecution

Running parallel to the rich development of life within the Church, in literature and liturgy, organization and the practice of spirituality, was a growth in numbers which gave Christianity at this period, even when viewed from outside, the character of a "great Church." The inner strengthening of the Church in this century created the conditions for her decisive missionary success in the world of Hellenic civilization right up to the beginning of the Diocletian persecution. This eminently important process in the history of the Church was influenced not only by such conditions, but also by the conjunction of further favorable factors of varying importance in their actual impact.

In the first place, the two long periods of peace in the third century offered the Church, to an extent unknown before, missionary possibilities of making herself known, and they were only disturbed by a few waves of relatively brief persecution. Moreover, the drive of Christianity toward expansion was furthered by developments in the paganism of antiquity itself. The crisis of the ancient world in the third century consisted not only of the threatening decay of the Roman Empire, but was also, and equally, of a crisis in the existing religious and cultural forces. New cults from the East gained increasingly larger followings even in the Latin world, until finally the Baal of Emesa, the Sun-God of Palmyra, Egyptian Sarapis and Persian Mithras burst the framework of the ancient Roman religion, and robbed it of its exclusiveness. In its place appeared a wide-ranging syncretism. Christianity could advance into this increasing vacuum, and with its claim to offer, in the midst of this religious confusion, both absolute truth and what was "new" and full of promise for the future, found a ready hearing among the pagan population. At the beginning of the third century the Alexandrian teachers Clement and Origen dared to attempt to win to Christianity not only cultivated people but culture itself. On the foundation of Christian revelation, they set up a new ideal of culture to which, they were convinced, the future belonged; and they were liberal enough to incorporate in this ideal those elements of pagan education and culture which did not contradict the fundamental truths of the gospel. Toward the end of the century there grew up in Antioch the second intellectual center of Christianity in the East; it influenced the Syrian hinterland as much as Alexandria did Egypt. In the West, also, Christianity produced writers of quality and reputation who are a striking testimony to the higher standards of Christian literary production. This brought Christianity an ever-growing number of adherents from the pagan upper class. Under the Syrian emperors, under Philippus Arabs and Gallienus, there were Christians in influential positions at the imperial court, and an increasing number of bishops sprang from the educated classes. At the beginning of the fourth century, a minority of such strength and quality professed the new religion, that its resistance could not be broken by the last onslaught under Diocletian.

Section Two

The Last Attack of Paganism and the Final Victory of the Church

CHAPTER 28

The Intellectual Struggle against Christianity at the End of the Third Century

When Emperor Gallienus (260–68), at the beginning of his reign, put an end to the persecution ordered by his father Valerian and adopted a series of measures favorable to the Christians, some of these, like Bishop Dionysius of Alexandria, indulged in extravagant hopes, that a new era was dawning for Christianity. Gallienus' rescript was, in fact, followed by a period of peace lasting about forty years during which the Christians did not suffer any centrally organized persecution. They were able in relative freedom to pursue and consolidate the internal and external development of their society into the "great Church" of early Christian times. Eusebius paid tribute to the years before the outbreak of the Diocletian persecution as a time of the most extensive toleration of Christianity and of the public expressions of its life, and emphasized three freedoms particularly which the Christian religion was at that time permitted to enjoy: freedom of belief, which allowed the Christians of all social classes to profess their faith publicly; freedom of worship, which allowed unrestricted access to Christian church services and made it possible everywhere to build great churches; and freedom of preaching to all, unhampered by anyone. As well as this, there was the markedly benevolent attitude of the civil authorities, who treated the leaders of the Christian communities with particular respect.

Seeing that such a phase of tolerance was followed by the Diocletian persecution, which brought the most violent wave of oppression Christianity had yet experienced, the question must be put whether many Christians did not overlook certain signs of the times and underestimate happenings which pointed to a development less favorable to Christianity and which make the turn of events under Diocletian intelligible.

143

In the first place, the situation of the Christians, even under the emperors since Gallienus, was in no way guaranteed by law. It was self-deception when some Christians thought that the tolerant attitude of individual emperors, and a consequently tolerant attitude of some high officials, had also brought about a definitive change in the mentality of the whole non-Christian population of the empire and already ensured final agreement with the pagan civil power. It was still possible for the hostile sentiment of an official to strike an individual Christian with extreme severity, for no law defended the Christian against such measures. This perpetual legal uncertainty shows that the period of toleration introduced by Gallienus was very far from a transformation of the situation as a whole such as was realized under Constantine.

It was inevitable that particularly serious consequences would in the long run flow from a new wave of intellectual intolerance toward Christianity which emerged among the educated, from Aurelian's reign onward, and which found its exponent in the neo-Platonist Porphyry. In Phoenicia, where he was born near Tyre, about 223, Porphyry had already come into contact with Christianity. He came to Rome, where he became the pupil, friend, and intellectual heir of Plotinus whose discourses he published in the *Enneads.* Plotinus himself, of course, did not engage in direct controversy with Christianity but in the second *Ennead* there are, nevertheless, some references which would seem to exclude a favorable estimate of it.

With Porphyry, a negative attitude to Christianity is perceptible, even in his early writings. The fifteen books *Against the Christians,* on which Porphry worked from about the year 268, are indubitably the most important contribution to the ambitious attempt of neo-Platonism to renew Greek wisdom and religious sentiment, in face of the increasingly successful advance of Christianity. The task demanded for its successful accomplishment far more than Celsus' project a hundred years before. Since that time Christianity had developed literary productions that commanded the respect even of an educated pagan. A comprehensive discussion of the Bible was now particularly necessary. To his plan for a comprehensive refutation of Christianity, Porphyry brought, as can be seen from the fragments which survive, genuine knowledge of the Christian Scriptures, a trained critical and philological mind, and a considerable gift of exposition. Porphyry's work immediately called forth Christian defenses against his design. The same fate has overtaken attacker and defenders, for all these works have completely perished. Constantine ordered, even before the Council of Nicaea, the destruction of the "godless writings" of Porphyry, "the enemy of true piety," the first example of the proscription of a written work hostile to Christianity by the civil power.

Porphyry finds in the figure of Christ many features which in his estimation are incompatible with a truly religious and heroic personality. In the first place, Christ does not show himself to possess the divine power which he claims for himself; he refuses out of fear, to throw himself from the pinnacle of the Temple; he is not master of the demons; he fails lamentably before the high priests and Pilate; and his whole Passion is unworthy of a divine being. After his resurrection, Christ should have appeared, not to simple unknown women, but to Pilate, to Herod, in fact to the Roman Senate; he should have given his ascension a much more grandiose setting; this would have spared his followers their harsh persecutions, for in face of such demonstrations of divine power, all doubt of his mission would have been silenced. The evangelists are severely rejected for their presentation of Jesus' deeds and words, which they themselves invented and did not experience. Their accounts are full of contradictions, inexactitudes, and absurdities and merit no belief. Porphyry felt the profoundest antipathy for the leading figures of the early Church, Peter and Paul.

The central doctrines of the Christian faith and the essential features of Christian worship are also decisively rejected. Christ's doctrine demands irrational faith, too large a demand for thinkers and philosophically trained persons. Christian monotheism is really only thinly disguised polytheism, for the angels also appear as divine beings. The doctrine of the Incarnation fills every Greek with abhorrence, and so does the Christian Eucharist, which Porphyry regards as a rite such as is not found even among the most savage tribes; for him the words of Christ at John 6:54, "Except you eat the flesh of the Son of Man ..." are bestial, and these words alone place St. John's Gospel far below the work of the Synoptics. Christian baptism, which is supposed by one washing to expunge all faults, even the worst, of adults, can only be considered an immoral institution inciting to new vices and wickedness. Christian esteem for the poor and sick meets with absolute incomprehension and for the ideal of Christian virginity Porphyry has nothing but mockery. The characteristic note and tone of Porphyry's controversy with Christianity, is bitter sarcasm; Porphyry is very definitely taking sides in a struggle between the civilization of antiquity and Christianity, which had entered its decisive phase. And here, the fate of the empire is far from being as much in the forefront of Porphyry's mind, as all that the intellectual and religious tradition of Hellenism meant to him.

Among the Christians, Porphyry's work was certainly felt to be important, or it would not have provoked the rapid and effective reactions it did.

Porphyry's book against Christians had serious consequences in pagan upper-class circles. To many, a religion could not but appear unacceptable which so sinned against the Logos, against clarity and against truth as, according to his account, the doctrine and practice of the Christians did. Above all, his work made the opposition between neo-Platonism and Christianity unbridgeable. The claim of the latter to exclusive possession of truth, was felt to be a denial of all that the World Logos had until then made known to mankind.

The possibility of literary polemic against Christians being linked with the will to actual persecution by the State was realized in the person of Sossianus Hierocles who as a high civil servant took up his pen and attacked Christianity in two works which he entitled *Logoi philalētheis,* with obvious reference to the work of Celsus. Hierocles took his material largely from Porphyry's work, that is evident from the most important arguments that he deploys against the Christian religion. Hierocles' only contribution from his own resources is his description of Christ as the leader of a robber band and the great prominence given to Apollonius of Tyana, that wandering philosopher with the aureole of legend of the first century, whose life had been written by Philostratus about the year 220. Perhaps in this biography Philostratus himself was trying to present his age with a religious figure who could compare favorably with Christ. That, in any case, was the sense in which the miraculous power of Apollonius was exploited by Porphyry, so that Eusebius of

Caesarea in his reply to Hierocles made the comparison between Apollonius and Christ the central point of the refutation.

As a last source of anti-Christian polemic and propaganda, the pagan priest-hood must be mentioned; it observed with understandable disquiet the powerful rise of the Christian movement, and inevitably felt itself threatened in its prestige and privileges. Diocletian, who still shrank from violent persecution, sent an augur to question the oracle of Apollo of Miletus; only the utterance of this oracle, which was unfavorable to the Christian religion brought about, he alleges, the decision.

About 270, a wave of anti-Christian polemic and propaganda set in which tried in the first place to win over the educated classes, but later also influenced wider circles.

CHAPTER 29

Outbreak and Course of the Diocletian Persecution Down to Galerius' Edict of Toleration (311)

The growing hostility to Christianity cannot itself explain Diocletian's relatively sud-den transition from liberally exercised toleration to the harshest of persecutions. The emperor practiced toleration for years, quite deliberately, for he could not have been unaware of the Christian religion's growing successes and its cease-lessly increasing power of attraction. A number of causes and influences were operative which profoundly influenced Diocletian's decision to use measures of State compulsion, but he made the decision with full freedom and personal re-sponsibility. The central motive for his action can most probably be found in a conviction that Christianity stood in the way of the work of reconstruction which he had so successfully undertaken in the most various spheres of life of the Ro-man Empire. After securing the frontiers, strengthening the civil government and eliminating financial difficulties at home, he now turned to the burning religious problem, the solution of which he envisaged solely in terms of a restoration of the old Roman religion. The renewed mood of hostility to Christianity in the educated upper classes and to some degree in the common people, too, seemed to him to recommend this course. But he undertook it on his own responsibility.

It is understandable that Diocletian began the fight against Christianity by a purge of the army, for the reliability of the army was the highest principle of Ro-man State power. But it was also suggested by some very recent disturbing events. Christians were not always opposed to military service as such; they refused to take part in an act of pagan worship, which is what the various forms of honor paid to the emperors signified for them, after the rulers had proclaimed themselves sons of Jupiter and Hercules. A decree issued by Diocletian as early as 300 aimed at removing such unreliable elements from the army; it laid down that all soldiers had to sacrifice to the gods or leave the army. The failure of the augury already mentioned, and the oracle given when the Milesian Apollo was consulted, then led him, after a consultation with the Senate, to publish the general edict of February 303. This ordered in the name of the four emperors, the destruction of all Christian places of worship, the surrender and burning of all their sacred books, and it forbade all their assemblies for divine worship. Extremely serious, too, was the degradation of the Christians which was laid down by the edict; if they were in the imperial administration, they were enslaved; notabilities among them lost the privileges of their rank, and their offices, and all Christians in the empire were declared incapable of performing legally valid acts. Two outbreaks of fire in the imperial palace whose authors could not be discovered, even by the harshest interrogation, made the situation worse; the Christians in the court administration were subjected to severe tortures, then burnt or drowned; in particular, distinguished Christians were compelled to offer sacrifice, among them Diocletian's own wife and daughter. And now the real impact of the persecution was aimed against the clergy; many clerics suffered imprisonment or death, presumably because they did not comply with a provision of the edict requiring them to hand over the sacred books. It is true that there were those among the clergy who failed in this, too, especially in North Africa and Rome, and they later were stigmatized as *traditores* The sources do not provide a survey of the outcome of the first edict in all parts of the empire. In the west, Emperor Maximian showed himself particularly compliant, while his *Caesar* Constantius carried out the decree very negligently in Gaul and Britain, for though he destroyed buildings he did not imprison or put to death.

Diocletian was soon driven further on the course he had begun. A second edict robbed the Christian communities of their pastors, and so struck the ecclesiastical organization at a vital spot. A third edict contained more detailed instructions for proceedings against the clergy; anyone who carried out the pagan sacrifices went free; anyone who refused was tortured and put to death. The fourth and last edict, early in 304, completed the imperial legal measures against Christians by imposing sacrifice to the gods on all of them without exception. Recourse was now had to the method of Emperor Decius, and the persecution was extended to a part of the population that numbered six to seven millions, bringing down unspeakable suffering on them by the most brutal methods of oppression. The intensity of the persecution did not alter when on the common abdication of the two *Augusti,* Diocletian and Maximian, there began on the first of May 305, the second tetrarchy which placed Constantius Chlorus in the West and Galerius in the eastern part of the empire in the highest rank and conferred the title of *Caesar* on Severus and Maximinus Daia, thus passing over young Constantine, son of Constantius, contrary to what the army had anticipated. Since Constantius as *Augustus* held firm to his previous tolerance, and as his *Caesar,* Severus, adopted this attitude too, it was only during the two-year rule of Maximian and in the territory under his jurisdiction that the edicts of persecution were systematically carried out. The later changes in the head of the government in the West did not cut short the toleration practiced there; both Constantine, who succeeded his father in 306, as well as Maxentius who, in the same year, ousted Severus from power, were averse to any persecution of the Christians though from different motives. The eastern part of the Empire, in contrast, was forced to bear the full burden from the first edict of the year 303 until Galerius' decree of toleration in 311.

The two chief witnesses on the Diocletian persecution, Eusebius and Lactantius, are unfortunately completely silent about the course and scope of Maximian's proceedings in the West. Consequently, definite details are often difficult to ascertain with certainty.

In the Balkans, and in the eastern provinces, the persecution raged for eight years, though with occasional local interruptions. There, Galerius and after 305 his *Caesar,* Maximinus Daia, supplied the impetus; they were also responsible for the cruel ingenuity of the methods of persecution. For Palestine and Phoenicia, some of Eusebius, reports are eye-witness accounts and he also collected reliable information about the martyrdoms in Egypt. In the Asia Minor provinces of Cappadocia and Pontus, the persecuted Christians were faced with particularly inventive torturers who ironically described putting out the right eye or maiming the left leg with red-hot iron as humane treatment and who tried to outdo one another in discovering new brutalities.

Eusebius gives us no actual information about the number of victims, except in Palestine. From his special account of this area, it seems that the number was less than a hundred. Elsewhere, however, the figure was considerably higher, certainly in Egypt, for example. Applied to the eastern provinces, with their relative density of Christian population, this reckoning gives a total of several thousand dead. In addition there were the numerous confessors of the faith who were tortured at this time and dispatched to forced work in the mines. It is striking that Eusebius is silent about those who failed in the persecution; both among clergy and laity there were those who did, as is shown by the re-emergence in Egypt of the problem of how to treat the *lapsi.*

Only in 308 there was a momentary lull. Some of the Christians condemned to forced labor in the mines were set free, or they were granted some relief. Among the Christians, people were already beginning to breathe again when Maximinus Daia introduced a new wave of oppression with a decree ordering the rebuilding of the ruined pagan temples and announced new detailed ordinances for the conduct of sacrifices to the gods. The real turning-point came with the serious illness of the *Augustus* Galerius, which seemed to the Christians only intelligible as an intervention of divine providence. The edict of the year 311 ordered the cessation of the persecution through-out the empire. The text of the decree still reveals the emotion that Galerius must have experienced when he realized that his policy of violence against the Christians had been an error and a failure. The edict begins with the affirmation that the emperors had in their earlier measures only the good of the State in view and had been striving for a restoration of the old laws and Roman manner of life and had wanted to win the Christians, too, back to these. For the Christians had fallen away from the religion of their ancestors and in revolutionary upheaval had made their own laws for themselves. However, the edicts of persecution had not been able to bend the majority of Christians, many of them had had to lose their life and others had become confused. The outcome was religious anarchy in which neither the old gods received appropriate worship nor the God of the Christians himself received honor. In order to put an end to this state of affairs, the emperors grant pardon and permit "Christians to exist again and to hold their religious assemblies once more, providing that they do nothing disturbing to public order." Another document addressed to governors is promised, which will provide more detailed instructions for the accomplishment of the edict. The Christians are charged to pray to their God for the welfare of the emperor, the State and themselves.

Galerius' edict was a document of the greatest importance; by it the highest representative of the power of the Roman State rescinded a religious policy which had been in force for more than two hundred years. From now on, the Christians were relieved of the oppressive legal uncertainty of the past; for the first time an imperial edict expressly recognized them; their belief was by an imperial juridical pronouncement of toleration, put on the same footing as other cults.

The two rulers in the West had no difficulties in proclaiming the edict in their dominions; it only gave legal foundation to a state of affairs that had already existed for some time. In the East, Maximinus did not in fact have the text of the edict published, but he gave instructions to subordinate authorities that no Christian was any longer to be molested or punished for the practice of his religion. They drew the immediate conclusion from this, at once liberated all Christians who were in custody and recalled those who had been condemned *ad metalla*. This toleration, legally guaranteed, rightly appeared to open to the Christians the gate to a brighter future.

C H A P T E R   3 0

The Definitive Turning-Point under Constantine the Great

Reverse under Maximinus Daia

In Galerius' mind the edict of toleration in 311 was intended to introduce a new state of affairs in religious matters. In his experience the God of the Christians had proved to be a real power which was to be recognized, together with its followers, and incorporated among the numerous religious beliefs of the empire so that the religious peace so attained might prove a blessing to the State and the tetrarchy ruling it.

Galerius died a few days after the publication of the edict and Licinius guaranteed that toleration would be observed in his dominions, but the joy of the Christians over the freedom they had acquired was short-lived in the eastern provinces and in Egypt. Maximinus Daia who had scarcely concealed his inner resistance to the policy of toleration, returned after a few months step by step to his earlier methods of oppressing the Christians. He began by forbidding the Christians to assemble in their cemeteries and tried to expel them from the larger towns. With harsh anti-Christian propaganda Maximinus combined energetic reorganization of the pagan cults. All these measures of the emperor quickly recreated an atmosphere in which the officials thought themselves justified in taking active steps against the Christians. The punishment of banishment from the towns was once more imposed, even if it was not fully implemented; leading Christians were once more arrested, imprisoned and condemned to death; death by wild beasts and by beheading were once again used as methods of execution. The situation which had become very serious again for the Christians was relieved, however, in a surprising way by a communication from the emperor at the end of 312. The same aim, it is true, is maintained in principle, that "of recalling the population of our provinces... to the service of the gods." Maximinus' new line of policy was determined by far-reaching events in the western parts of the Empire which had made Constantine master of Italy and Africa after his victory over Maxentius in October 312. The victor had immediately intervened with Maximinus in favor of the Christians and the new political situation made it advisable for him to veer into a more tolerant course. The young *Augustus* of the West thus became active in religious policy in a way that extended far beyond his own dominions. We have now to consider his attitude to Christianity.

Constantine's "Conversion" to Christianity

The question of Constantine's turning to Christianity, the fact, its course and its date, was and is hotly disputed among historians and this is partly due to the nature of the sources capable of providing an answer. Constantine's own historiographer, Bishop Eusebius of Caesarea, a friend of the emperor from 325 onward, was profoundly convinced of his hero's providential mission and he views all the events of his life, which changed the complexion of the age, in the light of this.

The second contemporary author, Lactantius, likewise sided with Constantine and his appointment as tutor to the emperor's eldest son, Crispus, shows the degree of trust that he enjoyed with the emperor. But for that reason he, too, is suspected of regarding Constantine in all too glowing and therefore distorting a light. Two characteristics stand out even in early tradition regarding Constantine; the passionate partisanship he aroused for and against himself, and a tendency to the formation of legends.

There is little in the sources about the childhood and youth of Constantine or of his religious development at that period. Constantius and Helena, his parents, were certainly pagans at the time of his birth in 285. His attachment to his mother was deep and lasting. The former inn-keeper was not Constantius' legal wife, for higher officers were not allowed to marry native women of the province. A few years after Constantine's birth, his father left her in order to contract a socially appropriate marriage with Theodora, the step-daughter of Maximian. The son presumably remained at first with his mother Helena and probably received his first religious impressions from her as a consequence. She was gifted above the average. Through her son she later made her way to Christianity; and when he became sole ruler, Constantine was able to give her the position of first lady in the empire and she filled it to perfection. It is questionable whether any marked influences of a religious kind came to Constantine from his father. The evidence however permits the inference that he deliberately rejected all compulsion in religious matters. Eusebius characterized Constantius as an adherent of monotheism and so probably viewed the emperor as a representative of the religious trend in the third century which gave increasing predominance to the one divine Being, the *summus deus* which transcended all other deities. The general atmosphere of Constantine's father's house was rather well-disposed toward Christians and that is how Constantine found it when in 305 he went to his father in the West after his flight from Nicomedia. When in 306 Constantine was elevated by his fathers troops to the position of *Augustus,* he maintained his father's religious policy, one of far-reaching toleration toward his Christian subjects and of conscious independence of the rulers in the East.

It was of fundamental importance that Constantine at this time was notably alive to the religious question. He linked his personal religious sentiment quite definitely to a mission entrusted to him by the divinity for the whole empire. The devices on coins show that Constantine at that time freed himself from the theology of the tetrarchy by choosing as his special patron-god, instead of Hercules, the *sol invictus;* this expressed a new political conception. The sun-god was worshipped in all parts of the empire in different forms. This was an announcement of the emperor's claim to universal dominion and his patron god was the *sol invictus* in the form of the Gallic Apollo.

Constantine took the first step toward the realization of his idea in the autumn of 312 when he took the field against the usurper Maxentius, then master of Italy and Africa, and whose troops outnumbered his. It would be a mistake to interpret the background to this conflict as though Maxentius were an oppressor of the Christians and Constantine their champion. Nor did Constantine's propaganda make out Maxentius to be a persecutor of Christians, but described him as a tyrant, plundering and oppressing his subjects and from whose yoke Rome ought to be set free. In a rapid onset Constantine overran Maxentius' defenses which extended in echelon as far as the Alps, brought the whole of Northern Italy under his sway and approached the city of Rome which his opponent intended to defend as his last stronghold. The decision turned in Constantine's favor at the battle of the Milvian Bridge to the north of the city on 28 October 312. Maxentius lost throne and life, and the way was open for Constantine into the Western capital consecrated by tradition. He was in possession of the whole of Western Europe and had victoriously concluded the first stage of his journey to universal rule.

This campaign was followed by Constantine's decisive turning to the God of the Christians, to which contemporary Christian writers, pagan panegyrists, and Constantine's behavior directly after the victory all testify.

The first report of it is given by Lactantius who says that Constantine had been exhorted in a dream to put God's heavenly sign on his soldiers' shields and so give battle. The emperor followed this instruction, he says, and made them put an abbreviation for "Christus" on their shields by bending the upper end of the letter

X placed sideways. This statement of Lactantius is in itself quite clear. It describes the sign drawn on the shields as a ✝, that is to say, a *crux monogrammatica*, a sign which at that time was not unknown to the Christians as well as their real Christ monogram ☧. Lactantius does not claim that what he relates was a miraculous occurrence. A dream of the emperor, which in view of the situation shortly before the battle was quite an understandable one, was the cause of the instruction, which was easy to carry out and the significance of which could be easily understood by all: emperor and army were not taking the field as usual, under a pagan magical sign, but under the protection of the God of the Christians. The victorious outcome showed that the Christian God had brought about this decision and that he now must be recognized as a divine patron. That was the picture of the remarkable event that was current in the emperor's entourage when Lactantius in 318 published his book *On the Manner of Death of the Persecutors*.

The same event is clearly at the bottom of the account given by Eusebius about twenty-five years later in his biography of the emperor, but how much more extensive it is now, in comparison with Lactantius' brief report! According to Eusebius, Constantine wanted to wage the campaign against Maxentius under his father's protector-god and prayed to him to reveal himself and grant his aid. Straightaway the emperor and the army saw in the late afternoon "in the sky above the sun the radiant victory sign of the cross," and near this the words: "By this, conquer: *Toutōi nika.*" The following night, Christ appeared to him with the cross and told him to have it copied and to carry it as protection in war. The emperor had a standard made according to his specifications; a long shaft with a cross-bar ending in a circle which bore in the middle the monogram of Christ, ☧, such as Constantine later had attached to his helmet, too. A rectangular banner hung down from the cross-bar and above this on the shaft were fixed the images of the emperor and his sons. The banner became the imperial standard, which was later called the *labarum*. It is noteworthy that Eusebius does not give this report of the vision of the cross in the last edition of his *Ecclesiastical History* (about 324). Consequently in the *Vita* he gives the version of what had happened as this took shape in Constantine's mind after a certain lapse of time from the event itself and in the transfiguring light of the memory of his victorious course. Constantine was convinced that the sign of the cross had been revealed to him at the beginning of his campaign against Maxentius; he had changed it into the monogram of Christ and with his help had triumphed over his opponent who trusted to the power of the pagan gods. His veneration for Christ as his protector-god was due to this event and it occasioned his turning to Christianity.

The triumphal arch in Rome, dedicated to the emperor after his victory by the Roman Senate and completed in 315, was naturally decorated with carvings which corresponded to the ideas of the pagan senate. Another monument is of greater importance; it too was intended to commemorate the victory and Constantine's view of it. This is the statue of the emperor in the Forum, bearing in the right hand, on Constantine's personal directions, "the sign of suffering that brought salvation." The inscription is due to Constantine's own initiative and explains the sign in his hand. "By this salutary sign, the true proof of power, I saved and freed your city from the yoke of the tyrant and gave back to the Senate and Roman people, as well as freedom, their ancient dignity and their ancient glory." It is the *signum caeleste dei* of Lactantius, the Christian cross, probably in the form of the monogram. Consequently this statue is not only a novelty by its form, being the first example of an emperor's statue with a standard, but it expresses in a particularly clear manner both Constantine's conviction that he had been led by this standard, and his will publicly to proclaim this.

Finally the process of turning toward Christianity, even in a very qualified way, is indicated in the coins Constantine had struck. Christian symbols gradually appear beside the images of the old divinities especially the *sol invictus,* which can be traced on coins down to the year 322.

Of considerable significance, too, for the emperor's attitude to Christianity were some measures directly connected with the victory of October 312. That very same year a letter must have gone from Constantine to Maximinus calling for an end to persecution of Christians in the eastern regions. It has already been shown how this wish was carried out. Similarly in the same year 312, he commanded in North Africa that confiscated Church property should be restored. Another letter was addressed directly to the Catholic Bishop of Carthage, Caecilian, who received quite a large sum for the clergy "of the lawful and most holy Catholic religion." Both measures go far beyond the intention of the edict of Galerius and the second already shows the emperor taking special interest in the liturgical concerns of the Catholic Church. The Church's worship forms the center of a third very important document which freed the clergy of the Carthaginian church from obligation to public service so that they might devote themselves unhindered to the performance of the liturgy. Constantine has become aware of the importance of Christian worship even if no understanding of its real content is perceptible. He feels obliged not merely to ensure freedom for this worship, but to ensure its exact and worthy accomplishment, because he sees in it a condition for the success of the work he has begun.

The features of Constantine's proceedings in regard to Christianity in the year 312–13 vary, it is true, in evidential force. Taken as a whole they nevertheless impose the conclusion that during this period Constantine had accomplished his personal turning to Christianity. Constantine's "conversion" must, it is true, only be understood in the sense of a "turning" founded on a recognition which perhaps had already been maturing in him for some time, that the God of the Christians alone had a claim to the worship due to the highest Being.

From the Convention of Milan (313)
to the Beginning of Sole Rule (324)

In February 313 Constantine and Licinius met in Milan to discuss the new political situation created by the former's victory. The marriage between Licinius and Constantia was also then celebrated. In regard to religious matters, discussions led to a settlement which, however, did not find expression in the form of an Edict of Milan, as was formerly thought. But it is clear that this agreement was not merely concerned with putting into effect the measure of toleration laid down by the edict of Galerius; it rather involved in principle a substantial extension of this as a comparison of the Galerian text with the content of two decrees of

Licinius published after his victory over Maximinus Daia will show. It is stressed in the first place that the emperor intends to settle the religious question by toleration: everyone, including Christians, had full freedom to follow the religion he preferred; that would be a guarantee for continued favor from the *summa divinitas*. Then, however, come a series of special ordinances for the Christian Church, which, by their content, intensity of insistence and tone of respectful goodwill, far exceeded Galerius' grudging grant of toleration. All places in which the Christians had been accustomed to assemble, that is, churches and cemeteries, were returned to them without charge, whether they were in public or private possession. Moreover this property was to be conveyed directly to the various Christian communities, whose corporate legal existence was thereby recognized. Finally a conviction is expressed which would have been quite impossible with Galerius; that through this treatment of the Christian religion, the divine favor, that the emperors had experienced in such great matters, would continue for ever in its beneficial effect on public welfare. The Milan agreement can be considered as the religious policy which Constantine was chiefly striving to carry out. The benefits it accorded could not, however, be enjoyed by the Christians of the eastern provinces and Egypt, until the conflict between Licinius and Maximinus, which still persisted, had been brought to an end. The latter sought a quick military decision when, early in 313, he moved to the Balkans at a moment when he knew that Constantine was occupied by his war with the Franks of the Rhine. Lactantius represents the battle between the two rulers as a religious war. Maximinus was decisively defeated at Adrianople and harried by Licinius in a rapid pursuit which struck deeply into Asia Minor. He still tried to win the sympathies of his Christian subjects by an edict of unrestricted toleration, and prepared for a new battle. His death in 313 abruptly ended the struggle and brought all the eastern territories under Licinius' authority and the Milan agreement.

The conquest of the oriental territories brought Licinius an enormous increase of power and Constantine had to postpone for the moment his ultimate aim of establishing a universal Roman rule. The two *Augusti* occupied themselves first with consolidating and strengthening what had been won. In the religious question, Licinius maintained the principles of the Milan agreement; Constantine, with his mental alertness, already saw the approach of a problem and a task which were to attract him more and more as time went on: that of bringing the Christian Church closer to the State, of discovering a form of mutual relation for them which would correspond to his view of their respective missions. He moved to a solution through the experience afforded him by his gradually deepening penetration into the specific nature of the Christian world and the questions belonging to it. He encountered them for the first time on a large scale through developments within the Church in North Africa which, shortly before his victory, had led to a profound split among adherents of Christianity there.

The superficial occasion of the Donatist schism was the question of church discipline regarding what judgment was to be passed on the action of Christians who had handed over the Holy Scriptures to the pagan authorities in the Diocletian persecution. One group among those who had remained faithful regarded it as grave betrayal of the faith and called the guilty *traditores;* among the latter were laymen, clerics, and even bishops. The question became theologically important when it was linked to the particular opinion traditional in North African theology, according to which the validity of a sacrament depended on the state of grace of its minister; consequently the sacraments conferred by a *traditor,* an apostate ultimately, could not be regarded as valid. In 312 when Caecilian, who had previously been deacon of Carthage, was called to the see, one group in the church which felt slighted because of the sharp treatment of one of its most influential members, whom Caecilian had criticized for his over-enthusiastic cult of the martyrs, pointed out that one of those who had consecrated him bishop, Felix of Aptungi, had been a *traditor.* The case was taken up by the first Bishop of Numidia, Secundus of Tigisis, and brought before a synod of seventy Numidian bishops, which declared Caecilian deposed. In this action of the Numidian episcopate, a certain rivalry with Carthage no doubt also played its part. First, Majorinus became rival bishop to Caecilian and then, after 313, Donatus, the real intellectual head of the opposition, from whom the rapidly developing schismatical church, the *pars Donati,* took its name.

When Constantine in 312 sought information about the situation in his newly acquired territories, he found himself faced by this complicated situation, very difficult for an outsider to grasp in its ultimate connections, and even more difficult to comprehend on account of the hostility of both groups, embittered by personal rancor. He probably received his first report from the point of view of Caecilian's supporters, perhaps from Bishop Ossius, who very early showed himself to be well-informed about the African clergy. Constantine immediately recognized its adverse effects on the unity of the Christian society and strove as occasion offered to restore that unity. In the first place he saw that by the dissension the correct accomplishment of Christian worship was no longer assured, and this, as has already been indicated, was of particular concern to him. Consequently he was ready to make the help of State officials available to bring back into line the disturbers of the peace, for that is how the Donatists chiefly appeared to him. Thereupon the Donatists addressed themselves directly to the emperor, and asked for the dispute to be settled by Gallic judges. Constantine accepted this suggestion and turned to the Bishop of Rome, Miltiades, informing him what he had decided in the matter: Caecilian was to come to Rome with ten bishops of his choice and so was his opponent; there an ecclesiastical court was to hear the case and give judgment. The emperor stressed that the inquiry into Caecilian must determine whether he answered to ecclesiastical requirements "which are to be held in high respect." Finally, he affirmed that he had the greatest reverence for the Catholic Church and did not wish any division to be found in it anywhere.

It is clear from this document that the emperor realized he was in a position which in many respects was completely novel to him. Constantine decided on episcopal judges, leaving the matter, therefore, in ecclesiastical hands and hoping that in that way peace would be restored. There can be no question, therefore, of any presumptuous intervention of imperial authority in the internal affairs of the Church, but the intense interest of the emperor in the restoration of peace within the Church is unmistakable. The unanimous verdict of the court pronounced Donatus guilty and confirmed Caecilian as legitimate Bishop of Carthage. The Donatists, however, contested the judgment on the ground of defects of procedure, and the emperor found himself obliged to have the matter dealt with once more. The proceedings were conducted this time in Arles in the summer of 314 on a much bigger scale and with the assistance of numerous bishops.

In the emperor's letter of invitation a double advance in his understanding of Christianity may be observed. He now sees the Church as a society which, in fraternal harmony, accomplishes by its rites the true worship of God. Anyone who does not respect the unity of this society endangers his salvation; so the Church is felt to be a means to salvation. He does not yet feel himself to be a complete member of the Church, but he fears for her reputation and her universal mission.

After the unsuccessful outcome of the Synod of Arles, Constantine decided after all to end the Donatist schism by his own means. In a threatening tone the emperor announced to both parties that he was going to come to Africa himself and proclaimed his aim of leading all men to the true religion and the worthy worship of Almighty God. Constantine did, after all, desist from a journey to Africa, but in a letter at the end of the year 316, plainly took the side of Caecilian and his supporters. When disturbances occurred, from 317 onward, he sent in troops, had Donatist bishops exiled, and their churches seized, but this only created martyrs and the sense of martyrdom until he resigned the struggle. At the same time, however, dangerous possibilities are already visible which arose for the Church from the sense of mission of a Christian ruler who thought himself justified by a religious call to intervene directly in the Church's own essential concerns.

This gradual and growing attachment of the emperor for Christianity was accompanied by certain laws which revealed the influence of Christian ideas or restricted the influence of pagan religious activity.

The general line of Constantine's legislation shows increasing regard for the dignity of the human person. A similarly humanitarian tendency combines with respectful recognition of those in charge of the Christian communities, in an ordinance addressed to Bishop Ossius which declares that Christians could free their slaves in the presence of the bishop with full legal validity, and clerics likewise, in certain cases, without written documents and without witnesses. As the liberation had to take place "in the bosom of the Church," it is treated as an action of religious significance. Similar regard for the episcopal office is expressed in the important decision allowing Christian bishops to set up a court of arbitration, even for civil cases. The law freeing those who were unmarried and without children from certain obligations may rightly be regarded as framed with the ascetics of the Christian Church in view. Of decisive importance was Constantine's Sunday law, March–July 321, ordering cessation from work in the courts and from manual labor on this "venerable day." A special favor granted to the Catholic Church is represented by the edict which allowed anyone the right to bequeath in his will whatever he liked to the Catholic community.

Certain legal provisions were necessary to protect the right to free profession of religion laid down in the Convention of Milan, in its detailed application to Christianity. Christian converts from Judaism who were molested by their former co-religionists receive the special protection of the law. It is significant that Constantine also here no longer designated the pagan religion as such by a neutral term, but characterized it pejoratively as *superstitio*.

Finally a restriction of the extent to which pagan religion could be practiced was introduced by the double decree on divination in 319 and 320, which forbade under strict penalties the practice of this custom in private. This cannot have concerned the abolition of an abuse, for divination in public remained permissible. But it was precisely in private life that divination made possible for pagans an effective propaganda for their religion and one that escaped all control.

These laws from the time when Constantine was sole ruler confirm the picture already drawn. The emperor was under the influence of Christian ideas, his concern for the accomplishment of Christian worship sprang from an inner personal interest and in this or that case a preference for the Christian religion is perceptible. Of particular importance is the unmistakable tendency of the emperor to call on the moral and religious values of the Christian religion and the authority of the Christian church leaders, for the benefit of the State. As a consequence, various features of the public life of the age already receive a Christian stamp. His attitude to paganism is in principle tolerant, but in the law against augury the first limitation of its freedom of action is seen.

The struggle for sole rule in the Roman Empire, which had been impending for some time between Licinius and Constantine, was to take the latter an important step further on the road to public and personal recognition of the Christian religion. A first military clash in Pannonia and Thrace in the autumn of 316 gave no decision, but the gains of territory in the Balkans that it brought to Constantine and the recognition of his two eldest sons as *Caesares* notably strengthened his position for the now inevitable final confrontation. The struggle assumed the character of a religious war that was finally to decide the victory or the defeat of Christianity. Licinius had maintained the provisions of the Convention of Milan in his dominions since 313. The marked favor shown to Christianity by the *Augustus* of the West, led Licinius gradually to diverge from the line of religious policy laid down in Milan, and after about 320 to exert pressure increasingly on the Christians in the East. It is not surprising that the sympathies and hopes of Christians in Asia Minor and the Near East turned to the *Augustus* in the West. The resentment of high officials was vented in violent measures. When after massive preparations, war broke out in the summer of 324, Constantine deliberately gave it a Christian stamp by giving the army the now fully developed *labarum* as a standard in battle, while Licinius questioned the pagan oracles and implored the help of the gods by sacrifices. Constantine's victories in battle at Adrianople and on the Bosphorus in July and at Chrysopolis in Asia Minor in September 324, forced Licinius to capitulate and accept negotiations with Constantine.

Constantine's complete victory and the position of sole ruler which it gave him, almost inevitably introduced a new phase of religious policy. The Christians, especially in the East, looked forward with intense expectation to what was to come. Eusebius speaks in the final section of his *Ecclesiastical History* of the days of rejoicing with which the emperor's victory was celebrated. The first proclamations of the victorious emperor were of such a kind as to confirm these hopes. A comprehensive decree concerning the inhabitants of the eastern provinces at once cancelled the wrong done to the Christians in the time of persecution, and provided generous compensation. More important still are those sections of the document in which Constantine explained the significance of recent events as the great battle for recognition of the Christian God who revealed his might in the success of Constantine's army. The earlier consciousness of a mission has now been replaced by a bold knowledge of his election which in future was to mark all the emperor's acts. He had a clearly defined aim, the restoration of the Christian Church. The document also shows the caliber of the victorious emperor as a statesman; he will not persecute adherents of paganism or force them to become Christians; freedom of conscientious decision is guaranteed: "Each must hold what his heart bids him."

CHAPTER   3 1

The Causes of the Victory of the Christian Religion— The Scope and the Import of the Turning-Point under Constantine

There is general agreement that the complete change in the relation between Christian Church and Roman State wrought by Constantine was an event of the first importance in the history of the world. This closer relationship had not, as a matter of fact, the radically revolutionary character that is sometimes attributed to it. Pre-Constantinian Christendom had already sought a tolerable relation even toward the pagan State because, as St. Paul had taught (Rom 13:1–7), behind every secular power the will of God was discerned. Religion and the State in late Antiquity were not known except as related to one another in principle. It would have been revolutionary if the Roman emperor and State had made absolute neutrality in regard to all religious cults a lasting principle of its policy and had thus been uninterested in any relations at all between the State and religions. Consequently, it was a perfectly normal way of thinking for Christians of the time to expect that under an emperor whose sincere conversion to their faith was not to be doubted, Christianity would soon take the place of pagan worship.

The positive as well as negative possibilities that presented themselves to the Christian Church at the beginnings of Constantine's period of sole rule may be summarized as follows. The freedom granted to the Church released strong forces that could be devoted to the unhampered building-up of life within the Church. Freedom of worship and of preaching within the Church was guaranteed by law. New conditions were created for the worthy performance of the liturgy through the possibility of reconstruction and the erection of new Christian places of worship which were very generously accorded by the State. The religious care for the faithful in the various forms of catechetical instruction, preaching and sacramental life was no longer subject to any restriction. New and attractive tasks appeared for ecclesiastical writers in unhampered work in pastoral and theological literature.

The missionary function of the Church was likewise no longer impeded by any restrictions and was able to develop in a particularly fruitful way, for freedom of conscience was guaranteed in the profession of a religious faith.

It was now also possible for the Church to undertake the enormous task of christianizing secular culture and public life and to develop and give a Christian stamp to an intellectual life of her own. Here the Church faced perhaps her most radical task of adaptation. Previously she had lived consciously at a distance from the cultural world around her and had withdrawn from the completely pagan public life into her own specific moral and religious domain which was easier to preserve in her complete isolation. When this new-found freedom enticed her out of that isolated ghetto-like existence, it also exposed her to greater risks, and it made her vulnerable to alien elements which could adulterate her beliefs and her morality. This imposed a heavy burden upon Christian leaders.

Again, the influx of vast numbers into the Church for political and religious social reasons posed risks to her high moral and religious standard.

Objectively, the most difficult task for the Church was the discovery of the right mental attitude to the new relation of Church and State. The double danger present was not consciously realized from the start. Even Eusebius was still quite unconcerned and full of praise for Constantine when reporting that now "the bishops received imperial documents and honors and subsidies" (*HE* X, 2). It would have been a temptation for many bishops especially in the East, after having been oppressed for so long, to sun themselves in the imperial favor and so lose their freedom. More dangerous was the tendency, deriving form the emperors view, not to consider the Church as a partner *sui generis,* but to make her serviceable to the interests of the State and so to stifle her independence and necessary freedom in the realm of internal Church affairs. Only the bitter experiences under Emperor Constantius could give the episcopate some idea of how exceedingly difficult it could be to achieve a healthy, fruitful equilibrium in the mutual relations between a State under Christian leadership and the Catholic Church.

Book Two

THE IMPERIAL CHURCH FROM CONSTANTINE TO THE EARLY MIDDLE AGES

Translated by Anselm Biggs

Part One

The Development of the Church of the Empire within the Framework of the Imperial Religious Policy

Karl Baus

C H A P T E R   3 2

From Christianity's Position of Equality to One of Privilege by the Favor of the Emperor Constantine I

Position of Church and Emperor in 324

Although, at the beginning of Constantine's sole rule, the adherents of the Christian religion in the Roman Empire constituted only a considerable minority, they were without any doubt infected by an unbounded optimism in regard to the future. To the Church historian Eusebius and his readers, Constantine was the servant and friend of God, who had had him "shine out of the deepest gloom and the darkest night as a great light and as a deliverer for all." "Now every fear that had once oppressed men was taken from them. Festive days were celebrated with splendor and pomp; everything was full of light. In the cities as well as in the country, in dancing and singing they gave honor first to God, the King of Kings, as they were instructed, and then to the pious Emperor and his sons, beloved by God" (Eusebis, *HE* 10, 8–9). Such a view and valuation of the future must have seemed well-founded to the contemporary Christians. For more than a decade the Emperor Constantine had assured to the Christian religion freedom to profess and proclaim its faith and, after giving it an initial equality with paganism, had shown it an ever more undeniable benevolence. Then, when he gave to his attack on Licinius the appearance of a war for the freedom of religion on behalf of the persecuted Christians of the eastern provinces, no one need further doubt the Emperor's personal conviction of the truth of Christianity. The Bishop of Caesarea was pondering in his heart more far-reaching possibilities, which were no doubt also anticipated by many of his colleagues. He stated that, by his victory over Licinius, Constantine had again created a single and centralized Roman Empire, in which all the territories of the earth from the east to the farthest west, together with the north and the south, were subjected to one peaceable scepter. Would this politically united Roman Empire not also profess the one same faith, be united in the exclusive acknowledgment of the God of the Christians? This hour of triumph was not likely to give rise in Eusebius or in his fellow-bishops of East or West any doubt that such a collaboration of Church and State could have for the former any hazardous consequences.

It is clear that the sole rule he had gained, which freed him from any concern with a coruler, merely strengthened Constantine's sense of mission: he could, in accord with ancient ideas, in looking back to his way thus far, see himself confirmed at the end of 324 as the Chosen One of God. He did not consider it to be "idle boasting" when, in the first decree after the overthrow of Licinius, he acknowledged to the eastern provinces: "God wanted my service and regarded as appropriate the carrying out of his resolve." Without doubt, for him this God was the God of the Christians, and hence his future attitude in regard to the Christian community could only be more and more cordial — he had to feel that he belonged to it in a unique way. But in the course of his consciousness of mission it was quite obvious that, if the Emperor felt a unique place was suitable for himself in or in regard to the Christian Church, this made it impossible for any other event or any other development of importance in the Christian world to be of no concern to him. If he himself stated that he was prepared, after the years of the persecution "to rebuild the most holy house [of God]," then of course the ecclesiastical leadership could hardly bear to deal with important questions of conduct without, not to mention against, the Emperor. Much depended on how far Constantine felt the innermost being of the Church was something so independent that here limits blocked the power of the State. The ineffectiveness of his exertions in the early phase of the Donatist troubles could have been a first lesson for him.

The Growing Privileged Position of the Christian Religion

Immediately after he had achieved sole rule, Constantine's religious policy entered externally upon a path which now led, circumspectly but nevertheless resolutely, from Christianity's equality with the existing religions, guaranteed as early as 312, to its clear and public preeminence. This became tangible in a whole series of laws and measures which were issued from time to time during the scarcely thirteen remaining years of his reign. They began with the decree to the inhabitants of the eastern provinces: their principal item can be summarized as regulations on the restitution to be made to the Christians for the injustices of which they had been the victims. The individual points — removal of all degrading and damaging judicial sentences, such as privation of earlier rank in the public service and reduction to the state of slavery, the restoration to individual Christians or their heirs of property that had been confiscated or sold, the restoration of Christian communities to their former property rights, even if such property was now in the possession of the *fiscus* (imperial treasury) or, through purchase or gift, had come into other hands — made clear that the Emperor's sympathy now belonged to the adherents of the Christian religion. The equality of all citizens before the law was abolished in practice when a later decree forbade to the high officials, provincial governors, and their immediate subordinates, if these still belonged to the old religion, the *external* profession of their faith by means of sacrifice, whereas Christian officials of the same rank could, as Eusebius stresses, "glory in the name of Christian."

Constantine's legislation remained thereafter open to Christian influence, although the existing social order, which was basically untouched by Constantine, and the esteem for the prevailing Roman law limited this influence. It becomes clearest in the fields of marriage and family life, as, for example, in the decrees which made divorce more difficult and forbade a husband to maintain a concubine, or those which decided that slave families were not to be broken up in a division of an inheritance. The Christian respect for human life is seen also in the prohibition of gladiatorial games, while the abolition of crucifixion as a death penalty also showed regard for the honor due to Christianity in public. Certain laws from the period before 324 which displayed a tone friendly to Christianity were again enacted, for example, the constitution which gave to a convert from Judaism clear legal protection against possible annoyance or persecution on the part of his former coreligionists. The fact that a state was bound to such protection — because the convert had, by his change of faith, dedicated himself "to the holy worship and opened for himself the door to eternal life" — clearly expresses the relationship felt by Constantine of the supreme legislator toward the respect due to the Christian faith even in the public sphere. The same attitude appears in the comment appended to the ratification of judicial decisions of the bishops in civil suits: the "authority of the holy religion," which constitutes the basis of the judgment given by the Catholic bishop, guarantees its fairness and assures it against any appeal. Finally, a general law gives to all the privileges assured in the decrees on religion their intrinsic value, of the utmost importance for the future: they were now for the benefit only of adherents of the Catholic faith, not of heretics and schismatics. A decree that left untouched the houses and cemeteries of the Novatians which had long been in their possession was not inconsistent with this: it proceeded from the principle that heretical or schismatic communities were ordinarily not to remain in possession of property that they had taken from the Catholic Church. This expression of a more positive valuation of the Novatians may have been based on the fact that they recognized the decision of Nicaea; but it may have lain in the hope of the Emperor's ecclesiastical entourage that an easier reconciliation with them was to be anticipated. Hence the decree on the Novatians was an exception in the field of law and, to this extent, a confirmation of the general edict against heretics which Constantine had published soon after his victory over Licinius. In it "Novatians, Valentinians, Marcionites, Paulicians, and Cataphrygians" were sharply attacked and subjected to harsh decrees; any gathering, even in private houses, was forbidden to them, their churches were confiscated and turned over to the Catholic Church, and their other property was awarded to the *fiscus.* Only one sentence contains the invitation to join the Catholic Church. Eusebius speaks also of a law which permitted the confiscation of heretical writings; according to him, the edict had the desired effect in its entirety, since "nowhere on earth did there remain an association of heretics and schismatics." In contradiction of this statement of Eusebius, both in substance and in tone, it should be noted that Constantine threatened no sanctions against individual members of an heretical community who persisted in their religious conviction, even if the Emperor's language is harsh in regard to heretics, because in his eyes they were already rebel Christians. He thought he had to proceed against heresy as such, because it upset the peace and harmony of Christianity and thereby not only caused great dangers for the calm and order of the Empire, but also impeded Christians on the road to salvation.

The Emperor displayed a greater toleration toward the adherents of paganism, especially since in this case there was a question of prominent persons in public life, such as, for example, the Neoplatonist philosophers Hermogenes, Nikagoras, and Sopatros or members of old and well-established families in the Roman Senate. But from 324 on, he made no effort to conceal his ever growing contempt for the pagan religion. As early as the autumn of 324 a letter to the inhabitants of Palestine let it be known that the Emperor regarded his victory as also a defeat of paganism; and even if the second edict to the eastern provinces of the Empire stresses toleration in regard to the adherents of the old faith as governmental policy and even justifies it as "Christian," nevertheless the overall tenor of the document must have made thoughtful pagans aware that the Emperor's clearly expressed sympathies for Christianity — whose adherents are contrasted as "believers" to "the erring" — implied no happy future for the pagan religion. Words were followed by deeds, which could also be interpreted by the pagans in no other way than as a repression of their religion in the public sphere. Here belongs the appointment of a bureaucracy consisting of a majority of Christians, when high administrative posts, left vacant by the change of ruler in the East, had to be again filled, although on the basis of the status of the religious confessions at least an equality in the distribution of positions could have been expected; furthermore, the public offering of sacrifice by the pagan minority among the officials was forbidden. Also the manner in which Constantine in 325 celebrated his *vicennalia* — the twentieth anniversary of his accession — in the East must have made the pagans anxious. The celebration took place in the midst of the bishops who had assembled for the Council of Nicaea and the customary panegyric was composed and delivered, not by a pagan *rhetor,* but by a Catholic bishop. Thus the Catholic episcopate gradually stepped into the place which the pagan upper class had hitherto occupied. The most intimate entourage of the Emperor at court reflected this new picture, an unmistakable sign of a changing world.

A special significance belongs, furthermore, to Constantine's measures which envisaged a steady suppression of pagan worship. In 324 he expressed the wish that pagans too might enter "into the brilliant house of [Christian] truth," but he clearly contrasted with it "the temples of delusion," which would be left to the pagans if they so desired. Soon, however, laws appeared whereby individual temples lost their revenues, were deprived of their images of the gods, or were completely done away with. In this connection it should be noted that both Christian and pagan writers report these measures with much exaggeration: the latter, in order, in their bitterness, to censure the conduct of the Emperor; the former, especially Eusebius, in order triumphantly to attribute to the first Christian on the imperial throne the complete overthrow of heathen worship. The following facts are sure: the famed and much visited temple of Asclepius in the Cilician Aegae was completely destroyed, as was the shrine of Aphrodite at Aphaca in Phoenicia, whose cult could have seemed especially offensive to Christians. This motive was all the more present in the elimination of the temple of Aphrodite which had been erected on the site of Christ's tomb. Phoenician Heliopolis (Baalbek) was also long a center of the cult of Aphrodite, which, according to Eusebius, was now forbidden by an imperial law that at the same time made known Constantine's missionary zeal, since it expressly invited the inhabitants of the city to accept the Christian faith. He sought to break down the totality of the pagan atmosphere of the city by erecting a church, which with its numerous clerics should become the center of a Christian community life. Eusebius also knew of a special decree of the Emperor which put an end to the liturgical honoring of the Nile, in whose service there was a priesthood consisting of eunuchs. Also, the oriental cults of Mithra and Cybele conspicuously declined in the years of the reigns of Constantine and his sons. But more than anything else the method by which the Emperor pillaged many a pagan shrine of the East in order to beautify his new capital on the Bosporus must have embittered every convinced heathen. No consideration was given even to objects so rich in tradition as the tripods of the Pythia in Apollo's shrine at Delphi. Eusebius reports that all this included mockery and derision of the pagan priesthood. But the bringing of the pagan religion as such into ridicule was unmistakable, since the images of its gods were now reduced to objects of exhibition, and only an artistic significance was thereafter attributed to it.

The imperial action gains in relief when it is considered against the background of the interest which Constantine devoted to building activity for the benefit of Christianity. Eusebius was very much attracted by this aspect of the Emperor's solicitude for Christian matters and spoke of it in detail in so far as it extended to the eastern part of the Empire. Constantine's view early turned to Palestine, which clearly played a special role in his religious and political plans, precisely because it could, as the beloved pilgrimage goal of Christians from all parts of the Empire, strengthen their awareness of belonging to one community. He wanted the sites of Christ's burial and resurrection in Jerusalem to be treated with special distinction; hence he had the burial grotto opened and rebuilt and then had a basilica erected, for which he had the money raised by the governors of the eastern provinces, and on the decoration of which he concerned himself even with details. Mount Olivet, as the place of the Ascension, also obtained a basilica, which was at the same time intended as a memorial of the Emperor's mother, Helena, since she had especially encouraged its construction. A decisive role in the erecting of the Church of the Nativity at Bethlehem is also attributed to her by Eusebius, and the Emperor likewise generously aided in its adornment. The Emperor, through a special circular, informed the episcopate of Palestine of his determination to build a basilica at the Oak of Mamre and invited them, together with the bishops of Phoenicia, to foster the work in every way. Precisely in this connection it is noteworthy how the Emperor considered church building as his personal concern. No doubt he urged the bishops to intensive cooperation, but since he demanded exact reports on the implementation of his orders and reserved the final decision to himself even in regard to details, it becomes obvious that he regarded himself as the real building contractor, who gave instructions through his officials to the chief architects, artists, and craftsmen. Outside Palestine it was especially the cities of Antioch and Nicomedia, populous and rich in tradition — the latter had been the eastern capital — which were distinguished by magnificent basilicas.

In the West the Christian congregation of the ancient imperial capital could take pleasure in the special generosity of the Emperor, which presented it with an abundance of grandiose church buildings and magnificently introduced the period of Christian architecture in Rome. The series of Constantinian basilicas was opened here with a church in honor of the Savior with a nearby baptistery (after 313) which would later receive the name of John at the Lateran. The property on which it was built was a personal gift from the Emperor to the Christian community of Rome. The first church erected as a memorial of martyrs, likewise encouraged by Constantine, was that of Saints Peter and Marcellinus, to which was attached the tomb of the Empress-Mother Helena. It was followed by the immense enterprise on the Vatican Hill, with which, despite all the technical difficulties, a worthy monument was to be erected to the memory of the Apostle Peter over the place of his burial. The memory of the two Apostles Peter and Paul together was also honored by a special church on the Appian Way near the present basilica of San Sebastiano, where decades earlier Christians had assembled to celebrate their memory. One more closely approaches historical truth if one attributes Constantine's zeal for building Christian churches to a religious notion, that is, to his idea of the Church, which he intended to express symbolically by the act of constructing a house of God adorned with all splendor. He understood, at least after the Council of Nicaea, the Church as the kingdom of God, which is ruled by divine law, and the earthly church building with its architectural arrangement and its height pointing heavenward was to him a reflection of that properly ordered kingdom, through which the individual human being and Christian finds the road to heaven. The Emperor aimed, by means of splendid basilicas in all the geographical areas of the Roman Empire, to insert the very Empire itself into the order created by God: the Empire entrusted to him should be Christian.

This becomes most clearly apparent in the greatest building enterprise which the Emperor undertook and was able to complete: the establishing of the new imperial capital on the Bosporus, which was to bear his name. There is no doubt that the new imperial residence, which was also the seat of the imperial government, was, by the will of the Emperor, intended from the start to have the character of a Christian city; hence, in contrast to old Rome, it must be free of the elements proper to paganism. It is true that he permitted the older capital in the West to retain its historical rank and hence preserved continuity by giving to the new foundation the name of Second Rome. He also borrowed many of its institutions, such as the Senate, the division into fourteen urban regions, and certain administrative forms. But what was really new lay in the religious sphere: the Empire received a Christian center, which thus in a sense made it an Anti-Rome. The city on the Tiber could cherish the old traditions, and the members of the esteemed senatorial families could still treasure their pagan cults, but the Emperor's interest was simply no longer directed to this city, which he seldom visited. The earliest coins with the *Tychē,* the personification of the new city, show the globe in her hand on the Cross of Christ. The constructing of new pagan temples was not considered in the planning of the new city, and the pagan priests at the cult sites existing in pre-Constantinian Byzantium lost their revenues. On the other hand, Christian churches in honor of the martyrs and several basilicas were, from the first, part of the Emperor's building plan, as, for example, a church in honor of Christ dedicated under the title of *Sophia* a church of peace (*Eirēnē*), and especially the Church of the Apostles, intended to correspond to the basilicas of the Apostles at Rome; it was destined to receive the remains of the Emperor in an adjoining room in the midst of the monuments honoring the twelve Apostles. He commissioned Eusebius to have fifty costly manuscripts of the Bible prepared for liturgical use. Monuments with Christian representations, such as that of the Good Shepherd or of Daniel, adorned the public squares of the city, and the sign of the cross was among the ceiling panels of the imperial palace. When, following intensive building activity, the city was solemnly dedicated on 11 May 330, four years after its founding, it had no Capitoline temple, no cult of Vesta, no pagan priestly college.

Without any doubt, Constantine was interested in seeing his personal position within the ecclesiastical community especially stressed. Hence he fully concurred when Christian writers of the time compared him with Abraham or Moses and addressed him as God's vicar on earth, whose palace was the earthly reflection of the heavenly throneroom. He himself once said that he felt himself to be *episkopos tōn ektos,* a bishop instituted by God to look after the people of his Empire in the religious sphere also, except in the area of the sacramental leadership that pertained to the priesthood of the Church.

Constantine's Baptism and Death

Some claim to see a continuation of Constantine's pagan convictions in the fact that he so long deferred the reception of baptism, until he felt his end approaching. To this it must be objected that the Emperor saw daily in his entourage or even on his journeys men of undoubtedly Christian convictions who likewise again and again postponed baptism, even though the Church itself disapproved such a practice. It was partly fostered by Christian teaching in regard to baptism: on the one hand, the sublimity of baptism, the exalted worth of baptismal grace, was extolled, and the difficulty of renewing it when it had been lost by sin was so solemnly described, that many a Christian was unwilling to expose himself to rick by a too early reception of baptism. That such considerations could carry weight with such a temperament as Constantine's cannot be disputed. But again and again Constantine stated that he regarded himself as a member of the Church.

Furthermore, if one considers the manner in which Constantine prepared himself for death, here too can be recognized a clearly Christian attitude of faith. The thought of his death had early occurred to him, because while he was erecting the Church of the Apostles, as earlier mentioned, he had had his tomb prepared along with it: his coffin was to be placed in a mausoleum attached to the church, between two rows, each of six burial slabs dedicated to the memory of the twelve Apostles so that he could share in the prayers which would be offered here in their honor. The Emperor seems to have celebrated Easter of 337 without any difficulties. A few weeks later he fell ill and at first sought a cure in the baths of the East. When he recognized the seriousness of the sickness, he called for some bishops to come to Nicomedia and asked them for baptism, which, according to Eusebius, he received in the spirit of the first Christians; then, after the rite, he continued to wear the white garments, "because he no longer wanted to touch purple." And the disposition of his soul was that of an authentic believer. The last words which Eusebius reports from him were uttered shortly after his baptism: "Now I know myself to be truly happy; now I know that I have become worthy of immortal life, a sharer in the divine life." After he had handed over the Empire to his sons and had taken leave of the high officials and the military commanders, he died on Pentecost, 22 May 337. His remains were brought to "his city" and first laid out in the imperial palace and later buried as provided for, in the presence of his second son, Constantinus, after the celebration of the liturgy.

With the recognition of Christianity as his own religion and that of the Roman Empire, Constantine had accomplished a deed of world-historical consequences. His memory lived on in East and West, and soon his image, like that of many of the great ones of history, was seized upon and glorified by legend. But in the good as well as in the questionable elements of his activity, this ruler continued to operate powerfully through the centuries in which there was a Christian Empire. Each time that a new Emperor ascended the throne at Byzantium, he was thereafter hailed by the magnates of the Empire as *Neos Kōnstantinos*. Since very few of his Byzantine successors measured up to the greatness, both as ruler and as man, of this exemplar, this appeal to their predecessor was more often harmful than beneficial to the Church of Byzantium. It also admitted him as the "equal of the Apostles" into its liturgical calendar and thereby from the start weakened its own position in later conflicts with the throne. In the Latin West, it is true, Constantine's memory was also often and at times unscrupulously appealed to in Church-State confrontations, but a remarkably surer instinct preserved the Roman Church from enrolling him among the saints. It thereby did the greatest service to itself and to the true significance of the first Christian Emperor.

CHAPTER 33

Origin and Course of the Arian Controversy to the Death of Constantine (337)

The Origin

Very soon after his entry into the eastern capital, Nicomedia, Constantine learned that the Christian community of the East, like the Church of North Africa, was torn by a conflict which had already reached threatening proportions. Eusebius characterized it as "a mighty fire," which had its beginnings in the Christian congregation of Alexandria, spread from there throughout Egypt, neighboring Libya, and other provinces of the East, and split both the bishops and the ordinary folk into two camps, which so fiercely attacked each other that the Christian fraternal strife had become the subject of jokes in pagan theatrical productions. This implies that the war in the fall of 324 already had a certain history and hence its beginnings are to be placed in the years before the instituting of measures hostile to Christians by Licinius.

The man under whose name the conflict has come into Church history, the priest Arius, was a pastor in the Catholic Church in the part of Alexandria known as Baucalis, but he came from Libya and had obtained his theological formation, not at the school of Alexandria, but in all probability in Syrian Antioch, since he counted himself among the pupils of the Antiochene priest Lucian, the founder of that city's theological school. These apparently found their former membership in this school a mark of distinction and through it they found themselves united in friendship in later life, when, not without pride, they acknowledged themselves as "Co-Lucianists" in allusion to their former teacher. Sources not well disposed to Arius attributed to him charming manners, a strictly ascetical manner of life, a general education, and a special talent for "dialectics." From 318 through 319 he expounded in his sermons and teaching an idea of the *Logos* and his relation to the Father, for which he found a considerable following within his congregation, in a part of the clergy, and especially among the consecrated virgins; whereas others decisively rejected it. When his bishop, Alexander, learned of the special views of his priest, he did not at first regard the matter as cause for alarm but believed that it should be examined in a theological discussion in which both sides could express and justify their ideas. And so, in the presence of Alexander, Arius stated that, in his opinion, "the Son of God was created out of nonbeing, that there was a time when he did not exist, that, according to his will, he was capable of evil as well as of virtue, and that he is a creature and created," while his opponents insisted on the consubstantiality and eternity of the Son with the Father. Alexander, who praised both sides for their theological zeal, finally accepted the second view mentioned and ordered Arius never to propound his opinion again.

Since Arius resolutely refused to comply, and Bishop Alexander could only fear that the peace of the Church of Alexandria was seriously threatened, because Arius could count on a certain following among the clergy, he excommunicated him and his clerical adherents. If Alexander believed that Arius was, by this action, condemned, together with his following, to the condition of an insignificant sect, he was greatly mistaken. The originator of the discussion did not intend to recognize the excommunication and leave the Church: instead, he wanted to bring his ideas to victory within the Church. For such an undertaking he could expect success, there being no unanimous opinion in this theological question, and a considerable part of the episcopate sympathized with his theses. Hence, when in a letter to the influential bishop of the imperial capital, Eusebius of Nicomedia, a "Co-Lucianist," he gave an account of the existing confrontation in Alexandria, he took the definitive step which deprived the conflict of its local limitations and could only gain for it an impact throughout the Church. Arius' making contact in this way with the episcopate outside Egypt now forced Bishop Alexander to a more decisive action. He summoned, probably in 319, a synod of all Egypt — apparently some 100 bishops. He made known the result of their deliberations in an encyclical to all bishops of the Catholic Church: Arius and his supporters in the Egyptian and Libyan clergy were excluded from the Church because of their "errors which dishonored Christ"; the supporters were six priests, the same number of deacons, in addition to Bishops Secundus and Theonas, both Libyans like Arius; later, two more priests and four deacons were included. The circular gave a concise exposition of the Arian propositions and a somewhat more detailed refutation; it also contained a sharp personal reference to Eusebius of Nicomedia, which declared that Alexander knew who would play a leading role on the opposite side in the now unavoidable expansion of the conflict. Not without alarm, Eusebius had replied to Arius in regard to the latter's letter: "You think correctly, but pray that all may think in the same way"; nevertheless, he at once set to work with energy and became the zealous propagator of the ideas of the Alexandrian priest. Arius had meanwhile left Egypt and finally — after a brief stay with Eusebius of Caesarea, who likewise supported him for a short time — arrived in Nicomedia, which now became a center of Arian propaganda, very effectively directed by the subtle Eusebius. As early as 320 a Bithynian synod that he had convoked sent a circular to all bishops which called for the restoration of ecclesiastical communion with those who had been condemned, since they were orthodox; pressure should be put on Alexander to receive them back. Arius drew up a profession of faith, which, in his own name and that of his friends who had been excommunicated with him, protested that their faith was that which they had heard Alexander proclaim within the Church of Alexandria: according to it, only the Father is eternal, he alone is without beginning, but the Son is God's perfect creature, he does not possess his being together with the Father, since the Father existed before the Son. Probably at this time he also wrote a work entitled *Thalia,* or *Banquet,* a mixture of prose and verse, in which he recruited for his ideas in popular form.

From many sides, Alexander was now pressed to issue a revision of his judgment on Arius, but he felt himself all the more obliged to warn others about him and his teaching. In a bulky treatise for Bishop Alexander of Thessalonica, which was, however, intended as a circular for other bishops, Arius and the priest Achilleus were branded as the real causes of the disturbance, who, with total disregard of the apostolic tradition, were, following the example of the Jews, waging war against Christ and denying his divinity. An encyclical sent by Alexander to all the bishops of the East, and preserved in a Syrian fragment, obtained the assent of some 200 bishops, not only the Egyptians but also those of Palestine, Asia Minor, Greece, and the Balkan Peninsula. Also, Pope Silvester I in Rome was informed of the events in Alexandria and of the excommunication of the Alexandrian clerics. These were merely examples of a much more copious correspondence on this question: Epiphanius was acquainted with a collection of some seventy letters of Alexander relating to this matter.

As a consequence of the literary feud, which was soon conducted in full vehemence, in which mutual distortions of the teaching and viewpoint of the one side were alleged by the other, and crude accusations of a personal nature were adduced against one another, the fronts quite early hardened into clear intransigence. At this stage the split in Eastern Christianity became known to the Emperor Constantine, probably through the bishops of the East, and it seems that at first, because of a certain embarrassment, he was not informed about the entire seriousness or about the theological significance of the quarrel. Otherwise, his first attitude is scarcely intelligible, as it appears in a letter to Alexander and Arius, which he had delivered at Alexandria by his western episcopal adviser, Hosius of Córdoba. Here the cause of the quarrel is seen in a completely unnecessary discussion of an unimportant point of the exegesis of a scriptural passage (Prov. 8:22), on which indeed there could be private, differing views, but which should not rashly be made public. Reference was made to the example of the philosophers, among whom quite often disagreement prevailed in individual questions of the systems represented by them without this leading to division among their followers. Hence the two opponents were summoned to become reconciled and to restore peace and unity in the Church so that general harmony, his political goal, could be assured in the Empire. The comparison of the Church with a school of philosophy and the evaluation of the essence of the discussion as an unimportant question of detail make clear how superficially at that time the Emperor had grasped the nature of the Church and the understanding of the figure of Christ; it likewise shows how very much he mistook the situation if he thought that it could be rectified by a summons to the two original spokesmen to become reconciled. In reality, a quite long-standing dispute over a fundamental question of Christian theology had cropped up once again: on its solution depended whether Christianity would lose or retain its deepest religious riches, whether it would remain a revealed religion or not.

A half-century before Arius the question of the relationship of Father and Son had been discussed by Greek and Latin theologians, and then too, by a striking parallel, a representative of the Alexandrian school and an Antiochene played a leading role, even though not in direct discussion. At that time theological terms and formulations which were characteristic of the discussions in the Arian controversy played a special role. At Antioch the bishop of that day, Paul of Samosata, declared around 260 that the biblical expression "Son of God' signified only the Man Jesus, born of the Virgin Mary, in whom the *Logos* had taken up his dwelling, but in order to safeguard the unity of God, Paul acknowledged in the *Logos* or divine *Sophia* no *hypostasis* of its own, but let it consist in God, "just as the human reason in the human heart." Hence to him the unity of God was the highest principle, and he was to be claimed as the representative of an emphatic Monarchianism. However, he conceded the designation of God to the Man Jesus, because the divine wisdom was operative in him in a special way, just as the prophets and saints were participants in the divine aid. At the Second Synod of Antioch (ca. 268) the expression *homoousios* played a role in the discussion; its improper use by Paul was condemned, but there was no intention of thereby entirely rejecting it in speculation on the Trinity. For, shortly before, Bishop Dionysius of Alexandria had been blamed by the Roman Bishop of the same name (259–68) because of his excessive reserve in regard to this terminology, and in a letter justifying his attitude he had to admit that the expression, even though it was not biblical, was nevertheless acceptable if properly understood. From these two discussions it is clear that in the third century the term *homoousios* was not yet so amply clarified that it could be used safely and without possible misunderstanding in theological statements on the Trinity; hence no exact terminology was yet available for dogmatic formulation.

The question of the relationship of the Son to the Father had also intensively engaged the most important theologian of the third century in the East, and Origen's view became everywhere discernible in its effect on the struggle over the orthodox understanding of the Trinitarian doctrine in the fourth century. He expressed very clearly and unequivocally that the *Logos* is a divine being, and when a bishop of his day, Beryllos of Bostra, on the frontier of Arabia, proposed the thesis that Jesus Christ was only a man, whom the Virgin Mary bore, at the request of the bishops of the province of Arabia Origen undertook a journey to Bostra in order to refute this thesis at a synod. But even Origen had not yet achieved the utmost clarity in the same question. There are numerous expressions of his which indicate that, while he ascribed to the *Logos* a divine dignity, he still subordinated him to the Father, perhaps under the influence of Neoplatonic ideas.

Finally, it is to be noted that the intellectual climate of Alexandria could still be under a certain influence of Gnostic ideas, which also taught a graduated hierarchy of divine beings, and, when Arius propounded his theology, many an Alexandrian

Christian may have been reminded of such Gnostic speculation. Later Athanasius accused Arius of being dependent on the system of the Gnostic Valentine.

The Council of Nicaea and Its Outcome

At Alexandria Bishop Hosius soon had to recognize that the way envisaged by the Emperor for a settlement of the dispute — reconciliation of Arius with his bishop and cessation of all public discussion of the controverted point — was not at all practicable. He hardly even encountered the already condemned Arius in the Egyptian capital, and it was not difficult for Alexander to convince the Emperor's theological adviser that the question was of the greatest theological significance and had definitively to be settled. And so Hosius probably went back directly to Nicomedia to see the Emperor in order to report to him on the failure of his mission. Soon both of them understood that there was only one possible way of restoring peace to the Church: to summon the entire episcopate of the Church to a great synod, which, after exhaustive consultation, would have to issue a binding decision.

The early sources all attribute to the Emperor Constantine the initiative for this solution, and they are to be believed. In the early phase of the Donatist controversy he had hit upon the convocation of the Synod of Arles (314) for a like procedure, so that the manner now chosen represented absolutely nothing new. Besides, in the meantime the Emperor must have learned that a second question, that of the date of Easter, also needed solving in order to put an end to varying practice in some provinces. It is certain that Constantine neither had negotiations with Rome on an eventual convocation of the great synod nor did he ask the consent of the Roman bishop.

The invitations to the bishops of East and West specified Nicaea in Bithynia as the place of meeting and May 325 as the date for beginning the deliberations. Many a bishop may have read in the text of the invitation, not without pleasure, that he might use the public post *gratis* for the journey and that he was the Emperor's guest during the sessions.

The number of participants in the Council is not clearly established. Eusebius says there were more than 250; Athanasius, also an eyewitness, on one occasion gives the round figure of 300, but elsewhere he gives 318. Later historians uphold this last number, especially since it had a biblical mystical prototype: Abraham's troop of retainers amounted to 318 (Gen. 14:14).

Among the Council Fathers were revered figures who, like Paul of Neocaesarea and the Egyptian Paphnutius, had distinguished themselves in the persecution of Diocletian by their constancy, but a leading role in the theological discussion was confined to a minority. To it belonged Alexander of Alexandria, who had hitherto taken the lead in the fight against Arius; Eustathius, bishop of the Syrian capital and splendid theologian, who as a staunch opponent of Arianism would later have to experience exile and would refute the erroneous doctrine in a large work that is unfortunately lost; Marcellus of Ancyra, whose hostility to the teaching of Arius would later drive him to extreme opposition and lead to his own condemnation at the Second General Council in 381. To the group of firm opponents of Arius belonged also Macarius, Bishop of Jerusalem. The faction of Arius' friends was led by Bishop Eusebius of Nicomedia; right after him is to be mentioned his name-sake, the head of the congregation of Caesarea in Palestine, who in dogmatic speculative questions did not reveal any of that special aptitude that would gain for him at Nicaea the favor of Constantine, which he later knew so well how to utilize again and again.

The Latin West was only poorly represented, but this is not difficult to under-stand: the long journey, even with the possibility of using the public post, must have caused many a bishop from Africa or Gaul, Italy or Britain to hesitate, and so only five complied with the Emperor's invitation. At their head stood Hosius of Córdoba, who had long been the Emperor's adviser but was very likely also the representative of the Pope, for he always comes first in the list of names of the bishops. Rome also sent two priests, Vitus and Vincent, who sat with Hosius. Of the remaining four bishops, only one is adequately known to Church history, Caecilian of Carthage, whose name is intimately related to the outbreak of the Donatist quarrel.

Even at the first general council there were men who would today be called *periti* theological advisers of the bishops, as, for example, the youthful deacon Athanasius of Alexandria, who accompanied Alexander and often intervened in the debates. In addition, there were present a number of interested educated laymen, who eagerly discussed the progress of the discussions among themselves.

Even before the solemn opening of the Council, conversations had started among the Council Fathers on the principal question which had brought them together; naturally in these the representatives of the "pro" and "contra" met and at times sought to strengthen their faction by gaining the as yet undecided. But the embarrassing spectacle of intrigues was also not absent from the first ecumenical council. The Emperor was presented with documents in which this or that bishop was accused of personal lapses, until Constantine called the bishops together, displayed the unread and probably also anonymous letters, had them burned before their eyes, gave them a few serious words on fraternal concord among bishops, and called upon them to turn to the real task that had brought them to Nicaea.

Since the church of the congregation of Nicaea scarcely offered adequate space for all the activities of the Council, the Emperor had placed his own palace in the city at its disposal for the entire period of the sessions. Eusebius enthusiastically and lyrically described the solemn opening, which took place on 20 May 325. The bishops had taken their seats along the two long sides of the meeting hall and eagerly awaited the entry of the Emperor, for whom a gilded chair had been set up. It made a strong impression on them when the tall figure of the Emperor, adorned in purple, strode through their ranks and did not take his place until by signs he had directed the bishops to sit. After a brief greeting by one of the bishops, the Emperor began a speech in Latin in which the admonition to peace and harmony within the Church was of unmistakable emphasis: an exhaustive discussion of the causes of the conflict should open the way to reconciliation and peace, and in this way the bishops would also render to him, their "fellow servant," a vast favor. Then he turned over the floor to the presidents of the synod.

Since the acts of the Council of Nicaea have not been preserved, neither a reconstruction of the order of business or of the exact chronological course of the debates nor an exact number of the sessions or even of the total duration of the Council is possible. Apparently, the faction friendly to Arius at once seized the initiative and proposed a formula of faith into which essential elements of Arian theology seem to have been incorporated. But it encountered the violent protest of the opposition, as did also the passages read aloud from Arius' *Thalia,* and it quickly became clear that his extreme formulations had no chance of being accepted by the Council. Then the supple Eusebius of Caesarea intervened in the debates with a compromise proposal and recommended to the Council the acceptance of the baptismal creed in use in his diocese. The bishops recognized fully the orthodoxy of this creed, and Constantine too regarded it as correct, as Eusebius stresses, not without self-satisfaction, but some held that certain supplements were indispensable whereby the statements just discussed should be made precise and an explanation of the creed in the Arian sense should be excluded.

It was precisely the supplementary propositions that produced the at times violent discussion to flare up again and again, and in it there was no lack of mutual recriminations on both sides. In particular, the acceptance of the word *homoousios* ("one in being"), which in the sequel was destined to become the keyword and slogan of Nicene theology, caused long debates. It not only seemed unacceptable to the expressly Arian-oriented bishops, but could produce uneasiness in many another eastern bishop, as its hitherto constantly varying history demonstrated. To the representatives of the Latin Church, on the other hand, it could seem quite appropriate, since they found in it the exact parallel to what in the West since the time of Tertullian was expressed by *consubstantialis* or *eiusdem substantiae.* Eusebius ascribes the acceptance of *homoousios* into the text of the Nicene Creed simply to the initiative of the Emperor, who exerted himself to the utmost in regard to the orthodox interpretation of the term by the Greeks and to the reconciling of the opposing viewpoints. It is very probable that it was suggested to Constantine by Hosius of Córdoba. The other individual formulas adopted in the definitive text of the Creed — "eternally begotten of the Father, God from God, Light from Light, true God from true God, begotten, not made, one in Being with the Father" — assured that the statements concerning Christ would not be susceptible of any Arian interpretation. The conclusion also contained an unequivocal rejection of the Arian theology: "But some say: 'There was a time in which he was not' and 'Before he was born, he was not' and 'He was created out of nothing,' or they claim that the Son of God is of another substance (*hypostasis*) or another being (*ousia*), or he was created or subject to change or alteration. The Catholic and Apostolic Church declares them excluded from its membership." This excommunication affected primarily Arius himself and his two episcopal friends, Secundus and Theonas, since, except for them, all the other Arians signed the Creed which had been unambiguously recommended for adoption by the Emperor. For Arius it must have been a bitter disappointment that the Co-Lucianists had thus abandoned him: for him there now remained the road to exile, and the ban did not spare his own writings and those of his adherents. When Eusebius notes that, through his diplomatic skill and his personal charm, the Emperor had brought it about that the bishops "were of one mind and one view on all points" this was surely not true of all those who had been Arians previously and was probably not true even of himself. Men like Eusebius of Nicomedia and Theognis of Nicaea still stood secretly at the side of the condemned Arius, but they did not dare to directly attack the Creed that had been so solemnly approved by the Emperor so long as he lived. However, they soon found ways and means to bring defenders of the Creed into discredit with the Emperor and thereby began the fierce struggle which the faith of Nicaea had to endure for decades in order that it might be accepted in the Universal Church.

After the adoption of the Creed, the Council Fathers took up the other points of the agenda. In the matter of the date of Easter they agreed on the practice of the greater part of the Church, which celebrated the solemnity of the Resurrection on the Sunday after 14 Nisan. Then disciplinary questions were discussed, and the decisions were set down in twenty canons. Finally, the Council decided on a generous solution for the schism caused in Egypt by Bishop Meletius of Lycopolis: Meletius was to retain his position as bishop and his see; the bishops and clerics ordained by him were received back into the Catholic Church after the imposition of hands, and the bishops could be promoted to sees as they became vacant, but only with the consent of the Metropolitan of Alexandria.

Constantine tried quickly and effectively to assure the newly won unity in the faith, first by means of a solemn and impressive closing of the Council. Probably after the adoption of the Creed and in connection with the twentieth anniversary of his accession, he gave a splendid banquet for the Council Fathers in his palace at Nicomedia; Eusebius, always so easily enthused, compared it to the glory of the heavenly kingdom. The bishops gladly accepted the presents which Constantine gave to each of them on this occasion. Before their departure he asked all of them to come to him once more, admonished them henceforth "to maintain peace among themselves, to avoid the envy that leads to strife," and recommended himself to their prayers. Soon afterward, he sent a comprehensive report on the Council "to the churches" — this probably meant chiefly those not represented at Nicaea — and in it he unambiguously attributed to himself the initiative for the great Synod. The Emperor assured the faithful that all questions had been carefully examined and unity in the Church had thereby been achieved. He devoted much space to the decree on the uniform date of Easter and stressed in surprisingly sharp words the necessity of holding Christianity at a distance from Judaism. A special letter went to the congregation of Alexandria in which Constantine expressed his joy over the restoration of unity of faith and once again rejected the errors of Arius. The above-mentioned special synodal letter of the Council probably went to all the larger communities. In the still extant copy to the Christians of Egypt and Libya the excommunication of Arius and his two episcopal friends is made known and especially justified by the condemnation of his teaching.

The Council of Nicaea, with its decision on the faith, was an event of the utmost importance for an understanding of Church history as a whole, especially the history of the councils. In it we find the first council in history which without any doubt possessed an ecumenical character, since to it were invited bishops from all the geographical areas of Christianity, and they attended, even though in varying strength. This first ecumenical council, with its adoption and promulgation of its Creed, made a decision in the area of faith which was equivalent to a dogmatic definition. For the entire course of the Council and the long struggle of the Council Fathers over a formula that as clearly as possible rendered the testimony of faith made clear their intention here to issue a definitive judgment that bound the Universal Church in a controverted question of belief. The manner of achieving the decision revealed at the same time a process that would be of the greatest significance in the history of dogma. The Church seeks to assure individual doctrines of faith from misinterpretation or heretical explanation in such a way that it clarifies the testimony hitherto accepted by complementary additions, elucidates them by more precise formulation, and for that purpose even takes philosophical terms into its service, if these seem appropriate. The guaranteeing of the threatened statement of faith in its orthodox sense is, accordingly, a decisive factor in the development of dogma. The goal of the Council was achieved despite all human shortcomings and meanness, despite all the risks which proceeded also from Constantine's pressure, which, while it really threatened the freedom of individual bishops, did not destroy it. The noteworthy remark in the Emperor's letter to the congregation of Alexandria exactly touches the theological reality here referred to: "What the 300 bishops have decided is nothing else than the decree of God, for the Holy Spirit, present in these men, made known the will of God." The validity of this statement is not lessened by the fact that in the next five decades of the fourth century there raged a struggle over the recognition of the Nicene theology, which convulsed the Church to its innermost depths and renewed the fear of its early dissolution into various denominations.

The Development to the Death of Constantine (337)

Only a few months after the ending of the Council it was plain that the Arian faction would not abandon the struggle for its understanding of the Trinitarian theology. Two of its leading bishops, Eusebius of Nicomedia and Theognis of Nicaea, informed the Emperor that they withdrew their assent to the Creed of 325. The Emperor, not accustomed to seeing decisions which he had solemnly approved treated in this fashion, regarded this step as self-exclusion from the ecclesiastical community, sent the two bishops into exile in Gaul, and gave their former sees to prelates loyal to Nicaea. A letter to the congregation of Nicomedia makes known Constantine's great displeasure with the malicious behavior of its bishop.

But from the beginning of 328 a reversal in the Emperor's attitude began to appear — not, it is true, in his position with regard to the Council, but concerning individual representatives of the pro-Arian faction. The reasons for the change are difficult to ascertain clearly. In that year the exiled Bishops Eusebius and Theognis were permitted to return from banishment and again occupy their former sees of Nicomedia and Nicaea. And now that same Eusebius, who three years previously had been condemned by the Emperor in the harshest terms, succeeded more and more in gaining the Emperor's ear and favor and finally in occupying that very position which earlier Hosius of Córdoba, who had probably returned to his Spanish see after the Council, had held as theological adviser and which automatically made him the effective promoter of the interests of Arius. Here one may probably take into account the influence of Constantine's stepsister, Constantia, who lived in Nicomedia and whose confidence the bishop of the imperial capital, a member of the upper class, had long possessed. Eusebius of Caesarea in Palestine had probably also contributed to the change of attitude, for his culture and his rhetorical talents strongly impressed the Emperor, all the more since his courtliness avoided any uncouth stressing of opposing views. It is also possible that the Empress-Mother Helena spoke in praise of him at court when she reported on her impressions of her journey to the Holy Land, where of course she met the bishop of the capital of the Province of Palestine.

Soon after his return from exile, Eusebius of Nicomedia energetically and methodically assumed the leadership of the Arian faction. He clearly understood that the fight must not be conducted directly against the Nicene Creed, because that would certainly provoke the Emperor's opposition. It was more important first to eliminate the leading personalities of the opposition. Following the close of the Council, Bishop Eustathius of Antioch had at first become the dominant figure of this group. Even at Nicaea he had played a strong role, opposing Arius by literary means, and through his sarcasm he had irritated Eusebius of Nicomedia by making fun of his new career. The Emperor was cleverly told that Eustathius was a morally doubtful character, again and again disturbed the religious peace, and had expressed himself disrespectfully in regard to the Emperor's Mother. The Emperor gave his assent to a synod held at Antioch ca. 331, at which the friends of Arius deposed Eustathius, whom the Emperor then exiled to Thrace. Before long, he was followed by eight bishops of his group; then, encouraged by this success, the Arian party directed its attack against Athanasius, who had been elected to the see of Alexandria after Alexander's death in 328. At Nicaea itself they had acquired a lasting impression of this new bishop's energy and constancy and could see in him the actual rising champion of the Nicene theology.

In his case too the Arians' accusation chose the route of insinuation and represented as the real cause of the still nonexistent religious peace the tyrannical character of the Bishop of Alexandria, who did not trouble himself about law and order and stopped at no methods of force to make his own interests prevail. Among other things, he was supposed to have murdered Bishop Arsenius, who, as a Meletian, had not submitted unconditionally; he had had other Meletian bishops flogged and had profaned a chalice used in the liturgy. The Emperor was so impressed by these charges that he gave instructions that the bishops whom he had invited to the dedication of the church he had built at Jerusalem over the tomb of Christ should treat the case of Athanasius at a synod in nearby Tyre (335). The Synod was completely dominated by the Arian faction, which admitted almost none but opponents of Athanasius. The Egyptian bishops in his retinue were turned away as uninvited; furthermore, the Emperor's representative, Count Flavius Dionysius, was a declared adherent of the Arian faction. At Tyre there also appeared for the first time two bishops from Pannonia who would often play a changing role in the later confrontations, Valens of Mursa and Ursacius of Singidunum, whom Arius had gained for his views, probably during his exile. At this Synod Athanasius was not only in the role of the accused; he also stood before men who almost without exception were his bitter opponents, so that here he could expect no just verdict and even had to fear for his life. Deciding to leave Tyre secretly, he went to Constantinople to meet the Emperor in person. The Synod at once decreed his deposition. Since Athanasius was not admitted to an audience, he addressed the Emperor directly when the latter had gone riding on horseback, described the proceedings at Tyre, and asked for justice. At first Constantine rendered no decision but commanded the participants of the Synod of Tyre to come to Constantinople; but only four of them, the two Eusebiuses, Ursacius, and Valens, appeared. They advanced a new charge against Athanasius, which amounted to high treason: that he sabotaged the imperial decrees in Egypt and prevented the export of the grain necessary for the capital's life. The Emperor could have decreed the death penalty for these crimes, but instead he ordered the exile of Athanasius to Trier. It is by no means clear why Constantine did not have this ridiculous accusation more thoroughly investigated. It seems to have been for him a welcome pretext for finally removing far from the East a troublesome man, who, in his view, stood in the way of reconciliation.

Now, of course, the Arian party had a free hand, and they wanted to crown their series of successes thus far with the full rehabilitation of Arius, hence with his absolution from censure and reinstatement in his priestly rights. For him too the situation had improved. It is true that as late as 333 the Emperor had issued an edict against him and his adherents and in a rather lengthy letter to Arius and his friends he had once more repudiated their doctrine. But at the latest in November 334 Arius received a letter from the Emperor, which urgently invited him to court for an exchange of views. Arius on this occasion presented to Constantine a profession of faith, which skillfully evaded the very point at issue but seemed to the Emperor to prove that Arius did not teach what his opponents attributed to him. Hence he referred him to a future synod, which should absolve him from excommunication. This possibility presented itself to the Arian bishops at the above-mentioned meeting in Jerusalem. They declared Arius' doctrine to be orthodox and for this purpose appealed to the profession of faith that he had presented. Then they lifted the excommunication pronounced against him at Nicaea and asked the Emperor to reinstate him in his priestly rights. This was intended to take place in a solemn ecclesiastical function, but Arius died shortly before. The Emperor's death the next year was to mean the beginning of further progress upward for the Arians. The eastern part of the Empire fell to his son Constantius II, who had chosen Arianism as his faith and would procure exclusive recognition for it during the twenty-four years of his reign, when necessary with any means available.

CHAPTER 34

The Struggle over the Council of Nicaea
under the Sons of Constantine

Constantine the Great believed he had made sufficient provision for the future of the empire when in 335 he informed his three sons of his planned division of its territory. To Constantine II went the West, to Constantius II, the East, and the central portion went to Constans, but within months of the accession of these three Augusti, a bloodbath in Constantinople had taken the lives of all of the male relatives of the Augusti, except for the brothers Gallus and Julian, nephews of Constantine, and within four years, Constantine II, preparing for war against Constans, was killed in ambush, and Constans had assumed control of everything from the Balkans westward, and the three had become two.

There was no reaction in favor of paganism by any of the young Emperors; all had been raised in Christian faith and their convictions accorded with it. Both surviving Augusti, in fact, departed from the relative religious toleration of their father toward paganism and its private practices, as witness a series of legislative measures. The year 341 C.E. proved decisive in this area. Constantius issued an edict which began: *Cesset superstitio, sacrificiorum aboleatur insania* (Cod. Theod. 16, 10, 2). What pagan sacrifices are meant here is unclear, but the harsh tone is unmistakable, and through it Christians felt encouraged to more bellicose reactions toward paganism. Occasionally this aggressive attitude exploded into actual measures taken by Christians against individual pagan sanctuaries in the East. That imperial officials had again and again to issue decrees enjoining the earlier prohibitions indicates the persistence of paganism and its worship practices, at least in secret. Constantius, of course, made the occasional compromise toward the senatorial faction in old Rome for political expediency, e.g., but his attitude was basically hostile toward paganism.

Christians, of course, awaited with bated breath the first expressions the new emperors in the conflict for or against the Nicene Creed, which had the faithful in the East split into two camps wholly at odds with each other. At first, Athanasius and the adherents to the creed were in favor: Constantine II, within three weeks of his father's death, had sent a letter to the Church in Alexandria to inform them that Athanasius was free to return from exile. Other bishops, Nicene loyalists, were permitted to return to their sees too. This occurred not without difficulty however. During the bishops' exiles, new incumbents had been elected, who, understandably, were reluctant to stand down in favor of those returning. Some social unrest ensued in many places.

The Eusebians — the faction surrounding Eusebius of Nicomedia — were naturally dismayed to see their most capable opponent, Athanasius, return to Alexandria and, through a council, tried to render his resumption of his cathedra canonically impossible (Synod of Tyre, 335). Athanasius responded with rigor and firmness. A synod of all the Egyptian bishops, convoked by him in 338, gave him a vote of confidence and, in a circular letter to all bishops throughout the Church maintained Athanasius' full right to return to his see. This encyclical provoked the

Eusebians to an ill-advised step. They asked the Pope to convoke a synod to decide Athanasius' case, abandoning, thereby, the validity of the decree the Synod of Tyre which they had so strongly stressed. They also elected — uncanonically — Gregory of Cappadocia as a successor to Athanasius. The Egyptian reaction was so violent that Gregory could not enter the capital until 339 and then under military protection. But the force was sufficient to coerce Athanasius back into exile. Meanwhile, Pope Julius had issued invitations for the synod initially requested by the Eusebians, but to which they now declined to come, and tried to hark back to their original position based on the Synod Tyre. With Athanasius and some of his fellow exiles present, the Roman council adjudicated in favor of Athanasius. The council's decision had no effect on the actual circumstances. Athanasius had to remain in the West and maintain contact with his loyalists in Alexandria by mail. The opponents of *homoousios* however met at the dedication of Constantius' new church in Antioch, 341. They sent out a circular letter in which they carefully avoided expressing allegiance to Arius, but in which they professed their faith by avoiding every formula which had been adopted into the Nicene Creed.

The Synod of Serdica and Its Sequel

Meanwhile, Pope Julius asked Constans to obtain his brother's consent to a new synod, to be attended by bishops from both parts of the Empire, which should definitively end the conflict. With Constantius' agreement, a council was summoned to Serdica (Sofia) in the Balkan Peninsula, a city within Constans' territory, but next to the border of the Eastern Empire.

Both factions arrived there in autumn, 342 or 343. At the head the approximately ninety western bishops were Hosius of Córdoba, now an elderly man, and two priests representing Pope Julius. The easterners were fewer in number (between seventy-five and eighty) and were led by Stephen of Antioch and Acacius of Caesarea in Palestine — Eusebius of Nicomedia, who had become Bishop of Constantinople, had died in 341 — but, characteristically, they were accompanied by two high officials of Constantius. Due to the intransigence of the eastern bloc, who insisted as a *conditio sine qua non* that the deposed eastern bishops, Athanasius, Marcellus of Ancyra, and Asclepas of Gaza, were not to take part in the synod, since, as the accused they might have neither seat nor voice in it, the two sides met only once in common session. The easterners then met and composed an encyclical for the whole Church in which they restated their views of the matter and condemning not only Athanasius and Marcellus, but also the leading western bishops (Pope Julius, Hosius of Córdoba, and Maximinus of Trier), because through them "Marcellus, Athanasius, and the other criminals" had been "received again into the ecclesiastical community." The easterners then departed the city by night on a pretext of a patriotic duty.

That left the westerners alone to complete the agenda of the Synod. After a documentary examination of the accused, the Synod found the charges unfounded and that the enemies of the accused, together with the successors in the sees of the accused, were guilty of many serious breaches of canon law. The westerners then cut off the leading men of the East from the ecclesiastical community.

Athanasius successfully opposed the inclination to promulgate a new creed on the grounds of the sufficiency of the Nicene Creed. The Synod then apprised the bishops of the universal Church of their conclusions, asking those not present to ratify it with their assent.

Perhaps the greatest importance of the Synod of Serdica lies in its having promulgated disciplinary regulations in twenty-one canons. Now some clarity and order came into the picture: a deposed bishop had the right to appeal the verdict, which might be made solely by a synod in his province in this form: his fellow-bishops had to submit the matter to the Bishop of Rome; it was up to the Pope to decide if the judgment were just or to refer the case for further consideration to a synod in a neighboring province where he himself might be represented (Can. 3, 4, 7). Bishops were enjoined from enticing clerics from other dioceses to their own, from ordaining a man without his own bishop's approbation, and from giving a parish to one who had been excommunicated by his own bishop (Can. 16, 18, 19). The bishop's duty of residence was strictly interpreted and his translation to another diocese prohibited (Can. 14, 15; 1, 2). Lengthy journeys of bishops to the imperial court were forbidden (Can. 8–12). The bishops then appealed to Constantius to end the intrigues and violence of individual bishops against their confreres and that government officials should not interfere in ecclesiastical affairs.

On the whole, except for its canons, the Synod of Serdica did not achieve, much positive result. The reciprocal excommunications of eastern and western leaders envenomed the atmosphere and the breach between East and West was already visible and became one of the first stages in the long process of alienation which would finally lead to the definitive schism. This alienation proved especially serious when the political power of one part of the Empire stood behind the notion that it acted for its episcopate in dogmatic or disciplinary questions. For instance, Constantius took sides against all who were in sympathy with Serdica, banished bishops and clerics, and took steps to ensure that those "rehabilitated" at Serdica not return home. Then unexpected help from the West arrived. Constans not only cared for the ecclesiastical peace in the West, but exerted pressure on his older brother to allow the Athanasians their rights in the East. Not until the death of Bishop Gregory in Alexandria (345), however, did Constantius actually invite Athanasius to return, although in the interim, he made life easier for Athanasius' adherents in Egypt. Athanasius returned in triumph and in communion with more than 400 bishops, including his old opponents, Ursacius and Valens, who had bowed to Serdica. All seemed ripe for a period of peace, until a political development frustrated the hope once again. Constans was murdered by mutinous troops, and it took Constantius three years to subdue the West and to emerge as sole Emperor. The religious policy of the state was once again in the hands of one man.

The Religious Policy of Constantius II as Sole Emperor (350–61)

It appeared at first that Athanasius' apprehensions about Constantius' religious policies were without foundation. But his reprieve was short-lived. The stronger Constantius grew in his war in the West, the stronger grew the hostile voices of Athanasius' opponents. Their voices grew more strident when in 352, one of Athanasius' most powerful supporters, Pope Julius died. The new pope, Liberius (352–66), also sided with Athanasius and appealed to Constantius to summon a synod to reestablish peace between West and East. The synod was held at Arles in 353, but there was no discussion, only a draft decision condemning Athanasius for the bishops to sign. Under imperial threat of deposition and exile for refusing signature, all save one of the Gallic bishops signed. The pope demanded of the emperor the summoning of another general council, and Constantius, sensing he could gain his way without serious opposition, readily acceded, and a council was convoked at Milan in 355. Once again the Emperor would brook no opposition and, countering every move by his opponents, he "persuaded" all save three bishops to sign the condemnation of Athanasius. The three were Eusebius of Vercelli, Lucifer of Cagliari, and Dionysius of Milan, who were exiled. Auxentius of Cappadocia, an Arian, was forced upon the Milanese Catholics as their bishop, despite the fact he could not even speak their language. After Milan, the emperor's agents tracked down other bishops for their signatures too. In Gaul, it was Hilary of Poitiers, who would during the next years play a crucial role in preventing the Latin West from becoming Arian, who led the opposition, and at yet another synod at Béziers (356), only he and one other refused to sign and went into Phrygian exile too.

Finally, there was still really only one western bishop whose attitude made a difference to the Emperor, the bishop of Rome, Pope Liberius. The Emperor sought to bring the Pope into line through bribery, and, being rebuffed, only later used coercion to bring Liberius to the court in Milan, where there were sharp confrontations between the excessively excitable Emperor and the Pope, who with dignified firmness refused to condemn the "godless Athanasius, whose insolence cannot be described," as the Emperor put it. Steadfast in his position, Liberius was sent into exile in Thrace. Liberius refused the Emperor's gift for his expenses as well as the Empress'. Liberius was "succeeded" by a deacon, Felix, who lacked the character to refuse the office. In this way almost every voice of effective opposition was silenced, save only the now almost 100–year old Bishop of Córdoba, Hosius, and when Hosius too stood his ground against him, the Emperor had him brought to the East and imprisoned, probably at Sirmium.

Having intimidated the West, the Emperor was freer to turn on Athanasius in Alexandria. When the wily bishop based his resistance on the Emperor's own letters to him of an earlier period promising him support and sympathy, and when an attempt to stir up a popular revolt failed, the Emperor sent his troops into St. Theonas Church during a liturgy where Athanasius was present. In the resulting tumult, Athanasius escaped and found his way to the monks in the desert who received him with great joy. Meanwhile Alexandria suffered through the vindictive episcopate of George, another foreigner, who gave the Catholics' churches to the Arians and ran a real regime of terror against any whose loyalties were with Athanasius. After eighteen months, the people put Bishop George to flight, but still Athanasius was not able to return. And the Nicene defenders were driven out of public view. In hiding among the Egyptian monks, Athanasius wrote several important works: *Apologia to the Emperor Constantius,* in which he refuted the calumnies being spread abroad about him; *Apologia for His Flight* was popular and addressed to the Universal Church. *Apologeticus against the Arians* is of inestimable value for the history of the years 339–57 because of the documents it contains. In his *History of the Arians,* which he dedicated to the Egyptian monks, he attacked his opponents pitilessly and occasionally violently.

In all these controversies, orthodox faith was not in the foreground so much as was the recognition or rejection of bishops, more precisely of Athanasius and his episcopal followers. Whoever acknowledged him was an adherent of the orthodox faith, so said his friends; whoever condemned him made a profession of peace and at the same time showed his loyalty to the Emperor, so said Constantius. Hence as soon as Athanasius' opponents acquired political influence, their primary concern seems to have been to drive from their sees all bishops who sympathized with Athanasius and to replace them with men of their own ilk. Thus it was that in the middle of the fourth century, there were very few among the bishops primarily interested in the dogmatic question. This situation changed however after 358 when Aëtius of Antioch took up the Arian cause with dialectical skill and verve. On the question of the relationship of Father and Son, he expounded the radical solution to it, namely, that the Son is neither equal to nor essentially like the Father, but at most only similar to him. Hence, he repudiated the formula use till then and came up with the formula *anomoios* [essentially unlike] to describe the relationship. He is regarded as the founder of the Anomoian or Aëtian school, the radical Arian wing. Finding little support in Antioch, Aëtius turned to Alexandria where Eunomius, later bishop of Cyzicus, came over to his views. These two men, however, by introducing a split within Arianism, became the unwitting cause of a weakening of the entire anti-Nicene movement.

Bishop Germanius of Sirmium shared Aëtius' views as well, and in 357 he sketched a new creed in which the expressions *substantia, consubstantialis,* and *homoousios* were disavowed. They sought and succeeded in obtaining the signature of the aged Hosius, who was in Sirmium, for this formula. But the centenarian, however, whose mental vigor had long ago deserted him, still retained sufficient clarity mind and energy that no condemnation of his long-time friend Athanasius could be wrung from him. Far more important was Pope Liberius' change of mind: in four letters of his he abandons his former attitude and now condemns Athanasius, accepted the communion of his opponents, and signed a creed which hitherto he had rejected, probably that of Sirmium, 351, which need not be interpreted in a heretical sense. Upon Liberius' return to Rome in 358, to which Constantius had affixed the requirement that he share with his "successor" Felix the office and dignity of the bishop of Rome, Liberius suffered bitterly for his weakness of character. Even when the Romans' sympathies were such that Felix felt obliged to leave the city, Liberius' reputation had fallen so precipitously that he was of no significance in the theological discussions of the ensuing years.

But the Sirmium creed of 357 did not meet with Arian approval in the East, to say nothing of Gaul and North Africa. Everywhere there was strong opposition to the attack on the divinity of the Son, clearly represented by the Anomoian position; and now a more moderate trend which came closer to the Nicenes was able to move into the foreground. Its leader was the theologian Basil of Ancyra, who around Easter, 358, invited several bishops to his city and in their name, he published an important document. It decisively rejected the Anomoian thesis and proposed as a new term *homoiousios.* The similarity in nature of the Son with the

Father that was thereby expressed meant without doubt a great movement toward the Nicenes. The Emperor, who had favored the Anomoian party, now approved of this formula, and a synod at Sirmium in 358 confirmed it. Pope Liberius also signed it. Both Athanasius and Hilary regarded the formula as susceptible of an orthodox interpretation and sought discussion of it in an affable atmosphere. But Basil was intent on seeing the Anomoian bishops defeated and sent into exile. Then he sought the greatest possible solemn sanctioning or his theology, which should occur at a great general council at Nicaea.

The Double-Synod of Seleucia-Rimini (359)

Meanwhile another group of bishops got the ear of the Emperor in favor of holding two synods simultaneously, one for the West and one for the East. Such a plan was uncommonly attractive to the Emperor: The eastern synod, despite splits, could count on an Arian majority; the bishops of the West could be presumed, based on his recent experiences, willing to sign one of the creeds he had recently proposed. Seleucia in Isauria was selected for the eastern meeting; Rimini on the Adriatic for the western. A preparatory commission was summoned to Sirmium in May 359 to draft an outline of a creed which should be laid before both synods. The still extant Greek version of the draft, on which the industrious and fickle Ursacius and Valens labored, must have been no slight surprise for Basil of Ancyra. The key word was not the *homoiousios* he was pushing, but *homoios tô patri,* which thus expressed only the *likeness* of the Son to the Father. Advocates of this theology had apparently won the Emperor's favor with the argument that so vague a formula, which excluded the question of substance, could win many participants in the synods who were of the most varied tendencies. After the double-synods, representatives were to report to the Emperor and at the court to give the decrees their definitive form.

So in the summer of 359, more than 400 western bishops converged on Rimini. Only Rome was not represented; there were two bishops of Rome, so the Emperor had sent no invitation. There was an Arian minority of about 20 percent at first, whose leaders were Ursacius and Valens, Auxentius of Milan, and Saturninus of Arles. The overwhelming orthodox majority set their own agenda. Without even considering the creed of Sirmium, they excluded the minority's leaders from the ecclesiastical community, professed the Nicene Creed again, and appointed a delegation to explain their views to the Emperor. The Arians did not submit, but sent a rival delegation to Constantius. The latter delegation obtained immediate access to the Emperor; the former were left to cool their heels waiting for access. The Arian minority's representatives came among them and so confused the Creed of Sirmium in their minds with further explanations, that finally in October 359 they signed it and solemnly ratified their union with the formerly excommunicated bishops of this group.

Meanwhile the rest of the 400 bishops in Rimini waited three months for the possibility of returning to their dioceses. They were informed that permission was contingent upon their signing the Creed of Sirmium. Thus the majority fell inexorably to pieces, and in the end all, save only the exiles, signed. Constantius now had in his hands a document signed by all of these western bishops which stood in irrevocable opposition to the Nicene Creed.

The eastern synod at Seleucia met in September 359. Its 150 bishops were unevenly divided among three parties: strongest were the Homoiousians, led by Basil of Ancyra and Macedonius of Constantinople, among others; then there were the Homoians, led by Acacius of Caesarea in Palestine, and hence called the Acacians; and finally there were the Arians represented by George of Alexandria and Eudoxius of Antioch, and by far the weakest party. In the course of the synod, there was contentious discussion among the parties, but the Acacians got the ear of Constantius, since their theology coincided with the position won at Rimini. Even the Homoiousian party cared in eventually, and the Creed of Nicaea was, externally at least, completely annulled, since with the acceptance of the Homoian theology a clearly Arian view had prevailed.

The Emperor wanted this assured by an ecumenical synod which met in Constantinople in January 360. Apart from eastern bishops, only a few from Thrace were represented. Once more the Creed of Rimini was ratified, to be valid for all time. All who thought otherwise were deposed, but for disciplinary infractions, not for heterodox doctrine. Thus all the Homoiousian leaders lost their sees, and Constantius added exile to their depositions. But the most powerful personality involved, Athanasius, had not yet been found by the imperial police, and he issued an encyclical which had the effect of holding Egypt as a whole for orthodoxy. Elsewhere there were individual bishops who preferred exile to denial of their faith. The vacant sees were filled by Acacius, and as a result, the major centers of the East — Alexandria, Antioch, Constantinople, Caesarea in Palestine, and Sirmium in the Balkans, and Milan too, all had convinced Arians for bishops. All of which led Jerome to make his pithy remark: *ingemuit totus orbis et arianum se esse miratus est.* ["The world groaned and was amazed that it had become Arian"]. Nevertheless a radical alteration in the political world led to a change in the ecclesiastical sphere.

CHAPTER 35

The Attempted Restoration of Paganism by the Emperor Julian (361–63)

In April 360 Constantius directed his cousin Julian, who as Caesar was at Paris with the legions of Gaul, to send him immediately his best troops for without them he could not control the continuous disturbances along the Persian border. The soldiers thereupon acclaimed Julian as Augustus. After some hesitation, Julian accepted and began to prepare for the now inevitable military showdown with his cousin. As he led his troops eastward, Constantius fell mortally ill at Tarsus, while coming to meet him. Constantius, like his father, had a death-bed baptism and bequeathed the rule of the entire Empire to the last member the Constantinian dynasty. A few weeks later, Julian received homage as Emperor in his birthplace, Constantinople. The Empire now found itself with a ruler, who in contradistinction to his dead cousins, was a convinced adherent of paganism and at once appointed as his advisers two renowned representatives of this religion, the philosophers Maximus and Priscus.

Julian, like the sons of Constantine, was raised a Christian. He lost his mother within months of his birth and his father and a brother at the age of seven in the bloodbath in Constantinople in 337. He easily connected Constantius with the latter event and harbored a profound antipathy for his cousin as a result. His education was at the hand of clerics, and was devoutly involved in the Christian faith as a young man. By his own admission, he was very impressed by the church's charitable activities, too. Julian read voraciously to satisfy his intellectual curiosity. Being geographically isolated at Macellum in Cappadocia, thanks to Constantius' suspicions, Julian found no one to turn to in his religious crisis, and so turned to the world of Homer and Greek religion of a Hellenistic sort. When in 347 he was permitted to leave Macellum, he studied rhetoric at Constantinople and then at Nicomedia, where he met the pagan rhetor Libanius. At Pergamum he met the philosopher Aedesius, and at Ephesus, he studied Neo-Platonism with Maximus, who also introduced him into the mystery cults which he grew so to esteem. Julian was captivated by their secret ritual, and in 354, when he spent several months in Athens, he had himself secretly initiated into the Eleusinian Mysteries. His relationship with Priscus, the distinguished pagan teacher of the Athenian academy, completed Julian's religious transformation: out of the young Christian of Macellum there had developed a convinced follower of the Hellenic religion. Julian's was a complicated character: his ascetical outlook made him abjure pomp and ceremony, but also personal comfort to the point of repulsive neglect of the body. He was very loyal to his few friends, but otherwise ill at ease, especially toward subordinates. In public he was nervous and restrained, but his bravery and unpretentiousness in warfare gained him the respect his soldiers. He clung stubbornly to decisions once taken, and was intolerant of dissent. He loved the praise of the mob. He had, on his own admission, no sense of humor. Finally, he had as a blot on his character the fact that he kept up the façade of being a devout Christian for almost a decade after he had abjured the faith.

With the death of Constantius, Julian removed the mask. He quickly embarked on a program of restoring a reformed paganism to its previous place. He reversed the religious policies of his cousin and uncle. In his appointees, Julian clearly preferred pagans. The *labarum*, the standard with the Christian symbols which Constantine had introduced, was replaced by the old pagan banners. Coinage was imprinted with pagan images again. All restrictions on pagan worship were annulled; temples were reopened, sacrifices permitted, and the veneration of the gods restored. Territory was to be returned and temples rebuilt, but Julian's wishes met stout resistance in many places, where Christians refused to participate as desired. Pagans often took advantage of the new situation to seek revenge on the churches and their people, and many found martyrdom. The bloody persecution of Christians was not countenanced by Julian, but its perpetrators went unpunished.

Julian's goal was the restoration of paganism to the leading position as religion of the State, so he set up a reform program to accomplish his ends. In a restored priesthood, Julian himself took the title of Pontifex Maximus, and actively exercised the functions of the office. Every province got a high priest and a high priestess, to whom all other priests and priestesses were subordinate. An ascetic style of life was imposed on them by Julian together with directions for their reading, preaching, charitable acts, and so forth. That Julian modeled this on the Christian Church's program and organization with view to attracting converts is possible.

Julian also worked to revive the pagan system of oracles and the mystery cults; he thereby reopened the door for the return of the soothsayers, the astrologers, and the magical forms of pagan folk religion. He himself too practiced his pagan religion assiduously.

It is important that Julian coupled his pagan reform program with a measure against Christianity, which though unbloody, was over the long haul designed to threaten the existence of the faith. The school law of June 362 effectively put up a religious test to prevent Christians from being appointed as teachers. They were moreover denied access to the highly esteemed rhetorical education and to public office. In short, the plan was to reduce Christianity to a religion of the uneducated. The exclusion of even esteemed Christian teachers such as Marius Victorinus at Rome from their profession aroused a great public outcry. The law was felt by Christians to be malicious and degrading, but it was also a source of uneasiness among pagans.

It may be assumed that the disappointment over the ill success of his efforts at religious reform drove Julian along the path of greater harshness. Apart from a small minority, the people received Julian's efforts with notable apathy. Few indeed were the conversions from Christianity to paganism. Julian responded to this state of affairs by trying to legislate Christians into second-class citizens. They were prohibited high state administrative posts and even from the army (on the grounds that Christian moral doctrine forbade their using the sword).

Finally, Julian launched an assault on the bishops as leaders of the Christian congregations. Till now, Julian had spared them for diplomatic reasons. In the beginning he had even allowed those in exile to return freely, perhaps with view to enticing Arian and Catholic into renewed squabbling and thus further to weaken the Church. Athanasius returned after six years in exile among the Egyptian monks. As there was no confrontation with the Arians, but more like a reconciliation instead, Julian issued an edict in October 362 ordering Athanasius' expulsion renewed. An appeal from Alexandria for his recall was met with extravagant fury on Julian's part. Other bishops were also harshly dealt with.

Julian's deep hatred for Christianity is given vent in his literary efforts. In *The Caesars or the Banquet,* he ridicules baptism, penance, and Jesus with extravagant polemic. In his *Against the Galilaeans* he summarizes everything he had negative to say about the hated faith. It seems likely to be accurately reported in some sources that after his Persian campaign in 363, Julian intended a bloody persecution of Christianity.

Julian did not survive the Persian campaign. He was killed on 26 June 383 and buried in Tarsus.

It was an illusion for Julian to think he could reinvigorate paganism by official decree and wipe out the work of his uncle, Constantine. Nor could he defeat Christianity by attacking it, even with recourse to the power of the state. And his failure on both counts only served decisively to weaken paganism.

Julian is difficult to categorize. To his fellow-devotees of Hellenic religion, he was a hero; Christians cruelly nicknamed him "the Apostate" for his initial allegiance to Christ and then turning his back on the faith.

CHAPTER 36

Collapse of Arianism and Definitive Recovery of the Nicene Theology at the Council of Constantinople (381)

Perilous though the situation of the Nicene Christians must have seemed after the victory of Arianism at the double Synod of Seleucia-Rimini in 359, a change quickly began when the death of the Emperor Constantius withdrew State support from the Arians. In both East and West, bishops loyal to Nicaea sought to rebuild their strength. In the West, Gaul became the center of orthodoxy under the tutelage of Hilary, bishop of Poitiers. It was Constantius himself who had allowed Hilary to return from banishment, feeling he would stir up less unrest in the West than in the East. Hilary summoned a synod of Gallic bishops to Paris in 360 from which went out a letter to the eastern bishops in which they deplored their earlier conduct, separated themselves from the Arianism of Ursacius, Valens, Auxentius, and Saturninus, and made unambiguous profession of the Nicene faith. Owing largely to Hilary's influence, the West was never again seriously threatened by Arianism.

In the East, Alexandria became the center of orthodoxy with Athanasius' return upon the accession of Julian as Emperor. Especially delicate was the task undertaken of filling sees with non-Arian bishops, and especially at Antioch, where circumstances had led the faithful into a three-way split of allegiance to separate men. Meanwhile, all of the Arian parties as well were currying favor with the Emperor. In the long run, the disunion among the Arians promised a better future for the adherents of Nicaea.

The Religious Policy of the Emperor Valens

In early 364, Emperor Jovian was succeeded by an officer of the guard, Valentinian I (364–75), who at the demand of the army selected his brother Valens (364–78) as second Augustus and gave him the East while retaining the West, North Africa, and the Balkans for himself. Valentinian, a convinced Nicene himself, adopted a hands-off policy toward ecclesiastical matters; whereas Valens, an Arian, sought alliance with his influential court bishop, Eudoxius, a Homoian, to promote Arianism to exclusive recognition in the East. At first the Homoiousians provoked his wrath when, at a Synod of Lampsacus, 364, they refused the Creed of Rimini, declared the *homoiousios* essential for distinguishing the divine persons, and demanded restoration of the bishops exiled by the Anomoians in 360. When Valens rebuffed them sharply, they appealed to the Pope and Valentinian for help. The Pope received them charitably, once they had renounced Rimini and professed Nicaea, giving them letters of communion for themselves and their orthodox colleagues in the East. Letters were also forthcoming from other western bishops. These results were reported at a Synod at Tyana in Cappadocia and were approved. Plans to carry forward this rapprochement at an expanded synod at Tarsus were thwarted by Bishop Eudoxius and Valens. Valens again cracked down on the Nicenes: in an edict of 365, all sees filled under Julian with Nicenes were declared to be vacant. This affected Athanasius too, but since disturbances broke out in Alexandria, Valens relented and let him return; Athanasius was now able to work unmolested in his episcopal city until his death in 373.

During the years 365–69, Valens' attention was so preoccupied first with the usurper Procopius and then after 367 with the Gothic War that he had to give the religious questions his benevolent neglect. The Nicenes used this breathing space considerably to strengthen their position through appointments to key sees. The rapprochement begun at Lampsacus got no further, partly because of the role of Liberius, but mainly because of the new theological question of the relation of the Holy Spirit to the Son and to the Father, which also became a dividing point.

The Nicene Creed simply stated the Church's faith in the Holy Spirit. Athanasius in his *Letters to Serapion of Thmuis* had rejected the thesis that the Spirit is a creature varying only in degree from the angels. And the Synod of Alexandria 362 confirmed its conviction of the true divinity of the Spirit. Some among the Homoiousians had reservations against this doctrine and, with varying nuances, came out against it. Among their leaders were the saintly Eustathius of Sebaste, Eleusius of Cyzicus, and Marathonius of Nicomedia, but in 365 was not yet possible to speak of a faction of "Pneumatomachoi."

A sharp persecution of Catholics and non-Homoians was instituted by the Emperor Valens in connection with a new appointment to the see of Constantinople in 370. Valens sent the Catholics' candidate into exile; they repulsed the Arians' candidate; Valens decided the time was now ripe for him to impose a monophonic profession of the Creed of Rimini and sent his men out to round up every episcopal signature to it. The recalcitrant lost their sees. The persecution was very severe. In Alexandria, however, no persecution broke out until after the death of Athanasius, when it exploded upon his designated successor, Peter. The Prefect Palladius had the Church of St. Thomas occupied under tumultuous circumstances and, by means of police power, inducted the Arian Bishop Lucius into office. Clerics and monks were imprisoned and then exiled or sent to the mines. Eleven bishops and 126 clerics were deported to Diocaesarea in Palestine, and not infrequently an effort was made to break the opposition by executions. Bishop Peter abandoned Egypt secretly and went to Pope Damasus I in Rome, from where he informed the episcopate of the Universal church about the happenings in Alexandria.

The Work of the Young or Neo-Nicenes

In the Asia Minor province of Cappadocia, Valens limited substantially the persecution of Catholics because of the moral reputation of Basil Caesarea, metropolitan of the province since 370. Basil was a profound theological thinker, had come from an esteemed Christian family, had had a splendid education, and was unflinchingly loyal to the traditional faith, and he combined these traits with the gifts of leadership and diplomatic skill. As a result, Basil was a man with great strength of character, and he impressed everyone who came into contact with him. The government wanted Basil on its side, and the Prefect Modestus set out to get him. As Gregory Nazianzen, his friend, described Basil's encounter with Modestus, Basil repulsed both Modestus' efforts at persuasion and his threats of punishment. And to the remark of the astounded prefect, that up till then no one had ever dared to speak so candidly to him, came the proud and cool reply: "Perhaps you have never yet had to deal with a bishop." As a result of his minister's report, Valens himself attended Mass on Epiphany 372 in Basil's church and was so impressed by his religious seriousness, that he gave up all exertions to win him for the Homoian confession, left him in his position, and even gave him large amounts of land for the charitable institutions Basil was having built. Thus the Bishop of Caesarea more and more became the protector of the persecuted Catholics for wide areas of the East. Basil tried in every way to profit by the possibilities open to him and worked tirelessly for the strengthening of the Catholics and the union of all groups that acknowledged Nicaea. When episcopal sees came vacant, he filled them with Nicenes or established new sees in order to enlarge the number of his suffragans. Basil suffered a bitter disappointment from Eustathius of Sebaste, with whom he had once been close. Eustathius, having worked through to acceptance of Nicaea, nevertheless found impossible the acceptance of the divinity of the Holy Spirit, and thus rendered impossible the union of Homoiousians and Catholics and even went so far as to accuse Basil of sharing the erroneous doctrines of Apollinaris of Laodicea. Basil was hurt most deeply, however, by his failure to solve the schism at Antioch between the faction loyal to Eustathius, now dead and succeeded irregularly by Paulinus, and the one led by Bishop Meletius. Theologically they were at one, but jurisdictionally they were two. The difficulty Basil faced was that Alexandria clung to Paulinus for emotional rather than theological reasons, and it was Alexandria from which Rome got all of its information on the ecclesiastical situation in the East. Hence no aid from the West was forthcoming for Meletius or for Basil's efforts in his behalf. This was unfortunate for many reasons, but not least for the fact that Rome thus was not fully aware that Arianism was not now the sole issue, but that now the new theological trend toward denying the divinity of the Holy Spirit deserved the greatest attention.

Hence people in the West were in no position to evaluate the theological work of the so-called Young or Neo-Nicenes — they were, in addition to Basil, his brother Gregory of Nyssa, Gregory Nazianzen, and their friend, Amphilochius of Iconium. These men understood two things: (1) that by the fundamental adherence to the statements of Nicaea a precise definition of terms for its correct understanding was achieved; and (2) the question of the divinity and personality of the Holy Spirit must be decided. They, Basil especially, resolved the first task by giving to the hitherto loose and hence still interchangeable concepts *ousia* and *hypostasis* an unambiguously defined content. *Ousia* now came to mean exclusively the "nature" of God, whereas *hypostasis* was reserved as an indication of the special being in which the divine nature is expressed in the Father, in the Son, and in the Holy Spirit: *mia ousia, treis hypostaseis* became the classical formula in the theology of the Trinity. Each of the three hypostaseis has its characteristic features: the first, that of fatherhood (*patrotēs),* the second, that of sonship (*hyiotês*), the third, that of sanctifying (*hagiasmos*). For the distinctions among the three persons, Gregory Nazianzen had already supplied the terms "unbegottenness" (*agennesia*), "going forth" (*poreusis*), and "mission" (*ekpempsis*). Though Basil does not expressly teach the *homoousios* of the Holy Spirit, he does declare his divinity and equality of nature; Gregory Nazianzen formally taught *homoousios*. In the question of the procession of the Holy Spirit, the Neo-Nicenes preferred the formula "from the Father through the Son." It was their merit through their theological work to have prepared for the decisions on the faith at the Council of Constantinople, to have brought the theology of the Trinity to its first settlement, and to have paved the way for the final break-through of the Nicene theology.

Externally, this development was facilitated by a political situation. A Gothic revolt in the Balkans in 378–79 forced Valens to go to war, for which he asked the help of his nephew Gratian, Emperor in the West since 375. Before departing for battle, Valens rescinded the sentences of exile against the Catholic bishops; hence Antioch and Alexandria got Meletius and Peter back. Without waiting for Gratian's assistance, he went into battle and on the 9 August 378 lost throne and life near Adrianople. In January 379, Gratian elevated the Spanish general Theodosius to co-Augustus, assigning him the East as his sphere of rule. Both Emperors professed the Nicene Creed and a more peaceful future now seemed to open up for it.

The Council of Constantinople (381)

Basil of Caesarea, in a 377 treatise, *To the Westerners* (with which he was addressing Pope Damasus I primarily), had said that West and East would need to make some decisions in "a common consultation" on questions of faith raised by the teachings of Eustathius of Sebaste and Apollinaris of Laodicea and Marcellus of Ancyra. He acknowledged however that the reign of Valens was not an appropriate *kairos* for such a meeting. Basil died in January 379 and subsequent leadership of orthodoxy fell upon Meletius, who summoned a synod at Antioch that autumn. There, consistent with Theodosius' desires, 153 bishops declared their unity of faith with Rome. Shortly before the synod, Gratian and his imperial colleagues Valentinian II and Theodosius I promulgated an edict in favor of the Catholic version of the faith. In his personal "official explanation" of the edict, *Cunctos populos* (28 February 380), Theodosius declared it the wish of the Emperors that the people should live in accordance with the religion handed down by the Apostle Peter to the Romans and which Pope Damasus and Peter of Alexandria both professed; "hence that we believe in the one divinity of the Father and the Son and the Holy Spirit in equal majesty and holy Trinity." Only those who so believed might call themselves Catholic Christians; others were branded as heretics, who might properly expect both divine and imperial punishment. The profession of faith which was the criterion was identified in 381 as the Nicene Creed.

The idea of a council intruded itself powerfully after the death of Valens, and Theodosius summoned a council to the eastern capital for May 381. The strongest group represented — some 71 in number — came from the East and were led by Meletius of Antioch. Included were the Neo-Nicenes, Basil and the two Gregories and their friend Amphilochius. Of the approximately 150 bishops in attendance, there were few from the coast of Asia Minor, hotbed of the Pneumatomachoi. Meletius was in the chair as the council began, and the sessions were not held in the imperial palace. Theodosius neither participated nor had himself represented, thus guaranteeing freedom to the deliberations.

As at Nicaea, no records of the sessions are extant; hence the exact course of the discussion cannot be determined with certainty. Probably the first agenda item was recognition of Gregory Nazianzen as the new bishop of Constantinople. During the first days of the council, however, Meletius died unexpectedly; he was succeeded in the presidency by the Bishop of Constantinople, Gregory of Nazianzen.

Early too would have been the discussion of the Holy Spirit. It was one of Theodosius' deepest concerns that there be an agreement between the orthodox majority and the Pneumatomachoi or Macedonians, but his hopes were frustrated. Despite all efforts, nothing could persuade the faction led by Eleusis of Cyzicus to confess the divinity of the Holy Spirit; these men left the council warning their members against recognizing the faith of Nicaea.

The Creed of Constantinople

It would have corresponded to the example of Nicaea and also to the situation of 381 if an attempt at negotiations had sought recognition of a creed in which the content of the Nicene Creed were accepted, but through which the question of the Holy Spirit would be adequately declared. The vehicle for this attempt was the not wholly aptly labeled Nicaeno-Constantinopolitan Creed. Important facets of the history of this creed, the so-called "Faith of the 150 Fathers," have found no scholarly consensus. Until the mid-nineteenth century, it was assumed to be from Constantinople; but then it was discovered in a couple of documents which ante-date the Council (Epiphanius of Cyprus' *Ancoratus*, 374, quotes it almost verbatim; and it seems to have been the basis of Cyril of Jerusalem's catechetical lectures of ca. 350). Perhaps the most recent views suggest that this creed goes back to Constantinople 381 after all, but there are major unresolved questions still vexing any solution.

An exhaustive analysis of the text of the Creed of Constantinople makes clear that the statements of the Creed of Nicaea were left intact. For the additions to the first and second article that went beyond this (maker of heaven and earth; eternally begotten; by the power of the Holy Spirit he was born of the Virgin Mary, and became man: for our sake he was crucified under Pontius Pilate; is seated at the right hand of the Father; his kingdom will have no end), are found here and there in other earlier texts and so are not new creations of the Fathers of Constantinople. It is rather the new statements on the Holy Spirit in the third article on which the great theological importance of this creed is based. Nicaea simply said, "We believe in the Holy Spirit," whereas the following amplifications are found here: "the Lord, the giver of life, who proceeds from the Father. With the Father and the Son he is worshiped and glorified. He has spoken through the prophets." With the profession of "Lordship" (*to kyrion*) with the title *kyrios,* the divine character is claimed also for the Holy Spirit, as for the Father and the Son, just as Basil of Caesarea had already concluded from 1 Thessalonians 3:13; 2 Thessalonians 3:5; and 2 Corinthians 3:17. And the designation "giver of life" intends to affirm that he is God, as the Neo-Nicenes stressed. By means of the formula "who proceeds from the Father" it was intended to oppose the thesis of the Macedonians, that the Holy Spirit is a being created by the Son; that the procession from the Father is instead an argument for his divinity had been stressed by Gregory Nazianzen in connection with John 15:26. However, the most decisive statement on the divinity of the Holy Spirit is: "With the Father and the Son he is worshiped and glorified." The same worship (*proskynêsis,* as the proper act of divine adoration) and the same honor (*doxa,* as the more ritual honoring in the liturgy) which belong to the Father and Son are also proper to the Holy Spirit. Orthodoxy had fought since the time of Cyril of Jerusalem for precisely this inclusion of the Holy Spirit in the doxological formula of divine worship. The Creed of Constantinople thus professed the equivalent of the consubstantiality of the Holy Spirit, and no convinced Macedonian could have signed it. Why *homoousios* was not incorporated can therefore only be surmised. In any case, the Council anathematized the Pneumatomachoi and other heretics of their ilk who did not conform to its creed. To that was added the Emperor's edict of 30 July 381 which ordered the immediate surrender of all churches to bishops "who confess that Father, Son, and Holy Spirit are of one majesty and power, of the same honor and dominion." The criterion of orthodoxy of these bishops consisted in their being in communion with Nectarius of Constantinople, Timothy of Alexandria, Diodorus of Tarsus, Amphilochius of Iconium, Helladius of Caesarea, Gregory of Nyssa, and some others — the representatives of defenders of orthodoxy at Constantinople.

With Constantinople 381 ends the long Trinitarian discussion in the Church with the faith of Nicaea finally being vindicated. Arianism no longer posed a threat to the faith within the Empire.

Also important for canon law and Church history are canons 2 and 3 of the Council. Canon 2 reinculcated from Nicaea's canons the view that matters in one province were to be dealt with by that province's synod and bishops are restricted to their own dioceses for the exercise of ecclesiastical functions. The political dioceses of the East are named: The East, with special privileges granted to the Church of Antioch by Nicaea reconfirmed, Asia, Pontus, and Thrace. Here we note a development on the route toward the eastern patriarchates.

Canon 3 was with its concise text by far the one most heavy with consequences: "The Bishop of Constantinople should have the Primacy Honor after the Bishop of Rome, for this city is the new Rome." Hitherto the special rank of Antioch and Alexandria had been seen rather in the apostolic origin of their congregations than in the political importance of these cities. Here the excessive elevation in rank of the episcopal see of Byzantium was unambiguously founded on the political importance of the new capital of the eastern part of the Empire, while indirectly the special position of the Roman Bishop was reduced to the political rank of Old Rome.

The Synod of Constantinople as an "Ecumenical" Council

As to the question of whether the participants at Constantinople 381 understood themselves as meeting in a Council of the entire Church, the answer must be a clear "no," based on extant sources. The western episcopate had not been invited and was not represented. It was not until the Council of Chalcedon 451 that Constantinople 381 was reappraised. There there was an emphatic recognition given to the Creed of Constantinople, the so-called canon 28 on the prerogatives the bishop of the imperial capital the canons of 381 were cited as "Synodikon of the Second Synod." In 545 Emperor Justinian I spoke in an edict of "the four holy synods" [Nicaea, Constantinople, Ephesus, and Chalcedon] whose dogmas are as esteemed as holy scripture. In the West, Pope Gregory the Great used a similar formulation in referring to the four councils as the four books of the "holy gospel." Thus Constantinople came to its place among the ecumenical councils.

C H A P T E R   3 7

Development of the Relationship of Church and State in the Fourth Century: The "Church of the Empire"

The discussion so far of the Church's struggles over Nicaea have made it abundantly clear that the imperial leadership of the Roman Empire had no thought whatsoever of remaining neutral toward the Church. The Emperors of this period showed a lively interest in the contemporary problems of the Church, especially the questions of unity of belief, of uniformity of organization, and of missionary work among pagans and often intervened with the greatest intensity in the search for the solutions of these problems. Thus it was with ever-increasing urgency that the question of the right relationship of Church and State obtruded itself. A solution tolerable to both sides had to be found. We shall glance briefly at the attitude of each of the Emperors to this problem and its evaluation by the Church, in order to follow the route that was pursued in the search for a solution until the end of the fourth century. It was a long and circuitous process which produced at its end the Christian "Church of the Empire" of late antiquity, which was, however, differently understood and evaluated in East and West.

Church and State under Constantine I

With Constantine's victory in 312 and his turn toward Christianity, the faith was not obliged to undertake too radical a reorientation of its attitude toward the State. There were and had been strong voices among churchmen speaking positively about the State. Origen, e.g., ascribed to it a providential mission for spreading the faith; Tertullian, and others, felt it a duty to pray *pro salute imperatorum.* Moreover, there were those two long periods of peace in the third century which had made possible contacts between churchmen and Emperors and others of the imperial families and entourage. When, then, Constantine gave the Church complete freedom of belief and of preaching, Christianity began to be ever more privileged, and in the exuberance of those halcyon years, the problem of Church and State did not yet present itself to either side in its full precision. Constantine's awareness of mission demanded a special position for the Church, but not such as would yet require a strict delineation of the boundaries for a Christian Emperor. When the Emperor sought to bring the Church closer to the State and to gain from it close collaboration in the interest imperial unity, only regard for the pagan majority of the inhabitants of the Empire prevented his overextending his special position. That Constantine shrank from intervening in specific internal affairs of the Church in an authoritarian manner and with full power to impose his decisions is demonstrated in his reluctant reaction to the approach by the Donatists for an imperial judgment in their conflict with the Catholics of North Africa. He referred them to a synod (Arles, 314). Even during the Arian controversy, Constantine saw himself as qualified only to urge peace and unity, not as the lord of the Church to whom pertained the final decision. At Nicaea he permitted full freedom of speech, seeking only by persuasion and diplomacy the most nearly unanimous possible acceptance of the creed formulated by the majority the bishops. Only by threatening the representatives of the opposition with exile, thus eliminating much of their freedom of choice, did he overstep his bounds. Hence the phrase attributed to him, that he was *episkopos tôn ektos,* seems a valid paraphrase of the attitude that he claimed and exercised toward the Church.

The right of the Emperor to summon synods as unquestioned; his efforts to steer the course of theological discussion through his ecclesiastical advisors were accepted as self-evident; even his use of exile was not regarded as out of line with his clear prerogatives, for we find no protests even from those upon whom he imposed it. Partly this was due to the sacred evaluation of the ruler in antiquity generally, but in Constantine's case, it also had a great deal to do with his victory over paganism, his legitimation of Christianity, and his own personal conversion to the faith.

However, it was important that it was Constantine, the first Christian Emperor, whom Eusebius of Caesarea took for his model in undertaking to establish theologically the position of the Christian imperial office in relation to and in the Church. In the panegyrical writings about Constantine, which belong to the last years of life, Eusebius outlined a political theology to which, again and again, especially at Byzantium, appeals would be made to try to justify the uniqueness of the Emperor's position within the Church. Writing in 335, Eusebius expounded the notion that the earthly *Imperium* is a reflection (*eikon*) of the heavenly kingdom, and as the latter has only one Lord, the Father, so also the reflection has only one Emperor, who receives his sovereign power and his virtues as ruler from the Father through the *Logos,* Christ. His task as ruler is to deliver mankind from the power of the demons, from idolatry, from polytheism, and to lead it to recognition of the true God. He is, thus, called upon to promote the realization of God's plan of salvation with human beings: and so he becomes God's vicar (*hyparchos*) on earth. In his writings, Eusebius applied this theory to the changes of his own times, experienced by him with a grateful heart. From this, Eusebius now deduces the place of the Emperor within the Church. Since *Imperium* and Church are both reflections of the heavenly kingdom, they are in practice identical in the now Christian *Imperium Romanum,* but this has only one supreme head, the Christian Emperor, God's vicar, who thus in a certain sense becomes Lord of the Church, and also a "sort of universal bishop" whose full power over the Church has a quasi-priestly character for it also extends to the right performance of worship and to the preaching of the Gospel.

Eusebius' political theology goes far beyond what Constantine did or claimed, and it proved a rich lode for later Byzantines to mine. Already, however, implications of this thought were present: *all* ecclesiastical factions of the fourth and fifth centuries sought to gain the favor of the ruler of the moment. They turned spontaneously to the State for aid in imposing their theological views, which was later to prove a problem, when this power became limitless.

Efforts to Subordinate the Church to the State by the Emperors Constantius and Valens

This power became limitless under Constantine's second son, Constantius, in whose reign is to be placed the second step in the progress of Church and State that pressed for a solution. This Emperor's inclination to exercise a strict control over the Church became apparent for the first time on the occasion of the Synod of Serdica (342). Whereas the group of western bishops arrived and functioned without an escort provided by the State, there were in the delegation from the East two high State officials, whom Athanasius sarcastically referred to as "their school masters and attorneys." When the western episcopate dared in an impressive letter to refer to the moral constraint which State officials were exercising on the faithful of his dominions and implored him to end this abuse and to guarantee complete freedom of judgment also in the religious sphere, Constantius reacted sharply, especially since he could not but feel the decisions of some of the canons issued at Serdica as a criticism of the methods of his religious policy, those, namely, whereby the frequent visits of some bishops to the imperial court were forbidden, an abuse which Athanasius had earlier censured. He undertook to subject the Church completely to his control when, after the death of his brother Constans, he had assumed sole rule. In the fall of 353 he submitted for their signatures to the bishops of Gaul meeting at Arles and to the legates of Pope Liberius a prepared decree, which condemned Athanasius and punished any resistance with banishment, while he rejected from the start any discussion of the question of faith. Constantius' claim to direct the Church reached its climax two years later at the Synod of Milan (355), called by him, at which he again demanded the condemnation of Athanasius by the bishops, whereas they demanded a clear decision in favor of the Nicene Creed. The resistance of the bishops finally elicited from him the ominous word that reproduced exactly his innermost attitude to the problem of State and Church: "What I want must be regarded as canon law." Thus was the complete subjection of the Church to the State demanded: it was to be a State-Church incorporated into the *Imperium* whose absolute sovereign was the Emperor. No Emperor of the fourth century expressed or outdid such a claim with the same precision. He cleverly avoided only one thing; to permit a bishop of independent mind to become a martyr by shedding his blood. Again exile was the fate of the few upright bishops, while the papal legates were shamefully ill treated. Even Pope Liberius, after a long, fruitless discussion with the Emperor, was exiled to Thrace. Likewise, the consent of the Gallic bishops who had not been present at Milan to the condemnation of Athanasius was extorted at the Synod of Béziers (356), and the two inflexible ones, Hilary of Poitiers and Rhodanius of Toulouse, followed the other opponents into banishment. The Synod of Rimini (359) offers the same picture: again a prepared creed is submitted to the bishops, not for discussion but for unconditional surrender. In the Emperor's letter to the members of the Synod occurs the statement: "No decree can have the force of law anywhere, if our will denies it any importance and obligation." Constantius claimed for himself the right of asserting his will, even in theological questions. The few subservient bishops exuberantly thanked him for having stricken the *homoousios* from the Nicene Creed: "Through the authoritative decision of Your Piety, we see all those defeated who use that word for God's Son." Lucifer of Cagliari reproached the Arian bishops with having acceded to Constantius' claim to be *episcopus episcoporum.*

In its confrontation with the claims of the Emperor Constantius to a leading role, the Church had to endure bitter disillusionments and an often distressing collapse of its own episcopate. The resistance was led by Athanasius of Alexandria, who, soon after his return from his first exile, in an encyclical to the Universal Church referred to the threat to the Church's freedom, which arose from the fact that forces external to the Church interfered, contrary to custom, in the filling of episcopal sees; hence he summoned all Catholic bishops to unanimous resistance. Thus Athanasius was the first bishop of the fourth century to formulate the Church's claim to freedom vis-à-vis the State. Pope Julius joined him when he complained that the freedom of ecclesiastical decisions was jeopardized by the threat of exile and death. The letter of the western members of the Synod of Serdica to Constantius drew an unmistakable line of separation between Church and State when they attributed to the latter only concern for the public well-being and rejected any interference in the ecclesiastical sphere; a deviation from this line takes liberty from men and leads necessarily to slavery. Equally spirited was the reply of the aged Hosius of Córdoba to the Emperor, when the latter still sought to gain him, after the tragedy of Milan, for his procedure: "Do not meddle in ecclesiastical matters . . . God has entrusted to you the imperial power, but to us the things of the Church. . . . It does not behoove us to rule on earth, nor you, Emperor, to offer sacrifice." This letter was followed by the fiery protest of Hilary of Poitiers, who in his exile wrote of his indignation of soul since the Emperor did not give him the opportunity to explain it to him in person. Above all, he pitilessly exposed the methods which Constantius employed to achieve his ecclesiastical political aims: he overwhelmed the bishops with honors in order to enslave them; he did not have them beheaded but killed with gold; he flattered in order to dominate; he exempted the Church from taxation but he thereby seduced it into denying Christ. No similarly strong opposition to any Christian Emperor of the fourth century had appeared on the side of the Church. Certainly the effort of Constantius to incorporate the Church into the State and to subject the former to the latter was shattered not only on this resistance but on the jubilation with which bishops he exiled were recieved on their return from exile after his death — a joy that resounded because of the freedom they now enjoyed.

Under the Emperor Valens (365–78) the Church in the eastern part of the Empire was again exposed for a time to similar stresses as in the days of Constantius. If he finally left Athanasius and Basil, the two champions of orthodoxy, in their sees, this was due not to any change of heart by the Emperor but to fear of possible political disturbances, which banishment could have evoked. Occasionally Basil had expressed his theory of the problem of Church and State. In connection with Romans 13:1–4, the Bishop of Caesarea was convinced that all the power of the State comes from God and therefore the Christian owes obedience to it, when its laws promote the welfare of society. But since the earthly *Imperium* is always subordinated to the divine law, the Christian's duty of obedience to it finds its limits at the spot where the State's power oversteps its competence and makes demands which oppose God's law. Therefore he let the Emperor Valens know that neither torture nor threats could induce him to put his signature, as commanded by the Emperor, to the Homoian creed. He thereby encouraged clerics and laymen to resist the State's might, if it armed to force them to the Arian faith. Both Latins and Greeks raised their voices for the liberty of the Church in the face of the power of the State.

Ambrose and Theodosius

The problem of Church and State entered a new and decisive phase when in the last quarter of the century two men confronted it: each in his own sphere tended to represent categorically and firmly his notion of the freedom of the Church or of the sovereignty of the State: Ambrose of Milan and Theodosius the Great. The Bishop of Milan had already made clear, in the confrontation between the Emperor Gratian (375–83) and the pagan faction at Rome, that he did not hesitate to appeal even to the conscience of an Emperor if it was a question of protecting the rights of the Church. He felt himself impelled to this all the more when Gratian's younger brother, Valentinian II (383–92), came under the influence of a faction of officials and clerics who strove to procure a strong position for Arianism in Milan at the expense of the Catholics. In resisting this effort, Ambrose took so fundamental a stand on the relationship of imperial power and Christian Church that he exercised the greatest influence on the future. First, Ambrose compelled the Emperor to cancel his decrees whereby he had ordered the sequestration of two Catholic churches, to be handed over to the Arians. When the Emperor then called upon the bishop to agree to an imperial court of arbitration, which should decide whether Ambrose or the Arian Auxentius was the lawful Bishop of Milan, the Catholic bishop twice in succession expressed his basic idea of the limits of the State's power in relation to the Church. In a letter to the Emperor he informed him in unambiguous language that he would not appear before the imperial arbitration court, because laymen cannot sit in judgment on clerics in questions of faith. On the contrary: according to custom, in such cases bishops would correct Christian Emperors, but Emperors would not correct bishops; he, the Emperor, who still had to earn admittance to baptism, arrogated to himself a decision in questions of faith for which only a synod of bishops in a church was proper. Even more decisive are the statements in the sermon in which Ambrose rejected the plan of Auxentius to make himself Bishop of Milan with the help of the State's power. For an Emperor who professed to be a Christian there was no greater honor than that he be called "son of the Church." "The Emperor is in the Church, not over the Church." This expression, which would never have occurred to a Eusebius, was, it is true, uttered as part of a concrete situation, but at the same time it proclaimed a principle which Ambrose and after him the Latin Church would always defend: the Christian Emperor is not the master of his Church but its beneficent patron; questions of faith, the discipline of the clergy, the form of the liturgy, the administration of ecclesiastical property, are, according to Ambrose, withdrawn in principle from the competence of even the Christian State.

For his principle that the Christian Emperor is not the master of the Church, but its son, Ambrose had to stand up to an Emperor of the stature of Theodosius the Great, who, like Constantine, was filled with an exalted consciousness of his sovereign position and who, because of his earlier unflinching stand for the Catholic creed, possessed the boundless sympathy of the Church. A first occasion for conflict arose when in 388 a group of fanatical Christians in the town of Callinicum on the Euphrates frontier, with the consent of their bishop, burned the Jewish synagogue, and the Emperor ordered the rebuilding of the synagogue at the expense of the Catholic bishop. Bishop Ambrose, however, saw in this command an unreasonable encouragement of a religious group hostile to Christianity and demanded that the Emperor annul his decree. When the latter hesitated, Ambrose spoke to him during Mass in the Milan cathedral and declared that he would not continue the Mass until the Emperor solemnly promised to act as Ambrose had requested. Theodosius finally yielded, but he long retained a deep resentment because of this humiliation at the hands of the bishop of his residence. On surer ground Ambrose made use of another incident to prove to him that a Christian Emperor is subject to the moral demands of his Church. When the people of Thessalonica murdered an unpopular imperial official, the Emperor, in a first fury, gave the brutal command to proceed with cold steel against the people assembled in the stadium. The Emperor, it is true, soon rescinded his order, but the counterorder arrived too late and a large number of inhabitants of the city were slain. For this serious crime Bishop Ambrose demanded public penance of the Emperor; he left Milan and declared in a letter to Theodosius that he would remain away from his episcopal city until Theodosius should accept the penance. Once again the Emperor submitted. The highest holder and representative of the power of the State subjected himself to the penitential discipline of his Church, which a bishop uncompromisingly required of him. Again a line was drawn which even an Emperor might not overstep. Questionable as Ambrose's argumentation was in individual cases, notably that of Callinicum, with his basic viewpoint he had created a sort of model which was to remain valid in the Latin West for the relations of the Church and the Christian State. Both powers stood in a basically positive relationship to each other, but the innermost sphere of the Church's life faith, the moral order, ecclesiastical discipline — remained withdrawn from the State's influence.

In the East the development followed another route. It is true that here there was later no lack of people who pointed clearly to the limits of the State's power in relation to the Church, as, for example, John Chrysostom, who in a striking parallel to Ambrose said that "the holy laws have subordinated the head of the *basileus* to the hands of the priests," who defended the Church's right of asylum and who, when the Gothic leader demanded a Catholic church of the capital for Arian worship, candidly reminded the Emperor Arcadius that it would be better to lose his imperial dignity than to become guilty of surrendering a church. But here finally the theocratic valuation of the imperial power, which Eusebius had introduced with his excessive glorification of Constantine, proved to be stronger and under Justinian I reached a height never again surpassed.

The "Church of the Empire"

To express the real situation of the Church in the constant ups and downs of the imperial religious policy of the fourth century the term "Church of the Empire" was coined, but this makes necessary some clarifying remarks in order to avoid possible misconceptions of the situation concerned. The term aims to characterize in compact form that total situation in the relations of Church and State which came to a first preliminary conclusion under the Emperor Theodosius I. Fundamental to this relationship was the fact that the State's power and the Church agreed in principle on a close collaboration in the public sphere. This became possible because the Emperor, personally and as representative of the State's authority, professed the faith which the Church preached and the majority of the Empire's inhabitants accepted. Since this faith had been proclaimed as the official religion of the Empire, the State accorded the Church manifold privileges and encouragement. For its part, the Church basically approved this *Imperium* that was now Christian and recognized the independence of the State's sphere. In its preaching it stressed that the power of this State came from God and depended on God. The criticism of ecclesiastical writers in the religious and political conflicts of the fourth century was directed not against the State as such and not against the imperial power as such: it was concerned with the interference by individual representatives of the State in the inner life of the Church. The extraordinarily close union of the two was not questioned.

But the enormous dangers which such an alliance of the two partners of the Church of the Empire implied were indeed seen and expressed by several representatives of the Church. They knew very well that the State's power was exposed to the constant temptation to abuse in relation to the Church. Others felt clearly that the privileges granted by the State and often all too eagerly claimed and sought by some bishops compromised the credibility of their preaching.

Finally, it is to be noted that the expression "Church of the Empire" reproduces only a very external aspect of the total reality of the Church at that time. It would, above all, be a serious misunderstanding, if one were to assume that the self-evaluation of the contemporary Church was expressed fully in what is included in "Church of the Empire." The best theologians of the time knew well that the Church in its innermost essence belonged to another area, namely, to that reality of the order of grace which was bestowed on mankind through Christ's redemptive act.

Part Two

The Theological Disputes in East and West to the Middle of the Fifth Century

Karl Baus

C H A P T E R   3 8

Christology to the Council of Ephesus (431)

The Christological Question in the Fourth Century

In the fourth century the problem of the Trinity so monopolized the forces of theology and the Church that, in comparison, a second very important question — that of the orthodox understanding of the union of God and Man in Christ — at first remained in the background. This Christological problem was, of course, quite familiar to the pre-Constantinian theologians, such as Hippolytus, Origen, or Novatian, but in their day there was as yet no exhaustive search for a solution. Only the Arian theology was unavoidably confronted with the Christological problem and made some very precise statements on it, but at first these led to no deeper discussion, first because the main interest was focused on the Trinitarian question, then probably because the opposing school had as yet no carefully thought out answer. To the extent that the inadequate state of the sources and the as yet incomplete research permit, the view of Arian theology on this question can be thus summarized.

1. In the Incarnation, the *Logos* assumed only the body of a man, but not a human soul, for in this case the *Logos* perfectly took the place of the soul. 2. This *Logos-Sarx* Christology was connected most intimately with the basic Arian thesis: that the Son is "a creature," in whom all the human traits reported by the evangelists — that Jesus was grieved, that he felt abandoned by the Father — had to be attributed to the *Logos;* the *Logos* would not have really become Man, if not he, but the human soul, had been the bearer of these "imperfections." 3. The unity of the Word with the flesh assumed was as closely understood as the unity of the soul with the body so that in the Logos-become-flesh there was basically only one nature. An Arian fragment, which is attributed to Bishop Eudoxius of Constantinople (d. 369), expresses it clearly: "we believe in one single Lord Jesus Christ...made flesh, not made man; for he did not take a human soul...not two natures, since he was not perfect man, but God was in place of the soul in the flesh, the entirety one nature through articulation." This Arian Christology has not only a Monophysite hue, but a Monophysite core, even if not the developed terminology of the later Monophysitism.

The Council of Nicaea took no position in regard to the *Logos-Sarx* Christology, probably especially because this was not yet presented in a formulation that would have clearly disclosed its dangers. But soon afterward some theologians, including Eustathius of Antioch, Marcellus of Ancyra, and, from the West, Hilary of Poitiers, recognized its weakness and for their part insisted that a human soul in Christ must be accepted, because otherwise the human traits ascribed to the *Logos* would force one to conclude that God was changeable. With this stressing of the complete Incarnation of the *Logos,* then, they opposed a *Logos-Anthrōpos* Christology to the *Logos-Sarx* Christology. The statement from the Prologue of John's gospel, "and the Word became flesh," was enough for Athanasius to believe in the real Incarnation of the *Logos.* Hence in him must be seen a representative of the

Logos-Sarx Christology, who, however, did not draw from it the same conclusions as did the Arians.

The Search of Apollinaris of Laodicea for a Solution

The theology of the day occupied itself somewhat more in detail with the effort made soon after the middle of the fourth century by a bishop closely bound to Athanasius to solve the Christological question, and after a rather lengthy discussion rejected it at the Council of Constantinople (381). Apollinaris the Younger, trained in philosophy and a keen thinker, had, following his theological studies at Antioch, become Bishop of Laodicea, the West-Syrian city of his birth, ca. 360. Throughout his life, he was a determined adherent of the Nicene doctrine of the identity of nature of the Son with the Father and clung also to the prevailing belief in the unchangeability of the divine *Logos.* But in Christology he upheld an idea which put him very close to the Arian notion just described. He also denied the existence of a human soul in Christ, but in so doing he sought to penetrate much deeper into the problem of Christ's humanity and to master it with the intellectual means of contemporary philosophy. According to him, Christ possesses a human body and a *nous* or a *pneuma,* a rational soul, which, however, is identical with the *Logos;* for it would be impossible that two natures, endowed with spirit and will, could coexist in one and the same being, since one must come into conflict with the other by means of its will and its individual activity. Hence this idea of the essential autonomy of the spiritual nature made it impossible for Apollinaris to assume a perfect humanity in Christ: in the God-become-Man there can be only *one* spirit, only *one* living efficacy — the *Logos.* Nevertheless, Apollinaris adhered to the prevailing expression — the Word became a Man. Even for the union of the Word with the flesh he found a unique answer: *Logos* and flesh became one, just as body and soul are one in the human being: after their union they form a single nature, which, however, comes about through a mixing of God and Man.

A discussion of the theses of Apollinaris seems to have first occurred at the Synod of Alexandria in 362; probably the problem was raised by representatives of Bishop Paulinus of Antioch. Agreement was reached on a formula, which seemed acceptable to both the followers of Paulinus and those of Apollinaris, but they interpreted it in a different sense. According to it, the Redeemer did not have a body without a soul, without sense-perception, without reason, for in the Word the redemption pertained not only to the body but also to the soul. But the Apollinarists understood this soul as the *Logos,* whereas the Paulinians saw it as the human soul of Jesus. After the Synod of Alexandria, the adherents of Apollinaris zealously made further propaganda for the doctrine of their master until in 374 Epiphanius of Salamis again pointed to the basic error of the Apollinarist solution: namely, that through it the redemption of the entire human nature is not assured. The two Cappadocians, Gregory Nazianzen and Gregory of Nyssa, both made a noteworthy contribution to the discussion of the Apollinarist Christology, since both decidedly demanded the existence of an intact human soul in Christ. In connection with Origen, Gregory Nazianzen constructed his Christology on the concept of the "mixture" (*krasis, mixis*), in which, however, the humanity of Jesus was not diminished but transfigured. Gregory of Nyssa also explained the unity of Christ by means of the concept of mixture and developed in detail the idea of the transfiguration of the humanity of Jesus; however, he deepened the doctrine of the soul of Christ when he said that the intact human soul must be postulated for the reason that the death of Christ could only be understood as a separation of soul and body. More so than Gregory Nazianzen, Gregory of Nyssa employed dyophysite formulas and thereby stood closer to the *Logos-Anthrōpos* Christology.

The disputed question was laid before Pope Damasus in Rome in 375 by the priest Vitalis, a follower of Apollinaris. At first, the Pope regarded as acceptable a cleverly worded profession of faith submitted by Vitalis, but later, in three letters to Paulinus of Antioch, he expressly repudiated the teaching of Apollinaris and in the summer of 377 solemnly condemned him and his adherents. When, two years later, a synod at Antioch under Bishop Meletius accepted the Roman judgment, the effort by Apollinaris to solve the Christological problem was definitively rejected in East and West. The Council of Constantinople in 381 repeated the condemnation when in canon 1, which enumerated the heresies of the day, it named also the Apollinarists. It is not known how Apollinaris himself acted in regard to the rejection of his Christology, but in any event he remained Bishop of Laodicea until his death (not before 385).

The Further Development of Christology to 428

The repudiation of Apollinarianism at first represented only a clarification in a negative sense: the route which aspired to find a solution of the Christological question in the denial of the human soul of Jesus was not passable. Soon the discussion of the issue was resumed, and the participants were almost exclusively theologians from the Greek-speaking world. Of course, one must no longer, as was formerly usual, combine some of these writers into a homogeneous faction because of their Christological statements and assign them to the "Theological School of Antioch." Diodorus of Tarsus, John Chrysostom, and Theodore of Mopsuestia represented such distinct outlooks that one cannot speak of a uniform Christological system among them. Hence it is more correct to speak in a broader sense of two currents that gradually became more sharply outlined: of these, the one represented rather the Christology of the assumed humanity and hence approximated the *Logos-Anthrōpos* system, whereas the Christology of the God-made-Man had its home in Alexandrian theology.

As a typical representative of a Word-Man Christology among the Antiochene theologians there loomed the figure of the former Bishop Diodorus of Tarsus (d. before 394), who as the outstanding teacher of theology at Antioch counted John Chrysostom and Theodore of Mopsuestia among his students and provoked the displeasure of the Emperor Julian because of his decisive defense of the divinity of Christ. This esteem of Diodorus was based on extracts from his single anti-Apollinarist work, *Contra Synousiastas,* but they came from the opposing faction and were later used against Diodorus by Cyril of Alexandria; hence they may have been subjected to distortion. To the extent that the very precarious state of the sources favoring Diodorus permits us to know, he was primarily interested in assuring the divinity of Christ, which he saw jeopardized by Apollinaris' idea of the unity between Word and flesh and which led him to formulations that had a very dualistic ring. He paid no attention to the human soul of Christ as a theological quantity and so the Antiochene Diodorus is rather to be regarded as a representative of the *Logos-Sarx* Christology.

John Chrysostom must also be understood as a representative of an Antiochene theology, but in his writings are found neither speculative presentations of the mystery of the Incarnation nor detailed remarks on Apollinarianism. To the preacher Chrysostom, Christ is in the traditional language the Word-made-flesh-and-man and the flesh is the dress or dwelling of the Word. The title *Theotokos* is not found in his works, nor any reason for it. At times he stresses that Word and flesh are a single entity, but that this union did not come about by mixture.

On the other hand, Diodorus' other pupil, Bishop Theodore of Mopsuestia (d. 428), developed new ideas and formulas on the Christological question, which were of great significance for the further completion of the doctrine of Christ. Of course, here the most recent research in the history of dogma had to establish several revisions in the traditional estimation of Theodore's Christology; his orthodoxy was, it is true, not questioned in his lifetime, but in the confrontation with Nestorius he, as his alleged teacher, became subject to the suspicion of heresy at the hands especially of Cyril of Alexandria, and finally he was condemned by the Fifth Ecumenical Council in 553 as a "Nestorian." His Christological thought must be seen, especially in his case, in the context of his total theology, which is not primarily speculative but rather "kerygmatic." It is based on the notion that God's plan of salvation has as its goal the immortality of human beings and that a preliminary participation in the eternal goods was given to those already on earth by Christ in baptism and the Eucharist, and after his resurrection this participation became full reality. Hence it was Theodore's chief concern to stress, against Arians and Apollinarists, the complete humanity of Christ, its total efficacy, and thereby to assure and make known its soteriological importance. In this he energetically distinguished two perfect natures in Christ, that of the "assumed" and that of the "receiver," so energetically that the impression was produced that their unity would seem only too loose, especially since he sought to make it understandable by the expression of the "indwelling" of the Word in the assumed humanity. But Theodore worked, in his constantly renewed point of departure, to show that this unity of the two natures was still no mere accident but an entirely unique inner relationship, which joined the divine *hypostasis* of the *Logos* with the human nature. He tried to describe it with the aid of the word *prosōpon* (not with *hypostasis*): the one *prosōpon* of Christ is the result and ultimately possible expression of the intimate union between the human nature and the *hypostasis* of the *Logos*. In Theodore *prosōpon* did not yet have the content of "person," first established by Chalcedon, and likewise *physis* and *hypostasis* were not yet ideally distinct in his thought. Theodore did not yet succeed in satisfactorily defining the unity of the two natures in Christ in the concrete, but through the formulations used by him he moved toward the solution which Chalcedon gave. They made it possible for him to worship the humanity of Christ together with the divinity in one adoration and to grant to Mary the title *Theotokos*. Accordingly, it is not permissible to designate Theodore of Mopsuestia as a "Nestorian before Nestorius."

The basic tenet of Alexandrian Christology after Nicaea was clearly stated by Athanasius in his words on the Incarnation: "Man did not become God, but God became Man in order to make us godlike" (*Adv. Ar.* 1, 39). Hence in this Christological thought the *Logos* is always the starting-point; he united the humanity to himself in the most intimate manner, not by elevating a man to himself, but by making himself a Man. Peter, the successor of Athanasius, was in Rome at the very moment when Pope Damasus had Apollinarianism condemned at the Synod of 377, and with it he professed his faith in the full humanity of Christ. In a letter to the exiled Egyptian bishops he speaks of the two natures as of two "persons." A further variation within the Alexandrian Christology is especially apparent in Didymus the Blind (d. 398), who in his youth, like Athanasius, first operated within the framework of the *Logos-Sarx* system, but after the condemnation of Apollinaris expressly professed the undiminished human nature in Christ. The commentary on the psalms acknowledged further that the soul of Christ could be exposed to anguish and perplexity and even ascribed to Jesus two *prosopa,* a divine and a human: here, then, *prosōpon* is still understood in its former meaning of "manner of appearing," no doubt a strong approximation of the Antiochene ideas and terminology.

Most intimately linked with the Christological discussion in the first half of the fifth century was Cyril, who in 412 was chosen to occupy the see of Alexandria. In his writings, however, must be distinguished two clearly contrasted phases in regard to the Christological question. The earlier covers the first sixteen years of his episcopate and shows Cyril as the undoubted heir of Athanasius, who, like the latter, came into confrontation with the Arian Christology and steadfastly upheld the immutability of the *Logos*-made-Man, but without proceeding to its disavowal of the soul of Christ or even mentioning Apollinarianism. Incidental remarks of Cyril, it is true, let us know that he presupposed a soul in Christ, but for him it had no theological or soteriological significance. It was his aim to emphasize that Christ possesses divinity *kata physin,* by nature, but not humanity, with body and soul, "by nature": instead, he made them his. Hence Christ is, indeed, God and Man, but in a certain sense more God than Man. Accordingly Cyril at first still represented a stage of the development in the Christological question, which as a whole had been already reached by Athanasius; the stronger emphasis on the divinity gives a presentiment as to how he would react if he was confronted with a theology which aspired to give a greater importance to Christ's humanity.

The Conflict between Cyril and Nestorius

Soon after taking possession of the see of Constantinople in 428, Nestorius ascertained that in his congregation there was in process a discussion of whether Mary should be called "Mother of God" (*Theotokos*) or "Mother of the Man" (*Anthrōpotokos*). He immediately took sides in his preaching and sought to bring about unity within the congregation by designating the title "Mother of Christ" as theologically the most appropriate. But since the title of *Theotokos* was customary even before Nicaea and in addition was employed without hesitation by many outstanding theologians of the fourth century and, most importantly, was consecrated in the consciousness of the faithful by its employment in the liturgy, the new bishop's attack on the word aroused shock and was regarded as a deviation from the preaching of the past. Opposition to Nestorius' view was first expressed in Constantinople, where the monks especially protested. Toward the end of 428 news of the happenings in the capital reached Alexandria also, where Cyril, without actually naming Nestorius, intervened decisively, first in letters to the bishops and monks of Egypt for the title of *Theotokos;* then in a letter to Nestorius himself, he requested enlightenment about his teaching, but from him he received only an arrogant admonition to Christian restraint. With this letter of Cyril's began the second phase in the Alexandrian bishop's Christology, which at the same time marked the beginning of the serious quarrel between him and Nestorius. Unfortunately, this conflict is encumbered also with features which are founded on the character of the two protagonists. In Nestorius an inclination toward intolerance of the views of others and a consequent inability to learn from them make a very unfavorable impression; Cyril sought to put across his ideas with adept and often highly questionable diplomacy, in which a certain antagonism of Alexandria with regard to the see of Constantinople may have played a role.

Nestorius himself immediately started a lively propaganda in behalf of his Christological theses, and it was also he who first informed Pope Celestine I (422–32) of the conflict in a letter which contained an exposition of his own standpoint and repudiated the view of his opponents as Arian and Apollinarian. For their part, his adversaries sent several of Nestorius' sermons to Rome; the deacon Leo, the future Pope, sent them on to John Cassian, Abbot of Saint-Victor de Marseille. Cassian thereupon wrote his *De incarnatione Domini,* which rejected the teaching of Nestorius, but without supplying a criticism that went deeper and farther. Cyril, meanwhile, was not inactive. His second letter to Nestorius, important for the history of dogma, must be dated at the beginning of 430. In it he asked Nestorius in his preaching to pay attention, "with all solicitude for the words, to doctrine and to loyalty to the faith" and to bring them into harmony with the doctrines of the Fathers. These last had unhesitatingly termed Mary the *Theotokos* because of her was born the body, with which the *Logos* had united himself "as regards the *hypostasis*" (*kath' hypostasin*); because of this union it may be said that the *Logos* suffered and rose. The retort, much sharper in tone, of Nestorius, rejected the title of *Theotokos* because it evoked the idea that the divine nature itself was born and died and hence was capable of suffering and mutable; but to intend to ascribe to the *Logos* birth, suffering, and death — such is precisely the madness of Apollinaris, of Arius, and of other teachers of error. Cyril also had recourse to the members of the episcopate and warned them against the suspicious teachings of Nestorius; with subtle diplomacy he especially approached the imperial family, which was well disposed to the Bishop of Constantinople, by means of theological essays to gain them to his side. Even in style, as Cyril informed Rome, he proved himself superior to Nestorius. In the summer of 430 Pope Celestine received from him a comprehensive dossier with a detailed description of the events thus far, with his personal evaluation of the Nestorian teaching, and with pertinent extracts from the Greek Fathers, — all this in a Latin translation, a gesture which Nestorius had neglected.

Rome had to take a stand. The Pope might have believed that in the report from Nestorius and in material transmitted by Cyril he had sufficient information to give a decision at the synod at the beginning of August. Cassian's work was also probably before him, and Cyril's deacon Posidonius was at his disposal for further information; but there was no one at hand to explain in more detail the position of Nestorius. But he was summarily condemned because, in contradiction of the tradition, he saw in Christ a mere Man, because he questioned Christ's virginal birth which had given to the world the true Son of God, through whom we have been redeemed. The Roman judgment displays no knowledge of the discussion of the Christological problem which had occupied the theologians of the East for years. True, it repulses the threat to tradition by the attack on Nestorius, but it shows no positive way to a deep understanding of the unity and diversity in Christ.

The Pope at once informed Nestorius, the clergy, and the people of Constantinople of the verdict of the Roman Synod and demanded of its bishop a public recantation within ten days; after that, judgment would be issued on him. Cyril of Alexandria was directed, in Rome's name, to see to the implementation of the synodal decree. This mandate was to have fateful consequences, for Cyril went far beyond his instructions. Instead of making the attempt to induce Nestorius to the required recantation in the appropriate form, he had him solemnly condemned also by the Alexandrian Church at a synod in November 430 and transmitted to him the judgment of the synod, which in the harshest manner blamed him for the "blasphemies" and the "scandal" that he had brought on the Church with his errors. In addition, Cyril claimed that Rome had recognized "that the letters sent to you by the Alexandrian Church reproduce the orthodox faith perfectly." And so he inclosed a profession of faith and twelve other propositions in which was contained what he was required to condemn. But in this letter and above all in the twelve anathemas were contained precisely the specific formulas of Cyril's Christology, which to Nestorius had always appeared dubious. He did indeed receive Cyril's letter, but at first he declined to comment and immediately apprised his friends at Antioch of Cyril's new demands. In these they saw new evidences of the Apollinarianism of the Alexandrian Christology, to which they must not submit. The fronts had again hardened.

Ephesus

While the envoys of Cyril, with the decrees of the Alexandrian Synod, were still en route to Constantinople, a letter had already been sent by the Emperor Theodosius II to Cyril: it made known that the Emperor had invited all the metropolitans of the East with some bishops of their respective provinces to appear at Pentecost 431 in conveniently located Ephesus for a general council. Invitations were sent also to Rome and Hippo, but Augustine was dead by the time the letter was sent, and Bishop Capreolus of Carthage designated the deacon Bassula to represent the African Church. Pope Celestine, whose decision in the case of Nestorius was now ready, had to consider how, in the new situation, to maintain Rome's authority so far as possible: he aimed to achieve this through letters to the Emperor and the bishops gathered in council, on whom he urged harmony. Once again, he saw his strongest support in Cyril, whom he appointed as his own vicar at the Council, since he expressly instructed his official legates to maintain the closest contact with the Bishop of Alexandria and follow his judgments. Thus Cyril regarded himself as the real master of the Council. That he wanted to fight for his Christological ideas was understandable. But the course of the Council shows that he was determined to promote the victory of these ideas with the most highly questionable methods. A strong escort of more than forty Egyptian bishops and of numerous clerics and monks would back him. Together with a group of bishops from Macedonia and the provinces of Asia Minor, Nestorius also had arrived on time. The Palestinian episcopate came late, but still absent were the Roman legates and the friends of Nestorius, the so-called Orientals — that is, the Syrian bishops with John of Antioch. In a letter John made known that they would soon be there: their arrival had been delayed by all sorts of travel difficulties.

It does not help Cyril's reputation that he awaited the arrival neither of the papal delegation nor of the Antiochene bishops, but on his own authority fixed the opening of the Council for 22 June, against the express protest of the imperial representative, Count Candidian, and a group of sixty-eight bishops. But they bowed to his will and thus about 150 bishops assembled in the principal church of Ephesus. To these — again under protest — Candidian read the Emperor's invitation to the Council, which was thereby regarded as opened. Only Nestorius, with a few bishops, stayed away from the meeting, despite repeated citations: he declared he would come when all the bishops had arrived.

The discussion in the first stage of the sessions proceeded in agreement with Cyril. After the reading of the Nicene Creed, the priest Peter of Alexandria moved that the so-called Second Letter of Cyril to Nestorius be made public, and after Cyril had made an appropriate intervention the bishops, one after another, noted that the content of this letter was in conformity with the Creed of Nicaea. The reply of Nestorius to Cyril's letter was also read but it was loudly condemned as blasphemous. The bishops likewise took cognizance of Celestine's letter to Nestorius and of Cyril's Third Letter with its Twelve Anathemas and, this time without a vote, put them into the acts. After some bishops had reported certain expressions used by Nestorius in private conversations, the sentence was issued that excluded him "from the episcopal dignity and from every meeting of priests." A letter "to Nestorius, the new Judas," informed him of the decision of the gathering. In a letter characterized by a powerful emotion of triumph, Cyril reported to his Alexandrian congregation that "the enemy of the faith" had fallen.

Nestorius and some of his friends issued a sharp protest against the proceedings of the meeting and blamed with special severity the local Bishop of Ephesus, Memnon. The Emperor's representative also reported to his master and declared the decisions of the episcopal gathering to be both illegal and invalid. Four days after this session, John of Antioch and the Syrian bishops arrived. When they had been informed of events, John summoned a countermeeting, in which about fifty bishops participated: for their part they now deposed Cyril and Memnon and so informed the Emperor as well as the clergy and people of Constantinople. Theodosius II declared that all the measures thus far taken were void and he would dispatch an official to make an investigation on the spot. Just the same, the majority of the Council met again, when, at the beginning of July, Celestine's legates arrived. These made known Celestine's letter to the Council, took note of the minutes of 22 June, and ratified by their signatures the condemnation of Nestorius.

When John of Antioch rejected Cyril's repeated citations, because he intended to await the arrival of the imperial officer, he and the Syrian bishops were excommunicated by the majority, so that now each of the two factions had visited anathema on the other.

Cyril's majority had thus completed its work, but the members could not disperse before the arrival of the imperial agent, who did not reach Ephesus until the beginning of August. Count John made known to the bishops of both factions a decree of the Emperor, which ordered the deposition of Nestorius, Cyril, and Memnon, and asked the other bishops to go home. When Cyril's adherents in particular protested, John had the three named confined in Memnon's residence. After a final attempt by the Emperor to arrange a compromise of the opposing positions — he had requested delegations from both groups to come to him at Chalcedon — remained fruitless, he declared in September that the Council was ended. But Cyril had already left Ephesus secretly, probably because he feared that in the meantime a successor would be given him in Alexandria. Nestorius, who had already received a successor in Maximian, had to return to his monastery at Antioch; later, he was exiled to Petra in Idumaea, and finally to the Libyan Desert.

But, just the same, the Council of Ephesus, in the midst of all the depressing human shortcomings, brought about theological progress in the Christological question. First, the bishops had, in their conscious renunciation of the claim to a new creed, indicated the Nicene Creed as the unchangeable norm, against which all future efforts at deepening the understanding of the faith must be measured. Second, by their solemn declaration that Cyril's Second Letter was in harmony with the statements of the Nicene Creed, they had recognized the *communicatio idiomatum* and the title of *Theotokos* for Mary as obligatory. Finally, with their condemnation of Nestorius, they warded off certain dangers for the faith of Nicaea which were contained in his new Christological starting-point. If, even through the approval of Cyril's Second Letter to Nestorius, no formula contained in it and no concept used by it was sanctioned, still the Council of Chalcedon could have recourse to it and utilize it for its clarifying and progressive statements on the faith.

The work of the Oriental bishops around John of Antioch was also not fruitless. As a justification of their attitude, they had presented to the imperial agent at Ephesus a profession of faith in which they confessed "one Christ, one Son, one Lord," in whom both natures are united without admixture, and that "on the basis of this union the Holy Virgin is *Theotokos.*" In the special situation prevailing at Ephesus, this significant formulation of the Antiochene faction did not have a direct effect, but when peace was concluded between Antioch and Alexandria two years later, this statement of faith constituted the basis on which the reconciliation became possible.

That Nestorius was branded as the "new Judas" and the "Blasphemer" casts a dark shadow over Ephesus. When later, in his exile, Nestorius obtained knowledge of Pope Leo's *Epistola ad Flavianum,* he at once swore in a letter to the people of Constantinople that he agreed with the theology of Leo and Flavian. His defense, contained in the retouched *Liber Heraclidis,* does not, however, make known any essential advance beyond the positions he had already achieved in 431.

CHAPTER 39

From Ephesus to Chalcedon

Reconciliation between Antioch and Alexandria

When in March 432 Pope Celestine, in letters to the participants in the Council of Ephesus, to the Emperor, and to the new Bishop of Constantinople, Maximian, expressed his congratulations on the Council's successful achievement, he was obviously only inadequately informed of the real situation in the East. The members had gone their separate ways completely unreconciled. The Antiochenes insisted on the withdrawal of the Twelve Anathemas by Cyril, who for his part demanded the express assent of the Orientals to the condemnation of Nestorius. And in the background there continued to lurk the still to be accomplished theological working out of the Christological problem. The fact, then, that relatively soon there occurred an essential rapprochement between Antioch and Alexandria was due, first, to the efforts of the Emperor and then to the energetic mediation of the aged Bishop Acacius of Beroea, who enjoyed the great respect of both sides. Theodosius II sent a special deputy to warn the two faction-leaders forcefully to resume the negotiations and also brought Simeon Stylites into the effort for peace. At the urging of the Bishop of Beroea, John of Antioch sent Bishop Paul of Emesa to Cyril with a letter into which the creed earlier formulated at Ephesus by the Orientals was inserted: it contained the recognition of the title of *Theotokos*. In addition, in the letter the deposition of Nestorius was approved, his teaching was condemned, and the ordination of Maximian as his successor was accepted. Cyril joyfully replied to this far-reaching accommodation of the Orientals with the declaration that now the same faith prevailed in the Churches of Antioch and Alexandria. For his part, it was a significant concession that in his answer he made absolutely no mention of the Anathemas against Nestorius and hence no longer insisted on their acceptance. The Emperor Theodosius and Pope Sixtus III (432–40) were at once informed of the completed union; the Pope sent his congratulations to the two leading bishops and thereby indirectly approved the formula of faith which had made possible the concluding of peace.

For the permanence of this peace, however, it was decisive to what extent the union proclaimed by the two spokesmen would be accepted by their respective followings in the episcopate. The Egyptian bishops made no difficulties. It was incomparably more difficult for John of Antioch to gain all the bishops of the Syrian region for the acceptance of the Union of 433. That finally the majority of the Orientals were actually ready to accept the Union was a consequence of the position which their most important theologian, who was also a man of the highest integrity of character and of deep piety, Bishop Theodoret of Cyrrhus, reached after a severe struggle. His hesitations concerning Cyril's Christology were ultimately founded on the latter's Anathemas against Nestorius, in which in the last analysis he saw Apollinarianism, since they spoke of a mixture (*krasis*) of the two natures, which would lead inevitably to Monophysitism. Once Cyril no longer insisted on the Anathemas, and Theodoret gradually understood that for Cyril the terms *physis* and *hypostasis* were not synonyms, he declared that, still urged by John of Antioch,

Acacius of Beroea, Simeon Stylites, and friendly monks, he was prepared to sign the Formula of Union. Theodosius II intended to draw the consequences of the position now gained, and in 436 he issued a severe edict against the Nestorians, which prohibited the possessing, reading, and disseminating of the writings of Nestorius and ordered them to be surrendered and burned.

The peace established with so much labor was again jeopardized when in 435 a violent discussion erupted over the orthodoxy of Bishop Theodore of Mopsuestia, dead since 428. The new Bishop of Constantinople, Proclus, promoted to that office in 434, then composed an essay in which he took a mediating position between the "Antiochene" and the "Alexandrian" Christology. In it he condemned some excerpts from Theodore's writings, but without naming him. But Bishop Ibas of Edessa, a resolute Antiochene, protested a condemnation of these propositions. But Proclus had recourse to John of Antioch, asking him to approve the doctrine expressed in the essay and the condemnation of Theodore's propositions. However, the Antiochenes declined to agree to the latter point because it seemed to them improper to sit in judgment on one who was deceased and had died in peace with the Church; furthermore, the excerpts from Theodore, torn from their context, were quite susceptible of an orthodox interpretation. But it was more significant theologically that John concurred with the Christological formula proposed by Proclus: "I know only *one* Son . . . and confess *one hypostasis* of the Word-made-flesh." Here the Cyrillan *physis* was replaced by *hypostasis:* the assent of the Antiochenes was an important step toward a formula that could be recognized by both sides. And since Cyril did not insist on an express condemnation of Theodore, the controversy ended and for several years peace prevailed among Alexandria, Antioch, and Constantinople.

Rise of Monophysitism

When a new phase in the discussion of the Christological question began in 446, some of the previous spokesmen were no longer alive. At Antioch Domnus had succeeded his dead uncle, John, in 442; Cyril died in 444 and his place was taken by Dioscorus, one of the most questionable figures of the century in the eastern episcopate; and in 446 Flavian became bishop of the imperial capital. Here had appeared some time earlier as herald of an extreme "Alexandrian" Christology the Abbot Eutyches. His basic thesis was that no one was permitted to go beyond the Creed of Nicaea and the decision of Ephesus — this was an allusion to the Formula of Union of 433. He expressed his own Christological doctrine in the obstinately repeated proposition: "I confess that before the union our Lord consisted of two natures, but after the union I confess one single nature." Since Eutyches had at his disposal a considerable following among the monks of the capital and maintained good relations with the scheming minister Chrysaphius, his godchild, it was not without peril to come out against his doctrine, which betrayed an unambiguously Monophysite tendency. But Theodoret of Cyrrhus, who in comparison with the weak Domnus was now more than ever the outstanding man of the Antiochenes, dared to launch the attack, when in 447 he published an exhaustive Christological work, to which he gave the title of *Eranistes* (*The Collector*). In this dialogue the collector expounded the idea that in Christ divinity and humanity constitute only one nature, since the divine nature has assumed the human into itself, as the sea absorbs a drop of water. The orthodox partner in the conversation objected that the two natures were not blended together at their union and that the divine nature is immutable and incapable of suffering; he supported his presentation with copious citations from the Fathers. Both in Constantinople as well as in Alexandria it was at once grasped that from now on Theodoret of Cyrrhus would be the opponent in any effort to assist a Monophysite Christology to victory. At once Dioscorus imperiously demanded of Domnus the removal of Theodoret from office and the approval of Cyril's Anathemas. The decisive reply of the two Antiochenes to Dioscorus, however, left no doubt that the Union of 433 would still not be sacrificed.

Naturally, Bishop Flavian was acquainted with the view of Eutyches, but he was not aggressive in character and at first he avoided taking any stand. However, in November 448 Eusebius of Dorylaeum, well known from his days in Constantinople under Nestorius, brought before the *Synodos Endemousa* the accusation that Eutyches rejected the doctrine of the two natures in Christ as set down in Cyril's Second Letter to Nestorius and in the Formula of Union of 433. After some evading tactics, Eutyches finally presented himself with a considerable retinue of monks and officials before the synodal court. At first he tried to parry by means of a neutral creed and a general assertion of his orthodoxy, but he was then asked directly whether he accepted the formulas "of two natures" and "the two natures." As a consequence of his refusal, the verdict of the Synod deprived him of his abbatial and his priestly dignities and declared him anathema. In a series of letters to the Bishops of Alexandria, Jerusalem, Thessalonica, to Peter Chrysologus of Ravenna, and to Pope Leo I, Eutyches emotionally complained that some people wanted to exclude him, a septuagenarian, from the number of the faithful, although he aimed only to adhere to the faith of Nicaea and Ephesus. In addition, he skillfully exploited his relationship with Chrysaphius, who influenced the Emperor entirely in favor of Eutyches and who finally succeeded in converting him to the idea of a new council, which probably sprang from Eutyches himself. Bishop Flavian, it is true, tried to thwart his plan and hence had recourse to Leo the Great, but it was already too late. A decree of the Emperor, dated 30 March 449, appointed 1 August for the opening of the Council: the place of the sessions should again be Ephesus. A special invitation proceeded to the Syrian Archimandrite Barsumas, because he had proved himself in the struggle against the heresy of Nestorius, and contrary to all custom he had the right to sit and vote at the imperial Synod. Dioscorus was asked to bring along twenty Egyptian bishops; at the same time he was told that Theodoret of Cyrrhus was forbidden to take part in the Council; the strongest theological force of the opposition was thus shamefully excluded. The purpose was clear: without any risk, Eutyches was to be rehabilitated, Flavian deposed, and all "Nestorians" rendered innocuous.

As soon as he had received the invitation, Leo the Great named as his legates Bishop Julius of Puteoli, the Priest Renatus, and the Deacon Hilary — destined to be his successor — and to them he gave letters to various personages of the capital as well as to the Emperor and Bishop Flavian. Since Bishop Flavian had again and again urgently alerted the Pope to the danger which could proceed from so well planned an imperial Synod, he tried to induce the Emperor to forgo the Council, but in vain. The letter to Flavian was the great *Epistola dogmatica ad Flavianum*, the so-called "Tome of Leo," the Roman decision on the Christological problem. Flavian's apprehensions received a further confirmation, when on 6 August 449 the Emperor designated Dioscorus as president of the imperial Synod, which met two days later in the same church as eighteen years previously. The Emperor had sent a strong police squadron. Eutyches had ordered his monastic following to come from the capital to Ephesus, Barsumas brought a group of Syrian monks, and Dioscorus had with him a detachment of Alexandrian *parabolani* — members of a guild of nurses of the sick, who could be used for other purposes also. As early as the first session, Dioscorus made known how he intended to preside over the Synod. He disregarded the desire of the papal legates, who wanted Leo's letter to be read aloud at the beginning of the proceedings. Then Dioscorus called for a vote as to whether Eutyches was orthodox: 113 of about 140 participants agreed that he was and hence rehabilitated him. Then the seventh canon of the Synod of Ephesus of 431 was read: it forbade adding anything to the Nicene Creed or making any changes in it. According to Dioscorus, Flavian and Eusebius had violated this prescription; hence they were deposed, and the bishops were expected to ratify this act by their signatures. When Flavian protested against this procedure, when the Roman deacon called out *contradicitur* into the church, and some bishops likewise expressed hesitations, Dioscorus had the church doors opened and soldiers, noisy monks, and a shouting mob streamed in. In the midst of this tumult the overawed bishops signed the decree of deposition of Eusebius and Flavian. He was at once banished and died soon after on the way to his place of exile. In another session, Dioscorus by the same means achieved his ultimate goal: the proscription of the Bishops Ibas and Theodoret, who were absent, and of Domnus of Antioch. By this deposition of the three leading Antiochenes, the Union of 433 was annulled and, to all appearances, the Monophysite faction had achieved a triumphal success. When Pope Leo had received the report of his deacon Hilary on the course of this imperial Synod, he could characterize it only with the statement that it was no *iudicium* but a *latrocinium,* the Robber Synod of Ephesus.

The Ecumenical Council of Chalcedon (451)

What little importance the Alexandrian Dioscorus attributed to Rome's attitude was ascertained, not without surprise, when he tried to make the Monophysite Christology alone valid. In this case also his actions clearly revealed his distance from the stature of his predecessor, Cyril. The affront to the papal legates and the condemnation of Pope Leo at Ephesus, managed by him, were to hurt him seriously when it came time to pass judgment on him at Chalcedon. He was perhaps still en route home when Flavian's appeal was sent to Leo the Great, soon to be followed by that of Theodoret of Cyrrhus. The Pope immediately fell in with Flavian's suggestion that a new council be summoned. After a Roman Synod had strongly condemned the decisions of Ephesus of 29 September 449, the Pope wrote to the Emperor, to the latter's sister Pulcheria, to the clergy, and to the monks of the capital who were loyal to Flavian. He urgently pressed the Emperor to annul the decisions just recently reached at Ephesus until a great synod in Italy, at which bishops *ex toto orbe terrarum* should be present, should restore unity of faith. Theodosius coldly replied that the law had not been violated at Ephesus and that, besides, the Patriarch of Rome should not interfere in eastern affairs. But Leo remained unyielding. In a letter to Bishop Anatolius of Constantinople, who had made known to the Pope that he had become Flavian's successor, he demanded from him a profession of faith that was in conformity with the teachings of the *Epistola ad Flavianum* and announced that a Roman delegation would again ask the Emperor for the convoking of a general council in Italy. The legates could not implement their assignment. Theodosius II died at the end of July as a result of a fall. The heir of the Eastern Empire was his energetic sister, Pulcheria, who four weeks later married the Illyrian officer Marcian and had him proclaimed Emperor. With this change on the imperial throne there at once occurred a complete reorientation of the total ecclesiastical and political situation.

Pulcheria had long disapproved the ecclesiastical-political line of her brother. The bishops deposed and exiled at Ephesus were recalled to their sees, among them Theodoret and Eusebius of Dorylaeum, who likewise at once called for a new council. Eutyches was sent to a monastery in the vicinity of the capital, and Bishop Anatolius held himself clearly aloof from Dioscorus of Alexandria, who thereby lost all support. In his first letter to Pope Leo, announcing his accession to the throne, the Emperor Marcian declared that he was in agreement with the project of a new council, and the Empress Pulcheria wrote in the same vein. In the meantime Marcian had already informed the Patriarch Anatolius that, in agreement with the Pope, he intended to summon an imperial synod to Nicaea. Leo I assented and made clear that he was determined to do everything to prevent the repetition of any occurrence such as the recent débâcle at Ephesus. He explained that this time his legates would preside over the Council in the Pope's name and as his only representatives. In a letter to those expected to participate he defined within a certain range the tasks which were envisaged for the episcopal gathering: it was to reinstitute solemnly in their offices and dignities the bishops punished at Ephesus because of their fidelity to the faith; it was to adopt as its own in the doctrine of the Incarnation what had already been expounded in detail in his *Epistola ad Flavianum;* under the presidency of his legates, everything was to be avoided that contradicted the faith and the canons. A large number of bishops had already arrived in Nicaea by 1 September 451 and were awaiting the Emperor, who had promised to participate. Since, however, state business too often required his presence in the capital, Marcian summoned the bishops to more favorably situated Chalcedon on the Bosporus, and there on 8 October 451 they met for the opening session in the Church of Saint Euphemia.

With some 350 participants, the Council of Chalcedon was until that time the most imposing ecclesiastical gathering in history. Although only six of its members came from the Latin West, its ecumenical character was established from the beginning, because Pope Leo I had guaranteed unequivocally his presence at the Council. Thus at the beginning of the first session Bishop Paschasinus, as legate, spoke and declared "at the instruction of the Bishop of Rome" that he moved that a seat and a vote at this Council be denied to Dioscorus. The discussion proceeded not entirely one-sidedly and peaceably, since the Egyptian bishops tried again and again to justify their behavior at Ephesus, and Dioscorus himself was able repeatedly to take the floor. When the bishops who had at that time condemned Flavian confessed their guilt and asked the Council's pardon, he declined to join them in this step and did not appear again at the third session, even though he was summoned to it three times. Finally, in the name of Leo I, Paschasinus declared that Dioscorus was deprived of his priestly and episcopal dignity. Anatolius was the first to accept this verdict; he was followed by 192 bishops of the same opinion. The decree of deposition was signed by 308 bishops. The Emperor received a report on the course of the trial, and shortly thereafter Dioscorus was relegated to Gangra in Paphlagonia, where he died in 454. Flavian had already been rehabilitated in the first session, and to Theodoret of Cyrrhus, whom Pope Leo had earlier justified, a place was pointedly allotted by the imperial commissioners.

These personal matters had to give way to the theological theme on which the Council had inevitably to take a stand. As early as the second session, on 10 October, it became clear that the Emperor had other ideas on the form of this stand than did the great majority of bishops. At the beginning of the session, his commissioners moved that the bishops be permitted to elaborate an exposition of the orthodox faith, hence a new creed. However, the Council Fathers were of the opinion that in the Nicene Creed, in the profession of the 150 Fathers of Constantinople, in the letters of Cyril to Nestorius, and in Leo's *Tome* the orthodox faith was so authentically formulated that no new statement should be sought. A few bishops, however, asked for elucidation of some of Leo's formulas, and so it was decided that Anatolius with a few bishops should seek to clarify these points in the next days. When at the fourth session the imperial officials took up the question of the formula of faith, the bishops again let them know that they regarded Leo's *Epistola* as an adequate document. Only thirteen Egyptian bishops declared they were not in a position to sign the *Tome* of Leo and return with it to Alexandria. Then the fifth session, on 22 October, brought the Council to an extremely critical position. On the one side was the express wish of the Emperor for a new creed, because he saw in one the sole possibility of a union and a settlement. On the other side were the overwhelming majority of the bishops, who were unwilling to go beyond the Nicene Creed.

At this point the Emperor intervened and again emphasized that he regarded the issuing of a creed as absolutely necessary. Either each metropolitan could present one or a commission could prepare an acceptable formula for the participants; if that should not be possible, he too would like to have a synod meet in the West. Thereupon the Council appointed twenty-three bishops, who after only three days were able to present the definitive Creed of Chalcedon: it could also be approved by the Roman legates because in it proper regard was had for Leo's *Epistola dogmatica*. And so the Council was able to publish its decree on faith at the sixth session on 25 October. In a Latin address, Marcian said that he had convoked this Council "in order to strengthen the faith," and after the reading of the decree he asked the assembly of bishops whether they approved this Creed. Since all the bishops gave an affirmative answer, he thanked them for the restoration of the unity of faith and asked them to complete at once the still unfinished business of the meeting. This included the especially important question of the orthodoxy of Bishops Theodoret of Cyrrhus and Ibas of Edessa, who had been condemned at Ephesus II as Nestorians. Both men were recognized by the Synod as orthodox and as the lawful holders of their bishoprics.

The first serious collision between Greek bishops and the papal legates occurred in the final session, on 1 November, when the latter filed a solemn protest against a decree which had been composed the day before, in their absence, by the eastern episcopate. In the so-called canon 28 of Chalcedon the precedence within the patriarchates was regulated, and the preeminence of Constantinople over the other eastern patriarchates was established. Since the legates did not prevail with their protest, they reserved to the Roman See the decision on this canon, which was destined to play a fateful role in the later relations of Rome and Constantinople. A solemn address of the Council to the Emperor constituted the final item of the acts of the Imperial Synod of Chalcedon, in which once again the importance of Rome for the success of the Council and of the *Epistola dogmatica* of Leo I for the clarification of the question of faith were underlined.

No council of early Christian times has met with so varied an evaluation as has that of Chalcedon. The direct participants — Emperor, Pope, and the majority — saw as, above all, the enthusiasm of the solemn concluding session shows, that through this Council the true faith in the God-Man Jesus Christ was assured and thereby ecclesiastical unity was restored in East and West. A comment on the significance of the Council demands first a concise analysis of its Creed. Its decisive statement reads:

> Hence we follow the holy Fathers and unanimously teach that the Son, our Lord Jesus Christ, is one and the same. The one and same is perfect in his divinity and perfect in his humanity, true God and true Man, consisting of a rational soul and a body.
>
> The one and same is equal in substance to the Father in his divinity and equal in substance to us in his humanity; he became like us in all things, except sin [Heb. 4:15]. He was begotten of the Father before all time in his divinity; in the latest epoch, however, the same was born for us and for our salvation of Mary the Virgin and Mother of God in his humanity.
>
> We confess one and the same Christ, the Son and Lord, the only-begotten, who exists in two natures, without admixture, without change, without division, without separation.
>
> The difference of natures was never annulled through the union; rather the special property of each nature is preserved as the two come together into one person or *hypostasis.*
>
> We confess, not one separated and mutilated into two persons, but one and the same only-begotten Son, the divine Word, the Lord Jesus Christ.

The first words themselves stress the principle from which the authors of the Creed would derive their conclusions: the basis of their statement was the tradition, as it was present in the Bible, the Creeds of Nicaea and Constantinople, and the decrees of Ephesus of 431; hence they intended to offer no revolutionary new formula, which would have, even in the slightest degree, violated the substance of this tradition. It was in accordance with this that, so to speak, each single formula was taken from the texts which were available to the Council; hence, in addition to the Second Letter of Cyril to Nestorius mentioned by them, these were the

Formula of Union of 433, elaborated by the Antiochenes and approved by Cyril, Flavian's profession of faith of the *Synodos endemousa* of Constantinople (448), and the *Epistola dogmatica* of Leo I. Here were found the concepts of nature, *hypostasis,* and person, but so widely clarified that they could be employed for a statement of faith that had now become necessary — necessary because the two dangers had to be repelled which most powerfully threatened the dogma of the person of Christ in the recent past: Nestorianism and Eutychianism. Since the then most important centers of ecclesiastical life each contributed to this conciliar definition, it could all the easier take rank as the expression of the faith of the Universal Church. The Creed of Chalcedon accordingly expressed, in its adhering in principle to the tradition, the Christological dogma in a form which corresponded to the real need. Its Fathers neither wanted to nor could do more in view of the contemporary state of theology.

CHAPTER   40

The Origenist Controversy
at the Turn of the Fourth and Fifth Centuries

Around the turn of the fourth to the fifth century there erupted a relatively brief but violent quarrel over the orthodoxy of Origen, in which Greeks and Latins took part. It represents the first phase of that development which would finally lead to the theological outlawry of the hitherto most important writer of Greek Christianity. In his lifetime the Alexandrian had experienced both rejection and recognition. Peter of Alexandria and Methodius, both of whom died in 311, raised questions especially about his doctrine of the preexistence of souls and his eschatological views, and the distinguished anti-Arian Eustathius of Antioch very sharply criticized the manner in which Origen used the allegorical method. But compared with these, the number of his admirers was far greater, beginning with his contemporaries, the Bishops Alexander of Jerusalem and Firmilian of Caesarea, his pupil Gregory Thaumaturgus, and down to Pamphilus and Eusebius of Caesarea, who dedicated to him a voluminous defense at the beginning of the fourth century. Above all, the teachers at the theological school of Alexandria regarded themselves as his spiritual heirs, for example, his pupil, Dionysius the Great, who defended Origen's allegorical method against the attacks of Bishop Nepos of Arsinoe, then Theognostus, who transmitted his views in his *Hypotyposeis,* and Pierius, who was nicknamed the Younger Origen because of the quality and extent of his literary works. Finally, Didymus the Blind attempted in a work of his own an orthodox interpretation of Origen's doctrine of the Trinity, but of course adopted the latter's teaching on the soul and eschatology as his own and hence fell under condemnation for these views in connection with the Origenist controversy of the sixth century. Basil and Gregory Nazianzen compiled the much read *Philocalia,* an anthology of the writings of the Alexandrian, and with them Gregory of Nyssa and likewise Athanasius appealed to his authority for one or another theological opinion; it was equally recognized among Latins such as Hilary of Poitiers, Eusebius of Vercelli and Ambrose of Milan.

The controversy over the orthodoxy of the Alexandrian theologian was again kindled to a bright flame in 394 by Bishop Epiphanius of Salamis, whose impetuous nature was united to a strong inclination to persecute all real or presumed theological errors. Since he had put the name of Origen in his catalogue of heretics, he was unremitting in his efforts to combat the influence of his writings. As the point of departure for his anti-Origenist activity, his Palestinian homeland had to intrude itself upon him, in particular Jerusalem and its neighborhood, since the city's Bishop John was well known as a zealous admirer of Origen, and the monks in some monasteries of his bishopric read Origen's works. Especially the superiors of two Latin monastic foundations, Jerome and his friend Rufinus, had, as translators of Origen's homilies, contributed greatly to the dissemination in particular of his ideal of piety in the Latin world.

Jerome says that at the beginning of 393 a certain Atarbius visited the monasteries of Jerusalem and its immediate vicinity and demanded of the monks their consent to a condemnation of Origen — perhaps by order of Epiphanius, but probably even without the latter's knowledge. While Bishop John and Rufinus firmly rejected this demand, Jerome, after some hesitation, assented to the condemnation of Origen. This 180 degree turn can probably be understood only as the fear of the monastic superior at Bethlehem that he might also fall under even the slightest suspicion of deviating from the orthodox doctrine. Finally the Bishop of Jerusalem had recourse to the Patriarch Theophilus of Alexandria to ask his help. Theophilus succeeded in settling the conflict at Jerusalem, and in the process Rufinus and Jerome became reconciled.

In 397 Rufinus returned to the West, first to Rome, where people showed a great interest in him, since he had lived for twenty-five years as a monk in the East. In his report on Palestine the discussion of Origen's orthodoxy naturally played a special role, and Rufinus decidedly represented the view that the theology and teaching on piety of the Alexandrian author had much to give to the Latin West. At the request of a friend he translated the first book of the *Apologia for Origen,* which Pamphilus and Eusebius of Caesarea had once composed. To the work he added an essay *On the Falsification of the Works of Origen,* in which he defended the really indefensible thesis that the contradictions and theologically doubtful opinions in Origen's works go back to unscrupulous falsifiers: for this he of course appealed to corresponding statements of the Alexandrian himself. In this he also alluded to the conduct of Epiphanius, who had seen it as his duty to defame Origen everywhere. Rufinus then set about translating Origen's theological masterpiece, the four books *Peri Archōn.* In a foreword he set forth the methodological principles which had guided him in his work: he had omitted specified passages of the work which he regarded as falsifications or had so modified them as to bring them into harmony with theologically correct expressions of Origen in his other writings. He further emphasized that he intended, by means of his translation of Origen's works and the method followed by him in it, only to continue the work of that great man who had already translated more than seventy of Origen's homilies into Latin and had announced further translations. Every informed reader knew that here Jerome was meant, but there is no justification to assume that Rufinus spitefully intended by this reference to injure him. Some Roman friends of Jerome had deceitfully obtained possession of the as yet uncorrected translation, which had not yet been released for publication by Rufinus, and sent it to Palestine with an accompanying letter. In this they expressed their amazement over the orthodoxy claimed for Origen by Rufinus and asked Jerome for a faithful translation of the *Peri Archōn*.

At once Jerome set to work, and before long his now really literal translation of the *Peri Archōn* reached Rome, omitting nothing, polishing nothing — unlike that of Rufinus, it is no longer extant — accompanied by two letters, one destined for the friends, the other directed to Rufinus, and of course both differing in tone and content. Apart from some ironically pointed formulas, Jerome assured Rufinus that, though he felt he had been attacked, he did not want to break again the friendship reestablished at Jerusalem. But the letter to the others attacked, sharply and irritably, the admirers of Origen and insinuated to them that they were also approving his questionable ideas and would in this way become heretics themselves. Jerome's friends did not send on the letter intended for Rufinus but saw to it that he received the second, sharp letter. Just as earlier, Theophilus, the Patriarch of Alexandria did an about-face and from being an admirer became a decided opponent of Origen and joined with Jerome in an alliance whose goal was the condemnation of the theologian, already dead for a century and a half, and the disparagement of all who treasured his writings. Theophilus had Origenism condemned at a synod early in 400 and in connection with this he undertook an anti-Origenist propaganda on a grand scale. In a series of Easter letters, which Jerome eagerly translated into Latin and disseminated, he warned the Christians of Egypt against the "blasphemies," the "madness," the "criminal error of Origen, this Hydra of all heresies," who equated the devil with the Son of God and forbade anyone to turn in prayer to the Son. In circulars to the bishops of Palestine and Cyprus, in letters to individual bishops, such as Epiphanius, he demanded the synodal condemnation of Origen and his heresies. Finally he had recourse in letters and through messengers to Rome in the effort to obtain also from Pope Anastasius I a condemnation of Origen. The circle of Jerome's friends was also active in the same sense, and so the Bishop of Rome also condemned "some blasphemous doctrines that had been laid before him, and still others put into writing for him, together with their author," and communicated this verdict also to Bishop Simplician of Milan.

Then in 400–402 Rufinus wrote his *Apologia contra Hieronymum*, which was intended first to be a reply to Jerome's *Epistula* 84 to the extent that it called into question Rufinus' orthodoxy, but became also a strong counterattack on the monastic superior at Bethlehem, whose inconsistency in his estimation of Origen was shown, as was the carelessness in regard to the truth of which his Roman friends had become guilty. In contradistinction to Jerome's method of working, who according to his own expression had dictated his letter *celeri sermone* and who had taken up his pen "as a result of a mere little rumor," Rufinus devoted much care to his work. Hence he pointed out to Jerome not only two acknowledged positive judgments on Origen, but quite a number of other and often more enthusiastic evaluations in his other works. He could also prove that he either had not or had not clearly held himself aloof from theologically questionable expressions of the Alexandrian, which he quoted. Out of Rufinus' whole work there is heard the deep disillusionment over a former friend, who, instead of discussing the defects and mistakes of his work in fraternal conversation by letter, had at once branded him as a heretic and besides had been the spiritual creator of the agitation stirred up against him in Rome.

The mere knowledge that Rufinus had composed an *Apologia* against him — again Jerome's informants were Pammachius and Marcella, who also gave him some details of the content — moved him immediately to write a reply in two books; to these he added still a third. In theatrical elegance and stinging irony Jerome's defense against Rufinus' *Apologia* is clearly superior, but in regard to content it is one of the most distasteful examples of theological polemics. He did not set himself to rebut the really sound criticism of Rufinus but tried to do so through mere sarcasm. His personal invectives against his former friend make painful reading. He unscrupulously questions the honesty of Rufinus' profession of faith to Pope Anastasius and compares his argumentation to the tricks of a fox. After reading the first two books, Rufinus sent Jerome a letter, which has been lost, and hence we do not know his final word in this matter — he kept silent for the last eight years of his life. And Jerome? When he learned of Rufinus' death in 410, he wrote in triumph that now the scorpion lies pressed flat under the earth of Sicily, now finally the many-headed Hydra ceases to hiss. No doubt Augustine expressed the view of many when he called this polemic of this former pair of friends a *magnum et triste miraculum*.

In the East the struggle focused ever more on the adherents of Origen; Theophilus of Alexandria had assumed leadership. And now John Chrysostom, Bishop of Constantinople, was also drawn into the conflict, because he had received some Egyptian monks in flight from Theophilus. He did not rest until he had arranged the deposition of Chrysostom and his relegation to the exile in which he died.

The controversy ended with a victory of the anti-Origenists. In his *Apologia* against Rufinus, Jerome had written that he had undertaken an absolutely literal translation of Origen's *Peri Archōn* precisely "to hand over the heretical author to the Church so that it could sit in judgment on him." He had achieved his goal. Rome and Alexandria had condemned the teachings and person of Origen; in Constantinople the unwilling bishop had to yield to such a verdict; and finally an imperial edict forbade the reading of the works of the Alexandrian. No formal condemnation of Origen as a heretic occurred until 150 years later at the Fifth General Council of Constantinople (553). But by then a consequence of the anti-Origenist strife that became deplorable for Church history was discernible: through the restricting of the view to the actually vulnerable theological ideas of the Alexandrian theologian, the remaining immense theological and religious wealth of his works was no longer seen and a stimulating aftereffect on the religious life and the work of theology was frustrated, especially in the Eastern Church.

CHAPTER   4 1

The Priscillianist Movement

In October 380 ten Spanish and two Aquitanian bishops met in synod at Zaragoza to discuss an ascetical movement which seemed in some parts of Spain and South Gaul to threaten ecclesiastical discipline and Christian morality. The outcome of the discussions was summarized in eight short decrees, which afford a first look at the unique character of this movement. Gatherings were forbidden in which women met with unfamiliar men, and certain writings were read or lectures were heard. It was forbidden to fast on Sundays or to stay away from the church during Lent for superstitious reasons. Persons were not to seek out hiding places in the mountains or go to unfamiliar farms for meetings. The custom of taking the Eucharist home from church was strictly censured. It was also not permitted to shun the church during the twenty-one days preceding the Epiphany on 6 January, to stay at home or in the mountains and go about with bare feet. One who had been excluded from the Christian community by his own bishop might not have recourse to another bishop for readmission. A cleric should not abandon his state in order to become a monk. No one should assume the title of "teacher" without the consent of the ecclesiastical authority. Virgins consecrated to God might not take the veil until the age of forty, after examination by the bishop. The censured behavior and practices were not designated by the members of the Synod as, for example, errors against the true doctrine: they were to be regarded as the expression of an eccentric and fanatical ascetical ideal, which was accompanied by a certain awareness of belonging to a chosen few, as appears in the claim to the title of "teacher." For the interior lifestyle of the community, this trend and the more prominent inclination to withdrawal from the community could represent a real danger in the eyes of the bishops. It is true that the synodal decrees of Zaragoza did not explicitly name any follower of this asceticism, but other sources leave no doubt that there was question of that movement whose leader in those years was a member of a well-to-do family, Priscillian, who also gave it its name. Priscillian must be regarded as the man who, on the basis of his background, education, and oratorical ability and because of his ascetical self-discipline and winning manners, from ca. 370 brought to the movement a strong following from all classes; among them were some Spanish bishops. The demand for the strictest asceticism is basic: it alone can really overcome the lusts of the flesh and the allurements of the world, and it is emphatically based on the Apostle Paul. The strong recommendation of fasting in Lent can in a sense render intelligible the decision of the Synod of Zaragoza in canon 2. The still obscure allusion of the Synod in canon 1 to "readings" in their gatherings is elucidated by the third Priscillianist treatise, which ascribes to the Apocrypha a kind of rank whereby they are, so to speak, likened to the canonical Scriptures and which marks as guilty before God whoever rejects them, because he repudiates the revelation of God made in them through "the Prophets." The Priscillianists' conviction of being a chosen few is strongly expressed when it is said that some of them are already proved to God as elect (*electi deo*) and when the author, as spokesman of all Priscillianist, loudly proclaims that he too possesses the Spirit of the Lord. This conviction of belonging to the chosen and the excessively high esteem for the Apocrypha could only appear to the bishops as suspicious.

The rapid spread of the Priscillianist sect into almost all of Spain finally induced Bishop Hyginus of Córdoba to indicate this danger to his metropolitan, who for his part turned to Pope Damasus I. Probably the Pope supplied the stimulus for the Synod of Zaragoza, since in his reply he stressed that no one may be condemned without having been heard. The reprimand expressed at Zaragoza in regard to the sect led directly to a hardening of the opposing views. Idacius of Mérida came ever more to the fore as the most determined opponent of the movement. He merely embittered the other side through his relentless pursuit. Another bishop stood not far behind him: Ithacius of Ossonuba, who was destined to play a pernicious role in the further course of the dispute. For their part, the Priscillianists' position was reinforced when Instantius and Salvian ordained Priscillian as Bishop of Avila, and two more bishops, Hyginus of Córdoba and Symposius of Astorga, joined them. Sulpicius Severus, who did not at all approve the tendencies of Priscillianism, blamed Ithacius for seeking now to suppress the sect with the power of the State and in fact, "through many odious machinations," secured from the Emperor Gratian an edict "against the Manichaeans," which deprived the Priscillianists of their churches and sent them into banishment.

The leaders of the sect — Instantius, Salvian, and Priscillian himself — utilized their exile for a journey to Rome in order to defend themselves before Pope Damasus, but they were not received; similarly later they were not admitted to see Ambrose of Milan: they could only conclude that both had seen the decrees of the Synod of Zaragoza as cutting off the Priscillianists from the ecclesiastical community. Now, for their part, the Priscillianists followed the same route that Ithacius had taken earlier and through bribery obtained a rescript from the *magister officiorum* Macedonius that gave them back their churches and enabled Priscillian and Instantius — Salvian had died at Rome to return to Spain. Here they could reorganize their forces. The free development of the Priscillianist movement seemed assured.

But the political development in the West unexpectedly promoted the plans for revenge entertained by Ithacius. Maximus had himself acclaimed as Emperor in Britain in 383, and, since the usurper made Trier his residence, Ithacius soon succeeded through mendacious representations in so injuring the Priscillianist leadership in the Emperor's eyes that the latter ordered that the principal persons among the accused had to present themselves to an ecclesiastical Synod at Bordeaux, ca. the spring of 384. When the first, Instantius, sought to defend himself, he was deprived of his episcopal office by the Synod. But Priscillian rejected the bishops as judges and, in a striking inconsistency, appealed — in one of the canons ascribed to him he had condemned the provision that clerics should have recourse to the secular court for their defense — to the Emperor, to his own undoing. Sulpicius rightly blamed the members of the Synod of Bordeaux, who, instead of passing sentence as the canonically appropriate judges, even on an unwilling Priscillian, or, if he rejected them as prejudiced, transferring their right to other bishops, freed the way for a civil trial. This could have very serious consequences in the future for the Church's claim to decide such matters as pertaining to its exclusive competence.

The conducting of the criminal trial at Trier — it had come to that since Ithacius had pushed the alleged criminal behavior of Priscillian into the foreground — took quite a long time. With Priscillian, several of his followers were brought to Trier, where the two bishops, Ithacius and Idacius, resumed with renewed vehemence their prosecution of the accused and also of all those suspected as sympathetic to the ideas of Priscillian. This suspicion even befell Martin of Tours, who during a stay at Trier earnestly entreated both Ithacius and the Emperor to withdraw the charges from the secular court and not to shed blood, for it was entirely sufficient if the accused were cut off from the Church by a sentence of the bishops. In fact, the beginning of the process was postponed so long as Martin stayed at Trier. After his departure, the Emperor yielded to pressure and authorized the trial. After the second examination, Priscillian was found guilty of the crime of magic (*maleficium*): he did not deny this or other moral lapses, such as participation in prostitution. He remained in prison until the Emperor, having received the Prefect's report, decreed the death penalty for Priscillian and some of his associates; it was to be carried out on him at once by beheading, but this was probably not done before 386. Further sentences of death were issued in processes immediately following; others accused were punished by banishment, which affected the Bishop Instantius, already deposed in Bordeaux.

The echo from the death penalty was vast and, happily, clearly disapproving among the most important bishops of the day. Even before the execution, Ambrose of Milan, during a stay at Trier, had coldly declined any meeting with the group of bishops who were demanding the death of the Priscillianists, and he thereby gained the disfavor of the Emperor. Martin of Tours likewise refused his *communio* to them and was only prepared for a gesture of accommodation when the Emperor promised to recall the officials he had already sent to Spain to proceed against allegedly refractory Priscillianists. Apparently Pope Siricius had also asked the Emperor for a report on the Trier proceedings; the latter sent him the acts of the trial and assured the Pope that the verdict was reached in a correct procedure on the basis of the confession of the accused persons. Ithacius lost his Spanish see of Ossonuba through deposition, Idacius preferred to abdicate his voluntarily. The incident had a further sequel for Felix, Bishop of Trier. Although, as Sulpicius Severus expressly stresses, his behavior was beyond reproach, many Gallic bishops denied him their communion because he had upheld the ordination of the friends of Ithacius and hence was regarded as a representative of their faction. Pope Siricius and Ambrose adhered to this view. This so-called Gallic Felician Schism, with its unhappy consequences for the Church in Gaul, only ended with the death of Felix or, more probably, with his renunciation of the see of Trier, which followed the Synod of Turin (ca. 398–401). The most balanced judgment on the affair of Priscillian was expressed by Sulpicius Severus when he said that he disliked both the guilty and the accusers, and among these latter most of all Ithacius, in whom was nothing holy, to whom, along with Idacius, what mattered was rather to overcome the hated opponent than the heresy.

The end of Priscillian and his companions by no means meant also the end of the Priscillianist movement. In Spain the execution of its leaders at first even evoked new sympathy. His adherents now honored Priscillian as a martyr and prepared an imposing funeral for him and the other dead after the transfer of their remains there; and to swear in Priscillian's name was regarded as a deeply religious act. Up to the Synod of Toledo, between 397 and 400, whose central theme was again Priscillianism, a group of bishops belonged to the movement who abjured their error only in connection with this Synod. Other bishops and clerics, who had compromised themselves after Priscillian's execution through their sympathy for the sect, were stripped of their offices; others, who were only convinced of the error of their doctrines through reading the works of Ambrose, were allowed to retain their sees. Naturally, such gentleness seemed inappropriate to some bishops, and there resulted a schism between a rigorist and a conciliatory wing in the Spanish episcopate, which only an energetic warning from Pope Innocent I, addressed to the rigorists, could heal. The Synod of Toledo, in addition to twenty disciplinary canons and a profession of faith, issued eighteen brief anathemas, which dealt exclusively with Priscillianism and made known that the movement was then more and more assuming heterodox characteristics. Thus to it were now ascribed, for example, a strong Sabellian doctrine of the Trinity (canons 2–4) and an incorrect Christology (canons 5–7, 13), as well as Manichaean and Gnostic traits, since they taught that there was one God of the Old Testament and another of the gospels (canon 8; cf. also canons 1 and 9). The excessive estimation of the Apocrypha was again condemned (canon 12), and likewise the rejection of marriage (canon 16), the refusal to eat flesh meat (canon 17), and astrological practices (canon 15). The Synod repeatedly based its judgment on the works and letters of Priscillian. The movement was considered to be still very dangerous and hence the bishops were admonished to the greatest vigilance. The sect was still alive in the sixth century. The last report of the existence of at least a few Priscillianists points to Braga in northwestern Spain. Pope Vigilius mentions them in 538 in a letter to the city's bishop. The Synod of Braga in 565 finally directed attention against their Apocrypha, took a position against them in seventeen anathemas, and urged the bishop to intense zeal in the struggle against the heresy.

CHAPTER 42

The Struggle with Donatism

Donatism under the Constantinian Dynasty

After 320 the Emperor Constantine I increasingly had given up his various efforts to restore the unity of the Church which had been shattered in North Africa by the Donatist Schism, permitted the banished Donatists to return to their homes in May 321, and in a letter to the bishops and Catholics of North Africa asked them to practice patience and leniency with regard to Donatist encroachments; in other words, in practice he had come to terms with the existence of two Christian Churches in this part of the Empire. But the moral condemnation of the Donatist leadership, finally expressed by him, in no way hindered the ranking Bishop Donatus of Carthage from using energetically and skillfully the now relative peace that had been provided for the organizational construction and inner consolidation of his Church. And so, undisturbed, the Donatists could erect their chapels, village churches, and even great basilicas, especially in Numidia and Mauretania. Only occasionally were there clashes with the Catholics, who were gradually reduced to the minority. Parallel with the building of the inner life of the Church ran an intensive propaganda by means of letters and sermons, which sought to make good the Donatist claim to be the pure wheat in the field, the true Church, whereas the community of the Catholics was to be despised as a growth of rank weeds. The success of the Donatists was considerable. Donatus could really feel himself to be Primate of Africa, when, toward the close of Constantine's reign, he gathered some 270 bishops around him for a synod at Carthage, where the conditions for the reception of Catholics into the Donatist Church were discussed. Donatus was flexible enough to dispense them from the otherwise strictly required rebaptism, if this appeared unacceptable to individuals. It speaks for their conviction that the future of Christianity in North Africa belonged to their Church when the Donatists dared to deprive the Catholics of Constantina in Numidia of the basilica that Constantine had built for them. The efforts of the Donatists to gain adherents also outside North Africa, however, had only slight success. At Rome alone did they succeed in founding a relatively small congregation, which, however, could meet only outside the city gates. Whether the Donatists on their own initiative applied for recognition by the Synod of Serdica (342–43) is unknown. In fact, the circular issued from there by the eastern bishops went also to Donatus and was later estimated by Donatist circles as a recognition of their Church; on the other hand, the successor of Caecilian, Bishop Gratus of Carthage, was present on the side of the western bishops at the Synod of Serdica. The Donatist Church thus remained a Christian sect substantially confined to North Africa.

In the first decade of the reign of the Emperor Constans, nothing changed regarding the reserve that his father Constantine had finally exercised toward the African problem of the Christian schism. The steadily growing consolidation of the Donatist Church and the much more impressive position of Donatus at Carthage in comparison with the pallid figure of the Catholic Bishop Gratus probably induced the supreme head of the Donatists to apply to the Emperor Constans in an effort to obtain from him a unification of all Christians of North Africa under Donatist leadership. At first the Emperor sent the officials Paul and Macarius with donations for the poor and the churches of both denominations in North Africa in the effort thus to gain more exact information about the possibilities of union and to create a favorable climate. However, this mission led to a serious clash between the power of the State and the Donatist Church. At once Donatus saw a favoring of the opposing side. When the two envoys appeared before him, he greeted them with the famed *Quid est imperatori cum Ecclesia?*, refused their gifts, and instructed the clergy not to receive the commission at all. Vague rumors of enforced union, alleged to be planned by the officials, quickly envenomed the atmosphere, and when the officials went to the province of Numidia the attitude of the population there had become so threatening that military protection seemed necessary for them. As a matter of fact, the Bishop of Bagai, also named Donatus, was organizing armed resistance, for which he summoned the Circumcellions, a religious and fanatical movement on the fringes of the Donatist Church, but one that was at the same time determined to fight; it appeared, from ca. 340 on, with growing strength.

The causes of the rise of the Circumcellion institution are insufficiently clear, just as the question of the ultimate meaning of the movement has still not found a unanimous answer. Their followers called themselves, with predilection, *milites Christi* or *agonistici* and thus aspired to be regarded as heirs and representatives of the early Christian view of martyrdom and of readiness for it; but their exalted esteem for it often amounted to a fanatical yearning for death, which they wanted to suffer in the bloody fight with the enemies of the faith, pagans as well as Catholics. Whoever found this death in the struggle was considered a martyr and hence was buried within the church building and honored by a special inscribed slab. In addition to this religious fanaticism, a social ingredient must also be kept in mind in the Circumcellion movement, for some of its adherents appear quite openly as enemies of the wealthy Roman landowners in the western provinces of Numidia and Mauretania; they attacked and plundered them or extorted blackmail from them. The Circumcellions were, without doubt, convinced followers of the Donatist Church and its ideas but especially supported by a fanatical enthusiasm, which could make of them either martyrs or terrorists. The Donatist leadership consciously exploited them for its aims when it seemed expedient to do so, but it also held aloof from them when their conduct could become injurious to the good name of their Church.

When in 347 Bishop Donatus of Bagai recruited the Circumcellions for armed resistance to the Roman troops who were accompanying Paul and Macarius on their visit through the province of Numidia, this was to have portentous consequences for the entire Donatist community. The resistance group was annihilated in a bloody battle, and Bishop Donatus of Bagai was executed as the ringleader. In the eyes of the Donatists, these dead were also martyrs, and their Church felt itself confirmed anew in its self-awareness as the community of the persecuted through this incident.

These occurrences quickly led to a radical about-face of the imperial religious policy on the African question. An edict of 15 August 347 abruptly ordered the uniting of the two Churches under the headship of the Catholic Bishop Gratus of Carthage. Donatus and the other chief personages of his community who had not fled with the lower clergy were sent into exile. This shocked the ordinary members of the Donatist Church, who submitted as a whole to the commanded merger; thus the Donatist Church also had its *lapsi* and *traditores.* Resistance was rare.

The union of Catholics and Donatists, ordered by imperial edict, existed in form for fourteen years — from 347 until the accession of the Emperor Julian. However, it is amazing how little the Catholic leaders did in those years to change a decreed union into one of hearts. Probably decisive, however, was the fact that the Catholic episcopate just then had no personality of strong religious powers of radiation, who could have fostered in the Donatists an inner consent to the union, or at least could have made it easier to accept. The successor of Gratus at Carthage, Bishop Restitutus, found his time also powerfully claimed by the conflict over the Creed of Sirmium under the Emperor Constantius; in this the leadership of the Synod of Rimini was entrusted to him. And so, outside Carthage, the position of the Catholics was only slightly strengthened. In their real spheres of expansion, Mauretania and Numidia, the Donatists soon remained largely unmolested.

The hope of a reversal was realized when the Emperor Julian came to power in 361. At once three of the exiled bishops, in the name of the Donatist hierarchy, appealed to the Emperor and asked him to permit all to return to Africa from banishment and to give them back their churches. Julian ordered the restoration of the situation as it had been before the Decree of Union of 347, but the Donatists used their newly acquired freedom for reprisal, which often assumed frightful forms. Expulsion of the Catholics from their own churches, ill-treatment of the clergy to the extent of even a few cases of death, desecration of the Catholic Eucharist, dishonorable treatment of Donatists who had gone over to the Catholic Church — these were the order of the day. Since many pagan officials witnessed these excesses passively, because they knew that the Emperor had no interest in halting the fights of Christians among themselves, the Catholic minority was thrown back into a state of demoralization and resignation. Among the bishops returning from exile was the highly gifted Parmenian, elected supreme head of the Donatists. Through his leadership the Donatist Church quickly came to a blossoming in which it seemed to become the unique denomination in North African Christianity.

The Golden Age of Donatism under Bishop Parmenian

During the period of exile under Constantius, the Donatist bishops had come to know the qualities of Parmenian, since they had chosen him to be the successor of Donatus in Carthage, even though he was non-African. Within a few years he created for himself a position which left no doubt as to his authority within the Donatist Church and also showed him to be a match for all situations with which he was confronted in his approximately thirty-years' episcopate. The ecclesiastical and political atmosphere, favorable to Donatism under the Emperor Julian, certainly made it easier for him to grow rapidly into his round of duties, and so also did the fact that Julian's successors, by reason of the Arian confusion, had to concentrate their ecclesiastical and political interests on the eastern and European provinces and thus let him work virtually undisturbed at rebuilding his community. But the deeper reasons for his unquestionable successes are to be found in his character and intellectual qualities. Praise was bestowed on him, not only by the Donatist side, on the ground that he was assured in his decisions, remained loyal to his convictions, kept himself aloof from intrigue and brutality, and in specifically Donatist concepts was a man of the middle course. His oratorical and literary endowment (*eloquentia*) was expressly recognized by Augustine.

The new supreme head of the Donatists also played a substantial role in the rise of the Donatist theological literature, which occurred at the period of Parmenian's episcopate. To his pen are due the "New Psalms," probably rhymed songs which were supposed to make the basic doctrines of their confession more easily understood by the laity and which were still popular in Augustine's time. In the first years of his activity he tackled a work which probably bore the title of *Adversus ecclesiam traditorum* and in five books presented a comprehensive and also original ecclesiology of the Donatists. The care which Optatus of Mileve devoted to refuting it gives an indication of the impression which it left on the Catholic side. According to Parmenian, the true Church can be recognized by this, that, as the Bride of Christ, it possesses a fivefold dowry: the *cathedra,* that is, the power of the keys entrusted to the bishops; the angel, who stirs the water at baptism (John 5:4); the Holy Spirit; the baptismal font (*fons*) and the baptismal creed (*sigillum*), without which the font cannot be opened. Since these five gifts can be found all together only in the Donatist community, the Catholics are branches torn from the tree of the Church. With a clear appeal to Cyprian's *De unitate ecclesiae,* Parmenian further argued that the Catholics had, through recourse to the power of the State against the Donatists, automatically betrayed the true Church; hence a return to it called for penance, which, however, was unthinkable without rebaptism. The cruelties blamed on them by the Catholics were not to be compared to the violence of the imperial soldiery but were a legitimate reaction against the persecutors of the Church, even if bishops were responsible for them.

More significant was the controversy which Parmenian had to engage in with a member of his own Church, the lay theologian Tyconius, who must be regarded as one of the most important writers of Donatism. His scriptural studies had let him achieve, above all, a universal understanding of the Church, as its own community reveals it. Even the non-African Christian groups were for Tyconius' churches, even if they were in communion with the *traditores* of North Africa. The biblical parable of the weeds which grew with the wheat induced him to question also the Donatist demand that, as the Church of the Pure, it must hold itself aloof from every staining contact with the wicked. Christianity would, on the contrary, be divided through a much deeper split into two parts, into a kingdom of God and a kingdom of Satan: to which of the two kingdoms the individual Christian belongs by virtue of his own voluntary decision will only be made known on Judgment Day. In an open letter Parmenian rejected Tyconius' dangerous theses: a review of the history of Donatism shows how, in fact, the entire non-Donastic Christianity became guilty through its communion with the *traditores,* so that only the Church of the Donatists, as the one persecuted by the Emperors, is the pure one, unique also in the possession of the true baptism of Christ. More than twenty years later, Augustine, at the urging of his fellow bishops, wrote a refutation of this *Epistula Parmeniani,* so powerful still was the influence it exercised. Tyconius, however, was not dissuaded from his views by it, and so Parmenian had him excommunicated from the Donatist Church at a synod. With the condemnation of Tyconius, Donatism gave up the possibility of a breakthrough into a greater theological breadth and became hardened in its sectarian narrowness, the creed of which was the cry: "Great is the Church of the Numidians: we are the Christians, and only we are."

Two episodes under Parmenian show how the relationship with the Roman State, necessarily poisoned by the notion of the Donatist "Church of the Persecuted," ultimately led, again and again, to damaging reversals for this church itself. At the accession of the Emperor Valentinian I in 364, Romanus became *comes Africae;* with his inclination toward corruption and avarice he did not spare even the predominantly Donatist province of Mauretania. When the Circumcellions resisted him and for their part also committed serious excesses, ten Donatist bishops under the leadership of Rogatus of Cartenna solemnly protested against them and finally separated themselves from the Donatists in order to realize the Donatist ideal as the Church of Nonviolence. More serious were the consequences for the Donatist Church, especially in Mauretania, when it openly sympathized with the revolt against Rome staged in 372. Rome did not leave unpunished the coresponsibility of the Donatists in this revolt: in 373 Donatist rebaptism had already been prohibited, and after the suppression of the revolt Donatist worship was forbidden in cities and village communities, and some especially compromised Donatist leaders went into exile.

Thus the last fifteen years of Parmenian's term of office became the period in which the Donatist Church achieved its fullest blossoming. Both the number of its members and its importance in the public awareness had clearly made it the strongest Christian denomination, to which the Catholic faction seemed ever more like a harmless sect. Also, the contemporary Catholic bishops were vague figures in comparison with Parmenian. This harmlessness of the Catholics caused even the animosity of the Donatists to die out and a certain patronizing manner in regard to the now apparently definitively beaten opponents to arise.

A change in this total situation, so advantageous to Donatism, only began in the first years of the last decade of the fourth century. It was occasioned especially by two factors, the one personal, the other political. After the death of Parmenian, the leadership of the Donatist Church was entrusted to Primian, a choice that was a serious blunder. Primian was the representative of an extremist group, who was also inclined personally to radicalism, appealed as a demagogue to the instincts of the masses, and had only a rudimentary feeling for what was genuinely religious. The harsh rule of Primian left with many Donatists a feeling of depression and facilitated for some their later passage to Catholicism.

A similar negative effect was produced by a second personality of the Donatist episcopate: Optatus, elected Bishop of Thamugadi (Timgad in southern Mauretania), in whom a bellicose religious fanaticism was joined with a strong inclination toward princely display. Under Optatus the Circumcellions became a paramilitary troop, which was at the bishop's disposal for every need, and for a decade it was the terror of the landowners of southern Numidia and especially of the Catholics.

Optatus took the fatal step in his career when he made an alliance with the Numidian Gildo. In 386 the Emperor Theodosius had made Gildo *comes Africae,* apparently because it was believed that his loyalty could be depended on because of his close relations with the court. His position was further strengthened when he was appointed *magister utriusque militiae* for Africa. But gradually Gildo yielded to the temptation to construct for himself in Africa a power independent of Ravenna. He saw the route to this in a closer connection with Byzantium, from where control over him could be exercised with greater difficulty than from Italy. To what extent Optatus was familiar with these plans can no longer be determined. From then on, he was allied with Gildo for better or for worse, even when in 397 Gildo moved to open rebellion against Ravenna by trying to stop the export of grain to Italy. Rome's commander in chief, Stilicho, immediately understood the magnitude of the danger, but craftily put Gildo's brother, Mascazel, at the head of the contingent of troops bound for Africa, since they had become bitter enemies because of a family feud. Since the deeds of violence against Catholics had again become so numerous that the Emperor had decreed the penalty of death against Numidian plunderers of churches, the military enterprise against Gildo and Optatus obtained also an ecclesiastical and political coloring. The Roman troops succeeded in stopping Gildo in the vicinity of Theveste and there annihilating him in the spring of 398. Nevertheless, the simple Donatist folk saw in the enthusiastically venerated Optatus a martyr, whereas his fellow bishops scrupulously held themselves aloof from him.

This defeat introduced at the same time the ruin of Donatist prestige in North Africa. The Catholic community could, it is true, after this compromising of the Donatists, build extensively again on the favor of the imperial government. But it could not be satisfied with that. It could only win over the humiliated Donatists interiorly if it succeeded in making clear to them the theological untenability of their position. Until now they had lacked men who had the qualifications for this. With the ordination of Augustine of Thagaste as Bishop of Hippo, a decisive change occurred here too.

Augustine and Donatism

When in 388, after an absence of five years, Augustine returned to his native city of Thagaste, the split of North African Christianity into two denominations had not directly induced him to become active for a recovery of the lost unity. Pastoral duty is the real key to the understanding of the tireless and versatile activity of the Bishop of Hippo, which for almost thirty years claimed his total spiritual and physical strength, at times to exhaustion.

It was first Augustine's conviction that the ideal route for the restoration of religious unity lay in the personal word, spoken and written — a route which was most in accord with his personal talent. A return of the Donatists compelled by forcible measures would have brought to the Catholic Church only *ficti christiani* and hence would have had unfavorable effects on the religious level of the community. Augustine's first efforts to make contact with the Donatists of his immediate vicinity were, then, supported by a strong faith in the strength of his enticing word. Wherever he saw the possibility of a personal conversation or of an objective discussion on the question of the schism, he courteously presented himself. When he noticed that a meeting with him was avoided because of his superior education or his oratorical gifts, he agreed to leave to the Donatists the choice of a partner in the conversation. His letters to Donatist personages are marked by a deep religious seriousness: knowing no insult. Without hesitating, he addresses them as brothers, since to a great extent they agree with the Catholics in doctrine and liturgy. In an effort to get beyond the armor plate of the hardened fronts, he proposed to leave aside the useless reproaches over the second-rank questions and to seek new ways. But the frost of disillusionment quickly fell on these exertions, begun with earnestness. They remained without important success especially as regards the bishops of the other side; only a few Donatist laymen were attentive to this new voice from the Catholic camp or even went to Augustine's sermons. The strongest effect of these first steps was verified within the Catholic community.

For Augustine this relative failure was only an occasion to seek new possibilities for the fulfillment of his spiritual function without at any time giving up the efforts for dialogue with the other side. He saw it in two courses: he must himself move out of the local confinement of Hippo and its surrounding neighborhood and draw the entire Catholic episcopate of North Africa into the solution of the task, and, second, the discussion of the theologically decisive questions must be pushed into the foreground. For the first element of the problem the ideal coworker was Aurelius, elected ca. 391 to the see of Carthage: his gifts of leadership and organization would be proved in a long episcopate — he died ca. 430 — and in a trouble-free lifelong friendship with Augustine. The theological assignment could at that time be undertaken by only one man in North Africa, the Bishop of Hippo.

The natural place for the consideration of the Donatist problem by the entire Catholic episcopate was the institution of the North African Episcopal Synod. It is to the merit of Bishop Aurelius to have infused new life into the episcopate, when, at the first Synod convoked by him to Hippo in 393, he had a decision taken to the effect that in the future the bishops of all the North African provinces were, so far as possible, to assemble annually for conciliar consultations. There is no doubt that this resolute leadership, after long years of resignation, gave the episcopate a new consciousness of its strength and at the same time enabled Augustine to explain his view of the tasks to his fellow bishops and gain them for it. Already in Hippo people were concerned with the question of the conversion of Donatist bishops and priests to the Catholic Church. The Synod of Carthage in September 401 left to the individual bishop the decision on the reception of Donatist clerics, but provided a new criterion for this: "when it seems useful for the pax christiana." It was further decided now to seek direct conversation with the Donatist bishops and congregations on a broader plane, this task being entrusted to selected bishops, who were to proceed *leniter et pacifice.* In all this it is easy to recognize the hand of Augustine, for whom direct dialogue was always a primary aim. Apparently encouraged by certain successes — by 402 three former Donatist bishops were heads of Catholic congregations — the Synod of Carthage in August 403 determined to try a religious dialogue on the highest plane. Every Donatist bishop received an invitation, which was delivered to him by state officials, to whom he was also to direct his reply. In the text of the invitation, the Synod asserted the sincerity of its intention and asked the bishops of the opposing side to appoint their representatives for a special synod of their own, with whom then the Catholic delegation wished to discuss *cum pace* every question connected with the split; a rejection of the invitation would, of course, be equivalent to an avowal that one was not sure of one's cause. But the eagerly raised expectations of the Catholic Synod were not realized. Primian of Carthage curtly declined the invitation with the original Donatist formula that "it is contrary to the dignity of the sons of martyrs to meet with the descendants of traditores," communicated his decision to all Donatist bishops, and thus anticipated the decision of his own Synod, which bluntly rejected the Catholics' invitation. The heightened activity of the Catholics and the partial success released, moreover, a new wave of acts of violence by the Donatists, whose victims were first the especially active Catholic bishops and Donatist clerics who had converted to Catholicism. Augustine's friend Possidius was attacked on a journey and cruelly mistreated, and an attack planned against Augustine himself was not actually carried out only because his guide took the wrong route.

When the Catholic Synod discussed the new situation at Carthage in June 404, there was basically a consensus that, in the face of such massive recourse to force, the protection of state officials would have to be requested. The Emperor Honorius had already made his decision. The Numidian Bishops had given him so impressive a description of the situation, with reference to their personal fate, that on 12 February 405 he issued an Edict of Union, which far exceeded the desires of the Synod. In this the Donatists were completely equated with heretics because they taught the necessity of rebaptism and also practiced it. To this corresponded strict sanctions: transfer of Donatist churches to the Catholic Church, prohibition of every sort of assembly, and exile for bishops and clerics who refused union. Carelessness in the implementation of the edict by the officials was to be punished by a fine. There was quick action in Carthage: Primian went into exile, and with him Bishop Petilian of Cirta. They went to Ravenna and surprisingly declared themselves ready to take part in a religious disputation with a Catholic bishop: the *praefectus praetorio,* as judge, should give the verdict on the outcome. But in the provinces there appeared everywhere strong resistance by the Donatists; the officials often withdrew in the face of it, so that in a series of decrees Honorius had to urge the implementation of the Edict of Union. The effects differed widely from place to place, and especially where the conversions were numerous one had to doubt the honesty of some of them. The fall of General Stilicho in 408, to whom the Donatists attributed a substantial role in the imperial policy of suppression, evoked among them the hope of a reversal. The report was spread that the prescriptions of 405 were annulled, and the Donatists sought to gain back by force what had been taken from them by law in property and respect. Aurelius of Carthage again had to ask help from Ravenna, and by word and deed it was made clear to the Donatists that the laws of 405 remained completely in force. The newly appointed Proconsul, Donatus, interpreted these very strictly and intended to impose the death penalty, but Augustine at once protested. Not until Donatus was replaced by the pagan Macrobius was the pressure on the Donatists lessened, and at the beginning of 410 an edict for North Africa surprisingly decreed that everyone could freely decide for one Christian denomination or the other. This declaration of toleration was, however, withdrawn by August of the same year at the petition of a delegation of Catholic bishops, which again explained to the Emperor the ideas and desires of the Catholic episcopate for a comprehensive and *definitive religious dialogue* of the two confessions. Thereupon, the Emperor on 14 October 410 officially commissioned the Senator Marcellinus to do the preparatory organizational work for this conference and at the same time appointed him as its president and arbiter. This time the Donatists could hardly hold themselves aloof, since two years earlier they had asked for such a conversation. At last Augustine's purpose, conceived years before and unwaveringly expounded, seemed to be fulfilled.

But had Augustine not long before turned against the idea of a peaceable discussion of a reunion by the fact that he was finally persuaded that a forceful solution was necessary and agreed to recourse by the secular power? A decision on Augustine's attitude in this question has to start with the incontrovertible fact that he himself repeatedly and frankly admitted a change in his views. He expressed himself equally clearly with regard to the motives which occasioned this change. First, it was the realistic insight, gained in the concrete and often cruelly harsh African workday, that both the life of individual Catholics and the free proclamation of the *veritas catholica* could be assured only thus against the force of the Donatist raids. Many Donatists, he further believed, would only then have the possibility of a free decision, when the pressure was taken from them to which they were exposed by their own leadership. Besides, state legislation in the past had led many Donatists to reflect and then to become convinced Catholics. And finally, he had acquired the insight that in the concrete African situation there was no more question of a mere schism, but of a heresy, which appeared most clearly in the Donatist doctrine of baptism, which made the effect of this sacrament depend, not on Christ, but on the moral quality of the one baptizing. Hence, against this heresy there must be recourse to the laws which the State, now guided by a Christian Emperor, had issued for such cases, with the restriction, of course, that in their application *caritas christiana* must always be assured and especially the death penalty must never be decreed. These laws, it is true, were understood as coercion by those whom they affected, but regard must be had for their purpose: they aimed to lead to the good, the holy, just as there was a persecution which led back out of error one who had fallen into the error. It was that persecution, as the workers practiced it in the gospel when they were sent by their master to the highways and hedges with the order "to coerce" the poor "to come in" (Luke 14:23), or as the shepherd is who "persecutes" the lost sheep, brings it back to the flock, even against its will, and thus saves it (Matt. 18:12–14). "Why should not the Church compel its lost sons to return, if the lost sons compel others to their ruin?" (*Ep.* 185, 6, 23).

Persons have aimed to explain Augustine's outlook by his inadequate view for the political quality and impact of religious questions also. If Augustine's anti-Donatist works are left to operate by themselves as a whole, if his pertinent correspondence and still more his sermons are examined, one can scarcely fail to hear that here speaks the voice of a man who was so driven and instigated by religious responsibility to bring back again to the Church the brothers who had fallen into error, that, compared with it, all other considerations moved to the background.

The Religious Discussion of Carthage (411) and Its Sequel

While the imperial rescript which ordered the holding of the religious discussion was not very conciliatory in what it said of the Donatists, the measures which the notary Marcellinus employed in preparing for it make clear the effort to win as many as possible of the Donatist bishops to participate. In a letter that invited all bishops of both denominations to Carthage on 1 June 411, he assured the Donatists that he would render his verdict in complete impartiality. For their part, they could still appoint a second arbiter, and they received the guarantee that after the conclusion of the conference they might return unmolested to their bishoprics. Until his verdict, all measures of compulsion against the Donatists were suspended. The response to this letter was everywhere gratifying for Marcellinus. The Donatist Primate Primian not only announced his own personal appearance: he also, through a circular, asked all his fellow bishops to arrive in Carthage as far as possible in full strength. A few days before the beginning of the conference Marcellinus was able to present both sides with a detailed agenda, to ask their approval and their disposal of the introductory procedures suggested in it. Even before the opening of the conference, seven bishops from each group were selected from all the assembled bishops as spokesmen, and an equal number of advisers were to stand at their side. The minutes of the debates, for the recording of which a bureau of stenographers was available, were to be edited by a commission of four representatives of each side and then published by being posted. The Donatists' reply did not commit itself in regard to the agenda but criticized very strongly the fact that only the elected representatives and not all the bishops present were to be admitted to the discussions, despite their having elected the delegates envisaged by Marcellinus. The Catholics not only gave their unconditional assent to the proposed agenda. They obliged themselves beyond it: in the event of a negative outcome of the conference, to relinquish to the Donatist bishops their episcopal sees; if the decision should go in favor of the Catholics, however, the Donatist bishops might retain their rank and office, if they joined the Catholic Church. Their effort to create a climate favorable to negotiations was unmistakable. In contrast to the Donatists, the Catholics also published their *mandatum,* the text with the names of their delegates together with the instructions imparted to these, in which was clearly staked out the line they were to adhere to in the discussions. The essential question must be and remain that of the true Church: questions of detail, such as "the case of Caecilian," must be sharply separated from it. A list of scriptural texts, probably assembled by Augustine, was appended for the theological argumentation. The accusations to be expected from the Donatists on the recognition of heretical baptism by the Catholics, on the employing of State power in the fight against the Donatists should always be rejected with reference to the entirely identical conduct of the Donatists on the occasion of the Maximianist Schism and under the Emperor Julian. For questions of historical facts, such as, for example, about whether Caecilian or his consecrator Felix had been a *traditor,* the documents of the official archives were to be referred to; Augustine had likewise carefully collected these. Every attempt of the Donatists to proceed to the discussion of individual questions of secondary importance was to be resisted from the start with the firmly stated demand to speak on the central problem of the conference — the true Church.

When on 1 June Marcellinus opened the conference in the Baths of Gargilius, there appeared for the Catholic side only their eighteen delegates, but for the Donatists the entire episcopate present at Carthage. From the first moment on it was their tactic, by raising ever more new questions of procedure, into which Marcellinus at first entered with great forbearance, to postpone or put aside the discussion of the basic theological questions. The first two days of sessions thus passed, whereupon the conference was interrupted in order to give the Donatists time for a study of the Catholic *mandatum,* to which they composed a systematic refutation. When, after the resumption of the debate on 8 June, they demanded that this refutation be read and at once discussed, Augustine immediately recognized his opportunity and supported their motion because thereby the possibility was given to him to proceed exactly according to the outline sketched by him and in a complete presentation to expound the Catholic standpoint in all important points. His supreme command of the subject, his certainty in the interpretation of the Bible, his exact knowledge of the acts, his quickness of repartee in regard to the Donatists' objections made him the dominant figure of this day. Late in the evening Marcellinus ended the debate and announced his verdict, according to which the Donatists had been refuted by the Catholics *omnium documentorum manifestatione.* A few days later he once again made known the result of the conference in the form of an edict, which was finally ratified by a rescript of the Emperor Honorius of 30 January 412.

Before long, the Donatist bishops filed with the Emperor an appeal against the verdict, which they based especially on the claim that Marcellinus had not only committed several mistakes in regard to form but had also made himself guilty of partisanship, even of corruptibility. But the state officials did not accept this and coldly and inexorably drew the consequences of the verdict. Marcellinus, in addition, ordered that all Donatist clerics who now still refused the union must at once surrender their churches to the Catholics, that the alliance with the Circumcellions was to be dissolved, and that all meetings of Donatists were thereafter forbidden. The imperial rescript of January 412 put all earlier prohibitions again in force, inflicted severe fines on the recalcitrant, if necessary the confiscation of a person's entire property, and threatened with exile from African soil the clergy who rejected the union. Again Augustine made himself the spokesman for *mansuetudo catholica,* which above all forbade the employment of the death penalty.

Although Augustine could claim for himself the decisive role in the issue of the religious debates in favor of the Catholics, he had no feeling of personal triumph. It is true that he once spoke of *evidentissima victoria nostra,* but by that he meant the victory of *catholica veritas.* When the mass conversions then got under way and he was praised as the author of such successes, he cooly parried this with *non sunt haec opera nostra, sed dei.* Besides, he was under no illusions in regard to the quality of some conversions and hence urgently emphasized the duty of the bishops through their pastoral exertions to procure the interior turning of the former Donatists to Catholic unity, as he tried this in an exemplary manner in his sermons. But a minority long refused to have anything to do with union. In 420 Augustine published his last anti-Donatist work; thereafter, the subject of Donatism is treated only occasionally in his correspondence and in general not at all in his sermons; and for decades from 418 it disappeared from the minutes of the North African Episcopal Synods.

Beside the solution of the practical pastoral task of restoring the unity of the Christianity of North Africa, there proceeded with equal poise the theological outcome of the intellectual confrontation with Donatism, which found its expression in Augustine's anti-Donatist writings. It is given, first, in the definitive explanation of the relationship of sacrament and minister, and, second, in a deepened grasp of the nature and mission of the Church. The Donatist practice of rebaptism originated in a concept of the sacrament that made its effect dependent on the "purity" of its minister. To Augustine this implied "placing one's hope in a man" and not in

Christ, the author of the sacraments, whose merits alone give them their efficacy. Hence it is not Peter or John who baptizes: it is always Christ who baptizes. The inner purity and sanctity of the sacrament is, therefore, attainable neither from the holiness nor from the impurity of the minister; it is neither enhanced nor decreased by such. Since Augustine again distinguishes between the sacramental act, which the minister performs, and the saving grace of the sacrament, which only the Holy Spirit, operating in the Church of Christ, grants, he is able also to recognize the existence and validity of the sacraments administered by schismatics and heretics, but they remain without salvific effect, since this is bound up with the presence of the Holy Spirit which, for its part, is found only in the communion with the true Church. As soon as a person who has been externally baptized has been incorporated into the one Church by the imposition of hands, he shares in the unity produced by the Holy Spirit and hence also in the sacramental grace bound up with it. It is true that Augustine elaborated these distinctions and principles chiefly in connection with the sacrament of baptism, but he extended them also to the other sacraments, especially to orders and the Eucharist.

Augustine enriched the doctrine of the Church through new, deep insights, which became possible to him through the distinction of the *ecclesia* as it now is and the *ecclesia qualis futura est.* Whereas the Donatists understood themselves as the Church of the Pure, which is without spot or wrinkle, Augustine perceived that in the "Church as it now is" good and evil live together until the judgment, which will produce the definitive separation. A person can belong to it *corpore* or also *corde:* in the first case, he indeed possesses the *communio sacramentorum* but does not belong to the *societas sanctorum* or *Spiritus,* and hence he also does not possess the *pax, unitas,* and *caritas* which are precisely gifts of this Spirit. The Church, it is true, is the community of those who hear the call of God in Christ or will still hear it, but the inner unity of this Church only becomes complete reality through the *pax* which the Holy Spirit operates in it. Thus, as this Spirit is the bond between Father and Son and hence perfects the community of the three in unity, so he is also the bond which enables the Church to become the "communion of saints." For Augustine, on the contrary, the Church is the spiritual mother of the faithful and, as such, holder of the power of the keys and of infallibility. Further to elucidate the reality of this *mater ecclesia,* Augustine with predilection grasped the image of the *columba.* He deepened and enriched the symbolic content of the Word when he called the Church itself *columba* and saw in this Dove the unique and faithful Bride of Christ; which, innocent and pure, groans for its sinful members and, groaning, calls to those who are separated from it, which received the Holy Spirit in order through him to give *pax* to all its members. Only one who possesses this *pax columbae* works out his salvation, and so Augustine holds in the deepest understanding to Cyprian's expression: *extra ecclesiam nulla salus.* Augustine thereby introduces the valid propositions in Cyprian's grasp of the Church into his own deepened ecclesiology, but there was in his days no theologian on the Donatist side who could have recognized this, taken it up, and so cooperated to restore the *pax ecclesiae* in contemporary North African Christianity in a less painful manner.

C H A P T E R   4 3

Pelagius and the Aftermath

The Ideal of Morality of the Pelagian Circle

The sources do not tell us when and why the Romano-Briton Pelagius left his homeland and went to Rome, where he lived from ca. 390 as a Christian ascetic, without, however, joining a monastic community in the strict sense. In the same circles of the Roman community in which Jerome in the days of Pope Damasus had recruited for the ascetical manner of life, successfully and against opposition, Pelagius gained the highest esteem and could gather about him a flock of the like-minded, among them a former lawyer named Caelestius, who was soon to become a zealous and versatile propagandist of the specifically moral principles of his master. Of his numerous works, only three are extant as to whose authenticity there is no doubt: a brief commentary on the thirteen Pauline Epistles, a formally very appealing ascetical treatise to the Roman lady Demetrias of the *gens Anicia*, and his profession of faith for Pope Innocent I.

The basic concern of Pelagius and his followers is suggested in concise form in the letter of a man who had joined the movement in his youth: he now knows *quomodo veras Christianus esse possim.* The Pelagians understood this genuine complete Christianity as the opposite of that attitude which was characteristic of the life of many average and half-Christians toward the end of the fourth century in the large Christian congregations, especially that of Rome. Many of these were all too gullible in regard to the view that the mere reception of baptism was a guarantee of salvation. Others excused their moral minimalism with the argument that it was in practice impossible to avoid sins in the allurements of each day; still others believed that the demand of a sinless and perfect Christian life was valid only for an elite. To this lethargy of resignation, Pelagius and his circle opposed a moral ideal which was characterized by a strong optimism in the evaluation of human nature and its capabilities and in a consequent appeal, corresponding to it, to the human desire to achieve. Only that Christian will assure his salvation who, by the exertion of all his powers, fulfills the *mandata* of God. God gave the capability for this when he endowed human nature with free will and the gift of distinguishing good from evil, gifts which, so to speak, represent a *naturalis sanctitas,* which qualified some pagan philosophers for moral capacity of a high level. In addition, God specially grants to Christians in the exemplary lives of the great biblical figures, but chiefly in the edifying life of Christ, a help based on grace, which stimulates them to the "perfect justice." Besides the *exemplum Christi* there is, furthermore, the constant reference to the heavenly reward which awaits the Christian after a perfect life, a distinguishing mark of the Pelagian preaching, which tirelessly called upon it to harness the capabilities proper to human nature for the supreme goal of perfection and which in this connection often appealed to feelings of pride and fame, which were accorded the goal achieved. The *verus Christianus* fulfills, however, not only each *praeceptum Dei* uncompromisingly — a distinction between greater and lesser importance is to him just as unsympathetic as that between venial and mortal sins — but he proves himself to be such precisely in the firm acceptance of definite attitudes, which the gospel praises as signs of perfection. *Continentia, castitas,* and *paupertas* are for Pelagius ideals which he would like to see lived not only by an elite but eventually by all Christians: in other words, he championed basically a moral Puritanism, which should realize itself in a Church without spot or wrinkle. Thus the Pelagian movement moved in a certain sense close to the moral rigorism of a Novatian, but in contrast to the latter Pelagius intentionally gave his following no organizational structure of its own. Thus, just as he neither entered the clergy nor attached himself as a monk to a religious community, so everyone should work and recruit for the program of an authentic Christianity by his life within the Church.

And so at first Pelagianism presented itself as a reform movement, which understood Christianity as a totality of the highest moral demands, which the individual Christian is called upon to realize in constant ascetical activity. The totality of these moral commands, the law of God, he finds in Scripture, which he must know and constantly reflect on. If, accordingly, Pelagianism does not offer primarily a theological system of doctrines, still it presupposes some theological notions and theses, which grew ever sharper in the course of later discussion. To these belongs a completely distinct evaluation of Adam's sin, which was only his personal guilt and could only operate negatively on the human race as an example of disobedience to God's command. The free will of man remained intact, and every man can, even after the fall of Adam, avoid sin by the strength of a free decision for good or evil. Similarly, grace, which God gives through Christ, is understood chiefly as the positive example of a Christian life, which strongly stimulates the disciples of Christ to follow him in the fulfilling of the *mandata dei.* Baptism blots out only personal guilt, and hence infant baptism must not be justified by absolute necessity for salvation. Even the efficacy of the sacraments and the necessity of prayer for a Christian lifestyle are undervalued by the Pelagian movement in favor of a moral accomplishment due to one's own powers.

The reform movement of Pelagius and his circle found a remarkable echo from the start. Even among many bishops of the day, the first impression was positive, and Augustine spoke constantly with appreciation of the ascetical reputation which Pelagius enjoyed. Caelestius especially displayed a busy propaganda for the spread of the Pelagian reform ideas, and soon there appeared a whole network of Pelagian groups, which kept contact with one another by a brisk correspondence, which, so far as it has been preserved, shows a striking inclination to remain anonymous.

The Discussion of Pelagianism within the Church

Hesitations about the demanding reform ideas of Pelagius were at first expressed more in the form of a diffuse uneasiness and, it seems, more in lay circles than in those of the official hierarchy. In North Africa it was Caelestius' theses regarding infant baptism that called forth the resistance of many Christians. The first official decision by bishops was brought out only by the intervention of the Milanese deacon Paulinus, who filed an accusation against Caelestius with Bishop Aurelius of Carthage in 411. Caelestius, questioned in detail before a synod as to what he thought of a guilt inherited from Adam even by children and of the necessity, then, of baptism for them, refused to give a direct answer and was condemned. Hence he had to abandon his plan of being admitted to the clergy of Carthage and go to Ephesus, where he received the priesthood. But the discussions continued, so that Augustine, who had not taken part in the Synod, as late as 413 delivered in Carthage two sermons on the meaning of infant baptism, in which he expressly asked that the other side not be branded as heretical.

The previous year, 412, Augustine, at the request of his friend, Count Marcellinus, had expressed his view of infant baptism in a special work, *De peccatorum meritis et remissione et de baptismo parvulorum,* and in it he made known that the Pelagian moral teaching threatened to compromise for him central truths of faith on the *gratia Christi,* the understanding of which he had gained in an unceasing exertion, strongly influenced by his personal religious route. He refrained from any personal polemic against Pelagius, whose commentary on the Pauline Epistles he had meanwhile read and whose entirely inadequate exegesis of the Epistle to the Romans he had at once ascertained with a sure look. His anxiety grew, the more Pelagian literature came into his hands. A Christian of Sicily had informed him of the activity of the Pelagians on the island and presented to him five of their theses on the question, three of which he discussed in a detailed reply: the alleged capability of man to achieve "justice" by his own power; the denial of an original sin in children, which moved him to a careful exegesis of Romans 5:12, and the obligation in principle on all Christians to renounce all riches. Two bishops had sent him a treatise which bore the inscription *Definitiones Caelestii* and also came from Sicily. Tersely and precisely, Augustine refuted the theses of the treatise in turn and then gave his exegesis of the biblical texts (*testimonia*), with which the author sought to support the Pelagian moral doctrine — *De perfectione iustitiae hominis.* He then elaborated with special care one of Pelagius' own works, the fundamental aim of which was to point out the high natural and moral dignity of human nature: in day-to-day life it is, he claims, of course, at times subjected to some rather fortuitous mistakes, but in principle it is capable of *impeccantia,* if one fulfills two conditions: (1) if he becomes aware that God has granted him the immortal gift of a rational will endowed with freedom of decision, and (2) if he makes firm use of this gift deriving from grace. In his *De natura et gratia* (415), Augustine tactfully did not name the author, although it was just this work that, by his own admission, had opened his eyes to the great danger which clearly threatened the salvation of Christians by its doctrine. All the more relentless was he in the case and he frankly exposed the basic error of the Pelagian system: it so highly commends the work of the creator — human nature, which was in no sense weakened by Adam's sin — that a redeemer is superfluous. To it he contrasted his thesis *of natura vulnerata, sauciata, perdita,* which makes a saving and redeeming grace, the *gratia Christi,* indispensable, and for it the Christian must pray unceasingly. Christ's redemptive act is intrinsically undermined by Pelagius, who also actually denies the necessity of prayer when he claims it belongs to the natural capabilities of man to achieve his salvation. With *De natura et gratia* Augustine offered what was up to then the most consistent refutation of the Pelagian understanding of human nature and at the same time the long authentic explanation of the relationship of nature and grace. Augustine also found a threat to the necessity of grace for salvation in the *Epistula ad Demetriadem* by Pelagius, against tendencies of which he strongly warned.

In 415 the discussion of Pelagian doctrine within the Church shifted to Palestine, where Pelagius had gone in 412–13 and had entered into close relations with Bishop John of Jerusalem. Toward the turn of the years 414 to 415 Jerome had tackled Pelagius in an unfortunate manner and claimed to bring his moral doctrine into relationship with various suspected ideas of Origen, Evagrius Ponticus, Jovinian, and others. Then in the summer of 415 the Spanish priest Orosius, who had spent some time with Augustine on his journey to Palestine, eagerly announced in Jerusalem the hesitations with which westerners regarded certain theses of Pelagius and his adherents, and thereby stirred such unrest that Bishop John arranged consultation for 20 July 415. But since Pelagius denied that he held the propositions attributed to him by Orosius in this form, John decided that the matter should be left to the Latin Church: here in the East the quarrel should end. Since Pelagius here too explained the propositions alleged against him in a sense which seemed orthodox to the fourteen bishops and since he clearly held himself aloof from the theses of Caelestius that had been submitted, the Synod decided that Pelagius "belongs to the ecclesiastical and Christian community." Pelagius saw in the verdict of the Synod not only a personal triumph over his calumniators, to whom he immediately made it known in the West also, but also a positive approval of his thesis that one can be without sin and easily fulfill the commandments of God.

In Africa the news that the episcopal Synod of Diospolis had rehabilitated Pelagius understandably evoked consternation. Augustine at once asked Bishop John of Jerusalem for a copy of the synodal acts, sent him at the same time a copy of Pelagius' work *De natura* with his own refutation, and implored him not to let himself be deceived by Pelagius. As a matter of fact, Augustine could no longer get rid of the suspicion that in certain situations Pelagius glossed over his real conviction, and his suspicion was further nourished when he ascertained some serious contradictions between a report coming from Pelagius and the text of the acts.

For Augustine it was first important to establish that the fourteen bishops at Diospolis could give an orthodox interpretation to the explanations supplied by Pelagius and, at least indirectly, also reject the theses of Caelestius that had been condemned at Carthage, when he at once saw that Pelagius would have inflexibly to give an exact definition of the ideas employed by him, as, for example, that of *gratia*. Thus he could henceforth deal only with what could be gathered from the works of Pelagius and Caelestius as their doctrine, and, now as before, this was in his eyes in contradiction to Scripture and the Church's conviction of faith. The two Synods of the African episcopate of the fall of 416, in letters to Pope Innocent I, asked him for his part to reject the Pelagian errors on free will and the fate of unbaptized infants. In addition, Augustine and some of his friends presented to the Pope their anxieties in regard to the growing spread of Pelagian ideas, to which a stop was possible only if Rome itself with its apostolic authority forced Pelagius to recant his *De natura* and the doctrine contained in it. Again Augustine attached a copy of this work and of his refutation, which he apparently regarded as an especially clear analysis of the Pelagian ideas.

Innocent acknowledged the three African writings in January 417. He approved the doctrine of grace expounded by the Synod of Carthage: Pelagius and Caelestius are *inventores vocum novarum* and should be excluded from the ecclesiastical community if they clung to their errors. He was, it is true, in possession of the synodal acts of Diospolis but could form no judgment as to what in them was true or false. He saw no possibility of summoning Pelagius to Rome for trial; he must come on his own to obtain absolution; the doctrines expounded in *De natura* are without doubt erroneous. The Pope's cautious decision did not perhaps correspond to all the expectations of the African episcopate, but nevertheless he condemned the Pelagian doctrines.

When Augustine spoke these words, a complete reversal had taken place at Rome. Pope Zosimus (417–18), successor of Innocent I, who had died in March 417, received still another letter addressed to Innocent by Pelagius with an appended creed; both were supposed to justify his previous conduct and teaching. Slightly later came a letter from the new Bishop of Jerusalem, Praylos, who very warmly took Pelagius' part. Soon after the death of Innocent I, Caelestius appeared in Rome and presented the new Pope with a *Libellus* containing a presentation of his doctrine; he demanded a review of the African judgment issued against him. In two letters to the African episcopate Zosimus reported on the events in Rome and the decisions reached by him: Caelestius should be regarded as rehabilitated if his earlier accusers could not demonstrate within two months in his presence that his confession was dissimulated. Letter and creed of Pelagius, the Pope said, had completely justified him in the eyes of the Roman clergy; it was incredible that a man of such genuine faith could be so calumniated. In Africa persons had acted imprudently and precipitately in the Pelagian question. Despite other attempts at interpretation, it is very difficult in the case of Zosimus not to admit an all too great gullibility vis-à-vis the constantly held protestations of Caelestius and Pelagius. In Africa people thereafter remained convinced of the danger of the Pelagian doctrine and probably sought also to gain the court of Ravenna for this view. Emperor Honorius on 30 April 418 after new troubles had been fomented by Caelestius, published an edict which banished Caelestius and Pelagius from Rome and forbade the further spread of their teachings. At the same time a synod at Carthage renewed the verdicts previously issued against the Pelagians and rejected their chief errors in eight canons. Finally, Pope Zosimus, who had already dissociated himself from Caelestius, expressed in an encyclical, the so-called *Epistula tractoria,* with the unambiguous approval of the attitude maintained in Africa, the definitive condemnation, which was to be signed by all bishops, and published in the entire Empire as an imperial Edict. Pelagius, soon driven from Palestine also and again condemned by a Synod of Antioch, perhaps ended his days in an Egyptian monastery, whereas Caelestius, now here, now there, preached further resistance or demanded his readmittance to the ecclesiastical community.

Julian of Aeclanum

A group of eighteen Italian bishops who declined to sign the *Tractoria* of Pope Zosimus included the young Bishop Julian of Aeclanum in Apulia, who now quickly became the spiritual head of the Pelagians. He had a good education, which included a knowledge of the Greek language as well as the study of Greek philosophy, in which Stoic doctrines and Aristotelian logic especially appealed to him. Quite early Julian let himself be converted to the Pelagian ideas, even though he substantially modified their ascetical harshness. His idea of Adam's life in Paradise is determined equally by the lifestyle of his circle and by Virgil's *Georgics,* which he loved to quote. His wit, his ease at sarcastic formulation, and his quickness of repartee in discussion had made him an esteemed figure in the South Italian upper class; they predestined him after the disappearance of the current leaders of the Pelagian movement to become the literary champion of their ideals. But to defend these meant not only to clash with Augustine but to make the latter's theology ineffective. Julian set up means and methods for this goal; they often left a painful impression, but here the contrast of the generations may have played its role. The young Julian sought irreverently to depreciate the achievement of the elders, while aiming to expose them to ridicule. He characterized Jerome's exegetical work summarily as childish and lacking in all originality; only with effort can one suppress laughter over it. His invectives against Augustine knew no limits, either of justice or of nobility. Like the Donatists, he did not refrain from pointing to Augustine's earlier manner of life, to represent him as an unconverted Manichaean, to point out his origin from a questionable family, to call his following a mob, and, accordingly, to brand him as *patronus asinorum.* If his remark that Julian was the architect who first put the ideas of Pelagius into a system was surely meant to be ironical, so also the long-drawn-out effort to refute this "young man" proves that Augustine regarded his work as noteworthy, at least as dangerous.

After the issuance of the *Tractoria,* Julian at once protested that here a signing by the bishops was extorted, whereas a council was needed to discuss the question. In a sort of manifesto the Pelagian opposition group developed its program: it would defend the freedom of the will as well as the essential goodness of human nature, which is free from any inherited stain; it would oppose the theses of the other side about a *peccatum naturae* as an attack on the sanctity of marriage, behind which stands ultimately a Manichaean heresy. In another place they formulated their theses in "Five Praises," which they wanted to proclaim: praise of the creature, praise of marriage, praise of the law, praise of free will, and praise of the saints. But at first the Pelagians had no possibility of realizing their program in the West: they suffered removal from office and banishment. Julian went to the East and found refuge with Theodore of Mopsuestia, where he busied himself with his literary works. These were especially his refutation of Augustine's *De nuptiis et concupiscentia,* to which he devoted two voluminous works, the *Libri quattuor ad Turbantium* (ca. 419), and the *Libri octo ad Florum* (ca. 421–22), which for their part are contained to a great extent in Augustine's *Opus imperfectum contra Julianum.* The essential issue of their confrontation is the question of *peccatum originale* and of the intimately related concupiscence. Augustine had proceeded from all men's need of redemption as this was expressed in Scripture. And since infants are not excepted from this need of redemption, despite their personal sinlessness, the explanation for this can be found only in the fact of an original sin, the sin of Adam, which was transmitted by him, as representative of the human race, to all his descendents. Augustine finds the fact of this original sin and its consequences for all mankind stated everywhere in Scripture, especially in Romans 5:12, which he explained according to the Latin text. He understands the nature of Adam's sin as the alienation of the soul from God to the visible world, as *amor sui,* which most powerfully manifests itself in *concupiscentia,* which in turn becomes most clearly tangible in sexual desire. The fact that since Adam the human race has been a *massa peccati* in need of redemption discloses to him further a glance at the concrete situation of mankind with its need, its distressing misery, even that of innocent children — a picture which the optimistic anthropology of Julian of Aeclanum treated with downright disdain. For his part he severely criticized Augustine's doctrine of original guilt and concupiscence in fiery words as Manichaeanism, without recognizing that Augustine's understanding of sin could in no sense be reconciled with the Manichaeans' material idea of sin and that it was exactly the Manichaean dualism as a whole that was for Augustine the decisive ground for abandoning the sect, even though he may unconsciously have retained from it individual but not especially striking modes of thought. In comparison to the naturalist and rationalist grasp of human nature and its possibilities, Augustine's theological anthropology is of incomparable religious depth, though also at times of a gloomy seriousness, especially in individual formulations. But this pessimistic basic trait never turns in him into a despairing fatalism, because the Christian Augustine was totally penetrated by a living faith in Christ's redemptive act, as it was expressed in prayer and the sacramental life of the Church, and to it he remained most intimately bound; Augustine the pastor, so filled with hope, proclaimed it, year in and year out, in his sermons to his congregation of Hippo.

The collapse of the Pelagian movement between 420 and 430 was obvious. Julian thereafter led an unending wandering life; in 439 he exerted himself to no avail with Pope Sixtus III (432–40) for restoration to his former see of Aeclanum; he was again condemned under Pope Leo I (440–61) and died in Sicily ca. 450. From now on Pelagian ideas persisted below the surface in various places.

Theological Augustinianism to the Mid-Fifth Century

In the last years of his life Augustine's doctrine of grace, which in its substantive form had long been fixed, obtained its final formation and at the same time its crudest formulation in his statements on predestination and God's salvific will. The occasion for renewed preoccupation with certain aspects of his teaching on grace was supplied by a letter from Augustine to the Roman priest Sixtus, the future Pope, in which he had sketched his idea of the total dependence of all justification on grace. The new position on this problem, requested of Augustine, was at hand in his *De gratia et libero arbitrio,* whose essence was the proof of the absolute necessity of grace and in which it was immediately explained in what sense the free will still endures under the operation of this grace. Augustine in a second work, *De correptione et gratia* took up the essential problem of the grace of perseverance: it causes with certainty the salvation of the one who receives it, but one to whom it is denied remains liable to a relapse. However, since it is at the same time an impenetrable secret, whoever belongs to the children of promise, every Christian, can and should be reprimanded and admonished to keep the commandments.

This very work brought about Augustine's final expression on the problem of grace. Letters of his adherents Prosper and Hilary from Gaul, both laymen, reported to him that in the local clergy and especially among the monks of Marseille opposition had developed to his doctrine of the separation of human beings into the chosen and the rejected at the creation, a doctrine which was contrary to the Church's tradition, in its consequences deprived every personal exertion for virtue and penance of its meaning, and placed the proclamation in sermon and catechesis in the presence of enormous difficulties. Moreover, these circles referred to the fact that Augustine was now proposing a new idea, since he earlier taught that election was based on God's foreknowledge, that man could of himself come to faith, and that an eternal punishment for infants dying without baptism was uncertain. Hence they held that a correction of his most recently proposed doctrine was necessary in the sense that the beginning of faith and perseverance in grace are attributed to the natural will of man, that predestination depends on the foreknowledge of God, and hence the number of the elect cannot be irrevocably determined. The determination of the calling must be so understood that God calls all men to the sacrament of rebirth, but that he intends to accept only the baptized into his kingdom.

Although Augustine felt that "he had done enough in this matter," he was at once ready with an answer to the difficulties of the Marseille monks, which he gave in the two treatises *De praedestinatione sanctorum* and *De dono perseverantiae;* they constitute a unity and were seen as such by him and by Prosper. The first was concerned chiefly with the problem of the beginning of faith, while the second placed predestination in the center. Free of any polemic against those who thought otherwise, but still very decisive in expression, Augustine here too insisted that grace is only grace when it is not bound to any ever so slight human preachievement; hence it is also necessary for the *initium fidei,* for the initial turning of man to faith, and then, as the grace of perseverance, leads to the perfection of sanctification. Far from taking away the free will of man, grace first gives him that quality by which he freely chooses and does the good. This radical lack of a need to merit grace and its universal effectiveness is, however, seen by Augustine exclusively against the background of a divine compassion for lost humanity, which, of course, can be understood, in connection with Romans 8:29f., only as predestining election for salvation. That this predestination embraces only a small number of souls, fixed from the start, was brought home to Augustine through the experience that only a minority live a real Christianity, but it seemed to him strictly demanded by Matthew 22:14: *multi enim sunt vocati, pauci vero electi.* Why the predestining call of grace goes out to these and not to other souls remains wrapped in the *mysterium* of the divine decree. Perdition strikes the rejected not through a positive act of predestination to sin, but as a consequence of their nonelection. God's righteousness is revealed in their fate, since they have no legal claim to his mercy. Since no Christian has any certainty whatever of his election, everyone can and should hope, pray, and love in humility. This so consistently operating system confronted Augustine inexorably with the universal salvific will of God, clearly proclaimed by Scripture — 1 Timothy 2 — but he did not succeed in solving this basic opposition despite his various attempts at exegesis.

Extreme Augustinianism, as expressed in his late writings, had its opponents, who came closer together after Augustine's death. John Cassian and Vincent of

Lérins turned definitely against his doctrine and now for their part represented ideas which overstressed the accomplishments of the human will in the first turning to grace. They thereby again called forth a defense of the Augustinian doctrine of grace, of which Prosper of Aquitaine especially made himself the leading spokesman. It was his aim, on the one hand to explain Augustine's theology of grace through extracts from his pertinent works — *Liber sententiarum ex operibus s. Augustini* or *Liber epigrammatum ex sententiis s. Augustini* — and on the other hand to demonstrate the weaknesses of the "Semipelagian" teaching of Cassian and Vincent of Lérins on grace — *Liber contra collatorem* and *Pro Augustino responsiones ad capitula obiectionum Vincentianarum.* In the question whether Prosper himself, in the course of the debates, separated himself from strict Augustinianism, opinion remains divided. Soon after Augustine's death, Prosper had personally intervened in his favor with Pope Celestine and sought to obtain a condemnation of his opponents: the Pope was indeed prepared for a summary praise of Augustine but refrained from any determination of individual questions of the Augustine doctrine of grace. There was never any ecclesiastical approbation of strict Augustinianism, but it still had enormous long-range effects.

Part Three

Inner Life of the Church between Nicaea and Chalcedon

Karl Baus
Chap. 44, Sec. 2: Eugen Ewig

C H A P T E R   4 4

Missionary Activity of the Church

The religious and political turning point of the years 311–24 meant also for the Church's missionary task hitherto unknown possibilities. The now favorable point of departure for gaining the pagan majority, however, concealed certain dangers for the Christian confession. One was that of conversions because of opportunism, which appeared almost automatically with the acceptance and encouragement of Christianity by the Emperors. Another, more pernicious in its possible consequences, was the temptation in evangelizing to employ, with the toleration or even the aid of the State, means and methods that aspired to effect the conversion to Christianity by pressure and force rather than conviction. Nevertheless, the outcome of the Church's missionary exertions lasting for more than a century was clear: around the middle of the fifth century the people of the Roman Empire professed and felt themselves to be Christians, except for a few pagan remnants, the closed group of the Jews, and some German tribes.

1. Christianization of the Population of the Empire

The mission of the Egyptian Church was ca. 325 in an especially favorable starting-place, since, with its approximately ninety episcopal sees at that time, it had already found its definitive organizational basis, from which the christianization of peasants, still mostly pagan, could be undertaken. In Athanasius it already had the supreme head of a territorial church, and he, aware of his goal, guided the evangelization from his center at Alexandria. The success of his missionary efforts motivated the still pagan circles of Alexandria to the resolute defense of their faith. The Emperor then had the great temple of Sarapis closed and transferred to the Christians, who remodeled it into a Christian church; the same fate later befell the temple of Isis at Menuthis. Beside the bishop there appeared also the monk as missionary in Egypt; he devoted himself especially to the conversion of pagan priests, since this usually implied further conversions.

For the external success of the missionary work of the Egyptian Church the assertions relating to the city of Oxyrrhynchus may be taken as typical. Circa 300, there were here, besides a synagogue and a dozen pagan temples, two Christian churches; a century later it shows twelve Christian churches, whose number increased still more into the sixth century. Soon after 400 C.E., only a minority professed paganism, and after fifty more years the christianization of the country was completed. However, many of the new Christians broke only with difficulty from the influences of their former religion. As late as 420 Bishop Cyril in his Easter letters repeatedly had to speak against superstitious practices.

Important stimuli for the Christian mission in Palestine went out from Constantine, who through his initiative for the erecting and adorning of Christian churches on the sites of Judaeo-Christian history, with their wealth of tradition, pushed the land of origin of Christianity powerfully into the consciousness of contemporary Christianity. Jerusalem especially, with its immediate neighborhood, obtained in the course of the fourth century — after a brief interruption due to the reaction under the Emperor Julian — even in externals the character of a fully Christian city, with the steadily growing number of its churches, monasteries, oratories, and hospices, which attracted even larger crowds of pilgrims, some of whom settled for long periods in Palestine and contributed greatly to the strengthening of the native Christianity. Even in Caesarea, the seat of the civil administration, there existed relatively early a rather strong Gentile Christian community. But in the countryside Christianity had as yet only a few adherents, since Judaism to a great extent refused to have anything to do with the Christian mission. The eighteen congregations of Palestine represented at Nicaea constituted only a minority of the total population of these sees. The powerful anti-Christian wave under the Emperor Julian revealed in the Palestinian provinces the stubborn resistance of Jews and pagans which the mission here encountered. Also in Palestine monks appeared as missionaries, such as Hilarion and Euthymius. The Christian mission in the three Palestinian provinces probably did not achieve its strongest impact until the fifth century.

The Christian community of the Syrian capital, Antioch, recovered rapidly from the reverses of the persecutions of Diocletian and Licinius, especially since it was able to enjoy the emphatic benevolence of Constantine. Up to the reign of the Emperor Julian, probably the majority of the city's population belonged to it, since the Christians could even dare public counter-demonstrations against the Emperor's measures of repression. Even the literary polemic of Julian and of the *rhetor* Libanius could not stop the progress of the mission, with which the atrophying of the pagan temple service ran parallel. At the end of the fourth century Antioch was regarded as Christian. This situation was also reflected in the number of the churches constructed at Antioch in the fourth century. Three factors conditioned this favorable missionary development of the Syrian metropolis: the greater power of radiation of the Christian message in comparison with the here especially questionable pagan system of worship; the intensive recruiting of man to man, to which the pastor Chrysostom tirelessly exhorted the congregation; and finally the attraction emanating from monasticism, highly esteemed in Syria, and from leaders of communities, such as Eustathius, Meletius, Flavian, and of preachers and theologians, such as Chrysostom, Diodorus, Theodore of Mopsuestia, and Theodoret of Cyrrhus.

Outside Antioch also the Syrian people accepted Christianity relatively quickly, since as early as the mid-fourth century there were churches in numerous cities and villages of the Syrian and Phoenician provinces, as appears from the reports of the Church historians on the pagan reaction under Julian. For the fourth and fifth centuries the existence of a notable ecclesiastical architecture can be shown in the entire Syrian area; moreover, the numerous Christian inscriptions permit the conclusion that at the beginning of the fifth century the majority of the Syrian peasants also professed the Christian religion. An informative piece of evidence for the situation in a single bishopric is provided by the famous letter of Theodoret of Cyrrhus to Pope Leo, whom he tells that his see embraces 800 *paroikiai*, by which can only be understood overwhelmingly rural pastoral districts. This complete evidence is corroborated by the status of the ecclesiastical organization in the territory of the Patriarchate of Antioch at the time of the Council of Chalcedon, which then exhibited some 130 episcopal sees. Once more a special rank belongs to monasticism, above all in the rural sections of the Syrian provinces. The early Stylites had already established their reputation among the people in the service of evangelization. Edessa itself needed in the fourth century only to give to the external picture of the city a Christian character by the erecting of new churches and martyrs' shrines within and without the walls, but the emphasis on the missionary duty of all Christians by Ephrem the Syrian still indicates the continued existence of paganism in the wider neighborhood. Missionaries from Edessa had made Christianity known in the Roman frontier province of Mesopotamia before Constantine.

Even in the fourth century the Antiochene mission embraced also the Arab nomads in the East Syrian frontier district. East Syrian Christians from the Sassanid Kingdom continued in the fourth to sixth centuries the missions begun earlier in North India and perhaps also took under their care the Christian communities of South India that had been founded from Egypt, as an exact analysis of the Thomas Tradition makes probable. The Nestorian mission achieved its greatest expansion when it pushed into Central Asia, to Tibet, China, and even to Manchuria, and could establish here the provinces "of the Outside."

To the fourth century (ca. 325–61) belongs also the conversion of the Georgians, on the southern slopes of the central Caucasus. At the beginning of the fifth century the Georgian Church had already gained a degree of autonomy, which was completed by the appointment of a *Catholicus* under King Wachtang I (446–99).

The completion of the evangelization of the island of Cyprus may have coincided with the recognition of its ecclesiastical independence in regard to Antioch at the Council of Ephesus of 431.

In Asia Minor as a whole the end of the age of persecution made public that the majority of the Greek and Hellenized population of the cities and of the larger rural centers of settlement had already been won for the Christian religion. Specifically missionary questions strikingly disappeared in the decrees of Asia Minor synods of the first half of the fourth century. The efforts of the Emperor Julian to restore paganism found only the slightest echo in Asia Minor. All the eagerness of his vicar for Asia, Justus, who had sacrificial altars again constructed at Sardes, sought to rebuild decayed or destroyed temples, and himself offered public sacrifices, remained as much without effect as did his displeasure that in Galatia the wives, children, and domestic servants of many pagan priests were Christians. Naturally, from now on, especially in the cities and among the upper class, some individuals still professed paganism or secretly adhered to it.

A special role in the process of the evangelization of Asia Minor may be attributed for the fourth century to Cappadocia. The bishops of the metropolis, Caesarea, from where the christianization of Armenia by Gregory the Illuminator started, maintained lively contact with their daughter churches; until 374 they ordained the Armenian chief bishop and claimed a sort of right of visitation in the communities of Asia Minor. The see of Caesarea became, with its organization of ecclesiastical community life social care, liturgy, organization of monasticism, elimination of pagan cult shrines and the type of public life allied with it in relation to Christian life, the missionary model for the congregations of the neighboring provinces. And the very openness of the Cappadocians among the bishops of

Asia Minor toward a profane education became a missionary factor of the first order, since it essentially facilitated conversion to Christianity on the part of the upper class, which stood close to these bishops socially. The receptiveness of Cappadocia to the missionary task is finally discernible in the series of important missionaries whom it produced, as, for example, the Bishop of the Goths Ulfilas, Eutyches, who labored among the Goths of the Crimea, and Vetranio, who became Bishop of Tomi in Scythia.

In the other provinces of the Diocese of Pontus the missionary task of the communities in city and countryside in the fourth century consisted chiefly in the deepening and elaborating of the religious life. Only occasionally were missionary enterprises or procedures mentioned in the sources for the fourth century in the heavily urbanized provinces of the west coast of Asia Minor.

In the southern provinces of the Diocese of Thrace — Europa and Rhodope — for the period ca. 300 one can pretty much assume the state of christianization which had been achieved in the Asia Minor provinces of Hellespont and Bithynia, which lay opposite. Their special interest was of importance to the Gothic tribes which had settled on the lower Danube. The most successful missionary was Ulfilas, who, after his episcopal ordination in 341, worked to the north of the Danube until persecution compelled the Christian Goths to flee ca. 350: they were then settled by the Emperor Constantius in Lower Moesia. Later missionaries were active among the nomadic Gothic tribes on the lower Danube, sent there by Chrysostom, who in Constantinople itself had exerted himself to win the Goths. In the last decades of the fourth century occurred the missionary work of Bishop Nicetas of Remesiana from the province of Dacia, who succeeded, after a full year's exertions, in gaining the tribes of Thracian Bessae in the mountains around Philippopolis; they became especially zealous adherents of the new faith.

For the Diocese of Macedonia as a whole, a clear missionary lag is established by a glance at the provinces of Asia Minor, despite the great tradition of the congregations founded there by Paul. To them, it is true, up to the Council of Nicaea had been added other communities in Macedonia proper, but paganism was long able to maintain itself here, not only in the country, but also in cult centers such as Delphi and Eleusis and especially at Athens itself. When Basil and Gregory Nazianzen studied at the Athenian school of higher learning around the mid-century, the city was still overwhelming pagan, the Panathenaea and the festivals in honor of Dionysus were still publicly celebrated, and Christian students were in the minority. At Athens the esteem and influence of paganism were kept alive especially through the teachings of the later Platonic Academy, whose staunch rejection of Christianity was permitted up to the time of Justinian I. Only Alaric's invasion of Greece in 395 and the gradual execution of the decrees of Theodosius I and his sons on the closing of the temples caused the decline and disappearance of the pagan cults. The transformation of many cult centers, including the complex of the Acropolis, into Christian churches in the first half of the fifth century seems to have succeeded without resistance. The increase in the number of episcopal sees between the beginning of the fourth and the middle of the fifth century from between ten and fifteen to almost fifty makes equally clear that the breakthrough in the evangelization of Greece only occurred after 400.

For the Danubian provinces of the Dioceses of Dacia and Illyricum, as well as for Dalmatia, a rather similar course of missionary work must be assumed. The unstable political situation of the frontier areas and also the Arian controversy, which was spirited precisely in the central Balkans, often obstructed a continuous mission. And the remarkably tenacious persistence of pagan cults restricted the progress of christianization. Nicetas of Remesiana must be again singled out as a missionary. The rich archeological finds in the Dalmatian coastal city of Salona make possible today an instructive glimpse into the sometimes stormy progress of Christianity in a rather large urban settlement. Here, for example, the missionary work was begun ca. 300 by merchants who, according to their grave inscriptions, probably came from Syria; according to the evidence of the first two bishops in the persecution of Diocletian, this young nucleus grew quickly into a flourishing community, as the basilicas, baptisteries, and burial grounds prove and the honorable treatment of the Bishop of Salona by Pope Zosimus in 418 confirms; it continued as a metropolitan see until the invasion of the Slavs at the beginning of the seventh century. From there were then evangelized the Dalmatian interior and Albania just to the south.

In Pannonia, Sirmium, quite early important in ecclesiastical politics, was the base from which in the last quarter of the fourth century proceeded an intensive missionary work among the peasants; it had largely achieved its goal by the time of the Avar invasion. For the two provinces of Noricum one must reckon with missionary undertakings which came from Aquileia to the south. Athanasius also mentions bishops from Noricum who approved the decrees issued in his favor by the Synod of Serdica, but he does not specify their sees. But episcopal communities certainly arose in Roman times. The efficacy of Saint Severinus in Noricum Ripense from 453 or 454 was no longer primarily missionary: it especially served charitable concerns, the organization of monasticism, and the peaceful association of Catholics and Arian Germans.

The christianization of Upper Italy and of the Raetian provinces (Italia Annonaria) first began on a broad scale likewise only in the fourth century. To the three episcopal churches of Milan, Aquileia, and Ravenna, which certainly belong to the period before 300, were added around the turn of the century Padua, Verona, Brescia, and Bologna, while the other bishoprics north of the Apennines originated only in the later fourth and the fifth centuries. The missionary importance of Milan, the sole metropolis of the fourth century, is brought into clear relief by the other sees. It was determined by the city's commercial situation as the starting-point of important routes, especially to the Alpine passages, through its character as the Late Roman administrative center and imperial residence, but also through the great esteem which the bishops of the fourth century had won for the community, starting with Mirocles, who took part in the Synods of Rome (313) and Arles (314), to Eustorgius and Dionysius, firm anti-Arians, down to Ambrose. Under the sure guidance of Ambrose, the early Christian Church of Milan gained its strongest missionary efficacy. It was accomplished first by the preaching of the bishop, who over and over reminded the members of his congregation of their personal duty through a pure life to make the Christian faith attractive to pagans of their neighborhood; in addition, he appealed directly to the pagans and Jews among his audience and sought to clear up their reservations in regard to Christianity. The impact of the Metropolitan Ambrose was determined just as strongly in relation to missionary activity. Personal relations between him and the Bishops of Como, whom he ordained, of Pavia (Ticinum) and Lodi (Laus Pompeia) make his collaboration in the erecting of these sees likely, and his correspondence with the Bishops Constantius and Vigilius treated the missionary task of preaching or the problem of marriage between Christians and pagans. Milan's missionary radiation is also made known by the fact that a series of Upper Italian bishops of the day came from the metropolis. In two important cases Ambrose finally assumed missionary tasks which extended far beyond his metropolitan province. When the Princess of the Marcomanni, Fritigil, asked him for more detailed information on the Christian faith, he wrote for her a catechism in the style of a letter. In the great confrontation with the group that was trying to restore paganism at Rome, he was the preeminent speaker on the Catholic side. Similar missionary initiatives are not known in connection with any of the contemporary Roman bishops.

Christianity had still not penetrated ca. 400 into the valleys of the southern Alpine strips, as, for example, in the Val di Non near Trent, where at that time three clerics, probably on instructions from Bishop Vigilius, first built a little church, from which they started their mission. They were killed by the pagan population when they refused, for themselves and their few converts, to take part in a pagan procession through the fields. But the death of the missionaries became the occasion for the quick conversion of the inhabitants of the valley. Bishops Zeno of Verona (ca. 362–72) Gaudentius of Brescia (d. before 406), and Maximus of Trier (ca. 397–415) found themselves in a genuinely missionary situation. They saw the members of their communities not only threatened by still continuing pagan customs; there still existed all around them a considerable pagan minority, especially among the peasants, who were often carelessly left alone in their veneration of idols and their sacrificial rites. Some came occasionally to hear the bishop's preaching; Maximus addressed them at the beginning of Lent and asked them to decide to accept Christianity. Christianity reached Ravenna by way of its port of Classis, which, however, was never the seat of a bishop. In the rural parts of the bishoprics subject to Ravenna the mission hardly got under way to any great extent before the sixth century.

The way into the Val d'Aosta, to the Valais, and to the Raetian provinces was shown to the Christian mission by the Roman roads, which proceeded all together from Milan. After Geneva, it is Gallic missionaries, from Lyon, who brought Christianity both into the Jura and to the *civitas Helvetiorum*, where Christians are demonstrable for the fourth and fifth centuries.

The pre-Constantinian community of Augsburg (Augusta Vindelicorum) grew so rapidly in the fourth and fifth centuries that here too one must reckon with an episcopal see in Roman times, whose existence is, moreover, made clear for the capital of Raetia Secunda. A great complex of former church buildings under the present Sankt Gallus Chapel with a basilica of three aisles and frescoes of a continuous illustration of the gospels point clearly to the previous existence of a cathedral.

In comparison with Milan, the missionary activity of Aquileia, which was a metropolis as early as the fifth century, left little trace in the sources, but the evangelization of the immediate vicinity, probably proceeded from Aquileia. However, paganism was still so self-assured here that as late as 388 its priests dared to greet the Emperor Theodosius in full official robes on the occasion of his passage to Italy. Finally, the fact that the sees of southern Noricum still belonged to the ecclesiastical province of Aquileia indicates early missionary relations with Aquileia; in the sixth century it was decisively upheld by the Metropolitan of that province.

The course of the evangelization of central and southern Italy is far less easily elucidated than that of Upper Italy because of the scanty sources. It is true that at the beginning of the fourth century there were at hand favorable starting-points for the Christian mission in Rome itself and in the communities of some commercial centers, such as Ostia, Terracina, Naples, Syracuse, and Cagliari, but precisely here it made a surprisingly slow advance. In the old imperial capital itself the number of Christians grew steadily throughout the entire fourth century, as the building of new titular churches under Popes Silvester I, Mark, Julius I, Liberius, and Damasus I makes clear, but on the whole Rome long presented the image of a predominantly pagan city, whose highest official, the Praefectus Urbi, did not usually belong to the Christian Church. The pagan religious calendar continued in use, pagan temples were still constructed or restored. The cults of Cybele and Mithras lasted into the 390s, the cult of Isis probably into the fifth century, and only toward the end of the fourth century did the problems of recruiting for the pagan priesthoods begin. The Christian mission encountered a powerful obstacle in the stubborn and often bellicose rejection of the new religion by the majority of the aristocratic upper class, which was unwilling to sacrifice all that the ancient Roman tradition meant for it, carried out a varied propaganda for it, intervened at the court in Milan, and finally, in cooperation with the usurper Eugene, even tried a decision by battle. Even the defeat thereby suffered did not mean the end of paganism in the city, since the government as late as the fifth century still took into consideration the susceptibilities of the reduced pagan senatorial aristocracy. However, a noteworthy missionary recruitment must be attributed to some ladies of this circle, who from 380 followed the ascetical movement in Christianity and through their activity assisted the upper class to a new understanding of their "Romanness," which now had a Christian basis.

Of the approximately 200 sees which ca. 600 are demonstrable for the territory of Italia Suburbicaria, hence also for Sicily, Sardinia, and Corsica, about half may have existed at the end of the fourth century; seventy-eight more bishoprics were founded in the fifth century, and the remainder only in the sixth century. A special importance for the evangelization of Campania may be assigned to the community of Naples. A few bishoprics from the first half of the fourth century indicate a relatively early christianization of southern Etruria, but Florence, Lucca, and Pisa also had episcopal congregations early. Except for Spoleto, known from 353–54, the episcopal sees in north-western Umbria are demonstrable with certainty only in the fifth and sixth centuries. Just as Syracuse was the entrance-gate for the gospel into Sicily, so it became also the point of departure for the evangelization of the interior, which proceeded rapidly after Constantine. The shepherds of several episcopal communities stood on Athanasius' side in the confrontation concerning him at the mid-fourth century. Letters from Leo I and Gelasius I were addressed to the entire episcopate of Sicily. In the correspondence of Gregory I the island seems to be entirely Christian, although there was still no episcopal see in the interior. In the course of the fifth century the Christians on Malta received a bishop.

In Sardinia the community of the port city of Cagliari was the bearer of the mission to the interior. And "bishops of Sardinia" were also mentioned among the supporters of Athanasius, but without precision of number and place-names. However, the northeast of the island still showed numerous pagans to the end of the sixth century, and Pope Gregory worked for their conversion. A somewhat slower development must, finally, be assumed for Corsica, whose bishops Athanasius also mentioned and who, according to Gennadius of Marseille, unanimously approved the *Expositio catholicae fidei* which Eugene of Carthage had composed in 483.

At the beginning of the fourth century a double missionary task was presented to the Church in the North African part of the Roman Empire. One had to do with gaining the adherents of paganism, on the defensive, it is true, in most cities, but nevertheless still influential. Second, the evangelization of the population on the *latifundia,* especially of the western provinces, and of the tribes in the southern frontier district, had to be tackled systematically, if one wished the achievement thus far to continue. The implementation of this task was no doubt aggravated for decades and partly impeded by the long confrontation between the Donatist and the Catholic Churches, which on both sides tied down the best forces, even if both denominations constantly received adherents from paganism. The Catholics had a strong support in parts of the upper class, who enjoyed a great influence in intellectual life, in the administration, or through their economic position. The preaching and correspondence of Augustine afford a glimpse into the missionary understanding and the day-to-day missionary activity of a North African bishop in the first decades of the fifth century. His preaching goes again and again into the objections of pagans of all classes, who indicated them as the reason for their rejection of Christianity; they were taken very seriously by him when they deserved to be, and he exposed their emptiness when they were accepted clichés. He candidly admitted that the life of many a Christian meant a no less serious hindrance for the Christian mission than the split of the North African Church into two bitterly warring denominations. Hence he called attention to the missionary duty of every individual Christian to lead his pagan acquaintances to Christ, as formerly the Samaritan woman had done with regard to her fellow townspeople. Augustine also used his contacts by letter with pagans in order to present to the correspondent, whose influence on the peasantry he by no means underestimated, in a manner mostly very courteous but in fact resolute, the inner emptiness of the pagan religion and the hopelessness of its current situation.

The further collapse of North African paganism was hastened by the legislation introduced by Theodosius and continued by Honorius, which here too decreed the closing of the temples, forbade public worship, had cult images and statues removed from the temples, and had temple property seized, but did not aim to trouble personally pagans who lived peaceably. In consequence of the now increasing State pressure there were bloody encounters between pagans and Christians. In 407 the Christians were permitted to make use of the temple of the Dea Caelestis at Carthage, which had been closed earlier, and Bishop Aurelius pointedly had his *cathedra* located on the place occupied by the statue of the pagan goddess. Some pagans even now still clung to prophecies which promised the imminent collapse of the Christian world in North Africa; eventually all they could do was to hide the images of the gods in caves and ravines and practice their worship underground.

All too meager are the reports on the Christian mission among the non-Roman population of the frontier zone of North Africa. Augustine knew that even ca. 400 there "were numerous tribes in Africa to whom the gospel has not yet been preached"; although he had also heard of conversions of individual members of a tribe. Here, however, he did not intervene personally, but expected their full conversion in the future. But there is evidence that evangelization was begun here even before the invasion of the Vandals. Missionary activity, of course, was not possible during the century of Vandal domination in the area controlled by them. Systematic missionary work was resumed only after the conquest of North Africa by the Byzantines in 533.

In the history of the evangelization of Gaul the fourth century presents espe-cially the phase in which Christianity established itself, in a virtually uninterrupted growth, in most cities of the Gallic provinces. At the first council on Gallic soil, the Synod of Arles in 314, sixteen Gallic sees were represented, and the existence at this period of ten others can be accepted with some certainty. The larger number of these bishoprics was in southern Gaul, where from the pre-Constantinian cen-ter, Lyon, a mission route upward through the Rhone Valley to the Rhine and into Belgica was marked off. Scarcely thirty years later Athanasius counted thirty-four Gallic bishops as his adherents, from the mid-century the bishoprics increased rapidly in the West and Northwest, and about a hundred years after the Synod of Arles there were episcopal congregations in almost all the more than 100 *civitates* of Gaul, mostly in the principal localities. This means that in all these cities a consid-erable part of the inhabitants professed the Christian faith. Since the metropolitan organization also established itself in the first decades of the fifth century, the basic ecclesiastical constitution of Gaul was complete soon after 390. By whom and with what methods this urban evangelization occurred in each case escapes us to a great extent.

The christianization of the peasantry of Gaul, on the other hand, began for the most part only in the last decades of the fourth century and reached its climax only in the fifth century. Since it was, first of all, the duty of the bishop in the territory of a *civitas,* for a time it remained dependent on the rise of the individual see, and practically and in its efficacy on the initiative of its leader, so that in a glance at the whole of Gaul one must reckon with a very much differentiated process. Except for a few allusions to a rural mission in the early period, the sources mention Martin of Tours (d. 397) and Victricius of Rouen (d. ca. 407) as the first bishops who devoted themselves systematically to the mission in the countryside, pushing on, each in his own bishopric and occasionally beyond its boundaries.

The course of the evangelization of the Iberian Peninsula in the fourth and fifth centuries can be determined only in the barest outlines. The lists of participants in the Synods of Elvira (between 306 and 314) and Arles (314) and some further indications make clear that at the beginning of Constantine's sole rule Christianity had its center of gravity in Baetica and southern Tarraconensis, since the majority of the Spanish members of the synods came from some forty places situated in these provinces. The decrees of Elvira, moreover, give acquaintance with a Christianity which still needed various forms of missionary work for its deepening;

apparently there was a definite desire to take up this task. With the flowering of
a noteworthy Christian literature, the spread of monasticism, the struggle over
Priscillianism, and the interest which Rome showed in the Spanish Church, it
becomes understandable that in the course of the century this Church gained in
expansion and in inner quality. That the mission took the route from the cities
on the Spanish east coast into the interior can be determined to a degree from
the churches and cemeteries with their sarcophagi. As in Gaul, so also on the
Iberian Peninsula Christian churches on the *villae* of owners of *latifundia* became
of importance for the origin of Christian congregations in the country. The Balearic
Islands were affected very early by missionary work, and the majority of their
inhabitants professed Christianity before the Vandal invasion. Especially in the
land of the Basques and in Cantabria can the mission be found first in an initial
stage ca. 400, since here no bishoprics are demonstrable even for the period
of Visigothic rule. Hence mission work among the peasants was by no means
everywhere completed even in the Visigothic period.

In the political Diocese of Britannia also there existed at the beginning of the
fourth century a certain ecclesiastical organization, as the participation of the Bishops of York, London, Lincoln or Colchester, and perhaps also the representative
of a fourth see — possibly Cirencester — the Synod of Arles proves. The number
of sees continued to grow up to the Synod of Rimini (359), but the Christians
in Roman Britain long stood in the shadow of paganism. Excavations at *villae*
in Lullingstone (Kent) and Hilton St. Mary (Dorset) with their private churches
reveal that the Christian religion also found entry into the families of well-to-do
landowners. But to what extent the peasants as a whole accepted it cannot be
determined. For a consolidation of the Church ca. 400 and later, especially in
the upper class, we have the witness of lively theological discussions in Britain,
which motivated the visit of the Gallic Bishops Victricius of Rouen (ca. 395) and
Germain of Auxerre (429 and perhaps again ca. 445); on this occasion Germain
also preached to the Christian peasants. That Christian communities also existed
in the western and northern frontier zones of Roman Britain is certain: from them
came the two missionaries, Patrick and Ninian, for whom the conversion of the
Irish and the Picts became their lifework. In these areas Christianity of a Roman
stamp could continue without a break, whereas in the southeast and center of
the island it was subjected to serious impediments when ca. 450 the still pagan
tribes of Jutes, Angles, and Saxons invaded in several waves and made themselves rulers of these territories. From the almost complete silence of the sources
for this time, however, one may not infer a total extinction of Christian life in the
Anglo-Saxon part of the island.

The presentation thus far makes clear that the evangelization of the peoples
of the Empire in the fourth and fifth centuries was by no means a uniformly developing process in all parts of the Empire; hence the usual wholesale judgment that
immediately after Constantine's turning to Christianity the pagan masses poured
into the Church requires a substantial differentiation. It must first be established
that in the missionary progress of this epoch several waves are apparent. The
freedom of worship granted by Constantine first revealed the real situation: the
number of Christians had grown so strongly, especially in the second half of the

third century, that in some urban congregations larger church buildings were necessary in order to hold the believers who were now able openly to profess their Christianity. After that, especially in the East, an active missionary work had begun, which brought to the Church a steady, though not spectacular, growth. Then, after the defeat of the anti-Emperor Magnentius (351–53), Christianity gained ground considerably in the cities of the western provinces. The failure of the Emperor Julian's effort at restoration introduced the concluding phase in the East, but also promoted the mission in the West, as Hilary of Poitiers emphasizes. Whereas for Chrysostom the end of paganism in the eastern part of the Empire, apart from a few frontier places, was a generally acknowledged fact, Jerome, Gaudentius of Brescia, Maximus of Turin, and others saw the period of the influx of the masses in the West only in the Theodosian age. The striking temporary and occasionally even qualitative lag in the peasantry of the Balkans, Italy, Gaul, and Spain in comparison to the East must have had an essential cause in the decline of civilization which existed precisely here between East and West, and which, for its part, was again conditioned by the different demographic situation. The greater population density of the eastern provinces with their many cities and their higher cultural level offered the Christian mission in the East the incomparably more favorable presuppositions also for the rural mission.

Christianity was able at this period to get a foothold also on the other side of the Empire's frontiers, especially among the peoples along its eastern boundary. Jerome was even of the opinion that the moment had already come when the gospel had been proclaimed to all peoples, and Augustine regarded a conversion of the as yet still pagan peoples as possible in the next generation. More important than the all too optimistic estimation of the missionary present and future was the fact that the "Church of the Empire," following the completion of evangelization in the interior, now became more keenly aware than earlier of the duty of evangelizing the "barbarians" also.

2. The First Contacts of Christianity with the Germans and the Conversion of the Goths

"The Churches established in the [two] Germanies have believed nothing other and transmitted nothing other than those in the Spanish provinces or among the Celts, than those in the east or in Egypt, than those in Libya or in the middle of the world." This much quoted sentence from *Adversus haereses,* composed ca. 180–82 by Bishop Irenaeus of Lyon, is the first testimony for the presence of Christianity in the Roman Rhinelands, the provinces of Mainz and Cologne. In the third century Christianity must have gained strength on the Rhine and the Danube, as the reports of the martyrdoms in these provinces indicate. In the second half of the third century the beginnings of an episcopal organization on the wide frontier of the Empire facing the Germans became visible. With this is included a *terminus a quo* for the first contact of the Germans with the Church.

Christianity appeared to the Germans as an element of late ancient civilization with which they had to come into conflict, and, indeed, in the West at first as one form of religion alongside others. Conversions of German officers to the Christian religion still remained the rare exceptions during the fourth century. Not until the fifth century were the Germans who had risen in the imperial service or their successors converted to Christianity in growing numbers. The successors of Germanic lords who had risen in the imperial senatorial aristocracy also assimilated themselves interiorly to the new faith.

The line between the Germans who had risen in the senatorial aristocracy and the princes of the *foederati,* who with their people had bound themselves to the Emperor by a *foedus,* was fluid. But the decision for Christ could not remain a private matter among the federate princes in view of the close fusion of religion with the total life of the people. It also automatically affected the group of people whom the prince governed and hence led more or less inevitably to a collective conversion. The confession of Christ probably implied at times also an acknowledgment of *Imperium* and Emperor: it was a question of a formal act rather than of a real conversion. Thus is explained how the Burgundians and the Sueves without difficulty exchanged Catholic for Arian Christianity when they fell under the influence of the Arian Goths.

Earlier and more enduringly than the Germans on the Rhine did the Goths on the lower Danube and the Black Sea coast come into contact with Christianity. Cappadocian war prisoners, perhaps also anonymous missionaries, were the first agents of the gospel, which at first probably found followers in the lower classes. Among the Visigoths the treaty concluded with Constantine in 332 may have favored contacts with the Christian religion. Very soon heterodox teachers also appeared. The Mesopotamian sectarian Audaeus worked among the Visigoths during his exile in Scythia. Alongside Audians and Catholics were the Arians, whose denomination was destined to become the Gothic form of Christianity, not least because of the considerable personality of the Gothic Bishop Ulfilas.

Ulfilas was born ca. 311. Through his mother he was a descendant of Cappadocian war prisoners, but his father was probably a Goth. As a cleric-lector he began to translate the Bible into Gothic. He went with a Gothic embassy to the court of Constantine I or of Constantius II. Eusebius of Nicomedia, Bishop of Constantinople from 338, ordained him Bishop of the Goths, perhaps in 341 at the Synod of Antioch. Ulfilas professed the moderate Homoian Arianism of Acacius and as bishop completed his translation of the Scripture. He escaped a first persecution of Christians in 347–48, and the Emperor settled him with his faithful near Nicopolis (Trnovo). Ulfilas died at Constantinople in 381 or 383. The Gothic group that had followed him remained permanently separated from the main body of their nation and survived in the Balkans as a peaceful tribe of herdsmen.

The persecution of 347–48, like the next one of 369–72, struck at all Gothic Christians, regardless of denomination. The second persecution was related to a new Visigothic-Roman conflict and probably also to a power struggle between the Visigothic Princes Athanarich and Fritigern. At that time both rivals were still pagans, but Fritigern, as the representative of a pro-Roman policy, may already have been leaning to Christianity. Athanarich at first held his ground in the leadership of his people. The persecution inaugurated by him was at the same time an anti-Roman reaction. The Audians were routed, and their remnant joined the Catholics. A group of Catholic Goths withdrew from the main body and migrated to Thrace.

Athanarich's position was shaken when in 376 the Huns attacked the Visigoths after they had overrun the Ostrogothic Kingdom. Under Fritigern's leadership bands of Visigoths trespassed on the soil of the Empire. At that time Fritigern seems to have embraced the Arian confession of his patron, the Emperor Valens; his passage was followed by the historically decisive mass conversion of his people to Arianism. The conflict with the imperial administration, in the course of which Fritigern finally led his Visigoths in 378 to victory over the Emperor Valens at Adrianople, made no change in the religious decision. If there were still destined to be anti-Christian excesses even after the treaty with Theodosius in 382, Visigothic paganism thereafter was without significance for the future of the people. Catholic Christianity also now moved to the background. It maintained itself as the popular religion only among the separated groups, such as the "Crimea Goths."

The origin and course of the Gothic mission can be understood only against the background of the Church history of the Greco-Roman East. The power of radiation of Greek Christianity, whose nucleus was Asia Minor, explains the early start of the work of conversion. The various denominations of the East met in missionary territory. The Goths accepted the diluted Homoian Arianism, which in the decisive moment of history was the denomination of the Eastern Emperor and of the court of Constantinople. Ulfilas' creed corresponded to the formula of Rimini (359), which for its part was based on the formulas of Sirmium (359) and Antioch (341). The Gothic Church also borrowed from the Church of the Empire the episcopal organization. The national liturgical language grew out of the needs of the mission: an important achievement of Ulfilas, but against the background of the relations of the East, where, in addition to Greek and Latin, there were also a Syriac and a Coptic liturgical language, it was nothing revolutionary. Ulfilas' translation of the Bible obtained the full recognition of the Church Fathers Jerome and John Chrysostom.

A deeper understanding of the controversies which occupied the theologians of the East in the fourth century may be presumed in any event in Ulfilas, but not in the new converts. The Goths did not choose the appealing Christian profession after a critical examination; they accepted the form of Christianity which Constantinople offered them. That, just the same, a Gothic national Church arose is explained by a rare coincidence: the death of the Emperor Valens on the battlefield of Adrianople sealed the fate of Arianism within the Empire. The Gothic Homoians were thereafter separated from the Church of the Empire by a deep ditch.

The isolated Gothic Church preserved the Homoian body of religious beliefs essentially unchanged. The Gothic theologians of the fifth and sixth centuries lacked originality. They fell to a certain degree under the influence of *Romania* when in the fifth century the Goths moved from the eastern to the western half of the Empire. Ulfilas' Bible was sporadically revised with a view to the Latin Bible, and there seem also to have been bilingual Gothic-Latin Bibles.

Except for the translation of the Bible and the liturgical language, it is possible to speak of a germanization at the earliest in the area of the ecclesiastical organization. The ecclesiastical classifications which could not be modeled on the urban districts had to conform to the organization of the people or of the army — hundreds, five-hundreds, thousands. Gothic Arianism early gave a place to the proprietary church system, perhaps under the influence of a Germanic proprietary temple system. Monasticism played no substantial role. Annual synods of the Arian clergy at Geneva are attested for the Burgundians. Only the Vandals, as *imitatores imperii,* established an Arian patriarchate.

At first the Gothic Church clung purposely to the universalism of the old Church and, like it, claimed alone to represent the true doctrine. But when the East Germans founded their kingdoms in the western provinces of the Empire it appeared that a missionary Arianism could only imperil the inner peace of the kingdoms. While the Vandals did not shrink from establishing Arianism as the religion of their kingdom, the Goths and the other Arian peoples accustomed themselves to regard their Church as a national institution while renouncing missionary exertions in regard to the Romans. Hence the "tolerance" relating to Catholic *Romania* was conditioned by a special political situation and finally led to stagnation.

The Ostrogoths probably accepted Ulfilas' Christianity even before their migration to Pannonia in 455. The Arianism of Ulfilas seems to have reached even the Thuringians and Bavarians.

Gradually Arianism established itself among all the Germans of the Danube: its area of expansion corresponded to a culture province defined by the Goths. It remained foreign to the Germans on the Rhine; however, the Goths finally carried it also to the peoples who migrated to Gaul and Spain, among whom now the Arian Gothic influence came into conflict with the Roman Catholic environment. Ostrogothic emissaries were active at the Frankish court in an effort to introduce Arianism, and not without success until Clovis' decision cut the ground from under them. Among the Burgundians and the Spanish Sueves Arianism never sank roots so deeply as among the Goths, Vandals, and Danube Germans.

CHAPTER 45

The Building of the Organization
of the Church of the Empire

The Local Episcopal Church

The rapid progress of evangelization of the population of the Empire after the Church obtained freedom led to a strong increase in the number of Christian congregations, which, as previously, continued to be local churches governed by a single bishop. The ordination of a successor even in the lifetime of the present bishop was, therefore, as in the case of Augustine, regarded as an illicit deviation from the norm. Whereas in the East the word *paroichia* established itself for the local church, the terminology in the West long remained unsettled: here, in addition to *paroecia, ecclesia, territorium, fines episcopatus,* and *dioecesis* were also used. The decision as to the necessity or opportunity for establishing new local churches lay usually with the bishops of an ecclesiastical province. The weightiest prerequisite for the new foundation was a sufficient number of faithful. And so areas with many cities had correspondingly high numbers of bishoprics of no great extent in size, while in areas of few cities their *territorium* was substantially larger. Ordinarily the episcopal boundaries coincided with the civil administrative boundaries of the cities, but numerous deviations and quarrels over jurisdiction between neighboring bishops show that no strictly obligatory law existed on this matter. Hence there were also episcopal congregations in settlements which had no city rights, in addition to bishoprics within whose territory lay two or more cities. Great exertions were required to establish the principle which restricted the bishop in the exercise of his functions to the territory of his own local church.

The connection of a bishop with a local church bound him to permanent residence in his community, from which he was to be absent only for serious reasons and ordinarily no longer than three weeks. This duty of residence was often disregarded, especially in the fourth century, because of the inclination of some bishops to be present personally at the imperial court in order to request material aid for their community and also at times personal privileges. Hence synods forbade these journeys or made them dependent on a written permission from the metropolitan. The unlimited duty of caring for his community also justified the prohibition to transfer a bishop to another see, which was motivated by patristic theology with the idea of a mystical marriage between bishop and local church, to be terminated only by death. From the beginning of the fifth century there appeared an easing of the prohibition, since reasons for exceptions were recognized — rejection of a new bishop by the community, prohibition of entering upon the office by the secular power, pastoral necessity. The provincial synod had to consider whether deposition was to be decreed because of serious lapses, but against its verdict the one concerned had the right of appeal to Rome. In the East, on the other hand, at times the Emperor, on his own initiative, decreed the deposition of a bishop.

The growing number of faithful in the city congregations and the success of the mission among the peasantry introduced, from the fourth century on, certain new features into the structure of the episcopal local church. In larger cities, such as Alexandria, Antioch, Rome, Carthage, and Milan, in addition to the cathedral, other churches became necessary in thickly populated urban areas. In Rome this led to the constructing of the so-called *titular churches,* to which members of the clergy of the city of Rome were assigned for the care of souls in these areas. However, these *tituli* remained parts of the one Roman local church; their clerics belonged, furthermore, to the *presbyterium* of the Roman community, whose unity was stressed by the liturgy celebrated by the Roman Bishop in the titular churches by turns. In the Greek East there developed for the care of the peasants belonging to a local church the institute of the *chorepiscopus* [lit.: "country" bishop; a suffragan]. Their regulations consistently emphasize the full dependence of the *chorepiscopus* on the real head of the community, who alone defined the sphere of his functions. As yet the West had not received the institute of the *chorepiscopus.* In the often quite extensive bishoprics of Gaul and North Italy special pastoral stations were erected in the rural settlements far removed from the cathedral, and these for their part represented a liturgical center for the inhabitants of the smaller villages and farms of the vicinity. Such subordinate places were, it is true, not parishes in the full sense of the word, since they did not yet administer their own church property, and the clergy working there had no real jurisdiction for an exactly defined territory, but the development toward the later parish was foreshadowed.

The Metropolitan Union

As early as the late second century initial movements toward a spatial organization within the Universal Church were clear: these would go beyond the episcopal local church. Various rules of the Council of Nicaea now show that out of these starts there developed a clearly organized structure of differing sizes. One of these consisted of the gathering of all local churches of one civil province into a union, which in the lands of Greek speech was called *eparchia,* in those of Latin speech *provincia.*

The Council of Nicaea took for granted the fully developed ecclesiastical province or metropolitan union in the East when is ruled that the ordination of a bishop should be performed, so far as possible, by all the bishops of a province, and the confirmation of his election should come from the "metropolitan." The very title metropolitan indicates that this chief of an ecclesiastical province had his seat in the metropolis, the capital of the civil province. Here too the boundaries of the ecclesiastical and of the corresponding civil sphere of administration generally coincided. The synods of the fourth and fifth centuries determined rights of the metropolitan in more detail: He led the episcopal synod of the province, which should meet twice a year, in discussing and deciding questions of more than local importance. Thus there belonged to the metropolitan a certain function of control over the religious and ecclesiastical life within the province and over the performance of their duties by the bishops. The Synod of Antioch in 341 stressed on the one hand that the local bishop was independent in his administration of his see, but on the other hand it called attention to the fact that the metropolitan was responsible for the care of the ecclesiastical province and without his consent and that of the other bishops he could not undertake anything that went beyond this.

The metropolitan organization established itself first and extensively in the Greek East, except for Egypt, which quite early showed a large area in which all bishops of the country as well as of Libya and the Pentapolis were apparently directly subject to the Bishop of Alexandria without the intermediate stage of the metropolitan. In the Latin West the development was still less uniform. In North Africa it exhibited certain differences quite early, in so far as the rank of metropolitan, who was here called primate, sometimes belonged to the senior bishop of the province according to the date of his ordination, thus he did not have to have his seat in the provincial capital. Besides, a special position pertained to the Bishop of Carthage, who was always Primate of the Provincia Proconsularis, and, in addition, as *Primas totius Africae* summoned and directed the African plenary councils, which possessed special authority. On the other hand, the metropolitan organization did not exist at all in the area of the civil Diocese of Italia Suburbicaria with ten provinces and the islands of Sicily and Corsica, whose relatively numerous local bishops were directly subject to the Bishop of Rome and so always appeared at the Roman synods. In Upper Italy the Bishop of Milan first appeared as metropolitan of an ecclesiastical province which comprised several civil provinces. This was first connected with the importance of Milan in the civil sphere, which it had gained as imperial residence since Diocletian and as seat of the vicar for the administration of *Italia Annonaria,* and then with the demographic situation of Upper Italy, which had far fewer cities than the South and the district around Rome. Likewise, the small number of cities in the provinces of Venetia, Istria, Raetia, and Noricum enabled the Bishop of Aquileia from ca. 425 to become the sole metropolitan of this extensive territory. In neighboring Pannonia a de facto preeminence belonged to the Bishop of Sirmium, which from time to time was the imperial residence and seat of a *Praefectus Praetorio.* But the development to a full metropolitan constitution here was at first impeded by the wandering of the peoples. In Gaul, on the other hand, the assimilation of the ecclesiastical organization to the civil administrative spheres is clear. With some divergences, from the late fourth century the provincial capitals of Gaul became also the seats of the metropolitan. For Spain in the fourth century there are no clear statements in the sources on the organizational development of the Church there. Only after the middle of the fifth century was the metropolitan organization found in Spain in particular features. The special situation of the Spanish Church under Visigothic rule induced its episcopate to lean more powerfully on Rome and to receive its canonical rules from there. It was not until the sixth century that the great age of the Spanish provincial synods began.

Also in the case of the ecclesiastical provinces did the boundaries in most cases coincide with those of the corresponding unit of civil administration.

Superior Organization of the Greater Churches

Finally, the Council of Nicaea also knew a form of classification of churches on a still larger scale, in which all the local churches of a quite extensive geographical area or unit of administration larger than the civil province were combined under the bishop of the most important city of this area. Canon 6 of the Council specified three of these structures: To the Bishop of Alexandria was acknowledged the ancient "customary right" which gave him the supremacy over all the local churches of Egypt, Libya, and the Pentapolis; the same "custom" held for the Bishop of Rome; and the privileges of Antioch were to be similarly maintained. In the last two cases, it is true, there was no delimitation of the geographical area within which the full authority of the Bishop of Rome or of Antioch was valid, just as the vague formulation in regard to the "privileges" of Antioch is noteworthy. But the context of the canon makes clear that in both cases there was question of a form of organization which extended far beyond the framework of a metropolitan union, but for which as yet no special designation had been found. By its canon 6 the Council of Nicaea basically recognized the classifications of the greater churches that were later termed "patriarchates."

Their development was completed in a rather lengthy process, whose course was determined by several factors. In the first place, both chronologically and in accord with their internal importance, the geopolitical and economic importance of the three cities, Alexandria, Antioch, and Rome, must be named: their local bishops became the leaders of these great ecclesiastical classifications. This factor had already to a certain degree determined the route of the early Christian mission, when the first missionaries sought to gain a foothold precisely in the great political centers of the Mediterranean world and in the congregations founded there gained the bases for mission work in the territory dependent on these cities. This assimilation of the ecclesiastical organization to the existing administrative division of the Empire, which presented itself virtually without alternative, was even the sole and unrestricted justification for the erecting of the fourth patriarchate, that of Constantinople, when the Synod of 381 conferred on the bishop of the eastern imperial capital his new rank, "because his city is the New Rome."

The development of the patriarchates was influenced by still another factor, which pertained to the popular and hence to the linguistic and cultural individuality of the inhabitants of those territories in which the greater Church classifications arose. This factor not only contributed to the origin of one patriarchate each in the Egyptian and Syrian cultural areas: it was likewise one of the causes why both in the properly Greek-speaking sphere and in the Latin area only one great patriarchate each was established, even though here several political dioceses existed as extensive units of administration. Initiatives toward several suprametropolitan groupings were, it is true, also present here. In the territory of the single Latin patriarchate an effort in the direction of a larger member Church of a certain autonomy is known only for Africa, where the Bishop of Carthage, as *Primas totius Africae* and president of the North African plenary council, functioned in a certain sense as the suprametropolitan. For this development both the political and cultural importance of Carthage and its position as mission basis for the evangelization of the North African provinces must be taken into account. The Vandal invasion prepared the end of this relative autonomy of the North African Church and occasioned its close union with Rome.

The special political circumstances under which Christians lived in Armenia and Persia caused, also outside the frontiers of the Empire, the rise of two large ecclesiastical structures, which in their organization must be equated de facto with the eastern patriarchates. The common conversion of the majority of the nation early favored the development of a national Church under a chief bishop of its own, who from the fifth century was called the *Catholicus*. The heavy pressure exerted on the Armenian kings by their powerful Persian neighbors motivated them to relax the ties of their Church with the "West" more and more, and the irresistibly progressing subjugation of Armenia by the Persians almost completely curtailed the contacts with Western Christianity just at the time of the great councils of the fifth century. Hence the definitive separation and independence of the Armenian Church was not the result of its own exertions but the consequences of political events to which the Armenian people were subjected. In Persia the beginnings of a leading role of the Bishop of Seleucia-Ctesiphon probably go back to the fourth century.

For the development and rights of the patriarchates of the East there was adduced relatively late a further factor, which was destined to gain considerable importance eventually: the apostolic origin of the leading episcopal sees or the Petrine principle of the founding of churches.

The principle of apostolic origin also played a role in the protracted conflict between the patriarchate of Antioch and the episcopate of the island of Cyprus in regard to its ecclesiastical independence. The Emperor Zeno assured for the island, with a series of distinctions for the archbishop, the definitive independence later called autocephaly.

Rome most effectively represented the principle of the apostolic origin of the patriarchal see as the basis of the higher organization of the greater churches. Even if in the pre-Constantinian period the political importance of Rome may also have had a certain influence on its ecclesiastical ascent, in the corresponding expressions of its bishops this played as little a role as in other writers before Chalcedon. When the political rank of Constantinople was urged as the motive for the establishing of a higher rank for its bishop, again and again recourse was had against this "political" argumentation, first by Pope Damasus, who would admit only the really "Petrine" sees of Rome, Alexandria, and Antioch, through Boniface I, who protested against an edict of Theodosius II in 421 which granted to Constantinople the privileges of Old Rome, down to Leo I and especially Gelasius I, who found in the Petrine Principle of the founding of churches not only the strongest weapon against the claims of Constantinople, but because of the unique relation of the Apostle Peter to the Roman community regarded themselves as justified in understanding Rome in an entirely specific sense as the *Sedes Apostolica* and themselves as the heirs of Peter's privileges. In the ninth century the apostolic character of the see of Constantinople was further supported by the thesis that it was the heir of Ephesus and hence of the Apostle John, and then by the connection with the legend of the Apostle Andrew, who through his disciple Stachys brought about the christianization of Byzantium and whose relics were venerated from the fourth century in the Church of the Apostles. Thus was the route opened for the theory of the Pentarchy, according to which five patriarchs were instituted by the Holy Spirit to govern the Church as successors of the Apostles and supreme Shepherds of equal rank.

Ecclesiastical Assemblies

The institution of the ecclesiastical assembly, familiar from the pre-Constantinian period and called *concilium* or *synodus* was further elaborated in the fourth century and completed by new forms. At Nicaea the dates for the holding of the provincial synod were established: twice a year, at the beginning of Lent and in the fall, all the bishops of an ecclesiastical province were to meet in order to discuss questions of Church discipline. It was the business of the metropolitan to invite the bishops to the synod, at which he also presided. The duty of all bishops to take part was enjoined, and unjustified absence was punished. The subject of the discussions was especially the disciplinary and liturgical regulation of the communities of the province, the examination of the legality of episcopal elections that had taken place, and the erection or division of bishoprics. The provincial council was functioning in the fourth and fifth centuries wherever the metropolitan organization had been introduced. Apparently it was in greater use in the East than in the West, where it was known in North Africa, Gaul, and, except in the fifth century, also in Spain. But it was not in use in Italy, where interprovincial forms of ecclesiastical assembly did not permit it to appear. As the lowest degree of all synods it knew no collaboration of the State officials, either in the summoning or in the execution of its decrees. The provincial synods of the early Church had a great significance for the regulation of the day-to-day life of the ecclesiastical communities.

The plenary council of the North African Church represents the organizationally most mature form of a synod comprising several ecclesiastical provinces. It was supposed to take place annually and thereby adopted the principle of the periodicity of the provincial synod. All the ecclesiastical provinces of North Africa had to send at least three representatives to this plenary council: they were elected from the members of the provincial synod. Under the presidency of the Bishop of Carthage, it concerned itself chiefly with questions which directly affected the entire North African Church, but it could also take a position on problems of the Universal Church and for weighty cause be convoked for an extraordinary session. The African plenary council distinguished itself in the confrontation with the Donatist Church, in the condemnation of Pelagianism, and in the discussion with Rome over the rights of the African Church, by a high degree of firmness and independence.

Among all the interprovincial councils a clearly unique position belongs to the Roman Synod, which represented the ecclesiastical assembly of all bishoprics which were subordinate to the Bishop of Rome as the single Metropolitan of *Italia Suburbicaria.* It not only dealt with questions which applied to the bishoprics of this territory but also intentionally made decisions on events and problems that primarily concerned other ecclesiastical spheres of jurisdiction, as, for example, the Donatist question, the case of Athanasius at the Synods of 340 and 353, the Antiochene Schism at several synods under Pope Damasus in 368, 377, and 382, the affair of Chrysostom under Pope Innocent I, and finally the question of Nestorius under Celestine I in 430 and the Synod of Ephesus of 449 under Leo I. Here the powerful role of the Roman Bishop is clear: as president, he used the Roman Synod as framework and forum for decisions that he intended to have regarded as binding on ecclesiastical territories outside his own metropolitan sphere.

Both the regularly recurring as well as the extraordinary interprovincial councils were, with few exceptions, summoned by the bishop of the current ecclesiastical center. The convocation of the great ecclesiastical assemblies, whether the episcopate of a part of the Empire or that of the entire Empire was invited to them, came directly from the Emperor, mostly at his initiative, at times at the request of the Roman Bishop. The first example of an imperial summons was present at the Synod of Arles in 314, to which Constantine I invited all bishops of his sphere of rule. The Emperors expected not only gratitude for a support given to the Church but obedience to a command. They not only created the technical presuppositions for the meeting of the council, which would, moreover, have overburdened the Church: they also determined the date and decided the exact group of participants and to a degree also the subject of the conciliar discussions. The imperial interest in the council convoked by him extended also to the course of the discussions, from which concrete results were expected. Hence, the Emperor was usually represented at the council by high officials, who, it is true, did not exercise the presidency, but saw to the orderly course of the debates and again set in motion business that had come to a standstill. The bishops' freedom of speech and of decision was in principle substantially respected, apart from the authoritarian interference of the Emperor Constantius II, who at the Synods of Arles in 353 and Milan in 355 sought to extort a condemnation of Athanasius by threat and physical strength. That the Emperors confirmed the decrees of the great councils and gave them the force of law in the secular sphere was, after all, only normal.

Of course, the conciliar decrees received their validity within the Church, not from the imperial confirmation, but from the council itself. It is true that the Pope did not take part personally in any council outside Rome, but he was represented by his legates. If the participants made known to him the outcome of their deliberations, this did not happen at first in order to procure for them their force in law. A new development is not apparent until the fifth century and thereafter. After the Synods of Carthage (416) and Mileve (417), the African bishops asked from Rome the confirmation of their decrees in order to obtain greater esteem for them; Rome more and more claimed the right to examine conciliar decisions and, if necessary, to reject them if they contradicted the Church's understanding of tradition and the faith. Leo I clearly regarded himself as the court which was set over the council and from which it received its authority.

A new type of synod developed from the second half of the fourth century in Constantinople, where the bishops who were just then staying in the imperial capital met with the local bishop, probably mostly at the suggestion of the Emperor, to discuss important ecclesiastical happenings or problems. Since the presidency devolved upon the bishop of the capital, this gathering of bishops, called *Synodus Endemousa,* became an important factor in the constructing of the authority of the see of Constantinople and, in a further development, an important administrative organ of the Byzantine Church.

C H A P T E R   4 6

The Further Development of the Roman Primacy from Melchiades to Leo I

Even in the pre-Constantinian period of Church history a position of preeminence of the Roman community and its head within the Universal Church had developed; it became especially obvious under Victor I and Stephen I. For the further growth of such a claim to leadership it had to be of decisive significance how the Empire, once it had become Christian, would react to this, since to it likewise was conceded a special position, based on religion, in the developing Church of the Empire. When in 313 Constantine I denied the proposal of the Donatists to have their quarrel with Bishop Caecilian of Carthage settled by a secular court and referred this task to an episcopal court under the direction of the Roman Bishop Melchiades (311–14), this was neither an unjustified interference of the Emperor into inner-Church matters nor, on the other hand, the recognition of a Roman claim to primacy, but simply regard for an already acknowledged preeminence of the Roman See in the Latin Church of the West, to which corresponded also the special treatment of the Roman community, as manifested in the gift of the Lateran Palace as the episcopal residence and in the encouragement of church construction, especially in the erecting of St. Peter's basilica by the Emperor. Since, however, the verdict of the episcopal court was not accepted by the Donatists, the Emperor regarded himself as justified, in the interest of peace, on his own initiative but without any objections on the part of the Church, in convoking a synod of the bishops of his area of rule to Arles in 314; at it Pope Silvester I (314–35) was represented by two priests and two deacons. The absence of the Roman Bishop was explained without difficulty by the pressing tasks which his office, just assumed, placed on him in Rome. But the members of the Synod themselves knew of a preeminence of the Roman See, since they first made known to Silvester the results of their discussions with the purpose that the Universal Church should be informed of them from Rome; hence they saw in Rome a sort of central office of information for the other churches. In the early phase of the Arian controversy Pope Silvester was surprisingly of little prominence, partly perhaps because the discussion occurred chiefly in the East and because another western bishop, Hosius of Córdoba, was the Emperor's adviser.

Bishop Mark (336) was succeeded by Pope Julius I (337–52), during whose pontificate the preeminence of Rome could develop in relatively greater freedom of movement, since the sons of Constantine were at first much less active in ecclesiastical political matters than was their father. Above all, in the confrontation over the person and affair of Athanasius the papal authority could strengthen itself considerably in East and West. It is significant that both the opponents and the adherents of Athanasius turned to the Roman Pope to obtain from him approval of their attitude.

The awareness of being obliged to act for the Universal Church was expressed in Julius I's initiative with which he asked the Emperor Constans to convoke an imperial synod which should definitively settle the conflict.

With the acquiring of sole rule by Constantius in 353 there also began for the Latin Church a decade in which the Church's freedom was not only curtailed but forcibly suppressed by the despotic imperial caprice. No bishop had to taste it so bitterly as did Julius' successor, the former Roman deacon Liberius (352–66), in whom the papacy of the fourth century experienced its deepest humiliation and hence strong damage to its authority. In the first three years of his pontificate he appeared throughout as the firm defender of the Nicene faith and its champion Athanasius and aimed to promote this twofold concern to victory at a synod in Aquileia, which he requested from the Emperor. When, instead of this, Constantius at Arles in 353 extorted the condemnation of Athanasius by the Gallic bishops and the Pope's representatives, Liberius bitterly deplored the collapse of his legates and of the Gallic episcopate and stated that he would prefer to die rather than to consent to decrees which contradicted the gospel. Two years later he had to experience again that the majority of the bishops at Milan (355) succumbed to the pressure of the imperial threats and assented to the condemnation of the Bishop of Alexandria. In the letter to the three bishops who had been exiled then — this time his legates also stood firm, despite abuse — he courageously declared his solidarity with them and asked their prayers that he might withstand the attacks falling upon him and maintain faith and Church intact. Then after the Synod of Milan the Emperor exerted an enormous physical and psychological pressure on Liberius in order to extort from him his assent to the verdict of condemnation on Athanasius — testimony of the high moral authority of the Roman Bishop. But neither threats nor presents, which an envoy of the Emperor alternately offered the Pope, nor the Emperor's violent fits of anger at a conference in Milan, where Liberius had been brought from Rome by night, could move the Pope to yield. Only a two-years' exile to Beroea in Thrace, thereupon decreed, combined with the persuasive tactics of the local bishops, adherents of the Emperor, and an agonizing homesickness, brought about the emotional breakdown, which caused the Pope to write those letters that were so seriously damaging to him, in which he broke off the Church's communion with Athanasius and with no sense of honor begged for only one thing — to be allowed to return to Rome. A fall of Liberius into heresy, such as Jerome claimed some years later, cannot be maintained, since, while the Pope did indeed sign the first and the third creeds of Sirmium, which excluded the *homoousios,* they otherwise permitted a quite orthodox interpretation. For the Pope's personal esteem, the disloyalty toward Athanasius weighed heavily enough; he was so compromised that Constantius could coolly disregard him in the following years. Rome was neither invited to the Synod of Rimini in 359 nor was any effort made this time to obtain its assent to the decrees: its voice now carried no weight in the Emperor's ears. Even if the sympathies of a majority of the Roman community were with the returning exile and forced Felix, who had been made Bishop of Rome by Constantius in Liberius' absence, to leave the city, Liberius knew that at first he had to be silent. He seems not to have tried to make a personal vindication of his conduct, but his eager exertions for a rapprochement and reconciliation of the strictly Nicene with the Homoiousian faction after the death of Constantius and his clear repudiation of the creed of Rimini-Nice may have been regarded by him as a sort of making amends. However, later Roman tradition harshly judged his failure and put, not him, but his temporary opponent Felix (II) in the list of legitimate Popes.

Popes Damasus I and Siricius

A consequence of the case of Liberius was, finally, the serious disturbances within the Roman community which broke out at the election of his successor. A minority, which rejected any reconciliation with the former adherents of Felix (II), quickly decided for the deacon Ursinus, whereas the majority chose the deacon Damasus (366–84) as bishop. Damasus later proposed to the Emperor a comprehensive new organization of spiritual jurisdiction. A Synod convoked by him in 378, submitted two proposals to the Emperors. In the event that clerics from Italy did not recognize a verdict pronounced against them by a spiritual court, the case should, with the aid of the State power, be sent to the court of the Bishop of Rome, but in the rest of the Empire to that of the metropolitan, while for trials of metropolitans the Bishop of Rome was exclusively competent. But he should be answerable only to the imperial council in the event of an accusation, in case the matter could not be settled by the sentence of the Roman Synod. With these proposals Damasus was certainly trying to expand and guarantee a special spiritual jurisdiction recognized by the State and to obtain for the Roman Bishop in particular a privilege that would clearly have underlined his preeminent position in the West. The reaction of the Emperors to these proposals was curious: in regard to the first they granted more than was asked, since they extended the cooperation of the State in the execution of episcopal judgments to the entire western part of the Empire, but they indirectly rejected the second, the specially requested judicial competence of the Roman Bishop, with the vague explanation that the well-known sense of justice of the Emperors made it impossible that frivolously slanderous charges would be brought against the Bishop of Rome. Damasus had to be content with a half-success.

In the final phase of the Arian disorders also the Pope displayed initiatives which indicate clearly his exertions to promote the importance and rank of Rome within the Universal Church. The criterion of the orthodoxy of a creed must be its approval by Rome, and this claim found expression a decade later in the well-known law of Theodosius I of 27 February 380, whereby the Christian faith was declared the State religion in that form which the Romans once received from the Apostle Peter and which was now professed by Bishop Damasus of Rome and Peter of Alexandria. Damasus had apparently not recognized how doubtful it was to claim state aid for establishing his preeminent position or even to permit it to grant it. Too easily could the privilege become an oppressing shackle.

In the East also Damasus sought energetically to have Rome's authority recognized, not always successfully of course, especially in the question of the Schism of Antioch, in which Rome, informed solely and inadequately by Alexandria, clung stubbornly to the person of the Old Nicene Paulinus and by which it evoked the strong displeasure of Basil of Caesarea because of the arrogant tone of several Roman documents, even though Basil assigned to Rome a deciding function in questions of faith. Damasus tried to influence the appointment to the See of Constantinople, and commissioned Bishop Acholius of Thessalonica to work at the approaching Council of 381 for the election of a worthy man who could assure the peace of the Church. It was, of course, precisely two canons of this Synod which gravely impeded any binding intervention by Rome into the inner ecclesiastical affairs of the East. While canon 2 defined the jurisdictional spheres of the eastern patriarchates, without even mentioning Rome, canon 3 gave to the Bishop of Constantinople "the primacy of honor after the Bishop of Rome, because that city is the New Rome." Hence it could not but be welcome to Damasus when persons from the East applied directly to Rome and in individual cases asked its help. He aptly esteemed such "appeals" as an expression of the reverence which belonged to "the Apostolic See," because Peter had once taught in this Church.

With this formula, which merely completed the identification of the Roman episcopal see with "the Apostolic See" — it is first met under Pope Liberius and was
used by Damasus with unambiguous frequency — the Pope claimed a rank which
was based not on Rome's political importance but on the quite special relation
of the Apostle Peter to this community. But since it also appears in letters to the
Greek East, which likewise exhibited apostolic churches, Rome intended to have
preeminence in their regard also. Among the ideas of Damasus on a Roman pre-
eminence within the Universal Church is to be included a text which is found in
the so-called *Decretum Gelasianum* and was probably formulated at a Roman
Synod under Damasus, perhaps in 382. Here the "Petrine" sees are presented in
the order of Rome, Alexandria, and Antioch, but at the same time it is stressed that
the Roman See owes its primacy not to synodal decrees but to the Lord's words in
Matthew 16:18, and that this rank was further reinforced by the double martyrdom
of Peter and Paul in Rome. Noteworthy grounds also give reason to see Damasus
as the author of a comprehensive letter to the Gallic bishops. Here he asks those
to whom he is writing, who have applied to the authority of the Apostolic See,
to pay attention to what he has to say, and he warns them not to tolerate certain
abuses in the Gallic clergy. He states impersonally that this or that is forbidden,
that a person is excluded from the communion of the Apostolic See if he does not
hold to what Scripture, apostolic discipline and tradition, the things handed down
by the Fathers, and the *regula ecclesiastica* have established. Hence in this letter
there is a sort of preliminary stage of the papal decretals, the content and form
of which was perfected only under the next Pope.

Another aspect of the many-sided activity of Pope Damasus is disclosed by his
correspondence with Jerome, whom he took for a while into the service of the
papal chancery: his interest in the Bible, in individual points of exegesis as well
as, especially, in a revision of the Latin translations of the Bible that were often
different from one another and faulty. That he entrusted Jerome with this task
marks him as a far-sighted initiator of a work which was destined in the future to
exercise a wide-reaching impact as the *Vulgata.*

Into the concept of the leadership role of the Roman Bishop as developed by
Damasus his successor Siricius (384–99) introduced no decisively new characteristics. The former deacon of the Roman community was, probably with an eye to
possible intrigues by the still living Ursinus, elected without delay and emphatically
recognized by the court. Surely the sarcastic remark of Jerome on the *simplicitas*
of the new bishop, who judged all others in accord with his own caliber, is full
of resentment, since Jerome himself, as he states, was regarded according to an
almost unanimous judgment as a worthy successor of Damasus. But it reveals
a grain of truth when Siricius was gauged against the figure of the contemporary Bishop Ambrose, of Milan. In the latter's hands, not in Rome, met the great
threads of Church politics: Ambrose corresponded with the bishops of the East,
guided important superregional synods, and was the decisive conversationalist of
the Emperors and of the imperial administration, whereas the activity of Siricius
remained confined to the inner sphere of the Latin Church. His importance lies in
the fact that he further developed, both in content and in form, into a serviceable
instrument, the initial steps achieved by his predecessor for an independent papal
legislation that embraced the entire Church of the West. Anyone who does not

adhere to the order given by him separates himself from the safe apostolic Rock on which Christ built his Church.

Pope Innocent I (402–17)

At the start of the fifth century stood the forceful personality of Innocent I (402–17) — his predecessor, Anastasius I, was in office only three years — who sought to realize his own high notion of the primacy of the Roman Bishop with methodical determination. The broad field of ecclesiastical discipline presented itself as an especially favorable area for the realization of his leadership task, perceived as a duty, since it gave occasion to manifold inquiries in Rome and made it possible for Innocent to use the now fully developed instrument of the decretals, controlled by him in a masterful way. The inquiries made known some abuses in these churches: encroachments of one bishop on the jurisdictional area of his neighbor, laxity in regard to heretics, admission of the unworthy to spiritual office, and frequent ignorance of the liturgical and canonical prescriptions. The position of Rome as the highest court of appeals was ably underlined and in regard to content was extended by his demand that all the more important cases (*causae maiores*) be submitted to the Apostolic See. Since it was not decided what at a given time was to be regarded as *causa maior*, the Pope assured himself the possibility of intervention as he saw fit, while on the other hand the reference contained in the formula *causae maiores* to the supreme judicial position of Moses (Exod. 18:22) gave a biblical consecration to the Roman claim.

Innocent I came into a direct confrontation with the eastern patriarchates in the course of the serious conflict centering on John Chrysostom. The latter, bishop of the capital since 398, had lost the favor of the court through his candid preaching, had become unpopular also with a part of the clergy because of his demand for an ascetic lifestyle, and finally had become the victim of the intriguing Bishop of Alexandria, Theophilus, who could never reconcile himself to the exalted rank given to Constantinople by the Synod of 381. When in 404, at the Emperor's command, Chrysostom was deprived of his office and exiled to Armenia, he turned to the Bishops of Aquileia, Milan, and Rome for help. Innocent I thereupon demanded the convocation of a general synod of the eastern and western episcopates at Thessalonica, adhered to this demand despite Theophilus of Alexandria, and sent to the Emperor Honorius the acts pertaining to the case, with the petition to protest in this sense to his brother at Constantinople. But the treatment of the delegation dispatched by Pope and Emperor to Constantinople it was treated en route without respect by the eastern officials, not admitted to the Emperor's presence, and forcibly sent back to Italy — clearly showed the limits which were set down for a Bishop of Rome in the Eastern Empire. The effort of the Pope to display an independent initiative in a conflict within the Eastern Church miscarried; he encountered serious difficulties from the leading bishops of the East — Alexandria and Antioch — and he foundered on the attitude of the Eastern Emperor, who claimed for himself the ultimate power of decision. Thus there remained to Innocent only the formal protest and the honorable and immovable maintaining of ecclesiastical communion with Chrysostom, whose restoration to the diptychs he stubbornly demanded of the Bishops of Alexandria, Antioch, and Constantinople even after Chrysostom's death in 407. He utilized the correspondence with Alexander of Antioch to expound to him his idea that the supremacy of Antioch over the episcopate of the political Diocese of Oriens was based, not on imperial marks of esteem but on the decrees of Nicaea; the sarcasm toward the higher valuation of the See of Constantinople by the Emperor was obvious.

A highly significant possibility of realizing Innocent I's grasp of his teaching authority in the strict sense was, finally, offered by his attitude in regard to the Pelagian controversy. In 416 three letters reached him from Africa — one each from episcopal synods in Carthage and Mileve, the third from Augustine and four of his fellow bishops — in which the fear was expressed that the suspected doctrines of Pelagius would continue dangerously in consequence of his rehabilitation by the Synod of Diospolis (415), unless their condemnation should follow from Rome. All three letters extolled the authority of the Apostolic See, which derived from the authority of Scripture and should confirm the verdict of the African episcopate on the heresy and thereby give it a special effect. In his reply of January 417 Innocent praised the bishops for following tradition founded, not on human, but on divine decree and for turning to the Apostolic See because they knew that all matters, even those of the most remote provinces, could not be definitively settled until they had been brought to Rome's attention. This was above all true in questions of faith, in which all bishops had to turn to Peter in order to obtain from this apostolic source an answer to their questions. Here Innocent expressed the conviction, the first to do so with such unambiguity, that the *Sedes Apostolica* possesses the highest teaching authority. It has been doubted that this conviction was shared by the African episcopate, especially since Innocent deepened and extended the notion of the authority of the Roman See. But it will have to be granted that the praise and the biblical justification of this authority, which the bishops bestowed on it, showed it on a route that would lead to its full recognition.

The satisfaction of the African bishops over the decision of Pope Innocent I turned quickly into dismay when in rapid succession there arrived two letters from the Greek Zosimus (417–18), who had been elected Pope; they made known that Caelestius had exculpated himself in person and Pelagius through a profession of faith presented in writing, and that in Africa these men had been condemned frivolously and precipitately on the basis of statements of extremely doubtful witnesses; they would be regarded by Rome as rehabilitated if no one could demonstrate their alleged errors within two months. But the African episcopate remained firm and forced Zosimus first to a revision, even though limited, of his verdict on Caelestius. When then an African general council in May 418 again rejected the Pelagian doctrines and stated concisely that the verdict of Pope Innocent an Pelagius and Caelestius was still in effect, and when at the same time the Emperor Honorius agreed with this view and banished the adherents of the heresy, Zosimus, in accord with a Roman Synod, published an anathema on the Pelagian doctrines. Although the Pope apparently had no appreciation of the theological achievement of Augustine in the Pelagian question, Augustine tried to explain in a conciliatory manner the Pope's fluctuating attitude from a pastoral care for those in error.

The crude way in which Zosimus sought to correct, in accord with the Roman view, the right of appeal hitherto prevailing in the African Church, had a similarly negative effect.

The dubious administration of Zosimus, which in his last months had even evoked opposition in his own clergy, had an impact in the confusion over the selecting of his successor. There occurred a double election, since one faction proclaimed the deacon Eulalius, probably favored by Zosimus, while the majority of the priests expressed themselves for the Roman Boniface I (418–22). Honorius finally decided that Boniface should assume the office. Boniface sent a petition to the Emperor, in which in a general form he requested his protection for the Church, whereupon Honorius issued a rescript prescribing that in a future double election in Rome a new election by the entire community should decide the Roman Bishop. This first papal election arrangement in history, decreed by the State, had, it is true, no influence in the later period, but the esteem and independence of the Roman See at first suffered because of it.

Boniface also faced the critical question of ecclesiastical supremacy in the Balkans. This was seriously threatened when the bishops of Thessaly, unhappy with an appointment arranged by Rome to the episcopal see of Corinth, applied to Constantinople and obtained from the Emperor Theodosius II an edict whereby all controverted cases of the Churches of Illyricum were to be submitted to the bishops of the capital of the Eastern Empire, since this city possessed the rights of Old Rome. In letters to Bishop Rufus of Thessalonica, whose vicariate was confirmed, and to the bishops of Thessaly, Boniface repeated in the language of Innocent I that the care for the Universal Church was laid on the Bishop of Rome as a duty and hence included also the Churches of the East, who accordingly had consulted Rome in serious questions in the past. Furthermore, the Pope induced the Emperor Honorius to write to Theodosius II, who thereupon instructed the *Praefectus Praetorio* for Illyricum to observe the previous order of ecclesiastical circumstances in his sphere of authority. The view of Rome was clearly formulated by Boniface: that, despite all recognition of the rank of the Churches of Alexandria and Antioch, Rome alone was the head, the others were the members (*Ep.* 14,1).

The understanding of the primacy by Pope Celestine I (422–32) found expression above all in the decisions which resulted from the controversy over the teaching of Nestorius. When the latter and Cyril presented to him in the summer of 430 their view of the Christological question and of the previous course of the discussion, he saw in this an appeal from the East to Rome, at once had a position adopted in regard to it at a synod, and made known its decrees to those directly concerned and to the clergy of Constantinople. Cyril was commissioned, "in his place," to see to the implementation of the Roman synodal verdict, which called upon Nestorius to recant and, in case of his refusal, excluded him from the ecclesiastical community. In the letter to Constantinople Celestine stressed that the Christians there were also his flock, for whom, in according with 2 Corinthians 11:28, his paternal care was intended. Here a repeated claim of the Pope became clear: the eastern Churches were also confided to his care, hence he could and must intervene in their affairs also, especially if, as here, there was a question of faith; he could make binding decisions and appoint a deputy. But the further development showed that, as previously, people were of a different opinion in the East in regard to such a claim. The decision of the Emperor to have the controversy over Nestorius settled at an imperial Synod, to which Rome too was invited, had put Celestine into a precarious position, since Rome had already taken a position and could not revise its verdict. And so the legates appointed for Ephesus received orders to consult there with Cyril, not to intervene directly in the discussion but only to express their view of the verdict rendered, and for the rest to be mindful of the authority of the Roman See. Of course, the letter to the Synod stated clearly that the legates had to carry out what had already been decided at Rome and that the Pope did not doubt that the Council would assent to these decrees. But since Cyril, appealing, it is true, to his function as Celestine's deputy, without awaiting the arrival of the papal delegation, had already accomplished the condemnation and deposition of Nestorius, the verdict of Rome could only be made known subsequently to the participants in the Council. But the Roman Legate Philip ably explained their acclamations as recognition of the head by the members and declared before the assembled Synod that "Peter, head of the Apostles, pillar of the faith and foundation-stone of the Church, up to this day and for ever lives and governs in his successors" and that Celestine is his successor and representative; this Synod took note of these explanations without objection. The Pope soon claimed for himself, in an assessment of the Council's work, the chief role in the outcome and stressed in regard to the clergy of Constantinople that Peter had not abandoned them in their need. Thus far no Pope had emphasized to the Eastern Churches as clearly as Celestine the rank of the Roman Bishop as head of the Universal Church, but an express acceptance of his claim did not follow at Ephesus.

Relations with the Eastern Churches also played a considerable role in the pontificate of Sixtus III (432–40). The Union between Alexandria and Antioch of 433, brought about after much exertion and not without Rome's collaboration, filled the Pope with great satisfaction; in a letter to John of Antioch he stressed how important it was to be of one mind with Rome, since in the successors of Peter was found the tradition which the latter had received. The cordial relations now existing between the Eastern Churches and Rome were temporarily overshadowed by an effort by the Bishop of Constantinople, Proclus, in 434 to recover influence in Eastern Illyricum, in which he had the support of some of the bishops of the area. Sixtus discreetly repulsed this attack, on the one hand calling attention to the position and rights of the Bishop of Thessalonica as *vicarius sedis apostolicae* and defining them precisely, and on the other hand making known to Proclus his expectation that he would not listen to the Illyrian priests or bishops who would apply to him contrary to the law.

Pope Leo the Great

In Leo I (440–61), who even before his official elevation as deacon of the Roman congregation had exercised a strong influence on his two predecessors, the consciousness of the primacy in the early Church achieved its first definitive climax. This Pope was deeply convinced that only Christ is the true and eternal Bishop of his Church; he can bear the burden of his office only in reliance on him who works in him and accomplishes the right that he does. But since Christ as the eternal Bishop granted to Peter an imperishable participation in his episcopal power, Peter always presides over his Roman See, and it is Peter who likewise works and acts through his heirs. Leo I deepened this notion of the Roman Bishop as Peter's heir already employed by Siricius, and saw in it the real justification of the primacy: just as the heir enters into all rights and duties of the one whose heir he is, so the current Bishop of Rome, as Peter's heir, assumes his function, full authority, and privileges. Not Peter's having worked in Rome, not the possession of Peter's tomb, but the legally understood succession of the heir permits the Roman Bishop to function as Peter's vicar. And furthermore, as, according to Matthew 16:18, more power was entrusted to Peter than to the other Apostles, so the same is true for the relation of his heir to the other bishops. On such a basis Leo understood himself as called to an office whose burden and dignity he likewise felt. It placed on him the duty of supervising in the Universal Church the purity of doctrine and standing up for a manner of life within this community which corresponded to the gospel and the tradition of the Fathers. As no Pope before him Leo I sought to do justice to this duty, in a seriously accepted responsibility and in the awareness of a high dignity, and at the same time with a watchful eye for the possible in the concrete individual case and with diplomatic skill.

In the territory of the Latin Church Leo's claim to leadership encountered no fundamental opposition: it was recognized, of course, without reserve by a relatively weak Western Empire. When the Pope learned of the existence in Rome of a not inconsiderable Manichaean community, he proceeded against it energetically and secured without hesitation an imperial edict which intensified the punishments already prescribed against it and for years he warned in word and writing against the Manichaean danger. When various congregations of the province of Venetia enlisted the services of former Pelagian clerics without adequate supervision, he admonished the Bishop of Aquileia to greater vigilance. Learning that Priscillianism was again flourishing in Spain, he supplied in a decretal concrete instructions for the action of the bishops. Abuses in episcopal elections in North Africa, which came about in consequence of the Vandal invasion, induced the Pope to write to the episcopate of Mauretania, to demand a comprehensive report on the measures adopted. Leo's jurisdictional power seems to have been questioned, and only temporarily, by a single Latin bishop, Hilary of Arles, a former monk of Lérins, in whom purely personal asceticism was joined to a strong inclination to a not always discreet supervision of ecclesiastical discipline in the whole Gallic Church. He derived the right to this from alleged privileges of the see of Arles, which he also personally defended before a Roman Synod. Leo quashed Hilary; he left him in office, but only as Bishop of Arles, whose metropolitan rights passed to the senior bishop of the province. In a masterfully formulated and measured letter to the bishops of the province of Vienne the Pope made known his decisions and emphasized expressly that he made them in his character as successor of Peter. He aptly utilized the case to have an edict, requested from the Emperor Valentinian III for Gaul, confirmed, to the effect that the primatial claim of the Roman Bishop was independent of any consent by the State. Since Hilary submitted to the Roman judgment, the case remained only an episode without that importance which is at times ascribed to it. Leo I had to call his vicar at Thessalonica to order when the latter exceeded his authority in regard to the metropolitans of his territory. In a formula become famous, the Pope made clear to him that the Roman Bishop had summoned him, in transmitting the vicariate, only to a share in his care as shepherd, not to the fullness of his power. Leo found an equally clarifying expression for the meaning and range of episcopal collegiality: all bishops are equal in dignity, but not in rank, as was already the case in the Apostolic College, since preeminence was given to one. From this pattern (*forma*) was deduced its measure in the pastoral care, which was different according to the importance of the individual see, but the care of all of them flowed together into the comprehensive care of Peter's see for the Universal Church: only a *concordia sacerdotum* thus understood guaranteed the unity of the Church.

However, the real and decisive testing area for the possibility of realization of Leo's understanding of the primacy was and remained the Churches of the East. Already in his letter of congratulations to Dioscorus of Alexandria, who had announced his election, the Pope in a cautious formulation mentioned that unity must prevail between Rome and Alexandria, since in the Roman Church the traditions of Peter, honored by the Lord with the primacy, were held in respect and in Alexandria those of his disciple Mark, and between teacher and pupil no opposition should exist. A direct reply from Dioscorus to Leo's letter is not extant, but what he really thought of Rome's position in the Universal Church was expressed clearly in the treatment which he accorded to Leo's legates at the imperial Synod of Ephesus in 449. He imperiously pushed aside their demand that the Synod at least let the papal verdict on the teaching of Eutyches, as contained in Leo's letter to Flavian of Constantinople, be read, and just as coolly he disregarded the Roman protest against the deposition of Flavian. This unambiguous nonrecognition of any special position of Rome by the Church of Alexandria was accompanied by the negative attitude of the Emperor Theodosius II, who bluntly rejected the combined petitions of the Pope, the Emperor Valentinian III, and the latter's mother Galla Placidia for the convoking of a new council in Italy. In his reply to Valentinian he consciously spoke only of the "Patriarch" Leo, whereas the letters of the Western imperial family clearly referred to Rome's universal rank. It is true, the Pope had often extolled in lyric terms the importance of the imperial office for maintaining the purity of the faith and had characterized its representatives as inspired by the Holy Spirit, but the real value of such formulations becomes discernible when it is established that Leo I by no means now abandoned the Eastern Church to the leadership of the Emperor. On the contrary, he was obliged to remind it continually of its duty to protect and be vigilant, did not hold back with pronounced criticism of the failure of Ephesus in 449 for which the Emperor was largely responsible, and demanded that a new council must correct "quae contra fidem facta sunt," and he even expressed his concern that the Emperor could in regard to a truth of faith become the victim of deception. Certainly, the bishops deposed at Ephesus in 449 — Flavian, Eusebius of Dorylaeum, and Theodoret of Cyrrhus — turned to Rome for help and to some extent expected or asked of the papal authority direct reinstatement in their former offices, but such voices remained isolated.

Like Pope Celestine earlier at Ephesus in 431, now Leo I had to be concerned that at the Council of Chalcedon his doctrinal decision contained in the *Epistola ad Flavianum* should not be again questioned. In keeping with this concern was the conduct of his legates, who repeatedly stressed the supreme teaching authority of Rome and intended to prevent any procedure that contradicted this notion. They could, like Leo himself later, find great satisfaction in the acclamation which greeted the *Epistola Dogmatica* — "Peter has spoken through Leo" — and interpret this in the sense of an approving confirmation of the Roman teaching authority. In reality the situation was by far not so clear. Without doubt, the letter to Flavian was once again discussed, and a group of the bishops had hesitations because of certain formulations, which had to be cleared up. The acclamations for the *Epistola* must obviously be understood as the Council's confirmation that Leo's teaching concurred with the tradition of the Fathers; hence the Council regarded itself as authorized, first to examine it and then to proclaim it. The Council acted even more independently in questions of jurisdiction, as, for example, the reinstatement of the deposed bishops, which it decided lay within its competence. This independence appears most strongly in the decree of the Council which is contained in the so-called canon 28 and granted to the see of Constantinople the same rights as the Roman See possessed, since they were of equal rank as the imperial cities. From this was derived for the Bishop of Constantinople the right to ordain all the metropolitans of the Dioceses of Pontus, Asia, and Thrace and of all bishops in the areas bordering these territories. The Council maintained this decree against the protest of the papal legates, but after the conclusion of the sessions turned to the Pope, again expressly recognized his teaching authority, explained the meaning of the canon, and asked him "through his recognition to honor" this decree also. The Emperor Marcian and Bishop Anatolius also petitioned Leo in the same sense. Leo's protracted comments in letters to the imperial pair and to the Bishop of Constantinople evaluated canon 28 as a serious affront to the decrees of Nicaea and solemnly declared it invalid, but achieved only a temporary suspension of the decree.

Glancing at this complex situation, one must say that the Council of Chalcedon did not express an unlimited and full recognition of Leo's understanding of the primacy, but the Roman teaching authority in the strict sense found a measure of assent previously unknown and later never again realized, whereas a competence of Rome in questions of ecclesiastical discipline and jurisdiction could not be established, but was only occasionally accepted by individual bishops. How unenduring was even this relative success was quickly revealed by the struggle that at once began in the East over the validity of the Council of Chalcedon. Of course, in the West the primacy of the Roman Bishop was no longer challenged in the full breadth understood and formulated by Leo I. Certainly, the surpassing personality of this Pope contributed to this: in the contemporary West no figure of similar importance could be set beside him.

C H A P T E R   4 7

The Clergy of the Church of the Empire

At the beginning of the fourth century there had long been a general conviction that, within the Christian community, there had to be a special clerical state with various ranks, to each of which were allotted specific duties in the service of the community. The synodal and papal legislation of the age, as well as the initiative of individual bishops, tried to assure to the mandate of this state the highest possible efficacy, especially by defining the conditions for admittance, more clearly distinguishing the spheres of activity of the individual offices from one another, and caring for the spiritual and intellectual formation of its members. Individual authors produced outlines of a priestly ideal, which could keep alive the seriousness and meaning of the priestly mission.

The Various Orders

The actual division of the clergy into two groups, characterized by Innocent I as *clerici superioris* and *inferioris ordinis,* was familiar to the fourth century. To the first clearly belonged bishops, priests, and deacons, whose ordination was reserved exclusively to bishops and whose special rank was also recognized by state legislation. The lesser ranks, on the contrary, were subject to wide variations, not only in regard to their number and esteem but also to their field of activity. The orders most often named in the sources — those of subdeacon, acolyte, exorcist, porter, and lector — were not actually found in all local congregations, nor was admission to the next highest order strictly related to the exercise of the preceding degree; there was not even agreement whether each of the orders named really represented a clerical function. In the course of the fourth century there occurred in the rapidly growing communities a further differentiation of the duties of deacons and priests; their more precise definition led on occasion to considerable difficulties. Since the deacons were in many respects the direct cooperators of the bishop, at times even his representatives — they played a special role in the administration of Church property, in the choice of candidates for ordination, and in liturgical functions — their reputation and influence were quite often greater than that of the priests. At Rome they constituted the *collegium* of the Seven Deacons, whose head was called the archdeacon by the end of the fourth century, and it was mostly from their number that the Pope (or also the Antipope) was elected. The sources make known that they rather often claimed liturgical functions that were reserved to the priests or in general sought precedence over these. And so various synods had to remind them of their real rank and clearly relegate them to the place behind the priests. These had full authority to administer baptism and celebrate the Eucharist in the event that they were appointed to a church of their own; otherwise, they supplied for the bishop in these functions in his absence. At times they were even entrusted with preaching, which was basically the bishop's responsibility.

In the fourth and fifth centuries attempts were made to reevaluate the priesthood with a view to the rank of the bishop and also to justify this in theory. Chrysostom saw as the sole difference between priest and bishop the full power of the latter to perform the ordination of clerics. In the West the Ambrosiaster and Jerome regarded the distinction between the two orders as not original, since priest and bishop are in principle *sacerdotes;* the later distinction in rank goes back, they said, to mere considerations of expediency. Tendencies of this sort were however rejected by Innocent I, who expressly calls priests *secundi ordinis,* and later by Gelasius I, who aimed to penalize with deposition the encroachments of priests.

While the Synod of Serdica enacted the general rule that the cleric should prove himself for a time in the individual orders before he could advance to a higher one, Popes Siricius and Zosimus established definite intervals — *tempora,* the later interstices — for remaining in one order, but the observance of this had again to be imposed by Leo I. Then Gelasius I championed the noteworthy idea that these prescriptions were to be treated flexibly and should be accommodated to the contemporary demands of preaching.

As regards the numerical strength of the clergy, both in individual communities and in entire provinces and countries, there are few reliable reports from this period, but no doubt in the Church of the Empire of the fourth century it grew considerably in proportion to the number of Christians.

Preliminaries for Admission to the Clerical State

In contrast to certain particular early Christian factions, such as Montanists or Priscillianists, the Church of the Empire on principle admitted only men to clerical orders. Deaconesses, who in the Latin West never achieved the same importance as in the East, were, it is true, inducted into their state by a special rite — imposition of hands and prayer — but the really sacramental sphere was not open to them. Their service was chiefly oriented to the women of the community, whom they prepared for baptism, took care of in the actual baptism, nursed in sickness, and acted as their contact with the clergy of the community.

Ecclesiastical legislation of the period in general required for admission to the individual orders a maturity corresponding to their importance, but in determining the age for ordination it was still fluctuating and not uniform. From the decretal of Pope Zosimus on the length of the interstices the following minimum ages result: for the acolyte and subdeacon, twenty-one; for the deacon, twenty-five; for the priest, thirty years. The most frequently mentioned age for the ordination of a bishop varied from forty-five to fifty years of age. The numerous exceptions indicate that these statements referred to standards whose observance could be disregarded if there was question of the ordination of an especially qualified man. For example, Ambrose of Milan became a bishop eight days after his baptism at the age of twenty-four, and Hilary of Poitiers before he was thirty-five.

The previously universally observed requirement of physical integrity and psychological health in the candidate for ordination was differentiated from the fourth century. Not only self-mutilation but strongly deforming scars or the lack of a bodily member excluded one from ordination, as did mental disorder and epilepsy. But more important for the Church was the fitness in moral character for the ecclesiastical state, and the testing of this was demanded with increasing urgency. This testing included a rather protracted probation of the previous layman in the faith and a moral life, and so the ordination of a neophyte was possible only by way of exception. This probation clearly had to be denied to those who had apostatized in a persecution. But a greater flexibility was shown to those who came to the Catholic Church from a schismatic or an heretical community, and on occasion their clerics might be left in their previous rank, as in the case of the Novatians at Nicaea and of the Donatists in North Africa. It was more difficult to determine an objective standard for the evaluation of moral qualities. The general view was that no fitness for the clerical state was present in those who had had to submit to public ecclesiastical penance because of serious sins. That these norms were often not observed is proved by the complaints, raised again and again, by the Popes on the ordination of *indigni* and the exclusion, decreed by them, of the guilty from the clerical state. That the clergy had to have at its disposal an extensive theological and pastoral knowledge because of its duty of proclaiming the faith and caring for souls was stressed by many authors and bishops of the time as well as by the Popes of the fourth and fifth centuries, but the sources provide only slightly varied statements on the contemporary educational program of clerics. The great majority of the lesser clergy at this time had at their disposal no theological institutions with a definite program of studies, and so the clerical aspirants were for the most part introduced by the contemporary local clergy into Scripture, the manner of administering the Sacraments, and the rest of pastoral activity. Under especially favorable conditions, as, for example, in large communities or under a bishop who welcomed initiative, a sort of scholastic instruction could develop, as was already foreshadowed in the Roman *schola cantorum* of the third century and then must be assumed in the beginnings of the *vita communis* of the clergy of the Church of Vercelli under Bishop Eusebius (d. ca. 371) and for some communities of North Africa. The clergy of the congregation of Hippo obtained an optimal formation under Augustine in his *monasterium clericorum,* but in his letters he had at times to complain in distress about the low level of knowledge of some clerics in the country. From the fifth century also some monasteries of the Latin West acquired a great importance for the education of clerics, as, for example, the South Gallic island monastery of Lérins, from which proceeded many bishops, who then sought to form the clergy in their sees on the Lérins model. The heart of the priestly education was generally considered to be the knowledge and understanding of Scripture, which was strictly demanded by all the contemporary "mirrors" for priests and bishops. The *Statuta ecclesiae antiqua* required that it be ascertained in a candidate for the episcopacy before his ordination that he possessed a satisfactory literary education, was familiar with Scripture and reasonable in interpreting it, that he knew the doctrines of the Church and concurred with the basic truths of faith. The cultural and economic crisis that accompanied the migration of the peoples and the consequent lack of recruits naturally caused these requirements often to be to a great extent disregarded.

Certain structures of the society of late antiquity also presented the Church and State of the fourth and fifth centuries with problems in regard to admittance to the ecclesiastical state, and both of them, at times from different motives, tried to solve them, for the most part in the same direction. For example: the slave

was basically an equal and full member of the Christian community, but his social and legal lack of freedom in contemporary society often made him seem as
unsuited for a clerical function as were the serfs bound to the soil on the State
domains or the estates of the owners of *latifundia* by the colonate legislation.
Even the freedman was to be included with them in a certain sense, since he
remained bound to his former lord through various obligations, and in certain
cases the lord could cancel the manumission. And so the Synod of Elvira (ca. 306)
forbade the ordination of freedmen whose *patroni* were still pagans, a prohibition which the First Synod of Toledo (400) modified to the extent that it made the
admission dependent on the consent of the former lord. Pope Leo I expressed
himself in a general way against the ordination of slaves and other dependents,
because their ties to their lords did not permit them to devote themselves totally to the service of God. Pope Gelasius I justified this regulation on the ground
that the ordination of these unfree would disregard the rights of others and the
state legislation, except in the case of the *colonus* who had obtained the written permission of his lord. Slaves ordained contrary to this rule had to return
to their lord, unless they were already priests; deacons could retain their office
only if they supplied a substitute to their lord. The state laws here mentioned by
Gelasius were, first, a decree of the Emperor Theodosius II, which forbade the
ordination of a *colonus* without the consent of his lord and only permitted one
already ordained to continue in the service of the Church if he paid the tax laid
on him and a substitute took over his former duties. Furthermore, a decree of
the Emperor Valentinian III forbade the ordination of slaves and *coloni* and left
bishops and priests from these classes in their offices only if they had already
occupied them for thirty years. In addition, state legislation sought to keep members of individual professions or holders of state or urban offices from entry into
the clerical state because they seemed indispensable for the operation of the
administration and the economy. For its part, the Church had hesitations about
the admission of former state officials, who after the reception of baptism could
have been forced, for example as soldiers or judges, to shed blood or to preside
over pagan feasts. Here the long existing Christian conviction that one in so "secular" a service could be freed of guilt only with difficulty came into operation in
a concrete manner.

Clerical Marriage and the Beginnings of Celibacy

At the beginning of the fourth century there were in the Church clerics of all ranks
of the hierarchy who continued, without any limitations, the married life they
had entered before ordination and others who, of their own accord, had decided
for continence in marriage or for the renunciation of any marriage. In the pre-
Constantinian source; married clerics are naturally mentioned more frequently
than the unmarried. From the third century, in the wake of the high esteem of
the ideal of virginity, the *continentia* of the clergy was extolled with great praise.
Tertullian and Origen made clear their sympathy for it, and justified it with the
greater efficacy of its prayer and the special purity required for intimacy with the
Christian mysteries. Clement of Alexandria adduced as motive for the continence

of the clergy, which he found in the Apostle Paul, the greater availability for the care of souls and the example proposed to *virgines*.

Of the married cleric it was at first required only that his marriage be spotless in every respect, that is, that both spouses enter into marriage as virgins and always maintain mutual fidelity. A second marriage did not measure up to this ideal, and so a man who had remarried or the husband of a widow was excluded from the clerical state. This rule at first lasted throughout the fourth century, but even so there were in the East discussions as to whether a marriage contracted before baptism should be considered here and whether the prohibition of the second marriage applied only to the higher orders. However, one who, when unmarried, had received one of these orders could not later enter into a marriage. The definitive legislation for the Eastern Church came from the Quinisext Council of 692, which required of the married candidate for the episcopacy separation from his wife and her entrance into a monastery, whereas it permitted to priests and deacons the continuation of their marriage and demanded continence only on days on which they celebrated or concelebrated the liturgy.

In the Latin West the development ran in another direction, since here from the late fourth century, under the authoritative leadership of Rome, the demand was made and firmly established by law that clerics of the higher orders were obliged, if they were married, to absolute continence after ordination. The first Roman document that was concerned in detail with the question was the letter of Pope Damasus I (366–84) to the Gallic episcopate. It justified the regulation by arguing that a bishop or priest, who preached continence to others, had himself to give an example and must not esteem physical fatherhood more highly than the spiritual fatherhood which his office so often bestowed on him. The violation of this "cultic purity" by the priest meant that he did not deserve this name and was not worthy to have the *mysterium* of God confided to him. Around the turn of the fourth to the fifth century the strict continence of married clerics in the three higher ranks of the hierarchy was a clearly decided question in the pronouncements of the Popes. Leo I (440–61) finally extended the law, without detailed justification, to subdeacons, whose growing approach to direct service at the altar brought them closer to the deacons.

Not only the papal decretals but the corresponding synodal legislation were motivated in their requirement of the sexual continence of the higher clergy most often by the cultic purity requisite for the administration of the Sacraments. In this unsatisfactory justification there operated, in addition to the Old Testament prescriptions of purity, especially the idea of the high dignity of the Christian priesthood, which was seen as fundamental in its relation to the Eucharist. A more exact investigation of the total picture of the contemporary priesthood can, however, establish a series of further essential motives for priestly continence: the greater availability for service in the preaching of the gospel; the exemplary life of the priest, who preaches continence and virginity to others the more efficaciously if he sets a convincing example; the spiritual fatherhood of the priest, who imparts the higher spiritual life through administering baptism and reconciling penitents; and finally, even if more indirectly, the imitation of the priestly model of Christ himself and the specific participation in his priesthood. The essence of this *lex continentiae* can be understood only against such a total background.

The episcopal recommendations of total continence in the higher clergy must have been suggested by the idea of uniting the clerical office and celibate monasticism, as was often the case in Egypt as early as the days of Athanasius. Probably this union was also true of the already mentioned *vita communis* of the clergy of the Church of Vercelli, which Bishop Eusebius introduced; Augustine implemented it in the *monasterium clericorum* of the community of Hippo, for which he also found sufficient recruits. It is clear here that at first individual bishops, going beyond the general ecclesiastical regulations, demanded the affirmation of total celibacy as a condition for admission to the clergy of their local churches.

Choice and Ordination of the Clergy

The vocation to an ecclesiastical office occurred in principle through election made by the entire community, clergy and people, but the manner in which the people participated showed considerable differences. Reflected most clearly in the sources is the manner of the election of a bishop. Generally the new bishop was called from the clergy of the local church because a candidate of this sort could best be evaluated by the electors; to be sure, exceptions were not at all rare. Since as unanimous a choice as possible was desired, the clergy of the community first agreed on a candidate, whom the people then approved and for whom the assent of the bishops of the ecclesiastical province, especially that of the metropolitan, was asked. To the decline of the lay element corresponded the growing influence of the bishops of the ecclesiastical province, which was often fostered by the lack of agreement of the community on the candidate to be elected or by its decision for a candidate who was canonically unsuitable. If the bishops themselves were divided in their choice, the final decision belonged to the metropolitan. Finally, the secular authority also interfered in the filling of vacant episcopal sees, either through high officials or through the Emperor personally, without thereby creating a legal basis for such a procedure. At times the unanimous will of the people may have been regarded as God's voice; sometimes the refusal of the one elected was more an initial reaction of terror in the face of the responsibilities which such a function imposed. But one also gets the impression that it pertained to the style of the age to utter a formal rejection of the office in order not to fall under the suspicion of seeking the episcopal dignity from ambition or greed.

Since the fundamentals of the rite and law of ordination were laid down in the pre-Constantinian period, especially by means of the *Traditio Apostolica* of Hippolytus, it is sufficient here to refer to the additions that completed them. Now in the Latin West *ordinatio* became in the colloquial speech of the Christians the designation for the rite of ordination, whereas *consecratio* was reserved for the ordaining prayer that accompanied the rite of the imposition of hands. Furthermore, definite times for ordination were developed: for episcopal ordination, Sunday, which Leo I designed as an ancient custom; for the ordination of priests and deacons, the Ember Saturdays and the Saturday preceding Passion Sunday. All ordinations were incorporated in the celebration of the Eucharist. Although Gelasius I emphasized the exclusive right of the bishop to ordain, by way of exception he granted to the priest the bestowing of the ordination of subdeacons or acolytes. Quite frequently the bishops of this period had to be reminded that they could exercise their right of ordination only within their sees and in regard to members of their own church. In principle, clerics were ordained for service in a definite local church; a transfer to another church should be possible only by way of exception, but, especially in the case of bishops in the Eastern Empire, it was more frequent than the ecclesiastical legislation envisaged.

Privileges of the Clerical State

Under the first Christian Emperor not only was the special status of the clergy, hitherto prevailing within the Church, also recognized by the State: in addition, it became a clearly privileged state by the granting of specific rights in comparison with the average citizen or the various professional groups. Constantine first freed it from the so-called *munera,* specified services performed for the State, such as the duty of assuming the office of *decurio,* properly provisioning the imperial retinue or troops passing through, or performing certain compulsory services (*munera sordida*), in order to make possible the unrestricted carrying out of its ecclesiastical duties. The exempting of the clergy from the *lustralis collatio,* a tax which merchants had to pay every five years, seems to have had an especially negative effect on the reputation of the Church. The numerous complaints about clerics engaged in business on behalf of the Church show that this privilege opened the door to abuses and obliged the State and the Church to repeated restrictions and prohibitions.

Of special importance for the credit of the Church in public life became the recognition of the judicial activity of the bishop in civil disputes, hitherto exercised only within the local episcopal congregation, that is, the incorporating of the so-called *audientia episcopalis* into the Roman civil law procedure. Constantine was convinced that an episcopal court, because of the high moral authority of the judge, guaranteed justice more and specifically protected Christians from the danger of being subjected to a prejudiced pagan judge, although now the pagan citizen could entertain the same suspicion with regard to the Christian bishop. In practice, then, this privilege proved to be for the Church a rather dubious gift. The majority of bishops were overburdened in this way because of a lack of juridical education; however, they could renounce the performance of this function as judge. Around the turn of the fifth century the *audientia episcopalis* was restricted to the merely mediating function of arbiter, which a Council of Carthage in 397 had already favored and which was far more suited to the meaning of the episcopal office. It seems that, for the Church's part, no one complained about this, and the same was true when the Emperor Valentinian III restricted this mediator's activity to purely ecclesiastical cases.

It is undisputed that the episcopal office in the fourth and fifth centuries, both through the development within the Church — growth of the spiritual authority in the numerous and increasingly strong local churches, at synods and councils, enhanced influence through economic and financial independence — as well as through the respectful and considerate treatment of its holders by the Emperors, the court, and the officials of the imperial administration and of the urban authorities gained an enormous social prestige. But a considerable gain in prestige accrued to the episcopal office from those manifold social welfare activities which so often made the bishops of the transition period from late antiquity to the Early Middle Ages the advocates of the poor and the miserable, the helpers of refugees, the spokesmen of prisoners, and even the defenders of the episcopal city in the threat of the migrations. The designations *pater populi, pater civitatis, pater urbis et pater patriae,* which did not signify the bishop's legal position, were the spontaneous echo which this aspect of the episcopal activity aroused in the hearts of those who experienced it in themselves.

The Collegiality of the Bishops

The *presbyterium,* which, according to the letters of Ignatius, assisted the local bishop in his duties, retained its function of service and of acting as deputy also in the fourth and fifth centuries. To be sure, at times the bishop was admonished to make use of the advice of his priests in specific cases, but the priests did not constitute a *collegium* which could act as such independently of the bishop by virtue of its own full power. The *ordo episcoporum,* for its part, maintained its independence, which since Irenaeus was based on the conviction that the bishops as a whole were the successors of the apostles and continued their function within the Church. The consciousness of the apostolic succession of the bishops remained also and was fully maintained under the primacy of the Roman Bishop that was at the same time achieving complete recognition and to a degree manifested itself in new ways. This could be observed especially in the development of the terminology, which the age employed for the episcopal office and its function. If the term *sedes apostolica* was used by the Roman bishops ever more frequently to denote their own see, this was true at the same time for other episcopal sees, even those to which no special rank pertained either from tradition or from their momentary organizational importance: every episcopal see was, therefore, *sedes apostolica.* The same idea is found in the application of the epithet *apostolicus* and of the noun *apostolatus* to the rank and activity of every bishop. The designation of a simple bishop as *summus pontifex* is even seen for the first time in a papal letter and appears especially in the address of letters to Gallic bishops.

An occasion on which the collegiality of the bishops especially appears was an episcopal ordination. Since in canon 4 the Council of Nicaea prescribed the presence of all bishops of the ecclesiastical province, but at least three of them, in this liturgical act, it was regarded as the norm, which was to be observed even under very difficult circumstances and which was again and again called to mind.

The concept of the apostolic succession also formed the basis for the idea of the collegiality of the bishops, which, especially in the fifth century, was decisively championed by the papacy itself in connection with the Christological controversies. Even before the Council of Ephesus, Pope Celestine referred Nestorius to the fact that, by his doctrine, he was excluding himself from the communion of the episcopal college, and his letter to the Council stressed that the proclamation of the gospel was entrusted to the episcopate in its totality, as it had once been confided to the college of Apostles, from which it had legitimately inherited this commission. Pope and bishops were obliged in their collegial responsibility to guard the true faith for the Universal Church and to stand up against error. For the bishops who continued to support Nestorius there was no place any longer in the episcopal college. Pope Leo I further deepened this understanding of episcopal collegiality when he emphasized that each bishop, in addition to his own see, bears a responsibility for the Universal Church, that in the ultimate analysis the Holy Spirit produces the inner unity of this college, and that of course no bishop can exercise his pastoral office in the Church if he is not in communion with Peter's successor. Collegiality thus understood was further expressed in the formula of the *consortium* and of the *communio episcoporum* and finally determined also the sense of the designations *fratres, coepiscopi, collegae,* and *consortes,* which the Popes liked to apply to the bishops.

CHAPTER   48

The Liturgy

The new situation consequent on the gaining of the Church's freedom and the turning of the imperial office to the Christian religion also influenced to a great degree the very heart of the interior life of the Church — the liturgy. These influences were for the most part directly related to the special missionary situation in which the Church then found itself. Now it had to prepare for its initiation a constantly growing flock which, for whatever motives, was requesting admission into the Christian community; hence the existing institution for this preparation, the catechumenate, was subjected to a severe test. Since, with the increasing number of Christians, more mediocrity also penetrated the congregations and with it the number of failures grew, the earlier penitential discipline was again examined in regard to its meaning and function. Furthermore, as always in periods of increased missionary activity, the Church was confronted with the problem of adaptation and hence with the question to what extent it could christianize certain forms of pagan celebrations and piety and incorporate them into its liturgical sphere. And so a series of new elements appeared in its sacramental liturgy, in church building, and in the liturgical year. The new relationship of the Church to the State and to public life made possible and likewise produced new forms, especially in the area of liturgical representation and the expansion of the liturgical calendar of celebrations.

Differentiation of Liturgies in East and West

From the fourth century there can be observed an increasing differentiation of liturgies, hitherto uniform in their basic features, but in principle free in the construction of word and rite: several factors contributed to this. Then, the development of much larger ecclesiastical structures supplied an impetus for the differentiation of the liturgies. The liturgy in use in the churches of the chief centers of these areas, especially of the developing patriarchal sees, acquired the character of a norm and gradually established itself in the sphere of influence of these ecclesiastical centers. In addition, the difference of languages and the cultural and national self-consciousness of individual regions produced by them in the areas of the expansion of Christianity repeatedly proved to be an especially effective principle of the differentiation, which included also the liturgical sphere. Finally, after the Councils of Ephesus in 431 and Chalcedon in 451, Nestorians and Monophysites went their own ecclesiastical ways and thereby promoted a special development of their respective liturgies. The process of differentiation naturally extended over a rather long period of time, at the end of which stands the codification of the liturgies, which took place for most of them only in the sixth and seventh centuries, but thereafter still admitted supplements and modifications.

Of the great eastern patriarchates — Antioch, Alexandria, and Constantinople — the first named displayed, with its proximate and remote hinterland, a richly creative liturgical activity. A more ancient core of it belongs to the so-called Apostles' Liturgy of the East Syrians, which first appeared in its complete form in the fifth century in the Syriac language and which remained the liturgy of the Nestorians, of the Uniate Chaldaeans, and of the Malabar Christians. The West Syrian Liturgy was distinguished for a special wealth in anaphoras (formulas of the Eucharistic Prayer or Canon). The Liturgy of James, originating in Jerusalem, must be regarded as their basis, as is testified both by the mystagogic catechisms of Cyril of Jerusalem and by Jerome. Known in the Syriac translation to the author of the *Testamentum Domini* of the fifth century, it became the normal liturgy of the Christians in the sphere of Edessa (Jacobites). Antioch itself or at least its immediate vicinity was the home of the so-called Clementine Liturgy and of the Syriac Anaphora of the Twelve Apostles, which is today generally regarded as the prototype of the Liturgy of Chrysostom, which was used in the Syrian capital probably even before the Council of Ephesus. In the so-called Liturgy of Mark, Alexandria created its oldest formula, which is attested by papyrus texts of the fourth and fifth centuries and influenced the prayers of the *Euchologion* attributed to Bishop Serapion of Thmuis (d. after 362); as the Liturgy of Cyril, it is still used by the Copts. Alongside the Liturgy of Mark there later appeared those of Basil and Gregory, which were taken over from Asia Minor or Syria and translated into Coptic. The Coptic liturgical formulas were finally passed on to the Ethiopians, who translated them into their national tongue and enriched them with several anaphoras. The two formulas of the Byzantine Liturgy — those of Basil and Chrysostom — were not original creations of the imperial capital. The first, long preferred to the second, must actually be linked with its namesake, who had elaborated a liturgy already in use at Caesarea. The second, named for Chrysostom only from the tenth century, could very probably have come to Constantinople before 431 in the form of the previously mentioned Anaphora of the Twelve Apostles and been reorganized by Bishop Nestorius. Of all the eastern liturgies, the Byzantine experienced the farthest expansion, especially among the Slavonic peoples, in whose evangelization it was used in the Old Slavonic translation. Among the characteristic features of the oriental liturgies, as these became known in the fourth and fifth centuries, must first be mentioned their understanding of the liturgy as a participation in the angels' heavenly service of God, which was further elaborated to a dramatically fashioned mystery celebration. In this the Christological discussion of the age found its expression in the stressing of the salvific deeds of the Redeemer and of the omnipotence of the divine *Logos:* the liturgy became the festive representation of the priestly action of Christ, and the liturgical acts became "pictures and symbols communicating the reality of the historical work of salvation, especially of the resurrection" (Schulz) an understanding of the liturgy which was especially promoted by John Chrysostom and Theodore of Mopsuestia.

Since Western Christianity at that time did not know any plurality of languages suited to the liturgy and, apart from Rome, no leading ecclesiastical see of the rank of Antioch or Alexandria could impose its authority, there were lacking here two of the factors, important in the East, for the differentiation of liturgies. Hence all western liturgies were linked by the one Latin language and it is natural to assume that before the completion of the two great liturgical types of the West — the Gallican and the Romano-African — there existed a general basic western form, from which Rome relatively early dissociated itself, whereas the Gallican Rite — to its subspecies belonged the Old Spanish, the Ambrosian, the Old Gallic, and the Celtic liturgies — later opened itself to oriental influences. To the general traits of the Gallic type belongs a relatively uniform order of the Mass, which knew prayers recurring virtually unchanged, and gave, not a fixed Canon, but a proper formula for every Sunday and every feast. In many prayers there appeared a deviation from old tradition. The effect of the confrontation with Arianism can be observed as a striking peculiarity especially in the Spanish and the Gallican liturgies: in this the idea of Christ's mediatorship was pushed into the background and the prayer addressed to Christ was more strongly emphasized. To this corresponded again a preferred worship of the Trinity, just as the Byzantine Liturgy knew it. Only in the Milanese Liturgy was Roman influence, in addition to these general Gallic features, found relatively early, since as early as the time of Ambrose it used the Canon of the Roman Mass. The originally Greek liturgy of Rome completed as early as the third century its translation, begun in the third century, into Latin ca. 370, with the introduction of the Latin Canon. Its most important characteristic was its adhering to the idea of Christ's mediatorship, which was manifested in the doxologies of the Mass prayers, which ended only "per Christum," and the prayer addressed to Christ was left to the sphere of popular piety. Furthermore, it gave up dramatic and poetic elements, such as the hymn, in the structure of the liturgy and thereby obtained a feature of objective and sober solemnity, which rather impeded a greater activity of the people.

New Features in the Sacramental Liturgy

The new missionary situation of the fourth century first operated in the broader area of the baptismal liturgy. Here especially the early institution of the catechumenate fell into an almost startling crisis, which, however, stood in a certain connection with the public recognition of Christianity. Whereas previously the acceptance of a pagan into the catechumenate presupposed in every respect a seriously intended and seriously undertaken commitment to the new faith, to which corresponded an immediately following intensive preparation, usually of three years, for the reception of baptism, now indeed the number steadily grew of those who asked admission to the catechumenate. But the number of pagans who made of it only a preliminary profession of Christianity grew also and at first deferred the reception of baptism, often until they fell into a sickness that endangered life or even, as Chrysostom said, "to the final breath," so that in a flagrantly abused development baptism became for them a sort of Sacrament of the Dead. The question as to the causes of this development permits several answers. Not only Emperors such as Constantine and Theodosius were among those who postponed their baptism, but also Basil, Gregory Nazianzen, Chrysostom, Ambrose, and others must be included: in their case, on the one hand their involvement with the perils of their profane calling, on the other hand the awareness of a lack of personal maturity made the postponement of baptism seem advisable. But in the case of the greatest number what was probably decisive was the fact that with admittance to the ranks of the catechumens a person was identified publicly as a Christian (with the accruing advantages) and that now one could evade the moral testing firmly demanded by Christian preaching after the reception of baptism. The consequence was a suspicious increase in the number of merely nominal Christians within the communities. The Church drew conclusions from such a situation and reconstructed the previous order of catechumens, separating the really serious seekers of baptism from the one large class of catechumens. But for one who joined the catechumenate the former manner of admission was complemented by an introductory catechesis, which was supposed to give him a first knowledge of the new way to salvation and place him in the position to receive with some profit the teaching supplied in the normal preaching to which he had access. To this catechesis was joined the rite of admission, which consisted of an imposition of hands, joined with a signing of the cross (*consignatio*) and, at least in North Africa and Rome, the presentation of salt. If the catechumen was not then induced to take part in the direct preparation for the reception of baptism, he belonged thereafter to the anonymous crowd of those to whom applied the bishops' annual admonition to have themselves enrolled at the beginning of Lent in the list of those immediately seeking baptism. For this group of *photizomenoi, competentes,* or *electi* (Rome) the Church supplied an instruction and a religious training intended for them; the baptismal catecheses preserved from East and West give information on the content and goal of this training. The instruction included, as earlier, an introduction to Scripture and the communicating of the Creed (*traditio symboli*) and of the Lord's Prayer, both of which were learned by heart so that they could be "given back" in the solemn baptismal profession. The instruction was accompanied by repeated prayer, impositions of hands, and signing with the cross, which were intended to strengthen the candidate on his way to baptism and shield him from demonic influences. The length of this preparation, despite the three years so often mentioned in the sources, was in practice reduced to one Lent, and hence, in spite of all the efforts of the bishops, a really effective "practice in Christianity" was often not realized. With the completion of the christianization of the Mediterranean peoples and the now almost exclusively practiced baptism of infants, this form of the catechumenate came to an end.

The growing number of Christian families involved at this period an increasing extension and importance for infant baptism, but not without discussion within the Church regarding the most appropriate time and a dispute with Pelagianism over its legitimacy. In the East Gregory Nazianzen and Chrysostom especially championed it on the ground that it bestowed on children as yet free of personal sins the status of children of God and "seal and consecration." In the West Augustine defended infant baptism as an old tradition and justified it theologically against Donatists and Pelagians in regard to the last-named especially through his doctrine of original sin. A proper baptismal ritual for infants was not developed; the rite of admission of the decaying catechumenate was retained for them — impositions of hands, signing with the cross, presentation of the blessed salt — and the sponsors or parents who took care of them during the baptism made the answers to the baptismal questions and the *redditio symboli.*

In the fourth and fifth centuries the importance of the so-called Discipline of the Secret increased; but, of course, its meaning was not entirely grasped when persons understood it as a mere keeping secret the sacred texts and rites. Moreover, the Creed and the Lord's Prayer were familiar from Christian literature and the Bible, and the publication of mystagogic catecheses also spread the knowledge of the baptismal and eucharistic liturgies. Rather, one should not speak of the mysteries in the presence of those not called or admit them to their celebration. The "not called" were all those who lacked the required means for the right understanding and experiencing of the mysteries. But this possibility was acquired only by "initiation," by the performance of the worship. The ultimate meaning of baptism and the Eucharist was only directly made known to the neophyte after his initiation.

The eucharistic celebration also admitted new elements in the fourth and fifth centuries and through continued development in individual points drew ever closer to the form of the "Mass." First, the Liturgy of the Word of God, usually with three readings from the Old Testament, the Apostle, and the Gospel and the sung texts interpolated between them, obtained its definitive structure. The readings, which began immediately after the entry of the clergy and the greeting of the congregation, were proclaimed by the lector or, in the case of the gospel, by the deacon, while the psalm between them was sung by a cantor from the ambo. In the psalm, after each segment, the response sung by the people was inserted; in the first chant it was taken from the psalm itself, but in the second it was the "alleluia verse," which led into the gospel. The homily of the bishop or priest was followed by the intercessions — prayers introduced by *oremus* for the catechumens, the penitents, the faithful, and the whole world, to which the community in the East — Jerusalem and Antioch — sometimes replied with the cry *Kyrie eleison.* The custom was adopted by the West and here in the form of the Kyrie-litany took the place of the customary intercessions; it was finally transferred to the beginning of the Mass, where it accompanied the entry of the clergy and ended with a prayer. The still remaining *oremus* of the intercessions thus became the introduction to the prayer over the gifts of bread and wine, which represented the transition to the Liturgy of Sacrifice.

Both the Anaphora of the East and the Canon of the Latin Mass at first display a uniform and obvious structure. The great Eucharistic Prayer of thanksgiving was proclaimed aloud to the silent congregation and it was interrupted only by the *Trisagion* (*Sanctus*), adopted from the East, ca. 400. In contrast to the East, the West at this time produced a large quantity of prefaces in the narrower sense, which called attention to one or another topical motive for the Eucharistic Prayer of thanksgiving. The central idea of the entire prayer of thanks was the presentation of the sacrifice, and was then completed with the words of institution, which at the same time effected the transubstantiation of the gifts of bread and wine. In the Antiochene family of liturgies after the words of institution, God was called upon in a special prayer, the so-called transubstantiation *epiclesis,* to send the Holy Spirit on the sacrificial gifts in order to make them the flesh and blood of the Lord, and thus they brought the recipient to salvation. The clear make-up of the Canon underwent a certain confusion through the placing of the intercessions before and after the *anamnesis,* for which again the East provided the model. In this the offering of the sacrifice was joined to prayers for the local and the Universal Church and their clergy and special martyrs and saints, with whom people understood themselves as constituting one great community.

While the Communion Rite of the eucharistic celebration in the eastern liturgies underwent considerable expansion through the acceptance of several new individual rites and of the accompanying prayers, it remained emphatically simple in the Latin Mass. The breaking of the bread, the kiss of peace, and the Lord's Prayer were followed immediately by the communion of clergy and faithful under both species, the deacon administering the cup. The reception of the Eucharist by all participants in the celebration was the normal thing in the West longer than in the East. After Communion the deacon, with the admonition "Bow your head," announced the prayer of dismissal, which was then a part of every Mass.

At first glance it seems surprising that the Church of the fourth and fifth centuries clung with a fundamental stubbornness to the externally strict penitential discipline hitherto in use, even though the growing throng of average persons of this period would lead one to expect instead a moderation here, just as in the catechumenate. But the testimony of the sources is clear: in addition to a certain further development in secondary details, the previous order was fixed ever more by canonical rules through episcopal letters, synodal decrees, and decretals, and thereby a flexible administration was rendered difficult; above all, the principle of the nonrepetition of penance remained inviolable. Even though a surer criterion was lacking as to which offenses in individual cases were subject to public ecclesiastical penance and which were not, and though Augustine also stressed that the gravity of the offense was to be determined by the intention of the sinner, in practice there was agreement on a rather uniform catalogue of such sins: idolatry, heresy and schism, murder, abortion, adultery, serious theft, implacable hatred, slander, drunkenness, attendance at immoral theatrical performances — these seemed more or less completely crimes deserving of penance.

And so, as earlier, the sinner who on his own initiative opened himself up to his bishop or whose offense was notorious, was initiated into the class of penitents at a public Mass by the formal sentence of the bishop. The date for the beginning of the period of penance was at first the Monday after Pentecost, then, probably from the fifth century, the Monday after the First Sunday of Lent. It ended with the solemn act of reinstatement, the *reconciliatio,* which, except in cases of necessity, was reserved to the bishop. It ordinarily took place on Holy Thursday, and was inserted between the gospel and the Offertory procession. After an address the bishop prayed that God would give the penitent back to the Church and then laid his hand on him as he knelt before him and raised him up.

Membership in the class of penitents involved for the one concerned, especially in the West, a heavy psychological burden and many restrictions in his private and professional life. The public nature of penance produced a demand that the average Christian of the day was often not equal to, even if the discretion of the bishop, the encouragement of the clergy, and the prayers of intercession of the community could provide help to him. The penitential duties, such as fasting, prohibition of marriage during the time of penance, the forbidding of marital relations among those already married, often lasted for five, ten, or twenty years, and in some cases, especially in Spain, which was inclined to rigorism, for the remainder of life. Any failure during the period of penance led to the permanent exclusion from the ecclesiastical community, which on occasion some were not even willing to grant again to the dying. The heaviest burden of all perhaps was the fact that his previous status clung to the reconciled penitent for the rest of his life. Hence, for example, not only was admittance into the clergy forever denied him, but as a husband he had also to refuse marital intercourse, he could not hold any public office or practice specified professions, including military service; in short, he was forever compelled to a lifestyle which otherwise only a monk would have freely adopted. Again, a nonobservance of these duties ranked as a relapse, which involved perpetual excommunication.

The cause of this rigorism, especially in the Western Church, must be seen most pressingly in the adherence to an understanding of the Church, which aspired to see the *communio sanctorum* in the strict sense realized in every community in the changed situation of the fourth and fifth centuries and to assure it with severe sanctions. Naturally, this attitude laid more stress on the exact execution of the penalties imposed than on the encouraging of the desire for atonement in the penitent. The consequences of such strictness were not absent. Alongside the postponement of baptism proceeded the postponement of public ecclesiastical penance, but now the Church, in contrast to the case of baptism, combated this only slightly, even to the extent of finally advising it in special cases, especially in still young men. Now the sinner was invited to make his entire life a constant preparation for penance. To be sure, the principle that ecclesiastical penance could not be repeated was saved, but its pastoral sense was undermined. The consequences of this development were, seen as a whole, so negative that eventually a basically new solution, private penance, became inevitable.

During the fourth and fifth centuries more energetic efforts of the Church become discernible to incorporate marriage and the wedding celebration into the liturgy, especially since they were included, more than other segments in the course of life, in pagan or profane custom. At the same time it was urged that the contracting of marriage be publicly blessed by bishop or priest. In this regard the first steps toward the development of a liturgical rite of marriage become clear. In the East the bishop or priest was invited to the celebration of marriage in a private house and there he pronounced a prayer of blessing over the bridal pair; it was surrounded by the singing of psalms, but definite liturgical texts are not to be found before the eighth century.

The Liturgical Year

The position of Easter, now as earlier the *mysterium praecipuum* and the *excellentior festivitas* of all celebrations which the liturgy observed, was now also brought to prominence in public life, since the Christian Emperors from Valentinian I honored the day by a special amnesty for prisoners. In the religious and theological understanding of the feast a certain change occurred in the East, since, following the Trinitarian and Christological discussions of the age, the suffering of the Redeemer was deemphasized in favor of the idea of the resurrection. In the West, however, its original meaning was still retained: in the Easter Triduum from Good Friday to Easter Sunday, "the mystery of the death and resurrection" was celebrated, whereby a new life was given to mankind.

With the fourth century the Easter season entered the final phase of its organization as a great Easter cycle, since now the feast was preceded by a rather long period of preparation — Lent. However, the exact number of forty fast days established itself only after a longer development.

The Pentecost, that is, the Easter Season, was concluded with the fiftieth day after Easter, which was at the same time devoted to the recalling of the descent of the Holy Spirit and the Ascension of the Lord. As early as the fourth century, however, the remembrance of Christ's Ascension was separated from this feast and given a feast of its own on the fortieth day of the Pentecost.

The liturgical year gained its most significant enrichment at this period through an exchange between East and West, in which the West took from the East the feast of the Lord's Epiphany and gave it Christmas; since both celebrations obtained a prolongation and a time of preparation, the basis was laid for the second festive cycle of the liturgical year. The first sure report on a feast which had as its content the birth of Christ and was celebrated on 25 December is found in a list of Christian feasts, the so-called *Chronographus* of 354, which took this notice from a model going back to the age of Constantine (336). The date of 25 December is one for which no one at all could appeal to a solid historical tradition. Most probably the choice of this date was motivated by the feast of the birth of the pagan Sun-god, which was observed as *dies natalis solis invicti* on this day as a high civil holiday. To this *Sol invictus* the Christians consciously contrasted their Lord as the new light, the new sun, the *sol iustitiae,* as the one whom the sermons of the Fathers and the texts of the liturgy celebrated on his *dies natalis.* The *sacramentum Christi nativitatis* was observed as early as ca. 360 in Africa. Christmas was first accepted in Cappadocia, Constantinople, and Syria in the penultimate decade of the fourth century, while it was not received until ca. 430 in Jerusalem

Egypt, that is, in the regions which first knew the Epiphany, and for this reason occasionally the mystery of the birth was separated from the festive content of the Epiphany.

Just as *epiphaneia* in the area of Hellenistic religions meant the arrival or public manifestation of a god or of a god-king, so the corresponding basic idea of the Christian feast of the Epiphany was the appearance of the Lord in the world, his divine manifestation before mankind. The fact that 6 January was chosen for the feastday was certainly conditioned by missionary considerations. Thus a feast of the winter solstice celebrated around the same date in Egypt, or that of a miraculous fountain in various cities of the East could be christianized by the declaration that in Christ the true sun has shone or that the water of baptism (*photismos*) has brought true enlightenment to man. Then, when the Roman Christmas was received into the local liturgies, the baptism of Jesus remained the central content of the Epiphany feast, which also made 6 January a baptismal day and was expressed in a second name for the feast (*ta phota*), while the celebration of the birth, joined with the adoration of the magi, was reserved for 25 December.

The reception of the Epiphany in the West occurred with no uniformity as to time and place and with differing emphases on the concept of the feast. It is earliest traceable for Gaul, where at first it was probably celebrated as *adventus salvatoris* in the original meaning of *epiphaneia*. Rome at the earliest accepted the Epiphany under Pope Innocent I (401–17) and, like the African and Spanish Churches, separated the adoration of the magi from the content of Christmas.

When both feasts were expanded through gradually growing celebrations in preparation and prolongation, the elaboration of a special Christmas cycle was introduced. Christmas obtained an after-celebration when its octave day was raised to prominence as the feast of the *Natale s. Mariae*. One may also speak of an after-celebration for the Epiphany, since before the seventh century the gospel readings of the following Sundays and, to a degree, of the weekdays, took up the basic theme of the Epiphany and reported the signs by which Christ displayed his glory (John 2:11).

A period of preparation for the Epiphany or Christmas respectively, in the sense of the later Advent, first appeared, not at Rome, but in Spain and Gaul. It was only in the course of the sixth century that Rome created an Advent liturgy in the strict sense by the introduction of five Advent Sundays, which Gregory the Great reduced to four and thereby brought to a conclusion the development of the second festive cycle within the liturgical year.

CHAPTER 49

Preaching and Piety

Catechesis and Preaching

Every attempt to answer the question of how the clergy of the Church of the Empire saw and carried out the pastoral duty of preaching must remain unsatisfactory because of the special situation of the sources. To be sure, approximately 3,000 sermons and catecheses are extant from the period between Nicaea and Chalcedon, but they come from only some thirty authors, hence from a fraction of those who labored as pastors in these 125 years. And more than half of the stock that has been preserved belongs to two bishops, Chrysostom and Augustine, and so it is not representative for a view of the entire clergy of the time. The criteria for this selection were mostly the quality of the sermons or at least the reputation of the author, but occasionally probably only chance preserved something. The average member of the pastoral clergy surely made frequent use of the models of recognized preachers.

The ecclesiastical catechesis was now also exclusively one for adults and embraced the totality of their instruction and practice, through which the unbaptized were made conversant by an official of the Church with the testimonies of faith and the moral demands which should determine the life of a real Christian. Apparently, there was no special catechesis for children before the end of the sixth century, although the practice of infant baptism was steadily growing.

Catechesis was determined, as regards its purpose, content, and method, entirely in relation to its missionary context. In his *De catechizandis rudibus.* Augustine gave a systematic guidance for the Carthaginian deacon Deogratias, which influenced practical catechetics down to modern times and has retained its freshness to this day. In the two models which he appended of a longer and a shorter introductory catechesis can be read how he wished to see his advice carried out. Augustine did not underestimate the difficulties and relapses which often tended to demoralize the catechist, but he felt they could be overcome if he let himself be led by the joy of the heart. In this the catechist must adapt himself to the individuality of his hearers, who often brought along very different assumptions, each according to his level of education, to their receptiveness to religious or other motives, which induced them to seek admission into the catechumenate.

The kernel of all catechesis, according to Augustine, had to be the history of salvation, as it was revealed by Scripture in the dealings of God with men. It must be made known to the hearer in its most striking events, in the creation of Adam, the deluge, the covenant of God with Abraham, the priestly kingship of David, the deliverance from the Babylonian Captivity, and the all-decisive Christ-event. This *narratio* of the *mirabilia Dei* should show not only the inner connection of the Old and New Testaments, but impart a universal view of all history, as it was framed in God's plan of salvation. When the catechist understood judiciously how to make the inner connection between the history of salvation and the religious route of the catechumen, he would represent to him the love of God for mankind and for him as the ultimate motive of the divine work of salvation, which reached its climax in Christ's death and resurrection. The Christ-event especially was to be made known with such warmth and forcefulness that the catechumen came to the faith by hearing, achieved hope by believing, found love by hoping. In a last *exhortatio* he should be admonished to guard faith, hope, and love from the allurements of that world out of which he came to the Church and not let himself be led astray by those baptized persons who again succumbed to this world. For the Augustinian catechesis it is also characteristic that it was entirely oriented to the positive exposition of salvation history and renounced polemic and rhetorical ornament.

In the baptismal catecheses attributed to Bishop Cyril of Jerusalem, however, there is realized Augustine's central concern: to make salvation history the center of the instructions in the preparation of the candidates for baptism. The dogmatic exposition was carefully joined to the moral catechesis, occasionally apologetic re-marks were inserted, and especially the concluding mystagogic catecheses were very clearly structured. The simple language, the appreciative entry into the situa-tion of the hearers, the clever, deliberate manner of the presentation make these catecheses an especially informative model of early Christian preaching.

John Chrysostom and Theodore of Mopsuestia, both outstanding representa-tives of the Antiochene catechesis, made prominent two aspects of it, since the first preferred the moral catechesis more in accord with his inclinations, while the other preferred the sacramental catechesis, which was apparently applied to hearers with a certain level of education. Chrysostom, the majority of whose extant catecheses come from Easter Week, untiringly inculcated in the newly bap-tized that they must remain *neophytoi* for the rest of their lives, and for this the Spirit given to them in baptism qualified them. The explanation of the rite of Chris-tian initiation by Theodore of Mopsuestia emphatically set off the eschatological character of baptism and Eucharist: with baptism the "new life" of the Christian begins, and the Eucharist nourishes it, while letting him participate in the death and resurrection of Christ and thus arrive at his own resurrection.

During the real catechumenate, now for the most part curtailed to one Lent, Christian preaching could not be satisfied with the catechetical introduction here provided. In addition to it, an intensive follow-up was necessary in order to extend the laying of the first foundation of a knowledge of the faith and of moral conduct and to deepen and consolidate it. This task was the lot of preaching, which for that reason long retained a missionary character and in an ever new onset had to free the newly won faithful from stubborn pagan custom and to seek to as-sure them in regard to pagan opposition that was still flaring up. In cities having a strong Jewish element in the population, such as Antioch, the anti-Jewish preach-ing was of great importance, and it too could display a strongly polemic tone. The Trinitarian and Christological controversies and the confrontation with Donatism and Pelagianism likewise found expression in preaching and occasioned a large number of dogmatic sermons. The topic of the sermon was expanded by the now powerfully developing cult of martyrs and saints, which introduced the laudatory sermon, the encomium or panegyric respectively, into Christian eloquence. Burn-ing questions of Christian behavior, raised by the day-to-day care of souls, confer on many a sermon a marked exhortatory feature. Finally, special occasions, such as church dedications, anniversaries of episcopal ordination, and funerals of individuals, mostly of high-ranking personalities, gave the bishop opportunity for sermons of a special type, which were often influenced by their model in the profane sphere. The highest rank of all forms of preaching belonged at this period to the homily in the strict sense, which interpreted either entire books or rather long sections of Scripture or even a single word of Scripture and thereby connected specific concerns of pastoral care.

The homiletic achievement of John Chrysostom represents the unquestioned climax of Greek Scriptural preaching of the age. In more than 700 preserved homilies he, for the most part when he was a priest at Antioch, interpreted from the Old Testament parts of Genesis, the Psalms, and Isaiah, and, from the New Testament, much of Matthew, John, the Acts of the Apostles, and, with special devotion, most of Paul's Epistles. He did not, it is true, express himself on the theoretical basis of his exegesis in the greater context, but the Scripture was to him wholly the inspired Word of God, to the service of which he knew he was called and to which he sought to do justice with a high sense of responsibility. In relation to Scripture he aimed basically to strengthen the community in its faith and to lead it to a piety which should hold up in the day-to-day life of the great city of Antioch.

In the sphere of the Latin Church Upper Italy produced a series of bishops who left a quite abundant homiletic legacy. Ambrose of Milan in his preaching displayed a decided preference for the Old Testament, from which he took the text for his numerous Scriptural sermons, apart from his commentary on Luke, on which likewise his homilies were based. Even in their book form, revised for publication, his rhetorical education becomes clearly visible: the dignified, solemn language displays the Roman aristocrat as well as the bishop of the contemporary imperial city of residence, who was quite conscious of his position. But on the whole, his preaching, as he required of it also in theory, was simple and natural, adapted to the subject as well as to the understanding of the hearers, and clear in its expression. During his stay in Milan, Augustine found the repute of Ambrose's eloquence confirmed and was deeply touched by the preacher's *suavitas sermonis,* which aimed rather to enlighten than to charm. The study of the Greek Fathers, especially of Basil and Origen, induced him to adopt the allegorical exegesis of the Scriptural text because it seemed so productive for the preaching of his Christocentric piety.

Jerome's homilies provide a surprise in the sense that these sermons on various psalms and pericopes from Mark and other New Testament writings renounce any rhetorical effect and linguistic elegance and show that the Christian preacher who has gone through the school of a profane education can thoroughly free himself from the rhetoric of late antiquity.

Precise in the range and quality of his homiletic achievement, Augustine represents the Latin counterpart of Chrysostom, from whom, however, he took so many individual features that he became a unique figure among early Christian preachers. The Bishop of Hippo also expressed himself in detail on the goal and form of the sermon and in so doing established the thesis that the Christian preacher need not have gone through the school of rhetoric in order to be able to perform his task objectively. He could model himself for this directly on Scripture and adhere to proved examples. More heavily than all rhetorical brilliance on the one hand or the displeasure of the grammarians because of unpolished diction on the other hand, there weighed on Augustine the duty of explaining the Word of God in so plain a manner that the less gifted could also grasp it. To this end he delighted to give to his preaching the character of a dialogue, of the intimate conversation between the bishop at his *cathedra* and the congregation, which hung on his words and ingenuously replied to his questions. Augustine's lively spontaneity, his superior gift of improvization, and his pedagogical skill were of uncommon benefit to such a manner of preaching. The deep effect of Augustine's preaching was not least of all conditioned by a unique relation of trust and sympathy which united hearers and preacher. They were glad to come because they loved him and knew they were loved by a shepherd, who, like them, wanted to be only one member in the flock of Christ the Shepherd, by a teacher, who wanted to be only their fellow-pupil in the school of the one Teacher, Christ, who placed significance neither on his intellectual superiority not on his episcopal authority, who might therefore even scold and reprimand, if the life of the community supplied the occasion. At bottom, Augustine was convinced that one who is not himself first a hearer in his inner being will be only a hollow preacher. Although not unaware of the strong echo which his preaching found in the congregation and which he sensitively recorded in all its nuances, he found the task of preaching a *magnum pondus* in the evening of his life, often deeply oppressed by the responsibility into which he knew he had been placed. The fertile soil of his preaching was almost exclusively the Holy Scripture: his intimate knowledge of it effortlessly put at his disposal every verse of the Bible for spontaneous use and made his language completely saturated with the Bible. Differing from Chrysostom, Augustine preferred the allegorical exegesis of Scripture for preaching, since it supplied more abundant opportunities to his gift for making clear his understanding of the Word of God, as the homilies on the psalms and on John's gospel attest with special vigor. While in the *Enarrationes in psalmos,* as well as in the general *sermones,* the great questions and themes of Christian life — the world as foreign, the meaning of suffering, Christian hope, life as prayer — are in the foreground, the figure of Christ, his message, and his Church are the dominant theme of the *Tractatus in evangelium s. Johannis,* which in its way represented an unsurpassed high point of early Christian preaching. The preaching of the Latin Church lived for centuries on his homiletic legacy as a whole.

The sermons of Pope Leo I are distinguished by linguistic elegance and solemn diction and are the first religious talks of a Pope of importance to come down to us. In them the consciousness of the rank of the Roman episcopal see is clearly reflected, but they do not cause one to forget the religious seriousness and the sparkling life of the Augustinian *sermones.*

Christocentric Piety

As the basic attitude and center of all piety, devotion to Christ in its various forms was pushed into the awareness of the faithful by Christian preaching even more powerfully than in earlier times. Christocentric baptismal piety, long stressed, still retained its rank, which could be noted in the thought and intensity which pastoral care devoted to the preparation for baptism and the elaboration of the baptismal liturgy. Naturally, the actuality of day-to-day Christian life often did not correspond to the untiringly extolled demand on the faithful to form their lives with regard to their baptismal promises. Eucharistic piety also now fell short, among the majority of Christians, of the ideal proclaimed to them, since, especially in the large communities of East and West, preaching had to complain ever more of the declining or fluctuating attendance at the liturgy. Here now, more and more, a nucleus of dedicated Christians stood in contrast to the bulk of the members of the community, who found their way to the church only on the solemnities of the liturgical year or for special occasions. Preaching clearly pushed devotion to the Passion to the foreground, as the numerous *sermones de passione domini* make known, and they prepared for the medieval devotion to the sufferings of the Lord. Their effect was a widespread veneration of the Cross, which was expressed as well in the popularity of the sign of the cross as a gesture of prayer in private and liturgical piety, especially in the *adoratio crucis* on Good Friday, as in the triumphal cross of the apses of basilicas and of sarcophagi, in the simple cross on the walls of a private house or in the cell of the monk, and finally in the keen interest in the fate of the true Cross of Christ. The popular pilgrimages to Jerusalem had one of their roots here. The sermon on the Passion was also the occasion on which the demand for the "following of Christ" was made with special urgency: this was emphatically understood as an imitation of the example which Christ gave in his Passion as *doctor humilitatis* and as physician of suffering mankind. Finally, Christocentric piety manifested itself impressively in prayer to Christ, which further expanded the start made earlier by Origen and the martyrs, and as a consequence of the stimulus which the Christological discussions since Nicaea gave it; the private piety of the prevailing attitude to prayer developed into it and received through Augustine its deepest theological justification.

The earlier arrangement of prayers with its set times for prayer in the course of the day and its basis, which found its first definite form in the *Apostolic Tradition* of Hippolytus, continued to endure under the influence of this writing: morning, evening, and mealtime prayer, prayer at the third, fifth, and ninth hours and once during the night, in order to be mindful at any given time of what the Lord did at these hours for the redemption of mankind.

An important further elaboration of the form of prayer is represented at this period by the change, effected in part under the influence of monasticism, of the earlier prayer-times from the private sphere into the liturgical prayer of the community in the church building. As regards content, an enrichment of the piety of the laity was thereby effected: they now came to know far more of the world of the psalms, Holy Scripture, and also ecclesiastical hymns and prepared texts, which they could also adopt in their private prayers. This daily liturgical prayer cannot be demonstrated for the fourth century in all areas where Christianity had spread; it was primarily the concern of the community and only in a rather long development became the obligatory *Officium* to be celebrated for the clergy of the cathedrals.

The great preachers spoke again and again on the meaning and content of prayer and essentially, even with varying stress, they expounded the same ideas: that prayer, as conversation with God, requires the proper altitude of soul; that it is first of all a thanksgiving for God's spiritual gifts and should express the desire for the *vita beata;* that it must not be restricted to set formulas, even if such are often recommended; that one may pray for earthly things only in so far as they are necessary for life and promote one's salvation.

Forms of Asceticism

"But we are not monks." Again and again Chrysostom had to meet this objection when at Antioch he proclaimed to the laity also the obligation to a life which should be in accord with the gospel. Apart from marriage, however, he and other pastors of the day preached that in principle monks and lay persons were called upon to strive for the same perfection, since there is only a single ideal of perfection for all Christians, which must be realized everywhere. Hence aloofness from the world is for all Christians the basic ascetical disposition which was staunchly emphasized by the Christian preaching and the ascetical literature of the time, which claimed to have been written not merely for monks or to recruit for the monastic life. Fasting was especially recommended as one possibility of its realization, understood not only as liturgical penitential fasting or as preparation for the reception of the Eucharist or even as mere hygienic fasting, but as a personal feat and attitude, which was oriented to man's goal in the next life. Then to all the propertied classes was directed by the pastors a continual admonition to almsgiving, which was not only regarded as a social duty of Christians toward the poor or as a form of expiation of the personal guilt of sin, but was presented as the way to interior freedom vis-à-vis wealth and property. Wealth, of course, was not considered in principle as sinful, but it was always described, at times with powerful rhetorical pathos, as highly dangerous to the individual's salvation. The total renunciation of often vast wealth and of a life of luxury, as was carried out not rarely in the fourth and fifth centuries by members of the upper class in Constantinople, Cappadocia, Rome, Gaul, Sicily, and North Africa, obtained unlimited praise from the ecclesiastical sector. For the most part this step sooner or later followed the entry upon a specific ascetical lifestyle, in which a person remained in his family or community as *continens* or *virgo* or joined an ascetic group or, more often, a community of nuns or monks or was admitted into the clergy. The Church at this time recruited intensely by word and writing in the lay world to urge a decision to this ascetical life, as the numerous works on continence or virginity respectively make known.

Cult of Martyrs and Saints

The freedom won through Constantine's conversion to Christianity gave to the already important cult of martyrs strong new impulses, which caused it to become, in the next hundred years, a very characteristic and, in its consequences, highly significant form of early Christian piety, in whose development both the private initiative of individual faithful and the Church as representative of public worship shared. The previous view of the martyr as the perfect imitator of Christ, who through the power of grace had given witness to his Lord with his blood and now as *coronatus,* as the contemporary Christian art liked to show him, united with him in the glory of the next life, underwent no substantial modification; only one feature was now stressed: his dignity and his nearness to the glorified Lord made him the advocate of the faithful on earth and the protector of the individual as well as of the community which chose him as its patron. Out of this esteem grew the strong interest in the grave of the witness to the faith and in the relics which it sheltered. In its direct possession was seen a special guarantee of the protection and intercession of the patron and it was distinguished from all other graves by a special cult building, erected as *martyrion* or *memoria* respectively or as a basilica over the grave, which in size and furnishing often vied with the churches of the community within the city walls. The community assembled in these cemetery churches on the *dies natalis martyris* to celebrate the Eucharist.

A new phase of the cult of martyrs began with the *translatio* of the remains of martyrs to the churches within the city walls, although at first this procedure encountered considerable doubt and difficulties, since it was contrary to a twofold law, binding in East and West, according to which the deceased might be buried only outside city walls, and graves were regarded as "inviolable." The corresponding laws were repeatedly inculcated by the Christian Emperors also, and exceptions required the authorization of the highest administrative officials.

The conviction of the intercessory power of martyrs led many Christians to want to be themselves buried as close as possible to a martyr's grave. From this burial *ad sanctos* people expected aid for themselves at the hour of the resurrection, because one was conducted before God's judgment seat by the martyr who rose with him.

The cult of martyrs as an early Christian form of piety was not promoted chiefly by the lay world or by monasticism, but in its essential features it was motivated, justified, and encouraged by the Church and its theologians. In scarcely any of the not very bulky homiletic legacy of a pastor of the time are there missing sermons in honor of a martyr, which extol his dignity, the power of his intercession, the example of his love of Christ, and the miracle-working efficacy of his relics. The Church not only allowed the interment of his body inside the house of God: it let its liturgical calendar be decisively determined by the memorial days of the martyrs and admitted their names into the text of the Eucharistic Prayer.

The cult of saints who did not rank as martyrs began somewhat hesitantly in the first half of the fourth century and reached full development in its last two decades; it was, after all, an extension of the cult of martyrs to a group of the dead whose life and actions enabled them to be compared to the martyrs in some degree, because it likewise represented an outstanding profession and witness for Christ. They included, first of all, those who in time of persecution had suffered for the faith in prison, under torture, or in exile, but the desired confirmation by a bloody death was denied them. With such *confessores* were soon associated individual ascetics and monks, whose life was willingly ranked as unbloody *martyrium,* and finally also those who especially proved themselves in the Arian troubles or in the missions as courageous adherents and zealous preachers of the orthodox faith. *Martyrium sine cruore* was granted to all those, and they were quickly celebrated in word and writing, like the other martyrs: the hermits Antony and Hilarion, the Syrian monks, especially the Stylites, the exiled Bishops Paulinus of Trier, Dionysius of Milan, Athanasius, the protagonist of Orthodoxy, Basil, Peter of Sebaste, Ambrose of Milan, the missionary Martin of Tours, and others.

The people were especially strongly involved in the spread and elaboration of the cult of this group of saints. The accounts of their life and activity were gladly filled in with that colorful detail which appealed to popular fantasy; the charismatic endowment of individuals was felt to be miraculous, and some lives of saints are mere collections of *miracula*.

In the Christian cult of saints were also included some outstanding figures from the world of the Old Testament, such as Moses, Abraham, David, some of the Prophets, and the Maccabee brothers, even though this was not without its difficulties for two reasons. The first was that thereby a certain recognition, if not commendation, of Judaism was expressed, and yet Christians were often still in polemical confrontation with it. Then, in the life of these persons the inner relationship to witnessing for Christ seemed to be lacking, and hence the decisive criterion for the dignity of martyr or confessor. Christian preaching theoretically countered this difficulty with the argument that these figures were Christians before the appearance of Christ, because their life served the ultimate goal of his coming, and thus the violent death of some Prophets, of Eleazar, of the Maccabees, could be understood as anticipated martyrdom and hence a Christian celebration in their memory was justified.

The cult of Mary had spread among the people long before theology had clarified the questions regarding her sanctity and virginity. People besought "the protection of the *Theotokos*" at least at the beginning of the fourth century. In the West her cult was theologically clarified and justified especially by Ambrose and Augustine. The oldest Marian feast was celebrated in Constantinople even before the Council of Ephesus as *mneme Theotokou* on 26 December and in title and content recalled the *dies natalis* of the martyrs; the first churches dedicated to her go back likewise to this time. The Council of 431 freed the way for the complete development of the cult of Mary.

Early Christian Pilgrimage

Another field of early Christian popular devotion is found in the pilgrimage system, the prototypes of which are represented by the pilgrimage to the places most significant for memories of the Christian past, which lie above all in the Holy Land, and the pilgrimage to the tombs and relics of saints. The initial steps toward the pilgrimage to Palestine are seen, after a period of caution conditioned by the critical contrast to the Jewish pilgrimage system, in the pre-Constantinian journeys of individual Christians, such as Origen and the future Bishop Alexander of Jerusalem, a native of Cappadocia: they were motivated by theological and exegetical interests or by the desire to pray at the holy shrines. As early as 315 larger crowds of pilgrims from all parts of the East were to be seen in Jerusalem, and the pilgrimage movement received new incentives when, with the beginning of Constantine's sole rule, the external circumstances of the journey became more favorable and when the visit to the holy shrines received encouragement from higher up because of the esteem which the imperial family, especially Helena and Constantine himself, gave to it. But that one should not see in Constantine's measures the basic cause of the pilgrimages to Palestine is made clear by the report of the journey of a pilgrim from Bordeaux in 333, who in Jerusalem came upon a situation quite in accord with the entire pilgrimage system, such as can have developed only in a rather prolonged period of time. In Jerusalem and its closest neighborhood, naturally, what was in the foreground for the pilgrims were the sites which had a relation to the events from the Redeemer's life; then followed the places of Old Testament tradition, while the cult of Christian saints began only with the discovery of Stephen's grave in 415, and the cult of Mary was discernible in Jerusalem still later. Hence the world of the Bible clearly determined the visits of the pilgrims: it was "the real Pilgrim's Guide" for the journey to the Holy Land.

Despite all external activity, as it showed itself occasionally at great pilgrimage centers, lasting effects were produced on the devotion of the pilgrims, which were passed on by them after their return home. The precious account of the journey of the pilgrim Egeria attests this, despite all the simplicity of the statements, as decisively as do the letters of Jerome, based on observations made over years.

The second type of pilgrimage, the visit to the grave and relics of the saints, naturally presupposed a certain progress in the cult of martyrs and saints, but it influenced its further expansion and intensification. In the course of the fourth century there developed, in the East a bit earlier than in the West, those great pilgrimage centers in all parts of the Empire, which always set large crowds of pilgrims in motion. In the Latin West no city could compete with Rome in the number of martyrs' tombs, among which those of the two Apostles Peter and Paul held the first rank also in the eyes of the numerous pilgrims.

As the basic attitude for the pilgrimage the preachers of the period required a disposition which would prove itself in the following of Christ and the imitation of his saints. The motives could differ in individual pilgrims. In the foreground stood the desire and hope to find healing or counsel in personal need, especially in sickness; thanks for help given was also an opportunity for a promised pilgrimage. The notion of penance and expiation was not yet emphasized, even though it would hardly have been missing in the often great hardships of the pilgrim's journey.

Survival of Pagan Customs in Christian Popular Piety

Like missionary work in all ages, so too that of the fourth and fifth centuries had to learn by experience that a relatively brief period of preparation for the reception of baptism did not suffice to supplant deep-rooted pagan practice in the newly converted. And so the pastors of all lands in East and West stood in a ceaseless struggle against various forms of pagan *superstitio,* which at times was mixed almost inextricably with what was Christian and seriously compromised the purity of devotion. People complained especially of the power of attraction of pagan magic, as practiced by astrologers, soothsayers, and faith-healers, who were again and again sought out by Christians, in spite of all the warnings of preachers.

An ingredient of the pagan cult of the dead was the *refrigerium,* a meal to which came the relatives of a deceased person on the third, seventh, and ninth days after the burial, on the anniversary of the death, and on the great memorial of the dead, the *Parentalia,* in February. The Christians retained this meal of the dead in a simple form without opposition from the Church and added to it a Christian feature when they had a part of the foods brought turned over to the poor.

Of course, it did not escape Augustine's watchful eye that a paganism of a subtler sort than that of the realistic popular devotion continued in some Christians, and he saw in it no slight danger. The traditional pagan vital feeling was carried like a subtle poison, as it were, in the blood: the desires for this world, the pride in one's own *virtus,* which so greatly opposed the understanding of Christian grace, the instinctive shrinking back, ever more revealing itself, from a crucified God, and finally the strong protest against the basic attitude of *humilitas.* Adherence to these features of paganism was the reason which made so many Christians of the upper class remain semi-Christian for years. Like no other preacher, Augustine spoke anxiously again and again of this basic danger to the Christian.

The Laity in the Church

The division of Christians, into the three groups of laity, clergy, and monks, actually already existing at the turn of the fourth century, became more precise in the course of the century and gradually found its fixed place in law together with the development of the corresponding terminology. In this process a clear change in the previous importance and position of the laity within the Church became perceptible, which went back to several causes. With the end of the persecutions the very intensely experienced community of the pre-Constantinian Church between clergy and laity, created by the same expectation of martyrdom, was relaxed everywhere. The glory of martyrdom now, in the opinion of many, passed ever more to asceticism and monasticism, the lifestyle of which was esteemed as an unbloody martyrdom, and, even unintentionally created a clear distance between itself and the mass of believers. Further, because of the differentiation of functions and still more because of the expansion of its tasks and authority in the care of souls and administration, the clergy gained such power in authority and public respect that the previous position of the laity could not remain uninfluenced by it. And monasticism, with its outlook of holding itself far aloof from "the world," promoted the idea according to which the effort to work out its salvation directly in this world was regarded as doubtful in principle; finally, the sort of lifestyle of many lay persons in the fourth and fifth centuries produced in some pastors a rather skeptical evaluation of the lay element.

The consequences of this change were, of course, neither the same in all areas of Christendom, nor was there always a question of a merely negative repudiation of lay influence, but often of a shifting within its previous spheres of duty. In the basilica the place of the people was now clearly distinct from the place of the clergy, which no lay person was supposed to enter. In procession there developed a certain order of precedence, whereby the clergy, the monks, and the virgins and widows went ahead of the "people." In the pastoral spheres, lay persons still took part in the preparation of the catechumens for baptism, especially widows in the instruction of the women; in cases of necessity lay persons could baptize, but women should not administer baptism, any more than they might instruct men.

The ancient right of the laity to cooperate in the choosing of their clergy continued in principle and was still especially exercised in the election of the bishop. Of course, the form of their collaboration was not precisely fixed: for the most part it consisted of an acclamation of the candidate proposed. The people were also supposed to be consulted in the possible transfer of a bishop to another see; however, at least in the deposition of a bishop they were usually ignored. The Emperors especially often intervened in the election of a bishop, without regard for this right of the laity. In the West lay persons occasionally could take part in the annual synods.

More and more the notion prevailed that the right "to teach" had to be reserved to the clergy. Thus lay preaching virtually ceased. Pope Leo I expressly forbade it and extended the prohibition to monks also, even if they had a certain level of education. Parallel to this limitation of an official teaching activity of the laity there developed, however, a growing sharing of the laity in the theological literary work of the time, which can be ascertained especially in the West.

Unmistakable also was the influence of lay persons in high official or private position on the many areas of ecclesiastical life. In the East ministers and high officials played a considerable ecclesiastico-political role. Well-to-do lay persons followed the example of Constantine as promoters of ecclesiastical construction and as founders of charitable institutions or supported the Church's care of the poor by corresponding bequests.

In East and West the importance and goal of the lay apostolate was clearly seen and urgently called for by the Church. It was seen as justified in the always recognized general priesthood of the laity, and hence it should be intended for the Universal Church. Chrysostom and Augustine precisely circumscribed the field of duties of this apostolate: they moved to first place the exemplary day-to-day Christian life, whereby a pagan would sooner be gained to Christianity than by any scholarly theological argument. Then, it should show itself in prompt and energetic help for the fellow Christian in religious or moral danger, who should be strengthened by the further giving of what one has learned in church from Christian preaching. To the unalterable content of such an apostolate belonged, finally, the missionary work of the layman among the pagans or heretics of his circle of acquaintances, who could be reached only with difficulty by the official preaching of the Church. The lay apostolate should be exercised in close collaboration with the clergy, who, according to Chrysostom, always need the prayer, the advice, and, at times, also the criticism of the laity, as, conversely, the Church prays especially for the laity.

CHAPTER   5 0

Early Christian Monasticism:
Development and Expansion in the East

The Religious and Historical Background

When, in the two decades preceding the turn from the third to the fourth century, individual Christians in Egypt and, perhaps quite independently of these, in eastern Syria broke with their previous life in their family and community and went into solitude apart from other human beings in order to lead a life there of voluntary poverty and sexual continence, the step was taken which was to move beyond early Christian asceticism to monasticism proper.

In a few decades areas remote from populous centers in Upper Egypt, later called the Thebaid from its geographical center of Thebes, and the region of the Nitrian Desert southwest of Alexandria, as well as the hilly country around Edessa in East Syria were settled by numerous anchorites, who built primitive huts for themselves or were satisfied with a cave. Many of them led their life in full isolation from one another and remained hermits in the strict sense for their lifetime; others, without any firm tie by means of a promise or a fixed rule, attached themselves to one of their number, who was to be their spiritual adviser and thus established a loose union of anchorites. History does not know any clearly outlined figure from whom, through his mere example or enticing word, the notion of realizing the following of Christ in such a way first proceeded. The young Egyptian Antony, who ca. 273 left his native village of Kome in central Egypt in order to live as a hermit, first in its vicinity, later in the Libyan Desert, and then on a hill on the Nile, is indeed often called "the Father of Egyptian monasticism" but he was not the first anchorite: he was only one of many, for whom, however, his charismatic endowment and the rank of his biographer Athanasius gained a very high repute. Since for the anchoretic life of East Syria, which was beginning about the same time, no clearly tangible founding figure can be named, the question of the causes of this unique phenomenon acquires special importance.

If early Christian monasticism is first studied according to its self-understanding, there can be advanced from the corresponding literature a whole series of motives by which monks justified their decision for the form of life that they selected. The idea of the following of Christ can, without difficulty, be recognized as the basic motive, which could be realized without compromise earliest in the radical estrangement from the "world," as Basil emphasized. The monk intended "to go the humble way of Christ," the narrow and painful way of which Scripture speaks, whereby he might some day repeat the words: "See, we have left everything and followed you." (Matt. 19:27). He was deeply permeated with the understanding that the following of the Lord forever placed him under the Cross, so that the Pachomian monks had themselves constantly reminded of the basis of their existence by a cross sewn on to their cloak, and Basil could define the existence of the monk precisely as "a carrying of the Cross." In a steady gazing on their crucified model, the monks took up the hardships of their life and intended thus to effect their dying together with Christ. Without doubt a strong influence on the origin of early monasticism was reaching back to the primitive Christian ideal whose theoretical rooting in the biblical world of ideas is already demonstrated. Since the days of Ignatius of Antioch the death of the Christian martyr ranked as the exalted form of the following of Christ; so the monks saw in the martyrs an inspiring prototype and made the latter's sacrifice of their lives for the Lord a constantly examined motive for their own attitude right down to the concrete demands of day-to-day asceticism. In the persecution of Diocletian some of them had themselves been able to experience the mood of death proper to Christians; they now esteemed as their immediate precursors the ascetics of the third century and their own struggles as an unbloody martyrdom, which likewise deserved the *corona martyrii,* since it was practiced from the same conviction as the bloody form.

The following of Christ, supported by the concept of martyrdom, was finally preferably identified by early monasticism on a broad plane with the angelic life, that catchword that so drew people to asceticism; it was already used by the early Alexandrian theologians and helped to characterize the premonastic asceticism of East and West. It was reached only by way of the *apotaxis,* the renunciation of the world, through *enkrateia,* to be practiced in body and soul, through the exercise of the specific monastic virtues of poverty, obedience, and virginity, which led to the height of *apatheia,* the peaceful security in the possession of monastic perfection. In its perfection the *vita angelica* of monasticism thus became a life in the community of the angels, an anticipated life in Paradise. With this a further motive for the monastic form of existence was touched upon: the eschatological outlook of monasticism, which not only embraced the constant thought of one's own death, but also meant the conscious and wakeful expectation of the Lord's *parousia.* A reawakening of the primitive Christian expectation of the *parousia* is unmistakable in the early phase of monasticism, and here there may be assumed at the earliest the influence of a certain disillusionment and sorrow over a legacy of the universal early Christian enthusiasm, as it undeniably appears with the numerical growth of large Christian congregations in the period of peace of the third century.

With the realization of the following of Christ, thus understood, the early Christian monk believed he could best fulfill two essential requirements of the Gospel — those of a genuine striving for perfection and of a true love of God. The Lord's words in Matthew 19:21, "if you wish to be perfect" not only directly produced in Antony the decision as to his vocation: to many monks of the early period they became a motive, always to be reflected on anew, for their way of life. Abbot Theodore designated the Pachomian system as the model for everyone who wanted to gather men around him in order to guide them to perfection. The motive of the love of God is sounded everywhere in the literature of early Christian monasticism: it is the source on which its asceticism is nourished.

Development and Expansion in the East

1. *Egyptian Anchoritism. The Pachomians.*
The Monasticism of the Deserts of Nitria and Scete.

The Egyptian Anchoritism.   The early form of Christian monasticism was anchoritism, practiced by those who, from the second half of the third century onward in rapidly growing numbers, added permanent withdrawal from family and community to Christian asceticism. This is a step beyond the temporary withdrawal of the ascetic into solitude, which was practiced elsewhere than Egypt as well. Egyptian anchoritism preexisted the great Antony's role, however, as is shown from the hermit whom Antony sought out and made his own model as he became an anchorite. Thus asceticism developed into anchoritism, which in turn led to the stricter forms of eremiticism in the Egyptian desert by about the year 300. When in some areas the numbers of hermits grew, there were formed anchorite communities, loose associations in which the hermits gathered around a monk of high repute who was to be their spiritual adviser and father, without his becoming a sort of "abbot" through a definite rule. There might be a considerable number of such hermits living in loose association with each other and one spiritual adviser. These "communities" formed in the Upper Egyptian Thebaid and in the wildernesses of Nitria and Scete southwest of the Nile Delta in Lower Egypt.

Antony the Great (ca. 251–356) overshadowed all of the others, and is regarded in early monastic literature as the father of anchoretic communities, both because he had a gift of charismatic leadership, which caused him to be sought out by hermits as a spiritual guide, and because of the biography of his life written by Athanasius, Bishop of Alexandria, who not only knew Antony personally, but who also ascribed to him a singular role in the development of monasticism. Of Athanasius' biography of Antony, it has been said that it offers no photograph of Antony, but rather the work of a painter, who, insofar as he is able, aspires to reproduce the reality in which the saint lived. From his earliest period in his anchoretic life, Antony sought certain characteristics in life: manual labor, prayer, and reading scripture. On each monk was also laid the task of struggling with the demon, who played an especially ample role in the life of Antony. It was ultimately a struggle with all of the forces opposed to God, which had to consist of an ever new start and could be endured only in faith. Since a man was most strongly exposed to the demonic in the extreme solitude of the desert, that was precisely where he took his stand and best proved his monastic character. Only one who had withstood this final test could be a guide and adviser to others in their struggles. Antony wrestled with himself and the demon, according to Athanasius, in an admirably Pauline sense: the demonic powers can be overcome only by faith in the power of Christ. Antony attributes ultimately to this power his insight into the nature of the demonic and its power.

Cenobitism of the Pachomians.   In fact, it was an anchorite who had gone through Pauline school who understood that many a monk was imperilled rather than protected by this severest type of eremiticism, and that therefore he needed a life in a community which gave him both a foundation and support through the brothers and through a spiritual adviser accessible at any time and at the same time made him equal to the numerous ascetical renunciations which a life in common imposed. Pakhôme, or Pachomius, born in the Upper Thebaid ca. 287, had come into contact with Christianity as a young soldier under Maximinus Daia; after his military discharge, he converted, as baptized, and then attached himself to a hermit. Between 320–25, he established a monastic community near the Upper Egyptian village of Tabennisi: members, by accepting a rule Pachomius had composed, bound themselves to realizing an ascetical manner of life in common that was the same for all, under the direction of a superior. Thus Pachomius became the founder of cenobitism, the form which gave Christian monasticism its specifically religious and cultural effectiveness.

The physical plant of a Pachomian monastery graphically displayed its differences from anchoritism: the entirety was surrounded by a wall, totally separating monks from the world: it could be entered only through the porter's quarters. At its center, the great room (*synaxis — ecclesia*) where the monks gathered for the liturgy. The refectory also underscored the communal character of the monks' lives. The community, directed by the "father of the monastery," did not live in one building, but in groups of thirty-forty in individual houses, each house being under its superior, a "second" (*deuteros — secundus*), respectively. The monastic community supported itself partly through the monks' practicing their former crafts and the sale of their products and partly through management of property which was acquired near the monastery. Inherent in the life-style were two real dangers: one, the numbers (hundreds) of monks made the spiritual role of the abbot almost unwieldy; and two, much property imperiled the ideal of poverty.

At first, the central religious idea upon which Pachomius based his foundation remained decisive: namely, that of a holy community, not only in separation from the world and the renunciation of personal possessions, but also and primarily in the common striving for salvation. "All should be a help to you, and you should assist all" is a famous saying of Pachomius which was taken up time and again by Pachomian abbots. An offense, thus, against charity was especially offensive to the Pachomian Rule; they seriously jeopardized the basic law of Pachomianism, the *hiera koinōnia*. The Pachomian community received the strength to realize its basic law from a life in and with Holy Scripture. Pachomius himself was well versed in Scripture, and he sought to inculcate the same in his monks; each was to memorize sections of it, and all were required to become literate for that purpose.

From the basic Pachomian law of *koinōnia* also issued the view of the fundamental equality of all monks in the obligation to the Rule. To all without exception applied its prescriptions in regard to food, clothing, furnishing of their cells, manual labor, as well as in regard to the form of the religious life. There was no place here for individualism of the anchoretic sort. It was this latter principle of equality which led Pachomius rarely to accept a priest into his community and to refuse priest's orders for himself. However, the uniformity in the Pachomian monastery was assured in the long run only if two conditions were met: the poverty of — the individual as a radical renunciation of any personal possession, of every ability to dispose even of things of daily use, and unconditional obedience toward superiors of every rank. The obedience here was qualitatively different from that of an anchoretic community: among the anchorites it was at times almost a technical training, which aimed to make the self-will and the private judgment so submissive that the monk, after achieving its highest form, could be sent forth into self-reliance; whereas for Pachomius it was to become an unalterably permanent attitude which should cause the monk to grow to perfection in and through his community. The prescriptions of Pachomius' rule on poverty and obedience were never essentially improved by other later rules, which indicates his creative significance. Pachomius' rule is also characterized by an emphatic simplicity, both in its goal and in its contents.

Given its elevated religious quality, Pachomius' Rule had a far-reaching impact on the future, although more strikingly in the Latin West than in the East. It may be assumed, e.g., that Basil, in his concept of cenobitism, was influenced by the Pachomian monasteries he visited in 357, but in his rule he is sharply critical of individual features and no literary dependence can with certainty be postulated. The impact of Pachomius' Rule is due especially to the translation of it by Jerome for the Latin-speaking westerners. After Jerome, it was John Cassian, who, as abbot at Marseille (d. ca. 430), through his *De institutis coenobiorum* directed interest to the Pachomian system. In the so-called *Regula Vigilii,* which probably originated in Italy ca. 500, there appeared a revision of Pachomius' Rule, and later in the sixth century, the rules of two bishops of Arles Caesarius and Aurelius clearly betray its influence. Benedict of Nursia made some use of it in his *Regula monasteriorum,* and in the ninth century, Benedict of Aniane (d. 821) used it in his reform of Frankish monasticism. Finally Pachomius' Rule was a model for details of the constitutions of the Society of Jesus.

The Pachomian ideal of *koinōnia* proved an uncommonly powerful attraction. A group of monks from Tabennisi began a new foundation down river at Phbow (Pabau). Two already existing communities (Scheneset [Chenoboskeion] and Tmuschons [Monchosis]) joined the Pachomian community submitting to the Rule. Pachomius assured observance of the Rule by placing monks from his own foundation into these monasteries. And he himself moved to Phbow in ca. 337, which thereafter became the chief monastery and the motherhouse of the Pachomian system. With the rounding of new monasteries and the accepting of existing monastic communities, Pachomius had taken the decisive new step of calling into being the first "Order" in the history or Christian monasticism, for all of the monasteries recognized his Rule as the basis of the *koinōnia* and saw in him the common superior-general of the monastic union. By Pachomius' death in 346, there were eleven such houses in the Order. Besides the Abbot-general was an *economus,* by whom the economic administration of all the monasteries was controlled. The unity of the Order was maintained by frequent visitation journeys of the superior-general and by a general chapter.

Down to the Council of Chalcedon (451), two other Pachomians were especially prominent: Horsiesi, whom Pachomius appointed superior of Scheneset. In 347 he became the Order's reluctant abbot-general; his attitude reflected his own recognition of his modest gifts for the post, and, when the Order began to slide spiritually (e.g., the erosion of the ideal of poverty with the acquisition of property, which led to the so-called poverty controversy) he appointed Theodore of Tabennisi his vicar and withdrew to Scheneset. Theodore, through discretion and energy restored discipline and saved the imperiled unity of the Order during his eighteen years as vicar. Upon his death, Horsiesi again took up the reins and nurtured the Order on his deep interiority and his biblically grounded piety. His work, *Liber Orsiesii,* which has been labelled his testament, sets forth his ideals for the monks: uncompromising poverty, preservation of the *koinōnia* through a joyful participation in the ordering of the monastic life, and finally living on Holy Scripture, which must be the foundation of their ascetical striving.

After Horsiesi's death (ca. 386), there is a paucity of information for the Pachomian Order. Of some import is the foundation of the Pachomian monastery of Metanoia, ca. 390, by Theophilus of Alexandria atop the ruins of the shrine of Sarapis, on the Egyptian coast of the Mediterranean, for here monks from the Latin West joined in. It was for them that Jerome translated the Pachomian Rule into Latin.

The Monasticism of the Deserts of Nitria and Scete.   In addition to the Thebaid, Egyptian monasticism had other centers of gravity, among which three are particularly significant in Lower Egypt on the northern border of the Libyan desert: near the village of Nitria, at the Kellia, and in the so-called Desert of Scete near modern Wadi-el-Natrûn.

A relatively abundant source material gives information about the monasticism of Lower Egypt also. The *Historia monachorum,* written in Greek ca. 400 (revised and translated into Latin by Rufinus of Aquileia a few years later), gives the impressions of a traveling party visiting the monastic sites in ca. 395. In 419–20, Bishop Palladius of Helenopolis in Bithynia published his descriptions of contemporary monasticism in Egypt, Syria, Palestine, and Asia Minor as the *Historia Lausiaca* in the form of brief edifying biographies which contain much that is legendary. Important for knowledge of the spiritual and religious atmosphere of Egyptian monasticism are the so-called *Apophthegmata Patrum* (Sayings of the Fathers), a collection of anecdotes, religious and ascetical instructions, and symbolic acts of the fathers, compiled ca. 500 from written and oral materials in circulation.

The first monk to settle on Mount Nitria, soon after 330, was called Ammun. By the close of the century, there were some 600 monks in Nitria, and many, desiring greater insolation, had migrated to Kellia. Nitrian monasticism enjoyed high prestige, and many bishops of Egypt were chosen from among them.

The highest esteem was enjoyed by the monasticism of Scete, for this was a rugged wilderness and one which taxed the physical and moral strength of the monks. Macarius the Egyptian, ca. 330, was first to go to the Scete, where he became the spiritual father over the next sixty years to the hermits who followed his example. This was anchoretic and semianchoretic monasticism, which from time to time had the ministrations of a priest. The "rule" of these monks came from the *gerontes,* the Old Fathers, whose "words" formed a living rule as opposed to the Pachomian written rule.

This monasticism flourished, particularly in the last two decades the fourth century, until they both lost favor with the Bishop Alexandria in a dispute over Origen's theology and the communities were attacked and plundered by marauding tribesmen and many monks were driven off, among them were John Kolobus (superior of one of the four anchoretic communities), Poimen, and Arsenius (to whom the *Apophthegmata* attribute the saying, when Rome had been captured by Alaric in 410: "The world has lost Rome, the monks, Scete").

2. Monasticism in Palestine and Syria

The biblical past of the Sinai Peninsula makes it understandable that from the fourth century, it became not only the goal of many pilgrims, but also a favored site for monastic settlement. The *Itinerarium Egeriae* [3–5] make clear that in the 380s the slopes of Sinai were peppered with monks' huts and its summit bore a small chapel where they celebrated the liturgy. This was monasticism of the anchoretic sort. The great age of Sinaitic monasticism began, however, with the founding there of a monastery of coenobites by Emperor Justinian I.

The Holy Land could not but exert an especially strong power of attraction on the budding monasticism. Its beginnings are shrouded in darkness, but with St. Chariton and his *laura* (ca. 330), the phenomenon emerges from the shadows. The *laura* was the specifically Palestinian form of monastery: the cells of the monks were situated close to each other, all encircling a center area with, perhaps among other buildings, a church, where, on Saturdays and Sundays, members of the *laura* gathered for worship. Three *lauras* are attested from the fourth century going back to St. Chariton: northeast of Jerusalem, at Duha near Jericho, and at Suka (south of Bethlehem?).

Euthymius, from Armenia, came to Palestine in 405, and, among other monastic developments linked to his name, initiated the peculiarly Palestinian relationship of *cenobium* and *laura,* namely, the use of the *cenobium* as the training ground for monks who will, upon a certain maturation, go on into the *laura* form.

Peter the Iberian founded in Jerusalem a hospice for pilgrims and the poor, yet another form of monastic life. Bishop Juvenal of Jerusalem also instituted an archimandrite of the monks in the person of a *chorepiscopus,* which led in part to the Chalcedonian canon which subordinated the monastic system in principle to episcopal supervision.

Later Monasteries in Palestine.   Sooner or later eastern monasticism had to exercise its power of attraction on the Latin West also. Athanasius, on his exiles to there, had borne attestation of and to it, and his *Life of Antony* did much to spark enthusiasm for it. Before long individuals from the West were in the East as monks, and in Palestine founded monastic houses with a peculiar Latin character.

Three important monastic foundations from the pre-Chalcedonian period were all founded through the good offices of aristocratic Roman ladies. The first was Melania the Elder (ca. 341–ca. 410), who, after being widowed visited monastic settlements in Nitria and then, with Rufinus of Aquileia, founded a double monastery on Mt. Olivet, for whose support she supplied the means. Thoroughly characteristic of this Latin settlement was the interest in ascetical and theological literature.

The second Latin monastic foundation was the common work of Jerome and the eminent Roman lady, Paula the Elder. Jerome had lived since soon after 372 as an anchorite in the desert of Chalcis southeast of Antioch but felt unequal to the demands of the life and returned to Rome, where he took care of an ascetical circle of prominent ladies. He departed Italy again in 385 with several monks because of a strong antimonastic movement. They went to Palestine, where some time later Paula and her daughter Eustochium followed. In 386, Jerome and Paula selected Bethlehem for their permanent abode, and in the next three years, a convent of nuns, a monastery and a hospice for pilgrims were built. The convent had the larger number of inhabitants, but the monastery was also tremendously important, thanks to the intellectual prestige of its founder, Jerome. With its retention of much of the Latin liturgy, the monastic house not only was a center of pastoral care of its geographical neighborhood, but also an island of Latin hospitality for pilgrims from the West in the Holy Land. The monastery also played a role in the theological confrontations of the day (the controversies over Origen and Pelagianism), and through the voluminous correspondence of its abbot became a major source of western information on eastern Christianity. With Jerome's death in 419/420, information on his monastery ceased.

The third Latin monastic foundation in Jerusalem had its origin in the noble Roman family, Pinian and Melania the Younger, granddaughter of Melania the Elder. The couple chose the monastic life after the early death of their two children. They fled before Alaric to North Africa, where they met Rufinus and Augustine of Hippo. They went to Jerusalem and initiated monastic foundations which played important roles in charitable activities as well as in theological interests.

Syrian Monasticism.   Early Christian monasticism found an eminently favorable climate in the greater Syrian area, whose Christian population quickly showed itself especially responsive to the ascetical ideal. The Encratite movement of the second century, with its stern demands for renunciation of marital rights and abstinence from wine and meat for every Christian, found a sympathetic reaction here. In East Syria, as late as the fourth century, reception of baptism was often joined to the commitment to a life of poverty and complete continence, so that the baptized, as "Sons and Daughters of the Covenant," represented the elite of the Church whereas other Christians continued in the catechumenate. Stemming from this strict asceticism of the pre-Constantinian Church, it is permissible to see early Syrian eremiticism as an autochthonous development, but the post-Constantinian anchoritic forms seem derived from Egyptian example. But the Syrian forms of monasticism exhibited certain peculiarities, such as the tendency to excessive severity, to striking and bizarre forms of asceticism, and to the uncritical and enthusiastic admiration of these by the Christian population, must probably be regarded as the expression of the Syrian cultural inclination toward religious exuberance.

In fasting and renunciation of sleep and of bodily hygiene the anchorites demanded results which often led to serious and permanent injury to health, even to mutilation. A specifically Syrian peculiarity in eremitism was represented by the so-called Stylites, whose first highly esteemed representative in the pre-Chalcedonian period was Simeon the Elder (ca. 390–459). Simeon, because of his kindness and amiability was sought out by innumerable pilgrims; in an effort to avoid the accompanying annoyances, he withdrew to a hut atop a pillar where he dwelt.

The community of anchorites with a hermit as a spiritual father was also manifested in Syrian monasticism as was Coenobitic monasticism. And in the second half of the fourth century, the numbers of Syrian monasteries grew remarkably.

Characteristic of early Syrian monasticism was the unbounded esteem it enjoyed among all classes, high and low alike. A correspondingly vast influence was therefore exercised by the monastics upon the religious conduct and piety of the people. From its circles, especially from among the coenobites, bishops were increasingly chosen.

As usual in the early monasticism of the East, so too in Syrian monasticism of the early period no special theological interest can be ascertained. Reading and writing were important means of providing access to Holy Scripture, entire sections of which, for example, the psalms, were learned by heart so that one could meditate on them and use them in the common prayer. Monastic schools in the proper sense, did not exist, and still a great space was allotted to theological study. This only became possible after cenobitism had left its founding phase behind it and the monasteries had obtained a secure economic foundation. Hence at this period monks as theological authors remained exceptional phenomena.

To the picture of early Syrian monasticism belong two more features, worthy of a positive evaluation: its social charitable activity and its missionary work. The early hermits, despite their modest resources, had an open hand for strangers and pilgrims who stopped at their cells and a helpful heart in regard to the needs of the poor and the sick. Individual monks courageously stood up for a fair treatment of the socially dependent vis-à-vis proprietors, tax collectors, or moneylenders. Monasteries soon organized their social activity through the constructing of hospices for strangers and hospitals.

Since the hermits' cells were mostly in the country, in the midst of an often still strongly pagan population, missionary work was offered a direct opportunity here. Still to be noted was the especially favorable relationship of Syrian monasticism to the official Church: there were no substantial tensions. A positive presupposition for this was the fact that the number of bishops taken from the monastic institute was relatively large. It is true that the heralds of Syrian monasticism, Ephrem, Chrysostom, and Theodoret, say little about an active participation of monks in the religious life of the congregations. Most hermits even seem to have participated only rarely in the eucharistic celebrations of the communities, but Communion was kept in one's dwelling and could have been given to oneself if a priest who happened by on occasion had celebrated the Eucharist among them; the Church took no offense at that. The priesthood for its own sake was not sought by monks, and even less the episcopal office, but the motive was clearly awe of the high responsibility thereby imposed. Hence the monk encountered priest or bishop with the greatest deference, and obedience to them was a matter of course. Chrysostom saw this relation of monasticism to the Church in a more profoundly theological context than did Theodoret. According to him, monasticism was called to be a sign for Christianity that it is possible radically to realize the gospel's ideal of perfection and through a life of poverty and virginity to proclaim the eschatological message of the coming kingdom of God in a way that could not be ignored. If the need of the moment demanded it, the monk must of course be prepared temporarily to give up his existence as a hermit or cenobite and assume a concrete task in the Church, that is, put himself at the Church's disposal as preacher or missionary or, if the aptitude were present, through accepting the episcopal office.

3. The Monasticism of Asia Minor and Constantinople

The beginnings of monasticism in Asia Minor are connected in the sources with the name of the later Bishop Eustathius of Sebaste. After his baptism, Basil of Caesarea became convinced that this sacrament obliged every Christian to the ascetical life in the meaning of the Gospel, and he moulded on it the life of the community of ascetics which gathered around him and his friend, Gregory Nazianzen, at Annesi in Pontus. Even as a bishop he remained united with it, but he also preached to his congregation at Caesarea the ideals of virginity and poverty, without, however, making them a law for all members of the community. When the group of ascetics at Annesi and probably also at Caesarea developed gradually by a sort of dead weight into a cenobitic community, there followed more and more from the questions posed by day-to-day life also the necessity of an "ordering" in writing. The origin of Basil's *asketikon* must be viewed in the light of this development; to it he brought not only the knowledge he had gained on a journey made for information to the monastic centers of Egypt, Palestine, Syria, and Mesopotamia, but in a second version he introduced the insights to which day-to-day practice in a cenobitic community led.

According to Basil the fundamental law of all ascetical life is the love of God, which demands a radical renunciation in regard to a world which despises God's commandments. This law is best realized in a specific community, which carries along and forms the individual. The eremitical life cannot give this help, and, besides, it contradicts man's social nature. Giving up of the world and its goods is turned by Basil into something positive as self-discipline of renunciation (*ekrateia*). The monk can still in certain cases personally manage his property that he has dedicated to the Lord, but it is recommended that the administration be turned over to an individual. Life in the community demands order and subordination, which is to be effected in obedience to the superior (*proestos*). The superior himself, with his vicar, at whose side is a council of seniors, is placed in a serious responsibility, first of all as spiritual father of those entrusted to him. Basil gives a high rank to manual labor, because, first of all, it should make possible to the monastery charity toward the poor and become the touchstone for the purity of the love of God. In so fundamental a deriving of the monastic existence from the word and spirit of the gospel, as the *asketikon* offers it, a definite dedication of the monks to the study of Scripture is self-evident. A further trait of the Basilian "Rules" is, despite all absence of compromise in what is basic, a deep discretion and magnanimity in things of second rank, which does not keep at hand a ready solution for all possible individual situations of everyday life but leaves them to the decision of the superior or of the individual monk. This should also be gained interiorly, in the case of a transgression of the rules, by mild punishment and loving reprimand for their true observance. The gradual maturing of he Basilian monastic life gave it an inner balance and elasticity that made essentially new forms superfluous in Byzantine monasticism. Its quality becomes discernible in the influence which, like the Pachomian Rule, it exercised on the Latin monasticism of the West, beginning with Rufinus and Cassian by way of Benedict of Nursia to Benedict of Aniane.

The sources are silent in regard to monastic foundations in the provinces of central Asia Minor in the period before Chalcedon. But on the Asiatic shore of the Bosporus, still within the limits of the capital, several monasteries arose around this time.

In regard to the beginnings of monasticism at Constantinople the sources give information that is partly contradictory. The capital certainly attracted monks from the eastern provinces of the Empire early, and at first they lived there as individuals or in rather small groups. To the Church historian Sozomen, Marathonius was already regarded as superior of a monastic community (*synoikia monachon*): he was a former official who had been won for the ascetic life by Eustathius of Sebaste ca. 350. On the other hand, the hagiographical literature attributes the founding of the first *monasterion* in Constantinople to the Syrian monk Isaac ca. 382. From the end of the fourth century other monasteries appeared in rapid succession. In 448 representatives of twenty-three monasteries signed the judgment of the Synod which repudiated the teaching of Eutyches. Among these monasteries that of the so-called *Acemetae* occupied a special place. A special force of attraction proceeded from the custom, brought along from Syria, of celebrating in the monastery uninterrupted prayer throughout the night — hence the name *akoimētoi* for these monks — for which groups of monks of different languages took turns. When jealousy and intrigues drove the *Acemetae* from the city, they went to Asia Minor. From this monastery in 468 the Patrician Studios summoned some monks for his new foundation in the capital that was later to be so famous.

The monks of this period did not always give joy and comfort to the bishops of the capital. They were eager to share, at times tumultuously, in the confrontations raging around the "orthodoxy" of their bishops, of whom Macedonius, Gregory Nazianzen, and Nestorius were able to experience their power and aggressiveness as much as John Chrysostom, who urged them to better monastic discipline and aspired to exercise a certain control over their life. In this attitude of the monasticism of the capital it becomes very clear that a framework had to be discovered which also incorporated it canonically into the total life of the Church. For the area of Eastern Christianity this momentous work was undertaken by the Council of Chalcedon in a series of canons. The most important norm was given in canon 4, which subjected every monastery to the supervision of the diocesan bishop. Without his knowledge neither a small colony nor a monastery could be established in the future. The canon further decreed that a monk remained bound for the duration of his life to the monastery in which he began his ascetical career: he could leave it only for a weighty reason and temporarily with the consent of the diocesan bishop. Canon 8 also strengthened the position of the bishop in relation to the monastery: monks who were clerics, and hence members of the hierarchy, remained explicitly subject to the bishop's jurisdiction. Other canons tried to guarantee the ideal of the vocation by forbidding the assumption of a secular function or military service and denying to monks and nuns entry into marriage. With this legislation of Chalcedon eastern monasticism, as an ecclesiastical state, obtained its official position in the total organism of the Church.

4. Messalianism

In the second half of the fourth century there appeared in Syria and Mesopotamia a movement led by monks, whose ascetical practice and teaching soon evoked opposition from ecclesiastical circles. The first to speak of them was Ephrem the Syrian; he called them Messalian — those who pray intensively — and spoke rather vaguely of their lack of discipline. Theodoret of Cyrrhus was the first to name some of the "authors of error," among them a certain Simeon. He states also that the Messalians, if necessary, avoided being cut off from the Church by disavowing their doctrines. According to his report, Bishops Letoius of Mytilene, Amphilochius of Iconium, and Flavian of Antioch especially fought against the movement. It was also Amphilochius who ca. 390 submitted the question of the Messalians to a synod at Side in Pamphylia, which, after adherents of the movement had been heard, rejected the following doctrines: baptism does not eradicate the root of sin, but only incessant prayer, which alone can expel the demon dwelling in the human soul; the Messalian pneumatic must reject work; he can foretell the future, see the Trinity with the eyes of his body, and physically perceive the descent of the Holy Spirit in his soul. A Synod of Constantinople of 426 raised basically the same objections against the Messalians, except that it now emphasized at the head of the propositions to be condemned their thesis that in each newly born person dwells a demon which drives him to his evil deeds.

This work, called *Asketikon,* was presented to the Council of Ephesus of 431, when, on the motion of Bishops Valerian and Amphilochius of Side, it took up the Messalian movement, which had then spread, especially in Pamphylia and Lycaonia. The decrees of the Synod of Constantinople of 426 were confirmed, the *Asketikon* was condemned, disavowal was demanded of persons suspected of the erroneous doctrine. Deposition and excommunication were decreed against clerics who refused to comply and excommunication against lay persons, and the Messalians were forbidden to have monasteries. Furthermore, the Council rejected eighteen individual propositions extracted from the *Asketikon,* which John Damascene placed in his *History of Heresies.* They refer to the binding of the human soul to the demon, to the effect of baptism, the importance of prayer, to the physically perceptible presence of Christ and of the Holy Spirit; the reproach of overesteeming dreams, of aversion to work, and of licentiousness was no longer raised.

As now presented, any moral laxity is condemned in the *Asketikon,* the work of the "brothers" is highly esteemed, and the phantasies of many a pneumatic no longer play a role. Here one encounters rather a refined theology of experience, in which a high but not an exclusive importance is assigned to prayer, in which ascetical training is a self-evident presupposition for the acquiring and preserving of the Spirit and his grace, and in which a devaluation of baptism is no longer traceable. Gregory of Nyssa and Diadochus of Photice regarded this Messalianism, after a tacit correction of its errors, as an ascetical attitude possible to them. Hence it seems that doubts are not to be excluded whether the *Asketikon* condemned at Ephesus represented such a Messalianism or whether extracts presented from it did not give a distorted picture of its doctrine. Of course, the negative verdict of Ephesus burdened it, without however being able to exclude the enormous influence of its writings on the mysticism of the future.

C H A P T E R   5 1

The Monasticism of the Latin West

While the Latin West, especially in Rome and North Africa, had its own early Christian asceticism on a considerable scale, a native monasticism in the proper sense, independent in origin and development from the movement in Eastern Christianity, cannot be demonstrated with certainty for the West. Both the eremitical life and the organized monastic system began in the West only after the middle of the fourth century — at a time, then, when the knowledge of eastern monasticism had long ago reached the West through various channels and could have a further stimulating impact, especially when the already lively relations between Eastern Christianity and the Christian congregations of the West became more intense in the early phase of the Arian struggles. The pilgrims from the West, who came to the East in growing numbers after 324 and were able to observe in Palestine the great interest of the imperial family in the holy places. The wholly credible report that Constantine and his sons sent letters to Antony in Egypt shows the significance which persons of the highest station attributed to monasticism. The repeated stays of Athanasius in the West — at Trier in 335, at Rome ca. 340–43, at Aquileia ca. 345 — gave him and his entourage the possibility of speaking as eyewitnesses of the powerful movement which had taken hold of the East. His testimony achieved its full impact when his account of the life and work of Antony, written ca. 357, became accessible to a larger Latin circle of readers in an early Latin translation soon after 360. A momentum favorable to monasticism certainly proceeded also from the itinerant eastern monks who appeared from time to time in the West, especially in Rome.

The knowledge of eastern monasticism at first, however, operated in the West only to reinforce the already existing ascetical communities, which, especially in Rome, saw themselves sanctioned in their ideals, gained further members, and were able to found new ascetical circles. The fact that a relatively long starting-time was needed in the West before an organized monastic system arose becomes intelligible when the state of the expansion of Christianity in the West ca. 350 is kept in mind. The real Christian centers were the cities with their relatively densely populated hinterland, but, according to the ideas of the time, these were precisely not the areas of settlement favorable to monasticism, which required solitude. Not until the conversion of a majority of the rural population was achieved were conditions advantageous to an organized monasticism of some magnitude created. A survey of the individual regions of the West makes clear at the same time important differences within Latin monasticism itself as well as in comparison with its eastern precursor.

Rome and Italy

The growing knowledge of eastern monasticism exerted its greatest influence in the circles of the Roman communities of Christians who were already open to the ascetic ideal. The correspondence of Jerome, who was especially active during his second Roman sojourn (381–84) as a zealous promoter and propagandist of the monastic ideal, informs us that the members of these circles were mostly ladies of the upper class, who, like Asella, Marcellina, sister of Bishop Ambrose of Milan, and Irene, sister of Pope Damasus I, at first led a life of virginity as individuals in their families or, like Marcella, decided on the ascetic type of life as widows. More and more they joined in larger ascetical groups or domestic communities respectively, among which those of the prominent Romans, Lea, Paula, Melania the Younger, and Proba played a special role. A substantial approach to the monastic form of life was indicated when ladies of these circles left Rome and continued their former community on one of their properties in the country. But some of them, such as Melania the Elder, Paula the Elder, and finally Melania the Younger, apparently saw that the possibility of a complete realization of the monastic ideal could take place only in the East and emigrated there. Augustine was the first to speak of a real monastery of Roman women ca. 387.

The ascetical ideal apparently found a far weaker response among the men of the Roman community.

For Rome it is only natural to raise the question of the position of the Roman Bishop in regard to the monastic movement of this period. Pope Damasus I (366–84) surely has to be considered as a definite promoter especially of women's asceticism: he encouraged it in word and writing. His successor, Siricius (384–99), was of the same mind: he expressed his opposition to a devaluation of the ascetical ideal. When, after the fading of the threat from the barbarian invasions in the early fifth century, the number of monks increased, Popes Innocent 1 (401–17) and Zosimus (417–18) intervened to issue regulations. The *Monasterium in Catacumbas* near the basilica of the Martyr Sebastian on the Via Appia owes its origin to Pope Sixtus III (432–40), and his successor, Leo I (440–61), founded a monastery near the Vatican basilica, later called that of Saints John and Paul; it was probably responsible for the liturgy in the basilica.

In a glance at the rest of Italy, what is first noteworthy is a relatively strong spread of the eremitical life on the coasts and islands of the Tyrrhenian Sea and, less often, in the Adriatic. The first island hermit known by name was Martin of Tours, who, after a brief time as a hermit in the vicinity of Milan, had to yield to pressure from the Arians and withdraw to the island of Gallinara off the Riviera, opposite the city of Albenga, ca. 357–60.

The first founding of a monastery on Italian soil is connected with the name of Bishop Eusebius of Vercelli, who gave this foundation a specific orientation. Before being called to become bishop of the North Italian city, Eusebius had been a lector at Rome and had already decided on a life of virginity and asceticism before he was banished to the East in 355 because of his fidelity to the Nicene Creed. It was probably only after his return from exile in 363 that he united the clergy of his cathedral in a monastic *vita communis;* hence he was the first founder of a *monasterium clericorum* in Church history, since, until then, there was in East and West no model for his institution, so far as the sources inform us. Ambrose mentions the singing of hymns, common prayer, study of Scripture, manual labor, and fasting as important ingredients of the life of the clerical community of Vercelli, which thus appears as the anticipation of Augustine's *monasterium clericorum* at Hippo and, with the requirement of the study of Scripture, already displays a specifically western element.

Milan under Bishop Ambrose must also be named as a further center of ascetic monastic effort in Italy. At the time of Augustine's stay at Milan there existed outside the city gates a monastery of men; the superior of the numerically not inconsiderable community was a learned priest, and Bishop Ambrose himself was its eager patron. Elsewhere too Ambrose stood up as the advocate of monasticism, when he praised the island eremitism, extolled the work of Eusebius of Vercelli, or bitterly reprimanded two former monks who now reviled what they had once vowed. But his care was directed in a special way to women who had vowed ascetical virginity. He put his word and his pen at the service of their ideal: from his efforts speaks the resolute seriousness of the Roman-become-Catholic-Bishop, who contrasted the exalted claim of Christian discipline with a lax pagan moral concept. While virgins came from Piacenza and Bologna, and even refugees from North Africa, to Milan in order "to take the veil" (*ut his velantur*) there.

In the rest of Italy, apart from Bologna, where the monastic community counted some twenty nuns, there existed in Ambrose's day one convent of nuns at Verona, on which Bishop Zeno expended his care. As early as 370 Rufinus was a monk in a monastery of his home town, Aquileia. When ca. 400 he translated Basil's *Asketikon* for the monks of a monastery of Pinetum, he asked that copies be sent "also to other monasteries" of the West. In South Italy asceticism first got a foothold with Paulinus, who came from Bordeaux and from 395 led a monastic life with his domestic community. The ascetical communities which Melania the Younger established ca. 408 on her properties in Sicily and Campania may also have been "domestic monasteries" of this sort. Later biographies ascribe to many a bishop of the fourth to the sixth century special interest in monasticism or even the founding of monasteries, but in individual cases this cannot be ascertained with certainty from other sources.

Gaul

For Gaul also we must presuppose a premonastic asceticism, even if the testimonies for it are relatively sparse and of a later date. A decree of the Emperor Valentinian I (ca. 370), which exempted the consecrated virgins of Gaul from a tax, assumes the existence of women's asceticism, just as does a canon of the Council of Valence (374), which dealt with the *virgines* who had abandoned their former state. Also at Trier there is known about the same time the institution of *virgines deo dicatae,* and even before the turn of the century a decree of Pope Damasus I (366–84) or of his successor, Siricius (384–99), expresses itself on the question of the treatment of such virgins who became unfaithful to their vows. The majority of these *virgines* in Gaul still lived with their families, but they occasionally gathered into rather small groups following the trend toward a monastic community.

The first reports on male asceticism in Gaul are connected with the name of the man who ranks clearly as the founder of Gallic monasticism — Martin of Tours. His discharge from military service was motivated by his decision for an ascetical existence, which, after a short stay with Hilary of Poitiers, he first put into practice as an itinerant ascetic in the Balkans, then outside the gates of Milan, and on the island of Gallinara off the Ligurian coast. After Hilary's return from exile in 360, Martin lived at first in a hermitage in the vicinity of Poitiers, with great probability on the site of the later monastery of Ligugé, eight kilometers south of the city.

By accepting a few disciples, this hermitage gradually became a colony of anchorites, and the same is true of the cell to which Martin withdrew soon after his call to be Bishop of Tours ca. 371; from it grew the monastery of Marmoutier. The rapidly growing number of hermits soon there were some eighteen caused the appearance here too of certain forms of common life, such as common meals and common prayer. Since manual labor remained forbidden to monks in an effort to keep from them a spirit of acquisitiveness — only some younger monks prepared the manuscripts needed for reading and prayer — the community's support had to be defrayed from the property supplied by brothers coming from well-to-do families and from the aid of the congregation of Tours. A series of traits of this monastic colony points unmistakably to like structures in Egyptian monasticism, as they are demonstrable in Antony's union of hermits or of those on Mount Nitria. Among these characteristics must be counted not only the loose, unregulated organization, but especially the basic ascetical concept that understands the monk's being as the following of Christ, as realized in apostolic poverty on the model of the primitive community — common possessions, clothing — and in constant warfare with demons. The essential ingredient of this struggle with demons was the destruction of pagan temples, the erecting of Christian churches in their place, the instructing of people through preaching, and the foundation of new monastic settlements. In this way Martin's monasticism received a decidedly pastoral and missionary trend, which gave it a specific character. Since new bishops were eagerly chosen from the circle of Martin's disciples and they promoted the monastic ideal in his spirit, the early monasticism on the Loire retained its special nature also in the future. Naturally, it aroused opposition among some bishops, to whom Martin's vast influence among the people was distasteful, but whose reputation, defended and propagated by the literature on him written by Sulpicius Severus, guaranteed a decisive and continuous impact, especially in southwestern Gaul. After renouncing his paternal inheritance, Sulpicius also personally sought to realize in practice Martin's ascetical ideal with some modifications, when he introduced for himself and his household at his country residence, Primuliacum, a lifestyle which united individual ascetical features, such as living in separate cells and a simple monastic garb, with intellectual activity and a ready hospitality to monks, especially those of Marmoutier. For this ascetic circle the memory of Martin was the unifying bond and the tomb of his pupil Clarus, whom Sulpicius Severus had buried at Primuliacum, was a constant stimulus for his veneration. The influence of Martin may also be assumed for the monasticism of the bishopric of Rouen, farther northwest, since the bishop of that see, Victricius, knew Martin personally, venerated him, and, just like him, had monasteries established near newly erected churches.

About a decade after Martin's death the second phase in the expansion of Gallic monasticism began, which especially included Provence and was to surpass Martin's form of monasticism in its significance for Church history. The starting-point and, for a century, also the center of this movement was the double island off the coast of Cannes, today called Lérins. On the larger island, Lerinum or Lerina, there settled, between 405 and 410, with his friend Caprasius, Honoratus, of a prominent family, after he had decided in his early manhood for the ascetical life against the opposition of his father. From its modest anchoretic beginning, there developed in the course of twenty years an *ingens fratrum coenobium,* as John Cassian called the foundation ca. 425. Honoratus, soon ordained a priest, remained, until his call to be Bishop of Arles in 428, the spiritual father of the monastery: while he perhaps did not supply it with a written Rule, he did give it an order of life entirely oriented to the Egyptian model. The reputation of the *coenobium* on this *beata insula* not only attracted many visitors but brought it a remarkably high percentage of recruits from the upper class families of Late Roman Gaul, which gave to the monasticism of Lérins a character clearly in contrast to that of Martin. Even more momentous for the Gallic Church of the fifth century was the fact that monks of Lérins coming from this very class were chosen as bishops and thus brought to their new circles of work the spirit that determined the religious and theological character of the monastery. There were also Maximus, second Abbot of Lérins, elected to the see of Riez, and Faustus, who succeeded him in both the abbatial dignity and the episcopal office. Apparently there was in progress here a development similar to that in the Eastern Church, in which the selecting of bishops from the monastic state became the rule. Thus the spiritual and theologically unique character of the island monastery is found again in the monastic community established by Hilary at Arles and in that existing at Lyon even before Eucherius' time. From Lyon the spirit of Lérins radiated also to the Jura monasteries, since Romanus, founder of the first of these, Condat (Saint-Claude, ca. 430), had learned "the life of the monks" in a monastery at Lyon, and at Condat under the later Abbot Eugendus the monks read, in addition to the ascetical works of Basil, Pachomius, and Cassian, also "what the holy fathers of Lérins" had published. Another important influence on the monasticism of the fifth century in southeast Gaul proceeded from the work of John Cassian. He came probably from the Romanized Dobrudsha (*natione Scytha*) and hence was a Latin-speaking monk. After a first stay in a monastery at Bethlehem, he had lived some ten years among the anchorites of Scete in Egypt until ca. 400; he was next a deacon under John Chrysostom at Constantinople and later, probably as a priest, a member of the clergy of the Church of Antioch. In the service of his bishops he was twice in Rome, where he became acquainted with the later Pope Leo I. For reasons that cannot be clarified with certainty, he came ca. 416 to Marseille, where Bishop Proculus gave him the Church of Saint-Victor outside the city. Here he founded the famed monastery of monks, dedicated to Saint Victor; it was followed by a convent of nuns, to which Caesarius of Arles later sent his sister for her formation. At the Church of Saint-Victor Cassian composed his two great works on the way of life and the spiritual world of eastern monasticism — the *Instituta Coenobiorum* ca. 424 and the *Collationes* ca. 426–28. Here too was displayed his collaboration in the theological discussion of his time on Nestorianism and Augustine's doctrine of grace.

    The Abbot of Marseille himself stated the goals of his monastic writings in the dedications, which were directed to the various bishops, monastic superiors, and anchorites of Gaul. He aspired to familiarize, in detail and reliably, the leadership of Gallic monasticism both with eastern cenobitism and also with the spirituality of the eremitism there. The proved cenobitic rules of the East, especially that of Pachomius, whose individual features were lovingly described in the *Instituta Coenobiorum*, should be a help to the Gallic monasteries, often founded rather haphazardly and still not sure of their way, for the preservation of the apostolic tradition, in which Cassian seemed to regard as advisable a certain adaptation to the climate and customs of life of the country. He assigned to anchoritism an objectively higher rank, it is true, since it presupposes a deeper ascetical discipline, but its high requirements could even become a danger. Although his admiration and secret love belonged to this form, he selected for himself, in a sense as a model for Gallic asceticism, the ordered life in the monastery within the city. Two characteristics of the monasticism of the Rhone certainly go back to Cassian's work: first, the decidedly high estimation of the eastern, really the Egyptian, model, which was here grasped more keenly and more profoundly than in the monasticism of Martin of Tours, and, second, the greater receptivity to a "theology of monasticism," which he brought as a legacy of the East from the circle around Evagrius Ponticus to Provence. From this resulted ultimately the lively interest in the theological discussion of the time on the validity of the Augustinian doctrine of grace, in which the monasticism of southeast Gaul took a laudable share. Still more important, of course, was probably the long-range impact of this abbot who had come to Marseille from the Balkan Peninsula. The discreet, intelligent judgment, the sure view for the ascetically possible, the winning purity of his ideals, and the attractive style of his writings decisively prepared for the great future of Latin monasticism in the Middle Ages. Finally, southeastern Gallic monasticism experienced certain impulses from the East which went back to the contacts of Jerome with the monastic circles in Toulouse and Marseille. Through the monk Sisinnius he was informed of the ascetical movements in Toulouse, which induced him to dedicate his commentary of Zechariah to Bishop Exsuperius and his exegesis of Malachi to the monks Minervius and Alexander. In a letter to a certain Rusticus of Marseille, who in 427 became Bishop of Narbonne, he recommended the ascetic life in a community of brothers, whereas he expressed himself rather critically in regard to Martin of Tours.

Spain

While premonastic asceticism is first attested for the Iberian Peninsula by the Synod of Elvira, reports on the existence of monasticism here do not occur until ca. 380, but then they of course make clear that it was not a question of an institution just coming into being there. Bishop Hosius of Córdoba, who stayed at Alexandria in 324 as Constantine's delegate, was able to report about eastern monasticism, so that he will be first thought of as the agent, in the reference of Athanasius, through whom Spain also had obtained knowledge of the life of Antony. The Synod of Zaragoza in 380 used the term *monachus* for the first time in a Spanish text in a special context: it decreed punishment for the passage of a cleric to monasticism because he thereby "aspired to appear [as] a more zealous observer of the law." Five years later, on the other hand, Pope Siricius (384–99) in a letter to Bishop Himerius of Tarragona expressed the wish that clerics should especially be chosen from monasticism; in the same letter monasteries of men and women are mentioned as a normal thing in the province of Tarragona.

A unique representative of Spanish monasticism in the last years of the fourth century was Bachiarius, of whom Gennadius reports that he chose the *peregrinatio* in order to preserve his asceticism; in fact, Bachiarius defended his itinerant monasticism spiritedly. In his *De lapso* he showed himself to be an ascetic of sound judgment and great knowledge who had studied Tertullian, Cyprian, and Jerome. Of course, his itinerant monasticism brought on him the suspicion of being an adherent of Priscillian ideas, which, however, he decisively repudiated in an *apologia.*

No doubt, however, the reaction to Priscillian's movement brusquely interrupted the further development of monasticism in the Iberian Peninsula. True, Priscillianism must be evaluated primarily as a dualistic heterodox theology, but from this theology its adherents developed an extreme and exaggerated ascetical practice, which brought even orthodox monasticism into disrepute and evoked in some bishops otherwise not unfriendly to asceticism a long-lasting distrust of it. This burden and the disturbances beginning after the turn of the century, which were connected with the occupation of the country by the Sueves and later the Visigoths, delayed until the beginning of the sixth century a stronger recovery of monasticism.

North Africa

Especially in North African Christianity the ascetical life had achieved a noteworthy expansion and a high esteem as early as the third century. From the days of Tertullian, the North African Church knew *virgines* or *continentes* of both sexes, who were encouraged by Bishop Cyprian with special care and often proved themselves in time of persecution. They continued to exist throughout the fourth century and apparently increased in number and importance, since the synods of this period were repeatedly concerned with them and issued rules which pushed them more and more in the direction of the common life. Perhaps the rank and spread of asceticism were a reason why in a glance at the rest of the development of the inner life of the Church in North Africa real monasticism appeared there relatively late. Augustine testified to the existence of several monasteries at Carthage ca. 400, and they could not have originated on his initiative because in them an understanding of monasticism was represented by at least one group of monks which was diametrically opposed to the Augustinian view. The characteristics of this group, condemned by Augustine with the utmost sharpness, their extraordinary coiffure, their rejection of all manual labor, their complacent appearance in public, and especially the subjectivity and capriciousness of their scripture exegesis apparently betrayed Messalian influences. And the itinerant monks, strongly condemned by him, whose unworthy conduct brought their entire state into discredit, clearly reveal eastern peculiarities. If, then, Augustine cannot be called the "father" of African monasticism, nevertheless to him belongs the credit for instituting a monasticism which bore the stamp of his spirit and through its quality was called to become a highly significant element of the inner life of the Church, first in that of North Africa, then through its continued operation in all of Western Christianity.

Augustine's Monastic Rule

Certainly decisive, first of all, for the formation of this monasticism was the personal direction of both monasteries founded by Augustine at Hippo the monastery of lay persons, of which he as a priest was superior, and the later episcopal *monasterium clericorum,* as he called it. The intensive study of the problem of the Augustinian Rule in the most recent period has led to the conclusion that Augustine put in writing his ideas on a monastic form of life. A comprehensive investigation of the manuscript tradition of all pertinent texts has shown that the so-called *Praeceptum,* earlier called the *Regula tertia* or *recepta,* can alone claim to be regarded as Augustine's monastic Rule. The question of the dating of the Rule is still open, since reasons can be adduced for a relatively early (shortly before 400) as well as for a later beginning (ca. 425–26).

An effort to put forward what was specifically Augustine's in his understanding of monasticism must not overlook that Augustine only gained his insight through a rather long development, determined by the stages on the way of his religious life. At times these became for him the opportunity to rethink his ascetical ideal and concretely to realize the insights thereby acquired. The *Confessiones* clearly show that Augustine's first encounter with monasticism in Italy forever stamped his understanding of Christian asceticism. But even then he knew that anchoritism in the real sense was not possible for him personally even if he spoke of it with admiration. In the *vita communis,* which, with some like-minded persons, he established in his paternal home at Thagaste after his return from Italy, an Augustinian peculiarity will be seen alongside certain features common to that cenobitism, such as seclusion from the world and renunciation of marriage: the high rank which was assigned to intellectual activity, the contemplative grasp of Christian revelation. Still, the community of Thagaste cannot yet be called a *monasterium* in the full sense, since apparently the renunciation of personal property was not yet required of all its members, who came chiefly from the educated class. These limitations do not occur in Augustine's two foundations in Hippo, in which he tried to realize the now definitively acquired monastic ideal. In the monastic life at Hippo the following features may be called specifically Augustinian: 1. The *vita communis* was understood as one of the highest possibilities for realizing the love of God and neighbor on the basis of a deeply Christian understanding of *amicitia,* which unites all. 2. The life of the community was supported by the atmosphere of a great inner breadth in the relationship to one another and to the superior, which was determined by the freedom bestowed in grace. 3. For *lectio,* spiritual study in the broader sense, a pride of place was demanded and maintained, which gave to the Augustinian monastery a characteristically intellectual alertness and receptiveness to all religiously significant questions. 4. The *monasterium clericorum* was put definitely at the service of the care of souls, so that the Augustinian monasticism was emphatically apostolically oriented and effectively bound to the *ecclesia.*

This Augustinian monastic ideal operated in the future in a double form: first, directly in the area of the North African Church in the monasteries which were founded here by friends and disciples of Augustine and were directed in his spirit; then, indirectly through the influence which the Augustinian Rule acquired on other monastic systems outside Africa. Augustine's biographer Possidius stressed that he personally knew some ten men, who were called out of the *monasterium clericorum* in Hippo to be bishops and founded monasteries in their sees. It can hardly be doubted that they gave to their establishments the Augustinian Rule as the norm of monastic life, just as Augustine by his personal contacts exercised a further influence on them. A prudent appraisal establishes that up to his death some thirty monasteries of men came into existence in North Africa which more or less bore his stamp. Even the foundations that occurred after his death in the later part of the fifth century for the most part referred back to the model he created. No less important was the later impact of the Augustinian Rule on the newly created monastic rules of the future. Caesarius of Arles and Benedict were under obligation to him in their new creations; the *Regula Monasterii Tarnatensis* of the sixth century was chiefly only an adaptation of the Augustinian Rule, the use of which can also be ascertained in the *Regula Pauli et Stephani* and in early Spanish monastic regulations.

Thus the most recent results of research prove that also in this aspect of the Church's inner life Augustine was a creative initiator and continuing force.

Anti-Monastic Currents

A phenomenon as striking as monasticism could not but immediately arouse the interest of pagan circles, which of course did not examine it according to its own self-awareness but for the most part condemned it only because of its external appearances and thus reached an often pointedly negative verdict. The Emperor Julian, it is true, admitted that Christians "in great number" decided for this form of life, but in their senseless asceticism, which drove them into the desert or burdened them with chains and iron collars, he could see only the activity of a demon, to whom they voluntarily subjected themselves. The *rhetor* Libanius attributed to them a dark life of wickedness, which concealed itself under their ascetical exterior, and attributed to them the ultimate responsibility for the destruction of pagan temples. A similar view was held by Eunapius of Sardes, who reproached them especially for the cult of martyrs — they had, he said, made gods out of slaves executed because of their crimes — and even accused them of high treason, since in 395 they had, so he claimed, facilitated Alaric's invasion of Greece via Thermopylae. The historian Zosimus formulated the reproach, often raised later, that monks, because of their renunciation of marriage, were worthless to human society and, under the pretext of wishing to support the poor, they made mankind poor because of the gifts they begged.

However, the Christian Emperors also occasionally had reason for criticism of the behavior of some monks and did not hesitate to take energetic legal measures because of certain encroachments. When monks from the Nitrian Desert took part in 375 in a riot of the population of Alexandria, which was directed against the installation of the Arian Bishop Lucius, the Emperor Valens forced them abruptly into military service and threatened severe punishments in cases of refusal. In 390 the Emperor Theodosius I forbade them to settle in cities, and six years later an edict by his sons sharply condemned their seditious intervention in favor of men who had been condemned to suitable punishments because of their crimes.

In the properly internal sphere of the Church there were often at first tensions between episcopate and monasticism, which had various causes. It could not but disturb the bishops that here an institution had come into being which at first escaped control by the hierarchy. The hierarchy could rightly point to the fact that at times monasteries had been established whose existence seemed not adequately assured; that questionable elements often found admission, whom a previous careful investigation would have excluded; that monastic superiors were chosen who were in no sense equal to their task. Thus are explained the exertions of the episcopate to incorporate monasticism as a state in the Church and to place it on the organized bases established by canon law, just as they were first secured by the decrees of the Council of Chalcedon. And the claim made, at least de facto, by some monks to belong to a state which was of higher rank than the episcopate occasionally produced friction.

The antimonastic movement proved to be strongest in lay Christian circles of the fourth and fifth centuries: it appeared as a reaction to the exuberant enthusiasm for monks at the time. Here also the discrepancy between the new ascetic ideal and the ordinary lifestyle of the upper class in the large cities of late antiquity was felt as a reproach, and people sought to counter it by a sort of defensive attitude. This is clearly attested for Antioch by John Chrysostom, according to whom local Christians branded monks as charlatans and seducers who enticed men from their previous environment to a dismal life in the desert. In Rome the ladies of the higher-class circles who had gathered into ascetical communities found themselves exposed to the caustic mockery of their former friends. At the burial of Blesilla, whose early death some ascribed to excessive asceticism, there were scenes of protest, in which it was demanded that "the monastic rabble" should be expelled from the city or thrown into the Tiber. Augustine likewise had to defend monasticism in Africa; its individual representatives themselves evoked much blame by their defiant appearance, which was later manifested at Carthage also. Finally, in both East and West the opposition of some parents, never entirely quieted throughout the later centuries, was also vigorous: they took precautions to prevent their children from exchanging a hidden life in the bosom of their family for self-burial in the monastery.

The antimonastic atmosphere of some circles expressed itself finally in a discussion, conducted at times with vast bitterness, simply about the justification of the ascetical ideal. Of course, an at times imprudent and all too enthusiastic exaltation of the ideal of virginity could be felt to be a devaluation of Christian marriage. In Rome the layman Helvidius in 382 published a work which attacked Mary, the model of all virginity, and denied her perpetual virginity by appeal to Matthew 1:8 and 1:25 and Luke 2:7 and 8:20. The refutation by Jerome, who was then living at Rome, became of enduring significance for the history of dogma because of its Mariology. A few years later occurred Jovinian's attack against some fundamental theses of Christian asceticism in his glance at the high estimation of celibacy he maintained the equality of the states of virgins, widows, and the married, since only the reception of baptism determined the rank of the Christian. To the high esteem for fasting he replied with the thesis that it is just as meritorious to eat with thanksgiving to God. Jerome's excessive reaction was followed by the condemnation of Jovinian by a Roman Synod ca. 390, with which Ambrose of Milan agreed. Once again Jerome put in an appearance when ca. 406 the priest Vigilantius from southern Gaul, censured, in addition to what he regarded as the excessive cult of martyrs and relics, especially the overestimation of the monastic ideal by the Christian people. What, he asked, was to become of an orderly pastoral care, who would win sinners and the children of the world for virtue, if everyone went into the monastery? Retreat into solitude from such duties was, he said, rather a desertion than a fight.

This antimonastic reaction, to which was denied a greater success than it intended, had, however, noteworthy positive effects. To the extent that it was aimed at actually existing abuses in the asceticism and conduct of some monks, it contributed to their elimination and helped to prevent other false developments. The ecclesiastical leadership was obliged to guide the at times impetuously enthusiastic movement along orderly paths and finally it provided the possibility of accepting monasticism as such without restrictions.

CHAPTER   52

Church and Society

In the process, extending over the entire fourth century, of the evangelization of the population of the Roman Empire, the Church was confronted with social structures, economic relations, forms of cultural life, and the daily habits of the society of late antiquity, which pressed for a confrontation under various aspects. The following account will show briefly on what especially relevant areas of the social life of the age the Church took a position, positive or negative, whether it sought or achieved a change — in short, in what respects the society of late antiquity experienced a transformation because of the existence and influence of Christianity.

Marriage and Family

A judgment on the esteem of the area of marriage and family by the Church of the fourth and fifth centuries must distinguish between the preaching of pastors and the writings of ecclesiastical authors, with their predominantly moralistic and exhortatory tendency, and the canonical regulations which were directed to this complex of questions. It must first be ascertained that the Church had to a great extent accepted the rules of the currently valid secular law of marriage, such as the legal contracting of a marriage and its consequences, the position of the *paterfamilias,* and the law of inheritance. When ecclesiastical writers indicated contradictions between the Christian order of marriage and profane laws on marriage, they were referring concretely to the different evaluation of individual questions and did not intend to reject the totality of the civil legislation on marriage. Also, the profane customs surrounding weddings were often retained by Christians and on the Church's part were challenged only in those features which were connected with pagan religious notions or in their occasionally coarse boisterousness, which contradicted Christian sensitivity.

However, those regulations of the Roman marriage law which employed a different standard in regard to the evaluation of adultery by the man and the wife did encounter a clear repudiation from the Christian side. People found unjust a law which penalized the adultery of the wife in every case but that of the husband only if it was committed with a married woman. It was further disapproved because it forced the husband to separate by a prescribed procedure from his wife when she was guilty of adultery and deprived him of the possibility for forgiving her and thereby saving the marriage. The Church came into still sharper opposition to the civil law of marriage with its definite defense of the indissolubility of marriage in principle and, based on this, its repudiation of remarriage of Christians divorced in accord with the current law. It is true that from some expressions of Christian writers and pastors it can be inferred that the Church permitted the remarriage of the man, not of the woman, if he was divorced from his wife on the ground of her infidelity. But a careful analysis of these passages and of their context and the consideration of all views of the writing of the period on the entire complex of questions make clear that the overwhelming majority of contemporary Christian theologians did not approve the remarriage of divorced persons. Some false interpretations of pertinent patristic texts are conditioned by the fact that they assent to the separation of the couple on the basis of the called Matthean clauses (5:32 and 19:9) but do not express themselves on the question of remarriage, which, however, in no sense means approval of it. Occasionally, Christians who were living in an unrecognized second marriage were, after appropriate penance, admitted to the ecclesiastical community and the reception of communion. But this practice is to be understood only as a pastoral, helpful measure in a complicated situation, not as a recognition of the legality of such a marriage. As the ultimate justification of this fundamental attitude of the Church, the really new element in the Christian understanding of marriage is given: it cannot be regarded only as a contract, again terminable for certain reasons, between the marriage partners, but as a union based on a divine ordinance, which obtains its indissolubility from that higher reality which Augustine termed *sacramentum* and in which he saw the sharing of the couple in the union which binds Christ and his Church. Even under the Christian Emperors the Church was unable in this question to change the civil law substantially. A decree of Constantine I of 331, which at least limited the grounds for divorce, may indeed have been influenced by Christianity, but it did not attack the principle of the dissolubility of marriage by *divortium* (separa-

tion by mutual agreement) or *repudium* (after the adultery of one party) and of
the then possible remarriage any more than did the constitution of his sons of
339, which made the punishment for adultery more severe. In a synodal decree
of 407 or 416, which unambiguously maintained the prohibition of a remarriage of
divorced persons, no matter which party was guilty, the African bishops required
that there should be a demand for an imperial law on this question, but as late as
449 a civil regulation still did not give up the principle of dissolubility by *repudium*,
but only made divorce more difficult "in the interest of the child" and in so doing
made husband and wife equal in law. Hence, in this matter, the "Constantinian
Turning-Point" meant no decisive change for the Church.

The enthusiastic recruiting of ascetical writers for the ideal of virginity led to
a reaction on the part of some Christians, who incorrectly saw it as eclipsing the
real worth of Christian marriage. This caused some Church Fathers to define their
view of the relationship of marriage and virginity and more deeply to establish the
understanding of marriage. Chrysostom and Augustine especially made clear that
the higher rank demanded for virginity was by no means to be understood as a
devaluing of marriage. Ambrose considered it necessary to deal with the scruples
which were asserted in the interest of the State against the strong ecclesiastical
propaganda for the ideal of virginity in a look at its possible demographically negative effects. The Church had no objections against regulations of the civil law
of marriage which in specific cases forbade the contracting of marriage, as, for
example, because of close relationship. But for its own part it decreed new marriage impediments, which followed from its understanding of the conjugal union
among Christians and here too it was able to influence civil legislation. Thus, more
and more in the fourth century it objected to marriages between Christians and
pagans or Jews, although such marriages occasionally brought missionary acqui-
sitions. The numerous canons of the synods of the time, despite the prohibition,
did not regard such marriages as invalid but merely inflicted canonical penance
on the parents or the married partners. The civil law here went beyond the view
of the Church in so far as it legally forbade marriages between Christians and
Jews and punished offenses against the law with the death penalty or with the
sanctions laid down for adultery.

While Roman law denied any juridical worth to marriage between slaves, the
Church regarded them as valid, but also had to have regard for the rights of the
slaves' master. Perhaps it must be attributed to ecclesiastical influence that a law
of Constantine I forbade the master to break up slave families in a partitioning of
his property. If the slaves did not belong to the same master, the Church made
the recognition of their marriage dependent on the agreement of both masters.
The real problem was that of marriage between slaves and free persons, which
the civil law forbade. The Church could and would recognize such marriages of
themselves, but demanded the emancipation of the slave before the contracting
of his marriage, thereby of course at the same time leaving it to the discretion
of the slaveowner.

The Church furthermore changed the meaning and extent of the rights which
the Roman *patria potestas* gave to the *paterfamilias* over the contracting of marriage by his children. It wanted this to be understood not so much as a right but
rather as concern for the child. Thereby it also gave the mother a voice and finally

allowed the child the right, if the occasion arose, to reject the spouse destined for him or her by the father.

Finally, the Church redefined the relations of the married couple to each other and hence gave to married life a much deeper basis than profane law had ever been able to do. This relationship was to be measured in principle against the model of the union which existed between Christ and his Church. Accordingly, its foundation was love, *caritas coniugalis,* which knew a thoroughly hierarchical ordering of marital and family life, but which abolished all legal inequality in a spiritual and religious community of life. This *caritas* took from the husband in his basically recognized role of leadership the harshness of the Roman *dominus* and *gubernator praepotens* in marriage; it made the *reverentia mulieris* a voluntarily assumed subordination of the wife, which was now based, no longer on the inequality of the sexes but on the position and role of the wife in the family life. Such equality of the partners bound them to equal fidelity and hence regarded failings against this as equally serious; in fact, the adultery of the man was even more serious, since he, as head of the family, was bound to exemplary behavior. When the Christian writers and pastors of this period in their preaching praise as virtues of the *wife pudicitia* and *castitas coniugalis,* display the figures of Susanna and Mary as models, and characterize care for husband and children as their foremost duty, this should be valued positively, especially with a glance at some features of contemporary social life, and no anti-emancipatory attitude of the Church should be seen, even if the reality more and more lagged behind the proclaimed ideal.

Likewise the relationship of parents and child experienced under the influence of Christianity a change, the effects of which were clearly perceivable in the society of late antiquity. Even the Church conceded to the paternal authority vis-à-vis the child the chief role, but it diminished its absolute character, since it esteemed it more as a duty than as a right, softened the *patria potestas* to *paterna pietas,* and especially sought to give the mother greater influence on the education of the child. There were ever more admonitions to parents to be understanding teachers and models in living for their children. The paternal authority found its limits when it sought to deprive the child of the free decision for the Christian faith or wanted to force the daughter to enter a convent out of material considerations. Parents who neglected their duty to support their children should be punished with ecclesiastical punishments, just as the children's duty of caring for their parents in need bound them too.

Just how much the Church's emphasis on the care of the child was justified is made clear from some rather melancholy features of the society of late antiquity. Augustine knew that parents with one to three children decided against any more because they did not wish to compel their offspring ever to beg. The Council of Elvira excluded for life from the ecclesiastical community "the mother or any other relative" who exposed their children to prostitution out of greed. The practice of the poorer classes of selling their children, and thus usually of depriving them of their freedom, was clearly condemned by the Church but maintained itself tenaciously: imperial laws as late as 391 and 451 still had to forbid it. The exposing of children, quite common in the ancient world, early encountered the strong condemnation of the Church, which saw in it a barbaric effect of the *patria potestas.* Ecclesiastical writers attacked the causes of this abuse, which must not be attributed chiefly to great economic need but to the utilitarian viewpoint of the head of the family, unwilling to share his means with a large group of children. They bewail even more the harsh lot of the exposed, who, in the event of escaping death, were mostly destined for the life of a slave, a catamite, or a prostitute. A law of Constantine I brought about in 331 the first limitation of the custom, in so far as it deprived the child's father of the right to demand the foundling back later from the foster parents, but the practice itself was still tolerated, and only under Valentinian I was it subjected to certain penalties under the influence of the Church. Basil, Ambrose, and Augustine make clear that it still occurred frequently in their days; Augustine reports that *virgines sacrae* occasionally gathered up such children and had them baptized. In 412 the Emperor Honorius once again had to emphasize that the exposure of children was deserving of punishment. The decrees of two Gallic synods required that a person should report the receiving of a foundling to his church, which saw to it that, after a period of ten days, he remained forever with the foster parents. Hence there was the individual Christian, who took an interest in such children, and the Church approved and encouraged this attitude of Christian *caritas.* Many Christian grave inscriptions make known what a good relationship had bound foster parents and *alumnus* or *threptos* in life. Under the Emperor Anastasius I (491–518) there were in the East orphanages (*orphanotropheia*) conducted by the Church; a law of the Emperor Justinian I was the first to speak of church homes which especially received and educated foundlings (*brephotropheia;*) hence they appeared at the latest in the second half of the fifth century. The State as such developed no initiative of its own in this matter: it left these, as in other cases also, to ecclesiastical *caritas.*

Likewise in the matter of the adoption of children, a practice influenced by Christian doctrine established itself. Whereas, according to Roman law, the possibility of adoption again was in the father's power, which however was usually conditioned by economic interests, now the wife also obtained the right of adoption, and acceptance as a child was seen primarily as concern for the orphaned child and was recommended by the Church as a work of mercy.

Just as did ancient medicine, so the Church too energetically attacked abortion, which in the late Roman Republic and throughout the imperial period had achieved a special expansion, and issued severe ecclesiastical penalties for it. Augustine saw facing him a theoretical difficulty, because one could not with certainty determine the moment when the fetus was infused with the soul, but his fundamental rejection of the ending of pregnancy at any time was unambiguous. Like Tertullian, he had, in conformity with the medical practice of the day permitted embryotomy by the physician in the event that this was the only possibility of saving the life of the mother. Ecclesiastical writers saw in it a double murder — the suicide of the aborting wife, whose deed often had fatal consequences for her, and the murder of the unborn child. The Church's synodal legislation was concerned from the early fourth century with the question and steadfastly defended the right to life of the unborn child. That the constant sharpening of the conscience of its members by the Church had a positive effect can scarcely be doubted.

Less numerous and productive are the statements in the sources on the situation of the illegitimate child, which was very unfavorable in Greece and Rome and could apparently be little influenced by the Church. Augustine regarded children born of incest Is unqualified to inherit. But Jerome was opposed to the illegitimate child's having to suffer for the sins of his parents.

The Social Sphere

The reform of the Empire, begun by the Emperor Diocletian and completed by Constantine I, had long-range consequences for the Empire's social structure. In the absolute monarchy established by them all political power was concentrated in the person of the Emperor, at whose disposal for exercising it was a tightly or-ganized central imperial administration, which in turn required a greatly enlarged bureaucracy in the provinces and an expanded control machinery. The power thus concentrated on the one side created new dependencies on the other. It be-came directly discernible in the effects of a tax system which had to produce the enormously high revenues demanded by a more than grandiose lifestyle of the court, the salaries of the officialdom, and the support of the army. The pitilessly collected taxes hit the small handicraft industries as well as the peasants and small tenants especially hard, above all since steadily rising prices placed an additional burden on them. In an effort to escape this compulsory situation, many small ten-ants surrendered themselves as *coloni,* with property and family, to the protection of the owner of *latifundia.* However, they only exchanged their former "freedom" at the cost of a still harsher dependence, for a law of Constantine I of 332 bound them and their descendants forever to the soil of their new master, and later laws left them the status of freemen only theoretically. Together with the State domains, a higher percentage of the arable land was concentrated in the hands of a numer-ically small upper class, which ruthlessly exploited its economic privileges in the fixing of prices and, on the basis of its power, was also in a position to ward off efforts at a stronger control by the provincial bureaucracy. The *decuriones* also, occupants of an originally honorable function in the administration of the cities, now had not only to bear the responsibility with their own property for the cities' tax yield, but were, together with their heirs, bound by law to this function. The workers in State factories — weaving and spinning, mints, arms, the great bak-eries of the capital — in so far as they were not already slaves, and the members of specified profession — retailers, smaller transport enterprises, and so forth — were subjected to still stronger compulsion. Their *collegia,* in which they were associated according to profession, were transformed into a sort of compulsory guild: any change to another calling, and in most cases even the change of the place of work, was forbidden to the members, and not even entry into the army was allowed. Hence in practice the possibility of social advance and social mo-bility was ended. Included in the compensation for work, as in the case of slaves, were food and lodging and minimal cash wages. The attempt to escape this sit-uation by flight was penalized by harsh punishments, which especially affected those who granted refuge to an escapee. The State tried to make up for the grow-ing decline in working class strength by sending those condemned by penal law and vagabonds to its factories. The series of laws quickly following one another shows, first, how very much the State was at this time overburdened by the eco-nomic problems, and also their content reveals a profoundly inhumane attitude toward the great mass of the socially unimportant. Thus the unsolved opposition between *potentiores* and *humiliores* became a powerful element in the process of the dissolution of the Western Empire. How did the Church react in this situation?

Magnates and Dependents

Neither the absolute monarchy of the Late Roman Empire nor its economic system nor the basic structures of contemporary society were questioned in principle by the Church of the time. True, it saw the harshness and injustices which were a part of the totality of these relationships and felt them as such, but considered them as the consequences of sin, which were to be endured. It neither envisaged nor sanctioned a change in the existing order, for example, by means of violence. This fundamental viewpoint becomes especially clear both in the theoretical evaluation of ancient slavery and in its attitude in practice to those subjected to it. According to Augustine, slavery certainly was opposed to the will of God, who had created man free, but injustice and force brought out inequality among men, just as sin made him as an individual the slave of his passions — which was even more severe. He believed this twofold form of slavery would continue to the end of time, "until wickedness ceases and all dominion and human power are empty and God is all in all." Whenever the Church Fathers spoke of the lot of the slaves, however sharply they criticized their inhuman treatment, they did not demand the ending of slavery by law or by revolution. They saw it partly as a necessary element of the contemporary economic order or as a form of property and hence, as a whole, respected the enactments of civil law applying to slaves. The Church even took slaves into its service and possession when they came to it through legacies and, if necessary, defended its right to own them.

At the same time, however, the Church stood up more decisively and comprehensively for the alleviation of the lot of slaves than any other institution or social group in the world. If master and slave were Christians, it could relax the relationship between them to a great extent by its preaching that no social differences carried any weight before God, since all the baptized are brothers, children of one heavenly Father, to whom emperor and beggar, slave and master pray. Hence in the liturgy there was no sequestering of slaves from the free, the marriage of slaves was regarded as valid, and a slave was admitted to offices in the Church if his master consented or even gave him freedom. Christian preaching ever more demanded that the treatment of the slave in a Christian home should correspond to this evaluation. Included here were not only clothing and food and the avoidance of every cruelty, even in the punishing of a guilty slave, but positive kindness and gentleness, and especially care for his religious welfare, instruction in the faith by the master of the house, and participation in the common prayer of the *familia*. It was due to the influence of the Church that from the fourth century the emancipation of slaves grew to a considerable extent. Since it regarded the possession of slaves as legitimate, it could only recommend their emancipation, but it did so energetically and purchased the freedom of slaves with its own means. However, freedom did not always seem to the slave a desirable goal since it did not automatically bring social security. Hence Chrysostom advised that, before emancipation, slaves be permitted to learn a craft which would assure them their livelihood. It is in this context that one must see the fact that some of their slaves expressed themselves against emancipation when Melania the Younger and her husband Pinian, after their turning to asceticism, freed several thousand slaves on their properties, and wanted to remain in the service of one of their relatives. Doubtless it must be attributed to this constant intervention of the Church for the voluntary emancipation of slaves that in 331 the Emperor Constantine I gave the Church the right of carrying out the emancipation by a special act within the church building with all the legal consequences which were united to the civil law procedure. In this *manumissio in ecclesia* the master presented his slave to the bishop; in the presence of the congregation the *libellus*, the charter of emancipation, was read aloud, the bishop was asked to ratify it, and then the *tabulae* were broken which contained the documents of the earlier act of purchase or the unfree status of the one to be freed. This officially recognized form of ecclesiastical emancipation established itself, it seems, over a rather long period of time in the Universal Church, and was finally adopted into the laws of the Burgundians and Visigoths which applied to the former Roman population.

A further possibility of assisting slaves was offered to the Church when the ancient right of asylum was extended to Christian churches, and thus slaves who fled to a church were under its special protection. But since the former master usually asserted his right of ownership, conflicts in such cases were not rare, and State laws sought to limit the right of asylum for slaves more precisely. A law of 398 seems generally to have ordered the restoration of slaves who had fled to the protection of the Church to their earlier position with Church cooperation. The right to sell the refugee slave to another master did not, of course, belong to the Church. The Synod of Orange in 441 decreed ecclesiastical penalties on one who, as a substitute for his own escaped slaves, forcibly took possession of other slaves of the Church.

The flight of the slave to a monastery was also the subject of a protracted quarrel between State and Church, since the former could not, for economic reasons, tolerate a mass flight of slaves to monasteries, but monasticism neither would nor could reject slaves when their motives for entry into the monastery proved to be unobjectionable. However, the Church had severely censured the sect of the Eustathians, who stirred up slaves against their masters, and Basil was willing to grant to a slave admission to the monastery only when his master compelled him to sin. Jerome and Cyril of Alexandria also stressed that the obedience of the slave to his master had its limits. The Emperors Arcadius and Honorius promised slaves freedom and the protection of the Church if they would abandon their Donatist masters, because they were said to be compelled there to rebaptism. Finally State and Church agreed at the Council of Chalcedon that slaves could become monks only with the express consent of their master, which had to be presented in writing.

Far less successful were the exertions of the Church to control the abuse of power of which the *potentes,* the high officials and the owners of great wealth, often the same group of persons, made themselves guilty in the late Empire. Augustine frankly said that many proprietors in North Africa had acquired their wealth through fraud and robbery. The proverb "You are what you have" was, he said, the slogan of these robbers, the oppressors of the peasants and small tenants, of those who forcibly took possession of others' goods and disavowed the goods entrusted to them. Many Christian senators in Africa did not concern themselves with the lot of their *coloni.* And Augustine had to admit: hardly anyone dared say it to their face because that was too dangerous. Salvian extended even to the bishops the charge that persons would keep silent about the violent deeds and exploitation by the ruling class or spoke of them only half-heartedly; the bishops, of course, did not so act out of cowardice but in order not to stir up the guilty to worse still, and so the poor, widows, and orphans had to keep on suffering. The few synodal decrees of the Church hardly altered anything in the total situation. The Council of Toledo of 400 wanted to cite before the episcopal court a magnate who pillaged a poor person or cleric and, in the event of his refusal, excommunicate him; the *Statuta ecclesiae antiqua* instructed the bishops to accept no gifts from those who oppress the poor.

Rich and Poor

Only a variation of the phenomenon of power and dependence in the society of late antiquity was the relationship of wealth and poverty, which the Church challenged to a decision in its crisis of these decades. Three features stood in the foreground in this matter: overwhelmingly unequal distribution of property and wealth, which made only the *potentes* also the *divites,* who wanted to see the disposal of their property unrestricted by any obligation toward the *pauperes;* the usually luxurious lifestyle of the proprietors, who placed no limits on themselves in the enjoyment of their wealth; the extensive lack of a purposeful concern of the State for a legal basis which would have ameliorated the situation of the economically and socially weak.

   Although the Fathers, with certain nuances in individual points, defended the opinion that the current distribution of property and wealth was not without sin, that is, that it came about through injustice, force and fraud, they accepted it as it was. They neither thought of a legal redistribution of property nor did they say a word about a change of this condition by force. Basically, they recognized private property and did not regard wealth in itself as sinful, even if their sharp words in the censuring of its abuse by its possessors could at times arouse the impression that they had championed the thesis that private property is theft. Quite the contrary: they stressed very definitely the social obligation of private property — and this is the really new element in the stand of Christianity on the social question of the day. Since God determined the goods of this world for the welfare of all, the present possessors are, in the last resort, only their stewards; private property is legitimate only when it is administered in the sense of its social bond. This means on the one hand to renounce every unchecked dependence on wealth and every injustice in acquisition and gain, every egoistic enjoyment, and on the other hand to use it for the alleviation of social hardships, to give to the poor what belongs to them. In the concrete question of what part of his property and income the individual must use for this, the views of the Fathers were not unanimous. Some, such as Basil and Jerome, certainly showed their sympathy for radical renunciation, as the Gospel recommends, but they knew that was only a counsel. There was agreement that "the superfluity" was intended to assure the necessities of life for the poor. Collectively, the expressions of the pastors and writers on the social bond of private property are so serious that one could not measure up to them by an occasional alms but only by a clear renunciation.

To the urgency of these demands corresponded the relentless condemnation of the behavior of some rich persons and of the methods and practices which had become common in economic and commercial life. The characterization of the well-off proprietors of Cappadocia by Basil is just as impressive as the pictures which Chrysostom sketched of the rich merchants or shipowners at Antioch. On the same level lay the blame for the inhuman believer who compelled his debtor to sell his children or even prevented his being buried until the debt was paid. The Church Fathers led a bitter struggle against every form of over-charging in business, against usury, as they regarded the request for interest on a loan. Their repetition lets us infer a continuing nonobservance, especially since the civil law in this matter in no way supported the Church's view.

The Church did not rest satisfied with appeals to the conscience of the faithful, but in the growing misery initiated a social welfare work which made its preaching credible. Especially in the communities of the larger cities the local *caritas* had to deal with an abundance of demands and duties. Chrysostom gave a vivid account of the conditions in Antioch. Of the already Christian majority of the population of the city, he says, 10 percent could be reckoned among the really wealthy, and equally great was the number of the poor "who possess nothing at all." On the list of poor of the community were some 3,000 names of widows and virgins, who received daily support. To them must be added "the captives, the sick and convalescing in the *xenodocheia,* the strangers, the cripples, the clergy, and still others, who appear by chance every day." The revenues of the Church of Antioch, however, were not greater than those of one rich man and of one man of the middle class combined, and ten times more was needed to be able really to deal with the poverty. Hence it was even more urgent to depend on the gifts of the faithful, whose right hands were, unfortunately, not too generous. It was true that now the congregations in a growing number were coming by means of legacies into the possession of landed property, but the revenues, from which the bishop had to support also his clergy and the churches, did not suffice at this time for all purposes. Augustine agitatedly told how the poor accosted him on his way to the church and asked from him a word in their behalf with the faithful, but he had to admit: "We give what we have, we give so far as we can, but we are not in a position to help according to need" (*Sermo* 61, 13). The same was even true for the Rome of Pope Leo I.

As the preeminent accomplishment of the *caritas* of this period may be reckoned the establishing of houses which saw to the care of the sick and the aiding of the poor, the orphans, and the *peregrini,* both because of their direct service to the needy of every sort and because of their signal importance for the *caritas* of the following centuries. The entirely unique justification of Christian social care, which was found ultimately in Christ, suffering need and a stranger had thus a uniquely religious foundation.

The first charitable institutions were probably inns for "foreigners" passing through; it had long been regarded as an *officium hospitalitatis* of each bishop to take care of them. They originated as real pilgrimage hostels on the occasion of the flourishing of this movement at the mostly more important pilgrimage centers, such as Jerusalem, the city of Menas, and Nola in Campania. The first known *xenodocheion,* which existed as early as 356 at Sebaste, accepted also the sick and lepers. This must have been generally the case in the smaller communities, which had only one house of this kind. The high estimation of hospitality by monasticism caused a *xenodocheion* to appear in every larger cenobitic monastery, and the receptiveness of Egyptian and Syrian monasticism for the needs of the poor and sick was early an object of praise. The drawing of monasticism into the Church's charitable work by Basil was to have an especially positive impact, since it not only provided new helping forces, but also brought about an enduring connection of monasticism with the Church's daily work. The most important undertaking in organizational planning and execution is connected with the name of Basil the Great, who had an institution built on the city borders of Caesarea, which included, besides a monastery and residences for the clergy, a hospice for pilgrims and a hospital for the poor, to which were attached all necessary services, physicians, nurses, workshops, and means of transportation. Its size even led to a gradual shifting of the center of the city around this new foundation, which in the fifth century was named for its founder Basilias. In Antioch also the community possessed a rather large hospital and a special hostel for strangers. In the Latin West the first works of *caritas* arose around the turn of the fifth century; the employing of the Greek names for them indicates the eastern model. Augustine likewise called the institution erected by him at Hippo a *xenodochium,* but remarked that the thing itself was known in Africa before the Greek loan-word.

The Church also included in its charitable care captives and prisoners. Visits by the bishops to prisons were already an established custom when in 409 the Emperor Honorius granted them control of the administration of penal institutes and of the treatment of captives.

At this time the State furnished the Church some support in its charitable work and granted privileges to individual establishments, and in the Early Byzantine period, of course, State supervision was assured. The fact remains that nothing of equal rank by the State could be set beside the comprehensive social concern of the Church of the fourth and fifth centuries, either in regard to its efficiency or its ethical and religious justification.

The Cultural Sphere

At the beginning of the fourth century Christianity represented only a minority in the society of late antiquity, the cultural life of which was still stamped by paganism in all areas. With the growing number of those Christians who, on the basis of their social provenance and position, had been formed by this culture, the Church was presented in an acute form with the question of what could be accepted or adapted from it from the Christian viewpoint and what was to be rejected. The answers which Christian writers gave to this question were very different, partly determined by their personal experience, partly depending on the significance which the individual attributed, negatively or positively, to a particular feature of this culture. The evaluations varied often in the course of time, as the trend toward dissolution became clearer in the cultural life of late antiquity and a Christianity that had become more self-conscious regarded as less serious the dangers threatening it from there.

The content of profane literature of antiquity was for the most part repudiated; the mythology that dominated it was rejected as immoral, and occasionally ridiculed, and the style of some authors was denounced as frivolous. But not quite every educational value was denied it. Gregory Nazianzen expressed himself positively: he thought that since, according to the Apostle Paul (2 Cor. 10:5), one should take all thought into the service of what is Christ's, the knowledge of profane literature could also lead to the strengthening of the faith. Ambrose saw that the works of pagan authors should be considered so that their errors could be refuted, but he attributed a proper value to some of their philosophers also. Jerome, on the contrary, usually expressed himself negatively, but he had to endure the charge by Rufinus that his facile repudiation of profane literature was opposed to his practice, since he constantly quoted its authors and in the monastery at Bethlehem read "his Virgil" and other pagan poets and historians with the young. Augustine himself indicated the development which his view in this question had gone through. His baptism was not, despite all the existential seriousness of his conversion, an absolute repudiation of everything that ancient culture had formerly meant to him, but the beginning of a critical process which only ended in his years as a bishop. Certainly, already at Cassiciacum, he gave up the *vanitas litteraria* of rhetoric and rejected the *curiositas,* the eagerness to know the new for its own sake, to which he had once succumbed. But ancient authors such as Cicero and Virgil still meant much to him; for his literary creations he retained the dialogue form and the stylistic laws of rhetoric, and his program of religious and philosophical studies was oriented to the old *artes liberales.* Augustine the pastor only completed the real break with ancient culture when in his day-to-day activity for souls he believed he experienced not only their insignificance for his work but even more he noticed their impeding effect on the final serious acceptance of the gospel by the faithful. Now his judgment on the formalism of rhetoric and the striving for oratorical elegance became coolly repudiating and his blaming of the immorality of this literature, whose effects he ever more encountered, became unrelenting. Corresponding to this was his almost sober outline of a properly defined course of education, which was conceived, it is true, primarily for the education of the clergy, but which he hardly would have presented differently for the Christian laity. According to the *De doctrina christiana,* the study of the Bible, based on the faith, is the *unum necessarium* for the spiritual work of the cleric; from the program of a profane education great importance belongs to the sciences, such as geography, history, natural science, and so forth, since they promote a better understanding of Scripture. A small circle, which possesses the compulsion and inclination for a *vita contemplativa* in the Christian understanding may pursue philosophical studies further. The final reason for Augustine's radical repudiation of profane culture is the knowledge, gained through personal experience, of the exclusive worth of the *summum bonum,* which more and more filled him with that deep skepticism in regard to everything that must be ascribed "to this world."

Augustine's theses certainly had their effects in the circles and relationships which he could directly influence. With all his distrust of the profane educational system of the day, still he, like the rest of the Fathers, did not require a properly

Christian school in which his program could have been realized. The children of Christians continued to go to the secular schools, the youth continued to attend the higher academies, at which for a long time yet the pagan teachers were in the majority, and they were still on familiar terms with pagan education. The Church hoped that the religious instruction in the family, as Basil and Chrysostom recommended it, would make it immune to the danger here threatening and that the gradually increasing number of Christian teachers in the schools would help to neutralize pagan influence in the framework of the instruction. Also lacking were all indications that the Church would have sought to gain at the State's expense influence on the form of the instructional program of the secular schools.

Thus it is not surprising that all important authors of the Church of this period made the formal influence of their profane education evident. Gregory Nazianzen could never hide his pride in his rhetorical training, Gregory of Nyssa was to a great degree dependent on it, Ambrose handled the literary genre of the *consolatio* in his funeral sermons just like a profane author, and the confrontation with his pagan opponent Symmachus over the Altar of Victory showed him to be quite equal to the latter in dialectics. Poets such as Gregory Nazianzen, Prudentius, and Paulinus of Nola bear comparison with the contemporary poetry, just as do Eusebius, Theodoret of Cyrrhus, Optatus of Mileve, or even Orosius with the profane historians. Christian epistolary literature had representatives in Basil, Jerome, and Augustine, who clearly left a Libanius and a Symmachus behind them. Certainly the superiority of the Christian literature of the Golden Age of the Fathers was based primarily on its content of ideas, on the freshness and power of conviction of its testimony, which knew that the future belonged to it, that in it was a new hope of awakening faith in a new-found meaning of human existence. Besides, the Latin authors could make use of a vocabulary which was at their disposal in Old Christian Latin and which gave a new life to the language of the West. In the Greek-speaking Church, it is true, it had not reached the point of forming a special Greek language, because the great writers here could make use of the standard classical tongue, which, if used flexibly, was understandable even by the audience of a Chrysostom and especially embraced the reading circle, the gaining of which was of ever greater importance to the Church. The total impact of this Christian literature on the society of the time would not have been possible without this recourse to the formal elements of the classical tradition.

In regard to a further sector of the cultural life of late antiquity the Church's attitude remained consistently implacable: that of the theater, the circus games, and the system of entertainment. The performance of the ancient tragedies had, from the Hellenistic age, been supplanted by mime and pantomime, the stage with cabaret and ballet now served for the relaxation of the people, the fights of gladiators and hunting of animals in the amphitheaters, chariot-racing in the circus of the big cities, on the numerous festivals of the year attracted thousands of often fanatically enthusiastic spectators. Chrysostom and Augustine complained strongly that on days of such entertainments the churches remained almost empty. The Church's criticism was directed against the waste of vast sums, which the arranging of the games required, but even more against the immorality which was propagated by the stage. To some degree the fight against gladiatorial combats was successful, since, because of their brutality and brutalizing effect, they were also objected to by pagans. As early as 325 Constantine I had had them forbidden in the eastern part of the Empire, but in the West, according to Augustine's testimony, they still enjoyed the greatest popularity until the Emperor Honorius definitively had them stopped here too at the beginning of the fifth century. At first the State did not attack the other forms, stage and circus, especially since a great part of the games was built into the official calendar of festivals. The ecclesiastical mission and preaching were, however, firmly convinced that here lay a substantial hindrance for the spreading and appreciation of Christian moral doctrine. In its opposition it went even to the extent of outlawing all professions which were in the service of the theater and of the contemporary entertainment industry. Not only prostitutes and pimps, but also actors of every sort, the organizers of the performances, gladiators and hunters in the pursuit of animals fell under the verdict. Augustine could appeal to ancient Roman tradition, which did not reckon the profession of actor among those socially recognized. Hence the performer had to give up his profession if he wanted to be admitted to baptism, and Communion was denied to Christians among them. The Emperors Gratian and Theodosius I supported the Church in so far as they wanted to remove Christian women from these professions.

Christian preachers of morals had to recognize that in this field a thorough-going success would be denied them unless they managed to eliminate the many profane feastdays with which the *ludi circenses* and *ludi scaenici* were connected or to neutralize their character, that is, to christianize the profane festive calendar and gradually replace it with a purely Christian one. The enormous difficulties of this project could not be mastered without the direct assistance of the Emperors. But the latter had to take into consideration the great popularity of the *ludi* of every sort with the masses, whose awareness of the pagan origin of such entertainment of the people was, moreover, very much missing. A series of feasts could be de-contaminated by dropping the names of the pagan gods and the sacrifices which had been connected with them, as was done ca. 357 by a decree of the Emperor Constantius II. The Church could hardly object to the feastdays on which the Emperor's or his ancestors' accession to the throne was commemorated, and hence in these cases the games continued. The designation of the Christian Sunday as a day of rest, ordered by Constantine I and later repeated, was a first step on the road to a christianized calendar of feasts. Then in 389 the Emperor Theodosius I in a decree published an arrangement of feastdays in which the Christian days of cele-bration already predominated over a series of neutral feasts, such as the birthdays of Emperors, harvest feasts, and so forth: all Sundays and the two weeks before and after Easter, Epiphany, and Christmas were here recognized by the State as Christian festival times, and the previous pagan feasts were no longer included in it. It was a further concession to the Church that the same Emperor also forbade the circus contests on Sundays, but, of course, only if the "Emperor's birthday" did not fall on a Sunday. And so only a half-success was on the whole gained by the Church here. The circus continued to maintain its fascination, especially in the East, at Constantinople, Antioch, and Thessalonica. Further progress could be expected only from a purely liturgical calendar of feasts.

If one should still ask, at the end of this presentation, what changes were accomplished in the society of late antiquity in the period between Nicaea and

Chalcedon from the aspect of Church history, the answer can be summarized roughly thus: the fundamental fact is the change in religious confession, by which this society moved from a pagan to a Christian majority. In this Christian majority two groups became socially relevant: the clergy, graded according to rank and sphere of function, and monasticism, which appeared as special states and exercised a powerful impact on society. Then, beside them were changing groups, which developed in the violent confrontations over the correct understanding of the content of the Christian faith, covering this whole period, and at times led to the formation of Christian sects. Out of this struggle over "orthodoxy" grew that serious hardening and establishing of religious intolerance, which marked this society as a whole and which is passed on as a legacy to the future. No group could allow the others the right to their own respective understanding of the faith; for the "orthodox," Arians, Donatists, Macedonians, and Monophysites, those belonging at the time to the other groups became heretics, whom people sought to combat with the aid of the State and also to curtail their civil rights. The victorious group was only more bitterly charged by the defeated with the flaw of erroneous belief, violence, and injustice.

This now Christian society did not aspire to alter anything in the basic organization of the State, and could alter very little in the economic and social structure. In some areas, such as that of the family, of the estimation of marriage and of the child, of the status of the slave, of the understanding of property, and of charitable concern, positive beginnings were created, at times with the modest support of the State. It is difficult to appraise the change in the moral conduct of this society. The moral preaching of the time leaves no doubt that here there was no radical modification. Only a minority, strong though it was, seems to have taken Christian ethics seriously in a genuine commitment. But the sources still indicate a change which did not call attention to itself very spectacularly: this was the gradual, quiet infiltration of Christian images, ideas, and subjects, which came from the world of the Bible and slowly altered daily speech; it was the becoming accustomed, still in progress, to Christian standards of value and ways of behaving, which preaching sought tirelessly to communicate. In some areas, not merely to be understood spatially, the Church was still in a missionary situation: the span of 125 years between Nicaea and Chalcedon was still the time of sowing rather than of the harvest.

Part Four

The Early Byzantine Church

Hans-Georg Beck

CHAPTER 53

The Henoticon and the Acacian Schism

The great ecclesiastical assembly at Chalcedon produced no peace, despite the exclamation of the Council Fathers: "We are agreed; there is only one faith!" On 31 October 451, without the assent of the Pope's legates, the Synod had issued that celebrated canon 28, which, following the precedent of the First Council of Constantinople, further consolidated the primacy of the "archsee" of Constantinople and thereby profoundly disturbed Rome — and, naturally, not only Rome. But it was also not to be expected that the dogmatic decisions of the Council would be readily accepted everywhere, and the fate of the Second Council of Ephesus of 449 had demonstrated that even imperial synods need not be unalterable. True, in their dogmatic decision the Fathers of Chalcedon had exerted themselves to praise Cyril of Alexandria, but they had made no effort to harmonize Cyril's famous formula *mia physis tou theou logou sesarkomene* with their own formula, *en duo physesi hen prosopon kai mia hypostasis.* Rather, with their definition they consolidated a conceptual development which was in advance of the contemporary state of the theological awareness of many bishops of the East and could only evoke the opposition of those to whom tradition was dearer than precision. It was not to be expected that the historically conscious Egyptians would submit to the renunciation of the Cyrillan theology parenthetically. Besides, the Synod had dared to depose the Patriarch Dioscorus, Cyril's successor, and to rehabilitate Theodoret of Cyrrhus, the *bête noire* of the Alexandrians.

In spite of a diplomatic letter of the Council Fathers to the Pope, especially in regard to canon 28, Leo the Great argued that the canon encroached upon the rights of Alexandria and Antioch and hence he tried to mobilize the eastern patriarchates. But in this he had no success: the two superior sees intended to enforce their claims without Rome's help and so the Pope had to address himself in his polemic chiefly to the Patriarch of Constantinople, Anatolius (451–58), who had to experience all its severity, whereas the Emperor was treated more considerately.

Because of all these questions of rank, the Pope neglected far too long to come out, officially and energetically, for Chalcedon's theological decisions. It was only on 21 March 453 that, under pressure from the Emperor, he could give a decision in their favor. And when, soon after, Anatolius gave his consent to a general letter, which expressed apologies and regrets, Leo had to regard this matter as settled — in any event he no longer returned to it with vigor. Of course, the loss of time could never be made up. If the recognition of the *Tome of Leo* at the Council had meant a climax of papal influence on the theology of the East, there now quickly followed a cooling of relations, from which the East-West connection would never recover. Above all, the old bond between Alexandria and Rome, which had made possible the conciliar politics at Ephesus, split. True, the Pope's last years did not witness the collapse of his work in the East, but after account had been taken of his authority at a critical moment, people now tried to get along without Rome.

The fate of Chalcedon was in principle decided in Egypt. Out of fear of the deposed Patriarch Dioscorus, the Egyptian bishops had refused to accept the *Tome of Leo.* Dioscorus was living in exile. Now the Orthodox had to concern themselves with selecting a successor to him who was qualified to pacify the enraged Egyptians, who already saw in their patriarch their recognized "national" leader. Thus a former intimate of Dioscorus, the Archpriest Proterius, was designated as his successor, without its being possible, however, to gain more than four bishops for him. This election resulted in a revolt of the people: the soldiers who were supposed to establish order were driven back and burned in the Sarapeion. Without new troops from Constantinople there was no hope of calm. Dioscorus died in 454, and in 457 he was followed by the Emperor Marcian, who had held Chalcedon very dear. Again there was rioting in Alexandria, and the leader of Dioscorus' adherents, the Priest Timothy the Cat, was ordained by the anti-Chalcedonians as their Patriarch on 16 March 457. The imperial governor immediately had him arrested, but the excitement among the people was so great that the measure had to be annulled. Nevertheless, the movement of revolt could no longer be checked, and a few days later the Orthodox Patriarch Proterius was murdered while he was officiating at Mass. Since the new Emperor Leo I (457–74) at first had to let go the reins in Egypt, Timothy the Cat was able to establish himself. He succeeded in filling the episcopal sees in the country with his followers, and a Synod at Alexandria excommunicated the Pope and the Patriarchs of Constantinople and Antioch. The Alexandrian Pope, conscious of his power, provoked schism, and all the complaints made against him in Constantinople could accomplish nothing against it. Only the punishment of the assassins of Proterius could be achieved. On the whole, the activities of Timothy the Cat probably had little to do with dogmatic questions. The censure against Rome, Constantinople, and Antioch was probably intended to avenge Chalcedon's refusal to take Cyril's formulas into consideration, but even more the deposition of Dioscorus, Timothy's predecessor. And the new position which Constantinople was now determined to assume in the Universal Church — a position which Alexandria had hitherto occupied in the East — was certainly also included. If the rest of the East came to terms with Chalcedon only partially, this was probably less a sign of genuine conviction than a certain display of weariness. Besides Egypt the chief centers of the opposition were the monastic circles in Palestine, to which the constant maneuverings of their Patriarch Juvenal, whose first concern at all ecclesiastical meetings was the independence of his patriarchate, supplied an occasion for discontent. The monks blamed him for betrayal of Cyril's theology. In the Empress Eudocia, widow of the Emperor Theodosius II, who lived and intrigued in Jerusalem, they found the necessary, even financial, support. It was due to her influence that soon there was no monastery in the vicinity of the Holy City which maintained loyalty to Juvenal. Under the leadership of a monk, Theodosius, they gave the Patriarch on his return the alternatives of repudiating Chalcedon or resigning. Juvenal fled, swarms of monks raged in Jerusalem, bishops were murdered, and vacant sees were everywhere filled with adherents of this Theodosius. Only military units, which engaged in a pitched battle with the monks, were able to relieve Jerusalem and restore quiet. The leaders of the monastic revolt fled, but Eudocia maintained her position.

The Emperor Leo I was a military man who held himself aloof from religious questions; he had quite enough to do to reach an understanding with his *Protector,* the powerful Aspar, and gave to Chalcedon only a part of that attention which his predecessor had devoted to it. Timothy the Cat thought he could demand of him

the revision of the decrees of Chalcedon by a new council. However, he had no
success with this. Nevertheless, the Emperor permitted an investigation to take
place, which he hoped would clarify how people stood in regard to recognizing
Timothy the Cat as legitimate Patriarch of Alexandria and whether the decrees of
Chalcedon should be maintained. The replies from most ecclesiastical provinces
of the Eastern Empire were unanimously against the recognition of Timothy, and
only one voice rejected the Council. The answer of those provinces whose letters
are no longer extant would be interesting. Perhaps they were more negative than
positive in regard to the Council. In any event, Leo, probably under pressure from
Aspar, long maintained a delaying policy, although the Pope did all he could to induce him to take steps against Timothy. It was only in 460 that the Emperor sent the
Alexandrian into exile in Paphlagonia and finally to the Crimea. Timothy Salofaciol
became Patriarch, but he did not succeed in restoring ecclesiastical unity in Egypt.

When the Emperor Leo I died in 474, the Isaurian Zeno, whom Leo had finally played off against the overmighty Aspar, had himself proclaimed Augustus
by the Empress Ariadne and their minor-aged son, Leo II. He probably had even
less interest in theology than his predecessor, but already, as *Magister Militum per
Orientem,* he had been under the influence of the personality of a priest, Peter the
Fuller, who, relying on the power of the *Magister,* had forced his election by a synod
as Patriarch of Antioch, contrary, of course, to all the canonical rules. The Emperor
Leo soon had him arrested and deported to Egypt, but Peter succeeded in fleeing
to Constantinople, and, since he promised to keep quiet, he was entrusted to the
rigidly orthodox Acemetae monks in the neighborhood of Constantinople. Zeno,
even as Emperor half-barbarian, did not know how to make himself popular. As
early as 475 he had to give way before a conspiracy, and Basiliscus, a brother of
Zeno's mother-in-law, the Empress Verina, tried to seize the throne — with no
more luck than Zeno. He believed he could dismiss Verina and thereby isolated
himself from both factions. Perhaps he was of the opinion that he could form a
strong following if he met the anti-Chalcedonians halfway. Without consulting a
synod, he issued an *Encyclion,* in which he decreed that people should be satisfied
with the Nicene Creed and its confirmation by the First Council of Constantinople
and that of Ephesus. The *Tome of Leo* and the *Horos* of Chalcedon were anathematized, and anyone who did not agree with this anathema should, if he were
a cleric, be deposed, and, if he were a monk or lay person, be banished. The
Encyclion was in no sense an innovation in matters of faith or even a Monophysite
document. The brief explanations of the faith which it offers are orthodox, but only
on the status of the period before the Council of Chalcedon: the tactic of backing
down in terminology. The decree made it possible for Timothy the Cat to return
to Egypt. He took the route via Constantinople, where the new Patriarch Acacius
gave him the cold shoulder, and a majority of the monks would have nothing to do
with him. On the other hand, he participated at Ephesus in a synod of the province
of Asia: this must have been a satisfaction for him, because here Constantinople's
detested patriarchal rights over the province were denied. Then he celebrated a
triumphal entry into Alexandria, after Timothy Salofaciol had tamely withdrawn
to a monastery. For the rest, Timothy the Cat adopted a moderate attitude and
did not push his triumph to extremes. Peter the Fuller returned to Antioch and
for some time again occupied "his" see. The Patriarch of Jerusalem also signed

the *Encyclion*. The opposition to it was concentrated at Constantinople, where the Patriarch Acacius (471–89) mobilized clergy and people. Success was quick in coming, because the position of Basiliscus became even more difficult. In his need he now had the *Encyclion* followed by an *Antiencyclion,* which annulled the former *pro forma* and ordered that every bishop should keep his place and that the drama of Nestorius and Eutyches must be definitely closed. With this the chaos was complete. In September 476 Zeno was able to march back into Constantinople, and Basiliscus went into exile. Likewise, the Fuller and the refractory Archbishop of Ephesus had to leave their sees, and Timothy the Cat was supposed to be deported a second time, but finally the old man was allowed to die in peace in June 477. His adherents acted quickly and chose as his successor his old friend, Peter Mongus, who, following the proved models, at once disappeared to a hiding place and from there ruled his flock, while Timothy Salofaciol was recalled by the authorities and ruled officially as Patriarch of the Church of the Empire. Whoever else had signed the *Encyclion* hastened to ask pardon and to accept the Council of Chalcedon. Everything seemed again in order, but anyone who watched more closely could hardly find this rapid pacification reassuring. Other means had to be thought of to give peace to the Church. The Patriarch Acacius of Constantinople took this task upon himself.

Acacius was certainly not a fiery adherent of the formulations of Chalcedon. But he knew that the privileges of his see depended on the recognition of this Synod; he was by no means a "Monophysite"; and also he saw clearly that the inextricable confusion in the Church of the East could not be corrected by formulas, because it had not originated in formulas, but that it was a question of dealing with personalities, and in this there was little promise of success by going too far into the past in examining such persons. It was important to rebuild a front of good will, to let *oikonomia* rule, and not to make any *theologumenon* into a shibboleth. It was especially urgent to understand that, despite Rome, the theological development could not be brought to a halt even with Chalcedon, any more than it had stopped with earlier synods. Experience had taught that nothing was gained in a situation where two bishops contradicted each other to choose a third — leading only to a third faction — that one must rather balance the two candidates at the favorable moment and test their good will — and do so *hic et nunc.* This was the policy of Acacius — a policy, depending on one's point of view, of cunning or of a desperate good will.

In 481–82 there came to Constantinople at the order of the Patriarch of Alexandria, Timothy Salofaciol, the monk John Talaia, with the request that, after the Patriarch's death, a successor be chosen who was an adherent of Chalcedon but also a member of the Egyptian clergy. The Emperor was in agreement, but he made John Talaia take an oath in the presence of the Patriarch and the Senate that, under no circumstances, would he, Talaia, accept the episcopal office. The Emperor was moved to this step because of Talaia's connection with the Isaurian Illus, in whose regard Zeno had reason to entertain suspicions. If Talaia became Patriarch of Alexandria, Illus would find in refractory Egypt, so the Emperor believed, an all too powerful partisan. Salofaciol died in February 482 and Talaia promptly became guilty of perjury by letting himself be elected as his successor. Rome was notified of the allegedly unanimous election, and the Pope was asked to confirm it. The furious Emperor Zeno had Talaia deposed, and since at the same time Egyptian monks in Constantinople vouched for the person of the Patriarch Peter Mongus, the Patriarch Acacius undertook the first attempt for a solution of the Egyptian question: Peter should be recognized in so far as he gave guarantees which were incorporated into an imperial edict, the manuscript of which clearly points to Acacius as its author. The *Edikton Zenonos* stressed first of all the inviolability of the decisions of Nicaea, Constantinople, and Ephesus. New was the canonical recognition of the anathemas of Cyril of Alexandria. It was modified by the acceptance of the Formula of Union of 433. There was no mention of Cyril's *mia physis* formula and its disavowal by Chalcedon was not annulled. Whoever did not accept this faith was punished with anathema, as was anyone who now or previously thought otherwise, whether "at Chalcedon" or at another synod. Accordingly, the edict formally glided over the Synod of Chalcedon, but it was no more rejected than was the *Tome of Leo*. It was not the Council that was rejected, but apparently an anti-Cyrillan interpretation of its decrees, whereas excessive "Cyrillanism" had been repudiated by the Formula of Union of 433 and the disregard of the *mia physis* formula. The edict thereby anticipated to a certain extent an interpretation of the Chalcedonian decrees which did not prevail in Orthodoxy until the sixth century, but then for ever. Naturally the die-hards could only view the *glissando* over Chalcedon as a treachery to the Synod, just as the die-hard "Monophysites" felt the failure to condemn this same Synod. Acacius, the composer of the edict, which has entered history under the title of the *Henoticon,* could nevertheless hope to establish peace on the basis of this document. He succeeded in gaining Peter Mongus for the *Henoticon* and received him into the communion of the Church. Of course, the monks who supported John Talaia upbraided him, as before, as a heretic. Many renounced communion with him; he agreed to a few concessions which satisfied no one, and it required all his shrewdness to keep the excesses within bounds. At Antioch the Patriarch Calandion refused to sign the *Henoticon,* but he was unwise enough to conspire with the faction of Illus against the Emperor and hence had to go into exile in 484. Once again Peter the Fuller found the opportunity to occupy the coveted See of Antioch. He signed the *Henoticon,* but Acacius did not for that reason see the possibility of accepting ecclesiastical communion with this scintillating personality. Jerusalem made no difficulties. On the other hand, it was ominous that Rome showed no appreciation for the personality politics of Acacius. Unfortunately the Emperor had failed to publish the *Henoticon* at Rome, probably because he saw in the document no new regulation but only an *explicatio fidei.* In any case, people at Rome were apparently pleased with it, for it presented no serious dogmatic confrontation but rested entirely on questions of law and discipline, which were essentially more congenial to the Roman mentality. The Emperor himself announced to Pope Simplicius the recognition of Peter Mongus. The Pope protested to the Emperor and exhorted Acacius to have the Emperor change his mind. Acacius shrewdly cloaked himself in silence. In 483 Felix II became Pope, and this vigorous defender of Roman interests did not let himself be put off. He wrote to Emperor and Patriarch and again represented the view that Peter Mongus was a condemned heretic. The fact that Peter had professed the orthodox creed of the *Henoticon* was not mentioned at all, nor was the perjury of Talaia. The last-named, meanwhile, had arrived in Rome and filed an official complaint against Acacius. In these circumstances the Pope decided on the extraordinary step, contrary to the tradition that a Patriarch could be condemned only by an imperial synod, of summoning Acacius before his court, spurred on by a letter from the Acemetae monks of Constantinople, who had at that time claimed a monopoly of Orthodoxy and now accused the Pope of being too remiss in the defense of the true faith. His legates received instructions first to get into contact with precisely these Acemetae and obtain advice from them. As would happen all too often later, Byzantine skill succeeded in bringing the papal legates to the right way "with pastry and the lash," as E. Schwartz expressed it. Soon after their arrival in Constantinople, they were seen going solemnly, with Acacius and the envoys of Mongus, through Constantinople to the church. They kept themselves aloof from the Acemetae and promised the Patriarch to push forward at Rome the case of Mongus against Talaia. After their return, Pope Felix had the unfortunate legates deposed by a synod. Peter Mongus was again refused communion as a heretic, and Acacius was declared deserving of the most severe penalties. Soon after, the Pope took the further step of formally excommunicating the Patriarch of Constantinople. The reasons were the Patriarch's interference in the affairs of the other Eastern Churches — hence, fundamentally, the exercising of his primatial rights on the basis of canon 28 of Chalcedon — and his measures taken by order of the Emperor, but above all his communion with Mongus. Nothing was said about his faith. By his not having obeyed the Pope's summons he had declared his own guilt. This was in 484 and, since Acacius did not submit, the so-called Acacian Schism was a *fait accompli* — a schism in which questions of faith were consciously evaded by both sides, and questions of personalities were tormented to the limits of the impossible. For this reason Acacius probably thought he should not reply, because the Pope had not at all looked into the explanations by the Emperor Zeno of Acacius' personal politics. What would he have been able to add to what had been said? The fact that Felix continued to uphold John Talaia gave little hope of the possibility of an agreement.

Acacius died in 489, and his policy seemed to crumble. His successor, Fravitas, was able, apparently under pressure from the Acemetae, to induce the Emperor to resume negotiations with Rome. However, the memory of Acacius was supposed to be spared, and the communion with Mongus to be maintained. Hence, Fravitas was evidently under the incorrect impression that at stake was the recognition of Orthodoxy and not of primatial rights. Pope Felix undeceived him and insisted on the deletion of the names of Acacius and Mongus from the diptychs. Fravitas died in 490 without having seen the Pope's reply. His successor was Euphemius, a Syrian, the man of the Acemetae — or so it has been assumed — but in any event a strict Chalcedonian. On his own authority he removed Peter Mongus from the diptychs and in a letter to the Pope acknowledged the Synod of Chalcedon without reservations. He was unwilling only to condemn Acacius, and in such a champion of Chalcedonian Orthodoxy this fact was a powerful testimony in favor of Acacius. It also prevents one from seeing in Euphemius an unscrupulous creature of the Acemetae, who roundly hated Acacius. Evidently Euphemius saw no Christian necessity to condemn Acacius after his death, as Rome demanded, even though the deceased Patriarch's policy may have been questionable to him also. Pope Felix remained obstinate and thereby prolonged the schism for some twenty years unnecessarily. The Emperor Zeno died in 491. The new Emperor Anastasius I (491–518) had been a high court functionary, not inexperienced in ecclesiastical matters and at one time even a candidate for the patriarchal See of Antioch. In contrast to the last years of his predecessor, he was determined not to stake the politically undeniable successes of the *Henoticon* in the East and not to sacrifice them even to a Pope who, in his eyes, living under the protection of an Ostrogoth outside the actual sphere of power of his Empire, was pursuing a policy which did not take into consideration the difficult circumstances of the Eastern Churches and the idea of imperial unity. But at Rome Pope Gelasius I (492–96) unflinchingly continued the policy of his predecessor; Euphemius did not receive the least support, and with each day it became clearer that, for Rome, not the question of Chalcedon but that of the primatial position of Constantinople represented the questionable heart of the matter. Even though the Patriarch informed the Pope that the condemnation of Acacius would inevitably lead to a revolt of the "demes," that is, the so-called circus factions, Gelasius persisted in his demand, and, even when the Emperor Anastasius sought to put pressure on him by means of King Theodoric, this was of no avail, probably because the King had at that time no interest in attaching the Pope to Constantinople.

In 495 Euphemius was succeeded as Patriarch of Constantinople by Macedonius (495–511), whom the Emperor invested only after he had signed the *Henoticon*. At Rome the intransigent Gelasius was followed by Pope Anastasius II (496–98), who apparently exerted himself to prepare for an end to the schism by a judicious policy. But he died in 498, and hence his plans could not mature. In addition, there now broke out in Rome the so-called Laurentian Schism, which made any eastern policy impossible until 502.

If the opposition at Rome to the *Henoticon,* or, more precisely, to Acacius, was thus impeded, the vacillation of Acacius' successors in the East strengthened the opposition to the *Henoticon,* which proceeded from theologians, to whom, it is true, the label of Monophysites can be simply attributed, but who energetically rejected the Synod of Chalcedon and saw in the *Henoticon* an all too compliant document. For them Cyril's theology was the starting point and the goal of Christological terminology: they rejected its explanation by Chalcedon. The most important men of this faction were Xenaia (Philoxenus) of Mabbug (Hierapolis) and Severus of Antioch.

Already as a teacher at the school of Edessa, Xenaia had bitterly attacked the theology of the old Antiochene School, which for him represented nothing but pure Nestorianism. Peter the Fuller promoted him to the episcopal see of Mabbug and here he developed in the Syriac language, with which he alone was familiar, an active literary activity not only against the Council of Chalcedon, but also against the old Antiochenes, Theodore of Mopsuestia, Theodoret of Cyrrhus, and Ibas of Edessa. He even sought to explain the "True" faith to the Emperor and for this purpose came to Constantinople, where, of course, Macedonius did not receive him, and so he soon angrily departed. Severus, a Greek from Pisidia, had considerably more success in the capital. He had first studied law and then was gained for the monastic life at Maiuma near Gaza. He employed the time in the monastery not only for the exercises of the ascetical life but also for a deeper study of all theology. Thus Severus became an opponent of the Synod of Chalcedon, whom the Chalcedonians could counteract only with difficulty. What led him to Constantinople was, first, the conflict with a certain Nephalius, who had originally belonged to his own faction but now vehemently defended the interests of the Chalcedonians and slandered the monastic groups around Severus to the Patriarch Elias of Jerusalem to such a degree that Elias had them driven out of their monasteries. Accompanied by crowds of monks, Severus traveled as their counsel to the Emperor, who received him with the greatest honor. Even when his case had been decided, he remained in the city from 508 to 511, and, in word and writing, developed a mighty propaganda against Chalcedon and, implicitly, also against the *Henoticon*. He gathered the opponents of the Patriarch Macedonius around himself, and people did not hesitate to spread falsehoods in order to compromise the Patriarch and to bring about his ruin. The shibboleth of Severus' cause became the so-called "Theopaschite Trisagion," that is, the *Hagios ho theos, hagios ischyros, hagios athanatos,* to which had been appended *ho staurotheis di'hemas* — hence a formula, which meant nothing more, if the *Trisagion* itself was understood Christologically and not in a Trinitarian sense, which was possible both historically and formally, but which could not but lead to misunderstandings if it was employed as a substitute for the controversial *mia physis tou theou Logou sesarkomene.* Macedonius was sacrificed by the Emperor because of all the difficulties caused him and the calumnies alleged against him, and replaced by Timothy (511–18), who could not really please any faction. The Monophysites wanted Severus in his place; the Alexandrians demanded of him an anathema against Chalcedon and the *Tome of Leo;* in Syria Xenaia continued to agitate and procured the deposition of the Patriarch of Antioch, Flavian, who had tried to champion the *Henoticon* in an orthodox manner. Severus was elected to replace him in 512, and he thoroughly exploited his new position of power to destroy all further opposition to his own *theologumena.* He solemnly declared, of course, that he accepted the *Henoticon,* but soon interpreted it in a way that could leave no doubt about his hostility to the Synod of Chalcedon. The Patriarch of Jerusalem, Elias, also fell victim to Severus. His successor, John, was ready to make any concession to Severus, but the great superiors of the lauras and cenobiarchs, Sabas and Theodosius, thwarted him, and, flanked by the two monastic superiors, he was compelled solemnly to condemn not only Nestorius and Eutyches but now Severus also. In the capital also an outspoken pro-Chalcedon opposition was constituted: it collected the adherents of the deposed Macedonius and even found powerful supporters in the imperial family. When in November 512 a procession of Severans once again marched through the streets with the "Theopaschite Trisagion," the opposition attacked, a revolt erupted, the statues of the Emperor were thrown down, and the rioters entrenched themselves in the *Forum Constantini.* Again the Emperor succeeded in restoring calm by prudent conduct, but now the opposition spread dangerously to the province. A Gothic officer in the imperial service, Vitalian, exploited the dissatisfaction of the imperial *foederati* in the Balkan Peninsula and marched on Constantinople. To acquire friends in the capital, he made use of pro-Chalcedon catchwords. At first the Emperor thought he could overcome the danger by proceeding tactically. When this did not succeed, he saw himself compelled to appoint Vitalian as *Magister Militum Per Thraciam* and to promise to invite the Pope to a council at Herachea, at which the schism should

be healed. A corresponding *Sacra* left for Rome. Pope Hormisdas, who had succeeded Symmachus in 514, took his time, evidently in order to consult Theodoric.
And so the date of the council, set for 1 July 515, passed. In the meantime Vitalian
appeared again before the walls of Constantinople. This time he was annihilated
by the imperial troops and so the council, in which no one else had testified to a
special interest, lost its *raison d'être* for the Emperor. The Pope twice sent legates,
it is true, but they had to turn back without success. And so the Acacian Schism
continued until the death of the Emperor Anastasius in April 518.

If one looks back to the years since 482, the period has a unique important
turning point in the pontificate of Pope Anastasius II. At that time appeared the
hope and the possibility of again achieving unity on the basis of an orthodox interpretation of the *Henoticon,* to which Acacius had always held. The death of
the Pope wrecked the hopes. Neither his predecessors nor his successors took
into account the difficulty of the situation in the East. They saw their obedience in
the Vicariate of Thessalonica imperiled; they did not know how to acquiesce in
a linking of the conciliar definition of Chalcedon with the notorious canon 28, although the latter had brought scarcely anything new in respect to the First Council
of Constantinople, and they built their policy on the only apparently stable foundation of Ostrogothic rule in Italy. The Popes failed to note that Constantinople and
its Patriarch had to remain victorious, precisely because they appeared, vis-à-vis
the Emperor, in an independence which they owed solely to the Ostrogoth and
Arian Theodoric. The *Henoticon* united the Eastern Churches in the face of Rome,
and Alexandria was no longer a point of departure for Rome. The first years of the
next imperial dynasty only seemingly justified the papal policy. John II and Vigilius
would soon have to pay for the policy of a Felix and a Gelasius.

CHAPTER 54

Justintan's Zigzag Course:
The Origenist Troubles

No one could maintain that the Union of 519, which Justinian concocted with the
Pope which gave to the papacy his unqualified support for the absolute primacy
of the Roman Patriarch, among other things, was a complete success. But despite all the severity of the antiheretical legislation, the refractory Monophysites
and opponents of Chalcedon never fully felt it. Justinian, who was certainly in no
way connected with Manichaeans, Novatians, and Montanists, was probably of
the opinion that he could come to terms theologically with the moderate Monophysites, especially these who followed Severus. In regard to them, it was also

not a question of any dwindling minority but of considerable proportions of the population of whole imperial provinces. Furthermore, now the Empress Theodora self-assuredly moved into the foreground. At the period of her roving life, she had apparently found Christian understanding only from Monophysite bishops, who were not rarely at loggerheads with the established society, and now, as Empress, she was prepared to forget this fact for their sake. Soon after he had begun his reign as sole Emperor, Justinian had recalled Monophysite monks and bishops from their exile, and in the summer of 531 he invited six of them to Constantinople. They guarded themselves against a surprise by imperial theologians by means of a forestalling dogmatic declaration and then came to the city, where, soon after the Nika Riot, following rather lengthy preliminary negotiations, a religious discussion was staged, the so-called *Collatio cum Severianis.* The outcome was jejune: the Severans acknowledged that Theodoret and Ibas of Edessa had rightly been rehabilitated by the Fathers of Chalcedon, and one bishop even let himself be induced to recognize Chalcedon. But that was all. The chief objection of the Monophysites against the decrees of Chalcedon was obviously the danger of a Nestorian interpretation of them, and this objection seems to have made a last-ing impression on the Emperor, who participated only indirectly in the *Collatio,* and motivated him to undertake something in return. In any event, the Mono-physites at first had a considerable breathing-space, and Justinian was ready to oblige them further. He published dogmatic letters to the people of Constantino-ple and the cities of Asia and to the Patriarch of Constantinople, Epiphanius, and his synod, which once again represented a remarkable gliding over the decrees of Chalcedon. Instead, the Theopaschite Formula was now expressly accepted, which had deeply interested the Emperor since 520. It goes without saying that the Acemetae monks were not pleased and, in keeping with their tradition, at once mounted a sharp attack against it, apparently without being clearly aware that the days of the Emperor Anastasius were past. They were said to have then gone so far in their "Nestorian" interpretation of Chalcedon that they even refused to Mary the title of *Theotokos,* which probably means no more than that the Acemetae did not want the *communicatio idiomatum* to be regarded as the *ultima ratio* of Christology. In keeping with their custom, they complained to the Pope. But Hormisdas was long since dead, and an imperial edict followed in their steps. Pope John II bowed to the imperial pressure and condemned the Acemetae on 23 December 534 and in so doing swallowed the Theopaschite Formula, which Hormisdas had loathed; in fact, in the letter to Emperor and Senate referring to this he even censured one of Cyril's Anathemas, in which the formula had been anticipated by way of suggestion.

Now, at the Emperor's invitation, even Severus came to Constantinople and found lodging in the palace, where he remained until March 536. And with Severus there came to Constantinople, as they had already come on their own initiative under Anastasius, all the monks possible, openly and secretly, most of them living on the hospitality of the Empress Theodora and behaving in Constantinople as though it was the metropolis of the opponents of Chalcedon. When in 535 the patriarchal see became vacant, the Emperor nominated a certain Anthimus, who had previously been Bishop of Trebizond but had given up that see in order to live at Constantinople as an ascetic. Now he also appeared from one of Theodora's palaces, which aroused the suspicion that it had been she who had made him acceptable to the Emperor as a candidate. Apparently nothing could be objected against his orthodoxy; but, having become Patriarch, he accepted the communion of Severus and sent his announcement of enthronement not only to the bellicose Orthodox Patriarch Ephrem of Antioch but also to his Monophysite colleague in Alexandria. The total situation undoubtedly recalled that under the *Henoticon,* and the question may be raised whether it was not precisely toward this situation that Justinian was purposely steering.

The turning point came surprisingly fast, not indeed as the result of an organizational development, but, as it were, *ex machina.* For the second time since Justinian was in power, a Pope came to Constantinople in the spring of 536, Agapitus I, successor of John II. He came as envoy of the Ostrogothic King Theodahad. For, in the meantime, Justinian, using the assassination of Amalasuntha, daughter of Theodoric the Great, as his reason, had decided to roll back Ostrogothic rule in Italy from the south upward: Belisarius had already landed in Sicily. Reluctantly the Pope undertook the King's errand to induce the Emperor to withdraw. The Pope's mission had no political success. But Agapitus did not make his journey only as a royal envoy. Informed from all sides in regard to the remarkable proceedings in Constantinople, he had decided to utilize his stay in the capital to affirm his primatial rights, which indeed Justinian had frequently solemnly averred that he highly esteemed. From the very start Agapitus refused his communion to the Patriarch Anthimus, formally on the far-fetched pretext that, as a transfer from Trebizond, he could not be a valid Bishop of Constantinople, but de facto probably because he suspected him of Monophysitism. Justinian at once abandoned the submissive Anthimus, who disappeared to where he had come from, probably into one of Theodora's hiding places. Menas, from Alexandria, became the new Patriarch and was ordained by the Pope after he had signed an expanded *Formula Hormisdae.* A synod should decide the future fate of Anthimus: at least, such was Agapitus' plan. But he died at Constantinople on 22 April 536 before it could be realized. Nevertheless, the Emperor also fulfilled this wish of the Pope and on 2 May of that year the Synod met under the presidency of Menas and with the participation of a whole group of Latin bishops and Roman clerics who had come with the Pope, at their head the papal Deacon Pelagius, the future Pope. Antioch and Jerusalem were represented by *apocrisiarii* and delegations. The formal charges against Anthimus were lodged by abbots from Constantinople. Since Anthimus did not appear, even though he had been summoned three times, and no one defended him, he was condemned *in absentia* and degraded. The Synod could have come to an end, but monks from Palestine also demanded the condemnation of Severus. Menas hesitated, but Justinian gave leave and so Severus also, together with his adherents, was anathematized. Hence the policy of Pope Agapitus bore fruit even after his death. The new *Henoticon* movement had ended.

What induced Justinian to this change of course is difficult to determine. It is certain that, for him, the Pope was always theoretically the highest court of the faith, but in practice the Emperor knew how to manipulate this court. It must not be overlooked that, after all, all his exertions to win back the Monophysites were without any particular success — even the Theopaschite Formula could not satisfy them. Perhaps the Emperor was content to leave the counteraction, which had to affect Theodora also, to the Pope, who was glad to undertake it. But presumably the situation in Italy also played a not unimportant role. We do not know how actively or carelessly Agapitus had represented the concerns of his King Theodahad. In any event, Belisarius was on the way to Rome, and perhaps the Pope was able to convince the Emperor how very much it would aid Belisarius' campaign, if, as representative of a blameless imperial Orthodoxy, he could confront the Ostrogoths, those heretics! It must not be excluded that at the time Italy was more important to Justinian than the recalcitrant Monophysites of the East. The success of Belisarius should not be jeopardized by an affront to the Roman Pope and his Catholic obedience in Italy.

After he had once made up his mind, Justinian drew the reins tight. Severus and the Severans were expelled from the capital, and Severus went again to Egypt as a refugee. Theodora did what she could to thwart these measures, but now her activity was solely defensive, no longer offensive. Pelagius, Agapitus' deacon, remained at Constantinople as papal *apocrisiarius* and seems to have played an important role as the Emperor's adviser. The Patriarch Ephrem of Antioch, a former general, occupied himself with the forcible conversion of Syria to Orthodoxy. In Egypt Monophysitism was already so much at home that it had split into factions, especially into that of the moderate Severans and that of the "Phantasiasts," the adherents of Julian of Halicarnassus, who saw in Christ's body an *aphtharton,* incorruptible being (Aphthartodocetists). The Patriarch Theodosius, a friend of Severus, had become Patriarch of Alexandria in 535 at Theodora's instigation, but he had had the greatest difficulties in establishing himself in opposition to the Julianists' man, Gaias. Now in 537 Theodosius was summoned to Constantinople; since he was unable to make up his mind to sign the *horos* of Chalcedon, he had to go into exile. After some time Theodora managed to have him come to Constantinople, where he enjoyed her protection and could do everything to govern his Egyptian Church from a distance. But, using his plenitude of power, the Emperor now named a certain Paul as Patriarch of Alexandria and supplied him with full authority, which corresponded to that of an imperial governor. Still, what the Emperor's theology had been unable to achieve, so also his policy of force could not do.

Precisely around this time the repertory of *theologumena* on which people could become alienated increased unnecessarily, but now concerning a new point which had been regarded as long dead — Origenism. After the first Origenist controversy around the turn of the fifth century, there had been silence in regard to the doctrine of the great Alexandrian. Here and there someone took up his pen to refute him, but the Christological controversy troubled spirits to such a degree that there remained no more room for the esoteric questions which had preoccupied Origen. In monastic circles, however, Origen, now as before, could not but exercise a mysterious power of attraction, to which Evagrius had already succumbed. And when the confrontation gradually hardened again in the first half of the sixth century, the difficulty seems to have been the same as it was a century and a half earlier: an extreme spiritualization of the spiritual life, seized upon by the *raptus* of the ascent to God in order to lose itself in him even to the loss of identity, in order to find again in him all that had fallen in one final transfiguration.

The starting point and center of the new movement was Palestine. Here, since the second half of the fifth century, monasticism in both its cenobitic as well as in its anchoretic (*laura*) form had known vast progress. One of the most important foundations was the *laura* of the monk Sabas from Cappadocia (d. 532), which was founded in 483 — Mar Saba. In 494 Sabas became Archimandrite of all the anchorites of Palestine, that is, representative of the Patriarch for these monastic groups. He was a great organizer, an eager builder, and a loyal champion of a problem-free Orthodoxy, but not the man who would be able, on the basis of his education, to evoke an understanding for Origenist currents. This tendency was present also among his monks, and, because Sabas was as he was, he faced opposition. Finally there occurred the exodus of the "cranks," of those dissatisfied with him, who ca. 507 gathered in a new foundation, the "New Laura." Their leader was a certain Nonnus. After some time, Sabas succeeded in getting the New Laura also under his control to some degree and in imposing his abbots on it. One of these abbots, Agapitus, finally expelled the strict Origenists from the new foundation. Only after his death in 519 did they return and follow the technique of silence and of the secret importing and cultivating of their doctrine. This apparently succeeded, especially when in 511 the aged Sabas, as deputy of the province, traveled to the imperial court with a petition for remission of taxes; he included in his retinue, from the monks of the New Laura, a certain Leontius, a native of Constantinople, who was one of the most convinced Origenists. At Constantinople, his home, Leontius saw no further reason to adhere to the obligation to silence of the New Laura and carelessly preached his doctrines. Now Sabas' eyes were opened and he indignantly expelled Leontius from his escort and very imprudently returned to Palestine without him; there he died in 532. Leontius received reinforcements from the Palestinian *Eremos,* notably the monks Dometian and Theodore Askidas. What they told the Emperor, to whom they gained access, and what he understood of it, we do not know. In any event, they gained him for their cause, and he made Theodore Metropolitan of Caesarea in Cappadocia and Dometian Metropolitan of Ancyra. But Theodore preferred to linger in proximity to the Emperor and left his bishopric to take care of itself.

Meanwhile, the Patriarch Paul of Alexandria had disappointed all the hopes which the Emperor had set on him. His acts of violence became intolerable, and even complicity in the murder of a deacon could be charged to him. Hence the Emperor had him banished to Gaza, where a Synod was supposed to depose him. The Synod did its duty, and the imperial delegates who had attended it were now confronted on the spot with Origenism. One of them, Papas Eusebius, influential at court, sought to finish with the problem by giving to the Abbot of the New Laura the order either to receive back the expelled Origenists or to drive the most determined anti-Origenists from the monastery. The Abbot Gelasius decided for the latter course. Those expelled now turned to the zealous Patriarch of Antioch, Ephrem, who at once anathematized the Origenists. Dometian and Theodore Askidas, who learned of this at Constantinople, sought to induce the Patriarch of Constantinople, Menas, to renounce Ephrem's communion. But in the meantime a detailed written complaint arrived from the anti-Origenists from Palestine, who spoke out against the intrigues of their opponents. The Patriarch sent it on to the Emperor Justinian, who soon issued a severe edict against the person and doctrine of Origen.

If the question is asked, who at court was sufficiently influential to put through such a measure against Papas Eusebius, against Askidas and Dometian, the answer is hardly the Patriarch Menas; most probably we may see the initiator in the Deacon Pelagius, who as *apocrisiarius* had taken part in the Synod of Gaza. Whoever it may have been, once he had been called upon, the Emperor completely plucked the strings of his theological instrument. His edict was not only the proclamation of measures but a theological treatise in the form of a conciliar decree. It not only proposed to refute Origen but also to defame him: with quotations, chiefly from *Peri Archon,* it made fun of the doctrine, which it then summarized in ten anathemas, to which the obedient theologians and prelates had only to submit. The edict may be dated at the beginning of 542. The Patriarch Menas was instructed to have it signed by all the clergy of the capital and to send the report of it to all other bishops for their signature. Neither the Pope nor any other Patriarch declined to sign. Of course, the leading Origenists refused to accept this decision and preferred to leave the *laura* for good and look for a place of refuge elsewhere. Dometian seems likewise to have rejected the edict after some hesitation, whereas Theodore Askidas apparently was able to force himself to sign it.

Origenism seemed to have received a mortal blow. But the appearance was deceptive, for under an assumed name the great mystics of the Byzantine Church again came under Origen's spell.

C H A P T E R   5 5

The Controversy over the Three Chapters and the Fifth General Council — End of the Age of Justinian

By the "Three Chapters" are understood the person and the work of three theologians who played a certain role in the period between the Councils of Ephesus and Chalcedon, and gradually, without the situation's having required it, became a bone of contention between the different factions in ecclesiastical politics. In the first place was a letter of Ibas of Edessa from the period after the Union of 433, which by no means defended Nestorius but expressed other than friendly feelings toward Cyril of Alexandria. The letter recognized the Union of 433, but its author was not inclined to see in the great exegete, Theodore of Mopsuestia, the father of Nestorianism and hence to condemn him. Next, Theodore of Mopsuestia himself. People had long ago begun to characterize his theology as Nestorian, and now efforts were made to condemn him and his work posthumously, even though neither Ephesus nor Chalcedon had been prepared to do so. In the third place were some writings of Theodoret of Cyrrhus, which were directed against Cyril's Anathemas. As early as 431 Cyril himself had exerted himself in vain for the condemnation of Theodore. But he was opposed on the ground that in his lifetime Theodore had not been accused of a heresy and that he had died in peace with the Church. It would not do to insult such a man after his death. Ibas as well as Theodoret had, it is true, been deposed by the Robber Synod in 449, but Chalcedon had rehabilitated both. The latter Synod had as little to find fault with in Ibas' letter as in the anti-Cyrillan writings of Theodoret. In other words: an attack on these three *kephalaia* was basically an attack on the authority of the Council of Chalcedon. To be obstinate in regard to the letter of Ibas and then to argue that it was not from Ibas and in this way to respect the authority of the Council, which had thus rehabilitated someone other than the author of the letter, was clearly hairsplitting, since the Council had also implicitly recognized the content of the letter. But Theodoret simply had to be sacrificed, because he had put his finger too well on Cyril's weaknesses. What could induce circles which pretended to stand for Chalcedon to make these Three Chapters the target of ruthless attacks and thereby shake confidence in the Council? Looked at as a whole, probably only the persistent anxiety of appearing in the eyes of the Monophysites as Nestorians, of abetting a Nestorian interpretation of Christological dogma with the formulas of Chalcedon, and of compromising the sincerity of the adherence to Orthodoxy with these personalities and their work. They might have been of the opinion that, if the Three Chapters were thrown overboard, the Severans could be induced to return. The backbiting of Church history, of course, gives more concrete motives. It knows the name of the man who had systematically prepared the attack and it knows his motives: Theodore Askidas, in the role of adviser of the Emperor, was exposed to the gravest risks through the attacks on Origenism, which were not least of all aimed at him, and he was intent on revenge, which should be aimed at the strict Chalcedonians, who had denounced Origenism to the Emperor. In the attack on the Three Chapters he found the way, under the pretext of purging Chalcedon of disagreeable concomitants, of striking at the very heart of the Council and at the same time of involving the Emperor in a theological conflict of such magnitude that, for its sake, he would have to forget about Origenism and would be happy to retain Askidas as adviser.

However matters may have proceeded, Askidas was successful in convincing the imperial theologian of his ideas. Justinian was quickly prepared to compose a scholarly treatise in which he explained the Three Chapters in detail. To it were appended anathemas against Theodore of Mopsuestia and his writings, against the works which Theodoret had composed against Cyril, and against the letter of Ibas and all those who claimed that Ibas was its author. Justinian explicitly felt he had to make sure that these anathemas had no other purpose than to confirm the decrees of 451. The treatise has been lost. It must have been composed and published in the period between 543 and 545. While one could acknowledge in the case of the imperial decree against the Origenists that a single one summarized the arguments of the first Origenist controversy and that therefore the condemnation produced nothing substantially new, in his decree against the Three Chapters — for the treatise claimed to be just that — Justinian acted in a totally authoritarian manner as master of the Church and of dogma, without the backing of a synod and even for a long time without envisaging a confirmation by a synod. The bishops received the formal command to sign the anathemas. But this time there were difficulties. The Patriarch Menas of Constantinople finally signed, together with his synod, but obtained the promise that he could withdraw his signature if the Pope refused to sign. Alexandria caused hardly any difficulties, but the Patriarch Ephrem of Antioch likewise finally yielded. More trouble came from Palestine, where especially the pro-Chalcedon monks put pressure on the Patriarch. A great number of the bishops of the West maintained a decidedly negative attitude. The Pope's *apocrisiarii* at Constantinople refused the communion of the Patriarch Menas because he had signed; the African episcopate and most of the bishops of Italy and Gaul made the most vigorous opposition. And so it had to be the Emperor's chief task to gain the Pope. Pope Vigilius had succeeded to the See of Peter in Rome in 537; his role in the deposition of his predecessor Silverius by Belisarius had given occasion for suspicions, and he seemed, in relation to the Byzantine government, to have always had a bad conscience. Now, for simplicity's sake, Justinian summoned him to Constantinople; only when he arrived there, in 547, was the new document officially presented to him for his signature. The conduct of the Pope now and in the sequel hardly requires commentary. At first everything appeared quite promising. Like his *apocrisiarii,* he refused the communion of Menas, who apparently did not bother any longer to speak of the assurance that he could withdraw his signature. Menas got his revenge by no longer mentioning the Pope in the liturgy. But Justinian employed every possible means of pressure to induce the Pope to give in. Thus in the course of 547 Vigilius resumed communion with Menas and in April 548 he issued his famous *Judicatum,* in which he abandoned the Three Chapters, even if not without qualifications. The agitation over this yielding by the Pope grew mightily and affected even his immediate entourage. Finally, Vigilius saw himself compelled to excommunicate even a group of deacons who had come with him from Rome to Constantinople, in order to defend himself from their disagreeable criticism. In return, he was himself excommunicated by a Synod of African bishops. The situation reached a dangerous climax for the Pope especially in the West, causing him to spread abroad that he had been induced by ignoble methods to publish the *Judicatum.* Justinian yielded for a moment and condescended to let the Pope abandon the *Judicatum* with the assurance that the matter should be decided at a synod. In return, he of course had the Pope give a written and sworn assurance that he would cooperate with all his power for the condemnation of the Three Chapters and undertake nothing without coming to an understanding with Justinian — a complete surrender of the Pope, which naturally was kept secret. The Synod was a long time in coming: bishops on whose appearance the court set great store did not arrive, and it was desired to keep others as far as possible from the capital. Thus it was not difficult for Askidas to persuade the Emperor again solemnly to condemn the Three Chapters by a decree with thirteen anathemas in July 551. Askidas himself undertook to deliver the decree to the Pope. But, now, probably under pressure from the western bishops, the Pope demanded the withdrawal of the edict and threatened Askidas and the Patriarch Menas with excommunication. At the same time he regarded it as necessary to seek security after this attack, and so he fled from his lodgings in the *Domus Placidiae* to seek asylum in the Church of St. Peter in the Palace of Hormisdas, where he then officially excommunicated Askidas. Justinian tried by means of police power to drag the Pope from his asylum but Vigilius literally defended himself with hands and feet. Only when the Emperor gave him a guarantee of his personal freedom could he be induced to return to the *Domus Placidiae*. However, since Justinian did not keep his promise, but treated him like a prisoner, he fled a second time, now across the Propontis to the Council Church of St. Euphemia at Chalcedon. Again there were on the Emperor's part all possible assurances, broken by roughness and acts of violence. Even Belisarius could not move the Pope to return. Here Vigilius published an encyclical, in which he sought to justify his behavior and declared the deposition of Askidas. The Pope's followers even succeeded in publicly posting in various places the bulls of excommunication against Menas and Askidas. A definitive break seemed to be in preparation, but Justinian did not want matters to go so far. He got Menas and Askidas to apologize to the Pope, who then returned to Constantinople. Soon after, in August 552, Menas died, and the new Patriarch Eutychius declared from the beginning his loyalty to the Pope. Now there was definitive agreement to entrust the final decision to a synod. There followed difficult negotiations on the make-up of the Council; the Emperor succeeded in imposing his own ideas, which aimed only at the condemnation of the Three Chapters, in such a way that there remained to the Pope slight prospect of letting the opposition of the West exercise its impact; he was de facto deprived of any power of decision and accordingly decided not to participate in the sessions of the Council. The Synod — the so-called Fifth Ecumenical Council — met on 5 May 553, with 166 bishops present, of whom only a dozen represented the West. For tactical reasons Justinian also stayed away, but he let the bishops know that they had already condemned the Three Chapters by their signatures on the imperial edict, that the Pope also had condemned them, and that now there was in principle only a question of a ratification of these decrees. The Council exerted itself to persuade the Pope to participate, but Vigilius was content with holding out the prospect of an official opinion. Now as earlier, he made his participation in the sessions dependent on a stronger representation of western bishops. The Council proceeded to the agenda and began with the preparation for the condemnation of the Three Chapters. At this moment, on 14 May, the Pope published a *Constitutum,* which he signed together with nine Italian bishops, two from Africa, two from Illyricum, and three from Asia Minor. "By virtue of his apostolic authority," Vigilius condemned sixty propositions from the writings of Theodore of Mopsuestia but strictly refrained from condemning this Church Father himself, just as he declined to anathematize Theodoret or the author of the Ibas letter, because thereby the decrees of Chalcedon would have been brought into question. The *Constitutum* forbade any polemic against the Three Chapters which went beyond this decree. True, the Emperor refused absolutely to receive the *Constitutum,* but nevertheless its content became known; causing the Emperor to pursue the route of publicity. He laid before the Council Fathers a packet of documents with letters of the Pope in which he defended his *Judicatum* and especially the minutes of his taking of his oath in 550. Thereupon the Fathers expunged the Pope's name from the diptychs, without excommunicating him. The authority of the Apostolic See as such was not to be impugned.

On 2 June 553, at the last session, the Synod finally accomplished, in fourteen anathemas taken from Justinian's decree, the condemnation of the Three Chapters in due form. Theodore Askidas seemed to have won all along the line: Justinian had indeed no longer spent any time in implementing his decree against the Origenists; they dominated in the monasteries and episcopal sees of Palestine. But in Abbot Conon of the Great Laura there now arose unexpectedly a dangerous opponent, who knew exactly that they had their protector in Askidas. In 551 he himself appeared at Constantinople and denounced their doings to the Emperor. Justinian awoke and decided by means of a letter to the bishops who had come to the Council to bring up the matter again. To facilitate the proceedings he garnished his treatise again, likewise with fifteen anathemas. Although we do not know the course of the negotiations, it is certain that the bishops made no difficulties. Their sentence was directed not only and not first against Origen himself, but against the Origenists of Palestine and concomitantly now also against Evagrius Ponticus. The negotiations must, in all probability, have been concluded in March 553 before the beginning of the Council, and Vigilius seems to have assented without hesitation.

After everything had thus been "settled," the Emperor demanded all bishops who had not taken part in the Synod to sign its decrees. In the East there were only slight difficulties. More important was the decision of the Pope. Rome, again firmly in Byzantine hands since 552, urgently called for the return of its Bishop. Justinian required as a preliminary that Vigilius recognize the condemnation of the Three Chapters. Once again the Pope yielded and on 8 December 553 uttered the condemnation. On 23 March 554 a new *Constitutum* was published by the Pope, in which he denied the authenticity of the letter of Ibas and his vindication by the Council of Chalcedon. Finally, in the spring of 555, the Pope was able to leave Constantinople. But en route he died at Syracuse. Thereby the opposition in the West obtained a still freer course and, despite severe police reprisals, stood firm. When finally the deacon Pelagius, who had again and again kept Vigilius on the path of the old convictions and hence had been imprisoned by the Emperor, also followed the route of recognition of the Council, this was now reason enough for the Emperor to impose him on the Romans as their Bishop in 556. The schism between the Apostolic See and important portions of the western episcopate could not be prevented any longer.

As regards the Monophysites, the decrees of 553 left them completely unmoved. Allegedly it was a Palestinian bishop who made him more conversant with the doctrine of Julian of Halicarnassus, the so-called Aphthartodocetism, according to which the body of Christ was an *aphtharton,* an incorruptible being, so that he could suffer on the Cross only because a special miracle made this possible. The representatives of this doctrine, also called Gaianites from one of their leaders, were especially widespread in Egypt, and perhaps once again the Emperor indulged in the hope of being able to gain, if not the Severans, at least this faction of Monophysites. He let himself be convinced of the correctness of Aphthartodocetism, and he then at once drew up a decree for a creed in favor of this doctrine, which was to be submitted to all bishops for their signature. The Patriarch Eutychius in the capital itself refused any sort of assent. But since the

Emperor knew better, the Patriarch had to go into exile in 565. Its content quickly became known and stirred up general displeasure, not only in the West but also in the East. Before the new conflict broke out fully, however, the Emperor died on 14 November 565, and no one was found who would accept and carry out his last idea.

CHAPTER   5 6

Justinian's Successors: Monoenergism and Monothelitism

It is not improbable that the Empress Theodora's niece Sophia, wife of the new Emperor Justin II (565–78), who until shortly before his accession to the throne is said to have sided with the Monophysites, had a hand in the affair when the Emperor began, after the start of his reign, to steer a course of meeting the Monophysites halfway. Imprisoned and exiled Monophysite bishops were permitted to return, efforts were undertaken through the mediation of imperial emissaries to settle intra-Monophysite dissensions, and finally Jacob Baradai was invited, together with the leading members of his Church, to a union conference at Constantinople. The discussions lasted for months without, of course, producing any concrete results. And so Justin II tried, as had the Emperor Zeno earlier, a new *Henoticon* in 567, which again imposed Zeno's formulas, condemned the Three Chapters, granted amnesty to the Monophysites, recommended the rehabilitation of Severus — and did not mention Chalcedon. But for the Monophysites this was not enough. An imperial agent was supposed to persuade bishops and monks to accept it at a conference held at Callinicum on the Euphrates. Jacob Baradai and his loyalists would have been inclined to agree with the document with a few clarifications, but the monks especially wanted to have nothing to do with an imperial effort at union, so that the meeting ended with a shrill dissonance within the faction. Now the Emperor prepared a new version of the edict, which recognized "the one nature of the Logos-made-Man" and spoke of a mental distinction of the natures, again without mentioning Chalcedon, but also without returning to the rehabilitation of Severus. The decree was to be implemented by force, and the Patriarch John the Scholastic of Constantinople (565–77) did all he could to let compulsion run its course. There were arrests and deportations in all areas. The persecution did not cease until Justin II gradually lapsed into insanity, and Tiberius II in 574 assumed control of the government in his stead and, after Justin's death, mounted the throne (578–82). The Patriarchs, including Eutychius, who had been called back from exile after John's death in 577, sought to continue the persecution, but the Emperor did not care to have much to do with it, and Eutychius himself soon became implicated in a doctrine on the resurrection of all flesh, which made him suspect of heresy. The policy of Tiberius was probably also influenced by the aim of not antagonizing the Monophysite Arabs on the important Persian frontier. He solemnly received their Phylarch, al-Mundir, at Constantinople and did much to oblige his demands for the release of persecuted Monophysites. The religious policy of Tiberius was continued by Maurice (582–602), who without doubt was personally a Chalcedonian. Under Phocas (602–10) and in the early years of the reign of Heraclius (610–41) the great attack of the Persians, who occupied parts of Asia Minor, Syria, and Egypt, made such demands on the policy of the Emperors that there remained little time for the old denominational quarrels. In addition, the Persian occupation withdrew especially the Monophysites more or less from the imperial power. The problems did not again appear until Heraclius in long campaigns had forced the Persians to their knees, even if the preliminaries lay further in the past. The Jews, who, even if they had not encouraged the Persian invasion, had warmly greeted it, could hardly hope for mercy. The imperial troops made short work of them, and the struggle against them culminated in the imperial edict of compulsory conversion. How should the Monophysites be dealt with, that is, not a minority but the population of entire provinces? Some of them, such as the Ghassanid Arabs, whom Maurice had treated so shabbily because of military distrust, may have done little to oppose the Persians, and the latter seem to have repaid this attitude. Could the imperial government further disregard the separatist tendencies of the heterodox Syrians and Copts? Heraclius reflected on a solution and again sought the remedy in ecclesiastical union. His loyal and outstanding assistant in this was the Patriarch Sergius (610–38), who had not the slightest interest in fishing in the troubled waters of Church policy. If it is said to have been the weakness of the Chalcedonian Christology that it did not clearly enough elaborate the unity over the duality, and if on the other hand the duality of natures in Christ could no longer be sacrificed, but the idea of person was still somewhat colorless, one could then seek the unity in Christ's will and activity. Already in some neo-Chalcedonian theologians were found formulas which referred to the *mia energeia,* the unique divine principle of activity in Christ. To the Patriarch this formula seemed promising, and very soon he worked on a patristic *florilegium* which could multiply the testimonies in favor of it. Bishop Cyrus of Phasis, who in 631 was appointed by the Emperor as Patriarch of the Church of the Empire in Alexandria, was prepared to forge out of this stock of ideas those formulas which should be presented to the Christian public as the basis of the common faith. In nine propositions, which had as content the fruit of the neo-Chalcedonian theology, that is, the reconciliation between Cyril and 451, the "Pact" was solemnly proclaimed at Alexandria on 3 June 633: its principal item was the doctrine of one and the same Christ, operating divinely and humanly, "with the one theandric energy" (*theandrine energeia*) — a term for which one could appeal to the "unquestionable" authority of the Pseudo-Areopagite. The Monophysites exulted. But the opposition was not slow to appear. The monk Sophronius, who soon after became Patriarch of Jerusalem (634–38), protested against the Formula of Union. He held to the Aristotelian principle that energy flows from nature, that hence in Christ two energies were to be admitted.

He journeyed to the Patriarch Sergius at Constantinople, and it was characteristic of the latter that he was prepared to negotiate. Agreement was reached that for the future it was proper not to speak of energies at all but of the one operating Christ (*heis kai autos energon*); in other words, the one Operator should be stressed, not the principle of operation or the agency. Sophronius apparently deviated from his two energies because he could not refer to any patristic passages for the use of this formula. In any case, he relied on the agreement with the Patriarch when he also in his encyclical left no doubt that in theory two natures have two principles of operation as their consequence. But now the Patriarch Sergius published a *Judicatum,* which likewise abandoned the abstract formula of the one energy in favor of the concrete personal energy of the one operating Christ. Even Maximus Confessor later regarded the formula as a good solution. For the Monophysites, of course, it could only be boring, for with it the problem of whether there was one or two natures was again wiped off the table. Sergius described the content and trend of his doctrinal decision in a letter to Pope Honorius. The Pope agreed that there should be no talk of two energies; that it had not happened up to now and could produce confusion in terminology. He accepted the Patriarch's formula and inferred from it that it is appropriate to speak of one will (*una voluntas*) in Christ. The vindication of the Pope needs no sophisms: He quoted the words of Jesus: "I have come, not to do my own will, but the will of him who sent me" and "Not my will be done, but thine," and so he somehow accepted a basic human principle of willing in Christ. If he then spoke of *una voluntas,* he obviously did not mean this basic principle but the concrete act of the will at a given time, which is determined by the divine will and only by it. The misfortune was that now again, instead of one word, an unclarified substantive was employed, which could be interpreted both as the basic principle as well as, in the final analysis, a decisive *arbitrium.*

Sergius was delighted with the initial help which the Pope offered him. And if the Pope preferred the formula *una voluntas,* then the Patriarch was prepared to put it in place of the *mia energeia,* which had anyhow already been abandoned; it became *hen thelema* in Greek. He gained the Emperor for a decree and in 638, the very year of the deaths of both the Patriarch and the Pope, there appeared Heraclius' *Ecthesis,* in which the prohibition was issued against speaking of one or two energies, and instead one will in Christ was decreed as the statement of faith, again with the reason that Christ in the flesh had never been separated from the will of the *Logos* or had willed anything against it; that is, *thelema* was not interpreted as a theoretical faculty but as the actual will. What was harmful here was not theology but terminology.

Maximus Confessor, who had once been in the service of Heraclius, had then become a monk, and had fled from the Persians to Africa, first revealed himself as the man who was competent to deal with the linguistic difficulties of a philosophical nature. After a long period of preparation, in which he did not pin himself down, around 640 he vigorously intervened in the controversy. For him, *thelema physikon* was a basic principle which belonged to the nature, and, since he was an enthusiastic adherent of the Council of Chalcedon, he was thus a Dyothelite. He had to reject the formula of Pope Honorius and the *Ecthesis;* true, he interpreted the Pope in an orthodox manner, whereas he did not do likewise with the Greek term. Otherwise, there was a predicament with the "gnomic" *thelema,* which was identical with the *arbitrium,* a property of the person; in Christ there can be only one since he subsists in the divine Person. The wretchedness of the following discussions consisted in this, that too little regard was had for this saving distinction, and probably also in this that Maximus demanded too much; that is, in the case of each one who spoke of one *thelema* without distinction he suspected that he thereby meant the physical faculty in itself. Hence, there arose in Byzantine Africa a center of resistance to the imperial policy. In view of the situation, the Emperor Constans II (641–68) decided on a new decree His *Typus* of 648 forbade any discussion at all of one or two energies and of one or two wills and abrogated the *Ecthesis.* Finally, Maximus turned to Rome, where the new Pope, Martin I, showed a complete sympathy for his train of thought. And so in 649 there was held a Lateran Synod which was entirely under the influence of Maximus' ideology. They defined the doctrine of the two wills in Christ and excommunicated Sergius, his successor Pyrrhus, and Cyrus of Phasis, as if the distinctions of Maximus had in their day been common property. The Emperor Constans reacted with extreme violence. In 653 he had Pope Martin taken from Rome to Constantinople, where he was tried for high treason. In any event, there was no further mention of the original reason for the arrest, and every effort of the Pope during the trial to bring the *Typus* and the Monothelite controversy into the discussion was rejected by the court. Finally, the Pope was condemned to death for high treason, and then reprieved with banishment, in which he died in 655. In 653 the imperial police were also able to take Maximus into custody and deport him to Constantinople, where he too underwent a trial for high treason. Mutilated in hands and tongue, Maximus died in exile in 662. With this the climax of the controversy was overstepped. Constans II still attempted personally to make his authority felt in the West, but he was assassinated in Sicily in 668.

Constans II was succeeded by Constantine IV (668–85). He had no interest in the continuation of the quarrel, which had reached a dead-lock. The Monophysites could not be gained back. The new orientation of Byzantine policy, which allowed greater weight to Byzantine Italy, made it seem appropriate to draw the Pope away from an opposition that was not without danger to the Empire. In 680 Pope Agatho could hold a preparatory Synod with 125 bishops, which in the spirit of that of 649 condemned Monothelitism. Then in 680–81 the Sixth Ecumenical Council was held at Constantinople, with the Emperor himself presiding. A letter from the Pope was submitted to the Council Fathers which indicated the route to be followed. Almost all the bishops accepted the papal decree. Only six constituted an exception. All were anathematized, and this censure was later extended to Theodore of Pharan, Cyrus of Phasis, the Patriarchs Sergius and Pyrrhus, and finally even to Pope Honorius. What was thereby condemned was a terminology, which could meanwhile be regarded as out of date. Historically, the verdicts were hardly justified. The definition of the Synod itself spoke of two physical faculties of will in Christ, whose goals were not directed against each other, because the human will was in everything subject to the divine, almighty will. The condemnation of the unyielding bishops produced no schism. The act was over, and no one wanted to go back to it. A question was disposed of, which had long ago lost its ecclesiastical and political meaning. After the Monophysites on the whole no longer belonged to the Empire, all these controversies had lost their threatening background: Orthodoxy withdrew into itself — Byzantium had become smaller.

CHAPTER   5 7

The Rise of National Churches
on the Frontiers of the Byzantine Empire

The Church of the Nestorians

The theological problem of so-called Nestorianism was first decided at the Council of Ephesus in 431. But for the Orthodox world only the Fifth Ecumenical Council of 553 at Constantinople, with its condemnation of the Three Chapters, drew the final conclusions, in part unnecessary, but in any case dogmatically not without danger. The decision of Ephesus would perhaps not have led to a breaking away of a separate Church, if, together with Nestorius, there had not also been a target in the great theologian of the Syrian Church, Theodore of Mopsuestia, the head of a school of exegesis which possessed canonical recognition for the East Syrian region and whose doctrines had found their domicile in the theological school of Edessa, one of the most exemplary educational institutions of Christianity. It is true that the Bishop of Edessa, Rabbula, sought by every means to enforce the decrees of Ephesus and the Union of 433, but Ibas, the head of the School of Edessa, continued in the opposition, so that the Bishop finally dismissed him from the school. But Rabbula died in 435, and the following of the expelled teacher was so large that Ibas could now be elected his successor. To call him a Nestorian presupposes some arbitrariness. What he did not want was that Alexandrian terminology of a Christological enthusiasm should simply drive Antiochene sobriety from the field. Ibas had quite a hard time during his episcopate. The Robber Synod of 449 deposed him, but Chalcedon restored him, and he died in 457. He was followed by a metropolitan who now sought strictly to enforce Chalcedon. The opposition of the school was a thorn in his side, and the head of the school, whom Ibas had appointed, Narses, had to quit the field. As early as 433, when the Formula of Union had come into existence, some bishops of the Antiochene patriarchate, who were unwilling to accept this compromise, had settled in Persia. Also condemned by the Robber Synod, a disciple of Ibas named Bar-Sauma (d. before 496) followed them and became Bishop of Nisibis. Narses now joined him and at Nisibis they established as an offshoot of the school of Edessa the "School of the Persians," in which Nestorianism found a new home. Nestorianism as a denomination with the ability to develop into a Church now found a home in the Persian Kingdom, where it grew into the Christian "territorial Church." The School of Nisibis was in great demand; the organization was exemplary, the resources abundant, so that here generations of theologians and clerics could be trained who gave the Persian Church its best framework and helped it overcome the dangers of its isolated position on the border of the Universal Church. Bar-Sauma himself was one of the most vigorous representatives of this territorial Church. He was a tireless missionary, opposed the spread of the Monophysites and Messalians, maintained a good relationship with the Great King of Persia, and knew how to use every means that could serve his ideas. That Nestorianism found entry into the Persian Church so easily is certainly connected with the fact that the School of Edessa had already established a reputation as a school whose graduates had for a long time spread their ideas in Persia; but probably also with the fact that the Church of Persia, which must have expressed itself emphatically in a Synod of 424 for its autonomy, that is, for its independence of Antioch, could develop in Nestorianism something like a theological self-awareness as opposed to West Syria and the Byzantine Empire.

At the head of this Persian Church there stood, at the latest from the beginning of the fifth century, a "Great Metropolitan," also called *Katholikos episkopos,* with his see in the twin cities on the Tigris, Seleucia-Ctesiphon. He soon had the position of a Patriarch: it was incumbent on him to determine the dates of the great festivities, to convoke synods, to summon the bishops to him every two years. On occasion, synods expanded his powers: then he intervened in the division of the bishoprics and probably also named the bishops himself, and at times an effort was made in important matters to supply him with a board by whose decisions he was to be bound. But in general he ruled monocratically, and not improperly the Synod of 424 designated him as "our Peter."

The *Catholici* gradually progressed into a position which was not unlike that of the Byzantine patriarchs. The Great King influenced their election and apparently also reserved to himself on occasion their confirmation and installation. In return the patriarchs had a high rank at court and were not rarely appointed to state functions. Now and then the King lent them his *bracchium saeculare* when there was question of pursuing heretics or of energetically settling other internal ecclesiastical matters.

The most important *Catholici* of the fifth and sixth centuries were Babai II (d. 502) and Aba Mar I (d. 552). The former governed in a period of peace between Byzantium and Persia, and so the latent Monophysitism promoted by the Emperor Anastasius I was able to have a missionary effect in Persia. Babai tried to keep everything about his Church pure, but the influence of the Byzantine Emperor on the Great King was strong enough so that the persecution of Monophysites was not too serious. Aba Mar was a convert from Zoroastrianism, the Persian State religion. He had made long journeys into the Byzantine Empire and he now tried to consolidate the canonical bases of his Church. For this purpose he did not hesitate to receive into the canonical collection of his Church even the canons of the Synod of Chalcedon in so far as they seemed pertinent to him. He founded new bishoprics and in addition to the School of Nisibis there now arose a special one at Seleucia, whose significance is clear from the fact that it could on occasion have a say in the election of the *Catholicus.* The activity of Aba Mar was all the more esteemed as it came in a period in which King Chosroes I imposed not inconsiderable restrictions on Christianity in Persia. Aba Mar himself finally fell victim to the persecution. He barely escaped death and had to go into exile, from which he tried to govern his Church with unbroken spirit. He died in 552, soon after having received amnesty. That Chosroes' personal physician was appointed as Aba Mar's successor was a singular expression of the circumstances. The position of the new *Catholicus* was for that reason substantially better than that of his predecessor, but he also misused it autocratically. Under King Chosroes II (590–628) the Christians long remained unmolested. He was under the influence of his Christian wife, Shirin, but probably more importantly, he owed his throne to the Byzantine Emperor Maurice. After the overthrow of this Emperor, he posed as his avenger against the Emperor Phocas, and there followed the great Persian-Byzantine war, which finally brought about the collapse of Sassanid rule. The more this war expanded, the more precarious became the situation of the Nestorian Christians. Apparently they were regarded as potential allies of the Greeks, and hence in 608 Chosroes forbade the election of a new *Catholicus,* and the Church remained without a head until 628. It was one of the most important theologians of the Church, Babai the Great, who, as a sort of abbot-general of the North Persian monasteries, found at this time the opportunity to assume the actual direction of the Church and to guard it against the worst. The difficulties increased, the more Byzantine territories came under Persian occupation. The population of Syria and Egypt was to a great extent Monophysite. Persecuted as Monophysites by the imperial central government, they apparently offered only slight resistance to the Persian occupation and hence won their sympathy. With this began a new wave of missionary propaganda of the Monophysites in regard to their opposites, the Nestorians, in Persia, and for a moment it even seemed that they would succeed in getting the Catholicate into their hands. In these circumstances the Persian bishops were glad to waive the election of a *Catholicus,* which would then have been possible. Not until 628, when Chosroes II was overthrown by his son with the help of a Nestorian Persian, was it again possible for the Nestorians to breathe freely, and a new *Catholicus* was elected. Chosen was Ishar Yahb (628–44 or 646). The years of his reign saw the collapse of Sassanid rule and the compulsory peace with Byzantium, in the concluding of which he took part as an official delegate. But they also saw the assault by Islam on the Persian Kingdom and thus the beginning of a new epoch for his Church.

The inner life of this Church in the period described was to a great extent determined by the development of the canonical foundations and of the organization. A series of synods was occupied with this task and sought to accommodate the legal prescriptions to the times. Still more important was the confrontation with the advancing Monophysites, who not only succeeded in gaining a number of monasteries for themselves but also in establishing at Tagrit an episcopal see, which became the center of their exertions. The Nestorians, who were not a State-Church in the sense that the Byzantine Church was, but a tolerated, not rarely encouraged, and occasionally also persecuted denomination alongside the Persian State-Church, saw themselves forced to the defensive. It could happen that they had to appear before the Zoroastrian Great King for religious discussions with the Monophysites, which, of course, like all such undertakings, yielded success to neither side. In the Nestorian Church there were even formed groups which reached the conviction that a certain union with Byzantine Orthodoxy, which for its part persecuted the Monophysites, could be practicable. Of course the factions soon fell between two fires, for the same Byzantine Orthodoxy had finally, under Justinian, just condemned the spiritual father of the Persian Church, Theodore of Mopsuestia. Thus all these exertions had no success, and finally at the Synod of 612 the Persian Church decided to make officially its own the Nestorian creed of Babai the Great. In this there was question of a proposition, which, translated into Greek, could be rendered with the doctrine of two natures (*physeis*) and two *hypostaseis* in Christ, but one single *prosopon*. A concise interpretation will assume that here *hypostasis* meant the complete existence of all characteristics of a nature, the divine as well as the human, while by *prosopon* was to be understood the actual historical manner of the total phenomenon. In other words, a formula which was only approximately covered by the corresponding Greek terms with which it could be rendered, and so it remained free for interpretation; a formula which could be interpreted not only as strongly Nestorian but perhaps even as approximately Chalcedonian. After the defeat of the Persians by Heraclius, on the occasion of the concluding of peace, religious discussions were also organized with the aim of a union of the two Churches. Accordingly, the *Catholicus* submitted a profession of faith which the Orthodox partners regarded as orthodox. Hence the formula of the Nestorian Church was interpreted in the sense of the Council of Chalcedon. But neither the Emperor Heraclius nor the *Catholicus* could make his view of such an agreement in faith palatable and credible to his respective Church. A long and differently proceeding ecclesiastical and political development of 200 years had long before erected barriers that were all too high. The Nestorian bishops would not accept the condemnation of Theodore and swallow the term "Mother of God."

And so the Nestorian Church was forced into a life of its own, which it kept closed against the entire West, hence against Europe and Asia Minor. For this reason the mighty missionary *élan* which especially characterized this Church in contradistinction to the Orthodox Church of the Early Byzantine period, pushed ever farther eastward. Even at this period there began that grandiose missionary activity which achieved its climax in the Middle Ages. As early as the sixth century Nestorian missionaries reached the western frontiers of India in Malabar. Cosmas Indicopleustes discovered them on the island of Socotra between the South Arabian and the African coasts and on the island of Sri Lanka. Even in Tibet the Nestorian mission probably dates back to the middle of the seventh century, and the first traces of Nestorians in China likewise extended to this time. The representatives of this mission were first of all monks. The origins of Persian monasticism are probably to be sought in the area of Nisibis, from which it spread powerfully.

If now, from the middle of the seventh century, this Church fell under Islamic domination, this fact produced no decisive changes. In fact, now Monophysites and Nestorians were again under one secular rule, the Caliphate. But this seems to have been the aim: to permit each denomination its status quo, so that the Nestorian Church could develop further relatively peacefully. If the *Catholicus* and some other Nestorian Christians enjoyed high dignities and offices under Persian rule, collectively the Nestorians were still second-class citizens in Persia, so that the Islamic system of government brought nothing new.

The Coptic Church

If it is desired forcibly to assign a date of birth to the Coptic Church as an unortho-dox Christian denomination in the sense of the later Byzantine Imperial Church, the year 536 could be designated, when the Emperor Justinian I, under the influ-ence of the Pope and probably out of regard for his war plans in Italy, put an end to his policy of friendliness toward the Monophysites and allowed the Patriarch of the capital, Anthimus, to be deposed and expelled Severus of Antioch from Constantinople. Of course, the period of incubation began in 451 with the then incipient resistance to the decrees of the Council of Chalcedon. Timothy the Cat and to some extent Peter Mongus represented the most important stages, and the activity of a Severus, of a Julian of Halicarnassus, and of similar figures consoli-dated interiorly what the ecclesiastical leadership of Alexandria carried through or tried to accomplish in relation to Byzantium. Then in 536 Justinian summoned the Patriarch Theodosius of Alexandria to Constantinople to demand from him submission to the decrees of the Synod of 536 — the condemnation of Severus and so forth. Theodosius refused to sign and was banished. Like so many other Monophysites, he touched down in a palace of the Empress Theodora, where, in the company of like-minded monks and clerics, he had full scope to supervise the Monophysite faith of his flock in Egypt by means of dogmatic treatises and pastoral letters until his death in 566. He could do this all the more effectively as the imperial central government had little luck with its Orthodox Patriarch, forcibly imposed on Alexandria: in 542 Paul had to be deposed by an imperial judgment at a Synod of Gaza; his successor Zoilus refused to conform to the imperial policy in the Three Chapters Controversy and hence lost his see in 551. John II (569–79) did not even obtain recognition from all his Orthodox colleagues. But this unhappiness did not in any way ease the lot of the persecuted Copts. In 551 the imperial Patriarch Apollinarius came to Alexandria with the full authority of gover-nor and high commissary and ruled with unprecedented violence. He confiscated all Coptic, that is, Monophysite churches and prevented the Monophysite clerics from even entering the city. In addition, the Monophysites were at odds among themselves. There was the powerful faction of the adherents of Julian of Halicar-nassus, usually called Gaianites from one of their first champions; there were the partisans of the middle line of Severus; then the Tritheists, for whom was claimed also the famous philosopher, John Philoponus; and there were others besides. If it could have been achieved, there would have been as many patriarchs as factions. Actually, the unity of the Church was based on the people and on monasticism, especially popular with the people. The really religious figures of monasticism were Monophysites because of the belief that only this confession guaranteed the Redemption through the Logos-made-Man, but they were more interested in the ardor of this faith and the purity of life corresponding to it than in the scholarly distinctions of the heads of the schools.

After the death in 566 of the Patriarch Theodosius of Alexandria, who was residing at Constantinople and who, while not uncontested in Egypt, had been something of an Ecumenical Patriarch of the Monophysites, it was not possible for some time to find a successor for him in Egypt itself. Jacob Baradai, the "Ecumenical" Metropolitan of the Syrian Monophysites, had sought during the lifetime of the Alexandrian to appoint a *locum tenens* for Egypt, without finding any requited love on the Nile. This meant that now also Jacobites and Copts were at one another's throats. When the Syrian Church believed it had to intervene and the Syrian Archimandrite Theodore was appointed as Egyptian Patriarch, he encountered decisive repudiation in Alexandria. Then the aged deacon Peter was elected as anti-Patriarch in 575. As his first act, he immediately ordained seventy bishops and thereby created not only a large obedience but also filled up the great gaps in the hierarchy that had been caused by the dissensions, and by this coup established a counterpoise to the Imperialists, the Melkites, against which the government could for a long time only exert itself in vain. However, because Peter was not the candidate of the Syrians, there were new discords. Finally Jacob Baradai himself arrived to see that everything was done properly, but he soon submitted to the majority which Peter had acquired. Peter died as early as 577. On the occasion of the election of his successor, which again was a long time in coming, something like a compromise with the Jacobites was apparent: the new Patriarch came from Syria but had been a monk in an Egyptian monastery. But he, Damian (578–605), also brought no definitive peace.

But if the Monophysite Church of Egypt was still so often split, if it could really agree so seldom on a patriarch, still the opposition to the Council of Chalcedon and to the Chalcedonian patriarchs imposed by Byzantium again united it. In addition, it even happened that the imperial governors, the *Augustales,* inclined to this confession, contrary to their official mandate, so that the outlaws could defy the imperial policy time and again. In any case, for the future the succession of Coptic Patriarchs continued unbroken, and if the Orthodox Patriarch had his seat guaranteed by troops in Alexandria in the Caesarium part of the city with the Cathedral of St. Mark, the monastery of Enaton in the vicinity of the capital constituted a more secure place for the Coptic chief shepherds because it scarcely curtailed their freedom of action. In the figure of the Orthodox Patriarch John III the Almoner (610–19) the Imperial Church once again had a representative whose pastoral zeal, whose blameless life, and whose legendary charity did not fail to make an impression also on the Monophysite population. Nevertheless, no union was achieved even under him. Besides, in 619 the Persians invaded Egypt and occupied it for almost ten years. The blow affected Monophysites and Orthodox equally, but if in the course of the years a certain alleviation occurred, in any case the Orthodox Church could not rely on any State privileges so as to persecute the Copts. And when the Emperor Heraclius, after the defeat of the Persian armies, also relieved Egypt again, he brought along that new "Monoenergist" creed which both sides could face with a common optimism. In 633 the Imperial Patriarch, Cyrus of Phasis, proclaimed this Formula of Union of the one divine energy in Christ. True, Cyrus reported a great success to Constantinople, but the Copts sneered, not that they had come to the Council of Chalcedon, but that it had come to them. In the long run this effort had no success, and soon Islam replaced the Byzantines. In 642 the same Patriarch Cyrus had to surrender Alexandria to the Muslim general Amr, and after a few years all Egypt was in Arab hands. The Patriarch Benjamin, the Chief Shepherd of the Copts, soon understood how to come to an arrangement with the Arab conquerors and to obtain for his Church a guarantee of that freedom for which the Islamic law of the Koran was always prepared. The same status would have been given to the Orthodox Church, but it was characteristic of the different treatment of the confessions that Benjamin could soon proceed to the reorganization of his Church, whereas the Melkites could not fill the See of St. Mark again for a long time. The Egyptian Church of the Middle Ages was the Coptic Church and no other.

The formation of a special Coptic Church can certainly be explained from the opposition to the decrees of the Synod of Chalcedon, in which people were convinced they had to see a condemnation of the theology and of the sacrosanct figure of the Patriarch Cyril of Alexandria. But even then this opposition was not of a purely dogmatic nature, but to a great extent the opposition of a proud self-awareness, residue of a time in which the Church of Alexandria, governed by its patriarch in a monarchical and autocratic manner, played the first role in the East, could always pride itself on the support of Rome, and had no serious competitors. But the Synod of Constantinople in 381 and, even more, canon 28 of Chalcedon had inflicted a blow on this position which the self-conscious patriarchs of Alexandria were not prepared to take. The people followed them blindly, for in the patriarch they saw not only the leader of the Church but also the representative of their Coptic individuality — a national individuality — in relation to which Byzantium and everything that came from Byzantium was regarded as foreign and inappropriate. This self-consciousness then led to a de-Hellenization of the ecclesiastical system, and it may be maintained that this de-Hellenization of the ecclesiastical system required a proper denomination in order to be able clearly to present itself, and Monophysitism was just the form for this. It led also to the development of a Coptic ecclesiastical literature. This consisted for the most part of translations, since, where it is original, there is almost always question of a literary plane which corresponds rather to a scarcely differentiated religious consciousness than to dogmatic or juridical definitions. An example is the whole monastic literature, the literature of monastic rules and of monastic sayings, which was then translated into Greek, Syriac, and Arabic, and this authentic Egyptian institution, in so far as it deserves the name of institution at all, spread throughout the world. Here belong also many sermons with a remarkable preference for angels and archangels, the vitae of monks and hermits, whose unconcealed Monophysitism bore the denominational opposition on the plane of the miraculous, but also serious catecheses and admonitions of provincial bishops and monastic superiors.

Behind this literature there more and more stands monasticism. This monasticism was Coptic in its origins and in Egypt remained Coptic to an eminent degree. It withdrew into the desert from the threatened economic world of Romanized Egypt of late antiquity, but the world pursued it, the entire contemporary world, and dragged it back into political publicity. The patriarchs of Alexandria, without regard for which dogmatic color they wore, saw in it their accomplice and used it unscrupulously. Not a few monks found pleasure in this role and gradually rose to positions of control over the religious and ecclesiastical life of the country, in fact not only of Egypt but far beyond. In any event, the Monophysite

Church of Egypt can be understood not only from its ecclesiastical leaders, the self-conscious patriarchs. It was likewise a Church of a self-conscious monasticism. In connection with the state of consciousness of these monks, it has to be self-evident that strict denominational boundaries could not always be drawn. The fronts changed, but the self-consciousness — and that was what was enduring — a Coptic self-consciousness made it more and more the backbone of the Monophysite opposition.

Just as was the case with the Nestorian Church, so too a strong urge to mission to the outsider was characteristic of the Monophysite Church. For the Coptic Church the region south of Egypt — Nubia and Ethiopia — offered itself as a principal mission field. Until the middle of the sixth century, the Nubians, in so far as they belonged loosely to the Empire, enjoyed, in opposition to the otherwise current laws against pagans, the privilege of still honoring, undisturbed, their goddess in the shrines at Philai on the Upper Nile. In 541 Justinian ended this privilege, and the Empress Theodora sent the Monophysite Priest John, who succeeded, with the support of a likewise Monophysite Bishop of Philai, in converting parts of the Nubians to Christianity. But Orthodox missionaries could also point to some successes. In the long run, however, the Monophysite propaganda was victorious, and Nubian Christianity was oriented totally in its organization to the Coptic Patriarchate of Egypt.

For Ethiopia this propaganda meant the second mission wave, following the first in the fourth century, But here too only this second wave seems to have included an intensive evangelization. That Monophysitism found a quite natural admission to Ethiopia was connected with the fact that since the fourth century the country had been ecclesiastically oriented to Alexandria. The doctrine of the Ethiopian Church from that time seems to have shown no special interest in the inner Monophysite controversies, but, considering the distances from the centers of the disputes, this is not surprising. In any event, people saw in the Coptic Patriarch of Egypt the supreme court, and from the seventh century they had their own supreme bishop, the Abuna, ordained by him.

The Jacobite Church

If the policy of Justinian had made its own contribution to enable the Coptic Church to become consolidated as an autonomous denomination, it was the same policy which, not only through its pressure, but also through its leaving matters alone, occasioned the rise of a Monophysite Church in Syria. After the Council of 536, the Emperor, as reported above, had had the Patriarch Theodosius of Alexandria come to Constantinople in order to gain him to the Council of Chalcedon. He had no success; but instead of being sent into exile, the Patriarch found secure lodging with the Empress Theodora and governed his Church as well as he could from his hiding place, which was one only in name. In 542 the thoroughly Monophysite Client King of the Arabs, the Ghassanid bar Harith bar Gabala, in the Syrian Desert, urged upon Theodora the appointment of some bishops for his territory. The Empress induced the Alexandrian Patriarch to ordain as bishops two Monophysites, who had been staying for some time at Constantinople:

Theodore "of Arabia" and Jacob Burdeana (Baradai). Jacob Baradai (d. 578) was entrusted with the entire East on a vast scale, beginning with the Greek islands by way of Asia Minor to Syria and Armenia, with his seat at Edessa. With immense enthusiasm, among all imaginable dangers and privations, disguised as a beggar, he evangelized wide territories, ordained thousands of priests, not always applying the strictest standards, and finally proceeded to organize for these priests a special Monophysite counterhierarchy that no longer concerned itself with the existing Orthodox hierarchy. The ground had long been prepared. As early as the first half of the century most of the Syrian bishops, especially in Syria Prima, in Osrhoene, in Euphratesia, and in Mesopotamia, had been adherents of Severus of Antioch. Now Jacob ordained some thirty new bishops of his denomination for episcopal sees that were mostly in the hands of the bishops of the Imperial Church. In 557–58 he appointed for his hierarchy in Sergius of Tella also a Patriarch with his "seat" at Antioch. He apparently regarded him as the sole legitimate successor of Severus. The succession of patriarchs was thereafter hardly ever interrupted, except through inner Monophysite schisms and quarrels. From a vague Monophysitism there had now come a Church in its own right. That neither the Patriarch nor most of the bishops could live in their cities mattered little. There were enough monasteries to give them shelter, and the imperial policy favoring Chalcedon was unable to harm them at all.

When Chosroes II, the Persian Great King, who had some votive offerings left over for the Christian churches, conquered broad areas of the Byzantine Empire, especially those territories in which the Monophysites lived could expect relief. In fact, the King expelled some Melkite bishops, but he felt it safer to fill the vacant posts with clerics from the Persian Kingdom. We do not know, however, whether there was a question here of Nestorians. Nevertheless, the Jacobites now succeeded in establishing themselves more firmly in Persia also and even obtained possession of a church in Seleucia-Ctesiphon, the Nestorians' stronghold. This, however, ended with the assassination of Chosroes. Soon after the victory of the Emperor Heraclius over the Persian Kingdom, Monophysite Syria came again under Byzantine rule. Now, here and there, the Byzantines were perforce greeted as liberators, but it happened that, as in Edessa, the bishop, a Monophysite, denied the Orthodox Emperor participation in the liturgy, which naturally only evoked fresh reprisals. Still, it was precisely Heraclius who, with the so-called Monoenergistic doctrine, sought ecclesiastical union for the last time, and for this end even convoked a special Monophysite Synod in which he took part. Since this attempt also miscarried, the persecution of the Monophysites was begun again by the imperial officials, so that they welcomed as deliverers from the ecclesiastical yoke of Constantinople the Muslims who arrived soon thereafter. With this began also for the Syrian Church a period characterized by legal relations which Islam had developed vis-à-vis the "Peoples of the Book," partly complemented by agreements between the conquerors and the bishops, who in the period of distress, as "city lords," had arranged the capitulation to Islam, but also interrupted by occasional persecutions, which of course were not basically of a dogmatic nature.

The supreme head of this Syrian Church remained, now as earlier, the Patriarch of Antioch, even if he did not succeed until 720 in establishing his seat in this city and even then only for a brief time. Ordinarily, the patriarchs, like the bishops, lived in the monasteries, from which they had for the most part come. What distinguished the new Church from the Imperial Church was certainly not in the areas of liturgy or canon law. Here no great break appeared. What really mattered was faith or, better put, dogma, and here not even so much a Christology which would have been essentially different from the orthodox, as rather the resistance to the Council of Chalcedon and its Christological formulas, a resistance which the Church shared with the father of its theology, Severus. This resistance was the real shibboleth, to which of course was gradually added an even stronger and stifling rejection of everything that the Greek imperial central government and its agents had to offer in ecclesiastical political ideas, that is, an awareness which, to be sure, cannot be termed a Syrian national mind, but represented a sort of preliminary of such a mind, a form which was essentially characterized by the linguistic distinction from Greek and not merely by an antipathy to the positive elements in the Greek intellectual world. Severus had written only Greek and hardly understood Syriac. But the longer, the more decidedly, the language of the Jacobite theologians became Syriac, there developed a literature which produced a time of flowering of the Syriac language. Here must be mentioned especially Xenaia of Mabbug (d. ca. 523), then James of Sarug (d. 521): the former was a classic author of Syriac literature, a dogmatician, a polemicist, a preacher, and an exegete at the same time, the latter was a representative of that metrical sermon literature which in similar form found admission even into the Byzantine world. No less important was the famous John of Edessa (d. ca. 586), whom Justinian in his time for obscure reasons had appointed as missionary of the pagan remnant in Asia Minor and who, until his expulsion from Constantinople by the Emperor Justin II, had governed the Monophysites there. We are indebted to him not only for a Syriac Church history but also for the *History of the Eastern Blessed,* that hagiographical collection which became at least as important for the self-evaluation of his Church as all the dogmatic treatises. One of the most important representatives of extensive scholarly interests was James of Edessa (d. 708). His educational road led him by way of Alexandria, he then became Bishop of Edessa, lost this see again, and taught in the monastery of Qennesrin, which was perhaps the outstanding Jacobite educational center of the time. He left a rich literary legacy. He gave lessons in Greek over the opposition of those who now chose to despise not only the Imperial Church but everything else Greek; he is said to have known Hebrew also.

In this world of the Jacobite Church monasticism played a significant role. It was multiform, as elsewhere in the East. There were many hermits in cells and mountain caves, on pillars, and in huts. But there was also a whole multitude of well-populated *cenobia,* where meditation was cultivated, where asceticism was, just as in Egypt, intensified to virtuosity, and where economic activities were to some extent regarded with very mixed feelings. Above all, the monastic settlements in the desert developed styles of life purely in relation to the environment; these were suited to those of the Bedouins and were not without an affinity to ascetical forms of Islam. Theoretically, each monastery was subject to the bishop, without whom there was no blessing of the abbot, no founding of a monastery, and no external activity. But it remains noteworthy that the community in the Jacobite Church never lost its influence: it was always in a position to oppose its own weight to an exaggerated hierarchization of the Church.

This Monophysite Church, frequently called "Jacobite" from its great missionary, became not only a Church of the Syrians but also of the Arabs. That it had its champions in the Ghassanid Princes in the Syrian Desert has already been mentioned. And this form of Christianity pressed forward along the caravan routes into northern and central Arabia, but these Arabian territories did not constitute a separate ecclesial body of their own. Their Christianity remained loosely united to that of the Syriac Church. On the other hand, the Arabs had long pressed forward from the heart of their country into the Syrian area, and indeed not only into the Syrian Desert, but also as settlers inside the walls of the cities in the country east of the Jordan. The centers of Arabian Monophysitism were the episcopal city of Bosra and the great Sergius Pilgrimage in Rusafa, the headquarters of the Ghassanids (Sergiopolis). The Byzantine Emperors of the second half of the sixth century were not always successful in their treatment of the nomadic masses of Arabs on the frontiers of their Empire. They especially all too readily accused the Ghassanid Princes of treason, and so it happened that Islam, storming forward, found allies in these Christian Arabs who very soon submitted to the new religion, whose styles of life and worship in some respects were not all too different from their own. This interaction between Christian and previously pagan Arabs was probably responsible for the fact that there are Christian elements in the Koran, which have been designated, with some probability, as substantially Monophysite.

The Church of the Armenians

In the Armenian Church may be seen a Jacobite denomination so far as the basic interests of the doctrine are concerned. Of course, the historical origins were different. They reflected in a special way the vicissitudes of this people between Byzantine and Persian domination on the one hand and their own peculiar political system on the other. The Armenian Church became as it is, less on the basis of dogmatic and ecclesiastical political succession of imperial synods than on the basis of just these historical dangers. If Nerses the Great, the chief Armenian Bishop (d. ca. 373), and the alleged great-grandson of the evangelizer of Armenia, Gregory the Illuminator, has rightly been called the organizer of the Armenian Church, this was an organization along the lines of the Greek Church, specifically the Church of Cappadocia, just as Nerses himself had been educated and ordained a bishop in Caesarea. In his organization was reflected the relation of respect of Armenian Christianity toward the point of departure of the Armenian mission, Cappadocia. Already his successor, a bishop of the King, had to have himself ordained, to the great annoyance of Caesarea, in the rival metropolitan see of Tyana, until finally the King definitively renounced the ecclesiastical connection with Cappadocia. The period of this separation cannot be exactly pinpointed. But the beginning of the ecclesiastical independence of Armenia had been made, even if not the beginning of a new Church of a different denomination. Soon after, the intellectual self-consciousness of the Armenians was also consolidated. Mesrop (d. 440) gave the nation its own handwriting, and this achievement very soon led to an independent Armenian literature. It is self-evident that at first this was a matter of translations from Greek and Syriac, and in this borrowing the orientation to the intellectual center of the Byzantine Empire acquired a new importance. Of course, ecclesiastically it was now no longer Caesarea that played the great role, but Constantinople, which meanwhile had acquired the supremacy over Cappadocia, to which the Armenians turned.

From 429, however, Persian pressure on Armenia was especially strongly evident, and the connection with the Byzantine Empire to a great extent ended. No Persarmenian bishops could take part in the Synod of Ephesus, and only by means of Nestorian missionaries was it learned what had been done there. In 435 there went to Byzantium an inquiry from the *Catholicus,* which was answered with the *Tomus* of Prochus. Chalcedon too took place without any Armenian representation worthy of mention, and the events of the second half of the fifth century brought no improvement of the situation. Meanwhile, in the Armenian Church people held fast to the doctrine of the unity in Christ. But Chalcedon had rendered decisions which, to Armenian ears, seemingly introduced scarcely familiar distinctions into this unity. The Armenians came in time to know of the *Tome of Leo,* but in a translation which was misleading. It was monks from the School of Severus who finally acquainted the Armenians with the *Henoticon* of the Emperor Zeno and interpreted it contrary to the Synod of Chalcedon. When in 505 and 506 the Emperor Anastasius could force the Persians to an armistice which again brought the Armenian Church a certain freedom, since the Byzantine Church was strongly oriented by this very Emperor to a Monophysite interpretation of the *Henoticon,* this interpretation was now also adopted by the Armenian Church. The *Catholicus* Babgen (490–516) in 506 convoked a Synod at Dvin with Armenian and Iberian bishops, who accepted the *Henoticon,* less, it is true, as a rejection of Chalcedon, which they scarcely knew, than to repudiate Nestorianism, which under Persian rule had evangelized powerfully in Armenia. Under the domination of Justinian there was no change in this position of the Armenian Church. In 554 a Synod again met at Dvin, which completed the break with the Imperial Church — an important decision, especially in view of the ever present threat from the Persians and the Persian Nestorian Church standing behind it; but also in so far as the self-consciousness of the Church vis-à-vis Byzantium was consolidated and new impulses were supplied to the Armenian striving for independence and a new latitude in the confrontation between the two great Churches.

It was the Byzantine Emperor Maurice who sought to put an end to this autonomy of the Armenian Church, as well as to the political freedom and exerted the strongest pressure to convert the Armenians to the Synod of Chalcedon. This produced a schism. The *Catholicus* Moses II refused to take part in a Synod at Constantinople, whereupon the Emperor in 590 appointed an anti-Catholicus for the Armenians under direct Byzantine rule. Only a new attack on Byzantine Armenia by the Persians settled the matter in 610 in favor of the Monophysite Armenians. At this time also the Iberian *Catholicus,* Kiurion, forced himself, as an adherent of the Greeks and thereby of Orthodoxy, out of the close connection with and dependence on the Armenian Church.

The great Persian-Byzantine war under the Emperor Heraclius again led to Byzantine domination of Armenia. The Peace of 629, which the Persians had to conclude after their defeat, relinquished the greatest part of the country to the Byzantines. On the whole, the Armenians were on the side of the Byzantine Emperor in these serious conflicts. But now the clergy of Armenia were again called upon to declare their adherence to the formulas of Chalcedon: if they would not, the Emperor would appoint an anti-Catholicus. The *Catholicus* Yezr yielded, and the Greek clergy offered a weak formula which culminated in the condemnation of Nestorianism, while Chalcedon was passed over in silence, apparently in order to gain the Armenians more easily. True, there was also resistance to this formula, but there can be no question of a real schism. That soon after, in the Monoenergist formula, Heraclius moved near to the ideas of the opponents of Chalcedon made the rallying easier. But from as early as 640 the Muslims were steadily advancing against Armenia, and with this the connection with the Byzantine Church was ended, even before the Arabs were definitively masters of the country. A Synod of Dvin under the Patriarch Nerses III in 648–49 completely rejected the formulas of Chalcedon, and the nation's leader at that time, Theodore Rechtuni, surrendered his country to the Caliph, who granted the Armenians a status of extensive autonomy.

The direction of the Armenian Church lay in the hands of a supreme bishop, a "Great Archbishop" or *Catholicus,* as he was frequently called — the title Patriarch gained the upper hand only relatively late. These *Catholici* were very firmly rooted in the feudalism of the country, and the ups and downs of their history is in some respects comprehensible only because of the rivalries of the tribes and tribal princes, the kings and sub-kings. Even the ecclesiastical organization, the erecting of honorary metropolises, and so forth, was not rarely determined by these political circumstances. The special way of life of the Church was expressed most purely in the literature, which to a great extent was restricted to the religious sphere. With Mesrop began the so-called Golden Age of Armenian literature. From Mesrop himself we know religious writings, talks, and circulars. What in individual cases is to be assigned to his pupils — biblical commentaries, homilies, sermons, and the like — can today be decided only with difficulty. Of special importance for the fifth century are Eznik of Kolb, who not only shared in the Armenian translation of the Bible but also turned against heresies in a polemic and published writings of a religious nature, and also John Mandakuni, the author of sermons and of hymns which were adopted into the liturgy. It was also in the fifth century that Mesrop found his biographer in his pupil Korium and that a man who called himself Agathangelus wrote a history of the evangelization of Armenia and of the missionary Gregory — the classic legend of the early Church history of the country.

The Church history of Armenia in Islamic times hardly differed from the history of any other Church under the domination of the Arabs. Noteworthy, to be sure, is the fact that many Armenians, under the pressure of the Arabs or because of the inner political situation of the country, migrated to the Byzantine Empire and there often achieved the greatest importance, so that the separation of the Armenian Church, despite the dogmatic differences, never meant that deep abyss between Byzantium and Armenia, such as had developed between the Jacobite Church and Byzantium or the Coptic Church and Byzantium.

CHAPTER 58

Early Byzantine Monasticism

The explosive growth of monasticism in the fourth and early fifth centuries was, it is true, accompanied by crises and setbacks, but its further expansion could not be halted by them. Egypt remained the mother country, goal of pilgrimages to the famed sites of the first enthusiasm, but gradually other imperial provinces also pushed themselves more powerfully into the foreground. Especially noteworthy was the power of attraction which Palestine exerted from the early fifth century. The stream of pilgrims from the whole world which hastened to the Holy Places brought along many a one who finally settled in Palestine for a life pleasing to God. Thus there arose here a monasticism which was less self-contained than in Egypt, more receptive in what concerned geographical provenance as well as social status.

The most important founders of the period were without doubt Euthymius the Great, Theodosius the "Cenobiarch," and Sabas. Euthymius (d. 473) founded a *laura,* whose church Juvenal dedicated in 429. Its very beginnings reflected "internationalism." Euthymius himself came from Melitene on the Euphrates, some of his first monks from the Sinai Peninsula, others were Cappadocians and Syrians, a "Roman" was mentioned, and finally a single Palestinian. The founder's life did not move only in the framework of monastic aims; no great abbot of the day could avoid the ecclesiastical political strife centering on the Patriarch Juvenal and ignore Chalcedon. The desert of Palestine was too near Jerusalem. Euthymius did not take part in the revolt of the monks around Theodosius in 452, and finally his exertions succeeded in inducing the ex-Empress Eudocia, who preferred to hatch her plots in Jerusalem if in this way she could thwart the Orthodox course of the Court of Constantinople, to become reconciled with Juvenal and abandon the propaganda against Chalcedon. The "Cenobiarch" Theodosius (d. 529) laid out his foundation east of Bethlehem as a monastery of cenobites from the start. His home was Cappadocia and he had early entered the service of the Church as a psalmist. This circumstance and his familiarity with the writings and aims of his great countryman, Basil, were probably the reason why, against the trend of the age, he established a strict *cenobium,* It was apparently regarded in Palestine as a model of its type, and finally the Patriarch appointed Theodosius as Abbot-General, or Archimandrite, over all *cenobia.* Abbot-General of the archorites and *lauras,* that is, of the isolated or loosely associated monastic settlements, was Saint Sabas (d. 532) son of a high official from Cappadocia. After some vicissitudes in various monasteries of the Holy Land, he withdrew into a hermitage in the vicinity of the west bank of the Dead Sea. Around 483 he made it into a *laura,* which soon attracted 150 monks — a "city in the desert," as it was called. Despite his gifts as an organizer, he had many difficulties, apparently because higher questions of spirituality did not interest him. When the controversy over the evaluation of Origen's doctrines flared up again, it led to a secession of a whole group of monks and the founding of the New Laura in 508, the center of the Origenist movement, and Sabas and his successors were able only gradually to assert their authority over it.

On the whole it can be said that, despite all difficulties, the three great founders

contributed much to make Palestine gradually a refuge of Chalcedonian Orthodoxy. The two named as archimandrites by the Patriarch found it difficult, of
course, to exercise their authority in the southwest of the country also: here arose
centers of Monophysite propaganda, which were oriented rather to Coptic Egypt
than to Jerusalem. The Georgian Prince Nabarnugi, who became a monk in Palestine under the name Peter — Peter the Iberian — had founded a monastery of
Iberians at Jerusalem but had then withdrawn because of Juvenal and moved
to this area. During the monks' revolt of 452 he was made Bishop of Gaza. He
was able to occupy his see only temporarily, but through his activity he made the
coastal strip of the country a refuge for Monophysites. It is significant that Severus,
the later Patriarch of Antioch, was his pupil and finally settled near Gaza as a
monk before he began his career in Constantinople.

The flowering of Palestinian monasticism left its mark also on the literature of
the age. Whereas the spiritual content of Egyptian monasticism found expression
in the collections of *Apophthegmata* of the great monastic fathers, Palestine gave
to monastic literature a great biographer in the person of Cyril of Scythopolis in
the sixth century. He devoted great biographies to Euthymius and Sabas and also
treated other monastic founders. He was able to describe the monks and their
life "from within" and to show how, despite all the politics, the great enthusiasm
of the past again and again found new life.

At this period the Sinai Peninsula also moved into the full light of the history
of the monastic life. In the vicinity of the episcopal city of Pharan on the east
bank of the Gulf of Suez the monastic settlement of Raithu (el Tor) is attested
from ca. 400. On Sinai itself rose the Brier Monastery, later called the Monastery of
St. Catherine, which Justinian had surrounded with a fortified wall and for which
he built the church.

In Syria around this time the village of Telnesin became a great pilgrimage spot
of Christianity, for here there arose around the column on which Simeon the Stylite
had led his ascetical life (d. 459) a mighty complex of churches, monasteries, and
pilgrims' hostels, which of course the Monophysites soon claimed for themselves,
just as they claimed the saint himself. The Orthodox attached themselves instead
to the younger Simeon the Stylite (d. 596), who had had his pillar on the *Mons
Admirabilis* near Antioch.

In the capital, Constantinople, monasticism made only slow progress. First,
it was established in Bithynia and in the Asiatic suburbs, and almost always it
was foreigners, especially Syrians, who appeared as founders: the hermit Auxentius (d. ca. 473), for example, who settled on Mount Scopus and organized other
colonies of monks around himself. The area around Prusa seems not to have
become a country of monks until the seventh century. In Constantinople itself,
despite all the legends, there were no monasteries from the time of Constantine
the Great. The most famous and, for the ecclesiastical political events of the capital, most significant foundation was that of the Monastery of the Acemetae by
the Syrian Alexander, who had already been active as a founder on the Euphrates
and came to Constantinople ca. 405. The Studium Monastery was founded in 463,
however, it did not experience its flowering until the early Middle Byzantine period.

The decades around and after the Council of Chalcedon saw monasticism
at a climax of its activity in Church politics and for this reason at the height of

the danger to its ideas and the ideals of the age of foundation. The peril was so obvious that people were concerned for a remedy. Characteristically, it was the Emperor who produced a corresponding proposal, which was then enacted by the Council Fathers of Chalcedon with slight modifications as canons 3 and 4. Canon 4 denounced those monks who, relying on the esteem for their state among the public, created disturbances in Church and State, moved from place to place without fixed dwelling places, and founded "monasteries" where they pleased. The canon prescribed that no one must establish a monastery or oratory without the permission of the local bishop, that every monk was subject to the bishop's supervision and had to stay in his monastery in quiet; further, that no slave might be accepted into a monastery without the consent of his master. For the first time also marriage was forbidden to the monk by canon law (canon 7).

It may be that in this way, for the first time, monasteries and monasticism were recognized at all in canon law or, respectively, were regarded as an institution of public law. However, the purpose which the imperial proposers had in mind was hardly achieved. At first it was often bishops themselves who misused monks for their own ecclesiastical political ends. After canon 4 granted them a power of dispensation, they continued unhindered in these activities. And the hierarchy itself was undecided in the midst of the struggles over the faith to the extent that "for the sake of the higher good" very religious but also fanatical and fanaticized monks again and again found reason to conduct themselves as saviors of the faith against the bishops. In any case, Church history after Chalcedon shows that the success of canons 3 and 4 was only meager. The monastic system of the Eastern Church was from the very beginning — if one excepts such as Pachomius and Basil, who, however, had only slight aftereffects as organizers — a movement rather than an institution. One was a monk by his own will, and an abbot by his own will. The action of the hierarchy always had to lag behind, since juridical concepts remained foreign to the essence of this movement. Without doubt, many educated men also found the way to the monastery. But to the great mass of monks, who rejected all culture, the enthusiastic awareness of a mission could always become a danger. But the *Apophthegmata Patrum,* those precious collections of monastic epigrammatic sayings, the great monastic *vitae* of the sixth century, the spiritual letters of a Barsanuphius in the sixth century, the conferences of the Palestinian Abbot Dorotheus, and the *Spiritual Ladder* of John Climacus of the seventh century say more on the heart of the movement than all the scandalous reports of fanaticism and squabblers in monasticism. In Maximus Confessor monastic mysticism found that height of synthesis which would never again be achieved in later Byzantium.

The legislation of the Emperor Justinian also tried to bring this monasticism under definitive control. It was due to him that more precise rules defined the details of vocation, of the reception, period of trial, and profession, and facilitated ecclesiastical control. But if he made the effort to make the strict *vita communis* generally obligatory, this was a failure, which disregarded the very nature of the "movement."

CHAPTER 59

Theological and Religious Literature

Mighty as may have been the dogmatic struggles which convulsed the Imperial Church from the mid-fifth century until the onslaught of Islam — this period by no means belongs to the great periods of classical theology. The formula of Chalcedon imposed on its champions rather the task of the masterly distinction than that of a synthesis, and the distinction had to keep separate what could be presented for religious experience only as a unity. Where there was question of unity, it found expression in a terminology which was not yet the common property of the age and in adjectives and adverbs — *adiairetos, achoristos* — which asserted the privative rather than the positive. An outstanding theologian would have been needed to make these necessarily colorless statements susceptible of religious experience. But for a long time the Chalcedonian theology had no such representative. And so philosophemes were sought with which to do justice to the distinctions. For the most part they lived on the vocabulary of the Aristotelian school, but no one who made use of them could without more ado be called an Aristotelian. In the *Tome* of Pope Leo I, this theology still had the powerful appeal with which the language of Latin rhetoric knew how to construct its antitheses in monumental precision. In the Greek syntax, more adept at modulation, it revealed its indigence very much more easily. Thus the strict Chalcedonian theology languished to some extent; it longed — to express it differently — for that Formula of Cyril, discriminated against at Chalcedon, of the one incarnate *physis* of the *Logos* or of the one *physis* of the Logos-made-Man.

That is not intended to mean that the history of theology of the age can supply no names. Perhaps Leontius of Byzantium may be mentioned here, even though his position in the framework of the totality of the theology of the epoch remains disputed. Of course, the majority of the theologians very soon began to give way to their yearning for Cyril. The occasion was provided by the so-called *communicatio idiomatum,* that is, the possibility of uniting the divine and the human in one single statement in regard to the Person of Christ, that is, with the *hen prosopon* of Christ as the real bearer of the predicates. In this manner of speaking, one could no longer join the *"qua hen prosopon,"* presuppose it as self-evident, or consciously pass over it in silence. What then appeared was the desire for "Baroque formulations," impressive antitheses, and a fascinating inexactitude. The tendency went farther. Partly in conscious, partly in unconscious approximation of the standpoint of the opponents of Chalcedon, persons insisted on these formulations as a shibboleth of Orthodoxy, whereby they were plunged into serious internal confrontations, such as that over the Three Chapters. Many theologians of the time followed this trend, the Scythian monks as well as John the Grammarian of Caesarea in Palestine or the Patriarch Ephrem of Antioch, and in the Emperor Justinian I they all found their powerful helper, who assisted their theology to its breakthrough in the Imperial Church. Purest in its point of departure and most exact in its formulation was probably the doctrine of Bishop John of Scythopolis, who characteristically was also preoccupied in detail with the writings of the pseudo-Areopagite. Furthermore, soon thereafter the champions of Monoenergism would derive precisely from the writings of the so-called Neo-Chalcedonians a part of their arguments, especially from Theodore of Raithu, in so far as he is not identical with the initiator of Monoenergism, Theodore of Pharan.

The attempted approximation to the standpoint of the Monophysites had, of course, no ecclesiastical political success. For these possessed in Severus of Antioch the greatest theologian of the day, to whom the Chalcedonian faction could oppose nothing of equal weight. Based above all on a biblical-patristic culture, without involving himself overly in the uncertainty of philosophical terminology, he again took hold of the theology of Cyril of Alexandria. He always kept in view the concrete, historical appearance of Christ, and, proceeding directly from this concrete idea, he identified *physis, hypostasis,* and *prosopon* to a great extent. The idea of unity was the predominating one; in relation to the unity, the concrete unity in Christ, there cannot be two natures. The Synod of Chalcedon had entangled itself precisely in this contradiction and so, despite all appeasing interpretations, no recognition could be given to its decrees. The terminus of the unity in Christ could always be only the one divine nature.

But what made Severus the undisputed Church Father of the Monophysites was not only his consistent dogmatic system, the fact that he had an answer ready for every attack on the part of the Orthodox theology, but also the circumstance that his comprehensive literary work was concerned with all aspects of religious life. An extensive correspondence, festive homilies and sermons, liturgical poetry, and so forth enriched the life of a Church which found with him its route to independence.

There were, to be sure, also in the Monophysite Church deviations from this classical doctrine; but, beside Severus, Julian of Halicarnassus, the father of the Aphthartodocetists, and the representatives of the Theodosianists, Aktists, and Agnoites, and whatever else they may have been called, were all poor examples. Only John, nicknamed Philoponus, could stand beside Severus for the period of origin. His work was intended as the balance between philosophy and dogma, and in it he of course fell into a sort of tritheism in the eyes of those who distrusted him — an interpretation which in its justification is dependent on how his notion of the Trinitarian nature and essence is interpreted. The Monophysites themselves, in the long run, did not admit the reproach but set him alongside Severus, whom he had himself always defended. Apparently he was one of the most important representatives of that philosophical and scientific viewpoint which so advantageously distinguished the higher schools of Alexandria from the teaching profession at Athens. Significant was his commentary on the biblical account of creation, which was based partly on the exegesis of the great Basil and, through his method of taking hold of problems, profitably contrasted to that *Topography* of Cosmas Indicopleustes, which was really only an effort to explain the work of the six days.

Outside the framework of the dogma and polemics of the age stands the figure of the obscure pseudo-Areopagite, an author with an indestructible preference for mystification and doubtless also with the talent for it. If he is not identical with Peter the Fuller, then the latter must be postulated as his twin-brother! Compared with the turbulent career of the Fuller, rarely blessed with success, his literary activity can be regarded as an attempt to construct an unreal view of life and to favor it with an indisputable authority — a cosmos which was ideally set off to advantage from the environment with which the author never got along, together with its everyday authority. And he succeeded to the extent that his centuries-long respectful acceptance cannot be explained by the pseudonym alone. The pseudo-Areopagite, with his treatises on the heavenly and earthly hierarchies, created a polished system of analogies which not only came halfway to meet the demands of the bishops of his own and later times but also gave to the liturgical achievement an in-depth focus which became very important for the liturgical theology, as well as for the liturgical art of the Byzantines of the future. With his work on the divine names, of course, he made the attempt, condemned to founder in its innermost essence, to create a system of negative theology. And if his terminology on the *via supereminentiae* in the statements on God caused him to become lost in linguistic impossibilities, nevertheless he thereby set a standard for the necessary breakdown of all talk about God. In other respects it spoke for his mystic instinct that, in addition to a system of illumination, which proceeded in a strictly hierarchical manner and separated the simple man from God by a protracted series of degrees rather than united him with him, he stressed again and again the notion of the "nearness" of God, compared to which the distances in his "hierarchies" became irrelevant.

In any case, the pseudo-Areopagite stands outside his age; and if Severus is disregarded, it can be said that only the Monoenergist Controversy of the seventh century again gave Byzantium a theologian of his rank — Maximus Confessor, who, of course, even less than Severus, can be restricted to dogma and polemics. It was certainly to his merit to have created, in the confusion over the definition of the energies and will in Christ, by means of a clear-sighted terminology, the presuppositions which were necessary in order to grasp the heart of the problem at all. Maximus was a Dyothelite as regards the physical faculty of willing in Christ, but in *thelema gnomikon* he saw a property of the *hypostasis* — a distinction which would have been suited to prepare a speedy end to the confrontation if attention had really been paid to it. But this was only one aspect of the importance belonging to the Confessor. It was probably decisive that in him exact dogma and mysticism achieved an insoluble connection. He hardly showed the importance of any new elements in the mysticism of the Byzantine Church: he was linked to Evagrius and through him to Origen, whereas pseudo-Dionysius, on whom, however, he wrote a commentary, remained rather on the fringes; he had incorporated Christology, which Evagrius was little concerned for, into this system, and out of the dialectics of the Christological formulas, which had hitherto been handled all too abstractly, not to say negatively, he constructed a mystical theology of the Cross, on which a suffering and glorified Christ collected all antitheses into an ultimate unity. He was the greatest master of the mysticism of Christ in the Byzantine sphere — never again equalled.

Besides Maximus there must be named the Patriarch of Jerusalem, Sophronius, one of the first champions of the two energies in Christ as opposed to the Alexandrian Union of 633; he must be mentioned also as preacher, hagiographer, and religious poet; then also Anastasius of Sinai, whose work and personality are still not sufficiently delineated, a sort of summit of anti-Monophysite polemics, but one who with some of his sermons determined the homiletics of the entire Byzantine period.

It is curious to establish that, alongside the great Christological controversies of the age, the newly popular Origenism of the same age — if one disregards official notifications and, perhaps, Maximus Confessor — found hardly a literary expression. The presumption is natural that the *pateres pneumatikoi* in the monastic settlements of Palestine and elsewhere could hardly extract much from the system of the great Alexandrian to the extent that they could understand it at all, and that there were probably only individuals among the Palestinian monks who were conversant with more than single basic elements of Origenism, while the mass of the "Origenists" were only their followers. Individual traces of Origenism can be discovered here and there, but they are of no great importance. On the other hand, we know some collections of simple instructions for the spiritual life of the monks, especially in community, who, far removed from losing themselves in speculations, displayed an astonishing knowledge of the deep psychological processes of life in seclusion from the world and from it drew their concrete conclusions for the guidance of hermits and still more of cenobites. The collection of questions and answers of, for example, the recluse Barsanuphius, who lived in Palestine in the mid-sixth century, with its very discreet method of direction of souls, the spiritual conferences of the Abbot Dorotheus, from the same period and the same environment, which later enjoyed a great repute in the monastery of Studium, to name only some, especially happily represent this trend. If there was danger, then Origenism was not the only answer for the spiritual life of the time. Messalianism, with its dualistic world view, at least in *praxi,* its exclusive concern for the "pure," and its longing for a physical experience of the state of grace, gave much trouble to the guardians of Orthodox monasticism. Of course, in the spiritual instructions of Diadochus of Photice they had a manual which came to meet the legitimate wishes as far as it staked out firm boundaries. Here a spiritual organ was discovered, the *aisthesis noera,* which should guide to the sure distinction between physically perceptible mystical phenomena and demoniacal delusions — a work of amazing psychological insight.

The classical Evagrian mysticism, here and there thoroughly indebted to Origenism, found only in the seventh century its revival in a form which made it acceptable to Orthodoxy. In addition to Maximus there must be mentioned here especially the Libyan monk Thalassius. Probably also under obligation to this system was that treatise of the seventh century which had the widest impact, the *Klimax* (*Ladder of Paradise*) of John of Sinai, even if in him the final stages of the union with God are rather hinted at than worked out. Interesting is the confirmation that in this work the famous Jesus-Prayer, the *mneme Iesou* more precisely, whose method goes much farther back, already appears as an integrating ingredient incorporated into the system of ascent, without the entrance into the spiritual behavior which this *mneme* presupposes as having already been simplified and rendered less demanding.

If the later Byzantine biblical exegesis again and again had recourse to the sixth century, this is so not because the explanation of Scripture at this period had been especially deep, but rather because in the sixth century the basis for those *catenae* was laid, which at the same time presented material and form in an outstanding way for the exegesis of long generations. Thus, as the dogmaticians collected ever more frequently anthologies of patristic passages for specific themes that interested them, finally to argue only from such *florilegia,* so now also the biblical exegetes began to assemble and arrange for every verse of a scriptural book the commenting texts of the most varied older authors. It remains noteworthy that these florilegists, consciously or unconsciously, in this always remained most strongly influenced by the great Antiochene exegetes even when these had fallen under the anathema of ecclesiastical synods as theologians, but this still speaks for the exegetical taste of the collectors.

One of the first compilers of *catenae* was apparently Procopius of Gaza in the sixth century, famed as head of a school of Christian sophists in the Palestinian city. His *catena* of the Octateuch became the model for all later ones. He also commented in this manner on other books of the Old Testament. The homiletics of the sixth and seventh centuries did not occupy in the whole of theological literature anything resembling the place it had had at the end of the fourth and the beginning of the fifth centuries. In the epoch of controversial dogmatic nomenclature rhetorical emphasis and amplification were apparently more dangerous than a collection of definitions! Only isolated oratorical talent appears. Then in the seventh century there emerged numerous preachers, whose more precise determination as to time and place still offers difficulties. Important for the future was also the homiletic legacy of the Cypriote Bishop Leontius of Neapolis, who was at the same time the most important hagiographer of the century. With his *Life* of the Alexandrian Patriarch John the Compassionate he created a monument of the ecclesiastical life of Egypt before Islam and, with the presentation of the "Fool in Christ," Simeon of Emesa, a precious document of bizarre popular religious life in the Middle East.

If the totality is surveyed, it may perhaps be said that the systematic theology of the age, apart from a few exceptions, lacked the trend toward the creative. On the other hand, a Peter the Fuller, identified with the pseudo-Areopagite, reveals what these querulous people were spiritually capable of and thereby discloses something of the disunited breadth of the talents of these men of late antiquity. And if the monasticism of the time was in general no better than the hierarchy, it must not be forgotten that here too for the most part only the hotheads of history have been preserved. The above-mentioned ascetical writers from the desert spoke another language. Here the theology of spirituality made Its supreme achievement.

CHAPTER 60

Organization and Inner Life
of the Eastern Imperial Church

The Council of Chalcedon — and no end. Even for the organization of the Imperial Church the Synod constituted a decisive date. The famous canon 28, to be sure, took up the decisions of the Synod of 381, but to a primacy of honor were now added jurisdictional privileges: the right of ordination in the ancient, hitherto autonomous great metropolitan areas of the provinces of Asia, Pontus, and Thrace, and beyond them a sort of missionary primacy for the frontier areas of the Empire that were until now subject to no metropolis. And if in 381 there was mention of a primacy of honor "after that of Rome," in 451 one spoke of an equal rank with Rome. But, basically there was no question of a novelty in this canon. We must not forget that at the latest from 421 we have to reckon with the political equalization between Constantinople and Rome. Finally in 421 the Emperors Honorius and Theodosius II had already attempted to establish the authority of the bishop of their capital in Illyricum. Hence it is not unlikely that Chalcedon with its canon only consolidated what had already begun promisingly as a development. In a decree of 477 the Emperor Zeno took a further step. When, on the occasion of the restoration of Orthodoxy in Constantinople in opposition to Arianism, the Emperor Theodosius I had decreed as the norm the faith of Rome and Alexandria, so Zeno called the Church of Constantinople "mater nostrae pietatis et christianorum orthodoxae religionis omnium." Nothing was said of Rome. Of course, the Emperor Justinian I again very strongly stressed the Roman primacy and in a critical situation took it into account de facto. But soon Rome's freedom of action was for political reasons no longer all too great, and the East quickly became used, not indeed to writing Rome off, but to exerting itself only when no alternative remained. Rome's primacy was in no sense denied, but apparently it was believed that the claims of this primacy were satisfied with "honorable mention." But the more the chief bishops of the Imperial Church in Asia Minor, Syria, and Egypt had to do to maintain themselves and prevail against the Monophysites, the more they were dependent on the protectorate of the Bishop of the capital. Then the occupation of broad areas of Christian territory by Islam only furthered this development. What canons and imperial laws prepared, what the activity of the Patriarch of Constantinople emphasized, was confirmed by the development of protocol, especially of the title of "Ecumenical Patriarch." From the Acacian Schism at the latest this designation was tendered to the Byzantine Patriarch. Only Pope Pelagius II, to whose ears it came that now even the synod officially used this title for the Patriarch, entered a protest against it with the Patriarch John the Faster (582–95). Gregory the Great, who in other respects, contrary to Leo the Great, in practice recognized canon 28, took up this protest. The Emperor Maurice thought he must urge peace, but Gregory argued that by his protest he was defending the rights of the other bishops, which were curtailed by such a title. He had no success. Of course, the title can be translated by a colorless "Patriarch of the Empire." But the Patriarchs of Constantinople themselves proved that it was susceptible of a weighty interpretation.

It is significant that Photius was the first to introduce the title into the protocol of the patriarchal charters, that Cerularius was the first to adopt it on his seal, and that the patriarchs included it in their signature only from the thirteenth century. In other words: the stages in the development of the title occur together with the stages of the strained relations between Rome and Constantinople.

Since the patriarchs of Constantinople were not content with the right of ordination in their new sphere, but exercised in it that jurisdictional and doctrinal authority which earlier the patriarchs of Alexandria called their own in Egypt and Libya, the development of their primacy was accompanied by a weakening of the old metropolitan organization. The entire life of the Imperial Church gradually concentrated on Constantinople. The weaker the attendance at synods in the province became, the more popular became the synod which assembled around the patriarch, the so-called *Synodus Endemusa,* which can be traced back to the fourth century and where all metropolitans met who were staying in the capital for any reason. The ancient structure of the metropolitan organization was upset also by the ever more frequent creation of autocephalous archbishoprics, that is, by the elevation of simple bishoprics to the rank of archbishoprics, which however obtained no suffragans. This exemption was mostly the outcome of political or personal rivalries. Basically, the most recent patriarch, that of Jerusalem, owed its origin to such an exemption. And the same is true of the autocephalous Archbishopric of Cyprus.

Again and again the effort was made to fix the status of the individual churches also in writing, and to these efforts we owe the so-called *Notitiae episcopatum,* which present the rank of the individual sees among themselves. Such a list for the Patriarchate of Constantinople may have come to a certain completion under the Emperor Justinian. Perhaps it was revised under the dynasty of the Emperor Heraclius. At that time it gave a number of thirty-three metropolises and now already thirty-four autocephalous archbishoprics.

All these problems strongly interfered with the legal status of the Church. If the Bible and the tradition of the Fathers were regarded as the primary sources of the canonical life of the Church, in the course of the generations the need arose for individual statements of norms and decisions, and soon the Imperial Church, like the Empire itself, saw itself faced with the problem of codifying the material as a whole. At Antioch there occurred the first extant attempt at a systematic collection of the valid canon law. The redactor was one John the Scholastic, who later became the Patriarch John III of Constantinople (565–77). He divided the matter into fifty categories (*titloi*), under which he arranged the pertinent canons or parts of canons of the synods held up to then and regarded as binding and material from the canonistic writings of the Fathers. In addition to his collection of canons, John now also arranged a collection of civil law enactments on ecclesiastical material by excerpting the most important Novels of Justinian. Today this collection is known as the *Collectio 78 capitum.* From there it was then only one step to collections which took into account also the canon and *nomos,* the so-called *nomocanones,* that is, collections which brought into a single system canon law as well as imperial law — the latter in so far as it affected the Church. The oldest *nomocanon,* the so-called *Nomocanon of Fifty Titles,* likewise perhaps originated at Antioch.

If the life of the Byzantine Church is gauged by the pitiless dogmatic struggles, the harsh personal rivalries of the bishops and patriarchs, the blood that flowed, and the hatred that produced this bloodletting, the question arises where was the Christianity of this Church. Perhaps this impression, which the external events convey, is to some extent softened if one turns to the liturgy of the period. How this is of significance to the origins of the so-called Liturgy of St. Basil and the Liturgy of St. John Chrysostom will long remain a puzzle. In all likelihood, both liturgies came from the Syrian area. But it was precisely our centuries in which they found at Constantinople their completion and a noteworthy enrichment. It is not useless to mention here a few small elements in the construction which were at that time inserted into the liturgy and which greatly account for its fascination. The fifth century enriched the liturgical formularies with the *Trisagion,* over whose Trinitarian or Christological interpretation there was so much wrangling, but which, as an element of liturgical rhythmization and intensification vigorously prepared for the scriptural reading. Again, without the dogmatically disputed background of the time, that hymn, perhaps composed by Justinian himself, with the opening words *Ho monogenes huios,* is unthinkable; it is one of the best examples of how in liturgical dress dogmatic strife could find the way back to its religious origin. The Emperor Justin II (565–78) is said to have introduced two hymns into the liturgy, which are probably older but in their new place incomparably reproduce briefly and deeply all that pertains to the essence of the Byzantine liturgy: first, the so-called *Cherubikon,* which presents all liturgical action in the Church as a duplication of the liturgy of the cherubim before the throne of the Most High, and then the communion song *Tou deipnou sou tou mystikou,* in which is expressed something of the humility of orthodox piety, which again and again, unobserved, cuts the ground from under the pageantry of the ecclesiastical organization. Also in this period the festal calendar acquired an important enrichment. The sixth century also gave to the Byzantine Church its greatest liturgical poet, Romanus the Melodist, the creator of the *Kontakion.* This form of liturgical hymn is, one may say, rhythmic prose, and, as rhythmic prose, nothing other than a sermon. But this literary definition cannot obscure the high poetic gifts of Romanus, in whom the stylized antithetical dogmatic statement is joined in a special manner with an almost picturesque talent of typical viewpoint. And what the Byzantine Church later produced in liturgical poetry lived on the not always sound amplification of this early creation.

Perhaps it is somewhat daring to designate another branch of the devout life of the Byzantine Church, which developed especially in this period, as a turning from the logomachy of the theologians of the time: the cult of icons. It can be pinpointed that the ancient Christian hostility to images came to an end precisely in the sixth century and that indifference in regard to icons could no longer be maintained. The people seized upon icons not as a *Biblia pauperum* but honored them with the fervor which belonged to the bearers of grace, and the icons came to meet the people by dispensing grace, doing signs and wonders, consoling, and helping wherever the trust of the faithful demanded this. If it has been said that the cult of icons was an expression of Orthodoxy as such, this is correct certainly at the earliest only from the seventh century, but from then on more emphatically. As escape from the dogmatic misery it was a religiously intelligible process, which of course introduced in a fatal manner the dichotomy which gradually would determine the Byzantine ecclesiastical system ever more strongly. But perhaps one may go a step farther. There is question not only of escape but probably also of a religious event which in a remarkable manner decided the dogmatic struggle in its own favor. Without using the slogan, "Monophysitism of the Byzantine icon of Christ," the notion cannot be rejected that that vacuum which the formula of Chalcedon left unresolved was again filled in the icon, in an icon which, although artistically it could represent only nature, went beyond this nature to a degree and deified it, so that if it is desired to add a postscript to the Byzantine icon of Christ, the Cyrillan formula would be more adapted to this than the Chalcedonian.

The religious life of the people was reflected also in the "life" of their saints. But it is interesting that the hagiographer Romanus made noticeable in this period that accumulating of legendary and not rarely piquant traits which occasionally even evoked the mistrust of the ecclesiastical authorities but apparently satisfied the taste of the people better than some of the labored expositions of hagiographical rhetoric.

If canonical decrees on discipline and order among clergy and laity are at all capable of giving information on the inner life of the community, this applies to the canons of the Synod of 691–92, which, because of the meeting-place in the imperial palace at Constantinople, is called the Synod "in Trullo" and regarded itself as an ecumenical completion of the Fifth and Sixth Synods, both of which had issued no disciplinary canons. Without any systematic arrangement, these canons, 102 in number, presented a comprehensive and very instructive collection of prescriptions on the inner life of the Church of the period — at the same time a reflection of the difficult situation into which the Byzantine Church had fallen through the invasions of numerous barbarian tribes, through imperial measures of resettlement, and through new heresies. It was in accord with the negative type of canons that almost only the shady sides of ecclesiastical life were mentioned. Behind them stood an inner ecclesiastical development, to which far too little thought has been given, in view of the denominational and dogmatic struggles that claimed all the interest. Without doubt the Synod intended to legislate for the Universal Christ, but it is also certain that it had in mind the specifically Byzantine canon law and in a series of canons took a stand *expressis verbis* against the usages of the Western Church, for example in canon 13 on clerical marriage, canon 55 against fasting on the Saturdays of Lent, and in canon 67 with its prohibition of the use of kosher meat, quite apart from the repetition of the anathema against Pope Honorius I in canon 1.

The Emperor Justinian II sought to compel Pope Sergius I (687–701) to sign, but his emissaries were frustrated by the Italian militia, and the Emperor himself soon had to go into exile. But in 705 he recovered the throne and now tried by peaceful means; finally in 711 Pope Constantine went personally to the East, and everything indicates that he agreed orally with the Emperor on the recognition of the canons while expunging those that were expressly directed against Rome. The tradition of the canons in the Eastern Church did not take this reconciliation into account, but in the West people were gradually content.

If the picture in these synodal decrees is not without spot and wrinkle, these shady sides were brilliantly covered over in the ecclesiastical art of the time. The age of Justinian represents in this respect a climax of secular importance. The most excellent expression is the ecclesiastical architecture, to which Justinian devoted enormous sums. In Hagia Sophia not only was a unique result achieved technically, but at the same time the mystical unity of God's Kingdom, Church, and Empire was expressed at one time. It was not only the Church which could do this. To architecture belonged the liturgy, and indeed ecclesiastical and imperial liturgy together in one interlacing, which means a sublimation of all that was called Byzantium — a sublimation which the Empire needed all the more, the more unfermented the juridical and canonical bases of just this interlacing were. Hagia Sophia is the expression of the Byzantine illusion of an Imperial Church, whose historical becoming and growing never measured up to the dream in stone. This flight from reality is, regarded from the viewpoint of Church history and not from that of art history also a *movens* within the Byzantine painting of the period, which more and more went in the direction of the icon, and in fact of the icon understood as a picture which bears grace and imparts graces. The revolutionary change of the times after the breakthrough of the Justinianean restoration policy in the sixth century — barbarians and war on all frontiers and into the heartland of the Empire — awakened a great longing for the visible and tangible Savior, and what had begun as painting technique emptied under the eyes of the believer into a sort of real presence of the thing represented, brusque echo of the idea of a "hypostatic union" in the dress of art. The theologians, in so far as there were any, resigned or tried, themselves carried away, to lag behind with likewise clumsy formulas of the development of popular piety.

CHAPTER 61

The Assault of Islam

In less than one generation Islam inundated great parts of Eastern Christendom and ended many quarrels simply by cutting them off from the capital of the Roman Empire. This storm did not arise by accident, and the permanence of its success lies to a considerable degree in the fact that large portions of the Christianity conquered by it were Arabic or already strongly infiltrated by Arabs. Along the commercial route which led from Damascus to southern Arabia, the so-called Frankincense Route, the city-system had considerably developed in the sixth century, due to the active traffic in goods in contrast to other provinces of the Empire. These cities played their role as stopping places and commodity depots for the caravans from Mecca, which at that time became the center of Arabian commerce. Outside the walls of the cities arose caravanseries with Arab personnel.

These centers of Arabic life more and more attracted seminomads from the nearby desert; and finally whole tribes, if they were not urbanized, were still drawn into the city's sphere of influence. This development became all the stronger, the more frequently the other commercial routes of the Byzantine Empire to the East were closed by the wars with Persia.

But also the great desert around the Dead Sea beyond the Jordan and south from Damascus to the Persian Gulf had long ago become the exercise-ground of Arabian tribes. They could only partly be kept under control by the great powers, Byzantium and Persia. To the extent that this succeeded, they served their respective overlord as vanguard against the other great power. Thus in the East, at the mouth of the Euphrates, the Arabs under the leadership of their sheiks of the Lakhmid family were again and again won by the Persians for service against the Byzantines. Their chief place was al-Hira, and from Persia they were partly gained for Nestorianism, even if the Lakhmids themselves accepted the Christian religion later than many of their followers. The "Byzantine" Arabs in the Syrian Desert had their chief place at Rusafa, east of Homs. Their leaders were the sheiks of the Ghassanid house, who had early been won for Monophysitism. Much depended for both Empires on their careful handling of these desert tribes. Monophysitism bound the Ghassanids to a denomination in which a self-consciousness in regard to the imperial central government could maintain itself more strongly than in Orthodoxy, and the Nestorianism of the Lakhmids was not the result of dogmatic considerations but of the mission of the Church of that country in whose direction the political ambitions of these Arabs moved. In addition, both denominations were united in the struggle against the ancient Arabian paganism, and the balance seemed to have been discovered especially happily in the monastic foundations in the desert. These monasteries became, presumably independently of their confessional denomination, popular halting places for all Arabs. The harsh life in the desert must not have differed substantially from the asceticism of the Christian monks. Simple cult forms, frequent genuflection, fasting, religious invocations arranged in litany form, and so forth, easily impressed the Arabs, and the famed formula *Heis theos,* which had found wide diffusion in the Syrian areas as a Christian religious invocation, placed on the believer no excessive demands. Many Arabs, drawn either by this religiosity or weary of their severe life as Bedouins, became monks in these monasteries, where people were prepared to accommodate their individuality. The best example without doubt was the treatment which very early in the fifth and sixth centuries Arabs who were devoted to the solitary life in the caves and *lauras* of Palestine found with the great monastic fathers, Euthymius and Sabas. Here, probably for the first time, the Arabs received a bishop of their blood, who was furnished no stable seat but, as Bishop of the Camps, was responsible for the evangelization of other tribes. And here also must be sought the beginnings of the further progress of a thus modified Christianity toward the South to the oases of North Arabia via the caravan routes to Mecca and Medina.

Thus for Muhammad at the time when he had his religious experiences and wrote them down, Christianity was just as well known as was Judaism, regardless of whether or not he himself had come to Syria as a commercial traveler. Christian elements have frequently been identified in the Koran, and an exact analysis of these elements probably indicates specifically Monophysite features, by which the

Christianity which was familiar to Muhammad was affected. That Muhammad at first saw his confederates in Judaism and Christianity is well known. This was not only naiveté but based on the common possession of a basic monotheistic attitude and on the strong doctrine of unity of the Monophysites, even if there cannot be denied what is much too little emphasized: that the position which the Koran assigns to Jesus, if it should be traced to Christian influences, looks to Nestorianism rather than to Monophysitism. Of course, in the long run both the Jews as well as the Christians refused adherence to the Prophet. They thereby fell under the verdict of persecution, but without the aim of compulsory conversion. As "Peoples of the Book," that is, possessors of revealed scriptures, they could, to the extent that they submitted and paid tribute, count on toleration and free exercise of their religion.

Nevertheless, the question remains whether this policy of toleration is sufficient to explain the enormous successes of Islam in the Christian area. One must certainly reckon with the unhappy treatment of the Christian Arabs by the Persians and the Byzantine Emperors. When the loyalty of the Arabs toward their former overlords was seriously harmed; a dangerous vacuum appeared, and Islam was prepared to fill it.

It is unlikely that Muhammad himself had planned the great predatory raids of Islam. But his looting expeditions reached ever wider circles, and in the struggle with the oases in the North he came for the first time into hostile contact with united Christian Arab tribes. Shortly before his death he risked the first attack on imperial territory and at the same time sought contact with the Ghassanids, but without success. Finally there occurred a defeat of Islam near Mu'ta east of the Dead Sea. An expedition for revenge did not take place, since the Prophet died in 632 before carrying out his plans. The relations between the Arabs and the new Emperor Heraclius (610–41) had meanwhile improved again, and this was probably the reason for the first successes of the Empire against the Prophet's forces. However, unfortunately the Empire now again failed to supply the confederated Arabs with the means of livelihood. The reasons are difficult to discover. In any case, in this critical situation the Empire could hardly count any longer on the loyalty of the Arabs. And so, after the Prophet's death, there began a mighty victorious advance. That these wars were begun is probably connected also with the fact that after Muhammad's departure the religious development in Islam was not yet concluded and hence his followers had to be kept at this task by every means. A diversion was necessary, and the weak flank of both the great Empires showed the direction. In the battle on the Yarmuk, a tributary of the Jordan, on 20 August 636, the fate of Byzantine Syria was decided, and it was not least of all the Ghassanids who turned the scales in favor of Islam. Jerusalem fell in 638, Mesopotamia was conquered in 639–40, from 640 the Arabs were in Armenia; Alexandria, the gate to Egypt, fell in 640, in 643 the Pentapolis, and as early as 647 began the raids into Cappadocia.

What was the situation of Christianity under the new rule? It was by no means without legal bases. The conquerors proceeded, apart from the inevitable cases of harshness under such circumstances, in accord with treaties of capitulation, and the besieged Christian cities seem to have known this well enough. The precedent for the Arabs was apparently the treaty with the Christians of South Arabia, which assured them the free exercise of religion and a certain self-government, while on the other hand it required the payment of tribute, provisions for the support of the troops, and, as needed, the supplying of auxiliary contingents. The basic lines of this treaty were employed also in the Syrian and Mesopotamian cities. The situation of the Christians was also eased by the circumstance that at first the conquest scarcely affected the administrative system. True, Muslim governors were installed, but the administration itself remained, after as before, in the hands of native powers, hence mostly of Christians. The same taxes had to be paid, and ecclesiastical life was not substantially upset. In principle, churches enjoyed a relative freedom. In individual cases, naturally, much depended on the attitude of the governors. Occasionally, churches were destroyed, and the building of new ones forbidden; occasionally there were compulsory conversions or even martyrdoms, and the election of bishops and patriarchs could be impeded and postponed. But by and large these were exceptional phenomena. Only under the Caliph Abd-al Malik (685–705) did the situation deteriorate. Christians were dismissed from the administration, the poll tax was introduced for them, a distinctive dress was prescribed, and so forth.

Seen in its totality, of course, the Arab conquest meant an enormous loss of territory for the Imperial Church. Provinces in which Christianity had spent its earliest youth, great patriarchal sees of the early Church, intellectually vigorous centers, such as Edessa, Antioch, and Alexandria, pilgrimage sites such as Jerusalem were forever lost to the Imperial Church. The fiction of the identification of Empire and Christian *Ecumene* was destroyed, just as the dream of one Emperor and one Church. This high price, however, brought to the Imperial Church a greater unity, for in so far as the denominations could then be kept apart geographically, the conquered territory to a great extent coincided with the country of the Monophysites and Nestorians, whereas the remaining imperial territory could in the main be claimed as orthodox. On the other hand, the Islamic law in the occupied territories brought in principle an equalization of the denominations and hence ended the ecclesiastical strife. The Melkites were no longer in a position to persecute the Monophysites.

In the course of time the Islamic rulers, each in accord with the situation, employed the Christians of their lands as agents in their political game with Byzantium and not seldom recognized the Byzantine Emperor as the born protector of these Christians. The Byzantine Church profited from this, for since the Melkite patriarchs of Syria and Egypt disposed of only slight means of power, the patriarchs of Constantinople in the retinue of their Emperors would likewise appear as protectors of these patriarchates and from this position unhesitatingly deduce papal claims.

Part Five

The Latin Church in the Transition to the Early Middle Ages

Chaps. 62–66: Eugen Ewig
Chaps. 67, 68, 71: Karl Baus
Chaps. 69, 70, 72, 73: Hermann Josef Vogt

Section One

The Missionary Work
of the Latin Church

C H A P T E R   6 2

The Origins of Christianity
in Ireland and Scotland

Around the middle of the fifth century a new note was heard in the ancient praise of the City of Rome. "That you, as a holy and chosen people, as a priestly and royal city, preside by God's religion over a wider circle than through earthly rule," said Leo the Great (440–61) in his sermon for the feast of the Princes of the Apostles, Peter and Paul. When the Emperors transferred their residence to Milan and Ravenna, Rome became the City of the Apostles. When the Empire reeled on its foundations, the Church carried the gospel outside the Graeco-Roman *Ecumene* to the barbarians. A new Western *Ecumene* arose on the foundation of the Christian faith and of Latin culture.

Since the Church of the East had the advantage in time over that of the West, it is not surprising that it also radiated first into the barbarian world. In other respects, however, the Celtic mission of the West offers a genuine analogy to the Gothic mission of the East. As in the East it was Cappadocian, so in the Hesperides it was British war-prisoners who were the first messengers of the gospel, which took root in Ireland in the fifth century. The Aquitanian, Prosper Tiro, a friend of Leo the Great, noted in his *Chronicle* for the year 431: *Ad Scottos in Christum credentes ordinatus a papa Caelestino Palladius primus episcopus mittitur.* "Scots" was the ancient name of the Irish. The notice assumes the existence of Iro-Scottish groups of Christians, who were, however, without a bishop.

The first Bishop of the Irish, Palladius, appears as early as 429 as a deacon: *ad insinuationem Palladii diaconi papa Caelestinus Germanum Autisidorensem episcopum vice sua mittit et deturbatis haereticis Britannos ad catholicam fidem dirigit.* There may have been a connection between the mission of the Bishop

Germanus of Auxerre to Britain and that of Palladius to Ireland. The mission of Germanus was intended for the fight against Pelagianism, which had numerous followers in Britain and from there may also have influenced the small groups of Irish Christians. Hence care for the orthodoxy of the Irish Christians may have been included in Palladius' commission.

Nevertheless, not Palladius but Patrick has gone down in history as Apostle of the Emerald Isle. Magonus Sucatus Patricius — this must have been Saint Patrick's full name — described his fate as a youth in the *Confessio,* composed by him probably toward the end of his life. He came from a Britanno-Roman curial family, which possessed a "villula" in the *vicus Bannavemtabernae,* a place not yet identified with certainty. Although his father, Calpornius, had been a *decurio* and deacon, and his grandfather, Potitus, a priest, the religious atmosphere in the paternal home was not of the best. Patrick was sixteen years old when Iro-Scots on a plundering raid kidnapped him and took him as a slave to Ireland, probably to Tirawley, Connaught. Here he found the way to God. After six years he succeeded in escaping and returning to his parents. A vision admonished him to proclaim to the Irish the Good Tidings. And so he finally went back to Ireland as a missionary bishop.

Unfortunately, the *Confessio* contains no chronologically fixed points. Later Irish annals, whose origin and trustworthiness have recently been strongly controverted, unanimously record the arrival of the apostle in the year 432 but his death in 461 or 491–92. The problem is further complicated by the fact that in these sources sometimes two Patricks with different dates of death are listed. It will probably have to be held that there was only one Patrick, who was apparently born ca. 390, came to Ireland as bishop ca. 432 or soon after, and died ca. 460.

The most obscure part of Saint Patrick's life is the period between his escape from his Irish captivity and his return to Ireland as bishop. According to the likewise controversial *Dicta Patricii,* Patrick journeyed *per Gallias ad Italiam,* and he also visited the islands in the Tyrrhenian Sea. Patrick's biographers from the late seventh and the eighth centuries connect the saint with Bishop Germanus of Auxerre and hence also with Palladius, who after a brief and unsuccessful activity had died on his homeward journey or had been martyred by the Irish. It is also said, explicitly or implicitly, that Patrick also proceeded from the school of Germanus and entered upon the succession to Palladius. On the other hand, Hanson has recently defended the opinion that Patrick remained in Britain during the entire time, became a monk there, and was sent by the British Church as missionary bishop to the Irish. Patrick's missionary work can, in fact, also be understood from British postulates, since it has a parallel in the activity of the British Bishop Ninian, who in the early fifth century founded the episcopal church of Candida Casa (Whithorn, Galloway) beyond the frontiers of Roman Britain and worked among the southern Picts. Still, it will not do to reject wholesale the sources of the seventh and eighth centuries on the history of the Apostle of the Irish without producing a convincing explanation for the origin of their statements. *Rebus sic stantibus,* it must be maintained that Patrick toured Gaul and Italy before his elevation to the episcopate, and at this time became acquainted with the Mediterranean Provençal monasticism. His being sent by Germanus of Auxerre may be subject to stronger doubts.

The remembrance of the perhaps only brief activity of Palladius soon faded in

Ireland. A note on three churches founded by him leads to the conclusion that Palladius was active chiefly in South Ireland and had perhaps established his chief seat at Cellfine (County Wicklow, Leinster). Patrick, on the contrary, seems to have worked chiefly in North Ireland from Armagh. The Bishops Auxilius, Secundinus, and Iserninus, mentioned in early Irish tradition, may have come to Ireland as companions of Palladius. But they must also have entered into contact with Saint Patrick; there seem to have been ritual connections between Cellfine and Armagh.

The oldest Christian groups in Ireland seem likewise, just as the first Christians among the Goths, to have belonged to the lower class. Patrick addressed all classes of the people, but naturally he also sought to win the toleration or the support of the dominant groups, whom he gained through gifts. The Irish mission, again like the Gothic mission, must have made use of the political and social structure of the people to be converted, and this differed considerably from that of the Empire. In Ireland there was a multiplicity of small tribal kingdoms (Tuathas), which were grouped into five areas — Connaught, Ulster, Meath, Leinster, Munster. In the fifth century there was not yet a central High King. The Tuathas constituted the basis for the diocesan organization, which was brought from the continent to the Emerald Isle. Armagh lay in the vicinity of Emain Maechae, the royal seat of the Ulaid in Ulster, with whom Patrick probably entered into intimate relations. The Irish bishoprics of the fifth and early sixth centuries did not differ in other respects essentially from those of the mainland. Not until the sixth century did the monastic element become ever more prominent in the ecclesiastical centers, while at the same time the aristocratic notion of kinship influenced the ecclesiastical organization.

The indicated transformation of the Church organization was noticeable also among the Celts of Britain, where it stood in close connection with the de-Romanization of the Britons. The de-Romanization of Britain was not based on a revolutionary repudiation of Rome. It was the consequence of the loss of the, for the most part, Romanized areas to the invading Angles and Saxons and of the isolation of Britain from the continent, caused by the wandering of the peoples. The Roman structures continued to operate for a while after the actual abandonment of the island by the imperial central government ca. 408–10 — the sub-Roman period. The decisive turning point came ca. 457. The great cities of London and York, attested as episcopal sees as early as 314, fell into the hands of the invading Germans, and the foundations of Roman Britain tottered. Latin, which hitherto had been the colloquial tongue of the urban population, was confined to the ecclesiastical sphere. The *civitates* were transformed into tribal kingdoms, which did not differ essentially from those of the Irish and the Picts. In this crisis the British population clung the more strongly to the Christian religion, which for Patrick had already become the sign of *Romanitas* and was now assimilated with the incipient Celtic culture. The fusion was completed in the symbol of monasticism, which was then in the process of establishing itself in Western Christianity, but appealed in a special way to the self-willed Celts. The details of this process elude our view. In the eighth century Illtud, Abbot of the monastic island of Calday (Ynys Pyr) on the south coast of Wales, was regarded as *Magister Britannorum*. He was the teacher of the next generation — the second third of the sixth century — of which David of Menevia St. David's (Wales), Samson of Dol (Brittany), and Gildas must be mentioned. Here was clearly apparent the development in which the monasteries became the chief center of ecclesiastical life. St. David's, like other foundations of its kind, was at the same time both monastery and cathedral under the direction of an abbot-bishop. The monastic transformation of the Irish Church followed, according to a tradition now questioned, under the influence of the British monastic culture, even under the direct influence of men like David and Gildas. In any case, it was the work of the great abbots of the sixth century, the saints of the second and third stages (after the first stage of the missionaries), among whom must here be mentioned Finnian, Comgall, Brendan, and Columcille (Columba the Older). The series of great monasteries was begun ca. 540 by Clonard in Meath, a foundation of the Abbot-Bishop Finnian, and other abbeys, such as Bangor (Ulster), Clonmacnoise (Connaught), Clonfert, Lismore (Munster), Moville, and Kildare (Leinster), followed. The Irish princes and kings supported these institutions, in which the abbatial dignity was usually reserved to the kin of the founder. The abbeys became centers of their own pastoral spheres (*parochiae*), which were grouped around the motherhouse and its daughter-foundations, but thereby broke up the territorial frame-work and grew beyond the older dioceses based on the small kingdoms.

Several old bishoprics, including Armagh, "reorganized themselves on a monastic basis" (Bieler), that is, under the direction of abbot-bishops; others were absorbed by the monasteries and monastic precincts. There were many abbeys, including those of the older Columba, whose abbots did not themselves receive episcopal ordination but had it conferred on one of their monks. The director of the ecclesiastical district in this case was not the bishop but the abbot. In these monastic *parochiae* jurisdiction and power of orders were separated: this contradicted the customary organization and from the viewpoint of the continent was an anomaly. Other anomalies are explained partly by the preservation of older customs — the method by which the Celts determined the date of Easter, which differed from the usage on the continent — and partly probably also by the acceptance of national customs — such as the Irish tonsure, extending from ear to ear.

The rules of the Irish monastic fathers were based on the tradition of monasticism up to John Cassian. Ascetical-moral instruction occupied much space in them. The penitential system was based in other respects on the practice of oriental and Provençal monasticism. In the area of worship the Irish showed a special preference for litanies and apotropaic prayers (*loricae*). The cult of all the saints had one of its roots in Ireland.

Instruction in the Irish monasteries served first of all the *lectio divina:* the reading of the pagan classics seems to have been not much pursued until the end of the eighth century. On the other hand, the Irish of the seventh and eighth centuries were masters in the fields of exegesis, grammar, and the *computus.* Despite the inner monastic orientation to the religious and ascetical life, the Irish monasteries were not only religious but also intellectual, professional, and economic centers. Their schools were open to children and youths from the laity, who, if their parents expressed no other desire, took part in the monastic life. From this often resulted lasting connections between monasteries and laity, which again were to the advantage of the monks' pastoral tasks. Thus the Irish stamped the spiritual life of the laity through the introduction of auricular confession and a graduated penitential system, which were adopted from monastic practice for the general care of souls.

Finally, not to be forgotten are the monks' charitable duties. To the circle of people that gathered around a monastery belonged also a not small number of the needy, who had to be cared for. All in all, it can be said that the great Irish monasteries were comparable to the little cities of the early Middle Ages. Excavations have shown that they were fortified by stone walls.

If, up to the middle of the sixth century, the Irish had learned from the Britons, they outstripped their teachers in the second half of the century. The most important personalities among the Old Irish abbots were the older and the younger Columba. Columcille (Dove of the Church) or Columba the Older (521–97) came of the royal house of the O'Neill of Connaught and became the Apostle of the Picts in modern Scotland (Caledonia). He entered Clonard as a monk and then founded the monastery of Derry in Ulster. After the battle of Culdranna (ca. 561), which Columba had contributed to because of a quarrel over a biblical manuscript, he is said to have vowed to win again for Christ as many men as had fallen in the battle. Thus he devoted himself to the mission to the Picts, which had been started ca. 400 by the Briton Ninian but had not advanced beyond the land of the southern Picts. In Caledonia toward the end of the fifth century Iro-Scottish princes had founded the little Kingdom of Dalriada or Argyle (Eastern Gael). A Pictish prince not far from Dalriada gave Columba the island of Iona in 563, on which the Irish Abbot founded a great monastery. From Iona the Picts and "Scots" of Caledonia were gained for the Church. At Columba's death in 597 the work had been completed. Iona remained the ecclesiastical metropolis of the newly won territory, although its abbots did not receive episcopal ordination.

The younger Columba, or Columban (530/540–615), was not related to his older namesake. He came from Leinster, became a monk of St. Comgall's Abbey of Bangor (Ulster), and in 592 with twelve companions set out for Gaul. He inaugurated the series of Iro-Scottish *peregrini* on the continent, and through his foundations of Luxeuil and Bobbio he belongs as much to Frankish and Lombard as to Irish history.

CHAPTER 63

The Conversion of the Franks and Burgundians: Origin and Organization of the Merovingian National Church.

The conversion of the Irish and the Picts was without parallel on the continent in the fifth and sixth centuries; the mission to the Germans did not at this time go beyond frontiers of the Empire but concerned only the peoples who had invaded the Empire. Thus it appeared as an especially important occurrence in the general process of the German-Roman assimilation on the soil of the Roman Empire. The leading classes took the lead in this. The old pagan faith demonstrated little power of resistance and asserted itself only in residual elements. But we observe that Gothic prestige at times competed with Roman in the barbarian world. The Goths succeeded in bringing the Burgundians, who had already gone over to Catholicism, and the Spanish Sueves to their own profession of Arianism around the middle of the fifth century. That statement underscores the historical change which Clovis produced in history of the West.

The country of the encounter between the pagan Germans and Catholic Christianity was Gaul. And it was not until the consolidation of Clovis' kingdom between the Meuse and the Loire that the Goths appeared at the court of Soissons. Theodoric the Great sought to incorporate the Franks into his political system and in 494 married Clovis' sister, Audofleda.

Clovis stood at a crossroads. It was difficult for him to separate religion and politics. The connection with Theodoric meant for Clovis acceptance into the circle of the great German kings, but at the cost of accepting the status quo, i.e., the leading position of the two Gothic peoples. It also meant following Theodoric's lead for Arian Christianity. But the Frankish leader did not wish to decide clearly for that option. He married a Catholic princess of the Burgundian royal house but he himself remained pagan. In fact, in 496 he was at war against the Visigoth King Alaric II, and had made a prior commitment to Catholicism in that his first two children were baptized Catholics. But the real die was cast rather in a battle with the Alemanni, which went against him, Clovis cried out to "Jesus Christ, whom Clotilda declares to be the Son of the living God . . . I implore your glory, your power: grant me victory over these enemies . . . and I will believe in you and have myself baptized in your name." Clovis was granted victory and was thus baptized.

But this baptism was for Clovis not more than a German ritual exercise, not dissimilar to others likewise attested. The Frankish victory over the Alemanni was taken as a sign from God to which Clovis responded as promised. This of course was similar to the experience of Constantine I and even the Apostle Paul's call at Damascus. So Clovis was baptized in Reims at Christmastime of 498 or 499 by Remigius.

This decision was not one of deep insight or of faith, but was simply belief in the power of the God to whom his wife, Clotilda, and his friend, Remigius of Reims, adhered. It was also related doubtless to the Petrine tradition, which the Gallic episcopate also employed in missions, of Peter as the Gatekeeper of Heaven, since Clovis dedicated a church to Peter and the Apostles and sent a crown to the pope at his death.

The Frankish-Visigothic war of 507–11 was no less significant for Church history than for profane history. The North Gallic churches, which had suffered severely during the wanderings of the peoples, now found a firm support in Catholic *Romania* of Aquitania. Out of the collaboration of the Gallo-Frankish episcopate sprang the Frankish "national Church." In July 511, at the instigation of Clovis, the bishops of the Frankish territory met in Orléans for the first Council of the Merovingian Kingdom. The Council, whose agenda was decided by Clovis, laid down, under the

King's influence, the fundamental law of the Merovingian Church and introduced ecclesiastical reorganization into the *Regnum Francorum*.

What was new in this plan was the fact that now bishops — who had been assembling on the level of the province, the diocese, and even the Empire were now to meet on the plane of a *Regnum*. The German kings who occasioned and permitted these "national synods" in some respect were taking the place of the Emperor. In these changes and others, were expressed the collapse of the *Imperium* and the vitality of the new *Regna*.

The Merovingian Church was only loosely united, however, for the practice of partition of the kingdom into subkingdoms militated against high unity's being exhibited either in politics or in Church matters. The resulting chaos wrought havoc with the synodal activity in the later Merovingian periods. The political rulers were able to legislate for ecclesiastical matters on their own however, and eventually the boundaries of separation between State and Church began to blur. Perhaps Clovis also instituted a higher *Wergeld* for bishops, but it is certain he also held the Roman canon law as competent for handling criminal cases against bishops. In reality the Merovingian recognized the juridical autonomy of the Church. This became especially important in view of the desirability of the episcopal office now. On the other hand, the episcopal organization of the early Church was here as well soon destroyed by the proprietary Church system. The principle that all churches founded by laymen should be conveyed to the bishop could not be maintained consistently. So that, as a matter of fact, the episcopate lost ground in the face of the ever more powerful proprietary church movement of the early seventh century. The proprietor felt quite free to appoint whomever he chose to "his" church and the benefice system thrived.

There was a hefty struggle among the episcopate and the lay proprietors of monasteries too. Radical change appeared with the entrance of Columban in 592 in the Frankish Kingdom on the southern edge of the Vosges where he founded the first continental monasteries of the Irish type. The most important of those houses was Luxeuil. Columban was a strong personality whose efforts produced powerful religious and moral impulses, but who also disregarded totally the existing Gallo-Frankish monastic law: he ruled his foundations in an authoritarian manner, traveled at will, had ordinations performed by bishops other than the local one, recognized no episcopal right to the monastic property, to taxes, or to lodging, and performed pastoral functions beyond the monastery's territory. Moreover, he refused to appear at synods 535 and arbitrarily threatened King Theodoric II with excommunication. So Columban was expelled from the Burgundian subkingdom in 610, and died in 615 in his Italian foundation of Bobbio. Luxeuil remained an important monastic foundation, nevertheless, and Columban's severe *Regula* was mixed with the *Regula Benedicti* to form a *Regula Mixta*. Although Irish rites and Celtic sorts of monastic unions did not last long on the continent, monastic strivings for autonomy radiating from Luxeuil did influence the political and spiritual leaders of the land. The monasteries obtained episcopal privileges which granted them not only internal autonomy under the Rule, the free election of the abbot, and the inviolability of their property, but often freedom from any authority of the local bishop. Episcopal privileges were often complemented by royal charters of immunity and of protection. These now almost independent churches under secular law, which, like the institution of proprietary churches, had a deleterious effect upon the ecclesiastical organization in the chaos of the late Merovingian epoch.

The first phase of the Frankish mission entirely took the form of an interior ecclesiastical restoration, which could make use of the existing congregations and probably be borne substantially by the clergy, even if monks and especially hermits were not entirely absent from it. The hermits seem to have worked especially among the rural folk. The ecclesiastical restoration was promoted by the Kings in regard to organization and probably also materially, but there was no compulsory conversion of pagans. Only the sanctification of Sundays and holy days was imposed under penalty at the end of the sixth century — a sign of the cultic and ritual view of Christianity.

The second phase of the interior ecclesiastical restoration began under Chlotar II (584/613–29) and Dagobert I (623/629–39). It was carried out predominantly by circles connected somehow with the monasticism of Luxeuil. Strong Aquitanian forces also poured into this monasticism.

The springtime of the country overrun by the Alemanni (i.e., Switzerland and the upper Rhineland) is connected with Columban's name after he was expelled from Luxeuil. Not that Columban personally had much success, but his pupil Gall, and Gall's little cella (which became later the thriving monastic foundation, Sankt Gallen) carried on the work.

When Winfrid-Boniface took up his activity in Hesse and Thuringia on the other side of the forest, there were already old bases of the mission in these two districts as well as on the Main. The evangelization of the Frankish strip on the right bank of the Rhine, Alemannia, and Bavaria was complete. The German mission had grown out of the ecclesiastical restoration, which had achieved its first successes on the Rhine in the sixth century, then in the Burgundian-Alemannian-Raetian frontier zone at the end of the sixth and the beginning of the seventh centuries, and finally in the North Gallic-Frankish territory in the first and second thirds of the seventh century. But its great triumphs are due extensively to the Luxeuil monasticism, which renewed the missionary impulse and was active in both the North Gallic-Frankish front and in the sphere of the South German tribes.

The Merovingians did not desire coerced conversions, but aided the clerics and monks involved in it with often considerable material support and with royal protection.

There was also present in the new mission work a different notion of faith from the tests of strength of the Christian God (as, e.g., with Clovis). Yet that notion was not entirely done away with either, as the "tests" of missionaries destroying pagan shrines and cult objects would illustrate; when the pagan god was unable to defend against the missionaries' violence to their sanctuaries, many Germans were convinced. The positive counterpart to the negative destruction was in the *prouesses ascétiques* of the monks of Columban and the older hermits, like Wulfilaich, which also made a great impression. And also of course the works of mercy, including the redemption of captives. There was moreover no absence of ethics and morals among the Christians. In the language of the Fathers, *pietas* was very strongly related to *clementia* and *misericordia*. There are indeed striking testimonies of genuine love of neighbor and of enemy, and the Church considered it to be its special task to protect the oppressed and the defenseless, the foreigner and underage children. But on the whole, there prevailed a formal understanding of Christianity which led to an overemphasis on cult and rite as opposed to moral principles. This would show itself in occasional attempts to outwit God by means of formal pilgrimages, or other exertions for the expiation of crimes. Donations to the Church, founding new churches, extravagant adornment of saints tombs, altars and of churches suggest the same motive.

To men of this sort, saints had to appear less as models than as helpers. A change of this kind was manifesting itself from the end of the fourth century as the cults of relics gradually covered up the cult of the saints as understood more symbolically and theologically as in the earlier periods. German ideas expedited this process.

In accord with early medieval thinking, canon law concerned with the *ritus* found earlier and more prominent application than the Christian moral law. But in the course of the sixth century, the Kings also gradually accepted ecclesiastical rules into their own capitularies. Ecclesiastical influence is manifestly obvious in the *Lex Allamannorum* and the *Lex Baiuvariorum* of the 720s to 740s. A great part of the earlier royal decrees was accepted into those legal systems: e.g., the special *wergeld* for the bishop as opposed to other clerics, sanctification of Sunday, marriage of blood relatives, law of asylum, ecclesiastical patronage of freedmen — all found acceptance.

The christianization of State and society, running parallel to evangelization, began at the earliest and most clearly with the kingship. Clovis had had at his baptism to renounce the divine origin of his family — *sola nobilitate contentus* (in the words of Avitus of Vienne). What changed here was less anything else than the view of the ruler's calling: here a constant influence of Christian moral principles is first to be recognized. The episcopate admonished the Kings to maintain *iustitia* in the sense of *aequitas,* to cultivate *pietas* in the sense of the personal fear of God as care for the Church and protection for the needy. As a special task of the ruler was the maintenance of external peace, especially in regard to pagans. In the seventh century the King was represented as God's vicar in the government of the world, and to him was even attributed the function of conferring the episcopal function.

Thereby was struck a new note that was attentively listened to. Many clues show that in the period from ca. 585 to 638 a new stage had been reached in the christianization of State and society: the boundaries between national councils and assemblies of magnates became blurred, Germans entered the episcopate in greater numbers, the Luxeuil monasticism radiated to the kingship and aristocracy in *Francia,* ecclesiastical decrees gradually found entry into royal and popular law. The development as such did not stop, but the organizing power of the Kingdom disappeared as a consequence of the hopeless decadence of the Merovingian dynasty, which since 680 was clear to the whole world. Only the Carolingians took up the threads and tied them again.

CHAPTER 6 4

The East Germans and Catholicism:
The Conversion of the Sueves and Visigoths
of Spain to Catholicism and the Second Flowering
# of Christian Antiquity in the Spanish Visigothic
National Church

The West stood under the aegis of the East Germans, especially the Goths, for scarcely a century — from the extinction of the Theodosian Dynasty in 455 to the beginning of Justinian's wars of reconquest in 533.

Politically and in Church history the Kingdom of the Vandals, whose Kings from Gaiseric to Thrasamund engaged in an active arianization, occupied a special position. Among the Vandals there occurred a real persecution of Catholics, which it is true did not lead to the ruin of the Afro-Roman Church but considerably impaired the importance and significance of that Church within the whole of Christianity. In the two Gothic Kingdoms and that of the Sueves in Spain which was under Gothic influence and that of the Burgundians in Gaul, the Catholic Church was spared trials of this severity. The structure of these *regna* was arranged in a double pattern. The dual construction was based on the Late Roman separation of military and civilian and made possible an on the whole peaceful and at times even friendly coexistence of Arian Germans (military) and Catholic Romans (civilian). Of course, it constituted an impediment for the German-Roman symbiosis, although the Goths opened themselves in a greater degree to Graeco-Roman culture than did the Franks. For the most powerful bond of community was not education but faith.

So long as the Arian Germans lived as *foederati* inside the *Imperium,* their relations to the Catholic Church were not problematic, since the Church, as an imperial institution, was withdrawn from their competence. True, there could be encroachments and plundering but not to the extent of a conflict of fundamental importance. Such a conflict first occurred when Euric dissociated the Visigothic Kingdom from the *Imperium,* by which the connection of the Catholic Church of his dominions with Rome and the Church of the Empire was severed, and the making of new appointments to vacant sees in his kingdom was thwarted. These restrictive measures crippled ecclesiastical life and naturally were felt as persecution, but they sprang from a new situation and had at bottom only a political, not a religious-ecclesiastical background. Euric's son and successor, Alaric II, replaced them with a positive policy of integration. The *Lex Romana Visigothorum* also called *Breviarium Alaricianum,* which was published under him in 506, contained the essential decisions of imperial law which regulated the life of the Church in the *Imperium* and were now sanctioned as Gothic royal law for the Romans. The Synod of Agde, which met in the same year under the presidency of Bishop Caesarius of Arles, inaugurated, five years before the Franco-Gallic Synod of Orléans and eleven years before the Burgundo-Gallic Synod of Yenne (Epaon), the series of early medieval "national councils," which were to meet in the future on the basis of a *regnum* at the order or at least with the assent of the German king of the moment. Ecclesiastical affairs in the Visigothic Kingdom became normal, and the Catholic Romans put up with a general, but in extent not more carefully defined, supremacy of the Arian King over the Church.

Alaric's solution was not at first effective in the Gothic area, since the Frankish war of 507–11 put the bases of life of the Visigoths in question. The Kingdom of Toulouse perished and the strongholds of the nation in western Aquitania were lost to the Franks along with the capital. The great Ostrogothic King Theodoric saved his Visigothic kinsfolk from destruction, but annexed Provence to the area under direct Ostrogothic rule and at the same time claimed the government in the interest of his Visigothic grandson, Amalaric, son of Alaric II. Under Ostrogothic protection the Visigothic capital was first transferred to Narbonne.

Not only as King of the Ostrogoths but also at the same time as *patricius* in the service of the Emperor, Theodoric was ruler of Italy. His position in relation to the Roman Church as well as to the Catholic Church of the West in general was therefore not comprehensible in the national-church categories. Even if the Amal was said to have exercised an influence over the Roman Church in far broader measure than was previously believed, in fact his domination was to the advantage of the ecclesiastical autonomy of Rome vis-à-vis the Emperor. In the entire Gothic area the relations of the Gallic-Spanish churches to Rome were again established, as the special mandate of Pope Hormisdas to the Bishop of Elne (province of Baetica) and the grant of papal vicariates to Arles for Gaul and Spain in 514 and to Seville for Baetica and Lusitania in 521 show. In Spain under Gothic rule the Church resumed its synodal activity of the old type: in the form of provincial, not of national councils.

Thus the rule of Theodoric the Great in the Gothic Kingdoms of the West meant for the Church basically a return to the situation of late Roman times. There was at first no change in this in the Visigothic sphere even after Theodoric's death. For when the restoration policy of Justinian spread to Italy, the *intermedio ostrogodo* in the Visigothic Kingdom still continued. Theudis was able to stop new Frankish attacks in 531 and 541. Gothic rule was maintained in *Narbonensis I* (Septimania without Toulouse) and in Spain. In Spain, the Goths could gradually spread beyond Tarraconensis and Carthaginiensis into Baetica (province of Seville).

Beside the Visigothic Kingdom there existed in Spain a second German Kingdom of the Sueves, which embraced the weakly romanized province of Gallaecia (Braga) and parts of northern Lusitania. The Sueves had become Arians in the fifth century under Gothic influence, but almost no reports concerning the history of their kingdom are extant for the last third of the fifth and the first half of the sixth centuries. The "sole genuine document" from this period, a letter of Pope Vigilius to the Metropolitan of Braga from 538, makes known that the Catholic Church was not then substantially impeded under Suevic rule, but opposed not only Suevic Arianism but also the Priscillianism which had been disseminated in wide circles of the province. From later sources it must be inferred that even paganism was not yet ended among the rural population of Galicia. A change in the Church history of the Suevic Kingdom began when King Chararic ca. 550–55, under the influence of miracles at the tomb of Martin of Tours, passed over to Catholicism and around the same time the Pannonian monk Martin, who had traveled to Spain, established the new mission center of Dumio near Braga. Martin of Dumio, who soon became Metropolitan of Braga (after 561–80), successfully united with the Suevic mission the fight against Priscillianism and pagan remains. He established the Catholic national Church of the Suevic Kingdom. Rightly was he celebrated even in his own day as the Apostle of the Sueves, even if at his death Arianism had not yet been completely extirpated.

Martin of Dumio's work of conversion did not radiate directly to the Visigoths. But the dualist structure of State and society, which had been the characteristic mark of the Arian German Kingdoms, had also already become an anachronism among the Visigoths. The cultural romanization of the Goths had already begun in the Kingdom of Toulouse. Marriages occurred among the magnates of both groups of people, although they were forbidden by law. King Theudis himself married a lady of the Hispano-Roman senatorial aristocracy. Although Goths and Romans still lived according to different laws, Theudis enacted laws which were valid for both peoples. Gothic aristocrats and military men, especially in the southern parts of the kingdom, came into intimate contact with Roman magnates, who adhered politically to the Gothic Kingdom. Ecclesiastical and cultural contacts with Latin Africa seem to have simulated Catholic controversial theology in the southern province around the mid-century and thereby released a missionary impulse which had an impact on the Spanish Gothic upper class. Important Goths were converted to Catholicism and rose in the Catholic hierarchy. Thereby new problems were created for the kings.

In the first decade of his reign Leovigild had to consolidate his kingdom and his own authority against internal and external enemies. Probably in 578–580 he tackled the interior reconstruction of the Kingdom. The prohibition of marriage between Goths and Romans, already much violated in practice, was abolished. In addition, Leovigild took the decisive step toward the unity of the Kingdom: he had the Gothic law of Euric revised and made the *Codex revisus* the law of the Kingdom.

If the *imitatio imperii* was the *signum* of Leovigild's reign, it benefited the reputation of the Goths, whose kingdom he enlarged, whose law he made the basis of the beginnings of Gothic Spanish unity. In the course of this work there was posed also the question of the ecclesiastical and religious unity of the Kingdom of Toledo, but it seems only to have been raised by a tragedy in the royal family.

In 579 Leovigild made his oldest son Hermenegild regent of the Gothic territories of Baetica with his seat at Seville. Hermenegild had as his wife the Frankish Princess Ingundis, who, despite her very young age, had clung at the court of Toledo to the Catholic faith of the Franks in opposition to the powerful pressure of Queen Goswintha, her own grandmother. In Seville Hermenegild himself now converted to Catholicism under the influence of the Metropolitan Leander. The young prince thereby brought on a conflict with his father, who at this time certainly had an entirely different idea about the solution of the religious question. A quarrel broke out. Hermenegild sought help from the Byzantines and Sueves but he could not hold out against his father. Leovigild conquered Seville and Córdoba in 584, and the son fell into his hands. Hermenegild could not be induced to recant. He was killed in Tarragona on Easter of 585 and the perpetrator remained unpunished.

It was in accord with the policy followed by him that Leovigild sought to realize ecclesiastical unity also on the basis of the "Gothic religion," but in doing so he made certain accommodations to Catholic views. In 580 the King convoked an Arian national Council to Toledo, which facilitated the conversion of Catholics by the abolition of the rebaptism hitherto practiced in conversions, something regarded as especially scandalous by the Catholics. Furthermore, Leovigild tried to efface the differences between Arianism and Orthodoxy by the accepting of the cult of Spanish saints and by his saying that he recognized the identity of substance of Christ with the Father, even if this expression must not be understood as an official formula of mediation. In an effort to achieve his goal, the King was not sparing in rewards but he also did not renounce external methods of pressure, such as exile and confiscation. However, there is no word of a bloody persecution. Also among the Sueves, whose kingdom he conquered in 585, Leovigild carried out an Arian reaction. The measures of compulsion, however, were by no means restricted to Catholic Germans. The goal of the ecclesiastical religious policy was also and especially the *transductio Romanorum ad haeresim Arianam*.

Despite temporary successes, Leovigild did not achieve this goal. His son and successor, Recared (586–601), embraced the Catholic religion in 587, ten months after his accession, and thereby at the same time inaugurated the conversion of the Visigothic nation, which was solemnly proclaimed in 589 at the Third Council of Toledo, the first national Council of the Spanish Gothic Church. Here Recared appeared as a ruler in the succession of the Emperors Constantine and Marcian: "In our time renewing the ancient and revered Prince, Constantine the Great, as he enlightened the holy Synod of Nicaea by his presence, and also the most Christian Emperor Marcian, through whose stubborn exertions the decrees of Chalcedon were established." Thus did the assembled bishops acclaim him in accord with the imperial style and at the same time in actual insinuation as Apostle of the Goths: "To whom belongs eternal merit with God, if not to the truly Catholic King Recared? . . . He truly deserves the reward of an apostle who has fulfilled an apostolic function."

The King eased the passage of the Goths to Catholicism by the fact that he accomplished the acceptance of the Arian clergy, including the bishops, into the Catholic clergy. Nevertheless, there was some resistance. But it has been noted that, of the eight Arian bishops who in 589 signed the acts of Toledo, four belonged to the Suevic area (Viséu, Porto, Tuy, Lugo) and, of the four Arian bishops of the Gothic area (Valencia, Tortosa, Barcelona, Palencia), only one (Palencia) had his seat in the heartland of Gothic settlement. Accordingly, a part of the Gothic Arian clergy right in the Gothic heartland must have still held itself aloof in 589 and been gained only in the future. But even here there was no serious opposition. In the Spanish literature of the early seventh century the Arian controversy no longer played a role. From 633 the episcopate was recruited from the circles of the Gothic aristocracy.

No source informs us about the motives for Recared's conversion. Hence the historian cannot throw light into the heart of the King and his Goths but only point to the concomitant circumstances and people: to the family tragedy of the royal house, which is said to have deeply affected Recared as mediator between father and brother, to the probably superior theological formation of the Catholic episcopate, to the impressive personality of Leander of Seville and other prelates. For the rest, religious and political motives may have been inseparably joined in Recared, as in Clovis, but at the same time the conversion was the decisive step to the unification of Spain under Gothic leadership. In this perspective Recared completed not the religious but probably the political testament of his father in the ecclesiastical sphere. The work of unification was continued after Recared's death by Sisebut (612–21) and Swinthila (621–32), who expelled the last of the Byzantines from the peninsula, by Chindaswinth (642–52) and Recceswinth (649/652–72), who, following Justinian's model, again stamped the *Lex Visigothorum* in a Christian sense and thereby created the most important legal work of their time in the Latin West. The anti-Jewish legislation of the kings was supposed also to serve the idea of unity but the episcopate partly opposed it and partly took a reserved stand. It cast a deep shadow over the Spanish Gothic Kingdom and ultimately only exacerbated the political crisis of the late seventh century. It had a parallel only in the Empire.

In his *civitas regia* of Toledo the orthodox King of the Visigoths could appear as successor of the Western Emperors — West, of course, which was restricted to the Iberian Peninsula and its Gallic appendage of Septimania. Toledo was the single royal city of the West which, like Constantinople, was also the ecclesiastical capital. In it from 589 met all the Spanish Gothic national councils. Like the imperial city on the Bosporus, Toledo had originally been only a simple episcopal city. The Church of Toledo definitively gained metropolitan rank at the time when Cartagena was in the hands of the Byzantines. As the royal city, Toledo would in time outstrip the other metropolises of the kingdom, including Seville with its rich tradition. As early as 646 it was decreed that the neighboring bishops should annually make a visit *ad limina* to Toledo *pro reverentia principis et regiae sedis honore vel metropolitani civitatis ipsius consolatione.* From 656 the Metropolitan of Toledo directed the national councils, over which previously the metropolitans had presided alternately, according to the date of ordination or reputation. In 681 he obtained the right to approve candidates designated by the King in episcopal vacancies in the entire Kingdom, and in 683 it was enacted that King and Metropolitan of Toledo could summon, under pain of excommunication, every bishop to prescribed liturgical or judicial actions at Toledo.

However, not the Metropolitan of Toledo but the King occupied the dominant position in the Spanish Gothic Church. Recared had already claimed the right to fill episcopal sees, which his successors apparently exercised in a much broader scope than the other kings of the time — even before it was expressly fixed in 681 and was easily restricted by the participation of the Metropolitan of Toledo. Recared not only convoked the first national council, but he directed it, decided the agenda, and signed the acts. In 681 it was set down as a custom that the kings opened the council, made known in the *Tomus regius* the agenda they wanted, and then withdrew. If the decrees of the synod were to obtain validity in the national law, they needed sanction by a royal law *in confirmatione concilii.*

From the beginning the bishops were also involved in secular matters, but strictly in the framework of the program laid down by the ruler in the *Tomus regius.* As early as 589 secular magnates also attended the consultations; the presence of royal dignitaries became in the future the rule, and in 653 they acquired the right of participation in the discussions and of signing the acts. Finally the Councils of

Toledo became in this way also national assemblies. They decisively stamped the Visigothic constitutional law, issued decrees on the election of the king, the rights of the crown, on high treason, on the legal status of the magnates. The bishops created a political ethics determined by the virtues of *iustitia* and *pietas* of late antiquity, objectified the royal domination into a royal function, and introduced the anointing of the king to strengthen the ruler's authority — first attested in 672. From 633 the episcopate took part, alongside the *seniores Gothorum* in the election of the king. Around the middle of the seventh century there appeared mixed ecclesiastical and secular commissions, which had to be consulted for the pardoning of rebels and in the publication of laws, and finally they became competent as a forum for political trials relating to the episcopate and the nobility. "Medieval" changes were thereby anticipated in the Gothic Kingdom of Toledo, otherwise still so strongly stamped by late antiquity.

The Spanish Gothic national Church was in itself much more compact and more strongly centralized than the Merovingian. The *Itio in partes,* which is characteristic of the entire western development in the sixth and seventh centuries, was apparent in Spain before the passage of the Goths to Catholicism — at the death of Theodoric the Great in 526, at which the vicariate for Gaul and Spain, granted in 514 to Caesarius of Arles, de facto ended. The canonical collections, which constituted the basis for the development of canon law in Gothic Spain make this break clear. The relations with Gaul came to a close, those with Africa moved to the foreground. As in the other countries of the West, Justinian's ecclesiastical policy aroused lively opposition in Spain also, but the Spanish attitude in the controversy over the Three Chapters was more strongly determined by the African polemic than elsewhere. The Spanish Church never recognized the Fifth Ecumenical Council, Constantinople II of 553. The connection with Rome lost in intensity on the basis of the general historical development, but the tensions between the Visigothic Kingdom and the Empire also reacted unfavorably on the relations of the Gothic national Church with the papacy. Add to this that the Spanish Gothic episcopate no longer attributed great importance to the support of Rome after the conversion of the Goths to Catholicism.

In 589 and 633 the Spanish Church acknowledged that papal synodal letters had the same authority as the ecumenical councils. Isidore of Seville saw in the Roman Bishop the head of the Universal Church, whom everyone is bound to obey, independently of the personal qualities of the successor of Peter: " . . . our duty of obedience is affected on no point except that he order something directly against the faith." The relations between Spain and Rome had, after a long suspension, been strengthened again under Gregory the Great, who was a personal friend of Leander of Seville and had also sent him the pallium, without however renewing the Vicariate of Seville. Recared had made known his conversion and that of his nation to Catholicism to Gregory as head of all the bishops.

In the future the connection between Rome and Spain seems to have been almost completely broken. In the period after Isidore papal decretals were no longer found in Gothic Spanish canon law. Contact was not renewed until Leo II communicated to the Gothic Spanish Church the decrees of the Sixth Ecumenical Council (Constantinople III of 680–81). Julian of Toledo, under whom the national primacy of the Church of Toledo was fully established, had the acts examined at provincial synods together with an *Apologeticum fidei*, which he had composed on his own. The decrees of Constantinople were received by the Spanish Church. The increasing gravity of the situation was to a great extent Julian's work, but the support which Julian found in the episcopate of the Visigothic Kingdom makes clear an estrangement between Spain and Rome. How far this estrangement went is difficult to say.

The inner structure of the Gothic Spanish Church was marked by an, on the whole, uninterrupted development on an early Christian basis. Ecclesiastical immunity, the right of asylum, the jurisdiction and legal status of the clergy were more strongly determined by late antiquity than elsewhere. The economic independence of the parish churches and monasteries was in accord with the time. The proprietary church system spread to the Iberian Peninsula and included also the monasteries, but the foundations of the episcopal organization of the early Church were only loosened by it, not convulsed. At the conversion of the Goths to Catholicism, the liturgy was enriched by the admission of the creed into the Mass *iuxta orientalium partium morem* at the order of King Recared. It received its characteristic formation in the seventh century through the collaboration of great bishops and abbots, who displayed an important literary activity and thereby also increased the self-consciousness of the Gothic Spanish Church.

An early sign of the ties with home was the pride in the native saints, who from the late fourth century appeared beside Mary and the Apostles.

Late Roman Spain was not rich in important ecclesiastical teachers, bishops, and abbots, but Visigothic Spain took the lead over other countries. After the confusion of the migrations, new life burst forth in the sixth century, often simulated by the influx of foreigners, especially of Easterners and Africans. In the first half of the sixth century Mérida had three eastern metropolitans. Justinian's restoration strengthened the Greek influence in the south of Lusitania, in Baetica, and in the territory of Cartagena, and it there survived the collapse of imperial rule. Very old relations existed between Spain and Africa. They were strengthened by two waves of immigration in the days of the Vandal King Hunneric (477–84) and the Moorish expansion toward the imperial province of Africa ca. 570, which also brought abbots and their communities to Spain. Episcopal and monastic schools replaced from ca. 500 the rhetorical schools that had disappeared. Many bishops came from these monasteries. In the last fourth of the sixth century Leander of Seville, Severus of Málaga, Eutropius of Valencia, Maximus of Zaragoza, and John of Gerona (Biclar) represented the intellectual life of Spain. From Leander's school proceeded Isidore of Seville, the country's Doctor of the Church.

Isidore stands beside Augustine and Gregory as one of the great teachers of the Western Middle Ages. He was born soon after 550 and succeeded his brother Leander as Metropolitan of Seville (599–636). His importance does not lie in the originality of his thought but in his encyclopedic scholarship, which he displayed especially in his masterpiece, the *Origines* or *Etymologiae*. The Middle Ages derived from it, among other things, the system of the *septem artes liberales*. A number of other treatises dealt with individual fields of knowledge, such as grammar (*Differentiae*) and astronomy (*De natura rerum*). In the succession to Jerome and Rufinus, Isidore wrote a history of Christian literature (*De viris illustribus*) and a world chronicle, which he completed by a history of the Goths, Vandals, and

Sueves. Not a few of his writings are devoted to exegesis. In the *Synonyma* Isidore appears as the father of the mystical theology of the Middle Ages. The *Sentences,* a manual of Christian doctrine involving also the lay world inaugurated the medieval Sentence-literature. The treatise *De ecclesiasticis officiis* and the *Regula monacho-rum* deal with ecclesiastical life; the apologetical work, *De fide catholica,* with the Jewish question, so acute in the Visigothic Kingdom.

The work of the Bishop of Seville was strongly engraved by antiquity — but of course by an already benumbed antiquity. Hellenistic natural science was known to Isidore only in fragments, philosophy only in condensations in the form of manuals. Thus, for Isidore, grammar with its methods (*Differentiae, Synonyma, Etymologiae*) became the basis not only of the trivium but also of the quadrivium, in fact of philosophy and theology. For him the "ancients" were no longer the classical writers but their late commentators who stood like a filter between him and the great authors of antiquity. Of course, through this filter Isidore also received the spirit of antiquity and made it so much his own that many regarded him as the last representative of the dying world. Through the Spanish Doctor of the Church Baetica became the 'Conservatoire de l'érudition grammaticale antique" (Fontaine) and in this function replaced Roman Africa, on which Isidore's scholarship was essentially based, which probably supplied him with no slight number of Greek works in Latin translation. Next to Africa, only Italy can be mentioned as mediator, but at a great distance. By means of Rome, which under Gregory the Great maintained lively relations with Spain, some codices may have reached Spain, among them the later writings of Cassiodorus, Isidore's kindred-spirit, which the Bishop of Seville included in his work.

With his copious work, Isidore intended to serve not only scholarship. In the *Synonyma* he speaks to us as the mystic; in the *Historia Gothorum,* as the Spanish patriot. As Metropolitan of Seville Isidore was also preoccupied with the great questions of Church and *Regnum.* The Fourth Council of Toledo in 633 and the definitions of kingship and law in the *Lex Visigothorum* bear the mark of his spirit. Apparently the *Hispana,* the best general collection of canons of the age which became so important for the canon law development of the entire West through the Carolingian Renaissance, goes back ultimately to Isidore. Beside Isidore's *Summa* of divine and human knowledge stands the canonical *Summa* as an equally important achievement.

After the death of the *Doctor egregius* the cultural centers moved from the Mediterranean zone to the interior of Spain. Málaga, Seville, Cartagena, and Valencia receded. Mérida and Zaragoza asserted their rank, while Toledo under the two Eugenes, Ildefonse, and Julian flowered anew. The Goth Fructuosus, who had grown up in Palencia, became in the years 640–50 the father of the monks of Spain. He wrote his *Rule* for the church in Bierzo, the hill country of Alcalá, where, after him, his biographer, Valerius of Astorga, also lived. King Recceswinth made Fructuosus Bishop of Dumio and finally Metropolitan of Braga. The leading churchmen of the time elaborated, as mentioned, the "Mozarabic" Liturgy. The *Liber de virginitate s. Mariae* of Ildefonse of Toledo constituted a landmark in the history of the cult of Mary.

The importance of the geographical shifting of the cultural centers in the seventh century becomes clear from archeological investigation, which has established a Gothic province of settlement north of the Tajo in Castile and León, to which in the west was added the Suevic settlement in Galicia. The Spanish lands north of the Tajo took little part in the cultural development of the Mediterranean zone in the sixth century. Goths and Sueves were Arians, under the Romans of Galicia Priscillianism was not yet dead, and in the Cantabrian Basque mountains there were still pagans. The northern advance bastions of the south were Mérida and Toledo, which lay in the radiation sphere of Córdoba. The Goths preserved, according to the evidence of the finds, their national customs until the turn from the sixth to the seventh century. At this time the Christian art of Baetica, dependent on Africa, lost its force. A new style of architecture and art arose at Mérida and Toledo, which had built the bridge from the south to the north. It spread via the Gothic area of colonization into Tarraconensis and to Septimania. This last epoch of Gothic Spanish culture no longer bore an African stamp, but was dependent on that of the Empire through its relations with Byzantine Italy. In it was reflected the Gothic Spanish national consciousness of the time of King Recceswinth and his successors.

CHAPTER 65

The Lombards and Italy

Late arrivals of the migration of the peoples, late also in embracing Arianism, were the Lombards, who, shortly before 490, entered "Rugiland" (Lower Austria) and occupied the country between the Enns, Danube, and March. Ca. 526 they moved into the first Pannonian province between the Danube and the Drave, long ago evacuated by the Romans, and thereby became the immediate neighbors of the Ostrogoths. Under their King Wacho (ca. 510–40) they entered into friendly relations with the Gepids, who lived between the Theiss and the Carpathians, and with the Franks, both of whom were opponents of the Ostrogoths. A change occurred in Lombard policy when, after Wacho's death, Audoin (ca. 540–60) assumed control, first as guardian of the heir to the throne, Walthari, then from ca. 547–48 as King himself. Audoin fell out with the Franks and ca. 548 sided with Justinian, who granted to the Lombards for settlement the country between the Danube and the Save as well as eastern Inner Noricum — hitherto Ostrogothic provinces.

According to Procopius, the Lombards had declared in 548 that they were of one faith with the Emperor. Although this was certainly a declaration of intention of the Lombard envoys, it must not have been taken entirely right out of the air. For, through the Franks, Catholic influence can have been at work, even if it would also have crossed with an Arian influence from the Gepid side. In the first years of

King Alboin (ca. 560–73) the religious decision was still undecided, as a letter of
Bishop Nicetius of Trier to Alboin's first wife, the Frankish Princess Clodoswintha,
shows. Only after the victory over the Gepids, immediately before the invasion of
Italy in 568, did Alboin decide for Arianism, perhaps with a view to the assimilation
of the Danubian remnants of Germanic peoples into the Lombard nation. Also the
desire to gain the Ostrogoths still remaining in Italy may have played a role. This
recently accepted Arianism did not go very deep. Portions of the people even
continued as pagans.

The Lombards entered Italy, in contrast to the Ostrogoths, not as *foederati*
but as conquerors. Alboin occupied the provinces of Aquileia (Venetia) and Milan
(Liguria), except for the coastal districts, and then had a part of his troops advance
via the La Cisa Pass into Tuscany in the direction of Benevento. After his death and
the brief reign of his successor Cleph there ensued an interregnum (573–85), in
which the Lombards lived only under dukes. At this time the Emperor succeeded
in attracting no small part of the Lombard *duces* into his service. Even after the
renewal of the monarchy in 584, the restoration of political unity was at first a
program rather than a reality. A Frankish-Byzantine coalition brought King Authari
(584–90) to the edge of the abyss. The imperialists, who still possessed strong
bridgeheads north of the Po, won back Reggio, Parma, and Piacenza and thereby
drove a dangerous wedge between Lombard North Italy and the Lombard groups
in Tuscany, Spoleto, and Benevento. Savior of the Kingdom was Agilulf (590–615),
who subjugated the hostile dukes, eliminated the Byzantine wedge in western
Aemilia, and conquered Cremona, Mantua, and Padua north of the Po (602–3).
King Rothari (636–52) carried out a further breakthrough against the imperial positions by gaining Oderzo in Venetia, Modena in Aemilia, and in Liguria the entire
coastal strip with Genoa. Now the Lombards possessed the entire province of
Milan, the province of Aquileia except for Istria and the Venetian lagoon, the western half of Aemilia, southern Umbria with parts of Sabina, Samnium, and parts of
Campania. The duchies of Spoleto and Benevento, separated by the Exarchate of
Ravenna and the Roman Duchy from the Regnum, stood in only a loose dependence on the crown. Benevento went into its own way and after 663 expanded
over Apulia and Lucania.

The vicissitudes of the Church in the Lombard Kingdom become understandable only against the background of the political history. Paul the Deacon reports
that, in contrast to the territories occupied under the rule of Alboin, the *civitates*
conquered by the Lombard dukes were treated very harshly. Modern research is
inclined to trust this statement of the historian of the Lombards.

Although the two Metropolitans of Aquileia and Milan fled to imperial territory
in 568–69 — the former to Grado, the latter to Genoa — for the most part their
suffragans remained in the two provinces occupied by the Lombards. On the basis of the privilege which Alboin granted to the Bishop of Treviso right after the
occupation of the city, it may probably be assumed that also the other bishops
who came to terms with the new situation obtained legal guarantees from the
King. On the other hand, the bishoprics in the sphere of Benevento were entirely
destroyed: Paul the Deacon may have been thinking of them especially when
he spoke of the devastations of the dukes. In retrospect one reaches the conclusion that greater disturbances occurred in the areas which were too remote

from the power of the king, or were conquered late, disputed or after severe struggles.

Before the eyes of the Lombard Kings stood the model of the Amals. Alboin chose Verona as the royal seat and thereby gave notice that he intended to follow Theodoric — "Dietrich of Bern." In 584 Authari was elevated to the throne at Verona and there in 589 married Theodelinda, daughter of the Duke of Bavaria; through her mother she came from the old Lombard royal house of Wacho, the tradition of which she introduced to the renewed Lombard kingship. Authari assumed the nickname Flavius, which the Amals had borne, as had also the Visigothic Kings since Theudis and Athanagild. Thus was a program of government imitated which promised to guarantee legal security also to the Italian population. The King was, of course, concerned strictly to maintain the separation between Lombards and Romans. At Easter 590 he issued a prohibition for Lombards to have their children baptized as Catholics.

That individual Lombards were converted to Catholicism in Authari's time is attested by Gregory the Great. The prohibition of Catholic baptism raises the suspicion that conversions were no longer limited to the smallest circles. The hopes of the Catholics of Venetia and Liguria may have been especially turned on Queen Theodelinda, who was likewise a Catholic and who, like them, did not recognize the Council of Constantinople of 553. The condemnation of the Three Chapters at this Council had led to schism in the provinces of Milan and Aquileia. The ecclesiastical alienation from Rome and the Imperial Church concealed from the start the danger of a political estrangement from the Empire. At first Narses had exorcised it by treating the Three Chapters with respect in North Italy, probably with an eye on the Franks, who also inclined to the schism and appeared still threatening even after their exclusion from the peninsula. The Emperor Maurice (582–602) adhered to this policy of Narses, but thereby encountered the opposition of the Popes, for whom naturally ecclesiastical unity had preference. The Roman influence operated more powerfully on the Metropolitan of Milan, a refugee at Genoa. The bishop-in-exile of Milan, Lawrence, secretly abandoned his opposition in 573, and his successor, Constantius, chosen in 593, was orthodox. But the suffragans of Milan in the Lombard Kingdom did not go along with this change. They adopted a position against Constantius at Lombard Brescia. The Metropolitan-in-exile, Deusdedit, elevated to succeed Constantius ca. 600, was recognized at Milan, but the union of the province was still quite far off. Como, which ca. 606 obtained a new bishop in Agrippinus, even joined the clearly schismatic province of Aquileia. For Aquileia the situation was only altered when, after the change of the imperial religious policy under Phocas (602–10), an orthodox Metropolitan was also installed at Grado in 607. The suffragans of Lombard Venetia, in contrast to the bishops of Lombard Liguria, consummated the break and elected their own Metropolitan, who took his seat at Cormons. The old province of Venetia was thus split into a Lombard metropolitan unit of Aquileia, with its seat at Cormons, later Cividale (Forum Julii), and an imperial metropolitan unit of Grado.

The clever policy of Narses and of the Emperor Maurice delayed the estrangement of the schismatics from the Empire but could not in the end prevent it, as the events of 607 show. The rapprochement of the schismatic Catholics in the Lombard Kingdom to the Lombard kingship became clear from the split of 593 in the province of Milan. It would hardly have been consummated so quickly if Queen Theodelinda herself had not been a Catholic and had found in her second husband, Agilulf, whom she had married after Authari's death, complete sympathy for the new policy, probably first conceived by her, of a close collaboration with the Romans of North Italy. Agilulf remained personally an Arian, but he transferred his residence from the "Gothic royal city" of Verona to imperial Milan, took Milanese Romans into his council, encouraged the restoration of the Milanese churches, and finally in 603 even had his son Adalwald baptized as a schismatic Catholic — totally contrary to the baptismal decree of his predecessor Authari. The office of godfather of Adalwald was assumed by Abbot Secundus of Nano in the diocese of Trent, the long-time confidant of the Queen and historian of the court. The schismatic mission that began ca. 600 among the Lombards of the *Regnum* took place under the aegis of Saint Euphemia of Chalcedon. Its route was reflected also in the dedication of churches to the martyrs of the Val di Non (Nano) among the Lombard settlements of the west and to the Norican martyr Florian, whose cult the church of Aquileia spread farther, among the Lombard fortresses of the east. The royal couple were also able to interest in their aims the Abbot Columban, who had fled to Italy in 612. They made over to him the Church of Saint Peter of Bobbio as the basis of his mission in the diocese of Tortona and tried through him to gain influence over the Pope at the same time.

The first phase of Agilulf's reign coincided with the pontificate of Gregory the Great, the initiator of the mission to the Anglo-Saxons, who at his accession was confronted also with the question of the conversion of the Lombards because of Authari's baptismal decree that had only just appeared. But Gregory saw in the liquidation of the Schism of the Three Chapters and in peace between the Lombard King and the Emperor the unalterable presuppositions for a corresponding Roman initiative. He staked all his energy on realizing these preliminaries, and in this sense especially tried to influence Queen Theodelinda. Complete success was denied him. After his death the Lombard royal pair even turned the tables by suggesting to Pope Boniface IV through Columban a new examination of the question raised by the Three Chapters.

Gregory's religious and peace policy, meanwhile, seemed to bear fruit when, after Agilulf's death, the imperial Exarch at Ravenna for his part adopted friendly relations with the Lombard court in view of the serious threat to the Empire from the Persians. Church union thereby again became urgent. The Queen-Mother and the young King Adaloald apparently let themselves be convinced that the Council of Chalcedon had not been jeopardized by the Second Council of Constantinople, and the exertions for the liquidation of the schism led ca. 625 to the reunion of the metropolitan territories of Aquileia and Grado. But the negotiations had apparently been carried out over the heads of the Lombard magnates and the schismatic episcopate. Both groups united against the court. Adaloald was overthrown in 625, Arian kings again ascended the throne, the residence was transferred to national Lombard Pavia, and the schism flared up again.

The wheel of history, nevertheless, did not let itself be turned back. Hence there cannot be any word of an Arian reaction worthy of mention, because the new ruler, Arioald, was also supported by the schismatic Catholics. Add to this that his wife, Gundeperga, daughter of Agilulf and Theodelinda, continued the Catholic tradition at court and in fact also under the next King, Rothari, whom she married as her second husband. Gundeperga, however, belonged not to the schismatic but to the orthodox faction. Still more important was the fact that the abbey of Bobbio under Abbot Attala, after Columban's death and indeed before 625, had clearly taken a stand on the side of Roman Orthodoxy and thereby became the first center of an orthodox mission among the Lombards. At the urging of its abbots, Bobbio was exempted from the jurisdiction of the local Bishop of Tortona by privileges of Popes Honorius I of 628 and Theodore I of 643 and directly subjected to Rome. The abbey still remained closely bound to the royal family, and its aspirations vis-à-vis Tortona were supported by Ariwald as well as Rothari and Gundeperga.

The actual state of peace between *Regnum* and *Imperium* under Adaloald and Arioald, which lasted into the first years of Rothari (636–52), facilitated the throwing of a bridge from the Lombard court by way of Bobbio to Rome. But then in 643 Rothari again moved to the offensive against the *Imperium:* relations between Old and New Rome had fundamentally changed because of the Monothelite quarrel that erupted in 640. This explains why the ecclesiastical cooperation between Rome and Pavia, established by means of Bobbio, was not interrupted by Rothari's war.

Hence, paradoxically, the Catholic orthodox mission in the Lombard Kingdom gained its first bases under the two Arian Kings Ariwald and Rothari. The representative of the dynastic and Catholic community at court had been Queen Gundeperga. After Rothari's death and the brief reign of his son Rodoald, in 653, when the crisis between Emperor and Pope had reached its climax, a cousin of the Queen was made ruler of the Lombards: Aripert I, a nephew of Theodelinda. Aripert (652–61) was an orthodox Catholic. He annulled the position of Arianism as the State religion and close to the older parish church of Saint John the Baptist at Monza he founded Saint Savior at Pavia. But he did not exploit the political opportunities present in the conflict between Emperor and Pope; hence he did not fulfill the hopes which the Lombards had probably placed in him. Thus, after Aripert's death, Duke Grimoald of Benevento was able to use a contest over the throne between the King's sons, Perctarit and Godepert, to gain the crown for himself with the aid of an Arian group, which probably supported Godepert.

It is significant that the Arian Lombards of the *Regnum,* from whom had probably come the initiative for the *coup d'état,* no longer felt strong enough to raise a king from their own ranks but turned to the Duke of Benevento. The Beneventan Lombards, just as those of Spoleto, had not been touched by the Catholic mission of North Italy, and the great questions of the *Regnum* had remained foreign to them. Their Arianism bore the marks of a strong, unreflecting popular faith, which did not exclude pagan and Catholic elements. Grimoald (662–71) was devoted to the Archangel Michael, whose sanctuary lay on Monte Gargano in the Duchy of Benevento. He ascribed to the Archangel a victory over the Byzantines and spread his cult to Pavia, where his Catholic followers took it up. Michael pushed the older cult of John the Baptist into the background and became patron of the kingdom and nation of the Lombards.

Grimoald's reign was basically an anachronism, which ran counter to an historical development introduced long before. Perhaps the King in his last years even returned to the course of his predecessors. When he died, the Lombards called back Perctarit.

Under Perctarit (661/671–88) and his son Cunincpert (678/688–700), made coruler as early as 678, decisions finally matured which had been so long in preparation. Bishop Mansuetus of Milan (672–81) was the first Metropolitan of Liguria — of Lombard "Neustria" — who can be proved to have resided again in the old capital of Northwest Italy. King, Pope and Metropolitan took in hand the reorganization of the ecclesiastical province. Anastasius, the last Arian Bishop of Pavia, converted to Catholicism. The days of the schism were numbered in the province of Milan. Ecclesiastical union was apparently achieved without friction, since the common position in the Monothelite question made the old controversy over the Three Chapters pointless. When the Emperor Constantine IV yielded in the Monothelite quarrel, and Pope Agatho in 679 called upon the national churches of the West for a great demonstration of faith, a Synod of the province of Milan again met for the first time and placed itself behind the Pope. The peace of the Church, which the Sixth Ecumenical Council ratified at Constantinople in 680–81, also brought about the first official conclusion of peace between the Lombards and the Emperor. On this occasion the obligation of loyalty to the *res publica* and the Emperor, which the Roman suffragans assumed in their oath of obedience to the Pope as their Metropolitan, was changed for the Roman suffragans in the Lombard Kingdom into the obligation to work for the maintenance of peace between the *res publica*, that is, the *Imperium*, and the *gens Langobardorum*.

The acts of the Synod of Milan were drawn up by the deacon Damian, who soon after, following the death of Anastasius, who had converted to Catholicism, was made Bishop of Pavia and missionary Bishop for the Lombards. Under Damian the royal city of Pavia became the real center in the last phase of the Lombard mission under Roman auspices, and as such, in an analogy to Bobbio, was withdrawn from the ecclesiastical province of Milan and directly subordinated to Rome. Damian had studied in Greece and was probably himself Greek. The wave of immigration from Greece, the East, and Africa to Italy, which the Monothelite controversy and the Arab invasion had produced, worked to the advantage of the conversion of the Germans.

At the same time the Roman-oriental mission made progress also in the sphere of Spoleto and — in keeping with the reconciliation of the royal family with the dukes of Benevento — in Lombard Lower Italy. Duke Romuald I of Benevento (662–87) was converted by Saint Barbatus. Near his residence arose a church of Saint Peter, and the bishoprics of Benevento and Siponto were reestablished. Not Benevento, but Lombard "Austria," the province of Aquileia, the chief bastion of the schismatics, was the last support of the opposition to the Catholic monarchy — an opposition, it is true, in which Arianism no longer played any role, and political motives were at least a match for ecclesiastical ones. A decade later a Lombard Council at Pavia sealed the return of the last schismatics of the province of Aquileia to Orthodoxy. The King sent the acts of the Synod of 698–99 to the Pope for confirmation. The separation of the ecclesiastical provinces of Aquileia and Grado, long ago hardened by the political boundaries between *Regnum* and *Imperium*, continued.

At Cunincpert's death the development begun under Agilulf and Theodelinda was essentially complete, but had been again and again thwarted not least by political vicissitudes.

The Catholic monarchy gained stature among the Lombards only under King Liutprand (712–44) in consequence of a dynastic crisis, which again suspended the development for a full decade. However, essential outlines had already been fixed under Perctarit and Cunincpert. The Synod of Pavia can be compared, *mutatis mutandis,* with the national Council of Toledo of 589. It was convoked by the King and, in keeping with the imperial model, met in the hall of the royal palace. Union was solemnly sworn in the Church of Saint Michael, patron of the Kingdom. Since Perctarit or Cunincpert the bishops of Pavia were exempt and seem in the eighth century to have occupied a mediating position between Rome and the *Regnum.* King Liutprand founded the court chapel near the Church of Saint Saviour and built Saint Peter in *Caelo Aureo.* Like the Frankish and Visigothic Kings, he exerted influence on the nomination to bishoprics and in his capitularies gave validity to ecclesiastical principles, once even expressly by appeal to the Pope as *caput ecclesiarum Dei et sacerdotum* [*in omni mundo*]. Many boundary disputes between sees of the *Regnum* during the ecclesiastical reorganization of the *Regnum* were carried to his forum. The episcopate was even bound to military service in the late period of the *Regnum.*

Meanwhile, Pavia, in contrast to Toledo, did not achieve primatial status, and in the Lombard Kingdom, also in contrast to Visigothic Spain, no national councils can be proved. The ancient metropolitan organization in Italy differing from that in Gaul and Spain — thwarted the full construction of the national Church. For only two ecclesiastical metropolises — Milan and Aquileia (Cividale) — lay within the *Regnum.* The Lombard sees of Aemilia belonged to Ravenna; those of Tuscany, Spoleto, and Benevento, to the ecclesiastical province of Rome.

The Visigothic Kings had "wedded" Spain, as Isidore of Seville said. The conversion of the Lombards and the liquidation of the schism seemed to offer the Lombard Kings the possibility of making Italy their "bride." After the reconstruction of the *Regnum* Liutprand set himself the goal of making his sovereignty really effective over Spoleto and Benevento and of including the Exarchate of Ravenna with the Pentapolis in the Kingdom of the *a Deo dilecta et catholica gens Langobardorum.* In regard to Rome he was satisfied with a *defensio.* But these ideas found no echo in Imperial Italy. The frontiers between *Regnum* and *Imperium* were too powerfully consolidated in minds, and Rome clung to the political status quo, although precisely at that time Iconoclasm had led to a new ecclesiastical conflict with the Emperor. The political conflict between Pope and King became thereby inevitable. The Popes had long clung to the Late Roman idea of the Empire, in which the welfare of the Universal Church was inextricably bound with that of the *Imperium;* now they felt themselves ever more clearly to be the protectors of Imperial Italy, indeed in a certain way even as the guarantors of the autonomy of Spoleto and Benevento. The sworn obligation of working for peace between *Imperium* and *Regnum,* which the Lombard suffragans of Rome undertook at their ordination, was reinterpreted as early as 740 as the obligation to defend the papal status quo policy with the Lombard King: at the very time when the first papal appeal went out to the Franks. In this way was created a conflict of conscience for the Roman suffragans in the Lombard Kingdom and, in addition, for all *viri devoti* in the clerical and lay states. The Lombard Kings tried for a while to settle the conflict only on the political plane. Even Aistulf in a politically critical situation carefully spared the ecclesiastical rights of Rome. Only Desiderius in 769 opposed Rome on the field of canon law, when he sought to withdraw the parts of Istria occupied by the Lombards from the obedience of Grado and had a layman of his choice uncanonically elevated to the metropolitan see of Ravenna. Five years later came the decision: the *Regnum Langobardorum* was wrecked in its conflict with Rome.

CHAPTER 66

The Conversion of the Anglo-Saxons and the Beginnings of the Anglo-Saxon Church

The age of the migrations meant for Britain a very much deeper turning point than for Gaul, Italy, and Spain. The German tribes of the "Anglo-Saxons" — Angles, Saxons, Jutes, and other national fragments occupied the most permanently romanized eastern provinces with the metropolises of London and York and thereby hastened the process of deromanization among the Britons who had withdrawn to the West and were more and more isolated from the continent. Hence the Celtic language and culture again filtered through among the old established population, even if the Britons clung to the Christian faith and to the Latin language in the liturgy; in fact for a long time still they regarded themselves as members of Romania. In their political and social structure the Britons and Anglo-Saxons did not differ substantially from one another. Both were, like the Picts of Scotland, organized in petty kingdoms, among which, it is true, one or the other occupied a position of hegemony. But no symbiosis of the two peoples took place. Especially in the south of the island there persisted a hostile confrontation, which did not allow a missionary impulse to appear among the Britons.

For the first Christian influences became noticeable among the Anglo-Saxons not from the British neighboring districts but from Gaul. Aethelbert of Kent, who as Bretwalda, "ruler of Britain," occupied a position of hegemony south of the Humber, before 589 married a Merovingian Princess, Bertha, daughter of King Charibert I of Paris (561–67): In her entourage came the Frankish Bishop Liuthard to the court of Canterbury. For the Queen's worship a cemeterial basilica of Roman Canterbury was furnished and presumably then dedicated in honor of Saint Martin of Tours.

The real initiative for the Anglo-Saxon mission proceeded from Gregory the Great. The universal mission mandate given by Christ had never entirely fallen into oblivion in the Roman Church. Leo the Great had still seen it in a connection with a providential mission of the Roman Empire: "For it especially accords with the work ordained by God that many kingdoms were united into the one Empire and [thus] the universal proclamation of the faith had quick access to the peoples whom the rule of the one City held under its control." Gregory the Great was in this tradition, but he lived in a changed world. Under Augustine's influence he had again established the biblical eschatological understanding of the universal mission to pagans and in so doing had progressed from the "basic affirmation of the Church's universal missionary commission" to the "planning and organizing of a missionary enterprise outside the boundaries of the Roman Empire" (W. H. Fritze).

If the intellectual background of the great Pope's initiative, of the greatest importance for the future of the West, was to some extent judicious, so too the particular circumstances by which his interest was directed precisely to the Anglo-Saxons still remain obscure. The question how Britain, removed from the Roman *ecumene* for a century and a half, came again into Rome's line of vision is answered tersely but in a simplistic manner, by the Northumbrian *Vita Gregorii* and the Northumbrian legends transmitted by Bede. The external beauty of Anglo-Saxon slaves, which struck Gregory on a visit to the Forum, made him recognize that the Angles were called to be coheirs of the angels. The impressive narration was probably based on the fact that in 595 Gregory gave the commission to buy up Anglo-Saxon slaves in Gaul, that is, probably in Marseille, in order to have them educated in the Christian faith with a view to a future mission activity in their homeland, even if it is not impossible that Anglo-Saxon slaves also came to the Roman market. As testimony for Northumbrian ideas of the beginnings of the mission, the narrative is worthwhile, but as a historical report it encounters critical doubts.

The story told by Bede is said to have occurred in the time of Pope Benedict I (575–79). A first reference to Britain is found in Gregory's *Moralia,* which was composed between 585 and 595. The question whether as early as 585 Gregory had conceived the plan of the mission and then intended to implement it personally — five years before his elevation to the papacy — is controverted. However, the mission had certainly been prepared long in advance, as the already mentioned mandate to buy Anglo-Saxon slaves of 10 September 595 shows. The recruiting of the first missionaries caused difficulties, for the Roman diocesan clergy evidently declined. Finally in the late spring of 596 Gregory sent the Prior Augustine with a group of monks from the monastery of Sant'Andrea al Monte Celio, which he himself had founded. The Roman missionaries landed in the spring of 597 on the island of Thanet, belonging to the Kingdom of Kent.

Gregory had not selected Kent as the starting point of the mission by accident. He must have been informed, at least in broad outline, about the possibilities of a missionary activity at the court of Canterbury. Nevertheless, the journey to the remote pagan country seemed at least to those involved as a dangerous adventure: they would have very much liked to have turned back soon after their departure. Gregory did not give in, but sent to his envoys letters of recommendation to the Papal Vicar of Arles, the bishops of Aix-en-Provence, Vienne, and Autun, the Abbot of Lérins, the Frankish Queen Brunhildis and her grandsons, Theodoric II of Frankish Burgundy (Chalon-sur-Saône) and Theodebert II of Austrasia (Metz). With regard to the Queen, the Pope motivated his missionary embassy thus: he had learned that the Angles wished to become Christians but no bishop of the neighborhood undertook to care for them. From this one could infer an initiative from Kent. But this was contradicted by, among other things, the distrust with which, according to Bede, the royal house of Kent first displayed toward the Roman missionaries. The Christian Franks in Kent seem not to have overbusied themselves in thirty years in preparing the King for Saint Augustine.

The first difficulties were, however, soon overcome, and the mission work made good progress. Aid came from the Merovingian Kingdom by means of Bishop Syagrius of Autun, who was close to Queen Brunhildis. In July 598 Gregory could report to the Patriarch of Alexandria great successes, which were climaxed by the conversion of King Aethelbert, baptized probably at Easter 601. Augustine, who had been ordained a bishop in the Frankish Kingdom, founded, with the King's assistance, Christ-Church, the Cathedral of Canterbury, and near the basilica of Saint Martin a monastery, whose Church of Saint Austin was to receive the tombs of the bishops and of the royal family of Kent. The episcopal church obtained the patronage of the Savior in imitation of the Roman cathedral at the Lateran, while the monastic church was dedicated in honor of the Princes of the Apostles.

The newly established Anglo-Saxon Church was, in accord with Gregory's wish, to be independent of the Gallic Church and the Papal Vicar of Arles, but was to be united with the Celtic British churches of the island. Augustine was to prepare for the founding of two ecclesiastical provinces with London and York as metropolises for twelve sees each, which were to be brought to completion after his death. As head of all the churches of Britain, he received the pallium in 601 with the permission to take his seat in London.

Gregory's plan of organization was based on the older Roman division of Britain. However, the plan of organization corresponded neither to the political circumstances of the early seventh century nor to the status of the mission. London belonged to the Kingdom of Essex, whose ruler was subordinate to the Bretwalda of Canterbury and, besides, was still a pagan in 601. Under these circumstances, Augustine's removal to the ancient Romano-British metropolis was impracticable, and the union of the Anglo-Saxons with the British churches foundered on the difference of ecclesiastical usages, on the national antipathy of the peoples, and on Augustine's imperious manner.

The proclamation of the faith could develop only on the basis of the existing situation, and thus for the time being the mission extended only to the kingdoms which were closely connected with Kent — to Essex and East Anglia (Norfolk and Suffolk). Augustine and his companions gained a firmer footing in Essex, where a nephew of King Aethelbert ruled. Circa 604 Rochester was founded as a second see in Kent, with its Cathedral of Saint Andrew, and in Essex the bishopric of London, with the Cathedral of Saint Paul near the Roman forum. As little pressure for the acceptance of Christianity was exercised there as in Kent: "The King had indeed learned from his teachers, from whom he received salvation, that the service of Christ is voluntary, and must not be compulsory" (*Hist. eccl.* 1, 26). Gregory had instructed the missionaries not to destroy pagan temples but to turn them into churches and to give pagan feasts a Christian content: "... so that, if some joys were preserved for them externally, they might the more easily assent to the inner joys. For it is doubtless impossible at the same time to cut away everything from hard hearts, because whoever seeks to mount to the highest place goes up by degrees and steps, not by leaps" (*His. eccl.* 1, 30).

Augustine's mission, geared to individual conversion, naturally did not exclude the idea that the conversion of outstanding princes should also involve the wholesale conversion of their retinues and clients, in which on occasion pressure may have been resorted to. Even so, at Augustine's death between 604 and 609 not even all the members of royal families of Kent and Essex had become Christians. And so after the death of King Aethelbert in 616 and of his nephew of Essex there could ensue a pagan reaction, which, it is true, produced only a temporary reverse in Kent, but in Essex and East Anglia it destroyed the first buds of Christianity. On the other hand, a decade later there opened up great prospects for the mission in northern England. King Edwin of Deira (Yorkshire), who also ruled Bernicia (Northumbria) and the Lindissi (Lindsey) and acquired the hegemony in Anglo-Saxon territory, in 625 married a daughter of Aethelbert of Kent. To northern England with the Queen went Paulinus, one of the missionaries from Kent, who was made a bishop. Edwin came into conflict with the West Saxons and in 626 held out the prospect of his conversion in the event of his victory. After the fortunate outcome of the battle he presented to the Witenagemot, that is, the meeting of the magnates of his kingdom, the question of whether Christianity should be accepted. The Witenagemot decided for collective conversion. The King had himself baptized at Easter 627.

Bede's report on the discussion at the Witenagemot is a significant monument from the history of the German mission, even if it cannot rank as a contemporary testimony in the strict sense. It shows that not only the God promising victory and success made an impression, but also the problem of the meaning and end of human life played a role.

> "The present life of men on earth, O King," said one of the magnates, "seems to me in comparison to the time which is unknown to us to be of this sort: as when a sparrow hurries through your house in flight, where you are sitting down during the winter with your dukes and servants for a meal around the hearth-fire in warm comfort — but outside the winter rain and snowstorms rage everywhere. The sparrow flies through the door and at once goes out again through another. So long as it is inside, it is untouched by the fury of the winter. But in an instant the tiny space of calm unconcern has been traversed and it is already withdrawn from your eyes, returning from winter into winter. Thus seems the life of men for a short while; but what may follow we do not know. Hence if this new teaching brings more certainty, it should be properly followed." (*Hist. eccl.* II, 13)

The second ecclesiastical province of York, planned by Gregory, seems to have become a reality after the publicly decided conversion of the Angles north of the Humber. Paulinus took his seat at York, where, soon after the baptism of King Edwin, there began the construction of a stone cathedral, which replaced the one erected before the King's baptism and the wooden church dedicated in honor of Saint Peter. Popes Boniface V (619–25) and Honorius I (625–38) maintained contact also with the Northumbrian mission. The connection between Rome and the *ultimi habitatores mundi* was consolidated, and Honorius even brought it about in these years (629–32) that South Ireland accepted the Roman calculation of Easter.

But the precarious political stability of Britain again led to a severe setback. In 632 King Edwin perished at Hatfield in a battle against Penda of Mercia and the British King Caedwalla of Gwynedd. The Northumbrian mission collapsed. When Honorius I sent the pallium for Paulinus of York, the latter was in flight to Kent with the Queen and her children. Penda, ruler of the central English Kingdom of Mercia — the "March Kingdom" of the Angles against the Britons — was until his death in 654 the "central figure of Anglo-Saxon history." He was and remained a pagan.

Paulinus ended his life as Bishop of Rochester (635–44). Canterbury and Rochester, the two Kentish sees, had weathered the storm, and in 624 the precedence of Canterbury in the Roman mission sphere was sanctioned with the sending of the pallium by Pope Boniface V. But Canterbury's mission area shrank considerably in the following period. Rome was distant and offered little help. In place of Roman support there came with the approval of the Popes support from the Merovingian national Church of Gaul, which had already offered shelter to the refugees of the first pagan reaction, Bishops Mellitus of London and Justus of Rochester.

South of the Humber there were in the time of Penda of Mercia (632–54) only two kingdoms which could be designated as Christian: Kent and East Anglia. In addition to them, Wessex must be mentioned as a third kingdom, but at that time it was only beginning to open itself to the new teaching. Christian influences had first obtained recognition in East Anglia by way of Kent (Canterbury) and then by way of Deira (York). But the *nova doctrina* was only established under King Sigebert (630–35), who was baptized in Gaul and on his accession to the throne brought in the Frankish Burgundian Bishop Felix. The Frankish Burgundian bishop, whose missionary activity was authorized by Canterbury, founded the see of Dunwich in the south of the East Anglian *Regnum* (Suffolk). In the north of the country (Norfolk) the Irish mission obtained a foothold, still under Sigebert, through Abbot Furseus at Cnobheresburg near Yarmouth. The two East Anglian missionary groups were apparently in friendly relations. They were united in a common work, and the difference of observances was at least moderated by the Irish influence on the Luxeuil circle.

From ca. 633 the Gaul (?) Birinus worked independently of Canterbury in Wessex, which up to then had not been included in the mission. Birinus had received permission to preach to pagans from Pope Honorius I and had been ordained a bishop by the exiled Metropolitan Asterius of Milan. In 636 he baptized the King of Wessex, Cynegils, and took his seat at Dorchester, at that time the center of the kingdom. Agilbert's nephew Hlothere (Clothar), at the desire of the West Saxon King and with the approval of the Archbishop of Canterbury, whose precedence was thereby acknowledged also in Wessex. Of course, there can be no question of a direction of the mission by the metropolitans at Canterbury either in East Anglia or in Wessex. Deusdedit (654–63), the first Anglo-Saxon on the archiepiscopal *cathedra,* was de facto restricted to Kent in his activity. The great turning point of the mission came from the north. The Angles north of the Humber had been again united after the defeat of Hatfield by the brothers Oswald (633–41) and Oswiu (641–70) of the royal family of Bernicia. In 641 Oswald fell in the struggle against Penda of Mercia, but in 654 in the battle of Winwood Oswiu was able to break Mercia's supremacy and restore the Northumbrian hegemony.

During the reign of Edwin of Deira (616–32) the two brothers had lived in exile among the Irish and Picts of Caledonia and there they had become Christians of the Irish observance. In 634, Oswald had the Irish Abbot Aidan come from Iona; with the King's help, Aidan founded the monastery of Lindisfarne and became the abbot-bishop there. Aidan was followed by Finnan (651–61) and Colman (661–64). After Oswiu's victory of 654, Finnan baptized Penda's son Peada, who married a daughter of Oswiu, and King Sigebert of Essex, a "friend" of the Northumbrian ruler. The Irish Diuma was sent to Mercia as missionary bishop, and his Anglo-Saxon companion Cedd was soon after sent to Essex.

Thus Irish influence grew in England in the second third of the seventh century. On the other hand, Roman and continental influences made themselves apparent even in Irish-oriented Northumbria by way of Essex and Kent. The mission circles overlapped in wide areas of the Anglo-Saxon world, and conflicts could not be avoided. Into the center of the controversies moved the differences in regard to determining the date of Easter and hence also of Lent, which greatly aggravated daily life in intimate circles. At the Northumbrian court King Oswiu celebrated Easter according to the Irish calendar; the Queen, raised in Kent, according to the Roman calendar. The disadvantages which ensued called peremptorily for a clarification, and so in 664 the King summoned a Synod to Whitby.

In the Kentish beginnings of the mission, the opposition between the Roman-continental and the Celtic-insular ecclesiastical systems, strengthened by the hostility between Anglo-Saxons and Britons, had occasionally assumed sharp forms. At Whitby a different climate prevailed. Roman influences had vindicated themselves in the Irish Church: the South Irish had accepted the Roman calculation of Easter a generation earlier. Irish churchmen did not question apostolicity of faith as the basis of ecclesiastical unity, they went as pilgrims to Gaul and Rome, and they also encouraged their pupils to go. Hence the decision of Whitby could hardly be in doubt. The Frankish Bishop Agilbert of Wessex and his Anglo-Saxon pupil, Abbot Wilfrid of Ripon, defended the Roman standpoint against Colman of Lindisfarne. When Wilfrid appealed to the authority of Peter and in this connection quoted Matthew 16:18, the King intervened:

> "Did the Lord really say this to Peter, Colman?" He replied: "That is so, O King." Thereupon the King asked: "Have you anything of such force to present for your Columba?" He answered: "Nothing." Then the King said: "And so you both agree that this was said in the first place to Peter and to him the keys of the Kingdom of heaven were given by the Lord?" Both answered: "Yes." Then the King thus concluded the debate: "And I say to you: This one is the gate-keeper, whom I will not resist; rather I want to obey his orders in every way according to my knowledge and ability, lest, when I come before the gates of heaven, there may be no one there to open to me, because he turns his back on me who obviously holds the keys." (*Hist. eccl.* 111. 25)

In this way the dispute was settled in favor of the Roman group. Colman abandoned Northumbria with a group of intransigents, but other Irish remained. The great abbatial bishopric of Lindisfarne was divided into the sees of Ripon and York.

No less important than the Synod of Whitby was the change of episcopacy which soon after occurred at Canterbury. When the Anglo-Saxon candidate chosen by the Kings of Kent and Northumbria died after his arrival at Rome, Pope Vitalian, after a painstaking selection, elevated the Greek Theodore of Tarsus. Theodore went to Kent in 669, accompanied by the Neapolitan Abbot Hadrian, an African by birth. During his long episcopate (669–90), Theodore, who was the first Bishop of Canterbury recognized in the entire English Church, gave shape to this Church. Seven bishoprics, among them two for Kent (Canterbury and Rochester), and one each for the kingdoms of Northumbria (York), East Anglia (Dunwich), Mercia (Lichfield), Essex (London), and Wessex (Winchester), were reorganized. New sees were erected in the relatively large kingdoms of Northumbria (Lindisfarne, Hexham) and Mercia (Lindsey, Worcester, Hereford). After the conversion of the South Saxons by Wilfrid (680–85), the see of Selsey arose in Sussex. After Theodore's death the number of Anglo-Saxon bishoprics was increased by only a few new foundations in Northumbria (Whithorn), East Anglia (Elmharn), Mercia (Leicester, Dorchester,) and Wessex (Sherborne).

Under the direction of the Archbishop of Canterbury, England became an ecclesiastical unity long before it constituted a political unity. The English Church assembled in provincial synods, which were at the same time "national synods." Since, as a consequence of the political pluralism, the councils could not be dated by regnal years, the episcopate adopted the era of the Incarnation, which soon began from England its triumphal procession through the West. The calculation of Easter was defined, and *stabilitas loci* was stipulated for monks, the clergy, and the episcopate. However, Theodore of Tarsus adopted basic elements of the Irish practice of penance, and for the first time he prescribed annual confession for all. A *Poenitentiale,* which was based on Theodore's instructions and was widely disseminated under his name, "acted so that the improved and individual penitential system of auricular confession became the common property of the Universal Church, with graduated expiatory acts even for secret sins" (T. Schieffer). On the other hand, the Roman influence spread from England to the Celts of the British Isles. In 704 and 716 the Northern Irish of Bangor and the Picts adopted the Roman calculation of Easter. Only the Celts of Wales held fast to Columba's old usage until 768.

For two generations England remained under the ecclesiastical direction of Canterbury. Then when the Bishop of York received the pallium in 735, Northumbria separated itself from the ecclesiastical province that had embraced all England. The bisection was not only in accord with the plan of Pope Gregory but also with the special development of the northern Anglo-Saxon Kingdom. And thus it remained in the future. But the tradition of the *sedes* of Augustine and Theodore of Tarsus already was too strong. In keeping with its origin and its character as an early medieval missionary Church, the Church of England was "more Roman" than those of the Frankish, Gothic, and Lombard kingdoms, which in their roots went back to antiquity and had a richer inheritance. The cult of Saint Peter was firmly anchored in all the German-Roman churches, but it acquired a special intensity in England.

> Saint Peter clearly became the national saint, to whom monasteries and churches . . . were dedicated in great numbers. The most obvious and best known characteristic of this religious devotion was the stream of Anglo-

> Saxon pilgrims to the thresholds of the Apostles...many a one closed his earthly life in Rome, such as two Kings...Caedwalla (d. 689) and Ine of Wessex (d. 726). (T. Schieffer)

In 679 the Anglo-Saxon Church met at Hatfield at the request of the Pope in order to station itself behind Rome in the Monothelite question. The attachment to Rome also received juridical forms in England. Here the right of the metropolitan was first connected by Gregory with the reception of the pallium, a vestment consisting of a strip of white wool, which the Popes had previously granted to their vicars. By means of the pallium the metropolitan obtained a participation in the rights of the Pope and the title of "Archbishop" which had previously denoted a super-metropolitan position. As in the Lombard Kingdom, where the Pope had shared in the Lombard mission and in the reorganization of the ecclesiastical province of Milan, there occurred also, in England the exemption of monasteries, which were freed from the power of the local bishop and directly subjected to Rome. True, these privileges of exemption, which were granted only in a few special cases on the initiative of the founder, were not an effort by Rome to interfere in the circumstances of the English Church. For the English Church was, no less than the Frankish, Gothic, and Lombard, a "national Church," even if united more firmly with Rome. The competence of king and archbishop, of Witenagemot (meeting of the magnates) and synod extended

> to such important tasks as the erecting of sees, ... the naming of the bishop by the king [was] not regarded as unusual, ... his assent to the election was taken for granted, the expulsion of the bishop from his church by the king was not unprecedented. The supremacy of the king was recorded in a legislation which assured the Church the state's protection, but also maintained an ecclesiastical disciplinary power over clerics and laity.... The bishops and abbots came from princely and noble families, which devoted themselves zealously to the founding of churches and monasteries, but also, in keeping with the custom of the proprietary church system, retained ownership of them. (T. Schieffer)

The phases of the christianization of Anglo-Saxon life can be clearly followed. The first Anglo-Saxon in the see of Canterbury was Frithona (654–63), who took the Christian name of Deusdedit. In the 640s and 650s are found the first Anglo-Saxons among the bishops of Rochester (Kent), East Anglia, and Wessex. Apart from Canterbury, all the episcopal sees of England were occupied by natives from the 670s. Earconbert of Kent (640–64) was the first Anglo-Saxon King to order the destruction of pagan shrines in his kingdom. King Aethelbert of Kent, who had the oldest Anglo-Saxon national laws compiled, had already established penalties for offenses against God, the clergy, and the churches. But the national laws which Ine of Wessex and Wihtred of Kent issued in 694 and 695 are the first witnesses of a stronger Christian influence. The system of records which the Church brought to England clearly began under the episcopate of Theodore of Canterbury. From the start, the Anglo-Saxon Church was most intimately linked to monasticism, and indeed both that of Ireland as well as that of Rome and Gaul. But the great Anglo-Saxon monastic fathers — Cuthbert of Lindisfarne, Wilfrid of York, Benedict Biscop, Aldhelm of Malmesbury — belonged to Theodore's generation or were younger contemporaries of the Archbishop of Canterbury. Cuthbert (d. 687) assembled the Irish usages of his monastery into a Rule. With the romanization of the English Church the Benedictine Rule found entry, for which Wilfrid of York and Benedict Biscop (d. 690) obtained recognition in broad areas of the country. The Benedictine abbeys were to a far greater degree centers of education than were the Irish monasteries, which were for the most part overburdened by pastoral work. However, the Benedictine stamp of Anglo-Saxon monasticism must not be overestimated. Augustine and his companions were not "Benedictines," and until the eighth century one can probably speak of a Benedictine dominant character, but not of an exclusively Benedictine monasticism among the Anglo-Saxons.

Section Two

Inner Life of the Church
to the End of the Seventh Century

CHAPTER 67

North African Christianity from the Beginning
of Vandal Rule to the Muslim Invasion

When Augustine's life was nearing its end, the Church of North Africa seemed to look forward to a peaceful further development. The majority of the population of the Roman provinces, especially in the cities, had converted to Christianity; the still pagan minority, including members of the intellectual and propertied upper class, could be gained through a prudent missionary work, as could the pagan tribes on the long southern frontier of the romanized territory, to whom thus far too little attention had been given, because all too many personnel were tied down by the conflict between Catholics and Donatists. True, the Donatist denomination still existed, but it was forced on the defensive by State measures and especially by Augustine's theological work. Here too a positive development could be anticipated, if Augustine's program was followed, which had as its goal the inner reconciliation of the two denominations. But all this depended decisively on a consolidating of the political situation in the Western Empire, which had fallen into a very precarious position because of the wanderings of the peoples.

The North African Church under Vandal Rule

Suddenly the relatively calm situation changed for North Africa also, when in May 429 the tribe of Arian Vandals, then numbering ca. 80,000 persons, under King Gaiseric (428–77) crossed from the southern Spanish coast to Tangiers and began its progress through the Roman provinces. Thus began for the North African Church a period, lasting more than a century, of suppression and persecution by the new rulers, which added to it severe material and even deeper-reaching moral injuries. This persecution, which probably affected Catholics and Donatists in equal measure, knew two phases of greater and lesser intensity; it also had locally circumscribed centers of gravity and occasionally was suspended for several years, but it can neither be questioned as a whole nor minimized in its brutal characteristics. The statements of the different sources, among them eyewitness reports, are too unanimous for this and are in part confirmed by archeological investigation.

The first, extremely harsh wave of persecution extended from the beginning of the invasion to the definitive establishment of Vandal power (429–42). Since the Vandals were preceded by the reputation of a special intolerance toward the Catholic clergy, many bishops and priests considered flight, but the aged Augustine at once intervened with a clarifying word and stressed firmly that it was the duty of the clergy to persevere everywhere, even if only a remnant of the congregations remained which would need the help of its priests then in precisely such a situation of misery. The first reports on the behavior of the conquerors which reached the eastern provinces were depressing: churches burned, monasteries destroyed, cemeteries desecrated, private houses plundered, and everywhere the corpses of the slain or of those tortured to death. The roads were inundated with refugees, and Bishop Capreolus of Carthage could not even gather the bishops for a synod in order to appoint the delegates for the Council of Ephesus. Only a few cities, such as Cirta, Hippo, and Carthage, which were moreover filled with refugee peasants, were able to hold out longer. A first agreement with Ravenna, which in 435 recognized the Vandals as *foederati,* was exploited by Gaiseric to prepare for new warlike measures, and the persecution of the clergy continued. A series of sermons give information about the situation and frame of mind of the Catholics, especially in Carthage before the conquest of the city in 439; with good reason they are attributed to the Bishop Quodvultdeus. He regarded the calamity which had overtaken the Church of North Africa as punishment for the tepidity of many Christians, who were even now to be found in the circus instead of letting themselves be guided by the heroic model of their martyrs, Perpetua, Felicity, and those who right then in the country were more gladly enduring death than betray their faith. An apparently considerable number of Christians had already succumbed to the pressure of the enticements of the Vandals and had gone over to the Arian profession. In the most severe expressions they were warned to attempts at blackmail and bribery.

After the fall of Carthage the wrath of the conquerors exploded in full force against the inhabitants because of their long resistance. So many people met death that they had to be interred in a mass-grave without ecclesiastical burial. Plundering affected especially the property of the Church: the principal churches of the city were given to the Vandal clergy, others were used as barracks. Bishop Quodvultdeus was banished with a part of his clergy and taken to damaged ships, which however still reached Naples. The senators and other members of the upper class were first expelled from the city, then banished from the country. Flight brought some of them as far as Syria, where Bishop Theodoret of Cyrrhus took care of them. An organized care of souls was not possible for years in the occupied territories, and the demoralizing consequences were not lacking. The pressure was partly alleviated when a new treaty between Gaiseric and the Emperor Valentinian III in 442 transferred to the Vandals the provinces of Proconsular Africa, Byzacena, Tripolitana, and eastern Numidia as an independent sovereignty — the so-called *sortes Vandalorum* — while western Numidia and the two Maureta-nias remained imperial. Pope Leo I at once tried to reconstruct, at least in these provinces, a Church government capable of functioning. After a vacancy of fif-teen years, the Vandal King also allowed the occupation of the see of Carthage by Bishop Deogratias in 454.

The political chaos produced in Italy by the assassination of Valentinian III in 455 was exploited by Gaiseric for a quick attack by his fleet on the Tyrrhenian Sea; he took Rome by a *coup de main* and subjected the city to a heavy contribution in art treasures and precious metals; Pope Leo I had to surrender liturgical ves-sels but obtained from Gaiseric in return that the city would be spared burning and bloodshed.

The first years of the reign of King Hunneric (477–84) seemed to introduce a change for the better, since Catholic worship was again allowed and the com-munity of Carthage obtained a new head in Bishop Eugene (481). Through his social concern, he quickly gained high esteem, but thereby aroused the envy of the Vandal clergy and of the Patriarch Cyrila, who gradually succeeded in inducing the King to a change of course. At first attendance at Catholic worship was forbid-den to all who wore Vandal dress, hence also to all Catholics in the service of the Vandals. A repulsive campaign of moral defamation of clergy and nuns ensued. Then all Catholics in the army and administration were given the alternative of accepting Arianism or giving up their positions; but the latter were punished by confiscation of property and banishment to Sicily or Sardinia. With the issuing of a decree in 483 which banished almost 5,000 people, clerics and laity of all classes, to the frontier district of the province of Byzacena, dominated by the Moors, the persecution under Hunneric reached its first climax. Victor of Vita described the march of the exiles to the desert, partly as an eyewitness; for many it became a road to death. Rediscovered inscriptions and the remains of a memorial chapel of their graves confirm his report.

Probably as a reply to the remonstrances of the Emperor Zeno, Hunneric sum-moned the Catholic bishops to Carthage for a religious discussion on 1 February 484, although the Vandal clergy, in contrast to the Catholic, had hitherto shown little interest in theological discussion. Bishop Eugene wanted also Catholic rep-resentatives from non-African countries, especially from Rome, to be invited to it, because a discussion between Arians and Catholics was not merely an inner Af-rican matter. The request was rejected, and before the beginning of the conference some Catholic bishops who were versed in theology were banished or intimidated by ill-treatment. What then took place at the sessions under the presidency of the Vandal Patriarch Cyrila was less a religious discussion than a passionate debate of both sides concerning questions of procedure; nevertheless, the Catholics were able to submit a detailed profession of faith, probably drawn up by Eugene. King Hunneric at once took up the charge of the Vandal participants in the meeting that the Catholic bishops were the real mischief-makers and issued an edict which placed the Catholic Church entirely under particular law. According to this, the ear-lier imperial laws against heretics were again declared valid against all who within a determined interval had not been converted to Arianism: all churches were to be closed, all Masses, baptisms, and ordinations were to be discontinued, the liturgical books were to be destroyed, the church property was to be conveyed to the Vandal clergy. After various tortures, a part of the bishops were deported to Corsica, the majority were degraded to the status of *coloni*, a remnant were forced to work in the mines. Now the harshest phase of the persecution also overtook the general population occasionally it had sadistic features. Add to this a severe famine, so that under the double pressure the number of conversions to Arianism from all classes rose sharply, while others bravely endured torture and death. Only the accession of King Gunthamund (484–96) brought a mitigation of the terror. The decrees of banishment were partly annulled, Bishop Eugene after his return in 487 could also resume Mass in the cemetery church of a suburb of Carthage, at his request Gunthamund in 494 finally allowed the return of all the exiles, and Catholic churches were again opened everywhere in the country. The African Church as a whole offered a picture of devastation, in which the spiritual and moral damage weighed far more than the material — a recovery had to last for years. Since the surviving bishops at first could not meet for a synod of the entire African Church, they turned over the question of the treatment of the numerous *lapsi* to Rome for instructions; the sources, however, supply no data on the number of those willing to do penance.

But no real reconstruction, within and without, came about, for the period of relative toleration ended after the first years of the reign of King Thrasamund (496–523). When the ecclesiastical leadership in the province of Byzacena began around the turn of the century to give new bishops, as far as possible, to the orphaned communities, in opposition, of course, to a royal edict, a new decree sent both consecrators and the newly ordained into exile. Again part of the bishops had to flee or look for a hiding place, again conversions to Arianism were recorded. Among the deported was the new Bishop of Ruspe, Fulgentius, whose theological learning soon made him the intellectual leader of the African episcopate. Through his extensive correspondence, which he carried on from Sardinia, partly as "secretary" of the exiled bishops, through his activity as superior of the monastery founded by him at Cagliari, through his preaching and lecturing, he became a factor in ecclesiastical politics whose importance the Vandal King could not neutralize by mere banishment. When ca. 515 Thrasamund let him be brought to Carthage to have him give his opinion in regard to the objections of the Arian clergy against the Catholic doctrine of the Trinity, he seemed to have had hopes of a disputation conducted in writing with Fulgentius alone rather than of a religious discussion on the model of 484. The Arian compiler of the *objectiones,* which the King had presented to Fulgentius, once in writing, the other time only read out, is unknown. Fulgentius replied in two works, which in their verbal respect toward the King corresponded to etiquette, but de facto represented the Catholic standpoint without any compromise; the second turned directly to Thrasamund and demanded of him that he accept the Catholic teaching. Since Fulgentius used the relative freedom granted him in Carthage for a successful activity among Catholics and Arians, under the pressure of the Vandal clergy he had to return to exile in Sardinia in 517. An abecedarian psalm from his pen, oriented on the Augustinian model and sharply anti-Arian, which urged the Catholics to remain true to the faith, belongs to this period. Thus ended in failure the attempt of King Thrasamund to take the Catholic Church of North

Africa into the service of the Vandal Kingdom, first by reprisals, then by more ecclesiastic-political procedures.

A lasting peace for the Catholic Church of North Africa was first brought about by the accession of King Hilderic (523–30), to whom hostility to Catholics was foreign, since he had spent years at Constantinople and regarded himself as a member of the Theodosian Dynasty through his maternal pedigree. His first measures, probably undertaken in agreement with the Emperor Justin I annulling of the decree of exile for the bishops, return of the alienated churches, permission for the filling of orphaned sees — gave back freedom of worship and of preaching to the Church and made it possible for it to tackle the reconstruction of a too deeply disturbed ecclesiastical life. Hilderic's ecclesiastical policy of friendliness to Catholics, however, evoked an ever-growing opposition among the Vandals, at whose head stood Gelimer, a great-grandson of Gaiseric. Then when Hilderic's troops suffered several defeats in battle against rebel Berbers, Gelimer had him imprisoned and himself acclaimed as King of the Vandals in 530. The ever more clearly apparent decay of Vandal power induced the Emperor Justinian I, in spite of some hesitations because of the technical difficulties of the enterprise, to bring the North African provinces again under the full authority of the Empire by a military intervention. In half a year, September 533 to March 534, the Byzantine expeditionary force under Belisarius, supported by the native population, succeeded in breaking the Vandals' resistance. In the victor's triumphal procession at Constantinople was seen their last King, Gelimer. The Emperor Justinian, who saw himself confirmed in his religious mission through the success of the North African undertaking, promised in the law which reorganized the administration of the Diocese of Africa that all inhabitants of these provinces would understand in what freedom they could live under his rule. Above all, the Catholic clergy could assume that they had special claim to freedom. They immediately began at a general Synod under Bishop Reparatus of Carthage in 534, in which 220 bishops were able to participate, discussions on the restoration of their so severely injured Church. In this, three problems occupied the foreground: (1) the restoration of all African clerics who were still staying in the other areas of the Empire, but now were needed for the rebuilding of an organized pastoral work in their homeland; (2) the procedure in the reception of Catholics who through force or seduction had gone over to Arianism, among whom were numerous clerics; (3) the reinstituting of the Catholic Church in its previous rights, which included both the return of its former possessions and the recognition of the special position of the Catholic denomination. For the first two questions the Council requested the confirmation of its decrees by Rome. According to these, only those clerics overseas should be received who could show in writing a special commission from their bishop. Further, every Arian cleric willing to return should be received only as a lay person, but the Church should see to his suitable support. For the regulation of the third question an imperial decree was required, and Justinian issued it in August 535. It ordered the return of all church buildings and liturgical vessels and confirmed the metropolitan rights of the Bishop of Carthage. Extremely severe were the measures which the decree laid down in regard to Arians, Donatists, Jews, and pagans: they had to close their churches and stop every cultic act; any gathering was forbidden; it sufficed that they were able to live. The Pope congratulated the Emperor for such zeal for the spread of God's Kingdom.

This harshness would take a bitter toll. When, soon after the return of Belisarius to Constantinople, the indigenous tribes in the south and west of the central provinces rose against the new regime, the Arian and Donatist clergy supported the rebels, so far as was possible, in their war, which lasted more than fifteen years and made a consistent and effective reconstruction of the Catholic Church impossible. But one gets the impression that the episcopate, on the other hand, had no comprehensive reconstruction plan sketched out on a wide view. Add to this the further burden of the controversy over the Three Chapters, in which the African episcopate took an active part. As its two spokesmen first appeared Facundus of Hermiane and the deacon Ferrandus of Carthage, both of whom repudiated Justinian's theology or called for opposition to it. In 550 the Synod of Carthage even withdrew its communion from Pope Vigilius in the event that he annulled his *Judicatum* and formally protested to the Emperor against the condemnation of the Three Chapters. Of the heads of the African ecclesiastical provinces summoned to Constantinople, only the Primate of Numidia proved to be submissive to the imperial wishes, while Reparatus of Carthage had to pay for his refusal with banishment to Pontus, where he died in 563. A second group of eight bishops, who were probably chosen as delegates for the Council of 553 by the successor of Reparatus, Primosus of Carthage, because they were loyal to the Emperor, likewise caused no difficulties. After the Council Primasius of Hadrumetum accepted the condemnation of the Three Chapters, in return for which Justinian rewarded him with the dignity of Primate of Byzacena. But on their return to Africa these bishops encountered the cold repudiation of their colleagues, whose resistance to the decrees of 553 they could break only with the aid of the State's power.

With the accession of Justin II (565–78) this theological strife gradually died out, but the authoritarian claims of the Byzantine Emperor left their mark on the African episcopate. In the Exarch of Carthage they constantly had the representative of imperial power close by; he had to foster the true faith, of course, but at the same time he understood this commission as control over the Church or as a right to interfere in its affairs. Thus more and more there spread among the bishops a certain resignation, and smaller and smaller grew the number of those who devotedly troubled themselves over the restoration of religious life.

In the face of the frequent encroachments of an often corrupt bureaucracy the African Church more than previously sought aid from the Roman Pope, but only men like Gregory the Great could occasionally secure remedies here. His correspondence with his Legate, Hilary, with some reliable bishops, and with the high State officials partly discloses serious abuses also in the higher clergy, which could only be regarded as signs of a progressively negative development. Tirelessly, Gregory sought to shake the bishops out of their lethargy, which showed itself especially in regard to the Donatists, who were becoming again very active in Numidia, since the Emperor Maurice had relaxed Justinian's strict decrees.

However, the resumption of missionary work among the pagan tribes in the frontier zones of the provinces represented a positive characteristic in the life of the African Church of this time. Here the Byzantine policy of securing the Empire's boundaries by the christianization of the population at the same time coincided with the Church's mission mandate. Already under Justinian the Moorish tribes in the south of the province of Tripolitana had been gained for Christianity. The year 569 brought the conversion of the Garamantes in the district of Fezzan in southwest Libya. And in the south of Byzacena Christianity found entry among the tribes in the oasis of Girba and in the southern slope of the Aurès Mountains. In the extreme west of Mauretania Caesariensis numerous Christians lived under the rule of King Masuna, and their bishops took part in the synods at Carthage. Even Arabic authors attest that the Islamic troops in their conquest encountered many native tribes that professed Christianity. Under the burdens of the Muslim invasion that soon occurred, the new faith possessed only slight and easily paralyzed powers of resistance.

The scanty sources on the interior situation of North African Christianity begin to flow somewhat more abundantly in the first decades of the seventh century, when the Monothelite Controversy made an impact here too. With the wave of eastern Christians who fled to Africa before the Muslim conqueror ca. 640 came also adherents of Monothelitism, whose propaganda was, of course, at first severely suppressed by the Exarch George with the approval of the Catholics. An opportunity for the African Church to reject the new theological doctrine just as decisively as once it had rejected the condemnation of the Three Chapters was the public dispute between Maximus Confessor and the former Patriarch Pyrrhus of Constantinople at Carthage in 645, in which Maximus overwhelmingly demonstrated the untenability of the Monothelite theology. The bishops informed Pope Theodore of their rejection of Monothelitism and at the same time asked him to induce the Patriarch Paul of Constantinople to the same view or to exclude him from ecclesiastical communion. They addressed a letter with the same content to the Emperor Constans II (641–68), and finally directly called upon the Patriarch to abandon the erroneous teaching at the beginning of 646. A delegation of African bishops took part in the Lateran Synod of 649, at which Pope Martin I solemnly rejected Monothelitism. With the episcopate of the other western countries the bishops of Africa adhered to Rome's verdict, which the Pope made known to all churches by an encyclical.

The Muslim Invasion
and the Ruin of North African Christianity

The tedious theological confrontations, along with other reasons, had led in the population of the North African provinces to a new wave of hostility toward Byzantine rule. When the Arabs again invaded the same province, they could without hindrance build the city of Kairawan as their religious and military center in North Africa; thereby a constant threat to Carthage and the rest of North Africa was created. Only when in 696 the Arabs under Hassan brought Carthage under their power did the Emperor Leontius send a fleet, which was at first able to relieve the city, but in the spring of 697 the Byzantines yielded without a battle rather than face another attack. In the next years, the Muslim troops broke the resistance of the Berber tribes in Numidia and Mauretania, and in 709 all of North Africa except for the bridgehead of Septem (Ceuta) was in their hands.

Unfortunately there is no eyewitness report from a Christian pen which would directly inform in detail of the conduct of individual Christians as well as of Church leaders during the Islamic conquest and of the situation of Christianity in the following decades. One may certainly reckon with a considerable decline of the Christian population in the years of the subjugation, which was caused by the flight of many Christians to Italy and Gaul as well as by the death of many inhabitants in the severe battles for the possession of the cities, which were in the majority Christian. However, the remainder of the Christians were at first treated according to the usual practice of the conquerors, that is, the exercise of their religion was allowed on the payment of a tax and the renouncing of any propaganda for their faith. But ca. 720 a heavy pressure began under the Caliph Omar II on the still Christian Berbers to convert to Islam, and most succumbed to it. Archeological investigation has been able, it is true, to bring to light a considerable number of Christian inscriptions and remains of Christian churches, which attest the continued existence of Christians in several places of North Africa long after the conquest. And reports of Arab writers and even letters from the papal chancery in the eleventh century testify to the continued life of at least small Christian groups up to this period. But these testimonies underscore ultimately the fact that North African Christianity, differently from the Egyptian or Syrian under similar conditions, perished relatively fast as a large organized community. The question often raised as to the causes of this process can be answered only with reference to many factors. A cause reaching far back was produced with the split of African Christianity into a Catholic and a Donatist denomination, which reduced their interior strength more and more. A further weakening followed from the Vandal persecution with its crushing permanent effect, from which the Church never really recovered. The rapid apostasy of the christianized Berber tribes, finally, was very much the fault of the African Christians themselves, who in the fourth century did too little and thereafter carried out an intensive mission activity too late among this part of the population and thus could not achieve an existential conversion. The rest of western and eastern Christianity in its total tragedy scarcely noted the ruin of a Church which had produced figures such as Tertullian, Felicity and Perpetua, Cyprian, and Augustine. There were no voices that would have given authentic expression to the shock of this loss.

CHAPTER 68

The Papacy between Byzantium and the German Kingdoms from Hilary (461–68) to Sergius I (687–701)

The relative understanding with the Christian East, especially with Byzantium, reached under Pope Leo I, continued under his successor, Hilary (461–68), who as Legate at the Synod of Ephesus of 449 had become acquainted with the East from personal observation. But a new topic of future papal concern was already intimated during his reign: the relationship to the Arian Germans. Hilary had to live with the fact that an Arian community had established itself in Rome and with the help of the German military commander Ricimer built a church of its own, from which grew the Church of Santa Agata dei Goti. His program, announced at his accession, that he would strive especially for the unity of the episcopate, caused him to intervene repeatedly in the questions of jurisdiction among the Gallic and Spanish bishops, and in these cases he preferred to have his decisions reached at Roman synods.

The extant correspondence of Pope Simplicius (468–83) shows that the post-Chalcedon development in the East was beginning to claim the special attention of the Popes. There, under the Emperors Leo I (457–74) and Zeno (474–91), the nascent Monophysite movement succeeded in filling the sees of Alexandria (Timothy the Cat) and Antioch (Peter the Fuller) with its own men, who enjoyed the special favor of the usurper Basiliscus (475–76). When the last-named, under their influence, condemned the creed of Chalcedon and the *Epistola dogmatica* of Pope Leo I in his *Encyclion,* and thereby intended to restore the Christological question to the position of Ephesus of 431, and when some 500 bishops, even though under pressure, assented to the edict, it was understood at Rome on what precarious ground the result gained with so much work at Chalcedon stood. In a series of letters Pope Simplicius implored the Emperor Zeno, restored to power in 476, and the Patriarch Acacius (471–89) to preserve the legacy of Chalcedon and to eliminate the people who were threatening it. The delaying tactics of Acacius, concerning whose failure to supply information the Pope repeatedly complained bitterly, led to a steadily growing mistrust on the part of Rome, especially when Constantinople elevated an open supporter of Timothy the Cat, Peter Mongus, to be Patriarch of Alexandria. This mistrust in Rome worked disastrously in regard to the *Henoticon,* composed by the Patriarch Acacius and issued by the Emperor in 482, which aimed to bring about a union of the factions by a compromise, avoiding an unambiguous acknowledgement of Chalcedon but expressly recognizing Cyril's anathemas. The *Henoticon* promptly obtained the consent of the Patriarchs of Alexandria and Antioch, who interpreted it in the Monophysite sense. The urgent warnings of the Pope against an obliteration of principle remained unheeded.

Since neither Emperor nor Patriarch even notified the Pope about the *Henoticon,* the far more self-conscious and energetic Felix II (483–92), in comparison to Simplicius, decided on crucial but momentous measures, especially since the abbot of the monastery of the Acemetae monks of Constantinople was complaining of Rome's hitherto hesitant attitude toward the Monophysite movement that was growing ever stronger. A papal embassy brought letters for the Emperor and the Patriarch, in which the latter was summoned to a Synod at Rome. When the papal legates were thereupon first imprisoned at Constantinople and then won over by bribes to accept the communion of Acacius and Peter Mongus, Felix II, in the setting of a Synod in July 484, had the Bishop of Constantinople solemnly deposed from his priestly office and any communion with him forbidden. In several letters to the clergy and people of Byzantium, to the monks of the city and its vicinity, but especially to Acacius and the Emperor himself, the decree of the Synod was made known and justified in sharp expressions. The chief reason for the condemnation of the Patriarch was, in Rome's view, the fact that he had again accepted the ecclesiastical communion of Peter Mongus, whom he had himself once condemned as a heretic, and whose condemnation he had also demanded of Rome. At Rome, despite Acacius' contrary assertions, people remained convinced that the Patriarch of Alexandria had never repudiated his rejection of Chalcedon, especially since his adherents in Rome confirmed this. Thus the Roman decision meant an open break between East and West, the Acacian Schism, which was deepened through the sharp and at times cutting instruction, never heard since the time of Ambrose, to the Emperor Zeno on the limits of imperial power vis-à-vis the Church: "the Emperor is a son of the Church, not a bishop of the Church. In matters of faith he must learn, not teach.... By God's will the direction of the Church belongs to the bishops, not the civil power. If this is a believer, then God intends it to be subject to the Church."

Pope Gelasius I (492–96)

The freedom of the Church from the tutelage of the State, here demanded, was also the primary goal of the activity of Pope Gelasius I (492–96), who as Felix II's deacon, had formulated the statements quoted. The erasing of the names of Acacius and Peter Mongus from the diptychs remained for Rome the *conditio sine qua non* for the restoration of unity: only thus, so it was thought, was a clear recognition of Chalcedon assured. This attitude was also maintained when Acacius' successor Fravitas, made known to the Pope the hope of an elimination of the schism, and also when the next Patriarch, Euphemius (490–95), held himself aloof from Peter Mongus, because the latter had demanded of Fravitas the rejection of the Council of Chalcedon and thereby had himself confirmed Rome's suspicion of his Monophysite connections. The reply of Gelasius I to Euphemius' notification of his election, which clearly aspired for peace and was not sparing in its praise of the Pope, was not only inflexible in the matter but even in form was a perplexing mixture of cold lack of courtesy and irony. The Pope utilized his first contact with the Emperor Anastasius I (491–518) for the presentation, more moderate in tone but portentous for the future in its content, of the task and rank of the two powers by which the world is ruled, the *auctoritas sacrata pontificum* and the *regalis potestas*. The competence of the latter is fully recognized for the secular sphere, and it also binds the bishops, but it remains subordinate to the former, so that the Emperor cannot direct the bishops, to whom *res divinae* are entrusted, according to his will, but is dependent on their judgment. Among the representatives of the spiritual authority, the occupant of that see is again preeminent whom the word of Christ placed ahead of all and whom the Church from time immemorial has recognized as its supreme head. The responsibility placed on this Apostolic See for the preservation of the purity of the faith has made necessary the exclusion of Acacius, since he maintained communion with those who rejected the creed of Chalcedon. In reality, the theological question so deeply troubled the Pope that he gave an account of it in several treatises, some of them quite detailed, especially in the work *De duabus naturis*, which went beyond Leo I's achievement, since it displayed a deeper knowledge of Greek theology and found more precise formulations, even if it could not define the exact relationship of nature and person. It must be admitted that Gelasius I understood that to a great degree he was responsible for preserving the heritage of Chalcedon from any falsification and depreciation, and since he saw it threatened also by the imperial power, he sharply pointed out the State's limits in relation to the Church.

As a deacon, Gelasius had defended this policy in respect to Constantinople, before Theodoric had firmly established himself in Italy, and as Pope he just as courageously warned the Gothic Count Teja not to interfere in ecclesiastical affairs, especially since he belonged to another denomination and his master, Theodoric, had recognized the autonomy of the Church. When he once enumerated examples for ecclesiastical opposition to State encroachments, he could with satisfaction refer to the fact that he himself had refused any obedience to the German King Odocer, when the latter demanded something unlawful from him. It is understandable that the Pope repeatedly turned to Theodoric from nonpolitical motives, since the Gothic King had expressly guaranteed to respect the Catholic Church and especially the Roman See. If Gelasius' understanding of the primacy, as it is manifested in word and deed, is compared with that of Leo I, two important further developments become prominent: the obligation of the Roman Bishop to watch over the purity of doctrine was drawn more strongly into the foreground and maintained without compromise, and the freedom of the Church with respect to the highest representatives of the civil power was thought out anew and more deeply and formulated with a precision which defined the relations of the two powers to each other for the West for centuries, in a sense that strongly deviated from the understanding of the Byzantine imperial power.

Because of this activity, another aspect in the total work of Gelasius I is occasionally unduly relegated to the background — his extensive pastoral work. In the heavy afflictions which the Ostrogothic conquest meant for the population of Italy, he exerted himself tirelessly for the alleviation of every misery. From Theodoric's mother, the Catholic Ereleuva, he asked support for his seeking of aid from the King. He repeatedly reminded the clergy that one-fourth of the revenues of a church must be used for the poor, that the bishops should maintain captives and strangers from their share, that a conscientious administration of Church property was a duty of the episcopal office. Concern for widows and orphans had to remain a constant aim of the clergy. He often protested the rather frequent violation in those disturbed times of the churches' right of asylum. An irrevocable presupposition for the pastoral mission of the Church was seen by Gelasius to be a zealous, conscientious clergy; in a comprehensive decretal he assembled guidelines for the selection of recruits, for their formation, for the active care of souls, for the building, endowing, and dedicating of churches. True, the Pope had far more to blame than to praise in his clergy, but he still had a sympathetic heart for their problems and needs; full of concern, he inquired after the state of health of a sick bishop, warmly interceded for a priest whom some wanted to deprive of his position after an accident, and threatened to report to the King an official who disregarded the rights of his clergy. Just as little did the Pope put up with a diminution of the rights of the lower clergy and of the laity by the bishops; when, during the election of a bishop, the bishops wanted to make the decision on the candidate among themselves, he decisively insisted that the clergy of all parishes and the entire community should take part in the election.

Liturgical activity did not occupy the lowest rung in the pastoral work of Gelasius I. He may be regarded as the compiler of the old Roman *Kyrie-Litany,* the *Deprecatio Gelasii,* which was probably introduced in connection with an adaptation of the Universal Prayer, related to it in content, in the Mass liturgy. Finally eighteen Mass formularies preserved in the *Sacramentarium Leonianum* go back to him.

Under Pope Anastasius II (496–98) a change in the relations between Rome and Byzantium seemed to be in progress, since he delegated an embassy to the East to carry notification of his election to the Emperor. In a letter, very humble in form, the Pope expressed his regret over the existing separation and unambiguously recognized the validity of the ordinations and baptisms performed by Acacius, but he still did not see himself in a position to confirm his orthodoxy by placing his name in the diptychs. Anastasius defended himself against the charge that the Apostolic See, for which he claimed the primacy of the Universal Church, had acted in the condemnation of the Bishop of Constantinople not out of concern for the faith but out of arrogance. The early death of the Pope prevented further discussion.

The split in the Roman congregation over the question of what attitude to maintain toward Byzantium led to a double election and hence to the Laurentian Schism, which for years crippled the activity of the Roman See. After hearing the bitterly feuding factions at Ravenna, King Theodoric first decided against the pro-Byzantine priest Lawrence for Symmachus (498–514), in whose favor the earlier time of his ordination and the greater number of adherents also spoke. At a Roman Synod in 499 Symmachus tried to prevent a repetition of such occurrences by a unique decree on the papal election, which aimed to assure to the reigning Pope a sort of right of designation of his successor and hence in practice excluded the collaboration of the community in the election of the Pope. Although Lawrence signed the synodal decrees and then assumed the see of Nocera, the pro-Byzantine senatorial faction continued its opposition to Symmachus and accused him to Theodoric of serious moral lapses, squandering of Church property, and disregard of the date of Easter, whereupon the King ordered an investigation of the accusations by a synod and appointed a visitor for the Roman Church until a clarification of the affair had been made. Despite repeated admonitions from Theodoric and pressure from the senatorial majority, the Synod, which met from early summer to late autumn 502, could not decide on a formal judicial process against Symrnachus because people were of the opinion that the occupant of the Roman See cannot be judged by his subordinates. Finally, it reached the uniquely formulated decree that a verdict in this case must be left to God, that Symmachus himself should be regarded as immune from judgment and able freely to celebrate the liturgy in all churches. But this outcome only hardened the resistance of the opposition, which brought Lawrence back to Rome and, in addition to the papal residence of the Lateran, was able to put him in possession also of most of the Roman titular churches, whereas Symmachus was restricted to Saint Peter's. The continuing disturbances in the city were accompanied by serious literary feuding, in which Ennodius, then still a deacon at Milan, and Avitus of Vienne intervened and in the course of which the so-called Symmachan Forgeries were launched, whose aim it was to prove by the example of alleged cases from the history of the papacy the principle that the first episcopal see cannot be subjected to any court — *Prima sedes a nemine iudicatur.* Not until the fall of 506, when Theodoric had to take into account the growing political tensions with Byzantium, did he decide, pointedly and definitively, for Symmachus, to whom he had all the churches of Rome given back, and thus caused the end of the schism, especially since the opposing faction soon lost its head through the death of Lawrence, whom Symmachus had excommunicated.

How very much this victory increased the Pope's self-consciousness in regard to Constantinople appears from his answer to a letter of the Emperor Anastasius, who saw himself betrayed by the Roman Senate and in his anger reviled the "illegally ordained" Pope as a Manichaean. Symmachus paid him back with equally gross coin, accused the Emperor of favoring every heresy, and branded him as a persecutor of the orthodox and a despiser of the Roman See. Also a letter, probably composed by Ennodius by command of the Pope, to the Illyrian episcopate is characterized by a like intransigence toward Constantinople; the gulf was not to be bridged under this Pope.

In the West Symmachus showed a special interest in the Church of Gaul. He not only restored the old vicariate rights of Arles in their full extent, but extended its jurisdiction even to the Spanish sees. A hitherto unusual distinction of a bishop was the granting of the pallium to Caesarius of Arles. The conversion of the Arian Burgundian Prince Sigismund of Geneva to Catholicism — he appeared also at Rome as a pilgrim — the first case of a change of denomination on the part of a German king, seems however not to have been clear in its significance to the Pope, any more than a Roman reaction to the baptism of the Frankish King Clovis can be perceived.

Pope Hormisdas (514–23)

For Pope Hormisdas (514–23), previously the trusted collaborator and the successor of Symmachus, reconciliation with the East was also a duty of the first rank, but he undertook its solution with much greater caution, flexibility, and genuine readiness for peace. In this he was favored by certain factors of the inner political development in the East, such as the growing discontent of the population of the capital with the pro-Monophysite policies of the reign and the revolt of the general Vitalian in 513–15, which forced the Emperor Anastasius at least temporarily to greater indulgence. To two letters from the Emperor, which invited Hormisdas to a Synod at Heracleia, the Pope replied with the sending of a carefully briefed delegation under the leadership of Ennodius of Pavia in August 515, which explained in Constantinople the Roman minimum conditions for a restoration of peace: recognition of the Council of Chalcedon and of the pertinent writings of Pope Leo by the Emperor and the bishops of the East; condemnation of Nestorius, Eutyches, and their adherents, including Acacius; signing of a *libellus,* the *Formula Hormisdae,* and treatment of the cases of the deposed or exiled bishops before a papal tribunal. In addition, detailed instructions were given to the papal embassy for the conduct of the negotiations. But the entire enterprise ended in failure, since the Emperor, after an abatement of the inner political difficulties, was not prepared to accept the Roman demands, especially the condemnation of Acacius. The same fate befell a second attempt of the Pope in 517, who this time had given to his legates a series of letters and propaganda writings for the Patriarch, the bishops of the East, and the clergy and people of the capital. Pope and Emperor maintained their basic positions, and in a crude letter Anastasius declared that further negotiations were meaningless, since he "was unable to accept any commands" from Rome.

Only the change on the throne in 518, which placed the Byzantine religious policy in the hands of the Emperor Justin I (518–27), a pro-Chalcedonian, and of his nephew and successor, Justinian I (527–65), brought a fundamental change. Since both men at once asserted their readiness for peace and asked for the sending of an embassy or, if possible, for the personal presence of the Pope, Hormisdas gave his legates the draft for a conclusion of peace, already worked out for Anastasius, in addition to letters to Justin, the imperial nephew, the Patriarch John, and other highly placed personalities of the capital; in these the glad and certain expectation of the restoration of Church unity was emphatically expressed. Immediately after the arrival of the delegation some bishops in the Balkan Peninsula accepted the *libellus* of Hormisdas and hence confirmed the Roman optimism. Surprisingly quickly, the legates were able to furnish the Pope with a detailed report of the union consummated on 28 March 519, when the Patriarch after initial hesitations signed the *libellus* amid the acclamations of clergy and people. An enthusiasm of joy and gratitude over the ending of the thirty-five-year-old schism runs through the letters on both sides, exchanged on this occasion; the Pope stressed with praise the share of the Emperor in the arrangement of the union, but also admonished him to be active for the full restoration of unity in Antioch and Alexandria.

There is no reason to doubt the sincerity of the "Gloria in excelsis Deo" in the letters of thanks and congratulations from Pope Hormisdas to the Emperor Justin.

Resistance to the restored unity came, as was to be expected, principally from Egypt, from where the exiled Severus of Antioch tried to sabotage it, and from the Metropolitan Dorotheus of Thessalonica, whose deprivation of office the Pope was unable to effect with the Emperor. A totally unnecessary threat to the peace was presented also by the so-called Theopaschite Controversy, which proceeded from a group of Scythian monks. They demanded the solemn recognition of the formula "One of the Trinity suffered in the flesh," because by it the Council of Chalcedon was really protected against any Nestorian interpretation. Neither the papal legates at Constantinople nor Hormisdas at Rome saw the necessity of the formula, correct in itself, and rejected it as inopportune, since the statements of Leo I and of the Council of 451 did not require such an interpretive addition, which would perhaps occasion new discussions.

Despite all his involvement in the question of union, Pope Hormisdas sought to maintain close contact with the Western Church, as his correspondence with the Spanish Bishops makes clear. He informed them, among other things, of the end of the Acacian Schism, gave guidelines in regard to the discipline of the clergy, inculcated the holding of annual synods, and confirmed and defined the sphere of the Vicariate of Seville, always guided by the effort to keep awake and deepen the awareness of a living connection of the Spanish Church with Rome, even under the rule of the Visigoths. His correspondence with Avitus of Vienne and Caesarius of Arles, with the reports on the status and progress of the negotiations for union with the East, aimed to stimulate interest in the fate of the Universal Church.

Hormisdas' successor, John I (523–26), opened the series of those strikingly brief pontificates, whose holders were necessarily caught up in the struggle which the mortally threatened Ostrogothic Kingdom had to wage against the superior Byzantine power. These Popes were partly not spiritually and morally, partly not even physically equal to the burdens connected with this struggle, and so the papacy of these years had to endure an unmistakable loss of authority. The descent began in the last years of the reign of King Theodoric, who, through the turning of the Burgundian Sigismund and of the Vandal King Hilderic in 523 to the Byzantine Emperor, was thrown into a political isolation, which caused him to end his hitherto tolerant attitude toward the Catholics of Italy. In his suspicions, he had the Patrician Albinus, his minister Boethius (524), and the latter's father-in-law, Symmachus, leader of the Senate, executed, one after the other, because of alleged conspiracy with East Rome or the abetting of high treason. When he learned that the Emperor Justin was applying the laws on heresy against the Arians of the Eastern Empire and turning over their churches to the Catholics, and that many Arians embraced their faith under pressure, he demanded of the Pope a shameful mission: John I, by a personal intervention with the East Roman Emperor, was to demand the repeal of these measures. The Pope, of course, even before his departure from Ravenna, refused to ask for a return of converted Arians to their former denomination. The humiliation imposed on him could not be offset by the manifold honors bestowed on the papal guest — the Emperor accorded him the *adoratio* proper in itself only to the imperial majesty, and at the Easter liturgy in 526 had the imperial crown placed on his head by the Pope instead of, as usual, by his Patriarch; they only increased the suspicion of the King, who after the Pope's return kept him at Ravenna because of the non-implementation of his chief demand, and there he quickly died. This treatment made John I a martyr in the eyes of the Roman Catholics, while only a few generations later legend made the Arian Ostrogothic King the melancholy persecutor of Catholics and had him, like Arius, the founder of his denomination, die a ghastly death, fancifully described.

In an effort to assure a man of his confidence in the Roman See, Theodoric contrived the elevation of the deacon Felix III (526–30) as Pope, but the King's death soon after, in August 526, did not allow a collaboration of any duration. Felix III's intervention in the final phase of the controversy over grace became of importance when he supported Caesarius of Arles in the warding off of Semipelagian tendencies, a help which the Gallic bishop used effectively at the Synod of Orange.

Nevertheless, after Felix's death a majority of the clergy decided on the pro-Byzantine former Alexandrian deacon, Dioscorus, who however died after a few weeks, and so Boniface II (530–32) quickly obtained general acceptance.

After a vacancy of three months, during which the papacy again lost respect because of the quarrel over the succession, in accord with the wish of the Ostrogothic King Athalaric the priest Mercury was elected Bishop of Rome — he called himself John II (533–35), the first example of a change of name by a Pope. He let himself be won by the Emperor Justinian I for the acceptance of the Theopaschite Formula, by which the latter intended to strengthen his policy of union in regard to the Monophysites. In this connection Justinian had, it is true, praised the doctrinal authority of the Roman Bishop in high-sounding words, but it became clear here that he would on occasion stress them for his own religious and political goals, an attitude which could easily bring the papacy into serious conflict or into unworthy dependence on the Byzantine imperial office.

Pope Agapitus I (535–36) showed himself to be equal to this danger to a certain extent: like John I a few years previously, he likewise had to make the journey to the Byzantine imperial court at the command of an Ostrogothic king, Theodahad, in an effort to induce Justinian to halt the already far developed preparations of East Rome for the liberation of Italy from Gothic rule. While the Emperor, who again did not fail in external reverence for the Pope, brusquely rejected Theodahad's request, he showed himself to be surprisingly accessible in the ecclesiastical-political sphere. When, in spite of all pressure, Agapitus stubbornly refused to accept the communion of the Patriarch Anthimus, transferred from Trebizond to the see of Constantinople, friendly to the Monophysites, and a favorite of the Empress Theodora, Justinian abruptly abandoned Anthimus and put in his place the former priest Menas, who even had himself ordained by the Roman Pope. Emperor and Patriarch again professed the Formula of Hormisdas, and Justinian also confirmed the verdict of a synod which came out against Anthimus, Severus of Antioch, and their adherents, even though Pope Agapitus had died at Constantinople, following a brief illness, a few weeks after the elevation of Menas. The sudden death of this strongly principled man, also very receptive to theological scholarship, introduced the most serious crisis of the papacy in the sixth century.

After the news of his death had arrived, Silverius (536–37), a son of Hormisdas, was quickly made Pope by Theodahad. The struggle between the Byzantines and the Ostrogoths for the possession of the City of Rome and the intrigues of the deacon Vigilius, who had counted on his own election, were to be fatal to the new Pope. Even though on his advice the Romans had surrendered the city without a struggle to the Byzantine general Belisarius, the Pope was accused of high treason, deposed in a disgraceful manner, and banished to Lycia. At the command of Belisarius, who was probably following a directive of the Empress Theodora, Vigilius (537–55) was elected his successor. True, Justinian had Silverius brought back to Italy for a new investigation, but Vigilius had him relegated by Belisarius to the island of Ponza, where he died the same year, 537. Vigilius believed he was now at the secure goal of his desires. For the methods he used to achieve it he was to do penance with a humiliation such as had hitherto befallen no Pope.

In 543 the Emperor Justinian had by decree condemned the so-called Three Chapters and now he sought to end the resistance of the West to this edict precisely by having it signed by the Roman Pope, whom he curtly summoned to Constantinople for this very purpose. The tragedy during the eight years of the Pope's stay at East Rome has been told: on the one side the figure of the authoritarian *Basileus,* who in opposition to the previous order disposed tyrannically of the doctrine and faith of the Church and played a repulsively cruel game with Vigilius' spiritual misery; on the other side, the equally depressing figure of the Pope, who, weak in character, changed his opinion with the lengthy pressure from the Emperor and entered into a secret, compromising agreement with him, and who ultimately lacked the courage to give the witness to which his office obliged him. In all this he should have been able to appeal for a clear, decisive attitude to the extensive support of the western episcopate, but instead he had to accept from it a stormy protest, which culminated in his excommunication by an African episcopal synod. Spiritually and morally broken, Vigilius died at Syracuse on the return journey to Rome.

The mortgage left by him heavily burdened the pontificate of his successor, Pelagius I (556–61), selected by Justinian. True, as papal *apocrisiarius* in Byzantium, he had first called upon his master to resist the Emperor's demands and had come out against them in a work of his own, but then he had accepted the verdict of the Synod of 553 against the Three Chapters. Only painfully and with slight success could he overcome the enormous suspicion which he encountered everywhere in the West. Again and again the Pope stressed his loyalty to Chalcedon and the doctrinal writings of Pope Leo I, to his predecessors John II and Agapitus I, and even sent a solemn profession of faith to the Frankish King Childebert. He was able gradually to overcome the opposition of the Romans by means of his grand-scale concern for the poor, the renovation of churches looted during the disturbances of the war, the reorganization of the administration of the papal patrimonies, and, not least, through his exertions on behalf of recruits for the clergy.

Only his successor, John III (561–74), was able to diminish the schism in Upper Italy when in 572 he gained the Bishop of Milan. But the ecclesiastical province of Aquileia again refused any union. In his pontificate occurred the invasion of Italy by the Arian Lombards in 568, whose pitiless warfare extensively limited the activity of his immediate successors, Benedict I (575–79) and Pelagius II (579–90). The appeals for help to Constantinople remained without an echo worthy of mention, since in the East people were tied down by the Persian war. But at that time Pelagius II saw in the Frankish Kingdom a possible support for the papacy, since he designated its kings as the helpers of Rome and Italy appointed by God, a concept which would be realized a century and a half later. Under Pelagius II occurred the first conflict with the Byzantine Church over the title of "Ecumenical Patriarch," which the Pope came upon as a designation for the Bishop of Constantinople in the acts of the Synod of 587.

Pope Gregory the Great (590–604)

With the great-grandson of Felix III there succeeded to the See of Rome a man who again so unmistakably represented the papal office by the uniqueness of his religious and priestly personality that to posterity he long appeared as the ideal figure of the papacy by which its later representatives more and more had to be measured. He came of a senatorial family and had risen in the civil service to be head of the city administration of Rome; after that he lived in the Roman monastery of Sant' Andrea al Monte Celio which he had founded, until he was ordained a deacon in 579.

Gregory saw the relationship of the papacy to the Byzantine imperial office and hence also the relationship of Church and State in fundamentally the same understanding as had his predecessors. For several years, until the end of 585, he had lived as papal *apocrisiarius* at the Byzantine court, and in his view the *Basileus,* even when he was so doubtful a character as the Emperor Phocas (602–10), remained in principle the supreme head of the Christian *Imperium,* called by God, and even the Pope could treat with him only in the established forms of court etiquette. If in regard to the Lombards Gregory regarded as necessary a different attitude from that of the Emperor Maurice (582–602), this was not an indication or a result of a basically new orientation of papal policy, but an insight gained from Italy's bitter, concrete situation and based in the final analysis on pastoral considerations. Since the Exarch of Ravenna was militarily not the equal of the Lombards, their pressure on the people and Church of Italy could be relieved only by the concluding of peace with them, and this again was only assured if there was success in gaining them for the Catholic confession.

It was also principally pastoral motives which caused Gregory's important correspondence with the Merovingian rulers, without whose consent and cooperation a change in the Frankish clergy, especially in the episcopate extensively infected by simony, could not be achieved. And so he had proposed an "eternal peace" between Franks and Byzantines, because in his eyes it was the precondition for the restoration of health to religious life, especially in Italy. If Gregory also did not thus intend the Frankish alliance, de facto by these contacts with the Merovingian Kingdom he created the initial moves toward a development in the course of which the Byzantine protectorate would finally be exchanged for the German.

Gregory's rank in the history of the papacy is also not based on an especially striking defense of the Roman Primacy or on a profound theoretical justification of the primatial idea. Like his predecessor, he also protested against the title of "Ecumenical Patriarch" to John the Faster at Constantinople, because it seemed to him to place in jeopardy the preeminence of the Roman Church. But he lodged his protest in the form of an unofficial discussion and referred the Patriarch to the non-biblical character of this title, just as for himself he refused the title *universalis episcopus.* When his objection remained without effect, he did not for this reason permit matters to proceed to break with the East, but, with recourse to a phrase of Augustine, he preferred in his letters the formula *servus servorum Dei,* which was later adopted by the papal chancery.

The real greatness of Gregory is based rather on his extensive pastoral activity, which made him one of the most important shepherds of souls among the Popes. Here must be mentioned charitable activity that shrank from no toil and no sacrifice; by means of it he sought to moderate the overwhelming misery of the people of Italy. Without hesitation he used for this purpose the patrimonial possessions of the Roman Church in Italy, Sicily, Dalmatia, and Provence, which, according to one of his most beautiful expressions, were "the property of the poor," and energetically reorganized the administration that had been shattered by the confusion of the interminable wars, so that a better yield would be forthcoming. He took the officials directly into the papal service, admonished them firmly to loyalty and justice, and especially protected the small farmers from exploitation. His warm-hearted care was directed especially to the socially weak, the orphans, the ashamed poor, those suddenly fallen into distress through misfortune. This aspect of his work, apart from the grateful devotion of the people, brought to Gregory a degree of esteem in the public life of Italy which elevated him far above the highest ranking official of the country, the Exarch of Ravenna.

Gregory devoted a great deal of time and energy to the improvement of the clergy, who everywhere, especially in the Frankish Kingdom, had sunk to a low level. For them he composed in his *Regula Pastoralis* an impressive mirror for shepherds, to which he added the happy motto: *ars est artium regimen animarum.* In addition to the duty of daily self-examination, he especially inculcated in the clergy responsibility for the orthodox proclamation of the faith. Preaching was to take place during the celebration of the Eucharist and especially should explain the gospel of the day. Gregory's forty extant *Homilies on the Gospels* supply an instructive glimpse into his special manner of preaching. They renounce any rhetorical accessories and aim to touch the heart of the faithful in their intentionally simple style and to impress themselves on the memory with their many examples taken from life.

The former monk Gregory gave, even as Pope, a preferred place in his thought and works to monasticism, provided effective aid for monasteries that had fallen into distress, and sought in every way to support and renew monastic discipline. He addressed himself to monks in his most voluminous work, the *Moralia in Job* originating in talks which he later retouched. Here and in the twenty-two *Homilies on Ezekiel,* which likewise presupposed a preponderantly monastic body of readers, Gregory set down his thoughts on Christian ethics, piety, and striving for perfection, gained from an allegorical exegesis of Scripture, which he preferred. What to today's reader seems a defect, precisely allegory, the breadth of the presentation, the numerous digressions, was regarded in another age as praiseworthy excellence and gained a deep-reaching aftereffect for these works in the medieval monasteries and, especially because of their content, in the moral theology of this period. In addition to Scripture, Gregory's personal piety was nourished on that of his favorite author, Augustine, even if for the reproduction of his thought at the end of the sixth century the same linguistic possibilities of expression were no longer at his disposal. By his innermost inclination totally devoted to *contemplatio,* like his model he did not refuse himself to service for his fellowman in and outside the Church. Although Gregory was deeply affected by the idea that an aging world was moving to an end soon, this conviction did not for a moment cripple his activity, which besides he had to wring from a usually sickly body. Rather, this eschatological tension impelled him to the undertaking which sprang from his initiative and was most pregnant in consequences both for Church history and universal history, the evangelization of the Anglo-Saxons. As no Pope before him, he understood the work of the mission as the first-ranking duty of the supreme head of the Church and in this connection he was the first Pope consciously to direct his gaze beyond the frontiers of the *Imperium.* His effort to gain the Lombards to Catholicism was partly determined by the severe distress of the Church in Italy itself, but in the Anglo-Saxon enterprise the biblical mission mandate operated in its original purity.

Popes of the Seventh Century

Gregory's immediate successors could not in their mostly brief pontificates maintain the papacy at the height reached by him. More than ever before, it fell into dependence on the Byzantine imperial office and into the tangled mesh of ecclesiastical politics, which operated especially ominously in the Monothelite quarrel. Only a few of its representatives are treated in what follows.

In the history of the City of Rome, Boniface IV (608–15) left his mark, for he obtained the Pantheon from the Emperor Phocas and consecrated it as the Church of *Sancta Maria ad Martyres,* and so in this way it has been preserved to the present. The Roman Synod of 610 saw the first Bishop of London, Mellitus, among its participants. The Schism of the Three Chapters, not yet liquidated in the ecclesiastical provinces of Milan and Aquileia, evoked new discussions when the Lombard King Agilulf patronized it and the monk Columban of the monastery of Bobbio let himself be induced by him to intervene in the quarrel. In a long letter he exhorted the Pope with Irish verbosity and very audacious formulations to that watchfulness in which, despite his name, Pope Vigilius had been deficient.

The pupil of Gregory the Great, Pope Honorius I (625–38), sought to carry out his office in the spirit of his model, with whom he shared a care for a correct administration of the Roman Patrimony and zeal for the winning of the Lombards. He had a partial success in his exertions to liquidate the schism in Upper Italy, since he contrived to fill the metropolis of Grado with a bishop loyal to Rome. Honorius also showed great interest in the progress of the Anglo-Saxon mission and granted the pallium to the Metropolitans of Canterbury and York. But his stand in the Monothelite controversy had a disastrous effect. When the Patriarch Sergius I of Constantinople reported in 634 on the divisions in this matter within the Eastern Church and proposed to him, in the interest of an elimination of the quarrel, that henceforth there be no further talk of one or two energies but only of one will in Christ, Honorius to a great extent followed this proposal, without seriously examining its theological significance and without considering the opposing view of, for example, the Patriarch Sophronius of Jerusalem. In this regard he commended the avoidance of the manner of speaking of one energy and professed "one will of the Lord Jesus Christ," but, of course, he stressed that in this question he intended to follow the plain faith of the Bible and rejected whatever in new formulas could become a scandal especially for the unlearned in the Church. The historic context of these expressions — approval of a suggestion of the Patriarch of Constantinople, who had not requested a decision of faith universally binding, inadequate examination of the theological problem — lets it appear as highly doubtful that here Honorius intended to render a decision *ex cathedra* in today's meaning. The "Question of Honorius" received its real importance rather from the fact that the Sixth General Council of 680–81 believed it should and must condemn the Roman Pope as a heretic because of his expressions and that Pope Leo II (682–83) confirmed the decrees of the Council and hence its verdict on Honorius, even if he tried to soften it by the hint that the Pope, through his negligent conduct in this question, had become an abettor of heresy.

How difficult it was to get free of entanglement with the imperial religious policy was to be learned, after the unsuccessful efforts of Pope Theodore I (642–49), especially by Pope Martin I (649–53/655), who as a former *apocrisiarius* had a good knowledge of the theological dispute and of the personalities involved in the discussion. Without awaiting the imperial confirmation of his election, he had himself ordained and convoked a Synod to the Lateran for October 649, at which he had Monothelitism, its leading representatives, and their writings condemned, and had the verdict circulated to the Universal Church. The Emperor Constans II (641–68), to whom the Pope had sent the synodal acts with the request that he assent to the anathema, intended to enforce his will in Italy, and, after a first failure, had the Pope arrested by his Exarch in June 653 and brought to Constantinople. Here he was condemned to death, not because of his rejection of Monothelitism, but for alleged high treason, then reprieved with relegation to Cherson in the Crimea, where after a few months he died of physical and spiritual exhaustion in September 655. What oppressed Martin most of all was the total silence of the Roman clergy, who as early as August 654, only too submissive to the imperial will, had elected as his successor Pope Eugene I (654–57).

Only under Pope Agatho (678–81) was reconciliation between Rome and Byzantium possible, when he acceded to the request of Constantine IV Pogonatus (668–85) and, following preliminary preparations by the Lateran Synod of 680, sent a delegation to a "conference" at Constantinople, which became the Sixth General Council. At the fourth session the Pope's dogmatic letter was approved and in the concluding decree on the faith Monothelitism was definitively repudiated. However, under the last Pope of this century, Sergius I (687–701) new tensions resulted, when the Emperor Justinian II (685–95 and 705–11) summoned a Synod at Constantinople — Trullan II or Quinisext of 692 — at which, without the participation of the West, under the almost exclusive use of eastern sources of canon law, 102 canons of a predominantly disciplinary character were issued, but Latin customs such as fasting on Saturdays or priestly celibacy were sharply rejected. When Pope Sergius decisively refused the assent demanded by the Emperor to these synodal decrees, it was intended that he, like Pope Martin earlier, should be made agreeable after a forcible kidnapping to Constantinople, but the plan foundered on the resistance of the militias of Rome, Ravenna, and the Pentapolis. The aborted action revealed unmistakably the current limits of imperial power on Italian soil and definitively introduced the process of the political and ecclesiastical separation of the West from the East.

C H A P T E R   6 9

The Ecclesiastical Organization and the Clergy

Papal Vicariates

Spain

Pope Simplicius (468–83) was the first to confer special full authority on a Spanish bishop, namely, Zeno of Seville. Zeno, because of his particular merits, was to take care, in place of the Roman See and with its authority in Spain, that the decrees enacted by the Holy Fathers were not violated. Pope Felix II (483–92),

Simplicius' successor, wrote in the same vein to the same Zeno of Seville. Thirty years later Pope Hormisdas renewed the full authority of the Bishop of Seville, who was now Sallust. However, this letter apparently contains a restriction: the power of vicar is valid only for the provinces of Baetica and Lusitania, hence for southern and southwestern Spain. Likewise, in regard to content the authority which Sallust obtained from Pope Hormisdas was not so great: the privileges of the metropolitans were not to be infringed. The papal vicar was to be concerned chiefly for the observances of ecclesiastical tradition and, if necessary, summon synods. Nothing more is known of disciplinary measures of the Papal Vicar of Seville. The sole testimonies are the papal letters themselves. Hence it is perhaps advisable not to speak of "vicariates" in the general sense, but merely to regard the bishops personally charged in each case as extraordinary envoys for very specific functions. Each individual Pope appointed them for the duration of his pontificate only, in the expectation that their zeal would be enhanced by the granting of the "vicarship." From the conversion of the Visigoths under King Recared in 586, the basis for a vicariate in Spain was eliminated. The Church felt itself to be safe under the protection of the King and flatly declined the care of the far distant pope. But this was not at all the granting of a vicarship.

Arles

We know more about the Vicariate of Arles, which went back to Pope Zosimus (417–18), and was confirmed by Leo the Great, than about the papal vicariates in Spain. Leo's successor, Pope Hilary (461–68), expected from the Archbishop of Arles reports from time to time on all important ecclesiastical events and problems and scolded him if such information arrived from elsewhere. The Bishop of Arles was to hold synods and issue letters of recommendation for traveling Gallic ecclesiastics. But Arles did not thereby gain precedence in southern Gaul; there persisted the old rivalry between Arles and Vienne, which possessed in Avitus a bishop towering far above the entire Gallic episcopate. Indeed, at the end of the fifth century there was an interlude in favor of Vienne. Pope Anastasius, whose letter is lost, gave Avitus of Vienne the right to ordain bishops in some churches which had hitherto belonged to the metropolitan territory of Arles. In 500 Pope Symmachus confirmed the rights of the Bishop of Arles, because Anastasius had acted against tradition. In the next year Symmachus appeased the Metropolitan of Vienne: he was to suffer no loss if he could supply documents from which the legality of the decision of Anastasius should be made clear. Only in 513 did Pope Symmachus definitively confirm the precedence of Arles, and that even though Avitus of Vienne a decade earlier had converted Sigismund, son of the Burgundian King, to Catholic Christianity, and the latter had turned up in Rome as the first royal pilgrim from a German kingdom. Symmachus not only again took up the old tradition: Caesarius, the Archbishop of Arles, on his visit to Rome, had personally taken care to ask for new papal decrees for questions which had long ago been in reality canonically regulated. Thus the Pope granted him the right, as the first western bishop, to wear the pallium. In the next year Caesarius was expressly made Vicar for all the Gallic and Spanish provinces. As Papal Vicar, Caesarius was to exercise the function of a supermetropolitan: he alone should issue letters of safe-conduct for all ecclesiastics traveling from Gaul, just as Pope Zosimus had decided, and Pope Hilary had renewed it. Thus Arles possessed a clear position of preeminence in southern Gaul, which would probably have devolved on this see even without the papal vicariate. True, there is mention already of special care in questions of faith, but Caesarius did not at all appear in the entire Semipelagian controversy as an ecclesiastical prince conscious of special authorization. Rather, he requested instructions from Rome and obtained them from Pope Felix III; besides, he even had the decrees of his synod confirmed by Pope Boniface II. It is probably to be understood from the example of Caesarius and his relations with the various Popes that the vicariate authority had no firmly determined dimensions and hence the vicariate was not an element of the ecclesiastical structure; the vicar had merely to act *ad nutum pontificis.*

Especially deserving of being stressed is the fact that with Pope Vigilius (537–55), the predecessor of Pelagius, a new element became noticeable in the granting of the vicarship. He obtained the assent of the Emperor Justinian before he agreed in 545 to the request of Auxanius of Arles, presented in 543, and transmitted special synodal jurisdiction to him, with the exception of *causae maiores.* In the next year Vigilius even joined the conceding of the dignity of vicar to Aurelian of Arles with the commission to work for a good understanding between their Byzantine majesties, Justinian and Theodora, and the Frankish King Childebert. Hence the papal vicar at Arles was expected to contribute to the political and military encirclement of the Ostrogothic King Totila in Italy.

In the following years the relations between Rome and Arles seem not to have been especially close; in any event, Gregory the Great had to have the Metropolitan of Arles warned by another Gallic bishop to send on to Rome the revenues which his predecessor had drawn from the patrimonies of the Roman Church but had withheld.

The clearest and most comprehensive account of the papal vicariate for Arles comes from Gregory the Great in his three letters to Virgil, the bishops in Childebert's kingdom, and Childebert himself. Virgil was to represent the Pope in Childebert's entire Kingdom; without his permission no bishop could undertake a journey of some distance; he was to decide questions of faith with a Commission of Twelve of the bishops. Only when a question could not be decided should it be submitted to the Pope, whereas hitherto in principle all *causae maiores* had been reserved to the Pope. The bishops were admonished zealously to obey the invitations to synods, to be expected from Virgil. Childebert, who had supported Virgil's request for the grant of the dignity of vicar, was called upon to give him all assistance so that the abuses that were prevalent in the Church of Gaul, namely, simony and the premature ordination of laymen, could be eliminated. One would expect success for this far-reaching project of Gregory, pushed with such effort. But, despite the great authority given him, his vicar acquired no important influence. Arles lay too much on the outer fringes of the Frankish Kingdom and had been incorporated into it too late. In the course of the sixth century the Bishop of Lyon obtained greater importance in the Frankish Kingdom; he was even referred to as Patriarch by the Synod of Mâcon in 585. At the great synods of the seventh century — Paris in 614, Clichy in 627, Chalon in 650 — the Bishop of Lyon presided unchallenged. The vicariate of Arles came to an end at the moment when it should have obtained its greatest authority.

Thessalonica

After the civil dioceses of Asia, Pontus, and Thrace had been subordinated to the ecclesiastical supremacy of New Rome by canon 28 of the Council of Chalcedon in 451, Western Illyricum was left under the supremacy of the sole Patriarch who could claim it, namely, the Bishop of Rome. True, a part of Western Illyricum belonged to the eastern half of the Empire, but through the delimiting of a sphere for Constantinople, it could, from Rome's viewpoint, appear less urgent to have a man of confidence in Illyricum than at the end of the fourth century, when precisely the Western Emperor had relinquished these provinces to the Eastern Empire and an ecclesiastical orientation of these sees to the East was to be feared. Thus the papal vicariate of Thessalonica apparently fell into oblivion in Rome itself ca. 500 and was again brought to mind there only through the appeal of Bishop Stephen of Larissa, who had been deposed at Constantinople and hence had turned to Rome for help. At the Roman Synod of 531 the representatives of the Metropolitan of Larissa, two of his suffragans, submitted twenty-seven documents, all of which referred to the vicariate function of the Bishop of Thessalonica. The reference to the vicariate function, conferred repeatedly on Thessalonica, served only to emphasize the competence of the Bishop of Rome, and not of that of Constantinople, for Illyricum. In this connection people were probably aware that on the one hand the Illyrian bishops were inclined to appeal to Constantinople, that is, apparently to the Emperor, not so often to the Patriarch. and on the other hand in Constantinopolitan circles appeals to the Roman See were very badly received.

But this Roman Synod of 531 did not involve, as might have been expected, a renewal of the papal vicariate of Thessalonica. Instead, the Emperor Justinian was soon busy; in 535 he raised his native city, under the name of Justiniana Prima, to the rank of an ecclesiastical supermetropolitan and assigned to it as its sphere of jurisdiction provinces for which Thessalonica had hitherto been competent. The assent of the Pope was not obtained nor was the papal vicariate of Thessalonica at all mentioned. Law 131 of the year 545 then gave the definitive version of the Novel of 535. In it there is at least a reference to an agreement with Pope Vigilius, which however did not mean much, since the Pope probably merely had to acquiesce. To the city of Justiniana Prima was now granted the position of Rome's vicar for the provinces definitely assigned to it. In all this, then, there was no question of a papal authorization of the Bishop of Justiniana Prima but of an elevation in rank of this city by imperial decree, for which a canonical status familiar in Rome, that of a vicariate, served well. This occurred at the same time to the prejudice of Thessalonica, whose area of influence was diminished. But neither the Bishop of Justiniana Prima nor that of Thessalonica seems to have exercised the power of a vicariate by a Roman mandate in the sixth century. Only Gregory the Great in one of his letters referred to the vicariate position of the Bishop of Justiniana Prima. He scolded Bishop John, because in a legal quarrel with Bishop Adrian of Thebes *occasione vicium nostrarum* he had dared to commit a wrong. True, judicial competence had been entrusted to John by the Emperor at Constantinople, but he had had a deacon turned over to the secular power and tortured. Gregory the Great examined the acts of the trial that were submitted to him and himself handed down a decision; hence he also did not bring in the Bishop of Thessalonica. He was apparently content with the transfer of the dignity to Justiniana Prima, for he bestowed it on the successor of the Bishop John whom he had blamed, who was also named John: *Pallium ... ex more transmisimus et vices vos apostolicae sedis agere iterata innovatione decernimus.* But not much authority is here discernible. John is admonished to be a good shepherd and to guard himself especially against simoniacal ordinations. Gregory apparently did not intend to be active in the Balkans by means of the Bishop of Justiniana Prima. On another occasion he addressed the metropolitans of Illyricum without distinction of rank or dignity. It was more in accord with his policy to intervene even in the Balkans through his stewards, assigning to them duties of supervision and representation even in jurisdictional questions. Thus the subdeacon Antoninus received instructions to arrange a canonical episcopal election in Salona, that is, to prevent a simoniacal election and completely to rehabilitate the Archdeacon Honoratus of Salona.

Gregory the Great was generally inclined now also to entrust with tasks of ecclesiastical discipline the *rectores* of the Roman patrimonies, whom he himself had appointed, in order to assure to his Church the necessary revenues — the local episcopate, which was earlier responsible for the administration of the goods, was really negligent in the transmission of the produce. The very first letter of Gregory that has come down to us speaks of the subdeacon Peter, who was to administer the Roman patrimonies in Sicily and in addition obtained the authority of a vicar with allusion to earlier models. If by these are meant the vicariates of Arles and Thessalonica, it is still clear that, as the papal stewards were appointed entirely *ad nutum pontificis,* so the vicariates were only to be thus understood and did not represent structural elements in the Church. In any case, in Church history they had as little future as the many new vicariates which Gregory conceded. In North Africa, in Britain, in Ireland, there were never papal vicariates. In Africa the position of the Primate of Carthage on the one hand and the exertions for independence on the other hand were so strong that there was a situation there similar to that of Spain in the seventh century. Ireland probably lay too far on the fringe of Europe, and England was at first to be cared for from Gaul.

Parish Organization

It is true that the future parochial organization could first be discerned not only in the country but also in the city as early as the fourth century, and in the great cities such as Rome, Carthage, and Alexandria even earlier, but what is today understood by "parish," which possessed a certain autonomy even vis-à-vis the bishopric, was first found in the epoch to be surveyed here. Churches in the countryside are attested as early as the First Council of Toledo, which in 398 required in canon 5 that every cleric, if there was a church in his place of residence, should go there every day for the *sacrificium.* In this connection also the *castella, vici* (villages), and *villae* outside the cities were also mentioned as places where there were churches, and hence where the clerics should fulfill this duty. This prescription appeared, it is true, in number 63 of the collection of *capitula* of Bishop Martin of Braga in northwestern Spain ca. 585 which states that clerics should come to the church morning and evening for the sacrifice of the psalmody, *psallendi sacrificium,* whereas participation in the celebration of Mass was required of all clerics only on Sundays (ibid., 64). The Council of Tarragona in 516 insisted on the daily celebration of Vespers and Lauds in all churches, but in this matter priest and deacon might alternate weekly. Probably the First Council of Toledo did not intend to oblige every cleric to the daily celebration of the Eucharist in his church, but only imposed on clerics attendance at church as a duty of their state not attached to a locality. The synod attests that churches with regular worship were no longer anything unusual even in the countryside. But whether they were parish churches, hence whether the clergy had pastoral responsibility and authority for a definite territory is not clear. The ordinary worship might represent a free offering for the people living nearby or correspond to the desire of the founder or even occasionally have served for the veneration of relics. In any event at Epaon in Burgundy in 517 a synod forbade in canon 25 the depositing of the relics of saints in a church in which there was not at least one cleric who could see to the regular psalmody. The rural parishes were apparently, in any case in southern Gaul, erected not in just any nucleus of a settlement but in a place which represented, even in pre-Christian times, a religious center for the surrounding peasantry. Thus it becomes clear that the organization of the parish system in the country coincided with the evangelization of the country. Thus Martin of Tours, during his long episcopate, consolidated the christianization of the peasantry by the erecting of parishes. True, he himself founded only six, and his successors to the end of the fifth century founded only fourteen more parishes. Thus the see of Tours, which ca. 500 still had the extent of a modern *département,* included only about twenty parishes. Around the same time the bishop of Auxerre had the same number of churches in the country, of which eight were in vici and twelve in *villae;* a century later there were thirty-seven — thirteen in *vici* and twenty-four in *villae.* In this regard not the entire area of the bishopric was divided into these pastoral centers, but they were responsible only for a smaller territory; the care of the rest of the territory was still directly incumbent on the bishop.

While the Council of Agde in 506 still expressly forbade priests in canon 44 to give blessings or penance to the faithful in the church, Isidore of Seville at the beginning of the seventh century saw it as precisely the duty of a priest to bless the people. Hence, in the meantime a decisive change must have occurred; the credit belongs to Caesarius of Arles, who it is true held the presidency at Agde, but at the time had had only a few years' pastoral experience. Twenty years later at the Synod of Carpentras in 527 he drew the canonical consequences from his experiences as bishop and established an administration of the property of the rural churches that was to a certain degree autonomous. Previously, the bishop received half the offerings in the cathedral — the rest of the clergy received the other half — and one-third of the offerings in the rural churches; their land and other property were on the whole administered by him. But now, in accord with the wish of Caesarius, the bishop could have recourse to the rural churches only when they were wealthy and his cathedral was in special need. The Synod of Vaison in 529, likewise presided over by Caesarius, expressly gave to the priests in the country the right of preaching, which at the same time meant the duty of preaching; if no priest was present, the deacon should at least read aloud the Lord's Prayer (canon 2). For Caesarius preaching was the chief means of the care of souls. True, Pope Celestine had reproached some South Gallic bishops for turning over the entire activity of preaching to their priests, but this seems to have referred to Masses in the episcopal church. But perhaps this papal admonition contributed to the fact that into the next century priests were regarded as unqualified to preach. Thus the decision of Caesarius of Arles was really a deeply effective measure and gave the rural clergy and hence the rural churches a real importance.

Caesarius wanted to go even further and oblige the rural priests to recruit their own successors, that is, first to educate young lectors, and in this he appealed to Italian customs which he had himself come to know on the occasion of his journey to Ravenna and Rome. He surely was also thinking of the example of the school in his own episcopal residence and in those of many of his educated colleagues. Thus here was the beginning of the parish school; indeed, it even appeared as a sort of seminary for priests. Caesarius himself seems not to have established any rural parishes; they were probably present in the territory of Arles in sufficient numbers. But the admonition to the pastors to be concerned for the young clergy seems to have been successful; in any event, his Vita (II, 20) reports that Caesarius miraculously cured an only eight-year-old cleric on one of his visitation journeys. Then in the course of the sixth century there arose parish schools in various places in Gaul, not only in the form of a boarding school, as Caesarius intended, but also for externs. But naturally these were to the advantage of the future clergy.

The requirement of canon 18 of the Synod of Mérida in southern Spain in 666 went, it is true, in a similar direction, but it had a lesser impact. There the pastors were admonished, on the basis of the wealthy church property, which also included slaves, *familia ecclesiae,* to raise such church slaves in their house and to train them as lesser clerics — today they would be called altar boys — and servants. It must not be assumed that they were regarded as recruits for the priesthood. Besides, it is not known how much success the canon had, so that one cannot infer from it the existence of parish schools in all Spain. It may be assumed that around the middle of the sixth century there were rural parishes in the entire Christian West, even if the network of the parochial organization became constantly thicker in the succeeding centuries. Even in the well documented districts of the Frankish Kingdom the number of parishes was then about five times smaller than today. Furthermore, the Arian Vandal Church in Africa seems to have known rural parishes as early as ca. 500.

The question of from when on parishes were also erected on *villae* cannot be easily answered. True, the First Council of Toledo in 400 presupposed churches in *villae,* and the First Council of Orange in 441 regulated the competence of the diocesan bishop for such churches; but precisely because the proprietors built these churches it seems to follow that it was not a question of parish churches. Many churches of *villae* became such only in the course of the sixth century; in every case they were such as early as 541, when a Synod of Orléans (canons 26 and 33) demanded adequate endowment for them and at the same time their subordination to the bishop. The first builders of "proprietary churches" seem to have been bishops, who in this way intended to care for the people of a *villa* belonging to their cathedral. They also regarded themselves as justified in such care if the *villa* lay in the territory of another bishop. Great proprietors from the lay state seem then to have followed this example of the bishops. In any event, canon 9 of the First Council of Orange in 441 let it be presumed, when it required that the dedication and the entire administration of such a church was reserved to the bishop who was responsible for this territory and not to the builder-bishop, and *a fortiori* it did not pertain to a bishop invited at pleasure. If by this was meant also the administration of the property, then the wish of this synod was not universally implemented. The Seventh Council of Toledo in 646 still had to defend parish priests against the greed of the bishops in canon 4. But synods had to deal much more frequently with proprietary churches in order to insist that they and especially the clergy serving them were under the direction of the diocesan bishop or of his archdeacon respectively. Such admonitions were directed to the clergy of the proprietary church or also to the proprietors.

The parish organization spread slowly from South to North. It gradually established itself in England, for example, in the eighth century. In Thuringia, Hesse, and Bavaria, on the other hand, it seems to have existed even before the arrival of Boniface. In any event, he encountered rural priests, whom he could only regard as half-pagan, as heretical, and as immoral (letters 68 and 91), and from this it must be inferred that a certain decay had already set in.

It needs to be observed also that, parallel to the increase in the number of churches in the country, the privileges of parish churches were stressed. At Easter, Christmas, Epiphany, Ascension, Pentecost, and the Birth of John the Baptist, however, the celebration of Mass should take place only in the cities (cathedrals) and parish churches; the clerics of the oratories had to come there, unless the bishop made an exception. In the Kingdom of Burgundy again the adult townsmen were admonished to seek out some bishop in the city at Easter and Christmas in order to receive his blessing. This prescription had, of course, nothing to do with the parochial principle. Instead, this was all the more clearly expressed then in 535 at the Auvergne Synod in canon 15, in which the rule of Agde was renewed, whereby all "canonical" ecclesiastics not in the parishes were to assemble around the bishop; the adult townsmen were to do the same. Hence Mass was to be celebrated in parish churches on these feasts, but not in private oratories. Finally, canon 3 of the Council of Orléans in 541 decreed that the first citizens must not celebrate Easter outside the city; if one did so without having expressly obtained the bishop's permission, he should be refused communion on this feast. Hence the Eucharistic celebration was also presupposed in the *villae* on these great feasts.

After the middle of the sixth century such instructions disappeared. Apparently people had to come to terms with the fact that all high feasts were celebrated in the private churches; in addition, the number of parishes in the country, that is, also in the *villae,* grew considerably. Behind all of this stands, of course, the self-evident assumption that the bishop or parish priest or the priest of an oratory respectively only celebrated once daily and that there were sufficient clergy. A totally different development occurred in Visigothic Spain. Although some churches were rich in land and serfs, others possessed nothing, so that the support of an ecclesiastic was not assured and several churches had to be assigned to one priest. But then he was obliged to celebrate on all Sundays in all his churches, and hence to celebrate several times.

Noteworthy in the history of the parish is the change of name: *parrochia* originally denoted the urban congregation ruled by the bishop. Rural congregations were so named for the first time by Pope Zosimus in 417. At first such a community that depended on the bishop was called *diocesis,* by which was expressed that the rural parish was an administrative unit of the local episcopal church. At the end of the fifth century it became customary to use both expressions interchangeably. In the course of the sixth century the current distinction of name established itself with a few variations; this was true for the Merovingian Kingdom as well as for the sources available from Spain and Italy, notably Gregory's letters. Then universally from the seventh century the territory of one bishop was designated as *diocesis,* the individual congregation subordinate to him as *parrochia.* The episcopal church had, so to speak, given up its honorary name and become a unit of administration; the religious life was moved into the parishes for the majority of the faithful. The consequence of this was that the parishes no longer felt so intimately joined to one another, as was the case in the unity of the episcopal *parrochia.* The bishop lost a good part of his religious authority and tried to compensate elsewhere by relying on the feudal lords. The Synod of Braga in 572 enacted an exact program for the visitation journey in canon 1, and the Fourth Synod of Toledo in 633 again imposed the duty of annual visitation in canon 36; in the latter case the bishop, if he was ill or hindered, could be represented by a priest. Hence it must be concluded that visitation journey were probably made, but not with the necessary regularity. Equally or even more important for the union of bishop and parishes would have been the diocesan synods. The oldest whose acts are extant took place at Auxerre between 561 and 605. But all together these synods also seem not to have been very frequent, so that the estrangement between bishop and rural clergy could gain ground.

Clergy

Formation

The Gallic councils especially have much to say about the essential morals, the financial resources, and the rights of clerics, in particular the *privilegium fori,* but very little about their formation and education. Apart from Caesarius' initiative in regard to encouragement of recruits, there were occasional references at councils to the effect that lay persons who were to become priests or bishops must study ecclesiastical discipline for at least a year. In 524, in canon 2 of the Council of Arles, Caesarius stated as a reason for the ordination of laymen as bishops and priests the fast growing number of churches. Nevertheless there was surprise that it was Caesarius who brought forward this argument, although he himself seems not to have established any parish but had found sufficient churches. When the Synods of Orléans of 533 in canon 16 and Narbonne of 589 in canon 11 demanded that only one who could read and write might be ordained a deacon, this was a sign of a quite low level of education of clerics. The Diocesan Synod of Auxerre, which took place between 561 and 605, said in canon 44 that lay persons must not disregard the instruction and admonition on the part of the archpriest, that is, probably generally on the part of their pastor; but it may be asked how these clerics were in a position to provide instruction and admonition. The overwhelming majority of pastors in the sixth century must not have been equal to theological confrontations, even if they had behind them the ideal career — ten years as lector, five years as subdeacon, fifteen years as deacon, twenty years as priest. But whoever had been a lector for ten years probably satisfied Caesarius' demand (*Vita*, I, 56) that every future deacon had to have read the entire Bible four times.

In Spain also conciliar legislation had to be concerned with the education of the clergy. Thus the Second Council of Toledo in 527 required in canon 1 that young lectors be trained in the bishop's house under a master and be introduced into the ecclesiastical sciences; at the same time Caesarius of Arles demanded that this be done not only on the level of the bishopric but, probably on a more modest scope, on the level of the parish. In canon 11 of Narbonne in 589 uneducated priests and deacons were obliged to learn to read and write. Knowledge of the canons was also demanded by the bishops in Gaul. The fact that in Gaul no complaints of synods over the ignorance of the priests are found probably does not prove that the clergy were generally better educated than in Spain. For if there were episcopal schools in some twenty episcopal cities of Gaul, it was the urban clergy who took advantage of them, hardly those in the country. The Spanish episcopal schools, which were the object of conciliar legislation, were, however, not the reason why there were bishops of outstanding literary merit in Spain; rather, they had obtained their education in monastic schools. So that the individual priest would not be left to his own devices in his parish, the Council of Toledo of 633 in canon 26 demanded that the bishop give him a *sacramentarium* or *libellus officialis*. In Gaul we hear nothing of such books, except of the one which Sidonius Apollinaris, that highly educated Bishop of Clermont, had compiled at the end of the fifth century, apparently only for his own use. But the clergy, even in Spain, should not be dependent on such books but know the entire psalter, the customary hymns and canticles, and the rite of baptism by heart.

Morality

The synods were even more concerned for the morals of clerics. In 583 it was decreed at Orléans in canon 30 that clerics from deacon upward must not engage in money-lending, which apparently was not generally forbidden for a Christian but only for clerics, who were supposed to separate themselves entirely from secular businesses. Thus at the Burgundian national Council of Epaon in 517 in canon 4 and at Mâcon in 585 in canon 13 the owning of hunting dogs and falcons was forbidden to them, as was participation in the hunt at Saint-Jean de Losne in Burgundy in 673. The Synod which met near Bordeaux in 662 forbade clerics in canon 1 to bear arms or wear extraordinary dress. Canon 1 of Narbonne in 589, which was at that time under Spanish Visigothic rule, similarly forbade clerics to wear purple dress. A few years earlier, at Mâcon in 581 in canon 1, it was enjoined on clerics to avoid secular dress entirely.

Clerics, more exactly priests and deacons, must not undertake a journey without a testimonial letter from their bishop; in any event, they must nowhere be admitted to sacramental communion. From the time of Pope Zosimus the Bishop of Arles was to issue the required passports for all clerics traveling out of Gaul. According to the view of the Council of Orléans in 533 in canon 9, priests must not even live together with so-called worldlings, unless the bishop has permitted this.

Celibacy

Celibacy occupied the most space in clerical legislation. The requirement of celibacy for the higher clerics was made as early as ca. 300 at Elvira, but this Council seems to have had no influence on the further development. The demand for celibacy again appeared toward the end of the fourth century with Popes Damasus I and Siricius. Then in the fifth century Innocent I and Leo the Great referred to Siricius, and Leo extended the requirement of celibacy also to subdeacons. However, this did not mean that married men would no longer be admitted to the higher ranks of the clergy, but only that, before their ordination, they must promise not to live any longer with their wives in the conjugal state. On the part of the Popes, however, there had always been hesitations about the ordaining of a married man, especially if he had children. Thus Pope Pelagius I (556–61) only very reluctantly agreed to the candidacy of a married man for the episcopal see of Syracuse. For each case he demanded that a complete list of his private properties be supplied in order to make certain that at his death he would not bequeath to his children a part of the ecclesiastical property. Here must be recognized an important root of the legislation on celibacy, namely, concern for church property. Celibacy was the surest guarantee that ecclesiastical office-holders would have no heirs. Under Pelagius II (578–90), however, it became clear that in any case the subdeacons in Sicily for far more than a century had not carried out the requirement made by Leo the Great, and the corresponding instruction of the reigning Pope appeared to them as a novelty. Gregory the Great expressed himself very urgently on the matter and declared that married men who received the higher orders must not dismiss their wives but must live with them, from then on, in complete continence.

In Gaul people willingly accepted the new legislation from Rome. In its canon 21 the Council of Orange of 441 had already prescribed that for the future married men were to be ordained deacons only when they began an ascetic life, that is, took the vow of perfect chastity. This vow was also required of the wives of these clerics, so that, if, for example, the husband died, they for their part could not remarry. But not all married men could be ordained to the higher ranks of the clergy: one who had married a second time or had married a widow was just as much out of the question as was one who had done public penance, for this excluded one entirely from the clergy. The vow of perfect chastity, in which in Gaul was seen the most effective protection of celibacy, was required in Spain only about two centuries later, namely, by the Fourth Council of Toledo in 633. In Gaul also the Roman motivation for celibacy was adopted, especially the exegesis of 1 Corinthians 7:5, in which Paul, really to limit overzealous asceticism and to guard his Corinthians against disillusionment, had instructed them to hold themselves aloof in order to devote themselves for a time especially to prayer. But now, after celibacy seemed required, this became the instruction: if lay people must live in continence so that their prayers may be heard, all the more then the priests and levites who constantly serve in God's presence and must pray for the people. Hence it is not surprising that almost all synods of the fifth and sixth centuries in Gaul imposed the obligation to continence on the higher clerics. In this connection it is interesting that the wife of the bishop was called *episcopa* and apparently occasionally played an important role in the administration of the see, for example, by undertaking the charitable activity. A bishop who had no *episcopa* seems, according to canon 14 of the Council of Tours of 567, to have clearly been an exception. He should have himself served by clerics; these should see to it that no woman came into the house. The same Council spoke of the wife of a priest, *presbytera,* and of the *diaconissa* and the *subdiaconissa* in canon 20; apparently they all occupied a worthy rank in Church and society, but could no longer live together with their men in the married state. But the decrees on penalties for transgressions of these prescriptions were frequent, just as the synods quite often had to take care that clerics who were not married were reprimanded because of intercourse with women and issue regulations as to how the household of a priest should be managed. Only close female relatives might be in the house of a bishop or priest, such as the mother, sister, daughter, or other persons who could evoke no suspicion of any sort. For the rest, the archpriests should especially see to it that other members of the clergy should always be in their company, who could give testimony to their continence. After the conversion of the Arian Visigoths in 586 there resulted for the Spanish Catholic Church a special problem due to the conversion of certain Arian clergymen who had up to now been married and now also wanted to continue their marriage, after they had been accepted into the Catholic clergy following a special examination. But canon 5 of the Third Council of Toledo in 589 decreed that such ecclesiastics, if they insisted on their marriage, were to be degraded to the order of lector. The same Council proceeded especially severely against concubinage: the ecclesiastic should submit to canonical penalties, that is, be deposed and sent to a monastery, the woman should be sold as a slave and the price of the sale distributed among the poor (canon 5). The Fourth Council of Toledo in 633, which was entirely under the influence of Isidore of Seville, demanded in canon 27 that the priests and deacons of rural parishes take a solemn vow of chastity before their bishop; in 666 the same was required at Mérida by the bishops in canon 4. In 655, the Ninth Council of Toledo in canon 10 had to state that the many decisions of the Fathers which were supposed to serve to restrict the licentiousness of clerics had had no impact up to now, and so it had recourse to the severest means: children born to a cleric, from subdeacon to bishop, after his ordination, were not to be entitled to inherit, in fact they were forever to be slaves of the church which the clergyman served.

Nevertheless it must be admitted that toward the end of the seventh century an intellectual and moral decline in the Spanish episcopate must be deplored, which went back to the strong involvement of Church and State with each other: the bishops belonged to the electoral body for the crown, and the King named all bishops. Also in Frankish Gaul the influence of the crown on the filling of episcopal sees had grown greatly in the sixth century. The consequence was that frequently laymen were ordained and simony flourished. The fact that in Gaul too the bishops became increasingly involved in politics in the seventh century must probably be attributed to this, that from the middle of the seventh century the parish system was established and the bishops had no further dynamic function within the

Church. On the other hand, there was a reason for this in the deficient education of the episcopate. True, ca. 575 Gallic bishops were pleased to be extolled by Venantius Fortunatus because of their stylistic skill. So that an awareness of style may be assumed in a majority of the episcopate, but the complaints on the decline of education are general. Gregory the Great especially tried to obtain bishops from monastic circles, because they guaranteed a minimum in intellectual and moral formation. Still one must guard against too dark a picture. In any event, for the sixth century in southeastern Gaul east of the Rhone and south of Lyon, of 148 bishops thirty-four at least can be named who were venerated as saints. And when it is seen how decisively Gregory the Great proceeded against violation of duty, it cannot be assumed that the entire episcopate had become corrupt.

Archpriest

With the completion of the parish organization, in any event in Gaul, the title of "archpriest," which hitherto had been reserved to a cleric of the episcopal church, came into wider use. These were now the archpriests appearing in the countryside — for the sake of clarity they were called "village archpriests," *archipresbyteri vicani,* in canon 20 of the Synod of Tours in 567. They were not, as later in the Carolingian age, competent for several parishes, but at times only for their own parish, but there they were responsible not only for the care of souls but also for the behavior of all the others of the parish clergy, to which, in addition to readers, singers, in any event in Merovingian Gaul, seem to have always belonged at least a deacon and a subdeacon. In many cases it seems that, besides the archpriest, there were still other priests in the parish. Since the number of rural pastors who bore the title of "archpriest" is very large, but still smaller than the number of pastors in general, it may be assumed that only those pastors did not bear the title of archpriest in whose parish there were no other priests.

In Spain, on the other hand, there continued to be only one archpriest in each episcopal church. He, or the archdeacon, according to canon 7 of the Synod of Braga of 563, which of course applied only to Galicia, had the duty of administering the third of the ecclesiastical revenues which was destined for the purposes of worship. And canon 5 of the Synod of Mérida of 666 decreed for all Spain that a bishop could be represented at a synod by his archpriest or another worthy priest but by no means by a deacon. Thus in Spain the archpriest appears alongside the archdeacon, in fact with a certain precedence. In Merovingian Gaul, on the contrary, the one archdeacon in each bishopric was placed over the many archpriests of the parishes, for lapses of the clergy were to be reported to him or to the bishop; in regard to jurisdiction he was the vicar of the bishop and during the vacancy of the see the ultimately responsible steward. Some Gallic councils apparently wanted to exalt the esteem of the archpriests: they should be deposed only with the consent of the other priests and only for a serious lapse; they were to take care that younger clerics were always with them to testify to their fidelity to celibacy.

Two synods of the seventh century, that of Clichy of 626 in canon 21 and that of Saint-Jean de Losne in Burgundy of 673 in canon 9, forbade without qualification the giving of the office of archpriest to a layman; hence this custom had probably crept in. But in this regard it was not greed that was blamed, as might be suspected. There seems to have been another reason. The Council already mentioned, which took place at an unknown locality after 614, forbade the installing of a layman as archpriest by the bishop, unless the candidate exhibited special personal superiority and was alone in a position to defend the members of the parish. The archpriest was competent, in fact, not only for the care of souls and the supervision of the rest of the parochial clergy but also for the defense or representation respectively of the parish clergy in public. The diocesan Synod of Auxerre (between 561 and 605) decided in canon 43 that no judge must bring a cleric before his court without the consent of the bishop or of the archdeacon or at least of the competent archpriest. Apparently it became difficult to defend the parish clergy in this manner in the course of the seventh century in the framework of the decay of the Merovingian Kingdom and its organization. In any event, this may still have been possible for people who had secular esteem and secular power and who for this reason were appointed as archpriests by the bishops. Here would be a comparison with the function of monastic *advocatus* that would come into vogue later; but this providing of the archpriest from the lay state had no future.

CHAPTER 70

Liturgy, Care of Souls, Piety

Liturgy

The period between the pontificate of Leo the Great and the beginning of the eighth century brought the Roman Liturgy to full development and in many features to its definitive shape. The oldest extant collection of Mass prayers bears the name of Leo the Great; another, which reveals a later stage of development, is attributed in tradition to Pope Gelasius I (492–96), and a third, in which the liturgy appears substantially curtailed and more rigid, to Pope Gregory the Great (590–604).

The oldest of these sacramentaries must have originated through the combining of individual booklets, Mass *libelli*, which collected various Mass formulas for the same feast of the Lord or of a saint. These *libelli* themselves are probably to be explained by the fact that Roman priests who preserved them in the archives of the Lateran compiled Mass prayers recently drafted from time to time by individual Popes. The Leonine, better called simply the Veronese from its place of discovery, extends only from the months of April to December: the beginning seems to have been lost. In April are found forty-four Mass formulas for feasts of saints, grouped together with different numbers of prayers; for Christmas there are nine formularies, not all of which, it is true, are complete, but all contain a proper preface.

One gets the impression that the compiler aimed to preserve every discoverable prayer of the Roman Liturgy, but occasionally there was a wrong classification. Thus we find in this sacramentary under the date of 2 August nine formularies for the old Roman feast of Pope Stephen I, killed in 258 in the Valerian Persecution and, under the indication of place, *in cymeterio Callisti in via Appia,* hence of the burial place of the third-century Popes, but all these formularies refer to the Protomartyr Stephen, who died in Jerusalem and whose feast was celebrated on 26 December from the time he was generally venerated in the West. In this connection, however, some of the formularies make known, through mention of the birth of Christ, that they were composed for the feast of this Stephen. Such a confusion would probably not have occurred to a Roman cleric.

The oldest extant manuscript of the sacramentary that is connected with Pope Gelasius comes not from Rome but from the Frankish Kingdom and is one of the many testimonies to the zeal with which Roman liturgical property was appropriated on purely private initiative in the Frankish Kingdom in the course of the seventh century. The Gelasian Masses are distinguished by this, that before the prayer over the gifts they provide two or three prayers which apparently are not optional, for then it is said: *item alia,* and hence one can infer more than merely two scriptural readings. In Gaul and Spain three readings were usual up to the adoption of the Roman liturgy.

The Gregorian Sacramentary is preserved substantially in two forms: first, as the so-called Hadrianum, which was sent to Charles the Great in response to his request by Pope Hadrian I, but which must have been supplemented in the Frankish Kingdom, since the Sunday Masses were missing, and then the Paduense, named from the place of finding, which was likewise written in the Frankish Kingdom but reached Padua via Verona, where the Mass of Saint Zeno was added to it. In the *Sacramentarium Gregorianum* the modern reader to whom the liturgy from the period before the reform of Vatican II is familiar immediately feels at home. The Mass formularies generally contain only three prayers, occasionally another optional one; the prefaces are strictly abbreviated. Here obviously there was at work a man to whom what mattered were clarity, purity, and intelligibility. People are quite prepared to recognize here the work of the great Pope, who reorganized the Roman ecclesiastical system at the turn of the seventh century. Probably for the sake of easier use, the Mass formularies were put into a continuous series, whereas the *Gelasianum's* were put in three books, first the *Proprium de tempore,* in the second book the *Proprium de Sanctis,* in the third book the Votive Masses. While the *Gelasianum* still gives no Mass formularies for the Thursdays of Lent, such are found from the start in the *Gregorianum-Hadrianum* — they were later added in the Paduense. But in fact, according to the information in the *Liber Pontificalis,* it was Pope Gregory II (715–31), who was also the first Pope officially to direct his energies to establishing the influence of the Roman Liturgy outside Rome, namely, through Boniface in Bavaria, who ordered these Thursday Masses and had texts created for them. The *Sacramentarium Gregorianum-Hadrianum* can thus have achieved its definitive form not under Gregory I but at the earliest under Gregory II; this also follows from the presence of Gregory's feast on 12 March, before the revision of the liturgical calendars. Hence when it is claimed in the title of the book that this sacramentary was *editum* by Pope Saint Gregory, this only means that

Gregory was the liturgical authority for the eighth century, probably because his creative liturgical activity was still best remembered, though probably with some exaggeration. A first redaction of the *Gregorianum* occurred probably as early as under Honorius (625–38). Especially characteristic, on the other hand again familiar to the modern person acquainted with the preconciliar liturgy, is the indication of the Roman churches in which Mass was celebrated, hence to which the Pope went on occasion, for example, on Christmas to Santa Maria Maggiore at night, to Santa Anastasia at dawn, to St. Peter's in the day. Hence it reveals the *Gregorianum* as clearly composed for the papal Mass, whereas the *Gelasianum* does not mention the stational churches but, for example, for the three Christmas Masses gives only the times of day, and so can thereby, among other things, be recognized as a Mass book for priests. True, the *Gelasianum* goes back to the time before Gregory the Great, but it cannot have received the form in which it migrated from Rome into the Frankish kingdom before 628, when the Emperor Heraclius brought the holy cross back from Persia to Jerusalem, for we find there on 14 September the feast of the Triumph of the Cross, which commemorates the victory of Heraclius.

Some references to the form of celebration of Mass can be inferred from the sacramentaries, but they contain no liturgical rubrics. This gap is closed by the so-called *Ordines Romani*, which give, among other things, the external course of the Papal Mass (*Ordo I*), of the preparation for baptism (*Ordo XI*), the celebration of Holy Week (*Ordo XXVII*), the ordination of clerics from acolyte to bishop (*Ordo XXIV*)

In *Ordo I* the solemn papal stational Mass is described, in which the entire celebration begins with the assembling of the Roman urban clergy at the Lateran Palace. It is stated from which of the seven regions of the city the clergy had to carry out the service in the papal Mass on the individual days of the week. In what order the clergy go to the stational church is also described; it is even decided in what manner someone coming down the road may present a petition to the Pope, the *Apostolicus*. On Easter Sunday, when the Pope goes to Santa Maria Maggiore, there comes to meet him on the Via Merulana the notary of this region to make known to him the number of children baptized on the vigil at Santa Maria Maggiore. The Pope rides to the stational church, and some other high dignitaries accompany him likewise on horseback, while the majority of the clergy precede on foot. Naturally, with so numerous an entourage, the entry of the Pope into the stational church was a very solemn procession, and it is not surprising that during it the *schola* executed a chant, the *introitus*. The Pope was preceded by a subdeacon with the censer and seven acolytes with candlesticks. The *Ordo* prescribed exactly how at which parts of the Mass the candlesticks were to be placed in the altar area. After the *introitus* the *schola* sang the *Kyrie eleison:* then the Pope, standing at his chair that had been specially brought along (*Ordo I*, 23) turned to the people and intoned the *Gloria*, but then immediately turned back to the East or the apse respectively. For the *Pax vobis* he again faced the people, but once more turned to the East to say *Oremus* and the prayer. This rubric seems to presuppose the, for the most part, de facto not real orientation of all Roman churches, hence it can probably be recognized as a Frankish interpretation. In regard to the direction in which the Pope prays there is also the important instruction (*Ordo I*, 87) that before the beginning of the preface the regionary subdeacons should station themselves opposite the

Pope on the other side of the altar — *retro altare aspicientes ad pontificem* — so that they can give the responses to the *Dominus vobiscum, Sursum corda,* and *Gratias agamus.* Hence it must not be excluded, though it is also not self-evident, that the celebrating Pope faced the people on the other side of the altar.

Contact with the crowd of the faithful, at least with those of senatorial rank, was had by the celebrating Pope at the preparation of the gifts and the communion. Following the *Dominus vobiscum* and *Oremus* after the gospel — they apparently had long served no purpose (*Ordo* I, 63, 69) the Pope, assisted on his right and his left by the first notary and the first *defensor,* went from his seat down to the nave in order to receive the gifts of the nobles (*principes*). He handed them to the regionary subdeacon and by the hands of the next subdeacon they arrived at the altar. At the same time that the Pope was receiving the gifts of bread, the archdeacon accepted the gifts of wine in little vessels and poured them into a larger chalice, which was then again poured into a larger vessel (ibid. 70). The gifts of bread and wine of the rest of the people were accepted by the bishop who performed the weekly service or the next deacon respectively (nos. 72 and 73). It is expressly stressed that the Pope also went to the women's side to accept their gifts. It is interesting that apparently all clerics taking part in the Mass brought gifts to the altar; even the Pope had his personal gifts of bread given to him by the archdeacon (nos. 74, 82, 83).

During the actual celebration of the Eucharist a paten and only one chalice with handles stood on the altar. Naturally the chalice did not suffice for the communion of the entire clergy and people. Furthermore, the Pope communicated, apparently for the sake of solemnity but hardly in accord with the meaning of the Eucharistic celebration, not at the altar but at the seat. While a deacon brought the apparently very large paten to the Pope seated on his cathedra, it should be noted that a piece of the Eucharistic bread remained on the altar so that during the celebration of Mass "the altar may not be without the sacrifice" (no. 105). After the communion of the Pope a small amount of wine from the consecrated chalice was poured into the large vessel containing unconsecrated wine, which the acolytes were holding. Then all clerics present communicated at the altar, during which the highest in rank of the celebrating bishops received the chalice from the hand of the archdeacon (no. 110). The consecrated wine still remaining after the communion of the clerics was likewise poured into the large vessel already mentioned. Then the Pope himself went down to the nave to give the consecrated bread to the faithful of senatorial rank. The archdeacon gave them the Precious Blood (no. 113), but apparently not from the chalice, which was in the meantime again put away (no. 112), but from the other vessel, which was filled from the large pitcher (nos. 111, 115). The wine which the faithful received in communion was therefore consecrated by contact with the Precious Blood poured into it. This seems to have been a peculiar Roman usage. In Gaul from the start there were apparently two or three chalices on the altar in order to have sufficient consecrated wine at the disposal of the laity. But later Pope Gregory II found fault with this custom in his fourteenth letter to Boniface: Christ took one chalice and said, "This cup . . . " and so forth; hence it is not fitting to have two or three chalices on the altar.

For the distribution of communion also the Pope went to the women's side (*Ordo* I, 118) and returned to his seat for the final prayer. The external course of the celebration of Mass is strongly characterized by the two ceremonies of the kiss of peace, which was passed from clergy to people (no. 96), and the breaking of the Eucharistic bread, in which all priests present took part (no. 102). In order that no particles might be lost, the consecrated breads were first put into small bags (no. 101). The ceremony of the breaking of the bread was accompanied by the singing of the *Agnus Dei,* which according to *Ordo* 1, 105, was sung by the *schola,* but according to *Ordo* XV, 53, by all. During this chant, the Pope dictated to a secretary the names of those who should be invited for this day to the noon meal with him or with his *vicedominus.* Then two clerics went down immediately to the nave and gave the invitation. Equally surprising is it to the modern reader that the archdeacon, with the Eucharistic chalice in his hand, announced where the next stational liturgy would take place (no. 108). The reason was perhaps that many left during the communion, so that this announcement could not be delayed until the end of Mass. It is also interesting that neither *Ordo* I nor *Ordo* XV attests a blessing at the end of Mass. Perhaps the deacon proclaimed *Ite, missa est,* but the Pope's last word was the concluding prayer, before which, furthermore, he did not direct the introductory *Dominus vobiscum* to the people, but said it toward the East or the apse respectively (no. 123). Of course, during the recessional the Pope blessed in order the bishops, priests, monks, *schola,* standard-bearers, candle-bearers, and sacristans (I, 126; similarly, *Ordo* XV, 65).

The description of the celebration of Mass in *Ordo* XV, it is true, lets the personnel appear less; but it is doubtful whether it is therefore to be regarded as older. It may for this reason deal with different degrees of solemnity. Both descriptions of Mass may probably belong to the seventh century, but then to its last years, for it was Pope Sergius I (687–701) who introduced the *Agnus Dei,* attested in both, into the Roman Liturgy. *Ordo* I especially shows a type of Mass so richly developed and at the same time so specific even in details and distributed among the different ranks of the clergy that probably Byzantine influence could rightly be responsible for it. More exactly, one may think of the pontificate of Pope Vitalian (657–72), who disregarded the dogmatic tensions of the Monothelite controversy and thought of a compromise with Byzantium. The fact that the papal singers were later called *Vitaliani* lets one conclude that Vitalian entrusted the new chants to the Lateran school, one of the two *scholae cantorum* founded by Gregory the Great, while that at St. Peter's continued to cultivate the traditional Roman urban chants.

Thus there developed in the second half of the seventh century the new typically papal rite and chant, which differed from the old Roman considerably, but was only codified and recommended for dissemination in the West by Pope Gregory II (715–31).

But allusions to the changes of rite, which had taken place as early as the sixth century, can also be obtained from the sacramentaries. Thus the Mass formularies of the *Gelasianum* contain, after the prayer designated as *post communionem,* very frequently another prayer which is entitled *ad populum.* Also the formularies of the *Leonianum* regularly provide after the preface two prayers, the latter of which asks God's protection for the Christian people, believers, the household of God, and the like. Hence it seems that into the sixth century no blessing was spoken at the conclusion of Mass in Rome, but the prayer over the people. The *Gregorianum* contains in both its Hadrianic and its Paduan versions a prayer over the people only for the weekdays of Lent, as this was preserved up to our own day. Apparently in the course of the seventh century the episcopal blessing took the place of the prayer over the people as the conclusion of Mass at Rome. Since this form probably represented a certain solemnity, it seems not to have been employed for the Lenten weekdays. That in the sixth century no other type of final blessing besides the prayer over the people was known appears from the report of the arrest of Pope Vigilius by the Byzantine police. He was dragged away from Mass; the people followed him and demanded to receive the prayer from him. After he had given the prayer, the people responded *Amen,* and the ship sailed off with the Pope. Later a series of fifty-two blessings for various occasions was added to the *Gregorianum–Hadrianum* in the Frankish kingdom. The difference which existed between the *benedictio* and the *oratio super populum* was not only that the *oratio* was very much more concise than the *benedictio,* but especially that the *oratio* addressed God, whereas the *benedictio* addressed the people and mentioned God in the third person. The blessings were especially popular in the Gallican and Spanish liturgies, but there they had their place before the communion. This blessing was especially favored by Caesarius of Arles; canon 44 of the Synod of Agde in 506 expressly reserved this blessing to the bishop. Furthermore, it was enacted in canon 47 that no one must leave Mass without having received the bishop's blessing. It was probably endured as inevitable that then many left the church and only those who were to communicate remained. The fact that at Rome the place of the next stational liturgy was announced before the distribution of communion seems to indicate that there too similar habits prevailed. The episcopal *benedictio* offered pastors the opportunity to enter again into the mystery of the feast and give the faithful a reminder for the journey. At the same time one could display all one's rhetorical gifts. In any event, this blessing seems to have been extraordinarily popular in Gaul and Spain with episcopate and people: all together 2,093 different formulas of benediction have come down to us, and this, even though Pope Zachary in 751 in his letter to Boniface cited against such a peculiar Gallic custom very serious but probably not appropriate exegetical arguments and compared the Gauls, desirous of glory, with people who preach another gospel. The *benedictio* was without doubt one of the elements of the Gallic or Visigothic-Spanish liturgies respectively which proved them to be more strongly pastorally oriented and popular than the Roman Liturgy.

The liturgical dress customary in Rome during this time was quite different from contemporary custom. *Ordo Romanus* I expressly testifies that at the end of the seventh century a distinction was made between the liturgical and the ordinary dress. In connection with *Ordo* 34, 10, it is known that with the exception of the deacon, who was clothed in the dalmatic, all clerics from acolyte to the bishop, hence also the subdeacon and the priest, wore the *planeta* during the liturgy, but it was probably not like the Mass vestments of modern times, but must have been very long and wide, probably also of flimsy material, so that the acolytes could hold the sacred vessels or the gospel book with hands veiled in the *planeta.*

The liturgy in use in Gaul and Spain not only differed from the Roman as regards the already mentioned episcopal *benedictio* before communion, in which, of course, one should speak rather of a divergence of the Roman liturgy from a probably extensively universal basic type. The three prayers at the beginning of the Mass in the *Leonianum* and in the *Gelasianum* seem to point to three readings at

Rome also. Of course, it must be taken into account that a wider reading attested in Rome, as also the first prayer, did not belong to the stational liturgy but were spoken in the church of the *collecta,* from which people marched to the stational church. The churches of Gaul and Spain in any case preferred three readings; regularly one from the Old Testament, one from the epistles, and one from the gospel. In this connection, on feasts of saints the Old Testament reading could be replaced by the *passio* or *vita* of the saint or at least by its last part, which had not been read in the solemn morning Office.

Canon 1 of the Council of Valencia in 549 decreed that the gospel should be read before the *inlatio munerum* and the *missa catechuminum* so that catechumens as well as the penitents could be edified by gospel and sermon, and others perhaps be even converted by them, as had occasionally happened.

In fact, Pope Vigilius at the beginning of his pontificate had in 538, at the request of the Bishop of Braga, sent him a baptismal ritual and an *ordo precum* and had indicated that the latter always remained the same in the celebration of Mass, that only on Easter, Ascension, Pentecost, Epiphany, and feasts of saints were *capitula* especially appropriate to these days inserted. From this it may probably be deduced that on the one hand at Rome in the days of Vigilius there were still no liturgical books in which the celebrations of one year or even only of a part of the Church year were collected, and on the other hand an official control of the variable prayers was not regarded as necessary. In fact, in contrast to the African Church, which very early knew prescriptions relating to the liturgical prayers, the Roman Church did not make the first efforts in this direction until the eighth century. Until then limits were hardly placed on the creative liturgical activity of the Popes. Thus, the oldest Roman collection of prayers, hence the so-called *Sacramentarium Leonianum,* contains several Mass formularies which Pope Vigilius probably composed. It is fitting to stress that at the Synod of Braga the texts that had come from Rome appeared as adequate models, hence that there was no wish to set limits to the free creative activity of the bishops for the variable prayers, whose volume in the Spanish Liturgy to a great extent surpassed the variable prayers of the Roman Mass.

If it is also questionable to speak of a Gallic Liturgy, because in Gaul there was absolutely no uniformity, still some common characteristic features can be emphasized. To be sure, we first have adequate sources only for the seventh century, for the letters of pseudo-Germanus, in which is found a description of the liturgy, are really an "edifying commentary on the liturgical decrees of an unknown Frankish council of the end of the seventh century." All the extant Gallic sacramentaries, for example, the *Gallicanum Vetus,* the *Missale Goticum,* and so forth, are already romanized. It has been pointed out that the Gallic, and likewise the Spanish, Liturgy shows a greater common character with the oriental than with the Roman. But it must be noted that in the variability of the Mass prayers Roman and Gallic Liturgies are in agreement against the oriental.

The Gallic pontifical Mass probably did not know a solemn entry of the bishop to the accompaniment of song before the seventh century; the bishop seems rather to have come in without any special ceremony so that the deacon first had to urge the faithful to silence in order that then the bishop could greet them. Then the *Trisagion* was sung in Greek and Latin; but it was probably adopted from the

East only in the seventh century, and then the older *Kyrie*-litany standing at this place, which for its part had been introduced by canon 3 of the Synod of Vaison of 529 not only for Mass but also for Lauds and Vespers, was reduced to a mere appendage. The *Benedictus* occupied the place which the *Gloria* had maintained at Rome since Pope Symmachus. Then the celebrant said the first prayer, the *collecta.* After the readings from the Old Testament and the apostolic epistles, the Canticle of the Three Children, called the *Benedictio,* was executed as the intermediate song. The gospel was read from the ambo, to which there was a solemn procession. After this, some of the faithful left the church, as Caesarius complained (*Sermo* 73, 2) and tried to correct, among other things by having the church doors closed. After the sermon the deacon recited a litany, which was concluded with the collect of the celebrant. The dismissal of the catechumens and of the penitents was followed by the Prayer of the Faithful, but probably, as at Rome, this had been severely reduced under the influence of the Gelasian Kyrie-litany. During the bringing of the gifts to the altar the so-called *Laudes,* that is, a triple *alleluia,* was sung. To this was added the mention of the names of the dead, for whom prayers were to be offered, and this was continued in a special prayer *post nomina.* Next the kiss of peace was given, introduced by a suitable prayer *ad pacem.* At Rome in the early fifth century the kiss of peace had found its position at the place in the Mass familiar to us today. Also at Rome there was occasional criticism that in Gaul the names of those for whom there were to be prayers were mentioned before the Canon. The preface, called *contestatio* in the Gallic Liturgy, was often a long description of the miracles of a saint. The further course of the Mass, namely, Canon, breaking of the bread, Lord's Prayer, was, except for the episcopal blessing before communion, very much like the Roman. But it should still be emphasized that in Gaul Psalm 34 was sung at communion, apparently because of verse 9: *Gustate et videte, quoniam suavis est Dominus.*

The Spanish Visigothic Mass, in any case, from the time of Julian of Toledo, knew a penitential act of the priest at the beginning. Isidore of Seville enumerates seven variable prayers, which were to be attached to the Mass of the Faithful. The first is a prayer of admonition to the people; the second, an appeal to God that he would accept the gifts and hence corresponds *to* the Roman Prayer over the Gifts, the former *Secreta.* The third prayer is the *Oratio post nomina,* hence an intercession for the deceased just named. The fourth prayer is related to the kiss of peace, that is, it asks that what is expressed by the external sign may be effective in the faithful. The fifth variable prayer, the *inlatio,* corresponds to the Preface. After the *Sanctus* there is also a variable prayer, which leads on to the consecration. The *Liber ordinum* gives as the seventh variable prayer one after the account of the Last Supper (*post pridie*) whereas Isidore gives it as the transition to the Lord's Prayer. Apparently, Isidore wanted to extol the sacred number of seven, and so the *benedictio* and the *conpleturia,* which are attested by the *Liber ordinum* and other liturgical documents, are left unmentioned.

Especially in comparison with the full mention of the names of the deceased and the prayers *post nomina* of the Gallic and Spanish Liturgies, it is surprising that no commemoration of the dead is found in the Canon in the *Gregorianum–Hadrianum.* However, this may be explained in this way, that at Rome on Sundays and solemnities, differing from Gaul, the deceased were not expressly named, and the model sent to Aachen contains only the solemn form of the papal Mass. Furthermore, the *memento mortuorum* seems, together with the *Nobis quoque peccatoribus*, to have been inserted into the Canon by Pope Gelasius when the *Oratio fidelium* was abolished and at least in part supplanted by the *Kyrie*-litany. If it is thought that the intercessions for the living and the dead must have been a special concern of the faithful, then, at Rome in any event, solemnity defeated popular appeal in the liturgy. Moreover, the papal rite and chant, newly introduced in the seventh century under Byzantine influence, made of the participants at Mass mere viewers and listeners. Both the Gallic and the Spanish Liturgies were, from the pastoral viewpoint, superior to the Roman Liturgy, but only so long as the people understood the liturgical language.

To the normal liturgical life belongs not only the celebration of the Eucharist but also the Liturgy of the Hours. Early Christianity took care, as Tertullian testifies, to sanctify the important hours of the day by prayer. Then this became the special duty of monks. But also in the episcopal churches these hour-prayers of the *Officium divinum* are found in the sixth century, probably through adoption from the monastic life. Surest is the testimony for Arles, where Caesarius, who during his long episcopate retained his monastic ascetical life, had the entire Office, namely, Lauds, Terce, Sext, None, Vespers, and, before the great feasts, Vigils celebrated by his clergy, but with the participation of the people, because these hours represented for him an important means of pastoral care, especially since he frequently preached at morning or evening prayer. In the sharing in these hours of prayer, which he presented as obligatory at least for Lent (*Sermo* 196, 2), he saw an essential manifestation of devotion. But there must also have been psalmody, that is, the hour-prayers, in the rural churches and chapels, at least a morning and an evening prayer: however, the more exact scope is unknown to us. In Spain, Isidore of Seville first attests the Little Hours as a duty of the diocesan clergy, but nothing is observed in regard to an obligation of participation by the people. Besides, Isidore, who was basically as monastic-minded as Caesarius, seems not to have succeeded in introducing the Little Hours as a fixed element of the cathedral office. Still, in the meantime the development had gone so far that Isidore attests Compline as a special hour-prayer after Vespers.

While in most areas of Christianity a distinction must be made for the seventh century between the monastic liturgy and the liturgy of the diocesan clergy, this was not the case at Rome, because there were monasteries at the great basilicas. In fact the monks who were on duty at Rome before Benedict had "so thoroughly replaced the cathedral prayer by their own arrangement that the modern Roman Office has an expressly monastic character." In the seventh century all the hours of prayer later customary took place, as can be learned from *Ordo Romanus* XII. It is expressly indicated that on Holy Saturday only the nocturns and *Matutinae Laudes* were prayed. Especially impressive in Rome must have been the customary double vigil celebration before great feasts. On the eve was held a vigil without *invitatorium* and without participation of the people, which included between five and nine readings and from six to nine psalms. Then around midnight began the second vigil, which was introduced by the *invitatorium* and took place with the participation of the people, and then to it were attached the *Matutinae Laudes*.

The order of readings for the Liturgy of the Hours began at Rome in the spring, seven days before the beginning of Lent, with Genesis, which was followed by the other books of Moses and then Joshua and Judges (*Ordo Romanus* XIV, 27). For the Franks, however, the liturgical year began with Advent, so that *Ordo* XVI, which witnesses to the adoption of the Roman order of readings in Frankish monasteries, begins with Isaiah, which was also read in Advent at Rome, but the books of Moses were allowed to remain in Lent. Thus it may be assumed that, from the time people thought at all about the question of the beginning of the liturgical year, the spring date was the oldest. True, both the *Gelasianum* and the *Gregorianum* begin the cycle of the year with Christmas, but the Advent Masses still stand at the end of the series in the Sankt Gallen Late *Gelasianum,* which on the one hand was under strong Frankish influence, and on the other followed the arrangement of the *Gregorianum.*

In Spain, on the contrary, it had become usual in the seventh century to have the liturgical year begin even with 17 November, hence with the start of the long period of preparation for Christmas. But the originally Gallic usage of beginning with a shorter Advent definitively established itself. While at Rome, besides the books of the Bible, also the treatises of Jerome, Ambrose, and the other Fathers were read at the nocturns; in Gaul also the accounts of the sufferings of the martyrs and the biographies of the Fathers acquired a place in them and were not displaced even at the adoption of the Roman order of readings.

The hymns, without which the Church's Liturgy of the Hours is hardly possible, had in the countries of Western Christendom a very different fate, which can easiest be illustrated in the office of Good Friday. While at Rome very early the *Missa praesanctificatorum* (of the bread and wine), coming from the East, was adopted for Good Friday, Isidore of Seville, who calls Palm Sunday also *Capitilavium,* because on it the heads of the children *qui unguendi sunt* were washed, and who reports expressly about the liturgical celebration of the *Cena Domini,* knows no Good Friday liturgy. It was first introduced by canon 7 of the Fourth Council of Toledo in 633. The fact that the hymn *Crux fidelis,* composed by Venantius Fortunatus, was sung in the Good Friday office was only possible after the decree of the First Council of Braga in 563, whose canon 12 had excluded all nonbiblical hymns from the liturgy, apparently out of concern that they might not be orthodox, had lost its meaning. Still, the Fourth Council of Toledo, just mentioned, saw itself required expressly to defend the newly composed hymns and to threaten their rejection with excommunication (canon 13). There would also be other "prayers" and "imposition of hands" composed for the liturgy. As a matter of fact, the Spanish Church in the seventh century produced some fifty hymns.

Care of Souls

Preaching

If occasionally a powerful means of pastoral care was seen in the publication of conciliar decrees or in the reading of the accounts of martyrs, sufferings, after which, for example, Braulio of Zaragoza permitted the omission of preaching, nevertheless the sermon was still the chief instrument of which pastors, especially of the sixth century, disposed. It was consistently composed of instruction for adults; we nowhere hear of a special catechesis for children.

If one bears in mind that at the end of the sixth century there were still many pagans in Spain and especially in Gaul in the rural areas, then one is surprised that absolutely no testimonies in regard to missionary initiatives are to be found. At most it was expected that pagans should come to Mass and be converted by hearing the Gospel and sermon. Gregory the Great, who inaugurated the Anglo-Saxon mission and gave his missionaries very useful instructions and also wanted to have the pagan or heretical Germans in Italy converted by preaching and admonition, recommended for the gaining of the pagan remnant still in Sicily only administrative measures, as it were: pagans who worked and lived on ecclesiastical property (*rustici*) should, if necessary, be compelled to convert by raising their rents.

When Caesarius of Arles declared that the word of God and hence its interpretation in the sermon was no less than the body of Christ, that is, the reception of communion (*Sermo* 78, 2), he then attested to the usual high estimation of preaching which was general in Gaul of the sixth century. In Rome too it was known that there were then capable preachers in Gaul. The *Statuta Ecclesiae antiquae* (no. 31) threatened with excommunication those of the faithful who went out during the bishop's sermon. Caesarius not only urged them to remain, he personally thwarted those who wanted to leave Mass early by even having the church doors closed and not opened again until after the blessing. But it would be false to conclude from these references that people had no interest in preaching; in sixth-century Gaul it was still quite usual that the faithful reacted to the sermon with applause or rejection; occasionally there was loud muttering, especially against purposeful moral exhortation. Caesarius demanded of his colleagues and of himself that they preach on all Sundays and solemnities; and in Lent he even did so daily (*Sermo* 230, 6), often even in the morning and evening, namely, at Lauds and Vespers. According to Avitus of Vienne also, preaching should be frequent. The normal sermon lasted, in any case with Caesarius, not more than a half-hour. In most cases the sermons must have been very simple, because the preachers had an all too meager education, but also because it was desired to make oneself understood by all the hearers. Of Caesarius it is known that he quite consciously preached on different levels, in each case depending on the state of education of his audience. Caesarius was probably not the first who put his sermons at the disposal of others; but he was the first who planned his own collections of sermons and dispatched them even to Spain.

The bishops preached not only in their cathedrals but also especially on the occasion of the visitation of parish churches. Thus the work on the improvement of the peasants of Archbishop Martin of Braga in northwestern Spain is nothing more than a model sermon for which he had been asked by his colleague, Polemius of Astorga, and which was to be given chiefly on the occasion of the visitation, regarded as annually necessary. There is also a visitation of Caesarius extant: *sermo in parrochiis necessarius.* Of course, such a sermon could hardly take into consideration the parts of the liturgical year; but it can be gathered from many sermons of Caesarius and Avitus that the Gallic pastors of the sixth century found abundant points of contact in the feasts of the Church's year and the biblical readings proper to them. The chief end of the sermon seems to have been to guide the thoughts of the hearers to eternity. But in this regard what mattered especially to Gregory the Great was to comfort the faithful so that they would not perish in the misery of this life (*Moralia* I, XIV, 27); Gregory lived in difficult times, which also marked his liturgical production. Caesarius, on the other hand, ascertained a rather careless attitude in his people and held before their eyes the picture of Christ the Judge. Indeed, he could even claim that the words of Christ on the Last Judgment would be completely sufficient of themselves alone; it was not necessary to have more of Holy Scripture (*Sermo* 158, 1).

In the decisive struggle against superstition and magic, especially for the sake of cures, as they had been preserved from pagan times, Caesarius and Martin of Braga were in agreement. The pastors of the whole Christian world must have seen themselves facing this task at the time. Caesarius of Arles, furthermore, saw himself forced especially to warn against drunkenness; for Martin of Braga, on the contrary, pride and vanity seem to have been the special dangers to the Christian life. Caesarius stressed that it is more important to have Christ before one's eyes as model than to ponder individual commandments (*Sermo* 35, 2). The name of Christian does not do it alone; even the sign of the cross does not help alone: necessary are alms, love, justice, and chastity (*Sermo* 13). On the other hand, Caesarius emphasized also the necessity of a minimal knowledge of the faith; at least one must master the Creed and the Lord's Prayer (*Sermo* 135, 1). But to an active Christian life also belong the gifts made at the altar (wax, oil, bread, wine) and attendance at Sunday Mass (*Sermo* 13). Later, canon 4 of the Second Council of Mâcon in 585 required that all men and women bring wine and bread to the altar every Sunday, because one may thus expect to be freed from sins and made a sharer in the communion of saints. Finally, the demand for Sunday rest was inculcated not only in sermons but also in synodal decisions.

The Sunday rest, was, of course, not demanded for its own sake. On the one hand, it was, so to speak, defined interiorly: good works, even long journeys to visit a friend, were permitted. Indeed, the earliest extant synodal decision on the question was directed first against "Jewish" exaggeration, which allowed no sort of journey, preparation of foods, cleansing, and so forth. Only the agricultural work should remain undone. In other respects, the Sunday rest was not only an element of religious culture, but a Christian profession, especially where it replaced the hitherto usual rest from work on Thursday, hence on Jupiter's day.

From the moral instruction which Caesarius provided for his hearers two points must be singled out, because they throw a piercing light on the situation in southern Gaul of the early sixth century. In spite of all the exertions of the pastors, the number of young men who early entered into concubinage and only later into lawful marriage was so large that it was not possible to excommunicate all of them (*Sermo* 43, 4.5). Naturally this evil custom prevailed only in the upper class. The second point lies in his opposition to both contraception and abortion by the involved.

Baptism

To the extent that, in the course of the sixth century, baptism was administered in ever greater numbers to children and no longer to adults, it took place more and more in the parishes and not only in the episcopal churches. However, there are accounts of the administration of baptism, for sixth-century Gaul, only in Caesarius. At most there are references that not only infants but also one-year-old to two-year-old children were baptized. True, an effort was made to keep the Easter Vigil as the sole date for baptism, but canon 3 of the Council of Mâcon in 585 had to complain that occasionally at most two or three children could be found for this date. Most children were baptized at Christmas or on the feast of Saint John or on that of another saint; even Clovis, the first Frankish King to be converted, had been baptized on Christmas, as appears from the letter of Avitus to the King. Caesarius adapted himself to the new situation not only by accommodating the old catechumenate, which had its most intensive phase in Lent, to the conditions of the baptism of children, but also by anticipating in brief form for each baptism the preparations formerly properly made in Lent. Even infants were registered among the *competentes* and received the imposition of hands and the anointing on the forehead. If at Rome the *scrutinia* were customary as examinations of the faith and life of the *competentes* and if in Africa exorcisms were seen in the *scrutinia,* the custom of Gaul, namely, that of exorcisms by breathing, was nearer to the African than to the Roman. The giving of salt to the *competentes* was a typically Roman usage and had no parallel in Gaul. In the framework of the longer, pre-Easter preparation for baptism, a particular role was played by special instruction, which was addressed chiefly to the godparents. They bound themselves to teach the child later the minimum profession of faith, that is, the Creed and the Lord's Prayer, and to assure his or her introduction into virtue. For baptism in the course of the year Caesarius required at least a week of preparation, during which the child received anointing and imposition of hands, and the parents were supposed to fast and at least take part in the morning Mass. Of course, he did not refuse baptism if the parents appeared in church with the child only for the baptism itself. An anointing administered immediately before baptism was not known in Gaul, but probably after baptism first the anointing with oil, then with chrism, and finally the *consignatio,* that is, the sealing with the sign of the cross. Very probably after the renunciation of the Devil the entire profession of faith was asked of the candidate or the godparents, perhaps in the way in which it was already attested in the *Church Order* of Hippolytus. As the final ceremony there took place in Gaul the washing of the feet of the neophytes. A further symbol of faith in the Trinity may have been seen in the three steps which led down to the baptismal font.

Baptistries in Gaul were occasionally flanked by a bath house, which served for cleansing before the baptism. Occasionally too there was another area furnished with an apse, in which confirmation was administered by the bishop. In Spain Ildefonse of Toledo, hence in the seventh century, like Martin of Braga in the sixth, still reckoned with adult applicants for baptism, to whom he gave the Creed on Palm Sunday and from whom he inquired about it on Holy Thursday. In this connection the adult applicants were probably not only Jews baptized under compulsion; however, the pastoral practice of the Spanish Church in the seventh century was powerfully overshadowed by the compulsory conversion of Jews. Canon 57 of the Fourth Council of Toledo in 633, it is true, tried to assure freedom of religion, but it did not allow the reversion to Judaism of those converted by force. Besides, canon 3 of the Sixth Council of Toledo in 638 brought back the old harsh language.

Penance

While in most parts of the Western Church the bishops reserved to themselves the administration of penance and the imparting of reconciliation, at Rome this, like baptism, was the affair of priests. For the *Sacramentarium Gelasianum,* intended for use by priests, contains rubrics and prayers for the treatment of the penitents on Ash Wednesday (I, XVI, no. 83) and their reception back into the community on Holy Thursday (I, XXXVIII, nos. 352f), whereas the *Gregorianum,* destined for papal use, contains a reference to the penitents neither on Ash Wednesday nor on Holy Thursday. The only prayer for penitents which is given (no. 989) is a later addition. Furthermore, the *Gelasianum* prescribed on Ash Wednesday a solemn confining of the penitents. It is not said where this was to happen; in every case it seems to concern a special Roman custom. On Holy Thursday the penitents were again released from their voluntary custody.

In the sixth century, even though in principle the ancient form of public penance was maintained, in Gaul the periods of penance were strongly curtailed in comparison with the earlier custom, and the bishops were clearly aware of this fact. But the ancient forms were kept: at the start of the period of penance the bishop imposed hands on the penitent and handed him the *cilicium,* a hood of goat's hair. The penitent himself was then obliged to cut off his hair and put on the penitential garb. Penitents were not allowed to take part in banquets and in trade; rather they were to spend their time in fasting and prayer; even military service was forbidden to them. Caesarius of Arles expected of penitents all the corporal works of mercy, such as to give alms, shelter strangers, care for the sick, bury the dead, and finally to clean the church. But the most incisive demand was that of perfect continence in marriage. This obligation continued even after reconciliation, and hence it pertained to the permanent consequences of penance, just like the inability to be accepted into the clergy. It was especially aggravating that even a penance accepted on one's deathbed had the same effect in the case of an unexpected recovery as every other public penance.

As regards admission to the clergy, evidently a very serious problem was seen here, which canon 1 of the Council of Gerona in 517 sought to solve: if a person had declared himself a sinner only generally in the most serious illness, but without actually confessing serious sins, he could later still become a cleric. Canon 54 of the Fourth Council of Toledo in 633 renewed this prescription. The problem of continence required in marriage by penance was solved differently. Avitus of Vienne advised younger people who had no *culpae capitales* to prefer to die without penance than to put themselves in the danger that, on recovering, they could not observe conjugal continence and for that reason would have to be regarded as apostates. Canon 27 of the Council of Orléans in 538 decreed in the same sense that the penitential blessing must not be entrusted to young people; the married might receive the penitential blessing only in advanced age and also with the consent of the other spouse. Only Fulgentius of Ruspe seems to have convincingly solved the problem as pastor. Even in his first letter he declared that the penance accepted in danger of death obliged to continence only when the other spouse had consented to this. But even in this case he wanted to show a certain mildness. Anyone who could not observe continence should abstain from all wickedness and guard himself especially against avarice, that is, give alms. Then, according to Fulgentius' assurance, he might count on not being damned. Canon 8 of the Sixth Council of Toledo in 638 apparently first found a synodal regulation of the problem, conceding as a favor that everyone who had undertaken penance in danger of death but had recovered might go back to conjugal life; if the other spouse died, then the penitent must not remarry; but in the case of the demise of the reconciled penitent, remarriage was permitted to the surviving spouse.

In other respects, a broad decline of public penance can be ascertained in the course of the seventh century in Spain; its place was slowly taken by private penance. In Gaul as early as the beginning of the sixth century Caesarius had to state that most persons put off penance to the end of their life (*Sermo* 60, 4); this situation was intensified in the course of the sixth century. Thus the time was clearly ripe for private penance. However, it did not come into practice first with the Celtic monks, disciples of Columban, but was spread by usages which can be ascertained as early as the sixth century in Gaul and Spain. This is true for both the laity and the clergy. Originally, there was no penance for clerics; they were deposed but might communicate as laymen; rehabilitation was not possible. But gradually a period of penance was also adopted for clerics, usually in a monastery, and after it restoration to office. Gregory the Great quite often prescribed a penance even for bishops, for example, he imposed on John of Justiniana Prima thirty days' abstention from the Eucharist, and on Spanish bishops six months', penance in a monastery. Such a penance was doubtless public, but it did not prevent the people thus treated from remaining in or returning to their office respectively.

Canon 11 of the Third Council of Toledo in 589 aimed to eliminate the abuse whereby in some churches of Spain people practiced penance in such a way that they demanded reconciliation just as often as they had sinned and to restore the old canonical form to force. It seems however to be much more certain that priests were acting in the exercise of their office and that in this there was question of sins which excluded one from the Eucharist. Less clear is a reconciliation, that is, absolution from serious sins, without public ecclesiastical penance in the writings of Caesarius of Arles. He first got around the difficulties which were connected with public penance by urging to frequent self-imposed penance and especially to examination of conscience (*Sermo* 50, 3). If he declared that *crimina,* hence serious sins, had to be effaced either by *elemosynarum remedia* or by *poenitentiae medicamenta* (*Sermo* 56, 2), he still seems to attribute to the private devotional exercise of almsgiving the same efficacy as he did to public ecclesiastical penance. The consequences would be that the penitent, after the verdict of his own conscience, would again join in the reception of the Eucharist. On the other hand, Caesarius speaks not only in his *Rule for Virgins* of confession through which guilt is made known, but he urges younger sinners against chastity to come quickly to confession and penance. If one considers how reserved he was otherwise with penance, especially for younger persons, there is probably not a question here of public penance with all its consequences. And when he finally declared expressly that penance, which a person publicly undertakes, could also be performed in secret (*secretius*), then he seems to have thought of a procedure which took place, not indeed before the community, but, however, could be considered as ecclesiastical in so far as it was under the supervision and responsibility of the bishop.

In the Vita of Bishop Desiderius of Vienne and in that of Bishop Siffred episcopal absolutions seem to be attested apart from public penance. It is most interesting that Bishop Philip of Vienne in 570 appointed the priest Theudarius as *poenitentiarius* of his diocese. That means that many came to him and confessed their secret sins; each left *medicatus sanusque... securior et laetior.* Here confession and the forgiveness of sins in entirely the modern sense seem already attested.

In this context attention should be directed to the Ninth Sermon of Gregory the Great on Ezekiel 40. He there requires (no. 18) the capability of distinguishing in penance: neither must discipline be too strict nor must mercy be too soft; neither must guilt be illegally remitted, because otherwise the guilty person would become more deeply involved in guilt, nor must guilt be regarded beyond the proper degree, because otherwise the penitent would become even worse, since he experienced no mercy. Indeed, it could even happen that a pastor, who lacked the spirit of discrimination, either was so easy on sins that he did not correct them, or, because he really injured in correcting, he did not remit the sins (no. 20). On this occasion Gregory reports that many are made aware of their sins by preaching and afterward come to the preacher and confess and ask his intercession for their sins; he should then extirpate by his prayer the guilt which he made known through his preaching. It is striking how often in this connection confession is stressed. If one recalls that the normal penitential care of souls, including excommunication and reconciliation, was provided at Rome not by the Pope himself but by the priests of the titular churches, then one is inclined to see here something like private or, better expressed, not public confession or penance. Perhaps one may even glimpse in the prayer of the holy teacher, which, according to Gregory, should efface sins, a deprecatory form of absolution, especially since Leo the Great declared (*Ep.* 108, 3) that the guilt of sin was absolved by the intercession of the bishop, *sacerdotalis supplicatio,* which brought the performance of public penance to an end. That finally around the middle of the seventh century penance was no longer connected with a class of penitents seems to be clear from canon 8 of the Council of Chalon (between 647 and 653), since there penance is characterized as a remedy for sins and necessary for all men.

Anointing and Imposition of Hands

It has already been pointed out that in Spain and Gaul as well as at Rome in our period the neophytes received an anointing, in some places even a twofold anointing. This anointing was not regarded at any time as the Sacrament of Confirmation or brought into connection with the Holy Spirit. We know from a letter of Eugene of Toledo to Braulio of Zaragoza that often even the deacons performed the anointing with chrism after the baptism. Anointing with chrism was ambiguous in so far as it could also be the external sign of the readmittance of heretics to the Church. Canon 16 of the Council of Epaon in 517 decided that heretics who wished to convert should request the chrism from the bishop; but if they were dying, the priest might come to their aid with the chrism. Hence there was question here not of the anointing of the sick but of an anointing which could be placed on a level with the postbaptismal anointing. Pope Vigilius in his letter to Profuturus of Braga (no. 3) introduced a careful distinction: the reconciliation takes place not by that imposition of hands which acts through the invoking of the Holy Spirit, but by that one through which the fruit of penance is acquired and the restoration of holy communion (of the communion of the Church) is completed.

Nevertheless, canon 7 of the Second Council of Seville in 619 still seems to make no distinction between these two impositions of hands, when in one breath it forbids the priests to give the Holy Spirit through the imposition of hands to baptized faithful or to those converted from heresy. Perhaps one may see in this the aftereffects of early African theology, for this view corresponds exactly to that of Cyprian's opponents, who did not rebaptize but only wanted to impose hands for the reception of the Spirit.

The anointing of the sick is attested for the sixth century in both Gaul and Spain. In Spain the oil for the anointing of the sick was consecrated on the feast of the holy physicians, Cosmas and Damian, with a prayer which asked the healing of body and soul by virtue of the sufferings of Christ. There are many testimonies in Gaul that this holy oil was used by lay persons to cure the sick or drive out demons. The faithful were even urged to this by the clergy, for example, by Caesarius of Arles, but apparently chiefly to draw them away from ancient pagan magical practices. Caesarius of Arles invited the sick to come to church to communicate and be anointed; thus would the admonition of the Epistle of James (5:14f.) be implemented (*Sermo* 19, 5).

Piety

At the turn of the fifth to the sixth century the frequency of the reception of the Eucharist sharply declined. As early as 506 the Council of Agde in canon 18 had to declare that whoever did not communicate at Christmas, Easter, and Pentecost could not be regarded as a Christian. But since the same Council demanded a strict preparation for communion, it could hardly have paved the way to more frequent communion. Caesarius of Arles in his sermons appealed besides for communion on the feast of John the Baptist and the other martyrs, but he did not venture to require a regular Sunday communion. The reason was no doubt the strict standard which was laid on the necessary preparation. Thus, for example, Caesarius required of those who wished to communicate at least several days of conjugal continence (*Sermo* 16, 2; 19, 3; 44, 3). He invited the newly married to stay away from church for a month (*Sermo* 43, 23). It deserves to be stressed that he emphasized the equality of rights and equality of obligation of both sexes according to Christian faith (*Sermo* 44, 5). In Spain continence was inculcated as a preparation for communion even in the marriage ceremony, and Isidore *(Eccl. Off.* 1 , 18, 9–10) required many days of continence, but perhaps in this lay a conscious exaggeration. In any event, even daily attendance at Mass did not yet mean frequent communion.

Christian piety is at times powerfully impressed by the saints, to whom special veneration belongs. In relation to the present-day understanding, one should ask first about the place which Mary occupied in the Christian consciousness. At Rome the name of Mary was introduced into the canon at the beginning of the sixth century, but the first Marian feasts in the West date only from the seventh century. The *Sacramentarium Veronense* (*Leonianum*), in which the first three months

are missing, knows, in addition to the feasts of local Roman saints, only the veneration of the Baptist and of the Protomartyr Stephen, and Mary is mentioned
only in a preface for the feast of the Baptist. Under Pope Theodore (642–49) the
feast of the Purification on 2 February was introduced, and before Pope Sergius I
(687–701) were added the feasts of the Annunciation (25 March), the Assumption
(15 August), and the Birthday (8 September). Here eastern influence is clearly to
be seen. In this it is noteworthy that Pope Sergius was apparently not satisfied
with the form and the Mass formularies of the three last-named Marian feasts, but
desired greater solemnity. He accomplished this by introducing a procession for
these feasts, on which the people set out from another church. The *collecta* was
recited in this church of the assembly. Thus these last three feasts obtained the
same solemnity as was already customary on the feast of the Purification. This
is revealed by the fact that the *Hadrianum* and the *Paduense* agree in the Mass
formulary of 2 February and both provide a *collecta* at the beginning. On the other
hand, in the *Paduense* the other three feasts have no *collecta* and hence no procession took place. The *Hadrianum* gives for the last three Marian feasts prayers
differing from the *Paduense* and for each a *collecta* at the beginning.

But the Marian feasts were not the oldest testimony to the veneration of Mary.
In Gregory the Great, for example, we find no Marian feast attested, but he does
mention churches dedicated to the Mother of God, not only Santa Maria Maggiore
at Rome but also several churches and oratories in Italy, and one in Gaul, at Autun.
Then in Gaul in the seventh century numerous convents of nuns are ascertained
whose churches were dedicated to Mary; indeed, this was the rule, while monasteries of monks were mostly dedicated to Peter and Paul. Circa 705 the seriously ill
Wilfrid of York was reproached in a vision of an angel that he had indeed erected
churches for Peter and Andrew but still none in honor of Mary, from which it
must probably be concluded "that Mary and the Apostles belonged together in
the piety of the age!" (E. Ewig). But the cult of Mary verified by patronages can
be pursued farther back. Circa 400 Nicasius seems to have built the first Marian
cathedral at Reims, and this so set a precedent that in the sixth century in many
episcopal churches a complex of three churches was characteristic, namely, with
one church for clerics dedicated to the Apostles, one church for catechumens
dedicated to Mary, and the baptistry dedicated to John the Baptist. In Spain the
cathedrals were mostly dedicated to Mary in the sixth and seventh centuries, but
there the cult of Mary is found in literature only at the middle of the seventh century
with the treatise of Ildefonse of Toledo on the perpetual virginity of Mary. The Tenth
Council of Toledo of 656 in canon 1 transferred the feast of the Annunciation, which
till then had not yet been celebrated uniformly on 25 March, to 18 December. The
day was certainly not only chosen because it comes a week before Christmas, but
also because at the Fifth Council of Toledo in 636 in canon 1 new rogation days had
been introduced for the triduum of 15–17 December. In this connection there was
probably only a question of accommodating King Chintila, who was seeking the
protection of heaven, but later these rogation days served to enhance the solemnity of this Marian feast now transferred to Advent. The fact that in the festal Mass
the treatise of Ildefonse, divided into six or seven sections, was read in place of the
Old Testament selection shows how movingly and in response to the demands of
the people and the time the Spanish Church of the seventh century fashioned its

liturgy. In many places the patronage of Peter seems to have succeeded a general patronage of the Apostles, so that the "cult of the Apostles obtained a more personal note." The Princes of the Apostles, especially Peter, passed over in the Early Middle Ages as the special patrons of the Roman Church into general awareness. The Latin episcopate of late antiquity, in order to emphasize the unity of the Empire against all appearances of collapse, had fostered the cult of the two Princes of the Apostles and thus passed it on to the newly converted Burgundians, Visigoths, and Franks. But in many places the cult of Peter in the later Merovingian period was overshadowed by the veneration of those saints whose remains were buried locally. This was not least of all connected with the fact that people could obtain only second-class relics from the Roman graves of the Apostles, whereas first-class relics corresponded more to the German mentality.

Like the cult of Peter, so the newly Christian German peoples also adopted the custom of the pilgrimage from Latin and Greek antiquity. The first Christian king of the Burgundians, Sigismund, was at the same time also the first Christian German king to make the pilgrimage to Rome. He brought back relics, which were apparently soon used up, for he sent a deacon to Rome to fetch new relics. In 590, Bishop Gregory of Tours likewise sent his deacon to Rome, and he brought back many relics. From him Gregory also learned how Peter's tomb was venerated at Rome. Especially impressive is the description that, if one prayed devoutly and piously enough, the little cloth which one was careful to let down to Peter's grave in order thereby to obtain a second-class relic was heavier than before after its contact with the tomb, and so one had proof of the grace of God. From the British Isles also pilgrims came to Rome even before the year 500. The new German rulers of the island, who were converted to the Catholic faith, also adopted the high esteem for Peter and the instinct for the pilgrimage. Some rulers laid aside their crown and went as pilgrims to Rome. In their own country they erected churches in honor of Peter as substitutes: one who could not go to Rome should honor Peter here. It is due to these eager pilgrimages of the Germans that in the fifth and sixth centuries, when Rome was gradually losing its external splendor, after it had lost its power, the former center of the Empire became the Holy City. In it during these centuries were honored the most famous martyrs of all Christendom; thus Rome became the agent and the distributor of these treasures. The pilgrimage to Rome for relics was of the greatest importance for the religious and cultural development of the West. Indeed it can even be said that pilgrimages created and developed a Catholic spirit, that is, a universal spirit for the whole of Christianity. Through the pilgrimages was spread a really fraternal attitude among the faithful in the most varied lands. In the seventh century there developed in Western Christianity, under the influence of the new penitential practice of the Irish monks, a new type of pilgrimage, namely, the penitential pilgrimage. It was chiefly undertaken by clerics, who were not admitted to public penance, for the expiation of serious sins; in this it was not a question of a specific goal, but of assuming homelessness as atonement. Of course, such pilgrimages also led to the holy places and contributed to the spread of the cult of saints and relics. But it must be remembered that the pilgrimage to Rome, which apparently received very early the character of a pilgrimage of expiation, occupied a special place, in so far as people went as pilgrims not only to the tomb of the Apostle but increasingly at the same time and in the course of years to the successor of the Apostle, the Roman Pope, in whom people were quite aware was the power of the keys, that is, Peter's full power of forgiving.

At Arles there were in the sixth century some twenty to twenty-five feasts of saints; in general, this century saw a powerful growth of the cult of saints, as can be inferred especially from the works of Gregory of Tours. Originally, of course, the veneration referred to the martyrs, but then it was extended to the ascetics, who through their austerity had shown that they were of the same rank as the martyrs. The saints were not only invoked at their graves, but also at a great distance away; then, of course, the effort was made to get into contact with them through relics. Gregory of Tours recommended their use in case of sickness, probably to wean the faithful from magical practices. It is noteworthy that Caesarius did not yet know this use of relics.

It was important to know the exact day of death of a saint, because his feast had to be celebrated on it. A vigil was held throughout the night, or at least a very early celebration of Lauds. The solemn Mass began around nine o'clock; in it the *passio* or the *vita* of the saint was read. The clergy who served at the shrine of a martyr were furthermore obliged to treat the people flocking there to wine. For their part the faithful sought the closest possible contact with the tomb of a saint. Thus they took along, for example, oil from the lamps burning there, in order to use it against sickness. The cult of saints must not only be regarded as a characteristic of popular devotion: it was rather a part of episcopal pastoral care. The picture of the saint might achieve more than the preaching of the bishop; indeed, it could even be said that the saint complemented the bishop's activity, but he was a mysterious, all-knowing power, which began to act where the bishop s action ceased. In general, the bishops seem to have had no reservations in regard to the cult of saints and relics: quite the contrary. Canon 5 of the Third Council of Braga in 576 saw itself obliged to check somewhat the zeal that probably promoted the personal vanity of the bishops. Only once is it attested that a bishop, namely, Serenus of Marseille at the end of the sixth century, took a stand against the cult of saints. He even had their images destroyed, because he assumed that the people adored them. Gregory the Great indeed praised his zeal for the exclusive adoration of God, but at the same time blamed the destruction of the images, since they could be of service to the faith of the uneducated.

It must be stressed that the cult of relics was in no sense only a characteristic of popular devotion. In fact, the Christian theologians of late antiquity were occupied with the question and assured the faithful that even the smallest part of the relic of a martyr meant a great treasure, for the power and grace of the saint were in some way in every tiniest particle as in the entire body. The distribution of relics, on the other hand, facilitated the collecting of relics of many saints, whereby people thought, probably quite naively, to assure themselves of the protection of many saints. In this way, the system of phylacteries, that is, the manufacture and use of amulets with relics, flourished. The fact that at Rome no bodily relics of the Apostles were given up, but only second-class relics, was based not only on the cult of the Apostles but also on the belief that every division of the relics of the Apostles would have weakened the position of the papal primacy, which for that age was founded not only on the succession of Peter but on the possession of the Apostles' tombs.

If it is now recalled that Isidore's monastic *Rule* (24, 1–2), hence a work from the seventh century, mentions for the first time an annual memorial on which the holy sacrifice was to be offered for all the deceased — Masses for the dead, which were celebrated partly at the exact hour of death of the deceased, were known in Gaul as early as the sixth century — then it may be said that the decisive monuments of Christian piety were formed in the period here surveyed. This applies especially if it may be assumed that auricular confession, only generally coming into practice under the influence of the Celtic monks, which is without doubt a characteristic of Catholic piety, was already spread in this period on the basis of the development of the ancient western practice of penance.

C H A P T E R   7 1

Latin Monasticism from the Mid-Fifth Century to the End of the Seventh Century

The further development of Latin monasticism from ca. 450 to 700 makes it clear that the episode of the wanderings of the peoples with its effects fostered the previously high estimation of the monastic ideal far more than obstructed it. The continuity with the monasticism of the fourth century was maintained, since both its ideal basis, the example of the East, and the earlier forms, cenobitic and eremitical, persisted. The latter experienced a certain variation, since, first, in addition to the strict eremitism of the individual, a type became more frequent which kept the hermit in the vicinity of a monastery and hence in contact with its abbot, and second, now itinerant hermits, at first predominantly of Irish origin, appeared, who joined to anchoritism *the peregrinatio,* the ascetical renunciation of home and all it meant. From now on, eremitism was valued as the chief form of monastic existence, to the demands of which only one who had previously been proved in a cenobitic community should expose himself.

The great majority of ascetics accordingly chose the cenobitic form of life, which in the period here treated acquired some characteristic features. Monasteries, growing vastly in number — their founders were, besides the individual monk, bishops, Popes, and also well-to-do lay persons, especially the Merovingian nobility and crown — first consolidated their inner organization, since they more and more lived according to a definite *Rule,* now fixed in writing. In such Rules, indeed, the ideal of eastern cenobitism was ever more decisive, but everywhere an adaptation to the concrete circumstances of Western European areas was undertaken. This is already noticeable in the *Institutiones* (1–4) of John Cassian and in the Latin form of Basil's *Ascetica,* and more clearly in the revision of the *Rule* of Pachomius and the two rules coming from Lérins, the *Regula quattuor Patrum* and the *Regula Macarii,* which belong to the fifth century. In southern Gaul abbots of several monasteries met on occasion for discussion of the inner structure of their monasteries, and from their decisions proceeded the so-called *Regula quattuor Patrum,* the *Regula secunda* and *tertia Patrum.* The sixth century was the age of the great Rules of the Master and of Benedict of Nursia in Italy and of the Bishops of Arles, Caesarius and Aurelian, in Gaul, who, however, made use of earlier works. Some of the new Rules were expressly mixed Rules, *Regulae mixtae,* such as the *Regula Ferioli,* the *Regula Tarnatensis Monasterii,* the *Regula Orientalis,* and the *Regula Pauli et Stephani,* which took over whole parts of existing Rules. Thus the Irish-Frankish monasticism acquired its own form through combining the *Regula Columbani* with the *Regula Benedicti.* In the monastic Rules of Spain from the seventh century, which were composed by Leander of Seville, his brother Isidore, and Fructuosus of Braga, even more eastern influence is detectable, in addition to that of the *Rule* of Augustine. The observance of the same *Rule* in several monasteries did not yet lead to their organizational union.

In so significant an element of the Church's inner life that the numerous monasteries represented, the contemporary episcopate showed an understandable interest and aimed, stimulated by the monastic legislation of the Council of Chalcedon, to see also in the Latin West the monastic system subjected in principle to its jurisdiction. This process of increasing episcopal control began in the fifth century, but, of course, it did not move everywhere at the same pace. In North Africa the oppressed situation of the Church under Vandal domination fostered an extensive independence of the monasteries. In Italy, following the Byzantine reconquest in 535, the eastern monastic canon law established itself especially in the area under Byzantine authority and thereby gave the bishop the possibility of calling upon the monks of the many smaller monasteries, especially in the South, for pastoral tasks. In the parts of Italy controlled by the Ostrogoths and then by the Lombards, however, the less numerous but often more important monasteries retained a greater freedom of movement with regard to the bishop. Then Gregory the Great subordinated them in general to episcopal supervision, which in the course of the sixth century was recognized also in Gaul and Spain, as the synodal legislation of the time makes known. The crucial points of episcopal control were influence on, or at least examination of, the election of the abbot and overseeing the administration of monastery property. A relaxation and limitation of episcopal jurisdiction, however, followed in the seventh century from the influence which the wealthy layman who had participated in the founding of the monastery could keep for himself, or from privileges which the landowner granted to a monastery. Monastic exemption, here under way, was first conceded in its full extent to the Upper Italian monastery of Bobbio by Pope Honorius I in 628.

A further important development in western monasticism of this period appeared with the undertaking of missionary activity on a scale hitherto unknown. From the thus far customary, often only occasional, mission among the population of the neighborhood of a monastery, the glance was directed to distant goals; there was a going over to the evangelization of unfamiliar peoples, which, as in the mission to the Anglo-Saxons, was planned and taken up on a grand scale. Then when the Irish-Scottish monks joined the ascetical *peregrinatio* with missionary work on the continent, the great missionary task was firmly anchored in the consciousness of western monasticism.

As a final characteristic of Latin monasticism of this age must be mentioned the monastic school, an institution now spread everywhere. True, it served exclusively for the formation of the monastery's own recruits, who had to be enabled to read the texts for the liturgical service and the Holy Scripture as material for the *lectio divina* and be able to prepare the manuscripts required for this; hence it purposely excluded the profane, especially the pagan, literature of antiquity from its program. But this monastic school was still not an ever atrophying remnant of the decaying school system of the Later Empire with its other institutions; rather, despite its elementary character, it was the viable germ from which, just as from the episcopal schools of the age, the medieval school would spring as the agent of Western Christian education. In the following geographically arranged survey the important facts, personalities, and tendencies in the monasticism of the period will be set forth.

Italy

The eremitical life, already noteworthy in Italy at the turn of the fourth to the fifth centuries, retained its esteem in the following period, but now it was encountered, not only on the preferred islands of the Mediterranean, but also in the interior of the country. The influence of Egyptian anchoritism here present was kept alive by the Latin translations of the *Apophthegmata* literature of the sixth century, the *Verba seniorum,* in which the future Popes Pelagius I (556–61) and John III (561–74) took part. But Italian cenobitism was also further oriented toward the eastern model, as, for example, with Lawrence, probably a native of Syria, who around the middle of the sixth century founded near Spoleto the monastery of Farfa, eventually to become famous. The *Regula Orientalis,* whose title indicated eastern influence, also had an Italian origin, apparently at the beginning of the sixth century. Certain impulses for the Italian monasticism of this period proceeded also from African monks, who abandoned their homeland under the pressure of Vandal rule. Thus the African Gaudentius founded a monastery at Naples, and Fulgentius of Ruspe assembled African monks in two settlements at Cagliari on Sardinia, in which theological study occupied no small position. In the course of the sixth century the number of monasteries in Italy grew vastly, as the correspondence and the *Dialogi* of Gregory the Great show, in which is mentioned an abundance of monastic settlement.

Today, almost without exception, the two most comprehensive monastic Rules of this epoch, which since 1938 have been the object of an intensive and still not finished discussion, the so-called *Regula Magistri* (RM) and the *Rule of Benedict* of Nursia (RB), are assigned to the sixth century. Between them exists so strong a relationship, in both content and form, that on the one hand the question of their reciprocal dependence, on the other hand that of the priority in time of the one over the other, urgently intrudes itself. The *Regula Magistri* is anonymous and in comparison with the *Rule of Benedict* about three times as large; in most manuscripts there is named as author of the latter a Benedict, who is apparently identical with that Benedict of Montecassino, whose signs and miracles Pope Gregory the Great described in the second book of his *Dialogi* and to whom he attributed a monastic *Rule* which was marked by *discretio* and clarity (*Dial.,* II, 36). True, Gregory supplied few chronological references to events in Benedict's life, but together with some credible criteria from the rest of the tradition about him they permit one to assign his life-span between 480/490 and 550/560. This tradition has him come from the old province of Nursia and study for a time at Rome in his youth. But he soon left the city in order to live as a hermit in a cave near Subiaco until disciples joined him, whom he is said to have gathered, according to the Pachomian model, into several communities. Then he sought to realize the experiences and insights gained here in regard to real cenobitism in a new foundation on Montecassino, where he must have died around the middle of the sixth century.

Today the priority of the *Regula Magistri* may be regarded as the established and also almost generally recognized outcome of the discussion just mentioned, and its origin ascribed to the first three decades of the sixth century, since, among other things, it represents a less developed cenobitism than that of the *Regula Benedicti,* since it also employs the apocryphal Scriptures to a degree that can only with difficulty be reconciled with the so-called *Decretum Gelasianum de libris recipiendis et non recipiendis* of the early sixth century, and finally since it was already used by Abbot Eugippius of Lucullanum (d. ca. 530) in his now identified *Rule.* On the other hand, there is less agreement on the homeland of the *Regula Magistri:* some would see its origin chiefly in the vicinity of Rome, others hold rather that it came from Provence.

With the priority of the *Regula Magistri* there is also established its employment by Benedict. These did not find their definitive form in their first versions, but were expanded in content (the *Regula Magistri*) or improved in form (the *Regula Benedicti*): very likely the *Regula Magistri* was in Benedict's hands in an intermediate stage. Among the sources common to both *Rules* Holy Scripture holds the first place; both also refer to Cassian, and Cyprian is familiar to them, while the meager use of the apocrypha by Benedict indicates, not a direct knowledge of them, but a direct adoption from the *Regula Magistri,* apparently even without more detailed knowledge of their character. As the special property of the *Regula Magistri* is knowledge of Julianus Pomerius, Caesarius of Arles, and Nicetas of Remesiana, while Benedict is acquainted with far more voluminous relevant works, such as the *Vitae patrum,* the "Rule of our holy Father Basil," the *Historia monachorum,* the *Rule* of Pachomius, and especially the *Rule* of Augustine, from which he gained some ideas, without expressly naming it. With the stock of ideas created from these sources Benedict put in order the knowledge acquired from his own experience and meditation, as this seemed to him essential for the cenobitic form of life and at the same time humanly possible. Thus, with a greater stylistic ability than the author of the *Regula Magistri* could call on, he created in a happy synthesis the hitherto most complete monastic Rule, which was to surpass for the next centuries in its greater power of attraction all other *Rules* from the early age of monasticism.

If one asks about the basic idea of the *Regula Benedicti,* its Christocentrism will have to be named. Already the decisive motive for the entry into the monastic community is the desire for the unconditional following of Christ. Service in the *militia Christi Regis* determines the entire manner of life of the monk (*conversa-*

tio morum). He gives obedience to the abbot, because in him he sees Christ; he takes up every renunciation because he wants to share in the Passion of Christ; nothing is dearer to him than love for Christ. To assure this central following of Christ is the purpose of the regulations on the liturgy (*opus Dei*), on the *lectio divina,* and on *stabilitas loci.* With the following of Christ as thus understood, Benedict's second fundamental concern is assured, *caritas fraterna,* which must be at the same time as the deepest Christian *humanitas* the basis of any monastic community, an insight which Benedict to a great extent owes to the reading of the *Rule* of Augustine. Some individual prescriptions of the *Regula Benedicti* are so flexibly composed that they could easily be adapted to various climatic conditions: hence its author reckoned on its spread. Whereas the testimonies for the existence of the *Regula Magistri* in the sixth century are relatively frequent, they begin only in the seventh century for the *Regula Benedicti.* Certainly the picture of Benedict in the *Dialogi* of Gregory the Great fostered its spread, and it appeared relatively early in the Merovingian Kingdom, until in the course of the eighth century it gained ground powerfully and through the combined efforts of the first Carolingian Emperors and of Abbot Benedict of Aniane (d. 821) achieved almost exclusive validity.

In the former minister of the Ostrogothic King Theodoric, Cassiodorus, born ca. 485, we meet a layman, who as a zealous promoter of monasticism founded on his South Italian estate of Squillace two colonies, a settlement of anchorites on the hill of Castellum and in the immediate vicinity the real monastery of Vivarium, which was intended to serve a specific task, namely, scientifically based and organized work on the Bible that went far beyond the previous *lectio divina.* In his *Institutiones divinarum et saecularium litterarum,* dedicated to the monks, Cassiodorus set down his ideas on this and developed a concrete program of studies. An important presupposition for this was a library in which faultless biblical manuscripts, introductions to the Bible, the exegetical works of the Church Fathers, and those works of profane literature were on hand which could not be dispensed with for a scientifically fruitful study of the Bible. A special *scriptorium* should undertake the production of the necessary manuscripts. New in this concept was, first, the demand of genuine scientific activity at all, and then the strong stress which was laid on the recourse to profane literary scholarship, but which Cassiodorus tried to justify again and again. In the realization of such exalted aims, of course, not all the monks of the monastery were involved; in any event a rather long starting-time was needed before a work force capable of such achievement was trained. But as early as the founder's death ca. 580 interest in the enterprise apparently began to flag, and thus from Vivarium came only one exegetical work, an *Expositio psalmorum,* and even this came from the pen of Cassiodorus himself, who in it relied on Augustine's *Enarrationes in psalmos,* without attaining its religious value even remotely. What were the most worthwhile, then, were, first, the stock of the library built by Cassiodorus and his program developed in the *Institutiones,* which of course would later gain a substantial share in the renewal of scholarly activity in the West.

Powerful impulses proceeded from Gregory the Great, himself a monk and founder of monasteries at Rome and on Sicily, to the contemporary monasticism of Italy. Many of his measures were intended for the external and internal reconstruction of the monastic system, which, like ecclesiastical life as a whole, had suffered because of the chaos of the Lombard invasion. It was further significant that Gregory more and more took monasticism into the direct service of the Church, called abbots to become bishops, sent them on important missions to Ravenna or Pavia, for example, or assigned to them the preaching among the Lombards and the evangelization of the Anglo-Saxons. Here is discernible an informative change in Gregory's view of the vocation of the monk, which was based on his own career. Whereas he at first regarded the monk's being and the exercise of an ecclesiastical office or function as incompatible, he later saw in the service of the Church a possibility for attaining the highest perfection, since in it could be joined together the *vita activa* and *contemplativa*. Soon after Gregory's death the Irish-Scottish monasticism acquired influence on the Italian, when in 612 Columban (d. 615) founded not far from the Trebbia, south of Pavia, his last monastery, Bobbio, which from the start enjoyed the rich encouragement of the Lombard royal family and in a certain sense was a royal proprietary monastery. Its rapid economic flowering allowed it an intensive activity in the cultural and theological sphere; especially by means of its *scriptorium* Bobbio became a first-class intellectual center in contemporary Italy, which with its numerous daughter-houses and through the spread of the cult of Columban, radiated not only in the area of Lombard rule but also into Byzantine territory. Columban's austere *Rule* remained in force under his first successors: only in the second half of the century did the influence of the *Regula Benedicti* gradually assert itself, to then become exclusively prescribed in the eighth century.

Monasticism in the Merovingian Kingdom

In what had been Roman Gaul there continued as the two centers of gravity for the expansion of monasticism in the fourth and fifth centuries: the area of the Lower Rhone Valley and Aquitaine, but in the sixth and seventh centuries they experienced important differentiations, partly coming from without. In Rhone monasticism the influence of Lérins at first still remained predominant. Bishop Caesarius of Arles (d. ca. 542) became the most important promoter of southeast Gallic monasticism; he himself was a monk at Lérins before he assumed the direction of a monastery outside the gates of Arles, until 502. In the two monastic *Rules* composed by him — the first was written for the convent of nuns of Saint John, founded by him as bishop, and his sister Caesaria was its superior; the second, a *Rule for Monks,* is probably only a revised abridgment of the *Rule for Nuns* — now, besides the Lérins tradition, the influence of Augustine's Rule becomes traceable. Both *Rules* of Caesarius worked to stimulate later authors of monastic rules, such as his successor Aurelian.

   The fact that the Rhone monasteries gave themselves a stricter organization so relatively early through the introduction of a *Rule* could not but have had a positive impact on the entire monastic life. It certainly contributed to the circumstance that precisely in the South Gallic monasteries there was a lively interest in theological and religious questions, as this became clear in the discussion on Augustine's doctrine of grace. It is furthermore striking that the very bishops who came from

Rhone monasticism showed a special readiness actively to shape public life both in the ecclesiastical and in the secular sphere.

In the central and western areas of ancient Gaul monasticism was at first still under the influence of Martin's ideals and retained its old inclination to individualism, which showed itself, in addition to other ways, in the rejection of *stabilitas loci* and of the introduction of a definite monastic Rule. Thus there occurred again and again the founding of monasteries by individual monks without a definite plan and often soon abandoned; hence the first Frankish national Council of Orléans in 511, in clear conformity with the monastic regulations of Caesarius of Arles, made the establishing of monastic settlements dependent on the consent of the local bishop and prescribed that monks settle down. That these decrees were implemented, however, only to a modest degree becomes clear from the reports of Gregory of Tours on the monasticism of the late sixth century, in which lack of discipline and organization was still characteristic.

The decisive impulse for a further development of Merovingian monasticism came when the Irish monk Columban (ca. 543–615) arrived there with twelve companions to the Frankish Kingdom ca. 590 and was able to put the monastic ideal of his homeland into effect on new soil. When the Irishman gave up the position of first teacher at the school of his monastery of Bangor in order to go far way, his motive was the *peregrinatio* in its religious understanding, as he emphasized in his letter to the bishops of the Merovingian Kingdom. Only when he came to know the depressing situation of the Merovingian Church from his own observation did he also decide on pastoral work among the people, in so far as this was possible in the framework of monastic community life. In this it was of the greatest importance that for his activity Columban quickly found the approval and support of King Sigebert and of the Merovingian upper class, who were powerfully impressed by the personality of the Irish monk. On the southeast slope of the Vosges he was able to establish, one after another, three settlements, Annegray, Luxeuil, and Fontaine, of which the second became the most important because of the magnitude of the plan — refectory, monastic school, guest-house and the rapidly growing number of monks. For these monasteries Columban wrote down his regulations, the *Regula Monachorum* in ten chapters, which rather determined the basic attitudes of the ascetical life of monks, and the *Regula Coenobialis,* a loose sort of notebook record of penances which were imposed for failings in the monastic life. Both reflect the theory and practice of the Irish home monastery of Bangor, which its Abbot Comgall had there introduced. To these belong especially the serious, strict characteristic of striving for interiority, to which the monastic Rule leads, the order of prayer (Chapter 7), and the detailed penitential regulations of the *Regula Coenobialis.* From the start, Columban's foundation had a strong power of attraction, which was expressed in two important traits. First, the Frankish nobility were attracted in a unique way by the Irish-Scottish monastic ideal: its sons were partly educated at Luxeuil or entered there as monks: monks of Luxeuil were summoned to be bishops, who then called into being monasteries on the model of Luxeuil or introduced the order of Luxeuil into existing monasteries; and finally laymen made numerous new foundations in both Neustria and Austrasia and North Burgundy, so that the number of monasteries oriented to Luxeuil rose to more than 100 in the course of the seventh century. The originally exclusive validity of the *Rule* of Columban was, of course, replaced in the course of the century by a *Regula Mixta,* into which it developed with parts of the gradually advancing Benedictine *Rule.* Second, there proceeded from these monasteries far-reaching pastoral activity, since auricular confession, which they recommended, and the stressing of a serious penitential attitude — in brief, the exercise of an individual pastoral care met a deep need in all levels of the population. This twofold success of the Luxeuil spirit, however, immediately became also an occasion for a serious conflict between monasticism and parts of the episcopate, as well as with King Theodebert II. The bishops were displeased by the relative independence of the Irish-Frankish monasteries, just as by the effective pastoral activity of Columban, and both the bishops and the King especially took a dim view of the candid words of the Irish monk, who unambiguously recalled to the diocesan clergy their duty as shepherds and sharply rebuked the King for his concubinage. Columban finally had to yield in 610 to the common pressure from both; after two years' missionary work among the still pagan population between the Duke of Zurich and Bregenz, he crossed the Alps in the fall of 612 and at Bobbio reached the last city of his *peregrinatio.* But the work of the Irish-Scots on Frankish soil began an important stimulus for the religious elevation of the population of the Merovingian Kingdom, which can be ascertained at the beginning of the Carolingian Age.

Spanish Monasticism

The development of Spanish monasticism in the fifth century was interrupted by the invasion of the Vandals, Sueves, and Visigoths, but after the consolidation of the political situation it knew a steady upswing, which led to a considerable flowering in the seventh century. Just as in Italy, here too eremitism retained its importance, especially on the Balearic Isles and in the mountains of Asturias and Galicia, but the center of gravity lay in the cenobitic colonies, rapidly growing in numbers, which at first owed their origin to bishops and monks and then, after the conversion of King Recared to Catholicism in 589, also to the reigning dynasty.

Soon after 506 the monastery of Saint Martin of Asan was founded on the southern slope of the Pyrenees, north of Huesca; its Abbot Victorian (d. 558) was active to the mid-century for the spread of monasticism by the erecting of smaller colonies subject to him. Even more important was the work of Martin of Braga, a native of Pannonia, who came from Palestine to Galicia ca. 550 and there established the monastery of Dumio, over which he presided as abbot until he was called to be Bishop of Dumio in 556. By means of a collection of sayings of Egyptian Fathers, translated and revised by him, which could be employed as a "Rule," he gave his monastery an eastern outlook, which made it similar to the Martinian monasticism of Gaul. Then, not without influence on Spanish monasticism, came the founding of the monastery of *Servitanum* in the Visigothic sphere by Abbot Donatus, who before 570 migrated from North Africa with seventy monks and a considerable library and soon acquired high esteem. His successor Eutropius, who became Bishop of Valencia after the Council of Toledo of 589, defended the stern discipline of his monastery in a special work. It must probably be assumed that the *Rule* of Augustine was followed in the *Monasterium Servitanum.*

The treatise *De institutione virginis,* which Bishop Leander of Seville (d. ca. 600) composed for his sister, the nun Florentina, made use of ideas from the writings of Jerome, especially his Letter XXII to Eustochium, but also of Cassian and Augustine; however, no traces of the *Rule of Benedict* can be found. The *Regula Monachorum* of his brother and successor Isidore (d. 636) is, in regard to content, dependent on eastern monastic writings — the *Rules* of Pachomius and Macarius, Cassian and on western work — Jerome, Caesarius of Arles, and perhaps also Benedict. His own achievement consisted in the clarity and balance with which he formed the material before him into a well-thought-out *Rule.* A helpful promoter of monasticism was also Isidore's friend, Bishop Braulio of Zaragoza (d. 651), a pupil of the monastic school of Seville. He maintained a correspondence with Fructuosus of Braga (d. ca. 665), who came from a prominent Visigothic family, used his wealth for the erecting of several monasteries in Galicia and on the southern coast of Spain, and later became Bishop of Dumio and Metropolitan of Braga. His *Regula Monachorum* is based on Pachomius, Cassian, and Isidore, but also displays certain parallels to Jerome and Augustine. Unique is the prescription in Chapter 22 that the monk, on entering the monastery, signs a *pactum,* in which he asserts the voluntary character of his decision and obliges himself in a sort of treaty to the fulfilling of the monastic statutes.

As a special characteristic of the Spanish monasticism of this period may be mentioned its receptivity to intellectual activity, in which the study of the Bible, which in Leander's view was also a duty in convents of nuns, retained its previous preeminence. For the daily prescribed three hours of *lectio* the monk obtained his reading matter from the *sacrarius* from the monastic library of Seville; it included also the works of profane authors to the extent that they were beneficial for theological study. Almost all the more important Spanish bishops of the seventh century obtained their considerable education in the monastic schools of Seville, Toledo (Agali), or Zaragoza, and as bishops, continued to use and foster their *scriptoria.* In this lively interest in intellectual activity may rightly be seen the influence of African monasticism at work, which proceeded from the monastery of *Servitanum,* under the African Abbot Donatus. It was the merit of the Spanish monasticism of this period to have given to its Church an episcopate which, measured by its ascetical and theological formation, occupied a high rank in the Latin Church of the seventh century. The religious self-evaluation of this monasticism was, of course, traditional, if it is compared with the zeal which it devoted to the practical shaping of monastic life by means of rules, synodal decrees, and other writings. It was extensively oriented to the stock of ideas which was offered by Jerome, Augustine, and Cassian, and at times a renovation and reform of monasticism were understood in the sense of a return to its original idea.

The Monasticism of Africa

African monasticism, which reached a rapid flowering chiefly through the initiative of Augustine, was affected in the last months of his life by the invasion of the Arian Vandals, just as was the African Catholic Church as a whole. In addition to churches and cemeteries, many monasteries were also destroyed, partly burned down, and their inhabitants expelled; some of them found death through the sword or torture, others were sent off into captivity. Probably those monasteries were chiefly affected which lay on the Vandals' route of march or in the province of Africa Proconsularis, the special territory of settlement of the Vandals. Since many African monasteries of men also had clerics in their community, these were also included in King Gaiseric's decree of expulsion against clerics. Going beyond his father's measures, King Hunneric (477–84) planned the total suppression of all monasteries, since by a decree of 484 he had them turned over to the Moors, but his death prevented the implementation of the project. Under the persecution of Hunneric, besides clerics, also monks and nuns went over to the Arianism of the conquerors, but the majority splendidly stood the test in difficult circumstances. When King Gunthamund (484–96) revoked in succession his predecessor's decrees of persecution and banishment, the expelled religious were able to return and put an end to the damage done in the persecution; even a relatively rapid renewal of monastic life can be ascertained, which is reflected, especially for the province of Byzacena, in the *Vita* of Bishop Fulgentius of Ruspe (d. apparently in 527). As earlier, there were, in addition to monasteries which had only lay persons as members and were in the minority, others in which also clerics and, with them at times, the bishop lived as monks.

A new feature was brought into the picture of African monasticism when, after the Byzantine reconquest of North Africa by Belisarius (533–34), Greek monks in flight before the Persians came to North Africa from Palestine, Syria, and Egypt, or later in consequence of the Monothelite quarrel, and settled in Proconsular Africa, where in the first half of the seventh century four Byzantine monasteries, among them a *laura* of Saint Sabas, can be demonstrated. Among the most famous representatives of this monasticism were, at least for a time, the Abbots Sophronius and Thalassius, Saint Sabas, and Maximus Confessor. The three last-named journeyed from Africa to Rome and took part in the Lateran Synod of 649, which occupied itself with the Monothelite controversy. When the Arab invasion began around this time, North African monasticism, with the African Church, was also drawn into the ever-changing struggles for the possession of these provinces and shared with it the fate of a long but inexorable death.

CHAPTER 7 2

Theological Discussions

The Church's Confrontation with the Arianism of the Vandals and the Goths

The confrontation was conducted on the part of the Vandals in Africa as a persecution, using all the State's means of power. This is attested by the *History of the*

Persecution in the province of Africa of Bishop Victor of Vita, published in 488–89, which was of course not only a historical record but at the same time an agency of the argument. Victor aimed (3, 62) to set right all who highly esteemed the barbarians and to show that the barbarians were still barbarians and had nothing else in mind than the annihilation of all Romans; hence he identified Catholics with Romans and conversely. Over and above this purpose, the work, despite its partiality, remains one of the most important sources, from which it follows that the Vandals indeed tried to gain the Catholic African population, but insisted on the rebaptism of those converted. The Roman Count Sebastian, for whom King Gaiseric personally exerted himself, rejected conversion and rebaptism thus: "As bread originates by the fact of flour's passing through water and fire, so I was baptized and cooked by the fire of the Holy Spirit. When bread is again cut up, soaked again, and baked again and in this way becomes better, then I will have myself rebaptized." Here it can be ascertained that the confrontation with the Arianism of the Germans was not only a matter for theologians and pastors, but also for the laity. The possibilities for the clergy were extraordinarily limited: Gaiseric forbade not only solemn Catholic funerals with chants and hymns, because he regarded them as effective propaganda, but he also received reports on the sermons of the Catholic clergy. Anyone who had spoken of Pharaoh or Nebuchadnezzar or a similar figure from the Old Testament was accused of having thereby meant the king and was sent into exile. Gaiseric's successor, Hunneric, in 483 again prescribed the creed of the Synod of Rimini of 359 for North Africa, because it was, he said, really ecumenical. The Vandals should be regarded not simply as Arians, but as adherents of the vague creed of Rimini, hence as Homoians. It is remarkable that King Hunneric appealed expressly to the anti-Arian legislation of the Emperors in order to use it against the Homoousians, the Catholics. When the Eastern Roman Emperor Zeno interceded with Hunneric to permit again the election of a Catholic bishop for Carthage, he demanded on his part freedom of worship and of preaching for the Arian bishops at Constantinople and in the eastern provinces; otherwise, the Carthaginian clerics would be exiled. Here can be recognized, at least in its initial stages, an Arian, or, rather, an anti-Catholic Germanic ecumenical conviction, which could not but appear threatening to the Catholic Church. Thus the clergy of Carthage preferred to renounce the election of a bishop, but had to yield to the wish of the people.

In his history of the persecution Victor included a book on the Catholic faith, in which, among other things, he presented the Christology of Chalcedon, that is, the doctrine of the two natures. Hence he was aware that only at Chalcedon was the definitive reply given to Arius. However, Fulgentius of Ruspe, Victor's younger contemporary, was first able to argue successfully from there. In addition to the scriptural arguments, which were known from the first Arian controversy, and were already developed in the lands of Greek speech, Victor profited from the text of the Old Latin translation. Thus he quotes from Jeremiah 9:10: "They do not hear the voice of the substance." What was meant was: "The hills no longer hear the sound of the flocks": in this way Jeremiah described the abandonment of the land of Israel, punished for its sins. In this passage Victor saw a proof that the heretical Arians, who would have nothing to do with the common substance of Father and Son, were facing damnation. Apparently the Vandals in Africa called themselves Catholics, while on the other hand they labeled both Roman Catholic

Christians and Donatists together as Homoousians. Thus Fulgentius could argue that the word "Catholic" was no more scriptural than was *homoousios;* the Arians would have to submit to being called the Triousians.

From the disciplinary measures which the Church had to adopt it appears that the struggle against Arianism was not always successful, but that many of the faithful, even clerics, let themselves be seduced to the Arian side. Thus in 487 Pope Felix II assembled at Rome a synod of the African episcopate to solve the problems of the apostates in the Vandal persecution. In his letter to the bishops of Sicily he made known the outcome: higher clerics who had gone over to the Arians should do penance throughout life; lesser clerics, monks, and lay persons should spend three years among the hearers and seven more years among the penitents, and for two years they must not take part in the presentation of gifts at the altar. Later, canon 9 of the Council of Lérida in Spain in 523 decreed that all who had had themselves rebaptized without compulsion might only pray for seven years among the catechumens and then two more years among the faithful before they were fully reconciled. It is noteworthy that no regulation was made there for those who had accepted rebaptism under compulsion, probably because the Visigoths in Spain did not resort to force. As a rule, the Arians, or, more correctly, the anti-Nicene Germans, insisted on the rebaptism of those converted to them. But as early as ca. 500 there were in Africa Catholics who went over to the Arians without rebaptism and expressed the hope that they had not sinned so seriously and would not incur the loss of eternal salvation. On the other hand, under the rule of the Catholic Clovis, who in 507 seized the greatest part of Gaul from the Arian Visigoths, there were conversions of Arian clerics. For then, canon 11 of the Council of Orléans, which met at Clovis' command in 511, decreed that they were to be restored to office through the laying on of hands of the Catholic bishop; Arian churches should be consecrated. The national Burgundian Council, which met at Epaon in 517, decided, on the contrary, in canon 33 that only such churches should again be taken into Catholic use which had been Catholic before their occupation by the Arians; the others should be thoroughly desecrated. Naturally, such decisions were possible only in the areas ruled by Catholic princes. Arian lay persons who converted to Catholicism should be admitted to the Church by anointing with chrism, which the priest might administer in cases of necessity; otherwise, the bishop. Gregory of Tours reports that both in Frankish Gaul and also in Spain it even happened that sometimes a new name was given to the convert. Gregory the Great, however, saw the reconciliation anointing for Arians only in the East; in the West the mere imposition of hands was performed. One will hardly have to reckon with a change of practice, but think of the Italian Roman custom, which Gregory regarded as general for the West.

In the first third of the sixth century Caesarius, Bishop of Arles, distinguished himself in southern Gaul as the opponent of Arianism. More important than his work on the mystery of the Holy Trinity and his Breviary against heretics was without doubt the fact that, due to his influence, canon 3 of the Council of Vaison in 529 prescribed the threefold *Sanctus* for all Masses. In this way it was probably intended to express that the three divine persons are holy in the same way, that is, they are of one being; for canon 5 decreed that, as hitherto in the East, Africa, and

Italy, so now also in the southern Frankish Kingdom the "as it was in the beginning, is now, and will be for ever" was to be added to the *Gloria Patri* in order to counteract the Arian "There was a time when he was not." No doubt such liturgical anti-heretical measures were especially successful and lasting. In this connection it must be mentioned that the insertion of the Creed of Nicaea-Constantinople into the Mass, which had taken place at Constantinople as early as the beginning of the sixth century, represented for the West an anti-Arian measure. The Visigothic King Recared decreed, in the introduction to the Third Council of Toledo in 589 immediately after he had converted to the Catholic faith with his people, that from now on this Creed was to be recited aloud at all Masses before communion. In the Spanish Visigothic Kingdom Recared also decided, as earlier in the Frankish Kingdom of Clovis, to retain celibacy for the reception of Arian clerics into the Catholic clergy, in case they were prepared. Here a new ordination seems, however, to have been required; in any event, there is mention that the "blessing of the priesthood" must be received again.

The encounter between the African Bishop Fulgentius, banished to Sardinia but briefly recalled to Carthage, and the Arian Vandal King Thrasamund ca. 515 represented an outstanding episode, which could indeed be likened to that between Ambrose and Theodosius. For this occasion Fulgentius composed his still extant three-volume work for King Thrasamund. It is not surprising that for the period of Justinian's wars against the Germans there were no reports of theological discussions.

The discussion with Oppila in 584 makes known that Gothic Arianism in Spain had meanwhile changed. Oppila professed himself to be orthodox — Father, Son, and Spirit are *unius virtutis* — and participated in the Mass but without communicating. But afterward Gregory took him to task, for he declared that he had stopped short because of the *Gloria Patri.* Glory must be given to the Father through the Son in the Holy Spirit. In this Gregory recognized him as a heretic and discussed at length but without success, in order to convince him of the correctness of the Catholic formula: "Glory to the Father and the Son . . ." If the report is included that the Arian Visigothic King Leovigild began to pray in Catholic churches and stated that the Son is *aequalis Patri* but he could not recognize the Holy Spirit as God, then it is seen how thoroughgoing was the change which King Leovigild imposed at the Arian Council of 580 — the only one of which we know: cessation of the demand for rebaptism, recognition of the equal divinity of the Son. Nevertheless, it is surprising that the King then clung so tenaciously to the Arian form of the *Gloria Patri.* From this it probably appears that the Arians, and a *fortiori* the Arian kings who ruled their Churches, were not really concerned with theologically pondered considerations, but rather with traditions, even with liturgical forms. In any case, Leovigild, of course without intending it, had prepared the conversion of his entire nation to Catholicism, by decreeing on the whole a decisive change which, in addition, already represented the half-way point to the Nicene profession; for, through it, Arianism, which lived only on the basis of the tradition, could not but be convulsed. On the other hand, through this deep intrusion into dogma and ecclesiastical discipline, Leovigild must have prepared the supremacy of the later Catholic kings over the Church, especially since one must reckon with the fact that among the bishops of the Third Council of Toledo in 589, at which King

Recared acted so authoritatively, were some who had taken part in Leovigild's Arian Synod of 580 but had meanwhile become Catholics.

Special doctrinal discussions of course occurred on the occasion of the marriages of princes, as, for example, when ca. 565 the Arian Visigothic Princesses Brunhildis and Galswintha went from Spain as wives of two Frankish kings and were converted as a result of "the preaching of the bishops and the urgings of the kings," professed the Holy Trinity, and were anointed with chrism. It is interesting that in the reverse case, that is, when a Catholic Frankish princess, Ingundis, came to Spain as the wife of an Arian Visigothic prince, Hermenegild, Gregory attributed the preaching to her. She thereby brought it about that Hermenegild became a Catholic, received the anointing with chrism, and in this connection even received a new name, John. Despite the threats and blows of her mother-in-law, who even had her thrown into the Arian baptismal font in an effort to force her rebaptism, the Frankish Princess Ingundis declared in Spain: "It is sufficient that I was once cleansed of original sin by the healing bath of baptism and professed the Holy Trinity in one equality." Ingundis' resolution may have contributed to King Leovigild's abandoning the demand for rebaptism. From the conduct of the three princesses, from the intervention of Leovigild and similar procedures in Vandal Africa, it may be concluded that Catholic Christianity developed an individual denominational moral sense among the newly converted German peoples, whereas Arian Christianity continued to be determined by the principles of the German *comitatus.*

The struggle against Arianism, however, easily operated to the other extreme. King Chilperic, who also on other occasions showed himself to be quite pretentious, composed a dogmatic decree on the Trinity and intended to oblige all bishops to it. Gregory of Tours at once recognized that in it Sabellianism was merely undergoing a revision, but only the Bishop of Albi was able to dissuade the King from his plan, which in any event had to be fitted into the total confrontation with Arianism. At the time a good share of this argument was borne by lay people, probably even by lay people of nonnoble rank, even if detailed accounts of this are lacking. Thus the merit for overcoming Arianism belongs not only to the outstanding figures among bishops and theologians, but to the totality of the Roman Catholic faithful.

The Arian German domination in North Africa and Italy, which had experienced in the sixth century a development working in the opposite direction, in the sense that the Vandals moved from intolerance to a certain toleration in regard to Catholics, whereas in the Kingdom of Theodoric the Great the converse was true, ended in both cases in the middle of the sixth century in Justinian's reconquest. The Visigoths' Arian domination in Spain, which had been rather tolerant until ca. 580, but then for a short time under Leovigild had exerted pressure on the Catholics, became Catholic under King Recared in 586, so that toward the end of the sixth century Arianism could really have been overcome everywhere if the Lombards had not produced a certain epilogue. It cannot be determined exactly what, as regards faith, they really brought with them to Italy; it is certain that many of them were still pagans, but they appeared not as persecutors of the Catholics but rather as brutal warriors. Religiously and ecclesiastically, the Lombards, though masters of Italy, felt themselves overcome by the people they ruled. True, under the Lombard King Rothari, hence in the second quarter of the seventh century, there was in many a city of Italy besides the Catholic also an

Arian bishop, but we hear nothing about theological controversies. From ca. 640 to 680 the Lombards converted to Catholicism, something that was facilitated from them by the circumstance that the Catholic Church was in opposition to Byzantium either because of the quarrel over the Three Chapters or because of the Monothelite controversy, so that they did not have to accept the religion of their political opponents.

What the Catholic writers transmit does not permit us to assume a very high theological level among the Arians. However, some important testimonies are still extant. Thus the famed *Codex Argenteus,* which is kept at Uppsala, a Bible manuscript written with silver ink, must have been written in Italy in the time of Theodoric and is proof of a high Arian religious culture. That there were also Arians of high theological and scientific rank can be deduced from a codex which was apparently written in Italy in the sixth century by an educated Goth. There is found on the wide, originally empty border of a *codex* of Ambrose, which contained the first two books *De fide* of the Bishop of Milan and the *Gesta Aquileinensia,* hence the acts of the Synod of Aquileia of 381, the *Dissertatio Maximini contra Ambrosium.* Hence the writer of the gloss attached importance to correcting the report on that Synod influenced by Ambrose by this means, that he wrote into the same *codex* the work of the Arian Maximinus against Ambrose. This theological level of Gothic Arianism may have survived the political dominance. In any event, the polemic which Bishop Agnellus of Ravenna composed ca. 560 against Arianism was directed against Arian Goths.

Accomplishment and progress, but at the same time also endangering and one-sidedness of the anti-Arian theology, which had an impact on the future and to a degree even today, are seen most clearly in Fulgentius. At the beginning of the sixth century bishop of the North African city of Ruspe, he was during most of his episcopate an exile in Sardinia. He stood forth not only as the greatest Latin theologian of his century, but also as the most determined and profound opponent of the anti-Nicene Homoian creed of Seleucia-Rimini upheld by the Germans. In his anti-Arian works he quoted especially Cyprian and Tertullian, hence pre-Nicene authors, but not, for example, Augustine by whom he was so strongly influenced that he could be called the abbreviated Augustine. He argued against the Germans, who had stopped on the position of the Synod of Seleucia-Rimini, from the height, meanwhile achieved, of Trinitarian theology and the development of Christological dogma. Thus, for example, he aimed so to speak that no one could impute to him either the idea of two Christs or the introduction of a fourth person into the Trinity. And so, in regard to this basically out-dated confrontation, he had at hand the anti-Nestorian concern of the fifth century and the anti-Apollinarist concern of the fourth. Indeed, he could even expound results of the purely theological development of the Vandals, not supported by ecclesiastical definition, as necessary for salvation. This was true especially of Augustine's psychological analogy of the Trinity, which in him is found as *memoria — intelligentia* (respectively *cogitatio* or *verbum) — voluntas.* For example, he declared against Fabian that whoever later wanted to learn the truth of the Creator himself now had to look at the picture of the Creator in the mirror of created man; through this faith one could ascent to the sight. But Fulgentius did not stop with Augustine: in some Christological questions he went far beyond him. For Augustine, the soul of the Redeemer was, as it were, the connecting link between his divinity and his humanity, so that at the moment of his death the divinity remained united only with the soul, but not with the body. Fulgentius, on the contrary, repeatedly stressed the idea that the divinity of Christ remained united with the body at his death; hence at least in this point he was influenced by eastern Christology, for the first to express himself clearly in this sense seems to have been Gregory of Nyssa. Fulgentius championed his doctrine probably not only to stress the omnipresence of the supernatural nature of Christ and from there to prove its divinity, but also to expound its incapacity to suffer, which for the anti-Nicene Germans was always unacceptable: in the biblical accounts of the Passion they found the proof of the inferior divinity of Christ. Fulgentius developed at least an elementary psychology of Jesus: It was of his human soul that it was said it did not yet know the good and the evil; of it was said that it grew in wisdom and grace. In this too appeared the significant progress of the Nicene position in relation to the Arian dispute of the fourth century. Even more it was the result of the Catholic Trinitarian theology, that had meanwhile become common property, that Fulgentius attributed all appearances and all supernatural effects to the entire Trinity and thus merged the divine persons to such a degree that their invocation became indistinguishable. Against the argument of the anti-Nicene Fabian, that the "Our Father" is addressed to the Father alone and the sacrifice of the Church is offered to the Father alone, hence Son and Spirit are of a lower rank, Fulgentius reacted decisively and maintained that not only the "Our Father" but also the sacrifice of the Church are directed to the entire Trinity; the same applies to the prayer of the prophets; the Father alone was named so that the danger of polytheism could be avoided; because the Trinity is only one substance and effects our salvation in inseparable power and goodness, it is invoked together, even under the Father's name. If Fulgentius rejects the view that Exodus 3:14f. refers to the person of the Father alone, and immutable being is attributed to him alone, with the argument that it would follow from this that the Father had appeared, then this sounds archaic and recalls the ideas of the apologists and the pre-Nicene theology in general. Hence it was expected that the appearance would be attributed to the Son, and Fulgentius thus interprets the divine appearance: God made himself visible by means of a *creatura subiecta;* hence Exodus 3:14 must refer to the entire Trinity. Of course, Fulgentius still knew that some (*aliquanti,* apparently not only anti-Nicenes) referred to the revelations of God in the Old Testament and the coming down of God to the Son: but the future did not belong to this interpretation.

The opponents of Fulgentius also, even though they appealed to the Council of Seleucia-Rimini, did not entirely stop in the first phase of the theological discussion of the Trinity, but included the question of the Holy Spirit with it. Fabian, for example, regarded the Holy Spirit as a subordinate essence of lesser rank, because one did not pray for his coming but that he be sent. Hence here an argument from the prayer practice of the Church was opposed to the argument from the baptismal form, usual on the Catholic side, for the divinity of the Holy Spirit. The sending of the Holy Spirit, however, according to Fulgentius, could not be compared to the sending of the angels, as Fabian did it; the Spirit is regarded rather as sent by Father and Son for this reason that he proceeds from the Father and the Son, *a patre filioque procedit.* Hence the later disputed *Filioque* had at least an anti-Arian root. But the procession gives to the Holy Spirit an entirely special rank. While essence of begotten or born can be transmitted from the one Son to the many adoptive sons, procession applies only to the Holy Spirit and cannot be stated of any creature. Fabian had appealed for the lesser divinity of the Son to this, that man was created according to his image, hence according to that of the Son. But Fulgentius insisted that man is an image of the entire Trinity. Without quoting the Augustinian analogy of the Trinity, he betrayed how very much he was dependent on it in this passage. But this meant, on the one hand, that only the intellectual part of human nature is understood as the image of God, namely, memory — understanding — love, as representation of Father, Word, and Spirit, and, on the other hand, that, without this being intended, the relation of God to man is no longer a personal relation but appears as a natural reflection. Each has considerable consequences for Christian morality and piety in so far as, on the one side, the entire Trinity is, as the one substance, the one addressed in prayer and sacrifice, and, on the other side, no positive importance can any longer be assigned to sexuality, for example. Of course, the ideas of Fulgentius and of the other Catholic defenders of Nicaea were not so much pushed in this direction by original hostility to the body as rather by the insight that all statements about God can be made only in analogy. On the contrary, the opponents of Nicaea wished to imagine the divine as they imagined the human. Indeed, Fulgentius blamed them for expressing thoughts of flesh and blood, which cannot inherit the kingdom of God (cf. 1 Cor. 15:50). Such argumentation no doubt made an impression, but it confused the requirement which must be placed on philosophical thought with the New Testament requirement of penance and conversion.

To the former Catholic monk, then Arian priest Fastidiosus, who thought that it would follow from the indivisibility of the Trinity that it had been born together, suffered together, and so forth, Fulgentius replied with the aid of Chalcedonian Christology: Just as in Christ there are not two persons, although the special character of each of the two natures persists, so too the assumption of human nature was not common to the entire Trinity. In this connection attention must be directed to a significant weakness of Fulgentius' theology, which clearly called for compensation. Although the unity of the person of the Redeemer was for Fulgentius an established theological possession, just as the duality of natures, it must be stated that he had no concept of person in the sense of personality, but understood *persona* almost as something natural: God suffered in the Man, because the person of God and of the Man is only one; God did not suffer with the Man, because the substance of God and of Man is not blended in the one Christ. Because of the unity of the person, Scripture attributes suffering to the Son of God, but the divinity of Christ itself, which suffered for us according to the flesh, must be regarded as immortal and incapable of suffering. Hence not the person is the subject, but the divinity of Christ. Finally, Fulgentius could even draw a parallel between the person-unity of God and Man in Christ, which signifies suffering and resurrection of the Son of God, with the nature-unity of Father and Son, in consequence of which the sacrifice of the Son by the Father is at the same time a self-sacrifice of the Son. If, however, he says that both priest and also sacrificial gift are accomplishments and names of Christ's human nature or the total Man offered himself or employed his soul respectively, then the humanity in the Redeemer appears almost as an autonomous subject alongside the divinity of Christ. Thus Fulgentius comes suspiciously close to Nestorianism, because he lacks Cyril of Alexandria's doctrine of appropriation, that the Son of God made the flesh his very own with all its sufferings, and he also thought that in the anti-Arian opposition he had to insist that the entire Trinity is the subject of the sacrifice. Nevertheless, he there succeeded, where he renounced the concepts of nature and person, in expressing himself not only as authentically Cyrillan but as completely orthodox in the sense of the Universal Church, by employing the slogan of Cyril, "one and the same," adopted by Chalcedon. One and the same Christ experienced in the humanity what was of man, but in the divinity he remained incapable of suffering and immortal.

The discussion of the idea that Christ suffered in his supernatural nature led Fulgentius to claim that Christ assumed a rational soul with its *passiones* for the purpose of freeing our souls from all *passiones*. There redemption is interpreted very one-sidedly, more Stoically than biblically. Hence the biblicism of the Arians evoked in the Catholics a moving away from the Bible in the direction of philosophical positions. This also operated exactly as one-sidedness in the theology of the Trinity. While the Nicenes of Serdica in 343 had still conceded that the Father is greater than the Son precisely on the basis of the name of Father, for Fulgentius the Son is subordinate to the Father only as the Incarnate One; indeed, the Father must not even be placed before the Son. Thus anti-Arianism led to the complete leveling of the theology of the economy of the Trinity.

A similar one-sidedness can be ascertained in the image of the Church: the true Church is characterized almost only by the faith in a Trinity undivided in substance; the saving faith seems to be only the profession of God one in substance. The proclamation of God's saving work in the historical Jesus moves into the background. For his ecclesiology, Fulgentius relied on Cyprian, but for Cyprian there was outside the Church, the one Mother, absolutely nothing worth recognizing, Christian, endowed with grace. Fulgentius, however, as heir of the Augustinian anti-Donatism, sought the following compromise: The Church as Mother is like Sarah, and the schismatic or heretical communities are to be compared to her maid. The children of the maid could also be saved, if they came to the true Mother; only then is the truth of the paternal seed of use to them, namely, baptism administered validly in heresy. However, it appears there when membership in the Church determines the effectiveness of the true divine gift of grace, when the Church stands above God or at least closer to the feeling of the believer or to the theological thinker. Thus this greatest theologian of the West in the sixth century is a proof of how fateful on the one side was an antiheretical position, especially then when the development of theology had proceeded beyond this controverted point, and on the other side how necessary was the acceptance of the total achievement of the past generations of theologians. The Spanish Liturgy especially displayed the effort again and again to stress the equal divinity of Christ and the Holy Spirit. That the language of prayer glides and it is often unclear which divine person is meant seems to be intention rather than carelessness. Something similar, if softened, could be found in the Gallic Liturgy. But the fact that the Spanish Bishop Braulio of Zaragoza (d. 651) spoke of the Creator Christ the Lord has in this connection not received the importance that similar expressions of Gregory the Great have. For example, in his seventh Sermon on Ezekiel 1–3 (no. 2) he called Christ both Judge and Creator; Christ is our Maker (*auctor noster,* ibid., no. 4); Christ is Maker and Redeemer of the human race (ibid., no. 12); Christ is the Creator of all, even of the angels (ibid., no. 19); Christ is the *sublimis Deus,* of whom there is mention in Ezekiel (ibid. 8, 2); Christ is the ever active God, who inwardly infuses grace, while outwardly he draws man to himself. Indeed, just where Gregory stressed against Pelagius that we can do any good only on the basis of the Lord's gift (ibid. 9, 2) it was clear that he was thinking of Christ as God. And so his viewpoint, also in this connection, was more strongly anti-Arian than anti-Pelagian. Since Gregory, with his letters, homilies, and scriptural exegesis was of such importance for all of medieval devotion, it is not surprising if this outlook was disseminated: the *Heliandlied,* for example, was entirely influenced by it. Perhaps that custom of our age still simply to call the Crucified One the Lord God — compare "carving of the Lord God," "shrine of the Lord God" — is a final offshoot of that anti-Arian exertion to stress the divinity of Christ by every means. In any event, it must be affirmed that the Western Church was never so enduringly influenced by any dispute as by the struggle with Arianism. The two controversies still to be treated were rather episodes.

The Semipelagian Quarrel

Fulgentius was also the one who completed the Augustinian doctrine of grace. With a view to the so-called Semipelagians, that is, those theologians such as the monk John Cassian and Bishop Faustus of Riez in southern Gaul, who had understood man's desire for salvation as the achievement of his own will and predestination simply as the result of God's foreknowledge, and whose view had prevailed at Gallic synods after 470, Fulgentius defended Augustine by pushing his doctrine to its most extreme consequences even if he did not overstate it. In Augustine are found contradictions, but not in Fulgentius. Augustine corrected himself several times — in his sermons he frequently withdrew, even quite far, from the theses which he upheld in his polemics. Fulgentius, however, came with inexorable logic, without letting himself relent through any sort of consideration, to the following chief doctrines.

The guilt of our first parents was transmitted through procreation. All men are unworthy of salvation and sentenced to damnation. The free will is fundamentally incapable of turning itself to the good. The grace of God is absolutely necessary to begin every meritorious work, to continue it, to bring it to a good end. The grace of God is absolutely unearned, all are undeserving of it, it is granted to men through pure mercy and in accord with God's discretion. God does not look at the future works of men to predestine them for heaven, but only to predestine them for eternal punishment. God's salvific will is universal (1 Tim. 2:4) only in so far as men are selected from all nations, all classes, and all ages. Children dying without baptism are condemned to eternal punishments. When it was objected to him that not only is baptism necessary for salvation, but also the eating and drinking of the Lord's body and blood, Fulgentius could thus interpret the reception of the Eucharist: Because all Christians are the one body of the Lord, one participates in this body at the moment when one is added to it, that is, baptized. Hence baptism bestows all that is the content of the Eucharist.

For the rest, it is not the sacrament of baptism as such which grants deliverance from sin, but children are freed by means of the profession of others, since they are also bound by the chain of the unrighteousness of others. They are cleansed when others utter the spirit-filled profession, since they are also tainted by the carnal intercourse of others. Hence, because children are destined by the agency of others for condemnation in a twofold manner — through the origin and the transmission of sin — they can also be externally destined for salvation through the faith and the profession of others. Hence, on the one hand, the sacrament is here spiritualized and made relative, and, on the other hand, *carnalis concubitus* and *spiritualis affectus* are as equally contrasted as spirit (=grace) and flesh (=sexuality) are directly natural contrasts. This impression is confirmed if the original sin of man is understood as the loss of the soul's health (*animae sanitas*) or of the garment of faith (*vestimentum fidei*), so that carnal desires inflict wounds on man. It seems to be forgotten here that the sin of Adam consisted in the wish to be like God, not that the flesh gained the upper hand. But this is not the only one-sidedness which can be ascertained in this great disciple and executor of the testament of Augustine. He interpreted the redemption so consistently as a new creation that man could contribute nothing at all to it, and God's salvific action had to precede in time every act proper to man. This constraint in the time-scheme and this clearly natural, indeed material, understanding of the power of sin and the grace of redemption did not facilitate an agreement with the opponents of such an excessively consistent Augustinianism; these doctrines were not then adopted unreservedly by the Universal Church, although Fulgentius was regarded in the whole of Christendom as the expert in the theology of grace, and people applied to him from Constantinople itself. Fulgentius maintained that the eternal punishment of sinners was fair because they did not even wish to stop sinning, indeed they took more pleasure in the sin than in life; however, he also regarded it as freely decided by God that pardon took place only here on earth, and thereafter only punishment; God could have decided otherwise, but he did not wish to. The eternity of the punishment seemed to Fulgentius to be such a concern that it falsified his exegesis. Thus for him the sentence from the Sermon on the Mount, "You will not come out until you have paid the last penny" (Matt. 5:26), curiously became a proof for the unending pains of hell. The fact that he so understood the resurrection of the dead that only the just acquired a transformed and transfigured body, while sinners, on the contrary, received a perishable one, capable of suffering, was of course not his fault but the fault of the textual development, which had turned 1 Corinthians 15:51, "We will not all fall asleep, but all will be changed" into "We will all indeed rise, but not all will be changed."

As much as the emphasizing of grace and hence of the all-causality of God served to make man humble and take from him all pride, for example for ascetical achievements, so too, an unprecedented claim to authority could flow precisely from this. Thus Fulgentius declared that he intended to write to Euthymius in regard to the forgiveness of sins whatever God suggested to him; it is then necessary for salvation to say that exactly; but then the addressee must accept it. But at least equally dangerous is the plain application of the doctrine of predestination to one's own experience, especially if it went hand-in-hand with antiheretical polemic. Thus it is said in Fulgentius' biography (XXI, 46), which came from one of his pupils and displayed his spirit, that the Arian Vandal King Thrasamund did not let himself be convinced by Fulgentius, because "he was not predestined to salvation." Later Gregory of Tours distinguished according to this standard between Arian Goths and Catholic Franks and regarded the possession of Gaul as proof of the divine favor for the Franks. As much as the intervention of Fulgentius on behalf of the Augustinian theology of grace was a necessary reply to Semipelagianism, which had again established all of salvation, with the *initium fidei* as its basis, on the will of man itself, just as little could this theology be the last word in the question. The Church followed Fulgentius less than Gregory the Great, or, at first, Caesarius of Arles respectively.

Caesarius of Arles, the somewhat younger contemporary of Fulgentius, had, in the conflict with Semipelagianism, not thought so one-sidedly of Augustine's doctrine as final, but, so to speak, had reduced it to the degree generally tolerable to the Church. Since the condemnation of Pelagius, it was the conviction of the entire Church that God's grace is necessary for every meritorious work. But it seemed, especially to some monastic circles, not only in Africa but also in southern Gaul, that human free will was abolished by Augustine's doctrine; by means of the theology of Fulgentius, such suspicions were even strengthened. Freedom seemed to be maintained only if at least the beginning of conversion, the first step to faith, was understood as the accomplishment of the human will itself. Even if especially Bishop Faustus of Riez, who had earlier been a monk on the island of Lérins, had expressed himself in this sense as early as the fifth century, this so-called Semipelagianism must still not be regarded as the characteristic attitude of mind of the island monastery, for Caesarius, who helped Augustine to victory against Semipelagianism, remained to the end of his life entirely under the stamp of Lérins. Of course we do not have from Caesarius a theological treatment of the problem, as we do from Fulgentius. But the expressions frequently coming from his pen, such as "with God's help" or "if the Lord grants it," make known that, like Augustine, he was convinced of the necessity of God's grace for beginning, continuing, and completing every good work. To the hearers of his sermons Caesarius did not appear to suggest any Pelagian or Semipelagian errors; in any event, he rather saw himself compelled to take a stand against those who denied the freedom of the human will, Manichaeans and astrologers (*Mathematici*). The will was so important for him because it could directly substitute for the external good work: fasting and almsgiving are doubly good; almsgiving alone is meritorious; fasting alone, without alms, is not meritorious, because it is, as it were, only a form of thrift, that is, of concern for self. But to one who has nothing at all from which he can give alms good will suffices, that is: "Glory to God in the highest, and on earth peace to men of good will." Sermon 199, in which these statements are found (Chapter 2), was regarded as the most widely read of all Caesarius' sermons, and this fact was surely no mere accident. It is shown in this, that the popular preaching tended rather to moralize than that the height of the Augustinian theology of grace could maintain itself. True, Augustine refers the words from the angelic hymn of Luke 2:14, which characteristically do not appear in his early anti-Pelagian writings, to the human will in the work On *Grace and Free Will* (2, 4), but he there understood them entirely as the gift of God, not as the least achievement of man, as Caesarius did. Caesarius took pains to rework, in the Augustinian sense, the material for his sermons, which he took wherever he found it. Our God feeds (*pascitur*) not on the abundance of alms but on the good will (*benevolentia*) of the giver, appears in *Sermo* 197, 4, which depended extensively on Faustus; indeed, Caesarius could even so express himself as though man had to care quite alone for his eternal salvation. In *Sermo* 198, 2, he indeed said that the soul is fed by the food of the Word of God, but he then explained: "If we each year fill barns, granaries, and cellars so that our body may have food for a year, how much must we then lay aside so that our soul may have support for eternity."

In the discussion with his colleagues, Caesarius put the accent differently. At the Synod of Valence in 528 he was attacked because of his standing up in principle for Augustine. It was characteristic of him that he did not compose a polemic against this Synod but turned to the Roman See. "A few (*pauca*) chapters" came from there as his answer, which he himself designated as extracts from Holy Scripture made by the Fathers. Caesarius submitted them to a synod of his suffragans at Orange in July 529, which adopted them as their own. In regard to form, these *capitula* appeared with surprisingly little claim to authority. True, the first eight, which deal with original sin (1 and 2) and grace (3 to 8), are presented in the form of canons, beginning with "if anyone . . . ," but they do not end with anathemas but with judgments such as: "contradicts the Prophet Isaiah" or "resists the Holy Spirit." It was the two chief errors of Pelagius — that only the body of man, not also the soul, was injured by sin, and Adam hurt only himself, not his posterity — that were shown to be contrary to Scripture. Then there was question principally of expounding that God does not await the decision of the human will for the good, that he not only increases faith but also grants the *initium fidei,* indeed even the devout desire for faith (canon 5); that his grace precedes every good human impulse (canon 6); that the nature of man, of itself, with the enlightenment and inspiration of the Holy Spirit, is capable of no good work deserving of salvation (canon 7). Hence here was made a sharp separation between every supernatural salvific activity and every natural thing unimportant for salvation. And this is true not only of a part of men, so that some would be saved only by grace, others by the decision of their own will, but of all (canon 8).

Canons 9–25 present extracts from the propositions from the works of Augustine that had been collected by Prosper of Aquitaine. In some passages the harmony is not perfect, but essential modification probably cannot be established. The choice is, of course, characteristic; there is found no single expression on predestination or on perseverance in good. Of course, this is not due to Caesarius but probably to that Roman cleric who had made the selection from the Augustinian *florilegium.* Nevertheless, this selection agrees with the views of Caesarius. In any event, he emphatically stressed in his accompanying letter the necessity of the prevenient divine grace and the incapacity of human nature to acquire salvation of itself. It was his desire to stress, however, that with the aid of Christ's grace the faithful should and could fulfill what was necessary for the soul's salvation. He came to speak of predestination only in the sense that he angrily rejected the idea that some are predestined by the divine omnipotence to evil. Of course, neither Augustine nor his overly consistent pupil Fulgentius had claimed that. The question to what extent predestination may and must be spoken of was not answered by the Second Council of Orange. Besides, even though Caesarius had requested and obtained from Pope Boniface II an express confirmation, in which divine grace, preceding every good work, was again emphasized, it very soon fell into oblivion and was not again brought to light until the discussions of the Council of Trent. But Gregory the Great followed Augustine, on whom he extensively depended, only so far as did the Council of Orange, and thus showed that the Roman tradition, as whose expression it must be understood, had maintained itself.

The Quarrel over the Three Chapters

The decree by which the Emperor Justinian I condemned Theodore of Mopsuestia, the anti-Cyrillan writings of Theodoret of Cyrrhus, and the letter of Ibas to Mari evoked a powerful rejection in the entire Western Church. The sharpest and most detailed repudiation of the imperial decree was the work of the African Bishop Facundus of Hermiane in his *Defense of the Three Chapters*. Although he was clear as to the authorship, he declared that he did not wish to regard Justinian as the author, because in it he discovered a contradiction of the faith already professed by the Emperor.

Facundus knew he was in agreement with Justinian in this, that on the one hand one must profess as a definition against both Nestorians and Eutychians that one of the Trinity was crucified for us, and on the other hand that Mary is truly and really called Mother of God. But it must still be added — he apparently missed this in Justinian — that the same Lord Jesus Christ exists in two natures, that is, that divinity and humanity are not diminished in him. True, Facundus occupied himself essentially with questions of form in order to show that the Three Chapters should not have been condemned, but he also offered a few noteworthy reflections of theological content. Thus in John 1:14 he found an adequate scriptural argument against Nestorians as well as Eutychians and their Apollinarist ancestors: "The Word became flesh" designated the one person, because the same one, who is God-Word, became Man; "he dwelt among us" shows that the two natures remain, because another is the one that indwells, and another is the one that serves as the dwelling. Despite this Johannine perspective, Facundus declared that one comes through the humanity of Christ to the knowledge of his divinity, and thereby expressed a basic rule always valid for theology and faith, even if often not sufficiently observed.

Facundus did not think that the Eutychians would really return to the communion of the Church when the Three Chapters had been condemned. The attack on the Three Chapters would not succeed in freeing Chalcedon from the charge of pro-Nestorianism and thus make it acceptable to the Eutychians, but only in burdening it and fighting it. If it was a question of the defense of Cyril, then people would also have to attack. Later the subsequent Pope Pelagius I also adopted this idea in his work, likewise called *Defense of the Three Chapters,* composed while he was still a deacon. He followed Facundus also in this argument: if praise of Cyril were the sole criterion of Orthodoxy, then the Eutychians would have to be considered orthodox. But in his argumentation Facundus surely went too far when he claimed that the letter of Ibas should not now be condemned because it had been approved at Chalcedon. No synodal verdict was issued at Chalcedon on this letter any more than on the works of Theodoret, but there was question there of the person of the two bishops just mentioned, namely, whether they might be recognized as full participants in the synod and retain their episcopal sees. Later it was declared on the part of Rome, in order to reconcile the Fifth Council with that of Chalcedon, that at Chalcedon there was question of the sessions of an ecumenical council only to the sixth session inclusively, hence only so long as the imperial commissioners supervised the agenda; the rest, in which Theodoret and Ibas had been rehabilitated, were not binding and were also not approved by Pope Leo.

One will perhaps not agree with Facundus, but still show a certain admiration for the keenness of mind with which he defended the letter of Ibas. Since Ibas attacked Cyril only because of an Apollinarist opinion imputed to him, but then praised him because of his alleged conversion from Apollinarist error, a condemnation of the letter of Ibas means nothing more than subsequently to make Cyril a Nestorian. In the case of Facundus, as of almost all opponents of the Second Council of Constantinople and moreover of the opponents of the Three Chapters — later theology has to a great extent adopted this simple legacy — a defect in historical reflection must be ascertained, when he wanted, for example, to defend Theodore of Mopsuestia with the allusion that he had been praised by such orthodox teachers as John Chrysostom and Gregory Nazianzen: Theodore outlived both of them long enough to have been able to fall into serious errors.

That Facundus, however, toward the end of his work, tried to reduce *ad absurdum* the strivings for union as they were being pushed in the East, especially by the Emperor Zeno, by the fact that he declared that where one God is, there can be only one Church and not, for example, different communities of the same Church, may indeed seem logical, but it causes one to suspect an inflexibility in the discussions, which then brought no honor to the Christian name in the course of Church history. Facundus himself in fact remained inexorably consistent; Pope Pelagius, on the contrary, who as a deacon had definitely championed the Three Chapters, but then had probably realized that Chalcedon had not been denigrated by the Council of 553, perhaps also by the hint that he was the only one under consideration as a successor for Vigilius, had been moved to a change of position, but had to let himself be reviled by the irreconcilable Africans, especially by Facundus, as *nekrodioktes* — persecutor of the dead — because he had accepted the condemnation of the long dead Theodore of Mopsuestia. In this connection, Pelagius in his great profession of faith, which he made on his assumption of office at Rome, passed over Theodore in silence but expressly defended the persons of Theodoret and Ibas.

Most strongly compromised was, of course, the memory of Pope Vigilius. Occasionally he incurred a plain *damnatio memoriae,* even there where his papal decisions remained in force. Thus the First Council of Braga in Galicia of 561 appealed four times to the letter of Vigilius to Profuturus of Braga in canons 4 and 5, but without mentioning Vigilius by name, although it otherwise cited all papal decrees by the name of the author.

The most significant theological achievement in the quarrel over the Three Chapters, important even for posterity, was produced by the Roman deacon Rusticus, nephew of Vigilius. He was deposed and excommunicated by the latter because of his obstinate championship of the Three Chapters, that is, because of his opposition to recognizing the Fifth Council as ecumenical, but he found refuge in a monastery of the Acemetae at Constantinople. There he compiled the Latin collection of the acts of the Council of Ephesus, which was to serve not only the purposes of documentation but as an argument in the theological debate. He himself intervened in this with great energy and deep professional knowledge. True, his work on the definitions, which he himself mentions, is lost, but the chief outcome seems to have been included in the extant disputation against the Acephalae. In it Rusticus offered the results of the theological discussions which he had conducted at Constantinople, at Antinoë in the Thebaid, and at Alexandria. He showed himself in these discussions to be well acquainted with the Aristotelian philosophy and with real skill developed the theological speculative argument which Boethius had made important. In the theology of the Trinity, it is true, he displayed a greater obligation to eastern thought than to that of Augustine and Boethius by basing the Trinity of the divine persons not so much on relations as rather on *proprietates;* but in Christology he relied on Boethius' definition of person and at the same time carried it farther. "Person" was for him not the individual substance endowed with reason, but the rational individual subsistence. In this regard he seemed to be aware that person could not be defined in opposition to nature but could at most be described. Thus the person is the coming together, *concursus,* of all that describes the rationally endowed subsistence.

Surely the individual human nature of the Redeemer, considered purely in itself, that is, apart from his divinity, could appear as a person; however, the true reality does not lead to such a view, but rather to the intellectual defect, namely, the forgetting of the union, that is, of divinity and humanity in Christ. But at the moment when the spirit is reminded that that which is Man in the Redeemer did not, so to speak, remain in itself, but through the union became the special property of the subsistence of God the Word, he can no longer be regarded as a person. Here, while Cyril's name does not appear, his doctrine of appropriation is employed. Thus Rusticus can further declare that the humanity of the Redeemer does not belong separately to itself, as is the case with us, but is so united with God the Word that it becomes his own just like garment and tool. Consequently the humanity of the Redeemer is not so much itself a subject as rather in a subject. It thereby becomes clear that for Rusticus subsistence means, beyond substantiality, the being of subject. Thus not only was a step taken beyond Boethius and that which was expressed as still missing in him, but even more that Leonine formula was tacitly corrected in which the Word and the flesh of the Redeemer appear as autonomous subjects and which had aroused such anger among the Cyrillans. Here it is clarified also by a Latin theologian; this clarification being gained precisely in the discussion with Cyrillans that the Redeemer is a single subject and not a composite, but that the divine person is to be regarded as the subject of the human nature. Expressed in Aristotelian terms, this means that the humanity of the Redeemer is, in comparison to God the Word, to be understood not as a subject but as an accident.

The fact that Rusticus described the relation between divinity and the humanity in the Redeemer again in analogy to the relation of soul and body in man, as the theology of the fourth century had already done, does not represent a relapse into pre-Ephesus methods of thought, but shows how consistently Rusticus employed the Aristotelian potency-act and matter-form schema respectively and thus at least for a moment anticipated scholastic theology, which then of course, to its own hurt, was based not so much on Rusticus as rather on the less perfect definition of person of Boethius.

Consequences of the Quarrel over the Three Chapters

The quarrel over the Three Chapters produced for the ecclesiastical organization of North Italy much more decisive and enduring consequences than the exemption of the see of Pavia as a consequence of the Arian controversy. On the invasion of Italy by the Lombards in 568, the Bishop of Milan transferred his seat to Genoa, where he felt safer under Byzantine protection; likewise, the Metropolitan of Aquileia fled to imperial territory, namely, to the island of Grado. Both metropolitans rejected the Second Council of Constantinople they defended the Three Chapters. At first the Byzantines apparently took no offense at this. But the Bishop of Milan, since he was dependent on the Sicilian property of his Church, was very quickly induced by the Roman Bishop to recognize the Second Council of Constantinople and to condemn the Three Chapters. This led the bishopric of Como, which really belonged to the ecclesiastical province of Milan, toward the end of the sixth century, to request from Aquileia the ordination of a bishop who upheld the Three Chapters. Como then remained a suffragan of Aquileia into the thirteenth century. In this it became clear that the question of the Three Chapters agitated not only the episcopate but also the clergy and people, at least those of the clergy and people who came into question as electors of a new bishop.

For the Catholic Queen Theodelinda of the still extensively pagan or, respectively, Arian Lombards, it was a matter of course from her Bavarian homeland to recognize the Three Chapters, so that she refused to accept the communion of the Bishop of Milan when she learned that he recognized the Second Council of Constantinople. Thus Gregory the Great saw himself forced to have an admonition sent to her in which he defended the Second Council of Constantinople. The letter, of course, did not reach the Queen's hands; instead, the Bishop of Milan, Constantius, in whose interest, among other things, it was written, held it back because he knew that the Queen would be only more enraged by this defense of the Second Council of Constantinople. Gregory wrote the Queen another admonition, in which there was no mention of the Second Council of Constantinople, and praised Bishop Constantius of Milan for his prudence. Hence Gregory was prepared to overlook the schismatic agreement of Queen Theodelinda with the Three Chapters because he saw in her a strong ally for the conversion of the Lombards to the Catholic faith. He also decisively defended himself against the reproach of having abandoned Chalcedon; rather, he condemned all those who had been condemned by the four Councils and recognized all who had been recognized by them.

Gregory proceeded much more decisively against Bishop Severus of Aquileia, who had been detained for a year at Ravenna by the Byzantine Exarch Smaragdus and during this time had maintained communion with the opponents of the Three Chapters, the adherents of the Second Council of Constantinople. The next year he had returned to Grado, where the patriarchate had taken refuge before the Lombards, and at a synod, yielding to the urging of his suffragans, he had repudiated the Second Council of Constantinople. Gregory now ordered him, with his supporters, the bishops who like him had maintained communion at Ravenna with the adherents of the Second Council of Constantinople, to Rome in order to hold there a synod on this question. From the long petitions of the ten suffragans of Aquileia living under Lombard rule to the Emperor Maurice of Byzantium it became evident that Gregory intended to have the Patriarch of Aquileia brought to Rome by police power, in regard to which he of course relied on a decision of the Emperor from the previous year. It appears from the Emperor's command to Gregory that Severus himself and his suffragans who were in Byzantine territory also wrote in the same sense. In this it is remarkable that these bishops did not intend to justify themselves before a synod directed by Gregory because they saw in him their antagonist, while on the other hand they hoped to gain from the Emperor a nonpartisan verdict. In the event that the Emperor did not intervene in their favor, they called to his attention that future episcopal ordinations in the ecclesiastical province of Aquileia would take place with the aid of the Gallic archbishops who were close by; this would then be to the detriment of the Church of Aquileia and to the harm of the *res publica,* hence of the Roman Empire, because thus far he ruled also churches in barbarian territory by means of the Church of Aquileia. In a pretty rough tone the Emperor commanded Gregory for the time being to leave matters alone until peace had returned to North Italy, until Byzantium had again won the upper hand. But this never happened: there was no victory of Byzantines over Lombards, but there was a change on the throne at Byzantium. Phocas toppled Maurice and exerted himself to solve the question of Aquileia in the sense of Gregory the Great. When Severus had died at Grado as Patriarch of Aquileia in 607, Phocas had Candidian, loyal to Rome, installed as bishop by the Exarch Smaragdus. The outcome was that the bishops in the area of Lombard rule repudiated this new Patriarch at Grado and in Aquileia itself — old Aquileia, as they said, elected an adherent of the Three Chapters, John, who then took his seat as Bishop of Aquileia at Commons in Friuli; later the seat was transferred to Cividale.

It seemed for a time that an adherent of the Three Chapters had succeeded to the patriarchal see even in Grado, but Pope Honorius I was able, after John's expulsion by the Exarch of Ravenna, to have the Roman subdeacon Primogenius elected and enthroned at Grado. The two patriarchates long remained separate, at least until that of Grado was transferred in the fifteenth century to Venice, where the patriarch had continuously resided since the twelfth century, and that of Aquileia was abolished in the eighteenth century. In all the rest of the Latin Church the opposition to the Second Council of Constantinople gradually died out without there occurring any too important controversies about it.

CHAPTER 73

The Epilogue
of Early Christian Latin Literature

The Golden Age of the Fathers came to an end in the Latin West in the fourth century, but the rich treasures of biblical exegesis and the great accomplishments of the Fathers in speculative theology were transmitted beyond the collapse of the ancient world to the Middle Ages. In the period here studied the ideas of the Fathers were reconstructed and rethought, especially by Fulgentius of Ruspe, and their works were collected and again and again copied and used for the care of souls and preaching, especially by Caesarius of Arles. There were far-seeing men of the ancient world who sought to save from the general decline all that was worthwhile; indeed they probably succeeded also, despite their view of what they believed was the approaching end of history, in preparing a new and permanent synthesis of the traditional treasures of faith and thought. Some Christian writers can be named, poets and authors of saints' *vitae,* but in this chapter after Fulgentius and Caesarius were treated extensively in the discussion of the controversies with the Arians and the Semipelagians, those four great men together with their theological achievement should be exhaustively presented and evaluated on whom all the intellectuality and piety of the Middle Ages was based as on four pedestals: Boethius, Cassiodorus, Gregory the Great, and Isidore of Seville.

Boethius

Boethius, who sprang from the noble Roman house of the Anicii, was at the beginning of the sixth century in the service of the Ostrogothic King Theodoric for several years. In 523 or 524 he was accused of high treason — for conspiring with East Roman circles — and executed. In prison he wrote for his own solace the *De Consolatione Philosophiae,* which has a thoroughly religious but not clearly Christian content. Boethius entered the history of the European mind through his translations of Aristotle's works, especially of the works on logic, and the commentaries he composed on them, as one of the great initiators of medieval philosophizing. Compared to the philosophical works, his theological writings are of clearly negligible importance. Nevertheless, they have acquired an extraordinarily great significance for Church history, especially for the history of theology and dogma. Through them Boethius became the founder of the argument from the *ratio theologica,* which then, scarcely a half-century later, the Roman deacon Rusticus used so skillfully in his fight against the decisions of the Fifth General Council, in his championing of the Three Chapters. In this connection the four works on the *Unity of the Trinity,* the *Three Divine Persons, How Substances Can Be Good,* and *On the One Person and the Two Natures* (in Christ) are rather occasional writings.

Boethius not only dedicated the first to his father-in-law Symmachus and the latter's other son-in-law Patricius, but he submitted it to their judgment. Because he discovered in all other contemporaries only intellectual sluggishness and subtle envy, he deliberately expressed himself concisely and introduced new words from the philosophical disciplines into theology, so that, besides himself and his two addressees, no one could understand the pamphlets, indeed would be scared off from reading them. Boethius was thoroughly aware of presuming something unprecedented, but he relied on the authority of Augustine and wanted also to be gauged by his works. In seven chapters he explained that the divine substance is pure *forma* that it is not subject to computation, that Aristotelian predicaments can be applied to God, that in God there must be talk above all of relations, because the names Father and Son express a reciprocal relationship, that finally the unity of God is based on substance, the Trinity on relations.

The three other pamphlets are dedicated to a Roman deacon John, probably the future Pope John I (523–26). Especially important is the treatise *On the One Person and the Two Natures against Nestorius and Eutyches*. In the introduction, Boethius reminded John that at a council, in which apparently both took part, a letter was read according to which the Eutychians confessed indeed that Christ is of two, but not in two, natures. Because Boethius did not speak at the meeting itself, he had agreed with John on a discussion which, however, both were then prevented from holding, so that Boethius had to write to John what he really had intended to present orally. To this accident the history of theology owes a definition of person, which in Scholasticism enjoyed the highest repute. Since in the controversy with the Nestorians and the Eutychians there was question of person and nature, Boethius first investigated, in Chapter 1, the concepts of nature and person. Nature is not only statically the manner of being proper to everything, but also dynamically the propelling power of the natural movement, *motus principium,* whereby, for example, fire presses upward and earth presses down. He tried to establish what a person is by exclusion: person cannot be in the accidents, but only in the substance, but likewise neither in nonliving bodies nor in irrational systems of life; besides, a universal idea cannot be a person. To personality, then, belong substantiality, rationality, individuality. And so there results the following definition: *persona est naturae rationalis individua substantia* (Chapter 3).

Boethius at once called attention to the fact that he here indicated not the etymology of person but an objective definition of what was meant by *hypostasis* to the Greeks. But he did not go on to the property of the person; he did not comprehend the idea of subjective being, because he proceeded from the question which natures really had person, hence which considered person as a characteristic of special natures and understood them himself as something natural.

Boethius' definition exercised, to be sure, a strong influence on all succeeding theology, but it provided no single argument for his own confrontation with Nestorius (Chapters 4–7). There person merely is that whose unity is maintained in the duality of natures of the Redeemer. The Christological speculation was only carried further by the definition of person of Leontius of Byzantium — being of itself . . . and of the Roman deacon Rusticus, who wrote at Constantinople — remaining in itself.

Especially noteworthy is Boethius' argument that the subordinate Two-Person-Christology of Nestorius did not do justice to the newness (*novum*), the greatness (*magnum*), and the singleness (*semel*) of the coming of the Redeemer. There was earlier intimate relationship of human persons with God; they were even for that reason called Christ. In this regard, Boethius referred generally to the authority of the Old Testament, but without quoting a single scriptural passage

In this it is made clear how with him the theological process of proof freed it-self from individual biblical arguments, but nevertheless remained convinced of being scriptural in general.

Cassiodorus

Cassiodorus, who had served as minister of three Ostrogothic kings in Italy, evi-dence of which is supplied by the edicts and letters of the rulers, the *Variae,* that came from him because they were formulated by him, in 535 left the service of the Gothic government that was becoming ever more anti-Roman and withdrew to private life. He had agreed with Pope Agapetus I to establish at Rome a theo-logical academy, in which professional teachers should see to it that "on the one hand souls could receive the preaching necessary for salvation and on the other hand the speech of the faithful should obtain the same care and development" as pagan philologists and poets had bestowed on their language, with the difference, of course, that everything that was presented should be "chaste and pure," and hence should be distinguished clearly from the myths and poetry of the pagans. Cassiodorus had been greatly pained that hitherto there was still no scholarly academy for Christian theology in the West, as one had existed earlier in the East at Alexandria and in his day was flourishing in Syrian Edessa. The Roman Church would share in the financing of the new Roman academy, which Cassiodorus him-self intended to help pay for to a great extent; but the war, that is, Justinian's recon-quest of Italy that had just begun, which led finally to the annihilation of the Ostro-gothic Kingdom, prevented the implementation of the project. After the conclusion of the war, Cassiodorus, who had meanwhile spent several years at Constantino-ple, returned to Italy. Although Justinian now gave new assurances of support to state professors at Rome in an effort to make good the damage done by the war to education, Cassiodorus did not again take up his earlier plan for an academy.

Instead, on his property in South Italy he founded a monastery which he called Vivarium, the center of whose life was represented by the library systematically established by him at great cost. For the monks he wrote two brief introductions to study or reading plans, by which they were to be introduced into the theological and philosophical literature respectively on hand in the library. He was aware that he thereby, on the one hand, entered of necessity upon the post of professor (*ad vicem magistri*) and that on the other hand his two introductory works could not replace a live college of teachers. Rather, this should be the task of the writings of the Fathers collected in the library, especially of the scriptural exegetes. Since only Latin works were available to his monks, he had pertinent Greek commentaries, of which no Latin translation yet existed, put into Latin and included them in the great commentary. This consisted of nine *codices* emended by Cassiodorus him-self, which contained commentaries on the following parts of Scripture: (1) the Octateuch, (2) the Books of Kings, (3) the Prophets, (4) the Psalter, (5) Solomon, or the Wisdom Books, (6) the Hagiographers, (7) the Gospels, (8) the Epistles, (9) the Acts of the Apostles, and (10) Revelation.

Among the exegetes were represented, besides the great Latin Fathers, also Greeks, such as Clement of Alexandria and Origen. At that time there were still no continuous commentaries on some books of the Bible, but only scattered remarks of the great Fathers. Thus in Volume II, that is, on the Books of Kings, and elsewhere, Cassiodorus collected the six questions and answers to Simplician by Augustine and three questions and answers of Jerome to Abundantius. Despite all his efforts, there remained gaps in the commentary. Cassiodorus sought to close them by, among other means, asking the priest Bellator to compose commentaries on various biblical books. But of all that Bellator contributed to Cassiodorus' work of collection — for example, two books on Ruth and the other outstanding women of the Old Testament — nothing has survived. The nine-volume commentary seems not to have been completely copied, but soon to have been lost. In addition to the commentators, Cassiodorus also collected in a special *codex* works of some of the Fathers that were introductions to the Bible.

In regard to this whole project, his work consisted not only in collecting the patristic texts that appeared to him to be important and helpful, but also in the preparation of a reliable scriptural text, which represented precisely a presupposition for the salvation of souls. The word of the two or three witnesses, by whom each matter can be decided (Matt. 18:16, Deut. 19:15b), which in Origen served as an exegetical principle — a theological statement is to be proved by two or three biblical quotations — became in Cassiodorus the basis of textual criticism: two or three ancient *codices* guarantee a text.

As regards the text of the commentaries, Cassiodorus in no way felt himself obliged to the true maintaining of what had been transmitted; instead, the orthodoxy and the value for edification of a work is the supreme standard. Thus he took care that on the occasion of the translation of the commentaries of Clement of Alexandria all his imprudent (*incaute*) expressions were suppressed. Cassiodorus was not impressed by the fact that a commentary on Paul was circulating under the name of Pope Gelasius but corrected, at least in the commentary on the Epistle to the Romans, all Pelagian errors which he discovered in it. Some texts with which he was not in agreement he let stand as they were but with a corresponding marginal note, especially, for example, in the commentaries of Origen and Tyconius. Cassiodorus also provided the biblical text with punctuation marks, so that it could better be read aloud. He himself revised the nine *codices* already referred to, but he left others to the work of notaries busy in the monastery. The mere spelling was to him so important for the understanding of the text that even at the age of ninety-three he composed for his monks a work on orthography, at the beginning of which he enumerated his earlier theological writings. The fact that here he began with the commentary on the psalms makes it obvious that he ascribed his work on the soul to an earlier, closed period of his life, to which also belonged his official letters, the *Variae*.

Although Cassiodorus found light from above in the entire Bible, nevertheless the psalter, the prophets, and the epistles meant the most to him, and at the same time they represented the deepest abysses and the summit of the whole Scripture. He felt beginners in the study of Holy Scriptures should first take up the fourth *codex* and so become familiar with the psalter. The monk should first fill himself with the reading of Holy Scripture, then apply himself to the commentators.

Theological knowledge is acquired in various ways: first, one should read the *introductores,* for example, Tyconius and Augustine, then the *expositores,* in the third place the Catholic teachers who have left question-and-answer literature. Finally one must carefully investigate the entire *corpus* of patristic literature that has been handed down. But it is not done with reading alone: there is knowledge which comes to the monk only in discussion with an experienced elder. Cassiodorus, it is true, sketched his reading plan for monks according to objective necessities, but the personal uniqueness of the individual must be respected. Thus he recommended to each of the monks to select one of the great Church Fathers, with whom he could engage in an inner dialogue. Cassiodorus hoped that his monks, through zealous study of the great biblical exegetes, would become capable of composing biblical commentaries themselves, so that the passages not yet treated by the Fathers might find their exegesis. He did not surrender the hope of being able to make scripture scholars of all his monks, but he reckoned that some would be capable of no intellectual work at all. They should devote themselves to horticulture, and for them the monastic library had on hand specialized works on that subject.

The simple man in the monastery, *vir simplex,* should, however, also come into the enjoyment of some knowledge of profane science and philosophy (*mundanae litterae*), because they contributed not a little to the understanding of Scripture; this is explained by the fact that, apart from some additions by learned men, they have their origin in Scripture, indeed they were directly stolen from it. Thus, for example, Abraham was the first to bring arithmetic and astronomy to Egypt. Hence the Fathers had recommended the reading of such works, because through them we are diverted from carnal things and led to things which could be grasped only by the heart. And so, abstraction is a means for the cultivating of spirituality. But for speculative theology Cassiodorus did not care: the Fathers interested him only as exegetes.

Cassiodorus did not devote himself to secular knowledge only because he was convinced that it served for the understanding of Scripture, but also because he found its rules and standards employed in Scripture itself; for example, in the book of Job, all the tricks of dialectics. Thus he felt himself to be justified and obliged to leave to his monks also a complete library of the *artes* and to introduce them into the study of the three linguistic disciplines — grammar, rhetoric, and dialectic — as well as the four mathematical sciences — arithmetic, geometry, music, and astronomy. This second introductory book actually represents a compendium of the accomplishments of ancient scholarship, and became the foundation for the medieval division of the *artes* into the *trivium* and *quadrivium.* The chapter on rhetoric, for example, would still be useful today as an introduction. Of course, it is surprising when Cassiodorus, who in this second introductory work was still addressing his monks, declared that, within the court speech — judicial trials were the chief field of activity for rhetoric — the narrative must begin with the description of the people involved, in which connection the person who belongs to "our side" must be fittingly praised, whereas a person of the opposite side (*aliena*) must be disparaged. The aged founder of Vivarium probably did not want to teach his monks such; instead, in these sentences one suspects a *verbatim* quotation from a work which Cassiodorus had in his library and which he excerpted for the introductory work. He seems on the whole, as must probably be inferred from occasional, unjustified repetitions, not always to have remembered the general view and to have simply followed a *codex* which he then had at hand.

It is surprising that this man, who ranks as a great statesman, to whom the politically successful decisions of the Ostrogothic government in Italy are attributed, and to whom, in contrast to the idealist Boethius, a more balanced realistic sense is adjudged, is said to have given to his monastery no constitution and prescribed no daily routine of life. Hence it is not surprising that in Cassiodorus some have sought to find the author of the *Regula Magistri*. But the fact that Cassiodorus, at the beginning of his last work, the one on orthography, in which he listed his religious and literary achievements, did not mention a monastic rule does not speak in favor of his being the author.

It must especially be stressed that Cassiodorus, in spite of all his preoccupation with ancient scholarship, still placed great value on emphasizing the differences in content and style between Scripture and profane scholarship. Indeed, he even meant that the Semiticisms, anthropomorphisms, and translation errors of the Bible were signs of the divine manner of speaking and therefore must not be subjected to the laws of profane language or literary scholarship. Thus, despite all his scholarly strivings, did Cassiodorus justify a fideist-authoritarian attitude, which long dominated the future.

Gregory the Great

Gregory the Great, the last of the four great Doctors of the Latin Church, lived in an age which neither required great intellectual achievements — there were no serious theological controversies — nor permitted them: anxiety over a vestige of calm and order, indeed over daily bread for the poor often monopolized the attention of the Roman Bishop. Gregory had to reorganize the administration of all the patrimonies of the Roman See, since these, for the most part in the hands of the local episcopate, had scarcely yielded any returns. He was concerned for the correct use of money; since the coins customary in southern Gaul were not accepted in Italy — they had a lesser gold content — clothes for the poor at Rome had to be bought on the spot and even in the hardest times Gregory was never only an almoner — young English slaves purchased to serve God in Italian monasteries. Gregory would have deserved his epithet "the Great" entirely from his ecclesiastical-political and practical pastoral accomplishments, but he was not only a practical man. Even his letters gave, where necessary, not only admonition but also clear replies in theological questions. Gregory's letters were clearly an inexhaustible mine for bishops and pastors who sought a model, but Gregory influenced the future more powerfully as the theorist of the pastoral office. Soon after the beginning of his pontificate he composed, as had Gregory Nazianzen, his *Regula Pastoralis* in an effort to show how justified had been his resistance to leaving the monastic life and accepting his election as Pope. In the first part he described the suitable candidate for the episcopacy, in the second the lifestyle which the office requires, in the third the necessary differences in preaching, and closed with a brief admonition to humility. When Gregory (I, 5) interpreted the Levirate Marriage (Deut. 25:5ff.) as the episcopal office and in the glorified Christ the dead oldest brother, but relying on Matthew 28:10, saw in the bishop the youngest brother, who must see to producing offspring or let himself be reviled by the wife (the Church), then this was not exegesis in accord with standards current today, but no doubt a suitable means for stimulating seriousness and zeal for pastoral care. Gregory attested and demanded an awareness of responsibility that is almost Donatist in color, when he asked: How can one request from God pardon for others who does not himself know whether he is reconciled with him? (I, 10). When, on the other hand, in Genesis 9:1f. ("fear and dread of you is on all animals") he found the rejection of any ownership of men over their fellowmen and thereby a limit to the blame and punishment necessary in pastoral care (II, 6), one may indeed agree with him in this matter today.

True, Gregory clearly saw in the bishop the superior, but he stressed that a candid word of a subject was to be regarded precisely as a sign of humble obedience, in any case by a pastor who is not full of self-love (II, 8). That Gregory equated preaching with admonition was probably solely conditioned by the time, but the third part of the *Pastoral Rule* offered in the enumeration of thirty-four pairs of opposites met in practice joyful and sad, bold and shy, obstinate and fickle, sinner in act and sinner in thought, those who do evil secretly and do good publicly, those who do good secretly but publicly have a poor reputation, and so forth — such a differentiated description and introduction to exhortation that even today profit can be drawn from them. In them Gregory's view of the bishop as physician of souls holds good; he would have had him understood only as preacher, if such an extensive listing of characteristics were neither necessary nor possible. Thus it is no wonder that the *Pastoral Rule* was everywhere enthusiastically received, as in Spain, where Gregory had sent it to his friend Leander of Seville, and even in the East, where the Emperor Maurice had it translated into Greek. In the Empire of Charles the Great several synods demanded the reading of the *Pastoral Rule* by all bishops. In England King Alfred the Great saw to its translation, together with the *Dialogues,* into Old English at the end of the ninth century and had a copy given to each bishop. It meant for the diocesan clergy what the *Regula Benedicti* represented for monks. Gregory formed for centuries the bishops who for their part formed the modern nations, and thus he became the great teacher of the West.

In exegesis Gregory is less original. He collected and passed on to the Middle Ages what the Fathers provided, without of course really intending it, because he was convinced of the approaching end. In this he is surprisingly nearer to Origen than, for example, Augustine and Ambrose, even nearer than Jerome. In his *Moralia in Job,* a commentary on the book of Job in thirty-five books, in the foreword the distinction of the three senses of Scripture is theoretically explained, and Gregory set out to demonstrate the threefold exegesis, but he did not stick with the three levels which he had so clearly distinguished in Book I; as early as Book IV the historical sense no longer interested him and from Book V the exegesis was only allegorical and moral, although Gregory was convinced that all meaning was lost if one did not take the historical sense seriously. The distinction of the various senses of Scripture could be found in Gregory by future ages, but their order is disputed. Most of the time, Gregory ranked second the allegorical-typical sense, which in part provides information on Christ and in part on the Church, and thus is twofold, and he ranked third the moral sense, that is, the exhortation to action contained in every scriptural word. Thus he used the deeper meaning only to justify the moral claims of the biblical word.

The ultimate goal in the context was action or, within preaching, admonition respectively. But the Bible was for Gregory not only the foundation of the sermon; it should also be read privately; the reader of the Bible is clearly the good man. In the framework of the sermons on Ezekiel the invitation to action seems not to be the highest and last; instead, the Word of God grows with the reader. The demands are only the external of the Bible; its interior, however, offers promises. Whether a person applies himself to the interior of Scripture is not placed fully in the preference of the interpreter; whoever neglects it deprives himself of the most valuable sense of the Word of God, which he owes to his hearers, because only thus does faith gain its fullness. In this regard Gregory was convinced with Origen that Holy Scripture itself compels appropriated exegesis: he counts all images, comparisons, anthropomorphisms, which would today be regarded as the literal sense, as allegorical statements. Nevertheless, he could be very tolerant in the exegesis of Scripture and concede that the one is satisfied with history, which will conduct him in the long run beyond himself, that another seeks the *intelligentia typica,* finally the third the *intelligentia per typum contemplativa,* that is, then, advances by means of typology to contemplation without having placed himself more deeply in the moral sense. But Gregory took into account that the way to contemplation leads by way of *historia, moralitas,* and the *intelligentia allegoriae.* This passage makes known that Gregory's piety is oriented not only to asceticism and moral activity but that his basically world-fleeing outlook revolves around the consideration of the eternal, around the vision of the promised good. Morality as the first step to knowledge was generally an ancient philosophical notion. If Gregory was really a man of antiquity, then for him morality could not be the highest and last. On the other hand, through this recognition of contemplation, springing from loyalty to the tradition, as the goal striven for in various ways, he protected the intellectual life of the future from having at once to prove itself by usefulness and thus becoming atrophied in pure expedience.

But Gregory exercised the widest influence on the future through his *Dialogi de vita et miraculus patrum Italicorum,* because they were read not only by clerics and monks, as were the *Moralia* and the *Regula Pastoralis,* but found their way to the laity. Gregory showed in these artificially arranged stories in dialogue form in four books that not only the East but also Italy displayed ascetics and wonderworkers. Besides Paulinus of Nola and Benedict of Nursia — the latter's deeds fill all of Book II — the heroes are scarcely familiar; thus the *Dialogues* must be used only very cautiously as historical sources. But in this is expressed not only an early Italian national pride, but also the insight of the pastor and promoter of the mission among the Lombards and Anglo-Saxons that the Word of God is only there highly esteemed where one is influenced by the life of saints. Thus Gregory sent his *Dialogues* to the Catholic Lombard Queen Theodelinda, in whom he saw his strongest ally for the gaining of this nation.

But Gregory not only narrated the edifying; he also introduced exegetical-dogmatic discussions, for example, on the question of how the saints, despite Romans 11:33 ("how inscrutable are his ways!"), have the knowledge of the divine decrees and express them (II, 16), or where hell is; whether the souls of the damned can be regarded as immortal (I, 42–44); whether there is a purification in the next world (IV, 25 and 39); how ecclesiastical burial and prayer are of use to the dead (IV, 51ff. and 55). Of course, such questions were not answered purely theoretically or exegetically, but with the aid of examples, visions and dreams from the lives of saints. The teachings on purgatory and on the expiatory power of the Mass thus found their securest place in Christian piety and from there in theology. That a priest secured eternal rest for a dead person by a week's penance and daily Mass did not influence the future as much as the thirty-days' celebration of Mass ordered by Gregory himself as abbot, by which a monk, who has sinned against poverty, after dying repentant was received into the company of the blessed (IV, 55); only this last usage continues as Gregorian Masses.

Gregory's teaching on penance and purgatory was based on the principle that no sin is forgiven without atonement, and hence was always in the danger of a certain notion of a balance-sheet, but this would of course be eliminated by the fact that the uselessness of external works without love was frequently emphasized. The basis for a certain intellectual imbalance of these doctrines on the last things lies in this, that on the one hand Gregory did not follow even the deeply revered Augustine in everything, and on the other hand, he first formulated views which up to now had prevailed in the Roman Church and thereby fixed them. Gregory's teaching on original sin was entirely in accord with Augustine's: all mankind is collectively responsible for Adam's sin, and children dying unbaptized go to hell. Sexuality is the refuge of sin, desire is already defilement. But in his doctrine of grace Gregory occupied an approximately middle position between Augustine and Semipelagianism: it is true that the gift of grace is the first beginning of conversion, but free will is not only, as in Augustine, the form of grace realizing itself but an agent which must be added to it. Thus Gregory understood Paul's sayings: "by the grace of God I am what I am" and "I have worked more than all" (1 Cor. 15:10). Hence Gregory tacitly dropped the idea of the irresistible grace and unconditional election and saw a certain merit in the assent of the human will to the prompting of grace. That God crowns his gifts when he crowns our merits means for Gregory that the free will acquires merits and finally God even imputes his gifts to man. Gregory arrived at no doctrine of predestination because the idea of *praedestinatio post praevisa merita* did not suit him. In him strict Augustinianism is limited by the demands of practical moral instruction; but Augustine himself had not remained entirely consistent in his sermons, and many a defender of Augustinianism at the beginnings of the fifth century had also not been able to be so. Gregory thus had the same convictions as the Synod of Orange, which was in fact only the expression of the Roman reception of Augustine. It was not known to the Middle Ages, but these obtained their ideas through Gregory. That he bequeathed to the future, besides important stimuli for spirituality and mysticism, also peripheral Christian subjects, has just been mentioned: an Augustinian-inspired feeling of unworthiness justified an intensive cult of the saints, especially then when Christ was seen as the Judge to come. Of course, Gregory did not go so far as to characterize the cult of the saints as an essential part of Christianity, as his somewhat older contemporary, Gregory of Tours, did. Finally, the Devil of the Middle Ages also appeared in that form in which he molested Dominic or Luther quite frequently in Gregory's *Dialogues* on the Italian Fathers. Thus Gregory passed on not only content to the theology of the future, but an abundance of ideas to the popular imagination and thereby to the plastic art and poetry, especially Dante.

Isidore

In the literary work of Isidore, Bishop of Seville from 600, which was impressive only because of its bulk and the abundance of its information, the question of the Three Chapters occupied only a little space, but it was, so to speak, a test question, with the aid of which Isidore's position is easily determined. In Book VI of his great encyclopedia, which treats of ecclesiastical books and duties, he spoke also of conciliar decrees and especially stressed the four synods worthy of veneration, which chiefly comprise the whole faith, without even mentioning a fifth synod. Of course, it need not have been expressly excluded in this way; Gregory the Great also occasionally kept silent about it. In Book VII of the *Etymologiae* (7, 12, 5), where Isidore speaks of God, the angels, and the orders of believers, he thus explains the title "patriarch": he is a patriarch who has an apostolic see, for example, the one in Rome or in Antioch or in Alexandria. Hence, Constantinople was not recognized as a patriarchate. In Book VIII of the *Etymologiae* (8, 5, 66) it is said that the Acephalae got their name from this, that no founder could be determined for them, they were opponents of the Three Chalcedonian Chapters, they denied the uniqueness of the two substances in Christ, and recognized only one nature in him. Isidore most clearly expressed himself in his catalogue of authors, in which he expressly vindicated Theodore of Mopsuestia: true, he was condemned by the bishops of the Acephalae at the instigation of the *Princeps* Justinian, but he was commended by praiseworthy men. Here, therefore, the Council of Constantinople of 553 is designated as a synod of heretical bishops of the Acephalae, that is, of irreconcilable Cyrillans. Thus any possibility of recognition of this Council was basically excluded.

That Justinian is named, not as king, but as *princeps,* seems not to be meaningless. For Isidore "king," is an honored name: one keeps the name of king only if one acts rightly; one loses it through sin. True, the title of *princeps* is also an indication of dignity and rank, but "king" (*basileus*) means very much more, namely, that kings support the people as a foundation. Hence, to Isidore, Justinian seems not to have been such a foundation. Apparently for Isidore whatever is connected with Constantinople did not rank as typical. Here not only theological evaluation but also the fate of Isidore's family became significant, because it was probably expelled by the Byzantines from Cartagena. However, Isidore seemed quite generally to reject the centralized world-empires, hence also the Roman Empire and *a fortiori* Justinian's work of restoration, for in his book on grammar he said that every people of whom the Romans had taken possession had brought to Rome, together with its treasures, also the blemishes of its language and of its morals. Hence so much that is wicked could never come together in national states as in a universal state.

In some respects Isidore is to be compared with Cassiodorus; but while the latter after his turning to the religious life attributed value only to Jewish and Christian historiographers, Isidore in his great work set Sallust and Livy on the same plane with Eusebius and Jerome. Thus to a certain extent in Isidore there can be ascertained a liberal assessment of ancient pagan scholarship in conformity with

Augustine. Isidore's works were hardly subject to a definite purpose; they were rarely apologetic and polemical and interested chiefly in knowledge as such. He himself had acquired great knowledge and he aspired to pass it on to younger clerics and his colleagues who expressly asked him for it. The most mature fruit of his willing acquiescence in such requests, of course, also of his own encyclopedic inclinations and perhaps also of the collaboration of a whole staff of secretaries, were the twenty books of the *Etymologiae,* which get their name from the face that Isidore offers a great many explanations of words — Book X is wholly devoted to explanation of words arranged alphabetically — but also occasionally and perhaps more correctly also called *Origines,* because Isidore expected to arrive at the basic origin of things through explanation of words. The work, in which all the knowledge available in Isidore's day is assembled, treats in its modern form grammar (I), rhetoric and dialectic (II), the four mathematical disciplines or the later Quadrivium (III), medicine (IV), laws and times with a survey of the six ages (V), ecclesiastical books and activities (VI), God, angels, and the orders of the faithful (VII), the Church and various sects (VIII), languages, peoples, military service, and degrees of kinship (IX), explanations of words (X), man and monsters (XI), living beings (XII), the world and its parts (XIII), the earth and its parts (XIV), architecture and estates (XV), stones and metals (XVI), agriculture (XVII), war and games (XVIII), ships, houses, and clothing (XIX), and finally domestic economy and storage (XX). The two books on the differences of names and things are like a preliminary study to the great encyclopedia. His different works on the Bible offer a number of *realia,* information on the biblical environment and times, but at the same time an abundance of allegories and possibilities of allegorizing, for example, on the numbers occurring in the Bible, so that the preachers of many centuries could obtain their equipment here.

Isidore could express himself quite naïvely on difficult theological questions, when, for example, in his *Differentiae rerum,* he speaks just as directly and simply about God as about things of daily life. Of course, he then appended a series of questions, such as: "How is the Father unbegotten?" or "Who will understand all this?" Thus he made clear that even in an encyclopedic presentation theology is not simply an exercise ground of the mind, but demands the highest respect and reserve. For the rest, Isidore was not only the expert on the Bible or books, but an observer of reality on earth. In his systematically theological work (*Sententiae*) derived almost entirely from Augustine, he had to speak of predestination and declared it a judgment of God which lets some people strive for the above and the inner, others for the below and the external; but then he stressed that in this great darkness man was unable to see through to the divine disposition (2, 6). Hence he distinguished between the order of experience and the order of theological statement of faith and thereby separated himself pleasingly from Fulgentius of Ruspe, for whom the Augustinian doctrine of predestination served to prove that clearly the Arian Vandals were not destined for salvation, and from Gregory of Tours, who saw in history the proof that the Catholic Franks were destined to expel the Arian Goths from Gaul. Certainly for Isidore the great experience which the Spanish Church had undergone, namely, the conversion of the ruling Goths to the Catholic faith, played a decisive role for his theological reflection. Probably it must also be stated that Isidore was no longer a man of late antiquity, that he

displays no longing for the old conditions, no enthusiasm for an empire, no faith in *Roma Aeterna,* no anxiety before the collapse of the world, as is the case, for example, with Gregory of Tours or, still more clearly, with Gregory the Great.

One understands that Isidore was admired by his contemporaries for his knowledge and that the future world willingly took over these rich treasures without making the effort to go behind Isidore. Thus to Isidore is due principally the break-through of the seven liberal arts in the early Middle Ages. His *Chronicle,* which was finished ca. 615, was used and expanded a century later in Gaul. As early as the seventh century some of his works had spread as far as Ireland. As in the case of Cassiodorus, so too Isidore's *Grammar,* that is, Book I of his encyclopedia, was by no means a grammar in our sense; rather, it is an introductory treatise to the various activities which pertain to a skill, to writing and expressing oneself. Isidore was the only one in whom in the seventh century almost all the wealth of classical antiquity once more resounds across the very limited period of late antiquity. For him the *artes liberales* were an express instrument of culture, that is, a tool for the cultivation of thought and word. In this he is distinguished also from his older contemporary, Gregory the Great, who could indeed express himself very properly in practice, for example, in the foreword to the *Moralia,* but in principle and theory rejected such efforts. Following the example of Augustine, Isidore counted historiography in grammar, because all that is worth remembering was written down. While in the other points he extensively followed the classical models, he showed himself independent in the definition of historiography and stressed that historiography, in contrast to the compiling of annals, was the work of eyewitnesses, who presented everything truthfully. Here the definition of historiography was gained by the aid of the idea of the gospels; hence it was defined in a Christian and theological manner. Even when Isidore emphasized that the ancient historians had written in order to instruct and educate later ages, he was influenced by the New Testament (Rom. 15:4).

In contrast to Cassiodorus, with whom he must be compared again and again, Isidore composed a monastic *Rule* and thus also showed the way for the practical organization of the life of monks. In this he was concerned for the divisions of the day, for the architectural plan of the monastery, for example, the location of the infirmary, for the publishing of books, and so forth. In Isidore's opinion, the monks should devote themselves completely to the spiritual life; but their life should be characterized chiefly by manual labor, though not by heavy fieldwork, which was left to slaves. If secular laborers sing unseemly songs during their work, then the monks must, *a fortiori,* praise Christ during their work. Hence, Isidore's monastery was not a monastery of intellectuals, like that of Cassiodorus, even though he was very much concerned for education. But the education of the clergy as a whole was a concern of his. For this reason the Fourth Council of Toledo in 633, inspired by him, complained in canon 25 especially of the ignorance of the clergy and imposed on the bishops the frequent reading of Scripture and the canons. Caesarius of Arles had also recommended the reading of the Bible as the means of education and of personal sanctification. The canonical regulations as obligatory reading were a new element, which was explained by the fact that meanwhile various canonical collections, such as that of Dionysius Exiguus and especially the so-called *Hispana,* had appeared.

In the *Liber Ordinum* (no. 43), which probably belongs to Seville, there is a special ordination for the cleric to whom is entrusted the care of the books and copyists. From the verses with which Isidore of Seville himself had embellished his library, it appears that external quiet was demanded in the *scriptorium*, and uninterrupted work by the writers was presumed. From this it becomes clear that no longer as in antiquity were multiple copies made by dictation, but merely individual copies, probably only on demand and by individual order.

Isidore himself seems to have taught orally also, but especially in his writings he supplied us with all that was then necessary for the education of a cleric, namely, the *humaniora* in Books I–III and X of the encyclopedia and in the two books of *Differences;* theology proper in Books VII and VIII of the encyclopedia and in Book I of the *Sentences* — Books II and III are concerned with morals and the guidance of souls — and furthermore in the book *On the Catholic Faith.* He passed on biblical knowledge in his work on the Fathers, in the allegories, and in the questions from the Old and the New Testament. If the *Collectio Hispana* really came from Isidore, he also took pains with instruction in canon law. Finally, pastoral theology is treated in the book on ecclesiastical duties and in the final chapters of the *Sentences.*

That Isidore was not an especially speculative thinker can be seen above all in his Christology, which, it is true, is thoroughly orthodox and takes pains to survey and preserve the doctrines of the Fathers, but which did not give attention to the achievements of the recent period, especially those brought forth in the dispute over the Three Chapters. Apparently Isidore knew no difference between *substantia* and *subsistentia;* if he says in Book VII of his encyclopedia (7, 4, 11) that in God there are three *hypostases,* it means in Latin either three persons or three substances, but in Latin substance is not expressed in the real sense of God but only *abusive,* for in the true sense of the word substance means in Greek person but not nature. It is interesting and, for Isidore, characteristic that in Book VII of his encyclopedia, where he enumerates the various names for the Son of God, he mentions not only the *homoousios* (7, 2, 14) but also the *homoiousios* (7, 2, 16); in this also it appears that he is in closer connection with the Christian literature of the fourth and fifth than with that of the sixth century, for Hilary had recognized the Homoiousians as orthodox.

Isidore forbade Christians to read pagan poetry, but he showed himself quite at home in it. Here one must not seek to discover an inconsistency. Perhaps Isidore was convinced of having provided for this work of reading and selecting once for all time for Christian education. In any case, he seems to have assumed that clerics must make the content of his works entirely their own. Thus he recommends the occasional reading and reflecting on brief sections. In this regard, one should read quietly because one can thus better grasp what has been read, and because the voice is spared. Of course, even better than the reading is the repeated discussion in common of what was read, because in this way what is obscure or doubtful becomes clear. Such discussion (*collatio*) was a custom in monasteries since the fifth century and in Isidore presupposes the community of monks or clerics. But Isidore definitely rejects the debate. Just as the *collatio* builds, so the *contentio* destroys. It loses the feeling for the truth, produces quarrels, even leads to blasphemy; for the sake of one's own glory the truth is often sacrificed; therefore sophistries must unconditionally be avoided. Hence even though Isidore transmitted to the Middle Ages a good part of his knowledge, he could not become the father of scholastic theology, for characteristic of it is the methodical new start of confrontation with opposing authors and even the debate.

If one surveys the work of the four Christian writers of late antiquity here presented — especially Fulgentius and Caesarius should also be reckoned with them — then one understands that they prepared the riches of the faith and of thought of Christian and pagan antiquity for a new unity to be created by the Middle Ages. In this connection it has already been said also that they were not yet able themselves to create such a unity. This literature is vastly inferior to the great accomplishments of the fourth and fifth centuries, not only in linguistic style but also in theological content. The reason for this must not be sought only in the general cultural decline, in the chaos of war, the destructions and daily miseries, but probably especially in the isolation in which these men existed. Cassiodorus and Boethius expressed it in saying that they found no debating partners; Isidore was admired by his contemporaries and was asked for new works and new instruction, but he was unable to obtain help and encouragement from them. But this situation is presented clearest in the *Dialogues* of Gregory the Great: true, there was a partner in conversation, but he really knew how to say nothing, and scarcely to pose real questions; Gregory himself alone had to see even to the progress of the discussion. Great new theological literature could not appear again until a new intellectually formed community had been born.

Book Three

THE CHURCH
IN THE AGE OF FEUDALISM

Translated by Anselm Biggs

Part One

The Church
under Lay Domination

Section One

The Papacy's Alienation from Byzantium and Rapprochement with the Franks

Eugen Ewig

C H A P T E R   7 4

Christendom at the Beginning of the Eighth Century

Dark clouds hung over the Christian world as the seventh century gave way to the eighth. The entry of the Anglo-Saxons into the circle of Christian peoples must have been of little significance to contemporaries, compared with the loss of the two ancient and highly civilized Christian lands which were buried in the second Muslim flood: Africa and Spain. The great age of Latin Africa was past when the catastrophe loomed. Justinian had recovered for the Empire provinces much reduced in size, but they had experienced an "Indian Summer" under Byzantine rule. In the controversies over the Three Chapters and Monothelitism the African Church had still had something important to contribute and many successes among the Berbers to record. The expansion of Islam, which at first had come to a standstill in Tripolitania, was resumed in 669. The Arabs occupied the province of Byzacena, where they founded Kairawan, the future capital of Muslim North Africa. Carthage fell in 698. Resistance by the Christian Berbers and the last imperial strongholds in the West was broken in the first years of the eighth century, and Africa withdrew from the Christian cultural community. What was left of the Christian minority grew smaller and lost all historical significance.

The Visigothic Kingdom had occupied a leading position in the Germano-Roman civilization of the seventh century. But domestic conflicts facilitated the adventure of the Berber Tarik, who crossed over to Spain in league with the Gothic claimants to the throne from the family of Witiza. At the battle on the Guadelete, at Jérez de la Frontera, on 19 July 711, the last Gothic King, Roderick, lost crown and life. The conquest of the kingdom was the work of Musa, Muslim governor of Africa. While the Arabs were also occupying Septimania, the Gallic province of the Visigothic Kingdom (719–21, 725), Pelagius, a swordbearer of King Roderick, tried to reorganize the Christian resistance in Asturias. Pelagius' victory at Covadonga in 722 assured the permanence of the small Asturian principality, but it did not acquire any real importance until the second half of the ninth century. The Church continued to exist in Muslim Spain, whose governor resided at Córdoba, but more and more lost contact with free Christendom.

The main power of the caliphate was, meanwhile, directed against the imperial city on the Bosphorus. The Byzantine Empire, convulsed since 695 by anarchy around the throne, seemed about to become an easy prey. The fall of Constantinople would, so far as one can judge, have opened up the pagan world of Central and Eastern Europe to Islam and thereby presented a mortal threat to Latin Christendom. The Arabs assaulted the walls of the imperial city for a solid year (15 August 717, to 15 August 718) but, contrary to all expectations, Constantinople held out. Its defender, the Emperor Leo III, became the savior of Christendom. Fifteen years later, in the Battle of Poitiers (733), Charles Martel brought the Arab advance to an end in the west also. Free Christendom had lost Africa and Spain but had repulsed the great offensive of the Muslim world and protected Central and Eastern Europe from Islam. The loss of provinces in the Mediterranean area was compensated by a mission in the interior of Europe. The center of gravity of the Christian world began to shift "to the inner West."

A presupposition for this change was the dissociation of Rome from the ancient Empire, which had become a Greek state and had its center of gravity on the Bosphorus. But to contemporaries this was an idea that could hardly be realized, since the Empire was not only a political but also a spiritual reality in which the Popes lived no less than the Emperors, despite the conflicts constantly breaking out since the *Henoticon* of 482. These conflicts were chiefly religious and ecclesiastical in nature, even if an Italian-Greek opposition stood out ever more distinctly in them. The Popes became Italy's spokesmen, but at the same time they spoke for a religious and ecclesiastical group which still saw the Empire as a unity. It should not cause surprise that Greek and oriental influence reached its zenith at Rome with the restoration of peace in the Church in 681. Of the thirteen Popes between 678 and 752, eleven were Sicilians, Greeks, or Syrians. Under Eastern influence the feast of the Exaltation of the Cross and the four great Marian feasts, Purification, Annunciation, Assumption, and Birthday, were introduced at Rome; they are first attested under Pope Sergius I (687–701). The *monasteria diaconiae,* all of them foundations of the sixth and seventh centuries and first mentioned under Pope Benedict II (684–85), displayed mostly Greek and oriental liturgical practices. They gathered in great numbers around the ancient *palatium* of the Emperors, which had become the Roman residence of the Byzantine Exarch.

The directors of the *monasteria diaconiae* probably played a role in the group of papal advisers, although they had not yet been admitted to the circle of deacons. The group of seven of the later cardinal bishops is first encountered in 732. The number of titular churches, whose rectors constituted the group of later cardinal priests, seems to have been raised from twenty-five to twenty-eight at this moment. Thus the circle of the future cardinals became gradually more distinct in the early years of the eighth century.

In addition to the clergy, the high bureaucracy of the *iudices* became much more prominent in the latter part of the seventh century. Already ancient dignitaries were the *primicerius* and *secundicerius notariorum,* who managed the chancery, and the *primus defensorum,* head of the Church's attorneys. These were joined by the *arcarius* (income), the *saccellarius* (expenditure), and the *nomenculator* (care of the poor and pilgrims). All the *iudices* belonged to the Roman nobility, which also naturally included the members of the imperial official nobility of non-Roman origin.

The Greek and oriental Popes were loyal subjects of the Emperor, but they represented the Roman viewpoint in ecclesiastical questions no less firmly than Popes of Roman or Italian origin. The Syrian Sergius I rejected the Quinisext Council of 692, which attached ecumenical validity to such Greek and oriental customs as clerical marriage and various details of fasting and liturgy. The anarchy in the imperial office, breaking out in 695, further weakened the imperial authority.

Iconoclasm, which, appealing to the divine transcendence, attacked the pictorial representation of God and the saints, emanated from the East, where in 723 the Caliph Yazid II ordered the removal of all icons from the churches. It then spread to Asia Minor. Germanus, Patriarch of Constantinople, opposed Iconoclasm, but the Emperor Leo III, who came from the borderlands between Cilicia and Syria, had meanwhile joined the opponents of images. He had the celebrated icon of Christ at the Chalke Gate pointedly destroyed in 726, thereby provoking a storm of indignation from the iconodule Greeks. The Emperor now sought to gain the Pope for his idea. Their correspondence, which was protracted through 728 and 729, led to no agreement.

The prohibition of 730 led to a bloody persecution of the opposition. John Damascene, a high-ranking Christian official at the court of the Caliph, became the theological spokesman of the iconodules. In 736 he entered the monastery of Saint Sabas at Jerusalem. In the eyes of John Damascene, who justified sacred art and the veneration of icons by means of the Incarnation, Iconoclasm was a final offshoot of Monophysitism. But the Pope firmly kept the ecclesiastical opposition in line and prevented the setting up of an anti-emperor by the troops of Italy. He did not give a thought to an alienation from the Empire. Nothing irrevocable had yet happened when Gregory II died on 11 February 731.

His successor, the Syrian Gregory III (731–41), again got in touch with the Emperor, but Leo III could no longer be diverted from the path he had taken. A Roman synod in November 731, at which appeared the metropolitans of Ravenna and Grado, "cum ceteris episcopis istius [He]speriae partis," expelled from the communion of the Church the despisers of ecclesiastical custom, who refused to honor sacred images and profaned them. What ensued is obscure. Perhaps, after a fruitless effort to subject Rome, Ravenna, and Venetia to his will by means of a naval demonstration, Leo III in 733 hit upon a decree which aimed to condemn Rome to insignificance. While confiscating the papal patrimonies in South Italy and Sicily, he cut off from Rome Sicily, Calabria, and the prefecture of Illyricum, comprising Thessalonica along with Macedonia and Greece, which had hitherto belonged to the Roman metropolitan and patriarchal jurisdiction, and attached them to the patriarchate of Constantinople. Or perhaps he simply disregarded the Italian opposition as unimportant and abandoned Old Rome, fallen from its former height, to its fate. Whatever it may have been, the Emperor took no notice of the warning already directed to him by Gregory II: "That the savages and barbarians had become civilized... The entire West offers fruits in faith to the holy prince [Peter]" (Gregory II to the Emperor Leo III).

Of course, it remained to be seen whether the "Western" basis would bear the strain.

C H A P T E R   7 5

The Revival of the Frankish Kingdom and the Crossing of the Anglo-Saxons to the Continent

The great Western power that united the Teutonic and the Latin genius was the Frankish Kingdom. At the beginning of the seventh century it had reached the first climax in its history, but from the end of the century it was menaced with inner dissolution because of the decay of the Merovingian Dynasty. This serious crisis was brought on by the assassination of King Childeric II in 675. Victor in the power struggle of the magnates was Pepin of Herstal. The kingdom was reinvigorated. This first *princeps Francorum,* dying at the end of 714, left no legitimate heir who had attained to his majority and who could have continued his father's lifework. And so the *Regnum Francorum* had to pass through the iron age of the bastard Charles Martel before reaching the great climax of its history under the Carolingians.

The illegitimate Charles Martel ruled Neustria to the Loire, but had to recognize Aquitaine as an independent principality. Only the victory over the Muslims near Poitiers in 733 opened up southern Gaul to him. In 733–36 he occupied Burgundy. Provence was conquered in 737–38. Thus the Frankish Kingdom was again constructed, and beyond the Rhine it was possible to incorporate Thuringia and much of Frisia. An effort was made to include Alemannia too, but it was not completed. In regard to Bavaria, like Aquitaine, Charles had to be content with a more or less effective suzerainty.

A second Frankish wave flowed over Gaul and Germany in the wake of the Carolingian reconquest of the Frankish Kingdom. The mayor's vassals from the Meuse, the Moselle, and the Rhine assumed the leading positions in the conquered territories and formed the matrix of the "Carolingian imperial aristocracy." The *princeps Francorum* provided new means of power for the central government. Since the crown lands and the confiscated property of opponents did not suffice, he had recourse to Church property, which had greatly expanded in the sixth and seventh centuries. The "secularization" was effected by direct confiscation or by the nomination of trusted laymen as bishops and abbots; they then placed the property of their churches at the disposal of the mayor for the equipping of troops. These brutal usurpations produced nothing less than chaos in the Church, and the metropolitan organization fell completely into ruins. Not the least consequence of the secularization was a powerful moral deterioration. The damage was least in the lands which constituted Charles' oldest center of support; worst in the territories which had been subjugated only after severe struggles. Charles' encroachments did not originate in an anti-ecclesiastical attitude. The Frankish *princeps* and his vassals were permeated with a strong religious emotion, which was powerfully stimulated by the struggle against the Muslims. They obtained their victories with Christ's help.

In the 730s Charles' position had become established to such a degree that he could leave the throne unoccupied and before his death divide the realm among his sons. In 743 the brothers again elevated a Merovingian to the vacant throne, but they quite frankly regarded the kingdom as their own. The subjugation of the Alemanni was completed in 746.

Roman missionaries had once journeyed to Anglo-Saxon Britain *via* the Frankish Kingdom, and since the mid-seventh century Anglo-Saxon pilgrims, churchmen, and kings had travelled the same road in the opposite direction.

Willibrord, born in Northumbria around 658, grew up in Wilfrid's monastery of Ripon. When in 678 his master was deposed from the see of York, the pupil left Ripon and spent the next twelve years in Ireland. There the Anglo-Saxon Egbert, who also had missionary ambitions, became his teacher. Since the Anglo-Saxon territories offered no further opportunities for missionary work following the conversion of Sussex and the Isle of Wight (681–86), Egbert in 688 sent his companion Witbert to the Frisians. The ultimate aim was missionary work among the closely related Saxons. But after only two years of frustration Witbert left. Radbod who was anti-Christian, had replaced Aldgisl as King of the Frisians. But Egbert did not become discouraged. At his bidding Willibrord sailed for the continent in 690 with eleven companions.

Willibrord went, not to Radbod, but to Pepin of Herstal, who had just re-established Frankish suzerainty over southwest Frisia. The earlier Frankish mission of Amandus, apostle of Flanders, had reached as far as Antwerp, which now became Willibrord's first base. Around 692 he went to Rome and obtained the Pope's blessing on the work he had begun. The mission then spread to other areas bordering on the Frankish Kingdom.

In these circumstances the Anglo-Saxon mission at first confined its attention to Frisia. At Pepin's suggestion Willibrord returned to Rome, where on 21 November 695, he was consecrated a missionary archbishop and given the name Clement by Pope Sergius I. The fortress of Utrecht, which had been again in Frankish hands since the beginning of the seventh century, became the seat of the Archbishop. During Pepin's lifetime the mission prospered, but on his death it completely collapsed. Only when Charles Martel had restored Frankish rule in southwest Frisia, could Willibrord resume the interrupted work. The church of Utrecht revived and was again endowed. Charles Martel's charter of 1 January 723, issued in regard to it, introduced a second phase of permanent missionary work, which, it is true, achieved enduring successes only within the Frankish frontiers west and south of the Zuyder Zee as far as the Yssel. His base was too restricted for a new ecclesiastical province such as the apostle of the Frisians had dreamed of. But when Willibrord died on 7 November 739, the foundations of the future see of Utrecht had been laid.

By that time Winfrid-Boniface was already the dominant figure among the Anglo-Saxon churchmen in the Frankish Kingdom. He came not from Anglian Northumbria but from Wessex. Born near Exeter in 672 or 673, he was sent for his education to the monastery of Exeter around 680. He later entered the abbey of Nursling near Winchester and was there ordained a priest. In mature life he decided upon the *peregrinatio propter Christum*. From the outset his aim was the conversion of the related Saxons of the continent.

It was just at that moment that Charles Martel had established his control of Frankish Austrasia. Winfrid, however, did not contact Charles; instead, he went *via* Neustria to Rome, where on 15 May 719, Pope Gregory II gave him a missionary mandate and at the same time the name Boniface, which from now on he used exclusively. And so Boniface went to Thuringia by way of Bavaria. He devoted himself to the mission in Frisia, laboring there for two years under Willibrord's guidance.

In 721 he again left Willibrord. By way of Trier, he proceeded to the upper Lahn in order to evangelize the still pagan Hessians around Fritzlar and Kassel on the Saxon frontier. He now went to Rome for the second time and on 30 November 722, he was consecrated a bishop by Gregory II. On this occasion he took the oath of obedience which the suffragan bishops of the Roman province were accustomed to take to the Pope as their metropolitan. The obligation of loyalty to the Emperor, which was included in this oath, was replaced by the engagement not to be in communion with bishops who acted contrary to the *instituta sanctorum patrum* and to take action against them, or, if this was not possible, to report them to the Pope. Thus Boniface's missionary diocese was intimately linked to Rome. Gregory II dismissed the new bishop with a recommendation to Charles Martel, who issued a safe-conduct for him at the beginning of 723. Boniface was now on the same footing as Willibrord.

Under the protection of the *princeps Francorum* the mission in Hesse made rapid progress. In 723 Boniface felled the "thunder oak" of Geismar and from its wood constructed the first church of Fritzlar, around which gathered a second monastic settlement. In 732 Pope Gregory III raised Boniface to the rank of archbishop by the bestowal of the pallium.

The Archbishop utilized the next years in consolidating his position. The arrival of Anglo-Saxon helpers made new foundations possible. In the Thuringian territory along the Main arose Anglo-Saxon convents. A great success for Boniface was the establishing of contact with the Bavarian Duke Hucbald (d. 736) and his successor Odilo. And Charles Martel's Saxon campaign, set for 738, even opened up the prospect of the longed for Saxon mission. In these years Boniface may have been tossed between hope and disillusionment until finally his third journey to Rome in 737–38 seemed to confirm all his hopes. Not only Thuringia and Hesse but also Bavaria and Saxony were entrusted to him. Gregory III extended the Archbishop's commission by making him his legate in Germany.

In 739, with the aid of Duke Odilo, Boniface was able to regulate the Bavarian situation and to establish the bishoprics of Regensburg, Freising, Salzburg, and Passau, which had been envisaged long before. Bavaria did not yet obtain its own ecclesiastical metropolis; Boniface retained the supreme authority. Ecclesiastical organization in Thuringia and Hesse was now an especially urgent question. Boniface had a free hand.

Carloman, heir of Frankish Austrasia, sought a close cooperation with the Anglo-Saxon Archbishop in Germany, but Boniface had to pay for this cooperation by renouncing his position in Bavaria.

The three Bonifatian reform councils sought the restoration of law and order in the Frankish Church and the renewal of moral and religious order among clergy and laity. Carloman subordinated the episcopate of his portion of the kingdom to the Archbishop-Legate Boniface. In Pepin's lands the ancient ecclesiastical provinces of Rouen, Reims, and Sens were to be restored. Annual provincial councils were to strengthen the inner structure of the provinces and promote moral reform.

Other decrees related to the restoration of diocesan structure. The subjection of the clergy to the diocesan bishop was reimposed. Priests were to report regularly to their bishop in regard to their conduct and the carrying out of their functions, while itinerant bishops and priests were not to be instituted without examination by a synod. But the ticklish question of the proprietary church was not taken up.

The restoration called for a guaranteeing of the material bases. A portion of Church property — the greater part — was excepted from the restitution because of the military necessities, but thereafter it was to be regarded as "tribute-paying loan land." This decree was of far-reaching significance for the development of Frankish feudalism.

Moral prescriptions for clergy and laity promoted inner reform. Priests were forbidden to carry arms and thus to engage in the chase and in war and they were required to practise celibacy.

The reform inaugurated in 743–44 profited not only the Church but also the reorganizations of the kingdom, as the regulations for the secularized Church property make clear. The two Carolingians acted as kings: they convoked and directed synods, appointed bishops, and created ecclesiastical provinces. "The principle of the territorial Church began to consolidate itself even in a monarchical and theocratic sense, not least under the stamp of Anglo-Saxon models" (Schieffer).

In these years Boniface was at the height of his creative activity. But the three reform councils meant only a beginning, not a completion, and the completion of the job was not granted to the Archbishop-Legate.

Boniface remained Archbishop and Legate, but the Frankish realm was no longer the scene of his activity. The closing years of his life were devoted to the care of the more restricted sphere of Hesse and Thuringia and of his mainly Anglo-Saxon assistants. More prominent now were the abbey of Fulda, founded in 744, and the bishopric of Mainz. Fulda had been planned from the start as a great monastic civilizing center and had been organized on the model of the Benedictine archabbey of Montecassino by Boniface's pupil, Sturmi. Fulda lay in the diocese of Würzburg but on the extreme northern edge, and, in accord with the intention of the founder, it was to serve especially for the Christian penetration of the dioceses of Büraburg-Fritzlar and Erfurt "prope marcam paganorum." In 753 Boniface set out on the Frisian journey on which his life was to reach fulfillment. In the exercise of his office of shepherd of souls in Frisia, when on 5 June 754, within the Pentecost octave, he was intending to confirm some neophytes in central Frisia, the eighty-year-old apostle met a martyr's death near Dokkum in a pagan surprise attack. His remains were recovered by a Frankish punitive expedition and, in accord with his desire, were deposited at Fulda. His martyrdom brought about a complete *volte-face* in the Frankish magnates, who now paid to the saint the reverence they had denied to the living Archbishop.

C H A P T E R   7 6

The Founding of the Carolingian Monarchy and the Progress of the Reform

From 747 the destiny of the Frankish Kingdom was in the hands of the Mayor Pepin. Born in 714, this second son of Charles Martel had been educated at Saint-Denis. His father had decided that he should inherit Burgundy and Neustria and in 740 had sent him to Burgundy with his uncle Childebrand. The young prince grew up in a Frankish *milieu* — he was a stranger to the Anglo-Saxons.

The men who directed Pepin's education at Saint-Denis are unknown to us. But under Charles Martel we encounter a churchman who can be compared with Willibrord and Boniface as a typical representative of the religious forces still alive in the Frankish Church Pirmin, "apostle of the Alemanni." Perhaps the father of Alemannian monasticism, who, in the manner of the Irish, had received episcopal consecration but represented the Benedictine rule and founded monastic congregations, was a refugee from Spain or Septimania. Pepin's election and enthronement in 751 complied with Germanic law, which, however, was now complemented and reinforced by the royal anointing, borrowed from the Old Testament.

The anointing of Pepin as King was of decisive importance for the development of the Christian notion of the king in the West. The ruler's position in the Church was thereafter sacramentally justified, for the royal anointing was regarded as a sacrament until the Investiture Controversy. The formula *Dei gratia rex* is first met under Charles the Great. The royal liturgy soon appeared not only at the king's anointing but also on great feasts, when he wore his crown. The triumphant "Christus vincit, Christus regnat, Christus imperat" began and concluded in the *laudes* the acclamations of Pope, King and Queen, royal family, and *exercitus Francorum*, joined with invocations of Christ, the angels, and the saints. In the basic version, determined under Charles the Great, the apostles were called upon for the Pope, Mary and the angels for the King, and the martyrs for the army. These groups corresponded in Visigothic Spain to the three divine Persons — the angels as the retinue of the Father, the apostles as that of the Son, the martyrs as that of the Holy Spirit. And so, despite the basically Christological character of the *laudes,* they symbolically expressed that the kingship belonged to the order of creation (God the Father), while the priesthood pertained to the order of redemption (God the Son).

In this symbolism the *exercitus Francorum* occupied the place of the Christian people, the *ecclesia* — the sphere of the Holy Spirit. Appealed to on its behalf were the great old Gallic bishops, Hilary of Poitiers and Martin of Tours, and the old Gallic martyrs, regarded as national patrons. Thus the Franks clearly appeared to be the new Israel. In addition to questions concerning episcopal authority in dioceses, the law of marriage was especially discussed. In order to provide material assistance again to the churches of the kingdom, Pepin imposed the tithe by law in 765. It was to be used exclusively for the care of souls; one-fourth was to go to the bishop, three-fourths to the parish clergy. The universal introduction of the tithe was of great moment for ecclesiastical organization, for, through the delimitation of tithe-areas, "the foundation was laid for a new system of small parishes." Chrodegang's rule for canons, composed, around 754 for the clergy of the Metz cathedral, promoted the reform of clerical morals. In it Chrodegang followed the Roman model but also borrowed most of the regulations of the rule of Saint Benedict and relied on the Frankish synodal law. In contrast to monks, canons retained the use of their private property. At the Council of Ver the *ordo clericorum,* based on the *canones,* was for the first time placed alongside the *ordo monachorum.* Chrodegang and Pepin also began the Romanization of the Gallican liturgy and chant, which was realized under Charles the Great.

C H A P T E R   7 7

The Beginnings of the Papal State

Since the conflict with the Emperor Leo III, Rome and Ravenna, though still parts of the Empire, had to depend on their own strength and devices in the face of the expanding Lombard Kingdom. The restoration of Rome's city walls, begun as early as 708 and resumed under Gregory II, was completed under Gregory III (731–41). Thereafter the basis of Roman politics remained that solidarity with Ravenna, Spoleto, and Benevento which had developed under Gregory II. The papacy found a more effective protection than city fortifications and alliances in the esteem which Peter, the prince of the apostles, was held in the Germanic-

Roman world, not least by the Lombard King Liutprand, who sought not only to incorporate the exarchate and the duchies of Spoleto and Benevento into his kingdom, but also to protect the Roman Church.

Gregory's successor, the Greek Zachary, in 742 again sent notification of his election and his profession of faith to the Emperor and the Patriarch of Constantinople. The Lombard King utilized the opportunity to neutralize Rome by a twenty-years peace. In 742 Zachary had to give up the alliance with Spoleto and recognize the royal conquests at the expense of the exarchate. In return, Liutprand restored papal patrimonies and even four frontier fortresses of the Roman duchy that had been seized in 739. The peace was maintained under Liutprand's successor, Ratchis (744). But it could hardly be kept secret from the Lombards that the independence of Ravenna and Rome depended entirely on their good will. King Aistulf occupied Ravenna in 750–51 and in the spring of 752 inaugurated economic warfare against Rome.

When the Lombard's intentions in regard to Rome became clear, Pope Zachary was dead. His successor, the Roman Stephen II, engaged in negotiations and in June–July 752 concluded an armistice. Aistulf expected the Pope to advocate the recognition of the Lombard conquests by the Emperor. But Stephen II sympathized with the people of Ravenna and implored the Emperor to send military help. When the Lombard King learned this news, he sent the Romans an ultimatum in October 752 to recognize his sovereignty and to pay a heavy tribute to Pavia. The Emperor sent, not an army, but an embassy under the *silentiarius* John. It reached Rome probably in November 752 and was then received by Aistulf at Ravenna. Negotiations continued. Envoys of King and Pope accompanied the *silentiarius* on his return to the imperial court.

The Pope understood that he could no longer expect any real aid from the Emperor. Constantinople was preparing for a new council, that could only aggravate the religious conflict with Rome. In this emergency Stephen II turned to Pepin. A first message depicted the precarious situation of Rome. Soon after the Pope sought an official invitation to the Frankish Kingdom. Aistulf now proceeded to a military attack on Rome, probably intending to present the Franks with a *fait accompli.* But he acted too late. In September the invitation to Frankland was delivered by two very exalted Frankish dignitaries. Archbishop Chrodegang and Duke Autcar, Pepin's brother-in-law. At the same time appeared the imperial *silentiarius* with an order to the Pope to negotiate with the Lombard King in the Emperor's name.

On 14 October 753, Stephen II, accompanied by the *silentiarius* John and the Frankish escort, left the Eternal City for Pavia. Stephan II left Pavia on 15 November. He was welcomed on Frankish soil at the abbey of Saint-Maurice.

No fewer than three Frankish embassies went to the court of Pavia in 754, but the Lombard King proved to be an obstinate and dangerous opponent. Aistulf backed up the opposition by getting Pepin's brother, Carloman, to undertake a journey into the Frankish Kingdom. This danger brought the Pope and the Frankish King even closer together. And at Easter 754, at the assembly of Quierzy near Laon, Pepin obtained a decision for the Italian campaign. The King apparently gave the Pope in writing a promise to guarantee the territorial status of Rome and Ravenna, of Venetia and Istria, and the autonomy of Spoleto and Benevento. The two partners concluded a pact of friendship. Shortly before the departure for the campaign, Stephen at Saint-Denis solemnly anointed Pepin and his sons Charles and Carloman as Kings.

While Pepin was moving into Italy *via* the Mont-Cenis in August 754, his brother Carloman died in a monastery at Vienne. The attempted revolution in the Frankish Kingdom collapsed. Aistulf began negotiations for peace when the Franks besieged him in Pavia. In the treaty of peace he recognized Frankish suzerainty over the Lombard Kingdom and obliged himself to give up Ravenna "cum diversis civitatibus."

Peace was concluded between "Romans, Franks, and Lombards," though neither the Emperor nor the city of Rome was represented at Pavia. Aistulf evacuated Venetia and Istria and turned over Ravenna to the metropolitan of the city. But he retained parts of the exarchate and likewise did not entirely carry out the restorations due to Rome. The undefined constitutional situation of Rome and Ravenna allowed him to defer fulfilling his engagements and play off Ravenna against Rome. And as Iconoclasm flared up again at that very moment, a Lombard-Byzantine coalition became a possibility.

But the Lombard King was lacking in patience. In December 755 he marched on Rome, which was completely invested on 1 January 756. Only the sea-route was still open. This the Frankish *missus* Warnehar took, together with three papal envoys, who in March delivered to the Frankish King a desperate appeal for help in the name of Saint Peter. In May an imperial embassy *en route* to Pepin arrived in Rome. It likewise took the sea-route to Marseilles, but when it got there Pepin was already before Pavia. The envoy George proceeded on to the King and made known his master's demand — the handing over of Ravenna and the exarchate to the Emperor. Pepin replied that he had embarked on the campaign only "pro amore beati Petri et venia delictorum," but he offered the Emperor a pact of friendship.

Aistulf capitulated at the end of June 756. The stipulations of the second peace of Pavia were substantially more severe than those of the earlier treaty. The Lombards had to surrender one-third of their royal treasury, renew the annual tribute of Merovingian times, and make the restitutions to the Pope through the agency of deputies of the Frankish King. Thus did the "Papal State" become a reality. It comprised the duchy of Rome and the exarchate of Ravenna with the Pentapolis. Officials and people took an oath to the Pope, and a papal administration was set up. In law the Papal State belonged, as before, to the Empire. And Stephen II and his successors made it clear by their coinage and the dating of their charters that they recognized the imperial sovereignty.

The events immediately following seemed to favor the realization of the full Roman program. King Aistulf died in December 756. His successor, Desiderius, was elevated to the throne in 757 in agreement with the Pope and with Abbot Fulrad of Saint-Denis, who had to supervise the implementation of the restitutions. But Rome's exaggerated expectations were not realized. Paul I succeeded his brother Stephen on the papal throne on 19 May 757 and sent notification of his election to the Frankish King after the manner of the earlier notices sent to the Exarch. Desiderius did not give a thought to observing his promises. In 758 he subjugated Spoleto and Benevento and got into contact with Byzantium, but King

Pepin declined to make another expedition to Italy. He was wholly absorbed in completing the Frankish state, to which Septimania was added as early as 759 and reluctant Aquitaine in 768 after long struggles. Pepin was obliging to Desiderius in order to prevent a Lombard-Byzantine coalition. Paul I gave in and in his demands for restitution agreed essentially to the stipulations of the second peace of Pavia. He had to yield also at Ravenna, where a direct papal administration was replaced by an indirect one conducted by the metropolitan.

A *modus vivendi,* unstable though it was, had been discovered with the Lombards. Then relations with Constantinople became Paul I's great concern. In the fateful year 754 there had met at Hiereia on the Bosphorus an imperial iconoclast council, which brought on the flood-stage of iconoclasm in the Empire. A new wave of Greek emigrants reached Italy, and the Pope placed at the disposal of the Greek monks the monastery of San Silvestro in Capite, founded in his own home in 761. Paul protested against the persecution of iconodules. He got into touch with the three oriental Patriarchs, who in the same year had taken a stand against the iconoclasts in a synod in Palestine. When, after a rather long interval, due to the Aquitanian war, another synod of the kingdom met again in 767 at Gentilly, there occurred at it a religious discussion in regard to images between Greeks and Romans. Paul's apprehensions were proved to be groundless, for the Franks remained on the Roman side.

Paul I died on 28 June 767. On 7 August Stephen III was consecrated Bishop of Rome.

Against the will of the new Pope the victorious faction let itself be carried into shameful excesses. The protection of the Roman Church in an extremely critical moment now devolved upon the young Kings, Charles and Carloman.

Section Two

The Greek Church in the Epoch of Iconoclasm

Hans-Georg Beck

CHAPTER 7 8

The First Phase of Iconoclasm (730 to 775)

Iconoclasm shook the Byzantine Empire to a degree that is comparable only to the Arian troubles after Nicaea I or the Monophysite struggles of the fifth and sixth centuries. But, differing from these, it ended without a new denominational split coming into existence as a lasting consequence. Despite its effects on the West, which were especially political in nature, it was to a certain degree a special characteristic of an Orthodox world which was closing and isolating itself.

It was only in the sixth and seventh centuries that icons entered on their victorious progress as cult images to any great degree, a progress which was powerfully accelerated by rampant popular credulity, legends, and miracles. If this development impresses us as being a straight and undisturbed growth, this is only partly correct, because the opposing literature was almost entirely destroyed at the command of Nicaea II in 787. But we can still hear voices calling for restraint and sobriety in scattered fragments of *catenae,* in Monophysite works, in citations from orthodox writings against Jewish propaganda, and so forth. There were whole areas in the Church which were opposed to images, notably Armenia, and it is significant that the most important Armenian sect which originated at that time, the Paulicians, made hostility to images their standard, apparently for the sake of the "pure Christian doctrine." The great iconoclasm of the eighth and ninth centuries meant only the effort to clarify this complex of controversial questions precisely and to enable Orthodoxy to arrive at a pure understanding of its own nature. Hence, at the beginning of the eighth century we have to inquire not so much into the causes of the controversy as into the external occasion for it.

The contemporary pious chroniclers and later historians — all of them iconod-ules — regarded as the initiator of the movement the Emperor Leo III the Syrian (717–41). What we really know from unobjectionable contemporary testimonies, the letters of the Patriarch Germanus I (715–30), is the fact that the initiative lay, not with the Emperor, but with ecclesiastical circles — the bishops of Asia Mi-nor. The ancient parallel tradition, hostile to images, of the Orthodox Church and concern for the purity of doctrine and worship were sufficient to explain their ac-tivity. Most prominently mentioned were Bishop Constantine of Nacolia in Phrygia, Metropolitan Thomas of Claudiopolis, and Metropolitan Theodore of Ephesus. In their dioceses, they began to remove cult images on their own responsibility and to forbid their veneration, apparently without encountering any great opposition. A first imperial announcement occurred most probably in 726; it consisted of, not a decree, but an exhortation to the people no longer to honor icons but rather to get rid of them. The Emperor set the example and had a celebrated icon of Christ at the Chalke Gate of the palace removed. The sequel was a popular riot; some of the soldiers directed to remove the image were killed. The Emperor's measures were limited to corporal chastisement of the guilty and to banishment and fines. There were no martyrs in defense of icons, and the Patriarch Germanus continued in office, despite his discreet opposition.

One cannot speak of an official iconoclasm until January 730, when the Em-peror, after a final vain effort to gain the Patriarch Germanus to his policy, published an edict against the cult of images. Germanus had to abdicate but was able to end his days in peace on an estate. The theological justification of this policy was ap-parently restricted essentially to the charge that iconodules were guilty of idolatry. It is only from this edict that the Patriarch Nicephorus dated the persecution by the iconoclasts.

Iconoclasm entered upon an acute and politically dangerous stage by virtue of the dispute with the Holy See. To be sure, economic and financial questions were crucial here alongside the religious, and these probably first brought the religious question to its special importance for Italy. In any case, the Emperor's intransigent attitude contributed essentially to alienate Italy from the Empire, to promote the *rapprochement* with the Franks, and to shatter the ancient Constantinian Imperial Church-*Oecumene*.

The intellectual basis for the dispute over Church practice very quickly ap-peared. The most weighty contribution to the iconodules came from a Syrian monk, John Damascene. His friends in the Empire enabled him to find a powerful response, while he provided the iconodules with the Christological and soteri-ological arguments on behalf of icons. The icon-theology of this period did not confine itself to reasons drawn from liturgy and morality but immediately lifted the subject to the highest dogmatic plane. It fought the war by means of argu-ments from the theology of creation and from Christology, against Manichaeism and Monophysitism respectively. The opponents were soon unable to remain con-tent with pointing to the danger of idolatry. What Germanus had already called for, a general council, appeared as a necessity.

Leo's son, the Emperor Constantine V (741–75), decided to hold the council, but at first he had his hands full, with the Empire's militant foreign policy and with maintaining himself against revolt. Soon, however, perhaps after John Damascene's arguments had become known to him, he came forth himself as a theologian. He denied the possibility of an adequate icon of Christ, an *eikōn,* which would not be an *eidōlon* with reference to the impossibility of portraying Christ's divine nature. Only the Eucharist, he said, was a true image of Christ, living by the equality of nature between prototype and copy. What else there was of iconoclast literature at this time has been lost. In any event, the ground had now been made ready for the general council.

It met on 10 February 754, at Hiereia, an imperial palace on the Asiatic side of the Bosphorus. Whether the Pope and the oriental Patriarchs had been invited is unknown. They were not represented, and in 787 this fact would constitute a chief argument against the ecumenicity of the synod. The Metropolitan Theodore of Ephesus, one of the first champions of iconoclasm, presided. The sessions continued until 8 August. It seems that the synod was not under any imperial pressure in regard to time and that its freedom of debate was not curtailed. In addition to the Emperor's theological works a *florilegium* of patristic passages hostile to images was apparently laid before the synod, and it seems to have made an impression. A whole generation later the iconodules still had to reckon with the arguments of the synod of 754, without being entirely capable of dealing with them.

The synodal decree is extant and shows clearly that the way of dogmatizing in the question of images, once entered upon, could not be abandoned. Christ is not capable of being represented; in fact, every image of Christ, according to what it intends to represent, presupposes either a Monophysite or a Nestorian Christology. Both the making and the honoring of icons were condemned. But the council warned against an indiscriminate destruction of existing works of art. Like the Emperor, the synod also discovered in the Eucharist alone an adequate image of Christ. On the other hand, the Fathers avoided the too bold ideas and formulas of the imperial theologian — another argument against the alleged subservience of the council.

Iconoclasm, hitherto supported by an imperial decree, was now a dogma of the entire Eastern Church. For there is no mention anywhere of any noteworthy resistance by groups of bishops.

The fact that the slowly hardening opposition proceeded from the monks so embittered the Emperor against them that before long it was impossible to determine whether the persecution was directed chiefly against monasticism or against the cult of icons. It may perhaps be supposed that monks were closer to popular devotion, more attached to icons, than were the bishops, and hence, then at least, they did not so much carry out the will of the people but rather formed it. For to all appearances monasticism did not from the start have behind it the overwhelming majority of the people. Instead, the monks' opposing stand vis-à-vis the executive authority of the state probably first obtained for them a following among the masses. Other charges correspond closely with the character sketch of that powerful but hot-tempered and unpredictable ruler, with his wrath and his animosity, which he gradually displayed. He is said to have refused Mary the sacred title of Theotokos, to have denied the saints even the term "holy," and to have forbidden the cult, not only of icons, but also of relics. Where he encountered resistance he confiscated the monasteries, transformed them into barracks, and enrolled the monks in the army. An occasional provincial governor went even further, forcing monks and nuns to abandon celibacy. The government went to extremes in inflicting torture and banishment and did not shrink from the death penalty.

Considerable time elapsed, however, before the Emperor drew the ultimate conclusions. It was only about ten years after the Synod of Hiereia that the persecution broke out in all its harshness. Leader of the opposition was Abbot Stephen the Younger of Mount Auxentius in Bithynia. The Emperor tried in every way to break his resistance, and his trial was long and protracted. It is possible that Stephen was actually not condemned to death but met death by being handed over to the rage of a mob. The monasteries of Bithynia, then the most important monastic settlement in the Empire, were depopulated, because the monks were either in exile or in prison. Churches were wrecked and profaned, and the monastic way of life was exposed to ridicule. But monasticism did not remain passive. From its circles proceeded violent pamphlets against the Emperor. Despite the persecution, monasticism built up a certain self-assurance and was recognized as the basic force of the whole Church, as a power which had the duty and the ability to represent the conscience of the Church in view of the lethargy of the episcopate.

The number of martyrs in the strict sense was probably not very great, even under Constantine V. The people's support of the monks left much to be desired. And the army stood beside the Emperor with unfailing loyalty. His policy, however, had become so clearly ill-advised in the course of time that at his death in 775 a reaction was not an impossibility.

CHAPTER 79

The First Restoration of the Icons

At the death of the Emperor Constantine V the tide of the persecution of the iconodules had begun to ebb at last, though the position of the iconoclasts was not lost. Bound up with the name of the dead Emperor and of his father, Leo III, in the minds of many self-assured Byzantines in the army and in the high bureaucracy was the memory of a period of energetic national self-defense against Islam and the barbarian world. Besides, the recollection of the iconoclastic persecution ceased to endure, however deep it may have been, and was interpreted, not so much as a struggle for "purity of faith" as a parallel to the fight for national self-assertion. In addition, at least one generation of Byzantine Christians had now grown up under iconoclasm and had perhaps been able to establish that Church life had suffered no particular harm through the removal of icons. Thus, a restoration of the cult of images could be accomplished only with the utmost discretion and with consideration for the memory of the dead Emperors.

Constantine V's son, Leo IV (775–80), apparently did not envisage any such restoration. Nevertheless, he seems to have abolished his father's excessive measures of persecution. Following his death, his widow, Irene, came to power for her minor son, Constantine VI, by outmaneuvering the brothers of Leo IV. She was determined to make the most of it. The cult of images was very close to her heart and no one doubted that she would work to restore it. *Rebus sic stantibus,* such a policy was pro-monastic. If anyone wanted to become a monk, he could do so without hindrance, and monasteries were reopened. At this time there was established in Bithynia the monastery of Sakkudion, first ruled by Abbot Plato, uncle of Theodore of Studion. It became the source of an ecclesiastico-political movement of large proportions.

But in reality any restoration of pre-iconoclast conditions was illusory, so long as the decrees of the Synod of Hiereia were in force, for the council had regarded itself as ecumenical. Restoration could be effected only by another council, and it also required, not only in law but in fact, a new and uncompromised Patriarch. The Patriarch in office, Paul, was certainly not an iconoclast of any great importance, but he had once sworn to obey the decrees of Hiereia. Was it a mere coincidence that he now asked to resign because of sickness and recommended the holding of a new synod? As always, no one forced him to stay in office, though it seems that even the Empress esteemed him highly. But now she had the opportunity of placing a new man at the head of the Church. It is a testimony to her good sense and her grasp of the actual difficulties of the situation that she did not select a representative of the monastic faction, despite its heavy pressure, but a high official who was still a layman, the *protoasecretis* Tarasius. He seemed to assure the Empress a course that was politically sensible and moderate, and he did not disappoint her. Well briefed, Tarasius also called for a new general council and made this a condition of his accepting his election as Patriarch. A large gathering at the Magnaura palace agreed to the demand, even though not without opposition. Tarasius was thereupon consecrated Bishop of Constantinople *per saltum* on 25 December 784.

Probably in the spring of 785 he contacted the Holy See by sending notification of his elevation in the so-called synodical. The letter explained his promotion to the patriarchal dignity from the lay state, included a profession of faith which contained the orthodox doctrine of images, mentioned his demand for an ecumenical council, and asked the Pope to send two representatives. About this same time Irene also made known to the Pope her plans for a council and asked him, probably in a second letter, to accept Tarasius' peaceful overtures. Pope Hadrian took exception to certain points in the letters which he received. In the Empress' letters there was indeed expressed the good intention of restoring orthodoxy, but not the readiness to annul the injustice done by her predecessors to the Holy See in the seizure of Illyricum. The promotion of Tarasius from the lay state to the episcopacy was certainly in need of a dispensation because it was uncanonical, and the use of the expression "Ecumenical Patriarch" was still offensive to the Roman view. But the prospect of an Ecumenical council that would destroy the memory of the pseudo-ecumenical Synod of Hiereia and could energetically restore an awareness of the papal primacy caused Hadrian to make light of his hesitations, recognize Tarasius with qualifications, and hail the Empress' plan for a council. He named two delegates for the coming synod in a letter which contained an exposition of his faith on the subject of the cult of images. His representatives were Peter, Abbot of the Roman monastery of San Saba, and the Archpriest Peter. He expressly emphasized his right to confirm the decrees of the council. The oriental patriarchates were likewise invited to participate. But their position vis-à-vis the Islamic authorities was such that Alexandria and Antioch could only manage to be represented by two *synkelloi* — and it is open to question whether these were really invested with full authority by their Patriarchs — while Jerusalem was unable to do even that much.

The iconoclasts must have been worried about their position but they did not give up. We hear of heated conferences among their bishops, and this agitation had its effect. Tarasius felt obliged to threaten with punishments such gatherings as took place without his authorization on the ground that they were uncanonical. At Nicaea the council was solemnly opened on 28 September 787.

In name the papal representatives occupied the presidency, but in the very first session the Sicilian bishops asked Tarasius to assume the direction of the discussions. The Empress was represented by observers. The number of participants vary between 258 at the beginning of the synod and 335 at its conclusion. The number of bishops was supplemented by a considerable crowd of monks and abbots. The most illustrious were Abbot Plato of Sakkudion, Theophanes Confessor, Nicetas and Nicephorus of the monastery of Medikios, and Abbot Sabas of Studion. The majority of the bishops came from Asia Minor, Thrace, and Macedonia. South Italy was represented by eight Sicilian and six Calabrian bishops. It is clear that a high percentage of the bishops, apart from the Italians, had come to some sort of terms with the preceding iconoclasm.

Among the Fathers of the Council there seems to have bee no theologian of rank. Only the *vita* of Theodore of Studion states that Tarasius made special use of the advice of Abbot Plato. The bold speculations of John Damascene's first discourse on images were not taken into consideration. Both the handling of the *ratio theologica* and especially that of the proof from tradition were appallingly inadequate in comparison with the Council of 680. The manner of using the old Testament would scarcely have obtained the approval of a single Council Father of the seventh century. In the demonstration of the Church's tradition all possible legends and miracle stories made a significantly deeper impression than the well-stated skeptical remarks of older Fathers, who were either not considered at all or were easily pushed aside. Hence it is also not surprising that, in contradistinction to the synod against the Monothelites, the adherents of the previous iconoclast doctrine did not lift a finger to make their earlier viewpoint even intelligible.

If the result of the debates in the *horos*, that is, the conciliar definition, seems so much more sound, theologically moderate, and worthwhile, this is one of those marvels encountered so often in the history of the councils. One must not forget that Pope Hadrian's letter, which was read and applauded at the beginning of the synod, represented that Western theology of images which had developed, not on the basis of dogmatic speculation, but of considerations of moral theology. It was the special merit of Tarasius, gathered from his incidental remarks in the discussions, that he tried time and again to shake the complacency of his fellow bishops in regard to legends and again and again brought the terminology back to the precise distinction between *latreia* (adoration) and *proskunēsis* (veneration).

The *horos* declared the veneration of icons to be the orthodox doctrine, condemned iconoclasm as a heresy, and ordered the destruction of iconoclast writings. The definition of "cult" itself was restricted essentially to its characteristic as "a mark of honor," a term which includes lights and incense. This veneration was sharply distinguished from *latreia,* or real adoration. Veneration itself was justified by its relation to the person represented by the image.

The Empress invited the Fathers to hold the closing session at Constantinople in the Magnaura palace. On 23 October 787, the *horos* was again read, this time in the presence of Their Majesties. After the Empress' question as to whether it met with universal consent had been answered in the affirmative, the Empress, in defiance of protocol, signed ahead of her son and then had him sign.

The Patriarch Tarasius furnished Pope Hadrian with a brief report of the synod. He obtained the acts through his legates, but in Rome they were wretchedly translated, and it was the defects of the translation that were taken over by the *Libri Carolini* and made the misunderstanding worse. Tarasius does not seem to have asked Rome to confirm the decrees.

Peace seemed to have been restored in the Orthodox Church. But iconoclasm was not yet dead, and the Patriarch's wise attitude toward the *lapsi* of the preceding period created among the monks a resentful opposition which waited only for an opportunity to break forth.

C H A P T E R   8 0

Interlude in Church and State

The Second Council of Nicaea was, not least of all, a triumph for the Empress Irene. She had managed to neutralize the army's opposition, bind the party of the monks to her, and find a Patriarch on whom she could rely. Her rule was based on the reconciliation of her Church with Rome. And even though the engagement of Charles the Great's daughter Rotrudis and her son Constantine VI was not realized, she was now able to renounce such an outside support for her policy in the Empire's domestic affairs.

Irene's exertions were directed ever more clearly toward sole rule. Her actually extraordinary position as ruling coempress was no longer sufficient, and Constantine VI had now reached an age which qualified him to assume the government. Since he could not expect that his mother would retire, he allied with army circles and elements of the official aristocracy in order by their aid — and this meant the help of iconoclasts — to enforce his claims. But the Empress-mother discovered the plot and took vigorous action. She demanded of the army an oath that guaranteed her position as coruler. The troops of the capital were persuaded to acquiesce, but the troops in the themes offered a bitter resistance and in 790 proclaimed Constantine VI as sole ruler. Irene yielded and withdrew. But only two years elapsed before her influence over her son had been re-established and her position as coempress was again a reality. Since Constantine VI did not live up to the expectations of the troops but performed without success, and to a certain extant with severe losses, on both the Bulgarian and the Eastern fronts, and likewise more and more sacrificed his adherents to the will of his mother, he so isolated himself that the troops sought to raise his uncles, brothers of Leo IV, to the throne. The attempt was suppressed in blood. Now the young Emperor had nothing more to hope for, from either his mother or the army. It was his mother's intrigues — the monastic chronicler Theophanes is the witness — that maneuvered him into conflict with the monastic party and thereby gave the *coup de grâce*.

The juridical situation is less clear than has usually been assumed. According to Theophanes there is no doubt that Irene in 788 brought about the marriage of her unwilling son with Mary the Paphlagonian, forcing him to break off his engagement to Rotrudis. In any event, the Emperor felt justified in divorcing Mary and inducing her to take the veil — and he was even more ready to do so, since he had decided to marry Theodota, one of his mother's ladies-in-waiting. Three canonical problems were thereby raised: the question of the grounds for divorce, that of the right to remarry, and that of the Church's treatment of successive bigamy. The development of the Byzantine matrimonial law was not yet final, even as far as the Church was concerned, and each of the three questions could be variously answered.

Confronted with the complex of questions, the Patriarch Tarasius had two alternatives — to prevent the Emperor from remarrying and hence to make the Emperor's iconoclast advisers his own declared opponents, with the risk of starting the Church conflict again, or of practicing dissimulation, thereby pushing a part of the zealot monastic faction, which had not agreed to his moderate policy at the Council of 787, into open opposition. At first he refused his permission for a remarriage of the Emperor and threatened excommunication. Nevertheless, Constantine VI married Theodota with the proper solemnities, the priest Joseph blessing the union. In other words, he did not impose ecclesiastical censures on the Emperor but only on Joseph, and then only after the Emperor's fall, and he let *oikonomia* prevail. They branded the Emperor's remarriage as adultery hence the label of "Moechian Controversy," — accused the Patriarch of laxity, and withdrew from his communion. Both the Emperor and the new Empress did everything to bring the monks over to their side. Thus the Emperor had alienated not only the army but also the ecclesiastical reform circles.

Irene's hour had struck. In 797 she had her son blinded — he lived only a few more years — and assumed the government as sole ruler of the Empire.

Tarasius died in 806, but the priest Joseph long continued to be the victim of the ambivalence which always characterized the notion of *oikonomia* in Byzantium. Tarasius' successor was another layman, the imperial chancellor Nicephorus, well known as chronicler and saint of the second period of iconoclasm. Nicephorus, Patriarch from 806 to 815, belonged to a family that had supplied defenders of the cult of images under Constantine V.

The point at issue was the question of simony. A perusal of the canons of the Seventh Ecumenical Council would cause one to believe that a great number of the bishops of that day had acquired their sees through simony. But if the canons are compared with later statements of the Patriarch Tarasius on this point, such as the decree of 787–88, mentioned by the *Vita Tarasii,* it seems to follow that the monks energetically labelled as simony all ordination fees, offerings made to the consecrating prelate, and the like. In any case, here too Tarasius first sought a *via media.* Bishops guilty of simony were not to be deposed forever, but, following a penance, that is, suspension for at least one year, they could be restored to office. The relevant decree was in keeping with the desire of the Empress Irene and was published in 787 or early in 788 in any event, with the participation of the papal representatives at the Council. The zealots among the monks, on the other hand, led by a certain Sabas, raised a storm and appealed to Pope Hadrian I. Eventually the Patriarch Tarasius had to give in. He was still, even now, accommodating to penitent simonists to a degree — and this too was taken amiss — but they were no longer allowed to exercise their office again. This is evident toward the end of 790, that is, after Irene had been forced into retirement, in a letter to the anchorite and Abbot John and in a further letter to Pope Hadrian I, in which he submitted the matter to the Pope's judgment.

The Church-State aspect of the conflicts consists in this, that the monastic party was apparently unwilling to recognize the real motive of the Patriarchs not to expose the precarious peace of the post-iconoclast period to any excessively strong tests. The Patriarchs, men of public life, could scarcely fail to note how weak was the consistently iconodule majority and how great the danger of a new flare-up of iconoclasm. In this situation a firm alliance of the monastic party with the iconodule hierarchy would have been the need of the moment. It was not realized.

C H A P T E R   8 1

The Second Phase of Iconoclasm (815 to 843)

The faith of the Byzantine nation almost always saw the destiny of its Empire intimately linked with its religion, with God's blessing or displeasure. From this point of view the divine mercy had apparently been rather on the side of the iconoclasts and their Emperors than on that of their successors, especially of the Empress Irene and the Emperor Michael I Rhangabe. One who did not share this popular belief could still make use of it for political ends, circumstances permitting. This seems to have been exemplified in the conduct of the Emperor Leo V.

Leo V (813–20) rose to power on a wave which clearly suggested the mentality prevailing under the first two Syrian Emperors, and he regarded it, if not as right, at least as advisable to undertake an attempt at a restoration in this direction. The theological approach that was assumed held that the cult of images was permissible only if it was ordered by the Bible; since this was not the case, it could not be allowed. The really appealing argument was that the rule of the iconoclast Emperors had been a blessing for the Empire. After this preparation, an approach was made to the Patriarch Nicephorus, probably in the late fall of 814. The imperial order was at first to the effect that he should remove the icons from direct veneration by the people; hence no general destruction of images was ordered. The Emperor felt that he could rely on the majority of the population. The Patriarch's reply was a decided negative. The veneration of images, he said, was an ancient Church tradition and so needed no express order in the Bible. The Patriarch also refused to have the question again discussed by a synod or an episcopal conference. However, he probably had a presentiment of the danger and sought to have the iconodules close ranks firmly. A number of bishops and abbots, the most prominent of the latter being Theodore of Studion, joined the Patriarch and swore to maintain their unity and to withstand the iconoclasts even as the cost of their lives.

It was especially important that at this moment of danger factionalism among the orthodox was resolutely put aside and peace was restored between the Studites and the hierarchy. Since Leo V apparently knew how to minimize his demands, he required only that the Patriarch should make one small concession — to remove from the immediate contact of the faithful the low-hanging icons in the church; there the matter should rest. As Nicephorus refused to agree even to this, he was deported to Asia Minor, where, in order not to become an obstacle to the peace of the Church, he resigned his office.

As early as 1 April 815, the Emperor appointed as the new Patriarch Theodotos Kassiteras (815–21), and in the same month there met at Hagia Sophia a synod which renewed the decrees of the Synod of 754, sharply criticized Nicaea II, and again forbade the manufacture of images of Christ and the saints. But there was intentionally no further reference to icons as idolatrous images, "for there are degrees of wickedness." Likewise, the Christological arguments were touched on only in passing. The patristic *florilegium*, which apparently served the participants in the synod as the basis of discussion, probably placed emphasis on the argument of "holiness." According to it, holiness is a quality imparted by God to the elect. No artist can, without blasphemy, claim to bestow similar properties on a material image. The practical implementation of the conciliar decrees provided for the removal of low-hanging images, which were too close to the devotion of the faithful, but to leave those higher up alone, in so far as no handling for religious purposes was attempted in their regard.

The council knew some success. In contradistinction to the first phase of iconoclasm, however, monasteries and monks no longer formed the core of the opposition to the same degree. The letters and laments of Theodore of Studion are clear — many abbots joined the iconoclasts. On the other hand, a considerable number of bishops can be named who now energetically represented the iconodule viewpoint. The best in monastic circles had already become bishops and as such had offered resistance. And, finally, no explicitly iconoclast declarations were demanded, so that many monks were in the position of pursuing their own type of devotion without any real cost. The officials seem often to have been satisfied if they were assured that persons would neither hold meetings nor publicly propagate the cult of images. The most famous exiles were the Patriarch Nicephorus and, once again, Theodore of Studion, whose relations to each other improved under the force of circumstances without becoming cordial.

Emperor Leo V, inaugurator of the persecution, was assassinated during the Christmas festivities of 820. The ex-Patriarch Nicephorus commented with the remark that the Roman Empire had lost a godless but otherwise important ruler. Theodore exulted that the winter was past, even if spring was still slow in coming. Leo was succeeded on the throne by Michael II the Amorian (820–29). He was not a friend of the cult of icons, but in this he was acting less in accord with religious convictions than with the *status quo* in which he had grown up and which he felt unable to change without wrecking the Empire.

The Emperor issued a *thespisma,* whereby the entire dispute was to be buried in silence and everyone was to follow his own conscience. If Michael did not consistently follow this policy thereafter, this was probably because there soon occurred a revolt which adopted as its own the catchwords of the iconodules. It was only in 823 that the revolt could be suppressed. But the Muslim power had allied, had again become fully active and did serious damage to the Empire.

Michael's son, Theophilus (829–42), witnessed the catastrophe of the fall of the strongest fortress in Asia Minor, Amorion, in 838. Theophilus was a more severe persecutor of iconodules than his father. He was a pupil of that John the Grammarian who in 815 had prepared the decrees of the iconoclast synod and who soon became the Patriarch John VII (837–43). He was the most efficient personality among the iconoclast bishops, and the defamatory hatred of the orthodox was directed at him to a much greater degree than at the Emperor. On instructions from the Patriarch, the persecution, especially of monks, was intensified.

When Theophilus died iconoclasm crumbled. The reasons for this collapse are complex. Keeping in mind the uniquely political theology of the Byzantines, for whom the prosperity of the Empire represented God's reward for the orthodox faith, the political failures of especially the last iconoclast Emperors had presented the iconodules with impressive arguments. The sources make known that precisely these political misfortunes were thoroughly exploited against iconoclasm. In addition, the iconoclasts of the second phase did not follow any strict line. Their *laissez-faire* deprived their policy of persuasive force, smoothed out the differences, and brought about a fatal indifference, in their own circles. And the group of iconodules was more united and no longer so theologically defenseless in the face of the outbreak of hostilities in 815 as had been the case in 730. The period of peace between 780 and 815 had procured for the monks the esteem of the people; they were able to regard themselves as the religious leaders of the masses. And even if these masses, as such, ceased to be their adherents in the period of the second persecution, this happened, not because of conviction, but out of weakness, and the masses were ready, at the very moment when the pressure was eased, again to make common cause with them. And so the government had no choice but to revise its current policy.

At his death Theophilus was succeeded by his three-year-old son, Michael III (842–67). The direction of the regency was assumed by the widowed Empress Theodora, a long-time devotee of icons. But the initiative for the restoration proceeded, not directly from her, but from her adviser and minister, Theoctistus. The

Empress gladly allowed herself to be convinced by the political necessity, just so long as the memory of her dead husband was not disparaged. A way was found to oblige her. The Patriarch John VII was induced to abdicate, and his place was taken by the Sicilian Methodius (843–47). Then in March 843 a solemn synod was held which re-established the cult of icons. Thus was ended a battle which had drained off the energies of the Orthodox world for generations. A peace was inaugurated which would no longer be troubled by this point. Orthodoxy was reunited in a new self-understanding, but at the price that religious attitudes which in the older Church had been entirely possible and lawful, even though perhaps not obligatory, now had to leave the inclosure of the Church.

CHAPTER 82

Theology and Monasticism in the Age of Iconoclasm

The single celebrity of the age was John Damascene, an Arab of distinguished family. He grew up at the court of the Caliph and eventually responded to the call to the monastic life at Mar Saba in Jerusalem. He died before 754. His work forces us to assume at Damascus, at Jerusalem, and in the lauras in the vicinity of the Holy City educational opportunities, especially a wealth of manuscripts, which surpass anything we know of the other metropolises of the caliphate. As the theologian of the cult of icons, John, like his successors, certainly took as his point of departure in his argumentation the questionable existence of authentic portraits of Christ and the saints and certainly confused the metaphysical image with the pictorial image. Thus for him the image became revelation and means of grace. Whatever one may think of these speculations, with John the totality expanded into a grandiose system of cosmic liturgy, into a hymn to the transfigured matter and world that God had created, into the visible expression of a theandric law which governs the whole redeemed world. Without realizing it and in a different connection he was thus continuing Maximus Confessor.

In the history of theology John's name is, of course, especially linked with his *Source of Knowledge*. In addition to a synopsis of the history of heresy, which presents many problems for the history of literature, this consists of a compendium of dialectics and of a compact exposition of the content of the orthodox faith. In this work John turns out to be, not an original thinker, but probably the most original mosaicist within the art of theology. To refuse him on this account a prominent place in the development of theology, as has usually been the case, is to overlook the theme of this mosaic, for which the *depositum fidei* is a model. In its first stage, Western scholasticism, which had early become acquainted with John through translations esteemed this work highly. And on closer examination one can also understand how deep are John's tracks in Byzantine theology. His work did summarize this achievement with special skill, with real erudition and theological instinct, and passed it on for use in a poorer age. It must not be forgotten that the separation of philosophical and purely theological topics, apparently first made by John, was a contribution to systematization, which was able to facilitate substantially the self-realization of theology on the philosophical bases of its thought. The influence of this theologian on the succeeding generations of Byzantine theologians can only be fully appreciated when one pictures to oneself the great importance attaching to liturgical reading in introducing young students of divinity to the world of thought of the theology of the past — the *vitae* of the saints sufficiently prove this.

The theology of the iconoclasts themselves is substantially less well known to us. However, from the extant fragments of the Emperor Constantine V and of the great Synod of 751 can be sifted trains of thought which are not without importance for the history of theology. The following is deserving of special note. The Quinisext Council of 692, and hence the orthodox complement to the great imperial Councils of 553 and 680–81, had in its Canon 82 attacked the pictorial representation of Christian symbols, such as the Lamb of God, because in these symbols it saw "shadows" of the New Testament fulness but not the fulness itself. It seems as though, for the iconoclast theologians, this train of thought, that is, the full reality of grace of the New Testament, was the decisive element. Only in this way can we understand why again and again they pointed out that images in the Church caused persons to forget that in the Church there is *the* authentic image of Christ, the Eucharistic Bread, and that, in comparison with it, nothing else can claim any true reality. The slight regard paid by the iconodule theologians of the second phase to this perhaps clumsily advanced argument may not have been without effect on the later and rather superficial Byzantine theology of the Eucharist. A synthesis was no longer sought in the heat of battle.

No slight role in the second phase was played by the Abbot of Studion, Theodore (759–826). His works on iconoclasm have come down to us only in truncated form. Theodore was a person who united the exaltation of the martyr with the vehemence of the politician — of a politician who, even in times of peace in the Church, was almost always driven into opposition or else forced himself into it. He took up John Damascene's ideas, but sharpened them, brought them to too fine a point, and made the cult of icons an essential element in the theology of the Incarnation. However, Theodore's importance lay not in the field of speculative theology but in that of monasticism, to be discussed later.

The greatest theologian of the second phase of iconoclasm was certainly Nicephorus, Patriarch from 806 to 815; he died in exile in 828. It only rarely occurred to the iconoclasts of the second phase to label the cult of images idolatry. All the more, then, they emphasized the patristic basis of their doctrine, which was now in fact not too complicated. What was characteristic of him was precisely that he, to a greater extent than John Damascene even, introduced this notion of tradition into the argumentation. The cult of images had to be lawful because it is the Church's tradition. However, as in the case of Theodore, in Nicephorus also the "viewing" as a basic theological element pushed itself to the fore; the Gospel of hearing was substantially perfected in a Gospel of seeing. For the first time there is decidedly encountered in Nicephorus the condemnation of iconoclasm as an heretical political theology, which sought to substitute the image of the Emperor, on coins, for the image of the heavenly *Pantokrator.*

In connection with John Damascene mention was made of the importance of the contemporary homiletics and hymnography. But Andrew of Crete (d. 740) also played a significant role in liturgical poetry as an early representative of that *Kanon*-poetry, which replaced the old *kontakion* and in which the poetic genius of the Byzantine Church found a congenial form.

The hagiography of the period began with the first *vitae* of the defenders of images, whereas canon law and exegesis attracted scarcely any notice.

Byzantine monasticism and its development are of particular importance in the period of iconoclasm. The struggle of the Emperors against the monks played no part in the beginning of the movement, but when the orthodox resistance solidified it was the monks who assumed the leadership. This circumstance gave them an ecclesiastical and political importance which they did not again achieve until the late Byzantine period.

Constantine V's persecuting measures did serious damage to some of these monasteries but were unable to prevent a rapid recovery. In this connection it is clear that we must imagine these monasteries as loose settlements consisting of primitive lauras or mountain caves, hence as institutions which were not firmly established in one particular place but claimed all the mobility that so long characterized the Byzantine form of monasticism. From this Bithynian monastic settlement proceeded also the new impulses of monasticism in the capital. In 794, Theodore took charge of the abbey, but in 798 he transferred the community, threatened by Muslim attacks, to the virtually abandoned monastery of Studion in Constantinople. Studion thereby became the headquarters of a circle of monks who were active and extremely interested in ecclesiastical and political affairs in the capital.

The norm for Byzantine monachism as regards organization was Justinian's legislation, which, with a few exceptions, had made the cenobitic ideal binding. But this ideal had long been violated by the principle of freedom of movement and by the permanently present ideal of the anachoretic life, as well as by the institute of the spiritual direction of the novices by charismatically gifted elderly monks, whose influence sharply reduced that of the abbots. Theodore now tried to restore the purest form of the cenobitic ideal. This goal was promoted by his monastic instructions, by the brief rules, composed in verse, for the individual of offices and occupations in his monastery, and above all by his rule, which we no longer possess in the original. Theodore, the type of the aristocratic Byzantine from the high official hierarchy, thereby transferred his qualities of leadership to the cloister and created for himself an instrument of ecclesiastical policy already discussed. The effort was limited to Studion and its success must have ended after a couple of generations. It was only two centuries later that Athanasius, the founder of the laura on Mount Athos, stirred the rule of the Studite to new life, but in an area remote from the capital and hence lacking the possibilities of excessively direct political ambitions.

The Age of Charles the Great
(768 to 814)

Eugen Ewig

CHAPTER 83

Charles the Great and Italy

At Pepin's death in 768 his older son Charles, was twenty-six, while the younger, Carloman, was seventeen. The magnates did homage to Charles at Noyon, to Carloman at Soissons, where in 751 Pepin had been made King. Charles obtained the Atlantic provinces, from Gascony to Frisia; Carloman, the central and Mediterranean territories. At the Roman Synod of 769, decrees determined the procedure of subsequent papal elections. An active vote was limited to the clergy; a passive vote, to the cardinal priests and cardinal deacons. To the laity was left only acclamation, but it was a legal requirement, for only after the acclamation was it possible to draw up the document of election, which had to be signed by the laity also. The election procedure thus determined continued to be an ideal. Practice quite often departed from it, but reformers had recourse to it later. Finally, the synod again expressed its views in regard to the question of icons, probably at the urging of the three oriental Patriarchs, who had condemned iconoclasm.

After a new attempt by the Queen-Mother Bertrada to bring about a settlement had proved unavailing with Carloman in June 770, Charles sought allies against his brother. Bertrada effected a pact of friendship between Desiderius and Charles. Charles married a daughter of the Lombard King, thereby becoming at the same time the brother-in-law of Tassilo of Bavaria and of Arichis of Benevento, who had shortly before married other daughters of Desiderius. Charles certainly had no intention of allowing his father-in-law a free hand against Rome.

Charles' newly consumated connection to the Lombards did not fit into Pope Stephen's plans at all well. And Stephen's own plans were so badly executed that he himself ended up under Lombard protection and died a short time later a failure. One can well imagine with what feelings Charles received the report of these happenings at Rome, which his *missi* had allowed to take place by their inactivity. The policy of the Lombard King had led him into a blind alley, for Charles could no more tolerate a Lombard protectorate over Rome than he could allow Carloman to intervene in Italy. Apparently even before the end of the year Charles dismissed his Lombard Queen and thereby broke completely with her father. Shortly before there had occurred an event which completely altered the situation and gave Charles all the trump-cards — his twenty-year-old brother Carloman died on 4 December 771. While Charles was reuniting the Frankish Kingdom, a change was also in process at Rome. As successor of Stephen III there was chosen the deacon Hadrian, who belonged to the city nobility of the Via Lata and, by origin and career, gave promise of bridging the opposition between the *proceres ecclesiae* and the *iudices militiae*. Very soon after Hadrian's consecration, which took place on 9 February 772, the Lombard King sent to the new Pope a demand for a pact of friendship with him. As a *sine qua non* Hadrian stipulated the fulfilling of the promise of restitution which Desiderius, had made to his predecessor. At the end of March he sent Afiarta to Pavia as his envoy, thus removing that dangerous man from Rome. Even before the arrival of the papal embassy, Desiderius had launched an attack on the exarchate; he seized Ferrara, Comacchio, and Faenza and laid siege to Ravenna.

The Pope protested against this violation of peace. Desiderius conspired with Afiarta for a repetition of the game of the previous year and demanded a personal meeting with Hadrian. But Hadrian, who had "a heart of diamond," did not let himself be intimidated. He insisted on his condition.

The crisis came to a head in the succeeding months, as the Lombards besieged Rome in the winter of 772–73, Hadrian, "necessitate compulsus," decided to appeal to Charles.

Like his predecessor, Desiderius drew up his forces in the defiles of the Mont Cenis, where Charles himself faced him. But the Frankish King had ordered a second army under his uncle Bernard to the Mon Jovis, or Great Saint Bernard. It went through the pass without much opposition and advanced to the Plain of the Po. Desiderius' army, seized with panic, fled in the direction of Pavia. The events of 754 and 756 were repeated, except that now was displayed the "Iron Charles," who abandoned his father's methods and demanded unconditional surrender from the Lombards.

Meanwhile, defections from Desiderius had also begun in Central Italy. Only Arichis of Benevento, son-in-law of Desiderius, remained loyal to the Lombard King.

The course of events in Central Italy appears to have worried Charles, and so he decided on a further step that led beyond what his father had done. With a large retinue he made a pilgrimage to Rome at the end of March 774.

Charles had not come to Rome merely to pray. On Easter Wednesday the decisive political agreements, which had certainly already been under discussion, were reached. The Pope, attended by the *iudices cleri et militiae,* went to Saint Peter's and asked the King to implement the *promissio* of Quierzy, which was now clearly interpreted as a promise of donation. The *promissio* was read. It received

Charles' approval, whereupon he had his chancellor draw up a second promise of donation similar to the first. In this Charles promised to Saint Peter and to his vicar, besides the duchy of Rome, which was not expressly mentioned, the island of Corsica, the exarchate of Ravenna, the provinces of Venetia and Istria, and also the duchies of Spoleto and Benevento. The northern frontier of the papal territory was designated by the line Luni–Sorgnano–La Cisa Pass–Parma–Reggio–Mantua–Monselice.

No less significant than the *promissio* were the consequences in regard to constitutional law that Hadrian drew from the new situation. Until Charles' Italian expedition Hadrian, like his predecessors, had dated his charters according to the Emperor's regnal years. The years of the pontificate and the Pope's name and image replaced them. The importance of this change is clear: the Papal State seceded from the Empire, the Pope became a sovereign.

This change may have been agreed upon with Charles, since about the same time he assumed an expanded title. The Lombard King surrendered to the Frankish ruler on 5 June 774. On 16 July is first encountered the triple style of *Rex Francorum et Langobardorum atque Patricius Romanorum* to express the constitutional structure of Charles' expanded realm. If Charles officially assumed the designation of *Patricius Romanorum,* which had already been conferred on his father by the Popes but which Pepin had never used, he was thereby making known that the protection of the Papal State had now moved from the moral into the juristic sphere and had gained a new constitutional importance.

The mention of Constantine must not be overlooked. The text of the papal letter is reminiscent of the so-called *Constitutum Constantini,* for the dating of which, in our view, Hadrian's letter provides a *terminus ad quem.* The famous forgery made use in its *narratio* of the legend of Silvester, which can be shown to go back to ca. 500. According to the *Constitutum* Constantine the Great handed over to Saint Peter and his vicars, whose universal primacy he sanctioned by imperial law, the imperial *palatium* of the Lateran, the insignia of imperial sovereignty, and "Romae urbis et omnes Italicae seu occidentalium regionum provincias, loca et civitates." The Roman clergy obtained the dignities and prerogatives of the Senate. The Emperor transferred his residence to Byzantium and abandoned Rome and the West to the Roman Church. The imperial ratification of the Roman primacy could only have been directed at Constantinople, for this point was not contested in the West. It was, of course, already in the Silvester legend. In addition, the *Constitutum* emphasized the quasi-imperial position of the Pope in the West, that is, the papal sovereignty, first claimed by Hadrian after 774, as well as the sovereign rights to the provinces of Rome and Italy "seu occidentalium regionum," which are probably to be interpreted as a claim to a large Italian ecclesiastical principality. The formal criteria of the forgery permit an even earlier stage in the time of Hadrian's three predecessors, but the legal content points clearly to the pontificate of Hadrian, more particularly to the years 774–78.

Hadrian was probably under no great illusions any more as to the success of his final appeal to Charles. The King of the Franks, who, following the set back at Roncesvalles, had to suppress a new Saxon revolt paid the long projected visit to Rome at Easter, 5 April 781. The time was ripe for an adjustment of the Italian question, especially since at Constantinople the Empress Irene, after the premature death of Leo IV on 8 September 780, had assumed the regency for her son, Constantine VI, who was under age. The Empress had resumed contact with the West. Solemn ceremonies, which served to secure the Carolingian Dynasty and to exonerate Charles, demonstrated at the same time the concord of Pope and King. Hadrian and Charles together sent an embassy to the Duke of Bavaria, Tassilo, with the admonition to remain loyal to the Frankish King. The Pope interred his dream of a large Papal State, which was now adjusted in size and was made more compact by Charles and now acquired its definitive shape.

C H A P T E R   8 4

The Completing of the Frankish Empire

Pepin had left to his sons a Saxon problem as well as an Italian one. The original Saxons made their home in Holstein. In the third century they had united with the Chauci, who lived between the Ems and the Elbe, and then they had advanced triumphantly to Britain as well as southward. Together with the Franks they had destroyed the Thuringian Kingdom in the sixth century and occupied the area south of Hanover between the Weser, the Elbe, the Unstrut, and the Saale. Finally, around 700 they conquered the territory of the Bructeri south of the Lippe, which belonged to the Frankish Kingdom. On the eve of Charles' Saxon wars the Saxon "state" appeared as a loosely organized aristocratic republic, with a strict class distinction between the chieftains of the original Saxon stock on the one hand and the *frilingen* and *laten* of the subjugated districts on the other.

Only more or less incidental features of Saxon paganism are known. The divine trinity, already transmitted by Tacitus, appears in the Saxon formula of abjuration as Wodan, Donar, and Saxnot (Ziu). The "Saxon steed" played an important role as a cult animal; it followed the chieftain to his grave, and its flesh was eaten in the ritual meal.

The earlier Carolingians put a stop to Saxon expansion and subjected the frontier areas of Westphalia and Eastphalia to tribute. Alongside the Frankish frontier fortresses churches were to be found quite early. Willibrord, Swithbert, and Boniface had started out here but had soon established new churches in the border zone. Important missionary centers were Utrecht, Swidbertswerth. At the time of Pepin the Anglo-Saxon centers of Frisia, Hesse, and Thuringia were often in competition with the old Frankish sees of Cologne, Mainz, and Worms. In the northern sector Utrecht, as the Anglo-Saxon center, continued to exist independently of Cologne.

In the Hessian and Thuringian frontier districts there was no longer any possibility of a "non-political" mission, that is, one not directed by the Frankish King. But in the northern section the situation had not yet hardened to the same degree. The Utrecht mission extended in Charles' first years into the Frisian-Saxon frontier area around Deventer. But the Saxons' hour of destiny had already struck; it was now too late for a real decision in regard to accepting the Christian faith. The political and ecclesiastical incorporation of Saxony into the Frankish Kingdom must have been one of Charles' first aims. He set about realizing it in 772, and again in 775. The Saxons formally submitted in 776.

Outside the march areas Frankish rule seems to have rested especially only on the pro-Frankish faction of the nobility. But there was also an anti-Frankish party and to it belonged the Westphalian Widukind, of a noble family native to the district of Münster and Osnabrück. Instead of appearing in Paderborn, he had fled to the land of the "Northmen." He returned in the autumn of 778, after the Franks' defeat at Roncesvalles, and stirred up the revolt that brought on the second phase of the Saxon war. Up to this time Charles had not advanced beyond Osnabrück–Minden and Wolfenbüttel–Schöningen, but now he proceeded for the first time all the way to the Elbe, where he made contact with the neighboring Slavonic tribes. The inhabitants around Lüneburg and the Northmen accepted baptism in 780. In that year all of Saxony was divided into mission jurisdictions.

Charles felt that the time had now come to bring all of Saxony under the Carolingian government. The country was divided into counties, most of which were entrusted to the pro-Frankish nobles. Probably at that time the King also extended to Saxony the ecclesiastical legislation of the Frankish state and issued the *Capitulatio de partibus Saxoniae,* which L. Halphen reduced to the dreadful formula: acceptance of Christianity or death. The only moderating effects were connected with the decrees on the right of asylum in churches and the rule that offences that were not public could be a matter of ecclesiastical penance.

To be sure, churchmen were not lacking even in the eighth century who opposed the harshness of the law and the crude religious ideas upon which it was based. Criticism of the *capitulatio* and of the missionary methods of these years is an imperishable title to fame for Alcuin and for Paulinus of Aquileia, and it had an effect on Charles.

The *capitulatio,* which could only appear to the Saxon as a violent enforcement of a foreign faith and a foreign law, caused revolt to flare up again. An army, to which the King, called back to Frankland, had entrusted the subjection of the Sorb tribes, was wiped out on the Süntel, where the Franks suffered the worst defeat in the Saxon war. Nevertheless, the Saxons did not risk battle when Charles himself appeared on the scene.

The Saxon war reached its climax in 783–85 and in 784 even spread to Central and Eastern Frisia. When, finally, in the spring of 785 Charles advanced to the Bardowiek, negotiations took place with Widukind and Abbio, who met Charles at the palace of Attigny and were baptized there. With Widukind's submission the second and bloodiest phase of the Saxon war ended. The King prescribed thanksgiving throughout his dominions. The peace was unbroken for seven years, during which the foundations were laid for Saxony's ecclesiastical organization.

The sees of Mainz and Würzburg and the monasteries of Fulda, Hersfeld, and Amorbach became the chief agents of the evangelizing of southern Saxony.

The ecclesiastical personnel on the front did not suffice for the evangelization of eastern Saxony, and so the King applied to the bishoprics inside the Frankish Kingdom.

Gradually there grew up self-sufficient bishoprics in the mission areas, but not before the beginning of the ninth century. The earliest to be established were those in Westphalia and Angria. The Eastphalian sees apparently did not obtain their autonomy before the time of Louis the Pious. The sees of Münster, Osnabrück, and Bremen were assigned to the province of Cologne, which also acquired the Angrian see of Minden that grew out of the Fulda mission field. The sees of Paderborn, Verden, Hildesheim, and Halberstadt were allotted to the province of Mainz. Cologne and Mainz, which shared Saxony, were not by mere chance the ecclesiastical metropolises of the two great deployment areas in the Saxon wars.

While the Saxon wars were in progress Charles was also faced with a Spanish problem. Ever since the annexation of Septimania (or Gothia) to the Frankish Kingdom in 759, the Pyrenees had formed a strong frontier between Franks and Muslims. The Muslims had internal problems of their own.

There appeared before Charles at the Paderborn Diet of 777 Suleiman Ibn al Arabi, *wali* of Barcelona and Gerona, to request the King's aid against the Emir of Córdoba. Charles accepted the offer and probably expected that success would come to him as easily in Spain as it had in Italy. He seems to have envisaged the establishing of a Muslim Spanish vassal state.

The mobilization became a grand-scale undertaking. In 778 the King in person led one army of Franks and Aquitanians via the western passes of the Pyrenees toward Pamplona. The second army marched via Septimania and Le Perthus toward Barcelona. The two armies united before Zaragoza around the middle of June. Thus far everything had proceeded smoothly, but now, for reasons unknown, the *Wali* Hussain refused to surrender the city. Charles finally gave up the enterprise and decided to withdraw. After destroying Pamplona, the Franks crossed the Pyrenees. On 15 August the army was attacked by Basques in the pass of Roncesvalles. Apparently the King was hurrying on ahead with a part of the troops. The entire army was thrown into confusion and many leaders fell. Sixty years later their names were still on everyone's lips, including that of Roland, Margrave of Brittany, glorified in legend.

The assailants were not Muslims but Christian Basques of Navarre or possibly Gascony, and Charles apparently feared a revolt in Aquitaine. He decided to make his son Louis sub-King of Aquitaine in order to oblige the separatist feelings of the Aquitanians and at the same time to relieve the central government. The sub-kingdom was established in 781, together with the sub-kingdom of Italy.

An attack by the Muslims across the Pyrenees was not to be feared, but Abd-ar-Rahman undertook campaigns into the Ebro basin and in 781–83 re-established his authority as far as the Pyrenees. These expeditions also involved measures of retaliation against the Christian population, and many Christians who had been compromised with the Franks emigrated during the next years, among them persons such as Theodulf and Agobard, who were to play a leading role in the Carolingian Renaissance.

On the inclusion of the Lombard Kingdom into Charles' empire the future of Bavaria and of Benevento was left undecided. Tassilo of Bavaria had managed to strengthen his position within his duchy. The ups and downs of Frankish power could for the future be clearly read in Frankish-Bavarian relations. The crisis did not mature until 787. Tassilo asked the Pope to mediate with the Franks, but Hadrian was already too closely bound to Charles, who rejected any mediation. A royal-papal embassy went to the court of Regensburg and demanded compliance with the obligations of a vassal, threatening excommunication. Tassilo submitted only as a result of a concentric deployment of the Franks around Bavaria. He got into contact with the Avars. Thereupon, the Frankish party among the Bavarian magnates instituted a process for high treason. It was deliberated in 788 at Ingelheim, where Tassilo had appeared.

Charles tackled the Beneventan question at almost the same time that he dealt with the Bavarian. When the Lombard Kingdom had been incorporated into the Frankish state, Duke Arichis had assumed the title of *princeps,* thereby claiming a royal position. Benevento was isolated. On the conclusion of the second Saxon war, Charles went to Italy in the winter of 786, and in January 787 he moved against the South Italian duchy. When he had advanced as far as Capua, Arichis made a peace proposal which the King accepted. At Capua appeared also an imperial embassy, which was to discuss the projected marriage of the young Emperor with Charles' daughter. But the marriage alliance had been concluded under different presuppositions. Not only the Beneventan question but also the new ecclesiastical policy of the Empress Irene, who had broken with Iconoclasm in 784, gave occasion for friction between her and the Western ruler. For Irene had invited the Pope, but not the Franks, to the council summoned by the imperial court to restore the cult of icons in the East and thereby ecclesiastical unity in Christendom.

After the ending of the Saxon war in 785 and the suppression of the Thuringian, or Hardrad's, revolt in the Main region in 786, the Frankish Kingdom experienced five years of relative quiet which were decisive for the progress of the Carolingian Renaissance. In this period Charles had secured the frontiers against the Bretons, the Wilzi of the Elbe, and the Greeks in Benevento and Istria and had annexed Bavaria. The incorporation of Bavaria made the Franks the immediate neighbors of the Avars and gave them new tasks.

Within just about five years all the dangers that had appeared so menacing in 792–93 had been exorcised. The peaceful pursuits of the 780s could now be taken up again. During the crisis Charles had not lost sight of the intellectual problems, and in 794 at the Synod of Frankfurt he had forcefully expressed the Frankish claim, vis-à-vis Byzantium and Toledo, to have a decisive voice in theological matters also. The *Regnum Francorum* was being transformed into the *Imperium Christianum.*

C H A P T E R   8 5

Reform of Empire and Church:
The Carolingian Renaissance

In the first decade of his reign Charles the Great was so preoccupied with the great questions of "foreign policy" that little leisure for the inner order of his realm was left to him. Not until the second decade of his rule was he able to resume his father's legislative activity. What has survived of the capitularies does not exhibit all the legislation of these years but does make known the growing intensity of Charles' domestic political activity.

The word *capitulare* was new; it refers to the dividing of the text into *capitula* and was probably adopted from Lombard-Italian usage. In content the capitularies corresponded to the old decrees and edicts. Their juridical basis was the royal ban — the King's right to command under penalty. Promulgation was made by the King orally (*verbum regis*), often in the form of solemn address (*adnuntiatio*). Hence the surviving capitularies are not legally binding law texts in the late Roman or the modern sense, but caption outlines of projects, or circulars, in most cases informally jotted down by secretaries *ad hoc.* Only in special cases were capitularies drawn up by the chancery.

The idea of peace again appeared in the *admonitio generalis*, probably formulated by Alcuin. Peace and order were promoted by organizational reforms of fundamental importance, which were implemented at this time, though the texts of the corresponding capitularies have not survived.

In the *admonitio generalis* Charles appears as a Church reformer of the type of King Josiah of Israel, who exerted himself, *circumeundo, corrigendo, ammonendo,* to lead back the kingdom entrusted to him by God to true religion. Apparently the capitulary was drawn up by Alcuin. The first part of its decrees is based on the canonical collection of Dionysius Exiguus, given to the King by Pope Hadrian in 774. It constitutes a sort of summary of canonical regulations for the clergy in the framework of diocese and province. The restoration of discipline among monks and clergy by means of the renewal of the diocesan law of the early Church had been a fixed goal of all Frankish synods since Boniface.

Despite recourse to the juridical arrangement of the earlier Church, the reestablishing of the ecclesiastical provinces in the Frankish Kingdom was no mere restoration. New was the combining of the archiepiscopal dignity with the office of metropolitan, which spread from England (Canterbury and York) first to the Frankish West (Sens) and then to the entire kingdom. In earlier times prelates superior in rank to metropolitans, such as patriarchs and papal vicars, were termed archbishops. Boniface and Chrodegang of Metz, as leaders of the Austrasian Church, were indeed archbishops but not metropolitans. Even under Charles the Great the archiepiscopal dignity was bestowed as a personal distinction. But thereafter it was regularly given to the bishops of the metropolitan sees. The archiepiscopal pallium became the sign of the metropolitans, who were now obliged to fetch the insignia from Rome within three months, presenting on this occasion a profession of faith. Before receiving the pallium they were not allowed to consecrate their suffragans. Thus the new archbishops were more closely attached to Rome than were the old metropolitans. At the same time, as sharers in papal authority they acquired a stronger position in their provinces. Alongside the Roman concept of the metropolitan power as a sharing in the universal primacy there persisted also the notion, coming from an earlier period, of a metropolitan constitution not created by the papacy.

The decrees of the second part of the *admonitio generalis* were very greatly modeled on the Ten Commandments, which were interpreted in the sense of the public peace. In one special chapter Charles imposed on the clergy the duty of preaching on faith and morals. The two groups, secular and regular clergy are mentioned in the chapter on the conduct of ecclesiastics but are not distinguished in any detail. The *cantus Romanus* was prescribed for the liturgy. Success was achieved only as a result of Charles' exertions. The liturgical books — sacramentary, lectionary, *ordines,* homiliary, antiphonary — were revised on the basis of Roman or Franco-Roman texts by the Carolingian court theologians and disseminated everywhere. Charles himself had asked the Pope for an authentic sacramentary and in 785–86 had received from Hadrian the *Gregorianum.* This, of course, contained only text for the papal liturgical rites; it had to be completed by Alcuin with recourse to the *Gelasianum* of Pepin. In Alcuin's recension this *Gregorianum* or *Hadrianum* obtained in regard to the Western liturgy the same importance that the *Dionyso-Hadriana* did in regard to Western canon law. Thus the consideration of Charles' liturgical reform leads in turn to the great teacher of the Carolingian Renaissance, who also had a decisive share in drawing up the *admonitio* of 789. It was not mere chance that the first allusion of certain date to Charles' concern for education is in the same *admonitio generalis*.

Charles' special gift for creating something new out of earlier modest beginnings appears also in an examination of the Carolingian Renaissance. The teachers at the court school in Pepin's time are unknown. At the beginning of Charles' reign we find two "foreigners," pupils of Alcuin of York: the Anglo-Saxon Beornrad, who obtained the abbey of Echternach in 777, and the Irishman Joseph the Scot. Dungal, another Irishman, famed for his knowledge of astronomy, may also have been in the King's circle at that time. To these men from England and Ireland were added Italians from the time of Charles' second visit to Italy: the Lombard Fardulf, who came to Gaul as an exile in 776, and the grammarians Paulinus and Peter of Pisa in 776 or soon after. The year 782 saw the arrival at court of the Lombard Paul the Deacon. That was an epoch-making year, for in it Alcuin, who had directed the cathedral school of York since 767, took up residence at the Frankish court. He assumed the direction of the court school; when he departed for Tours in 796 it passed to Einhard and thereafter was held by Frankish court chaplains. The last great representative of the early Carolingian Renaissance, the Visigoth Theodulf, may have come into the Frankish Kingdom with the wave of Spanish emigrants in 780. Some time before 790 he was admitted to the circle of the court scholars.

The early Carolingian Renaissance came to an end with Alcuin's removal to Tours. By then the older teachers at the court school had already departed. The education imparted at the court school was based on the *Septem Artes,* handed down from late antiquity. The emphasis lay on the *trivium* (grammar, rhetoric, dialectic) but the *quadrivium* (arithmetic, geometry, astronomy, music) was not entirely neglected. Instruction comprised both the elementary and the higher levels, but was constituted differently according to the several groups of individuals. Only one group of them was being prepared for an ecclesiastical career; another group, for a career in the world. Teachers and outstanding pupils were gathered under the presidency of the King into a sort of "academy" with regular meetings. In these they had common discussions on learned topics, solved riddles, and read poetic letters.

The members of this intimate circle bore pseudonyms, marks of *familiaritas*, but not selected by caprice. First of all was Charles, known as King David. Then came the Archchaplain Hildebald, Archbishop of Cologne (ca. 791–819), who, as the foremost ecclesiastic of the realm, represented the High Priest Aaron. The abbots bore the names of ancient monastic Fathers or of prophets. The classical pseudonyms of the secular dignitaries had no importance of their own, but were merely taken from Virgil's *Eclogues*. The same is not true, however, of the literary pseudonyms. Horace, Homer, Ovid, and Virgil indicated scholars and poets. These nicknames expressed not only a veneration for the classical authors, but also ambition to reproduce them in a changed world, out of a Christian spirit.

The renewal of the *Septem Artes* was undertaken, not as an end in itself, but in subordination to Charles' concern for reform. The study of the *Septem Artes* was the indispensable prerequisite for the emendation and exegesis of the sacred texts and for the proper ordering and organization of the liturgy. Reform had to begin with the simplest things — handwriting and orthography. Thus it appears in the *admonitio generalis.* It is said elsewhere that, while knowledge without works is dead, the prerequisite for right acting is right knowing.

Hence the first fruit of Charles' exertions for the reform of education was the new Carolingian script, which was distinguished from the older scripts by the clarity of the letters and the preciseness of words and sentences. Its first example — the poetic dedication of the Godescalc evangeliary, produced at court in 781–83 — is a landmark in the history of the Carolingian Renaissance. Refining of script and refining of language were intimately connected. The linguistic emendation led, not to a revival of classical Latin, but only to an elimination of vulgarisms. From the Carolingian reform proceeded Medieval Latin, based on the Bible and the Fathers and already foreshadowed in England.

Around the same time began the wider manuscript transmission of classical authors.

The "authentic text" of canon law, presented to Charles in the *Dionyso-Hadriana* in 774, inaugurated the series of these *libri canonici*. Shortly afterward other canonical collections of the "Gelasian Renaissance" found admittance into the Frankish Kingdom. The *Hispana Gallica* too was circulated.

The "authentic" sacramentary, the *Gregorianum* or *Hadrianum* sent to Charles in 786, Alcuin completed by recourse to Pepin's *Gelasianum*. Alcuin also published a lectionary containing the Mass readings, which was in accord with the *Hadrianum.* The Roman *ordines,* containing the instructions for the rites, were revised by an unknown scholar. Charles entrusted to Paul the Deacon the task of compiling a homiliary — patristic readings for the Office — which was introduced universally by the *Epistola generalis.* Between 758 and 763 Pope Paul I had sent King Pepin a Roman antiphonary. It was edited by Amalarius and published under Louis the Pious — the last liturgical book to be prepared. The Roman texts were the basis of the *libri canonici* in canon law and liturgy. In this context must be mentioned also the *Rule* of Saint Benedict, since from as early as the seventh century it was regarded in Gaul as the "Roman" monastic rule. In 787 Charles had an "authentic" copy of it made at Montecassino. The Roman calendar of saints was also received, along with the Roman liturgical books. Alcuin inserted it into the *Hadrianum.*

Charles the Great was also concerned about the text of the Bible. What Charles was mostly concerned with was to have manuscripts that were correct in regard to orthography and grammar.

From the court proceeded the initiative for the renewal of cultural life. The Carolingian Renaissance spread from the court, and new centers of culture took their place beside the older ones. Teachers and pupils carried the spirit of the court school to the places where they assumed new duties. In the old and the new centers *sapientia saecularis* and *divina* were not cultivated only for their own sake. The pastoral care of souls was also to be renewed from the great churches. There had been parish schools as early as the sixth century. They gave elementary instruction in reading, writing, and arithmetic, and in particular a cate-chetical instruction. That the faithful should learn the creed and the "Our Father" by heart was a demand made by the Carolingian capitularies ceaselessly from the *admonitio* of 789.

Preaching and catechetical instruction could take place only in the vernacular. Hence it should not cause surprise that the baptismal vows, "Our Father," and creed, and later the doxology, the list of sins, and formulas of confession are among the oldest texts in the German language. In general, the *admonitio generalis* forms the *terminus a quo* in dating them. From them developed a literature of translation, which included the psalter, hymns, and the Benedictine *Rule* (interlinear glosses), and reached their climax in a translation of works which were grouped around Isidore's *De fide catholica.*

If Old High German literature began earliest in Bavaria and Fulda, its development took place in a clear relationship to the Carolingian Renaissance. To be sure, none of the extant linguistic monuments came from the court itself. Without exception they lay in the area connected with Boniface, with Bavaria, and with Pirmin's Alemannia. Old High German was given its phonetic characteristics by an older Bavarian and a younger Rhine-Frankish linguistic movement.

CHAPTER 86

Iconoclasm, Adoptionism, and Filioque

With astonishing rapidity the Frankish Kingdom rose to the position of the ranking Christian political power from the middle of the eighth century, and at the end of the century it was also about to assume intellectual leadership in the West. The *Imperium,* still involved in difficult struggles with the caliphate and overrun by Slavonic immigrants in its European provinces, was relegated to the frontier of the *orbis christianus.* But the Emperors had maintained their claim to be the rulers of this *orbis.* As had once happened in the Frankish Kingdom, so now in Christendom itself *auctoritas* and *potestas* had separated. So long as Iconoclasm kept Rome and Constantinople apart, this may have seemed unimportant, especially since the imperial claim was scarcely recognized in the West any more. The reconciliation of Pope and Emperor at the Council of Nicaea in 787, however, could not fail to pose the question of the position of the Frankish King in Christendom. The attitude of the Franks to the decrees of Nicaea was thus encumbered with this question from the outset.

The acts of Nicaea reached Charles in a poor Latin translation that had been made in Rome. In 790 the King commissioned the Visigoth Theodulf to undertake a detailed refutation. Theodulf's first draft was discussed at court. Then Charles sent the Pope a memorandum in which he bluntly rejected the Council; this was the *Capitulare de imaginibus,* drawn up in the form of theses. Hadrian replied with a defense of Nicaea. His answer was also discussed at court and taken into account in the final redaction of Theodulf's work, but the viewpoint peculiar to Theodulf's treatise was maintained essentially unchanged. Thus originated in 791 the *Libri Carolini* — the embodiment of the Frankish view of the quarrel over images, composed by Theodulf, discussed and corrected in the court circle, and bearing the name of the King himself.

Theodulf had not contented himself with a superficial refutation of the Latin translation of the acts. He had developed a theology of word and image of real value, and in addition he had taken up the question of the Emperor's position in the Church. In the question of images he established the Western view, following Gregory the Great. At the outset he defined its limitations against the iconoclasts, who confused image and idolatry. Essentially Theodulf completely agreed with the authentic acts of Nicaea, when he clearly distinguished *adoratio,* belonging to God alone, from *veneratio,* the honoring of the saints and their relics. But he was unwilling to allow even *veneratio* to images. The Platonic notion of art held by the Greeks, who honored the prototype in the copy, was foreign to him. It may indeed be able to make past deeds and happenings present, but not to represent adequately a religious content, in contradistinction to the revealed word. Hence, such revealed signs as the ark of the covenant and the cross were, in his view, superior to the religious picture. Thus Theodulf's rationalistic notion of art ended in a spiritualism based on the revealed word.

In the very first chapter the *Libri Carolini* sharply attacked the forms of the imperial cult that had been passed on to the Christian world. The polemic was aimed at the formula "per eum qui conregnat nobis deus," for God reigns in us, not with us. The honoring of images of the Emperor was directly connected with the theme of the cult of images, "nullam enim hoc scelus fecisse legimus gentem, nisi Babylonios et Romanos." Here the ancient equation Rome-Babylon for the *Imperium* was again dragged out. But the imperial authority as such was not for this reason to be depreciated. In another passage it was explained that, according to Scripture, emperors, like kings, are to be honored, but in due form and not *propter se vel propter ordinem*. In the attack on the Empress Irene, whose right to speak at the Council was severely criticized because of her sex, the question of the legitimate imperial authority could perhaps be faintly heard.

Connected with the polemic against the imperial office was that against the universal character of the Second Council of Nicaea. According to the *Libri Carolini* the universality of a council could be determined quantitatively and qualitatively. Quantitatively, a council should be regarded as universal if the totality of Christian churches was represented or consulted; qualitatively, if two or three churches (Mt. 18:20) issued decisions in the framework of the Catholic tradition. But the authoritative guarantee of tradition was the Roman Church, which "nullis synodicis constitutis ceteris ecclesiis praelata est, sed ipsius Domini auctoritate primatum tenet." Thus was the ground cut from under the older view of the ecumenical council as convoked by the Emperor and justified by the participation of Rome and of the four eastern patriarchates. Charles, in whose name the *Libri Carolini* were issued, stressed with pride that the Church in his realm had never swerved from the "sancta et veneranda communio" with Rome; that this bond had been recently strengthened by the acceptance of the Roman liturgy; that he not only ruled Gaul, Germany, and Italy, but had also led the Saxons to the faith. Thereby, indirectly but unmistakably, was registered a Frankish claim to a voice in the great affairs of Christendom.

The fact that the *Libri Carolini* sharply emphasized the Roman primacy and at the same time challenged the validity of the Nicene decrees, which had been issued in agreement with the Pope, is not without irony. Charles sent the final redaction to the Pope, but shortly thereafter the great crisis broke and the matter was not pursued further for the time being. The King did not take it up again until 794, together with the question of Adoptionism, which ran parallel to it.

After his failure at Zaragoza Charles did not completely lose sight of Spanish affairs. Around 782 a certain Egila, whose name was Gothic and who had been consecrated by Wilchar of Sens as a bishop without a fixed see, went to Spain with the errand of propagating the Frankish ecclesiastical reform beyond the Pyrenees and of uniting Spain more firmly to Rome. Egila's mission was compromised by his overzealous helper, Migetius, who not only attacked mixed marriages between Christians and Muslims but also eating with Muslims and who by his Trinitarian doctrine made himself vulnerable to attack. The Spanish Primate, Elipandus of Toledo, who is said not to have been himself favorable to the intermingling of Christians and Muslims, had Migetius condemned by a synod at Seville before October 785. At this synod Elipandus described the relationship of the man Jesus to God by means of the image of adoption: "Christus adoptivus filius Altissimi humanitate, et nequaquam adoptivus divinita."

Elipandus' formula should not be understood as an echo of older heresies. In the Spanish Church the struggle against contrary heretical doctrines — Arianism and Apollinarianism, Priscillianism, Monophysitism, and Monothelitism — had led to a sharp contrasting of the two natures of Christ, and hence among the Spanish Church Fathers there appeared formulas similar that of Elipandus for explaining the Man Jesus. The key expression was transmitted by the Mozarabic liturgy, which bore the stamp of Elipandus' predecessors. The problem in which the Metropolitan of Toledo was in sympathy with Nestorius was the safeguarding of Jesus' true manhood, perhaps because of the association with Muslims, for whom the God-Man was a stumbling block . The distinguishing of the two natures of Christ in the image of *filius adoptivus* (humanity) and *filius proprius* (divinity) was not heterodox, but outside Spain it could be misunderstood, for in Germanic law adoption signified a very loose bond, in contradistinction to the *Lex Romana Visigothorum.*

The formula of Elipandus would hardly have been attacked had there not developed in Spain itself an opposition between the free Christians of Asturias and those of the Emirate of Córdoba. The conflict originated with Abbot Beatus of Liébana, famed for his commentary on the Apocalypse, and his pupil, Bishop Etherius of Osma, who accused Elipandus of destroying the unity of the person of Christ and of denying the divinity of the Redeemer. In 785 Elipandus replied with anathema against his opponents. Thereupon Beatus and Etherius composed a polemic, which they published in March 786. The Pope, who had been informed by adherents of Beatus and regarded Elipandus as a Nestorian, called upon the Spanish episcopate to bring the Primate back to the unity of faith. But, except for Teudila of Seville, the bishops of the Emirate of Córdoba ranged themselves behind the Metropolitan of Toledo.

The Franks were also dragged into the conflict by the Asturians, who around 790 denounced the adoptionist attitude of Felix, Bishop of Urgel, an esteemed prelate in the area under Frankish rule south of the Pyrenees. The formula of Elipandus could not fail to give special offense in the Frankish sphere, for in the Carolingian view of Christ the stress lay on the divine nature, and the Roman notion of adoption, with its strong bonds, was unfamiliar to the Franks. In the summer of 792 Felix was summoned to a synod at Regensburg. Paulinus of Aquileia seems to have been entrusted with the refutation. Felix recanted at Regensburg and a second time at Rome. He then returned to his see but fled to Muslim Spain, where he again professed the formula of Elipandus. The Muslim attack of 793 enabled him to return to Urgel, and now the adoptionist propaganda reached formerly Visigothic Septimania.

In 792–93 Elipandus and the episcopate of the emirate protested to Charles and the Frankish episcopate against the treatment of the Bishop of Urgel. Charles sent the Spaniards' documents to Hadrian, who condemned them, whereupon the King summoned a general assembly and synod of his realm to meet at Frankfurt on 1 June 791. The Council of Frankfurt was content, in so far as the Greeks were concerned, with condemning one proposition, which was indeed heterodox in the completely distorted Latin translation. Clearer and more comprehensive was the rejection of the Toledo adoptionist formula. A detailed refutation of Adoptionism was provided in two memoranda of the Frankish and Italian episcopates. The Frankish memorandum and a related letter from the King were composed by Alcuin, who had just returned from a rather long stay in England. Alcuin countered Elipandus' formula "Filius adoptivus" with the formula "Homo assumptus," which was intended to express that the human nature of Jesus had never had an autonomous existence. Whether or not the Toledans grasped the nuance is doubtful, since *adoptivus* and *assumptus* were very often used synonymously in Spain.

In regard to images the Council of Frankfurt did no more than condemn *adoratio,* and hence it did not touch the real kernel of the Nicene decrees. For the moment the controversy over images was concluded by the Frankfurt decree; it did not flare up again in the West until the reign of Louis the Pious.

The case was different with regard to the procession of the Holy Spirit, which Theodulf had used against the Greeks, presumably for the first time, in the *Libri Carolini.* At issue was the *Filioque* in the Creed of Nicaea-Constantinople, "qui ex Patre Filioque procedit," which was lacking in the original text but had appeared from time to time, first of all with Ambrose. It was present especially in the Creed of the Council of Toledo of 589, adopted probably as a clarification of the Catholic view vis-à-vis Arianism. From the Mozarabic Creed the *Filioque* had passed into the Gallican, and was in Charles' Creed of 794 with which the royal letter to Elipandus concluded. But Theodulf had incorporated the question of the procession of the Holy Spirit in his polemic, and Hadrian's rejection of the polemic had included this point also. The question had played no role at Frankfurt. But Paulinus of Aquileia took up the matter again at a provincial synod at Cividale in 796–97, which justified the Frankish stand in greater detail. What was involved at the moment was a mere echo of the Frankish-Byzantine confrontation. The explosive force of the disputed question would not take effect until later.

Adoptionism was likewise treated again at Cividale, and afterward Paulinus also composed a polemic against Felix. It was especially important to win back the adoptionists in Septimania and in the district south of the Pyrenees, reconquered since 798. Pope Leo II condemned Adoptionism at a Roman synod in October 798.

In Asturias the circle around Beatus and Etherius won out with the accession of Alfonso II to the throne in 791. The Frank Jonas, later Bishop of Orléans, toured the country at this time, and at the latest in 799 Beatus was in friendly contact with Alcuin. With the establishing of the archiepiscopal see of Oviedo in 811 the small Christian Kingdom of Asturias withdrew from the obedience of Toledo. Adoptionism lingered on for a while in the Emirate of Córdoba, but basically its fate was sealed here too with the death of Elipandus.

CHAPTER 87

From Frankish Kingdom to Christian Empire

The Carolingian Kingdom had survived the crises of 778 and 792–93; it came out of the last and most severe crisis stronger and greater than it had been previously. The efforts of the 780s for inner order and the intellectual renewal could be taken up again and bear fruit. The King's "project for a capital" show that after the crisis he again addressed himself to the plans and measures of 786–91. From the conclusion of the Saxon War in 785 Aachen took the place of the previously favored villa. It was not the change from Herstal to Aachen that was of historical significance, but rather the related plan of building the new residence as a stable center of the empire. On his Italian journey of 786–87 Charles took the preliminary steps for realization of this intention. From the end of 794 Aachen clearly and unambiguously appeared as the center of the empire, even though the buildings had not yet been finished.

In legislation too Charles continued to build on the foundations laid in the 780s. In the Frankfurt Capitulary there occurred for the first time a regulation in regard to the proprietary Church law, which the Carolingians had not previously dared to touch. Charles did not infringe on the right of alienation belonging to the lords of churches, but he ruled that churches once erected had to be maintained and that the divine worship conducted in them must not be jeopardized. The proprietary church system was indirectly affected by the prescriptions on ecclesiastical discipline. Thus already in 743 Carloman and Pepin had, decreed the universal obligation of the clergy to give an accounting to the bishop, to receive him on the occasion of the visitation and of his confirmation journey, and to get the chrism from him every year.

A circular letter of 794–800, the *Epistola de litteris colendis,* imposed on the cathedrals and abbeys of the empire the obligation of establishing schools. But the finest sign of the maturing process of these years was the new missionary method, which was defined at a synod held in Bavaria in 796 under the direction of Arn of Salzburg and Paulinus of Aquileia.At the out set the bishops mentioned that conversion is God's work, not man's. They demanded an accommodation to a *gens bruta et inrationalis,* which needed instruction. Mass baptisms and force were rejected. The instruction which had to precede baptism should aim at understanding and not at fear of man. The new principles were based on old insights of Gregory the Great. They were intended for the mission among Avars and Slavs, which belonged to the sphere of the Archbishops of Salzburg and Aquileia, but they were also to be applied to the Saxon mission. In this connection Alcuin's criticism of the previous mission, including the condemnation of the overhasty introduction of the tithe, brought about a change. The *Capitulare Saxonicum,* issued at Aachen in 797, introduced the new policy of reconciliation.

The age of the great conquests was concluded with the Avar war; it was now necessary to assure the gains against external attacks. Frankish might did not suffice to take possession of the entire Avar Empire. The Theiss became the frontier against the Bulgars, who annexed the eastern part of the former Avar realm. But even on the other side of the Theiss the Avars and the Moravians, Slovenes, and Croats, once ruled by the Avars, were now only under the supervision of the Prefect

of Bavaria and of the Margraves of Friuli and Istria. In 796 King Pepin of Italy specified the Drave as the frontier between Bavaria and Italy, between the ecclesiastical
provinces of Salzburg and Aquileia, and Charles ratified this in 803 and 811.

There were no changes in Italy. As earlier, the Dukes or Margraves of Spoleto
provided the border patrol vis-à-vis Benevento and the Byzantines. In the Pyrenees, on the other hand, the situation was not stabilized until the turn of the
century. Envoys sent by Spanish Muslims to ask Charles' aid against the Emir Al
Hakam of Córdoba turned up in Aachen in 797 and 798, but the King had become cautious. The Frankish offensive, resumed in 798, had only limited goals,
which were achieved when Barcelona fell into the hands of the Franks in 801 after
a two years' siege. The conquered strip of Spain, later the County of Catalonia,
was attached to the existing March of Septimania (or Toulouse) and subjected
ecclesiastically to Narbonne.

The expanded Frankish realm, now strengthened on its frontiers, did not have
an equal in the Christian West. Only the British Isles, the Kingdom of Asturias, and
the Principality of Benevento were not included in it.

Irish history is quite obscure at this period. The see of Armagh, founded by
Saint Patrick, achieved a sort of primatial rank in the Emerald Isle around 800 but
it is uncertain whether it also entailed a political concentration.

The *amicitia* of the Frankish ruler with the other Christian kings of the West
had become a reality, even though it might often have appeared in a somewhat
different light beyond the Frankish frontiers from the way it appeared at Aachen.

But the juridical step to the imperial office had not yet been taken. It was
only in the final climax which the *imitatio imperii* achieved in the "Paderborn
Epic" around 799 that a poet dared to seize upon the special titles reserved to the
Emperor: Charles appears as Augustus, Aachen as *Roma secunda*. By then the
crisis in Constantinople and Rome was already evident to all the world: the gates
to the imperial dignity had opened.

A state of war had existed since 788 between Byzantium and the Franks. Support at the imperial court enabled Duke Grimoald of Benevento to evade Frankish
sovereignty in 791. In 797 the Emperor Constantine VI commissioned the Patrician of Sicily, Nicetas, to extend peace feelers. The young ruler, who was weary
of the tutelage exercised by his mother Irene, reverted in the ecclesiastical sphere
to Iconoclasm. It has been suggested that his new policy toward the Franks was
determined by his religious policy.

The conflict between mother and son ended in tragedy. On 15 August 797,
Irene had Constantine VI deposed and blinded. She assumed the government
herself and thereby created a precedent in the history of the *Imperium* that was
extremely vulnerable from the point of view of constitutional law. Since the internal political situation remained precarious, Irene also needed peace. In the
autumn of 798 there appeared at Aachen an embassy sent by the Empress to offer
the renunciation of Istria, then under Frankish occupation, and the surrender of
Benevento. Although the deposition and blinding of Constantine VI were regarded
in the Frankish state also as an unprecedented crime, Charles accepted the offer. The peace still awaited ratification, but before this came about a new and
dramatic event occurred — the revolt against Pope Leo III.

Leo III had succeeded Hadrian I on 27 December 795. Einhard relates that

Charles mourned the dead Pope as a brother. Relations between Charles and Hadrian had not always been untroubled. The Pope had had to give up his dream of a large Papal State in Italy and had stood up to the King when the latter attacked the Second Council of Nicaea. But throughout his life Hadrian had been loyal to the Frankish alliance and in particular he had maintained order in the Papal State. The King probably did not forget this.

The change in the Holy See in December 795 was the first since the incorporation of the Lombard Kingdom into the *Regnum Francorum*. The Romans carried out the election and consecration of Leo III without apprising the King of the Franks, thereby declaring their sovereignty. The new Pope sent to the *Patricicus*-King not only the document of election, but also the keys to the *confessio Sancti Petri* and the standard of the city, with the request that the Romans' oath of obedience and loyalty be received by a representative. It may be doubted whether Hadrian would have offered the oath-taking in this form. But Leo, not belonging by birth to the city nobility, needed the support of the royal protector, since, probably from the outset, he had to deal with a powerful opposition, which included the family of his predecessor.

Charles' reply to Leo III contained fundamental statements regarding the duties of the two powers. They show to what a great extent power had shifted to the side of the King, whom Paulinus of Aquileia had panegyrized as *Rex et Sacerdos* in 794. The often quoted passages run as follows: "It is incumbent upon us, with God's help, to defend Holy Church outwardly with weapons everywhere against attacks by pagans and devastations by infidels, and to consolidate her inwardly through the understanding of the true faith. It is your task, Holy Father, like Moses, to lift up your arms in prayer and so to aid our army that by your intercession the Christian people, under God's guidance and guarantee, may always be victorious over the enemies of his holy name, and the name of our Lord Jesus Christ may be glorified in the whole world."

This passage certainly must not be considered in isolation; it must be seen together with the expressions of the *Libri Carolini* on the Roman primacy. By his remarks on the inner strengthening of the Church Charles certainly meant first of all his concern for ecclesiastical order, for the education of the clergy and the religious instruction of the people, just as Alcuin explained the *Rex et Sacerdos* formula by *Pontifex in praedicatione*. But concern for the inner consolidation of the Church had extended at Frankfurt also to questions of faith and it did not exclude the Pope, as the admonition shows: "Hold fast to the holy canons and carefully observe the rules of the Fathers... in order that your light may shine before men." It may be assumed that Charles had already heard complaints about Leo personally, for the instruction to the *missus* Angilbert contains the following sentences: "Admonish the Pope to lead an honorable life, to observe the sacred canons zealously, and to rule Holy Church in piety.... Above all he should fight the simoniacal heresy, which only too often stains the body of the Church...."

Gregory the Great had once written in a similar vein to the Frankish Kings, but now the roles were reversed.

It can be noticed that in these years the influence of the *patricius* was increasing also in the Papal State. In 798 Leo III adopted Charles' regnal years in papal dating. He also had the cooperation of Pope and King represented pictorially in Rome.

The founder's mosaic in the apse of Santa Susanna shows the Pope on the right, the King on the left of Christ. More significant were the two great mosaics which were set up by Leo in the *triclinium* of the Lateran, the papal hall for the holding of synods, legal proceedings, and receptions. The first of these showed Christ with Peter and Constantine the Great; the second, Peter with Leo and Charles, in the same arrangement as at Santa Susanna.

The leaders of the Roman opposition to Leo were relatives of Hadrian I. An inquiry from Alcuin to Arn of Salzburg in June 798 reveals that there was anxiety in the Frankish Kingdom in regard to events in Rome. The revolt broke out on 25 April 799. The accusations against the Pope were perjury and adultery.

A new papal election did not take place, perhaps from fear of the Franks, who were already presented with the *fait accompli* of the revolution against Leo. The Frankish Duke Winigis of Spoleto hurried to Rome. Matters took an unexpected turn for the conspirators, since Leo succeeded in fleeing from Sant'Erasmo to Saint Peter's, where he met the Franks. After a Frankish attempt at mediation had failed, Winigis took the Pope with him to Spoleto and reported to the King.

Events had taken a course which seriously endangered the papal sovereignty in Rome. The dramatic turn is clear from a letter of Alcuin to the King in June 799: "Until now there were three men who counted in Christendom: The Vicar of Peter, Prince of the Apostles, and you have apprised me of what has happened to him; the holder of the imperial office, the temporal ruler of New Rome, and how he was toppled, not by outsiders, but by his own, is in all mouths; and finally you, the King, whom our Lord Jesus Christ has appointed head of the Christian people and who surpass the other two in power, wisdom, and dignity. See, the safety of the Church of Christ depends entirely on you alone."

The question was how the King could help. A mere restoration of Leo seemed impossible in view of the accusation. The Pope could have taken an oath of purgation according to Germanic law or declared his abdication. But it was not only Alcuin who had misgivings in regard to these solutions. Only the Emperor, if anyone at all, could act as judge of the Pope. But even the Emperor's competence was questionable according to the canonical principle formulated at the beginning of the sixth century: "Prima sedes a nemine judicatur." And so Charles finally postponed a decision. He had Leo conducted back to Rome and through his *missi* introduced a process for gathering information.

The "Paderborn Epic," describes the reception of the Pope by the Frankish King according to imperial etiquette and thus shows that the imperial question was in the air.

The Pope was back in Rome on 29 November. In December royal agents held a *placitum* in the Lateran *triclinium,* to which Paschal and Campulus were invited. But the accusers had, in accord with Roman law, the burden of the proof, and apparently they were unable to adduce adequate evidence. The royal agents had no authority to render a final decision of the case, and so they restored Leo temporarily. The accusers were arrested and sent across the Alps.

The King took his time. He spent the winter at Aachen and in 800 at the beginning of spring set out for the North Sea. Here he look preventive measures of security against the Vikings, who shortly before had directed their first raids against Northumbria, Scotland, and Ulster. At the end of April he went via Rouen to Tours, where he received the submission of the Bretons and discussed with his son Louis the progress of the operations in Spain and the protection of the coasts of Aquitaine and Septimania from Muslim pirates. He surely also conferred here with Alcuin on the Roman question. Alcuin accompanied Charles back to Aachen.

The journey to Rome was not arranged until the general assembly of Mainz at the beginning of August. Again time elapsed before it got under way. At the middle of November Charles was in Ravenna. On 23 November he arrived at Mentana, twelve leagues from Rome. The Pope welcomed him at Mentana with a banquet. At the first milestone a solemn procession was formed, the mounted cavalcade of ruler and court, passing amid the acclamations of the Roman corporations and the foreign *scholae,* which had stationed themselves along the King's route. The ceremonial accompanying Charles' first entry into Rome in 774 had been quite different. This time it displayed the marks of honor rendered to the Emperor, and Charles could not but know that.

In Rome the King convoked a council on the model of the Frankish general synods. In addition to the higher clergy of Rome and of the Frankish Kingdom, the Roman Senate and the Frankish magnates were also invited to take part. The council held plenary sessions in Saint Peter's under the King's presidency on 1 and 23 December. But the first plenary session had already been preceded by preliminary discussions. The members of the council were not in agreement: a part upheld Alcuin's viewpoint that the Pope could not be judged, while the others demanded that Leo exculpate himself. The outcome of the preliminary discussions was a compromise. In the opening address on 1 December the King declared that the purpose of the meeting was to examine the accusation against the Pope. The assembly replied that it was unwilling to sit in judgment on the Pope, whereupon Leo declared his readiness "to purge himself of the false charges in the presence of the assembly, following the example of his predecessors." At the plenary session of 23 December the Pope took an oath of purgation, which referred only to the points of the accusation.

Following the conciliar session the participants, according to the *Annals of Lorsch,* demanded the transfer of the imperial dignity to Charles on the ground that the imperial throne among the Greeks was vacant, while Charles already possessed the imperial city of Rome as well as all the other imperial capitals in Italy (Ravenna was meant and perhaps also Milan), Gaul (Trier and Arles), and Germany (probably Mainz), so that he was really already an Emperor without the title. Charles is said to have agreed. There is no reason to doubt this report. Was it mere chance that on that same 23 December the court chaplain Zachary returned from an embassy to Jerusalem accompanied by two monks of the monasteries of Mount Olivet and Saint Sabas, who, on the orders of the Patriarch, delivered the keys of the Holy Sepulchre and of the City of David as well as a banner, thereby recognizing Charles as the protector of the Christians of the East? The imperial position of the great Frankish King could not have been more clearly demonstrated.

According to custom, the Pope celebrated the third Mass of Christmas 800 in Saint Peter's, where the conciliar session of 23 December had taken place. After the *oratio,* during which all bowed low, the *laudes* were intoned on solemn festivals. But before they were begun, Leo III took a crown and placed it on the King's head with a brief formula of blessing. At once the Romans acclaimed Charles as

Emperor, and the imperial title was also included in the *laudes* by the congregation: "Carolo Augusto, a Deo coronato, magno et pacifico imperatori Romanorum, vita et victoria!" Leo III rendered *proskynesis* to the new Emperor, just as it had been due to the former Emperors. It was the first and last *proskynesis* of a Pope before an Emperor of the medieval West.

Still controverted is the interpretation of the celebrated passage in Einhard's *Vita Caroli,* that Charles felt such an aversion for the *nomen imperatoris* that, despite the great feast day, he would not have gone into the church, if he had foreseen the Pope's intention. If Charles wanted the imperial office — and today this is certain — then he also had to accept the only possible form in which it could have been validly created: that of Roman constitutional law.

A few days after the imperial coronation Charles sat in judgment on the Roman opposition. The leaders of the rebels were, in accordance with Roman law, condemned to death as *rei maiestatis,* but then, on Leo's intercession, the sentence was commuted to exile. The judgment on the Roman opposition shows that, as Emperor, Charles had become overlord of Rome and of the Papal State.

That the Roman-Christian imperial ideology was adopted along with the imperial dignity appears from the imperial style, which was determined at the latest during Charles' stay at Ravenna in May 801. The imperial title was now: "Karolus serenissimus Augustus, a Deo coronatus, magnus et pacificus imperator, Romanum gubernans imperium, qui et per misericordiam Dei rex Francorum et Langobardorum." The *Imperium Romanum* is to be understood here, in the sense of a theology of history, as "an institution with a mandate from God as the Ruler of the World." The King of the Franks and Lombards executed the mandate as Emperor. The position of the Franks as the predominant people in the state was thereby maintained, and at the same time the imperial office was defined as dominion over Christendom.

C H A P T E R   8 8

The Development of the Carolingian Theocracy

The imperial years of Charles the Great were a time of relative external peace for the Frankish world.

Much greater anxiety was certainly caused the Emperor by the piratical raids of Spanish and African Muslims, who regularly visited the islands and coasts of the western Mediterranean from 806 to 813. Charles' security measures extended also to the North Sea and Atlantic coasts. However, the Viking peril was not yet apparent in these years. The Emperor's chief task lay in the sphere of domestic politics. Peace stood at the center of Augustine's *Civitas Dei. Iustitia,* which realized *ordo, ordo,* whose fruit is *pax,* and *pax* itself were no longer understood as referring to the static internal life but were related to Christ; they were capable of increase, open to God.

The Germans did not know the universal peace of the Roman and Christian type. Their peace was of various forms and degrees, like the circles of law in which the German lived. The law circles of the house, the kinship, the confederation were regarded as autonomous communities, not derived from the state, which the King must not violate. Hence even the King's peace had no universal validity. It referred to definite aspects of public life — worship, court of justice, army. The King could not exclude the feud *infra patriam;* at most he could settle it. If he wished to impose universal peace, this was possible only by means of the *pax christiana.* The Christian peace, basically the concern of the Church, thereby became the business of the ruler. Thus is explained the remarkable admixture of religious, political, and social aspects of peace in the Carolingian capitularies.

The Christian royal dignity had made the ruler the representative of the *pax christiana.* The ruler's sphere of jurisdiction was considerably expanded by the acceptance of the *pax christiana,* and memories of the ancient imperial office probably contributed to a further expansion. In Charles' imperial capitularies the *Lex scripta* was stressed in a novel way as the basis of justice.

A special importance attaches to the Imperial Assembly of Aachen of October 802 in both secular and ecclesiastical legislation. Just as the relevant tribal law was prescribed for the laity, so the *Dionyso-Hadriana* and the Benedictine *Rule* were prescribed for the clergy. The *Dionyso-Hadriana* was, then, to occupy in Church life the same position as tribal law in secular life. But within the ecclesiastical sphere a clearer distinction was made between the diocesan and the regular clergy. The *vita canonica,* modeled on Chrodegang's *Rule,* was set off more clearly than before from the Benedictine *lex* of monasticism. The introduction of the Roman office among the diocesan clergy and of the Benedictine Office among the regular clergy brought about a separation also in the liturgical sphere. At first, it is true, none of this went beyond decrees. The implementation of the new order was reserved for Louis the Pious, who again took up the work of the synod of 802.

The dogmatic discussions had come to rest. Only the controversy over the *processio Spiritus Sancti* flared up again in 809, since in Palestine there had occurred dissensions between the Frankish and oriental monks on this question. Charles once again involved the Pope in the matter. But the usually weak Leo clung to the position of his predecessor and refused to admit the *Filioque* into the Roman Creed.

In these years the capitularies were further concerned with questions of law, of ecclesiastical discipline, of education and pastoral activity. Legislation in regard to the proprietary church was further developed. While the bishop's participation in the nomination of the clergy serving such churches and his right of direction had already been established, now the episcopal right of supervision of the buildings belonging to proprietary churches was laid down (803–13), the simoniacal granting of such churches was forbidden, and the removal of the clerics serving them was subjected to the bishop's approval (813).

There are indications that the monarch's strength waned after 806; a grave chronic illness befell him in 811. In the capitularies of this period there were complaints that the *concordia* between the spiritual and the temporal magnates left very much to be desired. Clerical immunities on the one hand and the proprietary church system and ecclesiastical *beneficia* on the other gave rise to conflicts. In 809 the Emperor planned to resume ecclesiastical legislation on a more elaborate scale but the Danish peril of 810 forced him to put it aside. In 813 he convoked synods of the entire Empire to Mainz, Reims, Tours, Chalon, and Arles, which were to correct deficiencies and discuss the prosecution of the reform. In this connection he raised the question of the penitential discipline and thereby supplied impetus to the struggle against the insular penitentials under the auspices of canon law.

War eventually broke out, and the coasts of the Adriatic Sea became the scene of the conflict. The Patriarch Fortunatus of Grado, the highest ranking ecclesiastic in Venetia, had presented himself to Charles in August 803 to have his privileges confirmed. He probably urged the reconstituting of the ancient ecclesiastical province of Venetia (Aquileia), which had been divided for 200 years into the Lombard province of Aquileia (Cividale) and the imperial province of Venetia (Grado). As a matter of fact, in January 805 Emperor and Pope reached an agreement at Aachen "de Aquileiense ecclesia velut una, quae suam sedem haberet." The Patriarch's Frankish policy at first encountered resistance from the people of Venetia, who expelled him; but then around the turn of 805–6 they appeared before Charles with the Dalmatians (Zara) to do homage to him.

The Frankish monarch certainly regarded Venetia only as a dead pledge. When the Byzantine Emperor sent an envoy to Pepin in 810, Charles seized the opportunity to end the war. The envoy, who found that Pepin was dead, was invited to come to Aachen, where Charles offered the renunciation of Venetia and the Dalmatian cities in exchange for the recognition of the western imperial office. A Frankish embassy went to Byzantium in the spring of 811 to negotiate on this basis. Nicephorus fell in battle against the Bulgars in July, but his successor, Michael I, accepted the proposal. A Byzantine embassy which reached Aachen in April 812 proclaimed the recognition of the Western Emperor, and at the beginning of 813 a new Frankish embassy went to Constantinople for the ratification of the peace. In the negotiations of 811–12 Charles had agreed to renounce the Roman setting of his imperial dignity, as demanded by the Greeks. The authentic "Roman" imperial office, which alone was anchored in the classical and the Christian theology of history as the world Empire, was reserved to the Eastern Emperor, who, after the peace with the Franks, adopted the expanded title of *Basileus tōn Rōmaiōn* (*Imperator Romanorum*).

Peace with Constantinople brought also peace with Benevento in the summer of the same year 812. Grimoald II, who had lost his Byzantine support, acknowledged Frankish suzerainty and obliged himself to pay tribute. The third peace of this year was concluded around the same time with the Emir of Córdoba. The Western Empire had discovered a *modus vivendi* with the Eastern Empire and the neighboring Islamic state.

The peace treaties of 812 crowned the work of Charles the Great. The future of the Western Empire was first definitely assured by the Byzantine recognition. A settlement had been found on the basis of the twofold imperial office, which remained from now on a fact in the history of Christendom. The renunciation of the universality of his imperial dignity, which was implied by the surrender of the Roman setting, was probably not difficult for Charles to make, for he was especially concerned for a position of equality with Constantinople, and this seemed to have been achieved with the recognition of the Western imperial office. It was hardly perceived at Aachen that the twofold emperorship could not but deepen the cleavage in Christendom, but was probably sensed at Rome.

The imperial coronation of 800 had proceeded, on the part of the Franks and of the Romans, from the assumption that the imperial throne was vacant. And the fantastic project of a marriage between Charles and Irene was based on the notion that there could be only one Emperor in Christendom. Irene's deposition, which could scarcely have become known in the West before the beginning of 803, compelled a rethinking of the imperial question. For Rome a solution certainly lay along the same lines as for Constantinople, since the Roman and Christian imperial idea was still a living reality in both cities: if it was necessary to come to terms with a second Emperor, he was permitted to be only an Emperor of a lesser order. If the Greeks intended to reserve the authentic "Roman" imperial office, the Pope was concerned to present the ruler of the West as the real world-emperor in the meaning of the theology of history. Charles the Great was unwilling to base the pre-eminence of the western imperial office on an interpretation of the *Constitutum* whereby that office would have been derived from the Pope; furthermore, he was neither able nor willing to consider the imperial question apart from the Frankish royal and dynastic law. His reply, given at Thionville on 6 February 806, was the regulation of the succession, the *Divisio imperii,* in which, following Frankish law, he divided the *imperium vel regnum* equally among his three sons. The already existing subkingdoms of the younger sons, Pepin and Louis, were enlarged in view of the succession: Italy by the addition of Rhaetia, Bavaria, and Alemannia south of the Danube; Aquitaine by means of the larger part of Burgundy to the line Auxerre-Chalon-Mâcon-Lyons-Savoy. The oldest son, Charles, was to receive the heart of the immediate ancestral area of dominion: *Francia* between the Loire and the Rhine, with northern Burgundy and northern Alemannia, with Frisia, Saxony, and Thuringia. The nucleus of this portion of the Empire was *Francia,* so that it is possible to speak of a division of the Empire into three subdivisions: Frankland, Italy, and Aquitaine. The pre-eminence of the oldest son was expressed by the allotting of *Francia* to Charles. A further characteristic of the *Divisio* lay in the uniform assignment of the most important Alpine passes to the three sons, who were to aid one another and to undertake together the protection of the Roman Church and of the other churches.

Charles the Great's two oldest sons died before the conclusion of the negotiations with Constantinople, which brought Byzantine recognition of the Western Empire. only Pepin of Italy left a son, Bernard, to whom his grandfather assigned the Lombard Kingdom in 812. Bernard could not rank as an equal partner in the succession with the Emperor's only surviving son; he was also invested only with the subkingdom of Italy, not with the expanded inheritance of his father Pepin. Now only King Louis of Aquitaine was considered as successor in the imperial office and in the entire Empire. Charles intended to make him coemperor in his own lifetime, following the imperial practice of Constantinople. After he had obtained the consent of the magnates to this project, he had Louis come to Aachen.

On 11 September 813, the Emperor, in his robes of state and attended by his son and the magnates, proceeded to the chapel at Aachen. After they had prayed together, he committed his son before the altar to the duties of ruler and lord. He then crowned Louis with a crown that had been laid on the altar and had him acclaimed as *Imperator et Augustus* by the people. There was no religious coronation. The act of 813 shows that, despite his renunciation of the Roman setting of his title, Charles regarded himself as a "genuine" Emperor in succession to Constantine. At the same time the imperial office was now firmly bound up with Aachen and *Francia;* the polarity of *Imperium christianum* and *Regnum Francorum* was neutralized at least for the next reign.

The Empire was provided for. As early as the beginning of 811, when Charles fell gravely ill, he had arranged by testament a division of the treasure of the *camera.* On 22 January 814, the Emperor, who was almost seventy-two years old, was attacked by a high fever. Pneumonia developed, and the Emperor died on 28 January. His remains were laid to rest, not at Saint-Denis with his parents and his grandfather, but in the Marienkirche at Aachen.

The order of the Church, the feudal system, the reform of currency and courts, the new Christian concept of ruler and state, the Carolingian reform of education — all these outlived Charles' Empire. Through these accomplishments Charles became one of the great builders of Europe: with all his "desire to rule and to exercise power" still not extravagant in conquest, in the prudent use of elements at hand, in the arranging and binding of these elements into a new comprehensive whole, he is quite comparable to Augustus.

Section Four

The Western Church from the Death of Louis the Pious to the End of the Carolingian Period

Eugen Ewig

C H A P T E R   8 9

The Frankish Empire from 840 to 875

The judgment that history would render on the Frankish Empire lay with Lothar I. The emperor could have been satisfied with the partition of 839 and could have enforced it even against Louis the German. Thus the Carolingian Empire would have been spared the rude shocks of the next few years. But that was not to be. The internecine intrigues and warfare among the sons of Charles the Great doomed that historic opportunity. "De-Frankization" in the East, elaboration of the Carolingian political theory in the West, stagnation in the Middle Kingdom — these were the characteristics of a process of individuation. But it must be remembered that, despite this, the Frankish *Imperium* was still regarded as a unity even in the late ninth century. Despite the fragmenting aspects of the various treaties which the brothers devised and imposed on each other, people still held on to the idea of one *Imperium* and of one *populus christianus*. But nevertheless it remains the case that with the death of Lothar I, on the 29 September 855 in the monastery of Prüm, there disappeared the last fighter for one *Imperium Francorum*, and it remained to be seen whether *fraternitas* could supply for the *Imperium*.

The several-mindedness of the brothers brought decay to the idea of the one Kingdom of the Franks. One of the more confusing facets of this complex story was the marriage of Lothar II. Lothar II seems to have married Theutberga, sister of the powerful Duke Hubert of Transjurane Burgundy — the districts of Geneva, Lausanne, and Sion — for political reasons only. The marriage's remaining child-less, he soon returned to his former mistress, Waldrada, by whom he had a son,

Hugh, and a daughter, Gisela. Hugh and Gisela were to be legitimated by his marriage to Waldrada, for in the course of the reform which had been transpiring since the death of Charles the Great, the ecclesiastical view had been upheld — that only legitimate children were entitled to inherit. The dispute over the royal marriage first took place before Lotharingian courts in 858 and 860. After an extorted confession of guilt, Queen Theutberga was condemned by the episcopate of Lothar's kingdom to public penance for incest. But in the autumn of 860 she succeeded in fleeing to Charles the Bald. Once free, the unhappy queen appealed to Rome, whereupon Lothar also sent an embassy to the Pope.

The marriage case had not only religious and ecclesiastical, but also political aspects. Lothar could count on the sympathy of his brothers, who were likewise without male heirs, especially as he had approached them with territorial cessions in 858–59. He thought he had also bound his uncles to himself by his mediation of peace in 859–60. But Charles the Bald wrecked the Carolingian solidarity and supported Theutberga's appeal. The papal reply was some time in coming, and Lothar II decided to act. A third Synod of Aachen, in April 862, authorized him to remarry. He communicated the decision to the Pope and requested papal sanction also. He did not, however, await a papal decision, but married Waldrada in the same year, 862.

Charles the Bald, the West Frankish King continued to support Theutberga. He agreed to the demand of Hincmar of Reims that the question of the marriage should be examined at a general Frankish synod. Pope Nicholas I did not intervene in the marriage case until November 862. He appointed two bishops to investigate the matter at a new synod at Metz, in which the kingdoms of the brothers should also each be represented by two bishops. But after considerable intrigue, the synod met at Metz in June, 863, without the bishops of the brothers' kingdoms present. The legates, bribed by another, published the papal instructions only in distorted form. The synod thus ratified the annulment of Lothar's marriage with Theutberga and declared the lawfulness of his marriage to Waldrada. The archbishop of Cologne and Trier were to convey the synodal decrees to the Pope. The Pope was furious at the course of events, but planned his countermeasures with the utmost secrecy. In October 863, the two archbishops were summoned to an assembly of clergy and laymen at the Lateran. There they received a staggering blow. Not content to annul the Metz decrees, the pope also deposed the Archbishops of Cologne and Trier and forbade their now vacant sees from being filled without his consent.

The Pope's sentences hit the two archbishops like a bolt from the blue. They had recourse to the Emperor, who appeared in Rome with troops early in 864. Nicholas I had formally put himself in the wrong, for his summary proceedings against the archbishops was counter to canon law. But the Emperor declined to use his force and merely imposed his own man as a permanent *apocrisiarius* in Rome. But the archbishops remained deposed.

Meanwhile the two uncles met and advised their nephew to make his peace with the Church. Lothar had no choice but to submit: he took Theutberga back again and handed Waldrada over to the papal legate. She however promptly escaped and returned to Lothar. But the Pope remained adamant. And with his uncles' pressure on him, Lothar II announced a trip to Rome. The Pope's reconditions were spelled out: dismissal of Waldrada; full rights for Theutberga; and canonical elections in Cologne and Trier. But then, suddenly, the Pope died in November 867, and his successor, Hadrian II, was regarded as a saintly man, one who would have a gentler touch in these sorts of matters.

Indeed, Lothar met Hadrian in 869 and even received communion at his hand. And the whole question was to be taken up anew at a Roman synod of all of the Frankish episcopate in 870. But synod never took place, for en route home, Lothar II died.

CHAPTER 90

Spain and the British Isles — The Muslim and Viking Attacks on the West

The Frankish *Imperium* represented Western Christendom into the ninth century. Not that its boundaries embraced the entire West. But even under Louis the Pious Carolingian influence still extended to Spain and England. It was the crisis of the *Imperium* that first produced a decline of Frankish prestige.

The King left his successors a still small but already firmly established kingdom, which laid claim to all of Spain as the continuation of the Visigothic Kingdom. The realization of this claim was, of course, in the still distant future. *Al Andalus,* the Emirate of Córdoba, was then experiencing its summertime under the Umayyads Abd-ar-Rahman II (822–52) and Muhammad I (852–86). The Arabic civilization of Andalusia was in flower and attracted many Christians, so that conversions to Islam increased. The Mozarab Christians enjoyed religious freedom, but as a tolerated ghetto community to which any public activity was prohibited. While the religion of the numerically relatively small conquering class was subject to no restrictions, all propaganda was forbidden to the Church. The death penalty was inflicted for efforts at conversion.

The bishops, who had to be confirmed by the conquerors, submitted, but toward the end of the 840s there was opposition in the ranks of the lower clergy, the monks, and the laity of Córdoba, the capital, to the increasing assimilation. Between these groups and the Muslims there occurred spirited confrontations in the decade 850–59. The integralist Christians did not evade discussions on the divinity of Jesus and Muhammad's office as a prophet. They even provoked them and accepted death in return. The episcopate of the province of Seville condemned their actions in 852 at a synod in Córdoba. The Córdoba martyrdoms reverberated even in the Frankish Empire. Audradus of Sens expected a Frankish intervention under the patronage of Saint Martin of Tours to liberate Spanish Christianity, but of course

Charles the Bald was unable to appreciate such hopes and maintained peace with the emirate. On the strength of this peace the monks of Saint-Germain-des-Prés asked and obtained relics of the Córdoba martyrs.

In default of the Franks, it was the Asturians who, continued to embody the *Reconquista*. Under Alfonso III (866–910) they reached beyond the Asturo-Cantabrian mountains and, despite the resistance of the Emirs, resettled the no-man's-land, created as a defensive measure by Alfonso I (739–57), as far as the Douro. Among the colonists were many Mozarabs from the emirate, especially from Toledo. The size of the kingdom was doubled by the newly erected Marches of León and Castile, which soon became the chief protagonists of the *Reconquista*. Alfonso III did not remain content with this, but turned his court into an intellectual center of the country, in this imitating the Carolingians. Still, one cannot speak of a Spanish branch of the Carolingian Renaissance, since the Spanish development was overwhelmingly focused on its Visigothic past.

The continuous rise of Asturias in the ninth century was unparalleled in Western Christendom. England at this time shared the fate of the Carolingian Empire. The supremacy of the Kings of Mercia had reached its climax under Offa (757–96) and came to an end in 825. Like the Carolingians, the Mercian Kings had convoked assemblies composed of both ecclesiastics and laymen, which met usually at the royal residences from 746 to 816 and regulated especially gifts of land to the Church, but also questions of the ecclesiastical order — the bishops' right and duty of supervision, monasticism, the proprietary church, liturgy and feast days, marriage and economic morality. Canterbury remained the metropolis of the southern province, which extended to the Humber. The assimilation of the Anglo-Saxon to the Frankish Church, which was inaugurated under Offa by a papal legation of 786–87, made further progress after Offa's death. Archbishop Wulfred of Canterbury (805–32) introduced the *vita canonica* in his cathedral.

Mercia's great age was past when the fury of the Vikings hit England. At the middle of the ninth century four independent Anglo-Saxon kingdoms coexisted: Wessex, Mercia, Northumbria, and East Anglia. The first Viking expeditions, proceeding from politically fragmented Norway in the late eighth century, had only grazed England. The main storm center of the Norwegian Vikings had fallen upon the group of islands in the North Sea and had flooded over to Scotland and Ireland. Lindisfarne was sacked in 793, Jarrow in 794. In 795 the Vikings destroyed the grave and church of Saint Columba on the island of Rechru; in 798 they ruined Saint Patrick's in Galloway and in 820 occupied the Isle of Man. Thereafter arose Viking states on the Orkneys, the Hebrides, and in Ireland at Dublin, from which the Norwegians also attacked the Scottish and British western coasts. They soon sailed the old sea-routes from Ireland to the west coast of Gaul and appeared early at the mouths of the Loire and the Garonne. Here they encountered the Danes.

Unification of the state had begun earlier in Denmark than in Norway. King Göttrik had opposed Charles the Great. King Horik (ca. 825–54), a descendant of Göttrik, showed himself to be well disposed toward Anschar's mission, though he himself remained a pagan. But in 854 he fell in battle against his nephew Guthrum, and with him the Danish Kingdom came to an end for the time being. The few mission stations which continued to exist in Denmark and Sweden were doomed to destruction.

The great Viking expeditions of the Danes began in 834–35 and were directed against both the Frisian-Frankish and the Anglo-Saxon coastal districts. In Britain it was Kent that was the most exposed, but the Vikings soon extended their operations to East Anglia and Lindsey. The situation was aggravated when around 850 they proceeded to winter in their areas of activity. The crisis reached its height when the various enterprises were coordinated under the leadership of Ivar and Halfdan, sons of Ragnar Lodbrok, and the "Great Army" prepared to overwhelm England in 865. One after the other, Northumbria, East Anglia, and Mercia fell into the hands of the Danes, who proceeded to settle down and established kingdoms of their own. Only Wessex stood firm. Alfred the Great (871–99) assumed the government of Wessex at the beginning of the crisis. Matters hung by a thread for almost a decade until 879, when Alfred achieved the decisive victory of Edington over the Viking King Guthrum, who had himself baptized as an admission of defeat. The mutual boundaries were established in the peace of 886. Alfred claimed the territories south of the city of London, but north of the Thames only the southwestern part of the former Kingdom of Mercia, which now became a province of Wessex. The reconquest of the Danish part of England, the Danelaw, began only with the victory of Tettenhall in 910 under Alfred's son Edward.

After a half-century of struggle and of the occupation of extensive parts of England by the Danish Vikings, complete chaos reigned in the ecclesiastical sphere. Bishops and abbots, with their clergy and communities, often led a fugitive existence for years, and many sees remained vacant for years, some for decades. Still, in the end the Church did not perish even in the Danelaw, and only a few episcopal sees, such as Lindisfarne, were so thoroughly destroyed that they could not be reoccupied. The immigrant Scandinavian pagans could be gradually assimilated. But the intellectual and moral retrogression was enormous, for the dispersal of chapters and religious communities meant the disappearance of the elite that had taken care of the candidates for the clerical state.

Alfred the Great recognized this critical situation and sought to remedy it. He summoned men to his court from areas that had been least affected by the devastation: his friend and biographer Asser from Wales; Waerferth and Plegmund, who became Bishops of Worchester and Canterbury, from eastern Mercia; and from the continent the Gallo-Frank Grimbald and the Old Saxon John. To the last mentioned he entrusted the abbey of Athelney, his "Saint-Denis." The King, who felt it to be a defect that in his youth he had received no training in the *artes* and theology, had fundamental texts of Christian literature translated into Anglo-Saxon: the *Regula pastoralis* and the *Dialogi* of Gregory the Great, *De consolatione philosophiae* of Boethius, Augustine's *Soliloquia,* which was expanded into an anthology on immortality, and finally the historical works of Orosius (*Adversus paganos*) and Bede (*Historia ecclesiastica*). In the prologue of his law code Alfred referred to the Jewish-Christian law. Bede and other sources formed the basis for the *Anglo-Saxon Chronicle,* a history of Britain from Caesar to Alfred in Old English. What was here hinted in its basic idea — the claim to an imperial hegemony in Britain — was stated *expressis verbis* by Asser in his Latin biography of the King.

Alfred the Great became the founder of Old English prose literature through the literary work of his court circle, in which, like his contemporary, Alfonso III of Asturias, he personally participated. In his translations the King had in mind the free youth of his kingdom, who in the future were to acquire a knowledge of reading and writing in the vernacular at the schools. The higher Latin education was prescribed for the clergy. In this field the Wessex court circle produced nothing, and hence its limits become visible here. Wessex did not experience a comprehensive intellectual and spiritual reform, such as that of Charles the Great; it lacked the external presuppositions in an age which had not yet recovered from severe struggle.

The sufferings of the Frankish Empire were not less than the trials of Britain and Ireland, especially since at the same time the Carolingians had to fight also against the Muslims, who, like the Vikings, made their appearance in pirate bands and launched their attacks against the mouths of the great rivers. The Vikings who invaded the Frankish Empire were entirely of Danish origin, like those operating in England. At times there were even mutual relations between the enterprises in the Frankish Empire and in Britain: the plundering bands concentrated at a given time at the points of least resistance.

The first goal of the Danish Vikings on the continent was Frisia. An iron ring extended along the Frankish coast from the Rhine to the Garonne.

At first the Frankish defense broke down completely. Dorestad, the chief Carolingian center for commerce with Scandinavia, was ruined in these struggles, having endured its seventh and final sack in 863.

In the years 856–62 western *Francia* experienced a great invasion staged by the Seine Vikings. Paris, already sacked in 843, was taken again in 856 and 861. The invasion first centered on the territory between the Loire and the Seine, then on the districts on the Somme, where its effects were particularly severe. Only with the aid of a group of Vikings whom he recruited was Charles the Bald finally able to redress the situation.

In the meantime, however, other Viking bands, which had returned from a Mediterranean expedition, fell upon the districts between the Loire and the Garonne and in 862–66 pushed deep into the interior, to Orléans and Clermont. Especially hard hit was Aquitaine, where numerous episcopal sees were abandoned and long remained vacant, including the metropolitan see of Bordeaux. On the Loire the Franks were more successful under the leadership of Robert the Strong, ancestor of the Capetians. In 864 Charles the Bald ordered the building of fortresses in the country and established marches on the Seine and the Loire. When the Frankish resistance stiffened, the Vikings departed for England, and the West Frankish Kingdom knew a full decade of quiet.

The final and most difficult trial for the Carolingian kingdoms began when numerous Vikings, with their wives and children, streamed back again to the continent from England after the victories of Alfred the Great. The chief blow by the "Great Army" was first directed at the area between the Rhine and the Somme. In 879 the "Great Army" entered the Scheldt. In 880 the Saxons suffered a severe defeat and toward the end of 881 the chief Viking forces pushed up the Meuse to Liège, Maestricht, and Aachen. From there they moved on to the Rhine and destroyed Cologne, Andernach, and Koblenz. But the news that the East Frankish King was missing troops in the district of Mainz caused them to proceed up the Moselle. Trier fell in ruins at the beginning of 882. The resistance of Count Adalard and of Bishop Wala of Metz at Remich induced the Vikings to withdraw to the middle Meuse. In 885 they transferred the center of their attack to Paris. The Emperor Charles the Fat purchased their departure by assigning them areas in Burgundy for the winter of 886–87 and thereby delivering a hitherto untouched land for plunder. Only the victory of the East Frankish King Arnulf near Louvain in November 891 brought a turning point and induced the chief groups to depart for England. From there in 896–97 a group again moved to the continent; their leader, Rollo, became the founder of Normandy.

On their voyages between 859 and 862 the Vikings also advanced far into the Mediterranean. They sacked Nimes, Arles, and Valence in 860, Pisa and Fiesole in 861. But the Mediterranean remained the domain of the Muslims, who from Spain and Africa terrorized the Christian lands. Their first expeditions were aimed at the Byzantine Empire. They got under way with an accidental success of the Spanish Muslims, who occupied Crete in 825. In 827 began the officially organized attack of the Aghlabids of Tunis on Sicily, a struggle that was protracted for a half-century. The Muslims' first success was the conquest of Palermo in 831. Messina fell in 843, but the old Sicilian capital, Syracuse, held out until 878. Palermo became the seat of the Arabic administration. Toarmina continued until 902 as the final, but isolated, Greek base.

Even before the Sicilian war had ended, Muslim bands also crossed to South Italy, at first as mercenaries in the pay of the mutually hostile Christian states. Internal struggles weakened the Lombard Principality of Benevento from 839 and led in 847 and 858 to the separation of the Duchies of Salerno and Capua. During these disturbances the Muslims seized Bari and then also Taranto. Muslim vessels appeared before Ancona in 840, before Ostia in 846. The amazing attack on Rome was of no particular consequence, and a second attack on the capital of Christendom in 849 was successfully warded off. But at the same time a Muslim state with Bari as capital arose in Apulia. Emperor and Pope contrived to stabilize the situation in Central Italy, but in South Italy all the exertions of the Emperor Louis II finally foundered on the disunity of the South Italian principalities. After the death of Louis II in 875 the Western Empire ceased to count as a factor for order. The Muslims entrenched themselves between Capua and Gaetà on the Garigliano, and from there they devastated Central Italy and the Papal State. They destroyed Montecassino in 882. As during the Viking attacks on England and Aquitaine, so now also many sees and abbeys in South and Central Italy were left desolate. Effective assistance came only from the Greeks, who under the important general, Nicephorus Phocas, recovered Calabria in the 880s and in addition conquered the parts of Apulia and Lucania that had been occupied by the Muslims. Under papal leadership the Christians in Central Italy finally formed a coalition, which liberated the countryside in the decisive victory on the Garigliano in 915.

While African Muslims were afflicting South and Central Italy, Spanish Muslims were operating on the Gallic and North Italian coasts. More serious raids began here too around 840, but the brigands did not become a real threat until toward the end of the 860s, when they proceeded to establish permanent centers on La Camargue. In the 890s the Muslims erected La Garde-Freinet, their most famous fortress, in the diocese of Fréjus. From here they desolated Provence and the district around Genoa, took possession of the Alpine passes, and extended their expeditions into the Valais and Sankt Gallen. The trials of the regions afflicted by them only reached their climax in the 920s. Here too many churches and monasteries were destroyed. Sees of the provinces of Aix, Embrun, and Arles remained vacant for decades.

Only North Italy, the East Frankish Kingdom, and southern Lotharingia were spared serious devastations by the Vikings and Muslims in the second half of the ninth century. But these regions were to fall prey to the Magyars, who broke into the Western world in the tenth century. Thus the storm created by Muslims, Vikings, and Magyars left the whole German-Roman West well nigh desolate. Of course, not all lands were equally affected. Naturally, the interiors had less to suffer than the coastal and frontier provinces. But even in the districts which were directly exposed to the fury there were differences of degree in proportion to the effectiveness of the defense. Thus the starting point of reconstruction differed at any given moment when the great storm let up. The differing situations led to a displacing of the political and cultural centers of gravity within the West. Another circumstance, however, was of still greater importance for the future. While in southern Europe the Christian and Islamic worlds remained strictly separated and in consequence the Muslim invasion had a purely destructive effect, in northern Europe there finally resulted a symbiosis with the Vikings, who accepted Christian civilization. In Central Europe a similar situation occurred, since missionaries soon found a way to reach even the Magyars. The men and the forces which kept alive the substance of German-Roman civilization in the catastrophe of the late ninth and early tenth centuries made ready, under severe trials, the incorporation of Scandinavia and East Central Europe into the Western world.

CHAPTER 91

The Papacy and the West from 840 to 875

The history of the Roman Church reached a climax in the ninth century in the pontificates of Nicholas I (858–67), Hadrian II (867–72), and John VIII (872–82). Fundamental changes in the relations between the papacy and the imperial office were under way.

The Emperor's suzerainty of the Papal State, the basis for which was the *Constitutio Romana* of 824, continued unaltered. Efforts at Rome to loosen imperial control were fruitless. When there was the threat of a double election in 844, Sergius II was consecrated before the imperial confirmation had been obtained. But Lothar I dispatched his archchaplain, Drogo of Metz, and his son Louis to Rome with a large escort, and Drogo insisted on a reexamination of the proceedings by a synod. Thereafter a papal election was to take place only when authorized by an imperial *iussio* and in the presence of imperial *missi*. The imperial authority was also made good within Rome. The throwing of a wall around the Leonine City was ordered by Lothar I in 846 and carried out by Pope Leo IV in 848–52.

A change of great importance set in as a result of the connection of the elevation to the imperial office with the imperial coronation by the Pope, a connection that made its appearance after the Treaty of Verdun. When the Frankish "monarchy" fell apart and the Emperor became only one sectional ruler among others, the protectorate over Rome remained the only sign which distinguished the Emperor from the Kings. The sanction afforded the Carolingian imperial line by the Pope thereby acquired an enhanced importance. Lothar I's oldest son, Louis II, was crowned King of Italy by Sergius II in 844 and coemperor by Leo IV in 850. Since, unlike his predecessors, Lothar I had not himself been crowned, the coronation at Rome had a legalizing effect, and Nicholas I regarded it as the decisive juridical element. In 871, in a polemic exchange with the Greeks, Louis II appealed to his dominion over Rome and his anointing at the hands of the Pope. Thus the imperial coronation by the Pope became a constitutive element of the elevation of the Western Emperor.

South Italy had been a field of common papal and imperial interest since the days of Charles the Great. Great changes occurred here when Muslim mercenaries were employed in the conflict between Benevento and Naples (834–39) and in the struggles over the succession to Benevento (839–47) and eventually established the Sultanate of Bari. At this same time the Carolingians were disabled by their own succession quarrels, and so the earliest steps toward arranging a united Christian front came from the Greeks.

It was not until 866 that Louis II succeeded in regulating matters in South Italy and in establishing a united Christian front. Louis II managed to take Bari in February of 871. The son of Lothar I was at the height of his power, when a conspiracy of the South Italian princes imperilled all the successes he had achieved. On 31 August the conspirators arrested the Emperor at Benevento and did not set him free until 17 September, after he had sworn not to attack them. From Taranto the Muslims again poured into the South Italian principalities. From Salerno and Capua requests for aid again reached the Emperor, who rescued both cities in 873. But Benevento and Naples continued to be hostile to him. The Duke of Benevento sought and found help among the Byzantines. In 873 he acknowledged the suzerainty of the Eastern Emperor Basil I, to whom the Lombards even delivered Bari. The power of Louis II was broken. He left South Italy in the autumn of 873 and died on 12 August 875. The Byzantines came forward in the place of the Franks as the leading power in the defense against the Muslims.

In South Italian politics the Popes staunchly supported Louis II, in particular his exertions for the establishing of a united Christian front, even though they continued to distrust the Greeks. On the other hand, the marriage case of Lothar II led to dissension between Emperor and Pope when, at the end of 863, Nicholas I quashed the acts of the synod of Metz and deposed the Archbishops of Trier and Cologne. Louis II increased his control of the Papal State but avoided imposing any solution of the crisis by force, even though in 867, at the height of the quarrel with Photius, the Byzantines suggested that he depose the Pope. For his part, Nicholas I abstained from any intervention in the secular sphere. He held to the

Gelasian theory of the two powers, which had been roused to new life by the Frankish episcopate in 829. It is true that he understood the imperial coronation as the autonomous right of the Roman Church and thus, according to Knabe, he "regarded the papal authority as being the equal of legitimate birth as a source of imperial power," but he recognized the crowned Emperor as his temporal ruler and claimed no *potestas in temporalibus.*

The death of Nicholas I on 13 November 867 resolved the crisis in the relations between Emperor and Pope. Close cooperation was resumed under Hadrian II, who in 872 released Louis II from his oath to the South Italian rebels and repeated his imperial coronation in order to wipe out the ignominy of the imprisonment at Benevento. Hadrian also supported his imperial master in the question of the inheritance of Lothar II. Only in one point did the views of Emperor and Pope differ: whereas Louis II destined as his successor Louis the German or the latter's oldest son, Carloman, at the papal court the succession of Charles the Bald was favored.

After 840 and *a fortiori* after 855 the imperial office no longer corresponded to the Frankish Empire, but the Frankish Empire, now as earlier, constituted the nucleus of Western Christendom and, as such, continued to be the Pope's proper field of action. Rome's relations with the non-Frankish states of the West were not intense or frequent. Nothing is known of contacts with Ireland. On the separation of Brittany from the Frankish Empire the Breton ecclesiastical province of Dol was established against the will of the Popes. When Asturias grew strong under Alfonso III, Pope John VIII may have consented to the elevation of Oviedo to metropolitan status in 876 and ordered the consecration of Santiago de Compostela and the holding of a Spanish council. The old connections between Rome and England did not cease, but they were impeded by the Viking attacks. Papal letters to the Archbishops of Canterbury and York of around 874 and to Canterbury of 878 and 891–96 are extant. They came from a period when Wessex was surmounting the crisis and the situation in South England was gradually re-establishing itself. As early as 853 King Aethelwulf of Wessex (839–58) had sent his son Alfred to Rome, where Pope Leo IV honored the boy with the insignia of the consulship. The consolidation of the papal primacy of jurisdiction was completed within the Western *Imperium.*

Ravenna, former residence of the Emperors, the Ostrogothic Kings, and the Exarchs, formed a counterpole to Rome within the Papal State. Thereafter, as before, the metropolitans of Ravenna were again consecrated at Rome, but they acquired greater freedom in the governing of their province.

The determining of the moment when pseudo-Isidore False Decretals first became known in Rome is made more difficult by the circumstance that one must reckon with the fluctuating interpretations of things of this sort. A papal letter of January 865 to the West Frankish episcopate, containing clear references to pseudo-Isidore, establishes the *terminus ad quem.* Haller feels that the first traces of a use by Leo IV can be demonstrated. It is not impossible that the opposition to Hincmar at Reims in 853 may have brought the forgeries to Rome, but the papal letter to Hincmar that refers to this matter does not contain an unequivocal allusion to pseudo-Isidore. Hence it must remain on open question whether Nicholas already knew the forgeries when in 863 he deposed the Archbishops of Cologne and Trier.

More probable is the assumption that Rothad of Soissons first brought the *corpus* of pseudo-Isidore to Rome. Rothad was one of the bishops of the Reims province who had acknowledged the deposed Archbishop Ebbo during his temporary restoration by Lothar I in 840–41. Open conflict between him and Hincmar broke out in 861, when Hincmar demanded the reinstallation, after the performance of penance, of a cleric whom Rothad had deposed. The Archbishop had his recalcitrant suffragan excommunicated at a provincial synod. Rothad appealed to Rome, but then agreed to answer to an episcopal tribunal, which in 862 deposed him and sentenced him to detention in a monastery. The matter was nevertheless brought before the Pope and in the autumn of 863 Nicholas finally demanded that Rothad be sent to Rome. In January 865 he annulled the deposition at a Roman synod. The proceedings were conducted entirely according to the rules of the False Decretals, to which Nicholas alluded in his letter to Hincmar.

It was to no purpose that Hincmar pointed out that, according to the existing canon law, the Pope could indeed accept an appeal, but the case had to be referred back to an episcopal tribunal. The Archbishop and the King, who had likewise opposed Rothad, bowed to Rome's judgment. Around the same time there occurred an estrangement between Hincmar and Charles the Bald. The assembled Frankish bishops urged the Pope to determine anew the rights and duties of metropolitans and their suffragans and to explain the principle of the competency of the Roman court in the cases of bishops. The juxtaposition of the old and the new law had produced so much perplexity that a papal statement of principles seemed necessary. But this did not take place. Nicholas did not receive the message of the council. Just before his death he had declared himself satisfied with Hincmar's justification and had thereby ended the conflict.

The third and last quarrel between Reims and Rome occurred in the pontificate of Hadrian II. The Archbishop's nephew and namesake, Hincmar of Laon, was summoned before a royal tribunal in the summer of 868 for having deprived royal vassals of fiefs belonging to his see of Laon. The Archbishop of Reims at first intervened in support of his nephew and brought it about that the younger Hincmar was cited before an ecclesiastical court and took an oath of loyalty to the King. But before his uncle's intervention, the nephew had already appealed to Rome. Before the end of the same year Hadrian II demanded the annulment of the confiscation of the property of the church of Laon, as ordered by the King, and the dispatch of the appellant to Rome. The King did not yield, but in April 869 summoned the Bishop to the Synod of Verberie. Hincmar of Laon decreed as a pre-cautionary measure an interdict on his diocese in the event that he should be arrested. Just the same, Charles the Bald had Hincmar of Laon arrested, while Hincmar of Reims lifted the interdict that had been ordered. Again the old and the new canon law confronted each other. The correspondence with Rome assumed a very bitter form, but King and Archbishop did not budge. The Bishop of Laon was deposed at the Synod of Douzy in August 871. Finally, Charles the Bald played off the Pope against the papal chancery. He decided that it was not Pope Hadrian but Anastasius the Librarian who was speaking in the sharp notes. When in 872 he applied directly to the Pope through his *missus,* he received a conciliatory reply in a secret letter: The King might send Hincmar of Laon to Rome, and the Pope would then appoint judges according to the old canon law. In addition, Hadrian declared that after the death of Louis II he would accept no one but Charles "in regnum et imperium Romanum." The Pope not only yielded; he had made an amazing change of course. The ten-year-old struggle between Rome and Reims ended with a victory for the old canon law — the hour for a centralized papal government of the Church had not yet struck.

Ecclesiastical conflicts of the type of the collisions with Cologne, Trier, and Reims did not take place between Rome and the East Frankish episcopate. In the East Frankish Kingdom there were, it is true, only three metropolitan sees, and of these only two, Mainz and Salzburg, really counted. The church of Hamburg was seriously damaged by the destruction brought in 845. Louis the German hoped to provide for the missionary work by giving Anschar also the see of Bremen, a suffragan of Cologne. The union was decreed at the Synod of Mainz in 848, and a few years later it received the consent of Archbishop Gunthar of Cologne. Pope Nicholas I approved the uniting of the two sees in 864 and at the same time detached Bremen from the Cologne province. Archbishops Anschar (d. 865) and Rembert maintained the mission stations of Schleswig and Rügen in Denmark and of Birka in Sweden. But the Scandinavian mission was lacking in any power of expansion, and in the 880s it completely collapsed.

Quite different was the situation with regard to the Slavic mission in the southeast, which was maintained by Regensburg, Passau, Salzburg, and Aquileia. Since the 830s it had expanded to Bohemia and Moravia and also included Croatia, where the Roman Christian influence had earlier been recognized *via* Dalmatia. The Slavonic princes who acknowledged Frankish suzerainty also accepted Christianity. In 850 the Croatian bishopric of Nic, in Aquileia's mission field, first emerged into the light of history.

The Moravian Duke Rastislav was a ruler of importance. He recognized that the new state would be consolidated by the acceptance of Christianity. Were Moravia, as a Christian kingdom, to be admitted into the Western community, its permanence could no longer be questioned. On the other hand, however, complete independence could not be achieved so long as Moravia remained a part of the Bavarian ecclesiastical province of Salzburg. And so it was that in 862–63 Rastislav applied to the Byzantine Emperor for priests.

The Greek missionaries arrived in the Moravian state in 863–64. At their head were two brothers from Thessalonica, Constantine-Cyril and Methodius. Constantine, the younger of the two, had been born in 827. In 842 he had gone to study at Constantinople, where Leo of Thessalonica and Photius were his teachers. When Photius was summoned to court, Constantine took over his professorship. But the younger scholar soon entered the service of the Church and became a deacon and perhaps a priest. In 860 he went as imperial envoy to the Chazars in what is today the Ukraine. After his return he received the commission to proceed to the Moravians. His brother Methodius, who accompanied him, had been born in 815. Around 840 he had been made imperial *strategos* on the Strymon, but had then entered a monastery and had been made abbot. As natives of Thessalonica, the brothers were familiar with the Slavonic language; this was true especially of the former *strategos,* Methodius. Since as yet the Slavonic dialects differed little among themselves, they were able to address Rastislav's Moravians in their mother tongue. Unlike the Western Church, the Byzantine Church did not know any single ecclesiastical language, and so Constantine and Methodius had no hesitation about translating, not only the Bible, but the liturgical texts, including the Roman Mass, known as the Liturgy of Saint Peter, into the vernacular. For this purpose they created the Glagolithic script, which was based on the Greek minuscule with the addition of a few signs for specifically Slavonic sounds.

For three full years the brothers taught in Rastislav's realm, and their successes soon pushed the Bavarian mission into the background. But, since they were not bishops, they were unable to confer ordination on the Slavonic candidates for the priesthood whom they were training. Hence they decided to journey to Constantinople and proceeded to Venice, where in 867 they received from Nicholas I an invitation to come to Rome. When the brothers reached Rome, Nicholas was dead, but Hadrian II prepared a triumphal reception for them, since Constantine was bringing along the relics of Saint Clement of Rome, which he had found in the Crimea at the time of his journey to the Chazars.

But opposition to the Greek missionaries was not wanting. It was not especially the Greek liturgy that was contested — in Rome there were plenty of Greek monasteries, which followed their own way of life — but rather the introduction of the vernacular into the Mass. Already in Venice Constantine had had to defend himself on this score, and the same charges were heard in Rome. Some circles would admit only three sacred languages — Hebrew, Greek, and Latin, sanctified by the inscription or Christ's cross. But Pope Hadrian was free from any narrowmindedness. He had the Slavonic liturgy celebrated in Roman churches, ordained Methodius a priest, and had some of the Slavonic disciples of the brothers ordained priests and others deacons. Constantine died in Rome on 14 February 869, and Methodius returned to the Slavonic mission lands with papal recommendations. The only restriction imposed on him was that he should read the Epistle and the Gospel in Latin before proclaiming them in Slavonic.

Since a political change had taken place in Moravia in 869–70, Methodius at first labored in the Slovene principality on Lake Balaton, where Kocel had succeeded his father, Pribina, in 861. Methodius very soon returned to Rome, where in 870 Hadrian II consecrated him Archbishop of Sirmium (Mitrovitza near Belgrade). The new ecclesiastical province was to embrace the entire Serbo-Croatian, Slovene, and Moravian mission territory. It was an event of special importance, for just at that moment Bulgaria was threatening to slip away from Rome, since Nicholas I had, for canonical reasons, denied the Khan's wish that Formosus of Porto be made missionary bishop of the Bulgars. Bulgaria returned to the Byzantine obedience in February 870. By making Methodius Archbishop of Sirmium, Pope Hadrian was underlining Rome's right to Illyricum, whose capital had once been Sirmium. But actually Methodius was unable to establish himself in the destroyed late Roman capital of Illyricum. He returned to Kocel and for the time being resided in his chief fortress, Szalavár.

The Archbishop's moving into a territory which belonged to the East Frankish Pannonian March, had been assigned by Leo III to Salzburg, and was already being evangelized by Salzburg could not but lead to a collision with the Metropolitan of Bavaria. The Salzburg archpriest who was functioning in Pannonia returned home in 870. Methodius was apparently arrested in the Moravian part of his diocese by Carloman, son of Louis the German, and in November 870 brought before a Bavarian synod, meeting probably at Regensburg. Methodius appealed to the

Pope's inalienable right, but was taken to Swabia, possibly to Ellwangen, and imprisoned. The priests of Hadrian II were fruitless, but John VIII intervened energetically. He demanded and obtained the release of the Archbishop but forbade him to use Slavonic in the liturgy. Methodius departed for the Moravians, who achieved their independence in 874. He became the Apostle of the Moravians, although John VIII also subjected to him in ecclesiastical matters the Serbian Duke Montemir of Slavonia. The principality of Kocel, who died at this same time, remained under East Frankish suzerainty and a mission district of Bavaria.

It is not unthinkable that the papal *rapprochement* with Charles the Bald already effected by Hadrian II was motivated by the clashes between Rome and the Bavarian episcopate in 870–73. The great project of making good the loss of Illyricum, of the papal vicariate of Thessalonica, by the establishing of an extensive Slavonic ecclesiastical province had been conceived by Nicholas I and pushed forward on a grand scale by Hadrian II. It was hurt by the loss of Bulgaria and the Bavarian opposition in Pannonia. But the founding of a Moravian Church was an important success. Methodius must be placed alongside Boniface in his effectiveness. In the Moravian Prince Svatopluk (870–94), whose morals he severely criticized, he did not find the support which Rastislav had given him, but he enjoyed the confidence of Pope John VIII, who upheld him against Svatopluk, and who lifted the prohibition of the Slavonic liturgy in 880. In 882 Methodius journeyed to Constantinople, where he was cordially received by Emperor and Patriarch. He died on 6 April 884.

The death of the Apostle of the Slavs brought about a crisis. Pope Stephen V summoned to Rome Gorazd, whom Methodius had recommended as his successor, forbade the Slavonic liturgy, and named Wiching administrator of the metropolitan see. The small group of Methodius' disciples were unable to maintain themselves and in 885 they escaped to Bulgaria. There they reverted to the Byzantine rite, but in the Slavonic language. By a new adaptation to the Greek alphabet they transformed the Glagolithic script into the Cyrillic, which is still used by the Orthodox Slavs.

C H A P T E R   9 2

The Degradation of the Papacy and the Empire (875 to 904)

The death of the Emperor Louis II presented contemporaries with difficult problems of law. The revived Western Empire was hereditary in the senior Carolingian line until 876, though since 850 coronation by the pope had played a constitutive role. Hence in this sense the *ordinatio imperii* of 817 retained its validity — the right of Lothar I and his heirs to the imperial crown was never debated. Only on the extinction of the line of Lothar did the question come up: Who was to award the imperial crown? The event occurred at a time of numerous confusing issues in the world of the West. Louis had promised the crown to one nephew, while the pope held out the prospect of the imperial dignity to Charles the Bald, Louis' brother. The basis for the pope's action may have been the ancient right of the *populus Romanus* and the papal right of coronation, but also the *ordinatio imperii's* regulation that in the event of Lothar I's death without sons, the *populus christianus* should choose a successor from among the surviving brothers.

At the death of the Emperor Louis II, the Holy See was occupied by John VIII, the last among the important ninth-century popes. John created a *fait accompli* by having Charles the Bald acclaimed Emperor and then by crowning him on Christmas 875: With the death of Louis the German, in 876, his most dangerous adversary was eliminated.

John VIII turned to the East Frankish line in April 879 and had first of all approached Charles the Fat. But the situation in *Francia* did not at the outset permit any of the sons of Louis the German to intervene in Italy. Not until the autumn of 879 did Charles the Fat appear in Pavia; he met the Pope at Ravenna in January 880. This move yielded to the King of Swabia only the Italian royal crown. Only on his second Italian journey, dating from December 880 to March 881, was there found time for his imperial coronation at Rome on 21 February 881. The Pope obtained as little real assistance then as he did on the occasion of a third encounter at Ravenna in February 882. At that very moment the Muslims were establishing themselves on the Garigliano, from where they terrorized Rome. The ghastly murder of John VIII on 15 December 882 indicates how low the imperial authority had fallen. It was also an omen of an approaching dark epoch in papal history.

John VIII was followed in rapid succession by Marinus I (882–84), Hadrian III (884–85), and Stephen V (885–91). Marinus was the first Pope to have been a bishop before his accession to Saint Peter's see. This violation of the canons was also a sign of the breakdown of the old rules. The new Pope pardoned the opposition of 876 and gave back to Formosus his see of Porto. In 883 Marinus obtained from the Emperor the deposition of the Margrave Guy of Spoleto, but this merely produced further confusion. In the pontificate of Hadrian III it seemed as though the situation of the Empire was finally improving. The Emperor obtained successes against the Vikings and sought to profit from this to assure the succession of his bastard, Bernard. The Pope — such is the irony of history — was ready to assist him in this project but died *en route* to the East Frankish Kingdom, and matters took a turn for the worse again. Hadrian's successor, Stephen V, was selected against the will of the Emperor. When Charles the Fat in 887 demanded his cooperation in regulating the succession in the Empire — the still underage grandson of Louis II, Louis of Vienne, Boso's son, was selected as heir — the Pope declined and perhaps thereby hastened the dissolution of the Empire. The fall of Charles the Fat must have left Stephen V indifferent.

The deposition and death of the Emperor Charles the Fat mark an epoch in the history of the Carolingian Empire. Regino of Prüm underscores this turning point with the statement that now for the first time non-Carolingians were raised to the kingship in the subkingdoms. Under Carolingian rule remained only the East Frankish Kingdom, including Lotharingia, and the lower Burgundian Kingdom of Vienne, whose King Louis, still a minor, represented the line of Lothar I by virtue of his being a grandson of the Emperor Louis II. The new East Frankish King, Arnulf of Carinthia, was a bastard of Carloman of Bavaria. The Robertian Eudes established himself as King of the West Franks; the Welf Rudolf, as King of Upper Burgundy, the province of Besançon. The Italian crown was disputed between Berengar of Friuli and Guy of Spoleto. Empire and dynasty had parted company. A last but weak bond of imperial unity remained in the suzerainty of the East Frankish King, which was recognized by all the partner-kings except Guy of Spoleto. For the moment Arnulf could not give a thought to the imperial dignity, because of the Viking peril and the struggle now being resumed with the Moravians. In 890 Stephen V did ask his aid against "mali christiani" and "imminentes pagani," but on 21 February 891 he had to give the imperial crown to Guy of Spoleto.

Stephen's successor in the Holy See was Formosus of Porto (891–96), even though his elevation was likewise contrary to the ancient rule that no bishop was allowed to pass from his see to another. His opponents accused Formosus of ambition; his personal conduct was above reproach, and he was a man of strict, even ascetical life.

Death spared Formosus severe trials but not a *damnatio memoriae* of a gruesome sort. In January 897 his corpse was disinterred and, in full pontificals, brought before a synod, where a deacon, as his proxy, confessed his guilt. The synod acknowledged the nullity of his elevation to the papacy and of his official acts. Finally, his corpse was cast into the Tiber. It was recovered by a hermit, who reinterred it. The gruesome trial was not unavenged. In the same year 897 the adherents of Formosus in Rome rose and Pope Stephen VI was deposed and eventually strangled. But the Formosans were not very lucky with the next two Popes: both Romanus and Theodore II died in quick succession. Encouraged by this, the anti-Formosans seized the initiative and in the spring of 898 brought about the election of Bishop Sergius of Caere as Pope. The fact that, by this change of see, Sergius was violating an ancient ecclesiastical prohibition probably did not much concern the Romans, for three promotions of bishops to the papacy within a brief period had virtually nullified the opposing rule. Hence it was not for canonical reasons but for reasons of party politics that the Formosans forcibly expelled the newly elected Sergius and elevated John IX (898–90). John's first efforts were directed to the restoration of order in conjunction with the Emperor Lambert. A Roman Synod, attended also by North Italian bishops, condemned the sentence passed against Formosus, anathematized those who violated corpses and the leaders of the anti-Formosans, especially Sergius, and sought to guarantee future papal elections by decreeing, among other things, that, as earlier, they must take place in the presence of an imperial *missus.* Then the Emperor Lambert and John IX held another synod at Ravenna, which confirmed the Roman decrees and provided for appeal to the Emperor in the event of conflicts among the Romans, thus renewing the *Constitutio Romana* of Lothar I.

All that was expected of the future was frustrated by the sudden death of the young Emperor. In Lambert the Roman Church lost its last support. No help could be expected from the Emperor Arnulf, who succumbed to his incurable illness on 8 December 899 at Regensburg, nor from his successor as King of Germany, Louis the Child. John IX's successor, Benedict IV (900–903), did, it is true, give the imperial crown to young King Louis of Provence in 901, but the latter was defeated in his struggle with Berengar of Friuli; blinded, he returned to Provence in 905. But, before this, important events had occurred at Rome. On the death of Benedict IV there ensued a split in the still dominant Formosan faction. After about two months, in September 903, the priest Christopher overthrew the legitimate Pope Leo V and usurped his place. But the intruder was not to enjoy his success. At the beginning of 904 Sergius of Caere marched on Rome with an armed force and seized power. His pontificate marked an epoch, not so much because of the now final elimination of the Formosans as because of the connections which Sergius had with influential families. With him began a new period of Roman history, that of the domination of the city and the papacy by the nobility.

C H A P T E R   9 3

Reform, Theology, and Education under the Later Carolingians

The Carolingian Renaissance did not come to an end with the end of imperial unity, but achieved its third and final climax under the grandsons of Charles the Great. Its effects were first clearly discernible in Rome in this phase. In the Frankish Empire decentralization, which had begun under Louis the Pious, made further progress after the Verdun partition. Instead of the single imperial court there now existed three and later even five courts of equal rank; but these were in no sense the only or even the outstanding centers of education in the partner-kingdoms. Only the court of Charles the Bald, at which was the great Irish scholar, John Scotus (before 845 to after 867), polarized the cultural life of the West Frankish Kingdom to a certain degree.

The sons of Louis the Pious, who had had the benefit of a first-rate education, were, like their father, interested in theological questions. The Emperor Lothar I, to whom Walafrid dedicated two works in 841 and Wandalbert of Prüm his martyrology in 848, asked Rhabanus and Angelomus of Luxeuil for scriptural commentaries. The *praeceptor Gemaniae* dedicated some of his writings also to Louis the German, who, following the estrangement during the war among the brothers, made him Archbishop of Mainz in 847. The East Frankish King consulted Hincmar of Reims on Genesis and the Psalms and acquired the works of Saint Ambrose. The widest range of intellectual interests was possessed by Charles the Bald, to whom some fifty contemporary writings were dedicated. The West Frankish King himself commissioned authoritative theological opinions.

The most important link between the court and the great ecclesiastical centers of culture at this time was still the royal chapel. The chapels at Aachen, Frankfurt, Regensburg, and Compiègne were made collegiate churches. Thereby the Kings fulfilled a long-standing desire of the Church reformers. The canons continued to be members of the palace clergy, but, in contradistinction to the chaplains, who were from now on bound to service in the immediate retinue of the King, they had a fixed residence and an ecclesiastical status. Moreover, a closer connection between the chapel and the most outstanding ecclesiastical metropolises was in preparation. Likewise, with the assigning of the highest spiritual functions at court to the most distinguished metropolitans in their realms the Kings seem to have acceded to the desire of the reformers for the inclusion of the palace clergy in the existing Church order.

A number of large monasteries were closely attached to the several royal courts as the endowment of queens, princes, and princesses. From the chapels and the royal monasteries abbots and, especially in the West Frankish Kingdom, bishops thereafter proceeded. But new educational centers seldom arose as a result of direct action by the court clergy. More clearly than in the preceding period the episcopate appeared as the representative of education. The bishops even took charge of the quasi-official historiography, which had hitherto been the province of the chapel.

The various lands of the Frankish Empire did not all participate in equal measure in the later Carolingian Renaissance; in an age of growing external perils several older centers ceased to be active. In the third quarter of the ninth century the centers of intellectual life were in the provinces of Sens and Reims, Lyons and Vienne, Trier and Cologne, Mainz and Salzburg. And, alongside the Frankish centers, Rome emerged again as an intellectual center in this period.

Compared with the age of Louis the Pious, the third phase of the Carolingian Renaissance was full of variety and color. The *artes* were represented not only by grammarians but also by philologists and "humanists" of universal knowledge, such as John Scotus. Nor was the age lacking in gifted poets: Sedulius Scotus, Gottschalk, and Wandalbert of Prüm. Most writers did not confine themselves to the *artes* but also tried their hand at scriptural exegesis. History and hagiography were likewise cultivated. The new type of "historical" martyrologies originated at Lyons and Vienne.

A mastery of Greek was acquired by two Irishmen, John and Sedulius Scotus, at the West Frankish and the Lotharingian courts, and by the papal librarian, Anastasius. John Scotus and Anastasius translated into Latin the writings of pseudo-Dionysius, which were to be of the greatest importance for the later intellectual formation of the West and already inspired the philosophical and theological concepts of John Scotus. This teacher at the court of Charles the Bald had no equal as an original thinker in his day. In his chief work, *De divisione naturae,* composed in 867, he describes the creation of the world, *natura creata et non creans,* by God, *natura creans et non creata,* through the agency of ideas, *natura creans et creata,* and its return to God as its final end, *natura nec creans nec creata,* through the mediatorship of Christ. The Christian teaching on creation and redemption was here given a Neoplatonic interpretation with no toning down of its dogmatic content.

For John God remains ultimately inaccessible — theology of negation — to the extent that he has not revealed himself directly or indirectly by means of ideas and creation. Man ascends to him by his senses, reason, and intellect. Sense knowledge became a necessary preliminary to rational knowledge only because of the fall; but it is at the same time a remedy for sins in so far as it leads from the sensuous external to the intellectual. *Ratio* is not comprehended as separate from faith, but as a God-given force for the illuminating of faith. It conducts to intellectual knowledge, that is, to the vision of God, which for its part presupposes a theophany. The return of man to God is possible only through Christ, God's self-revelation, and his grace. Sin is explained neoplatonically as perseverance in the present state; its punishment lies in itself. Death appears as progress to the higher form, as return to the ideas, which are to be understood, not as emanations from God, but as an expression of the divine will, and which have their eternity in the Logos. To the extent that ideas exist virtually also in man's mind, the entire creation is also redeemed together with man by Christ.

John Scotus was one of the most important representatives of Carolingian intellectual life in the West Frankish Kingdom, but he was not its only witness. Carolingian theology reached its climax simultaneously in the discussion on the Eucharist and on predestination. In Christian antiquity the Eucharist had been understood as the "representation (*anamnesis*) of Christ's real person and of the salvation connected with it." The great mystery was left undefined. The presence of the Redeemer in the Sacrament was referred to the Logos, to the historical Jesus, and to the *Corpus Christi mysticum,* all at the same time, but the various theological schools stressed different aspects.

Paschasius Radbertus of Corbie had composed his *De corpore et sanguine* in 831–33 for the edification of his confrères at Corvey. In this he stressed the full identity of the Eucharist with the body of Christ that was born of Mary and expounded the reality of the Mass as the repetition of Calvary. The Abbot of Corbie followed Ambrose, whereas Carolingian theology was under the standard of Augustine, who had, it is true, understood the Eucharist as the "substantial image of the *res ipsa,*" but at the same time stressed its "function of sign as *sacramentum corporis* at a distance from the *res ipsa.*" The first opposition to Radbertus came after 845 from Rhabanus Maurus, who defined communion as union with Christ into one body by faith. Likewise the Saxon monk Gottschalk adopted a stand against the Abbot of Corbie in a work composed around 850. He likened the presence of Christ in the bread and wine to the hypostatic union of the two natures of the Son of God, just as John Damascene had done a century earlier. Hence Gottschalk saw in it an objective reality, but only in the form of a divine power inherent in the Eucharist. He rejected the interpretation of the Mass as a real repetition of Calvary. Gottschalk's fundamental notion was shared by his friend and teacher, Ratramnus of Corbie, who, like several early Christian theologians, compared the presence of Christ in the Eucharist to the operation of the Holy Spirit in the baptismal water.

Paschasius Radbertus defended his doctrine. He again maintained his explanation of the Mass, but defended himself against misinterpretations springing from a far too materialistic idea of the Lord's glorified body, and especially rejected the thesis attributed to him of a dismembering of Christ's body in communion. He wanted transubstantiation to be understood as a mysterious re-creation, repeated at any given moment, of the body and blood of the Lord. With this the controversy came to an end and was only taken up again, under different circumstances, in the eleventh century.

The discussion of the Eucharist had been confined to a relatively small group. Matters were far more stormy in the controversy over the teaching of the monk Gottschalk on predestination, in which even the episcopate took sides. Son of a Saxon Count Bern, Gottschalk was born around 804 and as a child was offered to the monastery of Fulda.

Gottschalk left Fulda but then returned to the monastic life. Finally he entered the monastery of Orbais, in the diocese of Soissons, where he was ordained a priest between 835 and 840.

Already in Italy Gottschalk, as a biased but highly gifted interpreter of Augustine, had expounded his doctrine of double predestination to salvation and to damnation, of the limitation of the redemption to the elect, as appears from letters written by Rhabanus in 840 and 845–46. After his return to *Francia* he was summoned in October 848 before a synod at Mainz, which was presided over by Louis the German. Here he defended his teaching against Rhabanus, now Archbishop of Mainz, but was condemned as a heretic and a vagabond monk, whipped, and sent back to Orbais. Rhabanus notified the metropolitan, Hincmar, who the next year summoned the monk to the Synod of Quierzy, which had been convoked by Charles the Bald. Here too Gottschalk refused to retract, was again flogged, perpetually silenced, and conveyed to the monastery of Hautvillers in the archdiocese of Reims, since Hincmar distrusted the proper local Ordinary, Rothad of Soissons.

Detention in a monastery was not the same thing as imprisonment. It is true that Gottschalk lived in a penitentiary apart from the monastic community proper, but in regard to maintenance and clothing he seems to have been treated like his confrères. He continued to write and found friends who would circulate his works. Hincmar opposed them with a brief treatise on predestination, and thereby began the great controversy. Ratramnus of Corbie entered the lists on behalf of his pupil and friend. Hincmar turned to five highly esteemed theologians, among them Amalarius of Metz, Prudentius of Troyes, and Lupus of Ferrières. But Prudentius and Lupus ranged themselves, apart from slight differences in detail, on the side of Gottschalk, who for his part dispatched a lengthy memorandum to the participants in the Synod of Quierzy. Even the court took notice, and Charles the Bald asked Lupus and Ratramnus for their opinion. Both complied in 850 with detailed discussions, Lupus in *Liber de tribus quaestionibus*, Ratramnus in *De praedestinatione*. Rhabanus and Hincmar had admitted only a predestination to good. Lupus adhered to double predestination, even though he made a distinction between *praedestinatio ad gloriam* and *praedestinatio ad poenam* and expressed himself cautiously on the question of the limiting of the redemption to the elect. Ratramnus characterized predestination to glory as a free act of the divine mercy, predestination to punishment as a being left in the state of reprobation.

Hincmar, theologically isolated, sought help from John Scotus. But Neoplatonic philosophy proved unable to solve the great theological mystery, and John's inadequate effort called the metropolitans of Sens and Lyons into the fray. Wenilo of Sens entrusted the refutation of the Irishman to his suffragan Prudentius, who presented his views in a new treatise written in 851–52. In the name of the Church of Lyons, whose Archbishop Amolo had thus far occupied an intermediate position, Florus attacked the doctor of the West Frankish court. Hincmar thereupon sought to play off Amolo against Florus, but Amolo died in 852 and was succeeded by Remigius. The new Archbishop of Lyons had a second treatise written, and this was directed chiefly against his fellow Archbishop of Reims.

Gottschalk was now almost forgotten as the quarrel moved to another plane. The controversy centered on the four *capitula* which Hincmar, with the aid of Charles the Bald, had had ratified by a small group at Quierzy. In these *praedestinatio ad poenam* was interpreted *as praescientia,* the recovery of free will was explained, in accord with tradition, as a gift of the grace of redemption, and God's salvific will and the redemption were expressly referred to all mankind, in opposition to the prevailing Augustinianism. Hincmar's *capitula* encountered criticism in a new polemical work from Lyons and in the Synod of Valence in 855, the canons of which specified the viewpoint of the episcopate of Lyons, Vienne, and Arles, which in many respects differed from that of Hincmar.

In 859 the Rhone bishops had referred the question to the Pope. Nicholas I had Hincmar and Gottschalk summoned to the Synod of Metz in 863, but neither of them appeared. Nicholas I, at that time heavily burdened with other kinds of anxieties, issued no decision — he died in the autumn of 867.

Around the same time, between 866 and 870, the monk Gottschalk also died. He was a fascinating personality of great brilliance. No innovator, he was a man of the most profound inner fervor, to whom worship and doctrine became so personal an experience that even deep mysteries appeared to him as evident truths.

The Eucharist and predestination were not the only problems occupying the theologians of the third Carolingian generation. The doctrine of the Trinity and questions referring to the nature of the soul and the vision of God were likewise discussed — and by the same persons: Gottschalk, Hincmar, and Ratramnus. More important apparently was the movement stimulated in the West by the Synod of Constantinople of the summer of 867 with its excommunication of Pope Nicholas I. Ratramnus of Corbie eclipsed the bishops with his *Contra Graecorum opposita,* in which he replied to the grievances of the East in detail. He especially took up the old controverted question of the *processio Spiritus Sancti* and defended the papal primacy against Byzantium. The renewed Greek-Latin controversy of 867–68 formed the final act of the great theological discussions which had begun after the Treaty of Verdun and had been conducted from the start predominantly. and, after the death of Rhabanus, exclusively, by the diocesan and regular clergy.

It was also in the West Frankish episcopate that the political impulses in questions of Empire and Church, coming down from the days of Louis the Pious, produced their strongest effects. The last great representative of the Carolingian "great church" was Hincmar of Reims, the most loyal assistant of Charles the Bald and his successors, for whom, nevertheless, the unity of the Empire in the form of *a fraternitas* continued to possess validity. The theocratic political ideology of the Carolingian period received its final formulation from Hincmar. The Archbishop proceeded from the Gelasian teaching of the two powers, which had impressed itself on the consciousness of the Franks in the reign of Louis the Pious. He clearly distinguished the political sector, the *res publica,* from the ecclesiastical. He defined the royal power, which in his view occupied the central place, as a *ministerium* instituted by God. But he rejected the unconditional duty of loyalty, especially for bishops, whom he wanted to keep uninvolved by feudal ties. Bishops, he said, owed fidelity to the King not "in omnibus" but "iuxta ministerium," on the basis of their office.

In his doctrine of the two powers Gelasius had attributed more importance to the *auctoritas sacrata pontificum,* with respect to its greater responsibility before God, than to the *regalis potestas.* Hincmar also based the higher authority of the bishops on the anointing of the King, the ritual for which he himself composed. The anointing was not only an external sign of the divine institution of the royal office but also a raising of the King above the laity. To attack the Lord's anointed was an especially serious crime. But by virtue of his anointing the King became no more irremovable than was the bishop, who, like him, was a *christus Domini.* The question of whether, in the case of tyranny, of serious offences by the ruler against the law of God, the bishops were competent to act as judges had been posed as early as 833. Hincmar answered affirmatively in principle. As appears from his attitude toward Louis the German in 858–60 and Lothar II in 860–83, he saw in the imperial synod, that is, in the all-Frankish council, the court before which Kings had to answer and which, in a case of necessity, could even depose a King.

Around the same time regional archdeaconries were also established, which often probably conformed to the former territories of *chorepiscopi.* The archdeacons supervised the delimiting and financial administration of parishes and controlled the archpriests and deans. With deanery and archdeaconry the medieval diocese acquired its shape. But it still required considerable time before these institutions were everywhere established.

If one's glance shifts from the parochial and diocesan organization to the monasteries and chapters, the balance is far less favorable. The abuse of the lay abbacy increased.

Although provincial synods were largely supplanted by synods of the several kingdoms, still the metropolitans played an important role in the ninth century. Since the time of Charles the Great they bore the title of archbishop and wore the pallium as the insignia of their rank. The assemblies and synods of the various kingdoms were dominated by certain archbishops — those of Sens and Reims in the West Frankish Kingdoms, those of Cologne and Trier in Lotharingia, of Lyons in Provence, of Mainz in the East Frankish Kingdom, and of Milan and Aquileia in Italy. The typical archbishop of the day, who energetically defended the rights of metropolitans against both rebellious suffragans and Rome, was Hincmar of Reims.

According to the ancient canon law the metropolitan was not the superior of the bishops of his province; he exercised over them only a right of supervision. He convoked and directed provincial synods. He confirmed the elections of his suffragans, thus possessing a right of veto, and had a right to be asked for his approval of the important decisions of his suffragans. From the time that metropolitans wore the pallium as archbishops, a right originally belonging only to the Metropolitan of Arles as papal vicar, they were also regarded as representatives of the Pope —

competent *in partem sollicitudinis* in a sense not defined in more detail in law. On the other hand, they were also intermediaries between the episcopate and the Emperor and were frequently appointed *missi* in their provinces. As such they had the task of publishing the capitularies and supervising their implementation in their provinces. But their powers were encroached upon in regard to the choosing of bishops, in which they had been concerned since the sixth century.

Strengthened by the reform of Empire and Church, the archbishops of the ninth century had frequently exerted themselves to transform the old right of supervision into a power of direction.

The exalted opinion which Hincmar had of his office. led to conflicts with his suffragans. The tensions in the province of Reims were aggravated by the opposition of the clerics and monks who had been ordained by Ebbo during his temporary restoration in 840–41 and whom Hincmar had suspended. To all appearances the Reims opposition was intimately connected with the great forgery *atelier,* from which proceeded the capitularies of pseudo-Benedictus Levita and the decretals of pseudo-Isidore. Of course, the intentions of the forgers were not simply identical with the aims of Hincmar's opponents; they were far more comprehensive and sought to guarantee the Carolingian reform work, threatened as it was by political developments.

The Carolingian reform had produced a uniform organization in the dioceses and provinces and had elevated the level of intellectual and religious education and moral consciousness, but it had been unable completely to disengage the Church from its involvement in the world. The restoration of the secularized Church property ceased. The proprietary church was regulated by law but thereby legalized. The lay abbacy was merely checked, not abolished. Despite the privileges granted by Louis the Pious, elections to high ecclesiastical offices were not really free. Since the confusion of the 830s retrogression was again noticeable in all these spheres. The moral deterioration of the lay aristocracy threatened the Church's marriage law, and episcopal authority over the clergy belonging to proprietary churches remained problematic. New secularizations struck at the material foundations of the Church. The main items of the reform program of the forgers corresponded to the ever recurring themes of the imperial assemblies: security of Church property from usurpation and secularization, freedom of the clergy for their religious and ecclesiastical duties, legal safeguards for the episcopate and the lower clergy by means of respect for canonical processes, and the extending of the *privilegium fori* to all clerics. But the forgers emphasized that the guarantor of the reform was no longer the Emperor since the Treaty of Verdun but the Pope. For them he ranked as the supreme judge in all *causae maiores,* that is, especially in the cases of bishops. In their view all synods received their authority from Rome, so that no conciliar decree possessed validity without the express or tacit consent of the Pope.

It is only possible to understand the forgeries when they are inserted into their historical context. Already in the ninth century Rome was regarded as the mother of many Gallic churches. Legends of apostolic foundations had spread from Arles throughout the south of Gaul in the fifth and sixth centuries, while in the early eighth and the early ninth centuries they can be traced in the Gallo-Frankish north, at Paris, Châlons, Trier, and Cologne. The Roman Church had supplied the doctrinal, liturgical, and canonical norms for the reforms of Pepin and Charles the Great. Persons had rights confirmed and exemptions granted by the Holy See. In the Middle Ages, reform was always understood as a return to the ancient law. And so the ninth century forgers regarded themselves, not as innovators, but as renewers. And so also they dressed up their ideas in capitularies of the great Carolingians and in decretals of the ancient Popes.

The forgeries were made between 847 and 852. For in 847 occurred the death of Archbishop Otgar of Mainz, already referred to as dead in the *Capitularies,* and 1 November 852 is the date of the diocesan statutes of Hincmar of Reims, in which some of the False Decretals are quoted for the first time. At approximately the same time, between 851 and 853, Archbishop Theutgaud of Trier claimed the primacy of Gallia Belgica, the ecclesiastical provinces of Trier and Reims, a thing he could have done only on the basis of forgeries. The immediate occasion for the making of the forgeries was probably provided by the royal assembly of Épernay in 846, at which the West Frankish episcopate and its reform program suffered a serious defeat at the hands of the imperial aristocracy.

The effects of the False Capitularies and False Decretals were limited in the ninth century. The forgeries provided Nicholas I with important tools but they did not give his pontificate its special character. It has been rightly stressed that the forgeries, far from establishing papal power, presupposed it. But they did give to Rome's authority a juridical form and in the eleventh century they became an essential instrument in the papal government of the Church, a basis of the Roman primacy of jurisdiction.

The great controversies of the Carolingian Age died out in the 860s, while the growth of canon law came to a standstill in the 830s and 890s.

At Rome intellectual life reached its peak in the pontificates of Nicholas I, Hadrian II, and John VIII. The outstanding scholar was Anastasius the Librarian, who was on friendly terms with the Emperor Louis III and in 855 even came forward as the imperial antipope, but afterward again had *entrée* to the Lateran. He wrote the *vita* of Nicholas I in the *Liber pontificalis* and, "as a sort of private secretary from 861 or 862," acquired great influence over papal policy. Hadrian II entrusted him with the direction of the chancery by making him librarian. Anastasius became famous not least of all for his translations from Greek — lives of saints, acts of the general councils of 787 and 869–70, documents of the ecclesiastical history of the seventh century, pseudo-Dionysius, and Theophanes. The quarter-century of cultural flowering at Rome also became significant for the development of the medieval idea of the Eternal City. It was ended by the collapse of the Carolingian papacy, made visible in the discontinuance of the traditional papal *vitae* in the *Liber pontificalis.*

Following the deaths of the Emperor Louis II in 875, Louis the German in 876, and Charles the Bald in 877, the Carolingian courts gradually lost their cultural importance. However, the *artes* and law were still cultivated at Pavia, which had a great tradition as the "capital" of Lombard-Frankish Italy and was one of the great school centers organized by Lothar I. At Milan, which in the Carolingian Age became a powerful rival of Pavia, a group of Irish monks even pursued Greek studies.

The Viking invasion of 879–91 had also seriously affected the very heart of

Carolingian *Francia*. In Champagne, however, the continuity of the schools of Laon was undisturbed. A group of Irish grammarians worked toward the close of the century in the strong city, whose walls defied every assault. The abbey of Saint-Amand in Hainaut had maintained its position in the midst of destruction and collapse. It was famed not only for its scriptorium but also as a refuge of the *artes:* from here proceeded the sequences, so significant for poetry and music. From Saint-Amand came not only the Eulalia Sequence, the oldest poem in French, but also the old High German song in praise of the West Frankish King Louis III, the victor of Saucourt (891).

In the likewise severely tried province of Cologne the most important late Carolingian culture center was the abbey of Werden, which had not been affected by the devastation and maintained close connections with Hainaut. It was the place of origin of the *Musica enchiriadis* of Abbot Hoger (d. 902).

The monastery of Saint Martin at Trier had also been destroyed. The ecclesiastical restoration at Trier was aided, however, by a textbook of harmony, with which Regino took his place beside Hoger of Werden and Hucbald of Saint-Amand, and by the manual of canon law, *De synodalibus causis*, which was completed in 906 and dedicated to Archbishop Hatto of Mainz.

The real centers of intellectual life in the East Frankish Kingdom now lay in Franconia, Swabia, and Bavaria. Under Charles the Fat there existed a close relationship between the royal chapel and the monasteries of Sankt Gallen and Reichenau on Lake Constance. Under Arnulf the imperial annals were continued at Regensburg and Niederaltaich. Sankt Gallen then experienced its first flowering with three luminaries, Ratpert (d. 890), Tutilo, and Notker (ca. 840–912). Tutilo was an important artist and musician noted for his tropes. But both were eclipsed by Notker Balbulus, who, despite a defect in speech, was a gifted poet. He determined the liturgical function and poetical laws of the sequence and showed himself to be a master of narration in his *vita* of Charles the Great, composed around 884. Sankt Gallen and Reichenau also appear at this time as centers of religious poetry in the Old High German dialect, which was carried to Freising by a pupil of Sankt Gallen, Waldo. Thus the monasteries on Lake Constance then replaced Fulda and Weissenburg in their function in connection with East Frankish education and German literature, for which the "more deeply historical" designation of *teutonica lingua* (in place of *theodisca lingua*) became customary at Sankt Gallen and Mainz around 880.

Seen as a whole, the accomplishment of the fourth Carolingian generation was not inconsiderable, even though it was confined to the *artes*. Especially in poetry works of high merit appeared. No less important than the individual achievements were the continuity of the schools in several old educational centers, the work of reconstruction that soon began in the great metropolitan sees, and the springing up of new educational centers in Saxony. Thus it came about that even under the most severe trials intellectual life did not die out, and the legacy of the Carolingian reform and renaissance was substantially preserved for a new age.

Section Five

The Church and the Western Kingdoms from 900 to 1046

Friedrich Kempf

CHAPTER 94

The New Kingdoms

The Church and the Carolingian *Imperium* had come together because of an inner affinity. Because both institutions strove for a supranational unity resting on their Christian character, the universality of the Church had contributed to the consolidation of the Empire, and, conversely, the wide expanse of the Empire had made possible a uniform organization of the ecclesiastical situation, oriented to the Roman tradition. The disintegration of the Empire, accompanied in France and Italy by the collapse of the royal authority, could not but hurt the Church especially seriously. The victory of the private powers caused her to fall more strongly than before under the influence of German-Roman juridical notions. Forced to adjust herself to the varying regional ways of life, she lost much of her own intrinsic energy, based on her unity and universality. And since scholarship needed supraprovincial cooperation, the theological studies that had been happily initiated decayed.

For that very reason the Church historian is not wrong when he calls the tenth century a *saeculum obscurum* or *ferreum*. But he should connect with it not so much the idea of decay as of transformation and reorientation, and be aware that much of what at first acted destructively helped to rebuild the new West and the new Church.

France

The West Frankish Kingdom had relatively little to suffer from outside enemies in the tenth century. The Magyar raids, beginning toward the close of the ninth century, seldom got farther west than Lotharingia. The Muslims, established at Freinet from about 888, chiefly harassed the neighboring lands. And it was possible gradually to master the various groups of Northmen from the time when the Seine Vikings, under Rollo, had received land in fief from King Charles the Simple, and, giving up their way of life, their language, and their religion, began to settle clown. But West *Francia* had to endure internal warfare, for there was no longer a strong crown which would have been able to curb the anarchy. The process of dissolution of the royal power, which had already started under Charles the Bald (840–77), went on all the more unchecked in the tenth century when the West Carolingian family could maintain its claim to legitimacy only with the greatest difficulty against the far more powerful Robertians, who were seeking the crown. A change occurred only after the death of the childless Louis V in 987. The Robertian who was then elected his successor, Hugh Capet, founded a dynasty which was to reign in the direct line until 1328 and in collateral lines until 1848. Hugh Capet did, it is true, take over a kingdom that was already smashed to pieces. While the independent principalities had already reached the considerable number of twenty-nine at the beginning of the century, this had grown to fifty by 987.

The result for the Church was a very ticklish situation. Since the feudal princes counts, marquises, or dukes — gradually usurped all rights of sovereignty, a considerable portion of the French bishoprics fell under their control. At the time of the Investiture Controversy the Capetians disposed of only twenty-five of the total of seventy-seven bishoprics. The princes' ecclesiastical sovereignty assumed to some extent the legal character of the proprietary church system and led, especially in the Midi, to serious abuses. Like any other object of value, bishoprics there could be given, in whole or in part, to members of the family, including wives and daughters, or sold to outsiders. Furthermore, they were useful to the princes who controlled episcopal elections as means of providing for their sons, with the result that in some dioceses there was an invariable dynastic succession for a long time.

Not rarely the churches became the playthings of political power struggles. The archbishopric of Reims, for example, which was, strictly speaking, directly under the King, had a particularly difficult time.

Nevertheless, the situation of the churches of France was better than one might think at first glance. The victory of particularism had as a consequence that the bishops and abbots did not, as in Germany, come into possession of important new rights of sovereignty. Hence they were less engrossed with the new forms of government. On the contrary, the arbitrary actions of so many lords of churches strengthened the forces of resistance of which the French churches disposed on the basis of a long tradition. Thus the old canon law did not fall into oblivion. Just as the French crown at the period by no means renounced its claim to supreme authority despite its actual powerlessness, churchmen also held firmly to certain basic principles, for example, to the right to free canonical election. Since they were not linked, for better or for worse, with a system of government, they were also able much more easily to develop a religious and ecclesiastical initiative of their own, and in this they not infrequently had the backing of pious princes. Here one need only recall the reform work of Cluny or the peace movements. And so when in the eleventh century the papacy had recourse to forces within the Church for the great reform, no country was so open to its exertions as France. It was not only the religious and ecclesiastical sense that had grown up among clerics and lay persons that contributed to this, but also the sovereignty over the Church as divided among King and princes. The princes were not powerful enough to maintain their rights against pressure from the reformed papacy, and the King could decide upon renunciation more easily than the German monarch could, because the political rights of the French ecclesiastical princes had a less pretentious range.

Italy

Italy's political and ecclesiastical situation provides an especially bewildering picture. In 951 the German King Otto I seized the Lombard Kingdom and thereby determined the fate of medieval Italy. In addition to the kingship there also arose great dynastic principalities in North and Central Italy. Farther south, the independent remnants of the Lombard Kingdom maintained themselves. After the death of the Emperor Louis II (875) the Byzantines had again established themselves in an energetic struggle with the Muslims and were again able to combine their themes of Calabria and Langobardia. Gaetà, Naples, and Amalfi were under nominal Byzantine suzerainty.

The political chaos invited enemies in. The Magyars invaded from 899 and soon extended their frequent plundering expeditions to the south also. The Spanish Muslims infested the northwest, while the Sicilian and African Muslims attacked South and Central Italy. In the devastated and fragmented country the Church found conditions that differed from one territory to the next. In the north, since inner feuds as well as the incursions of the Magyars forced the cities to self-defense, the Lombard bishops gained a preeminent position through the expanding of the power of *missi,* which in 876 Charles the Bald had granted to all Italian bishops for the territory of their cities. By incorporating important parts of the rural area into the urban territory, soon also gaining comital rights over the city or even over whole districts, and forcing the secular nobility into vassalage, they developed real city-state territories. In the great maritime cities, such as Venice, dominion was acquired by a secular patriciate.

In Rome there was in preparation a development similar to that in the territories of Benevento, Capua, and Naples, where the rulers of the moment disposed of the bishoprics. The anarchy getting under way from 882 had constantly increased the influence of the Roman aristocracy and of the neighboring princes.

The first step toward a greater concentration of strength was taken in 904. In that year there returned to the Eternal City Sergius III, elected in 897 but forced to yield to the Formosan John IX. His return was effected by the aid of the Frankish upstart, Duke Alberic of Spoleto, and of a faction of the Roman nobility led by Theophylact.

The pontificate of Sergius III meant the final victory of the anti-Formosans. They compelled the Roman clergy, all assembled in synod, to declare invalid the ordinations conferred by Formosus. This measure, which took effect far beyond Rome and even in South Italy, evoked sharp protests and malicious charges on the one hand, while on the other it posed the theologically important question of the validity of the ordinations, which was discussed with real competence especially by the Formosan Auxilius, a Frank living in Naples. But Sergius III was too firmly in control to have to worry about his opponents, who lived outside Rome. Belonging to the Roman nobility, he relied on Theophylact, since 904 financial director (*vestararius*) of the Holy See and at the same time commander of the Roman militia (*magister militum*).

The papacy's position at first still depended on the ability of the Roman Bishop of the moment. The next Pope, John X (914–28), transferred to Rome from the archiepiscopal see of Ravenna, was without doubt a strong personality. John X, who, with Theophylact and Alberic of Spoleto, was one of the chief promoters of the league against the Muslims and took part personally in the battle on the Garigliano in 915, was not subservient to the Roman nobility. After the deaths of Theophylact and Alberic (ca. 924), he even began to pursue an independent policy, allying with King Hugh of Italy, to whom he promised the imperial crown, and seeking to assure the greatest possible power to his own brother, Peter. But here he ran afoul of Marozia, now head of the house of Theophylact and, since 926, wife of the Margrave Guy of Tuscany. Peter was killed in 927; in 928 John X was shut up in prison, where he died, probably strangled. His successors were of no importance: the papacy had lost its freedom.

Marozia's fall brought no change. Free to marry again because of the death of Guy of Tuscany, she offered her hand and, with it, rule of Rome to Hugh of Italy, who was then at the height of his power. Incited by Alberic, son of Marozia and Alberic of Spoleto, the Romans stormed the Castel Sant'Angelo, where the wedding was being celebrated. Hugh fled ignominiously, Marozia landed in prison, and Alberic assumed power, which, outdoing the achievement of his grandfather, he brought to its peak (932–54). Merely the titles used by him — *senator omnium Romanorum, patricius,* perhaps granted by the Byzantine Emperor, and finally *princeps* — and then his coinage, bearing his own name and that of the Pope, reveal the enhanced and now undisguised claim to princely authority. Thanks to a shrewd policy, which was not oriented to expansion or to recovery of territory, except for the Sabine country, but to the security and order of the existing territorial possessions, Alberic's position remained unshaken. Even the condition of the Church was improved. Personally pious, the *princeps* called upon no less than Odo of Cluny to reform the monasteries in and around Rome and on his family property built the monastery of Santa Maria all'Aventino. Naturally, he kept the Popes in strict dependence. But it was clear to Alberic that this situation could not continue forever, because of the uncontestable right of the papacy to rule Rome and the *Patrimonium.* In an effort to assure his family the rule in the future also, shortly before his death he had the Romans swear to select his son Octavian as the next Pope. This was agreed to, and, after the death of Agapitus II (946–55), Octavian mounted the throne of Peter, putting aside his original name and styling himself John XII (955–64). In this union of *princeps* and *pontifex* Alberic's goal seemed to have been realized.

And yet his calculations included an error. Oriented to the dimensions of a city-state, they caused the universal element, and hence the real essence of the Eternal City, to come out the loser. The Christian West still looked upon Rome as its capital, as the seat of the *vicarius Petri,* who was entrusted with the care of the Universal Church, and at the same time as the place where an Emperor, to be anointed by the Pope, had to assume the protectorate of Christianity. Since the imperial office was vacant and the papacy had fallen prey to the Roman nobility, the call for a *renovatio imperii* gained momentum. As soon as a strong ruler answered it, Alberic's system was done for. That ruler appeared in the King of Germany, Otto I.

Germany

Henry I (919–36), founder of the Saxon Dynasty avoided the alliance with the Church and sought a federal union of the tribes under Saxon leadership. But he slowly came around again to the Carolingian policy, especially after the recovery in 926 of Lotharingia, which in 911 had gone over to France. It was important to the Church that Henry again instituted the politically important palace chapel and regained the disposal of all the bishoprics, except those of Bavaria, whose duke did not have to renounce his ecclesiastical sovereignty until the reign of Otto I. The Carolingian tradition came to life again in full force under this same Otto the Great, Henry's son. The severe struggles which Otto had to endure with the nobility and the tribal dukes may be passed over here. But they had an effect on the Church too. Otto was motivated by the understanding that the crown would not master the inner political opposition without a complete domination of the Church.

The King's will was regarded as virtually unlimited in the State Church that thus came to birth. The nomination of the bishops, who were mostly not connected with the tribes, was determined by political viewpoints. In order to be able to demand of the churches achievements of greater consequence for the state, the rulers were sparing neither in donations of crown property nor in privileges of immunity, which gave the bishops full jurisdiction, even over serious criminal cases, and hence made the ecclesiastical *advocatia* the equivalent of a countship. From the time of Otto III even whole counties with all their rights were bestowed upon episcopal sees or royal abbeys. Usually connected with jurisdiction were other profitable rights — tolls, market, ban — so that the Ottonian privileges laid the foundation on which an episcopal territorial power could be erected. The celibacy of the ecclesiastical princes made it possible to regrant vacated offices freely, as the occasion arose.

So strict a dependence of the prelatial churches on the King was conceivable only in an age which did not yet know the essential distinction between state and Church, but merely the functional distinction between *Sacerdotium* and *Regnum*. Since both powers, as members of one superimposed unity under the rule of Christ, regarded themselves as bound to the same religious and political goal, royal service, secular administration, and divine service could all be conceived as one and the same religious and moral accomplishment. The ruler, from whose hand the bishops, at their investiture by ring and staff, received, not only the property and the secular rights of sovereignty, but also the ecclesiastical function, was in the view of that age not simply a layman. His anointing, which, given the state of contemporary theology, could be regarded as a Sacrament, raised him to the sphere of *vicarius Christi* and made him, according to the anointing formula in a Mainz *Ordo,* a participant in the episcopal office and an intermediary between clergy and people. Thus the theocratic form of dominion, elaborated under the Carolingians, gained new force and validity. It reached its climax in the religious and political ideas of Otto III and motivated both Henry II and Henry III to serious reform efforts.

Since at the time there was no free Church, it was basically more advantageous for the bishops to be under the rule of a king rather than of a prince. The theocratic king pursued an objective religious and political general policy, whereas the princes were motivated by selfish interests. Hence the German episcopate in the tenth and eleventh centuries presented on the whole a really favorable picture; in fact, there were in it not a few exemplary and saintly ecclesiastical princes. Naturally, the Ottonian system could not last forever. As soon as the Western mind began to distinguish more carefully and hence to surmount the primitive phase of the relationship, the Church had to lay her hand again on the episcopal office and attack the theocratic form of investiture. The collapse of the Ottonian State Church that actually occurred weakened the crown considerably. For the German bishop continued to be a Prince of the Empire until 1803 and from the time of the Concordat of Worms (1122) was on the way to constructing his territorial power in competition with the secular princes and to the disadvantage of the imperial power.

The Ottonian-Salian State Church was never a real national or territorial Church. The presuppositions for the concept of a national state were then lacking, particularly in the Carolingian successor states, in which the awareness of the earlier unity disappeared only slowly. Otto I intended to be, not so much a German King, as successor of Charles the Great. For this reason it was in the Aachen chapel, the burial place of the great Charles, that he had himself acclaimed and anointed as King and seated upon Charles' throne, with its many relics. It is true that Charles' *Imperium* could not be re-established, but the Western concept of unity, fed by the Carolingian and the Christian traditions, impelled Otto beyond the German area of his authority, as his position of hegemony expanded and consolidated itself.

The struggles in the north and east also and the related political expansion did not concern merely Germany. A new missionary movement, conducted by German and other priests, expanded the Church's territory. Otto apparently did not intend to attack the independence of the neighboring Western states, but he occasionally intervened in their affairs. Thus he saved the crown for Conrad of Burgundy, the underage son of King Rudolf II. And in France Otto supported the Carolingian, Louis IV, once the latter had renounced Lotharingia, against the Robertian, Hugh of Neustria, not only in several campaigns but also by his exertions to have the Reims schism settled at the Synod of Ingelheim in 948 in accord with Louis' desires.

The position of hegemony which elevated the German King above the Western monarchs hinted of itself at a final enhancement, at its sanction by the Pope in the imperial anointing and coronation. Since this presupposed the possession of Italy, the politics of the Saxon Dynasty was oriented to the conquest of the Lombard Kingdom. Henry I had probably thought of an expedition to Italy and Rome in his last years. Perhaps it was for this reason that, probably in 935, he acquired at great cost from King Rudolf II of Burgundy the holy lance, a relic adorned with nails from the cross of Christ, which was thought to be Constantine's lance; it was therefore regarded as a symbol of imperial authority and could signify a claim to Italy. In any event, Otto I was thereafter determined to acquire the Italian royal crown and the Roman imperial crown.

C H A P T E R   9 5

Rome, the Papacy, and the Empire: 962 to 1002

The desire of Otto I, King of Germany, to gain the Lombard royal crown and the Roman imperial crown was entirely within the realm of the possible. It was important only to wait for the proper moment. This seemed to have arrived when, after the death of King Lothar of Italy in 950, his young widow, Queen Adelaide, daughter of Rudolf II of Burgundy, was unwilling to give way to Berengar of Ivrea, who had forced himself into power; she was therefore thrown into prison. Probably appealed to for aid, Otto entered Lombardy with a strong army, assumed the royal authority at Pavia, unelected and uncrowned, and married Adelaide (951). Envoys sent on to the Pope discussed the question of the imperial coronation with him, but the ruler of Rome, Prince Alberic, did not want a new Emperor, and so Pope Agapitus II had to refuse.

His attention claimed by difficulties within Germany, Otto soon relinquished even the Lombard Kingdom, assigning it to Berengar of Ivrea and his son Adalbert in exchange for vassalage, except for the northeastern part of Lombardy, which was placed under the Duke of Bavaria. Without knowing it, Otto had thereby smoothed his route to Rome. For Berengar, involved as early as 956, because of a violation of the territorial arrangements, in a war which was directed by Otto's son Liudolf and which was temporarily ended by Liudolf's death in 957, constantly extended his sphere of power. By conquering the Duchy of Spoleto in 959 and, in that connection, plundering or occupying small frontier districts belonging to the Papal State, Berengar became a threatening neighbor of Pope John XII. The youthful Pope had to fear Berengar's expansionist drive all the more, since his own position had been shaken by a foolish and miserably ruined attempt against Capua and by his religiously frivolous and even immoral life. In his distress, therefore, he sent two agents to Germany in 960 to ask Otto's help and to invite him to receive the imperial crown in Rome. Some Lombard princes and bishops also appeared at the German court and demanded war.

Otto made the most of the propitious hour. In a treaty concluded with the papal envoys he promised on oath, apparently in imitation of a formula submitted to Charles the Fat in 881, to protect the person of the Pope and the *Patrimonium*

Petri, the territorial extent of which was to remain inviolate, without the advice of the Pope neither to sit in judgment nor to issue orders in Rome which would affect the Pope or the Romans, and to oblige the future regent of the Lombard Kingdom to defend the *Patrimonium.* He then made ready his journey to Rome. To guarantee the succession he had his six-year-old son and namesake elected and crowned King. In the late summer of 961, accompanied by Queen Adelaide, he appeared in Lombardy with a strong force, restored his sovereignty there temporarily almost without striking a blow, and at the beginning of the new year set out for Rome. On 2 February 962, he and Adelaide received the imperial anointing and were crowned in Saint Peter's.

This solemn act bound Church, Empire, and Christendom into a unity heavy with consequences for the future. In so far as the altered circumstances would allow, the *renovatio imperii Francorum* had become a reality. The extensive territory under his rule, comprising two kingdoms, his position of hegemony, and his victories over the neighboring pagan peoples had pointed out Otto as the successor of Charles the Great and had led him to Rome to have his preeminence ratified sacramentally. Except for certain rights in Rome and in the Papal State, the imperial coronation could add nothing to his power of government, which remained fundamentally his power as King, even if, because of the possession of two kingdoms — to which in 1033 Conrad II would be able to add a third, that of Burgundy it had a quasi-imperial character. Hence, Otto and his successors did not, by virtue of their imperial title, demand any subjection from the other Christian Kings of the West. The rights of suzerainty which they acquired from time to time over neighboring rulers to the north or the east were the results of a policy independent in itself of the imperial office. But the anointing and coronation at Rome transmitted the imperial title and the imperial dignity.

The conferring of the imperial dignity, of course, would not have meant much unless it was destined for a ruler endowed with power. Here there was involved a fundamentally important double relationship The quasi-imperial power of the German monarchs and its hegemonial radiation gave importance and esteem to the imperial dignity, while the imperial dignity surrounded what was basically a royal power with a mysterious glamour supported by a genuine symbolic force and made it appear as an imperial power. Surpassing all other rulers in dignity and authority, the German Emperor appeared to occupy the throne of the world and to be charged by God in the first place to espouse the cause of Christianity, just as he was entrusted in a special manner with the protection of the Pope, the father of Christendom. The universal characteristic, present in the Christian essence of the imperial office, would be consolidated by the fact that the German Empire would be more and more regarded as the continuation of the world-wide Roman Empire. This development owed its origin to the rivalry, soon to begin, with the Byzantine Emperor as well as to the current ideas of renewal, harking back to antiquity and Rome, and to the theology of the four world-empires.

On the juridical questions posed by the union of the German kingship and the Roman imperial office Otto I and his successors, except Otto III, seem to have had no misgivings. Things developed, so to speak, automatically. It is true that the anointing and coronation at Rome, since 850 the unique means of imparting the imperial dignity, continued to be reserved entirely to the Pope as his prerogative, but it lost its importance by virtue of the fact that the Popes could no longer, as John VIII once did, select an Emperor from among the Western Kings. In his own lifetime Otto I had his son and namesake crowned as Emperor in 967 and enhanced the imperial prestige of his house by the marriage of Otto II to the Greek Princess Theophano, probably a niece of the Byzantine Emperor John I Tzimisces.

Although the elevation of the heir to the throne to the rank of coemperor did not take place after that, still the power substantially claimed by the German monarchs of the tenth and eleventh centuries guaranteed, even and especially in Imperial Italy, the claim to the imperial dignity and made it slowly into a *ius ad rem*, into a legal reversion. *Regnum* and *Imperium* became thereby so correlated that the election and anointing of the German King already implied the elevation of the future Emperor, and, conversely, the imperial anointing denoted the climax and finale of the progressive elevation of the German monarch. So long as the Saxon and early Salian theocracy endured, the imperial office was, for all practical purposes, not subject to the influence of Pope or Romans. If one disregards the ideas of Otto III, it was not the Romans but the Germans who appeared as the Imperial Nation. The German kingship and its power assumed an imperial character, and the Pope, in the imperial coronation that was his right, had only to ratify sacramentally what had already been decided and acted upon in ruling. While the Germans, like the Franks before them, might have felt that their rulers owed the *Imperium,* next to God, to their own inherent strength, the Romans and the Pope clung to the conviction that the *Imperium* was at their disposal. The Roman people were unable to carry their claim, but the Pope had a strong basis for his. It was he who conferred the imperial dignity by the anointing and coronation, and, according to Roman and ecclesiastical tradition, this meant, not an action to be undertaken, as it were, blindfolded, but an act somehow free and presupposing the examination of the one to be anointed — the doing of a favor. Thus supported, the papacy, once it had acquired its freedom in the Investiture Controversy and had assumed the leadership of Western Christendom, was to make demands which, because of the entanglement of the *Imperium* with the German *Regnum,* touched the foundations of German rule and contributed to the dramatic conflict with the Hohenstaufen.

Soon after his imperial coronation, Otto I, following the example of the preceding Emperors, issued a *privilegium,* for the Roman Church in his own name and that of his son. Despite the disappearance of almost all the earlier imperial *privilegia,* the regulations of the *Ottonianum* may safely be traced back to one text, which was slowly elaborated in the pacts of the ninth century and eventually reached its final form, probably in the pact of Charles the Bald of 876, from then on to pass, virtually unaltered, from one imperial *privilegium* to another. The producing of one or more such pacts may have induced Otto in the first part of his *privilegium* to confirm in favor of the Roman Church a downright fantastic territorial possession involving about two-thirds of Italy, although the poorly composed text contained obvious contradictions.

The to a great extent utopian statements need not, of course, have troubled the Emperor. He was, however, bound to procure its property for the Roman Church only to the extent that he was able. It would take years for Otto to control Italy to some degree and to be able to think of restitution. The more he became conversant with the territorial situation in Italy, the more exactly he learned to distinguish, even in the *privilegium,* between appearance and reality, between the never realized wishful thinking and the genuine legal claims of the Roman Church in regard to territorial possessions. But even in the restitutions that were to be effected in justice, there was no question of an absolute alienation. The Emperor remained the sovereign lord even in the Papal State.

Back in Lombardy, Otto began the struggle against Berengar, who fell back upon a castle in the former exarchate. When, during the siege, the Emperor brought the neighboring populations under his sovereignty, John XII regarded his rights as having been violated and, disregarding the oath of loyalty he had sworn to the Emperor, conspired with Berengar's, son Adalbert. Otto thereupon returned to Rome in 963. The Romans had to swear for the future not to elect a Pope without the authorization of the Emperor. Then, contrary to the fundamental legal principle that the Pope can be judged by no one, Otto had John, now in flight, summoned before a synod and, on his non-appearance, deposed. Leo, *protoscriniarius* of the Roman Church, was then raised to the papacy as Leo VIII. This notorious violation of the law not only led to an uprising but, following Otto's departure, also enabled John XII to take hold of the reins again. A few month later he was carried off by a stroke, allegedly in a liaison. As his successor the Romans elected the blameless Benedict V. But once again might prevailed: Otto forced Leo VIII on the Romans and banished Benedict V to Hamburg. John's perfidy had cost the Roman Church dearly. The Emperor's new right to confirm the papal election reduced the Bishop of Rome to a momentous dependence.

In addition to the Emperor, the papacy had also from now on to reckon with the Roman nobles and their rivalries. A first revolt, of short duration, against John XIII (965–72) was severely punished by the Emperor (966). It was followed by a second, after Otto's death in 973, led by Crescentius de Theodora. Pope Benedict VI was overthrown in 974 and replaced by Boniface VII, who had Benedict strangled. Then, hard-pressed by the imperial *missus,* the usurper fled to the Byzantines with the Church's treasury. His attack on Rome in 980–81, by which he intended to strip the reformer, Pope Benedict VII (974–83), of power, failed. But when the Emperor Otto II died at the end of 983, the adventurer emerged victorious against the unloved John XIV (983–84), who had been transferred from the see of Pavia at the Emperor's wish. John XIV was starved or poisoned in prison, while the hated and despised Boniface died in 985. The next Pope, John XV (985–96), relied strictly on the nobles, to the dissatisfaction of the lower clergy. Under him the two sons of Crescentius de Theodora, John and Crescentius II, rose to high position. John was entrusted with the administration of the Church's property and bore the title *patricius.* The power-mad and avaricious Crescentius II did not hold any office but, especially after his brother's death, exerted a tyrannical pressure on the Roman Church.

The tragic end of Benedict VI and John XIV indicated once again how badly the Popes, threatened by Roman factional strife, needed protection. But the German Emperors were certainly to be preferred as protectors to a Roman noble family that had gained power. The Ottos assisted the papacy out of its difficulties at Rome and brought it back into a larger context. And if the imperial protectorate also encroached upon the freedom of the papal election and of papal political activity, still, apart from the different course of Otto III, it did not attack the papacy's power of spiritual leadership in itself, quite in contrast to the rule of Charles the Great, who to a great extent had united the supreme direction of Church and Empire in his person and allowed the Pope hardly more than the position of a supreme Imperial Bishop. The German Imperial Church never attained to the compactness of the Carolingian territorial Church. More firmly even than before, it was to become a part of the Universal Church, once the Church's center of gravity at Rome showed itself more markedly along with the renewed imperial office.

Otto I and his successors not infrequently had important questions affecting the German Church decided at papal synods, meeting in Rome or elsewhere in Italy, now and then even in a sense opposed to the wishes of the German prelates. And even the wishes of the Emperors did not have to be unconditionally complied with. Thus John XIII, in his *prilvilegium* of 967, seems to have restricted the jurisdictional sphere of the archbishopric of Magdeburg, about to be established, out of consideration for the Poles and contrary to the intentions of Otto I. Brought face to face with entirely new missionary problems by the German Emperor in his struggles with pagan frontier peoples, the papacy began to focus its gaze beyond the Empire on nations with which it had hardly concerned itself earlier. Now the Pope not infrequently had to deal with the spiritual affairs of France, because they were referred to him no longer only from France but also, in specific cases, by the German monarchs.

Italy naturally constituted an especially important topic of discussion between the two chiefs of Christendom. Only his third Italian expedition (966–72), which put the Emperor in touch with the Lombard princes of South Italy and enabled the imperial frontier to be assured vis-à-vis the Byzantines, produced a somewhat orderly situation. This finally made it possible gradually to restore to the Roman Church, at least partially, the districts usurped by Italian nobles. The restitutions, begun in 967 and continued by Otto II, had to do with Ravenna and the counties of the old exarchate. John XIII, to be sure, seems to have again turned over Ravenna and Comacchio to the Empress Adelaide, and later Gregory V had to cede the greatest part of his rights in the exarchate to the Archbishop of Ravenna.

The Roman Church lacked the means of administering a somewhat extensive territory with its own resources. In the tenth century things were in a bad way in general with regard to the landed property of the Italian churches. The German Emperors observed with great anxiety how everywhere great and petty lords were taking possession of ecclesiastical property in an increasing measure. So long as this involved monastic property, the bishops also helped themselves. Further losses occurred because of the widespread disregard of celibacy. Bishops, abbots, and priests provided for their illegitimate children as far as possible with clerical property. For political reasons alone the Ottos came out for the preservation and restitution of ecclesiastical property, especially in the strategically important zones and in the royal monasteries, which were bound to the imperial service. From 967 they treated of Church property at synods and diets. They issued laws, such as the *Capitulare de duello iudiciali* of 967, which introduced the duel as the method of proof in conflicts over property and excluded the sons of those obliged to celibacy from holding public offices, and the *Capitulare de praediis ecclesiasticis* of 998, which set a time-limit to the enfeoffing of property. They granted monasteries the right of inquisition, privileges of immunity, charters of protection, and confirmations of their property, and brought the complaints of plundered monasteries before their tribunal. Meagre as this reform was in regard to depth, the problem of reform that was thereby thrown open was to have further effects in Italy.

Meanwhile, another danger loomed in the south. Provoked by a Byzantine raid on Messina, the Sicilian Muslims attacked Calabria and Apulia from 976. The Byzantine Emperor Basil II was too much preoccupied with the revolt of Bardas Sclerus to be able to help. Otto II assumed charge of the defense against the infidel. From this time on he designated himself as Emperor of the Romans, in open rivalry with the *Basileus,* with whom he had been on bad terms ever since the death of John I Tzimisces. His campaign ended with defeat at Cape Colonna in Calabria in July 982, but the battle cost Abul Kasim his life and hence induced the leaderless Muslims to quit the mainland. Otto had already decided on a second military expedition, but in 983, at the age of twenty-eight, he died at Rome and was buried in the atrium of Saint Peter's. (Today he rests in the grottoes.) He left a son of the same name, not yet four years old but already crowned as King. The regency was conducted by Theophano and, after her death in 991, by Adelaide, until the young King was declared of age in 994.

In 996 Otto III set out on a journey to Rome. The Romans sent envoys to consult Otto about the imminent papal election. To their surprise he designated a German cleric, his relative Bruno, son of Otto of Carinthia, as Pope. He ascended the throne of Peter as Gregory V (996–99). Having received the imperial crown, the young ruler was ready with a second surprise. He declined to renew the *pactum* which Otto I had issued in his own name and that of his son, and would have nothing to do with the restitution of the Pentapolis, which Gregory V asked for.

Remaining in Rome, Otto III began in earnest the *renovatio imperii,* as he conceived it. The highly gifted ruler, just eighteen years of age, was in no sense a well-rounded personality. The young Emperor possessed an exalted consciousness of his position as ruler, aiming at universal recognition, political passion, and an enthusiasm for the *Imperium Romanum* that was nourished by his literary pursuits. Not the least influence on him was that exercised by Gerbert of Aurillac, his friend and the greatest scholar of the day.

Educated in his monastery of Aurillac, then at Vich in mathematics and science, and finally at Reims, and appointed *scholasticus* of the Reims cathedral school, Gerbert had made such a name for himself through an amazing mastery of all branches of the trivium and, the quadrivium that in 980 he was asked by the intellectually curious Emperor Otto II to engage in a scholarly disputation at Ravenna with the learned German, Otric. In 982 he was appointed Abbot of Bobbio. Because of the impossible situation in his monastery he returned to Reims in 984 and acted as adviser of Archbishop Adalbero (969–89). When Adalbero's successor, Archbishop Arnulf, was deposed in 991, Gerbert was elected. The controversy thereby sparked, brought him in 996 to Rome, where the Emperor Otto III got to know and admire him. This determined his future. When in 997 he fled from Reims, Otto III welcomed him at his court. In 998 he had him chosen as Archbishop of Ravenna and in 999, on the death of Gregory V, as Pope. Gerbert called himself Silvester II. He thereby fell in exactly with the renovation idea of his imperial friend. Set at the head of Christendom, Otto and Gerbert strove, as the new Constantine and the new Silvester, to lead the corrupt world back to its origin, to the idealized times of the first Christian Emperor and the contemporary Pope.

This cooperation occurred, it is true, in the form rather of a subordination than of an equality of the Pope. The mere fact that Otto III established his permanent abode in Rome could not fail to encroach painfully on the freedom of the Roman Church. If the autonomy once aspired after by Stephen II and his successors, which had found expression in the *Constitutum Constantini,* had remained in force only to a limited degree since the imperial coronation of Charles the Great, the basic principle proclaimed in the *Constitutum,* that authority over Rome was abandoned to the Popes, and the Emperor had to reside elsewhere, had been recognized time and again in the imperial *privilegia* of the ninth and tenth centuries. But Otto III felt that he was bound neither by the *Constitutum* nor by the imperial *privilegia.* He even declared the *Constitutum* a forgery, appealing to the deceptive maneuver of the Cardinal Deacon John, who had shown Otto I, at a time and for a purpose that can no longer be determined, a magnificent, especially prepared document of the donation as an allegedly genuine charter. And he did not hesitate to accuse the Roman Church of having bartered away the property of Saint Peter and then seeking to recoup her fortune with the Emperor's goods and rights. He bestowed not on her but on the Church of Ravenna the last three counties of the exarchate which had not so far been restored, and, spontaneously and with an express protest against any obligation of restitution, he bestowed on Saint Peter in the person of his successor, Silvester II, those eight counties which constituted the greatest part of the Pentapolis and which Gregory V had demanded in vain on the basis of the *Ottonianum.* The constitutional sovereignty which Otto III vindicated in regard to the papacy, to a higher degree than had his predecessors, was not without consequences in the spiritual sphere. On occasion the Emperor participated in purely ecclesiastical discussions. While he may have claimed no real jurisdiction in such cases, still there were also questions in which not only the papacy but also the *Imperium* had a substantial interest.

Thus Otto III had certainly played a decisive role in the, establishing of contact with the Christian West by Poland and Hungary. In the winter of 999–1000 the Emperor undertook a pilgrimage to the tomb of his friend, the martyr Adalbert, who was buried in Gniezno. That the carefully discussed journey was intended to satisfy not merely personal devotion but at the same time expressly political and religious goals is clear especially from the devotional formula, "Servus Iesu Christi," which Otto attributed to himself in the charters issued during the journey. Assumed by the Apostles, it must probably be placed parallel to the Byzantine imperial attribute of *isapostolos.* Like the Byzantine Emperors, Otto III was claiming an apostolic mission. As a matter of fact, he brought along for the Polish Duke Boleslas a papal privilege which made Gniezno the metropolitan of a Polish territorial Church that was yet to be constituted, and thus drew Poland, in the first stages of its Christianization, into the sphere of the Roman Church. But Otto was also thinking of an expansion of his *Imperium.* Boleslas was presented by Otto with a replica of the holy lance, was accepted *as frater et cooperator imperii* into the rank of an ally and *feodalis imperii* and thereby was somehow incorporated into the Western *Imperium.*

After Otto's return a similar decision was to be made for Hungary. In 1000 or

1001 Silvester II established the metropolitan see of Esztergom, with the right to found a Hungarian ecclesiastical province. Furthermore, the ruler, Vajk-Stephen, was honored with the royal dignity, possibly along with the dispatch of a royal crown. To whom the last mentioned act is to be attributed from the juridical point of view — to Emperor or to Pope or to both — may continue to be controverted, but is probably going too far to deny any share of the Emperor or even of the Pope. And so a second country was definitely gained for the West.

Otto's plans went still farther. If the young Emperor visited the Doge of Venice, Peter II Orseolo, incognito in 1001, the real reason may probably be sought in the victorious naval expedition which had gained for Venice the rule of the Dalmatian coastal cities. Apparently Otto wanted somehow to add to his *Imperium* the growing area of Venetian domination, which pertained to Byzantium, but he did not find the Doge kindly disposed to the idea. The oldest Russian chronicle reports furthermore for 1001 about envoys of Otto who arrived in Kiev, while at the synod held at Todi at Christmas 1001 it was decided that Bruno of Querfurt should be consecrated as Archbishop in charge of the missions to the east. The consecration occurred at Rome in the autumn of 1002.

The exalted position occupied by Emperor and Pope in 1001 in the Christian West, which had now expanded eastward, reposed on a base that was much too weak. Neither the Germans nor the Romans were sympathetic with Otto's imperial ideas. In fact his eastern policy, which was supported by the imperial idea, differed considerably from his grandfather's course, which was directed to the interest of the German Kingdom, and encountered resistance in Germany, especially from the Archbishop of Magdeburg. Far more questionable, however, was the shifting of the center of the *Imperium* to Rome. The decisive element in the *Imperium* being now the German royal power, this could be maintained only by a ruler moving about in the Empire, not by one residing in Rome. A conspiracy was hatched and in February 1001 Pope and Emperor were forced to leave the city. The revolt would probably have been crushed eventually, but the Emperor, calling for reinforcements, fell seriously ill and died on 24 January 1002, at the castle of Paterno near Citta Castellana, at the age of twenty-two. Perhaps if he had lived longer he would have better adapted his imperial idea to the existing realities. The Crescentians immediately seized control again and made the Popes their creatures.

And yet the footprints of Otto III and Silvester II were not simply effaced. With the incorporation of Poland and Hungary the Roman Church had achieved a permanent gain. The prestige of the Holy See had increased, and its supranational task had been clearly stressed through the elevation of two non-Italian Popes. And even though the Emperor had sought, by exploiting the Roman Church's possibilities of universal radiation to consolidate his imperial position as "sanctarum ecclesiarum devotissimus et fidelissimus dilatator" and as "servus apostolorum," the preeminence of the Church was by the same token admitted by him in principle, however unintentionally. To the extent that the Christian West formed a unity at all, this rested on the *imperium spirituale et ecclesiasticum* of the Roman Church. As yet the Popes were in no position to do without an Emperor. However, as soon as they were able to use freely the power belonging to them and make it respected by the Christian peoples, the leadership of the Christian West would fall to them.

CHAPTER 96

The Church in Spain, Ireland, and England: 900 to 1046

So long as the states that emerged from the fragmented Carolingian *Imperium* had to fight for their existence, Spain, Ireland, and England were left, even more than before, to their own devices. Now and then, of course, there were contacts, but it was the ecclesiastical reform, only getting under way around 1050, that released the energies which were to affect also the churches on the periphery and incorporate them into Western Christendom, then in process of reconstruction.

Spain

From the time when the small Christian Kingdom of Asturias began to regard itself as the successor of the Visigothic Kingdom and the flourishing cult of Santiago at Compostela provided it with the conviction that it was under the heavenly protection of an Apostle, there had germinated the idea of the *Reconquista.* Conceived in the reign of Alfonso II (791–842) at a time of perpetual defensive against Muslim attacks, it was soon to produce its earliest fruits. The opportunity was provided by a dangerous political crisis into which the Emirate of Córdoba fell in the last quarter of the ninth century, the result of political, religious, and probably also social causes. Revolt broke out everywhere, and as a consequence the power of the Emir Abd-Allah (888–912) was often confined to the limits of his capital. The revolt was the work especially of *Muwallad,* that is, of Spaniards who had adopted Islam. In the hill country between Roda and Málaga a purely Spanish state could be founded. Its ruler, the *Muwallad* Oma ibn Hafsun, deepened the opposition to the foreign rulers by returning to the Christian faith of his ancestors in 899.

The Asturian Christians did not let the favorable opportunity slip unexploited. Not content with sending aid to rebellious Toledo, they proceeded themselves to a frontal attack. Under the leadership of Alfonso III (866–910), they enlarged the kingdom in the west, in what became Portugal, to the Mondenego, in the center to the Douro; in Castile, to the east, they gained so much ground that there too they reached the Douro under Alfonso's first son, García. Then King Ordoño II (914–22) was able to transfer the capital from Oviedo to León.

Settlers poured into the conquered territory — Asturians and Basques and also Mozarabs, that is, Christians from al-Andalus who wished to exchange the Islamic yoke for Christian rule. Since freer economic methods could develop in the new area than in tradition-bound Galicia, it became the supporting pillar of the kingdom. Castile acquired special importance: here arose an individual and high-minded people, who were to play a decisive role in the future history of Spain.

The weakness of the Emirate did not continue. The government at Córdoba emerged victorious from a stubborn fight that did not end until the subjugation of Toledo in 932. The disunited Christian front could not stand firm when the Muslim commander of genius, the vizier Ibn Abi Amir, attacked. He quite rightly called himself al-Mansur, the victorious. León, Pamplona, Barcelona, the national shrine at Compostela itself fell into his hands and were destroyed. The Douro frontier was lost. What was left to the Christians was a ravaged territory.

This final display of Muslim power was followed by a sudden crash. After 1009 the Umayyad realm slowly broke up into numerous small principalities — the age of the wrens, the *reyes de taifas,* had arrived. But a grand-scale *Reconquista* was prevented by dissensions among the Christians. The balance of power was upset when Ferdinand I of Castile (1035–65) conquered León and united it with Castile in 1037. Rendered powerful by a wise administration of the two territories, Ferdinand slowly resumed the *Reconquista* from 1054, but he often preferred to accept tribute from the Muslim *taifas* instead of engaging in wars of conquest. His work was to be continued successfully by his second son, Alfonso VI (1065–1109). Meanwhile the Count of Barcelona had become the most powerful person in the Spanish March. He too now attacked the Muslims with a growing determination.

Wherever Christian rule was established, the Church flourished once more. Ancient extinct bishoprics were restored and new monasteries were founded. Attention was devoted to the continuity of the Church's inner life. The Spanish Church had its own, the so-called Mozarabic, liturgy, an important synodal legislation coming down from the Visigothic period, and a theological literature. The Muslim civilization, which developed so grandly in the tenth century, was transmitted especially by immigrant Mozarabs; it especially stimulated ecclesiastical learning in the branches of the quadrivium.

In the eleventh century, Spain emerged from its isolation. Compostela itself had contributed to this by attracting pilgrims from France, England, Germany, and Italy. The influx seems to have been not inconsiderable around 950, and it grew beyond all limits in the eleventh and twelfth centuries. Furthermore, from the turn of the tenth century Cluniac monks crossed the Pyrenees and steadily gained influence in the Christian kingdoms, especially in regard to Church reform, which had begun there and found expression at important reform synods. Spanish Kings formed marriage alliances with princely dynasties of France, and the crusade notion, slowly awakening outside Spain, induced French knights to participate in the *Reconquista* in the second half of the eleventh century. Hence, Christian Spain was adequately prepared when Alexander II and the succeeding reform Popes sent legates to organize the Spanish Church according to Roman and Catholic principles and thereby to draw it into the great community of Western Christendom.

Ireland

The situation of the Irish and the Anglo-Saxon Christians was fundamentally different from that of their Spanish coreligionists. Whereas, from 711 on, Islam conquered almost all of Spain in a rapid victorious march and in the following centuries yielded only a step at a title to the Christian *Reconquista,* the expansion of the Vikings, beginning in the ninth century, had a far less powerful military as well as intellectual impact. Wherever they obtained a foothold in the Christian West, the Northmen, confined to relatively small areas, had to incorporate themselves slowly into the surrounding civilized world.

Of course, during the ninth century this was scarcely discernible in Ireland. At that time the island not only had to suffer from the general Viking danger, but also had to endure the establishing of a small kingdom at Dublin. But from 873 this caused no great concern. It was only at the beginning of the tenth century that matters became really critical. The Vikings launched new attacks and thereby inaugurated a hundred years' war (914–1014). On the entire coast extending from Liffey to Shannon there arose Norwegian colonies with the fortified towns of Dublin, Wexford, Waterford, Cork, and Limerick. Dublin was one of the busier ports of the worldwide northern trading area. Since the intruders came into closer relations with the Irish through marriages, political agreements, and cultural assimilation, the endless wars ceased to follow any clear lines. Finally two men broke the power of the foreigners: in the north the King of Meath, Mael Seachlainn, in the south the national hero, Brian Boru. The latter ruled all of Munster from 976, and in 1002 he acquired the High Kingship of Ireland. In 1014 at the Battle of Clontarf he forever put an end to the Viking terror, but at the cost of his own life.

Although the Norwegians even after 1014 retained the small coastal Kingdom of Dublin and the cities of Waterford, Limerick, and Cork, and by no means completely gave up their national peculiarities, they still incorporated themselves into the Irish community in language, civilization, and politics. This naturally implied their Christianization. Missionary efforts had long been made, particularly from England. The Irish Vikings were in closer connection with England from the time they conquered Cumberland, and the princely family dominant in Dublin had succeeded also in ruling the Danish Kingdom of York for a short time.

The contact established with the Anglo-Saxon Church led to closer ties, but just when is uncertain. In any event the first known Bishop of Dublin, Duncan, was consecrated and obliged to obedience by the Archbishop of Canterbury in 1028. This connection of the young Church of Dublin with the see of Canterbury, first evident in 1028, fell in the reign of Knut, whose extensive realm, embracing England, Denmark, and Norway, provided the English Church with unique possibilities for the evangelization of the North. Hence it was in accord with the existing situation that on the one hand the Archbishop of Canterbury should bestow his attention on the Dublin Viking state, and on the other hand the new Christians in Dublin, mindful of their Nordic origin, should prefer to have their Church established by an Anglo-Saxon metropolitan rather than by Irish abbots. What thus developed was, of course, different from that to which people in Ireland were accustomed. Organized according to the principles of Roman canon law, the Church of Dublin represented a genuine diocese, administered by diocesan priests and bishop and having clear territorial limits. An important assignment thus devolved upon it. The more the Dublin political creation expanded into an all-Irish kingdom, the more carefully was the Roman and Catholic form of its Church to be considered by the Irish reformers.

As a matter of fact, Church reform was urgent in Ireland. The Celtic monastic system had become antiquated. Many flourishing monasteries and monastic libraries had been reduced to ruins by the Vikings. The brutalization of spirits, a consequence of the ceaseless struggle, likewise fostered a movement of secularization, which had begun independently of the Viking peril. It was connected with the increasingly wealthy holdings of the monasteries, which must have enticed especially the founding families. For these possessed the right of having one of their members elected as abbot. In the event that they could not produce a qualified candidate, the law provided for the electing of another monk, but the founding families gradually expanded their privileged position into a real hereditary right. Unconcerned about the qualities required by the high office of abbot, they installed in their monasteries one of their members. He did not have to be a monk, and it actually came about that by far the greater number of monasteries were ruled by lay abbots. This development affected the very heart of the Irish Church, for the entire care of souls had become the province of the monasteries. Monks exercised priestly functions in a defined area belonging to the monastery; bishop-monks officiated at ordinations and consecrations; and ecclesiastical jurisdiction was in the hands of the abbots. Since the abbot did not necessarily have to be a bishop, and very often was not, all authority, including ecclesiastical jurisdiction, now belonged to numerous lay abbots, most of them probably married. Celtic family law had stifled canon law and created a situation that could hardly be tolerated any longer.

The founding of the Church of Dublin must be seen against this background. The advantages which the diocesan and parochial organization there set up offered in comparison with the now problematic Celtic monastic system were not to be overlooked. Since the only too firmly consolidated right of the laity did not give hopes of a reform of the monastic constitution, the Church of Dublin seemed to point out the only possible remedy. Not merely receptive Irishmen, but also the Archbishops of Canterbury were interested in a reform; these last hoped in this way to be able to extend their metropolitan and primatial authority to all of Ireland. Once the Gregorian Reform was encouraged in England more powerfully than earlier by William the Conqueror, the Archbishops of Canterbury, Lanfranc and Anselm, sought to introduce it also on the neighboring island. Though their exertions were ineffectual, a native Irish reform movement got under way. Making progress only laboriously, it was presented with a new situation by the Anglo-Norman invasion of 1172, which violently closed the "Celtic" period of Irish history. Unjustly as the conquerors at first dealt with the Irish Church, they forced it to incorporate itself definitively into the Universal Church.

Since the daughter Church of Scotland was organized according to the same Celtic monastic system, it knew the same portentous development. However, it had the good fortune to find a reform-minded Queen in the Anglo-Saxon Princess Margaret, who had fled to Scotland after the Battle of Hastings (1066) and there married King Malcolm III. It was due to her energetic efforts and those of her sons that Scotland exchanged the outdated Irish-Scottish ecclesiastical organization for the Roman.

England

Under the concentrated attacks of the Vikings in the second half of the ninth century, Anglo-Saxon England had far more to suffer than did Ireland. Without the heroic struggle of Alfred the Great, King of Wessex-Sussex-Kent (871–99), the whole country would probably have fallen to the conquerors, mostly Danes. But there continued to be a Viking Zone, known as the Danelaw because of the Danish law there prevailing. The frontier ran right through Essex and Mercia. But Alfred had not merely saved southern England; he had also united it more efficiently by strengthening the power of the state and by awakening a genuine national spirit. Sustained by these forces, his descendants in the tenth century were able to gain back what had been lost and to construct a strong single Anglo-Saxon Kingdom.

The reconquest began under his son, Edward the Elder (899–924). Danish rule was pushed back to the mouth of the Humber, and hence to Northumbria. In 927, on the death of Sihtric of Dublin, Alfred's grandson, Aethelstan (824–39), acquired the Kingdom of York. His authority, now expanding through Northumbria, was endangered when Olaf Guthrithson, crossed over from Ireland and was supported by the Scots, the Britons of Strathclyde, and the Danes of Cumberland and Northumbria, but Aethelstan's victory at Brunanburh in 937 crushed the resistance. There were still other attempts to render all or part of Northumbria independent, but they had no lasting success and from 954 they ceased completely. Thus King Edgar (959–75) was able to complete in peace the work of his predecessors the inner organization of the Anglo-Saxon state.

We must pass over what had been accomplished since Alfred for the government, the administration of justice, and the constitution. Growing consistently stronger, the kingdom, even in the first half of the tenth century, gained a position of hegemony vis-à-vis the other peoples living on the island. This found significant expression in the title *imperator totius Britanniae,* which the royal chancery not infrequently used in this or a variant form for the charters of its rulers from the time of Aethelstan. The Dynasty of Wessex was so highly esteemed on the continent that politically important family ties were formed.

The Vikings who attacked England were pagans. If they preferred to direct their attacks against churches and monasteries, this was not merely for the sake of the treasures accumulated there, but also because of a hatred for Christianity. King Edmund of East Anglia had to pay for his loyalty to his faith by a cruel martyrdom in 870. But the blessing which, from the days of Alfred the Great, obviously rested on the military and political enterprises of the Anglo-Saxons made the Vikings reflect that the God of the Christians proved to be the greater bringer of prosperity and peace. But during the tenth century Christianity made progress irresistibly in the Danelaw; it merely needed time.

The rise of the Anglo-Saxon Kingdom would hardly have prospered without the cooperation of the Church. It was for this very reason that the Kings took an interest in the reform of religious and ecclesiastical life. There were the exertions of Alfred the Great, which went beyond the purely religious sphere to include education in general and hence even provided for the translating of Latin works into old English. However, the time was not yet ripe for such a grand-scale undertaking. Hence Alfred's successors sought more accessible goals: they continued the ecclesiastical legislation, had extinct dioceses restored, and made gifts to the churches.

With the betterment of ecclesiastical conditions the inner forces also began, of course, to move and to press for a reform of both monasticism and the diocesan clergy and of the care of souls. The desolate state of the monasteries — most of them had been abandoned or destroyed or had passed to the possession of more or less easy going canons — affected the Anglo-Saxon Church all the more unfavorably since it had previously been a monastic Church to a great extent. Receptive prelates, such as the Dane Oda, Archbishop of Canterbury (942–60), and Aelfheah, Bishop of Winchester (934–51), thus had high hopes of a revival of the monastic spirit. What they dreamed of was carried out by younger men whom they inspired — Aelfheah's pupils, Dunstan and Aethelwold, and Oda's nephew, Oswald. All three became monks. In their serious efforts for a renewal of the Benedictine way of life they encountered difficulties. The venerable Anglo-Saxon monastic tradition, which had meanwhile decayed, was in some respects out of date, and so the three young reformers obtained inspiration from the new monastic movements in France and Lotharingia. The sources of this inspiration were, on the one hand, Fleury-sur-Loire, reformed by Odo of Cluny in the 930s, and, on the other hand, Ghent, with the two monasteries of Saint Peter and Saint Bavo, which from 954 bore the clear stamp of Gorze with a strong admixture of the customs of Brogne. Dunstan eagerly studied the Lotharingian reform when he spent a period of exile lasting until 956 with the Ghent Benedictines. Oswald and Aethelwold sought a more exact knowledge of the customs introduced at Fleury, Aethelwold by sending his pupil Oscar there, whereas Oswald himself spent several years at Fleury.

Hardly had Anglo-Saxon monasticism in this way resumed contact with the monastic reform movements on the continent when its great hour struck. King Edgar, a zealous reformer, assumed the government and placed the three monks in leading positions. Dunstan first became Bishop of Worcester, then of London, and finally Archbishop of Canterbury (960–88) and chief adviser of the King. Oswald received the see of Worcester in 961 and from 971 to 992 was Archbishop of York. Aethelwold was Bishop of Winchester from 963 to 984. Monastic renewal, already begun and chiefly promoted by Glastonbury and Abingdon, now moved at full speed. Existing monasteries were reformed, new ones were founded. In an effort to provide a more secure orientation for the now flourishing monastic life, a council meeting at Winchester between 965 and 975 drew up the celebrated *Regularis Concordia,* probably at Oswald's urging. In it Dunstan and his two friends, after long consultation with bishops, abbots, and monks, took up the Lotharingian and the Cluny-Fleury reform initiatives and adapted them to Anglo-Saxon monasticism.

The reform was by no means confined to the monasteries. Since originally the majority of the Anglo-Saxon sees had been connected with monasteries, it seemed natural to restore the old situation. Overzealous monk-bishops, such as Aethelwold, abruptly expelled from their cathedrals the canons who had established themselves there, while Dunstan and other Benedictine bishops sought to bring them back to a monastic mode of life or introduced monks among them, but avoided the use of force. In any event the monastic element was systematically strengthened in the English episcopate by King Edgar and Dunstan in an effort to get on with the urgently necessary reform of clergy and people. What had been prepared by Archbishop Oda of Canterbury and others was continued by Dunstan, who did all he could to put an end to clerical marriage, which had become almost the rule, and to remedy the defective education of priests and the abuses in the care of souls. Edgar seconded him by means of an extensive legislative activity that regulated both ecclesiastical and religious life, even in details. His cooperation was of course indispensable. A wholesome influence on clergy and people could, it is true, be expected from the monasteries and their schools — a hope which Aelfric, monk of Cerne, for example, sought to satisfy toward the close of the century by his masterly Anglo-Saxon version of homilies and of parts of Scripture — but the King and the episcopate continued to be the real leaders of reform.

Hence it was profoundly significant that Dunstan composed his celebrated coronation *ordo* for the unusually long delayed coronation of King Edgar in 973, a rite that was to be used again and again in England, and thereby stressed the religious functions of kingship in a rich symbolism, borrowed from Anglo-Saxon and continental customs. Edgar's death two years later and the subsequent collapse of the Anglo-Saxon Dynasty could only have shaken him all the more. The family of Alfred the Great had more and more lost its vitality since the death of Aethelstan, a fact that it was only too easy to conceal during Edgar's prosperous reign. The doom now approaching did not come without warning. The egoism of the magnates, the incompetence of Aethelred II, who in 978 had taken the place of his murdered half-brother Edward, and the new Viking invasions beginning in 991 — all these so weakened the kingdom that in 1013 Aethelred fled to his brother-in-law, Duke Richard II of Normandy, while the Danish King Svein Forkbeard, who had undertaken the conquest of England, took possession of the throne (1013–14). Aethelred and his son Edmund Ironside both died in 1016, whereupon Svein's son, Knut, was able definitely to secure the throne for himself (1016–35). This mighty monarch, who also ruled Denmark from 1018 and Norway too from 1028, did not regard himself as the conqueror of England but as its lawful ruler, bound by the laws of his predecessors. Neither the magnates nor the people nor the Church — Knut was loyally attached to her — could complain.

Shrewd as it was to rule England according to its own laws, the forces which since Edgar's death were effectively undermining the state would have had to be fought more energetically. Knut's failure to do so would soon take its toll. The English recalled Aethelred's son, Edward the Confessor, who was living in Normandy, and made him King (1042–66). The pious but scarcely qualified monarch was pretty much helpless against the higher nobility, which had become independent. The opposition grew when, following continental models, he sought to establish a central administration and as far as possible filled offices at court and in the Church with Normans or other Frenchmen. It was not very helpful that he succeeded in banishing his chief opponent, Earl Godwin of Wessex, for a short time, for the victory of the Norman faction that was thereby achieved gave a new impulse to the national opposition. Behind the national faction stood Godwin's son, Earl Harold; behind the Norman party, Duke William of Normandy. Since Edward was childless, both of these princes sought the crown. Following the King's death on 5 January 1066, Harold took it in a *coup d'état* and so brought on a war with Duke William, which was to bring England henceforth under Norman rule and thus into closer contact with the continent.

Edgar's death in 975 hurt the English Church even more than the state. The opponents of the monastic reform immediately raised their heads. Magnates took possession of monasteries, canons demanded the restoration of the position they had previously occupied in the cathedrals. Under Aethelred II Dunstan and his friends lost their influence at court. And so the reform that was in progress stopped half-way. Its strong dependence on the Kings and the earls led after Knut's death to serious abuses. Bishops were arbitrarily installed and deposed. Pluralism in high ecclesiastical offices and brazen simony were not rare. The state of stagnation made itself all the more conspicuous when the reform movements or the continent accelerated their rhythm from the beginning of the eleventh century and in 1049 the papacy assumed the leadership of the great reform. The English Church had fallen into a state of isolation.

Edward the Confessor had apparently sensed this and perhaps that is why he filled high Church offices with Normans and other Frenchmen. But he merely succeeded in enkindling a national English opposition to the foreign prelates. The most hated among them, Archbishop Robert of Canterbury, had to flee the country in 1052 and helplessly allow Bishop Stigand of Winchester to take his place. The closer the life of the childless Edward drew to its end, the more pressing became the choice between the two claimants to the throne, Earl Harold, chief of the national English party, and Duke William of Normandy. Stigand clearly belonged to Harold's faction. His defiant attitude could only confirm the view of the reform papacy that nothing could be expected from Harold and his adherents with regard to the renewal of the English Church. And so the future decision was prepared. In 1066 the Roman Church supported William's invasion in order to enable the continental reform to penetrate the Church in England.

C H A P T E R   9 7

The Papacy and the Empire
from 1002 to 1046

After the death of Otto III the situation both at Rome and in the Lombard Kingdom gradually reverted to what it had been before the days of the Ottos: domination by the nobles at Rome, and an Italian kingship handed over to the Margrave Arduin of Ivrea. In Germany too there were not lacking efforts to transfer the government to other hands, but the last scion of the Saxon Dynasty, going back in the direct male line to Henry I, Duke Henry of Bavaria, was able to enforce his claim and, as King Henry II (1002–24), to strengthen the Empire again by recourse to the sound principles of Otto I. Not Rome and the universal *Imperium* were regarded by him as the foundation of his throne, but rather the royal authority in Germany, in Italy, and eventually in Burgundy. The crown of Burgundy was only to devolve upon his successor, Conrad II, in 1033, but this was prepared for the German kingship by Henry II through an agreement on the inheritance with his uncle, King Rudolf III of Burgundy, and by the assumption of feudal suzerainty. Since the royal power in Italy was really quite limited, and the Burgundian kingship promised little increase of real power, though it did assure the Alpine passes, Germany remained the essential basis. Henry II built it up solidly, especially by having recourse to the Church.

The Ottonian State Church was the essential prop of the kingship, but until the reign of Henry II there were really only rudimentary stages in constructing it. He was the first to develop it logically and to connect it to a system. As none of his blood relatives before him, he monopolized the nomination to episcopal sees and forced upon the electors candidates he designated, chosen mostly from the royal chapel, so that there was very little of that free assent which constitutes the essence of the *electio canonica.* On several occasions he convoked synods or intervened in ecclesiastical matters. Episcopal sees were subjected to the additional burden of hospitality, which Henry claimed to a greater degree than had been the earlier practice, for himself and his court on his ceaseless journeys.

The royal monasteries had to put up with more serious interference, for in their regard the King was acting as the lord of proprietary churches. Abbots were deposed or installed without regard for the right of election of the communities concerned, and Henry disposed of the monastic property as of any other goods of the Empire. He assigned abbeys or parts of their property to other churches, usually to cathedrals; all monasteries had to pay fixed dues, the *servitium regale,* and even the enfeoffment of secular vassals with monastic property was at times ordered. In these measures the personally pious monarch was motivated not solely by the material interest of the Empire but by a genuine desire for reform. A monastic reform movement had begun long before in Lotharingia and had radiated into the interior of Germany. Influenced by it, Henry II sent at first South German and Bavarian and later Lotharingian reform monks as abbots to not a few royal monasteries. The friendship which the Ottos had cultivated with the great monastic personages of their day became under Henry II a co-operation in the top echelon in Germany. Behind this religious and political activity there stood, of course, the early medieval theocratic idea of kingship. Under Henry II and then under Henry III it experienced an exaltation that was to have a decisive effect on the reform of the Church.

His attention claimed by inner and outside struggles, Henry II left it to Duke Otto of Carinthia to go to Italy and attack Arduin of Ivrea. Only Otto's ill luck caused him to cross the Alps himself and to proclaim his taking possession of the Lombard Kingdom by being solemnly crowned at Pavia. Since Arduin had retired without fighting to a powerful castle, he was undefeated but his rival kingship was based on such a weak foundation that it posed no serious danger for Henry.

The restored rule of the nobility at Rome led of necessity to rivalries among the families. As a matter of fact, power was wrested from the Crescentians by the comital house of Tusculum. The victory of the Tusculans was complete. For decades now they ruled Rome and the *Patrimonium* as a sort of hereditary principality. Unlike Alberic they based their power, not on that of a *princeps,* but on that of the Pope; a member of the family assumed it each time and then assigned the most important secular functions to his brothers. Since other noble families, including the Crescentians, were given a share in the administration, there were no disturbances.

　　　The Tusculans were smart enough not to oppose in principle the *Imperium* that had been restored in 962. And so, after preliminary negotiations, Henry II was able to receive the imperial anointing and coronation at Saint Peter's on 14 February 1014. Just how he and Benedict VIII then defined their respective competence is not known. It is probably to be attributed chiefly to the Pope that the imperial *privilegium* of Otto I was not renewed at that time. The rights of sovereignty there assigned to the Emperor may have been annoying to Benedict VIII. But on the other hand Henry II did not renounce every right in Rome. The judicial sessions which he held during his brief stay show this, and it is probably not an accident that the title *patricius*, usurped by the Crescentian John, no longer appeared officially among the Tusculans. Basically, however, Henry II, Conrad II, and Henry III allowed a completely free hand to the Tusculans, who ruled until 1045. And the right of approval, which Otto I had acquired for papal elections and which his successors had augmented to a right of designation, apparently played no role in the elevation of John XIX and in that of Benedict IX, both of them falling in the time of Conrad II. The spirit of a really independent Rome was expressed in the *Graphia aureae urbis Romae,* the archaeological and political work, written around 1030, of an unknown adherent of the Tusculans, probably a layman but in any event a scholar, who sought to recall to memory the glory of the ancient Roman Empire and, in Schramm's words, "to take the government of the city out of the hands of the Emperor and transfer it to those of a deputy, of a Roman *patricius.*"

　　　Without disturbing each other, Henry II and Benedict VIII pursued their goals. Both on his journey to Rome and later Henry sought to tighten his control of the Lombard Kingdom. Since in Lombardy "and in Central Italy he had especially favored ecclesiastics, after his return to Germany there occurred a revolt of the secular princes, which drew Arduin of Ivrea from his lair and had him assume leadership. Boniface of Canossa, in alliance with the loyal bishops, thoroughly defeated the rebels. But Henry had little power in Italy. He strengthened it by beginning systematically to fill the episcopal sees with Germans, first of all in the metropolitan provinces of Aquileia and Ravenna.

　　　It cannot be determined whether Benedict VIII came to the papacy from the clerical or the lay state. But no matter: his ability quickly brought him prestige and influence. It is true that his interests were chiefly in politics and administration. After he had crushed the early opposition of the Crescentians and other families with the aid of his brothers, things in the *Patrimonium* could be put in some kind of order. But his glance went beyond the *Patrimonium.* The Muslims were causing anxiety in the Tyrrhenian Sea. Pisa was plundered in 1004 and 1011, and in 1015 Spanish Muslims under the Emir Mogehid conquered Sardinia. When in 1016 they destroyed the old maritime city of Luni from there, Benedict VIII intervened. Pisan, Genoese, and papal troops boarded ships, defeated the Muslims in a sea battle, and freed Sardinia. The Pope, moreover, paid close attention to the revolts which broke out against Byzantine rule in 1009. The victory of the Catapan Basil Bojoannes near Cannae in 1018 brought a turning point: the Byzantines advanced into Lombard territory and threatened Rome. Melo and, soon after, Benedict himself thus went to see Henry II in order to ask help. At Easter of 1020 Pope and Emperor took counsel at Bamberg in regard to their common tasks. On this occasion the Pope received from Henry an imperial *privilegium*, which reproduced the *Ottonianum* word for word and added a few gifts, and also the promise to go to Italy.

Henry II finally set out for Italy in the autumn of 1021, and in the following year moved directly south in three army columns. The Pope had to be content that at least the progress of the Byzantines came to a stop.

Of greater importance was the reform synod which the Pope and the Emperor held at Pavia in March 1022 before the campaign. The Ottos had earlier exerted themselves to protect ecclesiastical and monastic property from expropriation, and in 1014 Henry II had returned to the subject at the Synod of Ravenna, arranged by him together with Benedict, by commanding the churches to draw up an inventory of their property. A Roman Synod immediately after the imperial coronation, whose decrees are unknown, may have discussed similar questions. But at Pavia in 1022 more radical decrees were prepared, at the urging of the Pope. They insisted strictly on the ancient requirement of celibacy for the subdiaconate and higher orders, a law that had to a great extent fallen into oblivion, and decreed that the sons of unfree ecclesiastics should remain in the father's condition. Involved here was not the inner reform of the Church but the preservation of Church property, which all too easily devolved by means of clerical marriage on the children. But, once formulated, the decrees were to gain momentum as the desire for inner reform grew strong.

Neither Pope nor Emperor was permitted to do much more. Benedict VIII died in April 1024, Henry II three months later. The good memory which people in Germany retained in regard to the Emperor, was enhanced into a cult by the zealous cooperation of the episcopal see of Bamberg, founded by him and charged with tending his grave, so that in 1146 Eugene III undertook his canonization. While this exaltation was based less on authentic historical than on idealizing and legendary tradition, it concerned a man who had taken seriously the Christian ideal of a king of his day.

Benedict VIII was succeeded by his brother, the Tusculan John XIX (1024-32); the childless Henry II, by the founder of the Salian Dynasty, Conrad II (1024-39). Conrad II, on the other hand, showed himself to be equal to the task entrusted to him. Henry II's constructive work was now to produce its real fruits. In 1027 Conrad received the imperial crown at Rome in the presence of King Knut of England and Denmark and of King Rudolf III of Burgundy. It acquired greater importance through the gaining of the Burgundian Kingdom in 1033 and the consolidation of the imperial power in Italy. The Emperor acted vigorously in both Lombardy and Tuscany. But, differing from Henry II, he did not chiefly favor the spiritual princes at the expense of the secular. In fact in 1037 he especially singled out the lesser vassals among the secular nobles, the so-called *vavassores,* and because of them came into conflict with the Lombard bishops, above all with Archbishop Aribert of Milan.

Though less devout than Henry II, the first Salian substantially maintained the ecclesiastical policy of his predecessor, on the one hand promoting the Lotharingian monastic reform, on the other hand bringing to a completion the constructing of a German State Church. The West was preparing to enter upon a new phase in its development. The Church reform movements were among the most important progressive forces. If the German monarch intended to maintain his leading position, he had to remain in vital contact with them. Conrad II probably lacked the true instinct for this, but such was not the case with his young son and successor, Henry III. Taking up the reform on his own, Henry was to release a movement heavy with consequences.

Few early medieval rulers were so convinced of the sublimity of the theocratic kingship and of the heavy burdens connected with it as was Henry III (1039–56). His very exertions in the first years of his reign for a general peace in the Empire revealed this. While in France the Church rather than the then quite feeble crown fought against private warfare and developed the idea of the Peace of God, Henry III made use of the religious demands for peace in complete consistency. Guided by a correct understanding that justice must be united with mercy and pardon if genuine Christian peace is to prevail, he did not rest content with a mere peace edict. At the Synod of Constance of 1043 he proclaimed pardon to all his enemies from the ambo or the altar of the cathedral and urged those present to do the same. He made a like declaration at Trier. Secular princes sensed the aim of a ruler intent on the constant extension of the royal power. Henry stood forth in the sight of the bishops with all the authority of the theocratic ruler. In fact, he invested them no longer with the staff alone but also with the ring, the symbol of the spiritual marriage between the bishop and his church.

His monastic policy was his own. Whereas Henry II liked to subject abbeys to bishops, Henry III was so favorable to monastic efforts for liberty that he withdrew a group of monasteries from the power of their episcopal or noble proprietors and took them under his direct protection. Of course, this protection also meant domination, but the domination of the supreme religious and political power, which was to assure the monasteries of freedom, for to medieval man freedom meant also the state of subjection and service, ultimately to God, and so Henry could designate the subjection of the abbeys under his obedience as their freedom. Much as this protectorate aimed at making financial sources of aid accessible to the imperial authority, its real and more fundamental goal consisted for Henry III in the maintaining and furthering of monastic discipline. Not in vain were Henry and his second wife, Agnes of Poitou, who came from a house closely linked with Cluny, in intimate contact with the leaders of the monastic reform, the Cluniacs, the Lotharingians, and the hermits of Central Italy. The deep effect produced on the King by the reform ideas of the time appears especially in his renunciation of the fees which not a few kings or princes of his day did not hesitate to demand of bishops or abbots who were to be invested. He regarded them as simony.

John XIX was succeeded by his nephew Theophylact, who became Benedict IX (1032–45). Although the reports concerning his having assumed the papacy at the quite uncanonical age of twelve and concerning his wicked life must have been at least greatly exaggerated, still Benedict did not measure up to the papacy as Christendom in its restless religious state was expecting. But his spiritual inadequacies had less to do with his downfall than did movements within Rome against the Tusculan domination. An uprising in September 1044 compelled the Pope to flee. He was replaced, but probably not until January 1045, by the Bishop of Sabina, Silvester III, who was supported by a collateral branch of the Crescentians. After a few months Benedict was able to drive him out again, but he found in Rome so dangerous a situation that he was prepared to abdicate in the event that someone would reimburse him for the money that he had distributed to make sure his own election. What ensued is, unfortunately, very obscure. Probably Benedict discussed the financial settlement with a rather small group of men who were on friendly terms with him and apparently respectable, including his godfather, the pious Archpriest John Gratian of San Giovanni a Porta Latina, and, before or after his official abdication, received the hard cash from the hands of the Jewish Christian Baruch, called Benedict after his conversion. Then John Gratian was made Pope under the name of Gregory VI (1045–46). He encountered no resistance in reform circle, if Peter Damiani, Prior of Fonte Avellana, may act as an example. On the contrary, he found enthusiastic assent, which, it is true, cooled off or, as in the case of Peter Damiani, became the very opposite, once the story of the money transaction leaked out.

At first Henry III also recognized Gregory VI. When he crossed the Alps in the autumn of 1046, he was probably motivated only by the intention of visiting the pacified Lombard Kingdom and of receiving the imperial crown at Rome. In any event, on 20 December a synod met at Sutri, near Rome, to sit in judgment on the three claimants, notwithstanding the fact that Benedict IX and Silvester III had long before retired. Silvester III and Gregory VI were deposed at Sutri; three days later Benedict IX was deposed at a Roman Synod. At Henry's suggestion Bishop Suitger of Bamberg was then elected. Enthroned on Christmas 1046 under the name Clement II, the new Pope conferred the imperial anointing and coronation on Henry III and Queen Agnes.

But what may Henry III, the real actor in all this, have aimed at by the deposition? It would be good from the outset to take note of the entanglement of the religious and political goals, without which the typically theocratic intervention here under consideration is unintelligible. The Emperor was concerned there can be no doubt about it with the reform of the Roman Church, of the spiritual pivot of Christendom. But, as the quasi-priestly ruler, he did not merely want to protect a movement of renewal radiating from Rome to the Universal Church; he wanted to guide and lead it, so far as he could.

The preliminary condition was that the papacy should be freed from domination by the Roman nobility. Hence Henry again had recourse to the old right of participating in the papal election, established by Otto I. It is true that from 1046 on he was careful to discuss the appointment of a new successor of Peter with Roman envoys, but it was he who made the designation and accordingly determined the subsequent election by the clergy and people of Rome. In order legally to establish this practice, which had not been made use of since Otto III, in 1046 he had the Romans confer upon him the patriciate, which the earlier masters of Rome had exercised at least *de facto,* occasionally while bearing the title of *patricius.* The second innovation was that the Emperor was not to designate a single Roman, not even an Italian, as Pope. In this he resumed the policy of Otto III, but even more pointedly, in that he nominated only German bishops. He had no intention of incorporating the papacy into the German State Church. Henry III fully recognized the unique primatial position of the Pope, once he had been installed, and did not meddle in the administration. However, the provenience of the new Bishops of Rome from the German episcopate was intended not only to assure the reform better; it was also to bind the papacy as closely as possible to the *Imperium.* At the same time the Emperor must have expected from the German Popes a furthering of his imperial policy in Italy, although this viewpoint was probably not to the fore in 1046, because of the then prevailing peaceful situation.

Henry III's reform initiative has been harshly condemned at times. One witness from that period may verify on what unhistorical presuppositions such verdicts are based. He followed the events at Sutri and Rome as an unassuming and scarcely noticed Roman cleric and then accompanied to Cologne the deposed Pope Gregory VI, whom Henry sent into exile for safety's sake. This was Hildebrand, who later was to mount the throne of Peter as Gregory VII and take up the conflict between *Regnum* and *Sacerdotium*. From a man who was on principle an opponent of theocratic rule, who even bore the pain of banishment with Gregory VI, one really ought to expect a violent repudiation of Henry III. In actuality, however, he preserved a kind memory of the Emperor throughout his life and in this he was in agreement with almost all the leading reformers of his generation. Hence Henry III's reform initiative must have been regarded by these circles as an action that favored the Church, and Henry's theocracy, despite criticism expressed here and there, must have corresponded so well with the views of his time that the future radical development, furthered by his all too early death and other adverse circumstances, could not be foreseen. During the Investiture Controversy itself William the Conqueror could govern theocratically in Normandy and England, just like Henry III, without coming into conflict with Gregory VII, a proof of how slowly the intellectual change beginning in the second half of the eleventh century was completed.

Constitution of the Church, Worship, Pastoral Care, and Piety: 700 to 1050

Chaps. 98–100: Friedrich Kempf
Chaps. 101–103: Josef Jungmann

C H A P T E R 9 8

Diocesan Organization

The more Germanic, Roman, and, to a degree, even Celtic ways of life in the Christian West blended into one distinct early medieval culture, the more powerfully did new institutions, based on Germanic and Roman juridical ideas, have to be developed in the Church. These relaxed the strictly hierarchical structure of the ancient Christian Roman episcopal constitution, and partly even dissolved it or covered it over. Prepared as early as the Merovingian period, this process got fully under way from about the eighth century. Accordingly, a new period of Church history, characterized *par excellence* by Germanic law, began. It lasted until about the end of the Salian Dynasty. It is true that even in the age of the Gregorian Reform there appeared a reaction, based on Roman constitutional principles, but it required serious work before a synthesis could be discovered in the rising canon law, in the *Decretum Gratiani* that was completed around 1140. This gave preference to the Roman element, so that in the future the Germanic influence was pushed back, even though it was never eliminated.

Rural Churches

The creative juridical initiative of the Germano-Roman nations had its roots essentially in a rural and feudal way of life that was different from the urban culture of antiquity. Even in late antiquity, the proprietary spheres of influence established by the senatorial nobility introduced a development unfavorable to the city, and this received a powerful stimulus from the wanderings of the peoples. Among other things, new churches arose everywhere in the country. The circumstance that they were built, endowed, and maintained by the owners of the property or by cooperative groups relieved the bishops of a duty which they would hardly have been able to satisfy, considering the means at their disposal, but at the same time it presented them with serious problems.

For since the founders of those churches asserted rights of ownership, there developed a new juridical form, opposed to the Roman constitution of the Church — the institution of the "proprietary church." It was probably not of specifically German origin. There had been more or less developed proprietary churches both in the West, for example in Gaul, and in the East of the Roman Empire — in the Byzantine Empire even with a centuries-long development culminating in the so-called *ktitoren* right — and finally, again in a special form, among the Slavs. In the West, however, the Germanic peoples were undoubtedly the propelling element.

The strongest influence proceeded from the Frankish proprietary church. In the Merovingian period there had been no lack of resistance in regard to the principle on the part of bishops. The little that had been accomplished by this means disappeared in the chaos that crept in from 639. When, at the turn of the seventh and eighth centuries, ecclesiastical property was secularized on a grand scale, even the baptismal churches that were still dependent on the bishop fell for the greatest part into lay hands. In order to guard against further losses, the bishops too now adopted the proprietary church system for the churches still left to them. And since the monasteries did likewise, and in fact even tried to increase the number of proprietary churches as much as possible, soon there was no church in the Frankish Kingdom without a secular or a spiritual proprietor. The more or less successful exertions of the Carolingians, summarized in the ecclesiastical capitularies of Louis the Pious of 818–19, for a juridically acceptable form and the recognition of the proprietary church, both by the Carolingian episcopate, despite repeated protests, and by Popes Eugene II and Leo IV.

The proprietary church was a product of property law. It was reduced to juridical form by virtue of the stone altar firmly connected with the earth. For the church building and its equipment, rectory and cemetery, the landed property donated to the church with its peasants, the income from the tithe, offerings, and stole fees, in short whatever the altar attracted around itself belonged to it as its appurtenances and was, like the altar itself, the property of the landlord. From the time of Charles the Great this estate could no longer be taken from the Church. It was destined first of all to serve the Church and her function. But since the surplus revenues belonged to the proprietor, the proprietary church was exposed to the danger of exploitation. To be able to carry out its function, it needed a priest, just as the mill which the landlord set up on his property, usually with compulsory use by his peasants, needed a miller. Not the bishop but the proprietor of the church appointed this priest. If it so suited him, he took him, just like the miller, from the ranks of his serfs or slaves and in any event he laid down conditions which assured him the greatest possible usufruct and often even humiliated the priest. Proprietary rights over churches could be conveyed to other persons, both in the form of a loan and by means of inheritance or of sale, gift, mortgage, and the like. Although the church property was supposed to remain a whole and passed in its entirety to several heirs, greed brought it about that the proprietor reserved to himself, at least partially, especially lucrative revenues, in particular the tithe and the offerings, by either receiving them himself or selling the right to them, in whole or in part. Once this inclined plane had been set foot on, no stop was possible thereafter: during the eleventh and twelfth centuries the institution of the proprietary church clearly fell apart into a loose bundle of individual rights. The process was expedited, not least of all, by the reform movement in the Church.

In several respects the proprietary church was opposed to the ecclesiastical constitution, as this had earlier been developed with the aid of Roman law. To be sure, the power pertaining to the bishop of disposing of church property had earlier become less comprehensive in so far as donations were made to individual churches, but churches that had become holders of their own property had still been incorporated absolutely into the episcopal constitution. For, in accord with Roman law, the Church represented an institution of public law. Its virtually monarchical direction was in the hands of the bishop. He ordained his helpers — priests, deacons, and clerics — and appointed them to the ecclesiastical ministry with delegated power. Obliged to support them, he provided them with *stipendia* or with church property in the form of a loan.

So centralized an organization could not but appear strange to the Germanic peoples, who had different ideas and were on a more primitive level of culture. Since they knew neither the underlying Roman legal distinction between *ius publicum* and *ius privatum* nor the Roman form of the official positions and constructed both state and society less from above than from below, private and property law obtained preponderance in their proprietary churches. In order to carry out an economic enterprise the proprietor took a cleric into his service. The priesthood was for him a means to an end, whereas in the ancient Christian Roman constitution of the Church the opposite relationship prevailed: the property bestowed upon the church was supposed to serve the needs of the priesthood.

The proprietary church was too deeply rooted in early medieval culture to be extirpated; only its excesses could be curtailed. The reform laws of Charles the Great and his son solved this problem to a degree. With the compromise then achieved between the interests of the laity and those of the clergy the Frankish proprietary church system was directed to a road which it was to cling to despite ceaseless violations of the law. Even though the church continued to belong to the proprietor, it was up to the bishop to supervise its maintenance. Furthermore, the priests of a proprietary church were expressly made subject to the bishop's jurisdiction. Not only did their appointment or removal require the bishop's assent, but the priests were obliged to make an annual report and to attend synods and court sessions. And so, on the one hand, there was required for priests the condition of freedom and the consequent right of not being deposed except by the sentence of a court, and, on the other hand, the rent-free use of at least one hide of glebe, usually thirty acres, of the necessary structures with garden, of a portion of the tithe, and of the offerings. In return they had to carry out the ecclesiastical functions, while rights of use over and above this had to be reimbursed through payments of taxes, special services, and so forth.

This relationship between a loan and compulsory service basically amounted to the Frankish feudal system that had meanwhile come into existence. Hence it was natural in the installing of the priests to have recourse to the current Frankish loan in benefice. Ordinarily, though this did not apply everywhere in France especially in the eleventh century, the proprietor thereby renounced the vassalage of commendation so that the priest, because he was not affected by the change of lord, acquired a right to a life-long usufruct. In the early Middle Ages the object of the loan was the proprietary church with all its appurtenances, so that a tax-free use should accrue to the priest for one portion of the undivided property in the sense of the capitulary of Louis the Pious. Accordingly, the Frankish proprietary church contributed in no small measure to the forming of the ecclesiastical benefice system, though the ecclesiastical benefice in the strict sense only grew out of the decay of the unity of the proprietary church's property in the eleventh and twelfth centuries, for then the loan relationship to the benefice property, which was specified for the support of the priest, became obsolete. In Frankish territory north of the Alps induction took place by word of mouth; to be more specific, by investiture with ecclesiastical symbols — book, staff, stole, bell rope, and the like. In return the priest had to make a gift or pay a fee. The right to the offerings, the tithe, and the stole fees continued to be disputed, but often, especially in France, there was established the custom of dividing these into three parts, which usually yielded two-thirds to the proprietor. If the church fell vacant, the proprietor acquired the usufruct until there was a new appointment, a right which was transferred also to the higher ecclesiastical offices, in which connection it was termed *ius regaliae.* Despite the opposition of the clergy the proprietors were also able to secure the *ius spolii,* that is, the right to confiscate the movable property left by the deceased priest, either in whole or in part.

In Italy there also grew up a benefice system, but from other and older roots, while the Frankish type infiltrated only very slowly and incompletely. Already for a long time Italian bishops had endowed priests dependent on them, especially the rectors of the great baptismal churches with the goods belonging to a rural church in the forms of loan customary there, but without any prejudice to the basic principle that the conferring of the office was performed by the bishop. But in Italy also in the ninth century the element of property law gained the upper hand. The appointment of the *plebanus* now took place by means of a contract of loan and lease, most often in the form of the libellar lease; indeed, even richly endowed churches were not infrequently granted to lay persons, who then, for their part, according to the circumstances, had to appoint a priest. In contrast to the Frankish priest of a proprietary church, the *plebani* of well-to-do churches had to pay a high tax. The contract, which was usually in writing, did not only regulate economic matters; it often specified exactly the official rights and duties of the priest. The ecclesiastical authorities — bishop, archdeacon, dean retained their claims to fees and their right of supervision and jurisdiction over the priests. Without doubt, the tradition of the Roman ecclesiastical organization was more influential here than it was on the Frankish benefice system.

Since the profit element in the proprietary church depended to a great extent on the tithe, the offerings, and the stole fees, their proprietors strove to acquire, as far as they could, the rights hitherto reserved to the baptismal churches: the right to the principal Sunday Mass, to burial, to baptism, and so forth. And they obtained them little by little. Of especially great consequence was the acquiring of the right to the tithe. The demand for the tithe, appearing in the fifth century and thereafter often urged by the Church, gained general validity in the Frankish Kingdom when it was made into law by the Carolingians, first by Pepin the Short and then definitively by Charles the Great in the Capitulary of Herstal of 779. Regarded as compensation for the great secularization of Church property, the tithe at first benefitted only the baptismal churches and those built on royal land. But under Louis the Pious this important source of income was also unlocked to the proprietors of churches, so that now the old and already riddled system of baptismal churches was even further weakened. Now, however, the bishops had to define the new limits of tithing. They did so in the so-called determining by ban, that is, in charters which, by virtue of the episcopal ban, assured to the church concerned the rights and revenues belonging to it.

And so there arose, especially in France, more slowly in Germany, many rather small parish territories, comprising a few places or even only one village, with more or less defined rights. The parish territory was based on the parish ban, a productive right which bound the parishioners to their church in regard to the reception of the Sacraments, attendance at Mass, and the paying of the tithe, offerings, and stole fees, just as specified groups were bound by the mill, oven, and occupation *banalités*. Italy had not, or only slightly, taken part in the dissolution of the baptismal church system. The old mother churches in the south resisted the most tenaciously. But the bishops took care also of the growing population of Central and North Italy chiefly through new baptismal churches, in which there was not infrequently constituted a collegially organized clergy with *vita communis* and a department *(schola)* of its own for the administration of the total property. The proprietary churches appearing beside them could, it is true, gain many parochial rights, but ordinarily they had to leave the baptismal fonts to the old *plebes*.

The development taken by the rural parishes in the early Middle Ages has now probably become understandable in some degree. One must proceed from the ancient baptismal churches, which had been merged by means of territorial division, from the seventh century in Spain and Gaul, from the eighth century in Central and North Italy, into a system of large parishes. In tradition-oriented Italy they continued on, though of course not without modifications, into the high and late Middle Ages, whereas the Germanic peoples, while they retained the original form of the large parishes in many cases and even brought it to Scandinavia as late as the tenth and eleventh centuries, in the case of the old baptismal churches loosened the essential connection with the bishop to a far greater extent then was true of Italy. The churches belonging to larger or smaller associations constituted a special type, extending, apart from England, from the Lombard South to Scandinavia and varying in rights and customs. But the more the country was settled and included in pastoral activity, the less the large churches sufficed. Hence, strongly promoted by the proprietors of churches, there arose smaller parishes, mostly with defined rights, wrested from the baptismal and original churches. The result was a variety no longer clear: each church had its proper history, and represented an individual juridical creation that could be classified only imperfectly.

Urban Churches and Chapters

The urban churches were also in movement, but they had a different development. From time immemorial not only the cathedrals but also other rather large urban churches were served by several clerics, who from the close of the fourth century began here and there to lead a common life under the influence of monastic ideals. The notion of a community of clerics obtained a stable form from Augustine, but because of the meager evidence supplied by the sources it cannot be determined how far its influence extended. The first organizations in Gaul go back to the sixth century. The term *clerici canonici* came into use in the West at that time to denote the bishop's clergy, and it was slowly applied to the members of the communities now arising, the so-called canons. Here we are concerned merely with the organizational merger into cathedral and collegiate chapters of canons. The terms *capitulum* and *capitularis* originated in the rule, which was read publicly, chapter by chapter, day after day. Clarity finally came out of the great reform legislation of Louis the Pious in 816–17: chapters and monasteries were clearly separated, and fixed rules were decided upon for both.

The cathedral chapters occupied the first rank. Their pertaining to the cathedral, the center of all the churches of the diocese, procured for them an increasing influence in the government of the diocese, which, however, was only fully developed from the thirteenth century. Cathedral chapters were at first under the archdeacon, then the provost and, for disciplinary matters, the dean, who was later virtually to assume the entire direction. As in every ordered community, there were special offices for specific functions. The *Primicerius* or *cantor* took care of the liturgy and the sacred rites; the *scholasticus* directed the cathedral school and sometimes the schools of the entire diocese; the church's treasure was confided to the *custos,* but his office could be divided between the *thesaurarius* and the *sacrista;* and the provost, responsible for the administration, was assisted by *camerarius* and *cellerarius.*

Along lines similar to those of the cathedral chapters, there were formed in the other larger churches both of the episcopal city and of other cities in the diocese collegiate chapters, as the collegial manner of life of diocesan priests flourished, especially during the eighth and ninth centuries in Lombardy, and spread even to the rural clergy. For all their monastic emphasis — common table, common property, choir service — the collegiate chapters had at the same time to see to the care of souls. This was the duty of the provost, who was later inclined to have the *custos* act in his place. The canons officiated at the liturgy by weekly turns; during his week a canon was known as *hebdomadarius.* At times the double function of care of souls and choir service led to the constructing of double churches. In the event that the cathedral chapters were obliged to the care of souls, cathedral parishes, often with their own churches, were established.

In certain regions — South and West Germany, France, here and there in North Italy — there arose not a few chapters of canonesses, always attached to a chapter of canons. The proximity of chapters of canons to the monastic life had as a consequence that monasteries could be transformed into chapters and *vice versa.*

In the cities the bishops could better hold together the ecclesiastical property than was the case in the country until in the ninth century the process of dissolution set in. Since the considerable demands made by the secular rulers, and at times also arbitrariness on the part of the bishops, jeopardized the support of the canons, there occurred a division of the property between the episcopal table and that of the chapter; a third part was sometimes set aside for the obligations imposed by the royal service. But even the *mensa canonicorum* was in time divided between the chapter as a whole, for the common purposes, and the provost and canons. A new situation arose when, from about the tenth century, many canons gave up the *vita communis* and therefore had their share of the income from the common property delivered to their houses. This right to an individual usufruct of the still commonly administered capitular property led to the notion of the prebend: every chapter from then on possessed a fixed number of canonical prebends. As time went on they were more and more conferred, no longer by the bishop, but by the chapter, at times subject to the bishop's confirmation, and from the middle of the tenth century the one to be installed had to pay a *xenium* or *venditio*. Thus the chapters too entered into the benefice system. They would not have been able to take this road if private property had not been permitted to the canons. The reform movement of the canons regular in the second half of the eleventh century was to start with precisely this central point.

The nobility was especially interested in the chapters of canons. Although in the abstract every priest of a proprietary church was supposed to be in a condition of freedom, his social position remained depressed, and hence in that feudal-minded age it was all but impossible for a nobly born person to act as pastor of a lesser church. He entered either a monastery or a chapter. In the course of time prebends were very much sought by the nobility as means of support for younger sons, and there even began the tendency to exclude non-nobles here and there. As a matter of fact, from the late Middle Ages there were, in addition to those of common folk, some noble chapters and a somewhat larger number of mixed chapters. Although the bishops no longer disposed of churches and clergy as absolutely as they once had and even had to have recourse to the forms of loan and lease pertaining to private law for the estate belonging to them and consisting in no small measure of proprietary churches and proprietary monasteries, still their authority over their dioceses remained substantially intact. In the Frankish Empire, of course, it had to be again enforced by the Carolingian reform. The picture emerges of the activity of a Frankish bishop: By virtue of the *potestas ordinis* he ordained and confirmed and at Easter and Pentecost he also baptized; he prepared the holy oils and consecrated churches, altars, and sacred vessels. As *magister ecclesiae* he had to see to the education of the clergy, preach, and extirpate superstition and pagan customs. As possessor of the *potestas iurisdictionis,* he determined the holy days and imposed the attendance at Mass, the observance of fasting, the duty of tithing, and other commandments of the Church. Furthermore, he took care of the poor, widows, orphans, and the unfree, supervised the morals of clergy and laity, and officiated as ecclesiastical judge, if necessary by imposing penalties, which could include excommunication and, in the case of malfeasance on the part of clerics, even suspension and deposition. In the last case, however, appeal to the synod or to the King was allowed.

The bishop made a visitation journey annually and in this connection he held the ecclesiastical court. Furthermore, he gathered the clergy for diocesan synods, an institution attested since the sixth century; it was supposed to be held once or twice a year. Lay persons, especially the episcopal vassals and officials, also took part. Although all possible questions of law, administration, and trials could be dealt with at the synod, the chief stress was on legislation. In the Carolingian period this consisted mainly in the application of the general capitularies, decreed by imperial and provincial synods, to the diocese in question.

This picture, drawn from Carolingian sources, of the rights and duties of the bishop remained standard for the succeeding period. It in no way implied a diminution of the episcopal power when from the middle of the ninth century it was understood in Frankish territory as *bannus episcopalis,* paralleling the royal and the comital ban. This meant the right to command and to forbid under penalty, so that, just as in secular law, a distinction may be made between the episcopal decree, court, peace, and administrative bans.

To be able to take care of his manifold duties, the bishop, in addition to the cooperation of all the clergy, needed special assistants as well as a division of the diocese into smaller areas.

Among the diocesan clergy the clerics active in the cathedral naturally stood closest to the bishop, at their head the archdeacon and the archpriest. Responsible for disciplinary matters, the administration of property, and the care of the poor, the archdeacon (of the more ancient form) accompanied his bishop on visitations. The archpriest, on the other hand, saw to the liturgy and care of souls at the cathedral and hence was more connected with the city.

The more the diocese grew in size as a consequence of more active colonization and of the permeation of the countryside by the Church, the more necessary it became to break up the diocesan territory into smaller districts. Thus was developed in the seventh and eighth centuries the system of territorially defined baptismal churches, whose direction was entrusted by the bishop to a rural archpriest. But as soon as many smaller parish territories appeared alongside the ancient baptismal churches they had to be combined in a new unity: hence the origin of the deaneries, often in connection with the boundaries of the old baptismal churches. Named by the bishop or the archdeacon, with the participation of the deanery clergy, the dean gathered his priests in the so-called "calendar chapters" to discuss pastoral and disciplinary questions, especially matters of penance. Wherever the old baptismal and original churches remained, a later form of the rural archpresbyterate developed. This was distinguished from the older form by the fact that it comprised a number of smaller parishes with limited rights. In Anglo-Saxon England and in Saxony there was no division into archpresbyterates or deaneries.

Above the deaneries, for matters of jurisdiction and later also of administration, were the archdeaconries, which were to limit the episcopal power of jurisdiction sharply. The more the zeal for reform lagged in the ninth century, the more oppressive the bishops felt the burden of their office to be — a burden they now had to bear on the part not only of the Church but also of the state. From the end of the ninth century they therefore proceeded to appoint archdeacons as ecclesiastical judges in several strictly defined territories and hence in specially created archdeaconries. The process began in the West and then moved slowly eastward until in the twelfth century it reached Salzburg in one direction and Saxony in the other and in the thirteenth century Poland. The new institution was introduced into England by William the Conqueror. There was an equal variety in regard to the appointing of the archdeacons.

Archdeacons of the later type rose to considerable power. Because important revenues were connected with the judicial system, their office could be regarded as a profitable right and hence as a benefice that could be conferred and handed over by investiture; as a matter of fact investiture did take place in the eleventh century. Once established, the conferring of the office and the ban assured the archdeacon the autonomous position of a *iudex ordinarius,* who possessed his own proper archidiaconal ban and disposed of a staff of officials. In consequence of his right of visitation he gradually intervened in matters of administration, so that he became a real competitor to the episcopal jurisdiction. It was only from the fourteenth century that the power of archdeacons could be slowly undermined by the bishop with the aid of canon law and finally broken.

CHAPTER 99

Prelacies and the Secular Powers

The State Church which Constantine the Great and his successors had set up did not simply disappear in the Germanic kingdoms of the period of the migrations but was assimilated to the political and social conditions of the individual countries. In the strict sense, of course, this is true merely of the bishoprics and abbeys, for the papacy stood outside the Germanic political world until the alliance with the Carolingian monarchs and even after the imperial coronation of Charles the Great lost only a part of the autonomy that it had meanwhile acquired.

Bishoprics and Abbeys

As with the lesser churches, so also in the case of the greater churches the development must be studied as it occurred in the area of Carolingian Frankish power. When the Carolingian *Imperium* collapsed, the essential had already been achieved: the elaboration of the forms which firmly enclosed bishops and abbots, with their churches, in the political organism. The occasions for this had been, and were to continue to be, on the one hand the state's claims to supremacy, and on the other hand the titles to proprietary churches. The last mentioned applied especially to monasteries, whereas bishoprics, because of their continuing position in public law, could only with difficulty become a part of the proprietary church system. Among the institutions that exerted influence on the incorporation of the greater churches into the political structure three were especially prominent: immunity, royal protection, and *advocatia.* They were all connected with the Church's real estate and manorial lordship.

But a definitive change appeared under Louis the Pious. Hitherto the greater number of bishoprics and monasteries that possessed immunity had not stood in the protection or proprietorship of the ruler. But now, by virtue of the connection of royal protection and immunity, they all fell under the dominion of the King, who could thereafter assert a supreme right of ownership, attenuated though it was. From the royal rights over the Church, thus prepared, was to emerge, at least in German territory, the greater churches' position as direct royal vassals and the spiritual principality.

This process began probably in the second half of the ninth century. If the immunity of churches had hitherto been restricted to the scope of the lordship of property, thereafter ecclesiastical immunists obtained public rights of a judicial and financial nature, even in places (markets, episcopal cities) and in districts (forests, occasionally entire counties) which they did not possess as manorial lords or possessed only in part. Thus alongside the manorial immunity appeared the ban immunity, which was to contribute substantially to the building of the Church's territorial sovereignty. Furthermore, the immune jurisdiction was strengthened. Hence, to be an immunity judge became in time a really rewarding and, accordingly, coveted duty. Attended to by the Church's *advocati,* it had a development of its own, differing according to the country.

Already in Roman imperial law the churches had to be represented in court by *advocati,* who, with the decline of the *Imperium,* more and more became episcopal officials. But in the Frankish German world they increased in importance as soon as the protective function proper to the office — in the late Roman period it had been related to the concept of *patronus* — brought into effect the Germanic notion of the *mund* or protectorate. In order to furnish the full protection of rights, the *advocatus* had to be a man capable of bearing arms and fighting and hence a layman; the bearing of arms was forbidden to clerics. Hence in 802 Charles the Great prescribed to all bishops and abbots the naming of *advocati.* As *advocati, agentes, defensores, causidici,* they represented the church in question and its real estate in matters of personal as well as of property rights before the public authority, protected it from without, and exercised the justice pertaining to the church over the peasants. Charles the Great had their activity, like that of the counts, supervised by his *missi.* Nevertheless, the Church's *advocati* functioned, not yet by virtue of the royal or of their own right, but at the order of the bishop or abbot.

Their protection, of course, meant at the same time domination. It is true that this involved a territorially limited development. In West *Francia* and, from the end of the ninth century, in Germany noble *advocati* exercised various sovereign functions, not seldom to the detriment of the churches concerned. France took the lead but pretty soon found tolerable solutions. In Germany, on the other hand, especially in the south and west, economic feudalism reached such a peak that the peasant had almost nothing more to do with the state judge but rather with the *advocatus* of the manorial, spiritual, or temporal immune district and in this way the *advocatia,* both as protective and as judicial *advocatia,* became the dynamic element in the constitutional history of the tenth to the twelfth centuries. To a great extent the formation of the future territorial state depended on whether the Church's secular means of power, conferred with the *advocatia,* assisted the noble *advocatus* in the building up of his own political power or the spiritual immunist when the latter withdrew the *advocatia* and had the administration conducted by officials.

Monasteries especially had to suffer much from *advocati.* During the period of the Gregorian Reform, it is true, a quite large number of them succeeded in placing themselves under papal protection and in restricting the hereditary *advocatia* of the founding families, still continuing in practice, to judicial rights, but this by no means ended the struggle. This is attested by the numerous forged charters of the twelfth and thirteenth centuries, with which German monks sought to attack, first the *advocatia* system and the proprietary church, then the spiritual proprietors of churches. The new orders had an easier time.

But the power struggle with the *advocati* had already recommended the appointing of nobles as bishops and abbots.

Nevertheless it is clear enough how different the juridical situation of the bishoprics and abbeys could be. The German royal bishoprics represented something quite different from those under the Capetians or the French princes, and these in turn were distinguished from the South French bishoprics, which were sold, given away, bequeathed, or granted in fief by the counts or viscounts as ordinary proprietary churches. There was a similar gradation among the monasteries, but the situation was the reverse for them. Whereas proprietary bishoprics in the strict sense were confined to the Midi, ordinarily every early medieval monastery, at least from around 700, had a proprietor, either from the lesser, middle, or higher nobility, all the way to the king, or from the ecclesiastical hierarchy — bishop or Pope. The higher the rank of the proprietor, the higher became the right, the so-called "liberty," of the churches subject to him. Because of the slight power which the Kings of France possessed in the tenth and eleventh centuries, it made little difference at that time whether a bishopric or monastery depended on him or on a great magnate. In Germany, on the other hand, it really meant something to be directly under the King, to be a church subject to the crown only. For since, after the extinction of the East Carolingians, the entire Carolingian inheritance, regardless whether it was patrimonial or royal property, passed to the now emerging German Kingdom and was entrusted for its administration to the currently reigning King, the Carolingian East Frankish Church, embracing all the bishoprics and the immune abbeys that were under the royal protection, entered as a whole into the new German tribal federation, so that these churches were not property but a part, a member, of the realm and their chiefs later acquired the position of princes of the Empire. It is true that in the Saxon and Salian period, up to 1045, new monasteries were placed under the royal protection, but these royal monasteries, likewise direct royal vassals, did not completely attain the privileged position of the old royal abbeys coming from the Carolingian hereditary estate.

The dependence of the greater churches is probably clearest in the election of the bishops and abbots, for it was precisely here that important sovereign rights had been elaborated in Frankish territory since Merovingian times. Ecclesiastical circles, of course, appealed time and again to the ancient canonical principle of the election of the bishop by clergy and people, *electio canonica,* which was occasionally expressly confirmed in writing for individual churches, especially abbeys, as free election, and in Germany had been granted to all bishoprics.

The absence of strict rules permitted a really varied practice, dependent on the concrete situation. Powerful princes virtually had full control of the election of a bishop. When the widowed church was to be again filled depended on their decision, and at times this took place by a mere act of nomination. But if there was an election, then the ruler could determine it by designation or by vindicating a right of confirmation after it had taken place; not infrequently the right of confirmation involved a rejection of the one elected and then, according to circumstances, an arbitrary naming of the bishop. Still, even for the princes there was an insurmountable legal barrier. Since the business of the election was still regarded as a full, active process in which clergy and people participated, an unwanted chief pastor could not be forced upon the diocesans. Regardless of the manner in which clergy and people assented, their assent had to be given somehow; otherwise, the election was uncanonical, invalid.

The situation in regard to abbatial elections was similar and yet different. On the one hand, the real electors, the monks, represented a much more closed corporate body than did clergy and people in episcopal elections, even if the monastery's vassals also had a word to say. On the other hand, an abbey ordinarily depended not merely on the proprietor but also on the diocesan bishop. The abbatial election turned out according to the way in which the various interested parties made their influence prevail. Here the local bishop appointed the new abbot, there the proprietor of the monastery, while only a right of assent was left to the monks.

Election was followed by installation in office and consecration, two separate acts, which in themselves could be carried out by different representatives of the law. Naturally only bishops were taken into consideration as consecrators, whereas installation in office and in possession presupposed an authority which held rights of domination or of property in regard to the church concerned. In the case of bishoprics these were the kings or the princes who had taken their place; in regard to monasteries, in so far as they had no privileged position, they were the proprietors, that is, kings, princes, nobles, or bishops.

The fact that there was so strong a dependence in law on secular institutions was connected with the circumstances of the time. The more the feudal-vassalage institutions were elaborated and combined into the feudal system under the Carolingians, the more were the bishops and abbots drawn into this system. The important functions which they exercised even in the political field of themselves suggested the idea of binding them to the crown by means of vassalage. A welcome pretext could be found in the royal protection, which was granted to the immune churches from the time of Louis the Pious. As a matter of fact, from then on all bishops and the royal abbots had to commend themselves to the King and in the customary form of the giving of self — the placing of the clasped hands in the open clasping hands of the lord, — which was then followed by the oath of fealty.

But the other propelling force of the feudal system, the *beneficium*, was also to be seen. Not merely Church property but also the office of bishop or abbot was drawn into the wake of the benefice system. Just as in the course of the ninth century, over and above the fiscal goods belonging to the endowment of an office, the very function of count was regarded as a *beneficium* to be conferred by the King and eventually hereditary and was by preference termed *honor*, so also in the ninth century the episcopal function became a profitable right, a domain, an *honor*. This materialization made it possible for the ruler thereafter to convey the *episcopatus*, that is, the office of bishop, with all its rights of ownership, administration, and usufruct, after the manner of a *beneficium* by delivering the symbol of the office, the pastoral staff — the ring was added under Henry III. In the course of time, regularly from the end of the tenth century, this act was termed "investiture." It is true that its juridical character remained a problem, despite the existing undoubted parallel to investiture with a fief. The religious and ecclesiastical essence of the episcopal office was here overlaid by the Germanic law process of materialization, but it was not annulled, so that the Gregorian Reform was able to expose it again to view and limit the crown's right to a mere investiture with the *regalia*. The early medieval investiture of bishops and of royal abbots could the more easily appear in a feudal law sense when the vassalage acts of homage and oath of fealty were connected with it. The vassalage entered into by the higher prelates was not the juridical basis for the conferring of the *beneficium*.

In a development similar to that of bishoprics, in the case of monasteries the investiture of the abbot by the proprietor came into use, but not a few abbeys succeeded in avoiding an outside investiture. In the latter event, either one of the monks — *praepositus, prior, decanus* — presented the abbot's staff or the newly elected abbot himself took it from the altar.

Investiture would cost something. Secular vassals on succeeding to their hereditary fiefs ordinarily had to pay to their feudal lord an inheritance fee, the *relevium*, the amount of which was at first decided by an agreement, but later became a fixed charge. In the Germanic notion of law there was no reason to stop short with the investiture of bishops and abbots and to exempt them from the demand for payment. As a matter of fact, such payments were often made. However, canon law was opposed to them; it forbade any introduction of money in the conferring of ecclesiastical offices and denounced it as simony.

Whoever had the right of investiture could, at the death of bishop or abbot, easily claim special rights to the property of the widowed church or of the deceased prelate. In fact, it was often in the interests of the church in question that the use of its property during the vacancy should not be exposed to arbitrariness but should lie in the hands of the King in accord with a somewhat orderly procedure. Appropriate rights were developed and took shape as the so-called *regalia* and *spolia*. Already exercised earlier, they were to play a not unimportant role in the twelfth century. Churchmen naturally felt the *ius spolii*, or right to the movable estate of a deceased prelate, to be particularly oppressive, but the *ius regaliae*, or right to the enjoyment of the church revenues during the vacancy, also contained dangers, in so far as the rulers were tempted to postpone the new appointment to the church for an excessively long time for the sake of the income. The Church thus tried to persuade rulers to renounce these claims and was successful to a great extent. But the rights as such were not annulled thereby. They were transferred to ecclesiastical offices and were to acquire a great importance for the papal financial system that was fully developed in the fourteenth century in the claim to *spolia*, to the income during a vacancy, and to annates.

The bonds created by homage on the one hand and investiture on the other gave rise to the performance of services, both personal and real. We may summarize all these under the notion *servitium regis*. Bishops and royal abbots were bound to attend court and supply their military contingent, and they had to be prepared to act as envoys of the King, as his chancellor, and the like. Their churches had to bear the expenses of all this. In like manner the royal churches had to supply all the palace clerics who were occupied in chancery and chapel with benefices. Of course, the royal churches were able to comply with their military obligations only by having vassals of their own. The King's right to be lodged by the royal churches on his travels could be very burdensome. Resorted to in Germany only from the time of Henry II but with increasing consistency, it led to the ruler's monopolizing all the rights of sovereignty — court, toll, coinage, customs — during his stay in an episcopal city. Such rights were first limited substantially by Frederick II in 1220. As other burdens could be added annual presents and, in the case of monasteries, precisely fixed annual payments.

So singular a development, running partly counter to the ancient Christian Roman episcopal organization, encountered certain opposition in its earliest phase, and hence in the Carolingian period. The Popes of that period also did not follow a uniform policy. To their not infrequent declarations in favor of the old electoral regulations, which in some few charters from the end of the ninth century, granting the right of election, among other things attacked the dominant share of Kings, there was opposed the recognition of positive royal rights, for example, the right to permit the election to take place or to permit the consecration — these were acknowledged by Hadrian II and John VIII. And so that John X could declare solemnly that, according to ancient custom, the conferring of a bishopric on a cleric pertained solely to the King and without his command the episcopal consecration might not take place.

No doubt the papacy and the West Frankish episcopate were so compliant because in those difficult times, gradually becoming chaotic, the Church needed secular protection and as a matter of fact was always best provided for under a King. The theocratic idea not only did not disappear with the dissolution of the Carolingian *Imperium,* but it was even consolidated in the coronation *ordines* which appeared in the ninth and tenth centuries, just as in the iconographic tradition and in general in the thought and feeling of contemporary men.

The Papacy and Papal Institutions

The constitutional status of the Pope differed substantially from that of the bishops and abbots. But this does not mean that the Roman Church was entirely independent. The imperial confirmation of the papal election, likewise the right of the German Emperors to participate in the election discussions in an authoritative manner that was capable of becoming actual designation were retained. However, it must not be forgotten that in the institution of a Roman Bishop the imperial rights did not go beyond the electoral act. No Emperor installed a Pope in his office by means of investiture, not to mention tried to bind him as a vassal by commendation. The views of sovereignty and proprietorship which in the

Frankish world more and more fitted bishops and abbots into the political organization were not applied to the Roman Church. Since there was for the Emperors no adequate legal pretext for nullifying the juridical immunity pertaining to the Pope, the above mentioned depositions effected by Otto I and Henry III remained only episodes. Though the Popes may have fallen on occasion into serious dependence, they held to the principle that they stood not under but beside the Emperor. They even possessed an important right in the imperial anointing and coronation, and from 850 on there was no other act whereby the imperial dignity could be transmitted.

What enabled the Roman Church to maintain her political freedom was, most important of all, the Papal State, that Central Italian remnant of Byzantine rule, which let the papacy take the place there of the *basileus* and even claim imperial symbols of sovereignty, such as robes of state or tiara and imperial court ceremonial. It is true there was a correlation involved: While the Papal State and the adoption of imperial characteristics greatly preserved the papacy from political subordination, the spiritual authority of the *vicarius Petri* protected the existence of the Papal State, for the motivation of the *Constitutum Constantini* that the earthly Emperor must possess no power in that place where the heavenly Emperor had installed the head of the Christian religion — had an importance all its own.

Despite imperial protectorate and despotic control by the Roman nobility, the Roman Bishops and their co-workers never gave up the notion of autonomy. Behind it, of course, were the ideas of the *Constitutum Constantini*. They likewise lived on in the catalogues of judges, — the "older," composed probably between 867 and 877, and the "later," from the first half of the eleventh century, two literary works which aimed to make the papal dignitaries equal to the officials of the Byzantine imperial court. The clearest sign for the claim to quasi-imperial and hence to an autonomous position must probably have been the imperial symbol of the tiara, expressly mentioned in the *Constitutum*. Liberated in the period of the Gregorian reform, the Roman Church set about elaborating a thoroughgoing claim to sovereignty over Rome and the Papal State.

The constituting of a strong central administration encountered the further insurmountable difficulty that there was no reliable nobility of office. Of course young nobles were expressly trained for the higher administrative career in the *sacrum cubiculum* and enrolled among the clerics by receiving the tonsure or even the lower orders, but this half-clericate remained in final analysis a mere form. The most profound cause for the weakness of the Papal State is ultimately to be sought in the papacy itself. The Popes would not have been able to force the disintegrated Byzantine provinces into a unity without disavowing their priestly ideals and exalting the desire for power above everything else. The papal election saw to it that such purely worldly-minded men did not ordinarily ascend the throne of Peter; it was concerned chiefly with the Bishop of Rome and not with the secular prince. It goes without saying that political and economic interests also played a great role in it, again to the detriment of the Papal State. At almost every change of pontificate they altered the balance of power. The attendant internal discords undermined the power of the central government. A consistent policy in the Papal State was virtually impossible.

This is the background against which must be viewed the history of the Papal

State as it has already been narrated according to the individual epochs up to the middle of the eleventh century. Already under Leo III inner discords led to the reestablishment of an imperial protectorate. Up to a certain point the ninth-century Emperors actually fulfilled the task intended for them, even though Louis II and then more crudely the Spoletan Dynasty more than once injured the interests of the Papal State. The catastrophe approaching from the death of Louis II in 875 set in completely with the death of the Emperor Lambert in 898. When Sergius III returned in 904 after a six-years' exile, the Roman landed aristocracy was definitely victorious. In all branches of the administration, so we may assume, the powers of government were, little by little, wrested from the hands of the Popes, while the manorial-feudal principle gained ground and was consolidated under Alberic. Thereafter the Roman Church was able to manage directly only a few fragments of the old patrimony, situated close to the city; almost all other estates and territories passed in actuality under the control of the nobility. The German Emperors were unable to change this situation; in fact, they probably did not even understand what had recently happened. For they ruled the German Kingdom, a feudally organized political association of persons, on principles different from those which the Byzantine and then the papal bureaucracy sought to apply in the territory of the Papal State.

Thus the Roman Church saw herself faced with a new situation. So long as Roman noble families exercised the secular power — by no means always to the detriment of the Church — the papacy had to let things take their course. But in the Pope's own house, the Lateran Palace, the collapse of the old order in the Papal State so hurt the prestige of the traditional offices that the Popes had to come to terms at least there with the exigencies of a changed age. This occurred most fully in the period of the Gregorian reform, but certain initial steps go back to the turn of the tenth and eleventh centuries. They concerned first of all the papal chancery.

As a matter of fact the history of the papal chancery reflects with special clarity the development of the early medieval administrative organization in the Lateran. There is no need to discuss here its origin, which perhaps goes back to the third century. The chancery staff was furnished by the ecclesiastical notaries, who had gradually merged into a *schola* under the direction of the *primicerius* and of his deputy, the *secundicerius.* The two chiefs of the *schola* and notaries who were probably expressly selected took care of the chancery business. In the first place were specifically ecclesiastical matters. But the more the patrimony grew and the Roman Church was entrusted with political functions for the city of Rome, the more frequently were questions of secular administration involved; not infrequently ecclesiastical notaries received the management of patrimonies. The notaries obtained their training in the *schola cantorum* or *orphanotrophium.* Although tonsured, they must ordinarily have led the life of married laymen.

The seventh and eighth centuries were an especially productive period for the chancery. The book of formularies, or *Liber diurnus,* must have been drawn up at the beginning of this period in its first version, later to be repeatedly expanded.

The process of decay affected the institution of chancery notaries in so far as there was at times less to do. It should be noted that at the end of the tenth century a *cancellarius sacri pallatii* appeared in the Lateran Palace. Like the chancellor functioning at secular courts, he is probably to be regarded as the actual director of the entire business of papal diplomatics, who left to the librarian little more than a sort of honorary presidency.

C H A P T E R   1 0 0

Metropolitans, Primates, and Papacy

The groupings of the ecclesiastical hierarchy above the diocesan level in the West fell victim to a great extent to the political chaos of the seventh and eighth centuries. The struggle with Slavs and Avars had dreadful consequences in Noricum, Pannonia, Illyricum, Thrace, and Greece, while in Gaul under the last Merovingians the churches were so ruthlessly plundered by the magnates that the metropolitan groupings crumbled and not a few bishoprics remained unoccupied. Western Christendom suffered its cruellest blows from Islam, whose domination produced in time the total ruin of the episcopal organization in North Africa and later in Sicily and its partial collapse in Spain. The withdrawal of Africa and Spain, with their self-conscious churches governed by their respective primates, meant for the Christian West the loss of a good bit of ancient Christian tradition. All the more strongly then there moved into the field of vision the institution which had held to its ancient right not merely in principle but had impressively emphasized it in the Anglo-Saxon, Frisian, and Central German mission held by the founding of bishoprics, and in England even of metropolitan sees: the papacy. Of course it was unable to develop freely. Hence, the relations between the papacy and the episcopate were subject to a certain amount of conflict. And yet substantial decisions were made at that time. Whereas the passage of time greatly weakened the ancient rights of metropolitans and did not permit any genuine supermetropolitan organizations, such as territorial primacies, to appear at all, it could do nothing that was essentially detrimental to the papacy, based on divine right. And so there was made ready the ecclesiastical development that was to begin with the Gregorian reform.

Metropolitan Organization

The ancient Christian metropolitan organization emerged, as such, out of the collegiality of the episcopate in the apostolic succession, without any direct action on the part of the Holy See, even though it had to be in communion with the successor of Peter and to that extent the unifying function of the Roman primacy was given recognition. The metropolitan organization was, at least in the West, preponderantly collegial. The highest tribunal was the provincial synod, at which the metropolitan was not much more than the chairman. He convoked it, directed it, and supervised the implementation of its decrees. But his right of supervision could be extended so that he visited the bishoprics and controlled the administration of a widowed diocese. The Western provincial synods were competent for legislation as well as for administration and justice. However, their activity could be limited by higher tribunals. In Italy the Pope's position as territorial primate conferred preponderance on the Roman Synods; in North Africa the same was true of those convoked by the Bishop of Carthage. A supermetropolitan synodal practice had also developed powerfully in Visigothic Spain. In addition to and above all these groupings there was the Holy See.

The decay of the Carolingian Empire induced the rulers to an even greater degree to make the instituting of bishops dependent upon themselves. They thereby deprived the metropolitan group of an important right. As late as the time of Hincmar of Reims the Frankish metropolitans used to dispatch one of their suffragans to the widowed diocese as visitor, and the election took place under his supervision. There followed the examination of both the election and the elect by metropolitan and suffragans, confirmation by the metropolitan, and finally consecration. At that time the West Frankish episcopate even sought to establish a sort of right of devolution: in the event of a misuse of the right of election by clergy and people, metropolitan and suffragans were to be permitted to designate the new bishop themselves. This claim was aimed chiefly at the designation by the King, which had meanwhile made its appearance. All such efforts were rendered ineffectual by the constantly growing chaos. The naming of the bishops became of so much importance for the secular princes in their power struggle that it virtually passed into their hands, while the rights of the metropolitan group were restricted in practice to the consecration of the bishop-elect, who had already been invested, and to the related ceremony of the *scrutinium.*

Not only the secular rulers but also the bishops contributed to the weakening of the metropolitan constitution. The decline of the practice of holding synods on the one hand and, on the other, the enhanced prestige which the metropolitans possessed by virtue of the new title of archbishop and of the pallium, now pertaining to them, caused the West Frankish archbishops to try to consolidate their position in the sense of a superiority of jurisdiction with regard to the *episcopi comprovinciales,* for whom the significant expression *suffraganei,* or assistants, began to come into use from the close of the eighth century. The compilers of pseudo-Isidore were at pains to limit the powers of archbishops from below and at the same time from above: from below, by making the synodal procedure for the trials of suffragans as difficult as possible; from above, by enhancing the papal authority. Referring to the Council of Sardica, which had provided the Holy See as the court of final appeal for accused bishops, and to the demand of Innocent I that all *causae maiores* were to be sent to Rome, they had recourse to forged texts to make the right precise in the sense that the bishop could appeal to the Holy See at any stage of the process, and the Pope thus appealed to could at once summon the case before his tribunal, that synodal judgments handed down in regard to bishops needed to be approved by the Pope, and that, by *causae maiores,* for which Rome was to be competent, were to be understood especially matters affecting bishops. They installed a further guarantee by giving the widest possible interpretation of the claim long made by the papacy to the convoking and confirming of general councils and thereby subordinated much that had to do with synods to the Holy See. Nicholas I did not neglect to make use of the new principles, which approximated his own ideas. Neither he nor pseudo-Isidore had his own way, but their claims continued to be influential. They left more or less strong, direct or indirect traces in almost every pre-Gregorian canonical collection, outside South Italy, not to mention the Gregorian reform movement, which took up pseudo-Isidore and to some extent the letters of Nicholas I and gave them special prominence.

Finally, the metropolitan right was turned in a new direction by the stronger connection of the archbishops with Rome by means of the pallium. This liturgical mark of honor, probably originating in the Byzantine court ceremonial, in the West belonged properly to the Pope, but was given by him to other individual bishops as a special mark of favor. Originally it possessed no juridical significance. It was only the custom, appearing from the end of the eighth century, of honoring all metropolitans with both the archiepiscopal title and the pallium, on the Anglo-Saxon model, that led to changes. The papacy now transformed the bestowing of the pallium on archbishops into an act which was the equivalent of confirmation and afforded the possibility of deriving the metropolitan authority from that of the Pope.

The new norms drawn up by Rome obliged every newly elevated archbishop to ask for the pallium within three months and in that connection to submit his profession of faith. Before the reception of the pallium — and we here touch the decisive point — he was neither to officiate at the consecration of suffragans nor to occupy the throne. The juridical sense of the last mentioned requirement cannot be determined exactly from the extant ninth-century sources, but in the tenth century several pallium privileges make known that by this symbol the Pope intended to grant the right to consecrate suffragans. In the same manner the right to the title of archbishop was also occasionally connected with the granting of the pallium, and in a privilege granted by John XIX rights typical of legates were appended for the first time: to have the cross borne ahead of one, to ride a horse caparisoned in red on feast days, to decide urgent cases that pertained of themselves to the Holy See. Thus the pallium developed in time more clearly into a symbol of metropolitan authority. The conferring of the pallium made the archbishop seem ever more like the Pope's deputy with a delegated share in the universal primacy, a view which was in fact slowly to establish itself after the middle of the eleventh century.

Primates, Apostolic Vicars, Legates

The missionary activity of Willibrord and Boniface and the beginning of a Frankish Church reform induced the Popes in the eighth century to bestow on individual bishops the supermetropolitan dignity of archbishop and the authority of a vicar. These expedients became unnecessary when Charles the Great re-established the metropolitan organization: metropolitan function and archiepiscopal dignity were united. The creating of supermetropolitan tribunals was thereafter thwarted, even though two Carolingian Emperors and later several archbishops tried it.

The Papacy

The more the Eastern and the Western halves of the Church drew apart, politically and intellectually, in the eighth and ninth centuries, the more clearly was the Roman Church confined to the Germanic-Romance West. This implied a decisive turn in the development of the Roman Primacy. In the West there was no longer an Emperor nor was there a Patriarch who could have played the role of a rival ecclesiastical authority vis-à-vis Rome. Due to the patriarchate of the West and at the same time to the universal primacy, which eclipsed and, so to speak, absorbed the patriarchal authority, the Roman Bishop occupied, without challenge, the first place within the Western hierarchy. The Germanic peoples felt a special veneration for the successor of Peter. From the fifth century there had developed, inside and outside Rome and not least of all in Merovingian Gaul, a Peter cult, which centered around the Petrine power of binding and loosing and honored the Prince of the Apostles as the gatekeeper of heaven; this cult was carried to the Anglo-Saxons by the Roman missionaries. It had an especially powerful appeal for the ingenuous Germans. Furthermore, it was of advantage to the Roman Church to be regarded as mother of all Western churches. All of them attributed their founding to men whom either Peter or his successor Clement had sent out or to disciples of Paul, until in the tenth century individual West Frankish sees proceeded to derive their origin, no longer from Rome, but from the group of the Lord's seventy-two disciples.

The legends pointing to Rome were able to attest virtually nothing, and the cult of Peter very little that was definite, in regard to the prerogatives of the Holy See. Even the universal primacy, based on divine right and resolutely defended by West Frankish theologians against Photius, needed a more exact formulation by the positive *ius ecclesiasticum* promulgated by man.

That this initiative was up-to-date is shown by the pseudo-Isidorean decretals, which, independently of Rome, were driving in the same direction. And still, insurmountable obstacles stood in the way. Even if the bishops did not presume to deny the basis in the divine law of the preeminence claimed by Nicholas, they were still aware that, as successors of the Apostles, they possessed a power which likewise went back to Christ. Thus was revived the ancient question, not clarified in early Christian times, of the relationship between the primatial and the episcopal power. The intellectual abilities then at hand were not in a position to solve it. The new claims of the Pope found all the less sympathy in that men of the early Middle Ages had a static juridical interpretation, which stubbornly defended the old law.

Typically Western compilations ordinarily hold fast to the Roman tradition; that is, they recognize in the Pope an ecclesiastical supremacy that was established by Christ. But with regard to the concrete rights of the papacy, they display considerable differences. There are even two views of the papal primacy to be met — an extremely papalist and a moderate. In order to find a firm support in the confusing picture, the viewpoint of Burchard of Worms, the most successful author, should be briefly sketched. There can be no doubt that Burchard did not represent an episcopalist system but accepted a genuine Roman primatial power as founded by Christ. In his view the Pope was the highest tribunal for *causae maiores* and in particular in regard to controversies among bishops; his decretals occupied a special place among the sources of the law; he had the right to summon and confirm general councils; the tradition of the Roman Church was binding; canonical books were subject to her approval; synodal judgments on bishops were subject to the reservation, *salva in omnibus apostolica auctoritate,* bishops could appeal to the Holy See, and the Pope could depose or appoint bishops; transfers of bishops needed the consent of the provincial episcopate or of the Holy See. On the other hand, Burchard was unwilling to admit a direct papal power of jurisdiction over the individual faithful, except to a limited extent.

Other collections went further, teaching, for example, the infallibility of the Roman Church; the immunity of the Pope from judgment unless he was a heretic; his right, in case of need, to modify old canons or to lay down new norms, to ordain the clerics of any church whatsoever, to absolve from all sins and from oaths, and so forth. What we are here listing concisely from sources of differing worth and of differing content must have shown at least that the stream of tradition relevant to the Roman Primacy divided to form a delta, but flowed on and, to a great extent, together with pseudo-Isidore and other more ancient sources, emptied directly into the Gregorian reform movement.

The canonical collections were the works of scholars, which did not by any means have to be in accord with juridical practice. Only the concrete activity of the Holy See can give us an idea of what the primacy then actually meant. Mention has already been made of a powerful increase in Rome's authority. While the endeavor, beginning in the ninth century, to bind the archbishops more firmly to the Holy See by means of the pallium was not a complete success, the papacy became the ecclesiastical court which, together with the secular rulers, decided the founding of episcopal and metropolitan sees, not always to the satisfaction of the episcopate.

Growing prestige no doubt brought about the relationship which the Holy See gained with regard to the monks. Even in antiquity the incorporation of the monastic communities into the diocesan organization had brought on difficulties with the bishops. It was universally recognized that the Church's sacramental and disciplinary power in regard to monks pertained to the episcopate; until the turn of the tenth to the eleventh century there was probably not a single monastery, not excepting Bobbio and Fulda, that had been withdrawn by a papal privilege of exemption from the ecclesiastical jurisdiction of the *ordinarius loci.* But from about the seventh century the Popes had issued charters of protection to individual monasteries in order to guarantee their property against alienation or pillage. Rulers did the same. The more the West Frankish royal power now declined, the more often did the monasteries of that kingdom seek papal protection; some of them, by commendation, even became the property of the Roman Church. This example was imitated. In the course of the tenth and especially of the eleventh century Italy, France, Germany, and the March of Spain were covered with a network of monasteries under papal protection or papal ownership. The initiative was taken, not by Rome, but by the monks, who especially looked for assistance against interference by bishops. Then when around 1000 the papacy began to exempt individual favored monasteries from the ecclesiastical jurisdiction of the diocesan bishop, Rome's primatial claim and monasteries' efforts for exemption coalesced into a real community of interests. In the monastic world, especially of France and to some extent of Italy, there now arose particularly zealous defenders of the Roman prerogatives, e.g., Abbot Abbo of Fleury (988–1004). Not only in his struggles for the privileges of his monastery, which he fought out with the episcopate, but also in the troubles at Reims, to be discussed later, and in his writings, above all his *Compilatio canonum,* he again and again stressed the authority of the Holy See.

An innovation of the utmost importance appeared in the field of cult at the end of the tenth century. In 993 Bishop Ulric of Augsburg (d. 973) was canonized by Pope John XV at a Roman Synod. Soon after, John XVIII canonized Martial of Limoges, and then Benedict IX did the same for the Trier hermit, Simeon of Syracuse. Thereafter the Popes elevated saints in increasing numbers to the honors of the altar; bishops and synods continued to do the same until under Innocent III the Holy See reserved this right to itself and firmly established it in the decretals of Gregory IX (1234). This was the final result of a two-centuries' development, which belief in Peter, living on in the papacy, had prepared.

The veneration of Peter had long been active in the penitential discipline. Not a few Christians felt themselves drawn irresistibly to Rome to ask absolution of their sins from the vicar of the keeper of the keys and of the gate of heaven. If there was question of serious crimes, bishops were glad to send the guilty to the Pope, because they attributed to him a more certain judgment or even a greater authority. Basically they acknowledged thereby that the Holy See possessed a jurisdiction over all the faithful. Of course, strict legal norms were lacking; there were neither sins that were reserved to the Pope at that time nor a rule about cases already decided by the local bishop and then sent to Rome.

Rome was not infrequently involved in difficulties occasioned by the deposition or installation of bishops. Ordinarily the initiative proceeded from one of the parties. Since almost always political interests were directly or indirectly involved, the secular rulers had an important and often a decisive word to say. In spite of this burdensome dependence in both the decisions and their execution, Rome turned her intervention to advantage. At the same time it was a further reminder of the primatial claims. Occasionally the Popes went quite far in this. Thus in 881 John VIII consecrated at Rome the Emperor's candidate for the see of Lausanne and seems eventually to have established him in preference to King Boso's adherent, whom the Archbishop of Vienne had consecrated. In the same way in 889 Stephen V thwarted the attempt of Archbishop Aurelian of Lyons, a partisan of King Eudes, to impose on the church of Langres a person agreeable to him in place of the bishop already elected, a sympathizer of Charles the Simple. In cases of this sort the Popes were glad to send legates who took care to preside over the synods that were summoned and thereby secured greater respect for the claims made by Rome to summon and direct synods.

Just how matters stood with regard to the Pope's competence in the trials of bishops was to appear toward the end of the tenth century. At issue was the tangled situation at Reims, brought about by the political treason committed by the Carolingian, Archbishop Arnulf of Reims, in 989. According to pseudo-Isidore the synodal sentence required papal confirmation. The principle must have been clearly recognized at the time, for both synod and King wrote to ask the assent of John XV. It was only when the Pope neglected to reply that many French bishops and several abbots met in the monastery of Saint-Basle at Verzy in 991 and definitively deposed Arnulf. Gerbert of Aurillac was chosen Archbishop of Reims in his stead.

The importance of the controversy lay, not in Rome's actual victory, which depended essentially on political circumstances, but in the attitude adopted by the French episcopate. It throws a clear light on the forces of opposition which could be brought to bear in regard to Rome by the bishops of the time. Since there was here involved a general principle, applied to the secular authority in a similar manner, the position assumed by the bishops declared a limit which the old fashioned concept raised — the impossibility of conceiving of a monarch able to dispose of positive law as its sovereign. If it is added that the episcopal authority is of divine law and that the relationship between the college of bishops and the papacy was not sufficiently clear, the resistance that was offered becomes even more intelligible. It was not directed against the primatial power as such. All involved, Gerbert included, were convinced that the vicar of Peter had received the universal primacy from Christ. And within the sphere of positive law in which even the primacy had to find its concrete elaboration, they fully recognized Rome's right to confirm synodal judgments on bishops, as demanded by pseudo-Isidore, and hence they conceded to the Holy See a very extensive supreme judicial sovereignty.

The anti-Roman reactions of particular groups of bishops are, then, not to be overestimated. If one examines the constitutional position taken by the hierarchy during the Carolingian and Ottonian periods, the picture favors the episcopate less than it does the papacy. Deep as was the papacy's humiliation, it still imperturbably kept the idea of its universal primacy before its gaze as its guiding idea. The concept of collegial unity, on the other hand, on which was based the canonical position of the bishops, had at that time been weakened to a considerable degree. It is true that under the Carolingians there was an imperial episcopate which, after the decay of the *Imperium,* survived energetically at least in Germany, but what mattered was not this old fashioned institution, mainly supported by imperial law. Far more important were the episcopal groupings fashioned by the ancient Church, and it was precisely these which were unable to develop properly. And so the papacy was much better prepared for the coming development of the Church that was to be set in motion by the Gregorian reform.

CHAPTER 101

The Sacraments and the Mass

At the beginning of the Carolingian period liturgical life in the individual areas of the West displayed that wide diversity which had developed in the centuries of transition. In addition to the Roman liturgy, which was also used in England since the evangelization of the Anglo-Saxons as well as in the greater part of Italy, there were the Old Spanish, the not very uniform Gallican, the Ambrosian, and the Irish-Scottish or Celtic, consisting for the most part of borrowings. All of the preceding were in the Latin language. Frequently they were contrasted with the Roman liturgy under the collective name of Gallic liturgy.

The suppression of these liturgies started in Gaul, where bishops and abbots, in view of the chaos in their own liturgy since the seventh century, began to prefer texts from the orderly Roman liturgy. These texts circulated in the form of the so-called later *Gelasianum*. The general change took place under King Pepin, who around 754 prescribed the transition to the Roman liturgy, and definitively under Charles the Great, who obtained a Gregorian Sacramentary for himself from Rome around 785–86; it was imposed at Aachen as the obligatory model.

Since the Roman liturgy now prevailed in the Frankish Empire, it also advanced into Spain with the *Reconquista* that moved forward from the north. The recovery of Toledo in 1085 and, even earlier, the pressure exercised by Gregory VII brought about the decline of the Old Spanish liturgy, called "Mozarabic" ("arabicized") since the time of the Muslim conquest, which from now on survived only in vestiges.

In Scotland the Celtic liturgy yielded to the Roman at the instigation of Queen Margaret (d. 1093), in Ireland in consequence of a decree of the Synod of Cashel in 1172. Only the Ambrosian held its ground in the face of all threats by Peter Damiani and Gregory VII; it adopted only particular features of the Roman liturgy.

The development within the Frankish Empire became of decisive importance for the future. On the one hand, the texts contained in the liturgical books were taken over with great fidelity — all the feast days of local Roman saints were retained — and, on the other hand, consciously and unconsciously various additions from the local tradition and adaptations to local needs were made, which later passed on to the Universal Church. In particular, the Gregorian Sacramentary received from Alcuin a supplement which was gathered from Gelasian, Spanish, and local material and in the later manuscripts was at once blended with the Sacramentary itself. The tenth-century Fulda Sacramentary can be regarded as typical of the definitive amalgamation.

A significant work brought about the maturity of the German Church in the age of the Ottos for the Pontifical Mass. A monk of Sankt Alban at Mainz around 950 created the Roman-German *Pontificale* which, among other things, included the renowned *Ordo Romanus Antiquus* as a part of it. This is the *Pontificale* which is the basis of the later *Pontificale Romanum*. Liturgical manuscripts from the northern lands then enjoyed a great reputation, even in their technical achievements.

The administration of baptism was only slightly affected by the changes. It should take place, as Charles emphasized in a decree of 789, "secundum morem

Romanum." Making an inquiry among the bishops, he received from them around 811 a more or less clear and in part detailed explanation of the rite as carried out in their territories, which in fact corresponded with the Roman tradition. Following the *exsuffatio* the signing with the cross, and the proffering of the salt, the *scrutinia* occupied a good bit of space. Holy Saturday and the Vigil of Pentecost were now regarded as the only permissible days for the baptism of children, whereas these days had originally been set aside for the baptism of adults. Baptism itself was administered by immersion.

The missionary work on the eastern frontier of the Frankish state brought it about that the baptism of adults continued to be a source of lively concern. After the unhappy experiences with forcible mass baptisms among the Saxons, people were ready to listen to Alcuin's voice, calling for an orderly procedure, without compulsion and with previous instruction. Augustine's *De catechizandis rudibus* was to serve as model for the instruction. The missionary conference on the Danube, arranged by Charles' son Pepin in 796, accordingly required a preparation of forty, or at least of seven, days, with real instruction, and then seven days of direct ascetical and liturgical preparation. The preparatory instruction was to be concerned with the articles of faith. It was felt, with appeal to Matthew 28:20, that moral instruction could be left substantially to the time after baptism. In such a manner and with a subsequent acclimating did the conversion of the Germans proceed.

Important changes occurred in this period in regard to the administration of the Sacrament of penance. For serious public offences, *causae criminales,* public ec-clesiastical penance, directed by the bishop, remained in use throughout this time. It began with the inauguration of the penance on Ash Wednesday. On Ash Wednes-day the penitents were not merely excluded from Mass; they were expelled from the Church, "as once Adam from paradise," and the church was forbidden to them until Easter, or in serious cases for a longer period, as prescribed by the Synod of Worms in 868; only individual churches, which had received the privilege, re-mained accessible to them. Strict fasting was especially taken into consideration as a penance, and it was to be connected with specific exercises of prayer.

But commutations now played an important role. By this term was meant the possibility of "buying oneself off" from the severe penance imposed by sub-stituting easier and shorter penitential works. Originally they were allowed only in justified cases, such as sickness or difficult work, but they soon became the general practice. Most favored was the converting of the strict fast into the pray-ing of psalms; for example, three days of fasting could be represented by three times fifty psalms, which were usually connected with one genuflection each. Alms and pilgrimage were also taken into consideration. The pilgrimage to Rome was popular, but for it the consent of the bishop was required. The far-reaching depersonalization of penance became clear when the *Poenitentiale Bedae* of the eighth century even allowed one to be represented by a substitute, who would perform the penance. While the Synod of Tribur in 895 even recognized money commutation, other synods fought with little success against commutations or particular forms of them.

In accord with Roman tradition, the public ecclesiastical penance was con-cluded on Holy Thursday by means of the reconciliation, the rite for which continued on at the cathedrals in an elaborate form throughout the whole of this period. The penitents were conducted before the bishop during the singing of *Venite, filii,* and he restored them to the community of the faithful with the imposition of hands and prayer.

For the rest of the faithful, confession once a year was now the general rule. A first testimony to this is provided by England around 670. Confession was to be made before the beginning of Lent. In England the day preceding Ash Wednesday thus acquired the name Shrove Tuesday, from "to shrive," that is, "to hear confessions," because the penance imposed according to the penitentials and also the name of the penitent had to be "written." As the pattern for the examination of conscience were mentioned the seven or eight capital sins, "without which hardly anyone is able to live." In accord with the tendency to transfer forms of public penance to all, thereafter the ashes were also imposed on all on Ash Wednesday. From the end of the ninth century excuses were more and more sought that would permit the reconciling of individual penitents at once, before the performing of the penance. This practice became general around the turn of the tenth century, and thus confession was no longer connected with Lent.

In the period under consideration the Anointing of the Sick becomes clearer. In fact it appeared in connection with the penance of the sick, that is, with the forms of public ecclesiastical penance that were adapted for the sick, which everyone was careful to receive on his deathbed, but which, because of the heavy obligations connected with them, were postponed by the faithful as long as possible. The Anointing of the Sick was inserted into the penance of the sick between the assigning of the penance and the reconciliation; but from the tenth century it was frequently imparted only after the reconciliation, as the "last anointing." If possible, several priests should participate.

A considerable change took place also in the forms of ordination. In books the old list of seven orders continued to be given, and they were now explained as developments of a general order. In the tenth century persons began to understand them as a ladder, on which the individual ascended to the higher orders. The *traditio instrumentorum* long customary for the lesser orders, was now adopted also for the higher orders. Ordination to the subdiaconate already approximated that to the diaconate in the Roman-German *Pontificale* except that before the twelfth century the subdiaconate was not reckoned as a major order.

In matrimony, which, in accord with the forms of Germanic law, took place in such a way that the father or guardian of the bride handed her over to the bridegroom, there was no ecclesiastical rite in this period except in so far as the married couple then attended the nuptial Mass and received the priest's blessing. However, there first had to be an ecclesiastical investigation to determine whether there was any matrimonial impediment.

Despite complete fidelity to the text of the traditional Roman prayers, a grand-scale adaptation took place in the very heart of the liturgy, the celebration of Mass. Dramatic elements were added — incensations, changing position of the candlesticks, the giving of special prominence to the Gospel by means of a solemn procession and the place of its proclamation. The simple popular chants of the ordinary, now usually tended to by a choir of clerics, were musically enriched and provided with tropes, that is, with texts which corresponded, syllable for syllable, to the notes of the melody. The *jubilus* of the Alleluia was elaborated into the sequence, and there immediately occurred the springtime of sequence writing, especially with Notker Balbulus (d. 912). The praying of the Canon in silence, attested around 800, was also esteemed as a dramatic element: following the model of the Old Testament, only the priest was to enter into the sanctuary of the Canon. The Gallican pontifical blessing after the Lord's Prayer continued in use. And the kiss of peace was expressly encouraged. It was often regarded as a kind of substitute for communion. However, the custom soon developed that it was received only by the communicants and in such a way that it now proceeded from the altar and was passed on. Communion was still received under both species. As a rule the Host was only dipped into the Precious Blood (*intinctio*); or, only wine was administered, which was "sanctified" by contact with the sacred Host. Although in the Carolingian reform the effort was made to impose communion on Sundays, at least in Lent, for the majority of the faithful it was soon necessary to be satisfied with the number of times required for communion by the canon of Agde in 506 — on Christmas, Easter, and Pentecost. This canon was inculcated by many ninth-century synods. But even this norm was little observed, and still less when at the same period there was raised a demand for confession each time.

The national character of the northern peoples had a share in bringing about the changes just mentioned in the liturgy. Individual usages arose directly out of the Germanic language of symbols, such as praying with hands folded, or the related custom that the newly ordained priest placed his folded hands within the hands of the bishop at the promise of obedience, or the blow on the cheek at confirmation. But the greater prominence given to the sensible and the tangible in the adopting of the Roman liturgy was connected with the circumstance that the Latin of the liturgy was no longer comprehensible to even the Romance-speaking part of the population. To disturb the traditional liturgical tongue and change to one of the national languages, as Cyril and Methodius did farther to the east, was regarded in the West as unthinkable, for it was defended as a principle that in the liturgy it was permissible to use only the three languages of the inscription on the cross — Hebrew, Greek, and Latin; it had to be expressly stressed at the Synod of Frankfurt in 794 that one may at least pray in any language. And so people and altar drew farther apart, soon in the very church building itself. The altar was ordinarily situated near the back wall, in the place that had hitherto been allotted to the bishop's *cathedra* in cathedrals.

The distance from the daily life of the people was emphasized also by a change in the kind of bread. The pure white form of unleavened bread came more and more into vogue from the ninth century. It was soon brought to the altar in already prepared particles for the communion of the people. The sacred Host was then no longer handed to the recipient but placed in his mouth.

For all that, the Carolingian reform was not indifferent to the task of making the liturgy meaningful to the people. In a capitulary of 802 Charles the Great declared it to be a duty of the clergy to explain to the faithful "totius religionis studium et christianitatis cultum." Allegorical interpretation — became standard for the future. In this the Mass is explained as a synopsis and copy of the whole of salvation history, beginning with the call of the prophets of the Old Testament, who were heard in the Introit and *Kyrie* and the *Gloria* of the angels, down to the last blessing of the Lord on his disciples at the Ascension, to which the conclusion of the Mass corresponded.

Thus in the details of its development did the Mass become exclusively the priest's business.

Connected with the greater independence of the celebrant was the growth in frequency of the private Mass. The faithful wanted votive Masses for their special needs. In the monasteries, whose monks were now for the most part priests, the prayer brotherhoods, with the obligation of repeated Masses for a deceased member, operated in the same direction. Persons also celebrated Mass several times a day and frequently even without a server. This last point was censured by various synods as early as the ninth century as a serious abuse. Individual bishops as well as the reform Synod of Seligenstadt in 1023 finally specified three Masses a day as the absolute limit. Then Alexander II (1061–73) declared the single Mass as the rule.

In this period the calendar of feasts also experienced a not unimportant enrichment. At the beginning of the ninth century in the Carolingian Empire the days of precept in addition to Sundays were, in accord with various synods, among others those of Aachen in 809 and Mainz in 813, and also the *Statuta Bonifatii* the following: Christmas, the three following days, the octave day, Epiphany, all the days of Easter week and Pentecost week, or at least the first three days, the Ascension, two feasts of Mary — that on 15 August: and that on 2 February or 8 September the feasts of John the Baptist, Peter and Paul, and Andrew. In addition, at times the anniversary of the dedication and the patronal feast might be included. Only a part of the lists of this period included Michael, Martin, Remigius, Lawrence, and All Saints. Two hundred years later, all the feasts mentioned, except Remigius, belonged to the general list of holy days. To them were added Silvester, the three Rogation days, and, in conformity with a decree of the Synod of Erfurt in 932, the feast day of each Apostle.

It is clear that in the details of liturgical life, even apart from the continuing influence of the earlier non-Roman liturgies in the various countries, there was no strict uniformity. In addition, we find all the more frequently, for example, in Fulbert of Chartres (d. 1029), a saying that goes back to Gregory the Great: If the faith is the same, differences of usage can do no harm.

CHAPTER 102

The Clergy and the Care of Souls

The question arises as to what concrete forms the life and work of the priest took in the early medieval bishopric. One of the most urgent problems was decidedly that of bringing the rural clergy together as far as possible. The danger of isolation was especially present in the case of the priests of proprietary churches, and it was above all they who were in need of constant supervision and encouragement, because of their very deficient training and their dependent status, both for liturgical and pastoral functions and for their moral conduct. Even this problem was capable of solution only if the demands made were reduced to the most necessary.

At first the situation of the urban clergy was better. Certainly the association in collegiate chapters favored the preservation of a religious spirit, though on the other hand, of course, it led to a distribution of offices, which withdrew the larger number of canons from real pastoral activity. Nevertheless, the basic idea proved to be so fruitful that it was taken up even outside the chapters.

The principle of union also found application among the rural clergy. With the deaneries, a new order was established. The priests of each deanery now had to meet at the beginning of each month, *per Kalendas,* as specified in detail in a capitulary issued by Hincmar of Reims in 852. On this occasion, later referred to as a calend, Mass was first celebrated for the group; then followed the conference (*collatio*) under the presidency of the dean. We learn from later prescriptions that the following subjects were treated at the conferences: the official duties of priests, parish activity, the Sacraments, questions of faith and of the spiritual life, correction of negligent colleagues. In particular, according to Hincmar, each time there should be a report on the public penitents of each congregation and their behavior and the bishop should be notified. Common prayer, with intercession for the King, the ecclesiastical authorities, and the living and the dead, also pertained to the program.

An important means of improving the care of souls, from which at the same time we learn details of its practice, were visitations. Great stress had been laid on them again since Carloman's capitulary of 742. Every year the bishop visited the places specified for this, usually the old parishes. This was, of course, every time a festival for the place in question, but it could also be a serious burden on the host, and for that reason various canons set limits to the expenses. The bishop administered confirmation, preached, and, assisted by the archdeacon or archpriest, who could also deputize for him, examined the state of the congregation. This examination became around 800 the synod or synodal tribunal, in which the assembled congregation or later selected synodal witnesses, were put under oath and invited to express themselves, even against the priest.

Toward the end of the ninth century the visitation of the priest was separated from it. For these visitations and synodal tribunals Abbot Regino of Prüm wrote his *De synodalibus causis* in two books. The first book is devoted to the visitation of the clergy. In the second are assembled legal regulations which were taken into consideration in regard to the laity and were of use in examining the moral and spiritual life of a congregation. We obtain abundant information on pastoral conditions, especially in the ninety-six visitation questions with which the first book begins and to a degree also in the parallel questions of the second book. The requirements expressed there coincide to a great extent with the *Admonitio synodalis,* originating around the mid-ninth century, also called the *Homilia Leonis* (Pope Leo IV), which from then on — and, incidentally, in an expanded form, still today in the *Pontificale Romanum* — was passed on as the bishop's closing address at synods.

Duties to which the priests were referred concerned the integrity of the parish property, the condition of the buildings, and the cleanliness of the church, which was not to be used as a granary, the neatness and care of vestments and vessels; the atrium of the church had to be inclosed, and women's dances were not to be permitted there. The pyx, with the Blessed Sacrament, lay on the table-shaped altar for the communion of the sick. Otherwise, only the four Gospels and, in contrast to the custom of previous centuries, relics of saints in a worthy setting were also on the altar.

Every day the priest had to rise for Lauds and during the day pray the canonical hours at the proper times, at each of which the bell was to be rung — Regino mentions Prime, Terce, Sext, and None. He was to have a cleric to sing the psalms with him and to read the Epistle and make the responses at Mass. He was to offer Mass daily at Terce, and then remain fasting until noon in order to be able to celebrate again for pilgrims who might arrive. The faithful were to attend Lauds, Mass, and Vespers on Sundays and holy days. In individual villages trusted men, called *decani,* were appointed to remind the others of this duty and of the obligation of ceasing from labor, which had to be observed a *vespera ad vesperam.* Even shepherds — *porcarii et alii pastores* — had to come to Mass on Sunday. Before Mass the pastor was to bless holy water and sprinkle the faithful. At the offertory the faithful were to present their offering; they gave candles and the like earlier. If there was no deacon or subdeacon present, the priest himself had to cleanse the vessels at the end of Mass. After Mass he was to distribute blessed bread (*eulogias*) from the offering of the people.

Books that the priest had to own were the sacramentary (or missal), lectionary, antiphonary (for the Mass chants), and homiliary, and also an orthodox explanation of the creed and the Lord's Prayer and a martyrology, in order to announce to the people the occurring feasts. Wherever possible, he should have the forty homilies of Gregory the Great. He had to know the psalms by heart and also the unchanging Mass prayers, the creed *Quicumque,* and the formula for blessing holy water. He should at least be able to read the other texts without making mistakes. He should also be capable of explaining to the people on Sundays and feasts something from the Gospel, the Epistle, or elsewhere in Scripture. He was to see to it that all knew the creed and the Lord's Prayer by heart. Children were to learn them from their godparents. The priest was to take care that no child died without baptism and communion; hence he should always take the holy oils and the Eucharist with him on excursions.

The penitential system played a not insignificant role. The pastor had to summon the faithful to confession at the beginning of Lent. To avoid imposing penance arbitrarily, he should possess a penitential. The priest was warned not to let himself be bribed by public sinners whom he ought to report for ecclesiastical penance.

On the other hand, he must not invite public penitents to eat or drink without at the same time making amends by an alms.

It goes without saying that good example was especially impressed upon the priest. He was warned not to have a *mulier subintroducta* in his house. He must not bear weapons, a prescription that was certainly not insisted upon by many an episcopal lord. He must not find diversion with dogs and falcons or visit taverns. He was asked whether he had pawned the church vessels to the innkeeper or a dealer. He must not take part in weddings. At wakes he was not to let himself be induced to drink to the guests in honor of the saints and become intoxicated. He should always wear his clerical dress, even on journeys, at least the stole. If a priest without a stole was killed, only the customary *wergeld* had to be paid for him, not the triple *wergeld*. The priest should be especially concerned for the poor, and he should be hospitable to travellers passing through. He should visit the sick, absolve and anoint them, and bring them the viaticum personally, not through a lay person.

It is clear that with this mirror of duties, which was held up to the priests at diocesan synods and on parish visitations in the ninth and tenth centuries, at first only a program was outlined that could leave the actuality far behind, but nevertheless a program behind which stood the full authority, not only of the Church, but also of the contemporary state.

This much is certain: pastoral activity moved in primitive forms but it had firm outlines. The traditional forms of the Mass and the Sacraments constituted the supporting framework for the guidance of what was especially a liturgical care of souls.

There was no ecclesiastical catechism for children. The religious initiation and guidance of the young must have taken place substantially by way of custom. However, parents and godparents were directed to impress on the children the creed and the Lord's Prayer, and at the annual confession the priest should begin by having each penitent recite them. Elsewhere the priest, according to the testimony of the confession *ordines,* asked at least the two questions about faith in the three Persons in the one God and in the resurrection of the body for judgment of good and evil. The sermon was required on all Sundays and holy days.

The lack of an extensive preaching of the faith must have been all the more detrimental to the education of the people when the language of the liturgy was no longer understood. Nevertheless, the reform synods of 813 and the Synod of Mainz in 847 had expressly demanded that the priest must preach to the people "secundum proprietatem linguae" and translate the models of homilies "in rusticam Romanam linguam aut Theotiscam." For the intercessory prayers for the living and the dead, which were added after the sermon in several series, the use of the vernacular is probable at least in so far as the invitation to prayer each time was uttered in the vernacular, whereupon everyone was to recite the Lord's Prayer silently. The use of translations of the *Confiteor* as frankly acknowledged guilt in the same place at the public Mass cannot be proved before the twelfth century, whereas such texts for use in the confession of the individual (*Glaube und Beicht*) go back to the Carolingian period.

But the people knew they were somehow included in the Mass. Bishop Herard of Tours presupposed in his *capitulare* of 858 that the people sang the *Sanctus* and only admonished the priest to sing it with them. The *Kyrie eleison,* as a repeated supplication, had then already become the starting point of the "Leise," from which later would grow the German liturgical song.

CHAPTER 103

Forms of Devotion

A first task in the religious instruction of the people was constituted, even as late as the turn of the millennium, by the fight against the remains of paganism and against superstition. The penitentials are quite clear in this regard. Those remnants extended from women who, while spinning and weaving, uttered secret sayings and from the wake at which "diabolical songs" were sung to real magic and to pagan sacrifices at wells, stones, and crossroads.

It was not to be expected, by reason of the condition of the preaching of the faith, that a religious life based on real spirituality was to be found in the broad masses of the people. The force of popular instruction lay in the institutional element. It had to be enough if what was indicated in law and prescription was observed. A religious impetus could be expected only gradually, through the example of monasteries and chapters, whose piety alone is in some degree accessible to us.

Like the cultural life in general, the devotional life of this period bore a monastic allure. This is true of the clergy, but even lay persons sought in associations of prayer, the forerunners of the later confraternities, contact with a monastery. The monastery was so much the model for the collegiate chapters of diocesan clerics that at that time it was not too unusual for a foundation of the canonical life to pass to the monastic life and conversely. The requirement of the full monastic office was from now on repeated everywhere on the continent and was also applied to parish churches, but frequently private recitation by those who were impeded was not demanded.

The common choral office made available an important factor of religious formation — common spiritual reading. In the Cluniac monasteries stress was laid on the importance of reading the entire Bible every year. In addition there came from the writings of the Fathers, from hagiography, and from the passions of the martyrs whatever the monastic or chapter library could offer. The reading in choir was frequently continued in the refectory. The spiritual reading of the individual was of secondary importance because of the cost of books. But it was cultivated and was especially recommended as *lectio divina,* reflective reading, which also contained the elements of contemplative prayer.

Alongside the reading in the choral office was the psalmody. The psalms occupied an important position even outside the choral prayer.

In this period there also began the history of the prayer book, which of course at that time could belong to few only. They borrow from the liturgy and from the Fathers, and the psalms are abundantly used. And then more personal viewpoints also came to the fore — *apologiae* and prayers for specific virtues occupy much space. Texts were provided in honor of the most holy Trinity and of the individual divine Persons. Of special fervor were the prayers in honor of the cross, which might be regarded as the most outstanding object of devotion of those centuries, next to the relics of the saints.

In the piety of this rough epoch external exercises had a much greater importance than at other times. Instructors in this were the Irish monks. The genuflection, fifty times in connection with fifty psalms or repeated in a multiple of this number, praying for hours with outstretched arms, standing in cold water through entire nights, and in addition the ascetical roaming and the pilgrimage to holy spots were favorite exercises of great men of prayer and at the same time accomplishments prescribed for penitents.

If we would characterize the devotion of the epoch as it becomes evident in these and like forms, we may term it a piety of transition. On the one hand, strong forces of the tradition from Christian antiquity were still active. These revealed themselves perhaps most clearly in ecclesiastical art. Romanesque, and all the more the age preceding it, breathes the spirit of a firm, objective order with clear relationships. It is the art which, for all its autonomy, was in the most perfect harmony with the Roman liturgy. In the principal apse of many churches of this period the *maiestas Domini,* Christ royally enthroned, was represented. Even the representation of the Crucified, which appeared quite often now, was still far removed from a realistic reproduction of the event on Golgotha. And then was elaborated the Romanesque crucifix, in victorious attitude, with the royal crown on the head. The cross as a symbol of victory, already illuminated by the glory of Easter, was a favorite theme of Carolingian designers and versifiers, just as it was a favorite subject of devout prayer.

But the transitional character of this epoch is seen, and very impressively, on the other hand, in the prominence of a new type of piety, one which came to maturity later in the Middle Ages and is still active in the popular piety of the present. The image of Christ which now came more and more to the fore was, as has been aptly said, no longer the "Christus passus et gloriosus" of early Christianity, but the "Christus patiens," in any event Christ on the borders of the Gospel reports.

It is amazing with what force the mystery of the Trinity began to dominate consciousness at this time. The Christian faith was termed with predilection *fides sanctae Trinitatis.* Not the mystery of Christ but the doctrine of the Three Divine Persons appeared now as the central object of faith.

This is in accord with the circumstance that at times Christ often stood simply for God and *vice versa.* Much as the human of the Gospels now came to the fore, and in this sense one could speak of a growing esteem of the Lord's humanity, his total figure was understood as a manifestation of divinity. Christ is the God King, to whom one renders the service that one swore to him in baptism.

The force of this manner of thinking is to be recognized by this, that it even had a modifying effect on the Roman liturgy. The conclusion of the Roman oration, *Per Dominum nostrum,* emphasizing Christ's mediatorship based on his humanity and extolling his glorified life with the Father and his reign, was not infrequently replaced by *Qui vivis,* which only left his divinity more in the field of vision. It was a necessary consequence of a presentation shortened in such a way that the obscuring of Christ's humanity also obscured the awareness of the nearness of God's grace, into which the Christian was admitted through the God-Man. Church and Christian order now appeared above all as a matter of law, not unlike the political order, from which the Church was distinguished only by vague boundary lines, and behind the law stood the divine tribunal. The progress of vehement self-accusations in the *apologiae,* which, for example in the so-called *Missa Illyrica* of the eleventh century, penetrated the entire Mass liturgy like a climbing plant, thus becomes understandable. Christianity acquired a moralizing feature and a melancholy mood.

On the other hand, if the one mediator Christ Jesus withdrew to some extent from sight in the glory of his divinity, afflicted man had all the more to look for other helpers. The early Middle Ages are the period of a greatly intensified cult of relics.

In addition to and above the martyrs the cult of the Mother of God acquired an increasing importance. A great many of the new churches, including the palace chapel at Aachen, were dedicated in her honor. Pictures of the *Theotokos,* coming from the East, were now much copied. One day of the week, Saturday, first appears in Alcuin as Mary's day. In particular the Cluniac movement fostered the cult of Mary, the *mater misericordiae,* as she was now called with predilection. In every monastery at least one chapel was dedicated to her. The daily *officium parvum beatae Mariae Virginis* was already widespread in the eleventh century. From this time also the *hymnus akathistus* from Byzantium, with its long series of honorary titles for Mary, exerted a growing influence, which manifested itself from then on in a springtime of Marian poetry and later, among other ways, was consolidated in the Marian litanies.

How did this striking shifting of stress, or, to use the language of the Fathers, this different sort of illumination of the one world of faith, come about? It is clear that no new content of belief is involved. Here we encounter the effects of that great agitation which had been evoked at the end of Christian antiquity by Western Arianism. The source of that tremor, whose vibrations continued through the centuries, must, in fact, be sought in Visigothic Spain in the sixth century. The conversion of the Visigothic nation to the Catholic Church, which was sealed at the national council of 589, had been preceded by repeated severe struggles and intellectual discussions, in which there was question of the correct Christology. To the Arian denial of the consubstantial divinity of the Son and its reference to the mediation formula, *Per Christum,* which had been used from time immemorial also in the Catholic liturgy and which was alleged to indicate a subordination of the Son in his divinity, the Catholic defense opposed the equally positive emphasizing of the oneness of essence of the Father with the Son, the unity of the divine being in the Trinity of Persons, and this not only in the carefully sharpened definitions of the Trinitarian formula of faith but also in the formulation of liturgical prayer, and not least of all in the practical abandonment of the misunderstood mediation formula. The reaction on the Catholic way of thinking had to be all the more lasting, since the flexible Spanish liturgy was then undergoing a phase of active development and then definitively stabilized itself in this phase. Creedal struggles of a similar kind were, as we learn from Gregory of Tours, among others, also fought out on Gallic soil, but the decisive influence must have proceeded from Spain, whose Church experienced a period of flowering in the seventh century with Saint Isidore of Seville and others and thereby assumed the leadership in Christianity.

If the religious life of the early Middle Ages lost not a little of the freshness and confidence of earlier centuries, we can still identify signs of a new flowering on the new foundation. The more the Easter range of ideas with the glorified Christ was deemphasized, all the more did the devout soul turn to the manifestation of the earthly Christ. Christmas with its cycle of feasts gained in importance and popularity, and the earthly and visible element in the Easter mystery of redemption especially occupied the devout person. This last now became the favorite subject of imitative performances.

Section Seven

Renewal and Reform from 900 to 1050

Friedrich Kempf

CHAPTER 104

The Renewal of Monastic and Canonical Life

Four principal causes had in the course of the ninth century led to an extensive decay of the monastic and the canonical life: secularizing usurpations by rulers, squandering of the property by lay abbots, lack of protection because of the growing weakness of the royal power, and the devastation wrought by Vikings, Muslims, and finally Magyars. But the vitality of Western Christianity was unbroken. There slowly arose monastic centers of strength whose effects soon reached beyond the cloister. The canons also were affected by the movement of renewal, though to a lesser degree.

Monastic Renewal

North of the Alps the impulse proceeded, on the one hand, from Lotharingia — Brogne, Gorze, Verdun, — and on the other hand, from France — Cluny in the Duchy of Burgundy and other abbeys, for the most part influenced by its spirit. While the Lotharingian centers influenced the German Empire particularly, Cluny and the other French reform centers spread to all the surrounding lands. To about 1050 monasticism was powerfully on the move. At the beginning of the tenth century most monasteries were living on the intellectual legacy of Benedict of Aniane, which of course had been modified here and there and was to be still further modified in the future, so that in the long run with regard to the constitution and the *consuetudines* various groups were formed. The differences that soon appeared were at first only nuances of one and the same striving for renewal; only later, especially after 1050, were they at times to cause conflicts among them.

The Lotharingian and German Area

The first efforts for a monastic renewal in Lower Lotharingia are connected with the name of Gerard of Brogne (d. 959). A member of a not especially powerful noble family, Gerard, probably in 913 or 914, founded on property of his own a monastic community, for which he acquired the relics of Saint Eugene from the French monastic cell of Deuil. In any event, Brogne under Gerard's direction must have been of some consequence, for in 931/32 Duke Giselbert of Lotharingia presented the Abbot with the totally decayed monastery of Saint-Ghislain in Hainaut, perhaps inhabited by canons. The work of reconstruction accomplished there moved Marquis Arnulf of Flanders (918–65) to entrust Gerard with the revival of the Flemish abbeys, those of Saint-Bavo and Saint-Pierre de Mont-Blandin at Ghent and Saint-Bertin at their head. Thus in Flanders Gerard stepped into a position similar to that which had earlier fallen to Benedict of Aniane in the Carolingian Empire. And if Benedict's initiative weakened after his death the same fate befell Gerard's life-work and for the same reason.

The connection with specific persons is also to be observed in the monastic regeneration which began in Upper Lotharingia and soon operated in lower Lotharingia and in Germany. Almost always it was produced, partly from religious, partly from economic reasons, by the proprietors of monasteries, laymen and bishops.

The happily inaugurated movement of renewal stimulated greater achievements at the beginning of the eleventh century.

In contrast to Cluny, in Lotharingia and Germany there were no congregations during the Ottonian and early Salian periods, but at most rather loosely constructed monastic groups, based on the notion of observance and on the association of prayer, which could be reorganized or even dissolved. The lack of any institutional stability had its drawbacks, of course; but in a movement of renewal it was not the organization that was ultimately decisive but the spirit, and many Lotharingians and Germans were affected by it. A further distinction from Cluny and other French reform monasteries lay in the relationship to the diocesan bishop. The lack of protection on the part of the public authority in France aroused among the monks there the desire to escape episcopal jurisdiction as far as possible and be directly subordinate to the papacy. Such a striving for exemption, proceeding from an unpropitious situation, was virtually non-existent in the Lotharingian and German monasteries, which were legally better guaranteed.

France

From unassuming beginnings the abbey of Cluny in French Burgundy developed into the most important reform center. It owed its establishment in 910 to William the Good, Duke of Aquitaine and Count of Auvergne. In the very foundation charter the monastery's property was removed from the clutches of every power, secular and spiritual, the abbey was placed under the protection of the Holy See, and the free election of its abbot was granted. William gave it to Berno, Abbot of Gigny and Beaume, well known as a father of monks because of his monastic austerity. Other lords did likewise; Berno received three other monasteries — Déols and Massay in the County of Berry and Ethice in Burgundy. Shortly before his death in 927 he divided the six houses between his nephew Guy, who obtained Gigny, Beaume, and Ethice, and his disciple Odo, who received Cluny, Déols, and Massay, with the obligation of preserving the same observance.

Under Odo (927–42) Cluny's still rather small monastic community quickly gained influence. Not a few proprietors of monasteries called upon its Abbot for the renewal of old and the direction of newly founded monastic houses, especially in Aquitaine. When Odo made personal contact with the Popes, he was even entrusted by Prince Alberic with the reform of Roman and nearby monasteries. The seventeen houses which were subject to him in 937 were, it is true, united only very loosely by the abbatial function (*abbatia*) which he exercised, even though one or the other house, such as Romainmoutier, was given to Cluny forever. Odo probably did not even seek the formation of a real union. Administered in Odo's spirit by the capable Aymard (942–54), Cluny was prepared for the prosperity which it was to experience, due to the superb qualifications and the extraordinarily long tenures of the next three Abbots. Mayeul (954–93), Odilo (993–1048), and Hugh (1049 to 1109) brought their monastery world-wide fame. Directly or indirectly, the Cluniac observance not only affected a large part of the French abbeys, but obtained entrance into Italy, with the beginning of the eleventh century into Spain, and from around 1050 into Lotharingia, Germany, and England.

Actually Cluny held to the same tradition that had been established by Benedict of Aniane and was followed by the Lotharingian centers of renewal. It did not add new intellectual or ascetical ideas, but continued certain basic tendencies of Benedict of Aniane, such as stricter observance of silence and lengthening of the choral office. The liturgy, elaborated in the direction of solemnity, became the dominant element. Precious vestments and vessels and splendid architecture heightened the brilliance. The piling on of additional prayers brought it about that, according to Odo's biographer, more than 138 psalms were prayed every day. The ritualistic excess left the monks little time for study, and manual labor all but disappeared. Because of the last mentioned circumstance even a highly born lord could be comfortable at Cluny, especially since clothing, food, cleanliness, and sanitation were suitably provided. The extraordinarily careful attention devoted to the remembrance of the dead must have attracted well-to-do families to make gifts and to show their good will in other ways. Two elements in the constitution especially prevented a relaxation of monastic discipline: the right of the Abbot to designate his successor, and thus to assure continuity, and the forming of a monastic order.

The beginnings of the Cluniac Order have not yet been cleared up. However, Cluny succeeded in bringing a great part of the monastic houses that were committed to renewal into a more or less strong dependence. The principal element contributing to this was the priory system. For the most part the priories resulted from small monastic communities situated on estates of the motherhouse and called *cellae.* Even when they grew up to the size of a monastery or even founded priories of their own, Cluny let them remain as far as possible in their subordinate position under a prior, whom the Abbot appointed and replaced at will. Besides the priories, there were subject to the motherhouse a group of abbeys, some almost entirely so, others to a certain degree. The dependent superiors had to make an oath of loyalty into the hands of the Abbot, like a vassal to his feudal lord. For all members of the order the ordination of monks, not their profession, was arranged at Cluny from the end of the eleventh century.

All in all there was a matter here of an imperfect type, soon outmoded by the Cistercians; its unifying bond consisted of the person of the Abbot. In a sense it recalls the manner in which a noble combined far scattered properties or rights, amassed in juridically different ways, into one estate in his person. And as a matter of fact the Cluniac union was constituted to a great extent for economic reasons. Without centralization it was impossible to avoid the fragmentation of property which began in France and Italy at the end of the tenth century. Of course, beside economic interests stood reform concerns: incorporated into the order, the monasteries of monks could be kept under discipline by the Abbot by means of visitation and other measures.

It is still a subject of controversy whether Cluny strove for a comprehensive reform of the Church over and above the monastic world and hence was at least one of the causes of the great movement that got under way around 1050. Great as were the liberties granted it by the founder, Duke William, there is little reason for interpreting them as a demonstration against the existing juridical order. And if Cluny had no *advocatus,* it must be borne in mind that the *advocatia* of the nobility was not customary in all of southern France up to where Cluny lay, whereas in northern France even Cluniac houses could have *advocati,* and here and there even wanted them. With all their exertions for guaranteeing the monastic spirit of the houses entrusted to them, the Abbots of Cluny were able on occasion to accommodate themselves to the legal claims of proprietors. They understood their concerns. Since they did not have their many estates worked by their monks and only later, from around 1100, as far as possible by lay brothers, their economic system in the period here under consideration differed in no way from that of the feudal lords. A very special connection was signified by the proprietary churches which the Cluniacs acquired, even from lay persons, in an increasing degree during the tenth and eleventh centuries. For rounding out their possessions they even had no difficulty in buying up entire churches or partial rights to them. The contradiction to the principles appearing in the Gregorian reform was plain here. It showed how much Cluny was bound up with the Carolingian and Ottonian epochs.

Within the Church, on the other hand, Cluny directly prepared for the Gregorian reform in one particular aspect: by its connection with Rome. From the first contact made by Abbot Odo, the papal protection envisaged in the foundation charter was again and again confirmed by the Holy See and as far as possible acted upon. Gregory V went beyond this by granting what became typical rights of exemption: only bishops invited by the Abbot were to be qualified to consecrate, ordain, or celebrate Mass at Cluny, and the monks could receive orders wherever it pleased the Abbot. John XIX not only confirmed the decree of Gregory V, but also exempted the monks of Cluny from episcopal excommunication and interdict. Thus the motherhouse achieved full exemption. Other Cluniac houses sought to copy this, but only realized various successes or even none at all. The striving for exemption was of great significance: the hopes in this regard that were centered on the Holy

See made the Cluniacs the promoters and defenders of the idea of the primacy before and during the Gregorian reform.

Cluny's radiation was by no means restricted to houses belonging to the order. Monasteries that were directed by Cluny's Abbots only for a short time and then given their autonomy also retained to a great extent a Cluniac stamp with the addition of their own special characteristics and transmitted this spirit to other monastic communities. Thus the monastery of Saint Benedict at Fleury-sur-Loire, renewed by Abbot Odo in 930, became a separate reform center, to which recourse was even had for the monastic renewal in England by Dunstan's friends, Aethelwold and Oswald. William's reform movement reached beyond its principal field of activity in France into North Italy, where his foundation of Fruttuaria was to be especially prominent, and into Normandy. There were also monastic centers which were not directly affected by Cluny. Of these the most prominent was Saint-Victor de Marseille. From the time the first monastery became subject to it in 1034, Saint-Victor in quick succession attracted a whole group of monasteries of the Midi and then of Catalonia and Spain, where it vied with Cluny, and extended its influence as far as Sardinia.

Italy

The Cluniac movement first gained a firm footing in Italy with Mayeul of Cluny and William of Saint-Bénigne de Dijon. The dependent houses that both centers then established were for the most part in the North. Abbot Odilo, probably on the urging of Otto III, was able to take up again Odo's reform work in Rome. At the same time the important royal monastery of Farfa, on its own initiative and with the reserving of its liberty, accepted the Cluniac usages.

Meanwhile, there grew up in Italy a special, eremitically oriented form, which was to release new impulses. Itself the origin of Christian monachism in general and heroic realization of the *fuga mundi*, the eremitical life always and everywhere attracted high-minded persons. Although the Benedictines permitted individual members, with the consent of the abbot, to live as recluses or hermits, they were on the whole dominated by the cenobitical idea. Wherever the latter was renewed and realized with strict discipline, eremitical inclinations went into eclipse. On the other hand, Eastern monachism gave the eremitical element a much greater scope. Hence it was no accident that the attraction to eremitism was especially alive in Italy, where the Latin and Byzantine cultures were in direct contact.

Romuald, son of the Duke of Ravenna, entered the monastery of Sant'Apollinare in Classe around 972, when about twenty years of age, in order to atone for a murder committed by his father. Dissatisfaction with the spirit prevailing there drove him into solitude. He spent the first years under the care of a hermit in the swampy district near Venice, then went with his teacher and a couple of Venetians to the Catalonian monastery of Cuxá, in the vicinity of which he lived for about ten years with his friends as a hermit. Having returned to Italy around 988, his unusual and charismatic personality excited amazement and the desire to follow him. Otto III, his enthusiastic admirer, had little success when in 998 he had him elected Abbot of Classe; a year later Romuald literally laid the crozier at his feet.

Even later he could not bear to remain anywhere for long. Wandering restlessly through Central Italy, he reformed existing monasteries or founded new colonies of hermits, among them the at first still unimportant Camaldoli. At his death in the solitude of Val di Castro in 1027, he left neither a written rule nor an organizational summary of the eremitical communities that he had founded, several of which quickly disintegrated. If, in spite of this, his work continued, this was in great measure due to Peter Damiani, who in 1034 entered Fonte Avellana and in 1043 became its prior; he died in 1072. Peter gave the Italian hermit movement both a theological and a firmer organizational and economic basis, even though the congregation he constructed included not many more than ten settlements. Under Prior Rudolf (1074–89) began the rise of Camaldoli; there the tradition going back to Romuald was defined in the *Eremiticae Regulae.*

Basically, Romuald strove for nothing more than a monastic way of life, intensified to extreme austerity but somehow continuing in the framework of the Benedictine rule. Hence he was interested in Benedictine reform centers and their *consuetudines,* especially those of Cluny, which he highly esteemed. There could be no question of an opposition in principle: Benedictines in the old tradition did not exclude the eremitical life, and Romuald and his disciples did not exclude the cenobitical life. In addition to the *eremus,* an isolated district with separate hut-like dwellings and a church in their midst, there was a monastery in Romuald's foundations. From the viewpoint of worth, of course, to Romuald's followers the eremitical life was incomparably higher than the cenobitical; the superior in charge of both communities had to be a hermit. Neither Romuald nor Peter Damiani regarded the monastery as the preparation for the *eremus* — both allowed fit disciples to be hermits from the outset — but rather they assigned it the function of intercepting the noise of the world and managing the economic affairs.

No doubt this shift of stress contained new and even revolutionary elements. Here the demands present in cenobitism, of fitting oneself into the whole, were less important than the personal striving of the hermit to find God in an heroic struggle against his own nature and the demons, in an excess of fasting, mortification, and prayer. From so subjectively oriented a training of the spirit issued fearless men who severely flayed the failings of the age. Their criticism struck at the monasteries with their great wealth as well as at the life of the laity and of the clergy, high and low, wherever it gave scandal. Small though the number of hermits was, the excitement which they caused was great.

The Canons

By means of the reform legislation of Louis the Pious the *vita canonica* was separated once for all from the *vita monastica* and in the Aachen *Institutio canonicorum* of 816 it was defined even in regard to details. In all this there were adopted the essential points which were contained in the rule for canons composed earlier by Bishop Chrodegang of Metz (d. 766). As with the monks, the chief duty of canons was to consist of the choral liturgy, and their life was to be bound up with cloister, including common dormitory and refectory, and with the prescriptions of the rule. They were distinguished from monks by better clothing (linen), by the differentiation of the community according to orders received, and by the right to private property; furthermore, under certain circumstances they were permitted to live in individual dwellings within the cloister.

In France, Lotharingia, Germany, and North and Central Italy — in the last mentioned especially from the beginning of the eleventh century — many cathedral and collegiate chapters can be identified, where both choral liturgy and common life in fidelity to the rule were carefully cultivated. The canons rendered inestimable service in the cathedral schools. And if from about 920 new foundations of chapters constantly occurred, the *vita canonica* must have been displayed in many places in a form worthy of credence, though it was often economic interests that settled matters.

Chapter reforms ordinarily originated with bishops or even rulers, such as the Emperor Henry II. This was also the case with not a few monastic reforms, but there the renewed spirit was assured more easily through the monarchical position of the abbot or even because of the formation of a congregation than it could be among the canons. The collegial organization among the canons limited the power of the provost, and unions similar to congregations were made virtually impossible by the juridical structure of the chapters. To this extent the great continuous progress was missing from the canonical movement of renewal. The deterioration of a chapter took place almost of necessity when it was no longer in a position to see to the adequate support of its members. And since from the end of the tenth century an extensive fragmentation of property and rights began in France and Italy, not a few smaller chapters, for the most part foundations of the lower nobility, fell into economic distress, which undermined discipline, whereas monastic congregations, such as the Cluniac and others, overcame the economic crisis.

C H A P T E R   1 0 5

Education and Learning

When persons set to work in the tenth century to restore monasteries and chapters or to found new ones, studies, which had also fallen into decay, were stimulated. Great achievements, however, were not to be expected. More than ever, scholarly effort withdrew into monastic and cathedral schools. It was they that, in a silent work of reconstruction, were preparing the future development of Western scholarship.

Every monastery possessed a school, at least for its own recruits. At the same time, however, not a few abbeys maintained a school for externs, in which pupils who were entrusted to them, but were not destined for the monastic life, were instructed. The teaching continued the Carolingian tradition. Among the masters who handed it on, three were outstanding at the turn of the ninth century: Remigius of Auxerre (d. 908), Notker the Stammerer of Sankt Gallen (d. 912), and Hucbald of Saint-Amand (d. 930). The greatest was Notker. Sankt Gallen owed it especially to him that it remained an important intellectual center for the next century. Revived or new monasteries had to start from the beginning. Their attitude to studies varied.

Less numerous but not of less quality were the cathedral schools operated by the canons. The cathedral school of Reims reached its climax under Gerbert of Aurillac. His pupil Fulbert (d. 1029) established the fame of Chartres; what he began as teacher and fostered as bishop was to outlive him, and as late as the twelfth century the school of Chartres still had its own special character. The German cathedral schools owed their flowering to the exertions of Archbishop Bruno of Cologne and his brother, Otto the Great. By preference it was in the cathedral schools that the Ottos and the Salians trained their future chaplains, chancery notaries, and bishops. Italy was a country of too ancient a culture for studies to be able to die out. In the tenth century they lived on especially in the Lombard Kingdom. Cathedral and urban schools, like those of Pavia, Milan, Vercelli, Parma, Verona, and also Ravenna, maintained a high level.

The details of scholarship were set into the traditional framework of the seven *artes liberales.* The *trivium,* consisting of grammar, dialectic, and rhetoric, was followed by the *quadrivium* — arithmetic, geometry, music, astronomy. Concentration was on the *trivium* and, more specifically, on grammar.

Far less happy was the situation of the mathematical disciplines of the *quadrivium.* Music offered a particular difficulty. It was studied as *musica speculativa, theoretica, practica.* Gerbert, the Reichenau school, and others still took into account the mathematical elements, but in the eleventh century the theory of music more and more gave way to practical instruction in singing and composing. One of the great didactic achievements of the time was the new system of lines attributed to Guido of Arezzo.

All these studies, for which, in addition to pagan authors, the Church Fathers, especially Augustine, Jerome, Gregory the Great, then Isidore of Seville, Bede, and the Carolingian authors were called into service, found expression in a series of treatises. They were too much the product of their age to require discussion here. Only very rarely did the mind move on from dialectics to authentic philosophical problems.

Theology was in a pretty sorry state. It lived on the store laid up in the Carolingian age. Basically, theological efforts were geared to the practical.

The predominantly practical interest called forth in the tenth century a relatively large number of works on canon law. The best of these appeared at the beginning and the end of the century.

We may skip over the canonical compilations that followed these works. All were surpassed by the *Decretum* of Bishop Burchard of Worms (1000–1025), composed in 1008–12. Geared to the requirements of practice, this canonical collection, divided into twenty books, instructed bishops on all questions of spiritual jurisdiction. It was no mere chance that the time of its origin fell during the reign of Henry II. The ecclesiastical juridical situation had stabilized itself and posed quite special reform problems; there was question here of a reform, which despite certain tensions to be noticed at times even in Burchard, still regarded *Regnum* and *Sacerdotium* as a unity. Inner balance and usefulness assured the work a circulation previously unprecedented in the entire Christian West.

The rise in the quality of studies stands out especially clearly in the field of historical writing. Not until more than a century after the death of Regino of Prüm did an unknown monk of Reichenau again venture upon a chronicle of the world and of Germany (1040 or 1044); it is known to us today only through those authors who copied it. On it is based, for example, the widely circulated brief world chronicle (to 1054) of Hermann of Reichenau. The history of the Saxon dynasty, produced in the reign of Otto I by Widukind of Corvey (to 957–58, with appendices to 973), found in Thiotmar of Merseburg a new reviser, who made use of Widukind and other sources and carried the account to 1018, while Wipo's *Gesta Chuonradi imperatoris* describes the history of the Empire from 1024 to 1039.

Among the numerous biographical works of the Ottonian and early Salian periods the following are outstanding for their content: the work of Ruodger, of Gerard, of Abbot John of Saint-Arnulf de Metz, the Roman Abbot John Canaparius and Bruno of Querfurt. The series was continued in the next period. In addition to the excellent *Historia Remensis ecclesiae* (to 948) by Flodoard (d. 966), there appeared in the first half of the eleventh century the precious histories of the sees of Cambrai and Liege, the former by an unknown writer, the latter by the canon Anselm (d. 1056).

Scholarly interchange and practical activity induced several learned men to engage in a brisk correspondence. The older Worms collection of letters was a product of the school but it includes political letters; those that are dated belong to the 1030s. In the next period letter-writing slowly became a special art, cultivated by special schools, and in the intellectual and political struggles from the period of the Gregorian reform people at times made greater use of it than of weapons. In the period under consideration there is no trace as yet of such a tendency, but the fact that people began at all to make collections of letters is important. It shows a growing awareness of the value of a literary influence and of intellectual interchange.

The peaceful picture presented by education and scholarship is not entirely in accord with the reality. In the first half of the eleventh century a certain uneasiness proceeded from the *artes liberales*. The real danger threatened from the dialecticians. Dialectical attacks on Christian dogmas followed in increasing numbers in the course of the eleventh century; they presented Christian scholarship with the problem of the relations between faith and reason, theology and philosophy, and prepared the way for the new scholastic dialectic method.

CHAPTER 106

Heretical and Reform Movements
among Clergy and Laity (1000 to 1050)

There is an unmistakable sign that, with the eleventh century, the Christian West was slowly entering upon a new phase of development. For the first time in its history heretical groups cropped up in various places: at Mainz in 1012, six and ten years later in Aquitaine, at Orléans in 1022, at Arras in 1025, soon after at Monteforte near Turin and in Burgundy, in the diocese of Châlons-sur-Marne in 1042–48, at Goslar in 1051. They probably had no connection with one another. Still we find the carefully attested communities in Arras to have consisted of *rustici,* those of Orléans of clerics, and those at Monteforte of lay nobles. The contemporary chroniclers include them mostly under the term "Manichaeans," but nowhere is the properly ontological Manichaean dualism to be found. Instead, there is present an ascetical and moral dualism, which in individuals could go as far as the rejection of marriage, of the eating of fleshmeat, or even of killing animals.

The heretics took their religious and moral requirements to a great extent from the New Testament and did not hesitate to attribute their scriptural interpretation to the inspiration of the Holy Spirit. The essential point of the Gospels — faith in Christ, Son of God and Savior — definitely took second place to the personal striving to lead a pious life, and could even disappear entirely from one's mental horizon. With such an outlook, any appreciation of the Church's sacramental life was of necessity lost. In the intellectually noteworthy centers of Orléans and Monteforte, as a matter of fact, the religious dynamism, with the abandonment of the Trinitarian and Christological dogmas, was directed merely toward God the Father as creator, and in almost all groups baptism, the Eucharist, confession and penance, holy orders, consecration of churches and altars, and the cult of saints, the cross, and relics were regarded as useless; here and there the imposition of hands, whereby the Spirit was imparted, was retained.

The intellectual source of these movements, difficult to grasp, differing among themselves in individual points, yet containing much that was common, is controverted. Some would see here influences of the old Bogomiles. The Bogomiles, appearing from around the mid-tenth century, get their name from the Bulgarian (or Macedonian?) village priest Bogomil, who lived around that time. He represented a dualism in so far as he attributed dominion over the world to the devil, whom he regarded as son of God and brother of Christ, and hence he demanded separation from the world. At least the more intimate circle of his adherents, the so-called theorists, were to lead a pure "apostolic" life, avoid marriage, manual labor, and the use of fleshmeat and wine, pray, fast, and go on pilgrimage. The Bogomiles attacked ecclesiastical pomp and worldly possessions and power. They spread in the Balkan peninsula, especially in Bulgaria, and, after the subjugation of Bulgaria by the Emperor Basil II in 1018, also in Constantinople, and obtained a stable organization. In time their doctrines became differentiated. When the specifically Manichaean distinction between a God of heaven and an evil creator of this world entered their teaching and to what extent the Paulicians, transported from Armenia to Thrace, had an influence on this can no longer be precisely determined. In any event, in the eleventh century there were two main tendencies: alongside the older and more moderate dualism of the "Bulgarian Church" stood the radically dualistic "Dragovisian Church" — Dragowitsa was a Thracian country district. Any influences of the Old Bogomiles, who likewise represented a predominantly ethical and religious moralism in opposition to the radical dualistic tendency, appearing in the eleventh century, of the "Dragovisian" Church, must have penetrated via Italy into the West; without them the many similarities of the heretical groups, which of themselves were not connected, are probably inexplicable. On the other hand, the heretics proceeded from a situation proper to the West. Since the development of the West had progressed to a definite maturity, gradually in all aspects of life few efforts to continue the progress of early medieval culture began. Hence, one must not be surprised if religiously oriented natures found the official Church unsatisfying and set about preparing a spirituality of their own. In certain respects, many men did the same even within the Church; especially in the monastic world the inclination to stricter asceticism increased, not to mention the hermit individualists, whose numbers now grew constantly. The heretical movement was only one, in a sense the negative side of a religiosity inclining to radicalism, which at that time took hold of Western Christianity.

The more men were attracted by religious and ascetical ideals, the more clearly did certain moral abuses of the early medieval Church enter into the reflexive awareness. Criticism was directed especially against clerical marriage and against simoniacal or quasi-simoniacal practices.

In actuality, celibacy, to which the Western Church had bound major clerics since the fourth and fifth centuries, had to a great extent fallen into oblivion. In almost all countries the rural priests cohabited with women, either in concubinage or in a real marriage. Not a few clerics or canons attached to urban churches followed their example. There were even isolated cases of bishops or, in decayed monasteries, monks, who had wife and children. Concubinage on the part of a bishop, monk, or canon was pretty generally held to be intolerable, whereas in regard to the rural clergy it was to a great extent tolerated. Their lower origin, inadequate theological and spiritual formation, a very limited supervision by the ecclesiastical superiors, the fact that rural life was extremely difficult without a woman's aid — all these circumstances had contributed to alienate the rustic priests from the idea of celibacy; it was too lofty to be understood by them and by a great many of their parishioners. If isolated bishops, such as Atto of Vercelli, Rathier of Verona, and Dunstan of Canterbury, or even synods, and finally the Council of Bourges (1031) again enjoined the obligation of celibacy, they were to a great extent speaking to the wind. The solicitude of the official Church was concerned in this regard not least of all for Church property, for as far as possible it was made use of to provide for priests' children. To meet this danger most of all the Synod of Pavia in 1022 issued strict decrees at the instigation of Pope Benedict VIII. Economic motives were, of course, powerless in the face of so elementary an impulse as lay behind clerical marriage. Celibacy had to be sincerely approved by more extensive strata of Christendom; its violation had to be abhorred. And this is exactly what gradually took place. Though the movement at first may have found only a few followers, it slowly grew to such strength that it could be applied by the reformed papacy in the second half of the century. At the same time "Nicolaitism," meaning "lechery," appeared as the shibboleth for clerical marriage.

Simony constituted a very complex problem. From Simon Magus, who wanted to obtain from the Apostles by money the power to impart the Spirit (Acts 8:18–24), simony was and still is understood as the buying or selling of spiritual goods. If in Roman times and the early Middle Ages fees were not infrequently required for consecrations, the sacraments, burials, the taking possession of office, and so forth, this was to a great extent connected with legal customs. There was, to be sure, the danger of slipping in this way into real simony. Hence, from the fourth century synods and councils issued strict prohibitions; they even condemned payments connected with temporal goods that belonged to the Church. Gregory the Great went a step farther. He distinguished three rather than merely one form of simony: the *munus a manu* (money or gift), *munus ab obsequio* (services, favors) *munus a lingua* (intercession). He likewise energetically took up the notion, already developed, of *haeresis simoniaca:* whoever sinned against the Holy Spirit by simony should be regarded as a heretic.

Despite so universal a condemnation, the real situation could be controlled all the less when the young Germanic nations developed for Church administration forms that corresponded to their agrarian culture: proprietary church investiture, and the rest. They slowly reversed the original relationship between function and ecclesiastical property. Whereas, according to the Roman and the ecclesiastical idea the function was in the center and the Church property constituted an appendage specified for the support of the minister and for other tasks, in the canon law as stamped by Germanic notions the property law aspect moved into first place, the priest necessary for the function of the Church into second place. As a consequence, churches could be sold or otherwise alienated in whole or in part and payments could be demanded in making an appointment to a church. Since investiture at the same time handed over the function, the payments connected with it had at least the appearance of simony.

With each investiture was involved the acceptance of specified services. According to circumstances additional obligations were also required, and often enough the candidates made use of the intercession of influential persons. Accordingly, the three varieties of simony as defined by Gregory the Great were everywhere in use. Since those invested cherished the understandable desire to recover their expenses from church and office, not a few demanded money for purely spiritual official acts and hence fell into real simony. Whoever applied the strict standards of Gregory the Great and of the ancient synodal laws could not but regard the simoniacal heresy as one of the worst ills of the time.

Hence, there was no lack of warning voices. Atto of Vercelli and Rathier of Verona called for correction. Abbo of Fleury even more decisively took up the ancient ecclesiastical legislation and Gregory the Great's statements against simony; he was actually the first to enter into the juridical problem. To the distinction, complete in his day, between the altar as the sphere of the bishop and the proprietary church as the sphere of the proprietor and the resulting conclusion that the financial operations had nothing to do with the grace of the Holy Spirit but with the ecclesiastical property, Abbo opposed the inseparable unity of altar and church; any commercial activity within this entire holy field was, in his view, simony. The more the conscience became refined, the sharper was the reaction against the juridical forms of the age.

When William of Volpiano, the later Abbot of Saint-Bénigne de Dijon, was supposed to take the customary oath of loyalty to the officiating bishop before his ordination as a deacon at Locedia, he rejected it as a simoniacal demand. An ordination, he said, must not be purchased by anything, not even by an oath of loyalty. In any case, William of Volpiano, from the time he ruled Saint-Bénigne and made it the center of a reform group, propagated his own special hatred of simony not only among his monks but on the outside. And he was not alone. Monastic circles, hermits, heretical communities — all contributed to the forming of an antisimoniacal movement. Their criticism found an increasing response in areas which were especially susceptible in regard to abuses, above all in Italy.

The danger from simony did not come merely from lay persons; clerics, high and low, even monastic circles contributed to it. Still, there was a distinction: clerics or monks could more easily be subjected to the ecclesiastical norms than could laymen. Hence a thorough reform could not escape a confrontation in principle with the rights of domination which the nobility, headed by the kingship, had acquired over many churches. Here basic principles of the Roman ecclesiastical constitution had been covered over with institutions of the Germanic type of canon law. Once persons became more keenly aware of this, the religious and political world of the early Middle Ages began to totter. Deep realization of the sort tends to mature slowly, and so in the period under consideration only isolated voices were heard in criticism. Hence Henry III and the German bishops could only feel that Halinard's refusal of the oath of loyalty was virtually an attack on the royal theocracy and the Imperial Church. It is to Henry's honor that, at the request of Lotharingian bishops, he dispensed Halinard from the oath.

Shortly after the Synod of Sutri the unknown author of *De ordinando pontifice* began the most radical attack on the royal theocracy in general, especially that of Henry III. No lay person, according to him, might appoint clerics and dispose of Church goods not even the Emperor; the election of Clement II, occurring at Henry's instigation, was invalid; moreover, the power of the sword belonging to kings pertained to the sphere of the devil rather than of God; in any event, Emperors were subject to the bishops and, like all the laity, to Church discipline. Even if this treatise were not of French but of Lotharingian provenance, it would be difficult to include it in the intellectual *milieu* constituted by Wazo, for it goes far beyond Wazo's attitude, which, despite everything, was loyal to the crown.

How much the Church was able to display of the new initiative from the turn of the millennium was apparent in the movement of the Peace of God and of the Truce of God. The Midi was their place of origin. The process of political decomposition, which was especially active there, which fragmented the counties into power districts of viscounts, *châtelains,* and lords and furthered club-law, caused the bishops to intervene. The first to undertake self-help was the Bishop of Le Puy. At a synod in 975 he compelled the nobility by force to promise under oath not to attack the goods of the Church and of the *pauperes* and to give back what they had taken. We hear nothing more about similar efforts until the Council of Charroux in 989, representing the ecclesiastical province of Bordeaux. With it began the long series of synods which were to exert themselves for peace throughout the entire eleventh century and into the twelfth and partly even into the thirteenth. Although the goal was sought in various ways, certain basic trends can be isolated. The eleventh century efforts were welcomed, on the one hand, by the great princes and the King and, on the other hand, by the lesser folk; the middle and lower nobility, on the contrary, from whose ranks proceeded to a great extent the brigandage and violence complained about, held back and, according to circumstances, offered resistance. Occasionally, such peace synods were convoked, not directly by the bishops, but by secular magnates.

The powerful popular participation gave to not a few councils the character of a mass demonstration. Monks or clerics took care to bring along the relics of the titular saints of their churches in solemn procession, miraculous cures took place, a religious enthusiasm seized hold of the crowd and broke out into the cry, "Pax, pax, pax," while the bishops, in confirming the peace decrees, raised their croziers to heaven. This has been correctly called the first popular religious movement.

The masses went along, because the proclaimed peace was to protect not merely the churches and their ministers but also the bodies and property of the peasants and at times also of tradesmen. The Church brought her spiritual penal authority to bear against violators of the peace. The interdict, laid on the territory ruled by the guilty person, proved to be an effective collective penalty. Entirely new was the peace oath, which many synods required of the nobility. Furthermore, there was taken up at various times the obvious idea of having legal proceedings take the place of the feud. People did not even shrink from recourse to compulsion by war. There also arose peace militias prepared for war. Probably no one exerted himself so much for them, at least until 1050, as did Archbishop Aimo of Bourges, and with their aid he put a stop to the activities of many a robber knight. The slogan "war on war" was successfully taken up in many places in the second half of the century.

The Truce of God constituted a special form of the general peace movement. It consisted of the prohibition of feuds on specified days of the week. In most cases the suspension of hostilities was to last from Wednesday evening till early on Monday, but there were also briefer periods of respite. Attempts to extend it to longer periods, for example from Advent to the octave day of the Epiphany or from the beginning of Lent to Low Sunday, as well as to special feasts had little success. In themselves the decrees issued for the protection of clerics and peasants remained in force, but the old and frequently recalled duty of carrying conflicts over property before the judge steadily declined.

The origin of the Truce of God is obscure. We first meet it in 1027 in the acts of the Council of Toulouges (Roussillon). The idea spread quickly in the 1030s, first in Burgundy and Aquitaine and from there throughout France. It entered Spain, chiefly by way of Catalonia, while in 1037 and 1042 appeals made by the French episcopate and the propaganda of Odilo of Cluny propagated it in northwest Italy; Germany accepted it only toward the end of the century. However one prefers to interpret the Truce as a giving way, in the guise of a compromise, vis-à-vis the all too tense earlier efforts, or simply as a new initiative alongside the other exertions in any event it gave the peace movement fresh stimulation, especially since recourse was had both to the commitment under oath and to warlike compulsion.

Although the movement of the Peace and Truce of God attained its real goal only very imperfectly and even then only for a limited time, it was of importance as a pioneer. The fact that the French episcopate not only, as earlier, supported the crown in its care for the public order, but also worked for peace on its own authority gained it a new relationship to the Christian world. In itself this had long been based on the religious and political cultural unity of the early Middle Ages and the resulting cooperation of *Regnum* and *Sacerdotium,* but up till now the *Sacerdotium* had had to leave the constructing of a Christian world first of all to the crown, for only a hard fist could create order. Meanwhile, however, the ratio of forces had shifted: in France the *Regnum* had become weak, while the *Sacerdotium* had increased in authority as a consequence of the continually growing Christianization of the West. Its endeavors for peace found all the more assent in that, for medieval men, standing under Augustine's intellectual influence, *pax* and *iustitia* were rooted ultimately in the religious and supernatural and so directly concerned the *Sacerdotium.* And since, on the one hand, at that time the awareness of natural law began to lose its force in connection with the land and the people and, on the other hand, the secular, rational law that could be effectively enforced by a sovereign was still to be created, people and princes were especially amenable to the religious guarantee provided for the peace. Thus in the question of peace the French episcopate was able to stress a law fundamental for the Church's future position of leadership: the competence of the *Sacerdotium* for the spiritual and political goals of Western Christendom. Also pointing to the future was the practice now appearing whereby the Church summoned high and low alike to arms against violators of the peace and set in motion small or large armies. Thus the idea of the holy war was already present basically and with it the legal claim of the *Sacerdotium* to be allowed to exercise armed compulsion by means of laymen when essential interests of Christianity were threatened.

The idea of the holy war was to find powerful expression in the crusades. These, it is true, especially concerned knights, but the Church began even in the tenth century to assume a new attitude toward this social class. If previously the liturgical prayers had envisaged the King as the defender of the Christian religion, and even occasionally the army which he led, they were slowly applied also to the knight and to his vocation to war and found expression above all in the blessing of the sword with which the young knight was girded at his investiture. Formulas appearing in the second half of the tenth century assigned to the individual knight the protection of churches, widows, and orphans, as well as the defense of Christendom against pagans hence specific royal duties — and in direct imitation of the texts of the anointing of a King. Soon after, at the latest in the eleventh century, there was a transition from the blessing of the sword as a thing to a dedication of the person of the knight; then regular liturgical *ordines* were composed, in which the knight was solemnly inducted into his armed vocation. This development, completed in various countries, and especially in Germany, could not but acquire an up-to-dateness of its own by means of the initiative of the French episcopate in the Peace of God. However, the Church in France more and more disregarded the hesitations which opposed the notion of war by recourse to the oldest Christian tradition, despite the protests of individuals, such as Fulbert of Chartres. In the emerging idea of the holy war ideals lay at hand which were able to inspire knighthood so long as it was directed to the great aim the defense of

Christendom from Islam. The crusade idea was in the making. There is no doubt that reform was brought about by abuses that had crept in, but its real motivating power was to be sought at a deeper level. Simony, clerical concubinage, a piety that was too external and too much oriented to a legalistic view of achievements, and other maladies had long been connected with Western Christendom. That there occurred a sharper reaction against them in the eleventh century was the consequence of a process of maturation: the West was slowly moving from the early into the high Middle Ages.

Until around 1000 the Roman-Germanic community of nations was in the stage of coherence typical of early cultures. It was permeated with spiritual and secular forms of life: *Regnum* and *Sacerdotium,* law morality, religion. Man felt himself to be hidden in this world, all-integrating, sacral-sacramental, even interspersed with magical notions, so long as it corresponded to his own inner condition and he accepted it without discussion as objective reality handed down by the ancestors. But as soon as he began to become intellectually more awake, he entered into a new historical stage: into that of diastase. This occurred from the turn of the millennium. The old unity of culture was not destroyed, but the eye now took in its individual components. In a constantly growing process of differentiation they became more clearly distinct, were contrasted with one another, were slowly completed as special spheres. Naturally, this did not occur without tensions and struggles.

Part Two

The Struggle
for the Freedom of the Church

Section One

The Gregorian Reform

Friedrich Kempf

CHAPTER 107

Beginning of the Reform:
The German Popes (1040 to 1057)

There can be no doubt that the Gregorian reform began with the German Popes. Even the unusual names assumed by Clement II, Damasus II, and Victor II revealed the desire to return to the old, pure Church, but this wish was directed merely to a moral renewal which attacked simony and Nicolaitism. It never entered the mind of these Popes, designated by the Emperor and loyally devoted to him, to undermine the foundation of the Carolingian-Ottonian cultural unity. And yet, once the reform got underway, it was to produce something like an avalanche. The future development was already in preparation under Leo IX.

The first two German Popes did not really get into action. A reform synod arranged by Clement II and Henry III did actually come out against simony on 5 January 1047, threatening the sale of ecclesiastical offices and consecrations with anathema and imposing the moderate penalty of a forty-days' penance on priests who knowingly let themselves be ordained by simonists, but for the time being its decrees remained merely a program. The Pope accompanied the Emperor on his expedition through South Italy, then returned to Rome, and in the summer heat caught malaria. As a consequence, he died on 9 October.

The new negotiations ended at Christmas 1048 with the designation of Bruno of Toul. A more fortunate choice could hardly have been made. The nominee was highly gifted and only forty-six years old. Born of the Alsatian family of the Counts of Egisheim, that was related to the Salian Dynasty, he was educated at Toul, of which he was made Bishop in 1026. He had been tested and proved in the service of both the Empire and Church reform. On 12 February 1049, he entered the Eternal City in the dress of a pilgrim, and, having been elected by clergy and people, ascended the throne of Peter as Leo IX; the reform thereby finally got under way.

The very election somehow indicated this, for Bruno had declared to the Emperor that he could enter upon the new post only if the Romans unanimously accepted him as Bishop. As little as this demand actually involved anything new — no contemporary doubted that a designation without an election following was contrary to canon law — it was still unusual to say as much to the Emperor. Bruno probably did not thereby intend to come out against the right of nomination but rather, in an authentic Lotharingian awareness of the freedom of the Church, to express that the election was an essential institution of canon law, binding in conscience, and not a mere formality. In the same spirit he caused the necessity of canonical election to be insisted upon universally at the Council of Reims in 1049. Neither here nor in his much discussed monastic policy did he display any taking of a stand against the laity or even a project of a Papal Church as opposed to the Imperial Church. Leo did not strive for any overthrow of the constitution but he was well aware of the independence of the ecclesiastical juridical order and hence of his own position.

The new Pope immediately collected around him a group of capable co workers, whom he got mostly from Lotharingia and neighboring areas. Apart from Halinard, who remained Archbishop of Lyons but was always at the disposal of the friendly Pope, these men were incardinated into the diocese of Rome and assigned functions. It was they who, even after Leo's early death, energetically pushed the reform work. It must suffice to name only the most important: Humbert, from the monastery of Moyenmoutier, in the diocese of Toul, Cardinal Bishop of Silva Candida from 1050; Frederick, son of the Duke of Lotharingia and Archdeacon of Liège, Chancellor of the Roman Church from 1051 to 1055, and eventually Pope as Stephen IX; Hugh the White, from the monastery of Rémiremont in the diocese of Toul, later Cardinal Priest; and Hildebrand, whom Bruno had brought with him to Rome, perhaps as the contact with the Roman reform circles, and there ordained a subdeacon and entrusted with the administration of the property of the monastery of San Paolo *fuori le mura*. Without knowing it, Leo IX thereby made ready a fateful development. While he and his successors involved outstanding officials of the Roman clergy ever more actively in the reform of the Universal Church over and above their liturgical duties, there slowly developed the stable institution of the College of Cardinals, as the liturgical functions connected with the titular churches and the papal Masses were de-emphasized.

Another innovation also appeared more clearly. Unlike his predecessors, Leo IX did not reside in Rome. Restless, like the secular rulers of the day, he travelled from country to country. From 1050 South Italy saw him every year, and his three long journeys across the Alps took him not only in all directions through imperial territory but as far as Reims and in 1052, in order to mediate peace, even to the Emperor's camp before Bratislava. Reform synods interrupted his movements. Since the Pope was everywhere approached for privileges but the chancery was localized in Rome, new methods of documentary authentication had to be found, which gradually detached the chancery from the city of Rome and allowed it to become an independent administrative organ of the papacy. And finally Leo's journeys meant incalculable gain for papal authority. While people had already always regarded the Bishop of Rome as head of the Universal Church, now this idea took on flesh and blood a great part of Christendom looked at the Pope with its own eyes and let itself be captivated by the spell of his very being.

Three heavy tasks were imposed upon Leo IX: the reform of the Church, the struggle with the Normans of South Italy, and the confrontation with the Byzantine Church, which was to end in schism.

Reform centered on simony and Nicolaitism. Because the disregard of celibacy was so widespread, especially among the lower clergy, whom the Pope could reach only with difficulty, Leo took rather strong action only in Rome and its environs, forbidding the faithful by means of Roman Synods to have anything to do with incontinent priests and having the concubines of Roman priests reduced to slavery for the service of the Lateran Palace. Otherwise he was content with general prohibitions of clerical marriage. His real fight was with simony. Simoniacal bishops of France and, to some extent, also of Italy — in Germany Leo evidently relied upon the Emperor's opposition to simony — learned by experience the total seriousness of the synodal decrees of Rome, Reims, and Mainz (1049). The investigations, punishments, and depositions that now began were not to stop for decades.

The struggle was by no means always successful. That it did not flag but was waged with increasing exasperation was due to a special reason. Leo IX and his friends were concerned with something much deeper than the extirpation of a vice: the substance of the faith and the sacramental life seemed to them to be in jeopardy. Their refined religious conscience was dead serious about the denunciation, familiar since the fourth century, of simony as heresy, regardless whether, with Humbert, they believed that the divinity of the Holy Spirit was directly denied in the selling of holy orders and offices or, with Peter Damiani, assumed only an indirect attack on the faith. Moreover, they saw the mystery of the Church betrayed. The simonists, they complained, obstructed the free operation of the Spirit, falsified the correct relationship of Christ to the Church, and degraded the *sponsa Christi* to a prostitute, while the Nicolaites dishonored the spiritual marriage of the priest and the bishop with his church. Leo IX was especially distressed for the pastoral care of the souls of the faithful. Convinced, with Humbert of Silva Candida, that a simoniacal bishop could not confer valid orders, he wondered whether in the Church, so infected with simony, there were still enough priests who were able to dispense to the faithful the Sacraments that were necessary for their salvation. His attempt in 1049 to have all simoniacal ordinations declared invalid collapsed on the opposition of the Roman Synod, but, to be on the safe side, he not infrequently had simoniacally ordained bishops and priests "reordained." However exaggerated or incorrect the theological motives of the reformers in their struggle were to some extent, they did not spring from blind fanaticism but from an honestly endured anxiety, which was justified to this extent that a whole network of economic and political interests had fallen upon the great and the lesser churches.

Leo's reordinations called theologians into the arena. Peter Damiani wrote his *Liber gratissimus,* in which he developed the theologically correct view of the validity of simoniacal ordinations, while Humbert of Silva Candida maintained their nullity in the first two books of his *Adversus simoniacos.* Thus sacramental theology fell again into a state of flux; it complicated the problem of simony and was complicated by it. It was no accident that shortly before this Berengarius of Tours had precipitated the eucharistic controversy, in which Leo intervened in 1050 against Berengarius at the Synods of Rome and Vercelli. The problem of simony was only one facet of a complete revolution: the forms of the life of the early medieval religious and political world had become questionable, so that from various sides the duty was imposed on the Church of exploring more exactly her proper activity in the world by virtue of the Sacraments and of their ministers.

In another matter also the reform of itself led beyond the purely moral sphere. Forced by the struggle against simony to use the papal rights more energetically, Leo IX opened a new period in the history of the primacy. Other circumstances intervened favorably. The decree of the Council of Reims reserving to the Bishop of Rome the designation "universalis ecclesiae primas et apostolicus" concerned only a title, but the conflict with the Byzantine Church gave to Leo's adviser, Humbert of Silva Candida, the opportunity to expound vigorously to Michael Cerularius the greatness of the Roman Church in two works of which only fragments are extant and in a long doctrinal treatise. The canonical collection in seventy-four titles, *Diversorum sententiae patrum,* composed in Leo's lifetime or soon after, perhaps also goes back to Humbert. It took up the reform ideas in their entirety, reorganized them, and elaborated the leading position of the papacy.

The reform so happily introduced was soon overshadowed by the anxiety caused to the Pope by the Normans of South Italy. Ever since Benedict VIII had introduced Norman warriors to the South Italian Melo, in revolt against Byzantine rule, more and more knights had come from Normandy across the Alps to seek their fortune in the service now of one, now of another lord. They slowly established themselves. When in 1047 Henry III ceded the territory of the rebel Prince of Benevento to the Normans, whom he probably confirmed in their holdings, they attacked and by 1059 brought the greater part of the principality under their power.

At first Leo IX was not hostile to them, and in 1050 he had even accepted their homage in his own name and that of the Emperor. In the justified hope of recovering by their aid the jurisdiction over South Italy and Sicily that had been lost to the Roman Church since the Emperor Leo III, he then named Humbert as Archbishop of Sicily. But in the long run he could not remain deaf to the complaints of the population about the injustices of the Norman lords. But when these died violent deaths, Drogo in 1051 and Waimar in 1052, he saw no other possibility than an effort to drive out the Normans forever, preferably in union with the Byzantines. Their governor, a South Italian and son of Melo, who had failed tragically, had offered an alliance.

And so in 1052 Leo sought out the Emperor in Germany. Henry fell in with his plans and, in exchange for the cession of his rights of proprietorship to the see of Bamberg and to Fulda and other monasteries, gave him the Principality of Benevento and other imperial holdings in Italy, either as his own or at least for the exercise of the imperial authority. He even wanted to send an imperial army against the Normans, but let himself be dissuaded from this project by the objections of his chancellor, Bishop Gebehard of Eichstätt. Since Leo thought that he could not wait any longer, he recruited a small army of German knights at his own expense, combined it with Italian troops, and led his men south. Before his army could join the Byzantines, it was overwhelmed near Civitate, south of the Frento, on 16 June 1053, and the Pope became the Normans' prisoner.

The miserable failure of the campaign, anxiety about reform, and the conflict with the Patriarch of Constantinople, which, with the departure of the papal legates, was now moving toward misfortune, broke the Pope's spirit. Escorted back to Rome, Leo IX died on 19 April 1054.

After long negotiations Henry III definitely designated as Pope his chancellor, Gebehard of Eichstätt, in March 1055. Styling himself Victor II, he took possession of the Roman Church on 13 April. Although he was more directly involved in imperial politics than his predecessor, Victor energetically championed the reform. Together with the Emperor he held a reform synod at Florence in 1055 and on other occasions also took energetic action with authoritative measures. In France in 1056 important reform councils were organized by the Archbishops of Arles and Aix, in their capacity as legates, at Toulouse, and by the Roman legate Hildebrand, probably at Chalon-sur-Saône. Hildebrand's appointment shows that the new Pope did not disregard the co-workers of Leo IX who were still in Rome; Humbert's influence even grew constantly. But the chancellor, Frederick of Lotharingia, had to escape the clutches of Henry III, because of the political tensions between his brother Godfrey and the Emperor, by entering Montecassino. Godfrey the Bearded, for years at loggerheads with the Emperor, had married Beatrice of Tuscany, widow of the assassinated Marquis Boniface, and thereby provoked the Emperor to make an Italian expedition. Godfrey fled to safety.

His intimate relationship with the Emperor enabled Victor to gain the administration of the duchy of Spoleto and of the marquisate of Fermo. While the vested rights of the Roman Church to specific territories there may have played a role, the Emperor was especially influenced by the motive of enlarging the area under the rule of the German Pope in the interests of the Empire vis-à-vis Tuscany and the Normans. The death of Henry III on 5 October 1056 was to involve Victor still more powerfully in imperial politics. Entrusted by the dying Emperor with the care of the Empire and of his son, not yet six years old but already elected King, Victor managed through his diplomatic skill to assure the succession of Henry IV and the appointment of the boy's mother as regent; for the Empress he also gained the right to designate a successor in the event of the death of her son, a service which Gregory VII was later to make use of. That he furthermore made peace between the imperial house and Godfrey the Bearded, by having Lower Lotharingia and Tuscany restored to Godfrey, gained the Duke's friendship for him and for the Roman Church. It was soon to be of the greatest use to the reformers.

When Victor returned to Italy in February 1057 his days were numbered. Visiting Central Italy after a Roman reform synod, he died at Arezzo on 28 July. With him ended the series of German reform Popes. His successor belonged also to the Empire, it is true, but his election took place under other conditions.

CHAPTER 108

Progress of the Reform: the Lotharingian and Tuscan Popes (1057 to 1073)

The unexpected death of Victor II confronted the reformers with the question of how they could preserve the papacy from a new Tusculan domination. The only one who was able to assure them of effective help — Henry IV and his weak mother, the Empress-Regent, were not considered — was Godfrey the Bearded, Duke of Upper Lotharingia and Marquis of Tuscany. The reformers knew how to gain his support. They chose his own brother as Pope and then selected the next two Popes from the Tuscan episcopate.

Nothing so clearly reflects the insecure situation of the Roman Church as does the elevation of the three Lotharingian and Tuscan Popes. The first election was the smoothest. The reformers forestalled any maneuver on the part of the nobility by quick action. Three days after receiving the news of Victor's death they elected Frederick of Lotharingia, who happened to be in Rome, and then had him consecrated and enthroned as Stephen IX on the next day, 3 August 1057. Time did not allow a consultation with the German court; apart from the emergency, the King's minority may have been a further excuse. In any event this unauthorized procedure was probably not based on the intention of excluding for the future any participation by the German ruler in the election. In the autumn Stephen IX sent Hildebrand to Germany; it may with good reason be assumed that he was supposed to justify the unusual papal election before the royal court and obtain its belated approval.

With Stephen IX there came to power a man from the school of Leo IX. After Henry III's death Victor II had brought him out of obscurity again, forced his election as Abbot of Montecassino, and made him Cardinal-Priest of San Crisogono. In accord with his most recent past, the new Pope strengthened the monastic element among the reformers. For decades thereafter Montecassino rendered valuable services to the Roman Church, and the hermit movement, especially at home in Central Italy and so important for the reform, now acquired an official influence in the sense that Stephen made its most important representative, the Prior of Fonte Avellana, Peter Damiani, Cardinal-Bishop of Ostia. But the pontificate was too brief for anything decisive to have taken place. Of a Roman Synod arranged in 1057 only strict decrees against clerical marriage are known today. The Pope entertained great plans for South Italy: resuming the policy of Leo IX, he thought of expelling the Normans. An embassy headed by Desiderius of Montecassino was to leave for Constantinople when, during a journey through Tuscany, Stephen died at Florence on 29 March 1058.

Having a foreboding of his death, Stephen, before leaving Rome, had had the clergy and people swear not to proceed to the election of his successor until Hildebrand had returned from Germany. This, however, did not prevent the Tusculans, right after receipt of the news of Stephen's death, from tumultuously elevating Bishop John of Velletri as Benedict X and, because Peter Damiani refused, having him enthroned by the Archpriest of Ostia. The reformers did not recognize the election. After Hildebrand's return they agreed, with the support of Godfrey of Lotharingia, on Bishop Gerard of Florence, a Burgundian by birth, and obtained the assent of the German court. Finally, the Pope-elect, who styled himself Nicholas II, escorted by the Tuscan army under Godfrey's command, set out for Rome with the cardinal-bishops and with Guibert, imperial chancellor of Italy, who was probably sent by the German government. He excommunicated the Antipope at a synod held at Sutri, and, because Benedict X fled, was able to enter the Eternal City, where he was enthroned on 24 January 1059.

With Nicholas II a new trend in the reform began to show itself. Five cardinal-bishops had dared, contrary to custom, to elect a Pope outside Rome in alliance with a few friends of reform and with the German ruler. In the third book of *adversus simoniacos,* probably composed in 1058, Humbert of Silva Candida shows that this was more than an exceptional case, that among the reformers the realization was then gaining ground that, for the sake of the freedom of the Church, they must be prepared to eliminate traditional juridical rights. If in the earlier books he had sought to demonstrate the invalidity of simoniacal ordinations and the absolutely heretical character of simony, he now investigated the causes of this evil.

What actually made it impossible to eradicate simony was its involvement with the contemporary world. The simoniacal gift, *munus a manu,* as well as the services and the interventions connected with the attaining of an office, which since Gregory I had been reckoned as simony, *munus ab obsequio* and *munus a lingua,* were not based really on a simoniacal intention but on juridical and lifelong habits, conditioned by the times and bound up with the proprietary church system. Selecting the chief cause, then, Humbert condemned lay investiture as an unlawful abuse and as a perversion of the proper relationship between priests and laity. He stressed the perversion especially in regard to episcopal elections: Whereas, according to the ancient rules, first the clergy, in agreement with the view of the metropolitan, then the people with the subsequent assent of the prince, were to elect, now the decision of the prince came first, and the rest of the electors, with the metropolitan in the last place, had to conform blindly. Humbert thereby indicated the aims of the reform, which were directed not merely at moral and religious abuses but against the religious and political world of the early Middle Ages in general. Despite specific differences, his attitude was also shared by other reformers. It led to a greater freedom of the Roman Church and to a more radical fight for moral reform.

The freedom of the Roman Church was arranged by the papal election decree, which Nicholas II issued at the Roman Synod of 1059 in order to legalize his own election and to guarantee future papal elections. It provided for a threefold act of election: the cardinal bishops deliberated and then brought in the cardinal clerics; the rest of the clergy and the Roman people assented to the decision reached by them. Just as Humbert assigned to the metropolitan the first place in the carrying out of an episcopal election, the papal election decree put the cardinal bishops in the leading place, calling them, significantly, quasi-metropolitans. Their right was so extensive that, in the event of a substantial encroachment on the freedom of the election by the Romans, they could arrange the papal election outside Rome, having recourse to a few religious clerics and lay persons; the Pope thus elected, even if he had not yet entered Rome and been enthroned there, possessed the full governing authority. With the new law, which again conceived of the Church as a hierarchically arranged authority, running from the top down, the papacy broke away in principle from its connection with the people of the city of Rome. During the vacancy, the real representatives of the Roman Church were the quasi-metropolitan cardinal-bishops. Wherever they and the Pope then elected stayed, whether in or outside Rome, there was the Roman Church. Although the decree was not always observed in the future, still the basic idea expressed in it was established and led in the twelfth century to the exclusive right of the College of Cardinals to take part in the papal election.

By this decree Nicholas II obviously intended only to regulate the specifically Roman situation; he spoke only incidentally of a right belonging to Henry IV and his successors, which he conceded to Henry IV through the intervention of Guibert, Chancellor of Lombardy, and which succeeding rulers were on occasion to secure for themselves. The content of the right was taken for granted. It certainly involved the imperial right of assent. The claim in the decree that the Pope had to grant specially to each succeeding German ruler such a right as a sort of privilege was new. There was here no thought of any arbitrary grant but rather of a confirmation of an old traditional prerogative, which it was not easy to annul. But since privileges could be forfeited, at least by misuse, the hierarchical feature of the decree again came to light in the papal grant of an imperial right: ecclesiastical authority was to be ultimately responsible for everything that concerned the papal election.

Naturally, the law alone was not enough. Benedict X, protected by the Count of Galeria, maintained himself in the vicinity of Rome. Since Godfrey of Lotharingia supplied no help, the Roman Church had to look elsewhere. Her distress induced her, probably at the urging of Abbot Desiderius of Montecassino and of Hildebrand, to make a decision of great portent. Visiting South Italy in the summer of 1059, Nicholas II received feudal homage and the oath of fealty from the Normans, Richard of Aversa, since 1058 Prince of Capua, and Robert Guiscard, Duke of Apulia and Calabria and in return invested them with the territories they had conquered. The new vassals turned over to the Pope the churches of their lands together with the estates and bound themselves to loyal aid and, in the event of a disputed papal election, to the support of the "better cardinals." They paid feudal *census* merely for the parts of the *terra sancti Petri* that they occupied, and Robert Guiscard also for his own property. Richard of Capua immediately took his duties seriously; he destroyed castles and strongholds of Roman nobles, including Galeria, and delivered Benedict X as a prisoner to the Pope.

Hence at one stroke the Roman Church had gained feudal suzerainty over much of Italy.

This time the Roman opposition acted more sensibly, sending to Henry IV the insignia of the dignity of *patricius* and asking for a new Pope. On the other hand, the reformers, led by Hildebrand — Humbert was now dead — on 30 September elected Anselm of Lucca, a Milanese by birth, who called himself Alexander II, and on the next day enthroned him with the aid of the troops of Richard of Capua. Then, at the end of October 1061, Bishop Cadalus of Parma was chosen Pope at the German court in association with the Roman envoys and with Lombard bishops, at the instigation of the Chancellor of Lombardy, Guibert. He called himself Honorius II. The struggle between the two rivals for possession of Rome led to no decision, so that Godfrey of Lotharingia was able to intervene and induce both to retire to their dioceses until a definite decision should be rendered by the King.

Contrary to expectations, the decision favored Alexander, for the *coup d'état* of Kaiserswerth, which removed Henry IV from his mother and made the reform-inclined Archbishop Anno of Cologne the real power, meant a change of policy. The Synod of Augsburg of October 1062, for which Peter Damiani composed his *Disceptatio synodalis,* sent to Italy an investigating commission that was well disposed to Alexander. Hence in 1063 Alexander II was able to enter Rome with Godfrey's aid. Cadalus' desperate attack on Rome was shattered on the weapons of Tuscan and Norman warriors. A synod meeting at Mantua at Pentecost of 1064, in which Anno of Cologne and other German bishops took part, definitively recognized Alexander.

Having emerged victorious from the struggle for her freedom, the Roman Church was able to dedicate herself to reform with redoubled zeal. The pontificate of Nicholas II had prepared for this with important decrees. Thus at the Roman Synod of 1059 clerics and priests were forbidden to acquire a church from lay persons, no matter whether with or without the payment of money. This first attack, undertaken in Humbert's spirit, against lay investiture was, it is true, only in the nature of a program: the decree lacked any sanctions. And so the Cardinal Legate Stephen, sent to France in 1060, did not try to apply it. Alexander II also, who renewed the prohibition in 1063, did not venture upon an open struggle. All the more sternly did the Synod of 1059 proceed against Nicolaitism. Its prohibition of attending the Mass of a married priest must have been all the more effective since already some of the faithful in Lombardy had risen up against Nicolaitism. Another decree suspended those clerics bound to celibacy who had retained a concubine since the regulations of Leo IX. A third law, issued at Hildebrand's urging, commanded the *vita communis et apostolica* for the clerics of one and the same church, thereby fostering the movement of the canons regular, that was destined to be so important.

Simony especially was to be the concern of the two following synods. The decree probably issued in 1060 distinguished among simonists: between those ordained simoniacally by simonists, those ordained simoniacally by non-simonists, and those ordained non simoniacally by simonists. One who belonged to the first two classes was to lose his office, but clerics of the third class, considering the difficulties of the time, might continue in office. Certain obscurities probably moved the Roman Synod of 1061 to explain this decree more precisely and especially to insist that the concession granted to the third class was valid only for persons already ordained and would not hold for the future. Hence, despite Humbert's radical position, the synod left open the theological question of the validity or invalidity of simoniacal ordinations.

Nicholas II reigned too briefly to apply the decree; fully, but a relatively long pontificate (1061–73) was granted to Alexander II, the first reform Pope of whom this is so. Under him the reform reached an unprecedented intensity and expansion. In France, since Leo IX the favorite battle field, papal legates proceeded with synods and processes from 1063 on in almost uninterrupted succession. But even the proud German bishops, who were also vulnerable in consequence of the reintroduction of simoniacal practices by Henry IV, now learned to feel the Pope's heavy hand. Even the young, immature King considered it advisable to abandon the planned repudiation of his wife, Bertha of Turin, when Peter Damiani, sent specifically for this purpose, opposed him and was supported by a German synod.

England too was affected by the reform. The political and ecclesiastical situation at the close of the reign of King Edward the Confessor has already been described. There were two rivals for the succession: Earl Harold of Wessex and Duke William of Normandy. William thought that he could support his claim on an express promise made by Edward. After Edward's death on 5 January 1066, Harold at once had himself raised to the throne, whereupon William invoked the Pope's judgment, accusing Harold of perjury. The difficult legal question was probably less decisive for the Roman Church than the consideration of which of the two claimants supported her in her reform exertions and to that extent was the more fit. From this point of view the choice had to be for William and against Harold, for William had distinguished himself by his zealous promotion of reform in Normandy, without in any way relaxing his control, whereas Harold, in consequence of the earlier related usurpation of the archiepiscopal see of Canterbury, carried out by his partisan, Bishop Stigand of Winchester, and maintained in defiance of specially dispatched papal legates, gave the Roman reformers little or no reason for confidence. Advised by Hildebrand, then, Alexander II decided for the Norman and even sent him a specially blessed banner of Saint Peter for the expedition. Under this banner William and with him the Roman Church were victorious in the Battle of Hastings in 1066.

Alexander's expectation that William would now give England to the Roman Church in fief was not realized, but the King paid Peter's Pence, which had fallen into oblivion, and laid the foundation for a new development of the English Church. That three legates came to England at his request in 1070, held synods, and gave the Anglo-Saxon sees to Norman clerics, and the archbishopric of Canterbury to Abbot Lanfranc of Caen, was, it is true, only an initial success, for William and his immediate successors allowed Rome no great influence, but the closer contact then gained with the Church of the continent remained a fact that was not lost and was capable of being further developed.

The papacy realized still another success in Spain. The monastic reform movement of Cluny and Marseilles had been able to penetrate slowly from the beginning of the century, and now Rome followed. From 1065 to 1067 the Cardinal Legate Hugh the White held reform synods in Castile, Navarre, and Aragón. King Sancho of Aragón went a step further; commended his country to the Pope in 1068 and introduced the Roman liturgy in 1071, whereas the other Christian kingdoms clung for the time being to the traditional Mozarabic liturgy, despite the zealous efforts of Roman legates. At the moment Christian Spain was in the process of gaining ground at Islam's expense.

Portentous decisions occurred in South Italy too. With the capitulation of Bari in 1071 the Byzantines lost their last foothold. Robert Guiscard had already ventured the crossing to Sicily and had taken Messina in 1061; Palermo followed in 1072. Robert's brother Roger, to whom Alexander had sent a banner of Saint Peter in 1063, was to subjugate the island bit by bit and thereby open up to the Roman Church a new sphere of jurisdiction.

Meanwhile, struggles of a different sort were occurring in Lombardy. The upward development of this land had produced a general ferment that affected the religious sphere also, especially in the cities, flourishing by virtue of their trade and industry. Instead of seizing upon the religious currents and leading them into the correct course, the urban clergy, belonging to the nobility and mostly married, persisted in their worldly manner of life and hence provoked the criticism of many of the faithful. This was a criticism supported by a genuine desire for reform, which of itself had nothing to do with tendencies related to class struggles, anticlericalism, or even heresy. In Milan it produced the revolutionary movement of the *Pataria*. Under the leadership of the priest, Ariald of Varese, and of the Milanese noble, Landulf Cotta, a revolt broke out there on 10 May 1057, in which priests were forcibly obliged to celibacy. Stephen IX, approached by both sides, directed Hildebrand, who went to Germany as legate in the autumn of 1057, to go to Milan and gather information. The Pope waited for this, while the opposing groups at Milan consolidated their positions. A synod of bishops at Fontaneto condemned Ariald and Landulf *in absentia,* while the *Patarini* swore not to recognize any married or simoniacal priest. They could feel that they were confirmed in their opposition when in 1059 the Roman Synod issued severe decrees against Nicolaitism.

Nicholas II was well aware of the dangers connected with the *Pataria,* and so toward the end of 1059 he sent to Milan Peter Damiani and Anselm of Lucca; the latter at least sympathized with the *Pataria.* Peter Damiani, by a brilliant exposition of the Roman primacy, succeeded in overcoming the initial resistance of the citizens, who insisted on the special position of the Ambrosian Church, and in establishing order. The clergy swore to give up simoniacal and incontinent ways and obediently accepted the mild penalties imposed for their simoniacal procedures. But Peter had ventured too much. In a clear correction of his too gentle method the Roman Synod of 1060 issued the above mentioned decrees against simony, but it ratified the peace that had been gained by favoring Archbishop Guido, who was present, and rejecting Ariald's complaints.

This submission of the Archbishop was not merely a valuable victory of the idea of the primacy but the best solution of Milan's reform problem. The hierarchically minded reformers could only regard a revolution rising from below as an emergency measure. But since the weak Archbishop Guido let things return to the old groove, the *Pataria,* under the impassioned leadership of Erlembald, a brother of the now dead Landulf, let loose bloody struggles in the summer of 1066 and gained its first martyr in Ariald, who was killed during them. Other cities were also agitated. The people of Cremona drove out married and simoniacal priests; those of Piacenza, their bishop. The peace proclaimed by papal legates in 1067 did not last long. When in 1070 Guido, weary of his office, sent his ring and staff to Henry IV, the King at once invested the distinguished priest Godfrey. This notorious disregard of their right of election induced the Milanese to war against Godfrey, in which Erlembald displayed the banner of Saint Peter that the Pope had sent him. After Guido's death the priest Atto was elected Archbishop of Milan in 1072 under the presidency of a cardinal legate. Schism was the result. Since Henry IV clung to Godfrey, the Pope at the Roman Synod of 1073 excommunicated five royal councillors on a charge of simony.

This conflict between the Pope and the German King in which the Investiture Controversy was already intimated, showed clearly the development that had occurred between 1057 and 1073: the struggle against simony and Nicolaitism had brought on the more serious struggle over the principle of the freedom of the Church. The signs pointed to the storm when Alexander II died on 21 April 1073, for now there mounted the throne of Peter the man who had guided Alexander's policy the Archdeacon Hildebrand.

CHAPTER 109

Pope Gregory VII (1073 to 1085)

The reform entered its critical stage with Gregory VII, who, on 22 April 1073, during the very burial of the deceased Alexander II, was acclaimed as Pope by the Romans in the Lateran basilica and only then was elected at San Pietro in Vincoli by the cardinals and urban clergy and enthroned. For now one of the greatest of Peter's successors took charge of it and breathed his own spirit into it, without altering its substance or goal.

Gregory's age and provenance cannot be precisely determined. Born in Roman Tuscany, possibly at Soana, between 1019 and 1031, the son of Bonizo, who was probably not poverty-stricken but was likewise not of the nobility, Hildebrand went while still young to Rome, where he was educated in the monastery of Santa Maria all'Aventino, ruled by his uncle, and in the *palatium Romanum,* which cannot be more precisely defined. Having received the lower orders, he served Gregory VI, who was on friendly terms with him, as a cleric and accompanied him into exile in Germany. Set at liberty by the death of the deposed Pope in the autumn of 1047, he probably entered Cluny or a Cluniac monastery, but after a few months was summoned by Leo IX, brought back to Rome, and entrusted with the administration of San Paolo *fuori le mura.* The rise of his prestige among the reformers is attested by legations to France in 1054 and 1056 and Germany in 1057 and by his appointment as archdeacon in the autumn of 1059. Under Nicholas II he was regarded as one of the chief advisers, under Alexander II as the most powerful man in the Lateran.

It is not entirely correct to speak of Gregory VII as the monk on the papal throne. Reluctant though he may have been to abandon the monastery he continued to wear the monastic habit and willingly as he made use of monks for the work of reform, he devoted himself resolutely to the apostolic activity imposed upon him; in fact he placed it above the purely monastic ideal in frank criticism of the excessively monastic concept of, for example, Peter Damiani or Hugh of Cluny. For Gregory was profoundly convinced that, ultimately, the great concern in the world was with the struggle between God's Kingdom and that of the devil, with the warlike efforts of God's children that peace, justice, and the love of God might fill as many men as possible. All Christians were summoned to this struggle, but especially the spiritual and secular rulers. Gregory clung to the old view of the world throughout: God's Kingdom was the *ecclesia universalis* with the powers of the *Regnus* and *Sacerdotium* instituted by the Lord; but he intended that God should be again able to act freely in his Kingdom.

Since priests were primarily responsible for divine things, for him the two powers were not simply side by side; the *Sacerdotium* possessed the higher rank, and Gregory did everything to free it again for God's work and to guarantee the authority belonging to it, but one alone could, in his view, claim to be the proper interpreter of the divine will — Peter's vicar in Rome. For Christ, who gave Peter supreme authority and bade him establish the Roman Church, prayed for Peter's faith so that the Roman Church cannot err, and Peter lives on by entering, as Gregory firmly believed, into a sort of personal union with every successor and elevating him, by virtue of his own merits, to a better and holier being. Hence all Christians must obey the Pope, who is responsible for their salvation, and under his leadership fight for the kingdom of God, not only priests and monks who are subject to his superepiscopal authority, but also secular rulers.

With this claim, oriented to the spiritual sphere, Gregory did not intend to strip the *Regnum* of power or to expel it from the *ecclesia universalis;* he only demanded that the ruler really belong to the *corpus Christi.* If by his evil deeds the ruler revealed himself as a member of Satan's Kingdom, then basically he was depriving himself of power; for then he was commanding, no longer in God's name, but in that of the devil, and this contradicted the nature of the *ecclesia universalis.* From this Gregory deduced the radical and then even unheard of conclusion: by virtue of the papal right to decide ultimately who is of God and who is of the devil, he claimed that he could depose an unworthy ruler and free his subjects from their oath of allegiance.

All the more directly did Scripture interest him, especially the New Testament and there, by preference, Saint Paul, a kindred spirit. In addition, he was naturally committed to the ideas which the ecclesiastical *milieu,* with its Augustinian coloring, and the contemporary reform movement brought him, but, apart from the claim to deposition, he neither enriched them with new ideas nor articulated them into a consistent reform program. Withal, Gregory's greatness is to be sought, not in his ideas, but in his religious, perhaps mystically gifted, personality, in the abundance of the divine experience given to him, taken up by his genius, and converted into action.

It would be going too far to say that the measure of his thought and activity could be deduced merely from his personal, religious experience. That Gregory intended to follow ecclesiastical tradition appears in his calling for the drawing up of new compilations of the law, which were to work out the authentic and venerable statements of ecclesiastical tradition that were inspired by the Holy Spirit. Before this wish could be more or less satisfactorily fulfilled by his friends, headed by Anselm of Lucca, he had himself collected canonical material dealing with the Roman primacy, mostly taken from pseudo-Isidore, arranged it in sections, and for each section composed a concise sentence, suggesting the chapter headings of a canonical collection. Thus originated the famed *Dictatus papae,* which was put into Gregory's *registrum* of letters. There in twenty-seven sentences were summarized the most important primatial rights, with no systematization but with the already mentioned prerogatives of the Roman Church — her foundation by Christ and infallibility — and of the papacy — the inherited personal sanctity of the Pope and his right of deposition: the honorary privileges, including that of having his foot kissed and the exclusive right to use the imperial insignia, this last probably directed against the Byzantine Patriarch; the supreme legislative and judicial power and its effects; superepiscopal authority with regard to the deposition and institution of bishops, ordaining of clerics, determining of diocesan boundaries, and so forth; and excommunication and absolution from oaths as a consequence of the papal coercive power. The listing was not oriented to a concrete goal, connected with the reform or with negotiations for union. It was supposed merely to provide a synopsis of the primatial rights as they could be identified in tradition. Its use depended on the situation of the moment, that is, on the question, to be constantly investigated anew in the concrete case, whether and to what extent the interests of God's Kingdom required an intervention.

Gregory's election was charged with the tensions in regard to Henry IV which, because of the Milanese question, had clouded the last days of Alexander II. They probably did not permit an application to the young King for his approval of the election. Since Henry continued to associate with the excommunicated advisers and hence fell under the ban himself, no notice of the election was probably sent to him. It remained to be seen whether the King would react, but he did not. And, when the Saxon revolt broke out, he threw himself, so to speak, at the Pope's feet in an extravagantly humble letter in which he acknowledged his failings. Gregory could breathe freely and turn to the great concern of his heart, the reform.

The Reform

The first Roman Reform Synod, that of 1074, renewed the old rules, decreeing exclusion from the ministry for simony, suspension for Nicolaitism. The synod of the following year drew the reins tighter: for simonists it now decreed permanent deposition, while in regard to incontinent priests it referred to the regulation of 1059, calling for a boycott by the people. Resistance was not lacking; in particular the requirement of celibacy encountered widespread rejection. Polemical writings appeared, and there were scenes of violence at Rouen and in several places in Germany. But Gregory was unmoved. The Roman Synod in the autumn of 1078 obliged every bishop, under pain of suspension, not to tolerate any *fornicatio* among his clergy. Furthermore, priests who sold their official functions were suspended. The most decisive blow had to do with ordinations. The spring Synod of 1078 declared all ordinations performed by the excommunicated to be legally invalid (*irritas*), the autumn synod of that year decreed the same thing for ordinations which were imparted for money or as a result of petition or services or without the consent of clergy and people and without the approval of the proper ecclesiastical superiors. Although both decrees most probably did not intend to decide the dogmatic question of the sacramental validity or invalidity of such orders, their obscure wording increased the existing uncertainty. This is to be observed in Gregory VII himself. On the one hand, he avoided taking a stand on the dogmatic question; on the other hand, he allowed his legate, Amatus of Oléron, to have his own way when at the Synod of Gerona in 1078 he declared the absolute nullity of simoniacal ordinations. Hence it should cause no surprise that the question came up in the polemics and in general caused much unrest.

But the question of investiture made the conflict more bitter. Here Gregory was probably led into a quarrel that he had not sought. At first he entirely disregarded the decree promulgated by Nicholas II and renewed by Alexander II but never enforced. He did not have recourse to it until the Lenten Synod of 1075. Even if he is supposed to have then duly published the decree, this was probably done at first without great emphasis. Perhaps it would have played no great role in Gregory's reform work, had not something unforeseen intervened — Henry IV's extravagant counterattack in 1076. For then Gregory became inexorable. He not only insisted on the prohibition for Germany. He had it promulgated in France by his legates in 1077 and more precisely formulated at the Roman autumn Synod of 1078: it was forbidden to clerics, under penalty of excommunication and annulment of the completed action, to accept from a layman the investiture of bishoprics, abbeys, and churches. The Lenten Synod of 1080 decreed the same but expressly extended the prohibition to lesser ecclesiastical functions and now also visited excommunication on the investing layman. The Investiture Controversy that thereby erupted but by no means affected all countries was not to be settled for decades.

Gregory was here concerned, not for a question of power, and far less for economic interests, but for reform, which, in his view, could only be achieved when the appointing of priests and bishops, freed from the smothering influence of kings and proprietors of churches, again took place according to the canonical rules, which gave scope to the divine activity. The free election envisaged by the old canon law required, of course, a further guarantee, and Gregory did not hesitate to set it up. A decree of the Lenten Synod of 1080 not only enjoined the control of elections provided by the old law, which was now to be exercised by a bishop named as visitor, and the confirmation of the election by the metropolitan or the Pope. It also laid the foundation for the hitherto unknown right of devolution: in the event of an uncanonical election the electors' right to fill the office was to pass to the metropolitan or to the Pope. What the papal election decree of 1059 had imperfectly attempted, by empowering the quasi-metropolitan cardinal-bishops to choose the new Pope outside Rome in an emergency, was in 1080 perfectly achieved for the instituting of bishops. The final decision no longer lay with the electors, among whom the secular ruler had spoken the decisive word, but with the ecclesiastical authority: the hierarchical principle, already applied in 1059, had gained a new and portentous victory.

The autumn Synod of 1078 also risked a first attack on the right of the proprietors of churches by desiring to enlighten the laity as to how much danger for the salvation of souls was involved in the possession of churches and tithes. In the same year the reform Synod of Gerona stated that lay persons must not really possess churches; wherever this could not be avoided, at least the taking of the offerings was forbidden. The moderate attitude of the reformers could count all the more on partial successes, since already for some time there had been in progress a movement that was seeking to transfer proprietary churches from the lay to the ecclesiastical hand.

Gregory VII did everything to translate his reforming laws into fact. Like his predecessors he made use of legates for this purpose but introduced an important innovation. While he entrusted hitherto customary legates, dispatched only for a specified time, merely with particular tasks or visitations of remote lands, he had the real reform activity attended to by standing legates, usually taken from the country in question. There was a shower of penalties on simoniacal bishops or those failing otherwise. Since Gregory reserved the final decision to himself, there were frequent appeals to Rome. The Pope had many important cases decided by the Roman reform synods, which annually proclaimed a series of excommunications, suspensions, and depositions. The final struggle with Henry IV naturally took the personal direction of the reform work more and more out of Gregory's hand.

There is no doubt that Gregory's pontificate was a turning point in the history of the Roman primacy. It is not to no purpose that people speak of the "Hildebrandine Church" that was now beginning. But if the individual activities are looked at, they show little that was fundamentally new. When Gregory complied with the request of Gebuin of Lyons, he honestly believed he was restoring an ancient institution, without realizing that he was actually converting an invention of pseudo-Isidore into reality for the first time. If he were concerned merely for centralization, he would have ignored Gebuin's request and thus spared himself the intermediate tribunal.

Actually, Gregory sought no constitutional changes for the benefit of the Roman primacy. What he contributed of his own was his *mystique* of Saint Peter. Profoundly convinced that no Christian could be saved who was not bound to Peter's vicar in unity, harmony, and obedience, he used all the rights assembled in the *Dictatus papae* to the extent that he regarded as necessary. Such a religious dynamism, entirely oriented to the personal responsibility of the Pope, brought about the definitive turning point. While Gregory's own personal charism may have been extinguished with his death, the monarchical form of government of the Roman Church had become a reality. There remained merely the task of justifying it more precisely and guaranteeing and perfecting it.

Gregory's *mystique* of Saint Peter affected not only priests but also the laity. He expected the princes especially to be loyal adherents of Saint Peter and his vicar. Words such *as fidelitas, fidelis, miles Sancti Petri* or *sanctae romanae ecclesiae* or *sanctae apostolicae sedis* constantly recur in his letters. Gregory did not fail to make use of Christian princes for the interests of religion and of the Church. Thus he authorized some of them to proceed with force against unworthy bishops who defied ecclesiastical penalties or he asked for their help when the Roman Church or specific areas of the Christian world were threatened. Convinced that genuine love demanded that the machinations of the *corpus diaboli* be obstructed by force of arms and that life be risked for the brothers, he had no hesitation about summoning the laity to a holy war. In fact, he even established a troop of his own, the *militia Sancti Petri,* and sought to turn it into a real army in times of crisis, by voluntary enlistments, by military aid which he claimed from bishops or vassals, or by mercenaries.

Hence it was very important to him to augment the loyalty of the *fideles Sancti*

Petri. Since *fidelitas* was based on the religious connection with Peter and hence lacked a clear juridical form, he strove to strengthen it further in the most varied ways — simple promises of obedience, payment of *census,* pledge of military aid, vassalage. All possibilities were used by him, often with appeal to genuine rights or rights so regarded. This very lack of any systematization and of juridical clarity should indicate how little Gregory was concerned for a secular system of government. It is true that his effort to make use of the princes somehow as co-workers led to a real entanglement of reform and politics. Hence, in what follows the two spheres, which in his view were not to be separated, will be discussed together.

Reform Policy in the Various Countries

Characteristic of Gregory II's broad view, embracing all Christendom, was his alert interest in the northern missionary area, where at last the definitive decision was made in favor of Christianity in Sweden also. How carefully he followed the development appears from his pastoral letters of 1080–81 to Olaf III of Norway and to the Swedish Kings Inge and Alsten, which, in addition to instruction on the faith and on the royal office, contained the suggestion that clerics be sent to Rome for study. Already Christianized Denmark, which counted nine sees around 1060, had secured closer tics with the Roman Church under Alexander II. King Svein Estrithson had at that time expressed the desire for an archbishopric of his own and for the *patrocinium Petri* and had begun to pay Peter's Pence. Like Alexander, Gregory too was entirely favorable to the idea of a Danish archbishopric, without presuming a decision; in addition, he sought to strengthen the friendly relations thus inaugurated. If he gladly clarified the *patrocinium Petri* suggested by Svein, he further proposed that one of the King's sons should come to Rome with a military force in order to be set over a rich province on the sea Dalmatia was probably meant — and there to undertake the defense of Christendom. The letter, sent in 1075, did not find Sven alive. The discord then ensuing in Denmark among his sons induced the Pope to urge neutrality on the Norwegian King.

There was also no dearth of connections with the countries to the east of Germany. Boleslas II of Poland paid voluntary tribute, Vratislav of Bohemia continued to pay the *census* which Nicholas II had stipulated when he allowed Duke Spitignev to wear the mitre. Gregory VII was concerned with Bohemia chiefly because of the controversy between the Bishops of Prague and Olomouc.

Michael had to yield in 1078 to Nicephorus III, and the latter in 1081 to Alexius I Comnenus. The first of these changes on the throne gave Robert Guiscard the notion of crossing over to the Balkan peninsula and attacking the Byzantines, as the alleged avenger of Michael VII. Gregory VII, who in the meantime had become reconciled with Robert, supported the undertaking, while the new Emperor Alexius, continuing the war with Robert, still regarded the Pope as an opponent of the Norman and sought to gain him to his side. Gregory, who seems even to have excommunicated Alexius, had profoundly miscalculated. Robert's Balkan adventure, happily inaugurated by the victory of Durazzo, ended in a complete fiasco. The Antipope Clement III, set up meanwhile by Henry IV, did not fail to establish good relations with the Byzantine world. Only the need of Alexius I and the surpassing diplomacy of Urban II led again to a *rapprochement* between the reform papacy and Byzantium.

In a class by itself was Gregory's attitude to the English Church and its master, William the Conqueror. The new King rejected the homage of vassalage which Gregory seems to have once demanded through legates, but he paid Peter's Pence and promoted the politically necessary reform of the Church, supported by Archbishop Lanfranc of Canterbury. Numerous reform synods saw to improved conditions. Furthermore, the English Church prepared to move into Ireland. As early as about 1028 the Bishop of Dublin had been consecrated at Canterbury and had obliged himself to obedience. Lanfranc of Canterbury and his successor Anselm considered the Irish Church as under their jurisdiction. Gregory VII's attention must have been called by Lanfranc to the reform tasks at hand in Ireland and under the circumstances he must have been motivated to send a pastoral letter to King Toirdielbach and the Irish. It was a small token but full of future promise. Under Paschal II papal legates were to attend a first Irish reform synod.

Since Gregory saw that what was essential was being achieved in England, he came to terms with William's outlook, which was that of a State Church now coming clearly into the light. The King named the bishops, invested them — there was no Investiture Controversy in England and Normandy during the entire eleventh century — confirmed synodal decrees, and decided the limits of ecclesiastical jurisdiction. The reform ideal of William and Lanfranc obviously continued in the old conservative notions, as these had inspired the Emperor Henry III and the German bishops. Only on one point did the Pope remonstrate: William did not permit the English bishops to go to Rome or to have any contact with the Pope without his knowledge. In this matter a serious conflict might have occurred. To the King it may have been only proper that Lanfranc was intent on maintaining his ecclesiastical rights against Rome and did not love the troublesome Pope. After the capture of Rome by Henry IV in 1084, Lanfranc even made contact with the Clementists. Without a real break actually occurring, the English Church for years maintained a neutral attitude in regard to the schism.

Spain had become accessible to the Roman reform under Alexander II. Gregory energetically carried the happy beginnings further by means of standing legates. Reform councils, such as that of Gerona in 1078 and that of Burgos in 1080, especially attacked simony and Nicolaitism. Gregory achieved his greatest enduring success when the Mozarabic rite was now replaced by the Roman even outside Aragón. Rome's reforming and liturgical initiative awakened among the Spanish Cluniacs the fear that they would lose their influence. Hence Robert, Abbot of Sahagún, their most important monastery, began to intrigue against the legate and to gain King Alfonso VI. Gregory VII became so exasperated that he threatened the King, not only with excommunication, but with war. The conflict, which cost Robert of Sahagún his office, ended at once, and the Council of Burgos in 1080 became a complete triumph for the legate.

In no country was the reform so energetically pushed as in France, but even here its successes were modest. The Midi proved to be relatively willing; several of the South French princes had earlier sworn special fealty to Saint Peter, and now Count Bertrand of Provence entrusted his territory in 1081 and Count Peter de Melgueil the country of Substantion in 1085 to the Roman Church as fiefs. Not a few feudal lords and their clerical relatives renounced their proprietary rights over churches, for the sake of their salvation or out of fear of excommunication.

Italy caused the Pope great anxiety. When he went south in 1073 he was able to take possession of Benevento and to renew his feudal relationship with Richard of Capua, but Robert Guiscard held aloof. He and Richard intended to bring the few remaining territories under their rule. An attack on Benevento was not the sole act which violated the territorial rights of the Roman Church. The two princes had during this whole time taken possession of papal property within and without the Papal State. The Pope had to look on helpless. Excommunication, several times pronounced, had no effect on Robert, and the war planned against him in 1074, in alliance with Gisulf of Salerno, Beatrice and Matilda of Tuscany, and Godfrey of Lotharingia, to which Gregory summoned the South French *fideles* of Saint Peter, without finding any response, got no farther than wretched beginnings. Only the Treaty of Ceprano in 1080 prepared the way for peace. Not only did Gregory have to accept the conquests tacitly; Robert guaranteed the *terra sancti Petri* only in so far as the Roman Church could prove her rights.

Beyond the continent Gregory's attention was directed to Sardinia and Corsica. Since he regarded both islands as the property of the Roman Church by virtue of the *privilegium* of Louis the Pious, he sought to vindicate this claim in cautious letters and through his legates.

His chief supports were the Marchionesses of Tuscany, Beatrice (d. 1076) and especially Matilda, wife of Godfrey of Lower Lotharingia. Between 1077 and 1080 Matilda even made over her considerable property to the Roman Church and received it back for her free disposal and lifelong enjoyment. Her life became the mirror of the reform struggle. Put under the ban by Henry IV in 1081, she lost a good part of her dominions for more than a decade.

The difficult situation in Italy obstructed Gregory VII in any effective reform activity. If the south had to be counted out almost entirely, because of the political chaos, in Central and North Italy the opposition of the clergy hostile to reform stiffened as the tension with Henry IV increased. Not the opposition of Robert Guiscard but that of Henry IV ultimately determined Gregory's reform policy in Italy. The first dramatic conflict of 1076, which forever estranged the Pope and the King, blazed forth on questions affecting the Church in North and Central Italy.

The relations of Gregory VII to Germany and the German King were objectively weighed down by the Ottonian-Salian Imperial Church system. The Church, gathered around the theocratic monarch, had thus far withstood every intervention of any importance by the reform papacy. Even Alexander II had not achieved more than individual successes and in the Milan conflict he had experienced how little he could enforce his wishes. Henry IV's yielding in the autumn of 1073, motivated by the Saxon revolt, caused Gregory to hope for a change in principle, and so in 1074 he sent two legates to Germany to hold a reform council. The project failed, not because of Henry IV, whom the legates restored to the Christian community, but because of the juridical standpoint of the German episcopate. If the head of the opposition, Archbishop Liemar of Bremen, had not possessed the courage to go to Rome and appease the enraged Pope, there would have been a collision. Henry IV restrained himself, although at the Lenten Synod of 1075 five of his councillors were again excommunicated and the prohibition of lay investiture was made known to him; in fact he even entered into negotiations as suggested by Gregory on the investiture question and in the autumn of 1075 abandoned the simoniacal Bishop of Bamberg.

In reality he did not intend to comply with the Pope's reform wishes. This was to be revealed by the Italian policy that he inaugurated after his victory over the Saxons on 9 June 1075. Then Henry assumed a more severe tone. Contrary to the promises made in 1073, he invested as Archbishop of Milan, not Godfrey, who had been first appointed but had not made any progress, but another Milanese cleric, Tedald, and designated for the sees of Fermo and Spoleto, disregarding Rome's metropolitan rights, men whom the Pope did not even know. Gregory quite rightly felt that he had been deceived and challenged. He sent Henry a letter of admonition which, in addition to the uncanonical appointment of the three Italian bishops, referred also to the unlawful association with the excommunicated councillors; by word of mouth the King was threatened with excommunication.

Neither Henry IV nor the German episcopate showed themselves equal to the strained but in no sense inextricable situation. Incited by the disgusting slanders of the disloyal Cardinal Hugh the White and laboring under the delusion that Gregory's position was not only undermined in Christendom and in Italy but even in Rome, where on Christmas of 1075 Cencius de Prefecto had perpetrated an assault on him, the German bishops at the Diet of Worms of 24 January 1076 sent the Pope a formal letter of defiance, while Henry IV, in a letter of his own, by virtue of his office of *patricius* declared that Gregory had forfeited his authority and called upon him to renounce his dignity. A recast manifesto proceeded from the royal chancery to the German clergy. At Piacenza the Lombard bishops joined with the German episcopate.

Gregory answered the extravagant attack when, at the Roman Lenten Synod, in a solemn prayer to Saint Peter, he suspended Henry from governing, annulled oaths of loyalty made to him, and excommunicated him. The condemning of the King, something unprecedented, was not to fail in producing its effect. It mattered little that Henry, for his part, had Gregory excommunicated. His political opponents, the princes of Saxony and South Germany, now met for common action. Their meeting at Tribur in October involved the King, who had come with an army and was encamped at Oppenheim, in even greater difficulties as a consequence of a growing defection, when a radical group of princes worked for an immediate new election. Gregory, who wanted to force Henry to obedience but not to sacrifice him, had sent two legates, whose mediation produced a compromise. A new election was prevented, and Henry even seems to have succeeded in evading the delicate question of investiture, but he had to dismiss the excommunicated councillors and in writing promise the Pope obedience and penance. For their own safety, the princes agreed not to recognize Henry as King if he had not been released from the censure by the anniversary of the excommunication and invited the Pope to the Diet of Augsburg, called for February 1077, where he should settle their quarrel with Henry.

Gregory accepted and set out. Henry, who wanted at any price to prevent a coalition between Pope and princes, now hurried boldly across the Alps in order to obtain absolution from Gregory. On three days he appeared in penitential garb before the castle of Canossa, to which Gregory had withdrawn as a precaution, while inside the castle Matilda of Tuscany and Henry's godfather, Abbot Hugh of Cluny, implored the Pope for clemency. Despite justified misgivings and the great prospect of the court of arbitration, Gregory eventually decided to discharge his priestly office. On condition that Henry should give satisfaction to the princes and grant the Pope a safe conduct for his visit to Germany, Henry was received back into the Christian community. Whether he was thereby also to be restored to the royal dignity and the oaths of loyalty were again to apply was apparently an incidental question to the Pope, who thought along spiritual rather than juridical lines. In any event he employed the royal title for Henry thereafter. Henry could, then, be satisfied with what he had achieved, but the act of submission, the complete reversal at Canossa of the early medieval relationship of *Regnum* and *Sacerdotium,* cannot properly be measured against this success of his. With the turning point at Canossa there was announced a new epoch in Western history, whose problems were to be thrashed out in the succeeding period, extending to Boniface VIII.

From the political viewpoint, Gregory had acted unwisely. His opponent, for so the King, struggling for his rights, remained, was free of his fetters; the King's adversaries, the princes, who had intended to make use of the Pope merely for their own ends, now went their own way. Having abruptly decided on a new election, at Forchheim in March 1077 they chose Duke Rudolf of Swabia as King, making him renounce hereditary right and the nomination of bishops to be elected, but probably not their investiture. As early as the autumn of 1076, when a new election was being considered, Gregory had reminded the princes of the right of designation which in 1056, at the suggestion of Victor II, they had granted on oath to the Empress Agnes in the event of an election of a successor to Henry IV and which Gregory, as successor of Victor II, intended to exercise together with the Empress if a new election were to take place. Since at Forchheim the princes had silently ignored this right and since Gregory was not interested in the elevation of an Antiking, he did not recognize Rudolf's election, although the legates he had sent to Forchheim took part in it and Rudolf offered all assurances.

The neutrality that he now maintained for years, connected with his claim to act as arbiter, gained him, then as now, much blame. Gregory did not let himself be guided by strictly political views. In his judgment, that one should be king on whose side was *iustitia,* and hence God himself. This religiously determined attitude alienated both factions. The princes, pursuing their selfish aims, feared that Gregory might decide for Henry; Henry would have had to make ecclesiastical concessions which he regarded as irreconcilable with the rights of the crown, if the Pope should act as arbiter.

And so the arbitration court did not materialize. Henry especially was able to prevent it time and again, and the time thus gained worked in his favor. The Antiking, virtually confined to Saxony, constantly lost ground. The stronger Henry grew, the more emphatically did he maintain his ecclesiastical rights. Gregory had to come to a decision; the adherents of reform in Germany no longer understood his hesitation, and both claimants to the throne pressed him for a judgment. The envoys sent by Henry in 1080 must have settled the question. Gregory finally gave his verdict at the March Synod of 1080. In a solemn prayer to the Princes of the Apostles he again excommunicated Henry and deposed him. Firmly convinced that he had carried out the judgment of God and of the Princes of the Apostles, at Easter he even prophesied that Henry's ruin was to be expected by the feast of Saint Peter in Chains. Matters were to turn out quite differently.

Henry, behind whom stood the greatest part of the German and Lombard episcopates, caused the Synods of Bamberg and Mainz to renounce obedience to the Pope and then at Brixen in June 1080 had Guibert of Ravenna elected as Antipope. When in the autumn his rival Rudolf remained on the battlefield after an encounter, Henry could make ready for armed conflict with Gregory. As early as the spring of 1081 Henry went to Italy and at once marched on Rome, his Lombard friends having opened the way by their victory at Mantua the previous fall over the troops of Countess Matilda. His efforts to take Rome, made only for brief periods, failed in this and the next year, but in 1083 at least the Leonine City fell to him.

Gregory's situation became increasingly hopeless. Matilda of Tuscany could not help, Robert Guiscard was carrying out his Balkan campaign, and Jordan of Capua had submitted to the German King in 1082. Henry IV, scattering Byzantine coins among the Romans, began negotiations. A synod held in Rome with his approval led to no result, since, having become suspicious, he not only sent no representative but even obstructed it. In any event, he was prepared to sacrifice the Antipope, if Gregory would give him the imperial crown. His moderate offer captivated all who thought along political lines, but for Gregory it was not a political question but a question of conscience. Henry in his view remained an enemy to the divine order so long as he did not do penance and did not thus disavow his acts. This unyielding attitude, heedless of danger, drove thirteen cardinals and other prelates as well as warriors into the enemy's camp in the spring of 1084 and induced the Romans to open the gates to Henry. While Gregory remained in the impregnable Castel Sant'Angelo, the Roman clergy and people on Henry's motion elected Guibert as Pope; he called himself Clement III and at Easter gave Henry the imperial crown.

Still, Gregory was not lost. Robert Guiscard approached with a powerful army. Henry abandoned the city, which Robert took at his first assault. But a new misfortune now occurred: as a result of the looting a great part of Rome went up in flames. Gregory could not stay. To the curses of the population he left the city with the Normans and, accompanied by a few loyal persons, went to Salerno, where he died on 25 May 1035. His well attested last words were: "I have loved justice and hated iniquity; therefore I die in exile."

Gregory VII, whom the Church canonized in 1606, rises up for all times as a sign of veneration and of contradiction. Even a scholarship intent on the utmost objectivity probably cannot settle the controversy. One thing, however, is not to be doubted: the Pope felt himself to be one seized upon by God and acted accordingly. If, even in the most extreme distress, he made no dishonorable compromise with Henry IV, it was not obstinacy that guided him but his faith, able to move mountains, in his mission. He assisted the reform in its critical hour to a definitive breakthrough; the opposition, driven to extremes, had to be worn out. Gregory's heroic example called forth the religious forces of resistance and animated them for the struggle. The defeated Pope conquered in his successors, fashioned the face of the West for more than two centuries, and determined the figure of the Church into our own day.

CHAPTER 110

Stubborn Fight and Victory:
From Victor III to Calixtus II

Victor III

For the reform party Gregory VII's death was a severe blow. It was only after a
year that it was able seriously to consider the succession at Rome, now abandoned by Clement III, and to elect Desiderius of Montecassino on 24 May 1086.
Desiderius, who came from the house of the Lombard Princes of Benevento, was
certainly an important personality. To him Montecassino owed a flowering never
again attained, and, made a cardinal by Stephen IX, he had rendered a number
of services to the reform Popes, especially in their dealings with the Normans.
But even he seemed doubtful that his nature, more inclined to diplomacy than
to struggle, and also sickly, was equal to his new tasks. Eventually he decided on
21 March 1087, to accept his election and to call himself Victor III. The consecration could take place at Saint Peter's tomb under the protection of the Normans,
but Victor soon had to leave the Eternal City. Then Victor III was carried off by
death on 16 September 1087.

Urban II

Half a year elapsed before the reformers elected the Cardinal-Bishop Eudes of
Ostia as Pope under the name of Urban II on 12 March 1088, at Terracina, where
they immediately enthroned him. Born about 1035 at Châtillon, the son of a noble,
he was educated for the clergy in the school of Saint Bruno at Reims and there he
was appointed archdeacon between 1055 and 1060. Probably between 1067 and
1070 he entered Cluny and rose to be prior. Abbot Hugh, from whom Gregory VII
had asked for some monks in 1078, had to give him up in 1079–80. The Pope
made him Cardinal-Bishop of Ostia and in 1084 sent him as legate to Germany. His
election to the papacy, recommended by Gregory VII as well as by Victor III, was
to prove fortunate. Fully assenting to Gregory's principles, but elastically adapting
their implementation to the present situation, Urban II led the reform papacy out
of the narrow pass and toward victory.

Nothing reflects the situation facing the new Pope better than the relatively
well transmitted polemical literature of the day. If in 1074–75 the prescribing of
celibacy and of a boycott of married priests had stirred intellects, since the decisions of 1076 and 1080 there were other themes for debate: Gregory VII's integrity,
his right to depose and excommunicate Henry IV and to absolve from oaths of
loyalty to him, his recourse to armed force, the strict prohibition of associating
with the excommunicated, the juridical immunity of the anointed King, Henry's
patriciate, the raising up of the Antipope, and so forth. Outstanding among the
Gregorians were: Gebhard of Salzburg, Bernold of Sankt Blasien, and Manegold
of Lautenbach, the last mentioned famous for his so called doctrine of "popular

sovereignty," which interpreted the kingship as an office transmitted by the people and hence terminable in the case of a defaulting ruler.

But more decisive were the accomplishments of the Italian authors. In the Antipope's own city of Ravenna appeared the work of the jurist Peter Crassus, which traced the irremovability of the king to the Roman law of inheritance. Here too another jurist fabricated false papal privileges, allegedly for Charles the Great and Otto the Great, and had Ulpian's *lex regia* worked in, in the sense of an irrevocable transmission of the authority of the Roman people to the Emperor, in favor of Henry IV. From the discussion of the schism, revived with the death of Gregory VII, proceeded the work of the Clementist Guido of Ferrara, which, gratifying by its moderate judgment of Gregory and its positive exertions in regard to the investiture question, was in great contrast to the approximately contemporary hate-productions of Cardinal Beno and of Bishop Benzo of Alba. Of the Gregorian, no less than Anselm of Lucca, Cardinal Deusdedit, and Bonizo of Sutri intervened in the last part of the controversy, but their real achievement, which gave their party the intellectual superiority, was in canon law. Anselm's highly significant canonical collection, compiled under Gregory VII, was now followed by the important collections of Deusdedit and Bonizo, undisturbed by the bleak situation.

Urban II had no need to despair. So profound an intellectual movement as the reform could not be suppressed by armed force; in fact he opposing camp itself was accessible to it. It was really only a relative opposition. Clement III fought simony and Nicolaitism straightforwardly. But since he approved of the old, ever more outdated, Imperial Church system and was burdened by the flaw of an uncanonical elevation, he maintained a position which was basically a lost cause. Some Clementists, not to speak of bishops who were laboring under the censures of the reformed Church outside the territory under German control, hence cherished the tacit wish to be united with the successor of Gregory VII.

Urban knew this and sought to accommodate them. Relying on his power of dispensation, he himself went to the limits of what was then possible. In individual cases he recognized bishops who had been invested by their king, including Archbishop Anselm of Milan, who had been canonically elected but invested by Henry IV. Milanese whom Archbishop Tedald, never recognized by Rome, had ordained could retain their function if their ordination had not been simoniacal and if Tedald's simony was not known to them, and the Masses of priests ordained in the Catholic Church who had gone over to the schism were not to be molested. The old zealots, Hugh of Lyons, Amatus of Oléron, and Richard of Saint-Victor, lost their function of legate and no new standing legates were named to replace them. And recourse to armed force met with little sympathy from Urban. Residing on the Tiber island at Rome from the autumn of 1088, he had in the succeeding summer taken the city by storm and, following the coronation Mass, was solemnly conducted through the streets, but the meager successes which the victory brought him caused him to renounce further struggles with the Roman Clementists. Money gained him entrance to the Lateran Palace in 1094 and it was probably the same means that won him Castel Sant'Angelo in 1098.

The first years of the pontificate were lived under the pressure of the imperial predominance. Urban sought to impair this by arranging in 1089 the marriage of his loyal comrade in arms, the forty-three-year-old Matilda of Tuscany, with the seventeen-year-old Welf V, son of the deposed Duke Welf IV of Bavaria, thereby producing an almost unbroken stretch of territory from South Germany to Tuscany, but this outcome only induced Henry IV to go to Italy and seek a definitive solution. Urban experienced the King's successfully conducted campaigns against Matilda's troops in 1090–92 to the extent that he had to flee to the Normans from Clement III, who now again took possession of Rome. But then catastrophe overtook Henry. It came about after a defeat suffered near Canossa in 1092 and the formation of a league of hostile cities — Milan, Cremona, Lodi, Piacenza with the defection in 1093 of his own son, Conrad, who had himself crowned King of the Lombards at Milan. Betrayed by almost all, even by his wife Praxedis, and cut off from Germany, Henry remained locked up in the territories of Padua and Verona until he was reconciled with Welf IV in 1096 — the unnatural marriage between Welf V and Matilda had broken up — and could go to Germany in 1097.

Urban II, who definitively returned to Rome at the end of 1093 and in 1094 again appointed the inexorable Hugh of Lyons as standing legate in France, now took hold of the reins resolutely. As early as 1094 he set out on a two-year journey via Tuscany and Lombardy to France. As a matter of fact the reform needed thoroughgoing consultation. Urban's mildness had especially caused a revival of the tiresome question of the validity of simoniacal and schismatic ordinations. It was all the more urgent to establish binding norms, at least for practical action. This was done at the well-attended Council of Piacenza, meeting under Urban's presidency in March 1095. With regard to schismatics it decreed the nullity of all orders conferred by Guibert of Ravenna since his condemnation and of the orders conferred by his adherents who had been excommunicated by name and by all bishops who had usurped the see of a Catholic bishop, unless the cleric ordained knew nothing about the condemnation of the ordaining prelate; on the other hand, orders obtained from originally Catholic bishops who had later gone over to the schism retained their validity. The Council proceeded more strictly against simoniacal ordinations. It declared them all to be invalid, except the orders of those clerics to whom the simony of the ordaining bishop was not known. It is obvious that the decrees, which were open to varying theological interpretations and were lacking in consistency, left the dogmatic problem unsolved.

As early as 1089 Urban had renewed the prohibition of investiture at Melfi. He returned to it at Clermont, where on 28 November 1095 he opened another brilliant synod. Not only were the appropriate decrees of Gregory VII repeated; the synod now forbade bishops and clerics to become the vassals of the King or of any other layman, thereby advancing the demand of the *Sacerdotium* for freedom to a point which not even Gregory VII's legislation had ventured to take up. Urban had it recalled to mind in a somewhat modified form in his last Roman Synod in 1099. The same synod also made stricter the prohibition of investiture, by threatening with excommunication, not only the one investing and the one invested, but also the one ordaining a person who had received lay investiture. Thus the reform struggle centered more and more on the problem of investiture.

The Cluniac Pope's special love and gratitude belonged to monasticism, as numerous privileges attest. Although Urban seldom granted full exemption, he was happy to lessen the authority of the local bishop and in addition placed many monasteries under papal protection. With a sure instinct for the spiritual forces of his age, he also assured the canons regular their due place in the Church by placing their ideal of the *vita apostolica* on par with the monastic ideal of perfection and forbidding the canon regular from entering a monastery without the permission of his community and his provost.

Urban intended to be more than a mere reformer working inside the Church. And so he did not shrink from proclaiming the Peace of God, which had been instituted in France and promoted by the Cluniacs. At Clermont in 1095 he covered with the Peace of God not only clerics, monks, and women, but the person and goods of crusaders, even on days when it was lawful to fight. The Council of Clermont is especially famed for a creative initiative of the Pope, incalculable in its effect on the immediate and later times — the summons to the First Crusade. While the Emperor, shut up in a corner of Italy, was in a sense forgotten, the Pope, spontaneously acknowledged by the faithful as the true leader of the Christian West, with no participation by kings, set in motion a supranational army for the defense of the Christian East and for the conquest of the Holy Land. From then on the final victory of the reform papacy was only a question of time, and this victory was permanent. For two centuries the Vicar of Christ, eclipsing the power of the Emperor and of kings with his spiritual authority, was to preside over Western Christendom.

The causes and the course of the Crusade will be discussed later, as will also the relations which the Pope instituted right after his elevation with the Emperor Alexius I and the Byzantine Church for the liquidation of the Schism. But it is time to examine his relations with the Western monarchs. The reform policy encountered little difficulty in Spain, especially since the Pope did not prevent the Spanish Cluniacs from recovering their old influence and sent Roman cardinals in place of the former standing legate, Richard of Saint-Victor. He elevated the new Archbishop of Toledo, a monk of the Cluniac monastery of Sahagún, to the dignity of primate, but at the same time he encouraged, with the Count of Barcelona, the reconstruction of the city and metropolitan see of Tarragona. Thus began the new ecclesiastical division of Spain.

The Pope had to deal with no slight difficulties in England. On the death of King William I in 1087 his lands were divided between two sons Robert acquired Normandy, while William II became King of England. Normandy recognized Urban II, but William II maintained neutrality and gave such free rein to his lust for money and power at the expense of the English Church that the fruits of reform achieved under his father were imperilled. Lanfranc's death in 1089 suited him very much. Only a serious illness moved the King in 1093 to fill the archbishopric of Canterbury again with Abbot Anselm of Bec. This great theologian, trained in Lanfranc's school, had no intention of simply accepting William's acts of caprice. After some lesser clashes he forced the King to a decision in the question of the schism by demanding to be allowed to receive the pallium from Urban II. When an attempt to have Anselm deposed failed, William dealt directly with the Pope, who sent the Cardinal Legate Walter of Albano to England. Walter obtained the definitive recognition of Urban but in return had to make all sorts of concessions, in particular to acknowledge the special law that papal legates could come to England only at King William's desire. Anselm took no part at all in the negotiations. He was summoned to court only after their conclusion to receive the pallium which the legate had brought along. It was suggested by some of the courtiers that he should take it from William's hand, but this manner of receiving it would have made the King seem to be a papal vicar, and so Anselm courageously refused. He carried the point that he should take the pallium from the altar and put it upon himself.

Urban seems not to have entirely approved the all too elastic proceedings of Walter of Albano. Soon Anselm came into a greater conflict. Indicted by the King for having supplied unfit troops, he reproached him for the secularization of ecclesiastical property and for his lack of a will to reform and intended to appeal to the Pope. Since he refused to take the oath demanded of him, that he would never appeal to the Pope, he had to leave England, while William confiscated the goods of his church. Anselm went first to Lyons and then to Rome. Urban did not permit him to resign and even had the quarrel discussed at the Synods of Bari in 1098 and Rome in 1099, but could not bring himself to take serious action until death relieved him of the decision he had finally promised.

Urban also displayed the greatest prudence in regard to Philip I of France when in 1092 the King repudiated his wife and presumed to marry Bertha of Montfort, wife of the Count of Anjou. The scandal of this double adultery was punished by Hugh of Lyons at the Synod of Autun in 1094 with anathema, to which personal interdict was added in 1097. Urban only confirmed the excommunication in 1095 at the Council of Clermont and thereafter allowed himself to be gained to mildness time and again by Philip's empty promises, but without yielding in principle. When Urban died, the King had again incurred excommunication. His marriage affair allowed Philip no intensive struggle against the demands for reform. From this point of view the Pope could be satisfied with France in general; in no other country, despite rather frequent interventions, did he find so much obedience.

In South Italy, the refuge that he sought time and again till 1093, Urban interested himself in the Church organization so far as the fluid political situation following the death of Robert Guiscard in 1085 allowed. Robert's son, Duke Roger of Apulia, who in 1089 became Urban's vassal, was too young and insignificant to keep the rebellious barons in check. And the rule of Richard II of Capua was on so fragile a foundation that in 1098 he had to call for the help of Roger of Apulia and in return place his principality under the latter's feudal suzerainty. Thus the political center of gravity shifted to Sicily, where Robert Guiscard's brother, Roger I, captured the last pocket of Muslim resistance in 1091 and set out to construct a firmly consolidated state. Hence Urban established especially close relations with Roger I, which led to a fruitful cooperation in rebuilding the Sicilian Church. It is true that Roger tolerated no independent action by Rome, and the nomination of Bishop Roger of Troina as legate without his consent even caused a conflict. It was settled by the portentous privilege of 5 July 1098, in which Urban renounced, during the reigns of Roger and Roger's successor, any appointment of legates without an understanding with the rulers, granted them legatine delegation, and left it to Roger's discretion whether to be represented at Roman synods.

Relations with Henry IV remained unsettled. Urban considered peace even less when in 1095 he had met Henry's rebellious son Conrad at Cremona, received from him an oath of safety, held out the prospect of the imperial crown, and arranged the engagement of the young King with a daughter of Roger of Sicily. Henry's return to Germany in 1097 hardly affected the ecclesiastical situation. The

Emperor did, indeed, succeed in reestablishing his political authority, but he was unable to prevent the dissolution of the Clementist unified front in the episcopate and the defection of individual bishops to the Gregorians. Urban's policy of the open door bore its fruits. To this was added the propaganda directed by the German Gregorians at the masses of the population, carried to them especially by the preachers sent out from around 1080 by Hirsau and the monasteries under its influence. Thus also in Germany the reform party was slowly making progress when, on 2 July 1099, two weeks after the taking of Jerusalem by the crusaders, Urban II departed this life.

Paschal II

Sixteen days later Cardinal Rainerio, born at Bieda in Romagna, became Pope under the name of Paschal II. He had been a monk of an Italian monastery, which cannot now be identified but was probably not Cluniac, before being made Cardinal-Priest of San Clemente by Gregory VII. The new Pope was basically different from his worldly-wise predecessor in his simpler nature, partly inflexible, partly timid. Inclined to intransigence, he was rather to stress than to reconcile the antitheses in the problems of the age, but actually in that way to prepare for their later solution.

It was the question of investiture that was especially at stake. It had been pretty generally established as a principle that simony and Nicolaitism were to be fought against. And the death of the aged Guibert of Ravenna on 8 September 1100 settled the difficulties inherent in the schism, for the two Antipopes set up by the Roman Clementists in 1100, the schismatic Bishops Dietrich of Santa Ruhna and Albert of Sabina, were captured in turn and confined in South Italian monasteries, while the Archpriest Maginulf, proclaimed as Silvester IV in 1105, had to flee Rome after a few days, despite the armed assistance of the Marquis Werner of Ancona; but he did not renounce the dignity until 1111. Thus at the Synod of Gulstalla in 1106 Paschal II was able to declare the restoration of unity and let all schismatic ecclesiastics retain their office, provided that there were no simoniacal or other offenses involved. There remained only the prohibition of investiture as a still unresolved problem; in fact, since the tightening of the regulations by Urban II it had acquired an actuality which it had not had under Gregory VII or under Urban. A settlement could no longer be avoided; the Investiture Controversy in the strict sense was now just beginning.

It is distinctive of the new state of affairs that now a real Investiture Controversy even broke out in England, occasioned by the change on the throne following the death of William II in August 1100. In order to secure his own succession, which was not beyond question, the new King Henry I, himself also a son of William the Conqueror, called Archbishop Anselm back from banishment, only to experience the surprise that Anselm refused to do the customary vassal's homage, appealing to the Roman Synod of 1099 that he had himself attended. Anselm, it is true, was concerned less for the question of investiture than for obedience to the laws of the Roman Church. Hence he supported the King's effort to obtain for England a papal dispensation from the prohibition of investiture and went to Rome for this purpose.

Paschal, who had just renewed the prohibition in 1102, denied the request. Henry then refused to readmit Anselm, returning from Rome, into England (1104) until the excommunication of English ecclesiastics who had accepted investiture and of the royal councillors, announced by Paschal in 1105, moved him to come to terms with Anselm. The settlement, approved by Paschal, between the two men, who held each other in esteem, was ratified at a meeting of the Great Council in London in August 1107: Henry renounced investiture with ring and crosier but retained the right to receive homage from the bishops before their consecration. Furthermore, he maintained his influence on the elections of bishops by being present in person.

In France too, meanwhile, a practical solution had been prepared, without there having been open conflict or an official concordat, as in England. In France, however, there ceased not only investiture with ring and crosier, but, differing from England, also the homage of vassalage; the French King was satisfied with an oath of loyalty. Just the same, he renounced neither his power to dispose of the temporalities of sees, with the legal consequences — usufruct during vacancies, possible seizure of the administrative authority, and so forth nor the customary services, and hence he conveyed the temporalities by means of an informal act, termed a *concessio,* to the bishop elected with his permission.

Thus in both France and England there was first made a distinction between ecclesiastical office and possession of temporalities. In itself the idea was not new, but the merit of having first pondered deeply over the investiture question and of having led to a solution belongs to the great canonist, Ivo of Chartres. The handing over of the episcopal office, so he explained, was certainly to be refused to the laity, since it implied a sacramental act; on the other hand, the *concessio* of the temporalities could be granted to the King without difficulty, for it was a purely secular act, to be performed in any desired manner, to which the King could make a certain claim in so far as, according to Augustine, property is based on constitutional law and hence the churches owed their goods to distribution made by the king. Ivo's ideas, expounded as early as 1097 in a letter to Hugh of Lyons, had an influence in France on the new arrangement that was in preparation, but they also won importance for the English Investiture Controversy, since at that time Ivo's pupil, Hugh of Fleury, made use of them in his important *Tractatus de regia potestate et sacerdotali dignitate,* dedicated to the English King.

Paschal was wise enough to tolerate the two compromises that had been reached without his direct participation. They did not actually mean a genuine juridical solution. In England the real problem, investiture with the temporalities, had been evaded, and the *concessio* of the French King was open to various interpretations. But the essential thing, the renunciation of investiture with the office, was achieved, and the rights conceded to the kings to the customary services of the bishops could be entirely reconciled with the inner union of ecclesiastical office and property as demanded by the reformers. But for Germany the compromises thus far reached, and tolerated rather than accepted by the reformers, did not suffice. Considering the great damage that the royal authority had suffered at the hands of the secular princes since the death of Henry III, the German ruler not only could not renounce the rights of sovereignty which the more important churches had received in the greatest abundance since the days of the Ottos; he had to insist, with regard to the reform, on a clear regulation of his relations to the churches and their goods. For the reform principle of the inseparable unity of office and ecclesiastical property could not be applied here without a careful distinction. If it were a question only of the goods donated by private persons and of purely ecclesiastical income, such as offerings, stole fees, and tithes, then the principle could probably have been carried. But what had counties, margraviates, and even duchies, what had important political rights of usufruct to do with the churches? No king with a sense of responsibility could admit that they simply became inviolable church property in the sense of irrevocable gifts.

These difficult questions were to be presented to Paschal as soon as he was confronted, no longer by Henry IV, who had been again excommunicated at the Roman Synod of 1102, but by his son, Henry V. Henry V's revolt in 1104, the perfidious imprisonment and forced abdication of his father at the end of 1105, the Diet of Mainz with its recognition of Henry V at the beginning of 1106, the struggle that then flared up and only ended with the father's death in the summer of 1106 this tragedy of the Salian Dynasty concerns us here in so far as Paschal II espoused the cause of the young King, who posed as a protagonist of reform by absolving him from his oath not to intervene in the government without his father's consent and sending legates to the Diet of Mainz. He himself departed for the north in the spring of 1106 in order at last to establish peace between papacy and *Imperium*. He was to be disillusioned: Henry V's envoy, who found him during the Synod of Guastalla in 1106, insisted on the right of the Empire. Thereupon, the Pope did not go to Germany, as people were expecting, but to France, where in fact he could anticipate only the best reception. In 1104 Philip I had finally yielded on the marriage question and had adequately met the desires of the reformers by the renunciation in practice of investiture with ring and crosier. He and his son, Louis VI, now concluded an alliance with the Pope at Saint-Denis in 1107. France and the papacy had come together in a friendship that was to endure for centuries. All the more obstinate, then, was Paschal's attitude in his conference at Châlons-sur-Marne with Henry V's embassy. To the German demand for the royal right of investiture he replied with a blunt refusal, which he then had ratified at the subsequent Synod of Troyes, just as he had done a year earlier at Guastalla, by a repetition of the prohibition of investiture.

Nevertheless, the cleavage was not completely irreconcilable. Thus in 1109 a perhaps semiofficial memorandum, composed in the Empire, probably under the direct influence of Ivo's ideas, distinguished between the spiritual function and the secular property and, while adhering to the right of investiture, declared that the form of investiture was unessential. This already more differentiated outlook was to influence the negotiations which Henry V undertook when in the summer of 1110 he began his journey to Rome. Paschal indeed again rejected investiture but recognized a royal claim to the *regalia*, that is, to the goods and rights of the Empire which had been transferred to the bishops, and hence he proposed the radical solution of leaving to the churches as their property only the purely ecclesiastical revenues, such as tithes and so forth, and goods originating in private gifts, while all *regalia* were to be given back in accord with a papal command; in return, Henry was to renounce investiture.

Well meant as the proposal was, it was a stranger to reality. As though a peremptory order from the Pope, opposed to the will, not only of the bishops who had an interest in the *regalia,* but also of the secular princes, who feared the overgrowth of the royal power that would accompany such a restitution, could have annulled so deeply rooted a political order! Henry V must have clearly seen through it; but since he wanted the imperial crown, he declared his acceptance and had the secret treaty that had been agreed to, the content of which was to be published before the imperial coronation, ratified at Sutri on 9 February 1111. When on 12 February Paschal began the coronation rite in Saint Peter's and had the reciprocal charters read, a real tumult broke out. Bishops and princes indignantly rejected the papal command, whereupon Henry V demanded the imperial crown and the right of investiture. Since Paschal refused both, Henry denounced the treaty, arrested Pope and cardinals, and led them prisoners out of Rome, which was in a state of wild excitement and filled with the clash of weapons. After two months he succeeded in the Treaty of Mammolo in extorting from the Pope investiture with ring and crosier, to take place after the canonical election and before consecration. In addition, Paschal had to promise never to excommunicate Henry and to put the concession of investiture in the form of a written *privilegium* and crown Henry as Emperor on 13 April. On the way back to Germany Henry won a further prize. Meeting Matilda of Tuscany, he had himself appointed heir of her patrimonial goods, which had been enfeoffed to the Roman Church, though in this a recognition of the papal right of proprietorship could hardly have been avoided.

With his brutally gained victory over Paschal Henry had won nothing. The Pope might have been weak, but the reformed Church, growing into a supranational power structure, tolerated no exception for the *Imperium.* Besides, the Emperor had committed the serious psychological error of clinging to ring and crosier as symbols of investiture, though he related investiture merely to the *regalia.* It was this that produced the greatest commotion among the reform circles of Italy and France. There was a demand for the repudiation of the "privilegium" and the excommunication of the "heretical" Emperor. The Pope, mindful of his oath, could not assent to he excommunication, and he was unwilling either to approve expressly or to reject the anathema which a synod meeting at Vienne under Archbishop Guy in 1112 and two cardinal legates in Germany in 1115 hurled at the Emperor, but he probably agreed to the annulling of the privilege by the Roman Synod of 1112. Having become more firm with the passage of time, he himself condemned the concession at the Roman Synod of 1116 and renewed the prohibition of investiture and the threats of excommunication included in it.

And yet an important decision had been made in 1111. The Roman Church could no longer revoke the recognition, given at Sutri, of the royal right of *regalia,* the idea of which was then more exactly defined for the first time. Thus a certain readiness for an understanding became evident in the Gregorian polemical writings that soon appeared. Even the intransigent Placid of Nonantula, who, like Guy of Vienne in 1112, condemned the royal investiture with the temporalities and clung firmly to the churches' free right of ownership, was willing to concede to the Emperor not only the due services of the bishops but also investiture with the special political rights, using of course other symbols than ring and staff, and the possibility of confirming by charter their possession by a bishop already consecrated. Even more clearly did the *Disputatio vel defensio Paschalis papae,* originating at the Curia, distinguish between *temporalia* and *spiritualia,* proposing for the investiture with the temporalities the symbol of the scepter, which was actually used later.

The adjustment thus prepared in learned discussion could not be translated into reality under Paschal. The Pope insisted ever more strongly on the disavowal of the privilege. Neither the threatening proximity of the Emperor, who came to Italy in 1116 to enter into the inheritance of the Countess Matilda — she had died in 1115 — nor Henry's efforts at negotiations were able to divert him from that. Then a revolt had broken out in Rome because of the growing power of the Pierleoni, who supported the papacy. Paschal regarded it as advisable to leave the city in the spring of 1117, whereupon, summoned by the opposing faction, the Emperor came to the city for a few months. It was only at the beginning of 1118 that Paschal could dare to fight his way back. Scarcely had he done so when he died in the stronghold of the Pierleoni on 21 January 1118.

Calixtus II

It was providential that the Bishop of Rome, Gelasius II, had left his church a widow while he was abroad, for in the hopeless situation the reform papacy needed outside help. The cardinals surrounding the death bed of Gelasius were therefore well advised when they at once proceeded to the new election at Cluny and selected as Pope on 2 February, not a Roman cardinal, but Archbishop Guy of Vienne. Since the curialists who had remained behind in Rome with their staffs approved the election, the new Pope, who took the name Calixtus II, was universally recognized. Son of the Count of Burgundy, whose family was related to the Salians and other royal houses, a zealous bishop for thirty years, filled with the reform ideas, far-sighted and energetic, Calixtus was the right man both to settle the Roman situation and to solve the German question.

Even before his journey to Rome he extended the hand of peace to the Emperor, whom Gelasius had excommunicated together with the Antipope. Henry V had too great difficulties in the Empire not to accept it. The negotiations begun at Strasbourg between him and the papal envoys, William of Champeaux and Pons of Cluny, reached a preliminary conclusion in the charter of a treaty which two cardinals drew up with the Emperor; it lacked only ratification. For this purpose Calixtus proceeded, during the Council of Reims, which he had just opened, to Mouzon, where the Emperor awaited him. Since there had been a failure in the preliminary negotiations, apparently on both sides, to expound the controverted points with the necessary clarity, Calixtus demanded of Henry the express renunciation of investiture with the temporalities and of the right to take possession of church property. Hence at the last moment he gave him to understand that he intended to allow him merely the French practice, that is, the continuation of the services owed to the King, but the abolition of any investiture, even with the temporalities. Henry V, on the other hand, sought at least the vassalage of the bishops as tolerated for England and, in addition, an investiture with the *regalia.* Hence he did not agree to the newly formulated papal demand, but called for a postponing of the decision. Thereupon the deeply disillusioned Pope rode back to the council, where he was to find another surprise. While the participants, convinced of the Emperor's guilt, decreed anathema of Henry and his adherents, they could not make up their minds to extend the prohibition of investiture, demanded by Calixtus, also to church property. Merely investiture with bishoprics and abbeys was forbidden, while the disposal of tithes that happened to be in lay possession and of ecclesiastical fiefs was left an open question. Calixtus did not become soured. He now knew the controverted points and was willing to consider them in new negotiations for peace.

Meanwhile, he was carefully preparing for his journey to Rome. After a really triumphal progress through Lombardy and Tuscany, he was joyfully welcomed by the Romans in the summer of 1120. At last they again had a ruler, under whose authority the factional quarrels would become silent. Not until April 1121 did Calixtus, who had visited South Italy, dispatch troops to Sutri to capture the Antipope, who was entrenched there. Stripped of his episcopal dignity, Burdinus vanished into a South Italian monastery. Now peace with the Emperor was not long in coming. Unnerved by civil strife, Henry decided in the autumn of 1121 to entrust the starting of the negotiations with Rome to the German princes. Calixtus agreed to this and sent three cardinals, including the future Pope, Lambert of Ostia, to Germany. After two weeks of complicated deliberations the Investiture Controversy was brought to an end by the Concordat of Worms on 23 September 1122.

In it Henry renounced investiture with ring and staff but retained the right to investiture with the *regalia* by means of the scepter, to be performed in Germany immediately after the election, but in the case of the Burgundian and of the Italian sees within six months after consecration. He also granted canonical election and free consecration. However, in German territory he retained a substantial influence on the election — it was to take place in his presence or in that of his authorized representative and in the event of a dissenting outcome it was to be decided by him, with the cooperation of the metropolitan and the suffragans, in favor of the *sanior pars*. The Roman Church's sphere of influence, the *Patrimonium Petri*, was excepted from the regulations of the concordat.

The concordat, which despite certain shortcomings ranks with the best negotiated settlements of Western history, consisted of two documents: the one contained the concessions made by the Emperor to Calixtus and the Roman Church; the other, those made by the Pope to Henry V. It should be noted that the papal concessions were made to Henry alone, a circumstance which in ecclesiastical circles favored the opinion that the papal privilege would cease with Henry's death. This thesis, entirely defensible under the formal aspect could not, however, prevail against the more deeply based nature of the treaty now concluded. In the *Calixtinum* there was involved not the granting of papal favors but an old imperial right, which the Pope, once harmony had been achieved, had to acknowledge along with the Church's juridical claims. Though later the representatives of the Church as well as the Emperors, according to the status of the power situation, might try to alter the arrangements in their favor, the substance of the concordat proved to be a stable juridical basis.

Measured by the compromises reached in England and France, Calixtus granted the Emperor more for Germany and less for Burgundy and Italy. Henry could accept the last point: in Burgundy the king played no great role, and in Italy the bishops were being more and more eclipsed by the growing power of the cities. But in Germany too the royal power had been essentially impaired. Basically the Ottonian imperial constitution fell to pieces with the concordat. The dependence of the bishops and of the royal abbots, assured not merely by the rights conceded in the *Calixtinum,* but also by homage, not mentioned there but actually performed, was weakened by the fact the prelates, in the process of German constitutional development, were changed from royal officials into vassals of the crown, into spiritual princes of the Empire, who aspired to strengthen their secular power, based on law and something that could no longer be arbitrarily taken away, and thus they came together with the secular princes in a community of interests. As holders of an ecclesiastical office, whose juridical identity Henry V had to recognize by renouncing investiture with the office, they also belonged to the supranational body of the ecclesiastical hierarchy. And since the papacy was ever more strongly making the Church into a genuine monarchy, they had two lords to serve for the future. Thus an entirely new relationship, founded on the principle of the distinction in the two public-law spheres of the state and the Church, was being prepared, and its difficulties were to become clear in the following 180 years.

Both contracting parties had the treaty ratified within their juridical spheres. Calixtus overcame the resistance which he found there among the strict Gregorians by declaring that the concessions made to Henry were not to be approved but tolerated for the sake of peace. Everything depended on how persons acted in the future in regard to the problems inherent in the treaty, problems that as yet could not be mastered by ideas. From the old fighters for reform, who thought in now bogged down categories, there was not to be expected the elasticity which the new age, announced in the concordat, required. The Roman Church needed younger energies that would push forward. Calixtus at least seems to have suspected as much, for shortly before the council he elevated, among others, the Frenchman Aimeric to the rank of cardinal-deacon and around the same time, before 8 May, entrusted to him the weightiest curial post, that of chancellor. This important man, friend of Saint Bernard and of the Carthusian Prior Guigo, was to lead the Roman Church into a new stage of the reform and, to achieve this goal, even to accept the responsibility for the Schism of 1130.

The Lateran Council of 1123 brought to an end the numerous general synods which the Popes since Leo IX had arranged, in order to issue, in union with the bishops of the various countries, decrees universally binding. Without being essentially different from them, it alone has been recognized as ecumenical, and as the ninth ecumenical, First Lateran Council, inaugurated a new period in this sense, that thereafter the Popes decided the more important ecclesiastical questions in consistory, with the cardinals and bishops who happened to be present, and only rarely convoked general councils. The definitive character of this Council also appeals clearly in the decrees. What the reform had decreed earlier against clerical marriage, against simony and lay domination of churches and church goods, what it had decreed in regard to the Peace of God or the rights and duties of crusaders all was here summarized impressively. In the decrees relevant to the care of souls and the administration of the Sacraments, what is striking is how much the power of the diocesan bishop was taken into account both in regard to his own clergy and in regard to monks, to whom pastoral work was forbidden. The age of the emergency, which had required so much intervention by the reform Popes against the right, of the local bishop and the granting of privileges to the monks who were fighting for the reform, was past. If the reform was to continue, it needed the cooperation of the bishops and of new forces emerging from the clergy and from monasticism.

In reality there was still much to do. Nowhere, not even in France, had a definitive result been obtained. Germany and, with it, Italy only opened themselves up completely to the reform from 1122. The Church in Spain was in the process of reconstruction. In England the State Church system had by no means been overcome: Henry I clung more firmly than ever to his remaining rights and after the death of Anselm of Canterbury in 1109 cut off the bishops from communication with Rome, regardless of the protests of Paschal II. Ireland found itself in a first irresolute change, after the Synods of Cashel in 1101 and Rath Breasail in 1111 had begun to free the Church from its entanglement with the lay powers; the second of these synods had even provided for a definite hierarchy with twenty-six bishoprics and two metropolitan sees, one of the metropolitans to be also the primate. Of the Scandinavian Kings, Eric of Denmark succeeded in obtaining in principle from Urban II, against Liemar of Bremen, the right to a Danish archbishopric, and hence a legate sent by Paschal II was able to elevate the see of Lund to metropolitan status in 1104. This arrangement actually continued in force, even when Archbishop Adalbero II of Bremen again obtained from Calixtus II and from Innocent II the confirmation of his metropolitan rights in the North. It was now only a question of time till Norway and Sweden received their own archbishoprics. The Christianization of the North could only direct missionary interest to the still pagan Baltic peoples.

The Byzantine Church from 886 to 1054

Hans-Georg Beck

C H A P T E R   1 1 1

The Byzantine Church
from Photius to the Tetragamy

The forced abdication of the Patriarch Photius in 886 still did not give a hint that the confusion within the Byzantine Imperial Church would end. The new Patriarch Stephen I (886–93), brother of the Emperor Leo VI, was unable to obtain recognition by the intransigent Ignatians, led by the Metropolitan Stylian Mapas, because he had received the diaconate from Photius. Again and again Stylian tried to win Rome to his side.

Reconciliation finally occurred under Pope John IX. It was probably the Patriarch Anthony Cauleas (893–901) who was able to convince Stylian of the senselessness of his opposition. Furthermore, the new Patriarch had been enrolled in the clergy, if not under Methodius, then at the latest under Ignatius, and hence he was not vulnerable in the way that Stephen was. We do not know whether a papal letter prepared or only ratified the reconciliation of the factions, nor can we say for certain whether it took place in the presence of papal legates. In any event, Rome and Constantinople now recognized "Ignatius, Photius, Stephen, and Anthony" as lawful Patriarchs, that is, at least the second patriarchate of Photius was no longer under attack. Stylian accepted the formula, and only a few of his former adherents persisted in schism.

Anthony Cauleas died not long after the conclusion of peace in 899. There now occurred what seemed to be a belated recognition of Photius, when, as a result of the Emperor's initiative, there mounted the patriarchal throne a relative of Photius, though possibly only by spiritual ties, in the person of Nicholas I Mysticus (901–7, 912–25). Nicholas was unquestionably one of the great Patriarchs of Constantinople, and much in his character and activity is reminiscent of Photius.

He too had first followed an administrative career in the service of the state. The fall of Photius made him dread disgrace at the hands of the friend of his youth, Leo VI, and so he withdrew to a monastery. But eventually the Emperor recalled him to court, where he became *mystikos,* or private secretary.

As Patriarch he displayed an uncommon zeal, and the dossier of his correspondence is among the most bulky in the patriarchal chancery. In his patriarchate the Byzantine Church extended its frontiers far to the East. In several circles in Armenia there was discernible a turning from Monophysitism to Byzantine Orthodoxy, which the Patriarch followed with interest. The Christianizing of the Chazars is said to have been furthered from Cherson. The Patriarch even directly contacted the Muslim Emir of Crete to obtain relief for the Christians of the southern Aegean; he finally turned also to the Caliph of Baghdad and assured him of the protection of the mosque in Constantinople and of the free exercise of their religion by Muslim war prisoners in the capital. Together with the Emperor he regulated the important relations of rank of the bishoprics of the Empire by including the ancient bishoprics of Illyricum and South Italy in the official *Notitiae episcopatuum* and sought to control the ecclesiastical system of fees. He gradually became the convinced champion of *oikonomia,* of clemency, of yielding, of patient waiting in all fields.

There were three situations especially in which Nicholas had to show himself as a politician. The first had to do with his role in the treason of Andronicus Ducas; the next with the revolt of the latter's son, Constantine Ducas. A judgment in regard to the Patriarch's attitude is not possible in view of the present state of our knowledge.

More important was the famous Tetragamy Controversy. In 901 Leo VI had lost his third wife by death, and he still had no son. But before long he was presented with a son and heir by his mistress, Zoe Carbonopsina; Leo was willing to legitimate this son, the future Constantine VII Porphyrogennetos, and designate him as his successor. The Patriarch Nicholas was prepared to administer solemn baptism, which he did on Epiphany of 906, and also to recognize the baby prince as legitimate, contrary to all state and ecclesiastical regulations, which of themselves were directed against a third marriage, not to mention a fourth. But the Patriarch laid down as a condition that Leo must separate from his leman. At first Leo agreed, but after a short time he broke his promise, married Zoe, and elevated her to the dignity of Augusta. The Patriarch thereupon forbade the Emperor to enter a church.

Leo countered by consulting Rome and the oriental Patriarchs as to the permissibility of a fourth marriage. In view of such an infringement of his autonomy, Nicholas seems to have been inclined to offer the Emperor a dispensation *motu proprio,* but the Emperor was no longer disposed to bow to his Patriarch. Rome sent legates whether Nicholas held himself aloof from them or the Emperor kept them away from him is not known — who brought the papal reply that there were no canonical considerations contrary to a fourth marriage. The legates of the oriental Patriarchs delivered the same verdict. Nicholas had to go into exile and submit his resignation.

Once again a "case" had been manufactured. It is easy to defend Rome's position by reference to the primatial idea, but more difficult to justify the absence of any regard for the development of canon law in the Byzantine Church. No adjustment and no understanding were attempted; each side exerted itself to carry its own viewpoint just as it was.

Leo's confessor, the monk Euthymius, succeeded Nicholas as Patriarch, and the Byzantine Church split into the unyielding factions of Nicholaites and Euthymians, even though the position adopted by Euthymius differed little from that of his predecessor. He regarded the Roman decision as a dispensation in a particular case, which in no way bound him to recognize a fourth marriage in principle. With his synod he rejected such a request and also declared that any third marriage was unlawful. He deposed the priest Thomas, who had blessed the Emperor's fourth marriage, and was unwilling to review this judgment even on the intervention of the Empress. He refused to perform the religious coronation of the Empress. Hence the schism within the Byzantine Church cannot be fastened onto the canonical outlook of Euthymius; it is connected rather with the fact that Nicholas was compelled to abdicate, contrary to the rules of the canons. And so Euthymius had to pay after the death of Leo VI in 912.

Leo's brother and successor, Alexander, restored Nicholas to his rights and drove the disgraced Euthymius into exile. For his part, Nicholas decreed anathema and deposition for the adherents of his supplanter. This judgment quite needlessly affected all those whom Euthymius had ordained. In a letter to Pope Anastasius III Nicholas reproached the Latin Church with having encouraged unchastity by tolerating a fourth marriage, contrary to the Apostle Paul. He demanded that the Pope excommunicate the authors of the Roman decision. As Rome did not go along with these demands, the Pope was deleted from the diptychs.

Meanwhile there fell to the Patriarch duties which deeply involved him in the most urgent questions of Byzantine foreign policy. It is possible that after the death of the Emperor Alexander in 913 he wanted to place at the side of the little Constantine VII a vigorous guardian and coemperor in the person of Constantine Ducas, but in the meantime he found out that he had himself been appointed regent together with a few senators. But worst of all was his meeting with the victorious Tsar Simeon of the Bulgars, who was quite frankly reaching for the Byzantine imperial crown. This invasion of the Bulgars called for all of the Empire's defensive forces, including those of a united Church.

And so the call for peace and unity was heard throughout the second patriarchate of Nicholas Mysticus. But, as always in Byzantium, imperial pressure was finally required in order really to establish it. In 920 there at length took place a Synod of Union. The document issued at its close is of noteworthy good sense: the cause of the controversy, the fourth marriage of Leo VI, was entirely excluded. New regulations were issued only for the future: from the eighth indiction of the year of the world 6428, that is, from 1 September 920, a fourth marriage was forever forbidden, while a third was possible but only with reservations and subject to ecclesiastical penance.

Union was effected without Rome's participation. The question was: what would be Rome's attitude to it? Shortly after the synod Nicholas condescended to write again to Rome, this time to Pope John X. He requested the sending of legates to condemn fourth marriages in accord with the common faith of all Christendom. But Rome would not agree to any stipulations. Again Nicholas had to give way. Only a letter, in which no conditions were laid down, was successful.

Once again a serious quarrel had been eventually adjusted. Apparently Rome had not given way on any point, and in Byzantium it was clear that a genuine ecclesiastical peace was unthinkable without Rome's participation. Rome had won, and more clearly than in the Photian affair. But the triumph had been purchased at a price that was to become increasingly expensive in the succeeding decades, a lack of interest on the part of the Byzantine Church in crossing the path of the Roman Church. Each held itself aloof, the alienation grew, and the later break was nothing more than drawing the final line.

CHAPTER   1 1 2

The Road to Schism

In the further course of the history of the Byzantine patriarchate in the tenth century there appear historical figures who, on the one hand, amazingly resemble the contemporary Popes, and, on the other hand, office again make very clear the special characteristic of the "Constantinian" ecclesiastical system — the intimate connection between Church policy and the politics of a ruler who regarded himself as Emperor of the world. In other words: the history of these decades cannot be understood apart from the violent quarrels between East and West over questions of the "Roman" imperial office.

The Emperor Romanus I Lecapenus (919–44) aspired by means of an unscrupulous family policy to supplant the Macedonian Dynasty represented by his ward, Constantine VII. He also intended to reserve the patriarchal throne for his house. So long as his son Theophylact was still a child, he appointed two successive Patriarchs, who were regarded only as caretakers and, accordingly, remained in total anonymity. When Theophylact was barely sixteen years old, his father appointed him Patriarch (933–56), and Pope John XI — according to Liutprand, under compulsion from Alberic — made himself a party to the farce, solemnly legalizing the grotesque canonical situation by the presence of his legates. It is not improbable that the same Pope by written explanations of the rank of the see of Constantinople furthered still more the striving for autonomy at Byzantium.

It is amazing that the church of the young Patriarch enjoyed the confidence of the Bulgarian Tsar Peter, who consulted it on the treatment of the sect of the Bogomiles, which had only recently appeared.

It is characteristic of the regenerative powers of the Byzantine Church that the pontificate of Theophylact was a mere interlude. In the person of the monk Polyeuctus (956–70) he obtained a successor of surpassing repute. Fearless in regard to all authorities, austere and unpolished, and concerned to maintain the purity of ecclesiastical discipline, he defended the notion of the charismatic character of the imperial office but at the same time opposed any "identification" of political with purely canonical and religious interests.

The tocsin in regard to the situation of the Empire and of the Church in foreign policy was rung with the imperial coronation of Otto the Great in 962, that is, the recurrence of an event which had already led to severe shocks in 800, because it was at the same time the sign of the determining influence of a rival "non-Roman" imperial power on the papacy, which thereby abandoned the relatively independent, and for Byzantium tolerable, position between the two world powers. Byzantium's reaction was more sensitive when the new Emperor of the German nation reached out for the Byzantine possessions in South Italy, and the Roman Church in his train raised its ancient patriarchal claim to this territory. The most striking countermove of the Byzantine Church was the elevation of Otranto to metropolitan status with the right to consecrate the Bishops of Acerentila, Turcicum, Gravina, Macceria, and Tricarium. Mistrust remained the dominant attitude.

The circumstance that the usurper of the papacy, Boniface VII, escaped with the treasure of Saint Peter's from the German Count Sicco to Constantinople and acted from there as his headquarters could not but strengthen this outlook. Ten years later (984) Boniface succeeded in recovering Rome.

At this time the Patriarch of Constantinople was Sisinnius II (996–98). Peace with Rome was again a fact in the days of Pope John XVIII (1003–9). However, it was not lasting. The combining of papal policy with the purely political interests of the Normans and of the German Emperor in South Italy produced in this area a new situation, which would continue to be decisive for the entire period of the crusades and would really only reach its climax under Charles of Anjou. On the other hand, the reaction of the Byzantines confused ecclesiastical and secular just as perversely as did the policy of their papal opponents. And this is the basis from which the Byzantine Patriarch Michael Caerularius drew his strength.

Michael was the successor of a Patriarch, Alexius the Studite (1025–43), who brought to the patriarchal throne little of the old spirit of his monastery. His patriarchal *acta* are full of canonistic notifications of a laudable reform zeal, but in fact he bowed, in the age of the decay of the last Macedonians on the imperial throne, to every public violation of the rights of the Church without protesting, so far as is known. And just as Theophylact was followed by a Polyeuctus, so now Alexius was followed by the masterful figure of Michael Caerularius (1043–58), who, characteristically, referred the *Constitutum Constantini* to his see and from it deduced quasi-imperial rights. It is difficult to do him justice, for his headstrong, not to say revolutionary, personality represents an exception in the history of the Byzantine patriarchate.

The good services rendered by the Norman intruders to the papacy soon changed, and the Popes themselves were interested in again getting rid of the specter. Here, then, Byzantine and papal policy suddenly agreed again on something. But the resources of both were, by themselves, too little to deal with the danger, and so the idea of a great alliance of the two Empires and of the papacy began to stir. One of the strongest advocates of this idea was that very Byzantine who had to be the best informed about the situation, Argyros, *catepan* of the Byzantine Empire's Italian possessions. The Emperor Constantine IX could be gained for the plan without difficulty, but in Michael Caerularius it found an implacable opponent.

The reasons for this opposition were probably complex in nature. Argyros was the son of that Melo who in 1009 had fought against Byzantium in Apulia under papal and German protection. The son had been raised in Byzantium but belonged to the Latin rite and at the beginning of the 1040s played a highly ambiguous role as Byzantine commander in South Italy. If not by virtue of his rite, then because of his political background and past, Argyros could impress a convinced Byzantine as someone quite suspicious. Michael hated him.

And so he began a campaign of discriminating against the Roman Church, of an acidity not attained even by that of Photius. Michael was not concerned about proceedings on the highest plane, with a tumult in the capital against the new direction of imperial policy. His propaganda had to do with ecclesiastical ritual, especially the use of unleavened bread in the Latin Church, its custom of fasting on Saturdays, and so forth. He only discovered the *Filioque,* so to speak, at the eleventh hour.

In any event, he began with drastic measures in his own episcopal city. On his orders the churches of the Latins were closed; the upshot was disorderly scenes, in which even the consecrated Hosts were not always spared. Propagandist for the Patriarch was Archbishop Leo of Ochrida, with his circular to the Bishop of Trani, a Latin. Fundamentally it was directed at the Pope and demanded no less than the removal from the Latin Church of all rites which were displeasing to Byzantium. It is noteworthy however, that this letter expressed no anathema. The Bishop of Trani sent it on to the Curia, and Cardinal Humbert of Silva Candida was commissioned to reply. Michael Caerularius thereby found an opponent who was his match and whose temperament vied with that of the Patriarch. The eventual elimination of Pope Leo IX by death left the field to two warriors, between whom no compromise was now possible. Humbert's reply to the Greek circular contained all the claims of the reformed papacy, but distorted by historically questionable amplifications, by the incorporating of the *Constitutum Constantini,* and by the claims of the papacy to South Italy. The Cardinal charged the Greek Church with "more than ninety heresies."

Meanwhile, the situation in South Italy had reached a crisis. Pope Leo managed to collect a contingent of troops, and at their head he marched against the Normans. Shortly before, Argyros had had to accept a reverse from these very Normans at Siponto, and he was unable to bring his troops to join those of the Pope. Leo IX suffered a severe defeat and became the Normans' prisoner in June 1053; from captivity he tried to take care of the Church's affairs as best he could. The Pope's defeat was by implication a defeat for Byzantine interests in South Italy. The alliance desired by Argyros was more urgent than ever, and the imperial court could only bow to this line of argument. The Emperor Constantine IX wrote to the Curia and expressed his desire for peace in the Church as the precondition of a political alliance, and even Michael Caerularius had to yield to pressure and make known to the Pope in moderate tones his wish for an understanding.

The Curia now decided to send an embassy to Constantinople to bring about peace. It was headed by Humbert, who was accompanied by the Roman Chancellor, Frederick of Lotharingia, and Archbishop Peter of Amalfi. Before the departure for Constantinople Humbert conferred at length with Argyros, who was probably not sparing with warnings against the Patriarch. In Constantinople the embassy was honorably received by the Emperor, whereas its visit with the Patriarch was more than chilly. The Romans felt that they were not properly honored, the Patriarch that he was not greeted according to protocol. The scene ended, so to speak, with a silent handing over of the papal letter, which, again written by Humbert, was not capable of banishing the Patriarch's fears that the political alliance could impair his authority in the Byzantine Church. There was no conversation, and Humbert devoted himself all the more zealously to political propaganda.

In this situation the Patriarch, in a violent polemic which did not spare the court, succeeded in making propaganda in his own favor, and the legates decided to leave without having accomplished their purpose, but not without first, in a solemn act, having laid a bull of excommunication of the Patriarch and his accomplices on the altar of Hagia Sophia on 16 July 1054. Its text went much too far. It anathematized the "pseudo-Patriarch" Michael Caerularius, Archbishop Leo of Ochrida, and other adherents of the Patriarch as simonists, Arians, Nicolaites, Severans, Pneumatomachoi, Manichaeans, Nazarites, and so forth, and thereby subjected to anathema not merely the Greek doctrine of the procession of the Holy Spirit, for example, but also such things as the marriage of Greek priests and other legitimate Greek usages.

Pope Leo IX had been dead for three months; whether the legates knew this cannot be determined. The questionable nature of their proceedings is underscored by the unspeakable misuse of dogmatic deductions. After this act the legates took their departure of the Emperor in a very amicable fashion — as always, he was helpless — and set out on their return journey. It may be that at the time of their leaving the translation of the bull had not yet been laid before the Emperor or he had not yet reflected on its import. But this was quickly rectified, and Constantine IX was induced to call back the envoys, probably to discuss the complex of questions in a common meeting. This was not in the interest of the Patriarch. He rallied the people and proposed a session under circumstances in which the legates could have felt themselves to be in personal danger. The effort to calm spirits thus misfired, and now the Emperor suggested to the legates on his own that they leave, after the mob had even begun to besiege the imperial palace. The Emperor ceased to resist and bowed to the Patriarch's propaganda: Argyros was sacrificed, and the Emperor's closest advisers had to leave the palace.

On Sunday, 24 July, the Emperor convoked a synod, whose *semeioma* presented the events in its own fashion. The legates were disqualified as being legates of Argyros, the text of their bull of excommunication was incorporated into the *semeioma* as a horrible example, it was interpreted as an excommunication of the entire orthodox Church. The excommunication was turned back on the legates and their supporters.

This, then, was the celebrated Schism of 1054. The historical evaluation scarcely needs to be covered over with the juridical. Whether the excommunication was legal, now that the Pope was long dead and as yet had no successor, is controverted. In regard to its content, it was to a great extent an unlawful amplification of Humbert's own personal resentments, even if the central question was included. But in form it did not, in any event, attack the Orthodox Church as such, and not its head, the Emperor, but only Michael and his abettors. Similarly, Michael did not excommunicate the Pope or the Roman Church, but only the legates and their backers, as Argyros and his circle were alleged to be. What was meant by both sides was, in any case, something different, and of this there can be scarcely any doubt. According to the formalities of law, no acts had been performed which would permit one to speak of a schism in the strict sense. But the vehemence in word and act was new and unprecedented, the repertory of mutual recriminations had been substantially enlarged in comparison with the Photian Schism, and the generalizations were grotesque.

The term "schism" cannot be rejected out of hand, but it would be false to designate the situation as hopeless from then on. Even then the Emperor was still basically in control of the government of the Church, and there remained the question whether another Emperor than the weak Constantine IX would not have suddenly changed course again. Besides, in Byzantium the violent character of the Patriarch was well known, and the extent to which all the events were the result of his own vehement policy was hardly underrated. And, finally, it was not to be excluded that in time Rome might enter upon a path which would no longer adhere to the subjective line of a Humbert.

The oriental Churches did not follow the policy of the Ecumenical Patriarch throughout with flying colors. Above all it was the Patriarch Peter III of Antioch, a former cleric of Constantinople, who pursued his own course and was not inclined to wheel around to Michael's direction. For a long time churchmen almost universally took no more notice of this "Schism" than did Byzantine historiography.

CHAPTER 113

The Inner Life of the Byzantine Church between Photius and Caerularius

It is becoming ever clearer that the charge of hostility to culture, which was raised in regard to the iconoclasts, sprang to a great extent from the polemics against the heretics and that, on the contrary, an Emperor like Theophilus, the last iconoclast, was one of the significant protagonists of a self-realization of the Greek mind after generations of stagnation. So too the Patriarch Photius, as the scholar of his age, must at the same time be considered as the first great representative of this self-realization, to which pertained love for the treasures of ancient civilization along with impartiality of thought, confidence in reason, and enthusiasm for form and its classical setting. In this regard, classicism for Photius referred to the pagan writings of antiquity as well as to those of the Church Fathers. This movement culminated in Photius but did not end with his downfall. Its tracks are found everywhere, and a generation after his death a circle of busy philologists and encyclopedic compiler formed around the Emperor Constantine VII Porphyrogennetos (912–59)). It stored up much, even if in epitome, in the granary of tradition and perhaps even reduced to the form of a means of education what in Photius had served education more impartially and more freely. This movement also prevailed in theology.

A philologist of great importance, a philologist of ecclesiastical literature too, was especially Photius' pupil, Arethas, Metropolitan of Caesarea in Cappadocia, a scholarly glossator and scholiast, not only of classical literature but also of the Bible and of the earliest Christian literature — Justin, Tatian, Athenagoras, Clement, and so forth. A younger contemporary of Photius, Nicetas Byzantios, opponent of the Armenian Monophysites, of Islam, and of the Latins, and, as such, scarcely original, still surprises by a scholastic method of argumentation, which for that epoch seems almost rationalistic. His type is encountered a century later in the Metropolitan Stephen of Nicomedia, author of brief summaries on philosophical propaedeutics and on particular questions of theology. He is of interest most of all because the opposition of the pneumatics and enthusiasts, represented by the great mystic, Simeon the New Theologian, caught fire on his works. And here may be mentioned a special sort of work, the *Chiliostichos theologia* composed around the turn of the tenth century by Leo Choirosphactes, in whom Arethas saw an odious "Hellene." We are referring to an exposition of theology in verse, which seems to feed entirely on the Hellenistic mystery theology and neo-Platonic terminology. Even the work of encyclopedic compilation that was going on around Constantine VII found expression in theological literature. Theodore Daphnopates, a high official under the Emperor Romanus II (959–63), produced the Chrysostom eclogues, extracts from the sermons of this Church Father, which, in the form of homilies on the most varied virtues and vices, like the excerpts of Constantine VII from profane literature, summarized the thought of John Chrysostom. To this group also belonged Simeon Metaphrastes, with his eclogues from Basil, Chrysostom, and homilies of pseudo-Macarius.

This Simeon owes his name Metaphrastes to his hagiographical activity. With this we reach a field of theological writing that was more intensively cultivated in this period than ever before. The sufferings endured in the age of Iconoclasm gave this *genre* an unexpected upsurge. Others, had their panegyrists. Patriarchal biography found revisers, who, abandoning the *genre* of real hagiography, became the chroniclers and pamphleteers of their age, so agitated in ecclesiastical politics. In addition the edifying hagiographical romance, without any historical background, represented a variegated wealth, partly of undifferentiated encomia, partly of fanciful stories, partly of still naive reporting in the spirit of the hagiography of the early seventh century.

But it was exactly this last type which was to achieve its destiny in the period under consideration, and indeed in the name of classicism of rhetorical form, for which the scholars of the age, including the theologians, became ever more enthusiastic.

At least as important as the contribution of this period to hagiography was its contribution to the history of Byzantine mysticism In Simeon the New Theologian it acquired a prophet of a unique sort. Merely from the viewpoint of phenomenology, his importance is based on his having made the breakthrough from the mystical treatise to the entirely personal mystical confession or even hymn. As regards the sociology of his mysticism it should be noted that he always sought to prepare the way whereby it should move out of the monastery to the laity in the Church. But in regard to content he pursued a course which had probably never been unfamiliar in Byzantium but at first had difficulty in asserting itself vis-à-vis the strict line of Evagrian mysticism: the mysticism of the metaphysical feeling. That Messalian ideas stood as sponsors here can be disproved with difficulty, but in Diadochus of Photice the doctrine of the empirical nature of the mystical grace found an orthodox herald, and the introduction of the so-called Macarius homilies of Messalian origin into the treasure of the tradition of orthodox mysticism did more than was necessary. The impetus of this mysticism, which wanted to "experience," and that as quickly as possible, united early with the method of the so-called "Prayer of Jesus," which was likewise not foreign to Simeon. It culminated in light visions, which were so uniquely formulated in Simeon's language that one is induced and forced to seek their locale in an area midway between spiritual and corporal, which can scarcely be defined. Because Simeon was a hymnographer and ecstatic confessor and not a theorist, areas of the classical mysticism, such as the so-called "physical theory," the contemplative effort to penetrate, in patience and hope, into the divine *rationes* of creation and of history, certainly come off badly.

In Simeon that enthusiasm of the old monachism again breaks out, which the hierarchy, probably incorrectly, thought had been expelled, the conviction of the special mediating role of the monk as the bearer of the Spirit between God and the sinner. Conflict with the hierarchy did not fail to occur: two interpretations of theology, an enthusiastic and irrational and a scholastic, opposed each other intransigently, because apparently neither Simeon nor his direct opposite, the above mentioned Stephen of Nicomedia, was willing to admit the limitations of his own "method," and correspondingly, two mutually exclusive interpretations of the nature and significance of the *charisma* in the Church. In the course of time the antitheses were smoothed away but their traces could not be entirely obliterated.

If in Simeon's lifetime there was already evident the withdrawal from the Studites' cenobitic ideal, interested in ecclesiastical politics and living in an alternating relationship of friendship and hostility to the hierarchy, on the other hand this period meant "topographically" a shift of the center of gravity of the Byzantine monastic world from Bithynia to Athos, the holy mountain of the future. With the Muslim raids into Bithynia around the turn to the ninth century there apparently began a devastation of the monastic settlements on and around Olympus. And when as a consequence of the Byzantine offensive of the tenth century this danger could also be exorcised, the Seljuk invasion in the second half of the eleventh century again brought new and intensified dangers. The progress of monasticism on Athos is certainly connected with this.

The origins of the Athonian monastic colonization are covered with a darkness which is ever more transfigured by legend. Colonies of anchorites more or less entered the light of history in the ninth century. Rarely of any size, they eventually joined in a loosely organized community and discussed the most pressing community matters under a *protos.* A significant turning point in this development came with the founding of the so-called "Great Laura" on Athos by Saint Athanasius. Athanasius was born in Trebizond. Encouraged by his patron, the Emperor Nicephorus II Phocas, around 961 he built the first large monastery on Athos and gave it a rule, which conformed to that of the Studites but also borrowed from that of Saint Benedict. Athanasius not only succeeded, thanks to the imperial authority, in establishing his monastery devoted to the common life on the mountain, against the ill will of the anchorites already there, but in 971 or 972 he was able to induce Nicephorus' successor, the Emperor John I Tzimisces (969–76), to grant the whole monastic territory a *magna carta,* the so-called *Tragos,* extant in the original. In this the existence of a new large abbey in the overall structure of the administration of the mountain was duly taken into account. Other foundations arose of these the national monastery of the Georgians, the *Iberon* should be mentioned which also followed the cenobitic ideal, and a charter of the Emperor Constantine IX Monomachus of 1046 confirmed in general, despite all still existing opposition, the regulation of the community made by John I. Thus was the foundation laid for the amazing development of a monastic republic, which was soon to become the protagonist of Orthodoxy.

Besides these very promising beginnings of a new monastic territory, the monastic idea at this period also experienced the most serious injuries, which can be summarized under the juridical notion of charistikariate — the presenting of monasteries to lay persons by bishops or Patriarchs and Emperors. In some cases there may have been no doubt that the intention of the *charistikarioi* was, through the assumption of the monastery, to assure it a protection against oppression from all sides, especially from that of the *fiscus,* to correct evils that arose, and, with the best of intentions, to relieve the monks of the burden of secular business. But more frequently such a gift ministered only to greed. And in its origin the charistikariate must be seen as a secondary aspect of the attempt by the magnates, the *dynatoi,* to extend their possessions and also to invade the small holdings of the free peasant communities an attempt with which imperial legislation had to contend again and again in the tenth century. The movement proceeded both from the top down and from the bottom up, that is, occasionally the peasants purchased the protection of a magnate from the pressure of taxation and the harshness of the state's impositions by a voluntary renunciation of their freedom and entry into a tenant relationship. And likewise in the case of the commendatory monasteries, at first the desire of the monasteries seems occasionally to have been directed to a protector. In any event, the movement established itself and led to serious harm to discipline in the monasteries and even to the monasteries' material substance.

The Abbot's power disappeared as the monks looked rather to the *charistikarios* than to their spiritual superior. The *charistikarios* now determined the number of monks in the monastery, the maximum provision for their material life, the necessities for the monastery's library and liturgy, ordinarily in the interest of his own income, which he intended to draw from the monastery. The invasion of the small farms of the peasants by the *dynatoi* could be achieved by some kind of legal fiction, such as adoption or bequest, but in the case of monastic property an ecclesiastical legal formality was needed, and this was supplied by the charistikariate. At first the grant was for a time, but it goes without saying that the *charistikarioi* sought to make the property hereditary. Thus were developed the intermediate forms, "for three lives," which only thinly concealed the yielding of the ecclesiastical authorities, whom one must probably regard as themselves allied to the *charistikarioi* by family ties. *De iure,* of course, there was never a transfer of ownership but only of authority. But since, despite some initial opposition, the right of the founders to the ownership of their churches was more and more firmly established even in the central Byzantine period, and the founder was more and more identified with the "benefactor" and "restorer" (*charistikarios*), the rights of ownership of the founder, even when conditioned by the purpose of the foundation, were easily transferred to the *charistikarios.* A Patriarch as energetic as Sisinnius II (996–98) flatly forbade any such donation, but a successor, Sergius II (1009–19), had to annul this regulation and recognize the charistikariate with slight restrictions. The Patriarch Alexius the Studite (1025–43) did indeed complain in great distress about the situation, but his regulations did not attack the roots of the evil and were content rather with quite general precautions. And so the situation persisted and came to flower under the Comneni.

The power of the Patriarch grew, not with regard to the internal affairs of his Church, but in connection with the neighboring churches and, in extent, through the gaining of new territories. The Byzantine advance against the Islamic East brought territorial gains of great importance. Ancient sees, which for centuries had figured only formally on the lists, could now be occupied again, and others, as new capitals of political provinces, were elevated also in ecclesiastical rank. In this process not even the frontiers of the ancient patriarchates were observed, but rather the primacy of the "Ecumenical Patriarch," who adopted this title even on his seal from the time of Caerularius, was powerfully stressed. Here imperial and patriarchal policy went hand in hand. Any rights of Rome in ancient Illyricum were ignored by Byzantium now as before.

As we have seen, it was Antioch especially that had to endure the encroachments of an Ecumenical Patriarch, thinking in terms of a primacy, on territories not his own. Following the reconquest of 969 the Emperors at first installed Patriarchs here at their discretion and had their candidates approved by the *Synodos endemusa* in Constantinople. The Patriarch John III (996–1020) even had himself consecrated at Constantinople, contrary to canon law, and then, as consecrated Patriarch, bestowed this right of consecration in principle on the see of Constantinople. Peter III (1052–56), who had made his career in the patriarchal service at Constantinople, protested against this spurious right, but unsuccessfully. The jurisdictional primacy of the Ecumenical Patriarch was advancing under the shadow of the imperial authority.

Section Three

Changes within the Christian West during the Gregorian Reform

Friedrich Kempf

CHAPTER 114

The New Shape of the Church: Law and Organization before Gratian

The struggle for the *libertas ecclesiae* aimed at something more comprehensive than a mere liberation from the power of the laity. The reformers wanted to find the way back to the ancient, pure Church, to the free play of the forces proper to her. For the sake of clarity it was especially necessary to investigate the juridical sources. Since the usual collections, especially that of Burchard of Worms, did not suffice for this purpose, they extracted from the papal *registra,* the *Ordines romani,* the *Liber diurnus,* from conciliar acts, from the writings of the Fathers and historical works, from imperial *privilegia* and the law of Justinian a wealth of hitherto unused texts, not to mention the pseudo-Isidorean forgeries, regarded as genuine, whose content was now for the first time entirely exploited. The material, combined into unsystematic collections, no longer extant seems to have been at the disposal of several canonists working from the time of Gregory VII; of itself it called for systematically arranged collections.

Thus, throughout the reform period new canonical compilations were coming into existence. The authors of these private works were confronted with the difficult problem of separating the authentic from the false or from what was valid only locally. Although in the general view the norm lay with the papacy, it still needed a more precise definition. The demand of a few radicals, that only those laws which had been issued or approved by the Popes should be adopted, proved to be inadequate. Hence the more judicious recognized all texts which did not contradict the laws of the Roman Church; accordingly, they envisaged the idea of a *ius commune* as the totality of a somehow coherent legal system that culminated in the authority of the Holy See, without implying that every particular had to be positively decreed by the papacy. Naturally in this abundantly unclear principle of choice there were some contradictions among individual canons. To solve them became at times the more urgent task. For this the canonists were not merely satisfied with a hierarchical gradation of individual texts; they also worked out important rules of textual criticism and eventually instituted the dialectical method in order to cancel the contradictions with distinctions and subdistinctions. The science of canon law began slowly to pervade intellectually the source material at hand in the collections, but the sought for *concordantia discordantium canonum* was not achieved until around 1140 with the *Decretum* of Gratian.

The struggle for an ecclesiastical legal system, motivated by the understanding that for canon law the early medieval awareness, rooted in customary law, did not suffice, announced a new age. Its onward pressing *élan* assured the Church a wide lead over what was possible to the states. Gradually recognized by all Christian countries of the West, the canon law, always assuming more stable forms, fashioned the Church into a truly supranational power structure. This had as a consequence that the supreme guardian and interpreter of ecclesiastical law, the Pope, grew to overshadow the ruling position of the Emperor and the kings, a position which from the time of Alexander III was consolidated and extended by a steadily increasing decretal activity. Nevertheless, it would be ill-advised to see the development of ecclesiastical law as directed merely to the exaltation of the papal power. What the reformers stressed, not without sharp criticism of the early Middle Ages, was the fundamental hierarchical principle of the Church, in no sense restricted to the Pope. By making it the juridical form of the Church, they achieved a sharper separation between laity and priesthood and prepared for a more compact and, so to speak, corporative association of clerics as the real representatives of the Church.

Despite the clericalization now getting under way, the laity did not simply become hearers and flunkies. Besides their right to the administration of certain Sacraments, which was ever more elaborated by the canonists, they possessed not inconsiderable powers in questions of the clergy or of ecclesiastical administration.

Proprietorship of churches was, it is true, taken away from the laity, at least in principle, after the attempt, made occasionally in the reform period, to distinguish between the temporalities (*ecclesia*) and the spiritualities (*altare*) in regard to the lesser churches also had failed. The first two Lateran Councils thus held to the principle that lay persons must not possess any ecclesiastical property and that the lesser benefices were to be granted by the bishop. Thus Gratian and his successors down to Alexander III were able to bring about a solution in keeping with the hierarchical principle. They replaced the right of proprietorship with the *patronatus* subject to ecclesiastical legislation as *ius spirituali annexum* (Alexander III). On the one hand this maintained the Church's right of proprietorship; on the other hand, out of gratitude for the foundation, it conceded to the previous proprietor the right of presentation of the cleric to be instituted and specified honorary rights, but it likewise imposed obligations, such as a subsidiary construction burden. Actually the whole thing remained to a great extent mere theory; in practice the old right of proprietorship lived on everywhere, more or less energetically.

The history of the proprietary church system probably shows how laboriously the reform made its way to the lower levels of the ecclesiastical organization. Thus the lesser clergy remained essentially bound by the old relationships, despite their greater dependence on the ecclesiastical offices above them. The hierarchical principle had a graduated operation: whereas it produced its full effect in the case of the papacy, its force was already diminished in regard to the bishops. Free episcopal election was undoubtedly a lasting achievement of the reform. The amount of influence still allowed to rulers could be eliminated later in some countries — by Innocent III in England and Germany. The people's share became insignificant during the twelfth century, so that the election was carried out chiefly by the diocesan clergy and, from the end of the century, by the cathedral chapter alone. And yet the frequent disputed elections, often due not to oppositions within the church but to those springing from state and family politics, show how much the election still depended on secular factors.

And the bishop's own authority was strictly limited. Competing with it was the growing power of archdeacons, reaching its peak in the thirteenth century, not only in jurisdiction but also in important administrative tasks, such as visitation of and appointments to parishes, holding of synods, and so forth. Episcopal authority suffered a more painful, because enduring, loss at the hands of the cathedral chapter, which was able in the thirteenth century to secure a share in the government of the diocese. Bishops would certainly not have completely excluded these rivals of theirs, but perhaps they would have been better able to limit them if they had not been distracted, especially in Germany, by state and territorial political interests. Thus they found themselves in no position to keep pace adequately, through the systematic completion of their own proper hierarchical position, with the new development of the ecclesiastical organization, beginning about the time of Alexander III, which was powerfully to display the Pope's monarchical power.

In the early twelfth century, now under consideration, the relations between Pope and bishop were as yet no real problem. Although the reform Popes had often dealt sternly enough with individual bishops, these emergency measures must not be regarded as aimed at episcopal power as such. The more the Investiture Controversy neared its end, the more the Popes endeavored to show regard for the rights of the bishops. Not only the First Lateran Council, but the noteworthy prudence of Calixtus II and his immediate successors in regard to monastic exemption clearly indicate this. And is it not characteristic of the spirit of the age that the mightily flourishing new orders of the Cistercians and the canons regular wanted to be subject to the local bishops, the canons regular because of their natural bond with the episcopate, the Cistercians because of the idealism of their period of foundation, and idealism that would quickly fade? In any event there could be as yet no question of a tendency to bind the whole episcopate directly to Rome as far as possible. If the Pope occasionally decided the disputed election of a bishop not directly subject to him, if he officiated at the consecration and then required the customary oath of obedience, the initiative here lay usually with the bishop and his faction.

Much less favorable was the position of the metropolitans. From the Carolingian period it had become the custom that they requested the pallium from the Pope. Proceeding from this, the reform Pope; began soon after the middle of the eleventh century to demand that new archbishops receive the pallium in person. With its solemn investiture was included gradually, more commonly from Paschal II, the taking of an oath of obedience, modelled on the oath of vassalage, that is, of an oath which earlier the suffragans of the Roman Church and a few other, mostly Italian, bishops had had to take according to an older formula. The new formula included also the obligation of the periodic *visitatio liminum apostolorum.* The new development meant the triumph of the old Roman view, already to be discerned in the later Carolingian period, that the exercise of the metropolitan right of consecration depended on the possession of the pallium. The connection with Rome, secured symbolically and juridically, made it easy to regard the metropolitan authority as a participation in the universal authority of the Pope. This did not necessarily involve a diminution of archiepiscopal powers. As a matter of fact, at first most rights remained intact, and they were even extended by the right of devolution, established in 1080 for irregular episcopal elections. Just the same, metropolitans meant less in practice than they had meant in the early Middle Ages. The reason must be sought in the bishops rather than in the Popes. Out of the old opposition supported by the spirit of pseudo Isidore, many bishops preferred, in juridical matters, to apply directly or by appeal to the Holy See.

The primates making their appearance from the time of Gregory VII possessed virtually no influence. It was conceived as a voluntary tribunal of appeals. Its origin was a scholarly pseudo-Isidorean invention, which, having recourse to the Roman provincial divisions in Gaul, ascribed to the metropolitans of the respective "first" provinces, such as *Lugdunensis Prima,* the position of primate or patriarch over the metropolitans of the subordinate provinces of the same name, for example, *Lugdunensis Secunda* and so forth. The idea did not acquire reality until the reform period. The initiative probably proceeded not from the papacy but from French archbishops of a *prima sedes,* who, on the basis of pseudo-Isidore, regarded as genuine, thought that they could reclaim an ancient right. It is true that honorary precedence was gained rather than real power. Little interest was displayed for the envisaged possibility of appeal. And if recourse was had to it, the metropolitans thus affected offered active or passive resistance.

Accordingly, since the bishops were not interested in a strong metropolitan authority nor the metropolitans in any kind of primatial authority, even only a weak one, the hierarchical principle, with its striving for a comprehensive juridical unity of the Church, especially benefited the summit — the papacy. The reform period brought the definitive change. In the struggle for the *libertas ecclesiae* the Roman Church had finally been able to realize the freedom proper to her, that is, her primatial claims based on genuine or what was regarded as genuine tradition. These comprised especially: free papal election, now sufficiently assured both in regard to the German ruler, who in the course of the Investiture Controversy lost the right of consent as recognized earlier by Nicholas II, and in regard to the Roman people and clergy, who still shared in the election but were restricted and slowly pushed aside by the prerogatives of the cardinals; then, the exclusive right to convoke general synods, which were arranged by the reform Popes at Rome or elsewhere in place of the earlier Roman provincial synods and constituted the preliminaries to the general councils of the Middle Ages — Innocent III was the first to identify the Fourth Lateran Council intentionally with the ancient ecumenical councils; and, finally, the principle of supreme legislative, judicial, and administrative authority, to the extent that it was possible to seize upon it in tradition. More or less the following rights were then valid for the supreme judicial power: the Pope's immunity from trial, except in the case of heresy, his judicial competence both for exempt monasteries and for all bishops and, in general, for all *causae maiores,* and, finally, the position of the Roman Church as the supreme court of appeals. The primatial administrative rights comprised chiefly the basic supreme supervision, the establishing, defining, and suppressing of dioceses, the transfer of a religious community to another Order, the granting of exemption to monasteries, the exerting of influence on the filling of sees, made possible by a process instituted at the Holy See or by use of the right of devolution, which the Roman Synod of 1080 had granted to the Pope as well as to the metropolitan for the case of irregular episcopal elections. Further possibilities of intervention were added from the end of the twelfth century by the legal stabilization of episcopal elections. In like manner, the rights to the filling of lesser benefices and the constituting of a papal sovereignty over finance and the religious orders belong to the later development beginning with the decretal law.

If the papal monarchy was completed only later, still the reform assisted it toward the breakthrough and brought to an end the extensive independence of the early medieval episcopate. To be sure, there was no lack of angry protests in regard to particular measures or even in regard to the basic attitude of Gregory VII, who, according to the repudiation of 1076, sought to wrest all power from the bishops so far as he could; particular rights of the Pope were questioned in principle; and even reformers like Ivo of Chartres occasionally wished for a careful defining of papal competence. But, on the whole, friends and foes were agreed, and strict anti-Gregorians recognized the Roman primacy as much as did its direct defenders. Only one writer was bold enough to lay the axe to the roots: the Norman Anonymous. According to him, the primacy was not a divine institution but one created by men because of Rome's being the capital of the world, and hence in no sense was it something necessary for salvation; all bishops were vicars of Christ and thus to be judged by no one. The real mother of all the churches was not Rome but Jerusalem. Whoever sought to create a higher authority split the one Church.

It was not so much the principle of the primacy as such as its practical application that the reform established. That this occurred was to a great extent due to the papal legates. Already in the earliest periods the Roman Church had dispatched legates with particular commissions, and from the fifth to the eighth century it had even maintained permanent representatives, the *apocrisiarii,* at the imperial Byzantine court and at that of the Exarch in Ravenna. Furthermore, it had elevated Boniface and other heralds of the Gospel as missionary legates and as early as the fifth and sixth centuries had entrusted outstanding bishops of remote lands with an apostolic vicariate. This stream of tradition, almost choked off, was put to use from about 1056 by the reform Popes for the system of legates.

While it is true that the old principle remained in force that legates should receive as much authority as their assignment required — still, since the comprehensive reform work demanded general powers, the legates appointed for this, usually cardinals or local bishops, were made vicars of the Pope and disposed of the full primatial authority to the extent that this was then claimed by Rome. Of course, there were also legates with special tasks; they were chosen preponderantly from lower clerics. The activity of reform legates consisted principally of visitations and the holding of synods, in connection with which the opposition was often broken by stern punishments, even deposition, and by interventions in the filling of sees.

A real differentiation of classes of legates had not yet been made. It began only with Alexander III and amounted to the following groups: *legati a latere,* equipped with a wealth of special rights, which developed into a *iurisdictio ordinaria, legati missi,* with less authority; *nuntii apostolici* for particular assignments; *vicarii apostolici* or *legati nati,* who were local archbishops and bishops.

Still more decisive was to be the effect of another product of the reform — the College of Cardinals. Its origin is disputed. From the fifth century the priests of the Roman titular churches had to provide a weekly liturgical ministry for the cemeterial basilicas of San Pietro, San Paolo, and San Lorenzo, and then also for Santa Maria Maggiore and San Giovanni in Laterano. In the eighth century probably, this service was altered to the extent that thereafter it was attended to in the Lateran basilica by seven bishops of the nearby dioceses and in the other four basilicas by the priests of the titular churches which had been increased, in groups of seven, to the number of twenty-eight. Since from the time of Gregory the Great clerics who were employed in, or incardinated into, another church than that from which they came were called *cardinales,* this title was now used also for the bishops and priests who were made use of in the Roman weekly ministry. Their functions were purely liturgical, and so they made no claim to any special position of authority in the Roman Church.

There were now also "cardinals" in many churches inside and outside Italy; they must not be confused with the Roman cardinals. The most important group among them was made up of the so-called *presbyteri de cardine;* their precedence consisted in this, that their churches, as opposed to private oratories and proprietary churches, belonged to the bishopric or to the cathedral and hence were attached to the pivot (*cardo*) of the diocese. Both ideas must be borne in mind in the formation of the College of Cardinals. Since the Popes had to provide the enthusiasts for reform whom they gathered around themselves with important Roman churches, they usually enrolled them among the cardinal bishops and cardinal priests. Occupied with reform duties, the new cardinals naturally dissociated themselves from the duties of the hebdomadal ministry, to which of itself the possession of their churches obliged them. As co-responsible representatives of the Roman Church, the pivot of the Universal Church, they thus became *episcopi* or *presbyteri cardinis romani.*

The beginning was made by the Cardinal-Bishops; the papal election decree of 1059 elevated them for the period of the vacancy to be the actual representatives of the Roman Church. The Cardinal-Priests, no less zealous assistants in the reform struggle, won their position in the time of the Anti-pope Clement III and of Pope Urban II. For virtually only the Gregorian Cardinal-Priests had gone over to Clement, with whom they acquired such influence that Urban II had to have the same consideration for the Cardinal-Priests who adhered to him. Finally,

Cardinal-Deacons also made their appearance under both claimants, and in the time of Paschal II they numbered eighteen. The deacons originally numbered seven but the suppression of the archdeacon reduced them to six. They had long pertained to the Lateran basilica and performed both liturgical and administrative functions for the Pope. In the course of the general development they acquired the rank of cardinals.

Under Paschal II the College of Cardinals reached its final complement with seven (later six) bishops, twenty-eight priests, and eighteen deacons. International in composition, it thereafter stood at the Pope's side as an advisory and assisting institution and was able to strengthen its influence in the succeeding period, especially during the Schism of 1130–38, but at the same time no clear regulation of its right as co-speaker with relation to the papacy was reached. The cardinals' advisory function became so important, at least in consistory, that the Popes felt they should dispense with more frequent general synods. The more stable organization that was slowly being prepared included a treasury belonging to the college and administered by the Cardinal *Camerlengo* and a more precise regulation of the revenues.

The centralizing exertions of the reform papacy necessarily had to transform the old administrative organs. The papal chancery gradually freed itself from any connection with Rome's *scriniarii.* The frequent papal travels, beginning with Leo IX, of themselves brought it about that the documents to be issued *en route* were engrossed by the chaplains accompanying the Pope — the *scriniarii* concerned with Roman private documents naturally did not come along — or by scribes of the country in question. The next step quickly followed: the librarian-chancellor appointed one and later two and on occasion more clerics of the Lateran palace as permanent *scriptores* and thus laid the ground for an official college of clerical *scriptores,* which in the long run, deprived the urban *scriniarii* of any possibility of participating. The new development also revolutionized papal diplomatics. The curial hand employed by the *scriniarii* was replaced by the Carolingian minuscule, soon elaborated to meet the chancery's requirements. A new formal language. resuming the forgotten rhythmic rules of the *cursus latinus,* arose and new types were added to the old, remodelled charters. When in 1118 the Chancellor John of Gaetà ascended the papal throne as Gelasius II, the new chancery tradition was firmly established, thanks to his thirty-years' activity. Its membership drawn from the Catholic world, headed by a cardinal until toward the close of the twelfth century and from time to time more carefully organized, into the fourteenth century the chancery represented the most important administrative office of the papacy.

Furthermore, the financial system was reorganized. Following the model of Cluny, Urban II subordinated it to a *camerarius* and thereby founded the *Camera apostolica.* The at first modest office acquired around 1140, in addition to the administration of the treasury, that of the library and archives, and Hadrian IV's *camerlengo,* Cardinal Boso, assumed the care of papal property in the Papal State. From then on progress was continuous. The *camerlengo* acquired the rank of highest papal court official, and in the thirteenth and fourteenth centuries the *Camera* was at least to limit the importance of the chancery, if it did not entirely surpass it.

There were perhaps papal chaplains even before the reform, but one may probably speak of a papal *capella* in the strict sense only from the end of the eleventh century. This institution, modelled on that of royal and episcopal courts, affected the development of the Roman Curia to the extent that the clerics associated in it could be employed in any service and in any newly created office. Thus the Pope at last had a separate court of his own, detached from the city of Rome, which he could organize at his discretion. Hence it was not pure accident that, from the end of the eleventh century, in place of the old terminology, *sacrum palatium Lateranense,* the term still current, *Curia Romana,* established itself. It placed the papal court on a footing of equality with the Germanic-Romance *Curia Regis.* With the possibility of the free development of its administrative apparatus, the reform papacy had taken a decisive step forward.

CHAPTER   1 1 5

The New Relationship of the Church to Western Christendom

The hierarchical principle of the reform had to do, not with the Church such as we understand her today as an institution distinct from state and society, but with the *ecclesia universalis* coming down from the early Middle Ages and including state and society. The reformers clung throughout to this religious and political structural unity, but in it they sought to bring eventually to full prominence the aspect of religious value. And since priests were responsible for religious matters, they demanded that the *Sacerdotium,* through its hierarchical summit, the Pope, should lead the Christian world.

They thus established a new relationship to Christian kingship. The theocracy exercised by secular rulers appeared to them to pervert the right order; it contradicted the higher value and the higher function of the priestly office. As proofs were again brought forth the ancient notions stressing priestly pre-eminence: the comparison of gold with lead, of sun with moon, of soul with body, or the distinction between the life-giving priestly function and the royal function linked with the terror of the sword, or the directly divine origin of the priesthood vis-à-vis kingship, made necessary by original sin, established by men merely with God's assent, and often misused under the influence of original sin. But all of this would have profited little, had not the sacramental character of the anointed kingship, in the sense of a specific participation in the priesthood and the kingship of Christ, been denied by the reformers. For them, thinking in strictly hierarchical categories, the secular ruler was a layman, who, even though he was the holder of an important function in the *ecclesia universalis,* had to stand, not over, not beside, but below priests.

Just how this relation of dependence was to be explained, concretely was not systematically worked out by Gregory VII and his friends — this was only done in the succeeding two centuries — but they claimed for the priesthood the right to decide on the qualifications of a ruler, especially if he proved to be intolerable because of a godless, tyrannical government. For this case Gregory VII demanded the judicial competence of the Pope, as the supreme shepherd of souls, endowed with the power to bind and loose, and also the right to excommunicate, to absolve from oaths of loyalty, and to depose. While his ideas were not unchallenged, they pretty generally prevailed, apart from the claim to depose, which encountered serious doubt even in ecclesiastical circles and was not again put into practice by a Pope until 1245. Nevertheless, rulers affected by the Church's coercive power again and again refused obedience.

The incisive initiative of the reform could not but shake violently the structure of the Western world. The adherents of kingship naturally showed fight. To the extent that they were defending the old theocracy, as especially the Norman Anonymous at the beginning of the twelfth century sought to do in far too bold dialectics, they were, of course, fighting a lost battle. The theocracy had become antiquated. But the West was in the process of out-growing the early medieval stage of development of the coherence and of perfecting new, differentiated social forms.

This process had an effect on the reform. The West was not disposed merely to accept a papal hierocracy in exchange for the obsolete royal theocracy, and Gregory VII's radically religious impetus moved without any doubt in a hierocratic direction. Gregory himself released the counter-forces which now appeared. In his one-sided spiritual thought what mattered basically was merely the spiritual and political will of the *ecclesia universalis,* and for it the ecclesiastical authority should thereafter be responsible. He thereby unintentionally split the striving for a uniform goal on the part of the earlier *ecclesia universalis;* for, previously, spiritual-political and secular-political aims had been so intimately interwoven that even a secular ruler could see to the religious and political total goal. Gregory, to be sure, wanted to preserve unity by demanding that kings entirely subordinate their interests to the spiritual-political goal, but the rulers agreed to this only under conditions. For their part, they now took up the secular-political aim and developed it to relative autonomy.

The course of the Investiture Controversy, the clearer distinction at times achieved by rulers between spiritual office and *temporalia*, is an example of what the development amounted to. Despite their only too conservative clinging to outdated theocratic rights, the German and Italian defenders of Henry IV showed a good instinct for the difficulty of their time when to the claim of the reformers they opposed the traditional Gelasian principle, never given up even in the early Middle Ages, of the twofold division of power and stressed that not only the priest but also the king received his power directly from God. Their position, which was by no means irreconcilable with that of Gregory VII and his followers, was further strengthened from time to time in the future.

Good assistance in this connection was provided by Roman law; already made use of in the Investiture Controversy, it would be further exploited by the schools of legists soon to flourish. And so the *Regnum* slowly transformed its earlier rule, based on anointing and service to the *ecclesia universalis,* into a kingship by divine right, into a rule over an autonomous sphere of law and action, to be governed by virtue of the *potestas* directly conferred by God, which it from time to time systematically built up during the twelfth and thirteenth centuries and began to lead toward sovereignty. Here it was competing basically with that striving of the papacy, becoming ever clearer in the post-Gratian period, to bring the juridical sphere subordinate to it together as firmly as possible into a *regnum ecclesiasticum* under its monarchical power. Rulers were unwilling simply to be inferior even in regard to the sacred. Their being degraded to the lay state within the Church caused them to elaborate a theory of divine right, which was no longer based on a specifically ecclesiastical foundation but was even partly fed by originally pagan forces, as these survived, on the one hand, in Roman imperial law with its sanctification of ruler, law, and Empire, and, on the other hand, in the Germanic magical ideas of the royal "healing power," attached to the royal family.

The process of the separation of *Regnum* and *Sacerdotium* took its time. If the early medieval "two-in-oneness" of the two powers, only functionally distinct and understood as if they were professions, was now slowly replaced by the sharper antithesis between two powers directly from God and ruling autonomous spheres of public law, the West still had to travel a long stretch before being confronted at the beginning of modern time; with the ontologically distinct communities of Church and state. Despite a progressive decay, the unity of the *ecclesia universalis, or christianitas,* overlapping and embracing both spheres of law, remained throughout the twelfth and thirteenth centuries a basic fact of social and political life.

Before the Investiture Controversy the German Emperors, in spite of the indifferent or even negative attitude generally assumed outside Germany, had somehow represented the unity of the West. Afterward they continued to insist that they were the leaders of Christendom, at least within the secular sphere, but the change that had meanwhile come over the West made their claim ever more questionable. The *regna,* growing stronger from the twelfth century and concerned for their autonomy, allowed the Emperor merely an honorary precedence but no encroaching jurisdiction power. And his relationship to the Roman Church had been reversed in the Investiture Controversy: the Emperor thereafter possessed no further rights over the Pope, but the Pope did over the Emperor, who stood in need of anointing and crowning and was obliged to protect the Roman Church. What the brilliance of the *Imperium* had hitherto eclipsed now emerged into full light: the unity of the West was based ultimately on the common faith and on membership in the same Church. This foundation gained from the time of the reform an entirely new solidity through the supranational unification of the ecclesiastical hierarchy and the constructing of a common canon law recognized in all Christian countries. Thus the Church became the real bearer, and the papacy at her head became the leader, of Western Christendom.

Not only the supranational extent of his jurisdiction but also the nature and manner of his exercise of power lifted the Pope far above Emperor and kings. While it took a long time in most kingdoms before the power of the state adequately permeated the feudal classes to reach every subject more or less directly, the papacy had it easier from the start. Its jurisdiction extended not merely to the bishops and through them to their diocesans, but also directly to each individual Christian. Priests, monks, and lay persons turned this to account from the beginning of the twelfth century by taking their legal cases to Rome, directly or by appeal.

And if there was a secular field of law, always acquiring greater independence, still pre-eminence belonged to the spiritual field of law. The always valid principle of the Catholic doctrine of the state, whereby state and society are bound by the divine and the moral law and the interpretation of this law pertains to the Church, could not but have a much more powerful impact in the twelfth and thirteenth centuries than would be possible today. The dependence of the secular sphere of law was then so extensive that royal decrees which contradicted canon law in important matters could be declared null by the Church. In this way the Church's influence extended far into what was earthly. The Church laid down the norms for fundamental problems of human social life, for example, for the lawfulness of interest, of commercial profit, or of levying taxes. Marriage cases were subject to her authority almost exclusively; likewise, the oath, then so important for public and private life, from which the Church alone could dispense in specific cases. The educational system and many institutions of charity were under her control. Sharing responsibility for the welfare of the Christian people, the Church had always taken an interest in peace among the faithful to the extent that she was able to compete with the secular authorities. The peace initiative which the French clergy had assumed since the beginning of the eleventh century was taken up by the reform papacy under Urban II; laws dealing with the Peace of God were proclaimed at general synod. In the succeeding period the Popes took a further step: they sought from time to time to make peace among warring princes and not rarely were even invited to do so by at least one of the parties.

Finally, the Church's penal and coercive power acquired an unusually great importance. Excommunication and interdict, now decreed even against kings, produced a considerable effect in the course of the legal situation that was being stabilized. It was all the greater in that since Frankish times excommunication also involved consequences in civil law. Although these prescriptions were not always observed, especially if they concerned princes, they were still recognized in principle in the secular sphere of law and were applied in their entirety against the heretics who spread so charmingly from the twelfth century; here ecclesiastical and secular penal authority united for a pitiless struggle. During the reform period the Church had also gained the right to defend the interests of Christendom with arms. The highest forms of penal authority were at that time comprehended under the image of the sword. While, then, the Church had previously possessed only the *gladius spiritualis* — excommunication, anathema — she thereafter wielded also the *gladius materialis* in the sense of the right to compulsion by war, either by summoning the secular rulers to use the material sword proper to them or by virtue of her own authority, as it were by the handing over of the material sword that belonged to her, calling knights and other laymen to arms. How this portentous extension of the Church's coercive power arose out of causes conditioned by the age will appear from the history of the origin of the First Crusade in the next chapter.

The papacy's spiritual and political power of leadership, based on the primacy and embracing all of Christendom, was reinforced by particular secular-political rights. Thus, with the formation of the Papal State in 756 was gained the political autonomy of the Roman Church, which, while it was curtailed by the Frankish and German Emperors and by the Roman nobility, was never actually suppressed and in the reform period acquired a new importance in so far as the Roman Church's consciousness of freedom no longer tolerated any political dependence. The seeking of autonomy had been expressed in the eighth century not merely in territorial demands but also in the assumption of imperial insignia and honorary right; a justification, so to speak, had been found for both in the *Constitutum Constantini*. The reformers, headed by Gregory VII, hence acted quite logically when, for proof of the quasi-imperial, or politically independent, position of the Pope, and, in this regard, for his pre-eminence over all other bishops, they referred to the *Constitutum Constantini*. As a matter of fact, in papal ceremonial thereafter the imperial honorary rights mentioned in the forgery played a greater role than formerly, especially the tiara and the scarlet mantle. In the twelfth century the mantle became the most important symbol in the investiture of a newly elected Pope, while the tiara, gained no new function but did acquire a greater symbolic value in the course of the growing spiritual-political authority of the Pope.

The new self awareness was expressed concretely: the emperor-like Pope began to pursue an independent state policy. The gaining of feudal suzerainty over the Normans of South Italy and of Gregory VII's attempt from the outset to attach politically to the Holy See as many countries as possible. Motivated by religious and political aims, Gregory still observed certain limits: he derived his demands, not from the primatial power, but from old juridical claims regarded as authentic and in the event of resistance let the matter drop. Hence it basically depended on the willingness of the princes whether they would enter into a relation of dependence with Rome; often enough they did so because they promised themselves political advantages as a result. Since England and Denmark were prepared only to pay Peter's Pence, and the feudal suzerainty over Croatia-Dalmatia, established in 1076, came to an end as a consequence of the union of Croatia with Hungary in 1091, the rights of the Roman Church outside Italy were restricted.

The papacy's international policy obtained an incomparably greater success in Italy. Gregory VII's claims to Sardinia and Corsica and to the Marches of Fermo and the Duchy of Spoleto were rather ineffective, it is true, and the great donation made by Matilda of Tuscany could not be taken possession of after the death of the Countess until the investiture of the Emperor Lothar III in 1136, but the feudal suzerainty over Norman South Italy continued, despite all difficulties, and for centuries to come influenced papal policy decisively. Interested originally rather in the armed protection afforded by the Norman vassals, which was necessary for the reform the papacy was led ever more powerfully to the territorial viewpoint. The three stages of the rise of Norman power — at first the absorption of all earlier areas of political rule, then the feudal dependence of Capua on Apulia and thereby the limiting of direct Roman feudal suzerainty to the Duke of Apulia (1098), and finally the Norman Sicilian state created by Roger II from 1127 — presented the Roman Church with what were at times delicate problems. Unavoidable as the Italian territorial policy may have been, the Roman Church had to pay for it in the future with difficult struggles that would gnaw away at the religious substance.

The proper task, before which the feudal political and territorial policy retreated, continued to be the spiritual-political guidance of Western Christendom. Its difficulties were to preoccupy the papacy throughout the twelfth and thirteenth centuries. Their source lay in a situation that was in many respects unclarified. If at all times the ecclesiastical obedience which is based on the faith contains an element of the voluntary to the extent that faith cannot be forced, how much more, then, did the medieval papacy's power, taking effect in the secular sphere, depend on the good will of the faithful! Involved were rights which flowed only indirectly from ecclesiastical authority and for the most part were not even necessarily connected with the essence of the Church, and were therefore conditioned by the time. The stronger the secular-political determination of kingship grew and the more it affected the people, the more was the spiritual-political will, attended to by the Pope, forced back to the relationship within the Church between *ecclesia congregans* and *ecclesia congregata*.

The papacy was again and again confronted with the question of how far to acknowledge the autonomy of the secular-political will and of its most important protagonist, the kingship. A decision was all the more difficult, since up to the late thirteenth century a justification of the state in natural law was lacking and the traditional teaching of political Augustinianism, which conceived the *regnum* only in its religious function, was not equal to the new uncertainty. A readiness to acknowledge the secular-political will of kingship, to the extent that is put forward genuine rights, was in no way lacking to the church. Effective in the Concordat of Worms, it grew stronger in the succeeding period. From the time of the reform the relationship of the Church and of the papacy to Christendom was determined not merely by a hierocratic but also by a dualistic ingredient.

CHAPTER 116

The Papacy, the Holy Wars, and the First Crusade

The papacy may be said to have assumed the leadership of Western Christendom with the First Crusade, but this was only the result of a long and by no means uniform development. Even though in earlier periods Popes, bishops, or abbots had occasionally summoned to arms for resistance to Vikings, Magyars, or Muslims, still war as such was reserved to the King. Only with the turn of the tenth to the eleventh century did the Church acquire a new relationship to war, especially through the movement, originating in France, of the Peace and the Truce of God. Compelled to self-defense, spiritual lords not infrequently conducted "holy wars" against violators of the peace.

But there also took place a transformation in the military class, the knights. There appeared a Christian ethos of knighthood, which obliged to the armed protection of churches and of oppressed fellow-Christians and hence to tasks which had hitherto been allotted to the crown. That new forces were here in readiness was discovered when the *Reconquista* began again in Christian Spain soon after 1050, reached its climax with the taking of Toledo in 1085, and was then checked by the Almoravids, coming from Africa. For from 1064 French knights took part in these struggles, which they looked upon as holy wars. Their aid became greater after the defeat of Alfonso VI of Castile at Sagrajas in 1086 and thereby, so to speak, readied France for the idea of a crusade. The Normans of South Italy were motivated by similar ideas and not merely by desire of conquest when, under the leadership of Count Roger I, they set about wresting Sicily from Islam. These pregnant ideas that were spontaneously making their appearance here and there were taken up by the reform papacy, which bound them together and eventually directed them to the Orient. No holy war was then waged in which the papacy did not have some share. The French knights who in 1063 made ready for the Spanish war for Barbastro obtained from Alexander II the first known crusade indulgence.

It did not matter whether the war was against unbelievers or Catholics — its religious goal was decisive. In fact, under Gregory VII the holy wars within Christendom for the benefit of the reform came entirely into the foreground and received a specifically hierarchical stamp through the idea that he entertained of an international *militia sancti Petri.* Great successes were, of course, denied Gregory; in fact, his militant outlook aroused opposition, and there ensued a lively discussion as to whether the Church or the Pope may wage war at all. This caused Anselm of Lucca to ponder the problem more deeply. Following Augustine, he expounded the lawfulness of the defensive war and the moral and religious principles to be observed in connection with it, and from this position defended the Church's right to prosecute her faithless members. He thereby laid the ground for the future teaching, developed by Gratian and the decretists, on the Church's power of material coercion in the sense of the right to armed force. The expansion here present of the ecclesiastical *potestas coactiva materialis* did not really take effect for the moment, since it was applied to the pursuit of opponents of reform, branded as heretics and schismatics, and was very quickly blended with Gregory's struggle against Henry IV. So complex an initiative, calling forth opposition even from the well-intentioned, was not capable of carrying away the masses of knights or of finding support in the entire clergy. But once the papacy turned the pent-up energies of Christian knighthood from crusades within Christendom to one against the infidel, it could be sure of a response on a broad front.

It was precisely this change that was made by Urban II. While he did make use of weapons at the beginning of his pontificate, he soon renounced this means. On the other hand, he had no hesitation about promoting with all his energy the holy war against Islam. The crisis of the age induced him to this: Christians had been forced to the defensive in both the Orient and Spain. Urban regarded the western sector as so important that he forbade Spaniards to take part in the crusade in the Orient. His special concern was for the rebuilding of strategically important Tarragona; in 1089 he granted for this work the same remission of ecclesiastical penance that was attached to a pilgrimage to Jerusalem.

Gregory VII had already planned a crusade for the liberation of the Eastern Christians, which was to help in liquidating the Schism. As a matter of fact, the Christian East was in an extremely critical situation since the great victory of the Seljuk Turks over the Emperor Romanus IV at Manzikert in 1071. Little by little, virtually all of Asia Minor came under Seljuk rule. The capable Emperor Alexius I Comnenus (1081–1118) could not exert himself because the Patzinaks were threatening Constantinople. In his distress he tried to hire as many Western knights as possible. Thus in 1089–90 he induced Robert the Frisian, Count of Flanders, who was returning home from a pilgrimage to Jerusalem, to send him 500 knights. Hence it suited him very much when Urban II, soon after his election, began negotiations for union. These were encouraged by Alexius, who for his part asked for troops. Urban promised them but at first was unable to send any. Although the Emperor contrived to exorcise the threat from the Patzinaks by a brilliant victory in 1091, in 1095 he again had his request submitted to the Pope at the Council of Piacenza, according to the trustworthy report of Bernold of Sankt Blasien. Confident of his enhanced prestige, Urban now proceeded to take action: at Piacenza he called upon Christian knights to defend the Eastern Church. But this was only the overture. Once in France, he took the real step after rather long preparation by issuing the summons to the First Crusade at the Council of Clermont on 27 November 1095.

So far as the motivating ideas are concerned, the secret of the success lay not only in the concept of Christian knighthood and struggle, but also in the taking up of the notion of pilgrimage. The journey to Jerusalem had been the tacit desire of many Christians from time immemorial; it freed one from all other penitential obligations. But penitents who were pilgrims were not allowed to bear arms. On the other hand, at the Council of Clermont Urban granted the same full remission of the canonical penalties that was gained by pilgrims to Jerusalem, and hence he proclaimed for the first time the idea of the armed pilgrimage. Its propaganda force would probably have remained limited if persons had adhered to the Clermont decree, whereby the armed pilgrimage was merely a commutation for the penitential exercises imposed by the Church, understood in the sense of the customary so-called "redemption." However, the preaching of the crusade, now getting under way and increasingly eluding the supervision of the Church, probably disregarded the moderate decree of the Council and held out to the crusaders the prospect of a plenary indulgence, that is, the remission of all penalties for sin that were to be expected from God either in this life or in the next, and in this connection there may well have been mention occasionally of forgiveness of sins in a quite crude way.

By means of the spontaneously germinating notion of the indulgence, which was to cost the theologians of the twelfth and thirteenth centuries much sweat until it found its speculative solution in the doctrine of the Church's treasury of merits, the crusade acquired an immeasurable religious worth in the eyes of the faithful. Its danger lost its terrors all the more as persons began to look upon death occurring in it as a kind of martyrdom. The association of expedition and pilgrimage was at once expressed symbolically, especially in the cloth cross which the knights even at Clermont had sewn to their garb; this was the sign of the crusade vow, a religious obligation, and at the same time the military symbol of an army resolved to fight. There also appeared a common battle cry, "Deus le volt," and a new ritual blessing, which added the sword to the old pilgrimage symbols that were retained, the staff and wallet. Inherent in all these forms was a special publicity value.

If Urban, with a keen psychological instinct, strongly emphasized Jerusalem as the goal of the expedition, this by no means meant that he was concerned only for the holy city or the holy sepulchre. Rather he clung steadfastly to the original purpose of liberating Eastern Christianity from the Turkish yoke. This referred not exclusively but to a great extent to the Byzantine world; the Pope intended to remain true to his promise of help to Alexius, although the nature and manner of the supplying of aid turned out quite differently from what the Emperor had desired. Selfish power projects envisaging the gaining of territories were probably remote from Urban's mind; in fact, at Clermont he specified that the churches of the conquered lands should be under the rule of the conquerors. No one could deprive him of the essential success: when, disregarding the kings and relying only on his apostolic authority, he summoned the knights to the holy war and found so powerful a response that for the first time in Western history a supranational army set forth for the defense of Christendom, he became the spontaneously recognized leader of the Christian West. The contact that the reform papacy had made with the Christian knights took effect fully now for the first time and led necessarily to a special crusaders' law. Ecclesiastical legislation extended the Peace of God and the protection of the Church to the goods of crusaders; on the part of the Church encouragement was given to the effort to free the possessions of participants from taxes for the duration of the crusade; and even a moratorium on debts was provided for.

The leadership of the enterprise by Pope Urban should have been expressed visibly in the person of the Papal Legate, Adhémar of Le Puy, who was entrusted with the political direction, while the military command was originally intended for Raymond de Saint-Gilles, Count of Toulouse. Both arrangements foundered in the swelling crusading movement. Since, besides Raymond, other great princes also took the cross and set out with their own troops, the single command failed to materialize of itself; Raymond was merely the commander of his own troops. The slack organization also caused Adhémar's eclipse. His function was restricted rather to the spiritual care of one contingent, for Urban had clearly provided a chaplain with spiritual jurisdiction for each of two other units and hence had in a sense made them legates also.

Although the direction of the entire undertaking slipped from the Pope's hands, he continued to be the supreme authority for the crusaders. But Urban had no influence on the crusade movement of Peter the Hermit of Amiens. One of those wandering preachers of penance who held up to the people the ideal of the *vita apostolica et evangelica,* Peter began right after Urban's appeal to arouse his followers in central and northwestern France for the armed pilgrimage. The time was more favorable than ever. Religious excitement of the masses, now probably enhanced by eschatological ideas, and economic difficulties, especially among the peasantry, had built up the hope of a better life to a high degree of intensity. This tension was relaxed by Peter's summons to go to the holy city of Jerusalem with a force such as the West had never yet experienced. The mob that followed him, consisting overwhelmingly of the lower strata of the population, received so many reinforcements *en route* through Germany, from the Rhineland, Swabia, and elsewhere, that from April to June of 1096 there set out from 50,000 to 70,000 persons, including women, in five or six large batches successively. Religious fanaticism and rapacity in the uncontrolled masses led to frightful persecution of Jews in German Free Cities and in Prague. Only the first two contingents, travelling via Hungary and Bulgaria, reached Constantinople. The crowds that followed, incurring hatred because of their plundering and other deeds of violence, were almost totally exterminated in Hungary. The Emperor Alexius at first received the new arrivals amicably but had so many unhappy experiences with them that he quickly transported the troublesome guests to Asia Minor. Instead of waiting for the knights, they attacked the Turks concentrated around Nicaea, against the advice of Peter of Amiens, Fulcher of Orléans, and some nobles, and as a consequence, with few exceptions, lost either life or freedom.

Urban II's appeal had been directed to knights of military experience; they were to make careful preparations for the expedition up to August and then set out. Of the many noble lords who took the cross the princes were, of course, the most prominent. Each collected for himself a more or less large fighting unit. Thus in the summer a whole series of army divisions set out by different routes: either via Hungary and Bulgaria or via Italy and the Balkan peninsula, reached by ship, to Constantinople. Large armies were led by Duke Godfrey of Lower Lotharingia, son of Count Eustace of Boulogne and nephew and heir of Godfrey the Hunchback of Lower Lotharingia, and by Count Raymond of Toulouse, while the brother of the French King, Count Hugh of Vermandois, to whom Urban delivered a banner of Saint Peter at Rome, Bohemond of Taranto, a son of Robert Guiscard, and Duke Robert of Normandy, Count Stephen of Blois, and Count Robert of Flanders, who travelled together, disposed of smaller units.

Alexius found himself in the greatest perplexity. His situation had improved. He was interested in Western mercenaries, not in Western armies of knights under their own commanders. In an effort to secure himself adequately against his un-invited helpers, he forced the princes into political subordination, taking some of them, according to Byzantine custom, into the imperial family as sons and re-quiring of all the oath of vassalage customary in the West. As a matter of fact the princes, more or less reluctantly, did enter the vassalage bond, except for Ray-mond de Saint-Gilles, who agreed merely to an oath guaranteeing the life and possessions of the Emperor.

A first success, achieved in association with the Greeks, was the conquest of Nicaea. The main army detoured via Caesarea in Cappadocia to Antioch, while Bo-hemond's nephew Tancred and Baldwin, brother of Godfrey of Lower Lotharingia, decided on conquests of their own. Baldwin acquired a wealthy lordship around Edessa. Antioch, the next tactical objective, cost the crusaders immense toil. Only after a seven months' siege were they able to occupy the city on 3 July 1098, and then they had to beat back a great Turkish relieving army. Since the princes re-garded themselves as no longer bound by the oath sworn to the Emperor because of the meager aid, and eventually no aid at all, rendered by the Greeks, each of them sought to gain territory for himself. Bohemond took Antioch. Byzantium had never got over the loss of this important city, which the Turks had not taken until

1085. After a long delay Raymond finally managed to get the crusaders moving toward Jerusalem. An offer of help by Alexius was repulsed: the crusaders intended to keep the districts to be conquered in Syria and Palestine. Jerusalem fell to the crusaders on 15 July 1099. The victors engaged in a frightful blood bath among the local Muslims.

Raymond de Saint-Gilles was first chosen ruler, but he declined; then Godfrey of Lower Lotharingia was elected. He did not assume the title of king but that of Guardian of the Holy Sepulchre. His juridical position was weakened by the claims to an ecclesiastical state, put forward by the new Patriarch of Jerusalem, Archbishop Daimbert of Pisa, in favor, not of the Roman Church, but of the patriarchate. Godfrey died in 1100 and was succeeded by his brother Baldwin (1100–1118), who put an end to all vacillation. He had himself crowned King and was otherwise able to consolidate his authority. The Frankish conquest spread to the interior as well as along the coast. Almost all the coastal cities had been taken by 1111; but Tyre held out until 1124 and Ascalon till 1153. The territory that had been acquired was broken down into four rather large states, united loosely under the King of Jerusalem. Their preservation and defense were to cost the West more heavy sacrifices. The very first years brought great losses. During and immediately after the crusade Western pilgrims and crusaders kept setting out, but the poorly organized expeditions almost all ended miserably.

Thereafter the papacy had to assume the chief responsibility for the crusader states. This brought it an enhanced prestige and, with the crusade tithe introduced under Innocent III, also financial power, but at the same time it made the limits of papal influence much clearer on occasion. The unsteady ground on which the Pope stood as leader of Christendom was perhaps never made so clear as in the history of the crusades. Momentous as was the effect of the First Crusade on the Christian West and on the papacy, its full importance in Church history can only be estimated if the reaction of the Byzantine world is understood.

C H A P T E R   1 1 7

The "Vita Evangelica" Movement and the Appearance of New Orders

From about the middle of the eleventh century the religious state began to differentiate itself once for all. There is no doubt that the Gregorian reform contributed to this change, occasionally by direct intervention, but basically it was a spontaneous religious movement, which had its own prehistory and its own dynamics. From the beginning of the eleventh century, there gradually emerged a critical attitude vis-à-vis the wealthy monasteries and chapters that had been incorporated into the economic and political system of feudalism. In the final analysis this was really the same striving as that of the reform papacy, struggling for the freedom of the Church, namely, the determination to return to the original *ecclesia apostolica et evangelica,* and the consequent protest against early medieval forms of life, stamped to a great extent by Germanic law. In the world of monks and canons this impulse was based especially on the idea of poverty.

To high-minded men it was no longer enough that the individual monk must possess nothing, whereas the monastic community could dispose of a large income. To them poverty meant the fullest possible renunciation of earthly assurances. And so, alone or with companions, they betook themselves to remote forests in order to be entirely free for God. They earned their livelihood by the work of their hands, as occasion demanded, turning sections of forest into arable ground and meadow. Their radicalism could go to the extent of maintaining that the possession of proprietary churches, of rights to tithes and altars and the like, was incompatible with monasticism and even of refusing documentary authentication of the land given them. In conflicts over possession they preferred to accept injustice rather than to institute a suit. Finally, their protest was directed against the grand-scale building activity which monasteries of the old type not infrequently displayed, the lavish decoration of monastic churches and the costly vestments and vessels; their own dwellings, oratories, and churches were kept poor and bare.

This movement, spreading ever further in the second half of the eleventh century, was not represented by monks alone. The principle of poverty had already been related in patristic times to clerics, with reference to the primitive community at Jerusalem, and in particular cases had been put into practice, for example by Augustine. And even if the Aachen rule for canons of 816 allowed private ownership, the stricter interpretation was not forgotten and in the eleventh century acquired an arousing force. It is difficult to determine when and where individual canons began to institute a genuine *vita communis* with renunciation of private ownership; the meager sources point overwhelmingly to Central and North Italy. As early as the Roman Synod of 1059 Hildebrand became their spokesman and, sharply criticizing the Aachen rule, demanded personal poverty for all canons. So radical an attack, of course, had little effect; the reform had to come from below. And in fact from time to time more canons adopted the principle of poverty and thus appeared as a special group, called canons regular, in contradistinction to the older type of canons who clung to private property. But the striving for evangelical and apostolic poverty urged to still more resolute efforts. Even diocesan clerics now sought out the *eremus.*

If till then the ideal of the *Vita evangelica et apostolica* had been oriented to the poverty of cenobites or hermits, toward the end of the century it acquired a broader meaning. As Christ, with the Apostles, went from place to place to proclaim the kingdom of God and called no place his own where he could lay his head, this most extreme self-denial for the sake of the Gospel was now translated into action by isolated monks, clerics, and hermits.

The relations between monastic centers and the laity changed considerably in the eleventh century. Since the monasteries of the older type maintained a manorial economy, they were involved, with their servants and maids, their serfs, rent-paying peasants, and vassals, with the most varied strata of the population. A special position was occupied by the so-called half-*conversi,* pious folk who settled on the edge of the cloister, renounced parts of their rights of ownership, and led a quasi-monastic life. From them emerged the institute of lay brothers during the eleventh century, especially at the instigation of hermits of Saint Romuald's type and of the Vallombrosans. The cause of this new form, which flourished powerfully in the twelfth century, is to be sought in the progress toward sterner asceticism, which, in addition to monks and clerics, also embraced lay persons and prepared them to undertake poverty, celibacy, and claustral discipline as serving brothers. Basically at stake here was a spiritual concern — the more effective isolation of the cloister from the world.

This world-fleeing characteristic, however, in no way impeded an influence on the lay persons living outside. On the contrary, the very hermits and the cenobitic proponents of a stricter asceticism were in a much closer contact with the broad masses of the people than were the monasteries, of the older order. To an ever greater degree their ideals appealed to the restless lay folk of the popular religious movements before and during the Gregorian reform. In France and Lower Lotharingia there occurred a *rapprochement* of ascetics and populace. The faithful penetrated even into the *eremus* to be edified and have their souls tended to or even to settle there. Conversely, protagonists of the *vita apostolica et evangelica* did not hesitate to leave the cloister and preach to the assembled people, sharply attacking abuses. Thus there appeared itinerant preachers toward the close of the century. How powerfully they influenced the masses was shown by the unfortunate crusade initiative of Peter the Hermit of Amiens.

Like many other itinerant preachers, Peter the Hermit acted without any ecclesiastical commission. No wonder that the bishops exerted themselves to correct the chaotic system of preaching. From the viewpoint of logic alone, the movement could only be neutralized by the founding of new preaching Orders, but apparently the time was not yet ripe for this, and so itinerant preaching more and more became an illicit activity, exercised by heretics. In general, within the orthodox Christian sphere the feverish search for new forms of the *vita apostolica et evangelica* slowly ceased. From time to time there emerged from the process of fermentation more clearly sketched, new religious communities, which adopted fixed customs, while other foundations did not cling to their original *élan* and reverted to the old monastic or canonical institutes. The situation was somewhat stabilized in the third decade of the twelfth century.

Differentiation in Monasticism

The search beginning in various places for new forms was not occasioned, apart from individual cases, by evil living on the part of the traditional monasticism, for this, thanks to the renewal in progress since the tenth century, was on the whole on a high level. Monastic centers expanded especially after 1050. Cluny reached its zenith at the same time under Saint Hugh (1049–1109). Its usages found entry into England, Lotharingia, and Germany, partly by the direct, partly by the indirect route. Still greater importance was gained by the abbey of Hirsau, revived in 1065, as soon as it adopted the reform ideas of Gregory VII for questions of principle and the *consuetudines* of Cluny for monastic daily life. In its steep rise, which it is true lasted only a few decades, Hirsau, with its many monks, lay brothers, and other adherents of both sexes, loosely bound to it, became not merely a center of monastic strength but a bulwark and refuge of the Gregorian reform, struggling against clerical incontinence, simony, lay investiture, and royal theocracy. Even itinerant preachers proceeded from Hirsau.

Only the more important of the new foundations can be singled out here from the complicated profusion. When Stephen of Thiers (d. 1124), founder of the Order of Grandmont, sought the solitude of Muret near Limoges and gathered disciples around him, he was basically influenced, with regard to the community that came into existence in 1080–81, by the impressions gained when he had lived in the society of Calabrian hermits. To a great extent he rejected the forms of Western monasticism. He did not allow landed property, herds of cattle, rents, and proprietary churches, and the Gospel was for him the sole norm of monastic life; his sons were to be called neither canons nor monks nor hermits, and they were to seek their task in nothing but penance. Although Stephen did not dispense with a type of profession and choir service and hence with a certain organization of the community into monks and lay brothers, still the strongly lay characteristics of his rudimentary constitution brought it about that the lay brothers occupied a leading position, which eventually produced strife. Much as Stephen scrupulously avoided fixed constitutional forms, he must have created a living monastic spirit. Supported by it, the community, which moved to nearby Grandmont, was able to condense its unique character in a rule under the grand prior Stephen of Liciac (1139–63) and develop into an esteemed Order.

Quite different was the origin of the Order of Fontevrault. Its founder, the diocesan priest, hermit, and itinerant preacher Robert of Arbrissel (d. ca. 1117), had such an effect on the masses that many men and women, on fire for the evangelical life, constantly accompanied him. In order to lodge them, he established double monasteries, which, shortly before his death, he united into a congregation under the direction of the first foundation, Fontevrault (1100–1101). He entrusted the supreme direction to the Abbess-General.

Whereas itinerant preaching exercised only a passing and isolated influence on the monastic movement, *eremus* and evangelical poverty had an enduring power of attraction.

La Grande Chartreuse owed its origin to the diocesan priest Bruno, originally from Cologne. Around 1056 he assumed the direction of the philosophical and theological studies at the cathedral school of Reims, but he ran afoul of Archbishop Manasses of Reims and of his successor and was thereby strengthened in his desire to abandon the world. For a short time he stayed with Abbot Robert at Molesme, but he then went with some companions into the solitude of Lêche-Fontaine. He soon left here with six friends and around 1084 began to live again as a hermit in the valley of Chartreuse. The founding of an Order or the like was not envisaged, and the community might even have broken up entirely when in 1090 Bruno had to obey the call of Pope Urban II, his former pupil, and go to Rome. A year later the Pope allowed him to look again for a solitude in South Italy. In the wooded district of La Torre in the diocese of Squillace he established the hermitage of Santa Maria dell'Eremo, into which in 1097–99 he incorporated the cenobitic daughter house of Santo Stefano in Bosco for sick companions.

That every trace of Bruno's earthly work — he died in 1101 — was not lost was due less to the hermits of La Torre than to those of Chartreuse, especially to the important Prior Guigues de Chastel (d. 1137), who in 1128 fixed by rule the way of life established by Bruno and probably further developed it. What characterized the Carthusian order, which spread slowly and within a modest range, was the peculiar combination of the eremitical and the cenobitic form, an extreme austerity, which, however, was linked with a healthy instinct for what was endurable, and finally an organization corresponding to the goal, in which the two achievements of the age — the institute of lay brothers and the Cistercian constitution — were made use of. Here the spirit by which the poverty movement of the eleventh century found a particular but so authentic expression that it has continued to the present in the Carthusians in its original strictness without any substantial mitigation and, a unique fact in the history of religious orders, has never needed a reform.

Like Chartreuse, Cîteaux too proceeded from a love for solitude and for a stricter poverty but with a far closer adherence to the Benedictine cenobitic tradition. The founder, Robert of Molesme (ca. 1028–1112), had lived as a monk since his youth in several Benedictine monasteries without finding contentment. Even the abbey of Molesme, which he founded with some hermits in 1075, moved into the old feudal pattern as a consequence of increasing property. The renunciation of proprietary churches and of the letting out of monastic property, connected with an economy of dues and rents; the principle, supplanting the preceding, of economic operation conducted by oneself, which the adoption of the institute of lay brothers fostered; the necessity present in time-consuming manual labor of restricting the far too extended choral service of the Cluniacs and other branches; the principle of poverty, related to clothing, table, church, and its adornment — this program linked the Cistercians to many other, in some cases older, communities. And yet they succeeded in outstripping all the monastic reform centers that were striving for the *vita evangelica* and in eclipsing the traditional monasticism headed by Cluny.

Cîteaux owed its rise especially to three circumstances: to its location in Burgundy, where a community representing the new ideas could establish itself vis-à-vis Cluny and the many other monasteries of the older type only with difficulty unless it had an aggressive spirit; to the entry, probably in 1112, of Bernard of Clairvaux, a charismatically gifted genius, who brought along thirty companions, the first fruits of his future impassioned recruitment; and to an elastic constitution, combining centralization with a relative autonomy of the monasteries. This constitution was based rather early on two main supports that were to be completed later: on the organic union between mother and daughter monasteries, with the duty of visitation by the abbot of the mother house, and on the annual general chapter at Cîteaux, the supreme authority for supervision and legislation.

The Canons Regular

The spread of the canons regular occurred in various ways. The most obvious idea was that of inducing the old communities, especially in the cathedral chapters, to renounce private ownership. Bishops or canons, especially in Italy and the Midi, and individuals elsewhere too, notably Archbishops Conrad of Salzburg and Norbert of Magdeburg, pushed this reform, but naturally with varying and often slight success. The situation was much more favorable if the canons who had opted for poverty withdrew and founded houses of their own. This happened everywhere. Existing houses not infrequently assisted houses that were being established to get over their first beginnings. Common customs, association of prayers, or even juridical dependence produced bonds that were sometimes loose, sometimes intimate. Additional recruits came from diocesan clerics, who sought out the desert and there formed communities. But others, including Norbert, the founder of Prémontré, adhered to the *ordo canonicorum*. To enumerate all their many foundations would be tedious. But the powerful, even though overrated, flowering of the Premonstratensian Order showed how very much this initiative was in harmony with the time. A final group originated in lay communities, which in the course of time became chapters of canons regular as their lay element became more and more eclipsed. Their origin was often connected with the aim of lodging travellers on dangerous or deserted routes and, if necessary, of escorting them. The most celebrated example is the hospice on the Great Saint Bernard, the origin of which is still obscure. Pilgrim routes became especially important, and canons regular acquired particular merit for their protecting of the pilgrimage to Santiago.

In contrast to Western monasticism, which possessed a Benedictine tradition that had applied to almost all monasteries since the eighth and ninth centuries, the canons regular still had to define their way of life more exactly. From the closing decades of the eleventh century the rule of Saint Augustine is repeatedly mentioned as its basis, but more recent research has shown that this must be understood relatively. The Aachen rule of 816, which, referring to the Acts of the Apostles, they amended in favor of the principle of poverty; conciliar decrees and patristic writings, including Augustine, especially the so-called *Regula ad servos Dei* (often called *Regula tertia* in the literature); his sermons on the life of clerics; and his own *vita* by Posidius. Thus arose between 1070 and 1130 those statutes of the canons regular that were soon known as the *ordo antiquus*. If we disregard the rule, formerly ascribed to Gregory VII, they are characterized by wise moderation. Only some of their authors are known. A far more popular *liber ordinis* originated at Saint-Ruf in 1100–1110.

But these usages were not in accord with the ascetical severity which the eremitically inclined canons regular observed. Their efforts to draw up their own *consuetudines* found an Augustinian basis of tradition in the so-called *ordo monasterii* or *Regula secunda*. Since the ascetics there found confirmation of their ideas of manual labor, fasting, abstinence, and so forth, there appeared among them the notion that this was the original rule of Augustine. Probably first used at the beginning of the twelfth century at Springiersbach in the diocese of Trier, and from there transmitted to Prémontré, the text acquired great importance. Relying on it, the eremitically living canons regular opposed to the previous practice, or *ordo antiquus,* an *ordo novus* and thus started a controversy like that between Cistercians and Cluniacs. Then mixed forms were developed in the immediately following period.

A further tension-loaded element sprang from the problem of the care of souls. If the Aachen rule was directed principally to the choral liturgy and claustral discipline, this basically monastic feature could not but be even stronger among the canons regular, especially since many of them sought solitude. On the other hand, the inner understanding between the heralds of the *vita apostolica* and the laity involved in the religious movement led to explicitly pastoral contacts and even to itinerant preaching. Furthermore, the new chapters not infrequently obtained proprietary churches, so that the question to be answered was whether the canons regular were themselves to assume the care of souls there or were to employ diocesan priests. Many older chapters, moreover, were attached to urban parishes, and the canons at the cathedral had to undertake specific tasks of the diocesan administration. Should not the idealistic fervor permeating the canons regular be used for the urgently necessary reform of the care of souls? Various answers were forthcoming. Among both the bishops and the canons regular there were voices that regarded the ascetical principle of flight from the world as irreconcilable with pastoral activity, while others maintained that no one was better qualified for pastoral labors than the canon regular, a view shared by the reform papacy. Both views were carried into practice. In Italy and France the contemplative principle was adhered to, though not exclusively, whereas on German soil it was without difficulty combined with pastoral work.

At least at the outset the types of canonical organization displayed a great diversity. In the new eremitical or hospital foundations the lay element, consisting of *conversi* or even of *conversae,* could play an important role. If women took part, double monasteries were formed, and the male element, whose superior was usually called abbot in France, prior in Italy, and provost in the Empire, was ordinarily divided into canons and lay brothers. Here, then, were no essential differences from the Benedictine monasteries. The same was true of the forming of congregations.

Norbert of Gennep (ca. 1082–1134), scion of a noble family from the lower Rhineland, quite early became a canon at Xanten and soon after a royal chaplain at the court of Henry V. At a moment of extreme peril he underwent a complete change of life and, after receiving the priesthood in 1115, began to work as an itinerant preacher, in Germany until 1118, then in France, where he was authorized to preach by Pope Gelasius II. At the request of the Bishop of Laon, Norbert undertook the reform of the local chapter of Saint-Martin and, when he failed, sought in 1120 a solitude not far away, where he founded Prémontré, but changes of this sort were by no means unusual for an itinerant preacher. It was only in 1121 that the eremitical life at Prémontré acquired a more stable form through the adoption of the canonical manner of life and was thereafter organized in the sense of the *ordo novus.* Though Norbert again and again went out as an itinerant preacher until his elevation to the archbishopric of Magdeburg in 1126, Prémontré, which became a double monastery because of the reception of *conversae,* retained its contemplative and ascetical character. In the daughter houses that soon appeared, however, the pastoral element frequently obtained greater recognition, especially in Germany. In any case, a preaching Order in the strict sense did not proceed from Prémontré.

The history of the Premonstratensians shows unmistakable parallels to that of the Cistercians. Both groups quickly spread, although the ideas they represented were not original with them. Prémontré was only one among many eremitically oriented canonicates, but in its founder, Norbert, it possessed an outstanding personality, as Cîteaux did in Bernard of Clairvaux. An unconditioned devotion to religion, coupled with the charism of impassioned preaching, a will keenly intent on a goal, and intimate relations with nobles, princes, Emperors, and Popes provided Norbert with an uncommonly powerful influence. When he went to Magdeburg in 1126, the continuation of his work was assured. In the same year Honorius II confirmed the order, which Norbert's pupil and friend, Hugh de Fosses, Abbot-General of Prémontré (1129–61), happily developed further, borrowing from the organizational form of the Cistercians but without adopting the notion of filiation.

The Military Orders

The communities, especially those composed of laymen, which were interested in conducting hospices and in caring for pilgrims, answered not merely an urgent need of the West. More than ever, Christians were seeking the Holy Land, ever since its recovery by the crusaders, and wanted to be taken care of there. From the effort to supply them with aid emerged the Templars and the Hospitallers.

Hugh of Payens (d. 1136), a knight from Champagne, joined with eight companions in 1119 in a religious community obliged to poverty, chastity, and obedience, with the added duty of providing armed protection to pilgrims *en route* from Jaffa to Jerusalem. Since Baldwin II of Jerusalem housed them in the royal palace, the so-called Temple of Solomon, the name "Templars" came to be applied to them. In their manner of life they conformed to the canons regular. The early difficulties were overcome when Hugh of Payens visited France and interested Bernard of Clairvaux. With the latter's help a religious rule was decided on at the Synod of Troyes in 1128 and the Patriarch Stephen of Jerusalem supplemented it in 1130. Bernard's propaganda — he composed for this purpose *De laude novae militiae ad militiae Templi* — assured the Order a powerful growth. Directed by a grand master, it was divided into three classes: knights, serving brothers, and chaplains. The more the crusade states had to maintain themselves against Muslim attacks, the more were the Templars, and soon also the Hospitallers, employed as an always available militia for their defense. This circumstance alone procured for the Templars rich gifts in all countries of the West and made them a powerful international society, conversant with finance, independent of the King of Jerusalem and of the ecclesiastical hierarchy, especially since the Holy See granted them important privileges of exemption.

Somewhat different was the history of the founding of the Hospitallers. Around 1070, and hence before the First Crusade, merchants from Amalfi, resuming earlier attempts, had founded a Christian hospital in Jerusalem and dedicated it to the Alexandrian Saint, John the Almoner, who was later unobtrusively supplanted by

Saint John the Baptist. Intended for the care of the sick, the community acquired an enhanced contemporary significance after the First Crusade, under its masters, Gerard (d. ca. 1120) and Raymond du Puy (1120–60). In East and West, and especially in France and the Italian port cities, arose foundations and excellently managed hospitals. Privileges of exemption granted by Popes and testimonies of favor on the part of lay persons gave the community a growing prestige. To the care of the sick was added from 1137 the duty of armed border patrol. This made the Hospitallers explicitly a military Order, divided, like the Templars, into three classes: knights, brothers, and chaplains. The hospital work was almost entirely turned over to the brothers. The new development was completed in the statutes, drawn up around 1155, and based on the life of canons regular.

The period treated here meant an epoch-making change in the history of religious orders. The concept of *vita apostolica et evangelica,* which caused the older forms of monachism to withdraw into the background, which broke the monopoly of the monks and set up Augustinian canons and lay communities beside them, retained its dynamic force. It assured the new Orders, especially the Cistercians and Premonstratensians, a brilliant development but without being bound to them. When, toward the close of the twelfth century, their fervor cooled, the *vita apostolica* again became a problem. It found the long desired up-to-date expression in the mendicants.

C H A P T E R   1 1 8

The Beginnings of Scholasticism

The difficulties already set forth in regard to canon law were true to an even greater degree in philosophy and theology. The more the scholars, attached to tradition, sought to appropriate the intellectual treasures that had come down to them, the more pressing became the question of how to reconcile the differences and contradictions that were brought to light there. Even in the Carolingian period the heterogeneous material in tradition had occasionally evoked violent discussions, but the problem of methodology became more and more familiar to Western scholars only from the eleventh century. It found a solution in scholasticism.

Among the dynamic forces of the time, dialectics played a decisive role. Some of its protagonists began to travel about in the eleventh century.

One of the spokesmen was the Benedictine, Otloh of Sankt Emmeram at Regensburg (d. 1070). Doubts about faith, which must have cost him a great deal during his studies before he entered the monastery, moved him to a radical return to the Bible, the Fathers, and hagiography. He did not absolutely repudiate secular knowledge but frankly regarded it as not permitted to monks and sharply rejected the tendency to prefer Plato, Aristotle, or Boethius to the teaching of the Church. The canon regular Manegold of Lautenbach (d. 1103) was even more severe with secular knowledge. In his *Opusculum contra Wolfelmum*, which is based on the commentary of the Neoplatonist Macrobius on the *Somnium Scipionis*, he sought to show that the teachings of Macrobius, Pythagoras, Plato, and of the Aristotelian logic were sophistry and error, irreconcilable with Christian doctrine and a danger to salvation. In his view the dogmas of faith destroyed the ancient philosophy.

To a great extent Manegold depended on Peter Damiani (d. 1072), and, as a matter of fact, the ardent superior of the hermits occasionally did make use of weighty arguments. He cared nothing for dialectical skill in proofs, once called grammar a work of the devil, warned against the *artes liberales,* which should be termed *stultitiae* rather than *studia,* and preferred to regard all human efforts for wisdom as foolish in the final analysis. To him the absoluteness and transcendence of God were above everything. They tolerated no limitation on the part of human understanding. Even the law of contradiction — Peter pushed it as far as the question of whether God could undo something that had been done, such as the founding of Rome — could not be applied vis-à-vis God's unlimited omnipotence. The last mentioned postulate, untenable in itself and advanced even by Peter with obvious hesitation, must not be taken seriously. The whole attitude of he so-called antidialecticians must be estimated with the same caution. It in no sense consisted of absolute negation. Otloh applied dialectics to theological problems, though quite clumsily; Manegold referred expressly to the harmony between philosophy and faith, especially in ethics and the doctrine of virtue; and the warnings of Peter Damiani were meant chiefly for his hermits, to a lesser degree for the laity, and not at all for the diocesan clergy, for whom he even required a solid scholarly formation. His real concern was for the right order between the secular and the spiritual, philosophy and theology; philosophy — and here he took up an old idea — was to exercise the serving function of handmaid to theology. As childish as the use of dialectics may often enough have been, it was not to be stopped. The course of the eucharistic controversy provides a clear example.

The eucharistic controversy did not come about by chance. The Western Church lacked a uniform eucharistic doctrine summarizing the patristic tradition, such as John Damascene (d. ca. 750) had worked out for the Eastern Church. It would have been all the more desirable in that the incompleted initial efforts of the Latin Fathers pointed in two directions. One group, going back to Ambrose, stressed rather the changing of bread and wine into the Lord's body and blood, while another group, with Augustine, gave special prominence to the dynamic symbolic power of the Sacrament, which incorporates the faithful into Christ and into the mystical body of the Church. The two viewpoints led in the Carolingian period to the doctrinal controversy between the realistic and metabolistic outlook of Paschasius Radbertus and an Augustinian-oriented opposition, headed by Ratramnus. This theme engaged especially Rathier of Verona and Heriger of Lobbes in the tenth century. Though Heriger took pains with a synthesis of realism and symbolism, he basically followed Paschasius Radbertus, whose explanation pretty generally established itself in the course of time. However, it was not entirely satisfactory. Since Paschasius had identified the eucharistic and the historical body of the Lord without more precisely explaining the eucharistic species, his teaching could and probably did promote a grossly materialistic "Capharnaitic" interpretation.

A reaction did not fail to show itself. A pupil of Fulbert of Chartres, Berengarius (d. 1088), since 1029 *scholasticus* at Tours and at the same time archdeacon of Angers, sought to restore the dynamic symbolic teaching of Augustine to prominence. The ensuing discussion differed from that of the Carolingian period, on the one hand by the much greater use of dialectic thought, progressing at times even to metaphysics, and on the other hand by the broad and deep effect which it produced: the problem never set the theologians free until it had been essentially clarified. Even in the first phase of the struggle Berengarius had to contend with a whole group of equal or even superior opponents. In addition, the official Church intervened. His doctrine was condemned by Leo IX at the Synods of Rome and Vercelli in 1050 and by the Synod of Paris in 1051. On the other hand the Council of Tours in 1054, presided over by the legate Hildebrand, accepted Berengarius' explanation that the body and blood of Christ are present after the consecration. In 1059, however, Berengarius was forced at the Roman Synod to sign a formula drawn up by Humbert of Silva Candida, in which the Lord's body contained in the consecrated bread was described crudely as: "sensualiter manibus tractari vel frangi aut fidelium dentibus atteri."

This introduced the second phase of the controversy. Ten years later Berengarius submitted the formula and the doctrine on which it was based to a comprehensive dialectical criticism and moved into a radically spiritualistic symbolism. The consecrated bread is body in so far as it is image, sign, pledge of the real body; it awakens a remembrance of Christ's Incarnation and Passion and leads the mind that reposes in these mysteries to mystical union with the Lord. The bread remains bread even after the consecration; that is, the substance appears in the accidents, they are the coconstitutive principle of form. In the last mentioned argument Berengarius directed the debate to the metaphysical, but without having correctly understood the Aristotelian basic ideas that he used — *materia, forma, accidens, substantia.* Nor did his opponents yet know their real meaning. Hence their achievement is to be all the more highly esteemed in that, undertaking the speculative way on their own, they explained the process of change ever more clearly in the sense of a transubstantiation. Lanfranc (d. 1089) began the task, Guitmund of Aversa (d. ca. 1095) completed the doctrine. When in 1079 Berengarius was again summoned to Rome by Gregory VII, he had to swear to a formula of faith that was far better thought out: "[panem et vinum] substantialiter converti in veram et propriam et vivificatricem carnem et sanguinem Iesu Christi." The post-Berengarian period brought nothing basically new, but only an assimilation of the individual aspects, which then found their first systematic recapitulation in the school of Anselm of Laon (d. 1117).

The papacy's playing an important role in the eucharistic controversy shows again the concentrated strength of the Gregorian reform movement. However, what was involved was rather an indirect relationship. The controversy as such was not caused by the reform, and it was the theologians who decided it, while Rome supervised its course. The situation was quite different in regard to the discussion of holy orders, which has already been frequently mentioned in connection with specific synodal decrees; this proceeded directly out of the struggle over reform. The severe measures in regard to simonists, who were branded as heretics, and the numerous excommunications, especially those hurled against antipope, and their adherents, of themselves raised the very old problem of whether heretics or schismatics could confer valid orders at all. Since Cyprian had bluntly denied that they could and Augustine had held the contrary and both views had entered into the tradition of the Church, a sure orientation was lacking. The controversy waged over the Formosan ordinations had produced excellent works at the beginning of the tenth century, especially the writings of Auxilius, who was influenced by Augustine. In the 1050s Auxilius was used by Peter Damiani and by Humbert of Silva Candida; Peter agreed with him, whereas Humbert roughly rejected him. Much as Peter's *Liber gratissimus* surpassed Humbert's *Adversus simoniacos libri III* in theological depth, he too left many points unresolved. The reason lay in the unsatisfactory state of sacramental theology. Clarification would come only with the doctrine, appearing in the twelfth century, of *character sacramentalis* and the later distinction of *sacramentum, sacramentum et res,* and *res sacramenti.*

Another circumstance that impeded a solution was the fact that, in addition to the power of orders, promotion to the priesthood and the episcopate also imparted a function to which jurisdiction was attached and that at the time orders and jurisdiction had not yet been clearly enough distinguished. Through the union of the power of jurisdiction with ordination and vice versa there belonged to the Church a decisive importance in so far as incorporation into her constituted the prerequisite for the effectiveness of the priestly function. By "Church" at that time was in no sense meant a community of love and grace existing only in Christ, but also a corporate body, defined in regard to jurisdiction. It was not merely accidental that from about 1060 canonists especially were interested in the difficulty. They no longer presumed bluntly to declare simoniacal or schismatic orders invalid, but, by virtue of the distinction between the Sacrament, which ordination communicates, and the *virtus sacramenti,* the overwhelming number of them reached the view that, if a person no longer belonged to the unity of the Church, his ordinations would have to be regarded not merely as illicit but also as ineffectual, for he did not possess the Holy Spirit. They thus required for every simonist or schismatic who returned to the Church the traditional *impositio manuum,* which they regarded as a giving of the Spirit. Only a few, such as Bernold of Sankt Blasien, explained the primitive ceremony in the sense of a reconciliation. For the moment matters remained in these modest and unsatisfactory initial doctrinal efforts.

While a whole group of talented men were going to great pains about specific timely questions, partly in harmony, partly in disagreement, what was really essential was being accomplished far away from daily strife by a lone worker: with the effortless ease proper to the nature of a genius Anselm was raising the problem of philosophy and theology to a speculative height never reached since the days of John Scotus Eriugena. Born not far from Aosta in Piedmont in 1033 and educated by Benedictines, he left his home and after three years sought the monastery of Bec in Normandy in order to study under the very famous Lanfranc of Pavia. In 1060 Anselm entered Bec as a monk and soon assumed the office of teacher. He became prior in 1063 and Abbot in 1078. His promotion in 1093 to the archbishopric of Canterbury involved him in the already described conflicts with the English Kings William II and Henry I. He died in 1109.

Like all Western theologians, Anselm steeped himself in the writings of Augustine especially, but in his case there was a genuine intellectual encounter based on congeniality of soul. The celebrated guiding principles which Anselm carefully proposed for the relations between philosophy and theology, between reason and grace, are basically Augustinian. He frankly admitted his ardent wish somehow to understand the divine mysteries within the limits set for man, but he wanted to know that it was always directed only to truths which his soul already believed and loved; he did not wish to understand in order to believe, but he believed in order to understand "neque enim quaero intelligere ut credam, sed credo ut intelligam." The idea urged inner understanding so that, according to circumstances, facts became clear to the thinking believer which were invisible in the merely accepted truth of faith, which at times could even make the faith itself clearer. The movement, summarized by Anselm in the brief formula, *Fides quaerens intellectum* thus went really beyond faith and, faith always presupposed, ended in reason. This is able at times to clarify in its existence a truth belonging to the divine sphere and hence to establish it on *rationes necessariae,* while the inner, inaccessible nature of the divine mysteries presents itself to the investigating human mind merely in image, parable, and relationship of suitability.

Anselm's speculation, proceeding from faith as a matter of principle, knew no real separation between philosophy and theology. This should be especially kept in mind in regard to his works composed at Bec. Except for *De casu diaboli,* they were all concerned with questions which would today be assigned to philosophy — *De grammatico, Monologion, Proslogion, De veritate, De libertate arbitrii.* Two of them especially stand out. In the *Monologion* Anselm tried to prove the existence of God by means of cosmology. In so doing he used the category of causality less than that of participation; however, he did not continue in a Platonic character but progressed to the sovereign divine nature, standing above all participation. All things are contained in the inner utterance of God which begot the Eternal Word, before, during, and after their created existence; everything that has become is a copy of the divine Word.

The *Proslogion* leads even more deeply into Anselm's specific thought. It contains the much admired, much attacked, so-called ontologic proof. The argument presupposes an idea of God that is immanent to human thought and hence from the outset it contains an existential factor. In this idea God confronts us as the greatest that can be thought of at all. But, continues Anselm, the greatest cannot be merely in our intellect, for when another could be thought of which would be greater in so far as it really existed outside our intellect. Hence, the greatest, that is, God, must be in our mind and at the same time in external reality. This was attacked on serious grounds by a contemporary, Gaunilo, monk of Marmoutier, and defended by Anselm in *Liber apologeticus.*

Toward the end of his life Anselm treated specifically theological questions. In *De fide Trinitatis et de incarnatione Verbi* he stressed the distinction between the divine nature and the divine Persons against Roscelin, who, on the basis of his problematic doctrine of universals, assumed in the Trinity "tres res per se separatim." The *De processione Spiritus Sancti* was produced in connection with

Urban II's efforts for union. *De conceptione virginali et originali peccato* and *Cur Deus homo* deal with the mystery of the Incarnation. The second of these not only displayed Anselm's method to perfection, it also made obsolete the patristic and early medieval theory of redemption — that of a buying back of fallen humanity by Christ from the dominion of the devil — by the deep idea that Christ became man in order to make satisfaction for all mankind to the divine honor, outraged by sin. Anselm's doctrine of satisfaction was further developed by the great scholastics of the thirteenth century and was thus firmly incorporated into Roman Catholic theology.

Anselm has rightly been called the Father of Scholasticism. It was he who, boldly and undismayed, showed his contemporaries how dialectics and metaphysical speculation could be applied to theological questions without violating the reverence due to mysteries of faith by rationalistic arrogance. Others emulated him in this, and with them really appeared Early Scholasticism. Anselm decisively contributed to making this possible.

Probably none of the many fruitful initiatives of the age of the Gregorian reform so definitely transformed the medieval world as did the intellectual development. Entering the stage of alert awareness, Western man began to reflect on basic questions of his essential Christian existence. While he still always looked with reverence to the tradition handed down to him, he now applied more strongly the critically distinguishing reason in order to take vital possession of the inherited intellectual property, to come to terms with it, and thereby to press on to new knowledge. The more absolutely he pursued this course, the more the minds separated. In a struggle that never again came to rest the West was thereafter to experience drastically the tensions implied in its form of existence.